OOSTERHOFF ON WILLS AND SUCCESSION

Text, Commentary and Materials

Fifth Edition

A.H. Oosterhoff

B.A., LL.B., LL.M.
Member of the Ontario Bar

Professor, Faculty of Law
The University of Western Ontario

CARSWELL

A THOMSON COMPANY

National Library of Canada Cataloguing in Publication Data

Oosterhoff, A. H.
  Oosterhoff on wills and succession: text, commentary and cases

5th ed.
Third ed. published under title: Text, commentary and cases on wills and succession.
Includes index.
ISBN 0-459-26129-0

1. Wills — Canada. 2. Inheritance and succession — Canada. 3. Wills — Canada — Cases.
4. Inheritance and succession — Canada — Cases. I. Title.

KE808.A7067 2001   346.7105'4   C2001-930701-2
KF775.A7067 2001

CARSWELL

A THOMSON COMPANY

One Corporate Plaza	**Customer Service:**
2075 Kennedy Road	Toronto 1-416-609-3800
Scarborough, Ontario	Elsewhere in Canada/U.S. 1-800-387-5164
M1T 3V4	Fax 1-416-298-5094

for Michael and Andrew

PREFACE

Much has happened in the law of wills since the last edition. This is true particularly because of new developments in substitute decisions and because of the impingement of the *Canadian Charter of Rights and Freedoms* on the law of succession. I have incorporated these and other developments in this edition. I have also updated the materials to the end of 2000 and have substantially rewritten significant portions of the text. The following is a summary of the major changes.

In chapter 1, on History and Terminology, I have inserted a new section on constitutional issues, which comments on recent cases and statutes that give effect to the requirements of the *Charter*. This is, of necessity, incomplete, as further developments are expected. I also address this topic throughout the text, as required. I have also inserted a new section on succession under the *Indian Act*. That topic was mentioned in previous editions, but not in any detail. I have added a brief section on costs in chapter 2 (Probate and Administration) and have clarified the materials on the duties of personal representatives. They now address specifically the duty to dispose of the deceased's remains, and the duties imposed by the *Income Tax Act*.

Chapter 3, on Intestacy, now contains a section on the definition of "spouse," since recent cases and statutes have included common law and same-sex partners in that definition. Chapter 4, on the Nature of Testamentary Dispositions, now specifically addresses the issue of expectancies, which has arisen several times in recent cases, and contains new sections on proprietary estoppel and the use of will substitutes to avoid probate fees. I have replaced *Re Gillespie* with the British Columbia Court of Appeal case, *The University of Manitoba v. Sanderson Estate*.

In chapter 5, on Testamentary Capacity, Undue Influence and Mistake, I have added a section on knowledge and approval and replaced *Eady and Waring* with the Supreme Court of Canada decision, *Vout v. Hay*. In chapter 6, on Formal Validity of Wills, I have rewritten the materials on the power to dispense with failure to comply with all formalities, since more and more jurisdictions have adopted such a power. In chapter 7, on Revocation of Wills, I have included a section on vitiating factors, that is, reasons why an attempted revocation may fail, to make clear that revocation is a testamentary act and may fail for the same reasons as a will. The chapter now also contains a section on the validity of marriage. This is in response to a number of recent cases, of which *Banton v. Banton* is perhaps the most egregious example, in which younger women entice much older men, who lack testamentary capacity, into marriage to gain control of their property. I raise the question whether the automatic statutory revocation of wills on the testator's marriage needs to be restricted to those situations in which the deceased had testamentary capacity and was not subjected to undue influence.

In chapter 9, on Capacity of Beneficiaries, I took out the statutory material on foreign beneficiaries, which was largely directed to beneficiaries behind the former Iron Curtain. Chapter 11, on Testamentary Gifts, contains a new section on the subject matter of testamentary gifts to clarify what a testator may dispose of. I have also replaced the old Supreme Court of Canada case, *Rosborough v. Trustees of St. Andrew's Church* with the recent Ontario Court of Appeal case, *Granot v. Hersen Estate*. In chapter 13, on Class Gifts, *Re Charlesworth Estate* has replaced *In re Ward*. The former is a recent Manitoba case which is directly on point, while the latter was only an exception to the first class closing rule.

In chapter 16, on Spousal Rights, I deleted *Re Fraser* as no longer necessary. In chapter 17, on Support of Dependants, I deleted *Re Pulver* and *Maldaver v. Canada Permanent Trust Co. (No. 2)* for the same reason. I have added a new section to this chapter which clarifies and explains the two different approaches to claims for support that exist in Canada, that is, the approach that restricts support to the persons and on the basis of criteria listed in the statute and the approach that allows the court to redistribute an estate on the basis of a moral obligation on the part of the deceased towards her or his children no matter what age they are.

I have combined the former chapters 18 and 19 on the solicitor's duty in taking instructions for a will and the solicitor's duty of care towards beneficiaries into a new chapter on Solicitor's Duties. The chapter now contains the House of Lords decision in *White v. Jones*, which was handed down soon after the last edition was published.

I am very grateful to my wife, Dawn, who is an expert on substitute decision making. She has completely rewritten Chapter 19, on Substitute Decisions. The chapter incorporates the much revised legislation in Ontario and new legislation in the other provinces and discusses this developing area of the law.

In addition, all the materials were updated to incorporate new cases and statutes. These are reflected in the materials and in the Notes and Questions.

Previous users of this book will know that I include comprehensive references to legislation in other provinces whenever statutory materials are reproduced. It was not possible to include such references for the new Territory of Nunavut, which was brought into being on April 1, 1999. Section 29 of the *Nunavut Act*, S.C. 1993, c. 28, am. S.C. 1998, c. 15, s. 4, provides that the laws in force in the Northwest Territories continue in force for Nunavut until repealed, amended, or rendered inoperable in respect of Nunavut. Pursuant to the Act and to accommodate modifications of Northwest Territories laws that were required to be in force when the new Territory came into being, the Northwest Territories did enact certain statutes on behalf of Nunavut. Further, the Nunavut legislature, in its first legislative session enacted a number of statutes. However, none of these appear to affect the law of succession. A revision of Nunavut statutes is expected to be completed in 2001 and I hope, therefore, to be able to include references to these statutes in the next revision. Meanwhile, they are available online.[1]

---

1 See the QuickLaw database of Nunavut statutes, NUST; *www.acjnet.org*, specifically *http:// pooka.nunanet.com/~ncjlib/statutes.html*; and *http://www.nunavutcourtofjustice.nu.ca/library/ library.htm*.

Indeed, as time goes on, it is likely that we may need to refer more and more to online materials. For example, recent announcements indicate that Ontario will not be publishing a new 2000 statute revision, but will maintain an online continuing consolidation of its statutes. These developments present frustrations, but also challenges and advantages for those of us who write books. Perhaps they will allow one more easily to live up to Qoheleth's injunction, "Of making many books there is no end."

I express my gratitude to my colleagues, Nicholas Kasirer of McGill and Cameron Harvey of Manitoba, who regularly keep me informed of developments in their provinces and in the law of succession generally. I have incorporated many of their suggestions in this edition. And I wish to express my thanks to my research assistants, Tricia Holmes and Ruth Dick, who did much of the tedious work of finding new cases and statutes, so essential to a book of this kind. I could not have completed this new edition without their meticulous work and their very helpful suggestions. I am also very grateful to the Faculty of Law, The University of Western Ontario, and the Ontario Law Foundation for making the necessary research moneys available to complete this book.

Albert H. Oosterhoff
Faculty of Law
The University of Western Ontario
London, Ontario
February, 2001

ACKNOWLEDGMENTS

The author is grateful to the following persons and organizations for permission to reproduce materials from the sources indicated below.

Report of the Proposed Adoption in Ontario of the Uniform Wills Act
Ontario Law Reform Commission
Ministry of Government Services (Ontario)

Succession Law Reform in Ontario
Canada Law Book Inc.
Aurora, Ontario

Uniform Presumption of Death Act
Uniform Law Conference of Canada

SUMMARY OF CHAPTERS

For a detailed Table of Contents see page xiii

CONTENTS

PART I
INTRODUCTION

PART III
PROVING WILLS

PART V
FAMILY PROTECTION

TABLE OF CASES

TABLE OF STATUTES

ONTARIO

PART I

INTRODUCTION

1

HISTORY AND TERMINOLOGY

1. OUTLINE OF THE HISTORY OF SUCCESSION

(a) Introduction

The Canadian law of succession derives primarily from the English common law, ecclesiastical law and equity. Of course, it has been modified by our courts and by statute. But, even today, Canadian courts will often refer to English wills cases, and English statute law on succession is sometimes still copied in Canada.

It is appropriate, therefore, that we begin a consideration of the law of succession with a brief outline of the history of that law in England. We shall then look at the origins of the Canadian law of succession and a short outline of the law of succession in Ontario. Then we shall discuss constitutional issues as they affect succession, and succession under the *Indian Act*.[1] The chapter closes with a definition of common terms used in the law of succession.

(b) The English Background

(i) *Personal Property*

In English law the succession to personal property has followed a different course from succession to real property. From early times and certainly after the Norman Conquest, the ecclesiastical courts exercised jurisdiction over the testamentary disposition of personal property. It has always been possible to dispose of one's personal property on death by testament; in fact, it was one's duty to do so, since it was believed that to die intestate was to die unconfessed. Since the confession and the making of the last testament normally occurred at about the same time, the church, having jurisdiction over the former, assumed jurisdiction, as a matter of course, over the latter. The right of a person to dispose of his or her personal property was, however, restricted. If a man left a wife and children, his wife and the children would each get one-third of the personal property and the

---

1 R.S.C. 1985, c. I-5.

testator could dispose of the other one-third. The latter was the so-called "dead's part", which originally went to the church and was employed for pious uses. If a man left a wife but no children, or children but no wife, he could dispose of one-half of his estate, the other half going to his immediate family. If a man died leaving no wife and no children, he could dispose of the whole. The shares to which his wife and children were entitled were their "reasonable parts," which were enforceable by them against the executor by means of the special writ *de rationabili bonorum*. In most areas of England, the widow's and children's rights to their reasonable parts fell into disuse after the reign of Charles I.

Testaments (of personal property) could be in writing but were, at any rate in the early stages, often oral (nuncupative). *The Statute of Frauds*, 1677[2] made important changes in this regard. The statute did not abolish nuncupative testaments, but made them subject to severe restrictions. They had to be proved on the oath of three witnesses present during the making of the testament; the testament had to be made during the testator's last illness and (subject to a few immaterial exceptions) in his or her dwelling; and no evidence to prove the will could be taken six months after the testament was made, unless the testimony was put in writing within six days after the making of it. Further, no written testament could be revoked by an oral one, unless the oral testament was reduced to writing during the lifetime of the testator and was proved by three witnesses. The statute did not, however, prescribe any requirements for the signing and witnessing of testaments.

The *Statute of Frauds* excepted the following from its provisions (and, therefore, continued nuncupative wills with no restrictions in this respect):

1. persons disposing of an estate less than £30,
2. mariners at sea, and
3. soldiers on actual military service.

These exceptions were continued by the *Wills Act* of 1837[3] and extended by the *Wills (Soldiers and Sailors) Act* of 1918.[4]

Married women could not devise their real property. Nor could they dispose of their personal property except in four situations:

1. A married woman's testament of personal property was valid if her husband gave his consent to the testament with knowledge of its contents, if he did not revoke his consent before the testament was actually probated, and if he survived his wife.
2. A married woman might, if she was the executrix under the will of a testator, make a will in her capacity as executrix and appoint an executor for the purpose of continuing the representation of the original testator.
3. A married woman could dispose of her separate property.

---

2 29 Car. 2, c.3.
3 7 Will. 4 & 1 Vict., c. 26.
4 7 & 8 Geo. 5, c. 58.

4. A married woman could make a will, testament or a similar instrument in execution of a power conferred upon her to that effect.

The *Wills Act* of 1837 continued the restrictions on the testamentary powers of married women, subject to the exceptions existing at common law, and this was not changed until the *Married Women's Property Acts* of 1882[5] and 1893.[6]

The ecclesiastical courts permitted minors to make testaments of personal property provided they were 14 years of age, if male, and 12 years of age, if female. This was not changed until the *Wills Act* of 1837, which fixed the age at 21 years, which was the age at which a person could make a will of real property.

(ii) *Distribution of Personal Property*

If a person failed to dispose of his or her personal property by testament on death, it was distributed according to certain rules of distribution which were administered by the ecclesiastical courts. These rules were codified in the *Statute of Distribution*, 1670,[7] which, together with a later statute[8] formed the basis for earlier statutory schemes of distribution in the Canadian provinces.[9] The present Ontario *Succession Law Reform Act,*[10] as well as the statutes of the other provinces incorporate a similar scheme of distribution.

Under the *Statute of Distribution* an intestate's next of kin were determined according to the civil law "gradual" scheme of succession as opposed to the "parentelic" scheme used with respect to real property. Under the "gradual" scheme each step in the ascending or descending line is a degree. To determine the relationship between a *propositus* and a relative, you would count as a degree each step from the *propositus* to the relative in question. The basic scheme of the *Statute of Distribution* remained unchanged until 1925.

(iii) *Succession to Land*

While for a brief period of time after the Norman Conquest, it was possible to devise real property by will, the primogeniture rule became firmly established in the 12th century. Thereafter wills of real property were no longer effective and land descended to the heir-at-law of a deceased person according to certain fixed rules. These rules or canons of descent were as follows:[11]

---

5 45 & 46 Vict., c. 75.

6 56 & 57 Vict., c. 63.

7 22 & 23 Car. 2, c. 10 (U.K.), am. by *Statute of Frauds*, 29 Car. 2, c. 3; and *Statute of Distribution*, 1 Jac. 2, c. 17 (1685).

8 *Statute of Distribution*, 1 Jac. 2, c. 17 (1685).

9 Such as ss. 31 and 32 of the *Devolution of Estates Act*, R.S.O. 1970, c. 129.

10 S.O. 1977, c. 40; now R.S.O. 1990, c. S.26.

11 See Blackstone, *Commentaries on the Laws of England* (15th ed., 1809), at pp. 208ff.

1. Inheritances descended lineally to the issue of the person who last died actually seised, *in infinitum*, but they never ascended lineally.
2. The male issue was admitted before the female.
3. If there were two or more males in equal degree, the eldest only inherited, but the females inherited all together.
4. The lineal descendants *in infinitum* of any deceased person represented their ancestor; that is, they stood in the same place as the ancestor would have done, had he or she been living.
5. On failure of lineal descendants or issue of the person last seised, the inheritance descended to his or her collateral relations being of the blood of the first purchaser, subject to the three preceding rules.
6. The collateral heir of the person last seised had to be his or her next collateral kinsman of the whole blood.
7. In collateral inheritance, the male stock was preferred to the female, unless the lands in fact descended from a female.

The *Inheritance Act*, 1833[12] amended these rules in that it abolished the principle that parents and other lineal ancestors could not inherit, and substituted the following order of preference:

1. Descendants.
2. Parents.
3. Brothers and sisters and their issue.
4. Grandparents.
5. Uncles and aunts, and more remote collaterals.

Land descended to collaterals according to the "parentelic" scheme. A "parentela" is the sum of those persons who trace their blood from a given person. Under this scheme you take a given *propositus* and exhaust all of his or her descendants before taking another *propositus*.

Various legislative changes were made in the law of descent of real property. However, primogeniture remained in effect until it was abolished by the *Administration of Estates Act*, 1925.[13]

(iv) Wills of Real Property

We saw that the right to devise real property by will was abolished in the 12th century. This happened because the king's courts usurped the jurisdiction of the ecclesiastical courts over succession to land. The common law courts took the view that a will operated as a conveyance, but since it was not accompanied by livery of seisin, it was invalid. To overcome the prohibition against wills, landowners began to resort to the use, which was enforced in equity. Thus, a person

---

12 3 & 4 Will. 4, c. 106 (U.K.).
13 15 & 16 Geo. 5, c. 23 (U.K.).

would convey land to a number of friends to the use of the grantor's immediate family after the grantor's death When the *Statute of Uses* was passed in 1535,[14] it was thought that it abolished the right to make such "testamentary" dispositions and, as a result of the general outcry, the *Statute of Wills* was passed in 1540,[15] which was supplemented by the *Act Concerning the Explanation of Wills*, 1542-1543.[16] Under these statutes all tenants in fee simple acquired the power to dispose of all land held in socage tenure and two-thirds of all lands held by knight service. The *Tenures Abolition Act*, 1660,[17] which converted knight service into free and common socage, meant that thereafter all land held in fee simple could be devised. Under the *Statute of Wills* of 1540 femes coverts, infants, idiots, and persons of unsound memory lacked capacity to make a will. In addition, aliens and persons convicted of a crime, as well as persons under various physical disabilities such as deafness, dumbness and blindness were unable to make a will.

The *Statute of Wills* of 1540 fixed the legal age for making a will of real property at 21 and the *Statute of Wills* of 1837[18] made 21 the legal age for wills of personal and real property. The latter Act also made the rules regarding the execution of wills and testaments uniform and continued the existing exceptions. As we saw, the *Married Women's Property Acts* enabled married women to devise real property by will.

(v) *Probate and Administration*

The ecclesiastical courts, presided over by the Ordinary, originally had complete jurisdiction over probate and administration of estates of personal property. However, the common law courts controlled the succession to freehold estates, including the probate of wills of real property.

From about the latter part of the 16th century onward, the chancery courts gradually obtained jurisdiction over the administration of the assets of a deceased person, for example, by compelling accounting against executors, giving various types of relief to legatees and compelling satisfaction of debts out of land. Eventually, in the 17th century, the courts of chancery took over the administration of estates completely and the ecclesiastical courts retained only the right to grant probate and letters of administration.

The *Court of Probate Act*, 1857[19] took away the jurisdiction of the ecclesiastical courts over probate and administration and gave it to the newly established Court of Probate. The *Supreme Court of Judicature Acts*, 1873-75[20] transferred jurisdiction over testamentary matters to the new Probate, Divorce and Admiralty Division of the High Court of Justice. In 1971 this Division was abolished and

---

14 27 Hen. 8, c. 10.
15 32 Hen. 8, c. 1.
16 34 & 35 Hen. 8, c. 5.
17 12 Car. 2, c. 24.
18 7 Will. 4 & 1 Vict., c. 26, s. 7.
19 20 & 21 Vict., c. 77.
20 36 & 37 Vict., c. 66; 38 & 39 Vict., c. 77.

contentious probate matters were transferred to the Chancery Division, while non-contentious matters were given to the Family Division of the Court.[21]

The law of succession and of probate and administration was changed substantially in England in the great property law reforms of 1925. These changes have not generally been adopted in Canada, however, and are not discussed here.

(c) The Law of Succession in Canada

The several provinces and territories of Canada were settled at different times. When an area was settled, the settlers brought with them the English law to which they were accustomed, including the law of succession. By common law rules or by statute, a specific date of reception was established for each province and territory. This was usually the date when the colony received representative government. English law in existence on that date only was received into the colony; subsequent law was not, unless required by Imperial legislation.

Since the dates of reception differed across the country, the history of the law of succession differs as well from province to province.[22] However, the modern law of succession in the common law provinces is largely uniform. This is so for three main reasons: (1) Although not required to do so, colonial and provincial legislatures often enacted English legislation respecting succession enacted after the date of reception. (2) Colonial courts tended to follow English case law after reception. Indeed, they were obliged to do so if the case was a decision of the House of Lords or the Judicial Committee of the Privy Council until appeals to the latter were abolished.[23] And (3) most of the provinces and territories have adopted, in whole or in part, model statutes on succession and related matters promulgated by the Conference of Commissioners on Uniformity of Legislation in Canada and its successor, the Uniform Law Conference of Canada.

The law of succession in Quebec is governed by the *Civil Code of Quebec*.

For reasons of simplicity, I shall only give an outline of the history of the law of succession in Ontario.

(d) The Law of Succession in Ontario

(i) *Early History*

For the purpose of this outline we may regard the history of the law of succession in Ontario as commencing in 1792 with the *Property and Civil Rights Act*.[24] It

---

21 By the *Administration of Justice Act*, 1970, (U.K.), c. 31.

22 On the reception of English common and statute law, and the dates of reception, see Anger and Honsberger, *Law of Real Property*, 2nd ed. by A.H. Oosterhoff and W.B. Rayner (Aurora: Canada Law Book Inc., 1985), ch. 3.

23 Criminal appeals to the Privy Council were abolished in 1931, civil appeals in 1949. See *ibid.*, p. 56.

24 S.U.C. 1792, c. 1. It was possible to make wills under the laws of Quebec or the law of England in that part of the country now called Ontario before 1792.

stipulated that "in all matters of controversy relative to Property and Civil Rights resort shall be had to the Laws of England as the rule for the decision of the same," such laws being taken as they stood on the fifteenth day of October, 1792, except insofar as they were altered or modified by Canadian statutes.

Since, at that date, the ecclesiastical courts still had jurisdiction over matters testamentary in England, and since it was inconvenient and undesirable to import such courts into this country, a new system was devised. By the *Probate and Surrogate Courts Act*,[25] a Court of Probate was established in the province of Upper Canada, presided over by the Governor or Lieutenant Governor. The latter had the right to appoint an Official Principal (judge) and a registrar of the court. Further, provision was made for establishing a surrogate court in each of the several districts then existing in the province, each presided over by a Surrogate. The Court of Probate had sole jurisdiction if the deceased possessed goods to the value of £5 or more in any district, other than the one in which he or she usually resided. An appeal lay from the surrogate courts to the Court of Probate.

Before the passing of this Act, the Governor was, by virtue of his commission and instructions, Ordinary of the province and had power to grant letters probate of wills and letters of administration of estates of persons dying intestate.

In 1858 the *Surrogate Courts Act*[26] was enacted. It repealed all former legislation regarding probate, abolished the old Court of Probate and vested all probate jurisdiction in new surrogate courts established in each county. This scheme existed until 1990.

You should note that the surrogate courts originally had jurisdiction only over the personal property of a deceased person, since at common law no probate of a will of land was necessary, production of the will being sufficient to satisfy title, although the *Registry Act*,[27] made provision for the registration of memorials of wills on title. It was not until 1886, when the *Devolution of Estates Act* was passed,[28] that the surrogate courts obtained jurisdiction over real estate.

Prior to 1886 the real property of persons dying intestate continued to pass to the heir-at-law under the primogeniture rule, or the statutory substitute of that rule, while personal property was distributed in accordance with the statutes of Charles II and James II,[29] pursuant to specific statutory direction.[30]

With respect to real property, the common law canons of descent applied in Upper Canada as received English law until July 1, 1834, when they were changed by the *Real Property Act* of that year[31] to conform to the changes made by the English *Inheritance Act*, 1833.[32]

---

25 S.U.C. 1793, c. 8.
26 S.U.C. 1858, c. 93.
27 S.U.C. 1795, c. 5.
28 S.O. 1886, c. 22.
29 *Statute of Distribution*, 1670, 22 & 23 Car. 2, c. 10; *Statute of Distribution*, 1685, 1 Jac. 2, c. 17.
30 S.U.C. 1793, c. 8, ss. 12 and 13.
31 S.U.C. 1834, c. 1.
32 3 & 4 Will 4, c. 106.

These rules were further drastically changed in 1851 by the *Inheritance Act*,[33] which abolished the right of primogeniture effective January 1, 1852, and substituted therefor certain rules of descent comparable, but not identical to those applicable to the distribution of personal property under the *Statute of Distribution*.[34]

Then, in 1886, the *Devolution of Estates Act* was passed[35] by which real and personal property were assimilated for the purpose of administration and the property of a deceased person, whether he or she died testate or intestate, was directed to vest in the deceased's personal representative as trustee[36] for those beneficially entitled which, in the case of an intestacy, were those persons entitled under, and in the shares set out in, the old *Statute of Distribution*, which was one of the English statutes received in Upper Canada.

The *Statute of Distribution* was made subject, however, to the *Devolution of Estates Act*. This was important because the latter Act preserved dower and curtesy, which were life estates in land only. The *Statute of Distribution* was also subject to the widow's right to her preferential share, which was given her by *An Act making better provisions for the Widows of Intestates in certain Cases*.[37] This Act is the forerunner of section 45 of the *Succession Law Reform Act*.[38]

Finally, after a number of intermediate legislative changes, the *Statute of Distribution* was incorporated into the *Devolution of Estates Act*,[39] which was itself considerably revised. The scheme of distribution on intestacy as so consolidated, basically remained unchanged until the enactment of the *Succession Law Reform Act*,[40] except for some important amendments respecting the spouses' preferential shares.

With respect to the law of wills, there was, until 1873, very little legislative activity in Ontario. The *Real Property Act* of 1834[41] made certain provisions affecting the nature of devisees' interests under wills taking effect after that date, namely:

1. When two or more persons take under a devise they take as tenants in common, unless a contrary intention appears on the face of the will.[42]
2. A devise purporting to pass all the testator's real estate passes after-acquired real property.[43]

---

33 S.C. 1851, c. 6.
34 22 & 23 Car. 2, c. 10 (1670).
35 S.O. 1886, c. 22.
36 The phrase "as trustee" did not appear in s. 4(1) of the Act of 1886. It appeared for the first time in the *Devolution of Estates Act*, S.O. 1910, c. 56, s. 3(1).
37 S.O. 1895, c. 21.
38 R.S.O. 1990, c. S.26.
39 S.O. 1910, c. 56.
40 S.O. 1977, c. 40; now R.S.O. 1990, c. S.26.
41 S.U.C. 1834, c. 1.
42 *Ibid.*, s. 48.
43 *Ibid.*, s. 49.

3. A devise passes all the estate the testator has in the land, unless a contrary intention appears on the face of the will.[44]
4. A will of land can be attested by two witnesses only, instead of three. They have to subscribe their names in the presence of each other, but do not need to do so in the presence of the testator, although their presence at the time of execution is required.[45]

By the *Chancery Act*,[46] jurisdiction was conferred upon the Court of Chancery to try the validity of wills both of real and personal estate, and to pronounce such wills void for fraud and undue influence or otherwise. This jurisdiction eventually passed to the Supreme Court of Ontario under the *Ontario Judicature Act*.[47] The surrogate courts had concurrent jurisdiction in these matters and, in practice, that is where such actions originated. They could be removed to the Supreme Court of Ontario if they were of sufficient importance.

Some minor changes were made in the law of wills thereafter.[48] Finally, by the *Wills Act* of 1873,[49] the law of wills was codified by substantial adoption of the English *Wills Act, 1837*.[50] The Act of 1873 is the forerunner of Part I of the *Succession Law Reform Act*.[51]

In addition, various changes were made regarding disabilities, namely:

1. *Alienage*: At common law an alien was incompetent to hold real estate in Upper Canada. This restriction was removed in 1849.[52]
2. *Coverture*: The property rights of married women were the subject of several statutes in Upper Canada. These were consolidated as the *Married Women's Property Act*,[53] and the *Married Women's Real Estate Act*.[54] A number of changes were made subsequently and, finally, both statutes were superseded by the *Married Women's Property Act, 1884*.[55] As a result of these several enactments married women were completely emancipated as regards their property rights and acquired the right to dispose of their property *inter vivos* and by will without any restriction.
3. *Criminality*: At common law felons were intestable for the simple reason that they had nothing to dispose of, since their goods were forfeited to the Crown.

---

44 *Ibid.*, s. 50.
45 *Ibid.*, s. 51.
46 S.U.C. 1837, c. 2; and see C.S.U.C. 1859, c. 12, s. 28.
47 S.O. 1881, c. 5.
48 Namely, by *An Act respecting the Law of Property and Trusts*; *An Act to Amend the Law of Wills*, S.O. 1868-9, c. 8, which concerned matters of construction and revocation; *An Act to amend the law respecting the powers of Executors and Administrators*, S.O. 1869, c. 18; and *An Act to further amend the law relating to Property and Trusts*, S.O. 1871-2, c. 15.
49 S.O. 1873, c. 20.
50 7 Will. 4 & 1 Vict., c. 26.
51 R.S.O. 1990, c. S.26.
52 S.C. 1849, c. 197, s. 12.
53 C.S.U.C. 1859, c. 73.
54 C.S.U.C. 1859, c. 85.
55 S.O. 1884, c. 19.

Since forfeiture and escheat for the commission of a felony have been abolished[56] this disability no longer exists.

4. *Minority*: As regards wills of real property, the age was always 21 as in England and this principle was adopted in Upper Canada in 1792. However, as regards a will of personalty, the old English ecclesiastical law referred to above, applied. This was changed in England by the *Wills Act* of 1837, but the age was not changed to 21 in Ontario until the *Wills Act* of 1873,[57] and then only for wills made after December 31, 1873. The age of majority was changed to 18 by the *Age of Majority and Accountability Act*.[58]

5. *Unsoundness of mind*: This, in addition to minority, is the only other disability that survives.

Regarding nuncupative and privileged wills, you should note that the former were originally valid in Upper Canada under the *Probate and Surrogate Courts Act*,[59] which repeated substantially the provisions of the *Statute of Frauds*[60] in this respect. However, the *Surrogate Courts Act*[61] restricted such wills to soldiers in actual military service and mariners or seamen while at sea. This provision was continued by the *Wills Act*, 1873[62] and by subsequent revisions. In 1919, by *An Act to Amend the Wills Act*,[63] it was declared that the privilege of soldiers, mariners and seamen to dispose of their personal estate by nuncupative will had always applied to such persons even though they were under 21, and the privilege was extended to their real estate as well. By the *Statute Law Amendment Act*, 1939 (No. 2)[64] the privilege was extended to cover members of all the branches of the armed forces. Finally, by *An Act to amend the Wills Act*,[65] nuncupative wills were abolished completely, but privileged wills (that is, wills made in writing signed by the testator without further formality) were continued for members of the armed forces, mariners and seamen.

(ii) *Succession Law Reform*

A major and comprehensive reform of the law of testate and intestate succession took place in Ontario with the enactment of the *Succession Law Reform Act, 1977*.[66] It came into force on March 31, 1978, together with two concomitant

---

56 *Criminal Code*, S.C. 1892, c. 29, s. 965. See now *Criminal Code*, R.S.C. 1985, c. C-46, s. 6(1)(b).
57 S.O. 1873, c. 20, s. 6.
58 S.O. 1971, c. 98, s. 4 and Sched., para. 36; see now R.S.O. 1990, c. A.7; and see *Succession Law Reform Act*, R.S.O. 1990, c. S.26, s. 8.
59 S.U.C. 1793, c. 8, ss. 7-9.
60 29 Car. 2, c. 3.
61 S.U.C. 1858, c. 93, s. 61.
62 S.O. 1873, c. 20, s. 9.
63 S.O. 1919, c. 29, s. 1.
64 S.O. 1939 (2nd Sess.) c. 11, s. 5(2).
65 S.O. 1942, c. 40.
66 S.O. 1977, c. 40; now R.S.O. 1990, c. S.26.

statutes, the *Children's Law Reform Act, 1977*,[67] and the *Family Law Reform Act, 1978*.[68]

The *Succession Law Reform Act, 1977* was a combination of the *Wills Act*,[69] the *Devolution of Estates Act*,[70] the *Survivorship Act*,[71] and the *Dependants' Relief Act*.[72] It repealed those statutes except for the administration of estates provisions in the *Devolution of Estates Act*.[73] In addition, the *Succession Law Reform Act, 1977* contained certain provisions respecting the designation of beneficiaries of interests in pension funds. It also made minor changes in the *Compensation for Victims of Crime Act, 1971*,[74] and the *Perpetuities Act*.[75]

The *Succession Law Reform Act, 1977* implemented the reports of the Ontario Law Reform Commission relating to wills,[76] and international wills.[77] In addition, it adopted various principles recommended by the Commission in its reports on children,[78] support obligations,[79] and family property.[80] The enactment of this legislation made the law of succession in Ontario more uniform with the law in the other common law provinces, most of which had reformed their law of succession earlier.

The major changes effected by the *Succession Law Reform Act, 1977* were:

1. Illegitimate children were treated on the same basis as legitimate children.
2. Holograph wills were allowed.
3. The uniform law on the form of an international will was adopted.
4. The rules respecting survivorship were changed to conform to the *Uniform Survivorship Act*.[81]
5. The spouses' preferential share on intestacy was increased to $75,000 and the right to a preferential share was extended to partial intestacies in certain cases.
6. Curtesy was abolished.

---

67 S.O. 1977, c. 41; now R.S.O. 1990, c. C.12.
68 S.O. 1978, c. 2; consolidated as R.S.O. 1980, c. 152, rep. S.O. 1986, c. 4, s. 71(1), except the title and ss. 27(1), 69, 70 and 71. However s. 71(2) repealed s. 27(1) and s. 71(4) repealed the title and substituted therefor: *Dower and Miscellaneous Abolition Act*, which was not subsequently consolidated, but remains in effect.
69 R.S.O. 1970, c. 499.
70 R.S.O. 1970, c. 129.
71 R.S.O. 1970, c. 454.
72 R.S.O. 1970, c. 126.
73 The remaining portion of this Act was renamed *Estates Administration Act*. See now R.S.O. 1990, c. E.22.
74 S.O. 1971, c. 51, now R.S.O. 1990, c. C.24.
75 R.S.O. 1970, c. 343; now R.S.O. 1990, c. P.9.
76 *Report on the Proposed Adoption in Ontario of the Uniform Wills Act* (1978).
77 *Report on the International Convention Providing a Uniform Law on the Form of an International Will* (1974).
78 *Report on Family Law, Part III, Children* (1973).
79 *Report on Family Law, Part VI, Support Obligations* (1975).
80 *Report on Family Law, Part IV, Family Property Law* (1974).
81 See Uniform Law Conference, *Uniform Acts of the Uniform Law Conference of Canada* (1978), p. 46-1.

7. The distributive shares of surviving spouses on intestacy were equalized and spouses were allowed to take to the exclusion of next of kin when there are no issue.
8. Dependants' relief was extended to intestacy and the classes of persons who may make a claim was enlarged, while the effect of the conduct of spouses upon their claims was equalized.
9. The estate against which a claim can be made for support was enlarged to include, *inter alia*, revocable *inter vivos* trusts and *donationes mortis causa*.

The *Children's Law Reform Act, 1977*[82] abolished the status of illegitimacy and treated persons born outside marriage on the same basis as those born within marriage. This Act further contained presumptions of paternity and provided means whereby paternity may be proved.

The *Family Law Reform Act*[83] abolished dower and replaced it with certain rights to family property, rights in the matrimonial home and inter-spousal obligations of support. In 1986 a further major reform took place in family law and succession when the *Family Law Act, 1986*[84] was enacted. It repealed the *Family Law Reform Act*[85] except for certain sections and renamed that statute the *Dower and Miscellaneous Abolition Act*.[86]

The *Family Law Act, 1986* provides for a deferred equalization claim of spouses' net family properties, both on marriage breakdown and on death. In the latter situation a surviving spouse may elect to take one-half the difference between the respective net family properties of the two spouses if the net family property of the deceased is greater than that of the surviving spouse. The election is in lieu of the survivor's rights under the deceased spouse's will or intestacy. The nature and effect of this legislation is discussed is a separate chapter.

(iii) *Court Reform*

A general reform of the court structure and an amalgamation of the courts took place in Ontario in 1989,[87] followed by further changes in 1996, which renamed the courts.[88] In Ontario there now exist the Court of Appeal for Ontario and the Court of Ontario. The latter consists of two divisions, the Superior Court of Justice

---

82 S.O. 1977, c. 41; now R.S.O. 1990, c. C.12.
83 R.S.O. 1980, c. 152, rep. S.O. 1986, c. 4, s. 71(1), except the title and ss. 27(1), 69, 70 and 71. However, s. 71(2) repealed s. 27(1) and s. 71(4) repealed the title and substituted therefor: *Dower and Miscellaneous Abolition Act*, which was not subsequently consolidated, but remains in effect.
84 S.O. 1986, c. 4; now R.S.O. 1990, c. F.3.
85 *Supra.*
86 R.S.O. 1980, c. 152, renamed by S.O. 1986, c. 4, s. 71(4), not subsequently consolidated.
87 By the *Courts of Justice Amendment Act*, S.O. 1989, c. 55. See now *Courts of Justice Act*, R.S.O. 1990, c. C.43, as amended, ss. 2, 10, 34.
88 By the *Courts Improvement Act, 1996*, S.O. 1996, c. 25, Part IV. The changes took effect on April 19, 1999.

and the Ontario Court of Justice.[89] The 1989 legislation abolished the surrogate courts[90] and conferred their jurisdiction upon what is now the Superior Court of Justice.[91] The Superior Court of Justice has all the jurisdiction, power and authority historically exercised by courts of common law and equity in England and Ontario.[92] Similar amalgamations took place in other provinces. This is discussed in the next chapter.

(iv) *Estate Administration Law Reform*

In 1991 the Ontario Law Reform Commission published its *Report on the Administration of Estates of Deceased Persons*.[93] In it the Commission recommended wire-ranging reform of the law of administration of estates. Some of the recommendations were implemented by the enactment of a regulation,[94] which added Rules 74 and 75 to the *Rules of Civil Procedure*.[95] These are the new rules governing the administration of estates. The regulation also adds new forms for use in the administration of estates. The new rules adopt the new terminology recommended by the Ontario Law Reform Commission. This is somewhat strange, since the statutes governing estate administration have not yet been changed and, therefore, continue to employ the old terminology. These changes are discussed in the next chapter.

2. CONSTITUTIONAL ISSUES IN SUCCESSION

Until the 1970s, it was rare for a statute to confer any rights on a common law partner. Beginning in that decade, statutes began to confer rights of support on the "common law spouse," both *inter vivos* and on death. Typically, the statute would define the term as a person with whom the deceased had been cohabiting for two or three years, or in a relationship of some permanence if they were the parents of a child. The statutes were understood to refer only to two persons of

---

89 Until 1989, the Supreme Court of Ontario consisted of the Court of Appeal and the High Court of Justice. The latter was the superior court of justice for the province. In addition there were the county and district courts and the provincial courts. The 1989 reforms amalgamated the county and district courts into the superior court. The Court of Appeal became a separate court and the other courts were coupled together as the Ontario Court of Justice. It had two divisions, the Ontario Court (General Division) and the Ontario Court (Provincial Division). By the 1996 legislation, the former was renamed the Superior Court of Justice and the latter the Ontario Court of Justice.

90 *Court Reform Statute Law Amendment Act*, S.O. 1989, c. 56, s. 48(1).

91 *Ibid.*, s. 48(10), repealing and substituting s. 26 of the *Surrogate Courts Act*, R.S.O. 1980, c. 491. Section 48(25) of the 1989 Act renamed the latter Act the *Estates Act*. See now R.S.O. 1990, c. E.21, s. 7.

92 *Courts of Justice Act*, R.S.O. 1990, c. C.43, s. 11.

93 Ontario Law Reform Commission (1991).

94 O. Reg. 484/94, effective Jan. 1, 1995.

95 R.R.O. 1990, Reg. 194.

the opposite sex. However, common law spouses were not accorded succession rights. Of course, it was always possible for the deceased to make provision for a partner by will, but partners had no such right on the deceased's intestacy. On their partner's intestacy, or if the partner did not provide for them, adequately or at all, they had to resort to the doctrines of resulting and constructive trust to obtain redress, or to their statutory right to apply for support.

This began to change in the 1990s. Partners of the deceased, both of the same and opposite sex began to bring actions to seek access to the deceased's pension and to the deceased's estate. The basis of these actions was that partners were being discriminated against in violation of the equality provisions of s. 15 of the *Canadian Charter of Rights and Freedoms*. In *Miron v. Trudell*[96] the Supreme Court of Canada held that the exclusion of common law partners from accident and loss of income benefits conferred on spouses under the *Insurance Act*[97] was discriminatory and the court extended those benefits to common law spouses. In *M. v. H.*[98] the court held that the exclusion of same-sex partners from the *inter vivos* support provisions conferred on spouses and common-law spouses under Part III of the Ontario *Family Law Act*[99] was discriminatory. In consequence, Ontario statutes were amended to include common law spouses and same-sex partners.[100] The amendments conferred pension and support benefits and various other rights on common law spouses and same-sex partners, but did not confer succession rights. At the federal level a number of statutes were also amended to confer similar benefits on common law spouses and same-sex partners.[101] Similarly, in Quebec, *An Act to Amend Various Legislative Provisions Concerning De Facto Spouses*[102] extended to same-sex spouses all the rights and obligations of opposite-sex *de facto* spouses.[103]

Subsequently, in *Walsh v. Bona*,[104] the Nova Scotia Court of Appeal held that provisions of the *Matrimonial Property Act*,[105] which entitle spouses to a division of assets on a breakdown of marriage (and on death), discriminated against common law spouses. In *Watch v. Watch*[106] the Saskatchewan Court of Queen's Bench held that s. 5 of the *Matrimonial Property Act, 1997*,[107] which permits a spouse to apply for an order granting absolute possession of the family home, discriminated against common law spouses. In *Ferguson v. Armbrust*[108] the Saskatchewan Court of Queen's Bench held that the exclusion of common law

---

96 [1995] 2 S.C.R. 418, 124 D.L.R. (4th) 693.
97 R.S.O. 1980, c. 218, ss. 231, 233.
98 [1999] 2 S.C.R. 3, 171 D.L.R. (4th) 577.
99 R.S.O. 1990, c. F.3.
100 See *Amendments Because of the Supreme Court of Canada Decision in M. v. H. Act, 1999*, S.O. 1999, c. 6.
101 See *Modernization of Benefits and Obligations Act*, S.C. 2000, c. 12.
102 S.Q. 1999, c. 14.
103 See Marilyn Roy, "Same-Sex Equality" (2000), 19 E.T. & P.J. 203.
104 (2000), 186 D.L.R. (4th) 50, additional reasons at (2000), 186 D.L.R. (4th) 50 at 83 (N.S. C.A.).
105 R.S.N.S. 1989, c. 275, s. 2(g).
106 (1999), 182 Sask. R. 237 (Q.B.).
107 S.S. 1997, c. M-6.11.
108 (2000), 187 D.L.R. (4th) 367 (Sask. Q.B.).

spouses from the right to share on their partner's intestacy and to apply for letters of administration is discriminatory. Finally, in *Grigg v. Berg Estate*,[109] in which a deceased partner had made a small provision for his common law spouse, the British Columbia Supreme Court held that s. 2 of the *Wills Variation Act*[110] discriminated against common law spouses because it permitted only spouses (and children) to bring an application to vary a will to seek support from the estate of the deceased partner.

Undoubtedly in response to this judicial activity, the British Columbia Legislature made amendments to a number of statutes to confer various rights on partners of the same or different sex.[111] To date, it is the only jurisdiction that has conferred the right on partners to inherit on the deceased partner's intestacy on the same basis as a spouse. It may be expected that other provinces will follow suit.[112] British Columbia did not, however, amend Parts V and VI of the *Family Relations Act*,[113] which respectively deal with the division of family assets and pensions. Section 1(1) of the Act defines "spouse" for the purpose of those Parts as persons who are married to each other. However, the *Family Law Act, 1997*[114] goes further. It permits spouses and persons who have been cohabiting to make a claim for an equalizing payment on marriage breakdown and on the death of the first to die. The definition of "spouse" in s. 1 includes common law spouses and "cohabit" is defined "to live together in a conjugal relationship, whether within or outside marriage". While the definition does not say so expressly, it could include same-sex partners.

Common law partners and same-sex partners are usually entitled to make substitute decisions and give consent to medical treatment for their partners.[115]

Further Reading

Brian A. Schnurr, "Claims by Common Law Spouses and Same-Sex Partners against Estates" (1997), 16 E. & T.J. 22.

Helen H. Low, "Entitlements of an Unmarried Person on the Death of a Partner" (2000), 20 E.T. & P.J. 61.

---

109 (2000), 31 E.T.R. (2d) 214, suppl. reasons 32 E.T.R. (2d) 218, 186 D.L.R. (4th) 160 (B.C.S.C.).
110 R.S.B.C. 1996, c. 490.
111 *Definition of Spouse Amendment Act, 1999*, S.B.C. 1999, c. 29, ss. 4-15, am. *Definition of Spouse Amendment Act, 2000*, S.B.C. 2000, c. 24, s. 17, amending the *Estate Administration Act*, R.S.B.C. 1996, c. 122, and other statutes.
112 In Alberta the *Marriage Amendment Act, 2000*, S.A. 2000, c. 3, defines marriage as a marriage between a man and a woman and provides that the Act operates notwithstanding ss. 2 and 7-15 of the *Canadian Charter of Rights and Freedoms* and the *Alberta Bill of Rights*.
113 R.S.B.C. 1996, c. 128.
114 S.N.W.T. 1997, c. 18, Part III.
115 See, *e.g.*, *Substitute Decisions Act*, S.O. 1992, c. 30, s. 1(2), as amended; *Health Care Consent Act*, S.O. 1996, c. 6, Sched. A, s. 20(9).

3. SUCCESSION UNDER THE INDIAN ACT

The *Indian Act*[116] and the *Indian Estates Regulations*[117] contain a complete code governing testamentary matters of status Indians, that is, persons who are registered as Indians or entitled to be so registered and who are ordinarily resident on a reserve or on designated lands. This code supersedes customary law and provincial legislation dealing with succession.[118] It vests all jurisdiction in relation to "matters and causes testamentary" of deceased Indians in the Minister of Indian Affairs and Northern Development. An appeal from the Minister's decision lies only to the Federal Court.[119] The succession rights of other aboriginal peoples are governed by the law of their province of residence. However, non-status band members are treated as Indians for the purpose of ss. 51 and 52, which deal, respectively, with the estates of mentally incompetent Indians and the administration of the estates of Indian children who are minors. Further, the Minister has power under s. 4(3) of the Act to direct that ss. 42 to 52 apply to Indians not ordinarily resident on a reserve.

Under the code, the Minister may hold a will valid, or declare it void for duress or undue influence, lack of capacity, or uncertainty. The Minister may also avoid a will if it would cause hardship to the testator's dependants, disposes of land contrary to the interest of the band, or is against the public interest.[120] The Minister may appoint and remove an executor and administrator, distribute an estate, and approve a devise of reserve land. In addition, the Minister may make any order, direction, or finding that is necessary in connection with any testamentary matter. Alternatively, the Minister has power under s. 44 of the Act to consent to a provincial court (that, but for the Act, would have had jurisdiction) exercising jurisdiction over an Indian estate, including land on a reserve, and to direct that a matter be referred to such a provincial court.

The code applies only to matters testamentary. Hence, if the claim is concerned with contract, tort, or trust issues, even if they arise in respect of an estate, the provincial superior court has jurisdiction.[121]

Indians may make wills in the same manner as non-Indians. Section 45(2) of the Act contains a dispensing power. It provides that the Minister may accept as a will any written instrument signed by an Indian in which the Indian indicates his or her wishes or intention with respect to the disposition of the testator's property on death.[122] In *Re Bernard*[123] the court held that this provision allowed it to accept a will witnessed by the spouse of a beneficiary. By the same token,

---

116 R.S.C. 1985, c. I-5, ss. 45-52.
117 C.R.C. 1978, c. 954.
118 *Re Bernard* (1986), 23 E.T.R. 15, 29 D.L.R. (4th) 133 (N.B. Q.B.).
119 *Indian Act*, s. 47(1).
120 *Ibid.*, s. 46(1). The Minister's decisions are subject to judicial review: *Pronovost v. Canada (Minister of Indian Affairs and Northern Development)*, [1985] 1 F.C. 517.
121 See *Sampson v. Gosnell Estate* (1989), 32 E.T.R. 164 (B.C. C.A.), a case involving claims in contract, trust and restitution against the administrator of a estate of a deceased Indian.
122 See also s. 15 of the Regulations.
123 *Supra.*

the Minister or a court can reject a will that does not express the deceased's wishes because the deceased lacked capacity, did not know and approve of its contents, or because the will was executed under undue influence.[124] Section 45(3) provides that a will is not effective until approved by the Minister or until a court has granted probate of it. A will cannot dispose of land on the reserve to anyone not entitled to reside on the reserve. If no will exists, or if it has been declared invalid, the estate will be distributed among the deceased's family in accordance with the rules set out in s. 48 of the Act. These are very similar to those contained in the intestacy statutes of the common law provinces. However, they contain restrictions on dealing with land on the reserve in order to ensure that the reserve is maintained for the Indians that are entitled to reside on it.

Further Reading

Zandra L. Wilson, "Wills and Estates of Indians: The Indian Act in Review" (1994), 13 E. & T.J. 129.

4. TERMINOLOGY

The following terms are those traditionally used. However, I have also incorporated the new terms introduced by the new Ontario Rules, referred to above.

The law of *succession* concerns itself generally with all transfers of property from one generation to another. The subject includes wills and intestate succession. This casebook is concerned principally with those two topics. But the law of succession can also refer to will-like dispositions, sometimes referred to as will substitutes, such as *inter vivos* gifts and trusts, joint tenancy arrangements, pensions, life insurance, and the like. It may also include para-testamentary topics such as powers of attorney and living wills. And it may include the law of probate. This casebook also touches on those topics.

The law of *probate* is concerned with the validity of testamentary instruments and the administration of estates. The law of *wills* is concerned with the validity of dispositions that take effect on a person's death and are contained in his or her will.

A *will* is a written, typed or printed document made by the person who wishes to dispose of his or her property on death and executed in the manner prescribed by statute. It has effect only upon his or her death; during the person's lifetime the will is revocable, or ambulatory. The will is ambulatory in that (a) it is inoperative until the person dies, and (b) because, by statute, it passes property acquired by the person making the will between its date and the date of death.

Formerly, the word *testament* described a disposition of personalty on death, while the word *will* referred only to a disposition of realty. Since under our present law of succession real and personal property are largely assimilated, the more

---

124 *Johnson v. Pelkey* (1977), 17 E.T.R. (2d) 242 (B.C. S.C.).

common word, "will," suffices, whether the property being disposed of be realty, personalty, or both, although many wills still redundantly begin: "This is the last Will and Testament of . . . ."

A *codicil* is a testamentary document which supplements, explains or modifies a will bearing an earlier date. It is normally used only for minor amendments to the original document. If major changes are required it is customary to make a new will.

The person who makes a will is called a *testator* (f.: *testatrix*; pls.: *testators*, *testatrices*) and if the will is valid and is upheld after the testator's death, he or she is said to die *testate*. A testator may, in the will, *devise* his or her real property and *give* or *bequeath* his or her personalty. Thus a testamentary disposition of realty is called a *devise* and a testamentary disposition of personalty is a *bequest*, while a gift of money under a will is a *legacy*. There is, today, no substantive difference between these terms since real and personal property are treated the same way on death for the purpose of administration. It all passes to the personal representative who distributes it to the persons entitled under the will, after payment of debts and expenses. Formerly, only the personalty was dealt with in this fashion, while the realty passed directly to the heir-at-law. Nevertheless, the historical differences might be resorted to if it became important to do so in the construction of a particular will. The new Ontario Rules and Forms avoid the term "testator" and its variations. They speak simply of "the deceased person."

The *personal representative* of a deceased is his or her *executor* (f.: *executrix*; pls.: *executors, executrices*) or his or her administrator (f.: *administratrix*; pls.: *administrators, administratrices*). An *executor* is the person named in the will to administer the estate, who is willing to act as such. An *administrator* is the person appointed by the court to administer the estate of a person who dies *intestate*, that is, without a valid will. An *administrator cum testamento annexo* (with the will annexed) is appointed if there is a will but it does not name an executor, or if the person named is unable or unwilling to act, or has predeceased the testator. An *administrator de bonis non administratis* (that is, of the goods not administered) is the person appointed to complete the administration of an estate when the administrator has died or has been removed from his or her office. This person is called an *administrator cum testamento annexo de bonis non administratis* if there is a will. The new Ontario Rules abolish these several terms and use a new term, "estate trustee," instead. The new term has a number of variations, including "estate trustee with a will" and "estate trustee without a will."

If there is a will, the personal representative must, of course, distribute the property according to its terms. The personal representative may or may not prove the will in the court of probate, which is now the Superior Court of Justice. A personal representative who proves the will, receives *letters probate* if he or she is an executor, or *letters of administration (with the will annexed)* if he or she has not been named in the will. An administrator takes his or her authority from the appointment by the court, but an executor derives his or her authority directly from the will itself. The letters probate serve as evidence to the world of the executor's title. Letters of administration are also obtained on an intestacy. The new Ontario Rules abolish these terms and use the terms, "certificate of appointment of estate trustee with a will" and "certificate of appointment of estate trustee without a will."

On an intestacy, the persons who are entitled to share in the estate are determined by statute.[125] Formerly the realty descended directly to the heir-at-law, while the personal property was distributed among the next of kin. The heir has long since lost that preferred status and, as outlined above, must share with the other next of kin. The distinction between realty and personalty has virtually disappeared for the purpose of administering the estate since dower and curtesy have been abolished, although the distinction remains relevant for the purpose of determining the order in which property is liable to pay for the debts of the deceased.[126]

---

125 See, *e.g.*, *Succession Law Reform Act*, R.S.O. 1990, c. S.26, Part II.
126 See, *e.g.*, *Estates Administration Act*, R.S.O. 1990, c. E.22, ss. 3-5.

2

PROBATE AND ADMINISTRATION

1. INTRODUCTORY NOTE

Experience has shown that students in the traditional Wills course have difficulty understanding some of the concepts dealt with in such a course, because it does not concern itself with the practice and procedure of estate administration, except incidentally. This chapter is designed to alleviate the difficulty. The purpose is not to give a detailed account of the subject, but rather to familiarize the student with the function of the courts, the terminology, the statutory material and the procedure, in order to facilitate the study of the law of wills. For the sake of simplicity the material uses the Ontario statutes and procedure as a model. However, reference is also made to other jurisdictions. For further detail the student is referred to the standard texts on probate and administration.[1] The substantive law of probate is discussed in subsequent chapters.

As noted in chapter 1, a partial reform of the law of estate administration occurred in Ontario in 1994. The province adopted new Rules, Forms and Tariffs as of January 1, 1995 for estate administration.[2] These form part of the *Rules of Civil Procedure.*[3] The new Rules adopt a new terminology, but the various statutes

---

1 In particular, *Williams, Mortimer & Sunnucks on Executors, Administrators and Probate*, 17th ed. (London: Stevens & Sons Limited, 1993); *Macdonell, Sheard and Hull on Probate Practice*, 4th ed., by Rodney Hull and Ian M. Hull (Scarborough: Carswell, 1996); Ian M. Hull, *Challenging the Validity of Wills* (Scarborough: Carswell, 1996); *Widdifield on Executors' Accounts*, 5th ed. by Frederick D. Baker (Toronto: The Carswell Company Limited, 1967); Anne E.P. Armstrong, *Estate Administration: A Solicitor's Reference Manual*, loose leaf (Scarborough: Carswell, 1994); Brian A Schnurr, *Estate Litigation*, 2nd ed., loose leaf (Scarborough: Carswell, 1994). See also Ont. Law Reform Commission, *Report on Administration of Estates of Deceased Persons* (Toronto: Ont. Law Reform Commission, 1991); Nova Scotia Law Reform Commission, "Probate Reform in Nova Scotia" (1998), 18 E.T. & P.J. 53.

2 By O. Reg. 484/94.

3 R.R.O. 1990, Reg. 194.

governing estate administration have not yet been amended to make correspond-ing changes. To reflect the changes, while at the same time recognizing the retention of the original terms in other provinces, I have inserted the new terms in brackets after the familiar ones when appropriate. The new Ontario definitions, contained in Rule 74.01, are:

> "certificate of appointment of estate trustee" means letters probate, letters of administration or letters of administration with the will annexed;
> "estate trustee" means an executor, administrator or administrator with the will annexed;
> "estate trustee during litigation" means an administrator appointed pending an action;
> "estate trustee with a will" means an executor or an administrator with the will annexed;
> "estate trustee without a will" means an administrator;
> "objection to issuing of certificate of appointment" means a caveat;
> "will" includes any testamentary instrument of which probate or administration may be granted.

2. THE ROLE OF THE COURTS

As noted in chapter 1, formerly in England the ecclesiastical courts had juris-diction in matters of probate and administration with respect to estates involving personal property, whereas the common law courts had jurisdiction over the succession to freehold estates in land, including the probate of wills of real property. However, the Court of Chancery gradually assumed jurisdiction over various matters, in particular, the construction of wills. The remaining part of the jurisdiction of the ecclesiastical courts was transferred to the Court of Probate in 1857 and later to the Probate, Divorce and Admiralty Division of the High Court of Justice. This Division acquired jurisdiction over wills of real property by the *Land Transfer Act*, 1897[4] which vested the real property of a deceased person in his or her personal representative. A deceased person's personal property vested in his or her personal representative apart from statute. The Chancery Division of the High Court retained the jurisdiction formerly exercised by the chancery courts.[5]

In Ontario a similar development took place. The Probate Court and the sur-rogate courts established in 1793 were given the jurisdiction exercised by the ecclesiastical courts in England and this jurisdiction was transferred to the sur-rogate courts established in 1858. The latter courts acquired jurisdiction over wills of real property in 1886 by the *Devolution of Estates Act*,[6] which provided that all property of a deceased person would thenceforth vest in the deceased's personal representative. The testamentary jurisdiction exercised by the courts of chancery and the common law courts in England was exercised by the several superior courts in Upper Canada and Ontario and this jurisdiction was transferred to the Supreme Court of Ontario by the *Ontario Judicature Act* of 1881.[7]

---

4 60 & 61 Vict. c. 65, s.1.
5 See the previous chapter.
6 S.O. 1886, c. 22, s.3.
7 S.O. 1881, c. 5.

A general reform of the court structure and an amalgamation of the courts took place in Ontario in 1989,[8] followed by further changes in 1996, which renamed the courts.[9] In Ontario there now exist the Court of Appeal for Ontario and the Court of Ontario. The latter consists of two divisions, the Superior Court of Justice and the Ontario Court of Justice.[10] The 1989 legislation abolished the surrogate courts[11] and conferred their jurisdiction upon what is now the Superior Court of Justice.[12]

In British Columbia, Manitoba, Newfoundland, the Northwest Territories, Prince Edward Island, Saskatchewan and Yukon Territory, the superior court in the province, variously called the Supreme Court or the Court of Queen's Bench, also has probate jurisdiction, but in the other common law provinces there continue to be two courts having testamentary jurisdiction, namely, the superior court and an inferior court, referred to as the surrogate court in Alberta and the probate court in the New Brunswick and Nova Scotia.[13]

---

8   By the *Courts of Justice Amendment Act*, S.O. 1989, c. 55. See now *Courts of Justice Act*, R.S.O. 1990, c. C.43, as amended, ss. 2, 10, 34 (hereafter referred to without further citation).

9   By the *Courts Improvement Act, 1996*, S.O. 1996, c. 25, Part IV. The changes took effect on April 19, 1999.

10 Until 1989, the Supreme Court of Ontario consisted of the Court of Appeal and the High Court of Justice. The latter was the superior court of justice for the province. In addition there were the county and district courts and the provincial courts. The 1989 reforms amalgamated the county and district courts into the superior court. The Court of Appeal became a separate court and the other courts were coupled together as the Ontario Court of Justice. It had two divisions, the Ontario Court (General Division) and the Ontario Court (Provincial Division). By the 1996 legislation, the former was renamed the Superior Court of Justice and the latter the Ontario Court of Justice.

11 *Court Reform Statute Law Amendment Act*, S.O. 1989, c. 56, s. 48(1).

12 *Ibid.*, s. 48(10), repealing and substituting s. 26 of the *Surrogate Courts Act*, R.S.O. 1980, c. 491. Section 48(25) of the 1989 Act renamed the latter Act the *Estates Act*. See now R.S.O. 1990, c. E.21, s. 7. (The *Estates Act* is hereafter referred to without further citation).

13 The relevant statutes are:

    Alta: *Judicature Act*, R.S.A. 1980, c. J-1, s. 6(1), Court of Queen's Bench; *Surrogate Court Act*, R.S.A. 1980, c. S-28, s. 9, The Surrogate Court of Alberta.

    B.C.:   *Supreme Court Act*, R.S.B.C. 1996, c. 443, s. 9, Supreme Court of British Columbia; and see *Estate Administration Act*, R.S.B.C. 1996, c. 122, s. 1 — prior to 1990 the county court had concurrent jurisdiction up to a value of 25,000: *County Court Act*, R.S.B.C. 1979, c. 72, ss. 21, 38(a).

    Man: *Court of Queen's Bench Act*, S.M. 1988-89, c. 4, s. 32, Court of Queen's Bench; *Court of Queen's Bench Surrogate Practice Act* R.S.M. 1987, c. C290, s. 6.

    N.B.:   *Judicature Act*, R.S.N.B. 1973, c. J-2, s. 9(1), Court of Queen's Bench of New Brunswick; *Probate Courts Act*, S.N.B. 1982, c. P-17.1, s. 2(1), Probate Court of New Brunswick.

    Nfld.:   *Judicature Act*, R.S.N. 1990, c. J-4, s. 3, Supreme Court of Newfoundland; Part VI confers jurisdiction over probate and administration to the trial division of this court.

    N.W.T.:*Judicature Act*, R.S.N.W.T. 1988, c. J-1, ss. 3, 9, 10, Supreme Court of the Northwest Territories.

    N.S.:   *Judicature Act*, R.S.N.S. 1989, c. 240, s. 4, Supreme Court of Nova Scotia; *Probate Act*, R.S.N.S. 1989, c. 354, s.109, courts of probate.

    P.E.I.:   *Supreme Court Act*, R.S.P.E.I. 1988, c. S-10, s. 2, Supreme Court of Prince Edward Island; s. 15(1) confers jurisdiction upon the Estates Division to deal with matters

In jurisdictions where the two courts have jurisdiction, the superior court is charged with the interpretation of wills, while the surrogate or probate courts are concerned with probate and administration. However, there is some overlap in jurisdiction. In jurisdictions where only the superior court exists, it has jurisdiction over both probate and interpretation, but those jurisdictions remain distinct.

Section 11 of the *Courts of Justice Act* provides that the Superior Court of Justice is a superior court of record having civil and criminal jurisdiction with the same jurisdiction as was historically exercised by courts of common law and equity in England and Ontario. This section derives from s. 13 of the *Judicature Act*[14] which provided that all jurisdiction vested in the Supreme Court on December 31, 1912 should be exercised by the High Court in the name of the Supreme Court, except the jurisdiction theretofore vested in the Court of Appeal and in the Divisional Courts of the High Court.

The testamentary jurisdiction of the High Court on December 31, 1912 was defined by section 38 of the *Judicature Act* as consolidated in 1897[15] as follows:

> **38.** The High Court shall have jurisdiction to try the validity of last wills and testaments, whether the same respect real or personal estate, and whether probate of the will has been granted or not, and to pronounce such wills and testaments to be void for fraud and undue influence or otherwise, in the same manner and to the same extent as the Court has jurisdiction to try the validity of deeds and other instruments.

Although s. 38 was repealed by the *Judicature Act* of 1913,[16] the testamentary jurisdiction of the High Court as defined therein continues in the Superior Court of Justice by virtue of s. 11(2) of the *Courts of Justice Act*.[17]

The jurisdiction of the Superior Court of Justice in probate matters is not inherent, but is entirely statutory. Mr. Justice Middleton said of its predecessor, the High Court of Justice,[18]

> [T]he High Court has no testamentary jurisdiction save that conferred by the Surrogate Courts Act[19] in matters commenced in the Surrogate Court and transferred to the High Court, and in actions to set aside wills in which jurisdiction is conferred by sec. 38 of the Judicature Act.[20] The

---

under the *Probate Act*, R.S.P.E.I. 1988, c. P-21, ss. 1, 2.

Sask.:   *Queen's Bench Act*, R.S.S. 1978, c. Q-1, as amended, s. 12(1), Court of Queen's Bench for Saskatchewan; the *Queen's Bench (Surrogate Procedures) Amendment Act*, S.S. 1992, c. 62, repealed the *Surrogate Court Act*, R.S.S. 1978, c. S-66, and conferred probate jurisdiction on the Court of Queen's Bench.

Yk.:   *Supreme Court Act*, R.S.Y. 1986, c. 165, s. 4, Supreme Court of the Yukon Territory.

14 R.S.O. c. 1980, c. 223, repealed by the *Courts of Justice Act*, S.O. 1984, c. 11, s. 187. The section derived from the *Judicature Act*, S.O. 1913, c. 19, s. 12.

15 R.S.O. 1897, c. 51. Section 38 was first enacted as the *Court of Chancery Amendment Act*, S.C. 1849, c. 64, s. 10. The jurisdiction of the Court of Chancery was conferred on the High Court by the *Judicature Act*, S.O. 1881, c. 5, s. 9.

16 *Supra*, s. 125 and Schedule.

17 *Giffen v. Simonton* (1920), 47 O.L.R. 49 (C.A.).

18 *I.e.*, the trial division of the former Supreme Court of Ontario.

19 10 Edw. 7, c. 21, ss. 32, 33.

20 R.S.O 1897, c. 51.

Court also has the power to determine the title to land possessed by the Courts of equity and law upon the issue *devisavit vel non*.[21]

The following summary gives an outline (not necessarily complete) of the testamentary and quasi-testamentary jurisdiction of the Superior Court of Justice:

Probate Jurisdiction

1. Granting letters probate and letters of administration [certificates of appointment of estate trustee]. This includes, *inter alia*, determining
   (a) whether the will was properly executed and attested;
   (b) whether the testator had the necessary capacity and that there was no influence or fraud;
   (c) that the testator knew and approved of the contents of the will;
   (d) that there are no mistakes on the face of the will and if necessary, expunging the mistakes;
   (e) that any alterations were properly executed and attested;
   (f) that a testamentary gift is void because the will was attested by the beneficiary or his or her spouse;[22]
   (g) whether any document has been incorporated by reference;
   (h) whether the will or any part thereof has been revoked; and
   (i) proof of death, including survivorship.
2. Revoking letters probate and letters of administration [certificates of appointment of estate trustee].
3. Appointing executors and administrators.
4. Passing of accounts of trustees, guardians and personal representatives [estate trustees] and awarding compensation to them on the passing of accounts.
5. Applications by dependants of a deceased person for support.[23]

Matters relating to the custody, access to or guardianship of a child when an issue concerning the same arises in a proceeding in respect of an estate are heard by the Family Court in those areas of the province where that court has jurisdiction. Otherwise, the Superior Court of Justice has jurisdiction.[24]

---

21 *Mutrie v. Alexander* (1911), 23 O.L.R. 396 at 401. And see *Re Hoover and Nunn* (1911), 2 O.W.N. 1215.
22 See *Succession Law Reform Act*, R.S.O. 1990, c. S.26, s. 12.
23 Under the *Succession Law Reform Act*, R.S.O. 1990, c. S.26, Part V.
24 *Children's Law Reform Act*, R.S.O. 1990, c. C.12, ss. 61ff (hereafter referred to without further citation). In other proceedings under this Act the Family Court if its geographical jurisdiction extends to that part of the province, or the Superior Court of Justice or the Ontario Court of Justice has jurisdiction: *Children's Law Reform Act*, s. 3, am. 1996, c. 25, s. 3; *Courts of Justice Act*, s. 21.8.

Common Law and Equity Jurisdiction

1. Applications to construe wills, including the determination of the validity of testamentary gifts.[25]
2. Actions to try the validity of wills.[26]
3. Actions for legacies or the distribution of residues.
4. Proceedings regarding the disposition of a minor's property.[27]
5. Declaring a person to be an absentee and appointing a committee of the estate.[28]
6. Applications for declarations of sufficiency of proof of death and of presumption of death for insurance purposes.[29]
7. Removal of personal representatives [estate trustees] and appointment of replacements.[30]
8. Applications for the opinion, advice and direction of the court on questions concerning the management or administration of the estate.[31]

3. PROBATE JURISDICTION OF THE COURT

The *Estates Act* defines the probate jurisdiction of the Ontario Court (General Division) as follows:

> **7.** (1) An application for a grant of probate or letters of administration shall be made to the Ontario Court (General Division) and shall be filed in the office for the county or district in which the testator or intestate had at the time of death a fixed place of abode.
>
> (2) If the testator or intestate had no fixed place of abode in Ontario or resided out of Ontario at the time of death, the application shall be filed in the office for the county or district in which the testator or intestate had property at the time of death.
>
> (3) In other cases the application for probate or letters of administration may be filed in any office.

Whether the court has jurisdiction to grant probate or letters of administration depends in part upon the rules of conflict of laws. Indeed, questions concerning conflict of laws may arise when a grant is being made, particularly if the will was

---

25 *Rules of Civil Procedure*, R.R.O. 1990, Reg. 194, R. 14.05(3)(a), (d) (hereafter in this chapter referred to without further citation). The Superior Court of Justice has two jurisdictions. In its interpretative jurisdiction it may construe a will to determine the testator's meaning. In its probate jurisdiction the court has a limited jurisdiction to interpret wills. Thus, for example, the court may have to interpret a will in the context of a question involving incorporation by reference, mistake, or passing of accounts. However, the parties are not estopped from raising the same matter subsequently before the court on a question of interpretation: *Re Tuckett*, [1954] O.R. 973, [1955] 1 D.L.R. 643.
26 *Courts of Justice Act*, s. 11(2).
27 *Children's Law Reform Act*, s. 59; *Rules of Civil Procedure*, R. 67.
28 *Absentees Act*, R.S.O. 1990, c. A.3.
29 *Insurance Act*, R.S.O. 1990, c. I-8, ss. 208-9.
30 *Trustee Act*, R.S.O. 1990, c. T.23, s. 37 (hereafter referred to without further citation); *Rules of Civil Procedure*, R. 14.05(3)(c).
31 *Trustee Act*, s. 60; *Rules of Civil Procedure*, R. 14.05(3)(a).

made in another jurisdiction. This topic is beyond the scope of this chapter.[32] However, you should note that s. 2 of the *Estates Administration Act*,[33] provides that all real and personal property that is vested in a person (except joint property) vests on the person's death in his or her personal representative in trust to pay the debts and to distribute the residue in accordance with law, does not apply to personal property, except chattels real, of a person who at the time of his or her death is domiciled outside Ontario.[34]

Another office involved in the administration of estates is the office of the Estate Registrar for Ontario. This office, formerly called the office of the Surrogate Clerk for Ontario, was created in 1971. Every registrar is required every month to send a list to the Estate Registrar for Ontario of the grants of probate and administration [certificates of appointment of estate trustee], and of revocations of grants,[35] and further to send him or her a notice of every application for a grant[36] and of every caveat [objection to issuing of certificate of appointment][37] upon receipt. Caveats against the grant of probate or administration may also be lodged with the Estate Registrar for Ontario.[38]   The purpose of the office of the Estate Registrar is to act as a clearinghouse and to prevent concurrent grants being issued from different court offices.[39]

While it is customary for a testator or the testator's solicitor to retain the executed will for safekeeping, you should note that the Act provides that the office of each local registrar is a depository for the wills of living persons given to him or her for safekeeping.[40] Details of probate practice and procedure are contained in the *Rules of Civil Procedure*.[41]

4. OBTAINING GRANTS

(a) Purpose of Grants

The question is often asked: Is it necessary to obtain probate or letters of administration [certificate of appointment of estate trustee] in each case? The

---

32 See the *Succession Law Reform Act*, R.S.O. 1990, c. S.26, ss. 34-41; *Macdonell, Sheard and Hull on, Probate Practice*, 4th ed. by Rodney Hull and Ian M. Hull (Scarborough: Carswell, 1996), ch. 16.

33 R.S.O. 1990, c. E.22 (hereafter in this chapter referred to as the "*Estates Administration Act*" without further citation).

34 *Ibid.*, s. 2(3).

35 *Estates Act*, s. 4.

36 *Ibid.*, s. 16.

37 *Ibid.*, s. 22.

38 *Ibid.*, s. 21.

39 See *ibid.*, ss. 17, 22.

40 *Ibid.*, s. 2.

41 These rules were formerly called the *Rules of Practice - Surrogate Court*, R.R.O. 1980, Reg. 925, s. 48 and later as the Rules of the Ontario Court (General Division) in Estate Proceedings, R.R.O. 1990, Reg. 197, as am. O. Reg. 398/91. The latter were repealed as of January 1, 1995 by O. Reg. 485/94 and were replaced by new Rules, Forms and Tariffs under the *Rules of Civil Procedure*. See Rules 74 and 75.

answer is, no. Generally, if the estate is small and uncomplicated, if there is no dispute as to the validity of the will (if any) and if the members of the family can agree to the division of the property, it is not necessary to obtain a grant. This is so also when land is involved which was held in joint tenancy by the deceased and a surviving joint tenant or tenants, and similarly in the case of a joint bank account. However, it will be impossible to deal with many other types of property without a grant to a person authorized to deal with it, that is, the personal representative [estate trustee]. Real property other than that held in joint tenancy, registered securities, bank accounts, choses in action in respect of which action must be brought or for which a receipt must be given, all fall in this category.[42]

Before the grant of probate or of administration is made, the personal representatives must pay the probate fee or tax. The amount of this fee or tax has increased dramatically in recent years. For this reason, testators now use a variety of devices to avoid payment.[43] Once such device is the multiple will. One will disposes of assets for which probate is required, while the other disposes of assets for which probate is not required, such as shares in private corporations. A question that has arisen is whether the courts have jurisdiction over unprobated wills. The question has been answered affirmatively. In *Re Silver*[44] the court held it had jurisdiction to pass the estate accounts under the unprobated will. Similarly, in *Carmichael v. Carmichael Estate*[45] the court held that it had jurisdiction to remove executors who had taken steps to administer the estate, but who had not taken out probate.

The purpose of a grant, therefore, is to invest a person with lawful authority to deal with the estate.[46] This entails in outline: getting in the assets and administering them, bringing and defending actions on behalf of the estate, paying all lawful expenses, taxes, debts and other claims, setting up any trusts directed by the will and, finally, distributing the balance to those entitled under the will or on an intestacy, or both, as the case may be.

Section 30 of the *Estates Act* provides:

> **30.** After a grant of administration, no person, other than the administrator or executor, has power to sue or prosecute any action or otherwise act as executor of the deceased as to the property comprised in or affected by such grant of administration until such administration has been recalled or revoked.

---

42 However, there is provision in Ontario for registration of an unprobated will on title under s. 53 of the *Registry Act*, R.S.O. 1990, c. R.20. If this is done, the executor has power to deal with the property and cannot be forced to obtain probate. See *Prinsen v. Balkwill* (1991), 41 E.T.R. 110 (Ont. Gen. Div.).

43 See the discussion of these devices in ch. 4, *infra*.

44 (1999), 31 E.T.R. (2d) 256 (Ont. S.C.J.).

45 (2000), 46 O.R. (3d) 630, 31 E.T.R. (2d) 33, 184 D.L.R. (4th) 175 (S.C.J.).

46 Note, however, that an executor derives authority, not from the grant, but from the will. The grant is merely evidence of the executor's authority.

(b) Time Lapse

There is invariably a time lapse between the date of death and the appointment of personal representatives [estate trustees]. A question that sometimes arises is: Who has authority to deal with the assets in the interim?

Section 2 of the *Estates Administration Act* provides:

> **2.** (1) All real and personal property that is vested in a person without a right in any other person to take by survivorship, on the person's death, whether testate or intestate and despite any testamentary disposition, devolves to and becomes vested in his or her personal representative from time to time as trustee for the persons by law beneficially entitled thereto, and, subject to the payment of the person's debts and so far as such property is not disposed of by deed, will, contract or other effectual disposition, it shall be administered, dealt with and distributed as if it were personal property not so disposed of.
>
> (2) This section applies to property over which a person executes by will a general power of appointment as if it were property vested in the person.
>
> (3) This section does not apply to estates tail or to the personal property, except chattels real, of a person who, at the time of death, is domiciled out of Ontario.

The section ensures that all property, including real property which formerly descended to the heir-at-law, vests in the personal representative [estate trustee]. But what happens until one is appointed?

When an executor [estate trustee] is appointed there is no hiatus in ownership, since the executor takes his or her authority, not from the grant of probate, but from the will and, thus, directly from the testator. The grant of probate is only evidence (really, the only evidence) which a court and others dealing with the executor will recognize that a person has authority to administer the assets of the deceased. For this reason, while an executor can do many acts of office before obtaining a grant the executor cannot obtain judgment before that time, although he or she can commence an action. Similarly, no action can be maintained against a named executor unless he or she has obtained a grant of probate.

The title to the real and personal property of the testator, therefore, vests in the executor from the moment of death. And with respect to land, the executor retains title until he or she conveys it, or until three years have passed, when title automatically passes to the person beneficially entitled to it, unless the personal representative has registered a caution against the title.[47]

When an administrator [estate trustee] is appointed, however, the situation is different. An administrator derives title solely under the grant and thus has no powers, except under the doctrine of relation back. This doctrine only permits the person who is in due course appointed administrator to bring actions, or otherwise to protect or preserve the estate from wrongful injury. Thus the title of the administrator, when appointed, is said to relate back to the death of the deceased for this limited purpose.

Until the appointment of an administrator, it is probable that the personal property and the real property (since the *Estates Administration Act* abolishes the distinction between the two for the purposes of administration) vests in the judge

---

47 *Estates Administration Act*, ss. 9-13.

of the court have jurisdiction over the estate, who delegates it to the administrator by the grant.[48]

(c) Types of Executors and Administrators [Estate Trustees]

(i) Executor [Estate Trustee with a Will]

If the deceased left a valid will and has appointed one or more executors, the court appoints him, her or them by the letters probate [certificate of appointment of estate trustee] as executor or executors [estate trustee(s) with a will] unless the named person or persons renounce (that is, decline to act), or is or are disqualified. A person is disqualified from acting as an executor during the person's minority. If a minor is appointed sole executor, the grant will be made to the minor's guardians until the minor attains the age of majority. Section 26 of the *Estates Act* provides:

> **26.** (1) Where a minor is sole executor, administration with the will annexed shall be granted to the guardian of the minor or to such other person as the court thinks fit, until the minor has attained the full age of eighteen years, at which time, and not before, probate of the will may be granted to the minor.
>
> (2) The person to whom such administration is granted has the same powers as an administrator has by virtue of an administration granted to an administrator during minority of the next-of-kin.

Similarly, persons of unsound mind are excluded, as are persons who are criminally responsible for the testator's death.[49] A person who has an interest adverse to a beneficiary, who is bankrupt, or who is serving a lengthy prison sentence[50] may be excluded.

However, the courts are not anxious to deny the named person the appointment. Thus, in *Re Leguia*,[51] Lord Wright said:

> There is no doubt at all that the passing over of an executor and granting administration to other parties is an unusual and extreme course, though it is within the discretion of the Probate Court; but to do so without citing the executor is indeed a most extreme course. I assume, and I think I rightly assume, that it is within the discretion of the Probate Judge to take this course if he is asked to do so and the circumstances are very unusual circumstances which make it desirable that this course should be taken.

Thus, for example, a named executor may be granted probate even if insolvent, at least if the testator knew of the insolvency when he or she made a will. However,

---

48 *Macdonell, Sheard and Hull on, Probate Practice*, 4th ed. by Rodney Hull and Ian M. Hull (Scarborough: Carswell, 1996), at p. 186.

49 See *Re Crippen*, [1911] P. 108.

50 However, a sentence of an indeterminate period of incarceration for a matter not related to the management or administration of property, is not a sufficient reason to pass over the named executor. See *Re Oughton Estate* (1991), 40 E.T.R. 246 (B.C.S.C.), a case involving an executor jailed for sexual assault.

51 [1936] L.J.P. 72 at 79 (C.A.).

the named executor will be passed over if he or she becomes bankrupt after the date of the will.[52]

While a person who is not resident in Ontario or elsewhere in the Commonwealth may be granted probate, he or she must normally give the like security as is required of an administrator.[53]

If a named executor does not apply for probate, the court may cite the executor to accept or refuse the grant [order to accept or refuse the appointment]. If the executor does not appear, his or her rights cease.[54] If the executor declines the appointment by renouncing, section 34 of the *Estates Act* provides:

> **34.** Where a person renounces probate of the will of which the person is appointed an executor, the person's rights in respect of the executorship wholly cease, and the representation to the testator and the administration of the testator's property, without any further renunciation, goes, devolves and is committed in like manner as if such person had not been appointed executor.

(ii) Administrator [Estate Trustee without a Will]

An administrator is the person appointed by the court by letters of administration [certificate of appointment of estate trustee] to administer the estate of a person who died intestate or who died testate, but who failed to name an executor, or the named executor cannot or will not act.

The persons entitled to the grant are prescribed by section 29 of the *Estates Act*:

> **29.** (1) Subject to subsection (3), where a person dies intestate or the executor named in the will refuses to prove the will, administration of the property of the deceased may be committed by the Ontario Court (General Division) to,
>
> (a) the person to whom the deceased was married immediately before the death of the deceased or person of the opposite sex or the same sex with whom the deceased was living in a conjugal relationship outside marriage immediately before the death;
> (b) the next-of-kin of the deceased; or
> (c) the person mentioned in clause (a) and the next-of-kin,
>
> as in the discretion of the court seems best, and where more persons than one claim the administration as next-of-kin who are equal in degree of kindred to the deceased, or where only one desires the administration as next-of-kin where there are more persons than one of equal kindred, the administration may be committed to such one or more of such next-of-kin as the court thinks fit.
>
> (2) Subject to subsection (3), where a person dies wholly intestate as to his or her property, or leaving a will affecting property but without having appointed an executor thereof, or an executor willing and competent to take probate and the persons entitled to administration, or a majority of such of them as are resident in Ontario, request that another person be appointed to be the

---

52 Macdonnell, Sheard and Hull, *supra*, at p. 155.
53 *Estates Act*, s. 6. *Cf. Re Diblee Estate* (1990), 37 E.T.R. 293 (N.B.C.A.).
54 *Estates Act*, s. 25.

administrator of the property of the deceased, or of any part of it, the right that such persons possessed to have administration granted to them in respect of it belongs to such person.

(3) Where a person dies wholly intestate as to his or her property, or leaving a will affecting property but without having appointed an executor thereof willing and competent to take probate, or where the executor was at the time of the death of such person resident out of Ontario, and it appears to the court to be necessary or convenient by reason of the insolvency of the estate of the deceased, or other special circumstances, to appoint some person to be the administrator of the property of the deceased, or of any part of such property, other than the person who if this subsection had not been enacted would have been entitled to the grant of administration, it is not obligatory upon the court to grant administration to the person who if this subsection had not be enacted would have been entitled to a grant thereof, but the court may appoint such person as it thinks fit upon his or her giving such security as it may direct, and every such administration may be limited as it thinks fit.

(4) A trust corporation may be appointed as administrator under subsection (2) or (3), either alone or jointly with another person.

The usual order of priority of entitlement to letters of administration [certificate of appointment of estate trustee without a will] is as follows:[55]

1. surviving spouse, common law spouse, or same-sex partner;
2. children;
3. grandchildren;
4. great-grandchildren or other lineal descendants;
5. father or mother;
6. siblings;
7. other next of kin in the same order as entitlement to an interest in the estate.

If there is a will, but there is no executor capable or willing to administer the estate, the person or persons who are named as beneficiaries under the will are entitled to apply for letters of administration with will annexed [certificate of appointment of estate trustee with a will]. Hence, the right to administration follows the right to the property.[56]

If a person with an inferior claim to a grant applies, those who have a superior claim to a grant of administration must renounce, or they must be cited (summoned) to show cause why the application should not be granted.[57]

The Act provides that administration shall not be granted to a person who does not reside in Ontario except in the case of resealing.[58] Moreover, the Act states that every person to whom a grant of letters of administration, including letters of administration with the will annexed, is given must give a bond to the Ac-

---

55 See Brian A. Schnurr, *The 1999 Annotated Ontario Estates Statutes* (Scarborough: Carswell, 1998), p.26 (revised). Thus, for example, the niece of the intestate's spouse is not entitled: *Re Butt* (1986), 53 O.R. (2d) 297 (Surr. Ct.). Similarly, the executrix of an intestate's sole heir is not entitled to letters of administration in the intestate's estate in her capacity as executrix, although she is if she is her testator's sole heir: *Re Clements Estate* (1998), 21 E.T.R. (2d) 269 (Sask. Q.B.).

56 See *Macdonnel, Sheard and Hull on Probate Practice*, 4th ed. by Rodney Hull and Ian M. Hull (Scarborough: Carswell, 1996), p. 240.

57 *Ibid.*, s. 13, and see *Rules of Civil Procedure*, R.74.05.

58 *Estates Act*, s. 5.

countant of the Ontario Court, unless otherwise provided by law,[59] in a penalty of double the value of the estate.[60] Trust corporations are not normally required to give a bond,[61] nor is the Government of Ontario or any of its agents required to do so.[62] A bond is also not required of a surviving spouse on an intestacy if the net value of the estate does not exceed the value of the preferential share ($200,000) and an affidavit is filed setting forth the debts of the estate.[63] Further, the judge may, in special circumstances, reduce the amount of, or dispense with the bond.[64] Similar disabilities apply in respect of the appointment of administrators as apply to the appointment of executors.

It has been pointed out that it is anomalous that common law spouses (and same sex partners) are entitled to a grant of administration when they have no interest in the estate if the deceased died intestate.[65] However, they are now being accorded rights to the estate. Thus, in *Ferguson v. Armbrust*[66] the court held that the exclusion of common law spouses from the right to apply for letters of administration and the denial of a right to inherit the deceased's intestate estate in the absence of issue in priority to the deceased's siblings, infringed the equality provisions of s. 15 of the *Canadian Charter of Rights and Freedoms*. Further, in British Columbia partners of the same or different sex have the right to apply for administration and to inherit on the death intestate of their partners.[67]

(iii) Administrator with Will Annexed [Estate Trustee with a Will]

An administrator with the will annexed[68] is a person appointed by the court to administer the estate of a person who has left a valid will but neglected to appoint an executor, or when the executor named has renounced, or is unable or unwilling to act, or has predeceased the testator.

---

59 *Ibid.*, s. 35.
60 *Ibid.*, s. 37(1).
61 *Loan and Trust Corporations Act*, R.S.O. 1990, c. L.25, s. 175(4).
62 *Estates Act*, s. 36(1).
63 *Ibid.*, s. 36(2), am. S.O. 1997, c. 23, s. 8(1).
64 *Ibid.*, s. 37(2).
65 See A[nne] E.P. A[rmstrong], "Application for Letters of Administration in Ontario: Affidavit Attesting to 'Common Law' Relationship" (1988), 9 E. & T.J. 86.
66 (2000), 187 D.L.R. (4th) 367 (Sask. Q.B.).
67 *Definition of Spouse Amendment Act, 1999*, S.B.C. 1999, c. 29, ss. 4-15, as amended by *Definition of Spouse Amendment Act, 2000*, S.B.C. 2000, c. 24, s. 17, amending the *Estate Administration Act*, R.S.B.C. 1996, c. 122, and other statutes.
68 Sometimes referred to as an administrator *cum testamento annexo*.

(iv) *Administrator* de Bonis Non Administratis *[Succeeding Estate Trustee without a Will]*

If an administrator dies, or is removed from office before his or her duties are completed, the court will appoint a new administrator of the property not yet administered with the above title.[69]

(v) *Administrator* de Bonis Non Administratis *with Will Annexed [Succeeding Estate Trustee with a Will]*

An administrator *de bonis non administratis* with the will annexed is the person appointed by the court to complete the administration of an estate when the sole or surviving executor dies intestate, or when the administrator with the will annexed dies, leaving part of the estate unadministered.[70]

If the sole or sole surviving executor of an estate, having proved the will, dies testate, having appointed an executor who is able and willing to act, the executorship under the original will devolves upon the latter when he or she proves the will, unless the original will provides otherwise, or unless the deceased executor appointed a separate executor for the original estate.

(vi) *Administrator Appointed Pending an Action*[71] *[Estate Trustee During Litigation]*

An administrator appointed pending an action is a person whom the court appoints to represent the estate when an action respecting the validity of the will or the right to representation is pending. The court will not normally appoint a person who has an interest in the outcome of the litigation.[72]

Section 28 of the *Estates Act* provides:

> **28.** Pending an action touching the validity of the will of a deceased person, or for obtaining, recalling or revoking any probate or grant of administration, the Ontario Court (General Division) has jurisdiction to grant administration in the case of intestacy and may appoint an administrator of the property of the deceased person, and the administrator so appointed has all the rights and powers of a general administrator, other than the right of distributing the residue of the property, and every such administrator is subject to the immediate control and direction of the court, and the court may direct that such administrator shall receive out of the property of the deceased such reasonable remuneration as the court considers proper.

---

69 *Cf. Rules of Civil Procedure*, R. 74.07.
70 *Ibid.*, R. 74.06.
71 Also known as an administrator *pendente lite*.
72 See *Salisbury v. Dell* (1993), 50 E.T.R. 19 (Ont. Gen. Div.). And see *Rules of Civil Procedure*, R. 74.10.

The duties of an administrator appointed pending an action continue until the action is completely disposed of. An administrator *pendente lite* is not entitled to distribute the estate.[73]

(vii) *Litigation Administrator*[74]

By statute, a personal representative may maintain an action for any tort, except libel and slander, committed against the deceased during his or her lifetime.[75] Similarly, a person wronged by the deceased may maintain an action for any tort, except libel and slander, against the deceased's personal representative. However, in the latter case, if no personal representative has been appointed, the court may appoint a litigation administrator to defend the action.[76]

Rule 9.02 of the *Rules of Civil Procedure* provides:

> **9.02**(1) Where it is sought to commence or continue a proceeding against the estate of a deceased person who has no executor or administrator, the court on motion may appoint a litigation administrator to represent the estate for the purposes of the proceeding.
>
> (2) An order in a proceeding to which a litigation administrator is a party binds or benefits the estate of the deceased person, but has no effect on the litigation administrator in a personal capacity, unless a judge orders otherwise.

(viii) *Executor* de Son Tort

An executor *de son tort* is a person who does not have the authority of a personal representative, but who intermeddles with the estate in such a way as to take upon himself or herself the function of an executor. In that capacity he or she has the obligations of a lawful personal representative and may be sued by a beneficiary or a creditor.[77]

(d) Special Types of Grants

(i) *Introduction*

The following is a list of grants made in special situations. The Ontario Rules do not address most of these specifically. However, since these grants have always been issued by probate and surrogate courts and the Superior Court of Justice has

---

73 *Cameron v. Twinn* (1999), 28 E.T.R. (2d) 173, 172 D.L.R. (4th) 156 (Alta. Surr. Ct.).

74 Also known as an administrator *ad litem*: *Courts of Justice Amendment Act*, S.O. 1989, c. 55, s. 160a.

75 *Trustee Act*, s. 38(1).

76 *Ibid.*, s. 38(2).

77 Concerning the rights of an executor *de son tort*, see generally *Charron v. Montreal Trust Co.*, [1958] O.R. 597, 15 D.L.R. (2d) 240 (C.A.); *Loewen Funeral Chapel Ltd. v. Yanz* (1999), 27 E.T.R. (2d) 269 (Man. Q.B.).

the jurisdiction historically exercised by courts of common law and equity in England and Ontario, it would appear that the court can continue to issue these grants.[78]

(ii) Cessate *Grants*

A cessate grant is made when the original grant of probate is issued for a limited time, for example, to an administrator during the minority of the named executor. When the child reaches the age of majority, he or she may then apply for a grant of probate, which is the cessate grant.

(iii) *Double Probate [Succeeding Estate Trustee with a Will]*

A double probate is granted when a named executor does not, for some reason, apply for probate and does not renounce and the original grant reserves to him or her the right to apply later. The later grant is the double probate.[79]

(iv) *Grants Save and Except*

Probate may be granted to a person who was appointed by the testator as executor of the estate except for a specific purpose or part of the estate, for which other executors, for example, literary executors, were appointed. In such a situation the general executor would receive a grant save and except the administration of the literary assets of the testator.

(v) Caetorum *Grants*

If a will appoints general executors and executors for a specific purpose and the latter apply first for a grant, the general executors would then receive a *caetorum* grant, that is, a grant of the rest of the estate. If the executors all apply together, only one grant will be made with their respective powers distinguished.

(vi) *Grants* ad Colligenda Bona

A grant *ad colligenda bona* may be made to a friend or creditor of the deceased when the person entitled to administration declines the appointment, or is abroad

---

78 See *Courts of Justice Act*, s. 11. *Cf. Macdonnel, Sheard and Hull on Probate Practice*, 4th ed. by Rodney Hull and Ian M. Hull (Scarborough: Carswell, 1996), pp. 248, 251. And see *Rules of Civil Procedure*, RR. 74.04 and 74.05.

79 See the former *Rules of the Ontario Court (General Division) in Estate Proceedings*, R.R.O. 1990, Reg. 197, RR. 15, 16. See now *Rules of Civil Procedure*, R. 74.06.

or absent from the jurisdiction, and if it is necessary to protect the assets of the estate. The grant will end when a general grant is made.

(vii)   *Grants of Temporary Administration*[80]

A grant of temporary administration may be made to a person while the person normally entitled to administration is outside the jurisdiction. It will be revoked if the latter, upon his or her return, applies for a grant.
Section 14 of the *Estates Act* provides:

> **14.** (1) If the next-of-kin, usually residing in Ontario and regularly entitled to administer, is absent from Ontario, the court having jurisdiction may grant a temporary administration to the applicant, or to such other person as the court thinks fit, for a limited time, or subject to be revoked upon the return of such next-of-kin to Ontario.
> (2) The administrator so appointed shall give such security as the court may direct, and has all the rights and powers of a general administrator, and is subject to the immediate control of the court.

(viii)   *Grants Pursuant to Powers of Attorney*

If the person solely entitled to a grant is out of the jurisdiction he or she may appoint an attorney, resident in Ontario, who will be entitled to apply for letters of administration. However, they may be revoked upon the application of the principal for a *cessate* grant.

(ix)   *Grants During Minority*[81]

Letters of administration may be granted for the duration of the minority of the sole executor named, or the sole person entitled to administration.[82]

(x)   *Grants while a Person is under a Disability*[83]

A grant *durante corporis aut animi vitio* may be made to the committee of a sole executor, or of the person solely entitled to administration who is incapacitated or, if there is no committee, to some other person interested in the estate, for the use and benefit of the person who is incapacitated, until he or she recovers. If several persons are entitled to the grant and one of them is unsound of mind, that person will be passed over and the grant will be made to the others.

---

80 Also known as Grants *Durante Absentia*.
81 Also known as Grants *Durante Minore Aetate*.
82 See *Estates Act*, s. 26, reproduced in part 4(c)(i), *supra*.
83 Also knows as Grants *Durante Corporis Aut Animi Vitio*.

(e) Ancillary Grants and Resealing

(i) *Ancillary Grants [Certificate of an Ancillary Appointment of Estate Trustee with a Will]*[84]

An ancillary grant of probate or letters of administration with a will annexed[85] is one which complements, assists, or is auxiliary to the main, that is, the original grant. An ancillary grant may be made to a personal representative to whom a grant was made in a foreign jurisdiction and if there are assets in Ontario which must be administered. Without such an ancillary grant, the foreign personal representative has no authority to deal with assets in Ontario.

An ancillary grant will normally be issued if the original grant was made by a court of jurisdiction, that is, by a competent court of the deceased's domicile. However, the making of the grant is in the discretion of the court and will not be made, for example, if the personal representative is a minor or a foreign trust company which would lack capacity in Ontario.[86] Nor will an ancillary grant be made to an administrator with the will annexed if that person is not resident in Ontario, but a grant must be made to his or her nominee.[87]

Additional problems may arise in the context of succession rather than administration. Thus, for example, a will which is valid in the testator's domicile may not be valid in Ontario, in which case it can not govern the succession to land in Ontario. This subject matter is too complex to be dealt with at this point.[88]

(ii) *Resealing [Confirmation by Resealing of Appointment of Estate Trustee with or without a Will]*

If the original probate or letters of administration were granted by a court of competent jurisdiction in the United Kingdom, another province or territory of Canada, or any British possession, it is not necessary to apply for an ancillary grant. Instead the original grant may be resealed by the court.[89]

---

84 See *Rules of Civil Procedure*, R. 74.09.
85 An ancillary grant can only be made if there is a will. See *Macdonell, Sheard and Hull on Probate Practice*, 4th ed. by Rodney Hull and Ian M. Hull (Scarborough: Carswell, 1996), p. 285.
86 See *Re O'Brien* (1883), 3 O.R. 326 (Ch. D.).
87 *Estates Act*, s. 5; *Rules of Civil Procedure*, R. 74.09
88 For a discussion of these problems, see *Macdonell, Sheard and Hull on Probate Practice*, 4th ed. by Rodney Hull and Ian M. Hull (Scarborough: Carswell, 1996) at pp. 290ff.
89 *Estates Act*, s. 52; *Rules of Civil Procedure*, R. 74.08.

(f) Procedure

(i) *Introduction*

Much of the procedure for obtaining grants is codified in the Act and the *Rules of Civil Procedure*. In all cases, probate fees or taxes must be paid before a grant is issued.

(ii) *Application for Letters of Administration [Application for Certificate of Appointment of Estate Trustee without a Will]*

On an application for letters of administration the applicant must file with the local registrar an application for administration, giving details about the deceased, such as his or her residence, marital status, the persons entitled to share in an intestacy and the value of the estate. The form is verified by the applicant's affidavit. The applicant must also file: (1) an affidavit attesting that notice has been sent to all persons entitled to share in the distribution of the estate; (2) a renunciation from everyone entitled to be appointed in priority to the applicant and who did not join in the application; and (3) a consent to the appointment by persons who together are entitled to a majority interest in the value of the assets. Finally, he or she must file an administration bond.[90] The bond secures the making of a true and complete inventory, the due administration of the estate, and the accounting and the payment of moneys to those entitled. Once these duties have been completed, the bond is cancelled.

(iii) *Application for Letters Probate [Application for Certificate of Appointment of Estate Trustee with a Will]*

(A) *Introduction.* A will may be proved in either common form or solemn form. Probate in common form is issued upon the *ex parte* application of the named executor if no one contests the validity of the will and it appears to be proper on its face.

(B) *Common form probate [Application for Certificate of Appointment of Estate Trustee with a Will].* In common form probate the applicant must file with the local registrar an application for probate which, as in the case of the application for letters of administration, gives details about the deceased and the value of the estate, together with details of the will and any codicils, including details of gifts to beneficiaries and their spouses.[91] The applicant must also file: (1) the original will and any codicils; (2) an affidavit attesting service of notice on all persons entitled to a share of the estate; (3) an affidavit of execution of the will and each

---

90 *Rules of Civil Procedure*, R. 74.05.
91 *Ibid.*, R. 74.04.

codicil by a witness; and (4) a renunciation by every living executor named in the will who has not jointed in the application. The will and codicils are filed as exhibits to the several affidavits. This affidavit may be made either before or after the testator's death. If an affidavit of execution cannot be made, such other evidence of execution as the court may require must be filed. In addition, if the will is holograph, an affidavit attesting that the handwriting is the testator's must be filed. Further, if the will or any codicil contains alterations, erasures, obliterations, or interlineations, the applicant must file an affidavit of condition of will or codicil.[92]

If the applicant was not named in the will, the consent of beneficiaries who together are entitled to a majority interest in the value of the assets must be filed. Further, in that event, or if the applicant resides outside the province, security in the form of a bond must be filed.[93] An executor who has misappropriated estate funds will be required to repay the amount to the estate or may be required to provide security.[94]

If the will was written in a foreign language, it may be admitted to probate, so long as the testator did not direct otherwise. The applicants should supply an authenticated translation of the will, for it is the translation that is admitted to probate.[95]

Common form probate is revocable at the suit of any interested person who afterwards requires proof in solemn form.

(C) *Solemn form probate [Formal Proof of Testamentary Instrument].* If the court is alerted to the fact that there may be something wrong with the will, because an interested party filed a caveat [objection to issuing of certificate of appointment] or a request for notice of commencement of proceedings, or because the will appears on its face to be improper, the will must be proved in solemn form, or *per testes.* This means that it must be proved in open court upon citation of (notice to) all interested parties and it will not be admitted to probate unless the court is satisfied of the due execution of the will, the testator's knowledge and approval of the contents, his or her capacity, and non-revocation. These facts are proved as in an ordinary trial, by examination of witnesses.

Probate in solemn form is irrevocable at the suit of any interested person who was privy to the original proceedings, or who was cited, or who was not cited but was aware of the proceedings and who had a right to intervene, unless a later will is discovered subsequently, or unless the judgment is the result of a compromise. In the latter situation, however, the court may direct that a party who was cited originally is bound by the compromise.[96]

---

92 This affidavit was formerly called an affidavit of plight.
93 *Estates Act*, s. 6; *Rules of Civil Procedure*, R. 74.04.
94 *Saunders v. Crouse Estate* (1999), 26 E.T.R. (2d) 250 (N.S. C.A.). See also *Saunders v. Crouse Estate* (1999), 28 E.T.R. (2d) 136 (N.S. C.A.).
95 *Re Berger (decd)*, [1989] 1 All E.R. 591 (C.A.).
96 See Macdonnell, Sheard and Hull, *supra*, at pp. 316-17.

(iv) *Contentious Proceedings*

All proceedings in which there is a contest between opposing parties, such as those in which persons have been cited (given notice), an appearance is entered, an application is made to revoke a grant [a motion is made for an order for assistance requiring the return of the certificate to the court], or an application is made by a dependant for support, are considered to be contentious. The *Estates Act* and the *Estate Rules* make provision for the conduct of such proceedings. However, pleadings are not normally filed. Instead, an application is made to the court for directions regarding the parties to be added and to settle the issues.[97]

There is provision in the Act for jury trials.[98] However, in Ontario, as distinct from England, it is seldom that a motion for a jury trial succeeds, the onus being on the party seeking a jury to show cause why the issues should be tried by a jury.[99]

(v) *Method of Proceeding*

(A) *Generally*. Most proceedings in estate matters are by motion, some, such as applications for dependants' support, being by application. There are, however, other ways in which persons may commence or participate in proceedings. These are by caveat, citation and intervention.

(B) *Caveat [Notice of Objection]*. If a person is interested in a particular estate and is concerned that the estate may be administered contrary to his or her interest, or if a person desires to contest the will and receive notice of all proceedings, he or she may file a caveat with the appropriate court office or the office of the Estate Registrar for Ontario.[100] The caveat is simply a notice to the court and other persons interested in the estate requiring that nothing be done in the estate without notice to the caveator. Hence, for example, no grant will be made to any person except on notice to the caveator and he or she will have an opportunity to contest the application by entering an appearance. A caveat lapses after three years, but a new caveat may be filed in its place.[101]

(C) *Intervention [Request for Notice]*. An intervention is similar to a caveat in that it is a notice filed with the court and thereafter notice of all proceedings is given to the intervener.[102]

---

97 *Rules of Civil Procedure*, R. 75.06.
98 *Estates Act*, s. 8.
99 See *Jarrett v. Campbell* (1912), 26 O.L.R. 83, 3 D.L.R. 763; *Re McKellar Estate* (1993), 2 E.T.R. (2d) 41 (Ont. Gen. Div.); *Bigelow v. Parra* (1999), 27 E.T.R. (2d) 182 (Ont. Gen. Div.).
100 *Estates Act*, s. 21; *Rules of Civil Procedure*, R. 75.03. A person who claimed to be adopted by the testator at common law by *de facto* adoption is not entitled to file a caveat: *McNeil v. MacDougal* (1999), 30 E.T.R. (2d) 244 (Alta. Surr. Ct.).
101 *Ibid.*
102 *Ibid.*, R. 74.03.

(D) *Citation [Order for Assistance].* A citation or summons is an order of a judge made by him or her upon the affidavit of the person extracting (requesting) it.[103] The citation is addressed to another person with an interest in the proceedings and requires that person to enter an appearance or do such other things as may be specified.

Thus, a citation may issue to a named executor to accept or refuse a grant of probate if the executor has not appeared or renounced.[104] Persons who have a prior right to administration than the applicant are also cited for this purpose. Similarly, a named executor may be cited to propound a will if he or she has taken no action to do so and any person having possession, or who may have possession of a will, may be cited to produce it.

Citations [Motions for Return of Certificate] are also issued against personal representatives to bring in a grant for revocation.[105] If the validity of a will is disputed, all persons having an interest in the property, including those entitled on an intestacy are cited to see (that is, be made parties to) the proceedings.[106] Finally, personal representatives may be cited to bring in their accounts to have them passed by the court.

5. COSTS

It is beyond the scope of this chapter to discuss the matter of costs in detail. However, it is important that the topic be introduced. In estate matters, as in most proceedings, costs are entirely in the discretion of the court.[107] In the past it was common that the costs of all parties were paid out of the estate. There were sound policy reasons for this practice. First, the problem giving rise to the litigation was often caused by the testator and, thus, it was appropriate to require the estate to bear the cost of the litigation. Second, parties contesting a will often have reasonable grounds on which to attack it and lack detailed knowledge of the circumstances, so it is appropriate that they be awarded costs out of the estate.[108] However, the countervailing policy is that parties should not be tempted into fruitless litigation in the expectation that the estate will bear their costs.[109] The courts will balance these policy concerns to determine how costs should be awarded.

Normally, the person propounding a will or seeking its interpretation will be awarded costs out of the estate, but persons who represent the same interest normally are not.[110] However, executors may be condemned to pay costs person-

---

103 *Ibid.*, R. 75.14.
104 *Ibid.*
105 *Ibid.*, R. 75.05.
106 *Estates Act*, s. 23; *Rules of Civil Procedure*, R. 75.06.
107 See *Courts of Justice Act*, R.S.O. 1990, c. C.43, s. 131(1), and similar provisions in other provinces.
108 See *Mitchell v. Gard* (1863), 3 Sw. & Tr. 75 at 78, 164 E.R. 1280; *Spiers v. English*, [1907] P. 122 at 123; *Atchison v. Inkster* (1983), 15 E.T.R. 1 (B.C. C.A.).
109 *Logan v. Herring* (1900), 19 P.R. 168 (Ont. H.C.)
110 *Ibid.*

ally in appropriate circumstances.[111] Further, persons who oppose a will are often denied their costs if they have acted unreasonably.[112] For example, nieces who acted because of family animosity and attacked a will on the ground of suspicious circumstances and undue influence when there was no basis for the allegations, were denied costs out of the estate even though they ultimately withdrew the allegations. Instead, they were required to pay the executor costs on a party and party basis until the end of the discoveries and on a solicitor and client basis thereafter.[113] Similarly, a caveator who attacked a will on the basis of fraud and undue influence on the part of the executrix and persisted in the allegations after the discoveries even though it was clear that there was no case, was required to pay the executrix's counsel fees.[114]

The solicitor for a party challenging[115] a will may also be required to pay costs if the solicitor was responsible for the unjustified litigation. Similarly, a solicitor who propounds[116] a will he prepared may be condemned in costs if the solicitor was the cause of the lengthy proceedings.

These examples illustrate that it is by no means certain that all parties will receive their costs out of the estate or, indeed, that any party will receive costs. They also illustrate an increasing tendency on the part of the courts to refuse to award costs out of the estate to unsuccessful parties. Further, although the foregoing comments concern principally the practice in obtaining probate of a will, they apply, with necessary modifications, also to applications for support and applications to interpret wills.

Further Reading

Macdonell, Sheard and Hull on Probate Practice, 4th ed. by Rodney Hull and Ian M. Hull (Scarborough: Carswell, 1996), ch. 25.

Mark M. Orkin, *The Law of Costs*, 2nd ed. (loose leaf) (Aurora: Canada Law Book Inc., 2000), § 219.3.

Brian A. Schnurr, *Estate Litigation*, 2nd ed. (loose leaf) (Scarborough: Carswell, 1994), ch. 19.

---

111 See, *e.g.*, *Eady v. Waring* (1974), 2 O.R. (2d) 627 (C.A.), in which the executors were ordered personally to pay the costs on an appeal from a finding against the will.

112 See, *e.g.*, *Orleski v. Reid* (1989), 31 E.T.R. 249 (Sask. C.A.), in which the party challenging the will made allegations of fraud that were unsupported by any evidence and was required to pay costs on a solicitor and client basis.

113 *Schweitzer v. Piasecki* (1998), 20 E.T.R. (2d) 233 (B.C. C.A.).

114 *Re Marshall Estate* (1998), 22 E.T.R. (2d) 255 (Ont. Gen. Div.).

115 *Ibid.*

116 *Johnson v. Pelkey* (1998), 23 E.T.R. (2d) 137 (B.C. S.C.), affirmed (1999), 127 B.C.A.C. 229 (C.A.).

6. CONTESTATION OF CLAIMS

It is customary for personal representatives, usually through the estate's solicitors, to advertise for creditors by placing an advertisement in the local newspaper. The advertisement states that anyone having a claim against the estate should notify the personal representatives or solicitors within a specified time, failing which the estate will be distributed without regard to such claim.

In order to facilitate the winding up of an estate, the *Estates Act* contains provisions which permit the summary contestation of claims if their validity is in doubt.[117] The procedure allows the personal representative to serve the claimant with a notice in writing stating that he or she disputes the claim in whole or in part. The claimant then has an opportunity to file a statement of claim with the court, verified by affidavit, and the judge, after hearing the parties, rules upon its validity. If the claim is for $800 or more, the claimant must bring an action to recover the amount of the claim, but the action may be tried by the judge with the parties' consent.

The advertisement for creditors, referred to above, protects the personal representatives against future claims by creditors. Such claims only include actual debts. The personal representative is not responsible for an unliquidated claim for damages.[118] However, if the personal representative is negligent in obtaining relevant reports, he or she may still be liable to the creditor. Thus, in *Canadian Imperial Bank of Commerce v. Foley Estate*[119] a bank told the administrator that the deceased's debts owed to the bank could be paid out of his life insurance policies upon delivery of the coroner's report and death certificate. The administrator paid the other debts and distributed the remaining funds to the beneficiaries before the coroner's report and death certificate were available. When the coroner's report showed that the deceased had been driving with blood level alcohol over the legal limit, the insurer refused to pay in accordance with an exclusionary clause in the insurance contract. In the circumstances, the bank was able to recover the amount of its debt from the administrator. Even if the personal representative is protected, a creditor can still follow the assets into the hands of the beneficiaries.[120] If an executor informs the creditor that the claim is denied, the creditor must bring action within the limitation period, or the claim will be barred.[121]

If the personal representatives have no assets in the estate to satisfy a debt upon which an action is brought, they may rely on the doctrine of *plene administravit* to defend the action. If they do not do so, they are conclusively deemed to have admitted to having assets to satisfy the judgment and will be personally liable for the judgment. If the personal representatives have some, but insufficient, assets,

---

117 *Estates Act*, ss. 44-47.
118 *O'Dwyer v. Dominion Soil Investigation Inc.* (1999), 25 E.T.R. (2d) 296 (Ont. Gen. Div.).
119 (1998), 22 E.T.R. (2d) 277 (Nfld. T.D.).
120 *Trustee Act*, s. 53.
121 *McKenzie v. MacKenzie* (1992), 48 E.T.R. 134 (Man. Q.B.).

they may plead *plene administravit praeter*, in which case, they are liable only for the assets under their control.[122]

Further Reading

Rodney Hull, "Yet Another Minefield to be Avoided when Claiming against an Estate" (1998), 23 E.T.R. (2d) 132.

7. PASSING OF ACCOUNTS

(a) Generally

It is the duty of personal representatives, as fiduciaries, to keep proper books of account and be ready to account when called upon to do so. A personal representative may do so voluntarily[123] and customarily does so on a regular basis in order to be able to be paid compensation. He or she may also be cited (ordered) to account.[124]

The procedure is as follows: The personal representative files an application setting out particulars of the accounting period and the persons interested in the matter with the court office from which the grant was obtained. The application is accompanied by: (1) the accounts, verified by affidavit; (2) a copy of the letters probate or administration; and (3) a copy of the previous judgment, if any, passing the accounts.[125] On the return of the appointment, the applicant also files the court's notice of the application and proof of service on all interested parties, including, as required, the Children's Lawyer (formerly the Official Guardian),[126] and the Public Guardian and Trustee or the committee or statutory guardian of a mentally incompetent person or a person incapable of managing his or her affairs.[127]

The accounts are passed before a judge in chambers and the judge has jurisdiction to make a full inquiry and accounting of all the property the deceased was entitled to, and its administration and disbursement.[128] He or she may also inquire into any complaint against the personal representative of misconduct, neglect, or default occasioning loss to the estate (a "devastavit") and award damages if the

---

122 See *Edwards v. Law Society of Upper Canada* (1998), 39 O.R. (3d) 10, 23 E.T.R. (2d) 46 (Gen. Div.), reversed on other grounds (2000), 48 O.R. (3d) 321 (C.A.).

123 *Trustee Act*, s. 23; *Rules of Civil Procedure*, R. 74.18.

124 *Estates Act*, s. 48; *Rules of Civil Procedure*, R. 74.15(1)(h).

125 *Rules of Civil Procedure*, R. 74.18. It is customary to file an affidavit proving publication of advertisement for creditors. The personal representative will also wish to file a statement of compensation claimed.

126 *Courts of Justice Act*, R.S.O. 1990, c. C.43, s. 89(1) rep. and subst. by S.O. 1994, c. 27, s. 43(1), which renamed the office.

127 *Estates Act*, s. 49(5)-(9); *Rules of Civil Procedure*, R. 74.18.

128 *Estates Act*, s. 49(2).

complaint is proved, or direct the trial of such an issue.[129] The judge may also permit surcharge and falsification of accounts and award interest against defaulting personal representatives. A surcharge is an omission for which credit ought to have been given, while a falsification is a false or erroneous debit item. In addition, the judge has power to award costs of the audit and the solicitor's fees on the passing of the accounts. These are normally awarded out of the estate, but the judge has a discretion not to charge the estate and indeed, to disallow them altogether.[130]

The court has jurisdiction to pass the accounts of an estate in which the will has not been probated. The court has jurisdiction to supervise executors with or without probate.[131]

(b) Compensation of Personal Representatives

Personal representatives, like other trustees, are entitled by statute to be compensated for their services and the compensation is fixed on the passing of accounts.

Section 61 of the *Trustee Act* provides:

> **61.** (1) A trustee, guardian or personal representative is entitled to such fair and reasonable allowance for the care, pains and trouble, and the time expended in and about the estate, as may be allowed by a judge of the Superior Court of Justice.
>
> (2) The amount of such compensation may be settled although the estate is not before the court in an action.
>
> (3) The judge, in passing the accounts of a trustee or of a personal representative or guardian, may from time to time allow a fair and reasonable allowance for his care, pains and trouble, and his time expended in or about the estate.
>
> (4) Where a barrister or solicitor is a trustee, guardian or personal representative, and has rendered necessary professional services to the estate, regard may be had in making the allowance to such circumstance, and the allowance shall be increased by such amount as may be considered fair and reasonable in respect of such services.
>
> (5) Nothing in this section applies where the allowance is fixed by the instrument creating the trust.

In *Re Toronto General Trusts Corporation and Central Ontario Railway Co.*,[132] Teetzel J. outlined the factors which the Court should consider in fixing the compensation of trustees as follows:

> (1) the magnitude of the trust; (2) the care and responsibility springing therefrom; (3) the time occupied in performing [their] duties; (4) the skill and ability displayed; [and] (5) the success which has attended [their] administration.

Subject to these rules, the usual practice in Ontario has been to allow 4 per cent as capital compensation (that is, 2 per cent on receipts and 2 per cent on disburse-

---

129 *Ibid.*, s. 49(3), (4).
130 *Rules of Civil Procedure*, R. 74.18(13).
131 *Re Silver Estate* (1999), 31 E.T.R. (2d) 256 (Ont. S.C.J.).
132 (1905), 6 O.W.R. 350 at 354.

ments), 5 per cent as income compensation (that is, 2 1/2 per cent each on receipts and disbursements in the income account), and 2/5 of 1 per cent per annum on the gross value of the assets as a management fee. A special fee may be allowed in exceptional cases in addition to the foregoing.[133]

If the executors waive interest on promissory notes payable to the them, they cannot include the waived interest in calculating the revenue fee, since it has not been earned by the estate. For the purpose of calculating the capital fee on the value of shares sold by the estate, the correct value to use is the value at the time of sale.[134]

In *Re Atkinson*[135] Aylesworth J.A. opined that the percentages should only be used as a rough guide. Moreover, in a number of recent cases the courts have objected strenuously to claims by executors for compensation based on these percentages. Executors and trustees may claim compensation on this basis, but they are required to justify their claims by providing sufficient particulars of the magnitude of the estate, the diversity of assets and the actual duties required of and performed by them.[136] Thus, for example, an executor will have the claim for compensation reduced if many of the typical executor's duties were performed by others.[137]

In a trio of cases in 1998,[138] the Ontario Court of Appeal endorsed the tariff approach to determining compensation, but held that the five factors of *Toronto General Trusts* should be used as a cross-check on the tariff approach. To permit a proper cross-check, personal representatives should keep proper records of their time spent in administering the estate.

Personal representatives will not be denied their fee for care and management when they hold on to a major asset when there is litigation over entitlement to a share of the property, even though the value of the property dropped during that time.[139]

Beneficiaries who acknowledge receipt of the accounts and waive formal passing of the accounts cannot subsequently demand that the executor pass the accounts.[140]

In *Re Welbourn*[141] the court held that if the trust instrument docs not fix the compensation, it is improper for an executor or trustee to pre-take his or her compensation, for until the court has fixed it, he or she is not entitled to it. All

---

133 See *Re Cohen* (1977), 1 E.T.R. 80 (Ont. Surr. Ct.).

134 *Re Lohn Estate* (1998), 22 E.T.R. (2d) 311 (B.C. C.A.).

135 [1952] O.R. 685, [1952] 3 D.L.R. 609 at 612-3 (C.A.), affirmed [1953] 2 S.C.R. 41 (sub nom. *Nat. Trust Co. v. Public Trustee*), [1953] 3 D.L.R. 497.

136 See *Re Welbourn*, [1979] 3 W.W.R. 113, 4 E.T.R. 122 (Alta. Surr. Ct.); *Re Sproule*, 17 A.R. 58, (sub nom. *Sproule v. Montreal Trust Co. (No. 2)*) [1979] 4 W.W.R. 670, 95 D.L.R. (3d) 458 at 471 (C.A.).

137 *Re Holt Estate* (1994), 2 E.T.R. (2d) 163 (Ont. Gen. Div.).

138 *Re Laing Estate* (1998), 41 O.R. (3d) 571, 25 E.T.R. (2d) 139, 167 D.L.R. (4th) 150 (C.A.); *Re Flaska Estate* (1998), 83 A.C.W.S. (3d) 532 (Ont. C.A.); *Re Gordon Estate* (1998), 83 A.C.W.S. (3d) 144 (Ont. C.A.).

139 *Re Proudfoot Estate* (1997), 19 E.T.R. (2d) 150 (Ont. C.A.).

140 *Leckie v. Mitchell* (1997), 20 E.T.R. (2d) 6 (B.C. C.A.).

141 *Supra*.

the executor may do is pre-estimate the amount and retain it in trust.[142] However, in *Re William George King Trust*[143] the court held that pre-taking of compensation is not objectionable in a continuing trust if the compensation is for services rendered and does not exceed the fair value of the services. It is appropriate in those circumstances, because it avoids the expense of frequent passings of account. Executors are not entitled to charge separately for preparing income tax returns.[144]

You should note that if the will or trust document contains an express provision for compensation, the provision is an absolute limitation upon the allowance that may be made. The court will not look into the reasonableness of the provision, since section 61(5) of the Act is a bar to its jurisdiction.[145] On the other hand, an agreement between a testator and the proposed executor (to which the "beneficiaries" are not parties), which was entered into before the will was prepared and which was not incorporated into the will, is not binding on the court or the beneficiaries. Compensation may then be claimed under section 61.[146]

A trustee who becomes a director of a company in which the trust has an interest is accountable to the trust for any remuneration received as a director. However, the court may allow the trustee to keep the fees if the effort and skill required of the trustee was over and above that normally required of such a director. The court will not, save in exceptional circumstances, make such an order with respect to future remuneration.[147]

A solicitor who acts as both the executor and solicitor to an estate, is not entitled to be paid for his work as a solicitor and claim executors' fees for the same work.[148]

Further Reading

Jennifer J. Jenkins, *Compensation for Estate Trustees* (Aurora: Canada Law Book Inc., 1997).

Brian A. Schnurr, 2nd ed. (loose leaf) *Estate Litigation* (Scarborough: Carswell, 1994), § 5.7.

Jordan Atin, "Executor's Compensation - Quantum - Principles of Determination - Trustee Act (Ontario)" (2000), 19 E.T. & P.J. 1.

Barry S. Corbin, "Tax Relief on Executors' Compensation?" (2000), 19 E.T. & P.J. 251.

---

142 See also *Re Prelutsky*, [1982] 4 W.W.R. 309, 36 B.C.L.R. 214, 11 E.T.R. 233 (S.C.); *Finbow v. Finbow Estate* (1997), 20 E.T.R. (2d) 165 (Alta. Surr. Ct.), to the same effect. And see *Adams Estate v. Keogh* (1992), 48 E.T.R. 140 (N.S. T.D.).

143 (1994), 113 D.L.R. (4th) 701, 2 E.T.R. (2d) 123 (Ont. Gen. Div.), noted (1994), 14 E. & T.J. 97 (Marni M.K. Whittaker).

144 See *e.g.*, *Re Campin Estate* (1992), 49 E.T.R. 197 (Ont. Gen. Div.); *Re Clowater Estate* (1993), 49 E.T.R. 184 (N.B. Prob. Ct.).

145 *Re Robertson*, [1949] O.R. 427, [1949] 4 D.L.R. 319 (H.C.).

146 *Re Taylor*, [1967] 2 O.R. 557 (Surr. Ct.).

147 *Re Keeler's Settlement Trusts*, [1981] 1 Ch. 156, [1981] 1 All E.R. 888.

148 *Re Henry Estate* (1998), 23 E.T.R. (2d) 121 (Ont. Gen. Div.).

(c) Solicitors' Fees

The fees payable to the estate's solicitor are also determined on the passing of accounts, the judge having authority to vary the bill of costs or to refer it for taxation.[149] Until 1982, the *Estate Rules* contained a tariff of fees to be allowed solicitors and counsel for their work in connection with the estate. However, this was repealed and only the tariff for services on the passing of accounts was retained.[150] The former tariff was defective since the repeal of succession duties and estate tax, because it included a reference to succession duty schedules and estate tax returns. As a result, solicitors' fees have been calculated in different ways for a number of years. The old tariff is still sometimes used as a rough guide. Alternatively, a bill of costs based on the time spent may be submitted.

8. DUTIES OF PERSONAL REPRESENTATIVES

(a) Generally

The essential duties of a personal representative are to:

1. get in the assets;
2. pay the debts and legacies, transfer the bequests and devises and set up any trusts required by the will; and
3. distribute the residue.

Once these functions are completed, the duties of the personal representative cease, although the office remains, so that if other assets are subsequently discovered, the same person is capable of administering them.

(b) Disposition of the Deceased's Body

It is a criminal offence to interfere improperly or indecently with, or to offer any indignity to a dead human body.[151] Accordingly, a person having control of a body is required to give it a decent burial or to cremate the remains. This includes the deceased's personal representative. Indeed, the duty of the personal representative is accompanied by a right to custody of the body.[152] This right does not confer a property right, for no one can have a property right in a corpse.[153] The

---

149 *Rules of Civil Procedure*, R. 74.18(13).
150 *Ibid.*, Tariff C.
151 *Criminal Code*, R.S.C. 1985, c. C-46, s. 182(b). See *R. v. Newcombe* (1898), 2 C.C.C. 225 (N.S. Co. Ct.). See also *R. v. Hunter*, [1974] Q.B. 95, [1973] 3 All E.R. 286 (C.A.).
152 *Hunter v. Hunter*, 65 O.L.R. 586, [1930] 4 D.L.R. 255; *Edmonds v. Armstrong Funeral Home Ltd.*, [1931] 1 D.L.R. 676 (Alta. C.A.).
153 *R. v. Handyside* (1770), 2 East. P.C. 652.

right to deal with the body continues after the funeral.[154] The personal representative is not bound to follow the deceased's funeral instructions, but may do so if they are not extravagant or unreasonable, in particular as regards creditors.[155] Further, the deceased's family cannot prevent the personal representative from, for example, cremating the remains, even if cremation is contrary to the family's religious beliefs.[156]

Further Reading

Richard P. Young, *Estate Practice* (Scarborough: Carswell, 1993, loose leaf), ch. 1.

(c) Income Tax

Personal representatives also have significant responsibilities under the *Income Tax Act*.[157] They must file a terminal income tax return and may have to deal with income tax liability for capital gains, including deemed realizations. In particular, you should note the effect of section 159 of the Act. Section 159(2) requires that a certificate be obtained from the Department of National Revenue stating that all taxes have been paid or that security has been given before distributing any assets. Failure to do so renders a personal representative personally liable under s. 159(3) for the amount of unpaid tax.

Further Reading

Anne E.P. Armstrong, *Estate Administration: A Solicitor's Reference Manual* (Scarborough: Carswell, 1994, loose leaf), ch. 5

9. PAYMENT OF DEBTS

It is the duty of a personal representative to pay the debts of the estate as soon as possible, that is, normally within the "executor's year." Secured debts incurred during the deceased's lifetime have priority.[158] Further, funeral expenses are a first charge on the assets, followed by testamentary expenses and the costs of

---

154 Thus, for example, the executor can prevent disinterment and reburial by a relative unless necessary for public health reasons or another public purpose: *Waldman v. Melville (City)* (1990), 36 E.T.R. 172 (Sask. Q.B.).

155 *Schara Tzedeck v. Royal Trust Co.*, [1953] 1 S.C.R. 31, [1952] 4 D.L.R. 529.

156 *Saleh v. Reichert* (1993) 50 E.T.R. 143 (Ont. Gen. Div.).

157 R.S.C. 1985, c. 1 (5th Supp.).

158 *Trustee Act*, s. 49. An unsecured creditor of the estate does not have an interest in the estate's real property so as to permit the filing of a caveat, even though the will contains an express trust for the payment of debts: *Helm Estate v. Udovitch* (1988), 30 E.T.R. 213 (Alta. Q.B.).

administration, including the personal representative's compensation.[159] Apart from these, there is no priority among different classes of debts. If the estate is insolvent, the unsecured debts of the deceased are payable *pari passu*.[160]

There are special rules to determine which assets bear the burden of the debts. The *Estates Administration Act*[161] provides that a deceased person's real property is subject to the same liability for debts as if it were personalty, but that this does not affect the order in which real and personal property are applicable to the payment of debts as regards real or personal property of which the deceased has made a testamentary disposition. However, unless a contrary intention appears by the will, the real and personal property comprised in a residuary devise or bequest is applicable rateably to the payment of debts.

The effect of this legislation is not to create one fund for the payment of debts consisting of undifferentiated real and personal property. Rather, it merely vests the real as well as the personal estate in the personal representatives for the payment of debts, but, except as regards a residuary devise of real and personal estate, the order in which the different classes of property are liable to the payment of debts is not affected by the Act.[162] That order appears to be as follows (subject to a contrary intention appearing by the will):[163]

1. The general personal estate not bequeathed at all, or by way of residue only.
2. Real estate devised in trust to pay debts.
3. Real estate descended to the heir and not charged with the payment of debts.
4. Real or personal estate charged with the payment of debts, and (as to realty) devised specifically or by way of residue, or suffered, by reason of lapsed devise, to descend; or (as to personalty) specifically bequeathed, subject to that charge.
5. General pecuniary legacies, including annuities and demonstrative legacies which have become general.
6. Specific legacies (including demonstrative legacies that so remain), specific devises and residuary devises not charged with debts, to contribute *pro rata*.
7. Real and personal estate over which the testator had a general power of appointment which has been expressly exercised by deed (in favour of volunteers) or by will.
9. Paraphernalia of the testator's widow.

The legislation does not seem to have changed the general rule that the personalty is still the primary fund for creditors. Hence, when a testator left all his personal property by general bequest to his widow and died intestate of his real

159 *Widdifield on Executors' Accounts*, 5th ed. by Frederick D. Baker (Toronto: Carswell, 1967), at p. 82.
160 *Trustee Act*, s. 50. See also *Re Mintz and Adams* (1985), 33 A.C.W.S. (2d) 287 (Ont. H.C.).
161 Sections 4, 5.
162 *Re Hopkins* (1900), 32 O.R. 315; *Re Swayze*, [1938] O.W.N. 524.
163 See *Widdifield on Executors' Accounts, supra,* at p. 86. See also Ont. Law Reform Commission, *Report on Administration of Estates of Deceased Persons* (Toronto: Ontario Law Reform Commission, 1991), pp. 184-5.

estate, and the will contained no direction about payment of the debts, the court held that the debts should be paid out of the personalty.[164]

The provisions of the *Estates Administration Act* do not apply if the deceased specifically devised real property or a leasehold that is subject to a mortgage. In that situation, unless the will directs otherwise, the property is primarily liable for the payment of the mortgage debt. Moreover, a general direction to pay debts, or a charge of debts upon the deceased's estate do not, by themselves, signify a contrary intention.[165]

10. SALE OF REAL PROPERTY[166]

(a) Generally

Before the enactment of the predecessor of the *Estates Administration Act*, a deceased person's real property passed directly to those entitled to it. The effect of section 2(1) of that Act is to vest the real as well as the personal property in the personal representative in trust to pay the debts and to distribute the estate. In order to remove any doubts about the personal representative's ability to deal with the real property for these purposes, the Act provides that the real property remains vested in the personal representative for a period of three years from the death of the deceased. Thereafter it vests in the persons beneficially entitled, unless the personal representative registers a caution in the land registry office to delay the vesting for three years from the date of registration, and he or she may reregister the caution every three years thereafter before it expires.[167]

If a personal representative wishes to register or reregister a caution after the time has expired, he or she may do so upon registering an affidavit stating that it is necessary to sell the real property, together with the consent in writing of all adult beneficiaries and of the Children's Lawyer (formerly the Official Guardian)[168] on behalf of children and mentally incompetent persons. Alternatively, an order of a judge of the Supreme Court, or the certificate of the Children's Lawyer is required. However, the caution, while it will vest or revest the real property in the personal representative, cannot affect rights acquired by third persons from a beneficiary for valuable consideration, or the equities of non-consenting beneficiaries or persons claiming under them for improvements to the property.[169]

---

164 *Re McGarry* (1909), 18 O.L.R. 524.
165 *Succession Law Reform Act*, R.S.O. 1990, c. S.26, s. 32.
166 See generally Howland, "The Sale of Lands of a Deceased Owner", in Law Soc. of Upper Can., Special Lectures, 1951, *Surrogate Court Practice*, at p. 57; Lamont, *Real Estate Conveyancing*, 1976, ch. 15.
167 *Estates Administration Act*, s. 9.
168 Renamed by S.O. 1994, c. 27, s. 43(1).
169 *Ibid.*, s. 11.

The personal representative may withdraw a caution before it expires.[170] Further, a beneficiary may apply to the court to have a caution vacated on the ground that vesting ought not to be delayed.[171]

(b) Powers of Sale

(i) Introduction

So long as the real property is vested in the personal representative, he or she has the power to deal with it, as if it were personal property.[172] However, his or her power to sell may be restricted. If there is a will, it is paramount and, if it contains a power of sale, that power will govern the personal representative.[173] If the will does not contain a power of sale or it is insufficiently wide, the personal representative may rely on the powers of sale under the *Estates Administration Act*, provided they do not conflict with the will. Finally, if there is no will, the personal representative can only rely on the statutory powers of sale.

(ii) *Testamentary Powers of Sale*

A testamentary power may be express or implied. If the personal representatives have been given an express power of sale, they may exercise it at any time, since the property does not vest in the beneficiaries,[174] and the consent of the beneficiaries or of the Children's Lawyer is not required. Moreover, a purchaser in good faith and for value takes free of the debts unless the purchaser has notice that the sale was improperly exercised.[175]

An implied power of sale also arises under the will and thus, if it exists, has exactly the same effect as an express power. An implied power arises if the will contains a direction to pay debts. Section 44 of the *Trustee Act* provides that if the land is charged with the payment of the debts and the land is devised to the executors, they have an implied power of sale for the purpose of paying the debts. Hence, if there is no devise to the executors, reliance cannot be placed on that section.[176] However, it is probable that so long as there is a direction to pay debts, the executors have an implied power to sell for that purpose, for the following reasons: First, under section 2(1) of the *Estates Administration Act*, the real and personal property of a deceased person vests in his or her personal representatives in trust, *inter alia*, to pay the debts. Hence they have the legal estate by statute.

---

170 *Ibid.*, s. 9(4).
171 *Ibid.*, s. 13.
172 *Ibid.*, s. 16.
173 *Ibid.*, ss. 10, 17(7); *Re Koch and Wideman* (1894), 25 O.R. 262 at 267.
174 *Shaw v. Fluke*, [1938] O.W.N. 346, 19 C.B.R. 389, [1938] 4 D.L.R. 770.
175 *Re McCutcheon and Smith*, [1933] O.W.N. 692 (C.A.); *Trustee Act*, s. 44(2).
176 *Re Jefferies and Calder*, [1951] O.W.N. 27, which decides otherwise, must be regarded as incorrect.

Second, it is well-established that if trustees are directed to do anything for which the legal estate is required, the legal estate vests in them and they have a power of sale to carry out the directions.[177] Finally, section 41 of the *Trustee Act* is apt to raise an implied power of sale. It provides that if a will, expressly or impliedly, directs the sale of land and no one is appointed to execute the direction, the executor may do so.

(iii) *Statutory Powers of Sale and Conveyance*

(A) *Introduction.* The *Estates Administration Act* contains certain powers of sale and conveyance which may be used by a personal representative if there is no will, or the will does not contain a power of sale, or the power of sale is inadequate.

(B) *Sales to pay debts.* The first power is a power of sale for the purpose of paying debts. This arises because, under section 16, the personal representatives are given the same power to deal with real property as with personalty and, as regards the latter, they have the power to sell in order to pay debts.[178] Moreover, section 17(1) provides that the powers of sale conferred by the Act may be exercised not only to pay debts, but also to distribute or divide the estate among the beneficiaries, whether or not there are any debts.

Under the registry system, if the recitals of fact in the schedule to the executor's transfer state that the transfer is made for the purpose of paying debts, a *bona fide* purchaser for value without notice may rely on the fact that the executor is acting honestly.[179] Under the land titles system it is the duty of the land registrar to ensure that the sale is for the purpose of paying debts, a fact which is proved by affidavit.[180] In both situations the *bona fide* purchaser for value is, therefore, protected.[181]

Although section 15(1) of the *Estates Administration Act*[182] requires that when a minor is interested in the property, notice be given to the Children's Lawyer before a sale, section 17(1) effectively overrides this requirement when the sale is for the payment of debts.[183] Thus, so long as the sale is partly to pay debts, the

---

177 *Davies v. Jones and Evans* (1883), 24 Ch. D. 190 at 194. *Cf. Re Nattress and Levy*, [1946] O.W.N. 640, [1946] 4 D.L.R. 156, holding that if the testator directed the payment of certain legacies which could not be paid without the sale of the real property in the estate, the executors had an implied power of sale, even though the property had not been devised to them.

178 *Reid v. Miller* (1865), 24 U.C.Q.B. 610 at 622 (C.A.).

179 *Re McCutcheon and Smith*, [1933] O.W.N. 692 (C.A.).

180 *Re Land Titles Act; Hurst and Guthrie* (November 1, 1940), Kelly J. (Ont. H.C.) (unreported), see (1940), 18 Can. Bar Rev. 799.

181 See also *Estates Administration Act*, s. 19.

182 *Ibid.* And see *Rules of Civil Procedure*, R. 67.01.

183 *Re Watson and Major*, [1943] O.W.N. 696, [1944] 1 D.L.R. 228; *Hilliard v. Dillon*, [1955] O.W.N. 621.

bona fide purchaser is protected and notice to the Children's Lawyer is not required, even though it is also partly for the purpose of distribution.[184]

(C) *Sales to distribute the proceeds among the beneficiaries.* Personal representatives also have the power, while the property remains vested in them, of selling the real property in order to distribute the proceeds among the beneficiaries. This power arises under section 17(1), (2) and (8) of the *Estates Administration Act.*[185] However, in this situation the consent of the majority of the beneficiaries, holding not less than one-half of the interests in the property, is required. Moreover, the consent of the Children's Lawyer is required if any minors have an interest in the property,[186] even though a majority of concurring beneficiaries, holding not less than one-half of the interests in the property, are adults.[187]

The Children's Lawyer may also consent on behalf of mentally incompetent persons, persons whose concurrence cannot be obtained because their place of residence is unknown and persons whose concurrence is, in the opinion of the Children's Lawyer, inconvenient to obtain, if the sale is advantageous to the estate and the beneficiaries. Failing the consent of the Children's Lawyer, the court may dispense with the consent of any person beneficially entitled,[188] although it is loath to do so, unless the withholding of consent is capricious or obstructive.[189]

If the statutory power has been complied with and the purpose of the sale is set out in the schedule to the transfer, a *bona fide* purchaser for value without notice is protected. It is customary to join all persons who consent as parties to the executor's deed or transfer. If the power has not been complied with, however, as where the necessary majority of beneficiaries has not concurred, the purchaser's title is subject to the rights of the non-concurring beneficiaries.[190]

An agreement to sell by the personal representative is not enforceable if the requisite number of beneficiaries do not concur.[191]

(D) *Division in specie among the beneficiaries.* Personal representatives also have power to convey the real property to the beneficiaries for the purpose of distribution. They may do so without a court order, but must obtain the consent of the Children's Lawyer on behalf of minors and mental incompetents.[192] In fact, the Children's Lawyer refuses to give this consent in these circumstances and,

---

184 *Re Ross and Davies* (1903), 7 O.L.R. 433 (C.A.). *Cf. J.D. Irving Ltd. v. Burchill* (October 14, 1994), Doc. S/M/97/94, S/M/98/94 (N.B. Q.B.).

185 The power exists even though all the outstanding debts have been paid: *Re Adams and Crowe,* [1946] O.R. 890, [1947] 1 D.L.R. 469.

186 *Estates Administration Act,* s. 15. Failure to comply with this section renders the sale void: *Re Leblanc* (1978), 18 O.R. (2d) 507, 2 E.T.R. 62, 83 D.L.R. (3d) 151 (C.A.).

187 If the only beneficiaries interested in the property are minors, a different procedure is followed. See below.

188 *Estates Administration Act,* s. 17(2).

189 *Re Logan,* 61 O.R. 323, [1927] 4 D.L.R. 1074 (C.A.).

190 *Estates Administration Act,* s. 17(3).

191 *A. Harvey Hacker Bldrs. Ltd. v. Akerfeldt,* [1965] 1 O.R. 369, 48 D.L.R. (2d) 119, affirmed without written reasons [1965] 2 O.R. 182n, 50 D.L.R. (2d) 130n (C.A.).

192 *Estates Administration Act,* s. 17(3).

hence, a court order must be obtained. If the property is conveyed without a court order, it remains subject to the deceased's debts.[193]

If the property is to be conveyed pursuant to a court order, the court will require proof that the personal representatives have advertised for creditors and that all creditors have been paid or that there are sufficient assets left to pay them.[194]

(c) Sale by Beneficiaries

Once the property has vested in the beneficiaries, or it has been conveyed to them, they can, if they are adults, dispose of it, but the creditors may retain certain rights.[195] If the property is conveyed to the beneficiaries without a court order before it has vested in them and they sell it, a *bona fide* purchaser for value without notice takes subject to the deceased's debts, but he or she is only liable for them if, within the three year period, the creditors have commenced proceedings and have registered a *lis pendens* or caution against the property.[196] However, the purchaser can recover from the beneficiaries and also from the personal representative if the latter conveyed with knowledge of the debt or without advertisement for creditors.[197]

On the other hand, if the conveyance was made pursuant to a court order, the purchaser will take free of the debts, except debts secured on the property. However, the creditors may still proceed against the beneficiaries and the personal representatives.[198]

After the property has vested in the beneficiaries, it remains subject to the deceased's debts,[199] but, once it is sold to a *bona fide* purchaser for value without notice, he or she takes free of the debts.[200] However, the creditors still have the right to proceed against the beneficiaries to the extent of the proceeds of sale of the property[201] and against the personal representatives if they allowed the property to vest to the prejudice of the creditors.[202]

(d) Sale of Minors' Lands

If minors are interested in real property, the personal representatives may proceed under a testamentary power of sale, if any, or under the statutory powers

---

193 *Ibid.*, s. 21(2).
194 *Re Allison* (1927), 61 O.L.R. 261, [1927] 4 D.L.R. 729 (C.A.); *Re Shier* (1922), 52 O.L.R. 464.
195 In fact, the beneficiaries may sell before the property is vested in them, in which case the doctrine of estoppel to feed the title will give the purchasers good title once it does vest.
196 *Estates Administration Act*, s. 17(8)(a), (c). See also *Rocovitis v. Argerys Estate* (1988), 8 A.C.W.S. (3d) 242 (Div. Ct.).
197 *Estates Administration Act*, s. 17(8)(b).
198 *Ibid.*, s. 21(1).
199 *Ibid.*, s. 21(2).
200 *Ibid.*, s. 23(1).
201 *Ibid.*, s. 21(2).
202 *Ibid.*, s. 23(2).

described above. However, if the only persons interested in the property are minors and there is no testamentary power of sale, it is the practice to proceed under the *Children's Law Reform Act*,[203] rather than under the *Estates Administration Act*. Moreover, it is necessary to proceed under the former statute whenever real property has vested in, or has been conveyed to, a minor.[204]

An application is made by the parent or next friend of the minor to the Superior Court of Justice with notice to the Children's Lawyer.[205] The court has power to require or approve the disposition or encumbrance of all or part of a child's interest in land.[206] However, it may only do so if it is of opinion that the order is necessary or proper for the support or education of the child or will substantially benefit the child.[207] Moreover, the court may not make an order contrary to the terms of the instrument under which the child acquired the interest.[208]

If the estate has not yet been fully administered and the personal representative has registered a caution on title indicating that it may be necessary to sell the property in the administration of the estate, only the consent of the Children's Lawyer is required; a court order is not necessary.[209]

11. DISTRIBUTION OF ESTATE

Once the personal representatives have taken control of the deceased's assets, have obtained probate or letters of administration and have paid the debts of the estate, they must distribute the property among the persons beneficially entitled to it. If there is a will, they must, of course, follow its terms. Hence, they must deliver or transfer specifically bequeathed or devised property to the beneficiaries named and establish any trusts as directed by the will. Further, they must either pay legacies out of available cash, or sell assets in order to pay them. Problems arising when there are insufficient assets, or when specifically bequeathed or devised property has ceased to exist, will be dealt with elsewhere in this text.[210] With respect to residue, the personal representatives are, absent a contrary direction in the will, under a duty to convert the assets into cash and then to distribute it. They have a similar duty in the case of an intestacy. However, with the consent

---

203 The provisions of section 50 of the *Children's Law Reform Act* respecting the disposition of minor's lands were formerly contained in the *Infants Act*, R.S.O. 1970, c. 222, renamed the *Minors Act*, R.S.O. 1980, c. 292 [repealed 1982, c. 20, s. 4]. See *Re Cavanagh*, [1938] O.W.N. 67; *Re Adams and Crowe*, [1946] O.R. 890, [1947] 1 D.L.R. 469.

204 See *Wilson v. Thompson* (1914), 30 O.L.R. 502. Failure to comply with the Act renders the sale void: *Re Leblanc* (1978), 18 O.R. (2d) 507, 2 E.T.R. 62, 83 D.L.R. (3d) 151 (C.A.).

205 *Rules of Civil Procedure*, R. 67.01.

206 *Children's Law Reform Act*, s. 59(1)(a). Applications under ss. 59 and 60 of this Act are made to the Superior Court of Justice, not to the Family Court, see *Courts of Justice Act*, s. 21.8, Schedule.

207 *Ibid.*, s. 59(2).

208 *Ibid.*, s. 59(4).

209 *783107 Ontario Inc. v. Hickson Estate* (1993), 50 E.T.R. 285 (Ont. Gen. Div.).

210 This is discussed in the chapter on Testamentary Gifts.

of the beneficiaries, they may appropriate assets and divide them *in specie* and this applies also to beneficiaries who have been given legacies.

Re Schippman Estate[211] illustrates that the executor may have regard to the tax implications of distribution. The testator was survived by his wife and two children. He left 50 percent of the residue to his wife and the rest equally to the children. He appointed his wife his executrix. She took the real estate in specie and paid cash to the estate for the excess thus allotted to her. She did this to take advantage of the spousal rollover provisions of the *Income Tax Act*.[212] Further, she valued the real estate at an amount discounted for the accrued capital gains tax. The court held that her actions were unexceptional.

If minors are beneficiaries, however, different considerations arise. Unless the will directs the personal representatives to establish a trust for a minor, or to pay the moneys due to the minor to his or her parent or guardian, the moneys must be paid into court to the credit of the minor, with notice to the Children's Lawyer.[213] The same applies to mentally incapable persons.[214] However, if the Public Guardian and Trustee is guardian of the estate of a mentally ill person, the moneys are payable to the Public Guardian and Trustee.[215]

Similar problems arise with minors who are beneficiaries under contracts of insurance. If the proceeds are payable to a trustee in trust for a minor, or any other person, they will be paid to the trustee.[216] If there is no trust, the moneys may be paid to the representative of the minor or other person under a disability,[217] or if there is no one capable of giving a discharge, they may be paid into court.[218]

The court has jurisdiction to order the payment of all or any money belonging to a minor, or the income from property belonging to a minor to a person, if it is satisfied that it is necessary or proper for the support or education of the minor, or will substantially benefit the minor.[219] Normally such payment would be made to the minor's parent or guardian. The guardian stands *in loco parentis* to the minor and is entitled to have management of the minor's income.[220] He or she may be required to account for his or her guardianship in the same manner as trustees under a will are accountable for their trusteeship.[221]

---

211 (1999), 26 E.T.R. (2d) 67 (B.C. S.C. [In Chambers])
212 R.S.C. 1985, c. 1 (5th Supp.).
213 However, the sum of 2,000 per year, up to a maximum of 5,000, may be paid to a child who has a legal obligation to support another person, or to the parent, or to the person who has lawful custody of the child: *Children's Law Reform Act*, s. 51(1). See generally Susan E. Greer, "Recent Developments in Probate Practice", in Law Soc. of Upper Can., Special Lectures, 1980, *Recent Developments in Estate Planning and Administration*, p. 87, at pp. 105-109.
214 *Trustee Act*, s. 36(4), (6).
215 *Ibid.*, s. 36(9).
216 *Insurance Act*, R.S.O. 1990, c. I-8, s. 193(1).
217 *Ibid.*, s. 221.
218 *Ibid.*, s. 220.
219 *Children's Law Reform Act*, s. 59(1)(c), (2).
220 *Re Lloyd*, [1949] O.R. 473, [1949] 4 D.L.R. 99.
221 *Children's Law Reform Act*, s. 52.

Further Reading

J. Albert Brulé, "Specie Distribution in Estates" (1976-77), 3 E. & T.Q. 28.

PART II

INTESTATE SUCCESSION

3

INTESTATE SUCCESSION

1. INTRODUCTION

A person who dies without leaving a valid will disposing of his or her estate is said to die intestate. All of the Canadian provinces supply a "statutory will" for that situation. In other words, a statute directs who is entitled to the estate of the intestate.

If a person leaves a valid will but it fails to dispose of the entire estate, whether intentionally, through inadvertence, or because residuary gifts in the will are void, the person is said to die partially intestate. In those circumstances the will governs the distribution of the deceased's estate to the extent that it is valid and effective and the statute governs the remaining portion of the estate. A will may be void because of improper execution, undue influence, lack of capacity, or for other reasons. A testamentary gift may be void because it is made to a person who, or whose spouse, has attested the will,[1] because it offends a rule of public policy, because it is uncertain, because it has lapsed, or for other reasons. Absent a contrary intention in the will, a failed gift, other than a residuary gift, falls into residue, whereas a residuary gift which fails goes out on intestacy.

The law of intestate succession in the Canadian common law jurisdiction is now largely uniform. Most provinces have, in varying degrees, adopted the *Uniform Devolution of Real Property Act*[2] and the *Uniform Intestate Succession Act*.[3] Further, the common law concepts of dower and curtesy have been abolished prospectively in all jurisdictions.[4]

Some differences inevitably remain. Thus, for example, homestead legislation in the Western provinces may confer additional rights on a surviving spouse, as may family property law legislation. In addition, spouses are sometimes disentitled to share in an intestacy for various reasons. Further, there are differences in the way in which persons born outside marriage and adopted persons are treated. I shall point out these differences in the following materials.

---

1 See the chapter on Capacity of Beneficiaries.
2 Uniform Law of Conference of Canada, *Uniform Acts of the Uniform Law Conference of Canada* 1987, p. 12-1.
3 *Ibid.*, p. 25A-1.
4 See chapter 1.

2. DEVOLUTION OF PROPERTY

Today, the administration of an estate, whether testate or intestate, is in the hands of the deceased's personal representative. At common law a deceased person's personal property also passed to his or her personal representative, but the real property descended directly to the deceased's heir at law.[5] However, in Ontario, since 1886 the administration of the real property has also been entrusted to the personal representative.[6] This is governed by section 2 of the *Estates Administration Act*,[7] set out below. The section provides that when a person dies, all his or her property, except that held in joint tenancy, vests in the person's personal representative in trust to pay debts and funeral expenses and then to distribute what remains among the persons beneficially entitled. Those benefici-aries are the persons named in the deceased's will, if any, to the extent that it is valid, or the persons entitled to take under the provisions of Part II of the *Succession Law Reform Act*,[8] or both.

ESTATES ADMINISTRATION ACT
R.S.O. 1990, c. E.22

2. (1) All real and personal property that is vested in a person without a right in any other person to take by survivorship, on the person's death, whether testate or intestate and despite any testamentary disposition, devolves to and becomes vested in his or her personal representative from time to time as trustee for the persons by law beneficially entitled thereto, and, subject to the payment of the person's debts and so far as such property is not disposed of by deed, will, contract or other effectual disposition, it shall be administered, dealt with and distributed as if it were personal property not so disposed of.

(2) This section applies to property over which a person executes by will a general power of appointment as if it were property vested in the person.

(3) This section does not apply to estates tail or to the personal property, except chattels real, of a person who, at the time of death, is domiciled out of Ontario.

Comparable Legislation

Chattels Real Act, R.S.N. 1990, c. C-11, s. 2; *Devolution of Estates Act*, R.S.N.B. 1973, c. D-9, s. 3; *Devolution of Real Property Act*, R.S.A. 1980, c. D-34, ss. 2, 3; R.S.S. 1978, c. D-27, ss. 4-6; R.S.N.W.T. 1988, c. D-5, ss. 3-4; R.S.Y. 1986, c. 45, ss. 2-3; *Estate Administration Act*, R.S.B.C. 1996, c. 122, ss. 77-78; *Law of Property Act*, R.S.M. 1987, c. L90 [added by 1989-90, c. 43, s. 14], s. 17.3(1)-(3); *Probate Act*, R.S.P.E.I. 1988, c. P-21, ss. 103-4; *Real Property Act*, R.S.N.S. 1989, c. 385, s. 1.

---

5 For a discussion of the history of descent and distribution see ch. 1.
6 *Devolution of Estates Act*, S.O. 1886, c. 22, s. 4.
7 R.S.O. 1990, c. E.22.
8 R.S.O. 1990, c. S.26, hereafter in this chapter referred to without further citation.

Notes and Questions

1. You should note that s. 2 of the Ontario *Estates Administration Act* speaks of property that is "vested" in a person on his or her death. Does the statute, therefore, not apply to rights of entry for condition broken, possibilities of reverter, contingent remainders and other future interests that are not vested?

2. Other statutes avoid the problem by deeming all lands, tenements and hereditaments to be chattels real,[9] or by providing that real property or land in which a deceased person had an interest not ceasing at his or her death vests in the deceased's personal representatives.[10]

3. DISTRIBUTION ON INTESTACY

(a) Introduction

The statutory provisions governing distribution of an intestate estate are contained in Part II of the *Succession Law Reform Act*. Comparable statutes are in effect in the other common law jurisdictions.[11]

For the purpose of discussing the present law of intestate succession it is convenient to divide the potential takers into the following three groups, namely (a) the spouse or partner, (b) issue, and (c) lineal ascendants and collaterals.

(b) The Surviving Spouse or Partner

(i) *Definition of Spouse*

Beginning in the 1970s, statutes were beginning to grant surviving partners of the opposite sex quasi-succession rights to pension and insurance benefits and support, as well as the right to administer the deceased partner's estate. Initially, such rights were granted only to common law spouses, but not to same-sex partners. The latter began to acquire similar rights in the late 1990s. However, until 2000 no statute conferred on partners of the same or opposite sex the right to inherit on the intestacy of their deceased partner. Changes came because of early legislation recognizing certain rights of common law spouses and of a number of cases holding that denial of such rights discriminated against surviving

---

9 *Chattels Real Act*, R.S.N. 1990, c. C-11, s. 2. *Cf. Estate Administration Act*, R.S.B.C. 1996, c. 122, s. 77(1). *Law of Property Act*, R.S.M. 1987, c. L90, s. 17.3(4).

10 *Devolution of Real Property Act*, R.S.A. 1980, c. D-34, s. 2(1); R.S.N.W.T. 1988, c. D-5, s. 2(1); R.S.S. 1978, c. D-27, s. 4(1); R.S.Y. 1986, c. 45, s. 2(1); *Probate Act*, R.S.P.E.I. 1988, c. P-21, s. 103(1).

11 The statutes are: *Intestate Succession Act*, R.S.A. 1980, c. I-9; S.M. 1989-90, c. 43; R.S.N.S. 1989, c. 236; R.S.N. 1990, c. I-21; R.S.N.W.T. 1988, c. I-10; S.S. 1996, c. I-13.1; R.S.Y. 1986, c. 95; *Devolution of Estates Act*, R.S.N.B. 1973, c. D-9; *Estate Administration Act*, R.S.B.C. 1996, c. 122, Part 10; *Probate Act*, R.S.P.E.I. 1988, c. P-21, Part IV. These statutes, as amended, are hereafter in this chapter referred to as the "Alta. Act", *etc.* without further citation.

partners, contrary to the equality provisions of s. 15 of the *Canadian Charter of Rights and Freedoms*. At the time of writing, only one case has specifically held that the exclusion of common law spouses from the right to share on their partner's intestacy is unconstitutional,[12] but others have reached similar conclusions about various quasi-succession rights.[13]

Undoubtedly in response to this judicial activity, the British Columbia Legislature made amendments to a number of statutes to confer various rights on partners of the same or different sex.[14] To date, it is the only jurisdiction that has conferred the right on partners to inherit on the deceased partner's intestacy on the same basis as a spouse. It may be expected that other provinces will follow suit. Section 1 of the *Estate Administration Act*,[15] Part 10 of which contains the provisions governing intestacy, now contains the following definitions:

> "common law spouse" means either
>   (a) a person who is united to another person by a marriage that, although not a legal marriage, is valid by common law, or
>   (b) a person who has lived and cohabited with another person, for a period of at least 2 years immediately before the other person's death, in a marriage-like relationship, including a marriage-like relationship between persons of the same gender;
> "spouse" includes a common law spouse;

Further Reading

Brian A. Schnurr, "Claims by Common Law Spouses and Same-Sex Partners against Estates" (1997), 16 E. & T.J. 22.

Helen H. Low, "Entitlements of an Unmarried Person on the Death of a Partner" (2000), 20 E.T. & P.J. 61.

(ii) *When There Are no Surviving Issue*

Under section 44 of the *Succession Law Reform Act*, when the intestate's spouse survives, but no issue, the surviving spouse takes the entire estate.

---

12 *Ferguson v. Armbrust* (2000), 187 D.L.R. (4th) 367 (Sask. Q.B.).

13 *Miron v. Trudel*, [1995], 2 S.C.R. 418, 124 D.L.R. (4th) 693, holding that the exclusion of common law partners from insurance benefits was discriminatory; *M. v. H.*, [1999] 2 S.C.R. 3, 171 D.L.R. (4th) 577, holding that the exclusion of same-sex partners from the *inter vivos* support provisions conferred on spouses and common law spouses was unconstitutional; *Walsh v. Bona* (2000), 186 D.L.R. (4th) 50, suppl. reasons *ibid.* at 83 (N.S. C.A.), holding that the right of spouses to claim a division of assets on a breakdown of marriage (and on death) discriminated against common law spouses; and *Grigg v. Berg Estate* (2000), 31 E.T.R. (2d) 214, suppl. reasons 32 E.T.R. (2d) 218, 186 D.L.R. (4th) 160 (B.C. S.C.), holding that the right of spouses (and children) to bring an application to vary a will to seek support from the estate of the deceased discriminated against common law spouses.

14 *Definition of Spouse Amendment Act, 1999*, S.B.C. 1999, c. 29, ss. 4-15, am. *Definition of Spouse Amendment Act, 2000*, S.B.C. 2000, c. 24, s. 17, amending the *Estate Administration Act*, R.S.B.C. 1996, c. 122, and other statutes.

15 *Ibid.*

44. Where a person dies intestate in respect of property and is survived by a spouse and not survived by issue, the spouse is entitled to the property absolutely.

This provision overcomes the "doctrine of the laughing heir," that is, the remote next of kin with whom there has been no contact and who stood to make a windfall under the former legislation.[16]

Legislation similar to s. 44 is in force in most of the other provinces.[17] Moreover, in the Yukon, a surviving spouse may apply to the court for an order that the entire estate be transferred to the spouse even though children survive.[18]

Notes and Questions

1. A court has held that, for the purpose of entitlement to property rights, the term "spouse" means a person to whom one is bound in a legal marriage.[19] However, s. 1 of the Act was amended in 1986.[20] Subsections (1) and (2) now provide in part:

1. (1)

. . .

(fa) "spouse" means either of a man or woman who,
    (i) are married to each other, or
    (ii) have together entered into a marriage that is voidable or void, in good faith on the part of the person asserting a right under this Act.

. . .

(1a) In the definition of "spouse", a reference to marriage includes a marriage that is actually or potentially polygamous, if it was celebrated in a jurisdiction whose system of law recognizes it as valid.

2. It is possible under the amended legislation in British Columbia, which allows common law spouses of the same or opposite gender to share on their deceased partner's intestacy, that more than one person may be entitled to the spousal share, whether that share be the whole of the estate or part, as discussed in the following subsections. For that reason, the *Estate Administration Act*[21] now contains the following provision:

85.1 For the purposes of section 85, if 2 or more persons are entitled as a spouse they share the spousal share in the estate in the portions determined by the court as the court considers just.

---

16 Section 31 of the former *Devolution of Estates Act*, R.S.O. 1970, c. 129, provided that when a person died, survived by a spouse but not by issue, the surviving spouse was entitled to his or her preferential and distributive shares, while the remainder went to the deceased spouse's next of kin.

17 Alta. Act, s. 2; B.C. Act, s. 83; Man. Act, s. 2(1); N.B. Act, s. 24; N.S. Act, s. 4; Nfld. Act, s. 6; N.W.T. Act, s. 4; Yukon Act, s. 4; Sask. Act, s. 8. If the surviving spouse is bankrupt, however, the moneys become available for the creditors: *Re Fox* (1980), 35 C.B.R. 234 (Ont. S.C.).

18 Yukon Act, s. 15.

19 *Re McFarland* (1987), 60 O.R. (2d) 73 (H.C.).

20 By S.O. 1986, c. 53.

21 R.S.B.C. 1996, c. 122, as am. by S.B.C. 1999, c. 29, ss. 4-15, and S.B.C. 2000, c. 21, s. 17.

(iii) *Preferential Share*

If issue survive, the surviving spouse is entitled in Ontario to a preferential share. If the deceased died partially intestate, the surviving spouse is still entitled to a preferential share, but the share is reduced by the amount, if any, he or she received under the will. The preferential share had been $75,000 since 1978. This amount was stipulated in s. 45 of the Act. However, s. 45 was amended in 1994[22] to permit the Lieutenant Governor in Council to change the amount of the preferential share by regulation. A regulation passed on Feb. 18, 1995 increased the amount to $200,000.[23] Section 45 now provides:

45. (1) Subject to subsection (3), where a person dies intestate in respect of property having a net value of not more than the preferential share and is survived by a spouse and issue, the spouse is entitled to the property absolutely.

(2) Subject to subsection (3), where a person dies intestate in respect of property having a net value of more than the preferential share and is survived by a spouse and issue, the spouse is entitled to the preferential share absolutely.

(3) Despite subsection (1), where a person dies testate as to some property and intestate as to other property and is survived by a spouse and issue, and,

    (a) where the spouse is entitled under the will to nothing or to property having a net value of less than the preferential share, the spouse is entitled out of the intestate property to the amount by which the preferential share exceeds the net value of the property, if any, to which the spouse is entitled under the will;

    (b) where the spouse is entitled under the will to property having a net value of more than the preferential share, subsections (1) and (2) do not apply.

(4) In this section, "net value" means the value of the property after payment of the charges thereon and the debts, funeral expenses and expenses of administration, including succession duty.

(5) The preferential share is the amount prescribed by a regulation made under subsection (6).

(6) The Lieutenant Governor in Council may, by regulation, prescribe the amount of the preferential share.

Similar legislation exists in most of the other provinces.[24] However, the Manitoba statute applies only if one or more of the surviving issue are not the issue of the surviving spouse. If the surviving issue are issue of the surviving spouse, the latter takes all.[25] In some provinces the preferential share is not reduced on a partial intestacy even though the surviving spouse has received benefits under the will.[26]

---

22 By S.O. 1994, c. 27, s. 63(1).

23 See S.O. 1994, c. 27, s. 63(1)-(3); O. Reg. 54/95.

24 Alta. Act, s. 3(1), (2), 20,000 if death occurred before January 1, 1976, 40,000 if thereafter; B.C. Act, ss. 82, 85(1), (2), 5,000 if death occurred on or after April 1, 1955, 10,000 if death occurred on or after April 1, 1963, 20,000 if death occurred on or after April 1, 1966, 65,000 if death occurred on or after October 1, 1983; Man. Act, s. 2(3)(a), 50,000; N.S. Act, s. 4(1), (2), 50,000; Sask. Act, ss. 4(1), (2), 5(1), 6(1), 10,000 if death occurred on or before January 11, 1978, 40,000 if death occurred after January 11, 1978, 100,000 if death occurred on or after June 22, 1990; N.W.T. Act, s. 2(4), 20,000.

25 Man. Act, s. 2(2).

26 Alta. Act, s. 12; B.C. Act, s. 94; N.B. Act, s. 32; Nfld. Act, s. 14; N.S. Act, s. 14(1); Sask. Act, s. 17; N.W.T. Act, s. 12; Yukon Act, s. 12.

Notes and Questions

1. The interest to which a spouse is entitled under the will is valued as of the date of the testator's death for the purpose of this section.[27]

2. Is the Manitoba provision, described above, a desirable one? Why, or why not?

3. The intestate habitually resided in one province, but also owned real property in another. The succession to the real property was, therefore, subject to the law of the province in which it was situate, while the succession to the other property was subject to the law of the province in which the deceased was domiciled. The preferential share provisions of the two provinces differed: one preferential share was larger than the other. Is the surviving spouse entitled to two preferential shares?[28]

(iv) *Distributive Share*

After the preferential share, the surviving spouse is entitled to a distributive share, which varies with the number of children or issue surviving. The distributive share is not reduced by any amount the surviving spouse received under the will if there is a partial intestacy.

The distributive share of the surviving spouse under the *Succession Law Reform Act* is described as follows in s. 46:

> **46.** (1) Where a person dies intestate in respect of property and leaves a spouse and one child, the spouse is entitled to one-half of the residue of the property after payment under section 45, if any.
>
> (2) Where a person dies intestate in respect of property and leaves a spouse and more than one child, the spouse is entitled to one-third of the residue of the property after payment under section 45, if any.
>
> (3) Where a child has died leaving issue living at the date of the intestate's death, the spouse's share shall be the same as if the child had been living at that date.

Virtually identical legislation exists in all the other provinces, except Manitoba since July 20, 1978.[29] In that province the present rule is that, if the surviving issue are not the issue of the surviving spouse, the surviving spouse receives one-half of the estate regardless of the number of children or their issue who survive the intestate.[30]

(v) *Other Rights*

In some provinces the surviving spouse has certain rights in addition to the preferential and distributive shares. Thus, in Nova Scotia the surviving spouse

---

27 *Re Oswell* (1982), 38 O.R. (2d) 71, 136 D.L.R. (3d) 672, 11 E.T.R. 283 (H.C.).

28 See *Vak Estate v. Dukelow* (1994), 117 D.L.R. (4th) 122 (Ont. Gen. Div.).

29 Alta. Act, s. 3(3), (4); B.C. Act, s. 85(5)(a), (b), (6) ; N.B. Act, s. 22(1)-(3); N.S. Act, s. 3(5), (6); Nfld. Act, s. 4; P.E.I. Act, s. 87; Sask. Act, ss. 4(3), (4); N.W.T. Act, s. 2(6), (7), Yukon Act, s. 2.

30 Man. Act, s. 2(3).

may take the spouse's principal residence in lieu of or as part of the preferential share,[31] while in New Brunswick the surviving spouse is entitled to any interest of the intestate in property that is marital property, in addition to the distributive share.[32]

In the Northwest Territories a surviving spouse who has no interest in the family home, but who is occupying it at the time of the other spouse's death, is entitled to remain in the home for sixty days after the spouse's death.[33] In British Columbia the surviving spouse is entitled to a life interest in the spouse's main residence and to the household furnishings.[34] Formerly in British Columbia the court could order that part or all of the estate be applied to or for the benefit of an intestate's common law spouse. However, that provision has been repealed, since common law spouses are now otherwise provided for.[35]

Under the homestead legislation in the western provinces, a surviving spouse is entitled to a life estate in the homestead.[36] The wife's dower right and the husband's right to curtesy have been abolished in Ontario[37] and the maritime provinces.[38]

Orders for division of assets or for exclusive possession of the matrimonial home in favour of one spouse under family law legislation take precedence over the rights of the beneficiaries of the deceased's estate.[39] Moreover under some of these statutes a spouse may make application for a division of assets after the death of the other spouse whether or not there was a marriage breakdown before death. An order for division in such a case also takes precedence over the rights of the beneficiaries of the estate and is in addition to the surviving spouse's rights of inheritance.[40]

---

31 N.S. Act, s. 4(4).

32 N.B. Act, s. 22(2)(a), (2.1)(a).

33 *Family Law Act,* S.N.W.T. 1997, C.18, s.57.

34 B.C. Act, s. 96(2).

35 B.C. Act, Part 8 (s. 76), repealed by S.B.C. 1999, c. 29, s. 9. For case law, see *Re Nelson; Re Coss* (1982), 28 R.F.L. (2d) 323 (B.C.S.C.). A person was only regarded as a common law spouse under this provision if the parties had the capacity to enter into marriage, of if the person was maintained by the deceased for not less than two years immediately before the deceased's death: *Desjarlais v. British Columbia (Public Trustee)* (1988), 31 E.T.R. 18 (B.C.C.A.); *Keddie v. Currie* (1991), 44 E.T.R. 61 (B.C.C.A.).

36 *Dower Act,* R.S.A. 1980, c. D-38; B.C. Act, s. 96(2) (matrimonial home); *Land (Spouse Protection) Act,* R.S.B.C. 1996, c. 246; *Homesteads Act,* S.M. 1992, c. 46, s. 21(1); S.S. 1989-90, c. H-5.1. There appears to be no similar legislation in the Yukon. The court cannot compel the surviving spouse to consent to a sale of the land and take a sum of money in lieu of the life estate: *Melnychuk v. Bassingthwaighte* (1990), 39 E.T.R. 296 (Alta. Q.B.).

37 See the Notes and Questions below.

38 By the *Married Woman's Property Act,* R.S.N.B. 1973, c. M-4, s. 8 (curtesy); *Marital Property Act,* S.N.B. 1980, c. M-1.1, s. 49(1), (2) (dower); *Matrimonial Property Act,* R.S.N.S. 1989, c. 275, s. 33; *Family Law Reform Act,* S.P.E.I. 1978, c. 6, s. 62 (not subsequently consolidated), see now *Family Law Act,* S.P.E.I. 1995, c.12.

39 *Family Law Act,* R.S.N. 1990, c. F-2, s. 15; *Matrimonial Property Act,* R.S.A. 1980, c. M-9, s. 15; S.S. 1979, c. M-6.1, ss. 30(3), 35; R.S.N.S. 1989, c. 275, s. 12(4); *Marital Property Act,* S.N.B. 1980, c. M-1.1, s. 4(4)-(6).

40 *Family Law Act,* R.S.N. 1990, c. F-2; *Marital Property Act,* S.N.B. 1980, M-1.1, s. 4(1), (2), (4)-(6); *Matrimonial Property Act,* R.S.N.S. 1989, c. 275, s. 12(4); S.S. 1979, c. M-6.1, ss. 30, 35.

The *Family Law Act*[41] of Ontario has a major impact on succession, both testate and intestate. Under this Act, a surviving spouse is entitled to an equalization payment of one-half the difference between the net family property of each spouse, if the net family property of the deceased is larger than the net family property of the surviving spouse. However, in order to take advantage of this right, the surviving spouse must elect to do so. The details and operation of this legislation are discussed in a later chapter.

(vi) *Spousal Disentitlement*

A number of statutes provide that if a spouse lived separate in adultery imme-diately preceding the death of the other spouse, the surviving spouse is not entitled to share in the deceased's intestacy,[42] but it is otherwise if the deceased left the surviving spouse.[43] In the Yukon the court has a discretion to make an order directing that the surviving spouse be entitled to share nevertheless, if children under age 19 survive.[44] In British Columbia a spouse who has lived separate from the deceased for one year or more is debarred from sharing in the estate unless the court directs otherwise.[45]

A general release of all claims against the estate of the deceased spouse in a separation agreement also bars the survivor from inheriting, unless there is a reconciliation.[46]

The Manitoba *Intestate Succession Act* provides that if the spouses were living separate and apart when the intestate died, but had divided, or had made appli-cation to divide their property, the surviving spouse is to be treated as having predeceased the intestate.[47]

Notes and Questions

1. Prior to the enactment of the *Succession Law Reform Act* in 1978[48] a surviving husband was entitled to elect to take curtesy, that is, a life estate in his deceased wife's

---

And see *Re Fraser* (1981), 130 D.L.R. (3d) 665 (N.S. T.D.); *Levy v. Levy* (1981), 50 N.S.R. (2d) 14, (sub nom. *Re Levy*) 131 D.L.R. (3d) 15 (T.D.); *LeBlanc v. LeBlanc* (1984), 59 N.B.R. (2d) 31, 154 A.P.R. 31, 18 E.T.R. 160, 43 R.F.L. (2d) 250 (Q.B.).

41 R.S.O. 1990, c. F.3.

42 Alta. Act, s. 15; N.S. Act, s. 17; P.E.I. Act, s. 99; Sask. Act, s. 20; N.W.T. Act, s. 13; Yukon Act, s. 14.

43 *Re Rudiak; Rudiak v. Public Trustee for Alta.* (1958), 13 D.L.R. (2d) 566, 25 W.W.R. 38 (Alta. T.D.); *Re Mullins* (1981), 9 E.T.R. 167 (Nfld. T.D.).

44 Yukon Act, s. 15.

45 B.C. Act, s. 98. See *Re Small* (1982), 12 E.T.R. 17 (B.C.S.C.). And see *Re Munro*, 47 D.L.R. (3d) 625, [1975] 1 W.W.R. 83 (B.C.S.C.), holding that the section applies only if the separation arose because of the spouses' joint intention to separate. See also *Tuomi v. Ungarian* (1992), 47 E.T.R. 17 (B.C.C.A.), to the same effect. The criteria to be used by the court are the same as on an application for support: *Law v. Tretiak* (1993), 50 E.T.R. 176 (B.C.C.A.).

46 *Watkin v. Smith* (1979), 5 E.T.R. 162 (Ont. H.C.).

47 Man. Act, s. 3.

48 S.O. 1977, c. 40.

real property not disposed of by deed or will in lieu of his statutory right to a preferential and distributive share. This estate was abolished by the Act.[49]

Similarly a surviving wife was entitled, as her primary right, to take dower, that is, a life estate in one-third of the real property of which her husband died solely seized, or to which he died beneficially entitled. She could, however, elect to give up dower and take her statutory rights of inheritance instead. The life estate was abolished by the *Family Law Reform Act*.[50] However, the old law remains important for titles to land, for s. 70 of that Act only abolished the right prospectively. Section 70(4) spoke of a right to dower that has "vested," such a right being preserved. The meaning of this provision is uncertain. It is probable that the Legislature intended to preserve the right to dower consummate where the husband died before March 31, 1978, the date on which the statute came into force. However, it is inaccurate to speak of dower consummate as being a vested right and thus, as an estate in land, until it has been assigned by metes and bounds. Until dower is assigned, dower consummate and, indeed, dower inchoate, are mere possibilities coupled with an interest in land.[51]

(c) Issue

After the surviving spouse's shares have been paid, the intestate's issue are entitled to the balance of the estate.

The former rule that lineal descendants always share in the estate of their intestate ancestor *per stirpes* has been modified by the *Succession Law Reform Act*. This was done on the recommendation of the Ontario Law Reform Commission that if all the issue are of equal degree they should share *per capita* and not *per stirpes*. The Commission operated on the assumption that if, for example, an intestate was survived by grandchildren only, he or she would probably prefer that they take an equal share each.[52] A stirpital distribution might have the effect of giving some grandchildren more than others if, for example, the children of one deceased child were less numerous than those of another deceased child. In fact, the *Succession Law Reform Act* may go beyond this recommendation. Section 47 provides as follows:

> **47.** (1) Subject to subsection (2), where a person dies intestate in respect of property and leaves issue surviving him or her, the property shall be distributed, subject to the rights of the spouse, if any, equally among his or her issue who are of the nearest degree in which there are issue surviving him or her.

---

49 *Ibid.*, s. 48. For the former law of curtesy, see *Anger and Honsberger, Law of Real Property*, 2nd ed. by A.H. Oosterhoff and W.B. Rayner (Aurora: Canada Law Book Inc., 1985), §§ 708-708.2.

50 S.O. 1978, c. 2, s. 70, consolidated as R.S.O. 1980, c. 152, rep. by S.O. 1986, c. 4, s. 71, save, *inter alia*, for s. 70, the retained sections being renamed as the *Dower and Miscellaneous Abolition Act*.

51 *Freedman v. Mason*, [1956] O.R. 894, 4 D.L.R. (2d) 576 at 586 (H.C.); *per* McRuer C.J.H.C, reversed on other grounds [1957] O.R. 441, 9 D.L.R. (2d) 262 (C.A.), affirmed [1958] S.C.R. 458, 14 D.L.R. (2d) 529. For the old law of dower, see Anger and Honsberger, *supra*, paras. 707-707.20.

52 Ont. Law Ref. Comm., *Report on Family Law, Part IV, Family Property Law* (1974), at p. 354.

(2) Where any issue of the degree entitled under subsection (1) has predeceased the intestate, the share of such issue shall be distributed among his or her issue in the manner set out in subsection (1) and the share devolving upon any issue of that and subsequent degrees who predecease the intestate shall be similarly distributed.

In order to effect a correct distribution under this section it is necessary to do the following: (1) identify the issue in the nearest degree who survive the deceased; (2) divide the estate into as many shares as there are living issue in the nearest degree and issue of the nearest degree who predeceased the intestate but left issue who survived him or her; and (3) give a share to each of the living issue of the nearest degree and divide a share among the issue of those of that degree who predeceased the deceased as if the latter had died intestate.[53] Consequently, a descendant can share in an intestate's estate only if the descendant's ancestor did not survive the intestate. Thus, if the intestate was survived by a child, A, and A's child, B, B is not entitled to share in the estate, because B's ancestor is alive and, unless otherwise disqualified, entitled to share in the estate.[54] Some examples showing how the section works follow.

Example 1

I died intestate, survived by his child, A; his grandchildren, D and E, children of his deceased child, B; and F, G and H, children of his deceased child, C. This may be represented schematically as follows:

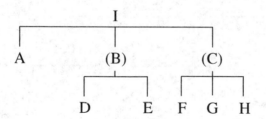

In this situation the balance of the estate is first divided at the level of I's children, since one of them survives. Hence it is divided into three parts and A will take one-third. The other two-thirds will be divided *per stirpes* among the families of B and C, so that D and E take one-sixth each and F, G and H take one-ninth each.

---

53 *Cf. Macdonell, Sheard and Hull on Probate Practice*, 4th ed. by Rodney Hull and Ian M. Hull (Scarborough: Carswell, 1996), p. 222.
54 *Re DWS (decd)*, [2000] 2 All E.R. 83 (Ch. D.).

Example 2

If, in example 1, A had also predeceased I without issue, the estate is divided at the level of the grandchildren. They will now share *per capita*, so that D, E, F, G and H will each take a one-fifth share.

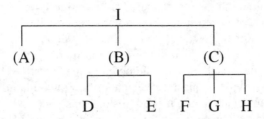

Example 3

I died intestate, survived by her child, A; her grandchildren, D and E, children of her deceased child, B; her grandchild, F, a child of her deceased child, C; and her great-grandchildren, H and J, children of I's grandchild, G, another child of C, who also predeceased I. Schematically this may be represented as follows:

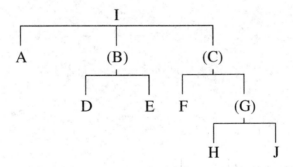

In these circumstances the estate is again first divided at the level of I's children, since one of them survives. Hence it is divided into three parts and A takes one-third. Another third is allocated to B's family and is divided *per stirpes* equally between D and E. The final one third is divided *per stirpes* among C's family, so that F will take one-sixth and H and J will share the one sixth interest to which G would otherwise have been entitled.

Example 4

If, in example 3, A had also predeceased I without issue, the first division of the estate would be at the level of the grandchildren, in which case D, E and F would take one-quarter of the estate and the remaining one-quarter would be divided *per stirpes* among G's children. Hence, H and J would take one-eighth each.

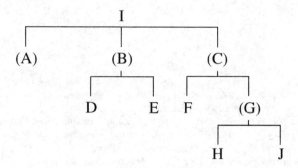

Most of the other provincial statutes provide that distribution to issue is always *per stirpes*.[55] However, the Manitoba legislation is like Ontario's in this respect.[56]

Children conceived before but born after the death of the intestate are treated by the *Succession Law Reform Act*[57] and the statutes in the other provinces[58] as though they were born in the intestate's lifetime and are, therefore, entitled to inherit on the death of the intestate.

Children of the half-blood probably share equally with those of the whole blood. We shall deal with this point in the next part.

Notes and Questions

1. It is clear that, except for the spouse of the intestate, and aside from adoption, the right to share on an intestacy depends entirely on the existence of a blood relationship between the claimant and the intestate. Thus, for example, the children of the partner of the intestate's brother are not entitled to inherit from the intestate.[59]

---

55 The provisions in the other provisions are: Alta. Act, s. 4; B.C. Act, s. 84; N.B. Act, s. 23; N.S. Act, s. 4(7); Nfld. Act., s. 5; P.E.I. Act, s. 88; Sask. Act, s. 7; N.W.T. Act, s. 3; Yukon Act, s. 3.
56 Man. Act, ss. 4(2), 5.
57 Section 47(9).
58 Alta. Act, s. 10; B.C. Act, s. 104; Man. Act, s. 1(3); N.B. Act, s. 30; N.S. Act, s. 12; Nfld. Act, s. 12; P.E.I. Act, s. 95; Sask. Act, s. 12; N.W.T. Act, s. 10; Yukon Act, s. 10.
59 See *Marcy v. Young Estate* (1998), 20 E.T.R. (2d) 274 (Man. Q.B.).

(d) Lineal Ascendants and Collaterals

Ascendants are the direct ancestors of the intestate; collaterals are the issue of the ascendants other than the intestate and his or her issue. The *Succession Law Reform Act* has simplified the rules of intestate succession with respect to ascendants and collaterals. Further, the Act has codified the manner in which degrees of relationship must be calculated. Subject to adoption legislation, entitlement is restricted to persons related to the intestate by blood.[60] Section 47(3)–(9) of the Act provides as follows:

47.

. . .

(3) Where a person dies intestate in respect of property and leaves no spouse or issue, the property shall be distributed between the parents of the deceased equally or, where there is only one parent surviving the deceased, to that parent absolutely.

(4) Where a person dies intestate in respect of property and there is no surviving spouse, issue or parent, the property shall be distributed among the surviving brothers and sisters of the intestate equally, and if any brother or sister predeceases the intestate, the share of the deceased brother or sister shall be distributed among his or her children equally.

(5) Where a person dies intestate in respect of property and there is no surviving spouse, issue, parent, brother or sister, the property shall be distributed among the nephews and nieces of the intestate equally without representation.

(6) Where a person dies intestate in respect of property and there is no surviving spouse, issue, parent, brother, sister, nephew or niece, the property shall be distributed among the next of kin of equal degree of consanguinity to the intestate equally without representation.

(7) Where a person dies intestate in respect of property and there is no surviving spouse, issue, parent, brother, sister, nephew, niece or next of kin, the property becomes the property of the Crown, and the *Escheats Act* applies.

(8) For the purposes of subsection (6), degrees of kindred shall be computed by counting upward from the deceased to the nearest common ancestor and then downward to the relative, and the kindred of the half-blood shall inherit equally with those of the whole-blood in the same degree.

(9) For the purposes of this section, descendants and relatives of the deceased conceived before and born alive after the death of the deceased shall inherit as if they had been born in the lifetime of the deceased and had survived him or her.[61]

In summary, therefore:

1. If no spouse nor issue survive, the surviving parents take all equally or, if only one survives, he or she takes all.

---

60 Thus, for example, a niece by marriage is excluded: *Re Butt* (1986) 22 E.T.R. 120 (Ont. Surr. Ct.); *Re Dunbar Estate* (1992), 49 E.T.R. 67 (N.S. Prob. Ct.); so are the children of the common law spouse of the intestate's brother: *Marcy v. Young Estate* (1998), 20 E.T.R. (2d) 274 (Man. Q.B.).

61 Virtually identical legislation exists in the other provinces: Alta. Act, ss. 5-10; B.C. Act, ss. 86-91; Man. Act, ss. 4-7; N.B. Act, ss. 25-30; N.S. Act, ss. 7-12; Nfld. Act, ss. 5, 7-12; P.E.I. Act, ss. 89-95; Sask. Act, ss. 9-14; N.W.T. Act, ss. 3, 5-10; Yukon Act, ss. 5-10. The Man. Act provides in s. 6 that a person who fails to survive the intestate by 15 clear days is treated as having predeceased the intestate.

2. If no parents survive, the brothers and sisters share the estate equally with representation being permitted among brothers' and sisters' children.
3. If no brothers and sisters survive, however, the nephews and nieces take *per capita*.
4. If no nephews or nieces survive either, any other next of kin of equal degree will take *per capita*.
5. If no next of kin survive, the property becomes the property of the Crown.

Traditionally, degrees of consanguinity are calculated by counting up from the intestate to the nearest ancestor and then down to the relative under consideration. This calculation is more readily understood by reference to the following table.

TABLE OF CONSANGUINITY

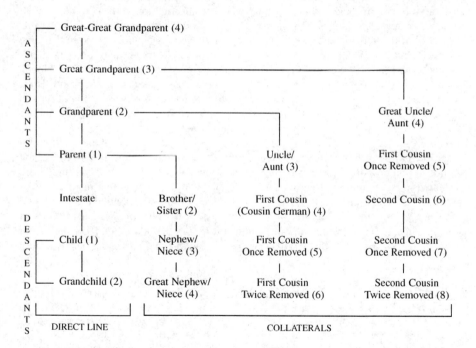

Thus, a parent would be of the first degree, a sister of the second, a nephew and an aunt both of the third, a first cousin of the fourth, *etc*. However, the statute does not always accord those of the same degree equal rights of succession. As we have seen, it prefers brothers and sisters over grandparents, even though both are of the second degree. It even favours nephews and nieces, who are of the third degree, over grandparents (second degree) and over great-grandparents and uncles and aunts (third degree). Apart from those exceptions, however, entitlement is on basis of the closest degree of consanguinity.

Notes and Questions

1. The legislation incorporates the old rule in *Winchelsea v. Norcliff*,[62] under which brothers and sisters took to the exclusion of grandparents.

2. You should note that while stirpital distribution is the rule for the intestate's descendants, save only if all are of equal degree, among ascendants and collaterals the rule is that those of equal degree take *per capita*. Section 47(4) contains the only exception to this rule. The subsection permits the children of a deceased brother or sister to represent their parent if they are competing with one or more living brothers or sisters of the intestate. Note, however, that only the *children* of the deceased brother or sister may take under this provision: remoter issue may not.[63]

3. Unborn next of kin of the intestate who are conceived before and born alive after the intestate's death may inherit as if they had been born in the intestate's lifetime and had survived him or her. This provision in section 47(9) was necessary, for, while section 1(1)(a) and (c) of the Act define "child" and "issue" as including a child or issue conceived before and born alive after the death of the *propositus*, those definitions do not expressly cover all relatives of the deceased. The provision is a codification of the common law.[64]

4. With respect to relatives of the half-blood, you should note that section 47(8) permits "kindred" of the half-blood to inherit equally with those of the whole-blood in the same degree. Because section 47 progresses through issue, parents, brothers and sisters, nephews and nieces and "next of kin," it is arguable that the reference to "kindred of the half-blood" in subsection (8) only refers to next of kin other than issue, parents, brothers and sisters and nephews and nieces of an intestate. But it is doubtful that this is the intent of section 47(8). Rather, it is probable that the provision was intended to be declaratory of the former law. The former law is not entirely clear either, however.

Relatives of the half-blood did share personalty[65] equally with those of the whole blood under the *Statute of Distribution*.[66] But under the common law canons of descent, which applied to real property, relatives of the half blood were excluded.[67] However, they were permitted to take under the *Inheritance Act, 1833*,[68] which provided that relatives of the half blood took next after relatives of the whole blood of the same degree if the common ancestor was a male, or next after the common ancestor if the common ancestor was a female. These rules were adopted in Ontario in 1834.[69] However, in 1851 they were changed further to provide that relatives of the half-blood should thereafter share equally

---

62 (1686), Freem. Ch. 95, 22 E.R. 1080.

63 See *Re Matthews Estate* (1992), 44 E.T.R. 164 (Alta. Q.B.); *Kiehn v. Murdoch* (1995), 9 E.T.R. (2d) 76 (Ont. Gen. Div.); *Farmer Estate v. Karabin Estate* (1997), 19 E.T.R. (2d) 66 (Ont. C.A.).

64 See as to personalty: *Wallis v. Hodson* (1740), 2 Atk. 114, 26 E.R. 472; *J.D. Irving Ltd. v. Burchill* (October 14, 1994), Doc. S/M/97/94, S/M/98/94 (N.B. Q.B.). With respect to taking land by descent, a child conceived but unborn was always regarded as in being: Challis, *Law of Real Property* (3rd ed., 1911), at p. 139. This was codified by the *Inheritance Act*, S.C. 1851, c. 6, s. 17.

65 See *Jessopp v. Watson* (1833), 1 My. & K. 665, 39 E.R. 832; *Re Green; Green v. Meinall*, [1911] 2 Ch. 275; *Doe d. Shannon v. Fortune* (1876), 16 N.B.R. 259 (C.A.); *Re Wagner* (1903), 6 O.L.R. 680; *Re Adams* (1903), 6 O.L.R. 697 (H.C.); *Re Branton* (1910), 20 O.L.R. 642 at 645 (H.C.); *Re Cummings*, [1938] O.R. 486, [1938] 3 D.L.R. 611, affirmed [1938] O.R. 654 (C.A.).

66 22 & 23 Car. 2, c. 10 (1670), am. by *Statute of Frauds*, 29 Car. 2, c. 3 (1677), and *Statute of Distribution*, 1 Jac. 2, c. 17 (1685).

67 Blackstone, *Commentaries on the Laws of England* (15th ed., 1809), vol. 2, at p. 228.

68 3 & 4 Will. 4, c. 106, s. 9.

69 By the *Real Property Act*, S.U.C. 1834, c. 1, s. 8.

with those of the whole blood of the same degree, unless the inheritance came to the intestate by descent, devise or gift from one of his or her ancestors. In that case any one not of the blood of such ancestor was excluded.[70]

It may be supposed that, since real property is now administered and distributed as if it were personal property,[71] the rule respecting relatives of the half-blood that formerly applied to personalty only now applies also to real property. However the legislation does not make this clear.[72]

5. What is the effect of the provision in section 47(8) that you must count upward to the common ancestor and then down to the relative under consideration to compute degrees of kindred? Is the calculation the same as under the former law? Or, if for example, the eligibility of a grandfather and an uncle are under consideration, is it necessary to count up to the great-grandfather and then down again to the grandfather? If so, that would make him of the fourth degree and the uncle, being of the third, would take priority.[73]

6. If some of the nearest next of kin, such as cousins, are related to the intestate in the same degree on both the maternal and paternal side of the family, do they take a double share?[74]

7. You should remember that the term "next of kin" does not include merely blood relations after issue, parents, brothers, sisters and nephews and nieces. The term is used in that sense in section 47. However in the normal sense it denotes the closest blood relative of a person and may thus refer to the person's child.[75]

8. Section 47(7) effectively abolishes the feudal doctrine of escheat for failure of heirs and, in so far as it applies to intestacy, the common law doctrine of *bona vacantia* and replaces them with a statutory rule that has the same result.

Problems

1. If a person dies domiciled in Ontario after March 31, 1978, without a will, how will the estate be distributed if the following persons survive him or her?
(a) Husband only.
(b) Wife, father and sister.
(c) Wife and child.
(d) Husband and three children.
(e) Children by two wives.
(f) Wife, one child and two children of deceased child.
(g) Husband, one child, two children of deceased child, A, one child of another deceased child, B, and two children of a deceased grandchild, C, a child of B.
(h) Three grandchildren.
(i) Three great-grandchildren.
(j) One child, two children of deceased child, X, one child of another deceased child, Y, and three children of a deceased grandchild, Z, a child of Y.

---

70 *Inheritance Act, supra.*
71 *Estates Administration Act*, R.S.O. 1990, c. E.22, s. 2, first enacted as *Devolution of Estates Act*, S.O. 1886, c. 22, s. 4.
72 Similar problems exist in the other provincial statutes.
73 For a discussion of this problem under the comparable Saskatchewan and Manitoba statutes, see *Re Cran; Western Trust Co. v. Forrest and Cran*, [1941] 1 W.W.R. 209, [1941] 1 D.L.R. 708 (Sask. C.A.); *Re Dixon*, [1948] 2 W.W.R. 108, 56 Man. R. 14 (K.B.).
74 See *Re Adams*, (1903), 6 O.L.R. 697 (H.C.).
75 See *Fasken v. Fasken*, [1953] 3 D.L.R. 431 (S.C.C.).

(k) Father and sister.
(l) Sister and four children of a deceased brother.
(m) Four brothers and sisters, three of the whole blood and one of the half blood.
(n) Six nephews and nieces.
(o) Four nephews and nieces and one nephew born of the intestate's brother's wife three months after the intestate's death.
(p) Grandfather, aunt and nephew.
(q) Two uncles and six nephews.
(r) Uncle, three nieces and six first cousins.
(s) Great nephew and five first cousins.

(e) Illegitimacy and Adoption

Persons born outside marriage and adopted persons have equivalent rights of inheritance with persons born within marriage in Ontario and substantial rights elsewhere. The details of the rights of inheritance of illegitimate and adopted persons are discussed elsewhere.[76] Persons who have been given up for adoption lose the right to share on the intestacy of their former parents and relatives.[77]

(f) Common Deaths

When two persons die intestate at the same time and they would otherwise be entitled to inherit from each other, questions arise about their rights of succession. These questions are discussed elsewhere.[78]

Further Reading

A.H. Oosterhoff, *Succession Law Reform in Ontario* (1979), pp. 61-80.

4. PARTIAL INTESTACY

We have seen that if a person dies partially testate and partially intestate, his or her surviving spouse is entitled to a preferential share, although it is reduced by the amount, if any, the spouse receives under the will. Apart from that the intestate portion of the estate is distributed in accordance with the rules discussed in the preceding part.

The fact that there is a partial intestacy may be apparent at the testator's death, or it may not be discovered until later. In the latter situation the question arises

---

76 In the chapter on Capacity of Beneficiaries.
77 See *Trombley Estate v. Rachow* (1988), 32 E.T.R. 157 (Ont. H.C.); *Oliphant v. Oliphant Estate* (1990), 38 E.T.R. 133 (Sask. Q.B.).
78 In the chapter on Lapse and Survivorship.

whether the persons entitled to take are to be determined as of the date of the testator's death, or as of the date when the partial intestacy occurs. Since this is primarily a question of interpretation of the will, it is dealt with in a later chapter.

5. CONTRACTING OUT OF LEGISLATION

Can a person who, in the normal course of events, would become entitled to inherit on another's intestacy enter into a valid contract by which that right is released? This question typically arises as a result of a provision in a separation agreement entered into by spouses in which they release their rights in the other's estate. In the past such a provision was often inserted in separation agreements to prevent a future dower claim by the wife. It has always been held that such a provision is valid, provided that it is clear and unambiguous.[79]

Such a provision is not contrary to public policy. In *Hyman v. Hyman*[80] Lord Atkin said in a passage often quoted in the Canadian cases:

> Full effect has therefore to be given in all Courts to these contracts as to all other contracts. It seems not out of place to make this obvious reflection, for a perusal of some of the cases in the matrimonial Courts seems to suggest that at times they are still looked at askance, and enforced grudgingly. But there is no caste in contracts. Agreements for separation are formed, construed and dissolved and to be enforced on precisely the same principles as any respectable commercial agreement, of whose nature indeed they sometimes partake. As in other contracts stipulations will not be enforced which are illegal either as being opposed to positive law or public policy. But this is a common attribute of all contracts, though we may recognize that the subject-matter of separation agreements may bring them more than others into relation with questions of public policy.

The effect of a provision barring dower, at least if it extended to rights of inheritance, was that the surviving wife was debarred not only from claiming dower, but also from electing to take her statutory rights instead of dower.[81]

As noted above, however, the provision had to be clear and unambiguous. Thus, in *Re Winter*[82] the surviving wife, had, in a separation agreement, covenanted to "release the husband...from all claims present, past or future against the husband for maintenance, alimony or separation allowance and acknowledge[d] that she ha[d] no further claims against the husband nor against the estate of the husband...." The court held that this provision merely covered claims for maintenance, alimony or separation allowance and that the wife was not precluded from claiming a distributive share in the husband's estate when he died intestate.[83] *Brant v. Brant*[84] is to the same effect. The spouses entered into minutes of settlement on

---

79 See, *e.g.*, *Re Schop; Cliff v. Schop*, [1948] O.W.N. 338 (H.C.); *Re Dalton*, [1939] O.W.N. 691 (H.C.); *Re Knoll*, [1938] O.W.N. 282.
80 [1929] A.C. 601 at 625-6 (H.L.).
81 See *Re Schop; Cliff v. Schop; Re Dalton; Re Knoll, supra.*
82 [1954] O.W.N. 726, [1955] 1 D.L.R. 134 (H.C.).
83 See also *Re Draper*, [1956] O.W.N. 106, 1 D.L.R. (2d) 366 (H.C.).
84 (1997), 16 E.T.R. (2d) 124 (Ont. Gen. Div.).

their separation. In the minutes the husband agreed to pay the wife a certain sum of money and she agreed to release all interest she might have by statute or common law in the assets then in his possession. When the husband died, his children contested the wife's claims to his estate. The court held that the release was made solely with reference to the property division on separation and that it was not broad enough to constitute a release of claims against the husband's estate as well. Consequently, the wife was entitled to a preferential share and to be appointed his estate trustee without a will.

It would seem that, since Part II of the *Succession Law Reform Act* (which deals with intestate succession) does not forbid contracting out, the same principles would apply under the new legislation. Indeed, they also apply to testate succession, since Part I of the Act similarly does not prohibit contracting out.

Re Saylor,[85] reproduced below, is concerned with the right to contract out of the present legislation and discusses the foregoing principles.

RE SAYLOR
(1983), 44 O.R. (2d) 188,
15 E.T.R. 253, 3 D.L.R. (4th) 434
Supreme Court of Ontario
[High Court of Justice]

The deceased and the applicant, his wife, entered into a separation agreement in 1977 in which the applicant barred her dower and both parties accepted the provisions of the agreement "in satisfaction of all claims and causes of action each now has...including...claims and causes of action for...possession of or title to property, and any other claims arising out of the marriage of the husband and wife." Pursuant to the agreement, the parties conveyed the matrimonial home which they owned jointly to the deceased. The husband, having complied with all his obligations under the agreement, died in 1982 with an estate of approximately $28,000 consisting of the former matrimonial home. There were no issue of the marriage. The applicant then brought this application claiming to be absolutely entitled to the estate by reason of section 44 of the *Succession Law Reform Act*.[86]

The applicant admitted and the court found that she would have been debarred from any rights on her husband's intestacy under the former law by reason of the provisions of the separation agreement.

KREVER J.:

. . .

Did the applicant's loss of the right to a preferential and distributive share of the deceased's estate under the repealed legislation deprive her of the right to the property conferred under s. 44 of the *Succession Law Reform Act*, bearing in mind

---

85 (1983), 44 O.R. (2d) 188, 15 E.T.R. 253, 3 D.L.R. (4th) 434 (H.C.).
86 Section 44 is reproduced earlier in this chapter.

that her husband died more than four years after the coming into force of the section? The answer, the respondents submit, is in the affirmative. Section 44, they argue, confers no right on the applicant notwithstanding that it is patently remedial and part of a deliberate reform of succession law. What prevents it from having the effect contended for by the applicant, they say, is the operation of s. 14(1)(c) of the *Interpretation Act*.[87] The relevant portion of the subsection reads as follows:

> **14.** (1) Where an Act is repealed...the repeal...does not, except as in this Act otherwise provided,
>
> . . .
>
> (c) affect any right, privilege, obligation or liability acquired, accrued, accruing or incurred under the Act...so repealed...

The language of this subsection brings me to the heart of the issue which is the question whether the applicant's act in the separation agreement and conveyance of the matrimonial home, of depriving herself of the right to share in her husband's estate, if he should predecease her, intestate, conferred any "right" or "privilege" on her husband or subjected her to any "obligation" or "liability", within the meaning of s. 14(1)(c) of the *Interpretation Act*. It seems to me that, as contemplated by the statutory language used, "right" and "privilege" have meanings that correspond to "obligation" and "liability" or, to put it figuratively the two sets of words are opposite sides of the same coin. I shall not cite cases interpreting these words because, even by analogy, I have found none of the cases decided under the subsection helpful, given the facts of this case. I have concluded, therefore, that this case must be decided on the basis of principle rather than authority.

When one considers what benefit, to use a neutral word, the intestate gained when the applicant lost her rights under the repealed legislation, two come to mind immediately. The first was the unqualified right to convey the real property during his lifetime, free of any claim the applicant might have had, but for her bar of dower. The second was, of course, to dispose of his property by will, again free of any claim by the applicant. Indeed, it may not be entirely without interest to point out that if the intestate had wanted to ensure that the applicant would have no claim to his property, he had more than four years after the effective date of the new law to become a testator. Turning to the other side of the coin, both "obligation" and "liability" import the concept of the state of being subject to the claim of another. To my mind it would be straining the meaning of the words to say that, in giving up her right under the *Devolution of Estates Act*,[88] the applicant subjected herself to an obligation or a liability. With respect, therefore, to this, the respondents' principal argument, I can find no justification for holding that s. 44 of the *Succession Law Reform Act* does not confer on the applicant a right to the property of the intestate's estate.

The respondents' secondary submissions are easier to deal with. The first is that the separation agreement entered into by the applicant and the deceased in

---

87 R.S.O. 1980, c. 219.
88 R.S.O. 1970, c. 129.

November, 1977, is a bar to the applicant's claim because it discloses an intention on the part of the parties to release each other and the estate of each other from any claims or rights they had or might have on the death of each other. Although I have no difficulty in discerning in the applicant an intention with respect to *inter vivos* claims and rights, the terms of the agreement leave much to be desired with relation to claims against the estates. Before it is concluded that a right as substantial as that has been surrendered one must find "direct and cogent" words to that effect. I adopt the words of Wells J. in *Re Winter*.[89]

The second point is that the separation agreement is a valid and binding domestic contract within the meaning of the *Family Law Reform Act*[90] and, as such, must prevail. It is impossible to give effect to this point in the light of the conclusion at which I have arrived in the immediately preceding paragraph. I have found that the language of the agreement was not clear enough to bring about the result contended for by the respondents with respect to the estate. This distinguishes this case from the decision of the Court of Appeal in *Bebenek v. Bebenek*,[91] which, in any event, dealt with the *inter vivos* relationship and claims of parties to a separation agreement and not with a claim under s. 44 of the *Succession Law Reform Act*.

Finally, it is said that the release contained in the conveyance of March 29, 1978, from the applicant and the deceased, as joint tenants, to the deceased to uses is a complete answer to the applicant's claim to entitlement under s. 44 of the *Succession Law Reform Act*. The deed, it will be recalled, was given pursuant to the *Short Forms of Conveyances Act*,[92] with the consequence that short form of release in the words of col. 1 of Sch. B of the Act bears the meaning of the extended form in col. 2.

> [His Lordship quoted the provisions of the short and long form of the release and continued:]

At first blush the argument that the extended form of the release disqualifies the applicant from making a claim against the estate with respect to the lands in which she conveyed her interest to the deceased has an appearance of attractiveness. With further reflection, however, it cannot withstand careful scrutiny. This is not an appropriate occasion for a definitive dissertation on the purpose of the grantor's release in a modern conveyance. Without an exhaustive release the alienability and the marketability of real property would be in jeopardy. But surely the release of a grantor should be interpreted as a release of interests arising out of, of by virtue of, the grantor's former ownership or interest in the land conveyed. No economic or social purpose would be served by interpreting it as extending to an interest the grantor may thereafter acquire under remedial succession legislation as the next of kin of the intestate grantee of the land conveyed by the deed

---

89 [1954] O.W.N. 726 at 728, [1955] 1 D.L.R. 134 at 137.
90 R.S.O. 1980, c. 152. [repealed except for title, ss. 69, 70, 71, 1986, c. 4, s. 71(1). Replaced by *Family Law Act*, 1986, c. 4 (am. 1986, c. 35)].
91 (1979), 24 O.R. (2d) 385, 98 D.L.R. (3d) 536, 11 R.F.L. (2d) 137.
92 R.S.O. 1980, c. 435.

containing the release. If the respondents' argument were to prevail the effect would be that if a child conveyed real property to his or her parent by deed prepared in pursuance of the *Short Forms of Conveyances Act* and containing the customary release, and the parent died intestate without having conveyed the land in his or her lifetime, the child would, notwithstanding the provisions of legislation entitling him or her to a share of the property or, indeed, to succeed to the entire property, be disinherited by the operation of law. Section 47 of the *Succession Law Reform Act* would be rendered ineffectual. That cannot be the effect of the release. Section 44 of the *Succession Law Reform Act* cannot be subordinated to the extended language in Sch. B of the *Short Forms of Conveyances Act* in the special circumstances of this case.

I should not conclude the matter without a brief reference to the inference which the respondents sought to have me draw from the fact that, pursuant to a provision in the separation agreement by which the applicant undertook to execute and deliver other documents to the deceased to give effect to the terms of the agreement, the applicant, in fact, gave the deceased a power of attorney. This, it is said, was evidence of an intention on the part of the applicant to release the deceased, in life and in death, from any claims she might have. I do not agree that such an inference is warranted. I repeat my earlier observation, that, had he chosen to do so, the deceased could easily have put his property beyond the reach of his widow under s. 44 of the *Succession Law Reform Act*. He did not do so.

. . .

Notes and Questions

1. If a spouse executes a release of claims against the other spouse's estate which is otherwise effective, is the spouse who executes the release debarred from taking any benefits under the other spouse's will? Is it relevant that the will was made before the agreement and was, for reasons not explained, left unrevoked?[93]

2. Suppose that spouses resolve property issues between them by minutes of settlement, which are incorporated into a judgment. The minutes contain a release which states that the release is a "full and final release to any future claim by either party to a further division of property or payment for net equalization pursuant to the *Family Law Act* or any other relevant statute." The husband later dies, intestate, survived by the wife and three children. Is the wife precluded from claiming her share of the estate?[94]

6. ADVANCEMENT

Sometimes a parent makes a substantial *inter vivos* gift to a child with the intention that the gift shall be taken into account in determining the child's share in the parent's estate. If the parent then dies testate this will occur if the will provides that the gift be taken into account or be brought into hotchpot, or if the

---

93 See *Pearson v. Pearson* (1980), 3 Man. R. (2d) 404, 7 E.T.R. 12 (C.A.), leave to appeal to S.C.C. refused (1980), 34 N.R. 459n (S.C.C.).

94 See *Cairns v. Cairns* (1990), 37 E.T.R. 264 (Ont. H.C.).

rule against double portions applies.[95] If the parent dies intestate, there are statutory provisions, which are sometimes (inaccurately) called hotchpot provisions, to govern the matter. Section 25 of the *Estates Administration Act*,[96] set out below, is one such provision. Its operation is explained in *Re Lewis*,[97] set out below.

ESTATES ADMINISTRATION ACT
R.S.O. 1990, c. E.22

25. (1) If a child of an intestate has been advanced by the intestate by settlement or portion of real or personal property or both, and the same has been so expressed by the intestate in writing or so acknowledged in writing by the child, the value thereof shall be reckoned, for the purposes of this section only, as part of the real and personal property of the intestate to be distributed under this Act, and if the advancement is equal to or greater than the amount of the share that the child would be entitled to receive of the real and personal property of the intestate, as so reckoned, then the child and his or her descendants shall be excluded from any share in the real and personal property of the intestate.

(2) If the advancement is less than the share, the child and his or her descendants are entitled to so much only of the real and personal property as is sufficient to make all the shares of the children in the real and personal property and advancement to be equal, as nearly as can be estimated.

(3) The value of any real or personal property so advanced shall be deemed to be that, if any, which has been acknowledged by the child by an instrument in writing, otherwise the value shall be estimated according to the value of the property when given.

(4) The maintaining or educating of, or the giving of money to, a child without a view to a portion or settlement in life shall not be deemed an advancement within the meaning of this Act.

Comparable Legislation

Devolution of Estates Act, R.S.N.B. 1973, c. D-9, s. 31; *Estate Administration Act*, R.S.B.C. 1996, c. 122, s. 92; *Intestate Succession Act*, R.S.A. 1980, c. I-9, s. 11; S.M. 1989-90, c. 43, s. 8; R.S.N.S. 1989, c. 236, s. 12; R.S.N. 1990, c. I-21, s. 13; S.S. 1996, c. I-13.1, s. 15; R.S.N.W.T. 1988, c. I-10, s. 11; R.S.Y. 1986, c. 45, s. 11; *Probate Act*, R.S.P.E.I. 1988, c. P-21, s. 96.

Further Reading

John Cunningham, "The Position of the Widow in an Advancement of Portion" (1988), 9 E.&T.J. 23.

---

95 This rule is discussed in the chapter on Testamentary Gifts.
96 R.S.O. 1990, c. E.22.
97 (1898), 29 O.R. 609.

Mary Louise Fellows, "Concealing Legislative Reform in the Common-Law Tradition: The Advancement Doctrine and the Uniform Probate Code" (1984), 37 Vanderbilt L. Rev. 671.

K. Thomas Grozinger, "The Ontario Law of Advancement on an Intestacy" (1993), 12 E. & T.J. 396.

RE LEWIS
(1898), 29 O.R. 609
Supreme Court of Ontario
[High Court of Justice]

George Lewis died intestate in respect of real and personal property. He was survived by several children and by the children of his son, George Edward Lewis, who predeceased his father. Differences had arisen between father and son and, in consideration of the father conveying certain lands to the son, the latter relinquished all claims he then had or might thereafter have against his father's estate. The agreement between the parties stated that the son accepted the conveyance as an advancement in full satisfaction of all such claims.

After George Lewis's death an application was made to the court to determine whether George Edward's children were allowed to share in their grandfather's intestacy, or whether they had to account for the advancement. The court held, first, that since the real property was to be distributed as personal property by statute and since the grandchildren would take by representation, that is, as representing their father, and not in their own right, they were precluded by the release in the agreement from sharing in the estate. The court then went on to consider the alternative argument that, since the conveyance represented an advancement, the grandchildren would have to account for it.

FERGUSON J.:

. . .

This, I think, is the proper view of the matter, and so it is not absolutely needful that I should say anything in respect to the other question, yet it may not be amiss to express the opinion that the conveyance of the land by the father to the son was an advancement to the son. An advancement has been perhaps fairly well defined as being a payment or appropriation of money or a settlement of real estate made by a parent to or for a child in advance or in anticipation of the distributive share to which such child would be entitled after his death. Yet there are many cases in which the payment or appropriation has been held to be an advancement in which it does not appear from a perusal of the decisions that it was done in anticipation of a distribution after the death of the parent. Here (in the present case) the agreement employs the word "advancement," and plainly speaks of such a distribution. The land was conveyed to the son by the father and I am clearly of the opinion that there was an advancement.

In the American and English Encyclopaedia of Law — a work in which the cases and authorities on the subject are excellently collected and arranged; a work that, as I think, cannot be overpraised — the definition given is:[98]

> An advancement is a transfer of property from a person standing *in loco parentis* towards another, to that other, in anticipation of the share of the donor's estate which the donee would receive in the event of the donor's dying intestate.

...[I]n the footnotes definitions are given in somewhat varying words and the sources of and authorities for them concisely stated. Amongst very many others that given by the Chancellor in the case *Re Hall*[99] is referred to. A transfer of property in consideration of a release of all interest in the parents' estate will be considered an advancement. A deed to a son in consideration of his renouncing all claims upon the other property of his father is valid. A father can impose as a condition to conveying the property to his son the release of all claims to his personal property, though the son claimed — but the father did not concede — that he was entitled to the conveyance as a matter of right. See the case *Kinyon v. Kinyon*[100] where the subject of such an advancement is discussed and a decision given....

A release in full of all claims against the ancestors' estate given on the receipt of the advancement by the heir, *sui juris*, is binding and bars any future claim, and this even though the value of the property received is much less than would be that of a share on distribution.[101]

When the advancement was one taking effect *in presenti* (as in this case) it is to be reckoned at its value at the time it was made. If to take effect *in futuro* it is, if necessary, to be reckoned at its value at the time the donee came into actual possession and enjoyment of it.[102]

A statement signed by the donee at the time of his taking the property that it is taken as an advancement is binding on him.[103]

Then, taking it to be an advancement, the law applicable seems to be plainly enough stated in Williams on Executors,[104] where it is said:

> If a child who has received any advancement from his father shall die in his father's lifetime leaving children, such children shall not be admitted to their father's distributive share unless they bring in his advancement, since as his representatives they can have no better claim than he would have had if living.

This proposition was laid down as long ago as the decision in *Proud v. Turner*.[105]

It was said in argument that the value of the lands conveyed to George Edward Lewis by his father was about equal to the distributive share that is claimed by

---

98   2nd ed. (1896), pp. 760 and 761.
99   (1887), 14 O.R. 557 at 559.
100   (1894), 57 N.Y. St. R., 850, 6 Misc. R. 584 (N.Y. Sup. Ct.).
101   *Quarles v. Quarles* (1808), 4 Mass. 680; *Kenney v. Tucker* (1811), 8 Mass. 143.
102   Am. & Eng. Encyc., *supra*, pp. 782 and 784, and cases referred to.
103   *Lockyer v. Savage* (1732), 2 Stra. 947.
104   9th ed., pp. 1370, 1371.
105   (1729), 2 Peere Wms., 160.

these grandchildren of the intestate; and, assuming this to be the case, it would make little difference if they were permitted to take, they bringing the advancement or its value into "Hotchpot"....[106]

I am, however, as already stated, of the opinion that these grandchildren cannot in all the circumstances appearing be permitted to share in the estate of the intestate at all.

Notes and Questions

1. It is clear from the legislation that there is no advancement unless the intestate refers in writing to the property transferred as an advancement, or the child acknowledges the transfer in writing as an advancement.[107]

2. Although the legislation covers advances to children only, it is clear from the *Lewis* case and, indeed, from the statute itself, that anyone claiming by representation through a child who received an advancement must account for it just as the child would have had to do if he or she had lived.

3. What is the purpose of the legislation? Is it to equalize the shares of any descendants, of the children only, or also the share of the surviving spouse? What happens if the intestate is survived by a wife and a child who had received an advancement? What if there were also other children who did not receive an advancement?[108]

4. Since, under section 47(1) and (2) of the *Succession Law Reform Act* the estate must be distributed equally among the issue of the nearest degree, that is, *per capita*, does an advancement have to be taken into account if only grandchildren survive?

5. In *Re Hall*,[109] referred to in the *Lewis* case, Boyd C., held that a loan is not an advancement, so that a promissory note given by a son to his father did not have to be brought into account by the son's child on the father's (the son's child's grandfather's) intestacy, the son having predeceased his father. Moreover, the Chancellor noted, the statute requires that the intestate must state in writing or that the child must acknowledge in writing that a donation is an advancement.

In this respect, the statutes of the other provinces must be distinguished from the Ontario legislation. None of the other statutes requires that either the intestate or the child indicate in writing that a donation is an advancement. Whether it is or not depends upon other evidence, therefore, the onus of proof being on the person claiming that there was an advancement. The fact that the donation was a large sum compared to the size of the estate is a relevant factor under those statutes.[110] Mere casual payments are excluded.[111]

6. The legislation in the other provinces derives from the *Statute of Distribution*,[112] whereas the Ontario legislation derives from the *Inheritance Act*.[113] Under the *Statute of*

---

106 Reference was also made to the *Devolution of Estates Act*, R.S.O. 1887, c. 108, ss. 50-52 and *Devolution of Estates Act*, R.S.O. 1897, c. 127, ss. 60-62.

107 See *Re Loipersbeck Estate* (1999), 27 E.T.R. (2d) 159 (Man. Q.B.).

108 See *Estates Administration Act*, R.S.O. 1990, c. 143, s. 24(2), set out above. And see *Kirkcudbright v. Kirkcudbright* (1802), 8 Ves. Jun. 51 at 64, 32 E.R. 269, 2 Ves. Jun. Supp. 81, 34 E.R. 1005.

109 (1887), 14 O.R. 557 (Ch. D.).

110 See *Blakeney v. Seed*, [1939] 1 W.W.R. 321, 53 B.C.R. 335, [1939] 2 D.L.R. 287 (S.C.). And see *Hardy v. Shaw*, [1976] Ch. 82, [1975] 2 All E.R. 1052 at 1056, *per* Goff J.

111 *Taylor v. Taylor* (1875), L.R. 20 Eq. 155 at 157, *per* Jessel M.R.

112 *Statute of Distribution*, 1 Jac. 2, c. 17 (1685).

113 (1833), 3 & 4 Will. 4, c. 106, ss. 20-23.

Distribution advancements had to be taken into account whether there was a complete or a partial intestacy.[114] This remains the case under the English legislation,[115] which also derives (with modifications) from the *Statute of Distribution*. The statutes of the other provinces apply expressly only to complete intestacies. The Ontario legislation does not say whether it extends to partial intestacies, but the opinion has been expressed that it does.[116] There appear to be no cases on point.

7. The value of the advancement under all the Canadian statutes is the value assigned thereto in writing by the intestate or the child or, if no value has been assigned to it, it is the value of the property when given. Under the English legislation[117] the value of the property at the time of the intestate's death is used.

---

114 *Stewart v. Stewart* (1880), 15 Ch. D. 539; *Re Ford; Ford v. Ford*, [1902] 1 Ch. 218, affirmed [1902] 2 Ch. 605 (C.A.); *Re Roby; Howlett v. Newington*, [1908] 1 Ch. 71.

115 *Administration of Estates Act 1925*, 15 & 16 Geo. 5, c. 23, s. 47(1)(iii). This provision differs substantially from the Canadian legislation and cases based on it should, therefore, be read critically.

116 Armour, *Essays on the Devolution of Land* (1903), at p. 271.

117 *Administration of Estates Act 1925*, 15 & 16 Geo. 5, c. 23, s. 47.

PART III

PROVING WILLS

4

THE NATURE OF TESTAMENTARY DISPOSITIONS

1. NATURE OF A WILL

(a) Generally

A will, it is sometimes said in a jocular fashion, is a dead giveaway. As with most forms of humour, there is much truth in this statement, although it is incomplete. In Anglo-Canadian law a will is an instrument by which a person disposes of property upon his or her death. Yet, this is also an incomplete statement, for there are many types of dispositions which effect that result which are not called wills. These, sometimes called will substitutes, are discussed in part 2 of this chapter. It is, however, first necessary to define the essential or intrinsic nature of a will.[1]

The intrinsic nature of a will in the modern sense is that it is an instrument which disposes of the testator's property, takes effect only upon the testator's death and neither before[2] nor after, is revocable until the testator's death, and is made *animo testandi*.[3]

---

1 Statutory definitions are unhelpful for this purpose. Thus, for example, s. 1(1) of the *Succession Law Reform Act*, R.S.O. 1990, c. S.26 defines a will as follows:
   "will" includes
       (a) a testament,
       (b) a codicil,
       (c) an appointment by will or by writing in the nature of a will in exercise of a power, and
       (d) any other testamentary disposition.
2 *Cf.* Hebr. 9:17.
3 *Page on the Law of Wills*, rev. ed. by William J. Bowe and Douglas H. Parker (Cincinnati: The W.H. Anderson Company, 1960), §5.1; *Williams on Wills*, 7th ed. by C.H. Sherrin, R.F.D. Barlow, and R.A. Wallington, assisted by Suzannah L. Meadway (London: Butterworths, 1995), pp. 7-9; *Mellows: The Law of Succession*, 5th ed. by Clive V. Margrave-Jones (London: Butterworths, 1993), pp. 6-7. See also *Milnes v. Foden* (1890), 15 P.D. 105 at 107, where Sir James Hannen P., stated:

The law also requires that a will be executed in accordance with specified formalities. These are not part of the intrinsic nature of a will, but rather of its form.[4] However, a will is invalid unless it is properly executed. Several of the above elements require further explanation.

When we say that a will must be an instrument, we recognize that formerly a will could be oral or nuncupative. More particularly, a testament of personal property could be oral. However, oral wills are no longer permitted.[5] We discuss the formal requirements of wills in a later chapter.

A will must make a donative disposition of the testator's property.[6] This, at least, is normally so. However, a will is nonetheless valid if it does not dispose of the testator's property, but rather the property of another. That happens when the testator exercises a power of appointment by will.[7] Indeed, it seems that a testamentary instrument which merely appoints an executor is a will and entitled to probate,[8] although it is difficult to see to what purpose, since the testator's property has not been committed to the executor.[9] In contrast, if an executor has been appointed but all the dispositions in the will are ruled invalid or cannot take effect, the executor has been entrusted with the administration of the estate and can assume the administration, although he or she cannot distribute the estate in accordance with the will.[10]

The foregoing suggests that, at the very least, a will should dispose of some property, not necessarily the testator's, but it may also deal with certain other matters, namely the appointment of a personal representative, the appointment of a guardian and the exercise of a power of appointment.

The right and need to appoint a personal representative is clear, for someone must be entrusted with the administration of the estate.[11] The right to appoint a guardian or custodian of one's minor children rests in statute[12] and the exercise

---

The true principle appears to be that if there is proof, either in the paper itself or from clear evidence *dehors*, first that it was the intention of the writer of the paper to convey the benefits by the instrument which would be conveyed by it if considered as a will; secondly, that death was the event which was to give effect to it, then whatever may be its form it may be admitted to probate as testamentary. It is not necessary that the testator should intend to perform or be aware that he has performed a testamentary act.

4   *Page on the Law of Wills*, rev. ed. by William J. Bowe and Douglas H. Parker (Cincinnati: The W.H. Anderson Company, 1960), §5.1.

5   The history of oral wills is mentioned in chapter 1.

6   *Ram v. Prasad* (1999), 28 E.T.R. (2d) 140 (B.C. C.A.).

7   See the definition of "will" in s. 1(1) of the *Succession Law Reform Act*, *supra*. And see *Barnes v. Vincent* (1846), 5 Moo. P.C. 201, 13 E.R. 468; *Re Tharp* (1878), 3 P.D. 76 (C.A.).

8   *Brownrigg v. Pike* (1882), 7 P.D. 61. This is so even if the executor renounces: *Re Jordan* (1868), L.R. 1 P.& D. 555. In contrast, a document that merely appoints a guardian, is not entitled to probate: *Re Morton* (1864), 3 Sw. & Tr. 422, 164 E.R. 1338.

9   A document that revokes an existing will, but does not contain any dispositive provisions, nor appoints executors, is not entitled to probate: *Toomer v. Sobinska*, [1907] P. 106.

10   *Blacksher Co. v. Northrup*, 176 Ala. 190, 57 So 743 (1912); *Trustees of House of the Angel Guardian v. Donovan*, 71 RI 407, 46 A. (2d) 717 (1946).

11   See 2 Pollock and Maitland, *History of English Law* (1898), 213.

12   See, *e.g.*, *Children's Law Reform Act*, R.S.O. 1990, c. C.12, ss. 61ff.

of a power of appointment is sanctioned by statute.[13] Apart from these matters, however, a will is concerned with the disposition of the testator's property.

It follows, therefore, that other of the testator's wishes, even if expressed in the form of directions, are of no effect and if the will deals only with such matters, it is not a will. Thus, for example, directions concerning the disposition of the testator's body are not binding, since the executor has the right to determine the manner of burial.[14] Similarly, a direction to the executors that they shall employ a named person as the estate's solicitor is not effective.[15] In essence, therefore, save for the exceptions mentioned above, a testator's directions have no legal effect except to the extent that they dispose of his or her property. Hence, a direction concerning any other matter, such as the conduct of a beneficiary, or the religious upbringing of a beneficiary, is effective only if the gift to him or her is made conditional. The validity of such conditions is discussed in a later chapter.

One of the most attractive features of a will is that it does not take effect until death.[16] Hence, the testator retains full control over the property while living and may do with it what he or she likes. In this respect it is different from other estate planning devices under which the donor is obliged to relinquish some or all control over the property during his or her lifetime. It follows, therefore, that even if an interest in property takes effect in possession on the death of the donor, but it was given by the donor during his or her lifetime in the sense that the donor no longer had absolute control over it, the method of disposition is not a will. If a testator directs that the instrument shall not take effect until some time after his or her death, it is not a will and cannot take effect as such,[17] unless the language can be construed as merely postponing possession by the beneficiaries.[18]

It is inherent in the nature of a will that it be revocable by the testator while he or she lives. This is because a will does not take effect until the testator dies.[19] Until then it is said to be ambulatory. Hence, a testator may at any time revoke the will and make another. The testator may also revoke the will in part by altering it. An instrument which purports to be irrevocable, therefore, is not a will. This is not to say, however, that an instrument cannot combine both *inter vivos* and testamentary dispositions, the former only being irrevocable, so long as it is executed with the formalities required for both forms of disposition.[20]

The word "ambulatory," therefore, denotes the same thing as "revocability." The word "ambulatory" is sometimes also used to refer to the property that passes under a will, namely, not only the property owned by the testator when he or she

---

13 See the definition of "will" in s. 1(1) of the *Succession Law Reform Act, supra.*

14 *Hunter v. Hunter*, 65 O.L.R. 586, [1930] 4 D.L.R. 255.

15 *Foster v. Elsley* (1881), 19 Ch. D. 518.

16 *Re Berger (decd)*, [1989] 1 All E.R. 591 (C.A.).

17 *Kavanagh Estate v. Kavanagh* (1998), 159 D.L.R. (4th) 629 at 636 (Nfld. C.A.); *State Bank v. Bliss*, 67 Conn. 317, 35 A 255 (1896). This is also true if the dispositions are to take effect before death: *Fletcher v. Fletcher* (1844), 4 Hare 67, 67 E.R. 564.

18 *Graham v. Graham*, 297 Mo. 290, 249 SW 37 (1923).

19 *Re Westminster's Deed of Appointment*, [1959] Ch. 265 at 271, *per* Lord Evershed M.R., [1959] 1 All E.R. 442 (C.A.); *Re Berger (decd)*, [1989] 1 All E.R. 591 (C.A.).

20 In that situation the testamentary provisions may be severed and admitted to probate: *Re Anziani*, [1930] 1 Ch. 407 at 424.

made the will, but also all property owned of the type described when he or she died.[21] However, this is an incorrect usage, since this secondary meaning arises only because subsequently acquired property is deemed to pass under a will by statute.[22]

The final requirement of a will is that it must have been intended by the testator to take effect as his or her testamentary wishes. From this requirement flows the rejection of wills which were obtained by fraud, duress or undue influence, or which were made while the testator lacked the necessary mental capacity to make a will.[23] The same reasoning applies to conditional wills, for a will that is conditional upon a certain event happening does not satisfy the requirement that a will has to be made with immediate testamentary intent.[24] Similarly, if the document in question contains merely an outline of a possible will[25] or is a statement of intention to make a future will, such as instructions to a solicitor,[26] it cannot be regarded as a proper will since the necessary *animus* is lacking. However, if such a document is properly executed and it can be proved that it is intended to have effect unless and until a more formal document is executed, it will be allowed to take effect.[27] A will written in jest[28] or, at the opposite end of the scale, one written at the importuning of another person in order to appease the person,[29] will also be ineffective.

A further aspect of intention is that the expressions of the testator must be imperative in form. This is a matter that normally only concerns particular dispositions in a will, although it may affect the validity of the whole will as well. In many home-drawn wills the testator may express certain wishes, hopes, exhortations and the like. This form of precatory language is normally insufficient to give effect to the testator's intentions. Rather, they are typically construed as mere wishes which do not have testamentary or binding effect upon the executors, but ones the testator would like to have carried out if possible. Thus, for example, in *Johnson v. Farney*[30] the testator left all his estate to his wife, but further on in the will he said, "I also wish if you die soon after me that you will leave all...to my people and your people equally...." The court held that this was no more than

---

21 2 Pollock and Maitland, *History of English Law* (1898), 315.

22 *Wills Act, 1837*, 7 Will 4 & 1 Vict., c. 26, s. 24.

23 These matters are discussed in the next chapter.

24 See *Corbett v. Newey*, [1996] 2 All E.R. 914 (C.A.). However, a will which is conditional on its face will be allowed to take effect when the condition occurs. Conditional wills are discussed later in this chapter.

25 *Bennett v. Toronto Gen. Trusts Corp.*; *Bennett v. Gray*, [1958] S.C.R. 392, 14 D.L.R. (2d) 1.

26 *Re Moir*, [1942] 1 W.W.R. 241, [1942] 1 D.L.R. 337 at 342 (Alta. C.A.).

27 *Re McNeil* (1918), 45 N.B.R. 479, 42 D.L.R. 449 (C.A.); *Borgen v. Borgen* (1973), 5 Nfld. & P.E.I.R. 275 (Nfld. T.D.).

28 *Page on the Law of Wills*, rev. ed. by William J. Bowe and Douglas H. Parker (Cincinnati: The W.H. Anderson Company, 1960), § 5.10; *Lister v. Smith* (1863), 3 Sw. & Tr. 282 at 288, 164 E.R. 1282, *per* Sir J.P. Wilde. And see *Josiak v. Setler*, [1971] 1 O.R. 724, 16 D.L.R. (3d) 490 (H.C.).

29 *Can. Permanent Trust Co. v. Bowman*, [1962] S.C.R. 711, 34 D.L.R. (2d) 106.

30 (1913), 29 O.L.R. 223, 14 D.L.R. 134 (C.A.). See also *Re Blow* (1977), 18 O.R. (2d) 516, 4 E.T.R. 209, 82 D.L.R. (3d) 721 (H.C.).

a suggestion which was not binding on the widow. However, it is clear that in all cases the court must first construe the will to ascertain the testator's intention and it may conclude that, although the testator used precatory language, he or she meant the wishes to be carried out. If that had been the construction in *Johnson v. Farney*, the wish would have been enforced as a trust.

A foreign will may be perfectly apt to dispose of property in the jurisdiction in which the testator died domiciled, so long as it contains directions for the disposal of the testator's property after his or her death, is revocable during his or her lifetime, and is executed in accordance with the required formalities. This is so even if the testator did not contemplate the enforcement of the will in the jurisdiction. Thus, for example, a Jewish religious will, or *zavah*, written in Hebrew, which meets the requirements set out above, may be probated, although a translation must be supplied to the court.[31]

Finally, it should be noted that the word "will" connotes all the valid testamentary instruments which the testator has made and which are unrevoked.[32] Hence, there can be only one will, but it may be contained in several instruments. These may include a "will" in the common sense of that word, as a document which purports to dispose of the testator's property generally, any other "will" which also does so and does not conflict with the first, a codicil, that is, a document which amends the "will" and any unattested document which may be incorporated by reference.[33]

(b) *Spes Successionis*

Since a will does not take effect until the testator's death, it follows that until the testator is dead the persons named in the will as beneficiaries do not own the property the will purports to give them. That is because the property still belongs to the testator who might have a change of heart and leave the property to others by subsequent testamentary document or by *inter vivos* disposition. Further, in order to take the property left to them the beneficiaries must survive the testator. If a beneficiary predeceases the testator, the property will not go to the beneficiary's estate, but to others. Thus, until the testator is dead the persons named in the will have merely a hope of succeeding to the property. Heirs of a person who lacks a will also have merely a hope of succeeding to the property of the intestate, because the intestate may dispose of the property *inter vivos* or by later will, or the heirs may predecease the intestate. Such a hope of succeeding to the property of a living person is known as a *spes successionis*, or as an expectancy. It follows, too, that the beneficiaries and the heirs cannot dispose or deal with the property,

---

31 See *Re Berger (decd)*, [1989] 1 All E.R. 591 (C.A.). On the Jewish law of succession, see I. Grunfeld, *The Jewish Law of Inheritance* (Targum Press, Oak Park, Mich., 1987).

32 *Douglas-Menzies v. Umphelby*, [1908] A.C. 224 at 233 (P.C.), in which the testator had separate wills to dispose of his property in two different jurisdictions. Bailey, *The Law of Wills* (7th ed., 1973) p. 64.

33 The doctrine of incorporation by reference is discussed later in this chapter.

since it does not belong to them. Nor have they a right to receive notice of dispositions of the property or of proceedings about the property.

These principles are well-known and of long standing. They hold true even though the testator can no longer change the will for lack of capacity. As Lord Eldon said in *Dursley (Lord) v. Fitzhardinge Berkeley*,[34] even if a person is *in articulo mortis*[35] an heir has no property interest.[36] Unfortunately, the courts sometimes fail to appreciate their importance. Thus, for example, in *Weinstein v. Weinstein (Litigation Guardian of)*[37] the court disregarded the principles (even thought the above cases were cited to it) and held that the heirs under the will of a woman who suffered from the ravages of Alzheimer's disease and was, thus, incapable of changing her will, "in practical terms" had "what amounted to a vested interest."[38] In fact, according to the established case law they had no interest at all, let alone a vested interest.[39]

Fortunately, other courts do recognize and apply the principles. *Del Grande (Litigation Guardian of) v. Sebastian*[40] is an example. The court held that the sole beneficiary under an elderly woman's will did not have power to veto a settlement reached between the Public Guardian and Trustee, acting as the woman's statutory guardian, and the woman's former attorney. Cullity J. affirmed the principle that a beneficiary under the will of a living person has no interest under the will whatsoever until the testator's death.

2.   WILL SUBSTITUTES

(a)   Introduction

Although this casebook is concerned primarily with the law of wills, a brief reference to other donative methods of disposition of property is in order. The student will have studied a number of these methods already. Hence, a brief statement of most of these will suffice. However, you should note that will substitutes are as much a part of a properly planned estate as the will itself. Indeed, today, the value of property disposed of by will substitutes is often much greater than by the will. Will substitutes are used for a variety of reasons, including: minimization of taxes, avoidance of probate fees, and attempts to evade obligations to one's dependants. It is important to recognize that while some of these objectives may be desirable, will substitutes do have disadvantages that a will

---

34 (1801), 6 Ves. Jun. 251 at 260, 31 E.R. 1036.

35 That is, at the point of death.

36 To the same effect, see *Midleton's Will Trusts (Re); Whitehead v. Midleton (Earl)*, [1969] 1 Ch. 600 at 607-8, *per* Stamp J.

37 (1997), 35 O.R. (3d) 229, 30 R.F.L. (4th) 116 (Gen. Div.).

38 *Ibid.,* at O.R. 234.

39 For further discussion of these principles and a critique of the *Weinstein* case see Albert H. Oosterhoff, "Great Expectations: Spes Successionis" (1998), 17 E.T. & P.J. 181.

40 (1999), 27 E.T.R. (2d) 295 (Ont. S.C.J.). See Albert H. Oosterhoff, Comment (2000), 19 E.T. & P.J. 257.

does not have. They involve a disposition of property which the grantor cannot reverse unless he or she retains a power to that effect. This can cause difficulties later if the grantor's financial needs change, or if relationships change, such as on a marriage breakdown.[41]

Further Reading

Page on the Law of Wills, rev. ed. by William J. Bowe and Douglas H. Parker (Cincinnati: The W.H. Anderson Company, 1960), vol 1, ch. 6.

(b) Gifts *Inter Vivos*

The *inter vivos* gift is one in which the donor parts with his or her property absolutely while living. In order for the gift to be valid, the donor must have had an *animus donandi*. If the subject matter of the gift is a chose in possession, manual delivery of the chose is normally essential, although constructive delivery is permissible if the object cannot be conveniently delivered itself. Gifts of choses in action are effected by an assignment or, in appropriate cases, by constructive delivery. Alternatively, personal property may be given by deed. An *inter vivos* gift of land must be made by deed in accordance with applicable statutes.[42]

When a creditor forgives a loan, he or she makes a gift to the debtor. If the forgiveness is to take effect at death, the question may arise whether the forgiveness has testamentary effect and must, therefore, comply with the statutory formalities for wills.[43]

(c) Gifts *Mortis Causa*

A gift *mortis causa* is an *inter vivos* gift of personalty, which is made in contemplation, although not necessarily in the expectation, of the donor's death. The subject matter of the gift must be delivered to the donee, although in appropriate circumstances constructive delivery is permitted. Finally, the gift, while it takes effect immediately, is dependent for its absolute effect upon the death of the donor. Hence, the donor can revoke the gift while living. Moreover, it is revoked automatically if the donor recovers from the feared peril.[44]

---

41 The use of will substitutes to avoid probate fees and the drawbacks of doing so are discussed later in this chapter.

42 Such as the *Conveyancing and Law of Property Act*, R.S.O. 1990, c. C.34, ss. 2, 3. For the requirements of *inter vivos* gifts see generally *Crossley Vaines' Personal Property*, 5th ed. by E.L.G. Tyler and N.E. Palmer, (London: Butterworths, 1973), ch. 13; Ray Andrews Brown, *The Law of Personal Property*, 3rd ed. by Walter J. Raushenbush (Chicago: Callaghan & Company, 1975), ch. 7.

43 See, *e.g.*, *Hutton v. Lapka Estate* (1991), 44 E.T.R. 231 (B.C. C.A.).

44 For the detailed requirements of *donationes mortis causa* see generally *Crossley Vaines' Personal*

(d) Deeds and *Inter Vivos Trusts*

A person may transfer his or her property to another absolutely by deed, or may retain an interest while also giving interests to others. Thus, for example, you may convey real property to yourself for life, with remainder to your children. Although the remainder interest takes effect in possession on your death, the deed is not regarded as a will, since it creates presently vested interests in the children, even though possession is postponed. The drawback of such a device is that it prevents the donor from recalling the property should he or she change his or her mind, except under recognized legal principles. Thus, for example, a grantor who by deed creates legal future interests can retrieve the property only if he or she retains a reversion, a possibility of reverter, a right of entry for condition broken, or a legal interest under a use executed by the *Statute of Uses*.[45] It is, however, impossible for the grantor to retain a power to revoke the grant. The foregoing is merely a short summary of the law of legal future interests which, I assume, the student has studied.[46]

A problem that sometimes arises with deeds absolute and similar transfers is that the grantor retains control over the deed and does not intend that it shall have effect until his or her death. If that is the situation, the deed is really a will, because it is "dependent upon his death for its vigour and effect"[47] but, unless it is executed with the appropriate formalities, it cannot take effect as one.

This problem is illustrated by *Carson v. Wilson*.[48] The deceased, Wilson, owned certain parcels of land and various mortgages. He executed deeds and assignments of mortgages in favour of named grantees and assignees and lodged them with his solicitor with instructions to hold them and not to deliver them until after his death. Moreover, it was understood that Wilson could demand the documents back at any time. Until his death Wilson managed the properties himself and collected the mortgage payments. The court held that the transactions were ineffective to transfer title to the grantees and assignees. They were not effective as *inter vivos* gifts since there was no delivery of the documents and they were, in any event, intended to take effect only on death. Hence, the gifts were testamentary in nature and, since the documents were not executed with the formalities required of wills, they failed.[49] It was also argued in the *Carson* case that the gifts could

---

Property, 5th ed. by E.L.G. Tyler and N.E. Palmer, (London: Butterworths, 1973), pp. 318-21; Ray Andrews Brown, *The Law of Personal Property*, 3rd ed. by Walter J. Raushenbush (Chicago: Callaghan & Company, 1975), pp. 130-145.

45 27 Hen. 8, c. 10 (1535).

46 For further detail, the standard texts on property should be consulted. See also Mendes da Costa, Balfour and Gillese, *Property Law: Cases, Text and Materials*, 2nd ed. (1990), ch. 16.

47 *Cock v. Cooke* (1866), L.R. 1 P. & D. 241 at 243, *per* Sir J.P. Wilde. See also *Wonnacott v. Loewen* (1990), 37 E.T.R. 244 (C.A.).

48 [1961] O.R. 113, 26 D.L.R. (2d) 307 (C.A.).

49 See also *Barnett v. Wise*, [1961] O.R. 97, 26 D.L.R. (2d) 321 (C.A.), to the same effect. And see *MacInnes v. MacInnes*, [1935] S.C.R. 200, 2 I.L.R 14, [1935] 1 D.L.R. 401; and *Re Beardmore Trusts*, [1951] O.W.N. 728, [1952] 1 D.L.R. 41 (H.C.). In *Re Beardmore* the court also held an *inter vivos* trust to be void because no property was to be transferred to it until the settlor's death and then only a part of his net estate. Hence, the subject matter of the trust was uncertain.

take effect as *inter vivos* trusts. However, this argument failed because Wilson retained complete control over the properties while he lived and, in any event, he did not intend to create an *inter vivos* trust.

On the other hand, a deed may be apt to create a valid *inter vivos* trust. In that event the interests of the beneficiaries under the deed take effect presently and are not dependent on the settlor's death, although they may not fall into possession until that time. A typical example of such a trust is a deed by which S transfers money or securities to T in trust for S for life, with remainder to S's children. In this situation, while S has not relinquished all interest in the property, he or she has given up control and, hence, the document is not testamentary. The same result would obtain if S declared himself or herself to be a trustee of the property upon the above terms. In that situation, however, S were wise to do so in writing so that, if the question is later raised whether S retained control over the property until death, there is evidence to establish that he or she did not.

The fact that an *inter vivos* trust is revocable does not mean that it remains subject to the control of the settlor so as to make the trust testamentary. However, this may be the result if the arrangement is informal and the evidence suggests that the settlor in fact retained full control over the property. *Anderson v. Patton*[50] aptly illustrates the use of a revocable *inter vivos* trust and the problems that this may cause. The deceased, Francis C. Costello, was afraid that he might be killed in a car accident. Therefore, he gave the defendant $5,000 and requested him to pay $4,000 to Mary Gertrude Patton and $1,000 to Mrs. R.L. Keiver if he should die. At the defendant's insistence the deceased wrote out the following receipt which the defendant signed:

> Received from Francis C. Costello the sum of $5,000 which I am to hold in trust for the said Francis C. Costello, and which I am to pay out as instructed to Mary Gertrude Patton and Mrs. R.L. Keiver, if anything should happen to the said Francis C. Costello. The money will be returned if the said Francis C. Costello should demand it.

Costello subsequently died in a car accident. The plaintiff, Costello's administratrix, claimed the money on the basis that the transaction was testamentary and failed for want of compliance with the necessary formalities. However, the court held that the transaction created a valid *inter vivos* trust, under which the defendant held the money in trust for the deceased for life, with remainder for the two named beneficiaries in the stated proportion. Hence, the latter's interests vested upon the creation of the trust and merely took effect in possession upon the deceased's death. Moreover, it was held that the reservation of a power of revocation (which is how the last sentence in the receipt was construed) did not have the effect of making the document testamentary.[51]

The reason why a power to revoke does not make an *inter vivos* trust testamentary is that, although the title may be recalled under the power, it passed to the

---

50 [1947] 2 W.W.R. 837, [1948] 1 D.L.R. 848 (Alta. T.D.), affirmed [1948] 1 W.W.R. 461, [1948] 2 D.L.R. 202 (Alta. C.A.).

51 See to the same effect *Campbell v. Fenwick*, [1934] O.R. 692 at 699-70, [1934] 4 D.L.R. 787 at 793-4 (C.A.), *per* Middleton J.A.

trustee when the trust was created. It follows that the beneficial interests also took effect at that time.[52]

The tax effect of this type of transaction should, of course, always be considered, but is beyond the scope of this brief introduction.[53]

(e) Joint Interests

You will recall that when title to real property is taken by two persons in joint tenancy, the *jus accrescendi* operates on the death of the first of the joint tenants to augment the interest of the survivor. Hence, it is possible to avoid having to make a will because the entire interest in the property passes automatically to the survivor. This form of title is, therefore, often attractive to spouses and others. Moreover, the property does not pass to the personal representatives first, but goes directly to the survivor.[54] Hence, it does not form part of the deceased's probate estate. It is, however, necessary to state expressly in the deed that the title is taken in joint tenancy, otherwise a tenancy in common is created.[55]

A transaction which creates a joint tenancy in which one of the parties does not pay any consideration is not regarded as testamentary, because the title vests in the donee immediately. The transaction may, however, be one of convenience only, in which case the donee may hold the interest upon a resulting trust for the donor. The principle is similar with respect to personal property generally.

With respect to joint bank accounts the situation is somewhat different, because the creation of a bank account establishes a debtor and creditor relationship between the bank and the depositor, so that the bank holds the legal title. In order to determine who has the right to the moneys in the account while both parties, that is, the depositor and the volunteer in the case of a joint account, are living and after the death of the depositor, it is necessary to reduce their rights to property interests and to have regard to the presumptions of advancement (or gift) and of resulting trust.

Traditionally, a presumption of advancement was raised when a father voluntarily transferred property to his child or children, or purchased property and had title taken in the name of his child or children, or when title was taken by the father and the child or children jointly. Modern cases have extended the pre-

---

52 *Stone v. Hackett* (1858), 78 Mass. 227 at 232, *per* Bigelow J., quoted by Frank Ford J.A. in *Anderson v. Patton, supra,* at [1948] 2 D.L.R. 203.

53 See John Arnold, "Revocable Inter Vivos Trusts" (1992), 11 E. & T.J. 44; W[olfe] D. G[oodman], "Is Settlement of Property on a Revocable Inter Vivos Trust a 'Disposition' for Income Tax Purposes?" (1994), 14 E. & T.J. 200. Formerly, when succession duty legislation was in force, any *inter vivos* gift, if made more than five years before the donor's death and provided that the donor divested himself of all interest in the property, was not subject to duty. All other gifts were brought back into the estate. See the *Succession Duty Act,* R.S.O. 1970, c. 449, s. 5(1)(g), repealed by S.O. 1979, c. 20. And see *Minister of Revenue (Ont.) v. McCreath,* [1977] 1 S.C.R. 2, (sub nom. *Re McCreath*) 67 D.L.R. (3d) 449.

54 See, *e.g., Estates Administration Act,* R.S.O. 1980, c. E.22, s. 2.

55 See, *e.g., Conveyancing and Law of Property Act,* R.S.O. 1990, c. C.34, s. 13.

sumption to the situation in which a mother voluntarily transfers property to her child or purchases property in the child's name.[56]

Prior to the matrimonial property law reform legislation in the 1970's and 1980's a rebuttable presumption of advancement was also raised when a husband voluntarily transferred property to his wife or into the joint names of himself and his wife. The same result obtained if he purchased property and had title taken in his wife's name or in the joint names of himself and his wife.

However, if a person voluntarily transfers property to any other person or into the joint names of himself or herself and that person, or purchases property and has title taken in the name of any other person or jointly with him or her, a rebuttable presumption of resulting trust is raised. That is, it is presumed that the transferor or the person who supplied the consideration did not intend to make a gift, but to retain the beneficial interest in the property. In order to give effect to this presumed intention, since the title has vested in the transferee, equity deems the latter to hold the legal title upon a resulting trust for the transferor, or the person who paid the consideration.[57]

By recent matrimonial property reform legislation the presumption of advancement as between husband and wife has been abolished and replaced with a presumption of resulting trust in some provinces. However, if any property is jointly owned by the spouses, that is *prima facie* proof that they intended to own the property as joint tenants.[58]

The presumptions cannot be applied to the rights of a depositor and as non-depositor of a joint account, however, unless they can be regarded as having property interests and, as seen above, they are mere creditors of the bank, or at least the depositor is. The problem was discussed in *Edwards v. Bradley*.[59] The deceased, Mrs. Edwards, had opened a joint account in the names of herself and her daughter, the defendant, the deceased being the sole depositor. The deceased drew a couple of cheques on the account in favour of the defendant to assist her in building a home. It was the deceased's intention to live with the defendant and her husband in her old age. Six months before the joint account was established, the deceased made a will in which she left the family farm to her son, the plaintiff, and the residue equally to all her children. Apart from the farm, most of the assets were in the joint account. The trial judge held that the deceased intended to give the balance in the account to the daughter, but that the gift failed because it was

---

56 See, *e.g.*, *Dagle v. Dagle* (1990), 38 E.T.R. 164, 70 D.L.R. (4th) 201 (P.E.I. C.A.), leave to appeal to S.C.C. refused (1991), 40 E.T.R. 75n, 74 D.L.R. (4th) viii (S.C.C.).

57 See generally D.W.M. Waters, *Law of Trusts in Canada*, 2nd ed. (Toronto: The Carswell Company Limited, 1984), pp. 301ff. In fact, the question whether a resulting trust would be raised consequent upon a voluntary transfer, as distinct from a purchase, has never been finally resolved. However, strong *dicta* in two Canadian cases suggest that such a trust is raised: *Niles v. Lake*, [1947] S.C.R. 291, [1947] 2 D.L.R. 248 at 252-3, *per* Kerwin J., and at S.C.R. 302, *per* Taschereau J.; *Neazor v. Hoyle* (1962), 37 W.W.R. 104 at 117, 32 D.L.R. (2d) 131 (Alta. C.A.), *per* McDonald J.A.

58 See, *e.g.*, *Family Law Act*, R.S.O. 1990, c. F.3, s. 14.

59 [1956] O.R. 225, 2 D.L.R. (2d) 382 at 386-8, reversed [1957] S.C.R. 599, 9 D.L.R. (2d) 673. See to the same effect *Russell v. Scott* (1936), 55 C.L.R. 440 (Austr. H.C.), and see *Re Levy* (1982), 50 N.S.R. (2d) 14, 25 R.F.L. (2d) 149, 131 D.L.R. (3d) 15, 12 E.T.R. 133 (T.D.).

testamentary. The Ontario Court of Appeal reversed, holding that the gift was not testamentary. The apparent problem was solved in the following manner by Mackay J.A.:

> With respect to the question whether the gift fails as being an attempted testamentary disposition, and therefore invalid because it does not comply with the provisions of the *Wills Act*, I think the legal effect of establishing a joint bank-account, in the circumstances that exist in this case, is as follows: Where A deposits money in a joint account in the names of himself and B the legal title to the money vests in the bank and the relationship between the bank and the depositor is that of debtor and creditor. The right of the depositor is the right to withdraw or demand payment of the money from the bank. It is a chose in action that may be assigned and by the terms of the joint deposit agreement with the bank, signed by both A and B, A assigns the legal right to withdraw the money to himself and B jointly, with the right to the survivor to withdraw the balance in the event of the death of A or B. The right of survivorship exists independently of any agreement in the case of joint ownership of personal property. Choses in action not yet in existence may be assigned;[60] so that the agreement operates as an immediate assignment of the legal right to withdraw any subsequent deposits that may be made in the joint account. The title to the chose in action being vested in A and B jointly on the execution of the agreement with the bank, each, under the terms of the agreement, has a legal right to withdraw the money during their joint lives and the survivor has the legal right to withdraw on the death of the other. B's legal title cannot be divested except with his consent or by his dying before A, although A may defeat B's title or interest by drawing all the money out of the account. Because of the application of the equitable doctrine of resulting trusts, the beneficial interest in the money does not necessarily follow the legal title to the right to withdraw or demand payment. Whether B takes the beneficial interest as well as the legal title, either during their joint lives or on the death of A, or both, depends on A's intention. His intention is to be determined from all the circumstances of the case, after applying the appropriate presumptions and considering the evidence. The legal right to take the balance in the account if A predeceases him being vested in B on the opening of the account, it cannot be the subject of a testamentary disposition. If A's intention was that B should also have the beneficial interest, B already has the legal title and there is nothing further to be done to complete the gift of the beneficial interest. If A's intention was that B should not take the beneficial interest, it belongs to A or his estate and he is not attempting to dispose of it by means of the joint account. In either event B has the legal title and the only question that can arise on A's death is whether B is entitled to keep any money that may be in the account on A's death or whether he holds it as trustee under a resulting trust for A's estate.

On further appeal, the Supreme Court of Canada held that the deceased did not have an intention to give the money in the account to the defendant, since that would nullify her stated intention in her will to benefit all her children equally. Hence, the daughter held the balance in the account upon a resulting trust for the estate. However, the Supreme Court did not disagree with the discussion in the Court of Appeal about the nature of a joint account, but came to a different conclusion on the facts only.[61]

A joint account to which only one person deposits money is, therefore, another method whereby a person may effectively pass moneys to another on his or her

---

60 *Tailby v. Official Receiver* (1888), 13 App. Cas. 523.
61 See also *Re Fenton* (1977), 26 N.S.R. (2d) 662 (T.D.), in which the presumption of resulting trust was rebutted. And see *Davies v. Bonnell* (1973), 39 D.L.R. (3d) 104 (P.E.I. C.A.), in which it was held that moneys withdrawn by the non-depositor shortly before the depositor's death were held upon resulting trust for the latter's estate unless it could be established that the depositor intended to make a gift to her *inter vivos*.

death without making a will. Moreover, the gift is revocable simply by the expedient of withdrawing the money.

A further device which has gained wide acceptance in the United States is the so-called Totten trust, named after the leading case, *Matter of Totten*.[62] The Totten or tentative trust arises when a depositor deposits money in a bank account in the form "A, in trust for B." Such a trust is regarded as revocable and the moneys can also be withdrawn by the depositor. The trust is revoked if the beneficiary pre-deceases the depositor, and may be revoked by the depositor's will.[63]

It follows from *Edwards v. Bradley*[64] and other cases[65] that transfers into joint tenancy are *inter vivos* transactions and not testamentary. I submit that the same applies to other will substitutes. Thus, for example, life insurance and pension benefits payble to a beneficiary are not testamentary dispositions, but *inter vivos* ones.

Further Reading

Jordan M. Atin, "Severance of Joint Tenancies" (1997), 16 E. & T.J. 225.

Ian M. Hull, "Joint Ownership on Death — Joint Accounts and Joint Assets in Estate and Capacity Litigation" (2000), 34 E.T.R. (2d) 151.

(f) Life Insurance

Today a substantial portion of the average estate consists of life insurance. Life insurance is a contract under which an insurer agrees to pay insurance moneys on death or a specified event. Since 1980, the term "life insurance" includes an annuity contract.[66]

A contract of life insurance may be an individual or a group policy. A group policy is common in an employment relationship. The individual insured and, normally, the member of the group have a right to designate a beneficiary of the contract, or of his or her benefits under the group contract. The insured may make a designation in the contract of insurance, by declaration,[67] or by will.[68] A des-

---

62 179 N.Y. 112, 71 N.E. 748 (1904).

63 See *Scott on Trusts*, 4th ed. by Austin Wakeman Scott and William Franklin Fratcher (Boston: Little, Brown and Company, 1987), vol. IA, §§58-58.6.

64 *Supra*.

65 See, *e.g.*, *Moskoff v. Moskoff Estate* (1999), 34 E.T.R. (2d) 57 (Ont. S.C.J.).

66 *Insurance Act*, R.S.O. 1990, c. I-8, s. 1. Prior to the amendment a number of cases held that annuity contracts issued by insurance companies were not life insurance and, thus, the proceeds were subject to the claims of creditors. See, *e.g.*, *Re Beck* (1976), 70 D.L.R. (3d) 760 (Man. C.A.).

67 *Insurance Act, supra*, s. 190.

68 *Ibid*, s. 192. Thus, a direction in a will that life insurance provided by the testatrix's employer should be used to pay immediate expenses was held to be a declaration sufficient to constitute a change in beneficiary designation: *Urquhart Estate v. Urquhart* (1999), 30 E.T.R. (2d) 310, 82 D.L.R. (4th) 249 (Ont. S.C.J.).

ignation that is made by will may be valid even though the instrument is itself invalid as a will. However, any later designation renders the designation in the will ineffective. Moreover, if the will containing a designation is subsequently revoked, the designation is also revoked.[69] The beneficiary may be more than one person, or it may be the estate of the person making the designation.[70] It is also possible to appoint a trustee for a beneficiary.[71] If you designate a trustee for a beneficiary, something you may wish to do if the beneficiary is a minor or otherwise lacks capacity, you can do so in the will without increasing the probate estate, while at the same time keeping the proceeds free from the claims of creditors.[72]

You may also designate a beneficiary irrevocably. That precludes you from changing the designation without the beneficiary's consent.[73] This kind of designation is useful, for example, to provide for a former spouse on a breakdown of marriage.

One of the main advantages of life insurance is that it permits you to avoid the claims of your creditors. If you designate a beneficiary other than your estate, the proceeds of insurance do not form part of your estate, but pass directly to the beneficiary. Hence, they do not come into the hands of the personal representatives and are not subject to the claims of your creditors.[74] Further, while a designation in favour of a spouse, child, grandchild, or parent of the insured is in effect, the rights of the insured in the contract are exempt from seizure.[75] Of course, if you designate your estate as the beneficiary, the proceeds will be subject to the claims of your creditors. They will also increase the size of your probate estate and, hence, the amount of fees that must be paid.

In the last decade the immunity from creditors that life insurance affords has come under attack in a number of ways:

1. As noted, until the Act was amended in 1980, some cases regarded annuity contracts as non-life insurance contracts which, therefore, were not protected from creditors.
2. Some courts have held that the voluntary settlement provisions of the *Bankruptcy and Insolvency Act*[76] apply to contracts of life insurance.[77] Such cases are incorrect, I submit, since section 67(b) of the Act provides that property exempt from seizure under provincial law is not available to creditors on a

---

69 *Ibid.*, s. 192.
70 *Ibid.*, s. 190.
71 *Ibid.*, s. 193.
72 See Barry S. Corbin, "Separate Insurance Trusts: Eating One's Cake and Having it Too" (1993), 12 E. & T.J. 104. *Re Brown Estate* (1993), 97 D.L.R. (4th) 163 (Sask. Q.B.), which holds that the proceeds form part of the probate estate, would appear to be wrong: see Pam Haidinger-Bains, Comment (1993), 13 E. & T.J. 205.
73 *Insurance Act, supra*, s. 191. Such a designation can not be made by will.
74 *Ibid.*, ss. 191(1), 196(1).
75 *Ibid.*, s. 196(2).
76 R.S.C. 1985, c. B-3 (renamed by 1992, c. 27, s. 2), s. 91.
77 See, *e.g.*, *Klassen (Trustee of) v. Great West Life Assurance Co.* (1991) 1 C.B.R. (3d) 263 (Sask. Q.B.); *Royal Bank of Canada v. Oliver* (1992), 11 C.B.R. (3d) 82 (Sask. Q.B.).

bankruptcy. However, it seems that insurance policies can be seized under the *Income Tax Act*[78] to collect tax that is owing, since (as distinct from the *Bankruptcy and Insolvency Act*) it does not contain a provision exempting property that is exempt under provincial law.[79]

3. Dependants of the deceased are sometimes able to gain access to the insurance proceeds, even though they are payable to a designated beneficiary. Thus, for example, s. 72 of the *Succession Law Reform Act*,[80] deems amounts payable under a contract of insurance effected on a person's life and owned by the person to be part of the deceased's estate for purposes of determining the value of the estate. Further, the proceeds are available to be charged with payment of a dependant's support order. This issue is discussed in a later chapter.

Thus, while the principle of immunity from creditors remains, substantial inroads have been made against it. However, insurance contracts receive better protection than pensions, another will substitute, which we shall consider next.

Further Reading

David H. McKee, "Debtor-Creditor Issues Affecting Annuity Contracts" (1993), 12 E. & T.J. 247.

Barry S. Corbin, "Separate Insurance Trusts: Eating One's Cake and Having it Too" (1993), 12 E. & T.J. 104.

Peter L. Biro. "The Erosion of Life Insurance RRSP Immunity from Creditor's Claims" (1994), 13 E. & T.J. 189.

David Norwood, "The Life Insurance Family Beneficiary" (1994), 13 E. & T.J. 256.

David McKee, "Creditor Protection: Basic Principles and Supreme Court Decision Impacts" (1997), 16 E. & T.J. 153.

Glenn Stephens, "Update on Creditor Protection" (1999), 18 E.T. & P.J. 119.

Edward A.J. Rothberg, "Life Insurance and Creditor Protection: Review and Update, 2000 (2000), 19 E.T. & P.J. 269.

Notes and Questions

1. The testator had validly designated the plaintiff as beneficiary under his insurance plan, by a contract of insurance. Later he made a will revoking all former wills and testamentary dispositions. The plaintiff claimed entitlement to the insurance proceeds since the words of revocation in the will were not valid as a declaration under the *Insurance Act*. The executors of the estate maintained that the designation of the plaintiff had been revoked by the will and the insurance proceeds were part of the estate. What result?[81]

2. *Shannon v. Shannon*[82] shows that persons may have rights apart from the *Insurance Act*. The deceased had promised, in a written separation agreement, that he would not

---

78 R.S.C. 1985, c. 1 (5th Supp.).
79 *M.N.R. v. Moss*, [1998] 1 C.T.C. 283, 50 C.B.R. (3d) 294 (F.C. T.D.).
80 R.S.O. 1990, c. S.26.
81 *Hurzin v. Great West Life Assurance Co.* (1988), 29 E.T.R. 51 (B.C. S.C.).
82 (1985), 19 E.T.R. 1 (Ont. H.C.).

revoke his wife's beneficiary designation under his insurance policy. He did not file this agreement in accordance with the provisions of the *Insurance Act*.[83] Subsequently, he broke this promise and named other beneficiaries. The court held that the Act does not specifically preclude the existence of rights outside its provisions. In finding a trust in favour of the wife, McKinlay J. stated:[84]

...the Insurance Act provides a statutory framework for the protection of the insured, the insurer and the beneficiaries; equity imposes duties of conscience on parties based on their relationship and dealings one with another outside the purview of the statute.

(g) Pensions and Beneficiary Designations

The pension plan is another will substitute by means of which wealth can be transferred on death. There is a great variety of pension schemes. Many pension plans are private and are a term of employment. In Ontario these are regulated in part by the *Pension Benefits Act*.[85] Private pension plans exhibit a great diversity, but generally provide for vesting and locking-in of pensions benefits after a designated period of employment and attainment of a specified age.[86] A pension normally begins upon retirement. It often takes the form of a life annuity and the annuity may be guaranteed for a specified number of years and made payable to the employee's estate or other beneficiary as designated by the employee.[87]

In addition to private employment pension schemes there are also retirement plans operated by individuals themselves which, if registered under the *Income Tax Act*,[88] defer income tax and entitle the owner to designate beneficiaries after his or her death. Finally, there are certain government insurance and pension plans, such as old age security[89] and the Canada Pension Plan,[90] some of which also permit the designation of beneficiaries.

There is a growing body of case law dealing with the right of employers to appropriate surpluses under pension plans. There is also a number of articles on the administration of private pension plans. These issues are beyond the scope of this brief introduction.

---

83 R.S.O. 1980, c. 218.

84 At p. 8 E.T.R.

85 R.S.O. 1990, c. P.8. The following are the comparable statutes in the other provinces: *Employment Pension Plans Act*, S.A. 1986, c. E-10.05; *Pension Benefits Act*, R.S.M. 1987, c. P32; R.S.N.B. 1973, c. P-5.1; *Pension Benefits Act, 1997*, S.N. 1996, c. P-4.01; R.S.N.S. 1989, c. 340; S.S. 1992, c. P-6.001; *Pension Benefits Standards Act*, R.S.B.C. 1996, c. 352. Before legislation respecting pensions was enacted pension plans which conferred benefits upon third parties after the death of the employee were liable to be found invalid as being testamentary unless the statutory formalities respecting wills had been observed: *MacInnes v. MacInnes*, [1935] S.C.R. 200, 2 I.L.R. 14, [1935] 1 D.L.R. 401.

86 *Pension Benefits Act* (Ont.), *ibid.*, s. 36, 10 years employment and 45 years of age.

87 *Ibid.*, s. 48. See also the *Public Service Pension Act*, R.S.O. 1990, c. P.48.

88 R.S.C. 1985, c. 1 (5th Supp.), as amended.

89 See *Old Age Security Act*, R.S.C. 1985, c. 0-9.

90 See *Canada Pension Plan Act*, R.S.C. 1985, c. 8.

In Ontario there is special legislation regarding the designation of beneficiaries under all pension and retirement plans, including registered retirement savings plans and registered retirement income funds. This is contained in Part III of the *Succession Law Reform Act*,[91] set out below.

This legislation does not govern beneficiary designations under all pension plans. The legislation itself excludes plans such as RRSPs issued under Part V of the *Insurance Act*.[92] Further, employees of the federal government are governed by the *Public Service Superannuation Act*.[93]

We saw that there have been encroachments on the principle that the proceeds of life insurance are immune from the creditors of the insured. It appears that pension plans are much less protected from the claims of creditors, unless they are issued under the *Insurance Act*. Only the statutes of British Columbia[94] and Prince Edward Island[95] contain protection similar to that afforded the proceeds of insurance. The Manitoba Law Reform Commission recommended that such protection by incorporated in the Manitoba Act,[96] but it was not adopted by the Legislature.

Case law in the other provinces is inconclusive. Early cases held that a designation of beneficiary is a testamentary disposition and the proceeds of pension plans, including RRSPs unless they are purchased through an insurance company, are paid to the personal representatives and form part of the plan holder's estate and are, therefore, subject to the claims of his or her creditors.[97] In principle, this is incorrect. A designation of beneficiary is not a testamentary disposition, but is intended to operate independently of the designator's will. Hence, the beneficiaries are the ones who have the right to collect the proceeds under the provisions of the plan and the personal representatives do not, unless, of course, the estate is the designated beneficiary. More recent cases have recognized that this is so, relying on legislation such as s. 53 of the *Succession Law Reform Act*, which authorizes payment to the beneficiaries and provides that the beneficiary is entitled to enforce payment.[98] Some of these cases have also held, however, that if the

---

91 R.S.O. 1990, c. S.26.

92 R.S.O. 1990, c. I-8.

93 R.S.C. 1985, c. P-36. See also the *Supplementary Death Benefits Regulations*, C.R.C. 1978, c. 1360. And see *Gagnon v. Sussex* (1992), 45 E.T.R. 309.

94 *Law and Equity Act*, R.S.B.C. 1996, c. 253, as am., s. 49(2)(c).

95 *Designation of Beneficiaries under Benefit Plans Act*, R.S.P.E.I. 1988, c. D-9, ss. 9, 10.

96 Man. Law Reform Comm., *Statutory Designations and the Retirement Plan Beneficiaries Act*, Report No. 73 (1990), Recommendation 7.

97 See, *e.g.*, *Canadian Imperial Bank of Commerce v. Besharah and Eaton Bay Trust* (1989), 68 O.R. (2d) (H.C.), the proceeds of a non-insurance RRSP devolve on annuitant's estate to be paid out to beneficiary as special legacy and was, thus, available to satisfy the claims of the annuitant's creditors; *Waugh Estate v. Waugh* (1990), 63 Man. R. (2d) 155 (Q.B.), following *Besharah*; *Pozniak v. Pozniak Estate*, [1993] 7 W.W.R. 500, 50 E.T.R. 114 (Man. C.A.), following *Besharah*.

98 See, *e.g.*, *Baltzan Estate v. M.N.R.*, [1990] 3 W.W.R. 374, 37 E.T.R. 111 (Sask. Surr. Ct.), R.R.S.P. proceeds paid to beneficiary not available to satisfy Revenue Canada's claim for income tax from annuitant's estate; *Clark Estate v. Clark*, [1997] 3 W.W.R. 62, 15 E.T.R. (2d) 113 (Man. C.A.), executor unable to recover funeral expenses from beneficiary to whom proceeds of RRSP had been paid; *Fekete Estate v. Simon* (2000), 32 E.T.R. (2d) 202 (Ont. S.C.J.), proceeds of RRIF

estate has insufficient assets to pay the deceased's debts, then the creditors can recover the balance from the beneficiaries to whom the proceeds of the RRSPs and RRIFs have been paid.[99] They reached this conclusion on two grounds: (a) that a distinction can be drawn between a contract of insurance, the proceeds of which never belonged to the insured but to the insurer, and an RRSP, under which the participant's money is invested on his or her behalf; and (b) that pension legislation in most provinces does not contain a provision like that which protects the proceeds of insurance from the reach of the insured's creditors.

Further Reading

Barry S. Corbin, "Designating Beneficiaries" (1989), 9 E. & T.J. 199, 349.
Stephen Stuart, "Locked-in RRSPs" (1990-91), 10 E. & T.J. 385.
Barry S. Corbin, "RRSPs: Partial Protection Against Creditors?" (2000), 20 E.T. & P.J. 33.

SUCCESSION LAW REFORM ACT
R.S.O. 1990, c. S.26, am. 1994, c. 27, s. 63(4), (5)
PART III
DESIGNATION OF BENEFICIARIES OF INTEREST IN FUNDS OR PLANS

50. In this Part,
"participant" means a person who is entitled to designate another person to receive a benefit payable under a plan on the participant's death;
"plan" means,
  (a) a pension, retirement, welfare or profit-sharing fund, trust, scheme, contract or arrangement or a fund, trust, scheme, contract or arrangement for other benefits for employees, former employees, directors, former directors, agents or former agents of an employer or their dependants or beneficiaries,
  (b) a fund, trust, scheme, contract, or arrangement for the payment of a periodic sum for life or for a fixed or variable term, or
  (c) a fund, trust, scheme, contract or arrangement of a class that is prescribed for the purposes of this Part by a regulation made under section 53.1,
and includes a retirement savings plan, a retirement income fund and a home ownership savings plan as defined in the *Income Tax Act* (Canada) and an Ontario home ownership savings plan under the *Ontario Home Ownership Savings Plan Act.*
  51. (1) A participant may designate a person to receive a benefit payable under a plan on the participant's death,

---

payable to testator's spouse as designated beneficiary passed outside estate and flowed directly to beneficiary; *Banting v. Saunders Estate* (2000), 34 E.T.R. (2d) 163 (Ont. S.C.J.), proceeds of RRIFs and RRSP payable to children did not form part of estate and tax liability arising from inclusion of amount of RRIFs and RRSP in deceased's income in year of death fell on estate.
99 See *Clark Estate, Fekete Estate,* and *Banting, ibid.*

(a) by an instrument signed by him or her or signed on his or her behalf by another person in his or her presence and by his or her direction; or

(b) by will,

and may revoke the designation by either of those methods.

(2) A designation in a will is effective only if it relates expressly to a plan, either generally or specifically.

52. (1) A revocation in a will is effective to revoke a designation made by instrument only if the revocation relates expressly to the designation, either generally or specifically.

(2) Despite section 15, a later designation revokes an earlier designation, to the extent of any inconsistency.

(3) Revocation of a will revokes a designation in the will.

(4) A designation or revocation contained in an instrument purporting to be a will is not invalid by reason only of the fact that the instrument is invalid as a will.

(5) A designation in an instrument that purports to be but is not a valid will is revoked by an event that would have the effect of revoking the instrument if it had been a valid will.

(6) Revocation of a designation does not revive an earlier designation.

(7) Despite section 22, a designation or revocation in a will is effective from the time when the will is signed.

53. Where a participant in a plan has designated a person to receive a benefit under the plan on the death of the participant,

(a) the person administering the plan is discharged on paying the benefit to the person designated under the latest designation made in accordance with the terms of the plan, in the absence of actual notice of a subsequent designation or revocation made under section 51 but not in accordance with the terms of the plan; and

(b) the person designated may enforce payment of the benefit payable to him under the plan but the person administering the plan may set up any defence that he could have set up against the participant or his or her personal representative.

53.1 The Lieutenant Governor in Council may make regulations prescribing classes of funds, trusts, schemes, contracts or arrangements for the purposes of this Part.

54. (1) Where this Part is inconsistent with a plan, this Part applies, unless the inconsistency relates to a designation made or proposed to be made after the making of a benefit payment where the benefit payment would have been different if the designation had been made before the benefit payment, in which case the plan applies.

(2) This Part does not apply to a contract or to a designation of a beneficiary to which the *Insurance Act* applies.

Comparable Legislation

Beneficiaries Designation Act, R.S.N.S. 1989, c. 36; *Designation of Beneficiaries under Benefit Plans Act*, R.S.P.E.I. 1988, c. D-9; *Income Tax Savings Plans Act*, R.S.N. 1990, c. I-2; *Law and Equity Act*, R.S.B.C. 1996, c. 253, ss. 49-51; *Queen's Bench Act*, R.S.S. 1978, c. Q-1; *Retirement Plan Beneficiaries Act*, S.M. 1992, c. 31; S.N.B. 1982, c. P-10.21; *Trustee Act*, R.S.A. 1980, c. T-10, s. 47.

Notes and Questions

1. Section 54.1 of the Act, as amended, retroactively validates designations made before or after the amendment came into effect, even if the person making the designation died before that date, unless that would change a judgment or order in a proceeding made before the date the amendment came into effect, or unless that would require a person liable to repay or account for moneys received.

2. The degree of capacity required to make a designation is the same as that required to make a will.[100]

3. X set up an RRSP through a financial institution. On the form provided by the financial institution, he designated his partner, Y, as his beneficiary to receive the proceeds of the RRSP payable on his death. Later X made a will in which he left all his estate to Y and designated Y as beneficiary under any RRSPs he may have. When X and Y split up, X made a new will, revoking the old. The new will left all of X's estate to Z. On X's death, who receives the proceeds of the RRSP, Y or Z? Why? Note that s. 52(2) of the Ontario legislation says that "a later designation revokes an earlier designation, *to the extent of any inconsistency.*"[101]

4. Is a beneficiary designation testamentary? Section 52(4) and (7) of the Ontario legislation would suggest that it is not. This has consequences for the validity of the designation. The issue arose in *Turner Estate v. Bezanson*[102] A pension plan contributor was dying of AIDS and was seriously ill when he signed a beneficiary designation in favour of a niece in suspicious circumstances. The execution of the document was defective if it was testamentary. The court held that the designation was not testamentary, so the formal requirements for wills did not have to be complied with. This was probably correct under the applicable legislation. However, the court then went on to say that the testamentary rules about onus and manner of proof of capacity and of knowledge and approval also did not have to be complied with, but the testamentary rule about the burden of proof respecting fraud and undue influence did. The latter, is wrong, I submit. A designation is either testamentary or it is not. If it is, then all the testamentary rules apply. If that was the case, then the designation would have been ineffective for failure to comply with the necessary formalities and failure to remove the suspicion. If a designation is not testamentary, none of those rules apply. However, then the *inter vivos* rules regarding undue influence applied and there would have been a presumption of undue influence against the niece and she failed to meet the onus of rebutting it.[103]

---

100 *Stewart v. Nash* (1988), 65 O.R. (2d) 218, 30 E.T.R. 85 (C.A.).
101 See Barry S. Corbin, "Practice Note: The Case of the Wayward RRSPs" (1995), 14 E. & T.J. 365 at 367.
102 (1995), 8 E.T.R. (2d) 169 (C.A.).
103 See Bernadette Maxwell, Comment (1996), 16 E. & T.J. 7.

(h) Use of Will Substitutes to Avoid Probate Fees

As noted above, one use of will substitutes is to avoid paying probate fees. This became a significant issue in Canadian jurisdictions in the 1990s when provinces began to increase their probate fees. Probate fees are fees charged by the province on the value of the so-called "probate estate," that is, the estate that is administered by the personal representative and in respect of which probate is sought. Ontario tripled its probate fees and began charging probate fees of approximately 1.5 percent of the value of the probate estate effective January 1, 1993.[104] British Columbia followed suit in 1997, doubling its probate fees to approximately 1.4 percent of the probate estate.[105]

The validity of the Ontario fees was contested in *Re Eurig Estate*.[106] Mrs. Eurig, who was her husband's executrix, argued that the fees were an indirect tax beyond the constitutional competence of the province. The lower courts held that they were, indeed, fees that were validly imposed as part of a regulatory scheme for the administration of justice. However, Mrs. Eurig's appeal to the Supreme Court of Canada was successful.[107] The Supreme Court held that the probate "fee" was in fact a tax because it was enforceable by law, levied by a public body, intended for a public purpose, and there was no correlation between the amount of the fee and the cost of the service provided. It was a direct tax and, thus, within provincial competence. However, it was invalid because it was imposed by regulation, rather than by statute, since only the legislature can impose a tax of its own accord. Further, the governing legislation only authorized the imposition of fees, not of taxes. Nor, assuming that is possible, did the governing legislation expressly delegate taxing authority to the Lieutenant Governor in Council. Accordingly, Mrs. Eurig was entitled to restitution of the moneys paid. The court suspended the declaration of invalidity for six months.

The Ontario Legislature took advantage of the suspension by enacting the *Estate Administration Tax Act, 1998*,[108] which was deemed to come into force on May 15, 1950,[109] thereby preventing claims for restitution of probate fees. However, the Eurig estate was specifically exempted.[110] The Act imposes the same amount in tax as was previously exacted in fees by regulation.[111] British Columbia followed suit by enacting the *Probate Fee Act*,[112] which also imposes the same amount in fees as were previously imposed by regulation. Further, a Nova Scotia case followed *Eurig* in holding that probate fees were an unconstitutional dele-

---

104 O. Reg. 293/92, s. 2 [am. O. Reg. 802/94, s. 1], imposed a fee of $5 per $1,000 on the first $50,000 and $15 per $1,000 on the value of the probate estate over $50,000.
105 By B.C. Reg. 10/96, amending App. C of the *Supreme Court Rules*, B.C. Reg. 221/90.
106 (1994), 20 O.R. (3d) 385 (Gen. Div.), affirmed (1997), 31 O.R. (3d) 777 (C.A.).
107 *Re Eurig Estate*, [1998] 2 S.C.R. 565, 23 E.T.R. (2d) 1, 165 D.L.R. (4th) 1.
108 S.O. 1998, c. 34, Sched.
109 *Ibid.*, s. 64(2).
110 *Ibid.*, Schedule, s. 7(1).
111 *Ibid.*, s. 2.
112 S.B.C. 1999, c. 4.

gation of the taxing power to the Governor in Council.[113] In contrast, Alberta is reducing its probate fees by a substantial amount.[114]

There is a number of ways in which probate fees may be avoided. For example, a person can make *inter vivos* gifts to persons to whom the person might otherwise have left testamentary gifts. Alternatively, the person can transfer property into the joint names of the donor and donees, or transfer property to trustees under an *inter vivos* trust for the benefit of the donees. There are obvious problems with these devices. The donor loses control of property disposed of by *inter vivos* gift, unless she or he retained a power to revoke. And putting one's property into joint tenancy with another person causes problems if the donee refuses to relinquish it, for example, after a separation. It also causes problems if the donee is sued by creditors or must account for the property on a breakdown of marriage to his or her spouse. Further, there are tax consequences to disposing of one's property before death. A solicitor should, therefore, carefully advice a client of these adverse consequences.

Another aspect of transferring property into the joint names of oneself and one's child that is often overlooked is that the donor may intend the donee to share the property with siblings or others when the donor dies. But unless there is evidence of that intent, a dishonest donee can hide behind the presumption of advancement and claim that the transfer was a gift to the donee.

Probate fees can also be avoided by the device of multiple wills. A testator may make a primary will of property in respect of which probate is desired or necessary, such as real property, publicly-traded shares, or life insurance,[115] and a secondary will of property in respect of which probate is unnecessary, such as shares in private companies. In *Granovsky Estate v. Ontario*[116] the court approved of this kind of scheme to avoid probate fees, holding that it was not necessary to submit the second will to probate.[117] The Rules have been amended to provide for new forms for situations in which probate of only one of the wills is sought.[118]

Finally, probate fees can be avoided by means of the "*alter ego* trust" and the "joint partner trust" proposed by Ways and Means Motion introduced in the House of Commons on June 5, 2000. The terms will be defined by s. 248(1) of the *Income Tax Act*.[119] An "*alter ego* trust" must satisfy the following conditions:

---

113 *Balders Estate v. Halifax (County) Registrar of Probate* (1999), 28 E.T.R. (2d) 288 (N.S.S.C.).

114 See John C. Armstrong, "From the Legislatures" (2000), 19 E.T. & P.J. 193 at 195.

115 Note, however, *Rozon v. Transamerica Life Insurance Co. of Canada* (November 30, 1999), unreported (Ont. C.A.), which held that the insurer could not require the executor to produce a probated will when the insurance proceeds were payable to the deceased's estate, rather than to a designated beneficiary.

116 (1998), 156 D.L.R. (4th) 557 (Ont. Gen. Div.).

117 See also *Re Silver Estate* (1999), 31 E.T.R. (2d) 256 (Ont. S.C.J.), holding that the court had jurisdiction to deal with an application by executors of an unprobated as well as a probated will to pass the estate accounts; and *Carmichael v. Carmichael Estate* (2000), 46 O.R. (3d) 630, 31 E.T.R. (2d) 33, 184 D.L.R. (4th) 175 (S.C.J.), holding that the court had jurisdiction to remove executors who had taken preliminary steps to administer the estate but had not obtained letters probate.

118 See *Rules of Civil Procedure*, R.R.O. 1990, Reg. 194, R. 74.04(1), (9).

119 R.S.C. 1985, c. 1 (5th Supp.).

(a) the taxpayer was alive and 65 years of age or older when it was created; (b) it was created after 1999; (c) the taxpayer was entitled to all the income before his or her death; (d) no person other than the taxpayer can receive or obtain the use of any of the income or capital of the trust before the taxpayer's death; and (e) the trust did not make an election under subpara. 104(4)(a)(ii.1) of the Act. A "joint spousal trust" must satisfy the following conditions: (a) the taxpayer was alive and 65 years of age or older when the trust was created; (b) it was created after 1999; (c) the taxpayer or the taxpayer's spouse was, in combination with the spouse or the taxpayer as the case may be entitled to receive all the income from the trust until the later of the death of the taxpayer and the death of the spouse; and (d) no other person can receive or obtain the use of the income or capital of the trust before the later of those deaths. Assuming that these amendments are in due course enacted, it is bizarre to have the federal government not only condone but actively promote tax avoidance at the provincial level.

Further Reading

Wolfe D. Goodman, "Re Probate Fee Planning for Ontario Estates" (1993), 13 E. & T.J. 301.

Barry S. Corbin, Practice Note: "How Not to Avoid Probate Fees" (1996), 16 E. & T.J. 169.

Wolfe D. Goodman, Tax Column: "Probate Fees — Minimizing Fees by Using a Separate Will for Registry Office Lands — Transfer of Such Lands to Land Titles System" (1997), 16 E. & T.J. 282.

Anthony P. McGlynn and K. Thomas Grozinger, "Joint Ownership of Property in the Context of Inter-Generational Transfers of Estates: Convenience and Conflict" (1997), 16 E. & T.J. 105.

Carmen S. Thériault, "Probate Fee Developments in British Columbia" (1998), 17 E.T. & P.J. 295.

Sharon E. Goldberg and Hillary E. Laidlaw. "The Vacation Property: How (Not) to Avoid Probate Taxes on Death" (1999), 18 E.T. & P.J. 341.

Paul LeBreux, Tax Column: "Eurig Estate: Another Day, Another Tax" (2000), 19 E.T. & P.J. 207.

Robert Spencely, *Probate Planning Through Will Substitutes* (Toronto: CCH, 2000).

3. CONTRACTS TO MAKE WILLS

(a) Introduction

The effect of support of dependants legislation on contracts to leave property by will is discussed in a later chapter. In this part we shall consider the law respecting such contracts generally.

An agreement to leave property to another by will may take two forms. A person may either promise to leave his or her property, some specific property, or an amount of money to another on death or, having already made a will in which he or she has left property to another person, agree with that person not to revoke the will. Such a contract may be merely under seal, or it may be supported by consideration. A common situation is one in which the promisor persuades the promisee to reside with the promisor and look after the promisor for the rest of his or her life, in return for which the promisor will leave property to the promisee. A promise may also be made to leave property to another in consideration of marriage or for some other reason.

The validity of a contract to make a will is determined by the law of contracts, not by the law of wills. Moreover, although, despite any agreement to the contrary, a will is always revocable, the contract, if otherwise valid, is not affected by the fact that the will is revoked.[120] The contract will be enforced outside the will. Whether the promisee is entitled to enforce the contract will depend upon the nature of the agreement, however. For example, if the contract is merely not to revoke an existing will, it is not broken if the will is revoked by operation of law,[121] unless the parties agreed that the property would pass to the promisee in any event,[122] even if the promisee predeceased the testator. Normally, if a legatee predeceases the testator, the legacy lapses[123] and a promise to leave property to a person by will is also not normally enforceable by the legatee's estate.[124] However, this is not because of the doctrine of lapse, but because that was the parties' intention. In other words, if the parties intended that the property should go to the promisee in any event, the latter's estate can enforce the contract if he or she predeceases the promisor.[125]

Since an agreement to leave property by will is a contract, the normal contractual rules regarding the existence and validity of the contract apply, including intention to enter into the contract, offer and acceptance, consideration or a seal, and certainty of terms and of subject matter.

Further Reading

Lee, "Contracts to Make Wills" (1971), 87 L.Q. Rev. 358.
Mellows, *The Law of Succession* (3rd ed. 1977), ch. 3.
Page on the Law of Wills, rev. ed. by William J. Bowe and Douglas H. Parker (Cincinnati: The W.H. Anderson Company, 1960), vol 1, ch. 10.
Sparks, *Contracts to Make Wills* (1956).

(b) Remedies for Breach

If the contract is breached, what remedies does the promisee have? Since it is a contract, the normal contractual remedies apply. Usually, therefore, the remedy

---

120 *Re Marsland; Lloyds Bank Ltd. v. Marsland*, [1939] Ch. 820, [1939] 3 All E.R. 148 (C.A.).
121 *Ibid.*, revocation by operation of law occurs when the testator subsequently marries.
122 *Robinson v. Ommanney* (1883), 23 Ch. D. 285, [1881-85] All E.R. Rep. 265 (C.A.).
123 Lapse is discussed in a later chapter.
124 See, *e.g.*, *Re Brookman's Trust* (1869), 5 Ch. App. 182.
125 Lee, "Contracts to Make Wills" (1971), 87 L.Q. Rev. 358 at 361-2.

will be damages.[126] However, if specific property was the subject matter of the contract, specific performance may be granted.[127] An injunction may also be awarded to prevent disposition of such property if the promisee learns that the promisor is going to dispose of it.[128] These several remedies are discussed in *Synge v. Synge*,[129] reproduced below.

Obviously a contract to leave property by will is fully performed if the promisor dies leaving a will by which the promise is carried out. A breach of a contract normally occurs on the death of the promisor, that is, when it is discovered that he or she has not left the property by his will as promised. However, the contract may be breached earlier if it concerns specific property and the promisor disposes of it in his or her lifetime. Moreover, if the contract is not to revoke a will, it will be breached when revocation occurs.

SYNGE v. SYNGE
[1894] 1 Q.B. 466
Court of Appeal

In consideration of and as an inducement to his intended marriage to the plaintiff, the defendant promised her in writing to leave a house and land to her for her life. After the marriage the defendant conveyed the property to a third person. The plaintiff then brought this action for a declaration that she was entitled to a life estate in the property after her husband's death and that the conveyance was subject to her right. In the alternative she claimed damages for breach of contract. The trial judge dismissed the action. The plaintiff appealed.

KAY L.J., delivered the judgment of the court:

The questions which arise in this court are these:—
1. Was there a binding contract?
2. Was it such a contract as could be enforced in equity, or was there a remedy in damages for the breach of it?
3. Has the time arrived at which such remedy can be asserted?
4. If the remedy be by way of damages, what amount of damages should be given?

The action was tried by a judge without a jury, so that all questions both of fact and law are open on this appeal.

It will be convenient to consider the questions in the order in which they are stated.

The alleged contract is contained in a letter of December 24, 1883, by the defendant to a lady whom he was desirous to marry, and is in these words:—

---

126 *Hammersley v. De Biel* (1845), 12 Cl. & Fin. 45, 8 E.R. 1312 (H.L.).
127 *Coverdale v. Eastwood* (1872), L.R. 15 Eq. 121.
128 *Synge v. Synge*, [1894] 1 Q.B. 466 (C.A.).
129 *Ibid.*

> You my love thoroughly understand the terms (and I daresay have told Mr. Woodruff on which we are to put a stop to all this bother by becoming one another) which are that I leave house and land to you for your lifetime....True it is possible but highly improbable that I might come in for the title and should be much better off. Should such a thing happen we could see what I ought and would do for you.

There seems to be no doubt that the house and land referred to were the house and a small piece of land at Ardfield in Devonshire, worth it is said about 60*l*. or 70*l*. a year, in which the defendant was then residing with two daughters by a former marriage. The defendant was not then Sir R. Synge. He succeeded to the title afterwards. The lady who is the plaintiff had some property of her own of which Mr. Woodruff was trustee. He was not a solicitor.

The construction of the letter is plain. It is a statement of the "terms" as to property on which the defendant proposed to marry the lady. The marriage took place on January 5, 1884, ten days after the date of the letter.

. . .

We are of opinion that the proposal of terms in this case was made as an inducement to the lady to marry, that she consented to the terms, and married the defendant on the faith that he would keep his word, and that accordingly there was a binding contract on the defendant's part to leave to his wife the house and land at Ardfield for her life.

Then, secondly, what is the remedy? Marriage is a valuable consideration for such a contract of the highest order, and where, as here, the contract is in writing, so that there is no question upon the Statute of Frauds, in the language already quoted,[130] a Court of Equity will take care that the party who marries on the faith of such a proposal "is not disappointed, and will give effect to the proposal."

In *Hammersley v. De Biel* the proposal was made on behalf of the intended wife's father, by his authority, and was reduced into writing, and was to the effect that the father would pay down 10,000*l*., to be settled on the intended husband and wife and their children, the husband to secure a jointure of 500*l*. a year to the wife if she survived him; and then followed the provision on which the question arose, by which the father "proposes for the present to allow his daughter 200*l*. per annum for her private use,....and also intends to leave a further sum of 10,000*l*. in his will to Miss Thompson, to be settled on her and her children." After the father's death, without having made the promised provision by will, the only child of the marriage — his mother having died before her father — instituted a suit in equity against his grandfather's executors to recover 10,000*l*. out of his assets. Lord Langdale, M.R., held that by acceptance the proposal had "ripened into an agreement," and that the plaintiff was entitled to the relief he prayed — i.e., to the sum of 10,000*l*., with interest at 4 per cent from the end of one year after the father's death, on the footing of a legacy. Lord Cottenham, L.C., affirmed his decision....

This was affirmed in the House of Lords by Lord Lyndhurst, L.C., Lord Broughham, and Lord Campbell, without calling upon the respondents. We have examined the case closely, because it is of the highest authority, not merely as a

---

130 From *Hammersley v. De Biel* (1845), 12 Cl. & F. 45 at 78.

judgment of the House of Lords, but it was decided by some of the best equity lawyers of that time. Lord St. Leonards has criticized the decision on the ground that the memorandum in that case might have been construed as a mere expression of an intention, not as a definite proposal which could by acceptance ripen into a contract.[131] But he does not intimate a doubt that the decision was right if the proposal was not merely of an intention which might be changed. Therefore, a definite proposal in writing so as to satisfy the Statute of Frauds to leave property by will, made to induce a marriage, and accepted, and the marriage made on the faith of it, will be enforced in equity.

Then, what is the remedy where the proposal relates to a defined piece of real property? We have no doubt of the power of the Court to decree a conveyance of that property after the death of the person making the proposal against all who claim under him as volunteers.

It is argued that Courts of Equity cannot compel a man to make a will. But neither can they compel him to execute a deed. They, however, can decree the heir or devisee in such a case to convey the land to the widow for life, and under the Trustee Acts can make a vesting order, or direct that someone shall convey for him if he refuses. And under the like circumstances, the Court has power to make a declaration of the lady's right.

But counsel do not press for such relief, or ask for a declaration to bind the house and land. The relief they ask is damages for breach of contract. It seems to be proved that the grantees of the property under the deeds executed by Sir R. Synge took without notice of the letter; they acquired, as we understand, the legal estate by the grant. If there was any valuable consideration moving from them, no relief in the nature of specific performance could be given against them....It is not necessary to examine this argument, as counsel elect to ask for damages only.

Sir R. Synge had all his lifetime to perform this contract; but, in order to perform it, he must in his lifetime make a disposition in favour of Lady Synge. If he died without having done so, he would have broken his contract. The breach would be omitting in his lifetime to make such a disposition. True, it would only take effect at his death; but the breach must take place in his lifetime, and as by the conveyance to his daughters he put it absolutely out of his power to perform his contract. Lady Synge...had a right to treat that conveyance as an absolute breach of contract, and to sue at once for damages; and as this Court has both legal and equitable jurisdiction, we are of opinion that such relief should be granted.

We have not before us the materials for assessing such damages. The amount must depend on the value of the possible life estate which Lady Synge would be entitled to if she survived her husband. Their comparative ages would, of course be a chief factor in such a calculation. There must be an inquiry as to the proper amount of damages.

. . .

---

131 *Sugden's Law of Property*, p. 53.

Notes and Questions

1. It is clear from *Synge v. Synge*[132] that the court will not grant specific performance if the deceased has, in his or her lifetime, conveyed the property to a *bona fide* purchaser for value without notice. Is such an order also precluded if the deceased devised the land to another?[133]

2. While damages would be the normal remedy for breach of a contract to bequeath specific personal property, it may be advantageous and possible to seek specific performance, particularly if the property has greatly increased in value.[134]

3. In *Synge v. Synge*[135] the court directed an inquiry into the amount of the damages and stated that these would depend upon the value of Lady Synge's life estate to which she would become entitled if she should survive her husband and upon the respective ages of the parties. Hence, in calculating damages for breach of contract during the deceased's lifetime, the promisee is entitled only to the actuarially determined present value of the subject matter of the promise.

4. Does a promisee under a contract to leave property to him or her by will take subject to the deceased's creditors? Does it matter whether the contract is performed or not, or that consideration was given for the promise?

It would seem that if the contract is to leave the residuary estate to the promisee, he or she will take subject to the deceased's creditors,[136] including, possibly, any claimants for dependant's support.[137] However, it seems likely that the promisee of specific assets would take in priority to creditors and also that a promisee of the residue would take in priority to legatees and devisees, since otherwise the promisor could defraud the promisee by making substantial dispositions under the will.[138]

(c) Part Performance

In order for a contract respecting real property to be enforceable, it must also comply with the *Statute of Frauds*,[139] that is, it must be supported by a note or memorandum in writing signed by the promisor or someone authorized by him or her. Indeed, since such contracts are not usually to be performed within one year, they must be evidenced by writing whether they concern real or personal property.[140] Alternatively, the contract may be enforceable under the doctrine of part performance. This doctrine was discussed in *Thompson v. Guaranty Trust*

---

132 *Supra.*

133 See *Devereux v. Devereux* (1978), 2 E.T.R. 164 (Ont. H.C.).

134 See *Phillips v. Spooner* (1980), 7 E.T.R. 157 (Sask. C.A.): the deceased had failed to bequeath to his first wife one-half of various securities listed in the separation agreement made with her.

135 *Supra.*

136 *Jervis v. Wolferstan* (1874), L.R. 18 Eq. 18 at 26, *per* Sir George Jessel M.R.; *Legeas v. Trusts & Guar. Co.* (1912), 4 Alta. L.R. 190, 1 W.W.R. 802, 5 D.L.R. 389 (T.D.).

137 This point is dealt with in a later chapter. See also *Phillips v. Spooner, supra*. At trial, [1979] 2 W.W.R. 473, 4 E.T.R. 178 (Sask. Q.B.), the court held that the first wife took her contractual rights in priority to the second wife's claim for support. That part of the judgment was not appealed.

138 See Lee, "Contracts to Make Wills" (1971), 87 L.Q. Rev. 358 at 360-1.

139 R.S.O. 1990, c. 481, s. 4.

140 *Ibid.*

Co. of Canada.[141] Thompson worked for the deceased, Copithorne, as a farm labourer for 48 years until Copithorne died. For the first two years Thompson was paid wages. Then Copithorne suffered a lengthy illness and was unable to pay further wages, so he promised Thompson that if he stayed on to work the property, he would leave all his property to him. Thompson not only worked the farm but nursed Copithorne back to health. Copithorne made similar promises in 1928 when he was injured. In 1942, when he suffered another injury that left him crippled for the rest of his life, he made what was thought to be a will, leaving all his property to Thompson. However this document, along with others, was later stolen. Throughout the 48 years Thompson faithfully worked and managed the farm and Copithorne fully relied upon him. During his final illness, Copithorne asked an insurance agent and notary public to draw up a document leaving everything to Thompson. In fact the agent prepared a power of attorney which was signed, but not read, by Copithorne. As a result, Copithorne died intestate. Independent witnesses confirmed Copithorne's promises to Thompson. Thompson brought an action for specific performance and relied on the doctrine of part performance. Spence J., who delivered the judgment of the court, quoted from the leading case, *Maddison v. Alderson,*[142] which held that the doctrine of part performance applies if the acts relied on are unequivocally, and in their own nature, referable to the agreement alleged by the plaintiff. Spence J. concluded that virtually every act of part performance on which evidence was given was unequivocally referable to an oral contract in reference to the deceased's property. Accordingly, the court granted specific performance of the contract.

Notes and Questions

1. The scope of the doctrine of part performance has been broadened in England in *Steadman v. Steadman.*[143] That case permitted the introduction of parol evidence to prove an oral contract when the promisee has relied to his detriment upon an act of the other party. There are some statements in recent Canadian cases which suggest a willingness to follow *Steadman,*[144] although none are decisive.

2. The doctrine of part performance in relation to contracts for the sale of land was effectively abolished in England by the *Law of Property (Miscellaneous Provisions Act) 1989.*[145] It requires that a contract for the sale of land be in writing and incorporate all the terms agreed to, and that the contract be signed by or on behalf of the parties.

---

141 [1973] 6 W.W.R. 746, 39 D.L.R. (3d) 408 (S.C.C.).
142 (1883), 3 App. Cas. 467.
143 [1976] A.C. 536, [1974] 2 All E.R. 977 (H.L.).
144 See, *e.g., Colberg v. Braunberger; Colberg v. Schumacher* (1978), 8 Alta. L.R. (2d) 73, 12 A.R. 183, (C.A.); *Shillabeer v. Diebel* (1979), 9 Alta. L.R. (2d) 112, 5 E.T.R. 30, 18 A.R. 173, (sub nom. *Re Shillabeer*) 100 D.L.R. (3d) 279 (T.D.); *Severin v. Vroom* (1977), 15 O.R. (2d) 636, 3 C.P.C. 183, 76 D.L.R. (3d) 427 (C.A.).
145 (U.K.), s. 2.

(d) Quantum Meruit

In many cases a contract cannot be proved or it is unenforceable. In those situations the promisee is not necessarily without a remedy, however. If unenforceability would work unjust enrichment, the promisee will be entitled to recover on a *quantum meruit* basis. This was discussed in *Deglman v. Guaranty Trust Co. of Canada and Constantineau*.[146] Constantineau was the nephew of the deceased Laura Brunet. In 1934-35, when he was 20, he attended a technical school in Ottawa and lived with the deceased for about six months at her apartment in a house at 550 Besserer St. She owned both 550 and the adjacent house, No. 548 and, other than her own apartment, rented them out to tenants. While staying with her, the respondent did chores around both houses. At the end of the school term he returned to his mother's home, also in Ottawa. He alleged that, while he lived with his aunt, she promised him that, if he would be good to her and perform such services for her as she might from time to time request during her lifetime, she would make adequate provision for him and, in particular, that she would leave the house at 548 Besserer St. to him. He never lived in that house. The respondent took a job in 1936 and was married in 1941. His services consisted of taking his aunt on pleasure drives and on automobile trips to Montreal, and doing odd jobs about the two houses and of doing errands and attending to her many personal needs. The deceased failed to carry out her promise and Constantineau brought this action for specific performance. The court held that the doctrine of part performance could not be applied because Constantineau's actions were not unequivocally referable to any dealing with the land in question. However, Constantineau was entitled to restitution. Although the contract between the parties was unenforceable because not in writing, the deceased had received the benefit of full performance of the contract and, thus, her estate was required to pay him the fair value of the services he rendered to her.

Further Reading

M. Jasmine Sweatman, "Claims of Compensation for Services Rendered: A Review" (1994), 14 E. & T.J. 143.

Notes and Questions

1. It would seem that in order for a person to succeed on a *quantum meruit* claim there must be some understanding between the parties, albeit not a contract, that the deceased did not intend the other party to render the services gratuitously and that the other party did not intend to do them gratuitously.[147] I submit, however, that this restricts the general restitutionary basis of a *quantum meruit* claim, which rests in unjust enrichment.[148]

---

146 [1954] S.C.R. 725, [1954] 3 D.L.R. 785.
147 See, *e.g., Rowe v. Public Trustee*, [1963] 2 O.R. 71, 38 D.L.R. (2d) 462 (H.C.); *Ross v. Ross* (1973), 33 D.L.R. (3d) 351 (Sask. Q.B.); *Garnett v. Armstrong* (1977), 20 N.B.R. (2d) 161, 34 A.P.R. 161, 83 D.L.R. (3d) 717 (C.A.); *Re Mandryk; Wegwitz v. Mandryk* (1980), 2 Sask. R.

2. To overcome the difficulties inherent in the enforceability of many contracts to leave property by will, the New Zealand Parliament enacted legislation in 1944[149] and re-enacted it as the *Law Reform (Testamentary Promises) Act 1949*.[150] This Act, as amended, provides that if a person, expressly or impliedly, promises to reward another person, by means of a testamentary provision, for work or services rendered, but fails to honour the promise, the estate of the promisor is liable to remunerate the promisee. Is such legislation necessary or desirable?

3. The deceased agreed, short of an enforceable contract, to make substantial provision for X by his will if X would care for him. The will made some provision for X, but not commensurate with the promise. Does X have a claim in *quantum meruit* against the estate?[151]

4. If the unjust enrichment is referable to specific property, the plaintiff may receive an interest in the property under a constructive trust.[152] Thus, if A improves property in the reasonable expectation of being able to remain indefinitely on the property and B, the owner, freely accepts the improvements in circumstances in which B ought to have known of A's expectations, A is entitled either to recover the value of the improvements on a *quantum meruit* basis, or to a declaration of an interest in the property under a constructive trust.[153]

(e) Proprietary Estoppel

The doctrine of proprietary estoppel can also be used by a person who has been promised all or part of an estate and who has acted to his or her detriment in reliance on the promise. The argument was raised and accepted in *Re Basham*.[154] The plaintiff had assisted her step-father for some 30 years in running his businesses without remuneration. She and her husband contemplated moving from the area on a number of occasions, but decided not to because they believed, a belief encouraged by the step-father, that he would leave his estate to the plaintiff when he died. He died intestate and the plaintiff claimed his estate. The court held that the plaintiff was entitled, having satisfied the doctrine's criteria, namely, (1) she believed at all material times that she would receive the deceased's estate on his death; (2) that belief had been encouraged by the deceased; (3) the plaintiff acted to her detriment; and (4) the acts done by the plaintiff were done in reliance on or as a result of her belief that she would receive the deceased's property on his death.

62, 6 E.T.R. 104 (Q.B.); *Brown v. Millett* (1979), 6 E.T.R. 88 (N.S. T.D.); *Milne v. MacDonald Estate* (1986), 23 E.T.R. 158 (B.C. C.A.).

148 See Jones, "Restitutionary Claims for Services Rendered" (1977), 93 L.Q Rev. 273; Fridman, "Annotation", 6 E.T.R. 105.

149 *Law Reform Act 1944*, c. 18 (N.Z.), s. 3.

150 C. 33 (N.Z.). See Coote, "Testamentary Promises Jurisdiction in New Zealand", in Northey, ed., *The A.G. Davis Essays in Law* (1965), ch. 1.

151 See *Leeson v. Brentz* (1978), 3 E.T.R. 161 (Ont. Surr. Ct.).

152 See generally *Oosterhoff & Gillese: Text, Commentary and Cases on Trusts*, 5th ed. by A.H. Oosterhoff and E.E. Gillese (Scarborough: Carswell, 1998), ch. 8.

153 *Gill v. Grant* (1988), 30 E.T.R. 255 (B.C. S.C.).

154 [1987] 1 All E.R. 405.

Another case to the same effect is *Gillett v. Holt*.[155] When he was 12 years old, the plaintiff became friendly with Holt, then a 38-year-old gentleman farmer and bachelor. At age 16 the plaintiff left school and began to work on Holt's farm at the latter's suggestion. The plaintiff worked for Holt for nearly 40 years. During that time he moved into a property owned by Holt's company and, through his wife and children, provided Holt with a surrogate family. Holt repeatedly assured the plaintiff that the plaintiff would inherit the farm and he made a will in which he made the plaintiff his residuary beneficiary. After 1992 the relationship between the two men began to fall apart. Holt summarily dismissed the plaintiff in 1995 and made a new will naming the defendant, Wood, as his main beneficiary. The plaintiff brought an action claiming an equity in Holt's property under the doctrine of proprietary estoppel. He argued that he relied to his detriment on Holt's assurances that the farm would be left to him. The detriment consisted of the fact that he failed to seek employment elsewhere or to go into business, carried out tasks beyond the normal scope of an employee's duties, and failed to take steps to secure an estate for himself. The court held that, for the doctrine of proprietary estoppel to apply, the detriment does not have to consist of the expenditure of money or other quantifiable financial detriment, but it has to be substantial. To determine whether the doctrine applied, the court should make a broad inquiry to determine whether the repudiation of Holt's assurances was unconscionable in all the circumstances, since equity is concerned with preventing unconscionable conduct. The court held that detriment was amply established.

An alternative way to approach the problem is to argue that the person who relied to his or her detriment on the promisor's assurances is entitled to a constructive trust in the property or, if a constructive trust is not an appropriate remedy in all the circumstances, to a money judgment for its value.[156]

4. MUTUAL WILLS

The mutual wills doctrine concerns a special form of contract to leave property by will. It is invoked when two or more persons make wills, which are similar in their terms, in accordance with an agreement to make the wills and not to revoke them. The doctrine typically arises when a husband and wife make reciprocal or mirror wills, or a joint will, by which they each give a life interest to the other, with remainder to a third party, or subject to a condition that if the other does not survive the property will go to the third party. If the will or wills were made pursuant to an agreement that they should be made and that they should not be revoked, the third party will be able to enforce the agreement. This court will raise a constructive trust in favour of the third party to enforce the agreement.

The doctrine originated with *Dufour v. Pereira*.[157] A husband and wife made a joint will disposing of their property on their respective deaths. The court found

---

155 [2000] 2 All E.R. 289 (C.A.).
156 See *Giumelli v. Giumelli* (1998), 196 C.L.R. 101 (Austr. H.C.)
157 (1769), 1 Dick. 419, 21 E.R. 332, 2 Hargr. Jurid. Arg. 304.

that the will evidenced a contract between the parties that these dispositions should not be altered. The husband died first, not having revoked the will and the wife enjoyed the property. Then she made a new will by which she disposed of the property in a manner contrary to the agreement. Lord Camden C., in the course of his judgment, said:[158]

> The instrument itself is the evidence of the agreement; and he, that dies first, does by his death carry the agreement on his part into execution. If the other then refuses, he is guilty of a fraud, can never unbind himself, and becomes a trustee of course. For no man shall deceive another to his prejudice. By engaging to do something that is in his power, he is made a trustee for the performance, and transmits that trust to those that claim under him.

This does not mean, however, that a joint will by itself proves the existence of the agreement, although the majority in the Ontario Court of Appeal in *Re Gillespie*[159] came close to drawing that conclusion. Nor does it mean that the mere simultaneity of two wills leads inescapably to the conclusion that there was such an agreement.

In *Gray v. Perpetual Trustee Co. Ltd.*,[160] the Privy Council said on this issue:

> In *Dufour v. Pereira*[161] the conclusion reached was that if there was in point of fact an agreement come to that the wills should not be revoked after the death of one of the parties without mutual consent, they were binding. That they were mutual wills to the same effect was at least treated as a relevant circumstance, to be taken into account in determining whether there was such an agreement. But the mere simultaneity of the wills and the similarity of their terms do not appear, taken by themselves, to have been looked on as more than some evidence of an agreement not to revoke. The agreement, which does not restrain the legal right to revoke, was the foundation of the right in equity which might emerge, although it was a fact which had in itself to be established by evidence, and in such cases the whole of the evidence must be looked at.

Hence, the agreement must in fact be proved, either from the will itself or from extrinsic evidence.[162]

You should note that, although we speak of an agreement not to revoke, that is an inexact reference. Since the agreement relates to a will and a will can always be revoked, it follows that a party to the agreement can revoke his or her will. Hence, if that party then makes another will, the latter, if valid, will be entitled to probate, but the property will be subject to the constructive trust.[163]

---

158 As reported in 2 Hargr. Jurid. Arg. 304.

159 [1969] 1 O.R. 585, 3 D.L.R. (3d) 317 (C.A.).

160 [1928] A.C. 391 at 399, [1928] All E.R. Rep. 7 (P.C.). See also *Re Cleaver; Cleaver v. Insley*, [1981] 1 W.L.R. 939, [1981] 2 All E.R. 1018. On the other hand, an agreement may be inferred from the circumstances: *Re O'Connell; Wadden v. Wahay* (1981), 45 N.S.R. (2d) 336, 9 E.T.R. 57 (C.A.), in which two persons who lived together as man and wife separated but made reciprocal wills after she returned to live with him at his request.

161 (1769) 1 Dick. 419.

162 *Patamsis Estate v. Bajoraitis* (1994), 2 E.T.R. (2d) 200 (Ont. Gen. Div.); *Bell v. Bell* (1998), 24 E.T.R. (2d) 169 (B.C.S.C.).

163 *Re Payne* (1930), 30 O.W.N. 314 (H.C.), affirmed (1931), 40 O.W.N. 87 (C.A.). See also Sheena Grattan, "Mutual Wills and Remarriage" (1997), 61 Conv. 153 at 155.

The juridical basis of the mutual wills doctrine was explained as follows by Sir John Latham C.J., in *Birmingham v. Renfrew*,[164] in which extrinsic evidence was held to be sufficient to establish an agreement between two spouses to dispose of their property in a particular way:[165]

> I think the legal result was a contract between husband and wife. The contract bound him, I think, during her lifetime not to revoke his will without notice to her. If she died without altering her will, then he was bound after her death not to revoke his will at all. She on her part afforded the consideration for his promise by making her will. His obligation not to revoke his will during her life without notice to her is to be implied. For I think the express promise should be understood as meaning that if she died leaving her will unrevoked then he would not revoke his. But the agreement really assumes that neither party will alter his or her will without the knowledge of the other. It has long been established that a contract between persons to make corresponding wills gives rise to equitable obligations when one acts on the faith of such an agreement and dies leaving his will unrevoked so that the other takes property under its dispositions. It operates to impose upon the survivor an obligation regarded as specifically enforceable. It is true that he cannot be compelled to make and leave unrevoked a testamentary document and if he dies leaving a last will containing provisions inconsistent with his agreement it is nevertheless valid as a testamentary act. But the doctrines of equity attach the obligation to the property. The effect is, I think, that the survivor becomes a constructive trustee and the terms of the trust are those of the will which he undertook would be his last will.

His Lordship further stated:[166]

> There is a third element which appears to me to be inherent in the nature of such a contract or agreement, although I do not think it has been expressly considered. The purpose of an arrangement for corresponding wills must often be, as in this case, to enable the survivor during his life to deal as absolute owner with the property passing under the will of the party first dying. That is to say, the object of the transaction is to put the survivor in a position to enjoy for his own benefit the full ownership so that, for instance, he may convert it and expend the proceeds if he choose. But when he dies he is to bequeath what is left in the manner agreed upon. It is only by the special doctrines of equity that such a floating obligation, suspended, so to speak, during the lifetime of the survivor can descend upon the assets at his death and crystallise into a trust. No doubt gifts and settlements, inter vivos, if calculated to defeat the intention of the compact, could not be made by the survivor and his right of disposition, inter vivos, is, therefore, not unqualified. But, substantially, the purpose of the arrangement will often be to allow full enjoyment for the survivor's own benefit and advantage upon condition that at his death the residue shall pass as arranged.

His Lordship continued:[167]

> In *In re Oldham*[168] Astbury J. pointed out, in dealing with the question whether an agreement should be inferred, that in *Dufour v. Pereira*,[169] the compact was that the survivor should take a life estate only in the combined property. It was, therefore, easy to fix the corpus with a trust as from the death of the survivor. But I do not see any difficulty in modern equity in attaching to the

---

164 (1937), 57 C.L.R. 666 (Austr. H.C.).
165 *Ibid.*, at pp. 682-3.
166 *Ibid.*, at p. 689.
167 *Ibid.*, at p. 690.
168 [1925] Ch. 75.
169 1 Dick. 419.

assets a constructive trust which allowed the survivor to enjoy the property subject to a fiduciary duty which, so to speak, crystallised on his death and disabled him only from voluntary dispositions inter vivos. On the contrary, as I have said, it seems rather to provide a reason for the intervention of equity. The objection that the intended beneficiaries could not enforce a contract is met by the fact that a constructive trust arises from the contract and the fact that testamentary dispositions made upon the faith of it have taken effect. It is the constructive trust and not the contract that they are entitled to enforce.

There is a number of problems that attend the application of the mutual wills doctrine which we will address in the notes and questions below. The general principles of the doctrine are discussed in *University of Manitoba v. Sanderson Estate*[170] set out below.

Further Reading

Abraham B. Davis, "Contracts to Make Wills" (1975), 2 E. & T.Q. 322.

Robert Burgess, "A Fresh Look at Mutual Wills" (1970), 34 Conv. (N.S.) 230.

L.A. Sheridan, "The Floating Trust: Mutual Wills" (1977), 15 Alta L. Rev. 211.

C.E.F. Rickett, "A Rare Case of Mutual Wills and its Implications" (1982), 8 Adelaide L. Rev. 178.

T. G. Youdan, "The Mutual Wills Doctrine" (1979), 29 U. of T.L.J. 390.

William A. Lee, "Contracts to Make Wills" (1971), 87 L.Q. Rev. 358.

Richard F. Double, Practice Note, "Legacies, Survivorship and 'Mirror' Wills" (1997), 16 E. & T.J. 274.

Keith B. Farquahar, "Mutual Wills — Some Questions Recently Answered" (2000), 19 E.T. & P.J. 326.

THE UNIVERSITY OF MANITOBA v. SANDERSON ESTATE
(1998), 155 D.L.R. (4th) 40
British Columbia Court of Appeal

In 1970, Mr. and Mrs. Sanderson entered into an agreement which provided that (a) they would make wills in the form attached to the agreement; (b) they would not alter or revoke the wills during their joint lives except with the written consent of both; (c) the survivor would not alter or revoke his or her will; and (d) if either will should be revoked by operation of law the survivor would make a new will leaving the residue upon the same terms as in the original wills. The wills, which were made on the same date as the agreement, declared that (a) the spouses had agreed to execute mirror wills and not to alter or revoke them; and (b) the wills were made in consideration of the agreement.

The wills left the estate of the first spouse to die in trust for the survivor for life, or until remarriage. The trustees were given a discretion to use the income and capital for the benefit of the survivor. The wills left the residue to the University of Manitoba in trust to establish a perpetual bursary fund for undergraduate student teachers. Mr. and Mrs. Sanderson made two mirror codicils in

---

170 (1998), 20 E.T.R. (2d) 148, 155 D.L.R. (4th) 40 (B.C.C.A.).

1973 and 1977. In 1984, Montreal Trust Co., their named executor, wrote the spouses suggesting a review of their wills. Mr. Sanderson replied asking that the wills be kept in force.

Mrs. Sanderson died in 1985. Almost all her assets were owned jointly with her husband. Accordingly, he became entitled to them by right of survivorship. This obviated the need to have her will probated. Mr. Sanderson made a new will in 1985, soon after his wife died. It was inconsistent with the original will in that it left part of the residue to certain named persons and the balance to the University of Manitoba. He died in 1994. Montreal Trust Co. obtained probate of the 1985 will.

The University brought an action for a declaration that Montreal Trust Co. held the assets of the husband's estate for its sole benefit. Arkell J. dismissed the action.[171] In the view of the trial judge, (1) the mutual wills doctrine was not attracted because Mr. Sanderson did not derive a benefit from his wife's estate; rather, he acquired the properties by right of survivorship; and (2) it could be presumed that the original agreement had been revoked from the fact that the parties purchased the properties as joint tenants and the fact that Montreal Trust, knowing of the original agreement and will, prepared the 1985 will. The University appealed.

ROWLES J.A.:

. . .

Issues on appeal

[22] The appellant argues that the learned trial judge erred: (1) in finding that the Agreement between the Sandersons had been modified, altered or cancelled by them prior to Mrs. Sanderson's death; (2) in finding that Mr. Sanderson had to receive a benefit before the court could find a constructive trust....

[23] The appeal raises these issues:

1. Was the Agreement not to revoke their mutual wills revoked by the Sandersons during their joint lives?
2. Does the obligation of the survivor not to revoke his mutual will depend on his receiving a benefit under the will of the first to die?

. . .

Issue 1: Was the Agreement not to revoke their mutual wills revoked by the Sandersons during their joint lives?

. . .

[30] In my respectful view, the trial judge was in error when he concluded that there was a revocation of the Agreement by conduct of the parties inconsistent with that Agreement. While it is true that mutual conduct inconsistent with a contract may be taken to show that the contract is no longer enforceable, that

---

171   *University of Manitoba v. Sanderson Estate* (1996), 17 E.T.R. (2d) 78 (B.C.S.C.).

conduct must be quite clear. Here the evidence would have to show that, by the purchase of assets in their joint names, the Sandersons intended to supercede the operation of their mutual wills.

[31] From the evidence in this case it is not at all clear what effect, if any, the Sandersons intended their subsequent purchase of jointly held assets to have in relation to their Agreement. The creation of a right of survivorship in their assets is not necessarily inconsistent with the operation of the mutual wills, and it has no bearing on the Agreement, which was simply not to revoke the wills.

[32] It is also my respectful view that the inferences drawn by the trial judge from Montreal Trust's involvement in the preparation of Mr. Sanderson's 1985 will are unsupportable. Montreal Trust's participation in the preparation of Mr. Sanderson's will after Mrs. Sanderson's death does not provide any foundation for drawing an inference that the Sandersons intended to revoke or modify their Agreement before Mrs. Sanderson's death.

[33] I am also of the view that the trial judge was in error in finding that the agreement not to revoke, which was contained in both the Agreement and the mutual wills, could be revoked by conduct or implication.

[34] The Agreement contained a provision allowing it to be revoked by written consent of both parties. In my opinion, anything less, such as conduct of the parties which might be construed as inconsistent with the continuance of the Agreement, could not be taken to revoke the contract in light of the clear mechanism for revocation contained within it.

[35] Quite apart from whether the Agreement could be revoked by conduct inconsistent with it, the mutual wills could not be so revoked. There are only a limited number of ways to revoke a will and the inconsistent conduct said to have occurred in this case is not one of them.

[36] The mutual wills clearly contain the parties' agreement not to revoke within them. Short of clear evidence that they were revoked prior to Mrs. Sanderson's death, I must conclude that the agreement not to revoke the mutual wills was still in force at the time of Mrs. Sanderson's death in 1985.

Issue 2. Does the obligation of the survivor not to revoke his mutual will depend on his receiving a benefit under the will of the first to die?

[37] The appellant argues that there are two conditions which must be met before the court will impose a trust as a consequence of joint or mutual wills: (1) a mutual agreement not to revoke the joint or mutual wills, and (2) the first to die must have died without revoking or changing his or her will in breach of the agreement.

[38] The question is whether there is a third condition, that is, a benefit flowing to the survivor from the will of the first to die. The appellant argues that a benefit is not required for equity to hold the survivor to his promise.

[39] The respondents' argument is to the contrary. The respondents contend that because the will of Mrs. Sanderson was never probated and Mr. Sanderson took no benefit under her will, the learned trial judge was correct in not imposing a constructive trust on any property of the Sandersons.

[40] In the respondents' submission, in all cases in which there is a constructive trust imposed in circumstances of mutual wills, the will of the first to die has been probated. Support for that proposition is said to be found in *Dufour v. Pereira*;[172] *Re Gillespie*;[173] *Pratt v. Johnson*;[174] *Re Kerr*;[175] *Re Cleaver*;[176] *Re O'Connell Estate*;[177] and *Re Grisor*.[178]

[41] The respondents further contend that even if Mrs. Sanderson's will had been admitted to probate, there would have been no basis for imposing a constructive trust because Mr. Sanderson received no benefit under Mrs. Sanderson's will, Mrs. Sanderson's assets having come to him by survivorship. In support of the proposition that a benefit must be received before a constructive trust may be imposed, the respondents referred to *Pratt v. Johnson*,[179] in which Locke J. quoted with approval the following passage from of *Snell's Principles of Equity*:[180]

> Until the death of the first to die either may withdraw from the arrangement, but thereafter it is irrevocable, at least if the survivor accepts the benefits conferred on him by the other's will.

Other cases said to support that proposition are *Denyssen v. Mosert*;[181] *Re Payne*;[182] and *Birmingham v. Renfrew*.[183]

[42] The respondents argue that the requirement of unjust enrichment is fundamental to the use of a constructive trust and that the three elements referred to in *Peter v. Beblow*[184] must be satisfied before a constructive trust is imposed: (1) an enrichment; (2) a corresponding deprivation; and (3) the absence of a juristic reason for the enrichment. The respondents submit that none of these requirements is met in this case because: (1) Mr. Sanderson took no benefit under the will of Mrs. Sanderson; (2) there was no deprivation to Mrs. Sanderson; and (3) even if Mr. Sanderson's taking assets of Mrs. Sanderson on her death constitutes an "enrichment", there is a "juristic reason" for it because of his entitlement by right of survivorship as joint tenant.

[43] According to the respondents, the unjust enrichment justification for the imposition of a constructive trust in the mutual wills context is set out in *Re Cleaver*,[185] where Nourse J. said:

> The principle of all these cases is that a court of equity will not permit a person to whom property is transferred by way of gift, but on the faith of an agreement or clear understanding that it is to

---

172 (1769), 1 Dick. 419 at 421, 21 E.R. 332 at 333.
173 [1969] 1 O.R. 585 (C.A.).
174 (1958), [1959] S.C.R. 102.
175 [1948] 3 D.L.R. 668 (Ont. H.C.), affirmed [1949] O.W.N. 70 (C.A.).
176 [1981] 2 All E.R. 1018.
177 (1981), 9 E.T.R. 57 (N.S. C.A.).
178 (1979), 26 O.R. (2d) 57 (H.C.).
179 *Supra.*
180 (24th ed.), p. 156.
181 (1872), L.R. 4 P.C. 236 (P.C.).
182 (1930), 39 O.W.N. 314 (H.C.), affirmed (1931), 40 O.W.N. 87 (C.A.).
183 (1937), 57 C.L.R. 666.
184 [1993] 1 S.C.R. 980 at 987, *per* McLachlin J.
185 *Supra,* at p. 1024.

be dealt with in a particular way for the benefit of a third person, to deal with that property inconsistently with that agreement or understanding. If he attempts to do so after having received the benefit of the gift equity will intervene by imposing a constructive trust on the property which is the subject matter of the agreement or understanding.

[44] With respect, I do not agree that either the probate of the will of the first to die, or a benefit flowing to the survivor from the will of the other, is a necessary condition for relief to be granted to the University on trust principles.

[45] This is a case in which there was an express agreement made that the mutual wills would not be revoked or altered during the joint lives of the parties to the agreement and that after the death of the first, the will of the survivor would not be altered or revoked. There was an exchange of promises and Mrs. Sanderson did not revoke her will, although she had the legal right to do so, before her death.

[46] The guiding principles to be applied in this case are to be found in *Dufour v. Pereira*,[186] in which the enforcement of an agreement in a joint will was held to be within equity's jurisdiction to prevent fraud. Equity considers it a fraud upon the deceased, who has acted upon and relied upon the mutually binding nature of the agreement, for the survivor to change the will and break the agreement. As the deceased cannot intervene to enforce the obligation, equity will enforce the survivor's obligation, despite the survivor's subsequent intentions.

[47] A very full account of *Dufour v. Pereira* appears in F. Hargrave, *Juridical Arguments and Collections*.[187] In that account, Mr. Hargrave quotes from a manuscript copied from Lord Camden L.C.'s own handwriting and, in view of the fullness of the account, it is to be preferred over the other report of the case. (In *Pratt v. Johnson*[188] Locke J. expresses a preference for the account in Hargrave's *Juridical Arguments*.)

[48] In *Dufour*, a husband and wife had made a joint will in which the residuary estate of the first to die was to be held for the survivor for his or her life with remainders over. On the death of the husband, the wife (who was one of his executors) proved his will. She had the benefit of his residuary estate together with her separate property for many years. On her death it was found that her last will was not in accord with the joint will and her estate had been left to her daughter, the defendant, Mrs. Pereira. The plaintiffs, who were the beneficiaries under the joint will, claimed that the wife's personal estate was held in trust for them.

[49] The significance in equity of the agreement that the mutual will should not be revoked after the death of one of the parties clearly emerges from Lord Camden L.C.'s judgment as it appears in the account in Hargrave's *Juridical Arguments*:[189]

[Her Ladyship quoted extensively from this text, and continued:]

---

186 *Supra.*
187 Vol. 2, (London: 1799) at pp. 304-11.
188 *Supra*, at p. 110.
189 *Supra*, at pp. 306-11.

[50] The essence of Lord Camden L.C.'s opinion on the question, "how far the mutual will shall operate as a binding engagement, independent of any confirmation by accepting the legacy under it", is contained in the following passage:[190]

> ... he, that dies first, does by his death carry the agreement on his part into execution. If the other then refuses, he is guilty of a fraud, can never unbind himself, and becomes a trustee of course. For no man shall deceive another to his prejudice. By engaging to do something that is in his power, he is made a trustee for the performance, and transmits that trust to those that claim under him.

That passage contains no suggestion that the first to die must have conferred a benefit on the survivor by his will for equity to intervene.

[51] Lord Camden L.C.'s opinion on the question, "whether the survivor can depart from this engagement, after she has accepted a benefit under it", is stated in this passage:[191]

> I HAVE perhaps given myself more trouble than was necessary upon this point; because, if it could be doubtful, whether after the husband's death his wife could be at liberty to revoke her part of the mutual will, it is most clear, that she has estopped herself to this defence, by an actual confirmation of the mutual will, — not only by proving it, but by accepting and enjoying an interest under it. She receives this benefit, takes possession of all her husband's estates, submits to the mutual will as long as she lives, and then breaks the agreement after her death.

The emphasis here is on the survivor proving the joint will and thereafter accepting and enjoying a benefit under it but those matters are not essential to the principles enunciated by Lord Camden L.C. on the first question. Proving the will and taking a benefit under it is simply evidence to support the survivor's acceptance of the joint will and the binding nature of the agreement within it. What is fundamental in *Dufour* is the finding that there was an agreement. The taking of the benefit under a joint or mutual will tends to support such a finding but it is not an essential element to the imposition of a trust on the estate of the survivor.

[52] Unlike the present case in which there is an express agreement between the testators not to revoke their mutual wills, the authorities to which the respondents referred all concern the question of whether there was, in fact, such an agreement.

[53] In one of these cases, *Re Hagger*,[192] Clauson J. of the Chancery Division in England explicitly rejected any benefit requirement, although the observation was obiter since a benefit was taken in that case:

> To my mind *Dufour v. Pereira* decides that where there is a joint will such as this, on the death of the first testator the position as regards that part of the property which belongs to the survivor is that the survivor will be treated in this Court as holding the property on trust to apply it so as to carry out the effect of the joint will. As I read Lord Camden's judgment in *Dufour v. Pereira* that would be so, even though the survivor did not signify his election to give effect to the will by taking benefits under it.

---

190 *Ibid.*, at p. 310.
191 At p. 311.
192 [1930] 2 Ch. 190 at 195.

[54] That an agreement is essential to the application of the principles in *Dufour v. Pereira* is clear from the decision in *Gray v. Perpetual Trustee Co.*,[193] the headnote to which accurately states what was decided:

> The fact that a husband and wife have simultaneously made mutual wills, giving each to the other a life interest with similar provisions in remainder, is not in itself evidence of an agreement not to revoke the wills; in the absence of a definite agreement to that effect there is no implied trust precluding the wife from making a fresh will inconsistent with her former will, even though her husband has died and she has taken the benefits conferred by his will.

[55] In *Pratt v. Johnson*,[194] a husband and wife made a joint will which contained these provisions:

> We desire that all property real and personal of which we may die possessed at the time of the decease of either of us shall be held by the survivor during his or her life to use as such survivor may see fit.
>
> Upon the decease of the survivor it is our desire that our property both real and personal shall be divided as follows:—
>
> To [five named beneficiaries] equally amongst them share and share alike.

[56] At the time of the husband's death, the will remained unaltered and no other will had been made, but thereafter the wife made a will disposing of her property to a differently constituted group of beneficiaries. The trial judge granted a declaration that the late Johanna Johnson "was bound by trust to leave her estate including all assets received by her from Arni Johnson, deceased, in accordance with the joint will of herself and the said Arni Johnson, deceased". Appeals to the provincial appellate court and the Supreme Court of Canada were dismissed. In the Supreme Court, Mr. Justice Locke, giving the majority judgment, said this:[195]

> The question to be decided is, in my opinion, not as to whether there was evidence of an agreement between the husband and wife not to make a disposition of the property referred to in the joint will in a manner inconsistent with its terms, but rather whether there was evidence of an agreement between them that the property in the hands of the survivor at the time of his or her death should go to the said five beneficiaries and, since nothing was done by Johanna Johnson to alter the terms of the joint will until after the death of her husband, the property received by her from the executor of her husband's estate and such estate of her own of which she died possessed were impressed with a trust in favour of the five named beneficiaries ....

[57] While the question of whether the survivor must receive a benefit before the survivor's property and any property received from the deceased spouse will be impressed with a trust was not directly before the Court in *Pratt v. Johnson*, I see nothing in the majority decision to suggest that a benefit was considered an essential element to the imposition of a trust.

---

193 [1928] A.C. 391 (P.C.).
194 *Supra*, at pp. 104-105.
195 *Ibid.*, at pp. 106-107.

[58] It is also my respectful view that the remedy of constructive trust rounded on the principle of unjust enrichment is not analogous to the principles enunciated in *Dufour v. Pereira*[196] and that the trial judge erred when he concluded that an unjust enrichment was required. A constructive trust arising from an unjust enrichment is imposed on property gained at the expense of another for no juristic reason, whereas the obligation created by an agreement not to revoke mutual wills binds not only that portion of the survivor's estate which may have come from the estate of the first to die, but also his or her own property.

[59] In my opinion, the requisite conditions for the imposition of a trust on the property of Mr. Sanderson have been met in this case and the University is entitled to succeed on the appeal.

[Cumming and Gibbs JJ.A., concurred. The court allowed the appeal.]

Notes and Questions

1. The trial judge in *Sanderson* stated that when the parties made their agreement any property then owned by them as joint tenants was converted into a tenancy in common. However, he concluded that the parties modified or revoked their agreement because they subsequently acquired a number of assets as joint tenants. It is, indeed, the generally accepted view that an agreement to make mutual wills converts a joint tenancy into a tenancy in common, at least if the agreement made such property subject to it. This is because the agreement (and the wills made pursuant thereto) are inconsistent with the survivor taking by survivorship, since the parties have made other arrangements for the succession of their property.[197]

The Court of Appeal took a different view. It held that the agreement had not been revoked by the parties' conduct in buying property in their joint names. Hence, one would assume that jointly-owned property would remain converted. However, in para. 31 of her judgment, Rowles J.A. noted that the creation of a right of survivorship is not necessarily inconsistent with the operation of the mutual wills. At first blush this might suggest that she is departing from the generally accepted view. But this is not so. She was referring to property acquired subsequently to the agreement. It may or may not be converted depending upon the terms of the agreement. If the parties intended to make subsequently acquired property subject to the agreement, presumably it would be converted, but not otherwise. The question which assets are subject to the agreement is discussed in a later note.

2. If a testator marries or remarries, his or her prior will is automatically revoked save for some minor exceptions.[198] If a testator, having agreed with his or her spouse to dispose of property by will in such a way as to cause the mutual wills doctrine to be invoked, remarries after the death of the spouse, are the beneficiaries under the agreement without a remedy?[199]

---

196 *Supra.*
197 See *Re Gillespie*, [1969] 1 O.R. 585 at 589, 3 D.L.R. (3d) 317 (C.A.), *per* Kelly J.A.
198 See, *e.g.*, *Succession Law Reform Act*, R.S.O. 1990, c. S.26, ss. 15(a), 16.
199 See *Robinson v. Ommanney* (1883), 23 Ch. D. 285 (C.A.); *Re Marsland; Lloyd's Bank Ltd. v. Marsland*, [1939] Ch. 820, [1939] 3 All E.R. 148; *Re Green; Linder v. Green*, [1950] 2 All E.R. 913; *Goodchild v. Goodchild*, [1996] 1 All E.R. 670; Sheena Grattan, Comment, "Mutual Wills and Remarriage" (1997), 61 Conv. 153.

3. Would the mutual wills doctrine, or a variant thereof, apply if the parties agreed not to make wills, but to die intestate because their respective estates would go to each other under the intestacy laws?

4. *Harvey v. Powell Estate*[200] illustrates the problems that can arise in trying to establish the agreement. A married couple made reciprocal wills leaving their entire estates to the other, subject to a survivorship provision. After the testator died, the testatrix changed her will to exclude the testator's children by a former marriage. The children brought an action claiming entitlement from a mutual wills agreement.

The court stated that the mutual wills doctrine is not to be inferred from the mere existence of two wills conferring mutual benefits. However, if they are made pursuant to an express agreement not to revoke, they remain revocable but the agreement against revocation can be enforced in equity. There was no evidence of a written agreement between the parties that the survivor would not revoke, and the dispositive provision was an absolute gift to the spouse if he or she survived for a specified period. In addition, the circumstances surrounding the making of the wills did not provide evidence that they were irrevocable.

5. Would the mutual wills doctrine apply if the parties have already made wills and then agree not to revoke them?[201]

6. Although a breach of the agreement normally occurs after one of the parties has died, there could be an anticipatory breach. Thus, if one party gives notice to the other that he or she will no longer be bound by the agreement, or revokes his or her will to the knowledge of the other, the latter should be able to sue for breach of contract.[202] The aggrieved party can only recover damages in such a case, however, since the court will not order a person to make a will.[203] Moreover, the damages will be discounted by the possibility that the plaintiff will not receive the property if he or she does not survive the other party.

7. Unless the agreement provides otherwise, it will normally be construed to enable the parties to deal freely with their property while both are alive and to enable the survivor to deal with the property as an absolute owner (unless he or she is restricted to a life estate). To hold otherwise would restrict the survivor unduly. This would not, however, allow the survivor to defeat the purpose of the agreement by disposing of the assets *inter vivos*.[204] Nor, of course, could either party make a testamentary disposition in conflict with the agreement.

8. You will have noticed from the material that parties often use a joint will. As explained in the introductory text, the common law does not recognize a joint will. A joint will is actually the separate wills of the two parties. However, in *Re Gillespie*,[205] Kelly J.A., writing for the majority of the court, concluded that a joint will makes it easier to find an agreement: the fact that both parties sign the document suggests an agreement. Laskin J.A. dissented. In his view the alleged agreement must be proved on a balance of probabilities whether the parties used a joint will or separate wills, because the consequences of finding an agreement can be quite onerous on the survivor. Laskin J.A. quoted[206] the

---

200 (1988), 30 E.T.R. 143 (N.S. T.D.).

201 See *Re Fox*, [1951] O.R. 378, [1951] 3 D.L.R. 337 (H.C.).

202 *Cf. Synge v. Synge*, [1894] 1 Q.B. 466 (C.A.).

203 *Ibid.*, at p. 471; *Birmingham v. Renfrew* (1937), 57 C.L.R. 666.

204 See *Birmingham v. Renfrew, ibid.*

205 [1969] 1 O.R. 585, 3 D.L.R. (3d) 317 (C.A.).

206 *Ibid.*, at O.R. 594.

following excerpt from the judgment of Latham C.J. in *Birmingham v. Renfrew*[207] on this point:

> Those who undertake to establish such an agreement assume a heavy burden of proof. It is easy to allege such an agreement after the parties to it have both died, and any court should be very careful in accepting the evidence of interested parties upon such a question. Perhaps most husbands and wives make wills "by agreement" but they do not bind themselves not to revoke their wills. They do not intend to undertake or impose any kind of binding obligation. The mere fact that two persons make what may be called corresponding wills in the sense that the existence of each will is naturally explained by the existence of the other will is not sufficient to establish a binding agreement not to revoke wills so made.

With this in mind, which opinion on the effect of a joint will is to be preferred, that of Kelly J.A., or that of Laskin J.A.? Why?

9. *Re Ohorodnyk*[208] is an example of a joint will. A husband and wife executed a joint will in which they gave their estates to the survivor absolutely and then went on to provide that upon the death of the survivor, his or her entire estate should be distributed equally among five named beneficiaries. The husband died first, having left the will unrevoked. The wife then made a new will in which she left her property to someone not named in the joint will. At trial, Hollingsworth J. admitted extrinsic evidence [the evidence of their solicitor] which proved the existence of an agreement not to revoke. However, he then held that the will forbade raising a trust, since it gave everything to the wife "absolutely."

On appeal, the Court of Appeal agreed and held, moreover, that the extrinsic evidence should not have been admitted since there was no ambiguity on the face of the will.

I submit that the latter point is wrong. The question at issue was not, in the first place, the construction of the will (in which case the principle applied by the Court of Appeal may be relevant), but whether or not there was an enforceable agreement between the parties. Moreover, previous binding cases have admitted extrinsic evidence,[209] and other cases have approved its admission.[210]

Further, as regards the point that there cannot be a trust since the property was given to the wife absolutely, this is contrary to at least two mutual wills cases.[211] The purpose of the word "absolutely" is to give the survivor a free hand over the property, that is, a right of enjoyment. Moreover, in construing a will in this manner, the courts are guilty of applying the repugnancy rule (that is, that if anything is given to A absolutely, there is nothing left for B), rather than trying to ascertain the intention of the testator and to give effect to all his expressed and implied statements.[212]

10. *Re Grisor*[213] also concerned a joint will. A husband and wife each gave the survivor a life estate in all the property owned at the death of either of them to be used as the survivor saw fit. One of the assets of the husband was a business and the will provided that the survivor had to carry on the business. On the death of the survivor all the property,

---

207 (1937), 57 C.L.R. 666 at 674-5.

208 (1979), 24 O.R. (2d) 228, 4 E.T.R. 233, 97 D.L.R. (3d) 502 (H.C.), affirmed (1980), 26 O.R. (2d) 704, 6 E.T.R. 215, 102 D.L.R. (3d) 576 (C.A.).

209 *Pratt v. Johnson*, [1959] S.C.R. 102, 16 D.L.R. (2d) 385, admitting an affidavit of a deceased party to the agreement. And see *Birmingham v. Renfrew, supra; Gray v. Perpetual Trustee Co.*, [1928] A.C. 391 (P.C.).

210 *Re Gillespie*, [1969] 1 O.R. 585, 3 D.L.R. (3d) 317 (C.A.).

211 *Birmingham v. Renfrew, supra; Re Green*, [1951] Ch. 148, [1950] 2 All E.R. 913.

212 See on this point *Re Shamas*, [1967] 2 O.R. 275, 63 D.L.R. (2d) 300 (C.A.).

213 (1979), 26 O.R. (2d) 57, 5 E.T.R. 296 (H.C.).

including the business, would go equally to the parties' two children. The wife died first and the husband subsequently sold the business. The two children then brought an application to construe the will. The court held that the business was not subject to the constructive trust, because such a trust can only bind the property of the deceased testator; it cannot bind property that did not flow to the survivor by the joint will.

I submit that this holding is erroneous. The subject-matter of the constructive trust depends upon the parties' agreement.[214] If they intended that the business should be subject to the trust, as they surely did, then that is the end of the matter.

11. In view of the divergent results reached in some of the cases, what is the duty of a solicitor in advising prospective testators? Should the solicitor ensure that the agreement is contained in the will, or that such an agreement is expressly denied, as the case may be? Should the property that is subject to the agreement and the trust be specifically identified?

12. The issue concerning the property subject to the agreement also arose in *Re Gillespie*. However, the parties conceded and the courts held that the agreement covered only the property owned by the wife at her death and the husband's property owned by him at that point. It did not encompass any property acquired by the husband thereafter. This, it would appear, is the usual result and for good reason. If the survivor is unable to dispose of property acquired after the first person died, he would be unable to deal with it by way of *inter vivos* or testamentary gift. Thus, for example, if he remarried, he would be unable to leave any property to his second spouse.

In *Pratt v. Johnson*[215] the Supreme Court of Canada held that the joint will did permit the surviving wife to deal freely with all the assets (both her husband's and her own, whether acquired before or after his death) during her life, but that the remainder of all those assets was subject to the trust. Hence, her subsequently- acquired assets were subject to the agreement.

Depending upon the parties' agreement, the property subject to the trust may extend only to the property owned by the first party to die. That was the case in *Re Green; Lindner v. Green*.[216] The parties had agreed, and included recitals of their agreement in their wills, that if the survivor of them had the use of the other's property during his or her lifetime, her or she would provide in his or her will for carrying out the wishes expressed in the will of the other. The wife died first and the husband, having received her estate, made a different will. The court held that his executors held the property he received from his wife upon trust for the persons his wife intended to be benefited. However, he could dispose of his own property as he wished.

13. A related question is whether the parties can dispose of their assets while both are living, or whether those assets are subject to the trust. This, of course, also depends upon the terms of the agreement, but if it is silent on the point, it is arguable that a disposition by one party of a substantial portion of the assets would be a breach of the agreement and would be actionable by the other. An analogous case is *Synge v. Synge*,[217] in which the defendant had promised that when he died he would leave certain real property to the plaintiff in consideration of her marrying him. When he subsequently sold the property, thereby putting it out of his power to perform the contract, she was held entitled to recover damages for the breach.

---

214 *Birmingham v. Renfrew, supra*, at p. 683, *per* Dixon C.J.; and see *Pratt v. Johnson, supra*.
215 [1959] S.C.R. 102, 16 D.L.R. (2d) 385.
216 [1950] 2 All E.R. 913.
217 [1895] 1 Q.B. 466 (C.A.).

It would seem that such substantial gifts by the survivor would also be a breach of the agreement. The point was addressed by Dixon J. in *Birmingham v. Renfrew*[218] in the following *dictum*:[219]

> The purpose of an arrangement for corresponding wills must often be, as in this case, to enable the survivor during his life to deal as absolute owner with the property passing under the will of the party first dying. That is to say, the object of the transaction is to put the survivor in a position to enjoy for his own benefit the full ownership so that, for instance, he may convert it and expend the proceeds if he choose. But when he dies he is to bequeath what is left in the manner agreed upon. It is only by the special doctrines of equity that such a floating obligation, suspended, so to speak, during the lifetime of the survivor can descend upon the assets at his death and crystallize into a trust. No doubt gifts and settlements, *inter vivos*, if calculated to defeat the intention of the compact, could not be made by the survivor and his right of disposition, *inter vivos*, is, therefore, not unqualified. But, substantially, the purpose of the arrangement will often be to allow full enjoyment for the survivor's own benefit and advantage upon condition that at his death the residue shall pass as arranged.

Analogous cases involving contracts to leave property by will hold that the promisor is precluded from making a disposition of property which is in substance testamentary and which has the effect of dissipating the assets subject to the agreement, unless the agreement provides otherwise.[220] American cases on mutual wills are to the like effect.[221]

14. When does the trust arise under the mutual wills doctrine? It would seem that it arises when the first party to the agreement dies and leaves a will in accordance with the agreement. This is because the third party beneficiaries have a right to its enforcement at that point.[222] Hence, unless the agreement provides otherwise, if a third party beneficiary dies after the death of the first party, but before the survivor, the third party's estate is entitled to his or her share.[223]

13. The main point decided by *Sanderson*, that the survivor does not need to benefit from the will of the first to die, would also apply if the survivor disclaimed her or his interest under will of the first to die. The point was also foreshadowed by a *dictum* in *Re Gillespie*.[224] The Ontario Court of Appeal did not have to decide the question, but Kelly J.A. stated that he would have been prepared to hold that the trust became binding on the husband when his wife died, even if he had not benefited from her estate.[225]

An English case, not referred to in *Sanderson* had earlier reached the same conclusion. *Re Dale; Proctor v. Dale*[226] involved wills by husband and wife in which they each left their respective estates equally to their two children, not to each other. The husband died first, not having revoked his will. The wife then changed her will. The court held that in order for the mutual wills doctrine to apply it is not necessary that the second testator to die received a personal financial benefit under the will of the first to die.

---

218 (1937), 57 C.L.R. 666.
219 *Ibid.*, at p. 689.
220 See *Fortescue v. Hannah* (1812), 19 Ves. 67, 34 E.R. 443; *Palmer v. Bank of New South Wales* (1975), 7 A.L.R. 671 (Austr. H.C.).
221 See L.A. Sheridan "The Floating Trust: Mutual Wills" (1977), 15 Alta. L. Rev. 211 at 230-40.
222 *Birmingham v. Renfrew, supra*, at p. 683, *per* Dixon C.J.
223 *Re Hagger*, [1930] 2 Ch. 190; but see also *Re Fiegehen*, [1942] O.W.N. 575 (H.C.).
224 [1969] 1 O.R. 585, 3 D.L.R. (3d) 317 (C.A.)
225 *Ibid.*, at O.R. 589.
226 [1993] 4 All E.R. 129.

5. INCORPORATION BY REFERENCE

The doctrine of incorporation by reference is a probate doctrine under which existing, unattested documents may be incorporated into a will. The statutory formalities, which are designed to ensure the authenticity of the will and to prevent fraud, are thought not to be avoided in these circumstances.

In order for the doctrine to apply, three requirements must be satisfied, namely: (i) the unattested document must be in existence when the will into which it is to be incorporated is executed, (ii) the will must refer to it as an existing document; and (iii) the will must describe the document with sufficient certainty so that it can be identified.[227]

With respect to the first requirement, the onus is on those seeking incorporation to prove that the document was in existence before the will was executed.[228] A document that postdates the execution of the will cannot be incorporated, because the testator would in that way, in effect, reserve to himself or herself the right to make an unattested future codicil to the will.[229] Hence, even if the document is properly referred to and identified, but did not come into existence until one day after the testamentary document, it cannot be incorporated.[230]

With respect to the second point, it is clear that a document which is referred to in the will as future cannot be incorporated, for the same reason as that given in the preceding paragraph. In many cases it is, however, a question of construction whether the reference is to a future or to an existing document. The rule in this respect is that if the will purports to incorporate either an existing or a future document, no document cannot be incorporated. This point is dealt with in *In the Goods of Smart*,[231] reproduced below. To the same effect is *Re Mihalopoulos*[232] in which the testator directed his trustees to distribute the residue of his estate to such charities "as they will find designated by me to share in this bequest among my papers." Similarly, if the reference is to an existing document which is subject to change, as when the maker of it has a power of revocation, the document cannot be incorporated.[233] If, however, the will refers to an existing document to be incorporated unless another document is substituted for it, it may be possible to incorporate the existing document if, in fact, it was not replaced by a later one.[234]

---

227 See *Williams, Mortimer and Sunnucks on Executors, Administrators and Probate*, 17th ed., by J.H.G. Sunnucks, J.G. Ross Martyn, and K.M. Garnett (London: Stevens & Sons, 1993), p. 153; *Croker v. Marquis of Hertford* (1844), 4 Moo. P.C. 339, 13 E.R. 334; *Allen v. Maddock* (1858), 11 Moo. P.C. 427, 14 E.R. 757 (P.C.). See also *Re Warren* (1930), 38 O.W.N. 358; *Re Poole; Stewart v. Poole*, [1929] 1 D.L.R. 418 (P.E.I. S.C.). And see *Re Saxton*, [1939] 2 All E.R. 418; *Re Spencer* (1975), 8 Nfld. & P.E.I.R. 345 (Nfld. T.D.); *Thomas Estate v. Gay* (1996), 14 E.T.R. (2d) 229 (Ont. Gen. Div.).

228 *Singleton v. Tomlinson* (1878), 3 App. Cas. 404 at 414 (H.L.).

229 *Re Currie; Labatt v. M.N.R.* (1978), 21 O.R. (2d) 709, 3 E.T.R. 196, 91 D.L.R. (3d) 559 (H.C.).

230 *Ibid.*

231 [1902] P. 238.

232 (1956), 19 W.W.R. 118, 5 D.L.R. (2d) 268 (Alta. T.D.).

233 *Re Jones*, [1942] Ch. 328; *Re Edwards' Wills Trusts*, [1948] Ch. 440, [1948] 1 All E.R. 821 (C.A.); *Re Bateman*, [1970] 1 W.L.R. 1463, [1970] 3 All E.R. 817.

234 *Re Jones, ibid.*

With respect to the third requirement, when the will refers to an existing document only, parol evidence is admissible to identify the document.[235] Evidence of the testator's intention is not admissible, however, unless there are two or more documents which satisfy the reference in the will equally.[236]

Apart from the foregoing restrictions, any document can be incorporated into a will, whether made by the testator or by another person. If the will is a holograph document, however, that is, one *wholly* in the testator's own handwriting and signed by him or her,[237] a problem may arise if the document to be incorporated is not in the testator's own handwriting. This problem is discussed in a later chapter.

The doctrine of republication may, in certain cases, allow a document which was not in existence when the will was made to be incorporated. This occurs when the document subsequently comes into existence and thereafter a codicil is executed which confirms the will. This matter is discussed in *In the Goods of Smart*.[238]

IN THE GOODS OF SMART
[1902] P. 238
Probate Division

By her will, made in 1895, the testatrix gave all her furniture, books, plates, linen, wearing apparel and personal effects of a like nature to her cousin for life. Then she directed her trustees

> ...to give to such of my friends as I may designate in a book or memorandum that will be found with this will the different articles specified for such friends in such book or memorandum,

and provided that upon failure by her to dispose of any articles her cousin would have power to dispose of them.

Affidavit evidence showed that there was no such book or memorandum when the testatrix died, but a book answering the description in the will was prepared by the testatrix in 1888-9. Then, in 1900, the testatrix made a codicil which did not make reference to the book, but made other dispositions and confirmed the will.

The executors applied for probate and sought the court's advice regarding the incorporation of the book.

GORELL BARNES J.:

. . .

The question is, therefore, whether the book, so far as it is referred to, if referred

---

235 *Allen v. Maddock* (1844), 4 Moo. P.C. 339 at 454-5. Applied in *Re Jackson* (1984), 18 E.T.R. 144.
236 *Paton v. Omerod*, [1892] P. 247 at 252.
237 Such wills are valid in most jurisdictions. See, *e.g.*, *Succession Law Reform Act*, R.S.O. 1990, c. S.26, s. 6.
238 *Supra.*

to at all, in that clause which I read from the will, is to be incorporated with the will and codicil. I have already practically intimated my view that it ought not to be incorporated, and I might have contented myself with saying that I come to that conclusion in consequence, principally, of a decision of the President in the case of *Durham v. Northen;*[239] but Mr. Deane argued that that case was inconsistent with other authorities, and that the authorities were in conflict amongst themselves; so I desired to look through them to see if that contention could be properly supported. Before referring very briefly to the cases, it seems to me desirable to state the principle upon which this matter ought to be decided appears to my mind. It seems to me that it has been established that if a testator, in a testamentary paper duly executed, refers to an existing unattested testamentary paper, the instrument so referred to becomes part of his will; in other words, it is incorporated into it; but it is clear that, in order that the informal document should be incorporated in the validly executed document, the latter must refer to the former as a written instrument then existing - that is, at the time of execution - in such terms that it may be ascertained. A leading case upon this subject is *Allen v. Maddock,*[240] and it is desirable also to refer to *In the Goods of Mary Sunderland.*[241] It will be seen from a statement of the principle in the form I have just given, that the document which it is sought to incorporate must be existing at the time of the execution of the document into which it is to be incorporated, and there must be a reference in the properly executed document to the informal document as an existing one, and not as a future document. If the document is not existing at the time of the will, but comes into existence afterwards, and then, after that again, there is a codicil confirming the will, the question arises, as it has done in a number of these cases, whether that document is incorporated. It appears to me that, following out the principle which I have already referred to, the will may be treated, by the confirmation given by the codicil, as executed again, and as speaking from the date of the codicil, and if the informal document is existing then, and is referred to in the will as existing, so as to identify it, there will be incorporation; but if the will, treated as being re-executed at the date of the codicil, still speaks in terms which shew that it is referring to a future document, then it appears to me there is no incorporation. I might put a clear concrete case. Suppose that the will said, "I wish certain articles to be disposed of by my executors in accordance with a list which I shall hereafter write", and the testator then wrote a list such as was contemplated, and then, after that, a codicil was made confirming the will, one of the conditions at the date of the codicil which is necessary for incorporation would be fulfilled, namely, the execution of a document; but the other condition would not be fulfilled, because the will, even speaking from the date of its so-called re-execution by that confirmation by the codicil, would still in terms refer to something which even then was future. I have, perhaps, stated a

---

239 [1895] P. 66.
240 (1858), 11 Moo. P.C. 427.
241 (1866), L.R. 1 P. & M. 198.

little more fully than is necessary what was very clearly and shortly said by the President (Sir F.H. Jeune) in the case of which I have referred.[242]

[His Lordship then made reference to other authorities and continued:]

Therefore, to my mind, it is clear that if the terms of the reference in this case indicate a document of a future character there is no incorporation. The words are: "I direct my trustees to give to such of my friends as I may designate in a book or memorandum that will be found with this will". That reference, made at the date of the will, was, I think, clearly made as to a future document. A document next comes into existence, and a codicil is afterwards made; but if you treat the will according to the cases, as speaking at the date of the codicil, the reference is still in terms to a document which, even then, is future, and therefore does not comply with one of the necessary conditions, namely, that it must refer to a document as existing at the date when the will is re-executed.

For these reasons I think there ought to be no incorporation of the book, or that part of it which it is sought to incorporate.

. . .

Notes and Questions

1. If the document is subsequent to the will, but prior to a codicil which confirms the will and if the reference is to an existing document only, the doctrine of republication operates to permit the document to be incorporated.[243]

2. An incorporated document is normally included in the probate.[244] However, if this is inconvenient, as when the document is extremely lengthy,[245] or if it affects other persons,[246] it is not necessary to do so.

3. *Re Jackson*[247] is an example of a case in which parol evidence was admitted to establish the testatrix's intention. The testatrix's will directed her trustees to distribute her personal goods in accordance with a memorandum filed with the will. The only memorandum found was one made three years prior to the will. The court admitted parol evidence to determine that the memorandum was intended to be incorporated by reference into the will.

4. It would appear that the doctrine of incorporation by reference does not require that the testator direct the incorporation. All he or she needs to do is refer with certainty to the existing document.[248]

5. The doctrine of incorporation by reference permits the incorporation of an invalid will into a subsequent valid will.[249]

6. Anglo-Canadian courts have not generally adopted the device of the pour-over trust, under which a testator may give money or property by will to an existing trust created by

---

242 *Durham v. Northen, supra.*
243 *Re Lady Truro* (1866), L.R. 1 P.& D. 201.
244 *Re Jones* (1920), 36 T.L.R. 294.
245 *Bizzey v. Flight* (1876), 3 Ch.D. 264.
246 *Re Jones, supra.*
247 (1984), 18 E.T.R. 144.
248 See *Re Chamberlain*, [1976] 1 W.W.R. 464 (Sask. Surr. Ct.).
249 *Re Berger (decd)*, [1989] 1 All E.R. 591 (C.A.).

himself or herself or by another. The advantage of this device is that if a beneficiary has a vested interest under the existing trust, but predeceases the testator, the beneficiary's estate will be entitled to the gift.[250] If, however, the existing trust is incorporated into the will, so that it is regarded as a referential trust, the gift to such a beneficiary would lapse, since the trust (except to the extent that it previously existed) takes effect as of the date of the testator's death.

The pour-over trust doctrine is not a probate doctrine, but rather concerns the construction of wills. It is based upon the doctrine of independent significance. Under that doctrine, if a fact or an entity exists which has significance independent of the will, extrinsic evidence is admissible to identify the fact or entity. A properly established trust is such a fact of independent significance.

The disadvantage of the pour-over trust is similar to that which attends the doctrine of incorporation by reference, namely that a reference to a trust which is revocable or which may be replaced with another is not acceptable, since the trust does not then have independent significance and the testator is purporting to reserve the right to make a future unattested codicil to the will. To overcome this difficulty legislation was enacted in many of the United States which allows the doctrine to operate even though the trust is revocable.[251] Similar legislation was recommended in Canada by the Uniform Law Conference of Canada.[252]

Even though it is clear that the testator does not intend to incorporate the trust in these cases, the Anglo-Canadian courts treat pour-over trusts, with the sole exception of *Re Playfair*,[253] as documents to be incorporated.[254]

7. Anglo-Canadian courts have also consistently confused the doctrine of semi-secret trusts with the doctrine of incorporation by reference. The secret trusts doctrine is, in fact, quite distinct. It is a doctrine of the law of trusts which raises a constructive trust when a person leaves property by will to another on the latter's undertaking to apply the property in accordance with the testator's directions. There are two kinds: the fully secret trust in which the legatee appears to take absolutely on the face of the will, and the semi-secret trust in which the legatee is given the property by the will and the testator then adds "upon terms which I have disclosed to him," or "to be disposed of in accordance with my letter to her," or words of similar import. While the cases hold that the communication to and acceptance by the trustee in the case of a fully secret trust may take place at any time before the testator's death,[255] in the case of a semi-secret trust they must occur before the will is made.[256] The reason for the latter restriction according to the cases is that to hold

---

250 See *Re Playfair*, [1951] Ch. 4.

251 See "Testamentary Additions to Trusts" (1967), Conf. Commissioners on Unif. of Legis. (Appendix U), p. 207.

252 *Uniform Testamentary Additions to Trusts Act, Uniform Acts of the Uniform Law Conf. of Canada* (1978, as rev.), p. 47-1.

253 *Supra.*

254 See, *e.g.*, *Re Currie* (1978), 21 O.R. (2d) 709, 3 E.T.R. 196, 91 D.L.R. (3d) 559 (H.C.); *Re Johnson* (1961), 30 D.L.R. (2d) 474 (B.C. S.C.); *Re Jones*, [1942] Ch. 328; *Re Edwards Wills Trusts*, [1948] Ch. 440, [1948] 1 All E.R. 221 (C.A.); *Re Schintz's Will Trusts*, [1951] Ch. 870, [1951] 1 All E.R. 1095.

255 *McCormick v. Grogan* (1869), L.R. 4 H.L. 82; *Re Boyes* (1884), 26 Ch. D. 531; *Ottaway v. Norman*, [1972] Ch. 698, [1972] 2 W.L.R. 50, [1971] 3 All E.R. 1325.

256 *Blackwell v. Blackwell*, [1929] A.C. 318, [1929] All E.R. Rep. 71 (H.L.); *Re Keen*, [1937] Ch. 236 (C.A.); *Re Mihalopoulos* (1956), 19 W.W.R. 118, 5 D.L.R. (2d) 268 (Alta. T.D.); *Re d'Amico*, [1974] 2 W.W.R. 559, 42 D.L.R. (3d) 759 (B.C. S.C.); *Re Poohachoff*, [1971] 1

otherwise would permit the testator to reserve the power to make a future unattested codicil to the will, at any rate if the will, by possibility or in fact, refers to a future communication.[257]

This reasoning is fallacious, since semi-secret trusts have nothing to do with incorporation by reference and the trust is not and, in fact, in many cases cannot be (because it is not in writing), incorporated into the will. The trust, if established, is enforced outside the will.[258] Nevertheless, the principle appears to be firmly established.

You should note that, if the beneficiary under a secret trust predeceases the testator, the beneficiary's estate can take the gift.[259]

Further Reading

Williams, Mortimer and Sunnucks on Executors, Administrators and Probate, 17th ed., by J.H.G. Sunnucks, J.G. Ross Martyn, and K.M. Garnett (London: Stevens & Sons, 1993), pp. 153-157, 309-311.

Macdonell, Sheard and Hull on Probate Practice, 4th ed. by Rodney Hull and Ian M. Hull (Scarborough: Carswell, 1996), pp. 81-87.

Theobald on Wills, 15th ed. by J.B. Clark and J.G. Ross Martyn (London: Stevens & Sons, 1993), ch. 6.

6. CONDITIONAL WILLS

Wills often contain conditions which affect particular dispositions. Such conditions may either render a disposition ineffective unless a stated event occurs or does not occur — a condition precedent — or it may render a disposition defeasible upon a stated event — a condition subsequent. This matter is dealt with in a later chapter.

A will may also be revoked upon a specified condition, for example, that the revocation is not to be effective until a new will is substituted for the revoked one. This will also be dealt with later.

Further, a will may be conditional in the sense that it is not to be effective except in a stated situation. The will itself is then subject to a condition precedent. If that is the situation and the contingency does not occur, the will is not entitled to probate.[260]

It appears that the courts prefer not to find a will to be contingent. They will hold it not contingent if the will is ambiguous and if admissible evidence shows that the testator regarded the document as a binding will even though the contingency was not fulfilled.[261]

W.W.R. 463 (Sask. Surr. Ct.). See also *Hayman v. Nicoll*, [1944] S.C.R. 253, [1944] 3 D.L.R. 551.

257 *Ibid.*

258 *McCormick v. Grogan, supra*, at 97, *per* Lord Westbury.

259 *Re Gardner*, [1923] 2 Ch. 230.

260 *Parsons v. Lanoe* (1748), 1 Ves. Sen. 189 at 190, 95 E.R. 597, *per* Lord Hardwicke.

261 *Re Vines*, [1910] P. 147.

There are many expressions which make a will *prima facie* conditional, but many of them can be construed as merely showing a motive for making the will, in which case it will be held not to be conditional. In this respect Sir. F.H. Jeune P., laid down the following principles in *Re Spratt*:[262]

> In cases of the character of the present, the difficulty which arises in determining the intention of the testator as expressed in his will is that an ambiguity is caused by the use of language which renders it doubtful whether the testator meant to refer to a possible event as his reason for making a will, or as limiting the operation of the will made. If the will is clearly expressed to take effect only on the happening, or not happening, of any event, cadit quaestio, it is conditional. If the testator says, in effect - that he is led to make his will by reason of the uncertainty of life in general, or for some special reason, cadit quaestio, it is not conditional. But if it be not clear whether the words used import a reason for making a will or impress a conditional character on it, the whole language of the document, and also the surrounding circumstances, must be considered. In such cases there are two criteria which are especially useful for determining the problem: first, whether the nature of disposition made appears to have relation to the time or circumstances of the contingency; and, secondly, where the contingency is connected with a period of danger to the testator, whether it is coincident with that period, because, if it is, there is ground to suppose that the danger was regarded by the testator only as a reason for making a will, but, if it is not, it is difficult to see the object of referring to a particular period unless it be to limit the operation of the will.

Parsons v. Lanoe[263] is an example of a conditional will. The testator intended to go to Ireland and to spend some time there. By his will, made before his journey, he provided that if he died before his return from his journey to Ireland, his house and land should be sold and the proceeds distributed.[264]

Re Govier,[265] was another situation involving a conditional will. The deceased, Mrs. Govier, and her husband, made a joint will in 1941 which stated in part that if they died, their estates should be disposed of in a particular way. The will did not provide for the eventuality of one spouse surviving the other. Extrinsic evidence showed that they resided in a part of the country that was then subject to severe enemy bombing. The husband testified that he regarded the joint will as merely being effective if he and his wife were killed together in an air raid. Mrs. Govier died in 1949 and letters of administration were granted to her husband. Subsequently he presented the joint will to the court for advice and directions.

The court held that the will was conditional upon the happening of the stated event and that extrinsic evidence of the circumstances in which the will was made was admissible to interpret the meaning of the condition. On the basis of that evidence, the court concluded that the condition was the simultaneous deaths of both parties caused by wartime bombing. Since the condition was not fulfilled, the will was ineffective.

---

262 [1897] P. 28 at 29-30.
263 (1748), 1 Ves. Sen. 189, 95 E.R. 597.
264 See also *Re Winn* (1861), 2 Sw. & Tr. 337, 164 E.R. 1026; *Re O'Connor*, [1942] 1 All E.R. 546.
265 [1950] P. 237.

Re Spratt[266] itself is an example of a will which was held not to be conditional. The deceased was a military officer on active service in the Maori War. He wrote to his sister in the following terms:

> My dear Robe, — This is the most important part of my letter. If we remain here taking pahs for some time to come the chances are in favour of more of us being killed, and as I may not have another opportunity of saying what I wish to be done with any little money I may possess in case of an accident, I wish to make everything I possess over to you. In the first place there is money at Cox's, over 100*l.* in New South Wales Bank, New Zealand. Keep this until I ask you for it. Your affectionate brother, C. Spratt.

The testator survived the war and died many years later without revoking the above military (that is, privileged) will.[267] The court held that the language of the testator suggested only a motive for making the will since there was no expression of any period within which the document would only be operative. Rather, the testator's request that his sister keep the letter until he should ask for it, suggested that the will should remain effective after his return. Further, the letter did not indicate that the disposition of the property was to be temporary or that it did not apply to any property which the testator might at any time in the future acquire.[268]

A further example of a will which was not conditional is discussed in *Re Huebner*,[269] reproduced below.

RE HUEBNER
[1975] W.W.D. 66, 53 D.L.R. (3d) 730
Manitoba Court of Appeal

The deceased, Peter Huebner, was about to make a trip to the Soviet Union in 1970. Shortly before he left, he made a holograph will which provided in part: "In the event of my death (on this trip) all my possessions and insurance monies, etc. are bequeathed to Patricia and Kevin Landolfo," and he instructed Mrs. Landolfo to pay any costs out of the property.

Huebner returned from his trip about a month later and died in 1973. Patricia Landolfo had been a close friend of his for many years. She applied for probate of the will. Huebner's next of kin opposed the application on the ground that the will was conditional and that the condition had not occurred. The trial judge admitted the will to probate. The next of kin appealed.

HALL J.A., delivered the judgment of the court:

---

266 *Supra.*

267 A privileged will is one made by a member of the armed forces while on active service or by a sailor while at sea. It does not have to be in the testator's own handwriting and requires only the testator's signature or the signature of some other person affixed in his or her presence. See, *e.g.*, *Succession Law Reform Act*, R.S.O. 1990, c. S.26, s. 8.

268 See also *Re Rempel*, 32 Man. R. 126, [1922] 2 W.W.R. 752, 68 D.L.R. 677 (C.A.); *Re Swords*, [1929] 2 W.W.R. 245, [1929] 3 D.L.R. 564 (Alta. T.D.); *Borgen v. Borgen* (1973), 5 Nfld. & P.E.I.R. 275 (Nfld. T.D.); *Re Schullman* (1984), 16 E.T.R. 271.

269 [1975] W.W.D. 66, 53 D.L.R. (3d) 730 (Man. C.A.).

· · ·

The principles to be followed in cases of this kind were well stated by Lord Penzance in the case of *In the Goods of Porter....*[270]

It is the common feature of wills in respect of which this sort of question arises, that the testator therein refers to a possible impending calamity in connection with his will; and the question arises whether he intends to limit the operation of the will to the time during which such calamity is imminent. *If the language used by him can by any reasonable interpretation be construed to mean that he refers to the calamity and the period of time during which it may happen, as the reason for*

· · ·

In that case the testator used the following language:

Being obliged to leave England to join my regiment in China...I leave this paper containing my wishes...Should anything unfortunately happen to me while abroad, I wish everything that I may be in possession of at that time or anything appertaining to me hereafter. . .to be divided....

It was held that the will was conditional, but crucial to the decision were the words "at that time" in the context of the will....Lord Penzance stated:[271]

The question then is, whether the paper before me comes within the principles of these cases. I think it does not. If it had stopped at the end of the first sentence, I think it would have come within it.

In the Goods of Mayd,[272] was a case of a will containing the following words: "On leaving this station for Thargomindah and Melbourne, in case of my death on the way, know all men this is a memorandum of my last will and testament". Lord Hannen, President of the Court, in admitting the will to probate stated:[273]

I am of opinion that I ought to grant probate of this will. The meaning of general phrases of this kind is, "knowing the uncertainty of human life, I make this my will", and the Court ought not to scrutinize such expressions with too great nicety.

Finally, reference is made to *Re Rempel Estate*[274]. In that case a testamentary document commences with the words: "Whereas I am going to go on a journey to Mexico, and should I die, I therefore certify by these presents...".
It was held that the will was not conditional and it was accordingly admitted to probate. Perdue, C.J.M., stated:[275]

Looking at the will in question in this appeal, I think it is clear that the contemplated journey to Mexico is referred to as a period of danger which operates as a reason why the testator should make his will. The operation of the will is not confined to that period.

---

270 (1869), L.R. 2 P. & D. 21 at 22.
271 *Ibid.*, at p. 24. The italics are mine.
272 (1880), 6 P.D. 17.
273 *Ibid.*, at p. 18.
274 (1922), 68 D.L.R. 677, [1922] 2 W.W.R. 752, 32 Man. R. 126.
275 *Ibid.*, at D.L.R. 680, Man. R. 129.

Applying these principles to the present case, it is my opinion that the language used by the testator, namely, "on this trip", refers to the occasion for the making of the will rather than to the condition for its operation.

The appeal is accordingly dismissed.

. . .

Notes and Questions

1. The Supreme Court of Canada affirmed *Re Huebner* without reasons.[276]

2. A and B, two sisters who lived together, made a joint will in which they stated that they intended at a later date to make their separate wills in favour of each other, but that in the event of death by a common accident or if one should survive the other and should die without making another will, the joint will should stand. Later both made wills in favour of the other, using a printed form which commenced with a revocation clause and in which each gave her estate to the other. A died first. After B's death the residuary beneficiaries under the joint will applied for a grant of administration with the will annexed. Did B die intestate, or was the joint will effective?[277]

3. A testator made a will in which he stated: "in case of any fatal accident happening to me, being about to travel by railway, I hereby leave..." Is this will conditional?[278]

4. A testatrix had a will in which she left a farm to a niece and one to a nephew and the residue of her estate equally to the niece and nephew. Later she decided to make *inter vivos* gifts of the farm to them and to change her will by deleting references to the farms and bequeathing the residue of her estate to the nephew's and niece's children. She did not want the new will to take effect until the *inter vivos* gifts were complete and when she signed it, she told her solicitors that this was her intention. The gifts were later complete by transfers to the niece and nephew. When the testatrix died, her executor sought to have the second will admitted to probate. Can it be? Is it conditional?[279]

Further Reading

Macdonell, Sheard and Hull on Probate Practice, 4th ed. by Rodney Hull and Ian M. Hull (Scarborough: Carswell, 1996), pp. 121-123.

Mellows, The Law of Succession, 5th ed. by Clive v. Margrave-Jones (London: Butterworths, 1993, pp. 48-9.

Thomas E. Atkinson, *Handbook of the Law of Wills*, 2nd ed. (St. Paul: West Publishing Co., 1953), pp. 416-8.

7. DELEGATION OF TESTAMENTARY POWER

Can you delegate your testamentary power? For example, can you make a will by which you appoint executors and then direct the executors to distribute the property as they see fit?

---

276 [1976] S.C.R. 4, [1976] W.W.D. 89.
277 See *Re O'Connor*, [1942] 1 All E.R. 546.
278 See *Re Dobson* (1866), L.R. 1 P. & M. 88.
279 See *Corbett v. Newey*, [1996] 2 All E.R. 914 (C.A.).

The principle that a person cannot delegate the power to make a will is of relatively recent vintage. It appears to have been enunciated first by Lord Penzance, although in a context different from the one in which the principle is usually stated.[280] The principle has often been repeated, however, in English cases, but only in *dicta*. Thus, for example, in *Chichester Diocesan Fund and Board of Finance (Inc.) v. Simpson*[281] Lord Simonds said:[282]

> It is a cardinal rule, common to English and to Scots law, that a man may not delegate his testamentary power. To him the law gives the right to dispose of his estate to ascertained or ascertainable persons. He does not exercise that right if in effect he empowers his executors to say what persons or objects are to be his beneficiaries. To this salutary rule there is a single exception. A testator may validly leave it to his executors to determine what charitable objects shall benefit, so long as charitable and no other objects may benefit.[283]

Other cases accept the principle, but also except from its operation, in addition to a power to select charities, general and special powers of appointment,[284] and more recent cases have added hybrid powers to the list of exceptions.[285]

If, therefore, there are so many exceptions to the principle, does it in fact exist? There are several Australian cases in which it has been applied.

The leading Australian case is *Tatham v. Huxtable*.[286] The testator created a special power which authorized his executor to distribute the residue to the beneficiaries named in the will or to others who, in the executor's opinion, had rendered service meriting consideration. The court held this power void because contrary to the principle against delegation. In *dictum*, the court also opined that

---

280 See *Re Smith* (1869), L.R. 1 P. & D. 717. The testator had made a codicil to his will in which he said that his wife should have the option of adding it to his will. Such a power is void because it enables a person, other than the testator, to revoke a testamentary instrument contrary to statute. See, *e.g.*, *Succession Law Reform Act*, R.S.O. 1990, c. S.26, ss. 15, 16.

281 [1944] A.C. 341, [1944] 2 All E.R. 60 (H.L.).

282 *Ibid.*, at A.C. 371.

283 To the same effect see *ibid.*, at A.C. 348, 349 and 364, *per* Viscount Simon L.C., Lord MacMillan, who also excepted special powers from the rule, and Lord Porter, respectively; *Blair v. Duncan*, [1902] A.C. 37 at 47, *per* Lord Robertson (H.L.); *Grimond (or Macintyre) v. Grimond*, [1905] A.C. 124 at 126 (H.L.); *Houston v. Burns*, [1918] A.C. 337 at 342 (H.L.); *A.G. v. Nat. Provincial Bank*, [1924] A.C. 262 at 264 and 268, *per* Lord Cave and Lord Haldane, respectively (H.L.); *A.G. of New Zealand v. New Zealand Ins. Co.*, [1936] A.C. 888 at 890, *per* Lord MacMillan, [1936] 3 All E.R. 888 (P.C.).

284 *Re Hughes; Hughes v. Footner*, [1921] 2 Ch. 208 at 212, *per* Sargant J., [1921] All E.R. Rep. 310; *Re Park; Public Trustee v. Armstrong*, [1932] 1 Ch. 580 at 583, *per* Clauson J., [1931] All E.R. Rep. 633.

285 *Re Manisty's Settlement; Manisty v. Manisty*, [1974] Ch. 17, [1973] 2 All E.R. 1203; *Re Hay's Settlement Trusts*, [1982] 1 W.L.R. 202, [1981] 3 All E.R. 786. A general power of appointment is one which the donee of the power may exercise in favour of such persons as the donee chooses, including himself or herself. It is, therefore, virtually the equivalent of ownership. A special power is one which permits the donee to appoint among a specified class of objects which may include the donee. A hybrid power is one which permits the donee to appoint to anyone except named persons or a named class of persons. See Hanbury and Maudsley, *Modern Equity* (13th ed., 1989), p. 165.

286 (1950), 81 C.L.R. 639 (Austr. H.C.).

hybrid powers of appointment offended against the principle.[287] In another case the court held that a power of distribution in favour of one object offended the principle.[288] Finally, in yet another case the court held that a power given to the executors to encroach in favour of the testator's widow without providing guidelines offended the rule as well.[289]

You should note that the cases recognize that such powers may well be valid in a deed.[290] You will also have observed that all of the cases concern various kinds of powers, including trust powers and mere powers.[291] Moreover, when you examine the cases, it is apparent that all of them involve cases in which the objects of the power, that is, the potential appointees, are, or could by possibility be, uncertain. It is a general rule that a power, whether a trust power or a mere power, is invalid unless the objects are described with certainty. Thus, the court must be able to say with certainty whether any person in the world either falls within the class of objects as described or does not.[292] The cases which hold that a power offends the rule against delegation are in fact cases which offend the rule against certainty of objects and, hence, could be decided on that ground alone. This is true also of cases involving purpose trusts which are non-charitable, since they are by definition uncertain.[293]

That being so, it is doubtful that there is, indeed, a rule against delegation. Moreover, historically wills have been regarded as the equivalent of deeds and a settlor may do as he or she wishes in the disposition of his or her property, subject to the certainty rule.[294] Nor can it be argued that the rule is based upon the statutes respecting wills, since those statutes do not confer the power to make wills. That power, as regards personalty, existed at common law and, as regards land, was conferred by the *Statute of Wills, 1540*.[295] Modern wills legislation is concerned principally with the execution of wills and contains enabling powers not otherwise held by the testator.[296]

Re Nicholls,[297] set out below, concerns the validity of delegation as it pertains to successive general powers of appointment and successive trusts.

---

287 *Ibid.*, at pp. 648-9, *per* Fullager J.

288 *Lutheran Church of Australia; South Australia Dist. Inc. v. Farmers Co-op. Executors and Trustee Ltd.* (1970), 121 C.L.R. 628 (Aus. H.C.).

289 *In re Will & Estate of Nevil Shute Norway*, unrep., Case No. 63/4731 (Vict., S.C., 1963), referred to in I.J. Hardingham, "The Rule against Delegation of Will-Making Power" (1974), 9 Melbourne U.L. Rev. 650 at 661.

290 See, *e.g.*, *Tatham v. Huxtable, supra*, at p. 649, *per* Fullagar J.

291 A trust power is one in which the donee of the power (the trustee) has a duty to appoint the property, but is given a discretion concerning quantum and the selection of the appointees. A mere power is one in which the donee of the power (the trustee) has the same discretion as in a trust power, but has no duty to appoint. It is usually followed by a gift over in default of appointment.

292 *McPhail v. Doulton*, [1971] A.C. 424, [1970] 2 All E.R. 228 (H.L.).

293 *Chichester Diocesan Fund and Board of Finance (Inc.) v. Simpson*, [1944] A.C. 341, [1944] 2 All E.R. 60.

294 See Hardingham, *supra*, at p. 664 ff.

295 32 Hen. 8, c. 1.

296 Hardingham, *supra*, at p. 667.

297 (1987), 34 D.L.R. (4th) 321, (sub nom. *Re Nicholls Estate*) 25 E.T.R. 228 (Ont. C.A.).

RE NICHOLLS
(1987), 57 O.R. (2d) 763, 34 D.L.R. (4th) 321, 25 E.T.R. 228
Supreme Court of Ontario
[Court of Appeal]

The testatrix was a member of an unorganized religious sect and had supported its missionary activities for many years. By her will she gave her estate to her executor upon trust and directed him to follow the directions of Carson Cowan for the distribution of the residue of the estate. She went on to provide that if Carson Cowan should predecease her, then John Richards should have the power to give such directions and if he should predecease the testatrix, Carson Wallace should have similar power. All three named persons were members of the sect.

Carson Cowan survived the testatrix and gave directions to the executor to distribute the residue among six members of the sect who were involved in its mission work. The executor applied for directions.

At first instance, O'Leary J., held that the will created a valid general power of appointment. The next of kin appealed.

KREVER J.A. delivered the judgment of the court:

. . .

The first issue between the parties is the correct characterization of the interests which cl. 2(c) of the will purports to create. Neither the executor nor the next of kin takes the position that the proper interpretation of the testatrix's language is that it creates successive outright bequests to Messrs. Cowan, Richards and Wallace. The real contest is between successive trusts on the one hand and successive general powers of appointment on the other hand. A trust requires the existence of three certainties, those of intention, subject-matter and objects. I find it impossible to discern in the language of the testatrix any intention to create a trust and am therefore left with the conclusion that the true character of the interest is that of a general power of appointment. As contrasted with a special power of appointment, a general power of appointment enables the holder or donee of the power to appoint to anyone and not simply in favour of certain described persons or classes of persons.

That the law raises no objection to a general power of appointment created *inter vivos* is accepted without argument. Equally well known is the fact, as D.M. Gordon pointed out in "Delegation of Will-Making Power"[298] that "[f]or centuries testators have been conferring both general and special powers of appointment by their wills; and this practice went on practically unchallenged until the turn of the century".

It is now contended that, notwithstanding this long-established practice, and the existence of many decisions of courts of first instance in common law jurisdictions upholding testamentary general powers of appointment, the validity of such powers of appointment is incompatible with the policy and formal require-

_____
298 69 L.Q. Rev. 334 at 334 (1953).

ments of the *Wills Act*.[299] It has been suggested that the continuing practice of inserting general powers of appointment in wills even after the enactment of the *Wills Act*, is to be explained by the fact that the practice was so thoroughly ingrained in the law by language that, again in Gordon's words, "it occurred to no one that the Act made a difference".[300]

It is conceded that as a matter of strict *stare decisis* there is no binding decision holding invalid a bequest creating a general power of appointment. However, it is submitted that in *obiter dicta* in several decisions of courts of last resort judges have expressed the view that such a power cannot be validly created by will because to do so would amount to the delegation of will-making power. The nature of the objection is illustrated by the following statement of Viscount Haldane in *Attorney-General v. National Provincial & Union Bank of England et al.*:[301]

> [A] man cannot disinherit his heirs by giving away his property unless he really gives it away; he cannot leave it to someone else to make a will for him, nor can he leave it to his trustees to give it for purposes which are to be completely in their discretion, unless these purposes are so indicated as in some sense to confer on a class of beneficiary an interest.

Similar *dicta* appear in speeches of the majority in the later case of *Chichester Diocesan Fund & Board of Finance (Inc.) v. Simpson et al.*[302] [where] Viscount Simon L.C. said:

> The fundamental principle is that the testator must by the terms of his will himself dispose of the property with which the will proposes to deal. With one single exception [not relevant here], he cannot by will direct executors or trustees to do the business for him.

To the same effect was the view of Lord Macmillan...:[303]

> ...the law, in according the right to dispose of property *mortis causa* by will, is exacting in its requirements that the testator must define with precision the persons or objects he intends to benefit. This is the condition on which he is entitled to exclude the order of succession which the law otherwise provides.

In Australia, courts have held some powers of appointment invalid because of the non-delegation rule but not general powers of appointment in wills: see, for example, *Tatham v. Huxtable*[304] and *Lutheran Church of Australia v. Farmers' Co-operative Executors & Trustee Ltd.*[305] In the light of Mr. Justice O'Leary's statement that there is no legal principle "that prevents a testator from giving another the right to direct that the testator's estate be paid to him personally for

---

299 R.S.O. 1970, c. 499, now Part I of the *Succession Law Reform Act*, R.S.O. 1990, c. S.26.
300 "Delegation of Will-Making Power," at p. 334.
301 [1924] A.C. 262 at 268.
302 [1944] 2 All E.R. 60 at 62.
303 *Ibid.*
304 (1950), 81 C.L.R. 639.
305 (1970), 121 C.L.R. 628.

his own benefit or be paid to such others as he directs", the following *dictum* from the reasons of Kitto J. in *Tatham v. Huxtable* is apposite:[306]

> Having regard to these principles, the proposition should, I think, be accepted that a testamentary disposition in favour of a person or persons to be selected by someone other than the testator himself, if it is not to fail as infringing the general rule forbidding the delegation of testamentary power, must either confer upon the person authorized to make the selection a general power equivalent to ownership or define with certainty a class or group from which the selection is to be made.

When one turns from the *dicta* on the subject, albeit *dicta* of a highly persuasive nature and from judges of courts of last resort, one finds decisions of courts of first instance holding valid general powers of appointment in wills in England, New Zealand and Ontario. *Re McEwen (Deceased); McEwen v. Day et al.*,[307] was a case in which Gresson J. of the Supreme Court of New Zealand had to determine whether a provision in a will created a trust or conferred a mere power of appointment and, if the later, whether it was invalid as a delegation of will-making power. He held that the provision conferred a general power of appointment and did so validly. Two passages from Mr. Justice Gresson's careful analysis of the authorities are instructive. After expressing respect for the *dicta* to which I have referred and pointing out[308]...that "[t]here are, however, decisions and judicial *dicta* (though not at so high a level as those cited in the article)[309] which recognize the validity of general powers of appointment as an established exception to the non-delegation rule", he reviewed these decisions and *dicta* and stated his conclusion. Part of his review...[310] read as follows:

There is, therefore, judicial recognition that a general power of appointment is either not truly a delegation at all or is an exception to the anti-delegation principle.

. . .

It appears to me that a power of appointment can be held valid as not offending against the prohibition upon delegating testamentary power upon either of two principles, one, that the giving of a power of appointment does not amount to a delegation if there is indicated with sufficient particularity the class of persons or objects to be benefited: that they are ascertained or ascertainable. *Re Ogden*[311] is an illustration where there was a class capable of ascertainment and in a specified area. Certainty can be secured either by an inclusive definition or by an exclusive definition, though it is difficult to treat the exclusion of only one person, or comparatively few persons, as affecting sufficient certainty. Nevertheless, in *In re Park, Public Trustee v. Armstrong*[312] the only exclusion was of the donee herself and *In re Jones, Public Trustee v. Jones*[313] all that were excluded were

---

306 *Supra*, at p. 655.
307 [1955] N.Z.L.R. 575.
308 *Ibid.*, at p. 580.
309 D.M. Gordon, "Delegation of Will-Making Power", *supra*.
310 *Ibid.*, at pp. 581-2.
311 [1933] Ch. 678.
312 [1932] 1 Ch. 580.
313 [1945] Ch. 105.

corporate bodies and individuals not in existence at the moment of the death of the appointor. Both were held to be permissible powers. The other principle upon which general powers of appointment have been supported is that it is equivalent to property and that such a disposition in accordance with the established practice as to general powers of appointment is to be treated as a disposition by the testator of the property: that, since the donee can give the property subject to the power to himself if he so chooses, the testator has in fact disposed of it by will. It would seem, therefore, that the anti-delegation principle is not flouted when either there is a power of selection from a class designated with certainty (and the whole world less one person has been held in *In re Park* to satisfy that requirement) or where there is power to dispose of favour of any person including the donee for that, is (as stated in *Jarman on Wills*)[314] "equivalent to property". The donee is for all practical purposes in the position of beneficial owner of the property since he can dispose of it as freely and effectually as if it were his own....

Mr. Justice Gresson set out his understanding of the result of the conflicting decisions and *dicta* as follows...:[315]

> My conclusions upon a study of the cases are that first, no Judge has held and no text-book writer has stigmatized a general power of appointment by will as invalid. There are, however, the furore of *dicta* earlier referred to, all by authorities of the highest eminence; but these were pronounced in cases in which there was a discretion given to trustees in the execution of their trust, in short, where there was a trust and not a mere power. I do not think these pronouncements should be understood as denying the well-established law with respect to powers of appointment by will, a power which, if delegation it be, is too firmly embedded in the law to be swept away in an oblique fashion. I do not think the passages cited should be torn from their context, divorced from the particular situation with which the Court was confronted, and treated as pronouncements true in all circumstances and with no qualifications save such as in some of the passages are mentioned. All the cases which gave rise to the observations cited were cases where the power was fiduciary; it was in each case a trust in the strictest sense - one which failed for uncertainty. It must ever be remembered that a trust and a power of appointment differ. There is no duty to exercise a discretionary power; it is not a trust; and the general principles which make a trust void for uncertainty since no one can enforce it, have no application. It must be remembered too, as was said by Lord Halsbury, L.C., in *Quinn v. Leatham*[316] that: "A case is only an authority for what it actually decides. I entirely deny that it can be quoted for a proposition that may seem to follow logically from it. Such a mode of reasoning assumes that the law is necessarily a logical code, whereas every lawyer must acknowledge that the law is not always logical at all".[317]

[His Lordship then referred to two Ontario cases which upheld testamentary general powers of appointment, *Higginson et al. v. Kerr et al.*[318] and *Re Heyes*[319] and continued:]

---

314 8th Ed., 500.
315 *Supra*, at p. 583.
316 [1901] A.C. 495.
317 *Ibid.*, at p. 506.
318 (1898), 30 O.R. 62.
319 [1938] O.W.N. 417, [1938] 4 D.L.R. 775 (C.A.), affirming [1938] O.W.N. 294, [1938] 3 D.L.R. 757.

It is fair to point out that in neither of these two Ontario cases was the question of delegation of will-making power discussed. It is also true to say that in the more recent and, with respect, entirely correctly decided case of *Re Lysiak*.[320] Goodman J. by way of *obiter dictum*...[321]suggested that if the will there in question had purported to empower the executors to dispose of the testator's assets by giving them to any persons other than the named beneficiaries it would have been void because "it would constitute an attempt to delegate his testamentary power".

[His Lordship distinguished *Klassen et al. v. Klassen et al.*,[322] which involved a trust power that failed because of uncertainty, and continued:]

I conclude from the preceding discussion that the authorities, in which term I include the decisions, *dicta* and scholarly commentaries, are in such a state of uncertainty that this appeal should be decided on the basis of principle or policy. Would any contemporary societal interest be prejudiced by permitting a general power of appointment created by will to be treated by the law in the same way as a general power of appointment created by an *inter vivos* instrument? I am unable to see how that question can be answered in the affirmative. I do not rest my answer on the general principle that prefers a construction that will avoid an intestacy. More appropriate, and a better guide, is the principle expressed correctly and succinctly in the "Report of the Ontario Law Reform Commission on The Proposed Adoption in Ontario of the Uniform Wills Act, 1968":[323] "The right of an individual to own and dispose of his assets is basic to our law. Any effort to restrict or circumscribe that right should only be permitted where the necessity for restriction clearly justifies interference with the basic freedom of the individual to dispose of his property". I am not persuaded that the formal requirements of Part I of the *Succession Law Reform Act*, formerly the *Wills Act*, are a sufficient justification. Indeed, the amendment in 1977,[324] making holograph wills valid is evidence of the existence of a less formalistic attitude towards testamentary disposition of property.

It has been suggested that it unrealistic or artificial to regard the giving of a completely unfettered discretion to the holder or donee of a general power of appointment, including, therefore, the power to appoint to himself or herself, as, in essence, not materially different from the gift of property. I do not agree with that criticism. It may be true that it is not clearly evident from the testatrix's language in this case that the testatrix contemplated that the donee of the power would ever direct that the residue be given to him. That, however, is not a complete answer. There is equally nothing in her language that indicates that she would have any objection to his direction that he be given the residue. Her words show that she intended an unfettered discretion, a discretion, so it seems to me, that an

---

320 (1975), 7 O.R. (2d) 317, 55 D.L.R. (3d) 161.
321 *Ibid.*, at O.R. 321, D.L.R. 165.
322 [1986] 5 W.W.R. 746, 50 Sask. R. 64 (Q.B.).
323 Toronto, Ministry of the Attorney General, at p. 9.
324 By c. 40, s. 6.

absolute owner would have. That, as I interpret his reasons, is what Mr. Justice O'Leary concluded. I have not been persuaded that he was wrong.

. . .

Notes and Questions

1. The *Nicholls* case was the subject of a comment.[325]
2. For a similar case which came to the same conclusion, see *Re Beatty's Will Trusts, Hinves v. Brooke*.[326]
3. The principle against delegation does apply when the testator tells another person to prepare his or her will but does not give that person any instructions concerning his or her wishes and signs the will without reading it. The will would then be refused probate on the ground that the testator lacked knowledge and approval of the contents.[327]

Further Reading

D.M. Gordon, "Delegation of Will-Making Power" (1953), 69 L.Q. Rev. 334.

D.M. Gordon, Comment (1955), 33 Can. Bar Rev. 955.

D.M. Gordon, Commentary (1955-6), 7 Res Judicatae 253.

F.C. Hutley, "The Delegation of Will-Making Powers" (1956), 2 Sydney L. Rev. 93.

I.J. Hardingham, "The Rule Against Delegation of Will-Making Power" (1974), 9 Melbourne U.L. Rev. 650.

M.C. Cullity, "Fiduciary Powers" (1976), 54 Can. Bar Rev. 229, at pp. 273-81.

I.D. Campbell, "The Enigma of General Powers of Appointment" (1955-6), 7 Res Judicatae 244.

J.F. Keeler, Comment, 4 Adelaide L. Rev. 210.

O.R. Marshall, "The Failure of the Astor Trust" (1953), 6 Curr. Leg. Prob. 151 at 160-3.

Ross A. Sundberg, "The Status and Authority of the Decision in Tatham v. Huxtable" (1974), 48 Austr. L.J. 527.

I.J. Hardingham and R. Baxt, *Discretionary Trusts*, 2nd ed. (Melbourne, Butterworths Pty. Ltd., 1984), pp. 54-70.

8. LIMITS OF THE POWER OF TESTATION

While most people consider the making of a will a most solemn act and, indeed, many refrain from making a will because of its morbid association with death, certain persons take a lighter approach to the matter and their resulting, often capricious, wills make interesting light reading. In addition, they are often productive of much litigation at the instance of disgruntled heirs who are passed over.

---

325 By A.H. Oosterhoff (1988), 9 E. & T.J. 1.

326 [1990] 3 All E.R. 844 (Ch. D.).

327 *Hastilow v. Stobie* (1865), L.R. 1 P. & D. 64. For an earlier case which held otherwise, see *Cunliffe v. Cross* (1862), 3 Sw. & Tr. 37, at 38, 164 E.R. 1185, *per* Sir C. Cresswell, which was adopted in *Re Johnson*, 32 M.P.R. 170, [1953] 4 D.L.R. 777 (N.B.C.A.).

One such will is that left by a Toronto lawyer, Charles Millar. The preamble to the will read as follows:

This will is necessarily uncommon and capricious because I have no dependants or near relatives and no duty rests upon me to leave any property at my death and what I do leave is proof of my folly in gathering and retaining more than I required in my lifetime.

In one clause of his will Millar gave a share in the Ontario Jockey Club to each of two opponents of gambling and to a competitor of the Jockey Club. In another clause, he gave one share of the O'Keefe Brewery Company to each protestant minister and to each Orange Lodge in Toronto, many of whom were firm proponents of temperance.[328]

In another clause of the will, Millar devised his house in Jamaica to three friends who hated each other.

Finally he left the residue "at the expiration of ten years from my death...to the Mother who has...given birth in Toronto to the greatest number of children".

The resulting "Baby Derby" contest was won by four Toronto mothers, each of whom had nine children born during the ten year period. The validity of this gift is discussed in the following case.

RE MILLAR
[1938] S.C.R. 1, [1938] 1 D.L.R. 65
Supreme Court of Canada

Charles Millar gave the residue of his estate upon trust to convert and accumulate and to give the capital and accumulated income to the mother or mothers who had, in the 10-year period following his death, given birth in Toronto to the greatest number of children. As noted above, four mothers won the contest, each having had nine children during the period.

Millar's next of kin contested the will on the ground that it was contrary to public policy. They were unsuccessful at first instance[329] and on appeal to the Ontario Court of Appeal.[330] They then appealed to the Supreme Court of Canada, which also agreed with the Ontario courts on this point and upheld the will.

Some of the children of the several contestants were illegitimate and it was held at first instance by Middleton J.A. that the word "children" included legitimate children only. His opinion was affirmed by the Ontario Court of Appeal and by the Supreme Court of Canada in this case. This portion of the appeal is not excerpted.

SIR LYMAN P. DUFF C.J.C.:

. . .

It has not been argued by the appellants that the disposition in question here is

---

328 For a case reported on this clause, see *Re Millar*, 60 O.L.R. 434, [1927] 3 D.L.R. 270 (H.C.), reproduced in a later chapter.
329 [1937] 1 D.L.R. 127.
330 [1937] 3 D.L.R. 224.

void upon any particular rule or principle established by judicial decision. Such being the case, we think, taking the most liberal view of the jurisdiction of the Courts, there are at least two conditions which must be fulfilled to justify a refusal by the Courts on grounds of public policy to give effect to a rule of law according to its proper application in the usual course in respect of a disposition of property. First, we respectfully concur in these two sentences in the judgment of Lord Thankerton in *Fender v. Mildmay*:[331]

> Generally, it may be stated that such prohibition is imposed in the interest of the safety of the state, or the economic or social well-being of the state and its people as a whole. It is therefore necessary, when the enforcement of a contract is challenged, to ascertain the existence and exact limits of the principle of public policy contended for, and then to consider whether the particular contract falls within those limits.

Secondly, we take the liberty of adopting the words of Lord Atkin in his judgment in the same case:[332]

> ...it (referring to Lord Halsbury's judgment in *Janson's* case)[333] fortifies the serious warning, illustrated by the passages cited above (among them is the passage, already quoted, from the opinion of Parke, B.)[334] that the doctrine should be invoked only in clear cases, in which the harm to the public is substantially incontestable, and does not depend upon the idiosyncratic inferences of a few judicial minds. I think that this should be regarded as the true guide.

. . .

We are asked to say that the tendency of this disposition is "against public policy" in the pertinent sense because, it is urged, its tendency is to give rise to a competition between married couples to bring about successive births of children in rapid sequence to the injury of the mothers' health, to the injury of the children, morally and physically, and to the degradation of motherhood and family life. It is even suggested that in cases in which the husband ceased to be fecund in course of the race, the contestants might be tempted to resort to other males to do his office.

. . .

We ask ourselves the question, is the second condition satisfied? Can it be judicially affirmed that for such reasons "the harm to the public" from such dispositions "is substantially incontestable?" Is it so clear that something like general agreement upon the point among Judges of this country could be judicially assumed? It will not be overlooked that the Ontario Judges unanimously held the opposite view.

It is the evil tendency of such dispositions in respect of some interest of the state, or of some interest of the people as a whole, with which we are concerned. We find it impossible to affirm from any knowledge we have that a policy of

---

331 [1937] 3 All E.R. 402 at 414.
332 *Ibid.,* at p. 407.
333 *Janson v. Driefontein Consolidated Mines Ltd.,* [1902] A.C. 484.
334 From *Egerton v. Earl Brownlow,* 4 H.L.C. 1 at 106, 10 E.R. 359.

encouraging large families by pecuniary rewards to the parents or donations to the children would have a tendency injurious to the state or to the people as a whole; still less than anything like unanimity in favour of such a proposition could be assumed. It is not sufficient to say that some people may be, or probably would be, tempted by the hope of obtaining this legacy to conduct themselves in a manner injurious to wife and children. That sort of argument is conclusively answered in *Egerton v. Brownlow*....[335] One could easily conjure up the possibility that similar temptations might be inspired by a bequest of a large fortune to the grandchildren of the testator, to be divided equally among them, as inviting each of the children to have a numerous offspring in order to secure for his family as large a proportion as possible of the inheritance.

Conceive[336] the case of a bequest of a large sum of money to each child of a given woman to vest at its birth. Such a bequest might, one could imagine, in some cases give rise to temptations similar to those whose possibility, it is said, is sufficient to invalidate the disposition before us. We do not suppose it would seriously be argued that in such a case the Courts could deny the claim of a legatee on grounds of public policy.

In *Egerton v. Brownlow*[337] Alderson B., states explicitly, and there can be no doubt about it, that "a sum of money or an estate left to the first son of that marriage if born within a year of the nuptials, would not be a void bequest or devise".

Would such a devise or bequest be void if given to the second son if born within two years?

The observations of Parke, B., in *Egerton v. Brownlow*[338] are so pertinent in this connection that we think it right to reproduce them textually:-

Suppose a large estate left to A., subject to the condition of his becoming senior wrangler and senior medallist at Cambridge. Would it be illegal, as tending to induce him to employ the money in corrupting the examiners, or betraying into idleness and profligacy or destroying his most promising competitors? If a large estate is left to a man conditioned that he should within a stated time marry a countess, would it be void, as tending to induce him to use improper means to effect such an alliance? Or if an estate was to be forfeited in case the devisee did not take holy orders, or become a dean or a bishop, or take a degree of doctor of divinity in a certain time, would it be void, as having a tendency to induce him to obtain those orders, dignities, or distinctions by bad means? So the case of a condition to obtain the royal licence to use a particular name and arms, a most common occurrence, might on similar grounds be impeached, as having a tendency to cause the royal licence to be obtained by corrupt means. So even also the clause, in the form in this will, which is to use "the utmost endeavours to obtain it", might be said to have a similar though a more remote tendency to the same end; and yet to object to either of such clauses, on either ground, seems to be utterly untenable. Nay, a limitation to one for life, remainder to another, might be said to be void, a tendency to cause the remainder-man to try to kill the tenant for life; a limitation to first and other sons successively in tail, to induce the second son to destroy the life of the elder by a direct act of murder, or a continued course of cruelty and unkindness, or to use fraudulent artifices to prevent him from marrying. Insurances on lives might be avoided on the

---

335 (1853), 4 H.L.C. 1.
336 Pun intended?
337 At p. 108.
338 At pp. 127, 128.

same ground. Insurances of property against fire, contracts by burial-clubs to pay sums of money for the funeral of wives or children; in short, there are few contracts in which a suspicious mind might not find a tendency to produce evil; and to hold all such contracts to be void would, indeed, be an intolerable mischief.

[The court dismissed the appeal. The concurring opinion of Crocket J., has been omitted. The other members of the Court agreed with the Chief Justice].

Notes and Questions

1. Sam Weir, who had practiced law in Toronto and London, Ontario, left a will in which he gave the sum of $3,500 to the Law Society of Upper Canada in trust to pay the income each year to the student graduating from the Bar Admission Course with the lowest marks. The testator said in his will that he knew many lawyers who became successful by "keeping their lack of knowledge in the dark." He strongly recommended that the winner spend the money on a night on the town. If the Law Society accepted the gift, it would also receive a further $10,000 to be spent on a series of "Weir Lectures."

The Law Society declined the gift on the ground that it (that is, the first part) was not charitable. If the Society had accepted the gift, could it have been attacked on the ground that it was contrary to public policy?

Weir is buried in front of his house in Queenston. Special permission was required for the burial. It was obtained because Weir had given his collection of paintings and antiques as well as his house to the public to be kept intact as a museum on condition that he be buried there. The museum has been established.[339]

2. A husband and his wife obtained a divorce and divided their assets. Not long thereafter, the former wife and the two daughters of the marriage were lost at sea and were declared dead. The former wife died intestate and under the relevant law, her estate passed to her children. The children also died intestate. Is it against public policy to have the former wife's estate pass, via her children to her former husband?[340]

3. A direction in a will that the executor arrange to have the testator's horses shot is contrary to public policy and void.[341]

9. DISPOSITION OF PARTS OF THE BODY

It is not possible to have property in a corpse.[342] Moreover, directions contained in a will with respect to the testator's remains are not legally binding,[343] the executor having the right to determine the place and manner of burial.[344] However, because human organs are important for transplant purposes, legislation has been enacted in the several provinces to govern gifts of human tissue both *inter vivos* and after death. The Ontario legislation is the *Human Tissue Gift Act*.[345]

---

339 Report in the *Toronto Star*, April 17, 1982, p. A-18.
340 See *Leach v. Edgar* (1990), 30 E.T.R. 65 (B.C.C.A.).
341 See *Re Wishart Estate* (1992), 46 E.T.R. (N.B.Q.B.).
342 *R. v. Handyside* (1770), 2 East P.C. 652.
343 *Williams v. Williams* (1882), 20 Ch. D. 659, [1881-5] All E.R. Rep. 840.
344 *Hunter v. Hunter*, 65 O.L.R. 586, [1930] 4 D.L.R. 255.
345 R.S.O. 1990, c. H.20.

Space forbids a detailed treatment of this matter, but the materials cited below may be found useful.

Further Reading

Castel, "Legal Implications of Biomedical Science and Technology in the Twenty-First Century" (1973), 51 Can. Bar Rev. 119.

Skegg, "Human Corpses, Medical Specimens and the Law of Property" (1975), Anglo-Am. L.R. 412.

Sugiyama, "Inter Vivos Transplantation and The Human Tissue Gift Act, S.O. 1971, c. 83" (1976), 34 U.T. Fac. L. Rev. 124.

Dickens, "The Control of Living Body Materials" (1977), 27 U.T.L.J. 142.

Dickens, "Legal Evolution of the Concept of Brain Death," 2 Transplantation Today 60 (1985).

"Uniform Human Tissue Act," Report of the Alberta Commissioners, Unif. L. Conf. 199 (1987).

Blumstein, "Government's Role in Organ Transplantation Policy," 14 J. of Health Politics, Policy and Law 5 (1989).

Prottas, "The Rules for Asking and Answering: The Role of Law in Organ Donation," 63 U. of Detroit L. Rev. 183 (1985).

Cotton and Sandler, "The Regulation of Organ Procurement and Transplantation in the United States," 7 J. of Leg. Med. 55 (1986).

E. Richard Gold, *Body Parts: Property Rights and the Ownership of Human Biological Materials* (Washington: Georgetown University Press, 1996).

5

TESTAMENTARY CAPACITY, UNDUE INFLUENCE, FRAUD AND MISTAKE

1. INTRODUCTION

When the executors named in the will make application for probate [in Ontario: application for certificate of appointment of estate trustee with a will], they must normally establish a number of matters, although some of these are presumed if no one contests the application and the will appears to be in good order.[1] These matters include proof: (1) that the testator satisfied the statutory age requirement to make a will; (2) that the will was executed in accordance with the statutory requirements and was not revoked; (3) that the testator knew and understood the contents and that the will was not affected by mistake; and (4) that the testator had testamentary capacity. If probate is contested, those opposing probate may allege that the will fails because one or more of these matters was not satisfied, but they do not have to prove their allegations. In addition, or in alternative, those opposing probate may allege that the will was procured by: (1) undue influence; or (2) fraud. They have the onus of establishing these allegations. Execution and revocation are discussed in the next two chapters. In this chapter we discuss the others.

It is rather obvious that a will cannot be probated if the testator lacked the mental capacity to make it. It is equally obvious that the will cannot be probated if the testator did not know and understand the contents of the will. For example, if a mistake was made in the will, either by the testator or the drafter, it may be that the testator did not know and approve all or part of the will and, if so, the will, or part of it, may be refused probate. Mistake is not the only aspect of knowledge and approval, however, so the two topics are discussed separately in this chapter.

It is also obvious that a will ought not to be probated if the testator was subjected to undue influence at the time it was made, or if fraud was practised upon the

---

1 There is a presumption that a duly executed will that is rational on its face is, absent evidence to the contrary, the will of a person of competent understanding: *Re Nelson Estate* (1999), 31 E.T.R. (2d) 230 (B.C. S.C.).

testator, for then the document does not represent the free expression of the testator's will.

It will be apparent that a solicitor who receives instructions to prepare a will is in a unique position to observe and form an opinion about the mental capacity of the testator. Similarly, the solicitor will be able to consider evidence of undue influence. The courts have on occasion criticised solicitors for failing to make note of such observations. A later chapter deals with the solicitor's duty when taking instructions for a will.

Further Reading

Macdonell, Sheard and Hull on Probate Practice, 3rd ed. by Rodney Hull and Ian M. Hull (Scarborough: Carswell, 1996), ch. 2.

Thomas G. Feeney, *The Canadian Law of Wills*, Vol. 1, *Probate* (3rd ed., 1987), chs. 2, 3.

Mellows: The Law of Succession, 5th ed. by Clive V. Margrave-Jones (London: Butterworths, 1993), ch. 5.

Albert H. Oosterhoff, "Testamentary Capacity, Suspicious Circumstances and Undue Influence" (1999), 18 E.T. & P.J. 369.

2. AGE REQUIREMENT

At common law, males of fourteen and females of twelve years of age were competent to make a will of personalty, this being the civil law rule which was adopted by the ecclesiastical courts.[2] In contrast, although the first *Statute of Wills* of 1540[3] did not address the question, an amendment two years later[4] provided that only persons 21 years of age or older could make a valid will of real property. The English *Wills Act* of 1837[5] made the age of 21 uniform for all except privileged wills and this provision was adopted in all the common law provinces of Canada.

Legislation in Canada has, however, reduced the age of majority and, accordingly the age at which a person may make a valid will.[6] Unfortunately the ages vary across the country. They are: 18 in Alberta, Manitoba, Saskatchewan and Prince Edward Island; 19 in British Columbia, New Brunswick, Nova Scotia, the Northwest Territories and Yukon Territory; and 17 in Newfoundland.

Most of the statutes make exceptions to the rule in the case of a person who is or has been married or is contemplating marriage, and of a person who is a

---

2 *Bishop v. Sharp* (1704), 2 Vern. 469, 23 E.R. 902.
3 32 Hen. 8, c.1.
4 *Statute of Wills*, 34 & 35 Hen. 8, c. 5, s. 14 (1542).
5 7 Will 4 & 1 Vict., c. 26, s. 7. The age was reduced to 18 by the *Family Law Reform Act 1969*, c. 46, s. 3(1) (U.K.), amending s. 7 of the *Wills Act*.
6 In Ontario the age of majority was reduced to eighteen by the *Age of Majority and Accountability Act*, S.O. 1971, c. 98, s. 1, which took effect on Sept. 1, 1971. See now R.S.O. 1990, c. A.7.

member of the armed forces or a sailor at sea. Section 8 of the *Succession Law Reform Act*,[7] reproduced below is representative.

SUCCESSION LAW REFORM ACT
R.S.O. 1990, c. S.26

8. (1) A will made by a person who is under the age of eighteen years is not valid unless at the time of making the will the person,

    (a) is or has been married;

    (b) is contemplating marriage and the will states that it is made in contemplation of marriage to a named person except that such a will is not valid unless and until the marriage to the named person takes place;

    (c) is a member of a component of the Canadian Forces,

        (i) that is referred to in the *National Defence Act* (Canada) as a regular force, or

        (ii) while placed on active service under the *National Defence Act* (Canada); or

    (d) is a sailor and at sea or in the course of a voyage.

(2) A certificate purporting to be signed by or on behalf of an officer having custody of the records certifying that he or she has custody of the records of the force in which a person was serving at the time the will was made, setting out that the person was at that time a member of a regular force or was on active service within clause (1)(c), is proof in the absence of evidence to the contrary, of that fact.

(3) A person who has made a will under subsection (1) may, while under the age of eighteen years, revoke the will.

Comparable Legislation

Probate Act R.S.P.E.I. 1988, c. P-21, ss. 60, 63; *Wills Act*, R.S.A. 1980, c. W-11, s. 9; R.S.B.C. 1996, c. 489, s. 7; R.S.M. 1988, c. W150, s. 8; R.S.N.B. 1973, c. W-9, s. 8; R.S.N. 1990, c. W-10, s. 3; R.S.N.S. 1989, c. 505, s. 4; S.S. 1996, c. W-14.1, ss. 4-6; R.S.N.W.T. 1988, c. W-5, s. 4; R.S.Y. 1986, c. 179, s. 4.

Notes and Questions

1. The statutes referred to above are not all identical. Thus, for example, they do not all provide for a will made by a minor in contemplation of marriage. Further, the Yukon legislation contains no exception for married minors and the Newfoundland statute contains no exceptions at all.[8]

2. The section dealing with the form of privileged wills[9] differs in some respects from the provisions of section 8(1)(c) and (2). Under section 5 only a member of the Canadian

---

7 R.S.O. 1990, c. S.26.

8 For the statutory references see above.

9 *Succession Law Reform Act, supra*, s. 5.

forces placed on active service, and not any member of a regular force, may make a privileged will. However, the right to make such a will is extended to members of the naval, land and air forces, while on active service, of other countries. It follows, therefore, that a will made by a member of a regular force which is part of the Canadian armed forces may make a valid will while under the age of eighteen, but, unless he or she has been placed on active service, it must either be holograph and executed accordingly, or formal and executed as a formal will.

3. Except for the disabilities of age, discussed in this part, and unsoundness of mind, discussed in the next, there are no other disabilities that would prohibit the making of a will. The former disability of alienage has been removed by statute.[10] Similarly, a married woman can now freely make a will.[11]

At common law traitors and felons could not make a will, since their real property escheated by reason of corruption of their blood consequent upon their being attainted of treason or felony and their personal property became forfeit to the Crown. This was abolished by the *Criminal Code*.[12]

3. KNOWLEDGE AND APPROVAL

A will cannot be probated if the testator did not know its contents. Hence, the propounders must prove that the testator knew and approved the contents of the will at the time of execution. However, they are aided by a rebuttable presumption that the testator knew and approved the contents once the propounders prove that the will was properly executed after it was read to or by the testator and the testator appeared understand it.[13] The presumption is rebutted if it shown that the testator did not really understand the contents of the will even though it was read to or by the testator.[14] On the other hand, if there are suspicious circumstances, such as when a beneficiary has prepared the will or has been instrumental in having the will prepared, the propounders must prove knowledge and approval affirmatively.[15]

The concept of knowledge and approval is separate from the concepts of testamentary capacity and undue influence, although these may and often do overlap. Thus, for example, a testator who lacks testamentary capacity may also not know and approve of the contents of the will. However, a testator may also

---

10 *Citizenship Act*, R.S.C. 1985, c. C-29, ss. 34-38; *Aliens' Real Property Act*, R.S.O. 1990, c. A.18, s. 1; *Property Law Act*, R.S.B.C. 1996, c. 377, s. 39; *Law of Property Act*, R.S.M. 1987, c. L90, ss. 1, 2; *Property Act*, R.S.N.B. 1973, c. P-19, s. 10; *Real Property Act*, R.S.N.S. 1989, c. 385, s. 2.

11 *Equality of Status of Married Persons Act*, S.S. 1984-85, c. E-10.3, s. 2; *Family Law Act*, R.S.N. 1990, c. F-2, s. 72; R.S.O. 1990, c. F.3, s. 64; S.P.E.I. 1995, c. 12 , s. 59; *Law and Equity Act*, R.S.B.C. 1996, c. 253, s. 60; *Married Women's Act*, R.S.A. 1980, c. M-7, s. 3; *Married Women's Property Act*, R.S.N.B. 1973, c. M-4, s. 2 (c); R.S.M. 1987, c. M70, s. 3(1); R.S.N.S. 1989, c. 272, s. 4.

12 S.C. 1892, c. 29, s. 965. See now R.S.C. 1985, c. C-46, s. 6(1)(b).

13 *Vout v. Hay*, [1995] 2 S.C.R. 876, 7 E.T.R. (2d) 209, 125 D.L.R. (4th) 432 at 440.

14 *Fulton v. Andrew* (1875), L.R. 7 H.L. 448; *Re Morris*, [1971] P. 62, [1970] 1 All E.R. 1057.

15 *Tyrell v. Painton*, [1894] P. 151 at 159, *per* Davey L.J.

know and approve of the contents of a will, but be subject to undue influence, in which event the document cannot be probated.

The consequences of lack of knowledge and approval vary with the circumstances. If the testator failed to understand the entire will, it cannot be probated. However, if the testator did not understand one clause, or made a mistake about part of the will only, the rest of the will may be probated. This is illustrated by *Russell v. Fraser*.[16] A bank manager suggested to an elderly testatrix, who had testamentary capacity, that she leave the residue of the estate to him. He knew the residue to be substantial, but was unable to show that the testatrix knew it, or that the solicitor who prepared the will on the bank manager's instructions discussed the size of the residue with her. The court concluded that the testatrix did not know the magnitude of the residue of her estate and, therefore, granted probate without the residuary clause.

The court may also refuse probate of parts of a will if the testator was mistaken about them, and probate the balance of the will. Mistake is discussed later in this chapter.

4. MENTAL CAPACITY

(a) Introduction

A person of unsound mind cannot make a valid will. This rule is designed to protect the person who suffers from unsoundness of mind and his or her assets, as well as his or her potential heirs. The state also has an interest in ensuring that the assets of a deceased person are disposed of properly on death.[17]

While it is clear that a person of unsound mind cannot make a valid will, it may be difficult to determine the degree of unsoundness necessary to invalidate a will. There will be no difficulty with the case of the raving lunatic or the case of a person of perfectly sound mind (although the definition of such a mind may be a matter of debate). However, between these two extremes, you are likely to find every degree of mental capacity and incapacity.[18] How do you determine that one testator lacks capacity while the next, who exhibits similar symptoms, has a sound disposing mind?

The problem is exacerbated by the fact that the law on unsoundness of mind in the context of capacity to make a will was laid down in the nineteenth century, well in advance of the development of the modern sciences of psychiatry and psychology. In reading the cases, however, you will discover that while the principles may be firm, each case must be decided on its own facts and references to the facts of similar cases is, in this area of the law, singularly unhelpful.

---

16 (1980), 8 E.T.R. 245, 118 D.L.R. (3d) 733 (B.C.C.A.).

17 See *Piasta v. St. John's Cathedral Boys' School* (1989), 35 E.T.R. 139 at 149, *per* Monnin C.J.M. (Man. C.A.).

18 *Boyse v. Rossborough* (1857), 6 H.L. Cas. 2 at 45, 10 E.R. 1192 (H.L.).

The classic statement of the law of unsoundness of mind is contained in the judgment of Cockburn C.J., in *Banks v. Goodfellow*.[19] His Lordship said:[20]

It is not given to man to fathom the mystery of the human intelligence, or to ascertain the constitution of our sentient and intellectual being. But whatever may be its essence, every one must be conscious that the faculties and functions of the mind are various and distinct, as are the powers and functions of our physical organization. The senses, the instincts, the affections, the passions, the moral qualities, the will, perception, thought, reason, imagination, memory, are so many distinct faculties or functions of the mind. The pathology of mental disease and the experience of insanity in its various forms teach us that while, on the one hand, all the faculties, moral and intellectual, may be involved in one common ruin, as in the case of the raving maniac, in other instances one or more only of these faculties or functions may be disordered, while the rest are left unimpaired and undisturbed; — that while the mind may be overpowered by delusions which utterly demoralize it and unfit it for the perception of the true nature of surrounding things, or for the discharge of the common obligations of life, there often are, on the other hand, delusions which, though the offspring of mental disease and so far constituting insanity, yet leave the individual in all other respects rational, and capable of transacting the ordinary affairs and fulfilling the duties and obligations incidental to the various relations of life. No doubt when delusions exist which have no foundation in reality, and spring only from a diseased and morbid condition of the mind, to that extent the mind must necessarily be taken to be unsound; just as the body, if any of its parts or functions is affected by local disease, may be said to be unsound, though all its other members may be healthy, and their powers or functions unimpaired. But the question still remains, whether such partial unsoundness of the mind, if it leaves the affections, the moral sense, and the general power of the understanding unaffected, and is wholly unconnected with the testamentary disposition, should have the effect of taking away the testamentary capacity.

We readily concede that where a delusion has had . . . or is calculated to have had, an influence on the testamentary disposition, it must be held to be fatal to its validity. Thus if, as occurs in a common form of monomania, a man is under a delusion that he is the object of persecution or attack, and makes a will in which he excludes a child for whom he ought to have provided; though he may not have adverted to that child as one of his supposed enemies, it would be but reasonable to infer that the insane condition had influenced him in the disposal of his property.

The Chief Justice further stated:[21]

It is essential to the exercise of [the power of testation] that a testator shall understand the nature of the act and its effects; shall understand the extent of the property of which he is disposing; shall be able to comprehend and appreciate the claims to which he ought to give effect; and, with a view to the latter object, that no disorder of the mind shall poison his affections, pervert his sense of right, or prevent the exercise of his natural faculties - that no insane delusion shall influence his will in disposing of his property and bring about a disposal of it which, if the mind had been sound, would not have been made.

Here, then, we have the measure of the degree of mental power which should be insisted on. If the human instincts and affections, or the moral sense, become perverted by mental disease; if insane suspicion, or aversion, take the place of natural affection; if reason and judgment are lost, and the mind becomes a prey to insane delusions calculated to interfere with and disturb its functions, and to lead to a testamentary disposition, due only to their baneful influence - in such a case it is obvious that the condition of the testamentary power fails, and that a will made under such circumstances ought not to stand. But what if the mind, though possessing sufficient power, undisturbed by frenzy or delusion, to take into account all the considerations necessary to the

---

19 (1870), L.R. 5 Q.B. 549.
20 *Ibid.*, at pp. 560-1.
21 *Ibid.*, at pp. 565-6.

proper making of a will, should be subject to some delusion, but such delusion neither exercises nor is calculated to exercise any influence on the particular disposition, and a rational and proper will is the result; ought we, in such case, to deny to the testator the capacity to dispose of his property by will?

It must be borne in mind that the absolute and uncontrolled power of testamentary disposition conceded by the law is founded on the assumption that a rational will is a better disposition than any that can be made by the law itself. If therefore, though mental disease may exist, it presents itself in such a degree and form as not to interfere with the capacity to make a rational disposal of property why, it may be asked, should it be held to take away the right? It cannot be the object of the legislator to aggravate an affliction in itself so great by the deprivation of a right the value of which is universally felt and acknowledged. If it be conceded, as we think it must be, that the only legitimate or rational ground for denying testamentary capacity to persons of unsound mind is the inability to take into account and give due effect to the considerations which ought to be present to the mind of a testator in making his will, and to influence his decision as to the disposal of his property, it follows that a degree or form of unsoundness which neither disturbs the exercise of the faculties necessary for such an act, nor is capable of influencing the result, ought not to take away the power of making a will, or place a person so circumstanced in a less advantageous position than others with regard to this right.

It may be here not unimportant to advert to the law relating to unsoundness of mind arising from another cause - namely, from want of intelligence occasioned by defective organization, or by supervening physical infirmity or the decay of advancing age, as distinguished from mental derangement, such defect of intelligence being equally a cause of incapacity. In these cases it is admitted on all hands that though the mental power may be reduced below the ordinary standard, yet if there be sufficient intelligence to understand and appreciate the testamentary act in its different bearings, the power to make a will remains.

It will be apparent from the foregoing that the law distinguishes two types of unsound mind in the context of capacity to make a will, namely: (1) a general insanity, whether caused by disease, congenital defect or advancing age; and (2) insane delusions. We discuss these two types separately below.

You should note, however, that lack of capacity may also arise for other reasons. Thus, for example, a person who makes a will while heavily under the influence of alcohol or drugs may be found to have lacked capacity.[22] Further, if death occurs shortly after the making of the will those who seek to prove the will must inform the court of the cause of death and the state of mind of the deceased before death. For the court must determine whether the deceased had capacity when the will was made.[23]

(b) General Insanity

The expression "sound disposing mind" connotes that the testator understand the nature and extent of his or her property, the moral claims of his or her dependants and the reasons for excluding any of those who have such a claim. As Lord Erskine said in *Harwood v. Baker*,[24]

---

22 *Re Bradbury Estate* (1996), 13 E.T.R. (2d) 67 (Alta. Surr. Ct.).

23 Thus, for example, the propounder cannot simply assume that a note left by the deceased was a suicide note. Failure to prove the cause of death or the state of mind of the deceased will result in a denial of probate. See *Arkley v. Nestoruk* (1996), 14 E.T.R. (2d) 93 (Y.T. S.C.).

24 (1840), 3 Moo. P.C. 282 at 291, 13 E.R. 117.

Their Lordships are of opinion that, in order to constitute a sound disposing mind, a testator must not only be able to understand that he is by his will giving the whole of his property to one object of his regard, but he must also have capacity to comprehend the extent of his property, and the nature of the claims of others, whom by his will he is excluding from all participation in that property; and that the protection of the law is in no cases more needed than it is in those where the mind has been too much enfeebled to comprehend more objects than one; and more especially, when that one object may be so forced upon the attention of the invalid as to shut out all others that might require consideration.

If the above test is not satisfied, the testator lacked the necessary capacity and the will must fail. On the other hand, if he or she had the necessary capacity according to the above test, it matters not that others would regard the exclusion of someone who had a moral claim upon the testator's bounty as unjust,[25] or that the will is eccentric.[26] Thus, in *Boughton v. Knight*[27] Sir James Hannen stated:

The law does not say that a man is incapacitated from making a will if he proposes to make a disposition of his property moved by capricious, frivolous, mean or even bad motives.... He may disinherit, either wholly or partially, his children, and leave his property to strangers to gratify his spite, or to charities to gratify his pride, and we must give effect to his will, however much we may condemn the course he has pursued.

The above principles were applied in *Leger v. Poirier*,[28] set out below.

LEGER v. POIRIER
[1944] S.C.R. 152, [1944] 3 D.L.R. 1
Supreme Court of Canada

The testatrix died in 1942 at age 79. From 1918, when her husband died, to 1936 she operated the business started by him. In the latter year she transferred it to her son, Hector Poirier. She had been a vigorous and capable woman, but her health began to fail in the fall of 1941. In 1939 Hector and his wife and large family moved in with her and remained there until her death. In August 1941, Hector engaged a grandniece, Rose Gosselin, aged 17, to help the testatrix look after herself and to get about the house. She testified that, in spite of the testatrix' protests, Hector kept the front door of the house locked and would admit no one to visit his mother until the visitor had passed his or his wife's scrutiny. The testatrix told the wife of her grandson, Adrien, and a Mrs. Lasnier, who had been brought up by her, to enter by the back door to visit her, but Hector showed such hostility to their visits that he ordered them out of the house on two occasions. The testatrix had objected to Hector and his family moving in with her and asked them to leave on a number of occasions and had spoken to her priest and her solicitor about it.

---

25 *Ibid.*
26 *Beal v. Henri*, [1950] O.R. 780 at 786, [1951] 1 D.L.R. 260 (C.A.), *per* Hogg J.A.; *Pilkington v. Gray*, [1899] A.C. 401 (P.C.).
27 (1873), L.R. 3 P. & D. 64 at 66.
28 [1944] S.C.R. 152, [1944] 3 D.L.R. 1.

In November, 1941, Hector arranged with his mother's solicitor, a Mr. Robichaud, to come to the house to prepare a will for her, although the evidence did not disclose who first raised the matter. Before Robichaud appeared, Hector had a conversation with his mother and Rose Gosselin was present during part of this conversation. She testified that Hector would suggest legacies and that the mother would repeat them and agree to them. The legacies included two gifts of $2,000 each to her grandchildren, Adrien and Yvette, of whom she was fond. However, she refused to leave her house to Hector. Robichaud testified that when he saw the testatrix, she was in a very feeble condition. The will named Hector executor.

Byrne, Probate judge, admitted the will to probate and the Supreme Court of New Brunswick, Appeal Division, dismissed the appeal by the testatrix's granddaughter, Mrs. Yvette Leger, and grandson, Joseph Adrien Michaud.

RAND J., delivered the judgment of Rinfret C.J. and Kerwin, Taschereau and Rand JJ.:

. . .

Shortly after three o'clock Robichaud was shown upstairs by the son who remained in his mother's presence at least until the gifts of $2,000 were mentioned. He told the granddaughter, Mrs. Yvette Leger, when the will was produced by him to be read, that he did not know its contents: but a letter to Mrs. Lasnier of December 1st in evidence, the fact that the document had been handed to him by Robichaud following its execution, and his complete assumption of authority over his mother's affairs thereafter, refute that statement.

Now, the mother had made a will in 1939 in which the son was bequeathed $2,000, the grandson $5,000, and the residue, less a small bequest for masses, left to the granddaughter. The executors were the last named and a Father Robichaud. This distribution was repeated in another drawn in 1940 in which a Father Poirier was named executor, the circumstances of the execution of which, however, on the objection of the respondent, were not allowed to be proven. Father McKenna, who drew both wills, says, apropos of having a lawyer, that she seemed "to have some kind of fear of lawyers and implicit faith in the clergy". The first of these instruments was executed in the home of the grandson. The will of 1941, of an estate of approximately $24,000, gave to each of the grandchildren $2,000 and, with a provision of $300 for masses, the residue to the son. This gives the latter about $17,500 more than he would receive under the prior instruments.

Apparently the will of 1940 was kept in a locked satchel, the key of which was carried by the mother in a small bag. Some time in October the Gosselin girl got it for the mother who kept it for a week or so and then had it locked up again. About the 14th of November, a date remembered by the girl in relation to wages due on the 13th which the mother, for the first time, forgot to pay, the small bag, in which money was also kept, disappeared. On the next day, when the loss was noticed, the mother, as she then so often did, began to cry. The girl went to Hector about it. He told her the bag had been dropped into the toilet from which he had recovered it and that he had put it in the safe in the store where it would remain. Whether the explanation given was true or not there is no way of deciding. This incident is clearly recalled by the girl as happening after the mother's mind and memory had become seriously weakened, from the effect of which her habits and controls, even as to natural functions, had become disorganized: and as the date is not disputed, it becomes a most material circumstance in her story. The satchel remained in the house and beyond doubt came into the possession of the son, but we know nothing more of its contents. This concurrence of circumstances, in which the son comes into control of the satchel containing the will and a new document appears within a week, while the mother is in or approaching a critical stage of illness, is too striking to be quite disregarded.

The mother had visited Yvette in Ottawa in 1940 and had written the grand-daughter if she might spend the winter of 1941-42 with her, but later on decided she was not well enough to travel so far and would have to put the visit off. There is no doubt of the affectionate regard in which she held the granddaughter: and on several occasions, when alone with the Gosselin girl, she had remarked that her "property" was "for Yvette".

The grandson had enlisted in 1940 and left Halifax for overseas on July 21st, 1941. About a week before this departure, his grandmother had visited him at Sussex, New Brunswick, in camp there and what passed between them can best be given in his words:

> Yes, when my grandmother was down to see me in Sussex, we were left alone about an hour and my wife and my mother-in-law were away. My grandmother mentioned at the time that even if I were going overseas, that she was looking after my family in spite of the fact that I mightn't return from overseas. She told me that she was leaving me $5,000. The way the conversation led to that was that she asked me if I would be very glad if she would keep an eye on my family. It was a young family and anything she would do to help them out would be very much appreciated by myself. That led to her statement, saying she was leaving me $5,000 in her will.

In 1935 or 1936 the mother had conveyed to the son the land adjoining her home on which the store building stood, with, so far as the evidence goes, the business carried on in it. There is nothing in the case to indicate what the value of this property was.

The deceased had been attended by Dr. Coffyn and during either November or the early part of December suffered a nervous disturbance which brought about a severe mental confusion. There are documents in evidence which purport to record visits on November 25th and December 3rd and he fixes the latter as the date of the minor stroke; but admittedly this was only his recollection of the occurrence in May, 1942. Admittedly, too, none of the documents brought forward by him were originals; they were said to be copies made in May, 1942, or later after the controversy had arisen; and the trial judge was quite justified in declining to place any reliance in them whatever. His comment, too, that "this witness displayed, in my opinion, some of those attributes of advocacy which, however unconscious, are not wholly devoid of partiality", was quite warranted. On the 15th of December, Mrs. Michaud, wife of the grandson, after having had almost to force her way into the house, found the mother dishevelled, "terribly failed", helpless in mind and body. Around Christmas Mrs. Leger paid a hurried visit to Bathurst but the son had given orders before she arrived that she was not to be left alone at any time with her grandmother and she was not. Mrs. Poirier was at the height of her confusion at this time and it is doubtful if she recognized the granddaughter. Later on, in January, when it is claimed she was somewhat improved, the son paid the Gosselin girl off before the month was up, ostensibly on the ground that his mother was then able to look after herself. Toward the end of February a more severe paralysis set in, from the effects of which she died in a few days.

Now, although the condition of the mother in August and September was fair, there is no doubt of marked deterioration as the fall wore on. The girl stresses the loss of memory, loss of initiative, a disintegration of habits, inability to carry on conversation, childishness, a tendency to repetition of words addressed to her, and apathy; "she would ask us something that had no sense. If we refused her she would cry"; "we would talk to her and she wouldn't answer". The girl tells us also that the failure of memory was commented on by the son's wife in connection with a remark, made by the latter, that the mother had asked the son "to make her will", but whether before or after November 21st is not clear. Neither is it wholly clear whether the marked change in memory, insisted upon by the Gosselin girl as taking place before the making of the will, was a result of the minor nervous seizure, "not exactly a stroke, although her face was twisted and her tongue refused to talk properly", as Dr. Coffyn puts it. Some time in November she presented a "glassy stare" to the wife of the grandson. No doubt to some degree she could be aroused but the picture is clear of a pronounced declension in her physical and mental condition. Although Dr. Coffyn spoke of "visits that I cannot remember the dates" of in November, his records show only one attendance. In any event, he would be concerned chiefly with questions as to which memory would play little, if any, part . . .

. . .

The veracity of this girl, the chief witness to the essential facts, is conceded; the only challenge is as to the accuracy of her recollection of the precise time when the breakdown in memory took place. But the fact on which she was most emphatic was that that collapse preceded the will; she felt the elderly lady was being put to something beyond her condition; "she had no commonsense in November".

Now, we know the intentions of this woman as to the disposition of her property at a time when she was in good health and able to look after her own affairs, and that those intentions, so far as the evidence discloses them, continued up to the day of signing the impeached will. Although the solicitor knew of her relatives, he made no enquiries of any sort regarding them, or her property, or an existing will. His opportunity to judge of her memory was of the most limited kind. According to the second witness, Meahan, throughout the time he was present, during which the will was read aloud and executed, not a word was uttered by Mrs. Poirier and she was unable to sign her name to the document.

These facts cast on the whole case such a doubt of the competency of the testatrix as, in my opinion, requires us to say that the onus of showing the document to be the will of a "free and capable" person has not been met. The direct evidence of Rose Gosselin remains uncontradicted by either of the only persons actually in a position to do it, the son and the wife. Neither took the stand;

and the sudden and radical reversal of benefits remains unexplained, save by the state of mind and memory portrayed by the girl.

The findings of the trial judge on the point of capacity are neither clear nor satisfactory.

[His Lordship quoted excerpts from the judgment of the trial judge continued:]

Throughout the trial he seemed to labour under the impression either that the prior wills and other evidences of intention were irrelevant or that they could be proved only by means that seemingly were not open to the appellants. He had previously stated that the evidence brought forward by the appellants had "not satisfied the onus placed on them of proving conclusively that the testatrix was unduly influenced".

Now, in the majority judgment below, it is clear that both Baxter C.J. and Grimmer J. were powerfully influenced by the view that a pronouncement against the will necessarily involved a reflection upon the integrity of Robichaud, which was repelled by both his standing as a solicitor and the finding of the trial judge. But there is no doubt whatever that we may have testamentary incapacity accompanied by a deceptive ability to answer questions of ordinary and usual matters: that is, the mind may be incapable of carrying apprehension beyond a limited range of familiar and suggested topics. A "disposing mind and memory" is one able to comprehend, of its own initiative and volition, the essential elements of will-making, property, objects, just claims to consideration, revocation of existing dispositions, and the like; this has been recognized in many cases:

Marsh v. Tyrrell and Harding.[29]

It is a great but not an uncommon error to suppose that because a person can understand a question put to him, and can give a rational answer to such question, he is of perfect, sound mind, and is capable of making a will for any purpose whatever; whereas the rule of law, and it is the rule of common sense, is far otherwise: the competency of the mind must be judged of by the nature of the act to be done, and from a consideration of all the circumstances of the case.

Quoting from the *Marquess of Winchester's Case,*[30] Sir John Nicholl adds:

By the law it is not sufficient that the testator be of memory, when he makes his will, to answer familiar and usual questions, but he ought to have a disposing memory so as to be able to make a disposition of his estate with understanding and reason.

Murphy v. Lamphier:[31]

Again the words of Sir John Nicholl are apposite: "To support a paper thus revoking and altering this will and substituting a disposition quite different from and the very opposite to it, would require the clearest and most indisputable evidence": *Dodge v. Meech.*[32]

---

29 (1828), 2 Hagg. Ecc. R. 84 at 122.
30 6 Co. Rep. 23, 77 E.R. 287.
31 (1914), 31 O.L.R. 287 at 308.
32 (1828), 1 Hagg. Ecc. 612, 617.

Menzies v. White.[33]

Merely to be able to make rational responses is not enough, nor to repeat a tutored formula of simple terms. There must be a power to hold the essential field of the mind in some degree of appreciation as a whole, and this I am satisfied was not present here.

I would, therefore, allow the appeal and direct that the judgment of the Probate Court be reversed and the document propounded be declared to be not the last will of the deceased. Because of special circumstances surrounding the controversy, however, all costs should be out of the estate.

[The concurring opinion of Hudson J., has been omitted.]

Notes and Questions

1. *Re Davis*[34] is also an instructive case on the issue of capacity. Mrs. Davis was a widow in her mid-sixties. After her husband died of cancer, she commenced living with her sister and brother-in-law, since she was unable to look after herself. She suffered from a cardio-vascular and a kidney condition and from arteriosclerosis. In consequence, she became forgetful, would leave taps running and was careless with fire. Further, her condition produced a complete personality change. Whereas previously she had lived a modest retiring and respectable widow, she became extraordinarily fond of the opposite sex and become infatuated with an old man who lived in a shack on the wrong side of town. The shack lacked all modern conveniences. She composed some verses in which she dignified his humble abode with the title "Ted's castle on the hill" and which she had set to music at her own expense. She assured all and sundry that she was in love and developed a compulsive urge to remove her clothing in the presence of male persons. She also spoke constantly of adopting a child and was obsessed with ridding the world of cancer.

Her previously loving attitude towards her family and close friends altered markedly, since they tried to restrict her untoward behaviour. In fact, she could not be left alone because of her loss of memory. Independent witnesses testified that she would talk incessantly about whatever happened to occupy her mind at the time, whether it was her old male "friend," cancer, or adoption.

The testatrix had made four previous wills, all of which divided her estate among her family. However, for her last will she instructed a different solicitor who did not inquire closely into her affairs. It left her estate to a non-existent cancer society.

The trial judge refused to admit the last will to probate and in considering the evidence, he gave little weight to the evidence of the attending physician and the solicitor on the ground that it was vague and unsatisfactory. Instead, he preferred the evidence of lay witnesses.

On this point, Schroeder J.A., who delivered the judgment of the Court of Appeal, dismissing the appeal, said:[35]

---

33 (1862), 9 Gr. 574.
34 [1963] 2 O.R. 666, 40 D.L.R. (2d) 801.
35 At D.L.R. 809-10.

A perusal of the evidence fails to convince me that the learned Judge's reasons for preferring the evidence of the lay witnesses to that of the doctor are not fully warranted. In the present case it appears from the judgment that the learned Judge made full judicial use of his opportunity of hearing the *viva voce* evidence. While his findings depend in part on inferences from proven facts, this is not in a case in which an appellate Court would be justified in substituting its view of the evidence for that of the learned trial Judge.

Whether a person has testamentary capacity, *i.e.*, whether he has a sound and disposing mind, raises a practical question which, so far at least as evidence based on observation and experience is concerned, as contrasted with evidence based on pathological findings, may be answered by laymen of good sense as by doctors.

His Lordship then addressed the issue of the difference between the first four wills and the last:[36]

In the present case the will of May 26, 1959, in which the deceased woman's whole estate was bequeathed to the Harriston Branch of the Ontario Cancer Treatment & Research Foundation, presents a marked departure from the scheme of her previous testamentary dispositions, and more particularly it stands out as an entire subversion of the dispositions made in the testamentary instruments of May 4th and May 6th, 1959. This is a circumstance of vital significance which raises *in limine* the question as to whether the deceased woman's capacity was adequate to the making of the subsequent and entirely varied disposition of her estate.

In *Harwood v. Baker*[37] Erskine, J., stated:[38]

If he (the testator) had not the capacity required, the propriety of the disposition made by the Will is a matter of no importance. If he had it, the injustice of the exclusion would not affect the validity of the disposition, *though the justice or injustice might cast some light upon the question as to his capacity.*

In that case emphasis was laid upon the fact that the will was a total departure from, and contrary to, the previous expressed intentions of the testator.

His Lordship also addressed the evidence and argument that Mrs. Davis was able to conduct her business affairs normally. On this point he said:[39]

While that evidence is entitled to careful consideration and must be given its proper weight, nevertheless, a person may have a mind of sufficient soundness and discretion to regulate his affairs in general, yet if in some manner dominion be obtained over him as to prevent his exercising his discretion in the making of his will, he cannot be considered as having such a disposing mind as will give effect to his will. He may be sane in the ordinary sense of the word and yet lack real testamentary capacity. . . .

In my opinion it is reasonable to conclude that when the testatrix stated that she wanted to leave her property to rid the world of cancer she was no longer thinking at all of the property which she at one time regarded as property which she was obligated to dispose of in favour of specific persons or in a particular manner. She was therefore unable at the time of making the impugned will to dispose of her property with understanding and reason, or with judgment and discernment, hence it was not the will of a person of sound and disposing mind and memory.

The onus of proving testamentary capacity where any dispute or doubt exists upon the matter is cast upon the proponents of the will. Where, as here, the will is an inofficious one and constitutes

---

36 At 40 D.L.R. (2d) 810.
37 (1840), 3 Moo. P.C. 282, 13 E.R. 117.
38 *Ibid.*, at P.C. 291.
39 At D.L.R. 817-8.

a marked departure from all prior dispositions and there is a history of progressive impairment of the mental faculties resulting from arteriosclerosis of the cerebral artery producing loss of memory and character changes, with other evidence suggestive of mental deficiency, that burden of proof is considerably increased. In my opinion the evidence falls far short of satisfying the heavy burden resting upon the appellants and I would affirm the judgment below and dismiss the appeal with costs.

2. It is common for the court to prefer the evidence of disinterested non-medical witnesses over that of physicians if the former had a close association with the testator and were able to form a sound judgment of the testator's capacity. This appears from *Leger v. Poirier* and from *Re Davis*, discussed in the preceding note.[40]

The evidence of the solicitor who took instructions for the will and attended on its execution can be particularly important in determining capacity. While the solicitor does not, indeed, cannot warrant capacity, she or he has an excellent opportunity to observe the testator and to determine, by means of probing questions, whether the testator has capacity. The solicitor should keep detailed notes of the discussions, which can be used in evidence when the issue of capacity is tried. Thus, if a solicitor carefully assesses the testatrix's demeanor and answers to questions, reviews the will carefully with her, and concludes that the testatrix has capacity, the solicitor's evidence will be accorded substantial weight.[41]

3. The deceased suffered from depression because of matrimonial problems which ended in a divorce. Her husband remarried. She attempted suicide on one occasion and threatened to kill herself several times. She gained a lot of weight and drank more than was good for her. She thought her family (her former husband and her son and daughter) were rejecting her and when they declined a dinner invitation from her she committed suicide by setting her house on fire. She had been drinking heavily at the time. She left a signed legible note in her purse hanging on a gate at the back of the house. The note was dated the day of her death. It said in part:

> Whenever I wanted something it was *no*. I was no longer good. $20,000.00 for Anne Gase and $20,000.00 for Bianca Gase. Whats [sic] left over you can do as you please.

The persons referred to in the note were her nieces, daughters of her sister in Germany. She corresponded regularly with the sister and had periodically sent her nieces money for Christmas and birthdays. Is the note a valid holograph will, or should it be ruled invalid for lack of capacity on the part of the deceased?[42]

4. A testator who has been declared incapable of managing property[43] does not necessarily lack testamentary capacity.[44] However, it is also true that a testator may be regarded

---

40 See also *Candido v. Ciardullo* (1991), 45 E.T.R. 98 (B.C. S.C.); and *Marquis v. Weston* (1993), 49 E.T.R. 262 (N.B.C.A.)

41 See, *e.g.*, *Stevens v. Crawford* (2000), 31 E.T.R. (2d) 268 (Alta. Surr. Ct.).

42 See *Re Pommerehnke* (1979), 4 E.T.R. 169, 16 A.R. 442 (Surr. Ct.). See also *Hollingsworth v. Boyle* (1926), 30 O.W.N. 413; *Re Wernicke* (1983), 25 Sask R. 120, 15 E.T.R. 197 (sub nom. *Quirk v. Wernicke*).

43 For the procedure to be followed on such an application, see the *Substitute Decisions Act*, S.O. 1992, c. 30, ss. 22-26. It replaced the *Mental Incompetency Act*, R.S.O. 1980, c. 264, s. 39, rep. S.O. 1992, c. 32, s. 21(1).

44 *O'Neil v. Royal Trust Co.*, [1946] S.C.R. 622, [1946] 4 D.L.R. 545; *Can. Permanent Toronto Gen. Trust Co. v. Whitton* (1965), 51 W.W.R. 484 (B.C.S.C.); *Royal Trust Co. v. Rampone*, [1974] 4 W.W.R. 735 (B.C.S.C.); *Allen (Committee of) v. Bennett* (1994), 6 E.T.R. (2d) 176 (B.C.S.C.).

as sane in the sense commonly understood and yet be incapable of making a valid will. This is because the testator may appear to be capable of exercising sound judgment and remembering the names of his or her relations, but, because of advancing age or other reason, does not have a sound disposing mind in that, for no apparent reason, except failure of memory, the deceased has not made provision for some of those who have a moral claim upon his or her bounty.[45] Further, if in the course of establishing inability to manage property, medical evidence also establishes that the testatrix lacks testamentary capacity, a will made at that time is invalid.[46]

5. A testator cannot revoke a will, made while sane, after becoming insane.[47]

6. A testator who suffers from manic depressive symptoms has capacity to make a will when not affected by those symptoms.[48]

7. If you wish to contest the validity of a will for lack of capacity, you must take care not to acquiesce in its validity. If you do acquiesce, you will be estopped from raising the issue of validity later. Thus, for example, if the executors bring an application to construe a will and you do not challenge the validity of the will at that time, but advance an interpretation of the will which the court rejects, the issue of capacity is *res judicata*.[49]

8. Although a person who lacks capacity cannot make a will, in New Brunswick the court has power to make, amend, and revoke the will of a mentally incompetent person, or to direct that the person's committee do so, subject to the court's approval.[50]

(c) Insane Delusions

A person may be generally sane and yet suffer from delusions which affect his or her capacity to make a valid will. An insane delusion is an irrational belief in a state of facts which are not true. *Banks v. Goodfellow*[51] is the *locus classicus* on insane delusions and the excerpts from this case reproduced above define the law on this kind of insanity.

In *Banks* the testator had at one time been confined to a lunatic asylum. He was discharged but remained subject to a number of delusions. He had a violent aversion to a man named Featherstone Alexander and, even though this person had died some years ago, he continued to believe that Alexander still pursued and molested him. He also believed that he was being persecuted and molested by

---

45 See *Lamb v. Brown* (1923), 54 O.L.R. 443. And see *Murphy v. Lamphier* (1914), 31 O.L.R. 287, affirmed 32 O.L.R. 19, 20 D.L.R. 906. The testator may, in fact, have testamentary capacity, but fail to understand and approve of the contents of the will, in which case it must fail: *Rhodes v. Rhodes* (1882), 7 App. Cas. 192 at 199, *per* Lord Blackburn (P.C.). Conversely, the testator may be able to comprehend the terms of the will and yet lack capacity: *Battan Singh v. Amirchand*, [1948] A.C. 161 at 170, *per* Lord Normand.

46 *Malcolm v. Rounds* (1999), 31 E.T.R. (2d) 97 (B.C.C.A.)

47 *Re Brechin* (1973), 38 D.L.R. (3d) 305 (Alta. T.D.).

48 See *Hamilton v. Sutherland* (1992), 45 E.T.R. 229 (B.C.C.A.).

49 See *Sigal v. Isenberg* (1992), 46 E.T.R. 13 (Man. Q.B.).

50 See the *Infirm Persons Act*, R.S.N.B. 1973, c. I-8, ss. 3(4), 11.1, 15(1) (enacted S.N.B. 1994, c. 40, ss. 1, 3, 4); Eric L. Teed and Nicole Cohoon, "New Wills for Incompetents" (1997), 16 E. & T.J. 1. For a case applying this legislation, see *M. (Committee of) H.C.* (1999), 27 E.T.R. (2d) 68 (N.B.Q.B.). Section 39 of the statute extends the legislation to persons incapable of managing their affairs. Such persons may or may not lack capacity to make a will.

51 (1870), L.R. 5 Q.B. 549.

devils and evil spirits and thought them to be physically present. His physician and minister testified to the testator's general insanity. However, he managed his money and affairs competently and there was evidence by lay persons attesting to the fact that the testator was capable when he executed his will. The will, which revoked an earlier one leaving everything to his sister who predeceased him, left his entire estate to his niece, Margaret Goodfellow. She survived him, but died shortly thereafter, leaving the defendant as her heir at law. Other nephews and nieces received nothing. The court held that, in the circumstances, the testator had capacity and that the will was valid. Although the testator was suffering from delusions, they did not have any influence on the provisions of his will and were not capable of having such influence. Moreover, the will was a rational one, since it left the testator's property to a niece who lived with him and who was the object of his affection and regard.

It is, however, apparent from *Banks v. Goodfellow* that if the delusion was one that could influence the dispositions in the will, the will might be invalid even if it was not manifest at the time the will was made, but was latent. This does not mean, however, that the will must be found to be invalid in those circumstances. It will only be invalid if the delusions in fact affected the dispositions made in it. These matters are discussed in *O'Neil v. Royal Trust Co.*,[52] reproduced below.

O'NEIL v. ROYAL TRUST CO.
[1946] S.C.R. 622, [1946] 4 D.L.R. 545
Supreme Court of Canada

The testatrix's husband died in 1919. By his will she was left furniture, $2,000, a monthly payment of $150 for life, and a power to appoint the residue. Her husband requested her in his will to leave the residue to his sister for life with remainder to his two grandnieces. In 1920 she made a will in which she carried out his wishes, but later she had second thoughts, determined that her husband's will was terrible, and made a new will in 1927 in which she left everything to her niece and nephew. In 1929 she became remorseful and made a new will which carried out her husband's wishes. At that time she was confined to a sanitarium, having voluntarily admitted herself, and she remained there until her death in 1943. The sanitarium was operated for the treatment of mental and functional nervous diseases.

The solicitor, Mr. O'Brian, testified that the testatrix appeared mentally clear and alert, with full capacity to appreciate the nature and extent of her estate, and a witness to the will, Mr. Watson, confirmed this evidence. Further, she was conversant with the details of her husband's estate and the contents of her earlier wills, and stated that she had deceived her husband by accumulating money from her housekeeping allowance and had not used that money to ensure that the testator's sister got proper nursing care. The solicitor was fully aware of the testatrix's nervous problems. The psychiatrist who treated her, Dr. McKay, testified that she "had certain peculiarities"; further, she had hallucinations and

---

52 [1946] S.C.R. 622, [1946] 4 D.L.R. 545.

delusions which "were never fixed at any time." The testatrix did speak to the psychiatrist about her worries regarding things she had done to her husband. He believed that she was fully competent to make the will.

On the other hand, in 1930 a court declared her incapable of managing her affairs by reason of mental infirmity arising from age or other reasons and appointed a committee of her estate. The psychiatrist had supplied an affidavit in support of the application in which he detailed her hallucination of taste and smell, and stated that she believed she could taste poison in her food and could smell gas which was forced into her room for the purpose of harming her. However, the psychiatrist drew a distinction between the testatrix's being competent to make a will in 1929 and being incompetent to manage her affairs in 1930. Further, he described the hallucinations as of a minor character, while he referred to her concerns about her husband as "worries" and stated that the two were not associated in her mind.

On other occasions she spoke to Mr. O'Brian, Mr. Watson, and her attending physician, Dr. Gillies, about how depressed she was; that the day seemed to be night at times and the night day; that she seemed to be going out of her mind sometimes; that voices seemed to speak to her at night as if from the grave, putting her in torment; that she felt she would never see her late husband and his sister because she had done them wrong; and that there was no hope for her in the next world.

The manager of the sanitarium office testified that she saw the testatrix every day, that she was bright and alert and a great conversationalist, had a good memory and often spoke of her late husband and sister-in-law, and was friendly with the staff.

The trial judge refused probate, but that decision was reversed on appeal. A further appeal was then brought to the Supreme Court of Canada.

ESTEY J.:

. . .

That Mrs. Brown possessed certain hallucinations and delusions of the type and character described by Dr. McKay must be conceded. The possession of such does not invalidate a will unless they have brought about the will or constituted "an actual and impelling influence" in the making thereof.[53] Dr. McKay describes her concern with respect to her husband's affairs as worries and does not associate the hallucinations and delusions therewith. The other witnesses make no reference to the hallucinations and delusions, and it may be that they looked upon her concern with respect to her husband's affairs in a manner that might be described as worries. Mr. O'Brian said she was "depressed and under great mental strain" and "tormented by her conscience". Mr. Watson said she "seemed to be distressed because she had neglected to bequeath the money and property as her husband had requested her to, and she now desires to make amends".

Messrs. O'Brian, Watson and Dr. Gillies, who heard her make the remarks the appellants so much rely upon, were definitely of the opinion that Mrs. Brown was

---

53 *Sivewright v. Sivewright*, [1920] S.C. (H.L.) 63.

competent to make a will. A perusal of Dr. McKay's evidence as a whole, including his admission, indicates that he believed she was competent to make the will. The credibility of all of these witnesses is admitted. Mr. O'Brian had known Mrs. Brown over a long period of years and had been consulted professionally by her as early as 1920. Dr. McKay had her under his care as a patient since July 1929.

It is possible that a person may conduct herself in a very rational manner, even making a rational will, and still be motivated and governed by insane delusions. That is the reason the authorities require that in such a case as this "we have to go below the surface" and determine if in fact the will be or be not the result of a "free and capable testator".

In 1920 Mrs. Brown complied with her husband's request. In 1927, under the stress of circumstances then obtaining, she disregarded his request. In the course of time and changing circumstances she concluded that she had made a mistake and her conscience now dictated that her husband's request should be complied with. In order to do so she made her will of November 1929.

The proved hallucinations and delusions are not upon the evidence connected with the motives and reasons that led to the making of this will in question. Dr. McKay did not associate her hallucinations and delusions with her worries. In this regard it is significant that Mrs. Brown did not discuss her will with Dr. McKay and never mentioned the taste of poison or the smell of gas to Mr. O'Brian, Mr. Watson or Dr. Gillies. This is an indication that in her mind they were not related. Her statements of November 28, 1929, and January 23, 1930, already discussed, when read in relation to all the other facts and circumstances, are not more than the extreme or extravagant expressions of one's thoughts and feelings who finds herself in some such position as Mrs. Brown.

In my opinion, when the evidence in this case is submitted to the test, so often quoted with approval, set forth in *Banks v. Goodfellow*[54] and which has been adopted in this Court, particularly in *Skinner v. Farquharson*[55] and *Ouderkirk et al. v. Ouderkirk*.[56] Mrs. Brown's will must be regarded as valid.

Counsel for the appellants, in a very forceful and exhaustive presentation of this case, contended that the learned Judges of the Court of Appeal "did not appreciate that there is a much greater burden of proof when the facts actually show insanity or mental derangement". It is true that some of the early authorities go far to justify such a statement. The decision of *Banks v. Goodfellow*,[57] makes it clear that these earlier authorities go too far. That while the burden of proof always rests upon the party supporting the will, and that the existence of proved hallucinations and delusions often presents a "difficult and delicate investigation", it remains a question of fact to be determined as in civil cases by a balance of probabilities. In the determination of this fact the contents of the will and all the surrounding circumstances must be considered by the jury or the Court called

---

54 (1870), L.R. 5 Q.B. 549 at 565.
55 (1902), 32 S.C.R. 58.
56 [1936] 2 D.L.R. 417, [1936] S.C.R. 619.
57 *Supra.*

upon to arrive at a decision. If satisfied that at the relevant time the testator was not impelled or directed by hallucinations or delusions and in possession of testamentary capacity, the will is valid.[58]

RAND J.:

. . .

Once there is shown the existence of a delusion which is calculated to influence the testator in making the dispositions of a will, then the Court must be convinced that in fact the delusion had no such effect. What then is the test by which we can say that a delusion is so calculated? Obviously its nature and subject-matter, and its relation in the mind of the testator to the matters material to testamentary disposition. Here, assuming that in the two respects mentioned there were real delusionary notions, they cannot be said, by themselves, to be so calculated and it does not appear that in her mind there was any connection between them and such matters. It is conceivable that the worry over what she looked upon as a moral dereliction gave rise to them — and there is a strange absence of evidence that from the making of the will until her death she was in the slightest degree disturbed — but they were not associated with such matters in her complaints, and nothing in her behaviour indicated that they were so associated either consciously or unconsciously in her mind. It was not fear but moral anxiety that actuated her. The principle, therefore, of *Banks v. Goodfellow*,[59] on the facts, is strictly applicable . . .

> [The concurring opinions of Hudson and Kellock JJ., have been omitted. The court dismissed the appeal.]

Notes and Questions

1. *Skinner v. Farquharson*[60] is an early Canadian case on the subject of delusions and is instructive on this issue. The testator had an estate of approximately $65,000. By his last will he left the family home, most of the furniture and the income on the sum of $15,000 to his wife. She was his second wife and was much younger than he. His daughter received $200 per annum until age 21, and $8,000, certain accumulated income and a piano at age 21. His son received $200 per annum until age 24, and $5,000 and accumulated income thereafter. The remainder interest in the $15,000 was divided among the families of the testator's brothers and sisters. The testator also gave other small legacies. The residue of the estate went equally to the son and daughter. The testator appointed his wife co-executrix with his solicitor and named her the guardian of the two children, who were minors. An earlier will was similar in content, but had left more to the testator's wife and son.

The testator's wife and son attacked the will on the ground that he was subject to the insane delusion that his wife and son were carrying on an incestuous relationship and that this perverted his judgment so as to render him incapable of making a will. Six months

---

58 *Boughton et al. v. Knight* (1873), L.R. 3 P. & D. 64; *Smee et al. v. Smee* (1879), 49 L.J.P. 8; 34 Hals., 2nd ed., p. 38.

59 L.R. 5 Q.B. 549.

60 (1902), 32 S.C.R. 58.

after the will was made, the testator was placed in an insane asylum, but he was not examined for insanity.

The testator did, in fact, speak of the subject to a number of persons, but the solicitor who drafted the will and who had been his adviser for many years, testified that the testator knew what he was about, recognized the claims of his wife and children and others and was concerned that his son did not show sufficient interest in becoming established in life.

The Supreme Court of Canada pronounced in favour of the will, principally on the basis of the solicitor's evidence and the will itself, which was not irrational or unjust. It seemed to the court highly unlikely that the testator would have given his wife and son such generous amounts and have appointed her co-executrix and guardian of the children if the delusion perverted his mind. They concluded that if there was a delusion, it did not affect him at the time he made his will.

2. Wills have been struck down for the following delusions which resulted in a partial or total disinheritance of the testator's family: a belief that the testator was the illegitimate son of George IV;[61] a belief that a relative was stealing his property;[62] a delusion that the testator's daughter had wired his chair and given him electric shocks;[63] and a delusion about the immoral character of the testator's wife at age 70 and his groundless suspicion that she was entertaining men for immoral purposes.[64]

3. A will cannot be set aside if the alleged delusion can be explained, as where a testator failed to leave anything to one son because he was displeased with that son on account of his business disputes with his brothers.[65] Similarly, if the testator has disinherited his

---

61 *Smee v. Smee* (1879), 5 P.D. 84. Such claims, delusional or otherwise, seem to have been common. There is a tombstone in Mount Pleasant Cemetery in London, Ontario, the inscription on which reads:

In
Memory of
LAVINIA HERMIONE
GERTRUDE AMANDA
GUELPH
Daughter of George 4th
and wife of
GEORGE WETHERBEE
— died —
Jan. 25, 1867
Aged 46 Yrs.

"Princess Amanda," as she preferred to be known, settled in London with her husband at the close of the American Civil War, after their plantation was destroyed by federal troops. She claimed to be the daughter of George IV and Mrs. Fitzherbert, his morganatic wife. Her claims were never proved, nor disproved. See Orlo Miller, *A Century of Western Ontario: The Story of London, "The Free Press," and Western Ontario, 1849-1949* (Westport, Connecticut: Greenwood Press Publishers, 1972 Reprint), pp. 177-8. It has been pointed out, however, that the claim is dubious. Mrs. Fitzherbert was born in 1756 and would, therefore, have been 65 when she allegedly gave birth to Amanda, which is highly unlikely. On the other hand, for the sake of vanity, Amanda may have lied about her age and pretended that she was 20 years or so younger than she was. See Herman Goodden, "The Madness of King George and the Mystery of Princess Amanda," *Scene*, vol. 6, p. 2 (Feb. 23- Mar.1, 1995).

62 *Re Wilcinsky; Schulze v. Ruzas* (1977), 6 A.R. 585 (Surr. Ct.).

63 *Re Barter; Corbett v. Wall*, 13 M.P.R. 359, [1939] 2 D.L.R. 201 (N.B.C.A.).

64 *Ouderkirk v. Ouderkirk*, [1936] S.C.R. 619, [1936] 2 D.L.R. 417.

65 *Re Schwartz*, [1970] 2 O.R. 61, 10 D.L.R. (3d) 15 (C.A.), affirmed (1971), 20 D.L.R. (3d) 313 (S.C.C.).

family and has given all his estate to a stranger because of an aversion to his family arising out of business disputes and because he did not care for them, the will must stand.[66]

4. If there is in fact no "delusion" in the sense defined in the cases, but merely a suspicion or doubt, or even an indifference about the matter, the will should be admitted to probate.

In *Royal Trust Co. v. Ford*[67] the testator's son challenged the will on the ground that his father had an insane delusion regarding his son's legitimacy. In the course of his judgment, Judson J., said:[68]

> Testamentary capacity and competence in general was attacked at trial. However, all allegations raised in opposition to the granting of probate of the 1958 will were dismissed by the trial Judge, excepting the existence of an insane delusion as to the legitimacy of the son. This was based on evidence which showed that the testator had no mental weakness prior to 1965, that his memory was excellent until 1963 or 1964, and that he was astute in business deals and in making numerous amendments to the 1958 will. These findings were affirmed on appeal, but the Court of Appeal substituted its opinion for that of the trial Judge on the issue of the existence of a delusion.
>
> The propounder of a will must prove by a preponderance of evidence that the testator was competent in every respect, and this includes negativing the existence of any insane delusions. On a consideration of all the evidence and in the light of dealing with an otherwise thoroughly competent testator, the trial Judge rejected the contention that a delusion existed. He found that the testator really believed the son to be legitimate, even though he expressed doubt. Although the 1933 will was largely in the son's favour, a separation for 31 years prior to the 1958 will and the reception of bad reports about his son were sufficient reason for a sane testator to change his will. Furthermore, a legacy of $50,000 was inconsistent with a testator having a poisoned mind resulting in the complete rejection of his son, and consistent only with belief in his legitimacy or, at most, doubt. Whether the testator's suspicions were reasonable or not, they were such as a sane man could hold.
>
> Throughout most of the son's life, father and son disregarded each other. The testator's wife undoubtedly played a major role in keeping them apart and in monitoring information concerning each of them. However, by the 1950's, father and son were strangers, and the father said so in very plain terms when he rejected the son's suggestion of a meeting. They would not have known each other had they met. What remained then was the bare fact of paternity. Whether the evidence shows merely an indifference to the son or, at most, a doubt as to legitimacy, this is not sufficient to establish a delusion, much less an insane delusion which motivated the testator to change his will.

5. As is apparent from the foregoing excerpt from *Royal Trust Co. v. Ford*, the onus is on the propounder of the will to prove capacity, including the onus of negativing the existence of an insane delusion. If it is proved that a delusion existed, it must be shown that the delusion did not affect the dispositions in the will.[69] If there is doubt about the matter, the onus has not been met.[70] However, the will itself may show that there was no delusion.[71]

6. Is the dislike of a particular ethnic group, if it has the result that a family member is excluded from the will, a delusion?[72]

---

66 *Beal v. Henri*, [1950] O.R. 780, [1951] 1 D.L.R. 260 (C.A.). See also *Re Darichuk; Darichuk v. Holaday* (1981), 8 Sask. R. 131 (Surr. Ct.).

67 [1971] S.C.R. 831, [1971] 3 W.W.R. 517, 20 D.L.R. (3d) 348.

68 *Ibid.,* at D.L.R. 359.

69 *Ibid.,* at p. 349.

70 See *Smee v. Smee* (1873), L.R. 3 P. & D. 64; *Ouderkirk v. Ouderkirk*, [1936] S.C.R. 619, [1936] 2 D.L.R. 417.

71 See *Skinner v. Farquharson* (1902), 32 S.C.R. 58.

72 *Dynna v. Grant* (1980), 3 Sask. R. 135, 6 E.T.R. 175 (C.A.).

7. The court has jurisdiction to admit part of a will to probate and reject other parts if, for example, a part was obliterated, or was inserted by mistake. Can this jurisdiction be invoked to reject a part of a will that is affected by a delusion?

The court did so in *Re Bohrmann*.[73] The testator made his will in 1926, followed by four codicils, the last of which was dated in 1932. The will made ordinary bequests to relatives servants and charities. However, the 1932 codicil changed the gifts to charities in the will by replacing the word "England" with the words "United States of America."

The testator was capable of managing his private affairs and showed exceptional ability in the investment of his assets. However, toward the end of his life he suffered from a delusion that the London County Council was trying to dispossess him of his house. The council wanted to expropriate it to build a hospital. The testator was found to be a paranoid psychopath. The evidence showed that he had little capacity for human affection and did not like, and dealt harshly with, his relations and acquaintances. In short, he was not a kindly or an affectionate man but, as the trial judge noted, a "most eccentric, very unreasonable, very spoilt and rather useless human being."

Langton J., held that because of the delusion, the part of the fourth codicil which made the changes referred to should be deleted, but that the will and the codicils should otherwise be admitted to probate.

In this technique defensible? Is it not the case that, if the delusion is shown to have affected the disposition, the testator lacked capacity, with the result that the entire instrument fails?

8. *Re Souch*[74] was similar to *Re Bohrmann*.[75] A conveyancer and friend of the testatrix drafted a codicil for her in which a life interest was left to the drafter. The friend prepared the codicil after the testatrix had suffered a number of epileptic fits. There were no delusions, but the court struck down the gift of the income to the drafter, while holding the remainder interest valid.

The correctness of the decisions in *Bohrmann* and *Souch* is open to serious doubt.[76]

9. *Montreal Trust Company et al. v. McKay*[77] is a case which illustrates that delusions may invalidate a will even thought its provisions are reasonable. The testator made provisions for his wife and children that appeared adequate. However, it was demonstrated that he was a paranoid schizophrenic and that his delusions concerning his wife and children resulted in an altered disposition of his estate. The court held that the testator was lacking in testamentary capacity and refused probate of the will.

10. Although a person's mind may be quite deranged in some respects, in other respects the person may be able to function at a very high level of ability. There is a famous story about Dr. William Chester Minor, an Assistant Surgeon (Ret'd), U.S. Army. He had served on the Union side in the Civil War and had been retired because of developing insanity brought on by his army duties. He went to England in 1871 for rest and recuperation and killed someone in London in 1872. Dr. Minor was found not guilty by reason of insanity and was incarcerated in Broadmoor Criminal Lunatic Asylum at Crowthorne, Berkshire, "until Her Majesty's Pleasure be known." He spent the next 38 years there. In 1910 he was released into the custody of his brother and returned to the U.S. where he spent most of the next 10 years in asylums. He died in 1920.

---

73 [1938] 1 All E.R. 271.
74 [1938] O.R. 48, [1938] 1 D.L.R. 563 (C.A.).
75 *Supra*.
76 For an illuminating comment on these cases, see (1938), 16 Can. Bar Rev. 405.
77 (1957), 21 W.W.R. 611 (Alta. S.C.).

While at Broadmoor, he was permitted to amass and keep a substantial library in his cell. When work on the Oxford English Dictionary began in earnest in 1879,[78] the editor, Dr. James Murray, sought the help of a vast number of volunteer readers to supply the many illustrative quotations for words used in the Dictionary. Dr. Minor became an enthusiastic and prolific contributor and in 1896 he and Dr. Murray met and formed a friendship based on their common intellectual pursuit. Dr. Minor's contributions (along with those of others) are acknowledged in the "Appendix to Preface" at p. xv of Vol. 1 of the Dictionary, which was published in 1888.

Dr. Minor suffered from a variety of delusions. For example, he had delusions about people coming into his room at night to molest him while he was sleeping. He believed that the person he killed had come into his room while he slept. When he awoke he went out into the street and seeing someone in the street, assumed it was the person he thought was in the house and shot him. Dr. Minor's condition was first identified as monomania and later as paranoiac dementia praecox. Today it is called paranoid schizophrenia.[79] Would Dr. Minor have had testamentary capacity?[80]

Further Reading

Kenneth I. Shulman, M.D., S.M., "A Psychiatrist Examines Testamentary Capacity"in *Special Lectures of the Law Society of Upper Canada 1996 — Estates[:] Planning, Administration and Litigation* (Toronto: Carswell, 1996), at 89.

(d)   Onus of Proof

(i)   *Generally*

The onus of proving capacity always lies on those who propound the will, that is, typically, the executors. In the leading case, *Barry v. Butlin*,[81] the rule was formulated as follows:[82]

> ...the *onus probandi* lies in every case upon the party propounding a Will; and he must satisfy the conscience of the Court that the instrument so propounded is the last Will of a free and capable Testator.

In many cases no issue of capacity is raised by the parties or by the will itself, in which case the will can be probated in common form, that is, without a trial. [In Ontario: a certificate of appointment of estate trustee can be issued in non-contentious proceedings]. However, if one of the parties raises the issue of capacity, or the will suggests a possible lack of capacity because of its condition,

---

78 Some work had been done before that, as the dictionary was first proposed in 1857.

79 Dr. Minor's story is told by Simon Winchester in his book, *The Professor and the Madman* (New York: HarperCollins Publishers, Inc., 1998).

80 For a case involving the issue of the testamentary capacity of a paranoid schizophrenic, see *Pike v. Stone* (1999), 29 E.T.R. (2d) 292 (Nfld. T.D.).

81 (1838), 2 Moo. P.C. 480, 12 E.R. 1089.

82 *Ibid.*, at Moo. P.C. 482, *per* Baron Parke.

or in light of the testator's circumstance and family, a trial is required and capacity must then be proved upon a balance of probabilities.[83] Thus the will must be proved in solemn form [Ontario: formal proof of testamentary instrument].

The operation of the onus of proof is discussed in *Robins v. National Trust Co.*[84] The testator had made a will in 1901 under which the appellant was a beneficiary. But the testator's last will made in 1914, gave most of his estate to the respondents, who were some of his trustees. The appellant attacked the will on the ground of lack of capacity, fraud and undue influence. He was unsuccessful at trial and in the Ontario Court of Appeal. The Judicial Committee dismissed his *per saltum* appeal, partly because of the rule that the court will not reverse concurrent findings of fact by lower courts save in exceptional circumstances. On the question of the onus of proof, Viscount Dunedin said:[85]

> Now the English Courts have gone what some might think pretty far on the question of what duty lies on those who propound a will. Those who propound a will must show that the will of which probate is sought is the will of the testator, and that the testator was a person of testamentary capacity. In ordinary cases if there is no suggestion to the contrary any man who is shown to have executed a will in ordinary form will be presumed to have testamentary capacity, but the moment the capacity is called in question then at once the onus lies on those propounding the will to affirm positively the testamentary capacity. Moreover, if a will is only proved in common and not in solemn form, the same rule applies, even though the action is to attack a probate which has been granted long ago.
>
> These propositions will be found to be settled by the following cases: *Barry v. Butlin*;[86] *Cross v. Cross*;[87] *Tyrell v. Painton*.[88]
>
> Now their Lordships will assume that these cases are right. The reason for this form of expression is that the appellant represented that the Appellate Division of the Supreme Court of Ontario in the case of *Larocque v. Landry*[89] had taken another view, in that it held that once probate was granted, though only in common form, the onus was on him who sought to set it aside, and the Court in this case held itself bound by that case. It is questionable whether that is the result of the decision. But assuming that it is, when an appellate Court in a colony which is regulated by English law differs from an appellate Court in England, it is not right to assume that the Colonial Court is wrong. It is otherwise if the authority in England is that of the House of Lords. That is the supreme tribunal to settle English law, and that being settled, the Colonial Court, which is bound by English law, is bound to follow it. Equally, of course, the point of difference may be settled so far as the Colonial Court is concerned by a judgment of this Board. But in the present case their Lordships do not consider it necessary to settle which of the two possible views as to the onus is right; they will assume, for the purposes of this discussion, that the English rule is right. But given the law the appellant in their Lordships' opinion fails in its application to the facts.
>
> Their Lordships cannot help thinking that the appellant takes rather a wrong view of what is truly the function of the question of onus in such cases. Onus is always on a person who asserts a proposition or fact which is not self-evident. To assert that a man who is alive was born requires no proof. The onus is not on the person making the assertion, because it is self-evident that he

83 *Re Barter*, 13 M.P.R. 359, [1939] 2 D.L.R. 201, 206-7; *Sherman Estate v. Sherman* (1989), 31 E.T.R. 254 (Sask. Q.B.).

84 [1927] A.C. 515, [1927] W.W.R. 692, [1927] 2 D.L.R. 97 (P.C.).

85 *Ibid.* at A.C. 519-20.

86 (1838), 2 Moo. P.C. 480.

87 (1864), 3 S.W. & Tr. 292.

88 [1894] P. 151.

89 (1922), 52 Ont. L.R. 479.

had been born. But to assert that he was born on a certain date, if the date is material, requires proof; the onus is on the person making the assertion. Now, in conducting any inquiry, the determining tribunal, be it judge or jury, will often find that the onus shifts. But onus as a determining factor of the whole case can only arise if the tribunal finds the evidence pro and con so evenly balanced that it can come to no such conclusion. Then the onus will determine the matter. But if the tribunal, after hearing and weighing the evidence, comes to a determinate conclusion, the onus has nothing to do with it, and need not be further considered.

Further Reading

Rodney Hull, "The Onus of Proof in Contested Wills Cases after Probate is Granted" (1974), 1 E. & T.Q. 122.

Rodney Hull, "Contested Wills and Proof in Solemn Form" (1979), 5 E. & T.Q. 49.

Ian M. Hull, "The Production of Medical Records in Estate Litigation Matters" (1998), 18 E.T.R. (2d). 187.

Ian M. Hull, "The Use and Admissibility of Retrospective Psychiatric Opinions on Testamentary Capacity and Undue Influence" (1999), 30 E.T.R. (2d) 52.

Notes and Questions

1. It is apparent from the opinion of Viscount Dunedin in *Robins v. National Trust Co.*, that there appears to be a different rule regarding onus of proof in Ontario than that in the other provinces. The Appellate Division in Ontario has held that a grant of probate in common form is *prima facie* evidence of testamentary capacity and that the onus is then upon those who later attack the will to displace this *prima facie* presumption and show lack of capacity. In other words, after probate in common form has been granted, the onus shifts to those attacking the will.[90] It is arguable, however, that the courts were influenced by special factors in these cases, including the lapse of time between the grant of probate in common form and the trial of the action to prove the will in solemn form. It cannot, thus, be said with certainty that the Ontario rule in this respect is different from the general rule.[91]

2. The supposed Ontario rule was considered and rejected in Alberta,[92] British Columbia[93] and Manitoba[94] in favour of the English rule.

3. If you are acting for a major beneficiary under a will which is being contested for want of capacity should you intervene or let the executor carry the action? In *Royal Trust Co. v. Ford*[95] two major beneficiaries sought to be added on the appeal to the Supreme Court of Canada since, while the trial court pronounced in favour of the will, the British

---

90 See *Badenach v. Inglis* (1913), 29 O.L.R. 165, 14 D.L.R. 109 (C.A.); *Larocque v. Landry* (1922), 52 O.L.R. 479 (C.A.). And see *Re MacKenzie*, [1944] O.W.N. 154, [1944] 2 D.L.R. 79 (H.C.), reversed [1945] O.W.N. 673 (C.A.), affirmed [1946] 4 D.L.R. 225 (S.C.C.); *Re Kaufman*, [1961] O.R. 289, 27 D.L.R. (2d) 178 (C.A.).

91 See Rodney Hull, "The Onus of Proof in Contested Wills Cases after Probate is Granted" (1971), 19 Chitty's L.J. 84, reprinted (1974), 1 E. & T. Q. 122.

92 See *Odynak v. Feschuk*, 23 Alta. L.R. 263, [1928] 1 W.W.R. 113, [1928] 1 D.L.R. 423 (C.A.).

93 See *Turner v. Rochon* (1980), 22 B.C.L.R. 319 (S.C.).

94 See *Re Kowalski*, 6 W.W.R. (N.S.) 165, [1952] 4 D.L.R. 117 (Man. C.A.).

95 (1970), 73 W.W.R. 1, 13 D.L.R. (3d) 351 (B.C.C.A.). The decision of the B.C.C.A. on the substantive issue is reported at (1970), 72 W.W.R. 646. It was reversed [1971] S.C.R. 831, [1971] 3 W.W.R. 517, 20 D.L.R. (3d) 348.

Columbia Court of Appeal decided that the testator lacked capacity. This court also denied the beneficiaries' motion. Fortunately for them, the Supreme Court of Canada restored the trial judgment.

See also *Royal Trust Co. v. Ford (No. 2)*,[96] on the issue of costs. At this stage the matter had reached the Court of Appeal a second time, so that the costs, all of which were directed to be paid out of the estate, must have been sizable.

4. Would you be entitled to costs if your client's interest was virtually identical with that of the executors?

5. You should always consider carefully the likelihood of costs being awarded against your party, whether that be the party propounding the will or the party opposing it. If the positions of the propounders and opponents are reasonable in the circumstances, costs are often awarded out of the estate. However, while it used to be common for the court to award all parties' costs out of the estate, that is no longer the case.[97] Depending upon the circumstances, the court will award the costs on a party and party, or a solicitor an client basis.[98]

(ii) *Suspicious Circumstances*

It often happens that a will is prepared, or its preparation is obtained, by a person who takes a benefit under it. In many situations this happens because the testator is unable to visit his or her solicitor because of a physical disability and asks a family member to give instructions to the solicitor for the making of a will. While the beneficiary may not be guilty of undue influence or fraud and, indeed, the gift may be perfectly proper, these are circumstances which arouse the suspicion of the court. For this reason, the court in the leading case, *Barry v. Butlin*,[99] held it ought not to pronounce in favour of the will unless the suspicion is removed.

The facts in *Barry v. Butlin* were these: The testator was 76 years old when he made his will. It was prepared by his solicitor. The will gave the solicitor approximately one-quarter of the estate, a substantial gift to the testator's long-time butler, and the residue to Mr. Butlin, a close friend. The testator appointed Mr. Butlin his sole executor. The testator's son and only next of kin received nothing under the will and he contested it, alleging, *inter alia*, lack of capacity and fraud on the part of the solicitor, the executor and the testator's butler.

The Privy Council pronounced in favour of the will. Although the testator was a peculiar person and addicted to drinking, he was not insane and did not harbour any delusions. Further, he was capable of transacting the ordinary affairs of his life. The testator had been on good terms with his son, but the latter had treated his father badly and had absconded because of a criminal charge against him. Thereafter, the two became estranged and completely alienated from each other. The testator was also estranged from his other relatives. The Board concluded that in these circumstances it was understandable that he wanted to make a will

---

96 [1972] 1 W.W.R. 731, 25 D.L.R. (3d) 114 (B.C.C.A.).

97 See Brian Schnurr, "Estate Litigation—Who Pays the Costs" (1991), 11 E. & T. J. 52.

98 For an example, see *McCardell Estate v. Cushman* (1991), 36 E.T.R. 104 (Alta. Q.B.).

99 (1838), 2 Moo. P.C. 480 at 482-3, *per* Baron Parke.

to exclude his son and bestow his bounty on those with whom he had regular social intercourse and who were his friends and associates. Further, there was no evidence that any of the legatees had exerted their influence upon the testator and everything had been done openly, without any attempt to be secretive.

In the course of his opinion, Baron Parke stated the following rule:[100]

> ...if a party writes or prepares a will, under which he takes a benefit, that is a circumstance that ought generally to excite the suspicion of the Court, and calls upon it to be vigilant and jealous in examining the evidence in support of the instrument, in favour of which it ought not to pronounce unless the suspicion is removed, and it is judicially satisfied that the paper propounded does express the true will of the deceased.

His Lordship explained the rule as follows:[101]

> The strict meaning of the term *onus probandi* is this, that if no evidence is given by the party on whom the burden is cast, the issue must be found against him. In all cases the *onus* is imposed on the party propounding a Will, it is in general discharged by proof of capacity, and the facts of execution, from which the knowledge of and assent to the contents of the instrument are assumed, and it cannot be that the simple fact of the party who prepared the Will being himself a Legatee, is in every case, and under all circumstances, to create a contrary presumption, and to call upon the Court to pronounce against the Will, unless additional evidence is produced to prove the knowledge of its contents by the deceased. A single instance, of not infrequent occurrence, will test the truth of this proposition. A man of acknowledged competence and habits of business, worth £100,000, leaves the bulk of his property to his family, and a Legacy of £50 to his confidential attorney, who prepared the Will: would this fact throw the burden of proof of actual cognizance by the Testator, of the contents of the Will, on the party propounding it, so that if such proof were not supplied, the Will would be pronounced against? The answer is obvious, it would not. All that can be truly said is, that if a person, whether attorney or not, prepares a Will with a Legacy to himself, it is, at most, a suspicious circumstance, of more or less weight, according to the facts of each particular case; in some of no weight at all, as in the case suggested, varying according to circumstances; for instance, the *quantum* of the Legacy, and the proportion it bears to the property disposed of, and numerous other contingencies: but in no case amounting to more than a circumstance of suspicion, demanding the vigilant care and circumspection of the Court in investigating the case, and calling upon it not to grant probate without full and entire satisfaction that the instrument did express the real intentions of the deceased.
>
> Nor can it be necessary, that *in all such cases*, even if the Testator's capacity is doubtful, the precise species of evidence of the deceased's knowledge of the Will is to be in the shape of instructions for, or reading over the instrument. They form, no doubt, the *most* satisfactory, but they are not the *only* satisfactory description of proof, by which the cognizance of the contents of the Will, may be brought home to the deceased. The Court would naturally look for such evidence; in some cases it might be impossible to establish a Will without it, but it has no right in every case to require it.

The rule in *Barry v. Butlin* extends not only to cases in which a beneficiary prepared a will, but to all cases in which

> ...a will is prepared under circumstances which raise a well-grounded suspicion that it does not express the mind of the testator.[102]

---

100 At 2 Moo. P.C. 482-3.

101 *Ibid.*, at pp. 484-6.

102 *Tyrrell v. Painton*, [1894] P. 151 at 159-60, *per* Davey L.J. (C.A.). See also *Riach v. Ferris*,

It has been said that the "suspicious circumstances"

...are not circumstances that create a general miasma of suspicion that something unsavoury may have occurred, but rather circumstances which create a specific and founded suspicion that the testator may not have known and approved of the contents of the will.[103]

It follows, therefore, that the rule is directed to proof that the testator knew and understood the contents of the will. This onus of proof also lies upon those who propound the will. Cases of this type are often brought before the courts on the basis of lack of capacity, lack of knowledge and approval, and undue influence.[104] While the onus lies on the propounders in respect of the first two matters, the onus lies on those attacking the will in respect of undue influence. This presents no difficulty, unless the onus decides the case. Many of the cases unfortunately have not kept a clear distinction between suspicious circumstances and undue influence. Hence it is not easy to discern what is meant by "suspicious circumstances."

The extent of the proof required to remove the suspicion varies with the gravity of the suspicion and the circumstances.[105]

Vout v. Hay,[106] reproduced below, discusses the circumstances in which the rule arises.

Further Reading

Walter Brenner, "Suspicious Circumstances, Undue Influence, and the Burden of Proof" (1991), 42 E.T.R. 63.

Rodney Hull and Ian Hull, "Suspicious Circumstances in Relation to Testamentary Capacity and Undue Influence" in *Special Lectures of the Law Society of Upper Canada 1996 — Estates[:] Planning, Administration and Litigation* (Toronto: Carswell, 1996), at 77.

VOUT v. HAY
[1995] 2 S.C.R. 876, 7 E.T.R. (2d) 209, 125 D.L.R. (4th) 432
Supreme Court of Canada

The testator, Clarence Hay, was murdered in 1988. He was 81 years old when he died, unmarried, and lived alone on his farm. His estate was worth about $320,000. The testator left a will, made three years before he died, in which he appointed the appellant, Sandra Vout, his executrix and made her the major

---

[1934] S.C.R. 725 at 727, [1935] 1 D.L.R. 118; *Re Martin; MacGregor v. Ryan*, [1965] S.C.R. 757, 53 D.L.R. (2d) 126; *Re Schwartz*, [1970] 2 O.R. 61, 10 D.L.R. (3d) 15 (C.A.), affirmed (1971), 20 D.L.R. (3d) 313 (S.C.C.); *Eady v. Waring* (1974), 2 O.R. (2d) 627, 43 D.L.R. (3d) 667 (C.A.); *Clark v. Nash* (1989), 34 E.T.R. 174 (B.C.C.A.).

103 *Clark v. Nash, ibid.*, at p. 193, *per* Lambert J.A.

104 See, *e.g.*, *Re Dorion* (1980), 27 Nfld. & P.E.I.R. 211, 74 A.P.R. 211 (P.E.I.S.C.).

105 *Clark v. Nash, supra*, at p. 194, *per* Lambert J.A.

106 [1995] 2 S.C.R. 876, 7 E.T.R. (2d) 209, 125 D.L.R. (4th) 431.

beneficiary. The will gave one farm to her and another to a nephew of the testator. It also gave $1,000 to Carl Hay, a brother of the testator, and $3,000 to each of seven nephews and nieces. Vout was 29 years old at the time of the trial. She was unrelated to the deceased, but had been his friend for the last years of his life and helped him with chores on the farm. It was not alleged that there was a sexual relationship between them. Members of the Hay family challenged the will and sought probate of a prior will made some 20 years earlier, in which the testator left everything equally to a brother and sister. The sister died before the second will was made.

The will was prepared in the office of Vout's parents' lawyer, but the evidence about Vout's involvement in the making of the will conflicted. It was drawn by a secretary in the lawyer's office and witnessed by that secretary and another. The secretary who drew the will testified that she received instructions, either by phone or by an attendance at the office, from a woman who identified herself as Vout. She stated that Vout attended with the testator at the time the will was signed and said that the testator hesitated at one point during the reading of the will and that Vout reassured him, saying that they had discussed the matter and that the draft will conformed with what he had decided. The secretary also said that Vout directed that the bill not be sent to the testator's house. She came in later to pay it.

Vout testified that she only became involved with the preparation of the will because the testator asked her, that she recommended her parents' lawyer to the testator, and that she was never involved in the instructions for the will. She said that she met the testator in town on the day the will was signed and waited for him at the lawyer's office while he signed it. She denied phoning in, or giving instructions, or driving the deceased to the lawyer's office. She also denied giving instructions that the bill not be sent to the testator's house, and stated that she came in to pay it with money given her by the testator. Earlier Vout had been interviewed as a murder suspect and told the police that she had given the testator a ride into town and that he went into the lawyer's office by himself. She explained the inconsistency between her testimony and her statement to the police by saying she was scared and under stress. Someone else was convicted of the murder.

Several witnesses testified at trial that the testator was eccentric, but alert, smart, independent, determined, and not easily influenced. Members of the Hay family testified that, except for Carl Hay, they had never met Vout and didn't know she existed until the day of the funeral.

Byers J., the trial judge, noted the suspicious circumstances, but concluded that the testator had capacity and that the suspicious circumstances described in the case law were not present in this case. The trial judge also held, however, that even if suspicious circumstances were present, the testator did exactly what he intended and that there was no undue influence. In a short judgment, the Ontario Court of Appeal allowed the appeal and directed a new trial, concluding that the trial judge failed to resolve discrepancies in the evidence and failed to consider properly the issue of suspicious circumstances, which would cast the burden of disproving undue influence on Vout. Vout appealed.

SOPINKA J. delivered the judgment of the court:

Analysis

Suspicious circumstances

[16] The Court of Appeal held that the trial judge had failed to properly consider the important issue of suspicious circumstances surrounding the execution of the will which, in their view, would cast the burden of disproving undue influence on the appellant Vout. The interrelation of suspicious circumstances, testamentary capacity and undue influence has perplexed both the courts and litigants since the leading case of *Barry v. Butlin*....[107]

. . .

[18] The order for directions provided as follows:

1. Sandra Florence Vout affirms, and Earl Hay and Carl Hay deny that the Will of the said deceased, dated the 11th day of July, 1985, was duly executed.
2. Sandra Florence Vout affirms, and Earl Hay and Carl Hay deny that at the time of executing the said Will, the said deceased had testamentary capacity.
3. Earl Hay and Carl Hay affirm, and Sandra Florence Vout denies that the deceased was procured to execute the said Will by undue influence.

[19] The first issue requires a finding not only that the formalities required by the *Succession Law Reform Act*[108] were complied with but that the testator knew and approved of the contents of the will. As the order indicates, these matters are affirmed by Vout, the propounder of the will, on whom lies the burden of proof.

[20] With respect to the second issue, testamentary capacity requires the propounder of the will, Vout, to establish that the testator had a disposing mind and memory.

[21] The third issue casts upon those attacking the will the burden of proving undue influence. This requires proof that the testator's assent to the will was obtained by influence such that instead of representing what the testator wanted, the will is a product of coercion. Although fraud is sometimes treated as a separate issue, "fraud and undue influence" are generally coupled and the burden of proof with respect to fraud also lies on those attacking the will.

[22] Any discussion of the role of suspicious circumstances must start with the statement of Baron Parke in *Barry v. Butlin*:[109]

[F]irst ... the *onus probandi* lies in every case upon the party propounding a Will; and he must satisfy the conscience of the Court that the instrument so propounded is the last Will of a free and capable Testator.

---

107 (1838), 2 Moo. 480, 12 E.R. 1089.
108 R.S.O. 1990, c. S.26 (formerly R.S.O. 1980, c. 488).
109 *Supra*, at pp. 482-3 Moo., p. 1090 E.R.

[S]econd ... if a party writes or prepares a Will, under which he takes a benefit, that is a circumstance that ought generally to excite the suspicion of the Court, and calls upon it to be vigilant and jealous in examining the evidence in support of the instrument, in favour of which it ought not to pronounce unless the suspicion is removed, and it is judicially satisfied that the paper propounded does express the true Will of the deceased.

[23] At least two problems are raised by this statement:

(1) whether suspicious circumstances impose a standard of proof that is higher than the ordinary civil standard; and
(2) whether the reference to a free and capable testator requires the propounder of the will to disprove undue influence.

[24] With respect to the first problem, in accordance with the general rule applicable in civil cases, it has now been established that the civil standard of proof on a balance of probabilities applies. The evidence must, however, be scrutinized in accordance with the gravity of the suspicion. As stated by Ritchie J. in *Re Martin; MacGregor v. Ryan*:[110] "The extent of the proof required is proportionate to the gravity of the suspicion and the degree of suspicion varies with the circumstances of each case."

[25] With respect to the second problem, although *Barry v. Butlin* and numerous other cases dealt with circumstances in which the procurer of the will obtained a benefit, it has been determined that the *dictum* in *Barry v. Butlin* extends to any "well-grounded suspicion."[111] This was reaffirmed in this court by Ritchie J. in *Re Martin*.[112] The suspicious circumstances may be raised by (1) circumstances surrounding the preparation of the will; (2) circumstances tending to call into question the capacity of the testator; or (3) circumstances tending to show that the free will of the testator was overborne by acts of coercion or fraud. Since the suspicious circumstances may relate to various issues, in order to properly assess what effect the obligation to dispel the suspicion has on the burden of proof, it is appropriate to ask the question "suspicion of what?"[113]

[26] Suspicious circumstances in any of the three categories to which I refer above will affect the burden of proof with respect to knowledge and approval. The burden with respect to testamentary capacity will be affected as well if the circumstances reflect on the mental capacity of the testator to make a will. Although the propounder of the will has the legal burden with respect to due execution, knowledge and approval, and testamentary capacity, the propounder is aided by a rebuttable presumption. Upon proof that the will was duly executed with the requisite formalities, after having been read over to or by a testator who appeared to understand it, it will generally be presumed that the testator knew and approved of the contents and had the necessary testamentary capacity.

---

110 [1965] S.C.R. 757 at 766.
111 *Per* Davey L.J. in *Tyrrell v. Painton*, [1894] P. 151 at 159-60.
112 *Supra.*
113 See Dr. Cecil A. Wright, Case Comment, "Wills — Testamentary Capacity — 'Suspicious Circumstances' — Burden of Proof" (1938), 16 Can. Bar. Rev. 405; and Rodney Hull, Q.C., *Macdonell, Sheard and Hull on Probate Practice*, 3rd ed. (Toronto: Carswell, 1981), at p. 33.

[27] Where suspicious circumstances are present, then the presumption is spent and the propounder of the will reassumes the legal burden of proving knowledge and approval. In addition, if the suspicious circumstances relate to mental capacity, the propounder of the will reassumes the legal burden of establishing testamentary capacity. Both of these issues must be proved in accordance with the civil standard. There is nothing mysterious about the role of suspicious circumstances in this respect. The presumption simply casts an evidentiary burden on those attacking the will. This burden can be satisfied by adducing or pointing to some evidence which, if accepted, would tend to negative knowledge and approval or testamentary capacity. In this event, the legal burden reverts to the propounder.

[28] It might have been simpler to apply the same principles to the issue of fraud and undue influence so as to cast the legal burden onto the propounder in the presence of suspicious circumstances as to that issue.[114] Indeed the reference in *Barry v. Butlin* to the will of a "free and capable" testator would have supported that view. Nevertheless, the principle has become firmly entrenched that fraud and undue influence are to be treated as an affirmative defence to be raised by those attacking the will. They, therefore, bear the legal burden of proof. No doubt this reflects the policy in favour of honouring the wishes of the testator where it is established that the formalities have been complied with, and knowledge and approval as well as testamentary capacity have been established. To disallow probate by reason of circumstances merely raising a suspicion of fraud or undue influence would tend to defeat the wishes of the testator in many cases where in fact no fraud or undue influence existed, but the propounder simply failed to discharge the legal burden. Accordingly, it has been authoritatively established that suspicious circumstances, even though they may raise a suspicion concerning the presence of fraud or undue influence, do no more than rebut the presumption to which I have referred. This requires the propounder of the will to prove knowledge and approval and testamentary capacity. The burden of proof with respect to fraud and undue influence remains with those attacking the will.[115]

[29] It may be thought that proof of knowledge and approval will go a long way in disproving undue influence. Unquestionably there is an overlap. If it is established that the testator knew and appreciated what he was doing, in many cases there is little room for a finding that the testator was coerced. None the less, there is a distinction. This distinction was aptly expressed by Ritchie J. in *Re Martin*. He stated:[116]

> There is a distinction to be borne in mind between producing sufficient evidence to satisfy the Court that a suspicion raised by the circumstances surrounding the execution of the will have been dispelled and producing the evidence necessary to establish an allegation of undue influence. The former task lies upon the proponents of the will, the latter is a burden assumed by those who are attacking the will and can only be discharged by proof of the existence of an influence acting

---

114 See Wright, *supra*; and Hull, *Macdonell, Sheard and Hull on Probate Practice, supra*, at p. 33.
115 See *Craig v. Lamoureux* (1919), 50 D.L.R. 10, [1919] 3 W.W.R. 1101, [1920] A.C. 349; *Riach v. Ferris*, [1935] 1 D.L.R. 118, [1934] S.C.R. 725; *Re Martin, supra*.
116 [1965] S.C.R. 757 at 765-6.

upon the mind of the testator of the kind described by Viscount Haldane in *Craig v. Lamoureux*,[117] where he says:

> Undue influence, in order to render a will void, must be an influence which can justly be described by a person looking at the matter judicially to have caused the execution of a paper pretending to express a testator's mind, but which really does not express his mind, but something else which he did not really mean.

The distinction to which I have referred is well described by Crocket J. in *Riach v. Ferris*,[118] where he says:

> Assuming that in the case in behalf of a plaintiff seeking to establish the validity of a will, there may be such circumstances of apparent coercion or fraud disclosed as, coupled with the testator's physical and mental debility, raise a well-grounded suspicion in the mind of the court that the testator did not really comprehend what he was doing when he executed the will, and that in such a case it is for the plaintiff to remove that suspicion by affirmatively proving that the testator did in truth appreciate the effect of what he was doing, there is no question that, once this latter fact is proved, the onus entirely lies upon those impugning the will to affirmatively prove that its execution was procured by the practice of some undue influence or fraud upon the testator.

A person may well appreciate what he or she is doing but be doing it as a result of coercion or fraud.

Application to the case

[30] The Court of Appeal allowed the appeal on the ground that the trial judge failed to deal properly with the issue of suspicious circumstances "which would cast the burden on the respondent [Vout] of disproving undue influence". In view of the foregoing, the Court of Appeal clearly erred in this respect. Moreover, the trial judge did consider the issue of suspicious circumstances. Byers J. listed the following matters which were alleged to constitute suspicious circumstances:

> (1) Clarence Hay went to the lawyer recommended by Sandra Vout, and that lawyer, Paul Russell, had been the lawyer for Sandra Vout's parents;
> (2) Sandra Vout is not to be believed as to her participation in the instruction and execution of the will, and her lies are suspicious;
> (3) Sandra Vout stayed with Clarence Hay and coached him when he hesitated, and confirmed her influence at the critical time of execution.

Although the trial judge expressed the view that these circumstances did not amount to the type of circumstances referred to in the cases to which he had been referred, he proceeded to deal with them on the basis that they did constitute suspicious circumstances. These circumstances did not relate to the testamentary capacity of the testator, but the trial judge made an affirmative finding on this issue. Apart from his express finding of testamentary capacity, he stated:

---

117 [1920] A.C. 349 at 357.
118 [1934] S.C.R. 725 at 736.

... Clarence Hay, on the evidence, was not a befuddled, senile old man whose mind had been captured by Sandra Vout and who, like the testator in *Eady v. Waring*,[119] was physically and emotionally controlled and isolated by those persons who stood to benefit. In fact, the reverse is true. Clarence Hay was self-reliant and independent, was not easily influenced, lived alone and visited all members of the Hay family regularly, and he was all these things both before and for three years following the execution of the Will.

[31] The Court of Appeal was critical of the trial judgment for failing to resolve the discrepancies in the evidence. They attributed this failure to the fact that the trial judge found that the testator was fully mentally competent. While the trial judge did so find, he also reviewed the evidence, pointed out the discrepancies and made a positive finding that the testator knew and approved of the contents of the will. In this regard, he stated: "In my view, Clarence Hay made his will *exactly the way he intended*. He did have testamentary capacity; it was duly executed and there has been no undue influence. The Will will therefore be admitted to probate."[120]

[32] While it would have been preferable for the trial judge to have made express findings with respect to the discrepancies and, in particular, as to whether the instructions for the will had been given by the appellant to the secretary..., I am satisfied that the trial judge scrutinized the evidence to the degree required. He obviously was of the view that this fully competent, self-reliant and independent-minded individual would not have made the will as he did if he had not appreciated fully what he was doing. The trial judge went further and negatived undue influence. This he was not legally obliged to do simply by reason of the presence of suspicious circumstances.

[33] I am unable, therefore, to conclude that the trial judge made any error of law or that he committed any palpable or overriding error with respect to the facts. The respondents also raised the issue of due execution but the Court of Appeal did not deal with this issue. Virtually no argument was directed to this point in this Court and I can find nothing to support this submission. The trial judge found the will was duly executed and there was ample evidence to support this finding.

Disposition

[34] I would allow the appeal and set aside the judgment of the Court of Appeal and restore the judgment at trial. The appellant as executor under the will is entitled to her costs of the appeal to the Court of Appeal and to this Court on a solicitor and client basis to be paid out of the estate. In my view, the respondents were justified in appealing to the Court of Appeal as well as responding to the appeal to this Court. I would direct that their costs be paid out of the estate on a party and party basis.

---

119 (1974), 43 D.L.R. (3d) 667, 2 O.R. (2d) 627.
120 Emphasis added.

Notes and Questions

1. Can you state the doctrine of suspicious circumstances? Does it affect the standard of proof? Is it simply the ordinary rules of proof that apply to civil cases? Is there still a doctrine of suspicious circumstances?[121]

2. The Supreme Court of Canada had earlier defined the scope of the "suspicious circumstances" doctrine in *Riach v. Ferris*,[122] referred to in *Vout v. Hay*. The testator's will was being contested on the grounds of lack of capacity, and undue influence and fraud, undue influence and fraud being the real ground of attack. The trial judge relied upon *Barry v. Butlin*,[123] *Fulton v. Andrew*,[124] which explains it, and *Tyrrell v. Painton*,[125] and refused to grant probate of the will, in effect casting the onus of disproving undue influence on the propounder. In particular, the trial judge relied upon Baron Parke's two rules in *Barry v. Butlin*[126] and the following *dicta* from the other two cases:

> There is one rule which has always been laid down by the Courts having to deal with wills, and that is, that a person who is instrumental in the framing of a will...and who obtains a bounty by that will, is placed in a different position from other ordinary legatees who are not called upon to substantiate the truth and honesty of the transaction as regards their legacies...But there is a farther onus upon those who take for their own benefit, after having been instrumental in preparing or obtaining a will. They have thrown upon them the onus of showing the righteousness of the transaction.[127]
>
> The rule in *Barry v. Butlin*...is not...confined to the single case in which a will is prepared by or on the instructions of the person taking large benefits under it, but extends to all cases in which circumstances exist which excite the suspicion of the Court; and wherever such suspicions exist, and whatever their nature may be, it is for those who propound the will to remove such suspicion.[128]

In affirming the decision of the Ontario Court of Appeal, which reversed the decision of the trial judge, Crocket J., who delivered the judgment for the Supreme Court of Canada stated:[129]

> It will be observed that in neither of Baron Parke's two rules nor in neither of the respective *dicta* of Lord Hatherley and Lindley, L.J., as quoted, is there any specific mention of the question of procuring the execution of a will by fraud or misrepresentation or undue influence of any kind, and that apart from Lord Hatherley's statement regarding the throwing upon those who take for their own benefit, after having been instrumental in preparing or obtaining a will, the onus of showing the righteousness of the transaction, the only expressions which can be relied upon to support the proposition that the onus resting upon a party propounding a will includes the negativing of undue influence in a case where circumstances exist which create suspicion, are the expressions "that the instrument so propounded is the *last will of a free and capable testator*", and "that the paper propounded does *express the true will of the deceased*". Both these expressions no doubt imply, not only that the testator was of sound and disposing mind and memory at the time he executed the will, but that he actually comprehended what he was doing when he executed

---

121 See S.M. Wexler, Annotation, (1995), 7 E.T.R. (2d) 211.
122 [1934] S.C.R. 725, [1935] 1 D.L.R. 118.
123 (1838), 2 Moo. P.C. 480.
124 (1875) L.R. 7 H.L. 448.
125 [1894] P. 151.
126 Set out above.
127 *Fulton v. Andrew, supra*, at pp. 472-3, *per* Lord Hatherley.
128 *Tyrrell v. Painton, supra*, at p. 157, *per* Lindley L.J.
129 *Riach v. Ferris, supra*, at D.L.R. 123.

it. Though it may be that they on their face comprise freedom from fraud and duress, we do not think that the three cases from which His Lordship [*i.e.*, the trial judge] quoted can properly be said to establish the principle that the *onus probandi* resting upon a party propounding a will for probate extends in all cases, where circumstances of suspicion are disclosed, to the disproof or negativing of an allegation or suspicion of undue influence or fraud.

His Lordship continued:[130]

That portion of Lord Justice Lindley's *dictum* in *Tyrrell v. Painton*,[131] which is above quoted, may perhaps well bear the construction, which the learned trial Judge has placed upon it. When, however, it is considered in the light of the language immediately following, it will be seen that what this eminent Lord Justice of Appeal had in his mind when he spoke of the onus lying upon those who propounded the will "to remove such suspicion" was the suspicion that the testator did not know and approve the contents of the will. His words are...:[132]

...to remove such suspicion, *and to prove affirmatively that the testator knew and approved of the contents of the document*, and it is only where this is done that the onus is thrown on those who oppose the will to prove fraud or undue influence, or whatever else they rely on to displace the case made for proving the will.

His Lordship continued:[133]

Clearly there is no suggestion in this *dictum*, when considered in its entirety, that any further onus lies upon a party propounding a will than to prove the testamentary capacity of the deceased and that when the testator executed the instrument he fully realized what he was doing. The *dictum*, of course, assumes that all the formalities required by law have been duly complied with. Indeed it is as positively stated as it could well be that, once it is affirmatively proved that the testator, being, of course, of sound and disposing mind and memory, did know and approve of the contents of the will, the onus is placed on those who oppose its admission to probate to prove that notwithstanding the fact that the testator fully knew and appreciated what he was doing when he executed the will, he was induced to do so by some fraud or undue influence having been practiced upon him.

The Supreme Court of Canada found that the propounder of the will satisfied the onus of proving testamentary capacity and that the testator knew and approved the contents of the will, thereby removing the "suspicion." The court further held that the opponents to the application for probate did not satisfy the onus of proving undue influence or fraud.

3. In *Eady v. Waring*,[134] Arnup J.A., referred[135] to a passage in the judgment of Ritchie J. in *Re Martin, MacGregor v. Ryan*[136] in which that learned judge "appears to consider certain suspicious circumstances from the standpoint of whether or not they constitute grounds for a suspicion that *undue influence* had been exercised". That passage is as follows:[137]

---

130 *Ibid.*, at pp. 127-8.
131 [1894] p. 151.
132 *Ibid.*, at p. 157.
133 *Riach v. Ferris*, [1934] S.C.R. 725, [1935] 1 D.L.R. 118 at 127-8.
134 (1974), 2 O.R. (2d) 627, 43 D.L.R. (3d) 667 (C.A.).
135 *Ibid.*, at O.R. 640.
136 [1965] S.C.R. 757, 53 D.L.R. (2d) 126.
137 *Ibid.*, at D.L.R. 140.

This is not a case in which the will was prepared by a beneficiary and it appears from the evidence that the first suggestion as to its preparation was made by the testatrix herself, but the age of the testatrix, the haste with which the instructions were carried out, the absence of Mr. Ryan from the witness stand and the failure of Mr. Sillery to discuss the changes made from the former will or to give any advice concerning them, are circumstances which standing alone might well constitute grounds for a suspicion that "undue influence" had been exercised, and there can be no doubt that Mr. Ryan was an "interested person". I am, however, of opinion that the evidence supports the finding that this will was the free act of a competent testatrix and having regard to the fact that there are concurrent findings of two Courts to the effect that there was no "undue influence" which are based on a careful and accurate review of the evidence called for the attacker as well as for the proponents of the will, I am unable to see that there is any room for the suggestion that the Court was not "vigilant and jealous" in examining the evidence so as to satisfy itself that any suspicion to which the circumstances might give rise was dispelled.

I submit that if this passage is intended to suggest that the propounder of the will must disprove undue influence, it is at variance with *Riach v. Ferris*[138] and, with respect, is wrong. It is clear, however, from the rest of his judgment that Ritchie J., appreciated the effect of *Riach v. Ferris* concerning the locus of the two onuses.

4. The facts of *Re Martin; MacGregor v. Ryan*,[139] also referred to in *Vout v. Hay*, were that the testatrix had revoked a will giving a life interest to her sister with remainder to her nephew and replaced it with one giving the entire estate to the sister and naming the sister's husband as executor. At the testatrix's request, the latter retained a solicitor known to her and the solicitor prepared the new will and attended to its execution. The will was admitted to probate and that decision was upheld on appeal.[140]

5. In *Eady v. Waring*[141] the court also held that the suspicious circumstances doctrine does not just apply when a beneficiary drafts the will, or is instrumental in having the will prepared, but arises whenever a will is prepared in circumstances raising a well-grounded suspicion that it does not express the mind of the testator.

While the testator boarded with his married brother, he made his will which left most of his estate to that brother. An earlier will had left a substantial legacy to his late wife's niece, who had lived with the testator and his wife for many years, and divided the residue equally between his married brother, a bachelor brother and a sister. The married brother's son, one of the executors, attended at the solicitor's office with the testator while instructions were given for the will and when it was executed. He also attended with the testator to close out his bank account and to open a new account in the joint names of the testator and the married brother. The evidence disclosed that the brother's family constantly supervised the testator and prevented him from associating with friends, neighbours and relatives, including his wife's niece. Nevertheless, the solicitor gave evidence to the effect that in his opinion the testator had capacity, and the attending physician confirmed this evidence. The court held that there were suspicious circumstances surrounding the making of the will, which were not removed, and dismissed an appeal from a judgment pronouncing against the will.

6. *Vout v. Hay* has been followed in quite a number of cases. *Doherty v. Doherty*[142] is an example. The testator's daughter, who assisted him in conducting his personal affairs,

---

138 *Supra*.

139 [1965] S.C.R. 757, 53 D.L.R. 53 D.L.R. (2d) 126.

140 See to the same effect *Re Harmes; Harmes v. Hinkson*, [1946] 2 W.W.R. 433, [1946] 3 D.L.R. 497 (P.C.).

141 (1974), 2 O.R. (2d) 627, 43 D.L.R. (3d) 667 (C.A.).

142 (1997), 19 E.T.R. (2d) 158 (N.B.C.A.), application for leave to appeal dismissed without

pointed out to him that his house would have to be sold in order to carry out the will he had just made, which left his property equally to all his children. He did not want that to happen, so he made a new will in which he left most of his estate to the daughter. However, he did so after consulting his lawyer and accountant. And the evidence showed that he had capacity. The court held that the testator had capacity and that any suspicions had been removed. The court also held that the onus was not on the daughter to disprove undue influence.[143]

MacKenzie v. MacKenzie Estate[144] is a different kind of case. The testator made a will five months before his death in which he left all his personal property to his wife and all his real property to his youngest son, subject to a life interest to his wife. The will purported to revoke a will made six months earlier (which was similar to one made five years before that) in which the testator left his house and farm to his youngest son subject to a life interest to his wife, and his personal property in trust to pay the wife a yearly income of $20,000 with the balance equally to all the children. The will made 11 months before death had been prepared by a solicitor who observed the duties of a solicitor taking instructions for a will very carefully. In contrast, the last will was prepared by a different solicitor at the instigation of the wife and youngest son. That solicitor did not inquire about the extent of the estate, about earlier wills, and about the reasons why the other children were being disinherited. The court considered the extensive evidence of suspicious circumstances and concluded that the propounder failed to remove the suspicions and, thus, failed to meet the onus of proving capacity.[145]

7. For an egregious case involving suspicious circumstances, see *Banton v. Banton*.[146] George Banton was 86 years old when he moved into a retirement home. He formed a friendship with a 31-year-old woman, Muna Yassin, who was a waitress in the home's restaurant. The relationship soon developed into a close attachment and in December, 1994 Muna persuaded George to marry her and the marriage took place in secret. Then they instructed a solicitor to prepare a will and power of attorney for George. The will left George's entire estate to Muna and the power of attorney purported to give her control over George's assets. Both were later replaced by identical documents. George had previously given a power of attorney to two of his children and his earlier will left his estate equally to his children. When he married Muna, George suffered from prostate cancer and had been castrated to inhibit the spread of the disease. He also had serious hearing problems, his physical mobility was restricted so that he required a walker, and he was

---

reasons, Apr. 2, 1998, S.C.C. Bulletin 1998, p. 584. The case is unremarkable on the issue of capacity. However, I submit that it is wrong on another issue. The testator had established joint accounts with the daughter, to which he had contributed all the funds, in order that she could assist him in conducting his personal affairs. The court said, in very brief reasons on this point, that the bank accounts were the daughter's by operation of law and did not form part of the estate. What the court should have found, I submit, is that there was a presumption of advancement in favour of the daughter, but that the presumption was rebutted. In consequence, the court should have concluded that she held the funds upon resulting trust for the estate.

143 For similar cases, see *McCullough Estate v. McCullough* (1998), 22 E.T.R. (2d) 29 (Alta. C.A.); *Fieldhouse (Litigation Guardian of) v. National Trust Co.* (1999), 27 E.T.R. (2d) 272 (Ont. Gen. Div.).

144 (1998), 24 E.T.R. (2d) 260, 162 D.L.R. (4th) 674 (N.S.C.A.).

145 For a similar case, see *Jackson Estate v. Nelson* (1999), 29 E.T.R. (2d) 34 (B.C.S.C.).

146 (1998), 164 D.L.R. (4th) 176, supp. reasons *loc. cit.* at 244 (Ont. Gen. Div.). See Albert H. Oosterhoff, "Consequences of a January/December Marriage: A Cautionary Tale" (1999), 18 E.T. & P.J. 261. See also *Banton v. CIBC Trust Corp.* (1999), 182 D.L.R. (4th) 486 (Ont. S.C.J.).

incontinent. The children were understandably upset about Muna's increasing influence over their father and about the marriage.

When George died in 1996 at age 89, the court directed certain issues to be tried, including testamentary capacity, undue influence, and the validity of the marriage. On the issue of capacity, the court applied *Vout v. Hay*. Cullity J. found that George was able to appreciate the nature of the testamentary act and the extent of his assets when he made the wills in favour of Muna. However, George no longer had the ability to understand and appreciate the moral claims of his children because of a delusion due to a mental disorder, which was activated by his relationship with Muna. Hence, George did not satisfy the test of a sound disposing mind. The court held that Muna failed to meet the burden of proving testamentary capacity. The court then went on to hold that Muna had exercised undue influence over George and that the two wills failed for that reason as well. I shall return to this aspect of the case in the next part of this chapter. However, the court also held that the marriage was valid. While the test for capacity to make a will is quite stringent, the test for capacity to marry is very simple. It only requires that the person understand the nature of the marriage relationship and its responsibilities. The court concluded that George had sufficient capacity to enter into the marriage and was not coerced into it. This was problematic because by statute a prior will is revoked by the testator's marriage. Hence, George died intestate and Muna was entitled to share on his intestacy. The part of the case dealing with the issue of the revocation of the will is discussed in the chapter on Revocation.[147]

8. On the matter of solicitors who prepare a will and receive substantial benefits under it, the case of *Wintle v. Nye*[148] is instructive. The solicitor, Mr. Frederick Nye, attended upon the testatrix, Miss Wells, to prepare a will for her. After many consultations with Nye and without independent advice, the testatrix executed a will by which she appointed Nye her sole executor and gave him her residuary estate. Miss Wells died in 1947 at age 76. Her estate was valued at £115,000, most of it being residue. Her sister and her companion, the sister of the plaintiff, received very little under the will. Nye obtained probate of the will. Then Colonel A.D. Wintle, the testatrix's cousin, decided to take matters in hand. He got Nye into an apartment by false pretences, took his clothes off, photographed him, made him sign a document and then threw him out.

Having served a short term in jail for this episode, Wintle then decided to contest the will. He lost at trial (with a jury) and before the Court of Appeal. Then he discharged his solicitors and appealed without legal assistance to the House of Lords, where he won on the ground that the trial judge had misdirected the jury and a new trial was ordered. The case was argued solely on the basis of lack of knowledge and approval, the issues of lack of capacity and undue influence not having been raised in the courts below. The House of Lords adopted the second rule in *Barry v. Butlin*.[149] Viscount Simonds, who delivered the major speech said:[150]

> It is not the law that in no circumstances can a solicitor or other person who has prepared a will for a testator take a benefit under it. But that fact creates a suspicion that must be removed by the person propounding the will. In all cases the court must be vigilant and jealous. The degree of

---

147 For a similar case, see *Barrett Estate v. Dexter* (2000), 34 E.T.R. (2d) 1 (Alta. Q.B.) in which the court held that the marriage was invalid because the man lacked capacity to enter into the marriage. See also Albert H. Oosterhoff, Comment (2001), 20 E.T. & P.J. 115.

148 [1959] 1 W.L.R. 284, [1959] 1 All E.R. 552 (H.L.).

149 (1838), 2 Moo. P.C. 480, 12 E.R. 1089.

150 *Wyntle v. Nye, supra*, at All E.R. 557.

suspicion will vary with the circumstances of the case. It may be slight and easily dispelled. It may, on the other hand, be so grave that it can hardly be removed. In the present case, the circumstances were such as to impose on the respondent as heavy a burden as can well be imagined.

At this stage Nye apparently had had enough, for he consented to a distribution as if there had been an intestacy. He was then charged by the Disciplinary Committee of the Law Society with taking advantage of his client for his own benefit. Colonel Wintle testified at the hearing. Nye was found guilty and was struck off the rolls in 1960.[151]

9. If the solicitor is being offered a legacy and counsels independent advice, but the testator refuses to obtain it, ought the solicitor to accept the benefit? If the solicitor does accept it, is he or she guilty of professional misconduct?[152]

10. T owned shares in a family business which he transferred to his three sons. One of the sons, J, had a disagreement with another son, M, over the business and J purchased M's shares as well as the shares of a third son under a buy-sell agreement. Before the agreement was concluded, T determined to disinherit J and his children. He asked his solicitor to draft a new will, but the solicitor refused to do so because of his relationship with the family. T then asked M's solicitor to prepare the will and he did so. Do these facts raise a suspicion? Ought the will to be set aside?[153]

11. T made a will by which he left everything to his housekeeper, B. His solicitor then informed B's son, S, that if B should predecease the testator, the estate would be distributed as on an intestacy. S thereupon instructed the solicitor to prepare a new will for T, leaving everything to him and his sister and, shortly after B's death, S and two friends attended at the hospital where T was being treated for pneumonia and skin cancer to obtain its execution. The will was read over to T and he indicated that he understood it, but asked no questions about it. He signed the will.

Are these circumstances suspicious? Ought the will to be probated?[154]

---

151 Some of the facts for this note were taken from James Comyn, *Lost Causes* (Collins), excerpted in *Canadian Lawyer*, Nov. 1982, pp. 21-3. For another case in which a litigant appealed to the highest court without representation, see *Campbell v. Hogg*, [1930] 3 D.L.R. 673 (P.C.). It involved an eminent Ontario lawyer who was ultimately found, by the Privy Council, to have failed to account for all the assets of a trust. The Board did not find the lawyer fraudulent or impute impropriety to him, but did saddle him with costs. The case is interesting because: (1) it was pursued by a beneficiary of the trust, who argued the case herself before the Privy Council; (2) the Board set aside concurrent findings of fact in three Ontario courts; (3) the Board itself audited the accounts; and (3) the beneficiary published a book about her experiences. In the book the beneficiary alleged something close to a conspiracy among the Ontario bench and bar, and a trust company, to protect the solicitor from the consequences of his conduct. See William J. Anderson, "Where Angels Fear to Tread" (1995), 29 Law Soc. Gaz. 14.

152 See *Re a Solicitor*, [1975] Q.B. 475, [1974] 3 All E.R. 853 at 858-9.

153 *Re Schwartz*, [1970] 2 O.R. 61, 10 D.L.R. (3d) 15 (C.A.), affirmed (1971), 20 D.L.R. (3d) 313 (S.C.C.).

154 See *Re Campbell; Slater v. Chitrenky* (1981), 10 E.T.R. 191, 28 A.R. 54 (Surr. Ct.), affirmed [1982] 3 W.W.R. 575, 11 E.T.R. 171 (Alta. C.A.). For other cases involving suspicious circumstances and the degree of proof necessary to remove them, see *Russell v. Fraser* (1980), 8 E.T.R. 245, 118 D.L.R. (3d) 733 (B.C.C.A.); *Re Mann* (1982), 33 A.R. 144 (Q.B.); *Friesen v. Friesen Estate* (1985), 24 E.T.R. 191 (Man. Q.B.).

(e)   Date as of Which Capacity is Required

It may happen that a testator is afflicted with a debilitating illness that affects capacity, but makes a will during a "lucid interval." Is such a will valid? Similarly, a testator may wish to make a will at a time when the mind is rapidly deteriorating. If the testator gives instructions for the will while capable, but executes it while incapable, is the will valid? The latter situation was considered in the leading case, *Parker v. Felgate*.[155]

The testatrix became affected with Bright's disease at age 28. She consulted her solicitor with a view to making her will and gave complete instructions to him while she had capacity, but before the will could be prepared, she became very ill and was often in a coma. The solicitor prepared the will and attended upon the testatrix. She was roused from her coma and was shown the will and asked, "This is your will. Do you wish this lady...to sign it?" and she replied "Yes".

In the course of summing-up to the jury, Sir James Hannen, P., said:[156]

If a person has given instructions to a solicitor to make a will, and the solicitor prepares it in accordance with those instructions, all that is necessary to make it a good will, if executed by the testator, is that he should be able to think thus far, "I gave my solicitor instructions to prepare a will making a certain disposition of my property. I have no doubt that he has given effect to my intention, and I accept the document which is put before me as carrying it out".

The jury found that when the will was executed the testatrix did not remember and understand the instructions given to her solicitor and would not have been able to understand each clause if she had been roused and they had been put to her. However, they found that she was capable of understanding and did understand that she was executing the will for which she had given instructions to her solicitor.

Re Bradshaw Estate,[157] reproduced below, is a Canadian example of this principle.

RE BRADSHAW ESTATE
(1988), 30 E.T.R. 276
New Brunswick Probate Court

The testator was 96 years old and a widower when he died. He was survived by a sister and a nephew and two nieces in England. He made a will in 1986, a codicil in 1987 and a codicil on the day he died in 1988. The estate was large. The will left a substantial legacy and furniture to the testator's housekeeper of 20 years, a gift of other furniture to remote relatives of his late wife, and another substantial legacy to his sister. The testator directed that the residue of his estate be divided between his nephew and nieces. The 1987 codicil gave a legacy to a

---

155   (1883), 8 P.D. 171.
156   *Ibid.* at p. 173.
157   (1988), 30 E.T.R. 276 (N.B. Prob. Ct.).

person who had worked for the testator over the years. The 1988 codicil left a $50,000 legacy to Audrey Robinson and a $25,000 legacy to Alice ("Robbie") Robertson, two persons who had been long-time friends of the family.

The will and codicil had been prepared by Mr. O'Connell, a solicitor, who had known the testator for about nine years and had been a neighbour of his. The solicitor and his wife visited the testator two weeks before he died. During the visit the testator gave instructions for the second codicil. Two weeks later the solicitor was called to the testator's house because the testator was dying.

The facts surrounding execution of the will are set out in the judgment. The court directed that the second codicil be proved in solemn form because of the incomplete signature and the physical condition of the testator at the time he signed it.

JONES J.:

. . .

Mr. O'Connell testified that on the morning of April 15th he and his wife attended at Mr. Bradshaw's home. This was at approximately 8 a.m. Mr. Bradshaw was in bed propped up slightly and he was using an oxygen mask. The evidence indicates that his health situation was declining essentially because of age. His lungs were filling up with fluid and thus the oxygen mask. He was at a stage where he would in due course be expected to go into heart failure. The evidence is that at this stage Mr. Bradshaw was not under any medication.

Mr. Bradshaw had difficulty talking but in Mr. O'Connell's opinion knew Mr. O'Connell, nodded to him and in response to a further question by Mr. O'Connell as to whether or not he knew why they were there Mr. Bradshaw nodded. Mr. O'Connell held up the document being the prepared codicil and asked Mr. Bradshaw if he understood what this was. In response he received a further nod. Mr. O'Connell asked if he wanted to sign it and Mr. Bradshaw also nodded. Mr. O'Connell did not read the codicil word for word but advised Mr. Bradshaw that it provided bequests of $50,000 to Audrey and $25,000 to Robbie to which Mr. Bradshaw nodded his assent.

The evidence is that the codicil was then held up and a pen placed in Mr. Bradshaw's hand and that he made an effort at starting his signature. This consisted of two diagonal strokes and a further mark by an obviously unsteady hand.

Mr. O'Connell stated that following this he again questioned Mr. Bradshaw as to whether or not he knew what he had signed and that he had provided $50,000 for Audrey Robinson and $25,000 for Robbie. He stated that Mr. Bradshaw nodded and that following this the two witnesses signed the codicil in Mr. Bradshaw's presence.

Mr. O'Connell testified that he and his wife stayed a short time further during which time Mr. O'Connell talked about matters of mutual interest and on several occasions Mr. Bradshaw nodded his understanding and in fact squeezed Mr. O'Connell's hand. Mrs. O'Connell who is the other witness to the codicil testified to like effect.

Mr. Bradshaw's housekeeper Theresa Farrell testified. She was not present during the time that Mr. Bradshaw put his marks on the codicil but described his condition essentially as outlined above and that he passed away early that evening. During the day he took liquid nourishment and spoke briefly to Mrs. Farrell as well as to one of the applicants Peter Emmerson and both testified that he was aware of his surroundings.

There was no evidence contra and no argument made contra.

. . .

On the evidence before me, I am satisfied that certainly at the time Mr. Bradshaw gave instructions with respect to the final codicil that he had a disposing mind and memory sufficient to take in the necessary elements referred to above. In fact while it is clear that Mr. Bradshaw was very frail on April 15, 1988, the evidence given indicates that his mind was alert and that he had testamentary capacity at that time. He certainly understood what he was doing. There is authority to the effect that the capacity of a person at the time of execution of a will need only go the extent of his understanding of what he is doing and that he is completing that which he has previously instructed.[158]

> The relevant time for having capacity to make a will is when instructions are given. If a person has capacity then, he may make a good will later, so long as he knows that he is executing a will for which he has previously given instructions and is physically capable of showing his assent thereto.[159]

I am satisfied that the testator had the requisite testamentary capacity both at the time that he gave Mr. O'Connell the original instructions with respect to the codicil of April 1988 and at the time it was presented to him for signature.

[The court went on to hold that the will had been executed properly.[160]]

Notes and Questions

1. The rule in *Parker v. Felgate* has been followed in Canada on many occasions.[161]

2. If the testator has given some instructions while he or she has capacity, but completes the instructions while he or she lacks capacity, can the part of the will that incorporates the latter instructions be severed and the part incorporating the former be probated, assuming that the first set of instructions were final and the case otherwise satisfies the requirements of the rule in *Parker v. Felgate*?[162]

---

158 Thomas G. Feeney, *The Canadian Law of Wills*, 2d ed. (Toronto: Butterworths, 1982) vol. 1 at 29.

159 See also *Parker v. Felgate* (1883), 8 P.D. 171.

160 The execution of wills and signing by a mark are dealt with in the next chapter.

161 See, *e.g.*, *Re Davis; Rogers v. Davis*, [1932] S.C.R. 407, [1932] 3 D.L.R. 351; *Faulkner v. Faulkner*, 60 S.C.R. 386, [1920] 2 W.W.R. 307, 54 D.L.R. 145; *Kaulbach v. Archbold* (1901), 31 S.C.R. 387; *Re McPhee; Can. Permanent Trust Co. v. Stewart; Can. Permanent Trust Co. v. Clare* (1965), 52 D.L.R. (2d) 520 at 525 (B.C.S.C.); *Re Seabrook; Dunne v. Dundas* (1978), 4 E.T.R. 135 (Ont. Surr. Ct.). See also *Re Fergusson* (1980), 40 N.S.R. (2d) 223, 73 A.P.R. 223 (Prob. Ct.), affirmed (1981), 43 N.S.R. (2d) 89, 81 A.P.R. 89 (C.A.).

162 See *Thomas v. Jones*, [1928] P. 162, [1928] All E.R. Rep. 704, 139 L.T. 214, in which this was done, but contrast *Re Seabrook; Dunne v. Dundas* (1978), 4 E.T.R. 135 (Ont. Surr. Ct.), in which this possibility was not considered.

3. Is the rule in *Parker v. Felgate* an exception to the rule that a testator must know and approve the contents of the will at the time the will is executed? This appears to be the consequence of the rule because solicitors normally insert a number of "boiler plate" provisions which the testator could not have known about or approved at the time of execution.[163]

4. If the instructions to the solicitor are communicated through an intermediary, the rule should be applied with caution.[164] The same caution applies if the testator gives instructions to two persons and their testimony differs.[165]

5. It is possible that a person who generally does not have mental capacity to make a will because of mental illness recovers sufficiently during lucid intervals to enable the person to make a will. The general rule is that if it has been shown that the testator has suffered from a long-standing mental illness which continues up until a time before the will is executed and also exists afterwards, it is not necessary to prove that the testator lacked capacity when he or she executed the will.[166] Nevertheless, if it can be shown that the will was made during a lucid interval, the will can be admitted to probate, the onus being on those who allege capacity.[167] Such proof is possible even if the testator is subject to delusions if it can be shown that he or she was not affected by them at the relevant time, even though his or her mind was directed to them.[168] Moreover, the will itself, if rational, may afford strong proof of capacity during a lucid interval.[169]

5. UNDUE INFLUENCE

It is quite common for wills to be attacked on the ground of lack of capacity, lack of knowledge and approval and undue influence, although a will may also be contested on one of these grounds alone. Undue influence is, therefore, not related to testamentary capacity, for a person may have the necessary capacity to make a will, but, because his or her volition was overborne by another, the will, if made, must be refused probate.

Sir J.P. Wilde defined it as follows in his directions to the jury in *Hall v. Hall*:[170]

To make a good will a man must be a free agent. But all influences are not unlawful. Persuasion, appeals to the affections or ties of kindred, to a sentiment of gratitude for past services, or pity for future destitution, or the like, — these are all legitimate, and may be fairly pressed on a testator. On the other hand, pressure of whatever character, whether acting on the fears or the hopes, if so exerted as to overpower the volition without convincing the judgment, is a species of restraint under which no valid will can be made. Importunity or threats, such as the testator has not the courage to resist, moral command asserted and yielded to for the sake of peace and quiet, or of escaping from distress of mind or social discomfort, these, if carried to a degree in which

---

163 *Cf. Kaulbach v. Archbold* (1901), 31 S.C.R. 387, and *Re Wallace*, [1952] 2 T.L.R. 925, to the same effect.

164 *Battan Singh v. Amirchand*, [1948] A.C. 161.

165 *Re Fergusson* (1980), 40 N.S.R. (2d) 223, 73 A.P.R. 223 (Prob. Ct.), affirmed (1981), 43 N.S.R. (2d) 89, 81 A.P.R. 89 (C.A.).

166 *Smith v. Tebbett* (1867), L.R. 1 P. & D. 354 at 398.

167 *A.G. v. Parnther* (1792), 3 Bro. C.C. 441 at 444, 29 E.R. 632, *per* Lord Thurlow.

168 *Nichols & Freeman v. Binns* (1858), 1 Sw. & Tr. 239, 164 E.R. 710.

169 *Ibid.*

170 (1868), L.R. 1 P. & D. 481.

the free play of the testator's judgment, discretion or wishes, is overborne, will constitute undue influence, though no force is either used or threatened. In a word, a testator may be led but not driven; and his will must be the offspring of his own volition, and not the record of some one else's.

Similarly, Sir James Hannen, in addressing the jury in *Wingrove v. Wingrove*,[171] said:

We are all familiar with the use of the word "influence"; we say that one person has an unbounded influence over another, and we speak of evil influences and good influences, but it is not because one person has unbounded influence over another that therefore when exercised, even though it may be very bad indeed, it is undue influence in the legal sense of the word. To give you some illustrations of what I mean, a young man may be caught in the toils of a harlot, who makes use of her influence to induce him to make a will in her favour, to the exclusion of his relatives. It is unfortunately quite natural that a man so entangled should yield to that influence and confer large bounties on the person with whom he has been brought into such relation; yet the law does not attempt to guard against those contingencies. A man may be the companion of another, and may encourage him in evil courses, and so obtain what is called an undue influence over him, and the consequence may be a will made in his favour. But that again, shocking as it is, perhaps even worse than the other, will not amount to undue influence.

To be undue influence in the eye of the law there must be — to sum it up in a word — coercion. It must not be a case in which a person has been induced by means such as I have suggested to you to come to a conclusion that he or she will make a will in a particular person's favour, because if the testator has only been persuaded or induced by considerations which you may condemn, really and truly to intend to give his property to another, though you may disapprove of the act, yet it is strictly legitimate in the sense of its being legal. It is only when the will of the person who becomes a testator is coerced into doing that which he or she does not desire to do, that it is undue influence.

The coercion may of course be of different kinds, it may be in the grossest form, such as actual confinement or violence, or a person in the last days or hours of life may have become so weak and feeble, that a very little pressure will be sufficient to bring about the desired result, and it may even be, that the mere talking to him at that stage of illness and pressing something upon him may so fatigue the brain, that the sick person may be induced, for quietness' sake, to do anything. This would equally be coercion, though not actual violence.

These illustrations will sufficiently bring home to your minds that even very immoral considerations either on the part of the testator, or of some one else offering them, do not amount to undue influence unless the testator is in such a condition, that if he could speak his wishes to the last, he would say, "this is not my wish, but I must do it".

If therefore the act is shewn to be the result of the wish and will of the testator at the time, then, however it has been brought about — for we are not dealing with a case of fraud — though you may condemn the testator for having such a wish, though you may condemn any person who has endeavoured to persuade and has succeeded in persuading the testator to adopt that view — still it is not undue influence.

There remains another general observation that I must make, and it is this, that it is not sufficient to establish that a person has the power unduly to overbear the will of the testator. It is necessary also to prove that in the particular case that power was exercised, and that it was by means of the exercise of that power, that the will such as it is, has been produced.

You will recall that, while the onus of proof rests on the propounder of the will to prove testamentary capacity and knowledge and approval (including the re-

---

171 (1885), 11 P.D. 81.

moval of suspicion), the onus of proof with respect to undue influence always rests on those who allege it.[172]

It often happens that the person who is in a position to exert undue influence over the testator is instrumental in preparing the will or giving instructions for it. If that is the case, the court must look at the evidence closely to ensure that the suspicion is removed and, if the issue is raised, that no undue influence was practised.[173] However, the different onuses that attend proof of undue influence and knowledge and approval are not always kept in mind.[174]

With respect to *inter vivos* gifts, if the person who receives the gift was in a position to exert undue influence over the donor and stood in a fiduciary or confidential relationship to him or her, a presumption of undue influence is raised.[175] However, even though the court will jealously scan the evidence in the case of a will if undue influence is alleged, the onus of proof (or disproof) does not rest on such a fiduciary, but remains with those alleging undue influence.[176] The onus is a heavy one and is not readily proved, although the onus is discharged by proof on a balance of probabilities. On this point, Viscount Haldane said in *Craig v. Lamoureux*:[177]

> There is no reason why a husband or a parent, on whose part it is natural that he should do so, may not put his claims before a wife or a child and ask for their recognition, provided the person making the will knows what is being done. The persuasion must of course stop short of coercion, and the testamentary disposition must be made with comprehension of what is being done.

The case involved the following facts: The testatrix and her husband were under the impression that the survivor would take all the estate of the one who died first. However, the parties had made an ante-nuptial agreement which provided that unless the parties died testate, the survivor would not be entitled to share on an intestacy. When the defendant husband was so advised, he informed his wife, who then expressed a desire to make a will. These discussions took place during the testatrix' final illness. The defendant husband had his brother, a lawyer, draw up a simple will which left everything to the defendant, except for some minor gifts and souvenirs which he was to give to her relatives. This will was read over to the testatrix and she asked that the will be changed so as to give something to her family, since that is what her deceased father had wished. The defendant took the will back to his brother, who redrafted the will to comply with the testatrix' wishes. The second will was then signed by the testatrix, but her signature was

---

172 See *Wingrove v. Wingrove*, *ibid.* at p. 83; *Maw v. Dickey* (1974), 6 O.R. (2d) 146, 52 D.L.R. (3d) 178 (Surr. Ct.); *Harmes v. Hinkson*, [1946] 2 W.W.R. 433, [1946] 3 D.L.R. 497 at 512 (Can. P.C.), *per* Lord du Parcq.

173 See, *e.g.*, *Goldsworthy v. Thompson* (1974), 46 D.L.R. (3d) 238 (S.C.C.).

174 See *Re Crompton; Crompton v. Williams*, [1938] O.R. 543, [1938] 4 D.L.R. 237 (H.C.).

175 See, *e.g.*, *Re Craig*, [1971] Ch. 95, [1970] 2 All E.R. 390; *Re Crompton; Crompton v. Williams*, *supra*; *Goguen v. Goguen* (1988), 31 E.T.R. 149 (N.B.Q.B.); and especially *Goodman Estate v. Geffen* (1991), 42 E.T.R. 97 (S.C.C.). See also *Dmyterko Estate v. Kulikowsky* (1992), 47 E.T.R. 66 (Ont. Gen. Div.).

176 *Parfitt v. Lawless* (1872) L.R. 2 P. & D. 462 at 468, *per* Lord Penzance.

177 [1920] A.C. 349 at 357, [1919] 3 W.W.R. 1101, 36 T.L.R. 26, 50 D.L.R. 10 (P.C.).

illegible. In addition, the witnesses did not sign in her presence. The defendant's brother informed the testatrix that the will was not valid for those reasons and she thereupon called for her first will, which was then properly executed and attested. This will was contested by the testatrix' sister who alleged that the will had been procured by the defendant through undue influence. The Privy Counsel held that the sister had not proved undue influence. In this connection, Viscount Haldane said:[178]

> ...in order to set aside the will of a person of sound mind, it is not sufficient to show that the circumstances attending his execution are consistent with the hypothesis of its having been obtained by undue influence. It must be shown that they are inconsistent with a contrary hypothesis.

Undue influence was proved in *Re Marsh Estate*,[179] reproduced below.

RE MARSH ESTATE; FRYER v. HARRIS
(1991), 41 E.T.R. 225
Nova Scotia Supreme Court
[Appellate Division]

The testatrix made a will in 1988 by which she devised her principal asset, that is, her house, to the respondents, Rev. and Mrs. Harris, and left the residue to her sister, the appellant, Hilda Fryer. In 1988, the testatrix gave a power of attorney to Hilda's husband, Frank, because he was managing her business and banking affairs. Later that year Frank learned of the devise, told the testatrix he didn't like it, and since she had given the property to the Harrises, she should give Rev. Harris a power of attorney to do all the work he had been doing for her. Apparently the testatrix then determined that she needed Frank and told him to contact the Royal Trust, which had been named the executor. Royal Trust requested a solicitor to prepare a codicil for the testatrix to change the devise from the respondents to Hilda, but to make sure there was no undue influence involved. The testatrix told the solicitor and her clerk when they attended on her at the time of signing that she was making the change because Frank had been good to her. The solicitor thought that the testatrix had capacity and she caused the codicil to be executed.

The probate court judge determined that the testatrix had capacity, but refused probate because she found that Frank exercised undue influence over the testatrix. Frank appealed.

CHIPMAN J.A.:

. . .

The finding of testamentary capacity is not disputed, and there is no question as to the relevant principles governing undue influence as a ground for setting aside a testamentary devise. Influence, to be undue influence, must amount to

---

178 *Ibid.*
179 (1991), 41 E.T.R. 225 (N.S. C.A.), varying (1990), 99 N.S.R. (2d) 221 (Prob. Ct.).

coercion. What is coercion in any given case depends on the circumstances. The burden of establishing undue influence rests upon those who attack the impugned transaction.[180] After expressing concern as to Frank Fryer's credibility, Judge Bateman said:[181]

> There is no question that Mr. Fryer exerted influence, nor any question that the exercising of that influence resulted in the change in bequest consistent with Mr. Fryer's wishes. The question is whether the influence was undue in this case.
>
> Mr. Fryer presents as a very opinionated, confident and outspoken man. He clearly felt that Reverend Harris had inappropriately procured the bequest and thus was justified in speaking strongly against it. Had he only spoken against the bequest to the Reverend Harris I would have had more difficulty in finding undue influence. On the facts before me, however, Mr. Fryer went farther than that. He implicitly, if not expressly, threatened to withdraw his assistance from Mrs. Marsh if the Will was not changed. In Mrs. Marsh's poor physical situation resulting in her complete dependence on Mr. Fryer for her business affairs and her minimal contact with other support systems, I find that the influence exercised by Mr. Fryer was undue, even accepting his version of the exchange between him and Mrs. Marsh.

Having reviewed the record, consisting of exhibits and the testimony of the witnesses, we are satisfied that there was no palpable error made by Judge Bateman in her finding that undue influence exerted by Frank Fryer brought about the execution of the codicil. This is so, even though her finding that Mr. Fryer gave specific instructions as to the change in the will is not supported by direct evidence. The evidence, particularly that of Mr. McGill, Mr. Fryer, and Ms. Whelton supports the conclusion that the testatrix was dependent upon Frank Fryer, and that there was an implied, if not expressed threat by him to withdraw the assistance that he had been giving her. His testimony, as well as that of the other witnesses, must be considered in the context of an unwell, elderly lady who was dependent upon her brother-in-law for the assistance which he had been giving her. All the evidence supports the finding of a threat to withdraw assistance, which in the circumstances amounted to coercion.

The appeal is dismissed.

. . .

Notes and Questions

1. In *Re Marsh Estate*, the trial judge found that Rev. and Mrs. Harris did not exert undue influence on the testatrix.

2. Frank Fryer was an appellant in the *Marsh* case. Did he have standing to be a party?

3. You will note that the person exercising the undue influence in *Re Marsh Estate* did not himself benefit from his actions. This is because of the reason equity intervenes when undue influence has occurred. Lord Lindley L.J. said in *Allcard v. Skinner*[182] that equity does not set aside gifts because "it is right and expedient to save persons from the

---

180 See *Wingrove v. Wingrove* (1885), 11 P.D. 81; *Re Harmes; Harmes and Custodian of Enemy Property v. Hinkson*, [1946] 2 W.W.R. 433, [1946] 3 D.L.R. 497 (P.C.).

181 At 99 N.S.R. (2d) p. 232.

182 (1887), 36 Ch. D. 145 at 182-3 (C.A.), quoted by Wilson J. in *Geffen v. Goodman Estate* (1991), 81 D.L.R. (4th) 211 at 220 (S.C.C.).

consequences of their own folly," but because "it is right and expedient to save them from being victimized by other people." Hence, it does not matter who committed the undue influence and whether that person obtained a consequential benefit. Because one person has victimized another, the gift must be set aside, or the will denied probate. Thus, for example, an *inter vivos* gift by a daughter was set aside on proof that her father had unduly influenced her to transfer moneys to which she was absolutely entitled into an irrevocable trust that provided only marginal benefit for the father and the settlor's brother.[183] Similarly, if friends or family members of the person who commits the undue influence are the ones benefited by a gift, the gift will be set aside, even though the friends or family members themselves were not party to the undue influence.[184] These principles appear also to have been adhered to, at least by implication, in *Keljanovic Estate v. Sanseverino*.[185] Two partners had acquired their home as joint tenants, but one of them later converted it into a tenancy in common. When the latter was dying, an acquaintance persuaded her to reconvert the title into a joint tenancy. The trial judge found that the conduct of the acquaintance did not amount to undue influence and the majority in the Court of Appeal dismissed the appeal. Thus, by implication the trial judge and the majority in the Court of Appeal must have been of the view that if the conduct of the acquaintance had amounted to undue influence, the transfer would have been set aside.[186]

3. Since undue influence is a species of fraud, the allegation of undue influence, if unsuccessful, can result in costs being awarded against the litigant, rather than out of the estate.[187] For this reason, counsel may prefer, if the allegation is unlikely to be successful, to attack a will by alleging only that the testator lacked capacity and did not know and approve the contents of the will.

4. T, a bachelor, was dying of a disease which, while it does not impair the intelligence, induces mental torpor and, in the end, coma. While he was in the hospital, his close friend and solicitor, H, visited him regularly. The attending physician suggested that H prepare T's will and H did so while he and T were alone in the room. The will contained a variety of substantial bequests to charities, to the testator's nephew in Toronto and his niece in Greece. However, the residue of the estate, which was substantial, was left to H, apparently at T's direction, H having suggested various other alternatives. The evidence shows that T had capacity at the time he executed the will. Should this will be refused probate for undue influence?[188]

5. The principles concerning undue influence are also applied when a person has poisoned the mind of the testator against a potential beneficiary, although this situation is really one of fraud. Typically, but not necessarily, a relative will allege things against another with a view to having the latter cut out of the will and thereby increasing the legacy of the accuser. It must be shown in these cases that the testator believed the accusations and acted upon them.[189]

---

183 *Bullock v. Lloyd's Bank Ltd.*, [1955] 1 Ch. 317.

184 *Bridgeman v. Green* (1957), Wilm. 58, 97 E.R. 22; *Huguenin v. Baseley* (1807), 14 Ves. 273, 33 E.R. 526.

185 (2000), 34 E.T.R. (2d) 32, 186 D.L.R. (4th) 481 (Ont. C.A.).

186 See also Albert H. Oosterhoff, Comment (2001), 20 E.T. & P.J. 115.

187 *Re Cutliffe*, [1959] P. 6 (C.A.). And see *Re Bisyk (No. 2)* (1980), 32 O.R. (2d) 281 (H.C.), affirmed (1981), 32 O.R. (2d) 281n, ed. note, in which costs were awarded against the solicitor for unfounded allegations of undue influence.

188 See *Harmes v. Hinkson*, [1946] 2 W.W.R. 433, [1946] 3 D.L.R. 497 (P.C.). *Cf. Goldsworthy v. Thompson* (1974), 46 D.L.R. (3d) 238 (S.C.C.).

189 *Pocock v. Pocock*, [1950] O.R. 734 (H.C.); affirmed without discussing this point [1952] O.R. 155 (C.A.).

Mayrand v. Dussault[190] is an example. The testator was suffering from a wasting disease when his brother suggested that the disease was caused mainly by the carelessness and lack of skill of the testator's wife in preparing his food. As a result, the testator revoked his former will, which left everything to his wife and made a new one in which the brother was named the principal beneficiary. The court held that the second will could not stand because of the brother's undue influence.

6. It may happen that the testator has executed a valid will and desires to change it, but is prevented from doing so by the undue influence of beneficiaries thereunder. In those circumstances, the will stands, but the beneficiaries in question will be held to take their legacies on a resulting trust for the estate.[191]

7. Two nieces of the testatrix, who were also major beneficiaries under her will, were instrumental in having her will drawn up. The testatrix had poor eyesight and no one had read the will to her prior to her signing it. The trial judge held that the will was invalid as it had been prepared and executed under suspicious circumstances. On appeal, the court stated that the proponents of the will had demonstrated that the testatrix had capacity and knew and understood its contents, thus discharging the burden of suspicion. There was no continuing onus upon them to disprove the alleged fraud or undue influence. Rather, the opponents of the will had failed to meet the onus of establishing their allegations. The will had been prepared in accordance with the testatrix's wishes, she had had ample opportunity to inspect it herself and she was an alert and independent woman who must have known she was executing a new will.[192]

Hubley v. Cox Estate[193] illustrates a clear case of undue influence. A mother had made an earlier will in which she left her estate equally between her two sons, D and P. D was married and had children, P was single, lived with the testatrix and looked after her, and was HIV positive. In 1996 the testatrix made a new will in which she left her entire estate to P. She felt obliged to P because he was looking after her and because D had shared in his father's estate from which P had been excluded. When D learned of the new will, he told his mother that it was illegal, stroked through all the pages, and wrote the word "void" on them. Then he and his mother signed the pages. The "revocation" was ineffective because the second witness signed later. However, the court held that, in any event, the revocation was invalid because of D's undue influence over his mother when she was sick, old, and upset by fighting in the family over her estate.

8. In an earlier part of this chapter we considered *Banton v. Banton*.[194] It involved a 31-year-old waitress, Muna Yassin, who persuaded an 86-year-old man, George Banton, to marry her and make two successive wills in her favour. His children contested the validity of the wills. Cullity J. assessed the evidence as follows:[195]

...Based on the evidence I heard, including the very strong impressions I received from her own testimony, I have no doubt at all that this influence was deliberately exerted to enable her to obtain control and, ultimately, the ownership of his assets. Her tenacity and strength of will is shown by her ability to deal with his doubts and the opposition of his family. After she consented to marry

190 (1907), 38 S.C.R. 460.
191 *Betts v. Doughty* (1879), 5 P.D. 26.
192 *Hall Estate* (1988), 50 D.L.R. (4th) 51, 52 Man. R. (2d) 1 (C.A.).
193 (1999), 31 E.T.R. (2d) 71 (N.S.S.C.).
194 (1998), 164 D.L.R. (4th) 176, supp. reasons *loc. cit.* at 244 (Ont. Gen. Div.). See Albert H. Oosterhoff, "Consequences of a January/December Marriage: A Cautionary Tale" (1999), 18 E.T. & P.J. 261. See also *Banton v. CIBC Trust Corp.* (1999), 182 D.L.R. (4th) 486 (Ont. S.C.J.). See Note and Question 7 in part 4(d)(ii).
195 *Banton v. Banton, ibid.*, at 164 D.L.R. (4th) p. 219.

him, her influence became overwhelming and irresistible. The speed with which she was able to procure a will and a power of attorney in her favour is testimony to this as well as to his weak and vulnerable mental condition.

His Honour described George Banton as "a lonely, depressed, terminally ill, severely disabled and cognitively impaired old man whose enfeebled condition made him an easy prey for a person like Muna with designs on his property."[196] He also found that Muna was not a credible witness[197] and concluded[198] that as a result of her influence George was not able to make an independent decision respecting the disposition of his estate when he made the 1994 and 1995 wills. Rather, when he made those wills, George was expressing Muna's will, not his own. Hence, the children met the onus that rested on them and proved undue influence.

9. Undue influence is a species of fraud,[199] although fraud is a wider concept. Thus, a will may be contested in the basis of undue influence as well as fraud. This is apparent from *Re Crompton; Crompton v. Williams*.[200]

The testatrix was a widow. Her husband died in 1927, intestate and the testatrix and the two children each got one-third of his estate. All three were well educated, but had little business experience. They placed full confidence in the husband's solicitor, Mr. Denison, who looked after their affairs. Since 1929, when the testatrix had a stroke, he would come to her house if any business needed to be transacted.

The defendant, Williams, was a solicitor in the office of Mr. Denison and he became involved with the testatrix and her daughter in connection with their income tax affairs. The defendant suggested that certain of their bonds should be checked over and that was done. Nothing was said about payment for this service, but it was later agreed that this would be $35 per night. The defendant asked the testatrix and her daughter not to tell anyone about this and he used an outside secretary for this service. The defendant also sold some jewellery for the testatrix and her children in order to pay taxes. He was handsomely paid for his services and did not report this to the firm. He gained the testatrix' affection by telling her that he was an orphan and that he was disadvantaged. He criticized the son, a spendthrift, who was supported by his mother and sister, and suggested that mother and daughter should make new wills and that he be retained by them on an annual retainer basis. When he suggested that he ought to leave Denison's firm, they disagreed and he then suggested that in order to make him secure they should each leave him $60,000 by will. The instructions for both wills were drawn up by the defendant, who inserted his name followed by gifts of $60,000, and the instructions were then copied out by the two ladies. The defendant informed them that another solicitor would have to draw the will and he obtained a Mr. Shaver to do so. Mr. Shaver asked the testatrix about the large gift and about possible undue influence and was informed that the ladies felt indebted to the defendant for various services performed by him and that the wills were drawn of their own free will. Nevertheless the testatrix reduced the gift to the defendant to $40,000, but said she would make a present gift to him of $15,000. After discussions between the testatrix and the defendant it was agreed that she would transfer $15,000 worth of Ontario bearer bonds to him. Mr. Shaver advised the ladies not to go ahead with this gift and confirmed his advice in writing. The defendant then told him that he would discuss it with

---

196 *Ibid.*, at p. 222.
197 *Ibid.*, at p. 208.
198 *Ibid.*, at p. 221.
199 *Allcard v. Skinner* (1887), 36 Ch. D. 145.
200 [1938] O.R. 543, [1938] 4 D.L.R. 237 (H.C.).

another solicitor, a Mr. MacDonald, who seems to have satisfied himself that Mrs. Crompton was competent to make the gift and that she was making it of her own free will. The bonds were accordingly transferred to the defendant. Mr. Shaver thereafter drew the retainer agreement, although objecting to it. However, the document was never signed.

The testatrix' will named the defendant and the son and daughter as co-executors, giving one-half of the residue to the daughter and the balance to maintain the son for life, with the remainder to his issue. At the time that instructions were given for the will, Mrs. Crompton was suffering from arteriosclerosis, but her doctor thought she had testamentary capacity.

Shortly thereafter, the transactions became public and the Denison firm fired the defendant. The son and daughter then brought proceedings to determine the validity of the gifts *inter vivos* and the bequest to the defendant in the will of the testatrix.

The court invalidated the *inter vivos* gift of the bonds on the ground that the defendant failed to rebut the presumption of undue influence raised by his confidential relationship towards the testator. In any event, undue influence was proved.

With respect to the will, the onus of proving undue influence lay on the plaintiffs and they were able to prove it easily. The court further concluded that the defendant had used fraudulent practices to obtain the gift under the will, having impressed secrecy upon the testatrix, having kept her from consulting her natural adviser, Mr. Denison, and having made various representations to the testatrix. Consequently, the court admitted the will to probate, except for the clause giving the $40,000 to the defendant.

Should the whole will have been denied probate?

6. FRAUD

If a testator is induced to make a will or a disposition in it because of fraud, the will or the disposition cannot stand.[201] However, it must be shown that the will or the disposition would not have been made apart from the fraud.[202] Thus, if the beneficiary goes through a form of marriage with the testator while already married and without informing him or her of it, the gift will be set aside,[203] but a gift to the beneficiary's child will stand if that person is not a party to the fraud.[204] A gift to a "wife" will be valid, however, if the "wife" practised no deceit, but thought that the marriage was valid.[205]

---

201 *Mayrand v. Dussault* (1907), 38 S.C.R. 460.
202 *Kennell v. Abbott* (1799), 4 Ves. 802 at 808, 31 E.R. 416.
203 *Ibid.*
204 *Wilkinson v. Joughin* (1866), L.R. 2 Eq. 319.
205 *In the Estate of Posner*, [1953] P. 277, [1953] 1 All E.R. 1123. *Cf.*, with respect to *inter vivos* gifts: *Rowse v. Harris*, [1963] 2 O.R. 232, 39 D.L.R. (2d) 29 (H.C.); *Re Isaacs*, [1954] O.R. 942, [1955] 1 D.L.R. 327 (C.A.).

7. MISTAKE

(a) Introduction

Since the propounder of the will must prove that the testator knew and approved its contents,[206] it follows that any part of the will may be refused probate if it was inserted by mistake. However, the law severely restricts the court of probate in this respect. The court does, indeed, have power to strike out passages inserted by mistake, but it does not have power to substitute words that the testator intended to use.[207] Moreover, it has power to strike out only for certain kinds of mistake, as will appear from the following materials.

The court's power to correct errors may be invoked in three types of situations, namely:

(a) when there is a patent mistake on the face of the will;
(b) when a drafting error has occurred; and
(c) when the testator has executed the wrong instrument.

Further Reading

P.M. Wood, "Rectification of Mistakes in the Inducement of Testamentary Dispositions" (1990 - 91), 16 U. of Queensland L.J. 196.

Stan J. Sokol, *Mistakes in Wills in Canada* (Scarborough: Carswell, 1995), ch. 3.

(b) Patent Mistakes

A patent mistake is one that appears from the will itself or from evidence of surrounding circumstances showing that the testator made an error about an existing fact. In such a situation the will, or the disposition in it is ineffective and denied probate, provided that it can be shown that the will or the gift was made in reliance upon the mistaken belief.[208]

Thus, in *Re Wright*[209] the testator stated in his will that he had no relatives and was, therefore, leaving his estate to X, a stranger. In fact, he had a wife and daughter living in England. The will was held to be inoperative because the court found that the testator believed them to be dead and that he would have benefited them had he thought they were alive.[210]

---

206 *Cleare v. Cleare* (1869), L.R. 1. P. & D. 655 at 657, *per* Lord Penzance.
207 *Re Schott*, [1901] P. 190; *Re Doner* (1931), 40 O.W.N. 120; *Alexander Estate v. Adams* (1998), 20 E.T.R. (2d) 294 (B.C.S.C.).
208 *Re Wright; Burrows v. Honeysette*, [1937] 3 W.W.R. 452 (Sask. Surr. Ct.).
209 *Ibid.*
210 The principle is similar to a revocation which, if made because of a mistaken belief in a state of facts, is treated as a *conditional* revocation and disregarded if the belief is *wrong*. This point is discussed in a later chapter.

(c) Drafting Errors

In exercising its function to correct errors, the court of probate is not as restricted in admitting evidence as the court of construction. Thus, for example, the court of probate may hear evidence of surrounding circumstances and even direct evidence of the testator's intention. However, in the leading case, *Guardhouse v. Blackburn*,[211] Sir J.P. Wilde circumscribed the admissibility of evidence on the ground that since the *Wills Act*[212] imposed strict formalities concerning the execution of wills, parol evidence ought not to be admitted to subvert the intention of the statute, save in clearly defined situations. His Lordship, therefore, laid down the following rules:[213]

> First, that before a paper so executed is entitled to probate, the Court must be satisfied that the testator knew and approved of the contents at the time he signed it. Secondly, that except in certain cases, where suspicion attaches to the document, the fact of the testator's execution is sufficient proof that he knew and approved the contents. Thirdly, that although the testator knew and approved the contents, the paper may still be rejected, on proof establishing, beyond all possibility of mistake, that he did not intend the paper to operate as a will. Fourthly, that although the testator did know and approve the contents, the paper may be refused probate, if it be proved that any fraud has been purposely practised on the testator in obtaining his execution thereof. Fifthly, that subject to this last preceding proposition, the fact that the will has been duly read over to a capable testator on the occasion of its execution, or that its contents have been brought to his notice in any other way, should, when coupled with his execution thereof, be held conclusive evidence that he approved as well as knew the contents thereof. Sixthly, that the above rules apply equally to a portion of the will as to the whole.

With respect to the fifth rule, however, later cases have held that it is not a rule of law, but merely a rule of evidence. It always remains a question of fact whether the disputed language was actually brought to the testator's attention and was adopted by the testator.[214]

The facts of *Guardhouse v. Blackburn* were as follows: The testatrix had disposed of certain parcels of real property by her professionally drawn will and charged several legacies against the real property. By a later codicil, she revoked some of these legacies and substituted others, and intended that the new legacies should be paid out of her personal estate. However, her solicitor drafted the codicil in these terms: "I direct that all legacies therein [referring to the will] and herein given (and not revoked) are to be paid out of my personal estate. In all other respects, I ratify my said will." He read the codicil to the testatrix. After her death the solicitor realized that the words "therein and" were inserted by mistake. However, the court held that the words could not be expunged because the will had been read over to the testatrix.

---

211 (1866), L.R. 1 P. & D. 109.

212 7 Will 4 & 1 Vict., c. 26 (1837).

213 *Guardhouse v. Blackburn, supra,* at p. 116.

214 *Fulton v. Andrew* (1875), L.R. 7 H.L. 448, at 469, *per* Lord Hatherley. And see *Re Morris,* [1971] P. 62, [1970] 1 All E.R. 1057; *Re Reynette-James,* [1976] 1 W.L.R. 161, [1975] 3 All E.R. 1037, noted (1976), 3 E. & T.Q. 105; *Re Phelan,* [1972] Fam. 33.

The force of the rule which, I submit, represents formalism in the extreme, has been much diminished over the years and, in light of *Re Morris*,[215] reproduced below, has now been virtually dissipated.

In any event, it appears that, if the drafter inserted words by inadvertence, which neither the drafter nor the testator intended to use, the fact that the will was read over to the testator is irrelevant and the error can, in certain circumstances, be corrected. The following dictum of Lord Blackburn in *Rhodes v. Rhodes*[216] explains this principle:

> When an instrument purporting to be the will of the deceased person has been executed by the deceased in the proper manner, but it is sufficiently proved that though he executed the instrument, yet that from fraud he executed that which was not his will there is no difficulty in pronouncing that the instrument is not his will. And it has been held that when it is sufficiently proved that the instrument comprised his will, but that from fraud, or perhaps from inadvertence, such as that *In the Goods of Duane*,[217] the instrument which he actually executed contained also something which was not his will, this latter part is to be rejected. And in such a case, if this latter part is so distinct and severable from the true part that the rejection of it does not alter the construction of the true part, it has been held that, consistently with the Statute of Wills, the execution of what was shown to be the true will, and something more, may be treated as the execution of the true will alone. A much more difficult question arises where the rejection of words alters the sense of those which remain. For even though the Court is convinced that the words were improperly introduced, so that if the instrument was inter vivos they would reform the instrument and order one in different words to be executed, it cannot make the dead man execute a new instrument; and there seems much difficulty in treating the will after its sense is thus altered as valid within the 9th section of the [Wills Act],[218] the signature at the end of the will required by that enactment having been attached to what bore quite a different meaning.

The correction may be made in the circumstances outlined by Lord Blackburn even if it leaves part of the will meaningless,[219] unless the correction qualifies or cuts down what remains.[220]

Another kind of problem arises when the drafter has selected particular language to carry out the testator's intention, but because he or she failed to understand the implications of the language used, a quite different result obtains. This is what happened in *Rhodes v. Rhodes*.[221] The testator was on his deathbed when he gave instructions for his will. His solicitor, thinking it impossible that the testator and his wife would have children, made no provision for them, but made provision for the testator's wife and others, and left the residue to the testator's natural daughter, all in accordance with a previous will. But when the testator heard the draft, he wanted provision made for possible children, since the former will contained a similar provision. The solicitor inserted the provisions for the testator's children, prefaced by the words "and from and after the decease of my said wife leaving issue of our marriage." He then united the new provisions to

---

215 *Supra.*
216 (1882), 7 A.C. 192 at 198 (P.C.).
217 2 Sw. & T. 590.
218 7 Will. 4 & 1 Vict. c. 26.
219 *Re Boehm*, [1891] P. 247.
220 *Re Horrocks*, [1939] P. 198, [1939] 1 All E.R. 579 (C.A.).
221 (1882), 7 A.C. 192 (P.C.).

those he previously drafted, but prefaced the latter by the words, "and from and after the decease of my said wife without leaving issue our said marriage." He inserted these words without specific instruction from the testator, had no particular reason for inserting them, but thought they should go into an ordinary will. In consequence, the daughter would have to wait until the testator's wife died before becoming entitled to the residue. The solicitor then read the will over to the testator, who executed it. The Privy Council opined that the testator probably had no intelligent appreciation of the effect of the expression used by the solicitor, but trusted his solicitor to carry out his wishes. In these circumstances, said Lord Blackburn:[222]

> Their Lordships think that there is no difference between the words which a testator himself uses in drawing up his will, and the words which are bona fide used by one whom he trusts to draw it up for him. In either case there is a great risk that words may be used that do not express the intention. There probably are very few wills in which it might not be contended that words have been so used. However this may be, the Court which has to construe the will must take the words as they find them.

In the end result, however, the Privy Council, when it turned to construe the will, was able to hold that the plaintiff's interest vested in possession immediately.

A similar type of case is *Re Horrocks*.[223] By her professionally drawn will, the testatrix devised the residue of her estate upon trust "for such charitable institution or institutions or other charitable or benevolent object or objects in Preston and district as my acting trustee or trustees may in his or their absolute discretion select." She died on March 29, 1929. Subsequently, her solicitor, Mr. Houghton, discovered that the use of the word "or" in place of "and" between "charitable" and "benevolent" rendered the residuary gift void for uncertainty. He alleged that the mistake was due to a typist's error. The trial judge granted probate after deleting the word "or."

The effect of the deletion was to render the gift certain, for the Court of Appeal held that the expression "charitable [ ] benevolent" should be read conjunctively in the same way as if the word "and" had been inserted between them. However, the law was quite clear that the use of the disjunctive "or" would make such a gift void. The reason is that the term "charitable" has a recognized meaning in law, whereas the term "benevolent" does not. In some respects it is wider, in other respects narrower in meaning than "charitable." But only gifts which are charitable are enforceable.

The Court of Appeal, allowing the appeal, concluded that the solicitor simply was unaware of this point of law, had, in fact, chosen the word "or" deliberately and only acquired the necessary knowledge later. In the course of his judgment in *Horrocks*, Sir Wilfrid Greene M.R. distinguished two cases in which the court of probate had struck out words, on the ground that the words omitted were self-contained and did not alter the sense of what remained: *In the goods of Boehm*[224]

---

222 *Ibid.*, at p. 199.
223 [1931] P. 198, [1939] 1 All E.R. 579 (C.A.).
224 [1891] P. 247.

and *In the goods of Schott*[225] In the first, the testator's drafter had inserted the name of one of the testator's two daughters twice so that she appeared to be receiving two legacies and the other none: the court struck out the name where it had been wrongly inserted. In the second, the residuary clause gave the "revenue of the said" proceeds of sale of certain property to named trustees. The court struck the incorrect words.

RE MORRIS
[1971] P. 62, [1970] 1 All E.R. 1057
Probate Division

By clause 3 of her will the testatrix left certain personal property to Miss Hurdwell, an employee. By clause 7, she left a large number of pecuniary legacies, each of which was preceded by a Roman numeral. Clause 7(iv) gave Miss Hurdwell £2,000 plus the equivalent of two years' wages.

Subsequently, the testatrix wished to change the gifts to Miss Hurdwell and wrote to her solicitor with instructions to prepare a codicil changing only clauses 3 and 7(iv). The solicitor did so and sent the codicil to her, and she had it executed. Unfortunately, he made an error. His draft purported to revoke clauses 3 and 7 (instead of 7(iv)) of the will and to replace them with other gifts.

In the probate action, the solicitor candidly admitted his error. The court found that the testatrix relied upon her solicitor and that she probably read the codicil over cursorily, but did not compare it with her will.

LATEY J.:

. . .

Now the law is that for a testamentary instrument to be valid, its contents must be known to and approved by the testator who executes it. That scarcely needs saying. Every canon of commonsense and justice establishes it.

Unless one or other of the two rules for which Mr. Holroyd Pearce contends covers this case, on the facts as proved it is not credible that any person of commonsense, any juror, any judge, using the English language in its ordinary meaning, could conclude that this testatrix knew and approved of the contents of this document. Of course, she did not. That some rule or rules of evidence or law could have been evolved by the court to require the court to hold by some fictitious or artificial reasoning that nevertheless she did know and approve is repugnant, to say the least.

Is there any such rule?

Mr. Holroyd Pearce argues that there are two and, if one looks at some of the cases and some of the dicta, it must be said in justice to his argument that it is not without support.

Before considering those two alleged rules, it must first be said that the law is clear that where there is absence of knowledge and approval (for example, because of mistake, as in this case) the court has no power to rectify by adding words to

---

225 [1901] P. 190.

the instrument. This has been so clearly stated judicially and for so long that it is not open to question in this court and can only be changed by legislation or, possibly, by a higher tribunal. Were it not so the defect in this codicil would be simply and entirely cured by the insertion of the Roman numeral "(iv)" after the numeral 7 in clause 1, thereby giving effect to the testatrix's intentions in their entirety.

Mr. Merrylees, indeed, advanced an argument to that effect. The court of probate has power in certain limited circumstances to rectify by excluding words from the executed paper. By so doing it alters the executed paper. Why, then should it not have power to alter it by adding words in certain limited circumstances? The Wills Act, 1837, after all, was designed to minimise the danger of fraud. It was not concerned with, and did not contemplate, mistakes, though it appears that the early authorities which establish that there was no power to rectify by addition must have assumed that mistake was also contemplated. If the matter were res integra it might not, to my mind, be a hopeless argument, but in the light of the long established law it is today an argument which must be rejected.

The two rules for which Mr. Holroyd Pearce contends are these: First, a rule of evidence: That a competent testator who has read, or has had read over to him, the instrument and has executed it must be taken to have known and approved of its contents, except where there is a suspicion of fraud. Against this Mr. Taylor contends that such a rule, if there ever was one, has been eroded by subsequent authority.

Secondly, a rule of law: That where a testator has delegated to an appointed draftsman (a solicitor, for example) the drafting of the instrument, and the testator executes the paper drafted by the draftsman acting bona fide the testator is bound by any mistake that the draftsman has made. Against this Mr. Taylor argues that an intending testator cannot delegate to another the task of making the will, and that knowledge and approval of what a draftsman has written is imputed to a testator in a strictly limited category of circumstances only.

I have done my best to consider all of the many cases to which counsel have referred, and to see whether a reconciliation is possible producing consistent principles. Such an attempt in the past has produced intellectual gymnastics, if not acrobatics. But I have not been capable of one which does produce such a reconciliation. I do not believe that all the decisions and all the dicta are reconcilable. What does seem clear is that there has been a developing trend (with perhaps an occasional regression) towards a more flexible and (dare one say?) more realistic approach. I refer to some, but by no means all, of the reported cases.

1. *The rule of evidence?* It is argued that a rule of universal application was enunciated by Lord Penzance in *Guardhouse v. Blackburn*.[226] The rule appears from the first, fourth and fifth propositions stated in the judgment.[227]

[His Lordship quoted these propositions, set out above, and continued:]

---

226 (1886) L.R. 1 P. & D. 109.
227 *Ibid.*, at p. 116.

That wording is clear and unequivocal and leaves no doubt that Lord Penzance intended to and did lay down absolute rules. If the testator is capable, had the will read over to him or otherwise had notice of its contents at the time of execution, then in the absence of fraud the court cannot have regard to other evidence showing that he did not in fact know and approve: he must be taken to have known and approved.

Lord Penzance himself so regarded it in *Atter v. Atkinson*.[228]

. . .

Shortly afterwards in *Harter v. Harter*[229] Sir James Hannen expressly accepted and agreed with Lord Penzance.

These three cases represent the high water mark of the rule. Presumably there were good reasons in the interests of justice nearly 100 years ago which impelled the court to fetter its own power to get at the true facts. But has not the more modern trend in many fields been to strike such fetters off, so that that court can make the best use of all materials available to ascertain the truth? At any rate, in this field there has been, in my opinion, a progressive erosion of the rigidity of the rule. This began in *Fulton v. Andrew*.[230] The material part of the headnote[231] reads:

> There is no unyielding rule of law (especially where the ingredient of fraud enters into the case) that, when it has been proved that a testator, competent in mind, has had a will read over to him, and has thereupon executed it, all farther inquiry is shut out.

. . .

In my opinion, the part of the headnote already quoted correctly distils the essence of the decision. Eighty years later, in another context but in similar general vein, Jenkins L.J. in *Martell v. Consett Iron Co. Ltd.*[232] said:

> But it is an abuse of authorities to extract from judgments general statements of the law made in relation to the facts and circumstances of particular cases and treat them as concluding cases in which the facts and circumstances are entirely different....

Looking at the cases which followed *Fulton v. Andrew*[233] some of which could not have been decided the way they were if the rule had continued to apply, it seems clear that eminent judges regarded the rule in *Guardhouse v. Blackburn*[234] as having received its quietus and as no longer binding the court.

Two further extracts from the speeches in *Fulton v. Andrew*[235] demonstrate that by "reading" or "reading over" there must be more than a mere literal, physical

---

228 (1869) L.R. 1 P. & D. 665.
229 (1873) L.R. 3 P. & D. 11 at 22 .
230 (1875) L.R. 7 H.L. 448.
231 At p. 449.
232 [1955] 1 All E.R. 481 at 498, [1955] Ch. 363 at 414.
233 (1875), L.R. 7 H.L. 448.
234 (1866), L.R. 1 P. & D. 109.
235 L.R. 7 H.L. 448.

fact of reading. Lord Cairns, spoke[236] of "the consciousness of the testator" regarding the contents of the will, Lord Hatherly said:[237]

> I do say that at least the jury should be satisfied that it was read over to him, and not only that it was read over to him, but that it was read over in such a manner as that the discrepancy between the instructions and the will was brought before the consideration of the testator.

In principle, surely, it is as necessary that this should be enquired into where the question is one of mistake, as where the question is one of fraud?

. . .

The testatrix was competent, did (as I have found) in a literal, physical sense read the codicil and did duly execute it, and if the rule in *Guardhouse v. Blackburn*[238] survived, I should be bound to find that she knew and approved of the contents of it. But that rule does not survive in any shape or form and on all the evidence I have no doubt at all that she did not in fact know and approve its contents.

That leaves the question whether there is a rule of law requiring that knowledge and approval must be imputed in certain circumstances and, if there is, whether this is such a case. To put it another way; should a testator be bound by a draftsman's mistake of which the testator is not aware?

2. *A rule of imputed knowledge and approval?* Without derogating from the helpful arguments and the review of the many cases, I can state my conclusion on this aspect and the reasons for it, more shortly.

Mr. Holroyd Pearce based his proposition primarily on what Lord Blackburn said giving the judgment of the Judicial Committee of the Privy Council in *Rhodes v. Rhodes*[239] Lord Blackburn said:[240]

> [His Lordship quoted the excerpt from Lord Blackburn's opinion reproduced above, and continued:]

From this and other cases that followed it is established, in my opinion, that there are cases where, though the testator did not in fact know and approve the effect of what he is executing, he is deemed to do so: he is bound by the draftsman's mistake. Here again it is not easy to reconcile all the decisions and dicta, but certainly the rule does not cover all cases where a draftsman had made a mistake; indeed, it applies to a limited class of case. Its basis is one of expediency, because without it confusion and uncertainty would produce worse results.

The fundamental principle is that an intending testator cannot delegate to another the task of deciding how his property shall be willed. He cannot "hand over the making of his will to another".[241]

---

236 *Ibid.*, at p. 460.
237 *Ibid.*, at p. 473.
238 (1866), L.R. 1 P. & D. 109.
239 (1882) 7 App. Cas. 192.
240 *Ibid.*, at pp. 199-200.
241 See *Hastilow v. Stobie* (1865), L.R. 1 P. & D. 64 at 67.

But though he cannot hand over the *making* of the will, he can entrust someone else with the task of *drafting* a will which he (the intending testator) wants to make. The scope of the draftsman's authority is to carry into effect the testator's intentions. In some cases (where, for example, an expert in law is needed to provide the appropriate wording to give effect in law to the testator's intentions) the testator has to accept the phraseology selected by the draftsman without himself really understanding its esoteric meaning, and in such a case he adopts it and knowledge and approval is imputed to him. If the draftsman in the use of the selected phraseology which he, knowing the testator's intentions, has deliberately and not *per incuriam* chosen, and thus himself known and approved, has made a mistake as to the effect of that phraseology, the testator, having adopted it, is bound by the mistake.

So far, I think, the law is plain.

I was much attracted by Mr. Taylor's argument that that is where the line should be drawn. He argued that, save in that limited class of case, the testator is bound only by what the draftsman writes on his instructions. If he puts in something which is contrary to the testator's instructions, he is acting outside the scope of his authority, and the testator is not bound unless, of course, the discrepancy is brought to his understanding and he adopts it. To enlarge the category of cases in which, although unaware of the draftsman's mistake, knowledge and approval is imputed to the testator and he is bound by it, would be to subtract unnecessarily and wrongly from the fundamental principle that it is for a testator and no-one else to make the will.

But whether the line can be drawn there so that it follows that in all other cases there is not knowledge and approval, and the court thus has power to intervene, is far from plain. There are decisions and dicta either way.

As is said in *Mortimer's Probate Practice*,[242] it is difficult "to extract a definite principle from the cases on this subject...." The author suggests that the cases establish the following propositions.[243]

> *First.* Where the mind of the draftsman has really been applied to the particular clause, then, whether the error has arisen from the fact that he misunderstood the instructions of the testator, or, having understood the instructions, has used inappropriate language in seeking to give effect to them, the testator who executes the will is - in the absence of fraud - bound by the error so made as if it were his own, even if the mistake were not directly brought to his notice; and the court will not omit from the probate the words so introduced into the will.
>
> *Secondly.* Where the mind of the draftsman has never really been applied to the words in a particular clause, and the words are introduced into the will *per incuriam*, without advertence to their significance and effect, by a mere clerical error on the part of the draftsman or engrosser, the testator is not bound by the mistake unless the introduction of such words was directly brought to his notice.

---

242 2nd ed. (1927), at p. 91.
243 *Ibid.*, at pp. 91-2.

There is nothing in this, so far as I can see, inconsistent with the decision and reasoning in *In re Horrocks*[244] and it is supported by the authorities cited in *Mortimer's Probate Practice*.

[The court then discussed the *Horrocks* case, and continued:]

But there is, so far as I can see, nothing in the judgment to vitiate the propositions in *Mortimer's Probate Practice*. Indeed, Greene M.R., used the word "selected" in the sense, I think, of consciously choosing, and he made it plain that the court could exclude words where there was a mere slip, and could do so where the effect was to leave what was left devoid of ascertainable content and thus inoperative (so altering the intention as expressed on the face of the instrument).

. . .

But whether the line is to be drawn as suggested by *Mortimer* or possibly, as submitted by Mr. Taylor, at a place which gives the court power in more cases, it is not, I think, necessary for me to decide in this case.

In my judgment, wherever the line is drawn, this case on its facts falls into the category where the court has power to do what it can by omission.

The introduction of the words "clause 7" instead of "clause 7 (iv)" was *per incuriam*. The solicitor's mind was never applied to it, and never adverted to the significance and effect. It was a mere clerical error on his part, a slip. He knew what the testatrix's instructions and intentions were, and what he did was outside the scope of his authority. And he did it, of course, without knowing and approving what he himself was doing. How can one impute to the principal the agent's knowledge and approval which the agent himself has not got?

Accordingly, I hold that the testatrix was not bound by this mistake of the draftsman which was never brought to her notice. The discrepancy between her instructions and what was in the codicil was to all intents and purposes total and was never within her cognisance.

Accordingly, the case is one in which the court has power to rectify, using that word in a broad sense, so far as it can. Which is the proper course? To pronounce against the instrument in its entirety? Or to exclude part and admit the rest?

Certainly to reject the whole instrument would come much nearer to giving effect to the testatrix's dispositive intentions (both in the number of beneficiaries and in the amounts involved) than would the admission of the whole instrument.

But is the instrument severable, and can one get nearer still by excluding part? In my judgment, I can.

I cannot add the numeral (iv) after 7 but if 7 is excluded, clause 1 of the codicil would read as follows: "1. I revoke clauses 3 and ( ) of my said will."

I agree with Mr. Taylor's submission that this would have one of the following effects. The chancery court as the court of construction might deduce from the two documents (the will and the codicil so altered) read together that the testatrix's intention was the other clause after the words "clauses 3 and ( )" should be 7 (iv).

---

244 [1939] 1 All E.R. 579, [1939] P. 198.

Or the court might decide from a reading of the documents alone that there was not enough intrinsic evidence to fill in the blank but that the revocation of clause 3 of the will, coupled with the reinstatement of the same gift in clause 2(a) of the codicil rebutted the presumption that the gifts in clause 3 of the will and clause 2 of the codicil were cumulative, and thus lead to the construction that those in clause 2 of the codicil were intended to be substitutional.

Either of those decisions would give full effect to what in fact the testatrix intended. Or the court might decide that the presumption prevailed and the gifts were cumulative.

[The court admitted the codicil to probate without the numeral 7 in clause 1.]

Notes and Questions

1. Another situation in which the court of probate may be asked to correct an error is one in which words have been left out of the will by inadvertence. It would seem that in such a case the entire clause in which the omitted words ought to have been inserted may be deleted. *Re Reynette-James*[245] is representative of this type of situation.

The testatrix gave instructions for her will to a solicitor's clerk. She wanted to give the income from the residue of her estate equally between her sister and a friend and if either of them died, that share of the income would be paid to the testatrix' son. The capital was to go to the son after the sister and the friend had died. At the clerk's suggestion, the draft will further provided that if the son predeceased the sister and the friend, his share of the income would go to the son's wife until both the sister and the friend died, after which the capital was to go to the son's wife and his three children. A draft of the will was sent to the testatrix who made some amendments. After it was returned to the clerk it was given to a secretary for engrossment, but in typing the engrossment the secretary accidentally omitted 33 words from the residuary clause. The effect of the omission was that the son would receive the capital only if the life tenants predeceased the testatrix, which they did not do.

The solicitor's clerk read the will, as engrossed, to the testatrix, but neither noticed the omission and the will was duly signed and witnessed.

In the result, the court omitted from probate all the gifts in the residuary clause except the two life interests. Any other action would not have cured the problem.

2. T made four wills in succession. He intended that they should together take effect as his last will. However, they were all on stationer's forms and the printed revocation clause contained in the last three had not been struck out. Can the revocation clauses be struck out?[246]

3. In his will, T disposed of the residue in seven numbered subclauses, but gave only one-eighth of the residue in each of these clauses. Can the references to "one-eighth" be struck?[247]

---

245 [1976] 1 W.L.R. 161, [1975] 3 All E.R. 1037.
246 See *Re Phelan*, [1972] Fam. 33; and *cf. In the Goods of Swords*, [1952] P. 368, [1952] 2 All E.R. 281; but contrast *Collins v. Elstone*, [1893] P. 1: the testatrix let stand a revocation clause in a printed will form, although she objected to it, on being assured by her executor that it had no effect since the subject matter of the two wills was different.
247 See *Re McKittrick*, 41 Man. R. 454, [1933] 3 W.W.R. 536, [1934] 1 D.L.R. 422 (C.A.).

4. The principle that the court of probate only has jurisdiction to strike, not to add words, has been applied in many cases.[248]

5. T went to a solicitor, Mary Doe, to have her will made and to execute it. Subsequently, T went to another solicitor, Richard Roe, who prepared a new will for her, revoking the first, and T executed it. Finally, T returned to Mary Doe and, without telling her of the will prepared by Roe, asked Doe to prepare a codicil to her will. Doe, on the assumption that T has only made the will prepared by her, prepared a codicil which confirmed that will and it was signed by T. Can the reference to the wrong will be struck out?[249]

6. The correction made in *Re Morris*[250] left an ambiguity in the will. It was then up to the court of construction to determine whether, as a matter of construction, the ambiguity could be resolved. Since the ambiguity was patent, however, the court of construction could not, on the traditional view of its function, admit direct evidence of the testator's intention. If the court of construction is unable to make sense of the provision as corrected by the court of probate, it will fail for uncertainty.

7. The dual jurisdiction referred to in the preceding note and the possibility that a provision may fail for uncertainty, even though everyone knows what was intended, is unsatisfactory and, I submit, an example of extreme formalism that brings the law and the administration of justice into disrepute.

There are several possible ways in which the law can be reformed. One that recommends itself is a power in the court to rectify a will. The equitable doctrine of rectification is used to correct *inter vivos* instruments when they fail to state the agreement the parties have reached correctly. It has never been used in the context of wills, because of the difficulty in ascertaining the testator's intentions after her or his death. However, if it is clear that the will does not contain the wording intended by the testator, and if it is clear what the testator did intend, there can be no serious objection to the court rectifying the will and admitting such evidence as may be appropriate to achieve the desired result.

The British Parliament adopted recommendations of the English Law Reform Committee that the court of probate be given the power to rectify a will for clerical errors and misunderstanding of the testator's instructions, but not for failure by the testator to appreciate the effect of the words used, to uncertain expressions, and to lacunae.[251] The reforms are contained in section 20 of the *Administration of Justice Act* 1982.[252]

The legislation was interpreted in *Wordingham v. Royal Exchange Trust Co. Ltd.*[253] The testatrix held a power of appointment under her father's will. In an earlier will she exercised the power by appointing her husband. Then she instructed her solicitor to make a new will. In drafting it the solicitor failed to include the clause exercising the power of appointment. The husband brought proceedings seeking rectification and was successful. The court held that the solicitor's omission was a clerical error.[254]

The Law Reform Commission of British Columbia went further. It recommended that both the court of probate and the court of construction should have power to rectify a will without a time limit, if satisfied that a will fails to carry out the testator's intentions because of an accidental slip or omission, a misunderstanding of or a failure to carry out the

---

248 See, *e.g.*, *Alexander Estate v. Adams* (1998), 20 E.T.R. (2d) 294 (B.C.S.C.).
249 See *Re Reade*, [1902] P. 75; *Re Chilcott*, [1897] P. 223.
250 [1971] P. 62.
251 Law Reform Committee (U.K.), *Nineteenth Report Interpretation of Wills*, Cmnd. 5301 (May, 1973), 17-33, 65.
252 C. 53 (U.K.).
253 [1992] 3 All E.R. 205 (Ch. D.).
254 See also *Re Segelman (decd)*, [1995] 3 All E.R. 676.

testator's instructions, or a failure by the testator to appreciate the effect of the words used. All relevant evidence would be admissible for the purpose.[255] Are the British Columbia proposals better than the English reforms?

8. In jurisdictions in which the superior court exercises both probate and interpretive jurisdictions, which is most of the provinces, it would be bizarre if the court's jurisdictions would have to be exercised separately. Although there is no law on the point, one would hope that the court could conjoin its jurisdictions in the area of mistake, so as more readily to be able to give effect to the testator's intentions.

(d)   Execution of Wrong Instrument

The third type of mistake occurs when the testator executes the wrong instrument while of the belief that he or she is executing his or her will. This presents no difficulty if the testator executes a completely different instrument, such as a mortgage, or a stranger's will. In these circumstances, the document cannot be probated, since it is obviously not the testator's will. However, a problem arises if the testator and his or her spouse have given instructions for reciprocal wills (not necessarily mutual wills), which are *mutatis mutandis* in the same form. That is, the husband appoints his wife as executrix and she him as executor, and they each leave their respective estates to each other for life or on some other basis, with remainder to others. Then, by mistake, they execute each other's will. Can the court of probate correct the error? Some cases in Western Canada have held that it can. *Re Brander*,[256] reproduced below, is an example.

Further Reading

Price, "Mistakenly Signed Reciprocal Wills: A Change in Tradition after *In re Snide*" (1981), 67 Iowa L.R. 205.

Gray, "Striking out Words of a Will" (1912-13), 26 Harv. L. Rev. 212.

Kennedy, "Comment" (1953), 31 Can. Bar Rev. 185, 444.

Lee, "Correcting Testator's Mistakes: The Probate Jurisdiction" (1969), 33 Conv. (N.S.) 322.

Stan J. Sokol, *Mistakes in Wills in Canada* (Scarborough: Carswell, 1995), ch. 2.

RE BRANDER
6 W.W.R. (N.S.) 702, [1952] 4 D.L.R. 688
Supreme Court of British Columbia

John Brander and his wife Margaret had their solicitor prepare a will for each of them, naming each other executor and sole beneficiary. By mistake they signed each other's will. John died first and Margaret sought to probate the will signed

---

255 Law Reform Commission of British Columbia, *Report on the Interpretation of Wills*, L.R.C. 58 (Nov. 1982), p. 50.

256 6 W.W.R. (N.S.) 702, [1952] 4 D.L.R. 688 (B.C.S.C.), noted (1953), 31 Can. Bar Rev. 185.

by him with deletion of the word "John" and its substitution by the word "Margaret" where necessary and with correction of related errors.

WILSON J.:

. . .

Any difficulty I might have in grappling with this matter is solved by the judgment in *Guardian, Trust & Executors Co. v. Inwood*,[257] where the Court of Appeal for New Zealand was confronted with an almost identical problem and solved it by granting the relief here asked for. In his judgment, with which I respectfully agree, Fair J. says:[258]

> It will be seen that although the document was signed by Jane Remington, it purports (*a*) in its opening words, to be the will of Maude Lucy Remington; (*b*) it is expressed to give a life interest "to my sister Jane Remington of 411 Hereford Street, Christchurch"; and (*c*) the attestation clause purports to be to the signature and acknowledgement of Maude Lucy Remington.
>
> Clearly, on the face of it, the document propounded as the will of Jane Remington appears to be irregular. There would, however, be no difficulty in clearing up the irregularity as to the attestation if evidence were available for that purpose, for an attestation clause is neither necessary nor is it an essential part of the will:[259] Obviously, too, the opening words are no essential part of the will, but if inappropriate, would call for consideration and, if necessary, explanation.[260]
>
> If the document can be admitted to probate, the reference to "Jane Remington" can be shown to be at least a latent equivocation and the person to whom it was intended to refer ascertained and if her name is not Jane Remington, and the identity of the person can be ascertained from the remaining words in the will the word "Jane"; or both words, can be struck out.[261]
>
> Then, too, it may be shown that clauses or expressions have been inadvertently introduced into the will, contrary to the testator's intentions and instructions, or, in other words, that a part of the executed instrument is not his will.[262] At the foot of that page it is said:

> *Under the modern practice*, the question whether the words have been introduced into a will by mistake is often considered by the Court of Probate and if it is found that they do not form part of the will, the Court directs them to be omitted from the probate.

I order that the will be admitted to probate with the alterations mentioned.

Notes and Questions

1. I submit that, although the result in *Re Brander* is eminently sensible, it is contrary to the law. A court of probate may strike out errors, but may not substitute new words.[263]

---

257 [1946] N.Z.L.R. 614.

258 *Ibid.*, at p. 622.

259 *Mortimer on Probate Law and Practice*, 2nd Ed. 1, 25, and R. 519 of the Code of Civil Procedure.

260 *Whyte v. Pollok* (1882), 7 App. Cas. 400, 424, *per* Lord Watson.

261 1 *Jarman on Wills*, 7th ed., 487 et seq., 492, 502; 2 *ibid.*, 1225; *In re Boehm*, [1891] P. 247; *In re Cogan* (1912), 31 N.Z.L.R. 1204; *Tartakover v. Pipe*, [1922] N.Z.L.R. 853; and *Isaac v. Mills* (1887), N.Z.L.R. 5 C.A. 122.

262 1 *Jarman on Wills*, 7th ed., 469.

263 See, *e.g.*, *Re Morris*, [1971] P. 62.

2. The case upon which Wilson J. relied in *Re Brander*, namely, *Guardian, Trust & Executors Co. v. Inwood*,[264] merely struck out the errors in a similar situation. It did not substitute new words and an English case, *In the Estate of Meyer*,[265] is to the same effect.

3. *Re Brander* was followed in each of the western provinces.[266] In a more recent case in Saskatchewan[267] the court admitted the incorrectly signed will to probate under the dispensing power contained in the *Wills Act*.[268] *Re Brander* was also followed in Ontario in a case in which the judge thought he had power to correct the will under the rules.[269] I submit that the case is wrong because it runs counter to established principles.

4. What would the result be if John Brander had signed the will of Jane Doe, whose will was in substance the same as the one he intended to sign?

5. The proposals for reform discussed above,[270] apply with equal force to the situation in which the wrong instrument is executed. Further, they seem particularly appropriate when the superior court exercises the jurisdictions of a court of probate and a court of interpretation, as it does in most of the provinces.

---

264 [1946] N.Z.L.R. 614 (C.A.).

265 [1908] P. 353.

266 *Re Thorleifson* (1954), 13 W.W.R. 515 (Man. Surr. Ct.); *Re Knott* (1959), 27 W.W.R. 382 (Alta. Dist. Ct.); *Re Bohachewski* (1967), 60 W.W.R. 635 (Sask. Surr. Ct.). See also *Matter of Snide*, 52 N.Y. 2d 193, 418 N.E. 2d 656 (N.Y.C.A., 1981), to the same effect.

267 *Re McDermid Estate* (1994), 5 E.T.R. (2d) 238 (Sask. Q.B.).

268 R.S.S. 1978, c. W-14, s. 35.1 [am. 1989, c. 66, s. 9].

269 *Re Malichen Estate* (1994), 6 E.T.R. (2d) 217 (Ont. Gen. Div.).

270 In Note and Question 7 to part (c), *supra*.

6

FORMAL VALIDITY OF WILLS

1. INTRODUCTION

To make a valid will, a person must observe certain formalities prescribed by law.[1] In this chapter we examine these formalities. We consider the formal or attested will first. Then we examine the holograph will, that is, a will wholly in the testator's handwriting and signed by him or her. After that we discuss the privileged will briefly. It is a will that may be made by a member of the armed forces and by those travelling at sea in certain circumstances. The formal requirements are relaxed for a privileged will. The chapter concludes with an examination of the international will.

Further Reading

Macdonell, Sheard and Hull on Probate Practice, 4th ed. by Rodney Hull and Ian M. Hull (Scarborough: Carswell, 1996), cc. 3, 16.

Feeney's Canadian Law of Wills, 4th ed. by James MacKenzie (Toronto: Butterworths, 2000 (loose leaf)), c. 4.

Law Reform Commission of British Columbia, *Report on the Making and Revocation of Wills* (L.R.C. 52, 1981).

Law Reform Committee, *Twenty Second Report (The Making and Revocation of Wills)* Cmnd. 7902, May 1980.

J.A. Brulé, Q.C., "Multiple Wills" (1979-81), 5 E. & T.Q. 200.

Robert C. Dick, Q.C., "Validity of Wills for Extraprovincial Assets" (1973-74), 1 E. & T.Q. 200.

Brian S. Lindblom, "The Forensic Examination of Last Wills and Testaments" (1988-89), 9 E. & T.J. 233.

Mary I. Duncan, "Estate Claims and the Document Examiner" (1982-84), 6 E. & T.Q. 366.

---

1 In New Brunswick the court has power to make, amend and revoke wills for mental incompetent persons under the *Infirm Persons Act*, R.S.N.B. 1973, c. I-8, ss. 3(4), 11(1) (enacted S.N.B. 1994, c. 40, ss. 1, 3). See Eric L. Teed and Nicole Cohoon, "New Wills for Incompetents" (1997), 16 E. & T.J. 1.

2. ATTESTED WILLS

(a) Introduction

The formal or attested will is a document which is signed by the testator at the end and attested by two witnesses. Because many wills are homemade, difficulties are apt to arise because the testator fails to comply exactly with the statutory requirements of execution. The statute itself recognizes that minor defects in execution ought not to invalidate a will. The statutory requirements are set out below. Also reproduced below are a sample will and codicil to illustrate some of the questions that arise in the context of formalities.

SUCCESSION LAW REFORM ACT
R.S.O. 1990, c. S.26

3. A will is valid only when it is in writing.

4. (1) Subject to sections 5 and 6, a will is not valid unless,

(a) at its end it is signed by the testator or by some other person in his or her presence and by his or her direction;

(b) the testator makes or acknowledges the signature in the presence of two or more attesting witnesses present at the same time; and

(c) two or more of the attesting witnesses subscribe the will in the presence of the testator.

(2) Where witnesses are required by this section, no form of attestation is necessary.

. . .

7. (1) In so far as the position of the signature is concerned, a will, whether holograph or not, is valid if the signature of the testator made either by him or her or the person signing for him or her is placed at, after, following, under or beside or opposite to the end of the will so that it is apparent on the face of the will that the testator intended to give effect by the signature to the writing signed as his or her will.

(2) A will is not rendered invalid by the circumstance that,

(a) the signature does not follow or is not immediately after the end of the will;

(b) a blank space intervenes between the concluding words of the will and the signature;

(c) the signature,

(i) is placed among the words of a testimonium clause or of a clause of attestation,

(ii) follows or is after or under a clause of attestation either with or without a blank space intervening, or

(iii) follows or is after, under or beside the name of a subscribing witness;

(d) the signature is on a side, page or other portion of the paper or papers containing the will on which no clause, paragraph or disposing part of the will is written above the signature; or

(e) there appears to be sufficient space on or at the bottom of the preceding side, page or other portion of the same paper on which the will is written to contain the signature.

(3) The generality of subsection (1) is not restricted by the enumeration of circumstances set out in subsection (2), but a signature in conformity with section 4, 5 or 6 or this section does not give effect to,

(a) a disposition or direction that is underneath the signature or that follows the signature; or

(b) a disposition or direction inserted after the signature was made.

Comparable Legislation

Probate Act, R.S.P.E.I. 1988, c. P-21, s. 60; *Wills Act*, R.S.A. 1980, c. W-11, ss. 4, 5, 8,; R.S.B.C. 1996, c. 489, ss. 3, 4, 6; R.S.M. 1988, c. W150, ss. 3, 4, 7; R.S.N.B. 1973, c. W-9, ss. 3, 4, 7; R.S.N. 1990, c. W-10, s. 2; R.S.N.S. 1989, c. 505, ss. 6, 7; S.S. 1996, c. W-14.1, s.7; R.S.N.W.T. 1988, c. W-5, ss. 5, 6; R.S.Y. 1986, c. 179, ss. 5(1), 6.

SAMPLE WILL

NOTE: This sample will is just that, a sample will. It should not be used indiscriminately. Other formats may be appropriate in particular estates and other clauses may be desirable, such as a provision for substitute executors. Further, when drafting a will, regard should be had to the provisions of the *Income Tax Act*[2] in order to minimize tax as much as possible, consonant with the instructions of the testator. In addition regard must be had to the provisions of the *Family Law Act*[3] in order to minimize its impact, if that is the wish of the testator.[4]

COMMENCEMENT
THIS IS THE LAST WILL of me, JOHN JAMES DOE, of the city of London, in the county of Middlesex, province of Ontario.

---

2 R.S.C. 1985, c. 1 (5th Supp.), as am.

3 R.S.O. 1990, c. F-3.

4 Reference may be made to published will precedents, such as *O'Brien's Encyclopedia of Forms*, 11th ed., Division V, "Wills and Trusts" (1988); Sheard and Hull, *Canadian Forms of Wills* (4th ed., 1982); and Scott-Harston, *Tax-Planned Will Precedents* (3rd ed., 1989).The drafting of wills is an art that requires great care. You must always ensure: (a) that you encapsulate your client's wishes in conformity with the law; and (b) that the will is intelligible, not only to the court, but to your client. Sadly, many wills fail on both counts. H. Rider Haggard, in *She* (Oxford: Oxford University Press, 1991 (World's Classics ed.)), at p. 18 refers to one such will as follows: "I . . . ran my eye through the Will, which appeared, from its utter unintelligibility, to have been drawn on the strictest legal principles."

REVOCATION

1. I revoke all former wills and other testamentary dispositions made by me.

APPOINTMENT OF EXECUTORS AND TRUSTEES

2. I appoint my son, TIMOTHY DOE, and my brother, WILLIAM DOE to be the executors and trustees of this my will, and I hereinafter refer to them as my trustees.

GIFT TO TRUSTEES IN TRUST

3. I give all my property wheresoever situate, including any property over which I may have a general power of appointment to my trustees upon trust to pay my just debts, funeral and testamentary expenses and

    (a) if my wife, MARY DOE, survives me for a period of thirty days to pay or transfer the residue of my estate to her for her own use absolutely;

    (b) if said wife should predecease me or should survive me but die within a period of thirty days after my death, I direct my trustees to divide the residue of my estate among my issue who shall then be living in equal shares *per stirpes*.

DEFINITION OF ISSUE

4. I declare that the word "issue" as used in my will, whether with reference to my own or any other person's issue, means issue born within marriage and includes legally adopted issue but not a person born outside marriage.

I further declare that any reference in my will to any person in terms of a relationship by blood or marriage to any other person shall include a person born within marriage or legally adopted, but shall not include a person born outside marriage.

INFANT BENEFICIARIES

5.(a) If any person should become entitled to any share in my estate before attaining the age of eighteen years, the share of such person shall be held and kept invested by my trustees and the income and capital, or so much thereof as my trustees in their absolute discretion consider advisable, shall be used for the benefit of such person until he or she attains the age of eighteen years.

  (b) I authorize my trustees to make any payments for any person under the age of eighteen years to a parent or guardian of such person or to anyone to whom they in their discretion deem it advisable to make such payments, whose receipt shall be a sufficient discharge to my trustees.

CONVERSION

6. I authorize my trustees to use their discretion in the realization of my estate, with power to sell, call in and convert into money any part of my estate not consisting of money at such time or times, in such manner and upon such terms, and either for cash or credit or for part cash and part credit as they may in their absolute discretion decide upon, or to postpone such conversion of my estate or

any part or parts thereof for such length of time as they may think best. My trustees shall have a separate and substantive power to retain any of my investments or assets in the form existing at the date of my death at their absolute discretion without responsibility for loss to the intent that investments or assets so retained shall be deemed to be authorized investments for all purposes of this my will. No reversionary or future interest shall be sold prior to falling into possession and no such interest not actually producing income shall be treated as producing income.

INVESTMENTS

7. I declare that my trustees when making investments for my estate shall not be limited to investments authorized by law for trustees but may make any investments which in their absolute discretion they consider advisable.

DIVISION IN SPECIE

8. My trustees may make any division of my estate or set aside or pay any share or interest therein, either wholly or in part, in the assets forming my estate at the time of my death or at the time of such division, setting aside or payment, and I expressly declare that my trustees shall in their absolute discretion fix the value of my estate or any part thereof for the purpose of making any such division, setting aside or payment and their decision shall be final and binding upon all persons concerned.

BORROWING

9. I authorize my trustees from time to time to borrow money upon the security of all or any assets of my estate in such manner, on such terms and conditions, for such length of time and for such purposes connected with my estate as they in their absolute discretion from time to time may deem advisable. My trustees may borrow from any person or corporation notwithstanding that such person or corporation may be a member of my family or a beneficiary or trustee under my will, and the person or corporation from whom my trustees borrow shall nevertheless be entitled to receive and be paid, for its, his or her own benefit, such interest as my trustees in their absolute discretion deem advisable.

TESTIMONIUM

IN WITNESS WHEREOF I have to this my last will, written upon this and preceding pages, subscribed my name this 2nd day of January, 2000.

ATTESTATION

SIGNED by the testator, JOHN JAMES DOE,)	
as his last will, in the presence of us, both present)	
at the same time, who at his request, in his presence)	
and in the presence of each other, have hereunto)	*John J. Doe*
subscribed our names as witnesses.)	
)	
Nellie-Marie Jones)	*Nellie-Marie Jones*

400 Ridout Street, London, Ontario   )

Armand Thomas Lachance   ) *A. Thomas Lachance*
30 Fiddler's Green Road, London, Ontario   )

SAMPLE CODICIL

THIS IS A CODICIL to the Will of me, JOHN JAMES DOE, of the city of London, in the county of Middlesex, and province of Ontario, which will is dated the 2nd day of January, 2000.

1. I revoke the appointment of my brother, WILLIAM DOE, as executor and trustee of my will, as set out in paragraph 2 of my will, and I appoint my sister, DOROTHY FRENCH, in his place as executrix and trustee.
2. In all other respects I confirm my will.

IN TESTIMONY WHEREOF I have to this Codicil to my will, written upon this page, subscribed my name this 1st day of February, 2001.

SIGNED, PUBLISHED AND DECLARED by the   )
testator, JOHN JAMES DOE, as a codicil to his   )
will, in the presence of us, both present at the same)
time, who at his request, in his presence and in the)   *J.J. Doe*
presence of each other, have hereunto subscribed)
our names as witnesses.   )
)
Nellie-Marie Jones   ) *Nellie-Marie Jones*
400 Ridout Street, London, Ontario   )
)
Ferdinand King   )   *F. King*
350 Waterloo Street, London, Ontario   )

Notes and Questions

1. The Newfoundland Act[5] lacks the equivalent to section 7 of the Ontario Act.
2. The Prince Edward Island Act[6] requires that the witnesses sign in the presence of each other.
3. Section 9 of the English *Wills Act 1837*[7] has been replaced[8] by the following:

   9. No will shall be valid unless—

---

5 R.S.N. 1990, c. W-10.
6 R.S.P.E.I. 1988, c. P-21, s. 60(2).
7 7 Will. 4 & 1 Vict., c.26.
8 By the *Administration of Justice Act 1982*, c. 53 (U.K.), s. 17.

(a) it is in writing, and signed by the testator, or by some other person in his presence and by his direction; and

(b) it appears that the testator intended by his signature to give effect to the will; and

(c) the signature is made or acknowledged by the testator in the presence of two or more witnesses present at the same time; and

(d) each witness either—

    (i) attests and signs the will; or

    (ii) acknowledges his signature, in the presence of the testator (but not necessarily in the presence of any other witness),

but no form of attestation shall be necessary.

How does this section differ from the typical Canadian legislation? What are its advantages and disadvantages?

4. For a document to be a valid will, must it necessarily follow the standard format? *Gertzbein v. Winer*[9] illustrates this point. A husband and wife negotiated an agreement. The wife signed and sealed the agreement and two witnesses attested her signature. In the agreement the wife promised that she would not sell or mortgage certain real property during her life, and she "devised" the real property after her death to her husband's two daughters by a prior marriage. The agreement said that it was irrevocable. The court held that the agreement was a valid will and, thus, revocable, and that it was in fact revoked by a subsequent will.

(b) A Dispensing Power

The materials in this chapter show that many wills founder on the shoals of the statutory formalities. To avoid that, the statutes in some provinces contain a provision that permits the court to order that the document be effective as if it had been executed in compliance with all the formal statutory requirements. Such provisions are sometimes, inaccurately, called substantial compliance provisions. Manitoba's legislation was the first to be enacted and is representative. It is set out below.

The legislation is useful since it allows the court to save wills in appropriate circumstances. We shall see other applications of this legislation in this chapter and the next.

Further Reading

W. Chris Martin, "Substantial Compliance: 'Where there's a Will there's a Way'" (1986-88), 8 E. & T.Q. 142.

Alberta Law Reform Institute, Final Report No. 84, *Wills: Non-Compliance with Formalities* (Edmonton: Alberta Law Reform Institute, 2000).

---

9 [1970] 3 O.R. 676, 13 D.L.R. (3d) 692.

WILLS ACT
R.S.M. 1988, c. W150

23. Where, upon application, if the court is satisfied that a document or any writing on a document embodies

(a) the testamentary intentions of a deceased; or

(b) the intention of a deceased to revoke, alter or revive a will of the deceased or the testamentary intentions of the deceased embodied in a document other than a will;

the court may, notwithstanding that the document or writing was not executed in compliance with any or all of the formal requirements imposed by this Act, order that the document or writing, as the case may be, be fully effective as though it had been executed in compliance with all the formal requirements imposed by this Act, as the will of the deceased or as the revocation, alteration or revival of the will of the deceased or of the testamentary intention embodied in that other document, as the case may be.

Comparable Legislation

Civil Code of Quebec, art. 714; *Indian Act*, R.S.C. 1985, c. I-5, s. 45(2); *Indian Estate Regulations*, C.R.C. 1978, c. 954, s. 15; *Probate Act*, R.S.P.E.I. 1988, c. P-21, s. 70; *Wills Act*, R.S.N.B. 1973, c. W-9, s. 35.1, added S.N.B. 1997, c. 7, s. 1; S.S. 1996, c. W-14.1, s. 37; *Uniform Wills Act*, Uniform Law Conference of Canada, s. 19.

Notes and Questions

1. In *Re Briggs*[10] the court upheld a holograph will under s. 23 which commenced with the words, "This is the last will and testament of me Lola Irene Briggs of . . . ." The will was not signed, but the court held that the document embodied the deceased's testamentary intentions, as required by s. 23.

Kuszak v. Smoley[11] is to the same effect. The testator filled out a printed will form in his own handwriting and signed it. The document was not valid as a holograph will, since the handwritten words required the printed words to be meaningful. But the court was satisfied that the document did embody the testamentary intentions of the deceased. Thus, it was fully effective as a will under s. 23.[12]

However, if the document is not signed or witnessed, it is unlikely to be probated. This is especially so if the document is not shown to be in the deceased's own hand.[13]

2. On the other hand, an unsigned, undated memorandum, found clipped to a stationer's will form, and which does not show a testamentary intention, will be denied probate.[14]

---

10 (1985), 21 E.T.R. 127 (Man. Q.B.).

11 (1986), 23 E.T.R. 237 (Man. Q.B.).

12 See also *Re Bunn Estate* (1992), 45 E.T.R. 254 (Sask. C.A.); *Martineau v. Manitoba (Public Trustee)* (1993), 50 E.T.R. 87 (Man. Q.B.).

13 *Belser v. Fleury* (1999), 27 E.T.R. (2d) 290 (Man. Q.B.).

14 See *Montreal Trust Co. of Canada v. Andrezejewski (Committee of)* (1994), 6 E.T.R. (2d) 42 (Man. Q.B.).

Similarly, in *George v. Daly*[15] the court denied probate of a document which did not clearly disclose a testamentary intention. The deceased had informed his accountant that he wanted to change his will. The accountant wrote a letter setting out the deceased's instructions to the deceased's lawyer. The deceased died before the lawyer could act on the instructions. The court held that the letter only constituted instructions for a will. In other words, the deceased did not have a fixed and final intention to make a will.[16]

3. It may also be possible to invoke the dispensing power in cases in which spouses execute each other's wills. *Re McDermid Estate*[17] is an example. The court ordered that the will signed by the husband (who died first) be attached to the will prepared for his signature, so that the latter, together with his signature to the former should be admitted to probate.

4. A Quebec court has even held a will which existed only on a computer diskette to be valid under the Quebec dispensing power. The testatrix had left a note which referred to the will on the computer. The will was clearly identified and was testamentary in nature.[18]

5. The Alberta Law Reform Institute has recommended the enactment of a dispensing power in Alberta, but has recommended against extending it to electronic records of wills.[19] However, the Uniform Law Conference of Canada has proposed that terms of reference be developed for a project to amend the *Uniform Wills Act* to accommodate new media and that materials be developed to that end.[20]

6. In *Sisson v. Park Street Baptist Church*[21] the court held that a will signed by only one witness was valid because the witness who signed testified that the other witness was present but forgot to sign. The court thought this amounted to substantial compliance, even though Ontario does not have substantial compliance legislation. I submit that the case is therefore wrong. The Newfoundland Supreme Court did not follow *Sisson* for that reason,[22] but the British Columbia Supreme Court followed *Sisson* in *Krause v. Toni*.[23] A husband and wife executed wills together at their lawyer's office. The secretary attested both wills, but the lawyer inadvertently witnessed only the husband's will. The court allowed the wife's will to be probated, holding that it had a common law jurisdiction to do so when there was no doubt about the will's authenticity.[24]

7. Arguably, a formal will granted probate in a foreign jurisdiction, although unwitnessed, might be allowed to be resealed in a jurisdiction having a substantial compliance provision, to permit administration of assets situate in that jurisdiction.[25]

---

15 (1997), 15 E.T.R. (2d) 1 (Man. C.A.).

16 See also *Re Mate Estate* (1999), 28 E.T.R. (2d) 103 (Sask. Q.B.), to the same effect.

17 (1994), 5 E.T.R. (2d) 238 (Sask. Q.B.).

18 See *Rioux c. Coulombe* (1996), 19 E.T.R. (2d) 201 (Que. S.C.). The case is discussed also in the Notes and Questions to the next section.

19 See Alberta Law Reform Institute, Final Report No. 84, *Wills: Non-Compliance with Formalities* (Edmonton: Alberta Law Reform Institute, 2000), pp. xiv-xv, 38-47.

20 See Uniform Law Conference of Canada, Civil Law Section, Draft 2000 Resolutions, *Uniform Wills (Non-Compliance with Formalities Amendment) Act*, http://www.law.ualberta.ca/ablri/ulc/2000pro/e2000res.htm.

21 (1998), 24 E.T.R. (2d) 18 (Ont. Gen. Div.).

22 *Re Murphy Estate* (1999), 26 E.T.R. (2d) 38 (Nfld. T.D.).

23 (1999), 28 E.T.R. (2d) 225 (B.C.S.C.).

24 But see *Bolton v. Tartaglia* (2000), 33 E.T.R. (2d) 26 (B.C.S.C.), in which the court refused to follow *Sisson* and *Krause* and struck down a will signed by only one witness. See further Ian M. Hull, "Due Execution: Is One Signature Really Enough?" (1999), 30 E.T.R. (2d) 23.

25 See *Re Knauff Estate* (1994), 7 E.T.R. (2d) 43 (Sask. C.A.).

(c) In Writing

The statute requires that the will be "in writing." What does this mean? It clearly includes the recognized forms of writing, such as handwriting, typescript and printing. Does it also include symbols that represent writing? *Murray v. Haylow*,[26] reproduced below, deals with this question.

MURRAY v. HAYLOW
60 O.L.R. 629, [1927] 3 D.L.R. 1036
Supreme Court of Ontario
[Court of Appeal]

The testator's will contained the following legacies:

```
I give and devise unto my grandchildren as follows:—
To Margaret Haylow ................................................................. $100.00
"  Leonard       " .................................................................   100.00
"  Edmund        " .................................................................   100.00
"  John          " .................................................................   100.00
I give & devise unto Rev. M.D. O'Neill $200.00 for High Masses
"   "  "    "      "      "      "      "     $100.00 "  Low  "
"   "  "    "      "      Genivieve Kenney, Oxford Co., my niece, $100,00
I give & devise   "      Mary McGuire, Hamilton, Ont. my niece,  $100.00
```

The Trial Judge held, *inter alia*, that since the statute does not mention dots and dashes, the will was not in writing and could, thus, not be probated. The case was appealed.

RIDDELL J.A.:

. . .

Of course the Wills Act does not require the will to be "in words." By [the *Wills Act*][27] the will is to be in writing—and the learned Judge seems to think that "dots and dashes" are not "writing."

Shorthand notes, even before being extended, are "writing".[28] But the matter is made clear by our own legislation.

The Interpretation Act[29] provides:—

(hh) "Writing", "written", or any term of like import, shall include words printed, painted, engraved, lithographed, photographed, or represented or reproduced by any other mode in a visible form.

That words already written may be and constantly are "represented" by a "do.," or "ditto," is familiarly known; and a word "represented" by " below it is just as effective as if written out in full.

---

26 60 O.L.R. 629, [1927] 3 D.L.R. 1036 (C.A.).

27 R.S.O. 1914, c. 120, s. 12.

28 *Nichols v. Harris* (1880), 32 La. Ann. 646, 648.

29 R.S.O. 1914, c.1, s. 29(hh).

The appeal must be allowed with costs.

. . .

[Latchford C.J. and Masten J.A., agreed with Riddell J.A. Middleton J.A. delivered a concurring opinion.]

Notes and Questions

1. You should note that the statute does not stipulate what the will must be written on. Thus, a will written on an eggshell,[30] and one scratched on a tractor fender,[31] if they otherwise comply with the required formalities (either of a holograph or a formal will), are perfectly valid.

2. Would a will typed and stored on a computer and signed, so that the signatures are also stored on the computer, be valid? Are there problems associated with this kind of medium?[32]

3. As mentioned in the previous section, in *Rioux c. Coulombe*[33] the Quebec Superior Court held a computer will to be valid under art. 714 of the *Civil Code of Quebec*, which is a dispensing power. The testatrix committed suicide. The police found a note, which led to the discovery of a computer diskette, labelled "this is my last will." The diskette contained what appeared to be the deceased's last will. It included her name, the date it was made, and testamentary dispositions. Is this a sensible decision?[34]

4. A will written in a foreign language can be admitted to probate, but the court must be furnished with an authenticated translation.[35]

(d) Signed by the Testator or an Amanuensis

The statute allows either the testator or some other person in the testator's presence and by his or her direction to sign the will. The provision which permits another person to sign on the testator's behalf is the amanuensis provision. It is often resorted to when the testator is unable to write, either because he or she has never learned to do so, or can no longer do so by reason of infirmity. If someone else signs for the testator, the attestation clause should state that this is done in the testator's presence and at his or her request and also, if the testator is unable to read, that the will was read over to the testator and that he or she appeared to understand it.

Questions sometimes arise about the validity of the execution of the will when the mental state of the testator has deteriorated and he or she must be assisted in making the will. This is discussed in *Re White*,[36] reproduced below.

---

30 *Hodson v. Barnes* (1926), 43 T.L.R. 71.
31 *Re Harris*, unrep., noted (1948), 26 Can. Bar Rev. 1242.
32 See Note and Question 5 to the preceding section.
33 (1996), 19 E.T.R. (2d) 201 (Que. S.C.).
34 See Nicholas Kasirer, "The 'Judicial Will' Architecturally Considered" (1996), 99 Revue du Notariat 3; *ibid.*, "From Written Record to Memory in the Law of Wills" (1997-98), 29 Ottawa L. Rev. 39.
35 See *Re Berger (decd)*, [1989] 1 All E.R. 591 (C.A.).
36 [1948] 1 D.L.R. 572, 21 M.P.R. 331 (N.S.C.A.).

RE WHITE
[1948] 1 D.L.R. 572, 21 M.P.R. 331
Nova Scotia Supreme Court
[Appellate Division]

The testator suffered a stroke in 1944. As a result, his power of speech was permanently affected and he required assistance in feeding and clothing himself. The testator's will, made in 1945, was prepared by a Mr. Binet, a Justice of the Peace, who was also Registrar of Deeds. He was requested to do so by Mrs. White, the testator's wife, who left him a list of bequests prepared by another person, but presumably with the testator's consent. Mr. Binet prepared the will and attended at the testator's house, along with two witnesses, Messrs. Morrison and Urquhart, the second of whom was known to the testator. The testator was unable to write his signature, so Mr. Binet helped him to make his mark. The testator died in 1946.

The application for probate was contested on the grounds of improper execution and lack of capacity. However, it was admitted to probate by the trial judge. The case was then appealed.

DOULL J.:

. . .

When Mr. Urquhart came in, the testator recognized him and although his speech was restricted by the paralysis, he spoke his name "Billie, Billie". Mrs. White said, "This is Mr. Binet, you know what he is here for," and the testator said "Yes". Mr. Binet then read every paragraph of the will and he said, "Yes, Yes" to it all and nodded his head. Mr. Binet then spoke to the witnesses: "Now, gentlemen, it is up to you to decide whether this man is of sound mind and understanding. I want this thing done above board as far as possible. He is a stranger to me."

It may be observed that neither Morrison nor Urquhart have a recollection of this speech in anything like the detail in which Mr. Binet gave it in his evidence. It is quite possible that Mr. Binet is more correct as he would be more certain to have it in his mind. At any rate, the witnesses were satisfied that the testator was capable of making a will, and while their opinion is not in itself of importance, they said they were satisfied and they proceeded with the execution. Apparently the will or parts of it were read over again and his answer was always "Yes, Yes". Mr. Binet then handed the testator a pen and asked if he would sign the will and he said, "No, No". He then asked him if he could make a mark and he said, "Yes, Yes". He tried to move his fingers but Mr. Binet helped him when he made the mark.

The witnesses then signed in the presence of the testator and of each other and of Mr. Binet.

Before considering other questions and the evidence of the testator's mental condition, it may be convenient to deal with the appellant's contention that the will was not properly executed.

. . .

The appellant argues that in this case the testator did not himself sign, but that Binet signed for him, and that in such a case it must be shown by the proponents of the will that there was a "direction" by the testator or an acknowledgment. I do not think that the cases cited in the appellant's factum mean more than this that where the signature is by "direction" of the testator, the direction is as much a part of the signature as the making of the signature and the "direction" must be given in the presence of the witnesses or the signature "acknowledged" in the presence of the witnesses.

In the present case whatever happened was all in the presence of the witnesses and even if it were held to be a directed signature, I would say that it was sufficiently directed. In my opinion, however, this is not such a case. I think that the testator himself signed and none the less if he were assisted by Binet even to a considerable extent.

The old case of *Wilson v. Beddard*[37] has always been cited in books of evidence as an authority. There the signature was made by a mark and a guided hand. The Vice-Chancellor (Sir L. Shadwell) said in part:[38]

Next, it was contended that what the learned Judge said with reference to the testator's hand being guided when he made his mark to his will was not law. The Judge said that it was necessary that the will should be signed by the testator, not with his name, for his mark was sufficient if made by his hand, though that hand might be guided by another person; and, in my opinion, that proposition is correct in point of law. For the Statute of Frauds requires that a will should be signed by the testator or by some other person in his presence and by his direction; and I wish to know if a dumb man, who could not write, were to hold out his hand for some person to guide it, and were then to make his mark, whether that would not be a sufficient signature of his will. In order to constitute a direction, it is not necessary that anything should be said. If a testator, in making his mark, is assisted by some other person and acquiesces and adopts it; it is just the same as if he had made it without any assistance.

I regard this case as one where the testator was trying to make a mark but could not effectively do it and received assistance. "It is just the same as if he had made it without any assistance."

[The learned Judge went on to hold that the testator had the necessary capacity to make the will and that any suspicious circumstances were removed. The court dismissed the appeal.]

Notes and Questions

1. If the will is signed by another person in the presence of the testator and at the testator's direction, how should that person sign, with his or her own name, or with the testator's?

I submit that it is preferable that the amanuensis write the testator's name and below it indicate that this was done by the amanuensis in the presence and at the direction of the

---

37 (1841), 12 Sim. 28, 59 E.R. 1041.
38 At pp. 33-4.

testator. However, there is ample case authority for the proposition that the amanuensis may sign his or her own name.[39] Such an execution should be accompanied by an explanatory attestation clause.

2. It appears, surprisingly, that the amanuensis may also act as one of the witnesses.[40]

3. The testator does not have to sign with his or her full name; a business signature is sufficient.

4. A signature consisting of other than the testator's name may also sufficient, such as "Mother," the testatrix being referred to by that term by her family,[41] and "Your loving mother."[42]

5. The signature does not have to take the form of a written signature, but may be printed if the testator normally "signs" in that fashion.[43]

6. If the testator has the required capacity and attempts to sign the will but is unable to sign it in a normal hand, a line or other mark will be a sufficient signature.[44]

7. If the testator signs with a mark, the attestation clause should state that the testator did so because he or she was unable to write, that the will was previously read over to the testator and that he or she appeared to understand it. The mark itself consists of an "X" and it should be identified further by someone who is present at the execution of the will in the following manner:

Joseph

His   X   Mark

Doe

8. A blind person can clearly make a will and sign it or have an amanuensis sign it. When applying for probate, the executors must prove that the testator knew and approved the contents. Evidence that the will was read to the testator in the presence of both

---

39 *Re Deeley and Green*, 64 O.L.R. 535, [1930] 1 D.L.R. 603 (C.A.); *In Bonis Clark* (1839), 2 Curt. 329, 163 E.R. 428; *In Bonis Marshall* (1866), 13 L.T. 643.

40 See *Re Bailey's Goods* (1838), 1 Curt. 914, 163 E.R. 316; *Smith v. Harris* (1845), 1 Rob. Ecc. 262, 163 E.R. 1033; *Re Ullersperger's Goods* (1841), 6 Jur. 156. And see *Theobald on Wills*, 15th ed. by J.B. Clark and J.G. Ross Martyn (London: Sweet & Maxwell, 1993, 44-5; *Williams on Wills*, 7th ed. by C.H. Sherrin, R.F.D. Barlow, and R.A. Walllington, assisted by Susannah Meadway (London: Butterworths, 1995), 125; *Jarman on Wills*, 8th ed. by Raymond Jennings, assisted by John C. Harper (London: Sweet & Maxwell Limited, 1951), 127. See also Robin Towns, "Execution of documents by an agent other than an attorney" (1998), 142 Sol. J. 676 at 677, who is of opinion that the old cases are unlikely to be overruled since the courts now take a more lenient approach to minor defects in the execution of wills. I am indebted to Prof. Cameron Harvey of the University of Manitoba for drawing this point to my attention.

41 *Re Smith*, [1948] 2 W.W.R. 55 (Sask. Surr. Ct.).

42 *Re Cook*, [1960] 1 W.L.R. 353, [1960] 1 All E.R. 689. See *contra Simms Estate v. King* (1995), 9 E.T.R. (2d) 40 (Nfld. T.D.).

43 *Re Clarke* (1982), 39 O.R. (2d) 392 (Surr. Ct.). See also *Hindmarsh v. Charlton* (1861), 8 H.L. Cas. 160 at 167, 11 E.R. 388, *per* Lord Campbell L.C. (H.L.), who stated:
    I will lay down this as to my notion of the law: that to make a valid subscription of a witness there must either be the name or some mark which is intended to represent the name.
    In *Re Blewitt* (1880), 5 P.D. 116 at 117, Sir James Hannan P. extended these remarks to the signature of the testator as well. See also *Re Chalcraft*, [1948] P. 222, [1948] 1 All E.R. 700, which held a partially completed signature of a testatrix to be acceptable on this basis.

44 See *Re Bradshaw Estate* (1988), 30 E.T.R. 276 (N.B. Prob. Ct.). And see *Re Chalcraft, supra*.

witnesses, present at the same time, and an attestation clause to that effect is desirable, but not essential.[45]

(e)   At the End of the Will

Although section 4(1)(a) of the *Succession Law Reform Act* states that a will is not valid unless it is signed at the end, section 7 takes account of the foibles of testators by permitting certain kinds of irregular forms of execution. There is a host of cases concerning incorrectly placed signatures. *Re Riva*,[46] reproduced below, discusses many of them and is itself illustrative of the kinds of problems that arise in this context.

RE RIVA
(1978), 3 E.T.R. 307
Ontario Surrogate Court
[County of Elgin]

The testatrix, Alma Riva, completed a printed will form in her own handwriting. The form consisted of one leaf (sheet of paper) folded in half to form four pages, with the dispositive provisions contained on the first two and the attestation clause and the signatures of the witnesses on the third. The form indicated that the testatrix should sign there as well, but insufficient space had been reserved for it. On the fourth page at the top there was a printed rectangle containing the printed word "Dated." The testatrix had filled in, in her own hand the date of the will, August 31, 1977, and the words "Alma V. Riva R.R. 9 St. Thomas, Ont. Canada."

The executors applied for probate in solemn form. The two witnesses could not be located.

McDERMID SURR. CT. J.:

. . .

I was assisted by counsel who referred me to several authorities and I adopt the general principles laid down in *Re Peverett*,[47] as expressed by Jeune P.:[48]

Two things may be laid down as general principles. The first is, that the Court is always extremely anxious to give effect to the wishes of persons if satisfied that they really are their testamentary wishes; and, secondly, the Court will not allow a matter of form to stand in the way if the essential elements of execution have been fulfilled.

That case involved a holograph document signed by the deceased and two witnesses, both of whom had died prior to the trial. The handwriting of one of the witnesses was proved by an affidavit of that witness' daughter. In addition, there

---

45   See *Brewster v. Brewster* (1989), 33 E.T.R. 204 (Sask. Q.B.).
46   (1978), 3 E.T.R. 307 (Ont. Surr. Ct.).
47   [1902] P. 205.
48   At pp. 206-7.

was no attestation clause whatever appearing in the document. The Court applied the principle "omnia praesumuntur rite esse acta" and granted administration with the will annexed. In doing so, Jeune P. stated,

> I am conscious that in this case where there is no attestation clause at all, I am going to the furthest limit of allowing the presumption to prevail.

In that case he found that one of the witnesses was "a person who was not unlikely to be a witness to a document for the deceased" and that "the signature of the other of whom is proved." In the case at Bar, it was not demonstrated that either of the witnesses was "a person who was not unlikely to be a witness to a document for the deceased", nor indeed was the signature of either witness proved.

In this latter regard, it was the evidence of Mr. Packard that the handwriting of the deceased, the handwriting of the witness R. Restwick and of the witness Lois Watts were all produced with different pens. Although he was unable to say who were the authors of the two witnesses' signatures, it was his opinion that it was extremely improbable that the deceased wrote the signatures of the two witnesses. In his opinion it was most probable that three different people, i.e. the deceased and two other persons signing as R. Restwick and Lois Watts, signed exhibit no. 1.

On the basis of this evidence, I have no difficulty or hesitation in finding that the purported last will and testament contains the handwriting of three persons namely the deceased and two other persons signing as "R. Restwick" and "Lois Watts".

In *Re DeGruchy*[49] the testator completed a will form and handed it to his wife who replied that it needed signing and witnessing. He left the form with her and four days later when "two old friends" were with him he called his wife to bring in "that paper", which she then did.

> The will was then completely folded so that the endorsement "will of" on the back was uppermost; and under it, *according to the positive evidence of one of the witnesses*, he then wrote his name. (Emphasis mine.)

The other witness testified that he was looking at a paper and could not be sure that he saw the testator write his name but believed that he did so as disposed by the other witness.

> Testator then opened the will and folded it so that the printed testimonium alone in the usual form was uppermost, and asked the witnesses to sign, which they did...Testator never signed in the usual place, or otherwise then by the writing on the back.

Robertson J. granted probate of the will.

The *DeGruchy* case is similar to the one at Bar in that in each case the testator completed a will form which consisted of "one sheet of paper folded in the middle, printed in skeleton form on the first, second and third pages" and endorsed "will

---

49 (1941), 56 B.C.R. 271.

of" on the back and the testator signed only on the back and not "in the usual place". However, the *DeGruchy* decision can be distinguished from the case at Bar in that in the former, there was evidence from at least one of the witnesses. In the case at Bar, there is no evidence whatsoever as to the circumstances surrounding the signing of the will either by the testatrix or by the witnesses.

> [His Honour then referred to *Re Eaglestone*,[50] which was virtually identical to *De Gruchy*. The court, having heard the evidence of a witness, concluded that the testatrix had written the will as one continuous act, concluding with her signature, and that her signature, although appearing on the back of the document, nevertheless appeared on the face of the will.
>
> His Honour also discussed *Re Mann*[51] in which the testatrix wrote out her will on a sheet of paper in the presence of one witness, while the second witness came in towards the end. When she was finished, the testatrix wrote on an envelope: "The last will and testament of Jane Catherine Mann." Then she asked the witnesses to sign their names at the foot of the sheet of paper, under an attestation clause which said: "In the presence of witnesses." The testatrix then placed the will in the envelope and kept it with her bankers for a time, after which she gave it to her executrix.
>
> The court admitted the sheet of paper and the envelope to probate, since the circumstances precluded fraud, the envelope had a close connection with the sheet of paper, both documents were written on the same occasion and in the presence of the attesting witnesses, and the safekeeping of the documents showed that they were genuine. His Honour continued:]

Although the decision seems predominantly concerned with the "rule as to attachment" of documents purporting to constitute a will, it is relevant as an example of the lengths to which the Courts have gone in holding a signature to satisfy the requirements of execution contained in the Wills Act that the signature of a testator must be "at the foot or end" of the will. Again, however, there was evidence that:

> both paper and envelope were written in the presence of the attesting witnesses, the first witness being present during the whole of the writing of both documents and the second during the writing of the envelope and the latter part of the dispositive paper.

As I have already indicated, there is no evidence of the circumstances surrounding the appending of the deceased's signature in the case at Bar.

Mr. Hull referred the Court to *Re Bean*.[52] In that case the deceased used a printed form of will which he completed in his own handwriting. The deceased did not sign the document in the space left in the form for a signature, but after he had filled in the form he wrote his name and address and the date on the back of the form and also filled in spaces on the envelope on which were printed the words:

> The last will and testament of......

---

50 [1950] S.A.S.R. 257.
51 [1942] P. 146, [1942] 2 All E.R. 193.
52 [1944] P. 83, [1944] 2 All E.R. 348.

To......Executor. Date......

by writing his name and address, the name of the executrix and the date. The attesting witnesses then signed their names and addresses in the spaces provided in the document for that purpose. The envelope was lying on the table at the time and the writing on it was seen by one of the attesting witnesses. After attestation, the deceased folded the will form and handed it to the executrix who had been present through the whole transaction and she kept it in a box until after his death. The Court held that the motion to admit the will to probate failed on the ground that the name written on the envelope was not the signature to the will.

Hodson J. had to deal with the question of whether or not the requirements of the Wills Act, 1837,[53] as amended by the Wills Act, 1852,[54] requiring a will to be signed by the testator "at the foot of the will" had been satisfied. He delineated two issues to be decided: firstly, "whether the name 'George Bean' written on the envelope, is a signature at all", and secondly, if so, "whether or not it makes any difference that the signature was written on a separate piece of paper."

There appears to have been evidence given by the executrix that she was unaware that the deceased had not signed the will form and Hodson J. concluded "that this omission on the part of the deceased was purely accidental" and that "the writing on the envelope was equally clearly, I think, put there for the purpose of identifying the contents of the envelope and not as a signature at all".

He goes on to state:

> He had written his name not only on the envelope, *but also on the endorsement which appears on the back sheet.* It is true that the endorsement was not visible to the attesting witness whereas the writing on the envelope was seen. Nevertheless, in my opinion it is impossible to be satisfied that the deceased intended to give effect to the will by writing on the envelope since in all probability, he, like the executrix, was under the impression that he had already signed the will on the form itself. (Emphasis mine.)

He added that if it had been possible

> to find as a fact that the name on the envelope was put there as a signature to the will, I should have regarded the facts in this case as indistinguishable from those in *In the Goods of Mann.*

The facts in *Re Bean* are similar to those in the case at Bar in that in both cases, the testator signed the back of the will form and the envelope. However, in the case at Bar there is, I repeat, no evidence of the circumstances surrounding the appending of the signatures by the testatrix or the witnesses. In *Re Bean* the case was decided on the ground that the signature on the *envelope* did not constitute a "signature" within the meaning of the Wills Act.

It appears that the effect of the signature on the back page of the will was not fully considered but was rather summarily dealt with and presumably considered to be of little import by the words, "It is true that the endorsement (on the back

---

53 7 Will. 4 & 1 Vict., c. 26.
54 15 & 16 Vict., c. 24.

sheet) was not visible to the attesting witness whereas the writing on the envelope was seen." This fact taken with the affidavit evidence of the executrix that she did not know that the deceased had not signed the will form, seems to have focussed the Court's attention upon the effect of the signature on the envelope to the exclusion of considering the effect of the signature on the back sheet of the will, and led the Court to conclude that the deceased's failure to sign the will "was purely accidental."

In the case at Bar, there is of course no evidence from anyone present at the time the signatures were appended to assist the Court in coming to a conclusion as to whether or not the deceased's omission to append her signature, in what might be considered the normal place, was purely accidental.

The question of the validity of a signature affixed to the envelope in which the will was contained rather than being affixed to the will itself was also dealt with in *Re Wagner*.[55] The Court there had the advantage of an affidavit from the executor who wrote the will at the request and upon the instructions of the testator. After this had been completed, the testator signed his name in the introductory clause to the will and it was duly witnessed by two witnesses, one of whom was the executor. The will was then enclosed and sealed in an envelope upon which the executor wrote "last will and testament of" and the envelope was then signed by the testator in the presence of the two witnesses but the two witnesses did not sign the envelope.

Hogarth Surr. Ct. J. had no hesitancy in holding that the signature in the introductory clause did not meet the requirement of the Saskatchewan Wills Act, which is similar in wording to that portion of s. 11(2) of the Ontario Wills Act which reads:

> but no signature is operative to give effect to any disposition, or direction which is underneath, or which follows it.

Hogarth Surr. Ct. J. considered the decisions in *Re Mann* and *Re Bean* and concluded:

> In the present case I do not find myself in the same position as Hodson J. in the Bean case. On the contrary I am definitely of the opinion that the signature "Adam Wagner Jr." on the envelope was put there by the testator as his signature to and for the purpose of authenticating his will and was so intended by him.

He explained that he came to that conclusion for the following reasons:

(1) "The signature on the envelope was the last act of the testator in making his will." This was obviously a finding of fact based on the evidence before Hogarth Surr. Ct. J.

(2) "If the signature of the testator on the envelope was not intended by him to be his signature to and in authentication of his will, why did he sign the envelope. It was not necessary for him to sign for the purpose of identification. If the writing on the envelope was for the purpose of identification only, I would expect the

---

55 (1959), 29 W.W.R. 34, 20 D.L.R. (2d) 770 (Sask.).

witness Shulz who wrote the words 'last will and testament of' to have completed the identification by himself writing the name of Adam Wagner Jr." Again, it is obvious that this reason was the result of inferences made by Hogarth Surr. Ct. J. from facts adduced in evidence before him as to the circumstances surrounding the appending by the testator of his signature to the envelope in which the will was contained.

(3) Hogarth Surr. Ct. J. stated that the deceased left a widow and nine children surviving him and that eight of the nine children were adults. He felt that the dispositions made by the testator in the will bearing in mind his estate and the fact that the adult children should be able to provide for themselves were "as it should be". In other words, it appears that he gave some weight to the reasonableness of the dispositions made by the testator in his will in light of his personal circumstances.

(4) As a further reason, he quoted from the judgment of Langton J. in the *Mann* case and stated that when dealing with an unattached paper an envelope "may reasonably be held to have a far closer relationship to a document which it encloses than a second and wholly disconnected piece of paper." One of the primary considerations, of course, where the testator's signature appears on a paper separate from that containing the dispositive clauses is that the possibility of fraud is more likely. In this case however, Hogarth Surr. Ct. J. was satisfied that "the facts and circumstances surrounding the preparation and execution of the documents before me, which so clearly expressed the intention of the deceased, in my opinion, preclude all possibility of fraud."

The other decisions to which counsel referred the Court dealt with the question of due execution as it relates to the witnesses of a will and the application of the principle of omnia praesumuntur rite esse acta.

In this connection, reference was made to the decision, *Re Peverett*,[56] in which case the headnote states:

> The Court (Sir F.H. Jeune P.) extended the presumption of law "omnia praesumuntur rite esse acta"—to the case of an informal holograph document containing no attestation clause whatever, and in regard to which there was no evidence to prove the handwriting of one of the persons (both of whom were dead) whose names appeared near the signature of the testatrix at the foot or end of the document.

As I have already indicated, the *Peverett* decision is distinguishable from the case at Bar since there the handwriting of one of the witnesses was proved by an affidavit of her daughter and the other witness was "a person who was not unlikely to be a witness to a document for the deceased."

> [His Honour then discussed *Re Phibbs*,[57] in which the contents of a lost will were proved by persons who had examined it, but not by the witnesses, since they were unknown, and in which the will was admitted to probate.

---

56 [1902] P. 205.
57 [1917] P. 93.

His Honour also discussed *Re Biggin, Bake v. McGregor and Public Trustee*,[58] in which a will was admitted to probate even though the witnesses could not recall that they were present at the same time when the testator signed. There was a proper attestation clause and the court relied upon the presumption of due execution. His Honour continued:]

In *Re Denning*,[59] it appears from the report that the document sought to be established as the deceased's last will consisted of a small single sheet of writing paper covered by the date, the dispositive words and the signature of the testatrix. There does not appear to have been any attestation clause and on the reverse side of the sheet upside down were written, each in different handwriting from the other and from that on the face of the paper, the names of two persons whom it had been proved impossible to trace.

During her lifetime the testatrix had told the plaintiff that she had made a will and that he was one of the beneficiaries and his sister the other and this was the effect of the purported will.

Sachs J., in finding the will to have been duly executed, felt:

In these circumstances the real issue for the court is whether the maxim omnia praesumuntur rite esse acta can be applied.

He referred to two general principles laid down in *Re Peverett* referred to above.

And notwithstanding the statement of Sir Francis Jeune P. that he was of the opinion that his decision in *Peverett* was "going to the furthest limit", Sachs J., "having taken into account all the factors" felt justified in taking "that step further" in *Denning* because it seemed to him that "there is no other practical reason why those names should be on the back of the document unless it was for the purpose of attesting the will."

Again, in this case, there appears not to have been any evidence as to the circumstances surrounding the execution of the will by the testatrix or the witnesses or as to the identity of

the witnesses or proof of their signatures. Notwithstanding that, the maxim of omnia praesumuntur rite esse acta was applied.

Having reviewed the relevant case law, I return to the facts of the case before me.

On p. 3 of the last will and testament form completed by the deceased Alma V. Riva, although the space provided for the signatures and a description of the occupation and address of the witnesses is quite adequate, the space in which the testatrix should sign, as indicated by an asterisk, is totally inadequate unless the signature were appended in a vertical as opposed to a horizontal position.

In addition, the attestation clause departs somewhat from that normally found and reads as follows:

---

58 [1949] O.W.N. 61 (H.C.).
59 [1958] 1 W.L.R. 462, [1958] 2 All E.R. 1.

Signed, published and declared by the said testator *"her"* last will and testament in the presence of us both present at the same time, who in *"her"* presence of each other have hereunto set and subscribed our names as witness.

The words appearing in quotation marks are in the handwriting of the deceased.

In view of the apparent deficiencies in the form it is not surprising that the name of the publisher does not appear anywhere on the will form and that on the envelope the words "V.B. Printing" appear without any address.

Although the lower half of p. 3, which contains the instructions for completing the will, designates by an asterisk where the testator is to sign, it would be physically impossible to do so unless the signature were appended in a vertical position and it would seem logical that the testatrix should sign on the back page of the will after the printed words in the form "Will of" where in fact she did sign.

I have therefore come to the conclusion that the writing on the fourth or back page of the will, which I find to be in the handwriting of the deceased, was appended by her with the intention of executing the document as her last will and testament.

I have come to that conclusion for many reasons:

Firstly, by reason, as I have already indicated, of the deficient fashion in which the will form was structured, namely the insufficient space for the signature of the testatrix in the place so designated by the form.

Secondly, by reason of the existence of letters written by the deceased expressing three main areas of concern, as outlined above, which are also expressed in the will form.

Thirdly, because these three main areas of concern would in her circumstances be reasonable and proper areas of concern.

Fourthly, because it would not seem necessary for her to have signed on the reverse of the will for the purpose of identifying the document as her will since the first few words of the document so identify it: "This is the Last Will and Testament of me 'Alma V. Riva RR #7 St. Thomas, Ontario County of Elgin'."Again, the words in quotation marks are in the handwriting of the deceased.

Fifthly, because it would appear curious to me that the testatrix would go to the trouble of obtaining a will form, completing it in her own handwriting, disposing of her assets in the same fashion as she had indicated in letters previously written that it was her intention to do, and of having two persons append their signatures to this document, unless she intended it to be her last will and testament.

For these reasons, taken together, I have no hesitation in concluding that the deceased affixed her signature on the fourth or last page of the will intending the document to be her last will and testament, notwithstanding the fact that there is no evidence available from anyone present at the time of execution as to the circumstances surrounding the appending of any of the signatures to the will.

The next question to be answered is whether such signature is "at the foot or end" of the will as required by s. 11(1) of The Wills Act.[60] Section 11(2) of The Wills Act refers to several circumstances with respect to the position of the

---

60 R.S.O. 1970, c. 499.

signature which shall not affect the validity of the will. One of those circumstances is where the signature is "on a...page...whereon no clause or paragraph or disposing part of the will is written above the signature...", subject to the overriding proviso that "no signature is operative to give effect to any disposition, or direction which is underneath, or which follows
it, nor does it give effect to any disposition or direction inserted after the signature was made."

I have no hesitation in finding that the signature of the deceased in its location on the fourth or back page of the will is a proper signature in so far as the position of the signature is concerned within the requirements of s. 11(2) of The Wills Act.

In addition, by s. 11(2) it must be "apparent on the face of the will that the testator intended to give effect by such signature to the writing signed as his will." I adopt the reasoning of Napier C.J. in *Re Eaglestone*,[61] with respect to his interpretation of the words "on the face of the will" and for the reasons already given find that the signature was appended by the testatrix with the intention of signing the document as her last will and testament.

I have noted above that the attestation clause is somewhat deficient, although the instructions at the bottom of p.3 of the form do state: "Testator sign here *in presence of witnesses and witnesses together in presence of testator.*" (Emphasis mine.)

As I have indicated, Sachs J. applied the principle omnia praesumuntur rite esse acta in *Re Denning*[62] and found the will to be duly executed in circumstances where there appears to have been no evidence adduced as to the circumstances surrounding the appending of the witnesses' signatures nor any evidence as to the identity or whereabouts of the witnesses. In addition, the signatures of the witnesses were found on the back of the will separate from the signature of the testatrix which was on the front of the will and the best that could be said was that "the handwriting on the back did not coincide with that on the face of the document" and that the names written on the reverse side were "in two different hands". I echo his observation that "it seems to me that there is no other practical reason why those names should be on...the document unless it was for the purposes of attesting the will." It should also be noted that in the *Denning* case, there was no attestation clause whatsoever.

There is a further anomaly in that the date of the will has been inserted by the testatrix as the 31st day of August 1977 whereas she in fact died on or about the 27th day of August 1977.   Having found the will otherwise valid, I must infer that the testatrix mistakenly inserted the date August 31st, 1977 on the first page of the will and on the fourth or back page of the will. On the envelope the printed form contained the words: "Dated.........19......" After the word "Dated" the word "July" had been inserted and crossed out with the word "August" written above and it appears that following those words there initially appeared "30th" and that

---

61 [1950] S.A.S.R. 257.
62 [1958] 1 W.L.R. 462, [1958] 2 All E.R. 1.

the "0" had been changed to a "1", with the number "77" having been inserted after the number "19".

From the other evidence adduced with respect to the dates or approximate dates upon which exhibits no. 2 and no. 3 were sent by the deceased to Mr. Wise and exhibits no. 5, no. 6, and no. 7 were sent by the deceased to Mr. and Mrs. Firmin, I think it is reasonable to infer that the deceased executed the will sometime in the month of July or August of 1977. Since there is no other will being tendered for probate, and there is, therefore, no contest as to which of two wills bearing different dates is the last will and testament of the deceased, it is my opinion that the fact that the will bears a date subsequent to the date of the testator's death, is not, in the peculiar circumstances of this case, fatal to its validity.

I therefore find that the document dated August 31st, 1977 was the duly executed last will and testament of the deceased Alma V. Riva and that letters probate shall issue to the executor named therein, John Wise, MP.

Since the cause of this litigation had its origin in the fault of the testatrix and there were reasonable grounds for requiring the will to be proved in solemn form, all of the parties shall have their costs as between a solicitor and his own client to be payable out of the estate, after taxation.

Notes and Questions

1. The testator wrote out his will on one side of a sheet of paper, but prepared a lined box on the right hand side, about half way down the page in which he wrote the word "signed" and his signature. Some dispositive provisions appeared opposite and below the box. The witnesses signed at the bottom of the page. Should the will be admitted to probate?[63]

2. A testator attempted to write his will on a four inch square piece of paper, headed "My Last Will and Testament." Underneath he listed various legacies. His signature and the date, followed by the witnesses' signatures were placed at the top in the right hand margin. Can this will be probated?[64]

3. Re Bean,[65] discussed in Re Riva, was followed in Re Beadle.[66]

4. In Re Long[67] the court considered the following facts: The will was written on two sides of a sheet of paper. On one side were the words "This is the Last Will and Testament of" the testatrix, with the address and date of execution and the appointment of an executor. A line was then drawn across the page and below the line were the usual attestation clause

---

63 See Re Hornby, [1946] P. 171, [1946] 2 All E.R. 150, 175 L.T. 161; and see Re Roberts, [1934] P. 102, 151 L.T. 79, signatures written sideways in margin because there was no room at the end.

64 See Re Harris, [1952] P. 319, [1952] 2 All E.R. 409; Re Stalman (1931), 145 L.T. 339.

65 [1944] P. 85, [1944] 2 All E.R. 348.

66 [1974] 1 W.L.R. 417, [1974] 1 All E.R. 493.

67 [1936] P. 166, [1936] 1 All E.R. 435. See also Palin v. Ponting, [1930] P. 185, in which the testatrix had written in the margin of page one of her will, made on a printed form, "See other side for completion". On the other side appeared the words "Continuation from other side," followed by several dispositions. Only the front of page one was executed and attested. The back of page one was not. It was held that the words "See other side for completion" interlined the words on the back and that the latter should be admitted to probate.For a related approach (that is, incorporation by reference), see Re Poole; Stewart v. Poole, [1929] 1 D.L.R. 418 (P.E.I.S.C.).

and signatures. On the other side of the sheet the testatrix had written, "I give and bequeath
. . . .," followed by a list of legacies. One of the witnesses was able to testify that when
they signed she noticed that the other side of the sheet had writing on it.

The court concluded from this evidence and from the fact that a line was drawn above
the signatures, which indicated the end of the dispositive part of the will, that the page
listing the bequests was written before the page containing the signatures. The court stated
that it was satisfied that the whole document was written before the signatures were made
and that that is the important point, so that the court will not insist upon proof that the will
was written in a particular order.

5. *Re Little*[68] illustrates another kind of problem. The testator's solicitor prepared a draft
will in accordance with his client's instructions and sent it to the client. Instead of taking
it back to the solicitor the testator filled in the blanks and executed it. The draft consisted
of four pages, plus a fifth blank page, on the back of which was written "Draft Will." The
four sheets were held together with a brass fastener. The fourth sheet ended with the
testimonium and attestation clauses, but when the will was signed and witnessed, all signed
on the bottom half of the fifth page, while the deceased pressed his hand on the top half.
One of the witnesses testified that the top half was blank at the time. Creases in the pages
next to the holes made by the brass fastener indicated that all pages were fastened together
when they were signed. There were some changes made in the body of the will and a
number of dispositive provisions were written in the blank space above the testator's
signature. The court held that it was a reasonable assumption that the first four sheets were
under the fifth at the time of execution so that when the testator pressed the sheets down
on the table with his hand, there was a sufficient nexus between all of them to establish
that it was one testamentary document. Hence the will as originally typed by the solicitor's
office was probated, but the handwritten additions above the signatures were excluded
from probate.

6. The signature should normally appear opposite and to the right of the attestation
clause. However, if the signature only appears in the attestation clause (in the place where
it is normally typed) the will is valid.[69] But if the will is signed and witnessed first and
then the testator completes the dispositive part of the will, it must be refused probate.[70]

If the testatrix's handwritten name appears at the top of the will, but not at the end, and
she did not acknowledge her signature to the witnesses, and they did not see her sign, the
will cannot be probated.[71]

7. When there is a question about the due execution of a will, the maxim *omnia
praesumuntur rite esse acta*, referred to in the *Riva* case, is often applied. The maxim
means that if an intention to carry out some formal act (such as the making of a will) is
established, an inference may be drawn that on reasonable probability the actor (testator)
did what he or she intended to do in the way in which the law prescribes that it should be
done. The maxim, therefore, operates so as to give effect to the intention of the testator.
Clearly you don't need to rely on the presumption if compliance with the statute can be
proved as, for example, by an affidavit or other evidence of a surviving witness. Conversely
it can not be applied if compliance is disproved. Thus, it can only apply if there is no proof
one way or the other, for example, if the witnesses are dead, or if they are disbelieved.[72]

---

68 [1960] 1 W.L.R. 495, [1960] 1 All E.R. 387.
69 *Cook v. Nova Scotia* (1982), 53 N.S.R. (2d) 87, 109 A.P.R. 87 (T.D.).
70 *Kennedy v. MacEachern* (1978), 27 N.S.R. (2d) 329, 41 A.P.R. 329 (C.A.).
71 *Ellis v. Turner* (1997), 20 E.T.R. (2d) 306 (B.C.C.A.).
72 For two cases in which the maxim was applied, see *Re Gardner*, [1935] O.R. 71, 1 D.L.R. 308

8. There is a presumption of due execution when the will contains a proper attestation clause.[73]

(f) Attestation

(i) *Generally*

Section 4 of the *Succession Law Reform Act* requires the testator either to sign in the presence of two witnesses who are both present at the same time, or having already signed the will, to acknowledge the signature in the presence of two witnesses who are both present at the same time. The two witnesses must then sign the will in the presence of the testator, although not necessarily in the presence of each other. The executors must prove due execution. If they are unable to do so, the will fails. Thus, for example, if the evidence of the two witnesses conflicts about the order of signing and the evidence is evenly balanced, the court can not grant probate of the will.[74]

Chesline v. Hermiston,[75] reproduced below, discusses the question whether the witnesses need to know they are attesting a will. It also considers problems caused by the order in which the parties signed.

CHESLINE v. HERMISTON

62 O.L.R. 575, [1928] 4 D.L.R. 786

Supreme Court of Ontario

[High Court of Justice]

The testator, Hermiston, entered the store of Mr. Petrie on Bloor St. in Toronto and asked him to witness a document which he said was an explanation of his income tax return. He brought Mr. Elliot, a neighbouring businessman, with him as a second witness. Elliott was in a hurry, so he signed as a witness and moved towards the door. Before he was gone, Petrie noticed that Hermiston had not signed and asked him to do so. By the time Elliott reached the door Petrie had started to sign. Elliott testified that the will was not signed by the testator in his presence or in the presence of Petrie and that he did not see the testator's signature on the document when he signed.

LOGIE J.:

. . .

It is not a question of acknowledgment, as contended by Mr. MacGregor, because, where a testator writes something on the will in the presence of the

---

(C.A.); *Re Laxer*, [1963] 1 O.R. 343, 37 D.L.R. (2d) 192 (C.A.). See also *Re Kane* (1979), 5 E.T.R. 44 (N.S. Prob. Ct.).

73 *Kirpalani v. Hathiramani* (1992), 46 E.T.R. 256 (Ont. Gen. Div.); *Beniston Estate v. Shepherd* (1996), 16 E.T.R. (2d) 71 (B.C.S.C.).

74 *Morris v. Morris* (1993), 2 E.T.R. (2d) 101 (B.C.S.C.).

75 62 O.L.R. 575, [1928] 4 D.L.R. 786 (H.C.).

witnesses summoned to attest the will, it will be presumed that he wrote his signature, though the witness may not see the signature and may not know that the document is his will.[76] And a request to sign a paper not declared to be a will, when the witnesses see the signature, is sufficient.[77] And there may be a sufficient acknowledgment if the testator's signature might have been seen by the witnesses if they had looked, although they may swear they did not in fact see it.[78] But a mere request to witnesses to attest an instrument, the nature of which is not explained to them and the signature of which they do not see, is not sufficient.[79]

On this conflicting evidence, it is impossible to hold that the will was executed in compliance with the Act.

The cases are clear, moreover, that the signature of the testator must be written or acknowledged by the testator in the actual visual presence of both witnesses together before either of them attests and subscribes the will.

In *In Bonis Allen*[80] the deceased signed her will by a mark in the presence of one witness who subscribed the will as attesting it, and on a subsequent day she acknowledged her signature in the presence of that witness and of another who also subscribed the will, but the former witness did not again subscribe the will, and Sir Herbert Jenner refused probate. The wording of the [Wills] Act,[81] the Act in force in 1839, when this case was decided, is the same as that of subsec. 1 of sec. 12 of [the present *Wills Act*].[82]

In *In Bonis Olding*[83] Sir Herbert Jenner rejected a motion for probate of a will signed by the testator after the witnesses had subscribed their names.

In *In Bonis Byrd*[84] Sir Herbert Jenner Fust said:—

My opinion is, that the witnesses should subscribe the will after the testator has signed it.

And in *Cooper v. Bockett*[85] the Court held that a will must be signed by a testator before it is subscribed by witnesses, but under the circumstances of that case the will was held to have been signed before the witnesses subscribed.

In *Hindmarsh v. Charlton*[86] the Lord Chancellor said:—[87]

The [Wills] Act...[88]requires that a will to be valid "shall be signed at the foot or end thereof by the testator, or by some other person in his presence and by his direction"; and such signature shall be made or acknowledged by the testator in the presence of two or more witnesses present at the same time; and such witnesses shall attest and shall subscribe the will in the presence of

76 *Smith v. Smith* (1866), L.R. 1 P. & D. 143, and other cases.
77 *Keigwin v. Keigwin* (1843), 3 Curt. 607, and other cases.
78 *In Bonis Gunstan* (1882), 7 P.D. 102, and other cases.
79 *In Bonis Ashton* (1847), 5 N. of C. 548, and other cases.
80 (1839), 2 Curt. 331.
81 1 Vict. c. 26, s. 9.
82 R.S.O. 1914, c. 120, now R.S.O. 1927, c. 149, s. 11(1).
83 (1841), 2 Curt. 865.
84 (1842), 3 Curt. 117.
85 (1843), 3 Curt. 648.
86 (1861), 8 H.L.C. 160.
87 At p. 167.
88 1 Vict. c. 26, s. 9.

the testator. It is settled by the case of *White v. The British Museum*[89] and other decisions to the same effect, that after the will has been signed or acknowledged by the testator in the presence of both the witnesses, there must be a subscription of the witnesses in the presence of the testator.

Lord Cranworth in the same case says:—

It has been determined, upon the construction of the last statute, and quite rightly determined, that there must be a subscription by two witnesses after the testator has signed the will in their presence, or acknowledged his signature in their presence.

The law has been so well settled that I can find no recent case exactly on all fours with the case at bar either in Canada or in England, but it is quite clear, that Elliot signed first, then the testator and lastly Petrie, and Elliott not having resubscribed, the will does not comply with subsec. 1 of sec. 12 of the Wills Act,[90] and is therefore invalid.

There will be a declaration accordingly and the action will be dismissed, but under all the circumstances costs of all parties will be paid out of the estate.

Notes and Questions

1. The requirement that the witnesses sign in the presence of the testator does not mean that the witnesses need to see what the testator writes, or even that the document he or she is writing on is a will. So long as they see the testator write something on the will, the court will apply the presumption *omnia praesumuntur rite esse acta* and presume that the testator wrote his or her signature.[91]

2. Not only must the witnesses see the testator sign, the testator must also see the witnesses sign, or at least have been able to see them sign, had he or she cared to look. If that is not possible, they are not signing in the presence of the testator. Thus, if the testator is unable to turn around because of a physical condition and the witnesses sign behind the testator, the attestation is invalid.[92] Similarly, if the witnesses sign after the testator, but in an adjoining room and out of the testator's line of sight (the door being open), they do not sign in the testator's presence and the attestation is invalid.[93]

3. Does the language of the statute, "in the presence of the testator," connote more than mere physical presence?

A few days before her death of cancer, the testatrix gave instructions to have a will prepared. One of her daughters did so, presented it to her and asked her if that was what she wanted. The testatrix nodded and attempted to write her signature, but was only able to write part of her name. The witnesses immediately signed their names. Earlier in the day the testatrix had been given painkillers and she was very drowsy. She did not regain consciousness. Assuming capacity, knowledge and approval and a proper signature by the testatrix, did the witnesses sign in her presence?[94]

---

89 (1829), 6 Bing. 310.
90 R.S.O. 1914, c. 120.
91 *Smith v. Smith* (1866), L.R. 1 P. & D. 143.
92 In *Re Wozciechowiecz*, [1931] 3 W.W.R. 283, [1931] 4 D.L.R. 585 (Alta. C.A.), noted (1932), 10 Can. Bar Rev. 55.
93 *Jenner v. Ffinch* (1879), 5 P.D. 106.
94 *Re Chalcraft*, [1948] P. 222, [1948] 1 All E.R. 700. See also *Re Bradshaw Estate* (1988), 30 E.T.R. 276 (N.B. Prob. Ct.), to the same effect.

4. Not all provinces are equally strict in the matter of attestation. *Simpkins Estate v. Simpkins*[95] is an instructive case in this regard. The testator went into a co-worker's office and signed his will in the presence of the co-worker, who then signed as witness. The testator then called another co-worker into the same office. That co-worker had seen the testator go into the first co-worker's office and saw that person sign a document. The testator showed the second co-worker the document with both signatures on it, told her it was his will and asked her to sign it, which she did. The court held that the will was properly attested. Do you agree? Would the same result obtain in Ontario?

The *Simpkins* case should be contrasted with *Bolton v. Tartaglia*.[96] The testator initialled the first two pages of her will and signed the last page in the presence of two witnesses. Both witnesses initialled the first two pages and one witness signed the last page of the will. The other witness inadvertently did not sign the last page. The court held that the failure to comply with the statutory requirement that two or more witnesses must subscribe the will in the presence in the testator meant that the will failed.

5. Although the *Succession Law Reform Act* and the statutes in the other Canadian provinces, except the Prince Edward Island Act,[97] do not require that the witnesses sign in the presence of each other,[98] most careful solicitors insist that they do so and the attestation clause then states that they have done so. Is this a good practice? Why?

6. Can a blind person be a witness to a will?[99]

7. Can a blind (or deaf-mute) person make a will?[100]

8. A Miami lawyer has been reported[101] to have devised a way whereby many of the questions that often arise about the due execution of a will may be avoided. For the trifling amount of $125 he is prepared to videotape the execution of a will in living colour. One testatrix who took advantage of this device thought that her children would appreciate such a message from her from beyond the grave. I doubt that those of her children whom she cut out of the will would view the message with the same equanimity.

(ii) *Acknowledgment*

If the testator has signed the will out of the presence of the witnesses, s. 4 of the *Succession Law Reform Act* requires the testator to acknowledge the signature in the presence of both witnesses, present at the same time. The witnesses must then sign the will in the presence of the testator, although not necessarily in each other's presence.

Re Gunstan,[102] reproduced below, is concerned with the formalities that must be observed when the testator acknowledges his or her signature. It deals with the question whether the witnesses saw the testator's signature.

---

95 (1992), 45 E.T.R. 287 (B.C.S.C.).

96 (2000), 33 E.T.R. (2d) 26 (B.C.S.C.).

97 *Probate Act*, R.S.P.E.I. 1988, c. P-21, s. 61.

98 This is confirmed in *Chester v. Baston* (1980), 6 Sask. R. 21, 8 E.T.R. 267, 118 D.L.R. (3d) 323 (C.A.).

99 See *Re Gibson*, [1949] P. 434, [1949] 2 All E.R. 90, *and* argument of counsel in *Brown v. Skirrow*, [1902] P. 3.

100 See generally Jarman, *Wills* (8th ed., 1951), ch. 7.

101 The London Free Press, Thursday, May 17, 1979, p. D3.

102 (1882), 7 P.D. 102 (C.A.).

RE GUNSTAN
(1882), 7 P.D. 102
Court of Appeal

The testatrix wrote out her will by hand and then asked the witnesses to come in to attest the document. As they came into the room, the testatrix was laying down her pen. The witnesses did not know what the document was that they were asked to subscribe and neither of them was able to see the signature and the writing above it.

The attestation clause and the signatures of the testatrix and of the witnesses were in the following form:

Signed by me in the	)	"Mary Gunstan,"
presence of the	)	Holdernesse House, Brixton Road.
undersigned, who in	)	"Ann Harradine,"
my presence and in	)	Holdernesse House, Brixton Road.
presence of each	)	"Susan Harradine,"
other, at the same	)	Holdernesse House, Brixton Road.
time signed their	)	
names as witnesses.	)	

Sir James Hannen P., dismissed the action for probate in common form and the executors appealed.

JESSEL, M.R:

I regret that I am unable to come to the conclusion that this will was properly executed. I say I regret, because from a mere accident, a want of form, that which was clearly the last will of this lady must fail of effect, and the persons interested under it be disappointed.

The real question is, what the law requires to be proved in order to support a will so that it shall be validly executed.

In this case it does not appear that the testatrix signed her name to this document in the presence of the witnesses . . . . [I]t is evident that the signature took place before they came in to the room. The question, then arises whether the testatrix acknowledged her signature before the witnesses. What is in law a sufficient acknowledgment under the statute? What I take to be the law is correctly laid down in Jarman on Wills[103] in the following terms:

> There is no sufficient acknowledgment unless the witnesses either saw or might have seen the signature, not even though the testator should expressly declare that the paper to be attested by them is his will.

And I may add, in my opinion, it is not sufficient even if the testator were to say, "My signature is inside the paper," unless the witnesses were able to see the signature. There is a great deal of authority on this point, several cases are referred to in the note to the passage which I have read, but I think it is sufficient to

---

103   4th ed. p. 108.

mention...only...*Hudson v. Parker*[104] where the matter is most elaborately discussed by Dr. Lushington. He tells us what in his view is the plain meaning of acknowledging a signature in the presence of witnesses; he says,

> What do the words import but this? "Here is my name written, I acknowledge that name so written to have been written by me; bear witness." How is it possible that the witnesses should swear that any signature was acknowledged unless they saw it? They might swear that the testator said he acknowledged a signature, but they could not depose to the fact that there was an existing signature to be acknowledged. It is quite true that acknowledgment may be expressed in any words which will adequately convey that idea, if the signature be proved to have been then existent; no particular form of expression is required either by the word "acknowledge" or by the exigency of the act to be done. It would be quite sufficient to say "that is my will", the signature being there *and seen* at the time; for such words do import an owning thereof; indeed, it may be done by any other words which naturally include within their true meaning, acknowledgment, and approbation.

. . .

I...agree with the ruling of Dr. Lushington, and therefore I hold that it is not sufficient to say "This is my will." The argument that that will do is founded on the notion that the statement by the testator "This is my will" implies that his signature is affixed to it; but that is not so, a will is not a valid will until it is attested, and there is no necessary implication that it already bears the testator's signature. It may be that the testator has not yet signed it, but may intend to do it, and it is quite possible that he may in that sense call it a will, inasmuch as it will, when executed, be a will. But I say that if he had distinctly said that he had signed the will, but yet the witnesses would not be able to see his signature, that is not sufficient acknowledgment.

. . .

If that is so, there is only one other point, and that is, did the witnesses see the signature? I am of opinion upon the evidence that they did not. Susan Harradine says in express terms that she did not; that there was a piece of blotting-paper over the signature. I have looked carefully at the original writing, and the appearance of the document strongly confirms the statement of this witness. The words, including the signature of the testatrix, are dull and blurred as if they had been blotted, and it would appear as if the blotting-paper reached down below the signature of the testatrix. The other witness says the same thing in the first instance, and then subsequently that she sometimes thought that she did see the signature, but she could not say whether she did or not. I must upon this evidence come to the conclusion that it is most satisfactorily, or rather most unsatisfactorily, proved that these witnesses did not see the signature.

. . .

[The concurring judgments of Brett and Holker L.JJ. have been omitted.]

---

104 1 Rob. 14.

Notes and Questions

1. With respect to an acknowledgment, the rule also is that the witnesses need not actually see the testator's signature, so long as they had an opportunity to see it.

In *Brown v. Skirrow*[105] the testatrix took her will into a store. She asked a clerk to act as a witness. The testatrix then signed, followed by the clerk. The proprietor was then asked to come to the same counter. Up until then he had not realized what was going on. The testatrix told him that the document was her will. At her request, the proprietor then signed the will. However, at that time the clerk was at another counter with a customer and did not see the proprietor attest the will. It was held that in the circumstances the acknowledgment was not made in the presence of both witnesses present at the same time and the will failed.

2. *Re Amos*[106] followed *Re Gunstan* in a similar fact situation. However, in *Beaudoin Estate v. Taylor*[107] the court held that a will executed by the testator, witnessed by two witnesses, and containing a standard attestation clause, should be admitted to probate. The witnesses did not see the testator sign and could not recall if the signature was on the will when they signed. The court found that their memory was faulty.

3. Can a witness acknowledge his or her signature to the other witness? A testatrix wrote out her will and signed it in the presence of one witness, who then signed it, and the two of them then went into another room to the second witness. The testatrix and the first witness identified their signatures and the second witness then subscribed her name as witness. Is the execution valid?[108]

4. The testator executed his will while in hospital. The witnesses were a patient in the next bed to his and a nurse. After the testator had started to write his signature in the presence of both witnesses, the nurse had to leave to attend to another patient and the testator completed his signature in her absence. The other witness then attested the will in the presence of the testator while the nurse was absent. The nurse then returned and the testator and the other patient acknowledged their signatures to her and she signed as a witness. Is the execution valid?[109]

5. What was wrong with the procedure in *Re Brown* and *Re Colling*, described in the two preceding notes, the fact that the testatrix/testator failed to sign in the simultaneous presence of both witnesses, or that, after the acknowledgment in the presence of both, the second witness did not resubscribe the will? Should a will fail because of such a technicality?[110]

6. Is it necessary that the testator acknowledge his or her signature (that being what the witnesses are asked to attest, not the will), or is it sufficient that he or she merely say to the witnesses that the document presented to them is his or her will and they see the testator's signature on it?[111]

A husband and wife made a joint will. Then they drove to the home of the witnesses, who came out to the pickup truck. The wife got out of the truck, while the husband

---

105 [1902] P. 3.

106 [1954] O.W.N. 545, [1954] 2 D.L.R. 574.

107 (1999), 27 E.T.R. (2d) 208 (B.C.S.C.).

108 See *Re Brown*, [1954] O.W.N. 301.

109 See *Re Colling*, [1972] 1 W.L.R. 1440, [1972] 3 All E.R. 729.

110 See Law Reform Committee (U.K.), *Twenty Second Report (The Making and Revocation of Wills)*, Cmnd. 7302, May 1980, § 2.11.

111 See *Brown v. Skirrow*, [1902] P. 3; *Re Balcom* (1978), 22 N.S.R. (2d) 707, 31 A.P.R. 707 (Prob. Ct.); *Ellis v. Turner* (1997), 20 E.T.R. (2d) 306 (B.C.C.A.).

remained in the driver's seat. The wife covered up the will, so that the witnesses did not see any signatures. The witnesses were not told whether the will had been signed. They signed the will on the hood of the truck. The court held that while the document was witnessed in the presence of the husband, it was not properly attested, because the testators did not sign or acknowledge their signatures in the presence of the witnesses.[112]

(iii) By Beneficiaries and Others

The formal requirements of wills are designed to prevent fraud. If a witness is a beneficiary under a will, there is a great potential for fraud and, as we shall see in a later chapter, as a general rule the gift to the witness is, therefore, void. The same rule obtains when the spouse of a beneficiary is a witness.

This does not mean, however, that the will itself is invalid.[113] The following are the relevant statutory rules.

SUCCESSION LAW REFORM ACT
R.S.O. 1990, c. S.26

11. Where a person who attested a will was at the time of its execution or afterward has become incompetent as a witness to prove its execution, the will is not on that account invalid.

12. (1) Where a will is attested by a person to whom or to whose then spouse a beneficial devise, bequest or other disposition or appointment of or affecting property, except charges and directions for payment of debts, is thereby given or made,...the person so attesting is a competent witness to prove the execution of the will or its validity or invalidity.

(2) Where a will is signed for the testator by another person in accordance with section 4, to whom or to whose then spouse a beneficial devise, bequest or other disposition or appointment of or affecting property, except charges and directions for payment of debts, is thereby given or made,...the will is not invalid for that reason.

. . .

13. Where property is charged by a will with a debt and a creditor or the spouse of a creditor whose debt is so charged attests a will, the person so attesting, despite the charge, is a competent witness to prove the execution of the will or its validity or invalidity.

14. A person is not incompetent as a witness to prove the execution of a will or its validity or invalidity solely because he or she is an executor.

---

112 See *Brandrick v. Cockle (Trustee of)* (1997), 160 D.L.R. (4th) 575 (Alta. C.A.).
113 Prior to the *Wills Act*, 1837, 7 Will. 4 & 1 Vict., c. 26, the *Statute of Frauds*, 1677, 29 Car. 2, c. 3, required that a witness to a will of freehold land be "credible" in order to prove the will. A beneficiary who attested a will was not credible, hence such a will could not be proved.

Comparable Legislation

Probate Act, R.S.P.E.I. 1988, c. P-21, ss. 64-67; *Wills Act*, R.S.A. 1980, c. W-11, ss. 12-15; R.S.B.C. 1996, c. 489, ss. 10-13; R.S.M. 1988, c. W150, ss. 11-15; R.S.N. 1990, c. W-10, ss. 6-8; R.S.N.B. 1973, c. W-9, ss. 11-14; R.S.N.S. 1989, c. 505, ss. 11-14; S.S. 1996, c. W-14.1, ss.12-15; R.S.N.W.T. 1988, c. W-5, s. 10; R.S.Y. 1986, c. 179, s. 9.

3. HOLOGRAPH WILLS

(a) Introduction

A holograph will is one written entirely in the testator's own handwriting and signed by him or her. It does not require attestation. See section 6 of the *Succession Law Reform Act*,[114] set out below. Holograph wills are now recognized in most jurisdictions.

The purpose of formalities of execution and attestation of wills is to eliminate fraud as much as possible. In view of the fact that holograph wills are now permitted, the question may well be asked to what extent the formal requirements concerning the execution and attestation of other wills remain necessary. It is at least arguable that, so long as the court is otherwise satisfied that there has been no fraud, a technical failure to comply with those formalities should not have the effect of causing the will to fail. The *Succession Law Reform Act*, however, continues the formal requirements in respect of attested wills. The English Law Reform Committee has considered and rejected the recognition of holograph wills.[115]

Holograph wills present problems peculiar to this type of will. These are examined in the following materials.

Further Reading

J. M. Sweatman, "Holographic Testamentary Instruments: Where Are We?" (1996), 15 E. & T.J. 176.

R. H. Helmholz, "The Origin of Holographic Wills in English Law" (1994), 15 J. Leg. His. 97.

Ronald G. Hopp, "Holograph Wills: Whether Handwritten Portions of Partly Printed Documents May be Admitted to Probate" (1979), 4 E.T.R. 1.

John Smith, "Validity of Holograph Wills on Printed Will Forms" (1979), 5 E.T.R. 83.

Cameron Harvey, "Stationers' Will Forms: Re Philip and other Cases" (1979-80), 10 Man. L.J. 481-6.

---

114 R.S.O. 1990, c. S.26.
115 Law Reform Committee (U.K.), *Twenty Second Report* (*The Making and Revocation of Wills*), Cmnd. 7902, May 1980, §2.22.

SUCCESSION LAW REFORM ACT
R.S.O. 1990, c. S.26

6. A testator may make a valid will wholly by his or her own handwriting and signature, without formality, and without the presence, attestation or signature of a witness.

Comparable Legislation

Wills Act, R.S.A. 1980, c. W-11, s. 7; R.S.M. 1988, c. W150, s. 6; R.S.N.B. 1973, c. W-9, s. 6; R.S.N. 1990, c. W-10, s. 2(1); S.S. 1996, c. W-14.1, s. 8; R.S.N.W.T. 1988, c. W-5, s. 5(2); R.S.Y. 1986, c. 179, s. 5(2).

(b) A Deliberate or Fixed and Final Intention

A testator must intend to make a will and give expression to his or her deliberate or fixed and final intention to do so. Since holograph wills are usually informal documents, however, such an expression is often lacking. The problem is discussed in *Bennett v. Gray*,[116] reproduced below.

BENNETT v. GRAY
[1958] S.C.R. 392, 14 D.L.R. (2d) 1
Supreme Court of Canada

The testatrix had made a formal will in 1949 by which she gave a life interest to her husband with remainder to her children. Her husband died shortly thereafter. In 1952 Mrs. Gray informed her solicitor, Mr. Dysart, that she wished to make a new will. As she was leaving Winnipeg for a period of time she wrote to Mr. Dysart giving him particulars of her wishes in the following terms:

Dear Mr. Dysart
    When I was in your office about a month ago I Promised to let you know how I would like my will to be made out. I have no Ida at all about such matters so Ill leave all that to you, but I do know its Important to have such matters settled before its to late. I will try to outline the way I would like to leave the little I have. the two boys are provided for and do not expect any thing from me. to Dixie her real name is Margaret Dorothea Beautrick Gray Bennett Wife of Charles Paul Bennett the sum of thirty thousand dollars.(30,000) my house if I own a house at the time of my death. Also all my furniture and my Car Also my Clothing and fur Coats.—to my daughter Jacqueline Dinnia Gray wife of Victor Fregeau the sum of ten thousand dollars (10,000). and to my Grand daughter, Joyce Gray, I leave five thousand dollars. and I also want to leave to my dearly Beloved Grand daughter Judith Ann Bennet fifteen thousand dollars and my summer home on Coney Island in Kenora Ont and also the furniture in the cottage my watch or any Jewellery and my diamond rings—To the Reverend A. X. MacAulay one thousand dollars to have holey Masses offered to God for the repose of my soul.

---

116 [1958] S.C.R. 392, 14 D.L.R. (2d) 1.

Dear Mr. Dysard I will be in Winnipeg in a few days I will call you. thanks for your trouble and for all your kindness to us.

Very sincerely,
Mary W. Gray

Upon her return to Winnipeg Mrs. Gray consulted with Mr. Dysart about the proposed will, but she could not decide on an executor. Some time later she changed one of the gifts set out in the letter (the guest house, from Judith to Dorothy). The question of the executor was still not settled; nor was the disposition of the residue. Nothing further happened until 1954 when Mrs. Gray made a gift of real property worth $10,000 to Dorothy and her husband. Mrs. Gray died in 1956.

The question was whether the letter could take effect as a valid holograph will. The trial Judge held that it should, but the Manitoba Court of Appeal reversed. That judgment was sustained in the Supreme Court of Canada.

FAUTEUX J.:

. . .

That the letter of September 27, 1952, satisfies the requirement, as to form, is beyond question; the point in issue being whether, as to substance, this holographic paper is testamentary.

There is no controversy, either in the reasons for judgment in the Courts below, or between the parties, that under the authorities, a holographic paper is not testamentary unless it contains a *deliberate or fixed and final expression of intention* as to the disposal of property upon death, and that it is incumbent upon the party setting up the paper as testamentary to show, by the contents of the paper itself or by extrinsic evidence, that the paper is of that character and nature.[117]

Whether the letter of September 27, 1952, contains *per se* a deliberate or fixed and final expression of intention must be determined by the phrases immediately preceding and following the intermediate part of the letter where the wishes of Mrs. Gray are expressed; for, read as a whole, the letter has one single subject-matter, indicated as follows by Mrs. Gray: "I Promised to let you know how I would like my will to be made out."

In the opening and closing phrases of the letter, Mrs. Gray conveys to Mr. Dysart sentiments of unreserved trust, reliance and dependence. Born, as admittedly shown by extrinsic evidence, out of an intimate relationship of many years between Mr. Dysart, on the one hand, and Mr. and Mrs. Gray and their children, on the other, these sentiments were those accompanying the mind of Mrs. Gray when, after expressing them, she wrote: "I will try to outline the way I would like to leave the little I have." And having done so, she closed the letter by informing Mr. Dysart that she would be in Winnipeg in a few days and that she would call him.

I am unable to dismiss the view I formed that, read as a whole and according to its ordinary and natural sense, this letter amounts to nothing more than what is

---

117 *Whyte et al. v. Pollok* (1882), 7 App. Cas. 400; *Godman v. Godman*, [1920] P. 261; *Theakston v. Marson* (1832), 4 Hag. Ecc. 290, 162 E.R. 1452.

a preliminary to a will. While Mrs. Gray indicated to Mr. Dysart the legacies she then contemplated her will to contain, it is clear, in my view, that she did not want that letter to operate as a will. Indeed, by her letter, she is committing to future consultation with Mr. Dysart both the finality of her decisions, if not of her deliberations, and that of the form in which they should eventually be expressed in a regular will, the preparation of which is entrusted to Mr. Dysart himself. If this interpretation properly attends the document, the letter has not *per se*, and cannot acquire without more, a testamentary nature.

. . .

What took place from the date of the letter, September 27, 1952, to the day of the death of Mrs. Gray, April 5, 1956, affords no evidence either that her letter contained a deliberate or fixed and final expression of intention or that it acquired such a testamentary character by subsequent and sufficient manifestation of intention on her part. Indeed the evidence shows that Mrs. Gray failed to pursue what she indicated in her letter she contemplated doing subject to consultation with Mr. Dysart, though there were, during this lengthy period of time, the fullest opportunities and facilities to do so, and that the most reasonable explanation for this failure is the abandonment of her original intention. No decision was ever reached as to the choice of an executor; nor was even the disposal of the residue of the estate ever considered; nor did she, at any time, decide to instruct Mr. Dysart to proceed with the preparation of the will, notwithstanding that both were perfectly aware that the formal will, executed by Mrs. Gray at the same time as that of her husband on January 6, 1949, was still in existence. There were, moreover, intervening facts affecting the contemplated apportionment of her estate. Thus there was, at a time unrevealed by the evidence, a change of mind as to the disposal of the guest-house, of which Mrs. Gray apprised Mr. Dysart on May 29, 1953, on the occasion of the second and last interview during which the matter of the will, amongst others, was considered. This change is cogent evidence of a still deliberating mind. There was also subsequently, in April 1954, the gift of $10,000 she made to her daughter Dorothy.

[His Lordship, therefore, held that the letter was not written *animo testandi*. The concurring judgment of Rand J., has been omitted.]

Notes and Questions

1. *Bennett v. Gray* may be contrasted with *Canada Permanent Trust Co. v. Bowman*.[118] The deceased left a document in her own handwriting and signed by her, which commenced with the sentence: "I would like Laura to have this property—house and lots," and continued with a list of gifts to other named persons. The document referred to the gifts as bequests. Some expressions in the document, including some amounts, had been crossed out and replaced by others. The court held that in these circumstances the deceased had

---

118 [1962] S.C.R. 711, 34 D.L.R. (2d) 106.

expressed a deliberate and fixed and final expression concerning the disposal of her property at her death, even though the document did not appoint an executor.[119]

It follows that so long as the testator has a deliberate and fixed and final intention to make a will, the document will be admitted to probate. Then the fact that a testatrix intended to see a lawyer about her testamentary dispositions afterwards does not mean that the document constitutes instructions only.[120]

2. Shortly before his death, A wrote a letter in his own handwriting and signed by him to his friend, B. In the course of the letter A told B his bank account number, "In case anything should happen to me." He told B to keep the letter safe and continued: "I have no will, and everything belongs to you anyways. This way there will be no Red Tape to go through." Is this a valid holograph will?[121]

3. The deceased left a suicide note hanging on the fence outside his house. The note said that he was leaving everything to his wife and children. A previous holograph will left his estate to his wife. Is the note a valid holograph will?[122]

4. The deceased had a safety deposit box which contained two envelopes. Each envelope contained four term deposit receipts of $50,000 each and a memorandum in the deceased's hand and dated and signed by him, stating, "Donations to...," followed by the list of certificates and the name of a charity after each one. Are the memoranda valid wills?[123]

5. The deceased had a formal will. Before he died, he had in his own hand written directions regarding his property on a pad of paper. The deceased's signature appeared at the top. The deceased asked his brother to take the pad to his solicitor and have the solicitor attend on him to make a new will. He died before this could be done. Is the document written on the pad of paper a valid will?[124]

6. The deceased has a holograph will. Then he made another holograph document with his name written at the top, and sent it to his solicitor. The solicitor prepared a draft will from the document and sent it to the deceased, who made some handwritten changes on the draft, but did not execute it. Is the second holograph document a valid will?[125]

7. In jurisdictions that have a dispensing power, a document cannot be probated unless it is shown that it incorporates the deceased's fixed and final intention to make a will.[126]

(c) Use of Printed Wills

Often a testator will use a printed form of will, available from a stationer and fill in his or her testamentary intentions on the form. The problem with this is,

---

119 See also *Re MacLennan Estate* (1986), 22 E.T.R. 22 (Ont. S.C.); *Caule v. Brophy* (1993), 50 E.T.R. 122 (Nfld. T.D.).

120 See *Janicki v. Janicki* (1997), 18 E.T.R. (2d) 301 (Man. Q.B.); *Dilts v. Roman Catholic Episcopal Corp. of the Diocese of London in Ontario* (1998), 22 E.T.R. (2d) 284 (Ont. Gen. Div.); *Lindblom Estate v. Worthington* (1999), 30 E.T.R. (2d) 106 (Alta. Surr. Ct.).

121 See *Re Henderson (Seekey)* (1982), 12 E.T.R. 118 (N.W.T.S.C.).

122 *Re Wernicke* (1983), 25 Sask. R. 120, 15 E.T.R. 197 (sub nom. *Quirk v. Wernicke*) (Surr. Ct.).

123 See *Re Steeden Estate* (1992), 48 E.T.R. 197 (Sask. Surr. Ct.), affirmed (1993), 50 E.T.R. 85 (Sask. C.A.).

124 See *Oliver Estate v. Reid* (1994), 4 E.T.R. (2d) 105 (Nfld. C.A.); *Hamill v. St. Luke's Church* (1996), 15 E.T.R. (2d) 184 (Ont. Gen. Div.).

125 See *Kavanagh Estate v. Kavanagh* (1998), 159 D.L.R. (4th) 629 (Nfld. C.A.).

126 *George v. Daly* (1997), 15 E.T.R. (2d) 1 (Man. C.A.); *Re Mate Estate* (1999), 28 E.T.R. (2d) 103 (Sask. Q.B.).

however, that the document is not then entirely in his or her handwriting. While it may be possible in some circumstances to admit only the handwritten portions to probate, this is not automatic as *Re Forest*[127], reproduced below, illustrates.

RE FOREST
(1981), 8 E.T.R. 232
Saskatchewan Court of Appeal

The deceased filled in, in his handwriting, all the blanks in the body of a printed will form, except the blanks in the attestation clause. He signed the will, but it was not attested. The two printed dispositive clauses in the form read, "I give, devise and bequeath all my real and personal estate of which I may die possessed in the manner following, that is to say:" and "all the residue of my estate not hereinbefore disposed of I give devise and bequeath unto." The first was followed in the deceased's handwriting by seven pecuniary legacies to seven persons, each of which was prefixed by the word "To." The second was followed, again in the deceased's handwriting by the names of his sister and brother and a direction that they share equally.

On the application for probate the trial judge held that the will could not be admitted since it was not wholly in the deceased's handwriting.[128] The Court of Queen's Bench[129] dismissed the appeal to that court. A further appeal was then brought to the Court of Appeal.

HALL J.A., delivered the judgment of the Court:

. . .

There have been many occasions upon which printed forms of testament with particulars filled in the blanks in the handwriting of the deceased have been tendered for probate. Cases with facts similar to the instant case were *Re Rigden*[130] and *Re Griffiths*.[131] In each case probate was refused.

In *Re Laver*[132] Davis J. said:[133]

> In the report of the *Rigden* case the will in question is set out in full. There, it will be found, that the dispositive words are part of the printed form. In the *Griffiths* case the will is not set out but I was able to examine it in the Surrogate Court files here. I find that in that will the dispositive words are likewise part of the printed form. In neither of these wills was it possible to formulate from the written words alone a valid testamentary document. With deference, I concur with the conclusions reached by the learned judges on the facts present in those cases. However, I am of the opinion they are clearly distinguishable from the will now in question. Here, it will be seen, all the requirements of a valid testamentary disposition may be found in the handwriting of the testator. Stripped of the printed parts and the non-essential written parts, the will reads:

---

127 (1981), 8 E.T.R. 232 (Sask. C.A.).
128 *Re Forest*, [1980] 1 W.W.R. 470, 5 E.T.R. 144.
129 *Re Forest*, [1981] 2 W.W.R. 289 (Noble J.).
130 [1941] 1 W.W.R. 566 (Sask.).
131 [1945] 3 W.W.R. 46 (Sask.).
132 (1957), 21 W.W.R. 209 (Sask. Q.B.).
133 At p. 211.

> I give, devise and bequeath all my estate both real and personal to James William Tandy. H.R. LAVER.

I agree with this portion of the reasons of Davis J. In my opinion it must be possible to find valid a testamentary document on the written words alone. However, as Davis J. points out, the handwritten words must include words of disposition. The will considered by Davis J. in *Re Laver* clearly met that requirement. There the printed form was not utilized. The writings which Davis J. admitted to probate could have been written on blank paper.

The need for dispositive words in the handwritten portion was referred to by Freedman J.A. in *Re Tachibana*[134] when he said:[135]

> The testamentary character of the document is clearly shown by the words which then follow:
>
> If I may die, please give my property — *I* — goods....
>
> The dispositive word "give" appears twice in the instrument.

The requirement of dispositive words was clearly met in *Sunrise Gospel Hour v. Twiss*[136] when the testator, after listing beneficiaries, wrote:

> To the above I bequeath $500 each.
> To the following institutions whatever is left divided equally.

The written words, standing alone, constituted a valid will. As with the *Laver* will, it was only incidental that the testator wrote upon the printed form. The form was not needed to make the words an effective will. Cairns J.A. speaking for the majority also distinguished *Re Rigden* and *Re Griffith*, when he said:[137]

> In *In Re Rigden*[138] McPhee, Surr. Ct. J., held that the will under consideration being on a printed form, and not being wholly in the handwriting of the testator, was invalid as a holograph will. This decision is clearly distinguishable from the one at bar in that the dispositive clauses of the will were printed and a complete will could not be made out from the handwriting portions.
>
> Again, in *In Re Griffiths Estate*[139] Hogarth, Surr. Ct. J., held that the printed form of the will, where the blanks were filled in in the handwriting of the deceased, was not a holograph will, as it was partly printed and partly written. The learned judge's decision may well be correct on the facts of that case, because in that case, as in *In re Rigden*, one has to look at the printed portions to find the words of disposition, which did not appear in the handwriting. This case is therefore clearly distinguishable on its facts from the case at bar.

Walker Surr. Ct. J. dealt extensively with *Re Philip*,[140] upon which the appellant relies strongly. I agree with the reasons which Walker Surr. Ct. J. gave for distinguishing that case from the instant one and for not following it.

---

134 (1968), 63 W.W.R. 99, 66 D.L.R. (2d) 567 (Man. C.A.) .
135 At p. 101 W.W.R.
136 (1967), 59 W.W.R. 321, 61 D.L.R. (2d) 582 (sub nom. *Re Austin*) (Alta. C.A.).
137 At p. 326 W.W.R.
138 [1941] 1 W.W.R. 566 (Sask.).
139 [1945] 3 W.W.R. 46 (Sask.).
140 5 E.T.R. 83, [1979] 3 W.W.R. 554 (Man. C.A.).

[His Lordship then referred extensively to a number of Scottish cases. In Scotland the law appears to be that dispositive words are required, but if present, the court can have regard to the printed parts of the document. His Lordship distinguished those cases on the ground that s. 7(2) of the *Wills Act*[141] required a holograph will to be entirely in the testator's handwriting. He continued:]

If only the handwriting is admitted to probate in the instant case, the document in addition to not appointing an executor would not dispose of the residue of the estate. The disposition of the residue may have been the most important and comprehensive part of the deceased's intent.

Indeed, as Noble J. pointed out in his reasons, if this document is held to be a holograph will, the effect would be that any printed form completed in the handwriting of the testator would have to be admitted to probate.

If the view which I have taken of the decided cases and the interpretation I have placed upon s. 7(2) of the Wills Act are correct it is impossible to grant probate.

. . .

I would therefore dismiss the appeal with costs.

Notes and Questions

1. A case such as *Sunrise Gospel Hour v. Twiss*,[142] referred to in *Re Forest*, does not seem to be objectionable, since the handwritten portions in that case could be severed from the written part and by themselves formed a complete expression of the testator's intentions.[143] In *Sunrise* the court deleted the appointment of the executor from probate, since the testator merely filled in the name after the printed words appointing an executor.

2. The situation was different in *Re Philip*,[144] which the court distinguished in *Re Forest*, although the facts were virtually the same. The court in *Re Philip* held that it is permissible to resort to principles of construction in order to give effect to the handwriting standing alone. Since the testatrix did not fill in some of the blanks and repeated the word "to" after the printed "unto," the court held that the testatrix did not intend to incorporate the printed words, but merely to use the printed form as a guide in assisting her in making a holograph will. Which of these approaches is to be preferred?

3. The Newfoundland statute does not require that the will be "wholly" in the testator's handwriting. Nevertheless, the case law requires that only the portions written by the testator that can stand on their own be admitted to probate.[145] However, it has also been held that since the will does not have to be wholly in the testator's handwriting the court may refer to the printed portions to determine that the testator intended to appoint a person as executor.[146]

---

141 R.S.S. 1978, c. W-10.
142 (1967), 59 W.W.R. 321, (sub nom. *Re Austin*) 61 D.L.R. (2d) 582 (Alta. C.A.).
143 See *Re Carr Estate* (1990), 40 E.T.R. 163 (N.B. Prob. Ct.), to the same effect.
144 [1979] 3 W.W.R. 554, 5 E.T.R. 83 (Man. C.A.).
145 See, *e.g.*, *Re McGettigan* (1996), 14 E.T.R. (2d) 283 (Nfld. T.D.).
146 See *Re Coish Estate* (1996), 136 D.L.R. (4th) 368 (Nfld. T.D.).

4. A dispensing power, such as s. 23 of the Manitoba *Wills Act*,[147] reproduced earlier in this chapter, will not save a will written on a printed form, unless the written portions embody the testator's testamentary intentions.[148]

(d) Formalities

The formalities of execution of a formal will are, *inter alia*, that it be signed at its end by the testator or by someone authorized by the testator and in his or her presence.[149] Clearly, another person cannot sign a holograph will for the testator, but does the requirement that the will be signed at the end also apply to holograph wills? This question is examined in *Re Clarke*,[150] reproduced below.

RE CLARKE

(1982), 39 O.R. (2d) 392

Ontario Surrogate Court

[Judicial District of Niagara North]

The deceased had used a printed will form which commenced with the words "This is the Last Will and Testament of me." He inserted his name in his own hand immediately following this sentence, but it appeared nowhere else in the document. A trial of the issue of the validity of the will was directed.

SCOTT SURR. CT. J.:

. . .

One of the initial problems with this alleged holograph is at the very beginning of the document, for after the printed words on the form "This is the Last Will and Testament of me" are the printed words "Harold K. H. Clarke".

There was evidence from a number of witnesses that due to his training and experience as an industrial chemist, the deceased had a habit of printing words for the sake of clarity and emphasis.

Black's Law Dictionary[151] defines (in part) the word "signature".

> The act of putting one's name at the end of an instrument to attest its validity....A signature may be written by hand, printed, stamped, typewritten, engraved, photographed...And whatever mark, symbol, or device one may choose to employ as representative of himself is sufficient.

---

147 R.S.M. 1988, c. W150.

148 See *Re Balfour Estate* (1990), 38 E.T.R. 108 (Sask. Q.B.) for an illustration. The deceased used a printed will form. After the printed dispositive clause she wrote "Whatever Brenda my daughter decides is O.K. if anyone else doesn't like it too bad." The court held that the document was not testamentary because there was no disposition in favour of Brenda or anyone else, but rather a delegation to Brenda of the power to distribute the estate. Is this decision at odds with *Re Nicholls* (1987), 25 E.T.R. 228 (Ont. C.A.), reproduced in chapter 4?

149 These formalities are discussed earlier in this chapter.

150 (1982), 39 O.R. (2d) 392 (Surr. Ct.).

151 5th ed. (1979), at p. 1239.

. . .

A Western decision, *Re Tachibana*,[152] was quoted extensively by Mr. Wilson on this issue of a signature in the body of a document and not at the foot. (See also for a similar result: *Re Moir*).[153] The following extracts from *Re Tachibana* deal not only with this question of the placement of the signature, but of much more importance due to the result that I have reached, a comparison with the then relevant sections of the Manitoba *Wills Act*[154] and the present *Succession Law Reform Act*....[155]

To make this decision intelligible and relevant to the issues herein the following should be noted:

(1) The commencement of this alleged holograph had as its opening word "will", written in Japanese. There then followed the handwritten words "This is Ritsuma Tachibana" and then his address and the date. This document consisted of three pages with Mr. Tachibana's signature on two of them; although neither of these signatures is at the end of the document.

(2) But, in my view, what is crucial to this action is a comparison of the then relevant Manitoba statute with the present Ontario one.

. . .

[His Honour set out ss. 6 and 7 of the Manitoba Act and ss. 4, 6 and 7 of the Ontario Act. The latter two sections are reproduced earlier in this chapter. Sections 6(1), 6(2) and 7 of the Manitoba Act corresponded respectively with ss. 6, 4 and 7 of the Ontario Act. However, s. 7(1) of the Ontario Act refers specifically to a holograph will and s. 7(3) of that Act further provides that a signature on any will (formal, holograph or privileged) does not give effect to a disposition underneath or inserted after the signature. Section 7 of the Manitoba Act did no contain similar provisions.]

Returning to the judgment of Freedman J.A. in *Re Tachibana*, the learned judge states:[156]

Counsel opposing the will takes the position that the express provisions of secs. 6 and 7 of *The Wills Act* invalidate the present instrument. Coupled with that submission is the argument that the statutory requirement for a signature at the end or foot of the will is to ensure that the testator intended thereby to finalize the document and to indicate that everything appearing above his signature represented what he wished done with his estate. In the present case counsel contends that the absence of a signature at the end leaves the document in an uncertain and inchoate state; that no settled testamentary intention should be attributed to its author; that at most this was a preliminary memorandum designed to serve as the basis of a formal will to be later prepared but which was never prepared; that accordingly the document fails to qualify as a valid will.

In support of this position counsel invokes the decision of Monnin, J. (as he then was) in *Equitable Trust Co. v. Doull*.[157] The effect of that decision was to hold that the phrase "every

152 (1968), 66 D.L.R. (2d) 567, 63 W.W.R. 99 (Man. C.A.).
153 [1942] 1 D.L.R. 337, [1942] 1 W.W.R. 241 (Alta. C.A.).
154 R.S.M. 1954, c.293.
155 R.S.O. 1980, c. 488 and amendments thereto.
156 At pp. 103-104 W.W.R. (Emphasis added.).
157 (1958), 25 W.W.R. 465, 66 Man. R. 253.

will" at the beginning of sec. 7(1) of *The Wills Act* includes and applies to a holograph will. Hence no signature is operative to give effect to dispositions which are underneath it or which were inserted after the signature was made. The learned judge came to this conclusion with regret, expressing the hope that some modification would be made to *The Wills Act* to clarify the law pertaining to holograph wills.

In my view Monnin, J.'s regret was well founded. A holograph will very properly stands on a different footing from that of an ordinary will and should not be subject to the formalities required of the latter. When a person proceeds to write out his will in his own hand one does not expect, nor does the law exact from him, the same strict compliance with statutory provisions of form as is imposed upon a testator who, in a much more formal manner and usually with the aid of a lawyer, has his will drawn up, to be solemnly executed in the presence of two witnesses. That is precisely why sec. 6(2) dispenses with any further formality beyond the requirement that a holograph will be wholly in the handwriting of the testator and signed by him. The subsection, it may be noted, is silent as to the location where the testator's signature must be placed. To say that the signature must appear at the end or foot of the will is only possible if we conclude that sec. 6(1) and sec. 7 of *The Wills Act* apply to holograph wills. In my view they do not.

And finally:[158]

...I would hold that the phrase "no will shall be valid unless...," appearing in sec. 6(1) does not apply to a holograph will. By the same token I would hold that the provisions of sec. 7 of *The Wills Act* do not, despite their comprehensive language, apply to a holograph will. In short, it is my view that the statutory provision relating to holograph wills (sec. 6[2]) stands by itself, unaffected by the requirements which the statute prescribes for ordinary wills.

On the basis of these and other authorities cited by counsel it is apparent that in other jurisdictions the position of the signature in a holograph will has been held not to be a bar to the document being valid.

But after a careful perusal of the various statutes as set out and a comparison of them, I have, albeit with some considerable reluctance, come to the conclusion that it is not possible to draw the distinction the western authorities have; and that, fundamentally, is that those courts concluded that the word "will" as used in the statutes they were considering did not, nor was it intended to, for reasons stated, include a holograph will.

In blunt terms I see no way of adopting these authorities in view of the explicit wording of s. 7 of the *Succession Law Reform Act* which specifically states that the formalities respecting the position of the signature apply to holograph wills; and, of course, of more particular importance is s. 7(3) of the Ontario Act from which it logically follows that the only interpretation is that a signature in an alleged holograph will (complying with s. 6) cannot give any effect to a disposition or direction that is underneath or after the signature.

The result here is that even if I recognized the signature all the directions and dispositions are underneath the signature and the only obvious and logical inference is that they were inserted after. Thus under s. 7(3) they have no effect.

[The court refused probate and then went on to consider an unrelated issue.]

---

158 At p. 105 W.W.R.

Notes and Questions

1. In *Re Williams*[159] the court followed *Re Tachibana*,[160] referred to in *Re Clarke*, in respect of a postscript to a letter, following the signature. However, in the end result, the court held that the postscript was not a testamentary document, since it only amounted to an expression of an intention to make a will in favour of the addressee at some future time.

2. The Manitoba Legislature amended the Act after *Re Tachibana*.[161] The statute now provides that a holograph will must be signed at the end.[162]

3. In *Wood v. Smith*[163] the English Court of Appeal held that the testator's name, written by him at the top of a holograph will, was capable of being a signature even though it is not the testator's usual signature, provided he indicated to the witnesses that he regarded the name as his signature and thereby showed that he intended to give testamentary effect to the document. The court also held that the signature does not necessarily have to be written after the dispositive provisions have been written, so long as both are written as part of one operation. The will failed for want of proof of capacity, however. Which is correct, *Re Clarke*, or *Wood v. Smith*?

4. *Re Schultz*[164] illustrates another aspect of the problem. The testator had made a will entirely in his handwriting, which concluded:

> Executors of this last Will and Testament of myself LIS shall be as follows: [words deleted] W.S.

The initials, L.I.S., were the testator's initials. The court held that s. 8(3) of the Saskatchewan *Wills Act*[165] which states that no signature shall be apt to give effect to any disposition or direction that follows it, also applied to holograph wills. However, the court also held that a signature consisting of initials was sufficient if intended to represent the testator's name. The court concluded that these initials were so intended. Hence, the will was properly executed.

5. In Quebec it is permissible to have dispositive provisions following the signature on a holograph will.[166]

6. When a testatrix died, two documents were found in an envelope identified as containing her will. The first document was wholly in her handwriting. It purported to dispose of her property, but was not signed or witnessed. The second was a printed will form which appointed executors and revoked former wills. It was signed and attested. The witnesses confirmed that when they attested the second document there were other documents present, but they did not know what was in them. Can both documents be probated?[167]

---

159 [1973] 5 W.W.R. 84 (Man. Surr. Ct.).
160 (1968), 63 W.W.R. 99, 66 D.L.R. (2d) 567 (Man. C.A.).
161 *Supra*.
162 *Wills Act*, R.S.M. 1988, c. W150, s. 6.
163 [1992] 3 All E.R. 556 (C.A.).
164 (1986), 21 E.T.R. 313, 24 D.L.R. (4th) 759 (Sask. C.A.).
165 S.S. 1996, c. W-14.1.
166 *Amyot v. Amyot* (1988), 32 E.T.R. 58 (Que. C.S.).
167 See *Re Bunn Estate* (1991), 41 E.T.R. 100 (Sask. Surr. Ct.).

(e) Holograph Codicils to Formal Wills

Although a formal will is normally changed by a codicil executed with the same formalities, this is not necessary. A holograph codicil is apt to amend a formal will as well.[168] However, although a holograph codicil may amend a formal will, in order to do so it must manifest a present intention to change the will; the expression of a future intention to do so is insufficient.[169]

(f) Incorporation by Reference of Non-Holograph Documents

Another issue that sometimes arises is whether a non-holograph document can be incorporated into a holograph will. You will recall that the doctrine of incorporation by reference, discussed in an earlier chapter, permits an existing document to be incorporated into a will if it is properly identified in the will. Whether this doctrine applies to a holograph will is examined in *Re Dixon-Marsden Estate*,[170] reproduced below.

RE DIXON-MARSDEN ESTATE
(1985), 21 E.T.R. 216
Ontario Surrogate Court

The deceased's alleged will consisted of a typewritten, single sheet of paper, which contained dispositive provisions and the appointment of an executor. The deceased had initialled each paragraph and had written the date in the top right hand corner of the page after it was typed. At the bottom of the page he had written, "the above-mentioned are in short those to whom my estate is left." Immediately below that appeared his signature and below that he had printed his name in his own hand.

The executrix argued that the handwritten words were a valid holograph will and that the doctrine of incorporation by reference permitted the typewritten portions to be incorporated into the holograph portion.

MISENER SURR. CT. J.:

. . .

I propose to comment briefly on those authorities and passages in due course,

---

168 This is so even though the holograph codicil predates the statutory recognition of holograph wills, provided the testator dies after such recognition. See *Re Chapman* (1959), 28 W.W.R. 145, 18 D.L.R. (2d) 745 (Man. Surr. Ct.); *Re Davis* (1979), 26 O.R. (2d) 348, 5 E.T.R. 174 (Surr. Ct.); *Owers v. Hayes* (1983), 43 O.R. (2d) 407, 16 E.T.R. 61, 1 D.L.R. (4th) 280 (H.C.); *Olson v. Olson* (1988), 30 E.T.R. 243 (Sask. Q.B.). See also the *Wills Act*, R.S.S. 1978, c. W-14, s. 12(2) [am. 1989, c. 66, s. 6], which permits holograph alterations to a will.

169 *Re Kinahan* (1981), 9 E.T.R. 53 (Ont. Surr. Ct.); *Hamill v. St. Luke's Church* (1996), 15 E.T.R. (2d) 184 (Ont. Gen. Div.), the handwritten document only contained instructions for a will; *Facey v. Smith* (1997), 17 E.T.R. (2d) 72 (Ont. Gen. Div.).

170 (1985), 21 E.T.R. 216 (Ont. Surr. Ct.).

but I shall proceed now to set forth my reasons for saying that the will does not qualify as a holograph will, and so fails completely as a testamentary instrument. I should say that counsel for the Public Trustee relied upon the same reasons so that in some ways at least I am simply adopting his argument.

In the first place, the document ought not to be viewed as two documents. The probability is that Mr. Dixon-Marsden typed or caused to be typed the typewritten portions of the document, and then proceeded, as essentially one act, to initial the clauses, put in the date, write in the handwritten statement, and sign and print his name. Viewed in that light, there is simply no room for the doctrine of incorporation by reference. It is one document, not two, even though I would be the first to agree with Mr. Thompson that the doctrine of incorporation by reference does not require two separate sheets of paper. See Doe d. Williams v. Evans.[171] If, therefore, it is right to categorize it as one document, how can one escape from the consequences of the Succession Law Reform Act.[172] Leaving aside the case of seamen and armed service personnel, that Act declares, in effect, that a will is not valid unless signed by the testator in the presence of two witnesses who also sign, or unless made "wholly by his own handwriting and signature." The one document here, tendered as a holograph will, is not "wholly in the handwriting of the testator. I am aware of the proposition that one document partly written and partly typed may well qualify as a holograph will, but it is only the handwritten portions that qualify, and only if those handwritten portions fully contain the testamentary wishes of the testator in the sense that the typewritten portions are irrelevant to the dispositive nature of the document.

In the second place, I have always understood that the doctrine of incorporation by reference contemplates the existence of a testamentary document that qualifies for probate, independent of the document sought to be incorporated. If that is so, the condition precedent to the argument that a typewritten document is incorporated is the tendering of a document wholly in the handwriting of the testator and bearing his signature that can be admitted to probate all by itself. Therefore, on the facts of this case, the handwritten words "the above-mentioned are in short those to whom my estate is left" must be capable of admission to probate. If I am right in that, the question as to whether or not those written words constitute a testamentary instrument must first be answered, and if the answer is no, then that is the end of the matter.

I am satisfied that the answer is no on the basis of both common sense and authority. At the very least, one would think, as a matter of common sense, that a document, in order to qualify as a testamentary instrument, must have something in it relating in some way to events that are to happen after the death of the maker of the document. The words in question here have no such reference. Authority compels that requirement and more.

. . .

So here, the words — "the above-mentioned are in short those to whom my estate is left", when viewed as a separate document from the typewritten portion,

---

171 (1832), 1 C. & R. 42.
172 R.S.O. 1990, c. S.26.

are both in form and in intention simply a declaration of what the deceased believed to be a fact. The case is no different from one in which the deceased writes a letter to a friend or a relative declaring that a certain piece of paper to be found in a certain drawer contains his will.

I made that very suggestion during argument. Mr. McIntyre disagreed. He submitted that the words — "the above-mentioned are in short those to whom my estate is left", viewed as a separate document, are the equivalent of "I hereby devise and bequeath all my estate to those persons above-mentioned." I simply say that such an interpretation conforms neither to the words used nor the obvious intention of the deceased when he used those words. He had already "devised and bequeathed" his property in the typewritten paragraphs. I can only repeat that, in my view, his handwritten words, isolated from the typewritten portion, are both in form and in obvious intention a simple statement of what the deceased believed had already been done.

And so I say that there is simply no testamentary instrument into which anything can be incorporated, and so no doorway for the admission of the doctrine of incorporation by reference.

Finally, if the assumption is made that my reasons so far stated are in error, and that the handwritten words constitute a holograph will and the typewritten portion an unexecuted "will", then in my view s. 4 and s. 6 of the Succession Law Reform Act preclude the doctrine of incorporation by reference in these circumstances....There is no difficulty with the doctrine of incorporation when the will into which the typewritten words are to be incorporated is a witnessed will. When those typewritten words are declared incorporated, the statutory requirement of the testator's signature duly witnessed is fully satisfied. In the case of a holograph will, however, incorporation of typewritten words does not meet the statutory requirement. The holograph will, to be valid, must be "wholly by his own handwriting and signature", and patently the incorporated typewritten words are not in the testator's handwriting. I am not prepared to ignore clear statutory words simply because I am completely satisfied — as I am — that the deceased typed the words or caused them to be typed, fully understood them, and intended them to have full effect as his last will. Nor do I think that I should make a specious attempt to circumvent the words of the statute simply because the purpose of requiring certain formalities in the making of a will is to prevent fraud, and no fraud here exists....On this ground then, only the handwritten words could be tendered for probate, and since, even viewed as a testamentary document, they mean nothing, probate would be refused.

[The court refused probate].

Notes and Questions

1. In *Dixon-Marsden*[173] the court refused to follow *Re Chamberlain Estate*.[174] The facts of that case were these: The testator executed a printed will form on August 19, 1972,

---

173 *Supra.*
174 [1976] 1 W.W.R. 464 (Sask. Surr. Ct.).

which appointed two executrices and purported to dispose of the testator's entire estate. Parts of it were in his own handwriting, but since it was not entirely in his own handwriting it was not a valid holograph will and, since it was unattested, it was not a valid will. However, another document, dated October 1972, written entirely in the testator's own hand was found with the will in his safety deposit box. This document recited that the testator had that day deposited certain documents in his safety deposit box, including the printed will of August 19, 1972. The document concluded with a disposition of a ring and a watch and a direction about the cremation of the testator's remains. It was signed by the testator and it was, therefore, a valid holograph will.

Without addressing the question whether a printed document could be incorporated into a holograph one, the court held that the doctrine of incorporation by reference was satisfied and admitted both documents to probate.

Tucker v. Tucker Estate[175] is to the same effect as *Chamberlain*. The court granted probate of a holograph will which incorporated by reference an earlier formal, but invalid will. The formal will failed because it was attested by only one witness.

2. In *Re Coate Estate*[176] the court followed *Dixon-Marsden*. The testatrix had, in her own handwriting, made annotations to her earlier (attested) will. She had also annotated and signed a typewritten letter containing instructions to her solicitor for the preparation of a new will. It was submitted that the handwritten portions of the letter constituted a valid holograph will or codicil, which incorporated by reference the typewritten portion of the letter and the annotations to the earlier will.

The handwritten portions of the letter did not contain the essential testamentary and dispositive language and, thus, did not constitute a valid holograph document. Moreover, there was no foundation upon which to incorporate the other documents. The will in its original form was admitted to probate.

3. Clearly, an earlier document cannot be incorporated in a later document if the later document does not refer to the earlier.[177]

Further Reading

W. Chris Martin, "Substantial Compliance: Where there's a Will there's a Way" (1986-88), 8 E. & T.Q. 142.

4. PRIVILEGED WILLS

A privileged will is one which, by statute, does not have to be executed with the same formalities as a formal will and which is made by a member of the armed forces while on active service or by a sailor while at sea or in the course of a voyage. The statutory provision is set out in section 5 of the *Succession Law Reform Act*, reproduced below. The legislation is discussed in *Re Booth*,[178] also reproduced below.

---

175 (1985), 56 Nfld. & P.E.I.R. 102 (Nfld. T.D.).
176 (1987), 26 E.T.R. 161 (Ont. Surr. Ct.); followed in *Facey v. Smith* (1997), 17 E.T.R. (2d) 72 (Ont. Gen. Div.).
177 See *Simms Estate v. King* (1995), 9 E.T.R. (2d) 40 (Nfld. T.D.).
178 [1926] P. 118.

SUCCESSION LAW REFORM ACT
R.S.O. 1990, c. S.26

5. (1) A person who is,

(a) a member of the Canadian Forces placed on active service under the *National Defence Act* (Canada);

(b) a member of any other naval, land or air force while on active service; or

(c) a sailor when at sea or in the course of a voyage,

may make a will by a writing signed by him or her or by some other person in his or her presence and by his or her direction without any further formality or any requirement of the presence of or attestation or signature by a witness.

(2) For the purposes of this section, a certificate purporting to be signed by or on behalf of an officer having custody of the records certifying that he or she has custody of the records of the force in which a person was serving at the time the will was made, setting out that the person was on active service at that time, is proof, in the absence of evidence to the contrary, of that fact.

(3) For the purposes of this section, if a certificate under subsection (2) is not available, a member of a naval, land or air force is deemed to be on active service after he or she has taken steps under the orders of a superior officer preparatory to serving with or being attached to or seconded to a component of such a force that has been placed on active service.

Comparable Legislation

Probate Act, R.S.P.E.I. 1988, c. P-21, s. 62; *Wills Act,* R.S.A. 1980, c. W-11, s. 6; R.S.B.C. 1996, c. 489, s. 5; S.M. 1988, c. W150, s. 5; R.S.N.B. 1973, c. W-9, s. 5; R.S.N. 1990, c. W-10, s. 2(2); R.S.N.S. 1989, c. 505, s. 9; R.S.N.W.T. 1988, c. W-5, s. 6; S.S. 1996, c. W-14.1, s. 6; R.S.Y. 1986, c. 179, s. 5(3); *Wills (Volunteers) Act,* R.S.N. 1970, c. 402 [not subsequently consolidated], s. 3.

RE BOOTH
[1926] P. 118, [1926] All E.R. Rep. 594
Probate Division

The testator served as paymaster in the 46th Regiment stationed in Gibraltar. He made a holograph will in 1882, in the following terms:

I leave everything I have to my wife absolutely.
I hope she will have regard to my sister Mary.

The testator signed the document and the Pay Sergeant witnessed it. The testator sent the document to his wife with a covering letter in which he said:

I am off to Egypt with the regiment and send my will with fond love. Will write when I get to Egypt.

His wife placed the will in a locked closet, but it was destroyed by fire in 1916, many years after the testator returned. After the testator's death, his widow sought to establish the will. Several questions were raised, including the question whether the will was a valid privileged will and whether the testator acquiesced in its destruction.

LORD MERRIVALE (President):

. . .

I come to the conclusion, in point of fact, that it was written when the 46th, in which the writer was, had received its orders for embarkation and was on the point of the embarkation, and I am as well satisfied as one can be on matters which depend to some extent upon inference that the point of time at which it was written was substantially nearer to the moment of the embarkation than to the time at which the orders to prepare for embarkation were received. We know when the orders for embarkation were received. That was at a time practically coincident with the opening of hostilities; it was either some time on July 10th, or early on the 11th. I do not think that is quite clearly determined by the evidence. It is stated at times to be on the 10th. But the orders were that the regiment was to be ready for embarkation on the *Mombasa* by dawn on the 14th. It was during the period when the regiment was under those orders and was preparing for embarkation on the trooper that this document was written, and my own belief upon the subject is that it was probably written some time on the 13th. That tallies with the facts as I appreciate them, and with the making by a man of education and position in life and of some substance of a military testament. It is quite clear that the man who wrote the document I find to have been written knew of the soldier's privilege of making a will. What is the result of those findings?

. . .

If "mobilization" were the test, Colonel Booth was "mobilized". He and his regiment were in the course of making ready under orders to go on board a troopship for the purpose of reaching the scene of operations. That, in my judgment, is actual military service within the meaning of the phrase in the Wills Act. He personally was involved actively in the military operations which were then in progress. That can safely be said.

[His Lordship referred to a manual of military law which was to the same effect and continued:]

And so on the debated question of whether Colonel Booth at the time he wrote this paper was on actual military service within the meaning of the expression in s. 11 of the Wills Act I find without doubt that he was.

[As to the other questions his Lordship concluded that the will:]

...was effectual at that time to pass his personalty; that it remained effectual to his knowledge until 1916; that the fire in 1916 accidentally destroyed it, but that its destruction was not a destruction which he intended or desired, or upon which he founded any subsequent conduct; that his conduct from 1916 to 1924 does not prove any intention to deprive the will of 1882 of any operation which by law it had; that that will was in operation at the time of his death, and that I ought, therefore, now to decree its admission to probate in the words in which it was proved by the plaintiff in her evidence in the witness box.

Notes and Questions

1. You should note that s. 5 of the *Succession Law Reform Act* does not require that a privileged will be holograph.

2. Section 5 of the *Succession Law Reform Act* should be compared to s. 8,[179] which empowers certain persons, including a member of the armed forces and a sailor while at sea or in the course of a voyage, to make a will while a minor. Wills made under the provisions of s. 8 may be either formal or holograph. That being so, is there a need for s. 5 at all, since s. 6 also provides for holograph wills? Note the differences in wording between ss. 5, 6 and 8.

3. The power to make a nuncupative, that is, oral will of personalty is retained for soldiers and seamen in Nova Scotia[180] and for sailors, fishers[181] and armed forces volunteers in Newfoundland.[182] The right to make a nuncupative privileged will also survives in England.[183]

4. The meaning of "active military service" was explored in *Re Jones, (decd).*[184] A soldier in the British Army was serving in Northern Ireland, the armed forces having been asked by the Northern Ireland authorities to assist the civil power to maintain law and order there. He was shot and killed during a military patrol by an unknown assailant. He made an oral testamentary declaration shortly before his death. The court held that the nature of the duties determined whether a soldier was on actual military service; that the service can be within or outside the country; and that it can be against a force that is not organized on conventional military lines but is in the nature of a clandestinely organized force causing insurrection. The court, therefore, admitted the nuncupative will to probate.[185]

5. Until the 1990 statute revision, s. 5(c) of the *Succession Law Reform Act* spoke of "a mariner or seaman." The Act did not define that expression, but it has been held that a female typist employed on an ocean-going liner comes within its ambit,[186] while a pilot on a ship plying inland waters does not.[187] Would a person employed on a Great Lakes steamer be a mariner or seaman? Is a female typist employed on an ocean-going liner a "sailor"?

---

179 Reproduced in the previous chapter.
180 *Wills Act*, R.S.N.S. 1989, c. 505, s. 9(2).
181 Section 2(2) of the *Wills Act*, R.S.N. 1990, c. W-10, says "This Act does not affect the disposal [*sic*] of [*sic*, by?] a sailor or fisher of his or her property while at sea." Was the drafter of this stunning piece of legislative prose perhaps at sea when drafting it?
182 *Wills (Volunteers) Act*, R.S.N. 1990, c.402 [not subsequently consolidated], s.3.
183 See *Re Jones*, [1981] 2 W.L.R. 106, [1981] 1 All E.R. 1 (Fam. D.).
184 *Ibid.*
185 See also *Re Wingham; Andrews v. Wingham*, [1949] P. 187, [1948] 2 All E.R. 908 (C.A.); *In the Goods of Tweedale* (1874), L.R. 3 P. & D. 204; *In the Will of Anderson* (1958), 75 W.N. (N.S.W.) 334.
186 *Re Hale*, [1915] 2 I.R. 362.
187 *Hodson v. Barnes* (1926), 43 T.L.R. 71.

6. The term "at sea" was considered in *Re Rapley's Estate; Rapley v. Rapley.*[188] An apprentice to a shipping company was on leave and awaiting orders to join a ship. He was a minor and purported to make an unattested will while on leave. The court held the will invalid, for although the deceased was a mariner or seaman, he was not at sea and had not received instructions to join a ship so as to be making preparations for sea.

7. A privileged will remains valid even though the active service or voyage ends;[189] it may be revoked by an informal act while the privileged situation continues, but must be revoked by formal act thereafter;[190] it is revoked by marriage;[191] and alterations made without attestation are presumed to have been made during a privileged situation.[192]

You should note that the power to revoke is specifically set out in s. 8(3) of the *Succession Law Reform Act.*

5. THE INTERNATIONAL WILL

The mobility of the members of modern society creates difficulties in the proof of their wills. Therefore, it would be convenient if wills could have international validity, so long as they were executed with certain prescribed formalities. In 1973 an international convention was concluded which makes provision for such a will. It is described in the following material. In addition, section 42 of the *Succession Law Reform Act,*[193] which adopts the provisions of the convention is reproduced. Section 42 was enacted upon the recommendation of the Ontario Law Reform Commission in its *Report* on the adoption of this uniform law,[194] and contains the "Convention Providing a Uniform Law on the Form of an International Will," adopted by the Diplomatic Conference on Wills in Washington, D.C., October 16-26, 1973, together with the Annex thereto.[195]

SUCCESSION LAW REFORM ACT
R.S.O. 1990, c. S.26

42. (1) In this section, "convention" means the convention providing a uniform law on the form of international will, a copy of which is set out in the Schedule to this section.

(2) The convention is in force in Ontario[196] and applies to wills as law of Ontario and the rules regarding an international will set out in the Annex to the convention are law in Ontario.

---

188 [1983] 3 All E.R. 248.
189 *Re Booth,* [1926] P. 118.
190 *Re Gossage,* [1921] P. 194, [1921] All E.R. Rep. 107 (C.A.).
191 *Re Wardrop,* [1917] P. 54.
192 *Re Newland,* [1952] P. 71, [1952] 1 All E.R. 841.
193 R.S.O. 1990, c. S.26.
194 *Report on the International Convention Providing a Uniform Law on the Form of an International Will* (1974).
195 *Ibid.,* p. 3. Hereafter cited as "Convention" and "Annex".
196 Since Sept. 15, 1978.

(3) All members of the Law Society of Upper Canada, other than student members, are designated as persons authorized to act in connection with international wills.

(4) Nothing in this section detracts from or affects the validity of a will that is valid under the laws in force in Ontario other than this section.

SCHEDULE
Convention Providing a Uniform Law
on The Form of an International Will

The States signatory to the present Convention,

DESIRING to provide to a greater extent for the respecting of last wills by establishing an additional form of will hereinafter to be called an "international will" which, if employed, would dispense to some extent with the search for the applicable law;

HAVE RESOLVED to conclude a Convention for this purpose and have agreed upon the following provisions:

Article I
1. Each Contracting Party undertakes that not later than six months after the date of entry into force of this Convention in respect of that Party it shall introduce into its law the rules regarding an international will set out in the Annex to this Convention.

2. Each Contracting Party may introduce the provisions of the Annex into its law either by reproducing the actual text, or by translating it into its official language or languages.

3. Each Contracting Party may introduce into its law such further provisions as are necessary to give the provisions of the Annex full effect in its territory.

4. Each Contracting Party shall submit to the Depositary Government the text of the rules introduced into its national law in order to implement the provisions of this Convention.

Article II
1. Each Contracting Party shall implement the provisions of the Annex in its law, within the period provided for in the preceding article, by designating the persons who, in its territory, shall be authorized to act in connection with international wills. It may also designate as a person authorized to act with regard to its nationals its diplomatic or consular agents abroad in so far as the local law does not prohibit it.

2. The Party shall notify such designation, as well as any modifications thereof, to the Depositary Government.

Article III

The capacity of the authorized person to act in connection with an international will, if conferred in accordance with the law of a Contracting Party, shall be recognized in the territory of the other Contracting Parties.

Article IV

The effectiveness of the certificate provided for in Article 10 of the Annex shall be recognized in the territories of all Contracting Parties.

Article V

1. The conditions requisite to acting as a witness of an international will shall be governed by the law under which the authorized person was designated. The same rule shall apply as regards an interpreter who is called upon to act.

2. Nonetheless no one shall be disqualified to act as a witness of an international will solely because he is an alien.

Article VI

1. The signature of the testator, of the authorized person, and of the witnesses to an international will, whether on the will or on the certificate, shall be exempt from any legalization or like formality.

2. Nonetheless, the competent authorities of any Contracting Party may, if necessary, satisfy themselves as to the authenticity of the signature of the authorized person.

Article VII

The safekeeping of an international will shall be governed by the law under which the authorized person was designated.

Article VIII

No reservation shall be admitted to this Convention or to its Annex.

Article IX

1. The present Convention shall be open for signature at Washington from October 26, 1973, until December 31, 1974.

2. The Convention shall be subject to ratification.

3. Instruments of ratification shall be deposited with the Government of the United States of America, which shall be the Depositary Government.

Article X

1. The Convention shall be open indefinitely for accession.

2. Instruments of accession shall be deposited with the Depositary Government.

Article XI

1. The present Convention shall enter into force six months after the date of deposit of the fifth instrument of ratification or accession with the Depositary Government.

2. In the case of each State which ratifies this Convention or accedes to it after the fifth instrument of ratification or accession has been deposited, this Convention shall enter into force six months after the deposit of its own instrument of ratification or accession.

Article XII

1. Any Contracting Party may denounce this Convention by written notification to the Depositary Government.

2. Such denunciation shall take effect twelve months from the date on which the Depositary Government has received the notification, but such denunciation shall not affect the validity of any will made during the period that the Convention was in effect for the denouncing State.

Article XIII

1. Any State may, when it deposits its instrument of ratification or accession or at any time thereafter, declare, by a notice addressed to the Depositary Government, that this Convention shall apply to all or part of the territories for the international relations of which it is responsible.

2. Such declaration shall have effect six months after the date on which the Depositary Government shall have received notice thereof or, if at the end of such period the Convention has not yet come into force, from the date of its entry into force.

3. Each Contracting Party which has made a declaration in accordance with paragraph 1 of this Article may, in accordance with Article XII, denounce this Convention in relation to all or part of the territories concerned.

Article XIV

1. If a State has two or more territorial units in which different systems of law apply in relation to matters respecting the form of wills, it may at the time of signature, ratification, or accession, declare that this Convention shall extend to all its territorial units or only to one or more of them, and may modify its declaration by submitting another declaration at any time.

2. These declarations shall be notified to the Depositary Government and shall state expressly the territorial units to which the Convention applies.

Article XV

If a contracting Party has two or more territorial units in which different systems of law apply in relation to matters respecting the form of wills, any reference to the internal law of the place where the will is made or to the law under which the authorized person has been appointed to act in connection with international wills shall be construed in accordance with the constitutional system of the Party concerned.

Article XVI

1. The original of the present Convention, in the English, French, Russian and Spanish languages, each version being equally authentic, shall be deposited with

the Government of the United States of America, which shall transmit certified copies thereof to each of the signatory and acceding States and to the International Institute for the Unification of Private Law.

2. The Depositary Government shall give notice to the signatory and acceding States, and to the International Institute for the Unification of Private Law, of:

  (a) any signature;

  (b) the deposit of any instrument of ratification or accession;

  (c) any date on which this Convention enters into force in accordance with Article XI;

  (d) any communication received in accordance with Article 1, paragraph 4;

  (e) any notice received in accordance with Article II, paragraph 2;

  (f) any declaration received in accordance with Article XIII, paragraph 2, and the date on which such declaration takes effect;

  (g) any denunciation received in accordance with Article XII, paragraph 1, or Article XIII, paragraph 3, and the date on which the denunciation takes effect;

  (h) any declaration received in accordance with Article XIV, paragraph 2, and the date on which the declaration takes effect.

IN WITNESS WHEREOF, the undersigned Plenipotentiaries, being duly authorized to that effect, have signed the present Convention.

DONE at Washington this twenty-sixth day of October, one thousand nine hundred and seventy-three.

ANNEX

Uniform Law on the
Form of an International Will

Article 1

1. A will shall be valid as regards form, irrespective particularly of the place where it is made, of the location of the assets and of the nationality, domicile or residence of the testator, if it is made in the form of an international will complying with the provisions set out in Articles 2 to 5 hereinafter.

2. The invalidity of the will as an international will shall not affect its formal validity as a will of another kind.

Article 2

This law shall not apply to the form of testamentary dispositions made by two or more persons in one instrument.

Article 3

1. The will shall be made in writing.

2. It need not be written by the testator himself.

3. It may be written in any language, by hand or by any other means.

Article 4

1. The testator shall declare in the presence of two witnesses and of a person authorized to act in connection with international wills that the document is his will and that he knows the contents thereof.

2. The testator need not inform the witnesses, or the authorized person, of the contents of the will.

Article 5

1. In the presence of the witnesses and of the authorized person, the testator shall sign the will or, if he has previously signed it, shall acknowledge his signature.

2. When the testator is unable to sign, he shall indicate the reason therefor to the authorized person who shall make note of this on the will. Moreover, the testator may be authorized by the law under which the authorized person was designated to direct another person to sign on his behalf.

3. The witnesses and the authorized person shall there and then attest the will by signing in the presence of the testator.

Article 6

1. The signatures shall be placed at the end of the will.

2. If the will consists of several sheets, each sheet shall be signed by the testator or, if he is unable to sign, by the person signing on his behalf or, if there is no such person, by the authorized person. In addition, each sheet shall be numbered.

Article 7

1. The date of the will shall be the date of its signature by the authorized person.

2. This date shall be noted at the end of the will by the authorized person.

Article 8

In the absence of any mandatory rule pertaining to the safekeeping of the will, the authorized person shall ask the testator whether he wishes to make a declaration concerning the safekeeping of his will. If so and at the express request of the testator the place where he intends to have his will kept shall be mentioned in the certificate provided for in Article 9.

Article 9

The authorized person shall attach to the will a certificate in the form prescribed in Article 10 establishing that the obligations of this law have been complied with.

Article 10

The certificate drawn up by the authorized person shall be in the following form or in a substantially similar form:

CERTIFICATE
(Convention of October 26, 1973)

1. I,.............................(name, address and capacity), a person authorized to act
   in connection with international wills
2. Certify that on ....(date) at .... (place)
3. (testator).......................(name, address, date and place of birth)
   in my presence and that of the witnesses
4. (a).............................(name, address, date and place of birth)
   (b).............................(name, address, date and place of birth)
   has declared that the attached document is his will and that he knows the
   contents thereof.
5. I furthermore certify that:
6. (a) in my presence and in that of the witnesses
   (1) the testator has signed the will or has acknowledged his signature pre-
       viously affixed.
   *(2) following a declaration of the testator stating that he was unable to
       sign his will for the following reason...........................
       — I have mentioned this declaration on the will
       *— the signature has been affixed by..........................(name, address)
7. (b) the witnesses and I have signed the will;
8. *(c) each page of the will has been signed by....................and numbered;
9. (d) I have satisfied myself as to the identity of the testator and of the witnesses
       as designated above;
10. (e) the witnesses met the conditions requisite to act as such according to the
        law under which I am acting;
11. *(f) the testator has requested me to include the following statement con-
         cerning the safekeeping of his will;
12. PLACE
13. DATE
14. SIGNATURE and, if
    necessary, SEAL

*To be completed if appropriate.

Article 11
The authorized person shall keep a copy of the certificate and deliver another
to the testator.

Article 12
In the absence of evidence to the contrary, the certificate of the authorized
person shall be conclusive of the formal validity of the instrument as a will under
this Law.

Article 13

The absence or irregularity of a certificate shall not affect the formal validity of a will under this Law.

Article 14

The international will shall be subject to the ordinary rules of revocation of wills.

Article 15

In interpreting and applying the provisions of this law, regard shall be had to its international origin and to the need for uniformity in its interpretation.

Comparable Legislation

International Wills Act, S.N.S. 2000 (1st Sess.), c. 7; *Wills Act,* R.S.A. 1980, c. W-11, Part 3; R.S.M. 1988, c. W150, Part III; R.S.N. 1990, c. W-10, Part III; S.S. 1996, c. W-14.1, ss. 41-51.

SUCCESSION LAW REFORM IN ONTARIO
A.H. Oosterhoff (1979), pp. 58-9

Under the Convention, each contracting party agrees to introduce into its law the new form of international will, which is the Annex to the Convention, within six months of the effective date of the Convention in that country. In countries such as Canada with a federal form of government, this is, of course, subject to the federal government ratifying and implementing the Convention on behalf of the several provinces that wish to adopt the uniform law.[197] Section 42(1)(b) and (5) of the Act so provides. Each participating State agrees to recognize the formal validity of the international will.[198]

The formalities required in the case of an international will are relatively simple and are similar to those required in the case of Ontario wills. In summary:

(a) The will must be in writing by hand or otherwise, by the testator or another, and may be written in any language.[199]

(b) In addition to two witnesses, the international will calls for the designation of authorized persons. The will must be signed and attested in the presence of an authorized person and he must attach a certificate to the will stating that the proper formalities have been observed. The certificate is conclusive evidence of the formal validity of the will in the absence of evidence to the contrary,[200] although the absence of the certificate does not affect the formal

---

197 Convention, Art II.
198 *Ibid.,* Art. III.
199 Annex, Art. 3.
200 Convention, Art. II; Annex, Arts. 4, 9, 10 and 12.

validity of the will.[201] The Act designates members of the Law Society of Upper Canada other than student members as authorized persons.[202]

(c) The testator must declare in the presence of two witnesses and an authorized person that the document is his will and that he knows the contents thereof.[203]

(d) The testator must then sign or acknowledge his signature in the presence of the same three persons who "shall there and then attest the will by signing in the presence of the testator".[204] Presumably the phrase "there and then" means that the witnesses and the authorized person must attest in the presence of the testator and in the presence of each other. It will be recalled that under *The Wills Act*[205] and under the [Succession Law Reform] Act[206] there is no requirement that the witnesses must sign in the presence of each other.

(e) If the testator is unable to sign, the authorized person is to make a note of that fact and the reason for it on the will. Provided the testator is authorized by the internal law of the place which designated the authorized person to do so, he may appoint an amanuensis to sign on his behalf.[207] Presumably if the law does not contain such a provision the will is still valid even without the testator's signature.

(f) The signatures must be placed at the end of the will and the testator or his amanuensis or, failing the latter, the authorized person, must sign each sheet of a multi-page will and the pages must be numbered.[208]

(g) The date of signature by the authorized person is the date of the will and is to be noted on the will by him.[209]

(h) The authorized person must satisfy himself as to the identity of the testator and of the witnesses, that the witnesses were qualified to act as such under the internal law under which he is acting and he must ask the testator whether he wishes to make a declaration concerning the safekeeping of the will in jurisdictions not having a mandatory rule in that regard such as Ontario. In that event, this must also be noted in the certificate.[210]

In view of the increasing mobility of the world population, one would expect that the international will will become a much utilized document. The provisions respecting international wills have been adopted in several of the other provinces.

---

201 Annex, Art. 13.
202 *Succession Law Reform Act*, s. 42(3).
203 Annex, Art. 4.
204 Art. 5.
205 R.S.O. 1970, c. 499, s. 11(1).
206 Section 4(1)(c).
207 Annex, Art. 5.
208 *Ibid.*, Art. 6.
209 *Ibid.*, Art. 7.
210 *Ibid.*, Arts. 8, 9 and 10.

Notes and Questions

1. The Convention is in effect in a substantial number of countries. For an up-to-date list one should write to the Department of External Affairs, or to the Secretary of State in Washington, since the government of the United States of America is the Depositary Government under the Convention.

2. To date, the convention has been extended to Alberta, Manitoba, Newfoundland, Nova Scotia, Ontario, and Saskatchewan.

The procedure to extend the convention to a province is for it to enact the appropriate legislation and to request the Minister of External Affairs to deposit a declaration extending the convention with the Depositary Government. The convention then comes into effect six months later.

Information concerning the application of the convention to states in other multi-state jurisdictions may be obtained from the Depositary Government.

7

REVOCATION OF WILLS

1. SCOPE OF THIS CHAPTER

A will can only be revoked in accordance with the provisions of statute. There are two main types of revocation: (1) those that arise by operation of law, namely upon marriage and, in certain limited circumstances, upon dissolution of marriage; and (2) those that arise by act of the testator. These two types are described first in this chapter.[1]

Instead of revoking the will, the testator may attempt to alter it by crossing out provisions and replacing them with others. The law concerning such alterations is also discussed in this chapter.

The last parts of the chapter discuss the law of conditional revocation and of revival of revoked wills.

Further Reading

Law Reform Commission of British Columbia, *Report on the Making and Revocation of Wills* (L.R.C. 52, Sept. 1981), Part IV.

Law Reform Committee (U.K.), *Twenty-Second Report (The Making and Revocation of Wills)*, (Cmnd. 7902, May 1980), Part III.

Macdonell, Sheard and Hull on Probate Practice, 4th ed. by Rodney Hull and Ian M. Hull (Scarborough: Carswell, 1996), c. 4.

2. VITIATING FACTORS

A revocation will be ineffective if it does not meet the statutory requirements for revocation described in this chapter. However, there are other reasons why a

---

1 In New Brunswick the court has power to make, amend and revoke wills for mental incompetent persons under the *Infirm Persons Act*, R.S.N.B. 1973, c. I-8, ss. 3(4), 11(1) (enacted S.N.B. 1994, c. 40, ss. 1, 3). See Eric L. Teed and Nicole Cocoon, "New Wills for Incompetents" (1997), 16 E. & T.J. 1.

revocation may fail as well. These are primarily those that cause wills and other documents to fail, such as mistake, lack of capacity, undue influence, fraud, and inadvertence. We shall look at instances of mistake later in this chapter.

With respect to capacity, it should be noted that revocation is a testamentary act. Hence, the testator must have same the capacity as is required for making a will.[2] Thus, if the testator lacks capacity at the time he or she destroys the will, the destruction will not effect a revocation.[3] A testator who destroys the will while drunk, lacks the capacity to form the intention to revoke. Hence, the destruction will not cause the will to be revoked.[4]

The effect of undue influence on a revocation is illustrated by *Hubley v. Cox Estates.*[5] The testatrix made a will in 1994 by which she left her estate equally between her two sons, D and P. D was married and had children. P was single, lived with the testatrix and looked after her, and was HIV positive. In 1996 the testatrix made a new will giving everything to P. When D discovered this, he went to his mother's home, told her that the new will was illegal, and drew lines over all the pages and wrote "void" on them. Then the will, as altered, was executed. Two months later the testatrix was diagnosed as mentally incompetent. The evidence showed that the testatrix knew she was depriving D of his share of her estate, but felt obliged to P because he had been looking after her and he had been excluded from his father's estate. The court found that the testatrix had capacity when she made the 1996 will, but that the "revocation" of that will was invalid because D exercised undue influence over his mother when she was sick and old and upset by the fighting in her family over her estate.[6]

A will destroyed through inadvertence is not revoked.[7] The testator lacked the intention to revoke.

3. REVOCATION BY OPERATION OF LAW

(a) Introduction

It often happens that there is a change in the circumstances of the testator, such as a marriage or a dissolution of marriage. It is more likely that the testator would want the will to be revoked in those circumstances that to have it remain in effect. Hence, it is revoked by operation of law. The two situations are discussed below.

---

2 *Re Beattie Estate*, [1944] 3 W.W.R. 727 (Alta. Dist. Ct.); *Re McGinn Estate* (1969), 70 W.W.R. 159 (Alta. S.C.); *Spence v. Spence* (1988), 87 N.B.R. (2d) 415 (C.A.); *Syrota v. Clark Estate* (1991), 74 Man. R. (2d) 116; *Re Sabatini* (1969), 114 Sol. J. 35.

3 *Sprigge v. Sprigge* (1868), L.R. 1 P. & D. 608; *Re Beattie Estate*, [1944] W.W.R. 727; *Eaton v. Heyman*, [1946] 3 W.W.R. 98 (B.C.S.C.).

4 *Re Brassington's Goods*, [1902] P. 1.

5 (1999), 31 E.T.R. (2d) 71 (N.S.S.C.).

6 In any event, as the court also held, the revocation by alteration was not executed properly, since the testatrix and D placed their signatures on the will while the other witness, who signed afterwards, was not present.

7 *Eaton v. Heyman*, [1946] 3 W.W.R. 98 (B.C.S.C.).

(b) By Marriage

(i) *Generally*

Since it is a moral duty, as well as a matter of public policy that a deceased person provide for his or her spouse and issue upon death, it is reasonable to insist that (subject to the comments made in the next section), if a person has made a will and then marries, the will is revoked. The effect of the revocation is that, if no new will is made, the spouse and issue will become entitled to the deceased's estate under the law of intestate succession. The law in effect presumes that, if the deceased does not make a new will, he or she intends this result. All statutes accordingly provide that a will is revoked by the testator's marriage.[8]

The statutes do provide for certain exceptions, however, namely, wills made in contemplation of marriage and wills made pursuant to a power of attorney. Some statutes also allow a surviving spouse to elect under a will that would otherwise be revoked. These situations are discussed below.

Further Reading

G.M. Bates, "Revocation of Wills on Marriage" (1979), 129 New L.J. 547.

Williams on Wills, 7th ed. by C.H. Sherrin, R.F.D Barlow, and R.A. Wallington, assisted by Susannah L. Meadway (London: Butterworths, 1995), c. 17.

Feeney's Canadian Law of Wills, 4th ed. by James MacKenzie (Toronto: Butterworths, 2000 (loose leaf)), c. 5.

Jordan M. Atin, "Revocation of Wills by Marriage" (1999), 18 E.T. & P.J. 13.

(ii) *Validity of the Marriage*

Since a will is revoked by the testator's marriage, it will be important for the beneficiaries under the will to know whether the marriage is valid. One would have thought that because of the testamentary consequences a marriage would be vitiated for the same reasons and on the basis of the same standard of proof as wills are. However, this does not seem to be so. A marriage may be either void or voidable. It is voidable if it the formal requirements of a marriage were not adhered to, if the testator was coerced into the marriage, or if there is an inability to consummate. A marriage is void if a party lacked capacity to consent to the marriage or is mistaken about the identity of the other party.[9] A voidable marriage can only be challenged by the parties and only while both are living.[10] A void

---

8   Note that under Quebec law a will is not revoked by marriage. See *Re Covone Estate* (1989), 36
    E.T.R. 114 (B.C.S.C.).

9   *Thompson v. Thompson* (1971), 81 D.L.R. (3d) 608, [1971] 4 W.W.R. 383 (Sask. Q.B.).

10 *Re Roberts*, [1978] 3 All E.R. 225 at 227 (C.A.).

marriage can be challenged by any person having a financial interest in the matter.[11]

It has been said that a marriage contract is "the essence of simplicity"[12] that does not require "a high degree of intelligence to comprehend."[13] Thus, marriage does not require a great deal of mental capacity. Consequently, a person may lack the capacity to make a will, but have the capacity to marry.[14]

The issue became important in *Banton v. Banton*.[15] George Banton had made a will in 1991, when he was 84 years old. It left his property equally among his five children. In 1993 George moved into a retirement home. Within the year, he became friendly with Muna Yassin, a 31-year-old waitress in the home's restaurant. The relationship soon developed into a close attachment. At this time, George was terminally ill with prostate cancer and was castrated in an attempt to halt the spread of the disease. In consequence, he became severely depressed. He was also in a weakened physical state, required a walker and was incontinent. In December, 1994, when George was 88 years old, he and Muna were married at her apartment. Two days later they met with a solicitor and instructed him to prepare a power of attorney in favour of Muna and a will leaving all George's property to Muna. Because of concerns about George's capacity, identical documents were prepared in May, 1995, after an assessment of George's capacity to manage his property and to give a power of attorney had been done. George died in February, 1996. Not surprisingly, George's children, with whom he had been close, took exception to what had happened, so the matter ended up in court. The court ordered a number of issues to be tried, including whether George had capacity to make the 1994 and 1995 wills, whether the wills were procured by undue influence, and whether George had capacity to enter into marriage with Muna. After an exhaustive examination of the facts and issues, Cullity J. had no great difficulty in finding that George lacked testamentary capacity to make the wills and that the wills were procured by undue influence. He described the situation as "the case of a lonely, depressed, terminally ill, severely disabled and cognitively impaired old man whose enfeebled condition made him an easy prey for a person like Muna with designs on his property."[16] However, if the marriage was valid, the earlier will in favour of the children would have been revoked. Cullity J. reviewed the law on the validity of marriage and noted that the threshold for finding capacity to marry is low. He found that George had capacity to enter into the marriage and that while he initially tried to resist Muna's "attempts to

---

11 *Capon v. McLay*, [1965] 2 O.R. 83, 49 D.L.R. (2d) 675 (C.A.); *Re McElroy* (1978), 22 O.R. (2d) 381, 93 D.L.R. (3d) 522 (Surr. Ct.); *Hart v. Cooper* (1994), 2 E.T.R. (2d) 168 (B.C.S.C.).

12 *Calvert (Litigation Guardain of) v. Calvert* (1997), 32 O.R. (3d) 281 (Gen. Div.).

13 *Durham v. Durham* (1885), 10 P.D. 80 at 81.

14 *Re McElroy* (1978), 22 O.R. (2d) 381, 93 D.L.R. (3d) 522 (Surr. Ct.).

15 (1998), 164 D.L.R. (4th) 176, suppl. reasons *loc cit.* at 244 (Ont. Gen. Div.). See also *Banton v. CIBC Trust Corp.* (1999), 182 D.L.R. (4th) 486, 30 E.T.R. (2d) 138, 148 (Ont. S.C.J.). The case raised a number of other issues as well. See Albert H. Oosterhoff, "Consequences of a January/December Marriage: A Cautionary Tale" (1999), 18 E.T. & P.J. 261.

16 *Ibid.*, 164 D.L.R. at 222.

seduce him into marriage . . . in November, he capitulated and consented to it."[17] Hence, he was not coerced into the marriage. Consequently, George died intestate and Muna became entitled to a substantial portion of his estate as his surviving spouse.

This result is surely problematic. If the law wants to take the position that it should not be too difficult to enter into marriage, that is one thing. But if the consequence of the marriage is that a spouse's carefully made estate plan is destroyed, that is quite another. Should the law not take into account that when there is a prior will the marriage is, in effect, a testamentary act and should, at least to that extent, conform to the requirements for a valid will? Indeed, the matter has wider implications, for surviving spouses have significant rights under modern legislation. They are entitled to an equalizing payment from[18] and to apply for support out of the estate of the deceased spouse.[19] Thus, society had an interest in ensuring that the surviving spouse has a legitimate right to such payments. Hence, for the purpose of a statutory revocation of a prior will, perhaps we need to change the statutory rule of automatic revocation by limiting it to situations in which the testator had *testamentary* capacity at the time of the marriage and was not subjected to undue influence (as measured for testamentary purposes) to enter into the marriage. Further, the estate of the testator and any person having a financial interest in the matter should be accorded standing to raise the issues of capacity and undue influence.

Notes and Questions

1. Would a statutory regime such as exists in Quebec where a will is not revoked on marriage be appropriate today?

2. For a case similar to *Banton*, see *Danchuk v. Calderwood*.[20] The deceased's care giver secretly married the testator. However, she was unable to claim his estate since his previous marriage had never been dissolved.

3. Another similar case is *Barrett Estate v. Dexter*.[21] It also involved a much younger care giver who persuaded an older man into marriage. However, the court held the marriage to be invalid because the man did not meet the very low threshold for the test of capacity to marry.

4. Note that a void marriage does not revoke a will. However, a voidable one does, unless it is avoided, since the avoidance, by a decree of annulment, relates back to the marriage and it is thereafter treated as if it never existed.

A marriage entered into without the consent of one of the parties is void at common law. However, in England such a marriage is now treated as only voidable, and voidable marriages are there now treated after annulment as having existed between the marriage

---

17 *Ibid.,* at p. 223.
18 Under Part I of the *Family Law Reform Act*, R.S.O. 1990, c. F.3.
19 Under Part V of the *Succession Law Reform Act*, R.S.O. 1990, c. S.26.
20 (1996), 15 E.T.R. (2d) 193 (B.C.S.C.).
21 (2000), 34 E.T.R. (2d) 1 (Q.B.). See Albert H. Oosterhoff, Comment (2001), 20 E.T. & P.J. 115.

and the decree of annulment.[22] Accordingly, it was held in *In re Roberts*[23] that a marriage which was voidable (because of lack of consent) and which was not avoided, operated to revoke a prior will.[24] Which is preferable, the common law position or the statutory one? If the testator lacked capacity to enter the marriage, is his or her prior will revoked?[25]

(iii) Will Made in Contemplation of Marriage

A person who is about to marry may wish to make a will containing provision for the future spouse prior to the marriage. The statutes permit such a will to stand, but only if it is clear that that is the testator's intention. The relevant statutory provision from the *Succession Law Reform Act*[26] is set out below. The problems concerning this type of will are discussed in *Re Coleman*[27] reproduced below.

SUCCESSION LAW REFORM ACT
R.S.O. 1990, c. S.26

15. A will or part of a will is revoked only by,

(a) marriage, subject to section 16 . . .

. . .

16. A will is revoked by the marriage of the testator except where
(a) there is a declaration in the will that it is made in contemplation of the marriage. . . .

. . .

Comparable Legislation

Probate Act, R.S.P.E.I. 1988, c. P-21, s. 68(1), 2(A); *Wills Act*, R.S.A. 1980, c. W-11, ss. 16(a), 17(a); R.S.B.C. 1996, c. 489, s. 14(a), 15(a); R.S.M. 1988, c. W150, ss. 16(a), 17(a); R.S.N.B. 1973, c. W-9 [am. S.N.B. 1991, c. 61, s. 4], ss. 15.1(2)(a), 16(a); R.S.N. 1990, c. W-10, s. 9(a); R.S.N.S. 1989, c. 505, s. 17(a); S.S 1996, c. W-14.1, s. 16(a), 17(a); R.S.N.W.T. 1988, c. W-5, s. 11(2)(a), (3)(a); R.S.Y. 1986, c. 179, s. 10(2)(a), (3)(a).

---

22 See *Nullity of Marriage Act, 1971* (U.K.), c. 44, ss. 1, 2, 5, now contained in the *Matrimonial Causes Act, 1973* (U.K.), c. 18, ss. 11, 12, 16. *Cf. Marital Property Act*, S.M. 1978, c. 24, s. 2(2).
23 [1978] 1 W.L.R. 653, [1978] 3 All E.R. 225 (C.A.).
24 See generally Hahlo, *Nullity of Marriage in Canada* (1979), pp. 43-57; Law Reform Committee, *Twenty Second Report (The Making and Revocation of Wills)*, Cmnd 7902 (May, 1980), §§ 3.19-3.25.
25 See *Hart v. Cooper* (1994), 2 E.T.R. (2d) 168 (B.C. S.C.), in which the beneficiaries did not prove lack of capacity.
26 R.S.O. 1990, c. S.26 (hereafter referred to without further citation).
27 [1976] Ch. 1, [1975] 1 All E.R. 675.

RE COLEMAN
[1976] Ch. 1, [1975] 1 All E.R. 675
Chancery Division

The testator made a will by which he gave certain real property, personal chattels, a stamp collection and a legacy, "unto my fiancée, Mrs. Muriel Jeffery." The will was drawn professionally. He married Muriel Jeffery two and a half months later. At issue was whether the *Law of Property Act 1925*[28] saved the will from revocation. Section 177 read as follows:

> A will expressed to be made in contemplation of a marriage shall, notwithstanding anything in section 18 of the Wills Act, 1837, or any other statutory provision or rule of law to the contrary, not be revoked by the solemnisation of the marriage contemplated.

MEGARRY J.:

. . .

There is a substantial body of authority on the section, or on similar provisions, and I have been carefully taken through the cases. They may be classified under three heads. First, there are the 'general contemplation' cases. In these, the will merely expressed a contemplation of marriage in general, so that the will could not be said to have been made 'in contemplation of a marriage' within the section. 'Marriage' and 'a marriage' are two different concepts; and this is emphasised by the concluding words of the section, 'the solemnisation of the marriage contemplated'. Thus in *Sallis v. Jones*[29] the last sentence of the will stated that 'this will is made in contemplation of marriage', and Bennett J. held that this did not satisfy the section. In *Re Hamilton*[30] the will made certain detailed dispositions by a long clause beginning 'Should I marry prior to my death', and Lowe J held that this did not satisfy a statutory provision substantially similar to s 177. These decisions, if I may say so seem plainly right, and neither side suggested the contrary, though counsel for the plaintiff did point out that the detailed clause in *Re Hamilton* appeared to relate to the particular woman whom the testator later married, and that this might have been said to remove the defect of generality. However, I need consider these cases no further, as they do not seem to provide any real assistance in the present case.

Second, there are the 'wife' cases, where in the will the testator describes as his 'wife' someone who is not in fact married to him. In the earliest of these cases, *Pilot v. Gainfort*[31] a gift to X 'my wife' was held to satisfy the section. The testator's wife had disappeared three years before he began to live with X, six years before he made his will, and seven years before he married X. Lord Merrivale P held[32] that the testator had made his will 'At a time when his marriage was

---

28 15 & 16 Geo. 5, c. 20, s. 177, rep. 1982, c. 53 (U.K.), Sched. 9.
29 [1936] P. 43.
30 [1941] V.L.R. 60.
31 [1931] P. 103.
32 *Ibid.,* at p. 104.

obviously within the contemplation of the testator, if he could validly contract it...' He said that the section 'prescribes that the solemnization of his marriage shall not revoke his will made in contemplation of that marriage...' and that 'the will was in contemplation of the subsequent marriage and practically expresses that contemplation...' It will be observed that these statements seem to give little emphasis to the statutory requirement that the will should be 'expressed to be made' in contemplation of the marriage, as distinct from there being a mere factual contemplation of it; and as counsel for the widow observed, there is some difficulty in discerning the exact sense in which the word 'practically' is used. The word 'wife', too, may be said to be an expression of the present rather than a contemplation of the future. For reasons of social conformity or otherwise a man may well describe a woman as his wife even if he has no intention whatever of marrying her. On grounds such as these, in *Re Taylor*[33] O'Bryan J refused to follow *Pilot v. Gainfort*[34] and held that when the testator married X, whom he had previously described in his will as 'my wife' X, that marriage was not 'a marriage in contemplation of which' the will had been 'expressed to be made'.

Then there is *Re Gray*.[35] There the will gave everything to 'my wife' X, whom the testator had previously 'married' bigamously. Many years later X executed a will benefiting the testator. Some while later the testator discovered that his wife was still living, and X then learned for the first time of her existence. However, the wife died shortly afterwards and the testator then married X. Within a year X died, and a month later the testator died. Sir Jocelyn Simon P held that s 177 saved neither will. When X executed her will, she did not contemplate marrying the testator, as she believed that she was already married to him; and when the testator executed his will he was unlikely to have had it in mind to tell X the truth when his wife died and then go through a second ceremony of marriage with X. The case is very shortly reported, and one may doubt whether the full reasoning emerges. Certainly, the report gives some impression that the actual intentions of the testator and X were being considered rather than the intentions expressed in their wills; but this may well have been part of the process of attaching a meaning to the words 'my wife' X, and so on. These three cases do not bear directly on the case before me, but I think they at least indicate that the courts are not at present inclined to spell out of a bare reference to 'my wife' X an expressed contemplation of marrying X. Certainly I do not think that a testator who is in fact married to X could possibly be regarded as expressing an intention to marry her again merely because he describes her in his will as 'my wife X'; and yet, as an expression, 'my wife X' is precisely the same whether or not the testator is in fact married to X. The third and most relevant category of cases consists of those where the will refers to a named person as 'my fiancée', or uses words having an equivalent effect. There are four of these cases, and in all save one it has been held that the statute was satisfied. The earliest case is *Re Knight*[36] briefly men-

---

33 [1949] V.L.R. 201.
34 [1931] P. 103.
35 (1963) 107 Sol. Jo. 156.
36 (1944), unreported.

tioned in *Re Langston* .[37] There the testator's will gave all his property to X 'my future wife', and this was held to be a sufficient expression of contemplation of marriage to X to save the will from revocation by the testator's subsequent marriage to X. The next case is *Re Chase*.[38] There the gift was of two-thirds of the testator's net estate to X 'my fiancée at present travelling to Australia on board the S.S. Stratheden due in Fremantle on the 8th June 1948', and the will was made on June 6, 1948, two days before the arrival date for X. On those facts Herring CJ held that the testator's marriage to X on 24th June 1948, was 'a marriage in contemplation of which' the will was 'expressed to be made'. Then there is *Re Langston*[39] itself. There the testator gave his entire estate 'unto my fiancée' X, whom he appointed sole executrix. Davies J followed and applied *Re Knight*.[40] He said[41] that the proper test was 'Does the testator express the fact that he is contemplating marriage to a particular person?' He applied that test, and held that it was satisfied.

The next case was decided some six weeks after *Re Langston*, and on the other side of the world. In *Burton v. McGregor*[42] the testator gave his whole estate 'unto my fiancée' X, and Adams J held that the will was not 'expressed to be made in contemplation of a marriage'. As one might expect from a jurist of Sir Francis Adams' standing, his reserved judgment contains the most substantial discussion of the subject to be found in the cases. He expressed his concurrence with the views expressed by O'Bryan J in *Re Taylor*[43] about *Pilot v. Gainfort*[44] and he then discussed *Re Chase*[45] at some length. He said[46] that he agreed that the question was one of construction of the language used in the will, and that extrinsic evidence was admissible in order to identify X and show that she was in fact the testator's fiancée. But he held that extrinsic evidence was not admissible merely for the purpose of ascertaining the testator's intention and showing that the will was made in contemplation of a marriage. That contemplation, he said, 'must in order to comply with the statute, be sufficiently expressed in the will itself'. With that, I would respectfully agree. I shall have to return to the question of evidence later. Adams J then both distinguished and dissented from the decision in *Re Chase*.[47] The will in that case had words in it relating to X's impending arrival in Australia which were lacking in the case before him; and in that latter case the question was whether the mere description 'my fiancée' was enough. He held that it was not. The testator might have been intending to provide for X only while she remained his fiancée, and the judge regarded the word 'fiancée' as a mere word

37 [1953] P. 100 at 103, [1953] 1 All E.R. 928 at 930.
38 [1951] V.L.R. 477.
39 [1953] P. 100, [1953] 1 All E.R. 928.
40 (1944), unreported.
41 *Supra,* at pp. 102 and 929, respectively.
42 [1953] N.Z.L.R. 487.
43 [1949] V.L.R. 201.
44 [1931] P. 103.
45 [1951] V.L.R. 477.
46 At p. 491.
47 *Supra.*

of description such as 'mother' or 'wife'. He held that it was going too far to hold that the statute was satisfied 'merely because the word "fiancée" signifies that the testator intends to marry the person so described'. The learned judge further held[48] that the statutory language meant that the will must be made in contemplation of the marriage 'in the sense that the testator contemplated and intended that the will should remain in operation notwithstanding the marriage'. I shall return to this point later. For these reasons, he held that the statute was not satisfied, and so the will was not saved from being revoked by the marriage of the testator to X.

It is plain from what I have said that there is a marked divergence between *Re Langston* and *Burton v. McGregor*, each decided in ignorance of the other: and while counsel for the plaintiff strongly relied on the former, counsel for the widow equally strongly relied on the latter.

. . .

I think that before I say anything further about the cases, I should return to the expressions used in the will, and the words of the section, and say what they appear to me to mean. First, the testamentary expressions to be construed consist of bequests 'unto my fiancée Mrs. Muriel Jeffery' and a devise 'unto my said fiancée Mrs. Muriel Jeffery'. 'Fiancée' is a word which means a woman who is engaged to be married, or is betrothed, and 'my fiancée'; must mean a woman engaged to be married to the speaker. When a man speaks of 'my fiancée' he is speaking of 'the woman to whom I am engaged to be married'. It seems to me that in ordinary parlance a contemplation of marriage is inherent in the very word 'fiancée'. The word 'wife' is a word which denotes an existing state of affairs, and one that will continue until death, or, these days, divorce: but I do not think that it could reasonably be said that there inheres in the word 'wife' any contemplation of a change of that state of affairs, whether by death or divorce. 'Fiancée' seems to me to be quite different, in that it not only describes an existing state of affairs but also contemplates a change in that state of affairs. No doubt some engagements last a long time, and others are broken off; but the normal future for an engagement is its termination by marriage, or perhaps I should say its sublimation into marriage. Provided the 'contemplation' is real, I cannot see that it makes much difference whether or not there is any particular degree of imminence about the marriage. Accordingly in my judgment, unless curtailed by the context, a testamentary reference to 'my fiancée X' per se contemplates the marriage of the testator to X, as well as describing an existing status.

Second, the statutory expression to be construed is 'a will expressed to be made in contemplation of a marriage'. Given a contemplation of the marriage, that has to be expressed in relation to the making of the will. The words 'will' and 'made' must be given due weight. It is the will, and not merely some gift in it, that must be expressed to be 'made' in contemplation of a marriage. The statute is not framed in terms of a will 'in which a contemplation of a marriage is expressed', or a will 'containing a disposition expressed to be made in contemplation of a marriage'. It is the will itself, which I think must mean the will as a whole and not just bits of it, that must be 'expressed to be made' in contemplation of a

---

48 [1951] V.L.R. 477 at 492.

marriage. An expression to this effect may appear simply enough if a clause is inserted which states 'This will is made in contemplation of my marriage to X', or contains some such words. That, of course, was not done in the present case. But I do not think that this is the only way of achieving the result. If each beneficial disposition made by the will is expressed to be made in contemplation of the testator's marriage to X, then it seems to me that the will as a whole must have been expressed to be made in contemplation of that marriage. What governs all the parts of a will must govern the will as a whole. I do not have to decide whether the absence of any such expressed contemplation from some non-beneficial provision, such as an appointment of executors, would prevent the section from applying; at present I would doubt it.

On the other hand, where some of the beneficial dispositions in the will lack any expression of such a contemplation, I find it difficult to see how it can be said that the 'will' is expressed to be made in contemplation of a marriage. To take an example that I put to counsel for the plaintiff in argument, if in cl 17(e) of a will disposing of an estate of £100,000 the testator left £100, or a gold ring, or something of the sort, to 'my fiancée Mary', but made no other provision for her, one could certainly say that the testator had expressed a contemplation of marriage to Mary in the will, and also in making that bequest; but it would be extravagant to say that the will was 'a will expressed to be made in contemplation of a marriage'. Counsel for the plaintiff was constrained to accept this: but his reply was that if it sufficed in substance, or to any substantial degree, the will was expressed to be made in contemplation of a marriage. The £100 or a gold ring he dismissed as being in the nature of de minimis: but he said that if, as in the present case, the provision made by the will for the fiancée was substantial, then the section was satisfied.

I do not think that this can be right. Under the section one is concerned not with what the testator actually contemplated, but what contemplation is 'expressed' in the will. If that contemplation relates not to the will as a whole but only to part of it, then even if that part is substantial I do not see how it can be said that it is the will which is expressed to be made in that contemplation. No doubt with the aid of the Interpretation Act 1889, s 1(1)(b), the expression 'a will' in the singular may be read as including 'wills' in the plural; but I know of nothing which in the present context would allow the expression 'a will' to be read as including 'bits of a will'. In my judgment, 'a will' means the whole will, and not merely parts of it, even if they are substantial; and the will that is 'made' is of necessity the whole will. It may indeed be that merely trivial parts can be ignored, so that 'a will' can be read as being 'the whole of a will, or substantially the whole of a will': but I cannot regard 'any substantial part of a will' as being 'a will'. In my view, the question to ask is, 'Was the will as a whole expressed to be made in contemplation of the particular marriage that has been celebrated?'

If that is right, as I think it is, it disposes of this case; for nobody could dismiss the residuary gifts as being merely trivial or immaterial, and in relation to them no contemplation of the marriage is expressed. In my judgment, the will before me is not 'a will' which is expressed to be 'made' in contemplation of a marriage, even though it contains provisions which are expressed to be made in such contemplation.

There remains, however, the question how far this view is consonant with the authorities, and especially with *Langston*. As I have mentioned, the test propounded in that case[49] was 'Did the testator express the fact that he was contemplating marriage to a particular person?' If all that Parliament required was something in the will which showed that when the testator made it he was contemplating a particular marriage, thereby demonstrating that he had the marriage in mind when he made his dispositions, I do not see why Parliament did not speak simply in terms of requiring the will to express such a contemplation. Instead, Parliament used the stricter and more specific language which requires that the 'will' should be 'expressed to be made' in that contemplation. If, of course, one accepts the test laid down in *Langston* and applies it to the present case, the answer must be that the test is satisfied, whereas on the test that I have suggested the mere expression of such a contemplation in some of the disposition made by the will, without more, would not suffice. However, one must remember that *Re Langston* was argued only by the applicant (the other parties consenting), and that in any case the will in fact gave the whole of the testator's estate to his named fiancée. By reason of that fact, the application of the test that I have suggested would have produced the same result in *Re Langston* as the test applied by Davies J. In other words, I would respectfully agree with his decision, though for somewhat different reasons. I would similarly agree with the result in *Re Knight*.

. . .

Notes and Questions

1. The Prince Edward Island Act requires that if a will is made in contemplation of marriage, the marriage must take place within one month of the execution of the will to avoid revocation.[50]

2. The New Brunswick legislation provides that a testator who subsequently marries shall be deemed to die intestate if the person dies while married or while issue of the testator are alive.[51] However, s. 16(a) provides that this rule does not apply if the will is made in contemplation of marriage.

3. Is the decision in *Re Coleman* too strict? It is arguable that if it is clear from the will that the testator intended the will to survive the marriage, effect ought to be given that intention.[52]

4. Is it necessary that the whole will be expressed to be made in contemplation of marriage, or should it be sufficient if you can discern that this is the testator's intention, as was argued in the *Coleman* case? Would it be possible to argue that part of a will only should be revoked if that is what the testator intended?[53]

---

49 [1953] 1 All E.R. 928 at 929, [1953] P. 100 at 102.

50 *Probate Act*, R.S.P.E.I. 1988, c. P-21, s. 68(2)(a).

51 *Wills Act*, R.S.N.B. 1973, c. W-9 (am. S.N.B. 1991, c. 62, s. 4), s. 15.1.

52 See Law Reform Committee (U.K.), *Twenty-Second Report* (*The Making and Revocation of Wills*), Cmnd. 7902 (May, 1980), §§ 3.13 - 3.17.

53 *Ibid.*, § 3.18. And see the materials on powers of appointment, *infra*.

5. The English legislation was amended in 1982. Section 18 of the *Wills Act 1837*,[54] which provided that a will was revoked by the testator's marriage except a will made in exercise of a power of appointment if the property would not in default of appointment pass to the testator's heir or personal representative as the person entitled as his or her next of kin, was replaced[55] by the following:

> **18.** (1) Subject to subsections (2) to (4) below, a will shall be revoked by the testator's marriage.
>
> (2) A disposition in a will in exercise of a power of appointment shall take effect notwithstanding the testator's subsequent marriage unless the property so appointed would in default of appointment pass to his personal representatives.
>
> (3) Where it appears from a will that at the time it was made the testator was expecting to be married to a particular person and that he intended that the will should not be revoked by the marriage, the will shall not be revoked by his marriage to that person.
>
> (4) Where it appears from a will that at the time it was made the testator was expecting to be married to a particular person and that he intended that a disposition in the will should not be revoked by his marriage to that person,—
>
> > (a) that disposition shall take effect notwithstanding the marriage; and
> >
> > (b) any other disposition in the will shall take effect also, unless it appears from the will that the testator intended the disposition to be revoked by the marriage.

The *Administration of Justice Act*[56] also repealed s. 177 of the *Law of Property Act 1925*.[57]

While the English statute has now reversed *Re Coleman*[58] in part, there has been no corresponding change in the Canadian statutes. Would *Coleman* still apply in Canada? Would legislation of this type be desirable in the Canadian provinces?

6. It seems clear from the language of the Ontario Act that the testator must contemplate marriage to a particular person. The English legislation says so expressly.[59]

Hence a will made "in contemplation of (a/the) marriage" without naming the intended spouse would be revoked upon the marriage.[60] Is this desirable, if it can be shown by extrinsic evidence that the testator intended to marry a particular person and did in fact do so?

7. *Re Pluto Estate*[61] is similar to *Re Coleman*. The testator devised his home and contents "to my wife, Mary Beatrice Pluto." He was unmarried at the time, but married a person who satisfied the description in the will, except for the term "wife" and the last name, the day after he executed the will. The court held that the marriage revoked the will. The relevant statute required "a declaration in the will that it is made in contemplation of marriage."[62]

Should a reference, such as "my wife," or "my fiancée," not be sufficient to prevent revocation, or would this require a statutory amendment?

---

54 7 Will. 4 & 1 Vict., c. 26.

55 By the *Administration of Justice Act 1982*, c. 53 (U.K.), s. 18(1).

56 *Ibid.*, Sched. 9.

57 15 & 16 Geo. 5, c. 20.

58 *Supra.*

59 *Wills Act*, *supra*, s. 18(3) as substituted by the *Administration of Justice Act 1982*, *supra*, s. 18(1). The amendment applies only to wills made on or after 1 January 1983.

60 See, *e.g.*, *Sallis v. Jones*, [1936] P. 43.

61 (1969), 69 W.W.R. 765, 6 D.L.R. (3d) 541 (B.C.S.C.).

62 *Wills Act*, R.S.B.C. 1960, c. 408, s. 16(a). See now R.S.B.C. 1996, c. 489, s. 17(a).

8. Some cases have been quite lenient in finding compliance with the statute. *Owers v. Hayes*[63] is an example. The testatrix wrote a letter to her daughter, stating that if she married X, he was to be entitled to live in her home. The court held the letter to be a holograph codicil which amounted to a declaration made in contemplation of the marriage that subsequently took place.

9. It would appear that the question of revocation by marriage for the purpose of the rules of conflict of laws is a matter of matrimonial law and not of the law of succession. Hence, the law of the testator's domicile at the time of the marriage and not his or her domicile at death (in the case of movables) or the *lex rei sitae* (in the case of immovables) governs the question.[64]

The point is further illustrated by *Allison v. Allison*.[65] The testator made a will in Quebec and then married there. As noted, under Quebec law a will is not revoked by the testator's marriage. The testator and his wife then moved to British Columbia and died domiciled there. The court held that Quebec law governed the validity of the will.

(iv) *Election*

It is possible that the will makes provision for a surviving spouse even though it is not made in contemplation of marriage. It would seem appropriate to permit the will to stand in these circumstances, at least if the spouse is prepared to accept the provision made for him or her. Some statutes, therefore, allow for an election by the surviving spouse in these circumstances. The Ontario legislation is set out below. *Re Browne and Dobrotinic,*[66] also reproduced below, discusses this issue.

SUCCESSION LAW REFORM ACT
R.S.O. 1990, c. S.26

16. A will is revoked by the marriage of the testator except where,

. . .

(b) the spouse of the testator elects to take under the will, by an instrument in writing signed by the spouse and filed within one year after the testator's death in the office of the Estate Registrar for Ontario; or

. . .

---

63 (1983), 43 O.R. (2d) 407, 16 E.T.R. 61, 1 D.L.R. (4th) 280 (H.C.).

64 *Re Martin,* [1900] P. 211 (C.A.); *Davies v. Davies* (1915), 8 W.W.R. 803, 24 D.L.R. 737 at 740 (Alta. T.D.).

   The principle can have significant consequences. For example, if the testator was domiciled in Quebec, but owned real property in another province, Quebec law govern the effect of the testator's marriage on a prior will and under Quebec law the prior will is not revoked. See *Re Covone Estate* (1989), 36 E.T.R. 114 (B.C.S.C.). However, there is some dispute on this matter since the conflicts rule regarding succession to immovables is that the *lex situs* governs the succession and that would lead to a different result: *Page Estate v. Sachs* (1990), 37 E.T.R. 226 (Ont. H.C.).

65 (1998), 23 E.T.R. (2d) 237 (B.C.S.C.).

66 [1958] O.W.N. 91, 13 D.L.R. (2d) 562 (H.C.).

Comparable Legislation

Wills Act, R.S.N.S. 1989, c. 505, s. 17(b). *Cf. Wills Act*, R.S.N.B. 1973, c. W-9 [am. S.N.B. 1991, c. 62, s. 4; S.N.B. 1994, c. 32, s. 1], s. 15.1(3)-(6).

RE BROWNE AND DOBROTINIC
[1958] O.W.N. 91, 13 D.L.R. (2d) 565
Supreme Court of Ontario
[High Court of Justice]

The deceased, Robert Dobrotinic, made a will in 1938 by which he left all his property to Katherine Dobrotinic if she survived him. He lived with her from 1937 until his death in 1956. In 1948 he divorced his wife, Maria Dobrotinic, and married Katherine in 1949. When the will was probated, Katherine filed a doctrine of election in the office of the Registrar of the Surrogate Court of the County of York and not in the office of the Registrar of the Supreme Court as then required by the *Wills Act*,[67] although it was transmitted to the latter office one year after the date of death by the Registrar of the Surrogate Court as required by statute.

Katherine then agreed to sell part of the real property she received from the estate and the purchaser objected to her title since she had filed the election in the wrong office. The purchaser brought a vendor and purchaser application. The testator's two children by his previous marriage, although served, did not appear on the application.

MOORHOUSE J.:

. . .

The purpose of s-ss. (a) and (b) of s. 20 of the Wills Act indicates a manifest intention on the part of the Legislature to protect a husband or wife of the testator, and s-s.(c), the testator's heirs, executor or administrator. Subsection (c) has been in the Act for a great many years and is in the English Act.

In the instant case the widow immediately indicated her intention to adopt the will. Before the expiration of one month from the date of death she caused her election to be filed in the Surrogate Court Office. This was a public office in which one might ordinarily expect such a document to be filed. In its wisdom, our Legislature has determined this document should be filed in the office of the Registrar of the Supreme Court. The Court has been informed by counsel that Ontario is the only Province in Canada providing such exceptions to the revocation of a will by the subsequent marriage of the testator. He has also informed the Court he has found no similar legislation elsewhere. Counsel have been unable to refer this Court to any case in which this statute has been considered.

It should be observed that in England the *Law of Property Act, 1925*,[68] provides that a will expressed to be made in contemplation of marriage is not revoked by

---

67 R.S.O. 1950, c. 426, s. 20(b).
68 (Imp.), c. 20, s. 177.

solemnization of the marriage contemplated. Were this Court to adopt the argument of the applicant it would be a clear case of a strict and literal interpretation of the statute defeating the purpose of the statute.

Having regard to the intention of the Legislature as this Court understands it from a reading of the Wills Act, it must be held that the matter of filing was a directory matter and did not go to the substance of the legislation. In the instant case all those parties who would inherit in the event of an intestacy have been notified and have failed to appear. This Court must find that the election was properly made and that the will is a valid will and was not revoked by the failure to file the election so made in the proper office and that, accordingly, a good title has been shown by the vendor.

. . .

Notes and Questions

1. The instrument of election must now be filed by the spouse in the office of the Estate Registrar for Ontario.[69]

2. Does the exercise of the right to elect save the entire will, or only that part in which property was left to the surviving spouse? A literal reading of the statute suggests that the entire will remains unrevoked. If a contrary interpretation were given to the legislation, would the surviving spouse be entitled to share in the resulting partial intestacy?

The point of partial revocation seems to have arisen only in the context of powers of appointment. We discuss that topic below.

3. Only the Ontario and Nova Scotia Acts provide for an election by a surviving spouse. The election provision is a useful one in that it can save a will that would otherwise be revoked because it does not contain a declaration that it is made in contemplation of marriage. Thus, for example, if a testator leaves property "to my wife, X," and later marries X and then dies, X can elect to take under the will, thereby saving the gift.[70]

4. The New Brunswick Act contains a provision which is somewhat similar to the Ontario and Nova Scotia legislation. It provides that a testator is deemed to have died intestate if he or she subsequently marries and dies while married or while any issue of a marriage of the testator subsequent to the will is alive. A beneficiary under the will who is not entitled on the intestacy may apply to the court within four months of the testator's death for an order giving effect to the gift to that beneficiary in the will, provided the order will have no undue effect on a person who would otherwise take any part of the deceased's estate on intestacy.[71]

(v) *Powers of Appointment*

A power of appointment is a right given by the owner of property, called the donor of the power, to another person, called the donee of the power, to dispose

---

69 *Succession Law Reform Act*, R.S.O. 1990, c. S.26, s. 16(b).
70 These facts are based on *Re Pluto Estate* (1969), 69 W.W.R. 765, 6 D.L.R. (3d) 541 (B.C.S.C.). Of course, the British Columbia statute did not and does not contain a right of election.
71 *Wills Act*, R.S.N.B. 1973, c. W-9 [am. S.N.B. 1991, c. 62, s. 4; S.N.B. 1994, c. 32, s. 1], s. 15.1(3)-(6).

of, or appoint the donor's property. One advantage of a power is that it delays disposition of the property and permits the donee to determine at a later time who should have the property. The power may be general, special or hybrid. A general power permits the donee to appoint to anyone, including the donee; a special power permits the donee to appoint among a specified class of persons; a hybrid power also permits the donee to appoint among a specified class of persons, but the class is defined to exclude one or more persons who would otherwise form part of the class. For example, a mother may give her daughter a power to appoint the corpus of a trust fund among the daughter's children. This is a special power and gives the daughter a discretion to appoint the property equally or unequally among her children, or to give all to one or more, to the exclusion of others. A power may be a trust, in which case it must be exercised, or it may be a mere power, in which case it does not have to be exercised. A mere power is often followed by a gift over in default of appointment. Thus, the mother in the above example could have added a clause such as, "but if she fails to appoint, then equally among all my grandchildren." Unless the exercise of the power is re-stricted, it can be exercised by deed or by will. If it is exercised by will, we say that the will is made pursuant to, or in exercise of the power. It is important to remember that the will, to the extent it exercises the power, disposes of the donor's property, not the donee's. However, the same will may also dispose of the donee's own property and most wills which exercise a power of appointment do.

If a will is made pursuant to a power of appointment given to the testator and if the will were to be revoked by his or her marriage, the property which is the subject matter of the power would not go to the testator's estate or those who would take on his or her intestacy, but to others. It would be regrettable to have the appointment fail in those circumstances and, therefore, most statutes allow that part of the will that exercises the power to stand in these circumstances. The Ontario legislation is set out below. This provision is discussed in *Re Gilligan*,[72] reproduced below.

SUCCESSION LAW REFORM ACT
R.S.O. 1990, c. S.26

16. A will is revoked by the marriage of the testator except where,

> . . .

(c) the will is made in exercise of a power of appointment of property which would not in default of the appointment pass to the heir, executor or administrator of the testator or to the persons entitled to the estate of the testator if he or she died intestate.

Comparable Legislation

Probate Act, R.S.P.E.I. 1988, c. P-21, s. 68(2)(b); *Wills Act*, R.S.A. 1980, c. W-11, s. 17(b); R.S.B.C. 1996, c. 489, s. 15(b); R.S.M. 1988 c. W150, s. 17(b); R.S.N.B. 1973, c.

---

72 [1950] P. 32, [1949] 2 All E.R. 401.

W-9 [am. S.N.B. 1991, c. 62, s. 4], s. 16(b); R.S.N. 1990, c. W-10, s. 9(b); R.S.N.S. 1989, c. 505, s. 17(c); R.S.N.W.T. 1988, c. W-5, s. 11(3)(b); S.S 1996, c. W-14.1, s. 17(b); R.S.Y. 1986, c. 179, s. 10(3)(b).

RE GILLIGAN
[1950] P. 32, [1949] 2 All E.R. 401
Probate Division

The testator executed a settlement in contemplation of marriage in which he retained the power to appoint half of the corpus in the event that there were no children of the marriage, the half to be held "in trust for such person or persons as would have been entitled thereto under the statutes for distribution of the personal estates of intestates on the death of the said [settlor] had he died possessed thereof intestate and without having been married," in default of appointment. After his wife's death, there being no children of the marriage, the testator made a will in which he gave a legacy to his executors and gave the residue to his nephews and nieces. Then he married again, but later predeceased his second wife. The question was whether the part of the will exercising the power of appointment remained unrevoked.

PILCHER J.:

. . .

The Wills Act, 1837,[73] s. 18, is in the following terms:

Every will made by a man or woman shall be revoked by his or her marriage (except a will made in the exercise of a power of appointment, when the real or personal estate thereby appointed would not in default of such appointment pass to his or her heir, customary heir, executor, or administrator, or the person entitled as his or her next of kin under the Statute of Distributions).

As I understand it, the meaning of s. 18, so far as I need consider its terms for the purposes of the present case, is that the only exception to the rule that a will is wholly revoked by subsequent marriage is in so far as such will exercises a power of appointment, and then only when the instrument conferring on the testator the power of appointment provides that, in default of the exercise of the power by him, the fund which is the subject-matter of the power shall devolve other than to the next of kin of the testator under the Statute of Distributions, 1670.[74]

The power of appointment which the testator purported to exercise by his will was conferred on him by the settlement of Nov. 29, 1890. The material terms of the settlement provided, in effect, that, in default of the exercise by the testator of the power of appointment granted to him, the trust fund should pass to the person or persons who would on his death have been entitled to it under the statutes for the distribution of the personal estate of intestates had he died intestate *and without having been married*. These last five words make it clear that, in default of the exercise of the power of appointment granted to him, the parties to

---

73 7 Will. 4 & 1 Vict., c. 26 (1837).
74 1 Jac. 2, c. 17.

the deed did not intend any widow of the testator to take the share to which she would otherwise have been entitled under the statutes of distribution. To this extent, therefore, the provisions of the settlement make it clear that, in default of appointment, the widow shall be excluded from the portion of the fund to which she would have been entitled on an intestacy. It would seem, therefore, that the words in the settlement "and without having been married" necessarily involve that the estate will not, to use the words of s. 18 of the Wills Act, "in default of such appointment pass to...the person entitled as his...next of kin under the Statute of Distributions" provided that a widow can be properly called a "next of kin under the Statute of Distributions."

. . .

In the circumstances I may, perhaps, be permitted to consider shortly the purpose and effect of s. 18 of the Wills Act. The section provides that wills shall be revoked by subsequent marriage except in so far as they exercise powers of appointment where the instrument creating the power provides that in default of appointment the fund subject to the power does not pass to the heir at law or "next of kin under the Statute of Distributions." If these last words are ambiguous, and it seems to me that they may be, it is right that consideration should be given to the whole purposes of the section and such interpretation given to the potentially ambiguous words as shall carry out the intentions of the legislature if these can be ascertained. The event which the section contemplates is the re-marriage of a person who has made a will, and the circumstances in which a will so made shall be revoked by such subsequent marriage. If the instrument creating the power of appointment provides that, in default of appointment the fund shall pass to named persons or, as in the present case, that a widow shall be excluded from all share in the fund, this manifests an intention by the settlor and grantor of the power that the fund shall not in default of appointment pass as on an intestacy. If, on the other hand, the instrument creating the power provides in terms that in default of appointment the fund shall pass as on an intestacy, the settlor has not thereby manifested any intention actively to control the ultimate destination of the fund. It is the marriage of the testator which revokes his previously made will, so that if after marriage he dies without making another will his widow will take her portion on an intestacy under the Statute of Distributions. In so far as the exercise by will of powers of appointment are concerned, there would seem logically to be no reason why a will exercising such powers should not be revoked by marriage where in default of the exercise of the power the after-taken wife is entitled to her widow's portion. Where, however, the settlor under the instrument creating the power has provided that in default of appointment no wife of the appointee shall take any portion of the fund, it seems not unreasonable to adopt a construction of the words in the Act which will give effect to the wish of the settlor, and will preserve such portion of the will as exercises the power of appointment.

I have accordingly, come to the conclusion that the meaning of the words in s. 18 of the Wills Act "next of kin under the Statute of Distributions" were intended to include a widow. The intention of the section was that a will exercising a power of appointment should only be wholly revoked by the subsequent marriage of the testator in those cases in which the instrument creating the power provides that in default of appointment the fund shall devolve as on an intestacy, in which event the widow of the testator will take her portion of the fund. This construction gives to the material words in s. 18 the meaning which has been assigned to them by BUTT, J., in *In the Goods of Russell*.[75] It is also the meaning which they necessarily have since 1925 in documents to which s. 50 (1) of the Administration of Estates Act, 1925, applies. I, accordingly, order a grant of administration to the applicant with that part of the will which remains unrevoked annexed.

Notes and Questions

1. Section 50(1) of the *Administration of Estates Act 1925*[76] abolished the rights of the heir to real property and the right of the next of kin to share in the personal property and replaced these rights with new statutory rights of inheritance.

2. For a case similar to *Re Gilligan* see *Re Paul*.[77]

3. Why, in the case of powers of appointment, is only part of the will revoked? Is this correct when the statute says that the *will* is revoked? If it is correct, does this result also apply to wills, or parts of wills, made in contemplation of marriage and to the right of a surviving spouse to elect? What is the purpose of the legislation?

4. As already noted, the English legislation was amended in 1982.[78]

(c) By Dissolution of Marriage

The law does not generally presume that a will was revoked by reason of a change in circumstances. The statute has reversed this rule for good reasons with respect to a subsequent marriage. But there are other situations in it is arguable that the testator would not have wanted the will to stand had he or she thought about it. Typically, this would be so when a testator has made a will benefiting his or her spouse and then obtains a divorce, but does not change the will. At common law a testamentary gift to one's spouse or to another's spouse was construed *prima facie* to refer to the person to whom the testator or the other person was married at the time the will was made, unless surrounding circumstances showed that a future spouse was intended. Thus, the fact that the testator's marriage was dissolved or annulled made no difference,[79] but a release by the parties of their rights to the other's estate might, at least if the release mentioned the will,[80] or if it was sufficiently broad.[81]

---

75 (1890), 15 P.D. 111.

76 15 & 16 Geo. 5, c. 23.

77 [1921] 2 Ch. 1.

78 By the *Administration of Justice Act 1982*, c. 53 (U.K.).

79 See *Re Posner*, [1953] P. 277, [1953] 1 All E.R. 1123; *Re Boddington* (1884), 22 Ch. D. 597, affirmed 25 Ch. D. 685 (C.A.); *Re Coley*, [1903] 2 Ch. 102 (C.A.); *Re Cameron; Cameron v. Toronto Gen. Trusts Corp.*, [1940] O.R. 49 at 52, [1939] 4 D.L.R. 581 (C.A.); *Re Marks*, [1945] O.W.N. 717 (H.C.); *Re Brechin* (1973), 38 D.L.R. (3d) 305 at 311 (Alta. T.D.). And see Ontario Law Reform Commission, *Report on the Impact of Divorce on Existing Wills* (1977).

80 *Eccleston Estate v. Eccleston* (1999), 30 E.T.R. (2d) 193 (N.B.Q.B.).

81 *Ward Estate v. Olds Aviation Ltd.* (1996), 29 E.T.R. (2d) 310 (Alta. Q.B.).

Since it may be supposed that a testator does not normally wish to benefit his or her former spouse, some Canadian statutes have reversed the common law in this respect. Section 17(2) of the *Succession Law Reform Act*, reproduced below, is representative.

SUCCESSION LAW REFORM ACT
R.S.O. 1990, c. S.26

17. (1) Subject to subsection (2), a will is not revoked by presumption of an intention to revoke it on the ground of a change in circumstances.

(2) Except when a contrary intention appears by the will, where, after the testator makes a will, his or her marriage is terminated by a judgment absolute of divorce or is declared a nullity,

(a) a devise or bequest of a beneficial interest in property to his or her former spouse;

(b) an appointment of his or her former spouse as executor or trustee; and

(c) the conferring of a general or special power of appointment on his or her former spouse are revoked and the will shall be construed as if the former spouse had predeceased the testator.

Comparable Legislation

To Section 17(1)

Probate Act, R.S.P.E.I. 1988, c. P-21, s. 71; *Wills Act*, R.S.A. 1980, c. W-11, s. 18; R.S.B.C. 1996, c. 489, s. 14(2); R.S.M. 1988, c. W150, s. 18(1); R.S.N.B. 1973, c. W-9, s. 17; R.S.N. 1990, c. W-10, s. 10; R.S.N.W.T. 1988, c. W-5, s. 11(1); R.S.N.S. 1989, c. 505, s. 18; S.S 1996, c. W-14.1, s. 18; R.S.Y. 1986, c. 179, s. 10(1).

To Section 17(2)

Probate Act, R.S.P.E.I. 1988, c. P-21, s. 69; *Wills Act*, R.S.B.C. 1996, c. 489, s. 16; R.S.M. 1988, c. W150, s. 18(2); S.S. 1996, c. W-14.1, s. 19.

RE BILLARD ESTATE
(1986), 22 E.T.R. 150, 50 R.F.L. (2d) 99
Ontario Supreme Court
[High Court of Justice]

The testator left the residue of his estate "to my spouse Gertrude Alva Billard." He made the will made after the parties had separated, but prior to the divorce decree. One issue at trial was whether the divorce decree revoked the bequest to

Gertrude or whether a contrary intention appeared by the will as specified in s. 17(2) of the *Succession Law Reform Act*.

ANDERSON J:

. . .

It is submitted on behalf of the respondent Gertrude Alva Billard that the making of the will after the separation of the parties and after the execution of the separation agreement evidences an intention contrary to the revocation of the bequest and that the bequest indicates that the deceased did not anticipate a reconciliation and intended that his former wife receive a bequest notwithstanding the separation. Reference is also made to the fact that the deceased, the petitioner in the divorce action, did not change his will at the time of the divorce. In other words, I am invited to conclude that, considering all the surrounding circumstances, the will should be read as indicating a contrary intention.

It is contended on behalf of the Official Guardian that the "contrary intention" must be one which "appears by the will", that is, by express provision or necessary implication. It is further submitted that the Court in determining the intention of the testator ought not to go to evidence of surrounding circumstances. In my view, the submission made on behalf of the Official Guardian should prevail.

What is involved is not really the interpretation of the will, in which the bequest is clear and unambiguous, but of the statute, which, in my view, is equally clear and unambiguous. If it were open to me to find, on the balance of probabilities, from the making of the will and all the surrounding circumstances, that a "contrary intention" was shown, I might do so. But, in my view, that approach is not open. What I must find, to avoid the effect of s. 17, is a "contrary intention" which appears "by the will". None does, and that is the end of the matter.

. . .

Notes and Questions

1. An interesting commentary on the interpretation of s. 17(2) of the *Succession Law Reform Act* is found in an annotation by T.G. Youdan, "The Meaning of 'Contrary Intention Appears by the Will.'"[82] The author criticizes the rationale in *Re Billard Estate* while agreeing with the result.[83]

2. The Manitoba, Saskatchewan and Prince Edward Island statutes define "spouse" to include a person purported or thought by the testator to be his or her spouse. The British Columbia definition includes a person "considered by the testator" to be his or her spouse. What is the purpose and effect of these definitions?

3. The legislation applies only after a divorce or nullity decree becomes effective. Under the present *Divorce Act*,[84] a divorce becomes effective 31 days after it is granted, unless a party appeals. Until the divorce becomes effective, therefore, the parties are still married.

---

82 (1986), 22 E.T.R. 150 at 151.
83 The legislation is retrospective in operation: *Page Estate v. Sachs* (1993), 49 E.T.R. 1 (Ont. C.A.).
84 R.S.C. 1985, c. 3 (2nd Supp.), in force June 1, 1986.

Section 17(2) speaks of a "judgment absolute of divorce". This is a reference to the former practice.[85]

4. In view of modern matrimonial property law reform legislation which entitles a spouse to an equalization claim on a breakdown of the marriage,[86] should the dissolution of marriage exception be extended to cases such as breakdown of marriage?

5. You should note that the legislation has only partially reversed the common law. Thus, for example, if a testator leaves a gift by will "to X's spouse" and X subsequently obtains a divorce, X's spouse is still entitled to the gift. Moreover, if X subsequently remarried, his or her second spouse would not be entitled to the gift in the absence of a contrary intention in the will. Is this appropriate? What does it suggest about drafting such gifts?

6. What is the purpose and effect of the last clause of section 17(2) of the *Succession Law Reform Act*, "and the will shall be construed as if the former spouse had predeceased the testator"? Would the former spouse otherwise have rights of inheritance? Consider this question in the context of a gift "To my wife for life, remainder to my children living at her death."[87]

7. The English legislation was amended in 1982. The new legislation is like s. 17(2).[88] The amendment was interpreted in *Re Sinclair (decd), Lloyds Bank plc. v. Imperial Cancer Research Foundation*.[89] The testator left all his estate to his wife but if she should predecease him or fail to survive him for one month, then to the appellant research foundation. The parties were later divorced. The court held that since the English legislation does not say that the will shall be construed as if the former spouse had predeceased the testator, but merely that the gift to the former spouse shall lapse, the gift to the research foundation could not take effect, since it was contingent on the wife predeceasing the testator or dying within one month after him. The word "lapse" was not sufficient to deem the spouse to have predeceased the testator.[90]

---

85 Under the former divorce practice, the successful applicant was first awarded a decree *nisi* of divorce, followed three months later by a decree absolute if the other party had not appealed. Hence, if the testator died after a decree *nisi* and before the decree absolute, the gift to his "wife" was not revoked: *Re Kindl* (1982), 39 O.R. (2d) 219, 31 R.F.L. (2d) 11, 13 E.T.R. 101, 140 D.L.R. (3d) 92 (H.C.). Until the decree absolute was obtained, the wife was still the wife of the testator and, if he died before the decree absolute, she was his widow: *Re Laur* (1975), 7 O.R. (2d) 385, 21 R.F.L. 159, 55 D.L.R. (3d) 321 (Surr. Ct.).

86 See, *e.g., Family Law Act*, R.S.O. 1990, c. F.3, Part I. Statutes in other provinces typically give the spouses a right to a share in the matrimonial property on a breakdown of the marriage.

87 See also *Succession Law Reform Act*, s. 57 (am. S.O. 1999, c. 6, s. 61) which defines "spouse" to include a former spouse and "dependant" to include a spouse. The effect of this legislation is that a former spouse can, in certain circumstances, claim support out of the deceased's estate.

88 By the *Administration of Justice Act 1982*, c. 53 (U.K.), s. 18(2), which added s. 18A to the *Wills Act, 1837*, 7 Will. 4 & 1 Vict. c. 26.

89 [1985] 1 All E.R. 1066 (C.A.).

90 See R.J. Mitchell, "Will Drafting after the Succession Act — Divorce, Survivorship and Second Death Legacies", [1996] Conv. 112.

4. REVOCATION BY ACT OF THE TESTATOR

(a) Generally

A will may also be revoked by the testator. The testator may revoke it by a subsequent document in which he or she declares an intention to revoke it, such as a new will, or a codicil. Alternatively, the testator my revoke the will by destroying it. Printed wills and professionally drawn wills invariably commence with a revocation of all previous testamentary documents.

These methods of revocation are discussed in the following material. The statutory rules regarding revocation by the testator are reproduced below.

SUCCESSION LAW REFORM ACT
R.S.O. 1990, c. S.26

15. A will or part of a will is revoked only by,

. . .

(b) another will made in accordance with the provisions of this Part; [or]
(c) a writing,
    (i) declaring an intention to revoke, and
    (ii) made in accordance with the provisions of this Part governing making
        of a will . . . .

Comparable Legislation

Probate Act, R.S.P.E.I. 1988, c. P-21, s. 72; *Wills Act*, R.S.A. 1980, c. W-11, s. 16(b), (c); R.S.B.C. 1996, c. 489, s. 14(1)(b),(c); R.S.M. 1988, c. W150, s. 16(b), (c); R.S.N.B. 1973, c. W-9, s. 15; R.S.N. 1990, c. W-10, s. 11(a), (b); R.S.N.S. 1989, c. 505, s. 19(b), (c); R.S.N.W.T. 1988, c. W-5, s. 11(2)(b), (c); S.S 1996, c. W-14.1, s. 16(b), (c); R.S.Y. 1986, c. 179, c. 10(2)(b), (c).

(b) By Subsequent Document

The statutory provisions regarding revocation by a subsequent document contemplate both a subsequent will (which includes a codicil)[91] and any other document, provided it is made in accordance with the statutory formalities required to make a will and the document declares an intention to revoke.[92] The legislation permits the revocation of a formal will by a holograph will, or a privileged will.[93]

Although the statute permits revocation by a writing declaring an intention to revoke, it is not necessary that the testator in a subsequent will or codicil declare

---

91 *Succession Law Reform Act*, s. 1(1)(g).
92 Such a document is not admitted to probate if it contains no dispositive provisions: *Re Fraser* (1869), L.R. 2 P. & D. 40.
93 *Re Gossage*, [1921] P. 194, [1921] All E.R. Rep. 107 (C.A.).

that he or she is revoking his or her previous wills. Most formal wills do so, but if a will does not, it is still apt to revoke a former will if that was the testator's intention. Such a revocation can be effective even though the subsequent will does not dispose of the testator's entire estate.[94] Evidence of surrounding circumstances and direct evidence of the testator's intention is admissible for the purpose of ascertaining his or her intention.[95] Normally, however, if there is no express revocation clause, both testamentary documents are admitted to probate and the first is regarded as having been revoked to the extent that it is inconsistent with the second. This is an implied revocation and the effect of such a revocation is discussed in *Re Davies*[96] reproduced below.

An express revocation arises when the testator states his or her intention to revoke a previous testamentary document. Such a revocation is normally effective. However, ultimately it depends upon whether the testator intended to revoke his or her former wills. If the testator did not intend to do so, the express revocation clause is disregarded.[97]

Clearly, a revocation, whether express or implied can revoke either a whole will or part thereof.

RE DAVIES
[1928] Ch. 24
Chancery Division

By clause 8 of his will, the testator devised "all my farms and lands in the parish of Bedwas in the County of Monmouth" upon trust for the defendant. Subsequently, the testator made a codicil in which he recited that he had bought further property (Farm A) in the parish of Bedwas. He devised it to his daughter for life, remainder to his grandson. The remainder failed.[98] The question was whether that farm passed under clause 8 or fell into residue.

ASTBURY J.:

. . .

Here the testator devises "all my farms and lands in the parish of Bedwas" on the trusts of clause 8. That must mean what it says — namely, that all the testator's farms and lands in Bedwas at his death so far as not otherwise disposed of are to pass under clause 8. By his codicil he recites the purchase of Farm A and devises it on trusts that partially fail. But Farm A being a farm in Bedwas not effectually otherwise disposed of has not ceased to be a farm at Bedwas within the meaning of clause 8.

---

94 *McPherson v. Can. Trust Co.*, [1941] O.W.N. 65, [1941] 2 D.L.R. 788; *Re Fitzsimmons*, [1939] 2 D.L.R. 50, 13 M.P.R. 429 (N.S.C.A.).

95 *Cottrell v. Cottrell* (1872), L.R. 2 P. & D. 397.

96 [1928] Ch. 24.

97 *Re Phelan*, [1972] Fam. 33. And see *Re Johannson* (1978), 3 E.T.R. 206 (Sask. Surr. Ct.).

98 The remainder was actually given to the grandson in tail. The remainder failed because the grandson predeceased his mother without issue and with the entail unbarred. The testator did not dispose of the fee simple estate.

There are numerous authorities on this point, but I need only refer to two.

In *Ward v. Van der Loeff*[99] a testator gave his residuary estate to trustees upon trust for his wife for life and after her decease, in default of children which happened, upon trust for his brothers' and sisters' children as his wife should appoint and in default of appointment upon trust for all those children in equal shares. By a codicil the testator revoked the wife's power of appointment and gave his residue after her death on trusts void for remoteness. It was held that, the gift in the codicil being inoperative, there was no implied revocation of the gift in the will, which therefore took effect. Viscount Cave said:[100]

> I conclude, therefore, that the gift in the codicil is void; and it remains to consider whether the gift in the will fails also. In my opinion it does not. The codicil, while it expressly revokes the power of appointment given to the testator's wife by the will, contains no words of revocation affecting the gift in default of appointment. No doubt, if the gift in the codicil had taken effect, it would have superseded and to that extent would have impliedly revoked the gift in the will; but the implication of revocation is found only in the terms of the substituted trust and if that trust falls to the ground the implied revocation falls with it.

That is exactly applicable to the present case. Lord Dunedin said:[101]

> If when a subject has been disposed of in a will and the same subject is again disposed of, either in a subsequent will or in a codicil, then if you can find, apart from the description of the subject, words expressly or impliedly effecting revocation, that revocation will stand, whatever the fate of the subsequent disposition; but if the only revocation is that . . . . to be gathered from the inconsistency of the subsequent disposition with the earlier one, then if the second disposition fails from any reason to be efficacious there will be no revocation.

That again applied to the present case, because the residuary legatees are faced with a devise of "all the farms" in Bedwas followed by a subsequent ineffectual disposition of Farm A in that parish.

I am really asked to read the codicil as a devise of Farm A and clause 8 as a devise of the rest of the farms in Bedwas. That is exactly what clause 8 does not say. It is a devise of all the farms in Bedwas. The codicil merely devises one farm there on trusts partially inoperative. To the extent that the codicil is effective, clause 8 is revoked but to that extent only, and I cannot see any ground for saying that Farm A, so far as not taken out of clause 8, does not pass by that clause.

. . .

In *Doe v. Marchant*[102] a testatrix gave the ultimate remainder of all her lands in the events that happened to her granddaughter Betty Jones in fee. By a codicil "instead of" that devise she gave her a life interest, with remainders over that failed, but with no ultimate remainder in fee. It was held that the ultimate remainder in the will was unaffected by the codicil. Tindal C.J., delivering the judgment of the Court of Commons Pleas, said:

---

99 [1924] A.C. 653.
100 *Ibid.*, at p. 665.
101 *Ibid.*, at p. 671.
102 6 Man. & G. 813, 826.

But the codicil does not go on to dispose of the ultimate fee, in case the intermediate remainders should, as the fact has proved, never take effect. But, as this ultimate fee is given by the will to Betty Jones, it appears to us that such disposition of the fee in the will being unaltered by the codicil, must still be considered as taking effect. The argument on the part of the plaintiff has been, that inasmuch as the devise in the codicil is expressly given to Betty Jones 'instead of' the devise and bequest contained in the will, it must be considered as an express revocation of the former devise, and the substitution of that contained in the codicil. But we think the force of that word will be satisfied without giving it so large an operation; and that it may well be interpreted to mean "instead of so much only of" the devise in the will as is incompatible with the disposition contained in the codicil. And this appears to us the sounder construction, as it is the manifest intention of the testatrix, both in the will and codicil, to make Betty Jones the principal object of her bounty.

In the present case clause 8 contains a clear and plain devise of "all my farms and lands" in Bedwas and so far as that devise is not altered by the codicil, the gift remains. The undisposed of interest in Farm A therefore passes under clause 8.

. . .

Notes and Questions

1. From the quotations from Lord Dunedin's speech in *Ward v. Van der Loeff*,[103] relied upon in *Re Davies*, it will be seen that His Lordship regarded an implied revocation not as one in which the provisions of the two documents are inconsistent, but as one in which it can be deduced from the testator's language (which falls short of an express statement, such as "I revoke") that the testator intended to revoke the previous will or part thereof. Hence, an implied revocation as that term was used by His Lordship is one that, after construction, is equivalent to an express one.

2. It also appears from *Re Davies* that once a will or part thereof has been expressly revoked, it remains revoked even though the subsequent gift fails, whereas, if there is merely an inconsistency between the two documents and the gift in the last one fails, the gift in the first stands unrevoked.

3. What is the effect of a gift in a subsequent will or codicil that is inconsistent with a gift in the first will if the spouse of the beneficiary in the subsequent document attests it?[104] Would there be any difference if the subsequent document contains an express revocation clause?

What effect would a subsequent document have upon an earlier will, either if the subsequent document contains an express revocation clause, or if it is inconsistent with the earlier will, if the subsequent document was improperly executed in that one witness signs first, then the testator and then the second witness?

4. A testator made three successive wills on printed will forms, intending them to have cumulative effect. However, each contained an express revocation clause. Are the first two wills revoked?[105]

5. The fact that a will commences with the words "This is my last will," or words of similar import, does not have the effect of revoking it, unless that is the testator's inten-

---

103 [1924] A.C. 653 at 671 (H.C.).
104 See *Re Robinson*, [1930] 2 Ch. 332.
105 See *Re Phelan*, [1972] Fam. 33.

tion.[106] However, if the second will disposes of all the testator's estate, even though it does not appoint an executor, while the first one did, the first is *prima facie* revoked.[107]

On the other hand, the second will may be construed as a codicil to the first. This occurred in *Matzelle Estate v. Father Bernard Prince Society of the Precious Blood*.[108] The testatrix had left the residue of her estate by her professionally drawn will to her nephews and nieces. Then she executed a handwritten will on a standard form. It listed bequests to religious organizations, followed by the words "and to all my nephews and nieces." Having regard to the surrounding circumstances, the court held that the later will was intended as a codicil to the first and that the revocation clause in the second did not express the testatrix's intention, so it could be ignored.

6. Section 23 of the Manitoba Act,[109] reproduced in the previous chapter, permits the court to make an order declaring that, if a document embodies the deceased's intention to revoke, alter or revive a will, it is effective, even though it was not executed in accordance with the statutory formalities. Is this kind of dispensing power a desirable provision?

7. A testatrix had made an attested will consisting of five pages. Several years later, she wrote the word "Cancelled," the date and her signature diagonally across each page. Is the will revoked?[110]

8. Clearly an oral declaration is insufficient to effect a revocation.[111]

(c) By Physical Act

(i) *Generally*

If a will is destroyed *animo revocandi*, it will be revoked. However, it must actually be destroyed. In other words, there must both be an actual destruction and an intention to revoke. Further, the two must coincide.[112] Thus, a testator cannot subsequently ratify a prior destruction.[113]

There are two ways in which a will may be revoked by physical act, namely, by the testator or by someone else on the testator's behalf. The statutory provision is reproduced below. The two methods are discussed in the following materials.

---

106 *Lemage v. Goodban* (1865), L.R. 1 P. & D. 57; *Re Dunfield* (1955), 63 Man. R. 293; *Re De la Saussaye* (1873), L.R. 3 P. & D. 42.

107 *Henfrey v. Henfrey* (1842), 4 Moo. P.C. 29, 13 E.R. 211; *Re Welburn* (1980), 8 E.T.R. 137 (Alta. Surr. Ct.).

108 (1996), 11 E.T.R. (2d) 78 (Ont. Gen. Div.).

109 *Wills Act*, R.S.M. 1988, c. W150. And see to the same effect, *Probate Act*, R.S.P.E.I. 1988, c. P-21, s. 70; *Wills Act*, R.S.S. 1978, c. W-14, s. 35.1 [am. 1989, c. 66, s. 9].

110 See *Bishop Estate v. Reesor* (1990), 39 E.T.R. 36 (Ont. H.C.); and see *Canada Trust Co. v. Foster* (1991), 40 E.T.R. 221 (Ont. Gen. Div.). For a similar case in which the testator wrote words of cancellation on his solicitor's account and signed it, see *Morrison v. Owen* (1991), 44 E.T.R. 290 (Ont. Gen. Div.).

111 *Re McLean Estate* (1992), 47 E.T.R. 310 (Sask. Surr. Ct.).

112 *Cheese v. Lovejoy* (1877), 2 P.D. 251 at 253.

113 *Gill v. Gill*, [1909] P. 157; *Re Booth; Booth v. Booth*, [1926] P. 118.

SUCCESSION LAW REFORM ACT
R.S.O. 1990, c. S.26

to be revoked

15. A will or part of a will is destroyed only by,

. . .

(d) burning, tearing or otherwise destroying it by the testator or by some person in his or her presence and by his or her direction with the intention of revoking it.

Comparable Legislation

Probate Act, R.S.P.E.I. 1988, c. P-21, s. 72; *Wills Act*, R.S.A. 1980, c. W-11, s. 16(d); R.S.B.C. 1996 c. 489, s. 14(1)(d); R.S.M. 1988, c. W150, s. 16(d); R.S.N.B. 1973, c. W-9, s. 15(d); R.S.N. 1990, c. W-10, s. 11(d); R.S.N.S. 1989, c. 505, s. 19(d); R.S.N.W.T. 1988, c. W-5, s. 11(2)(d); S.S 1996, c. W-14.1, s. 16(d); R.S.Y. 1986, c. 179, c. 10(2)(b), (c).

(ii) *By the Testator*

A testator who is minded to revoke a will does not have to execute a new one in order to revoke it, but can destroy it. There must normally be a complete destruction, however. If there is not, the will may not be revoked. Thus, for example, if the will is partly torn, but the contents remain legible, there is a presumption that the tearing was done by the testator, but the burden of proving that it was done *animo revocandi* is on the person alleging revocation.[114] Similarly, if portions of the will are cut out, the will is not revoked (except to the extent of the parts cut out),[115] unless the rest of the will cannot stand without the parts cut out. Cutting off the testator's or a witness' signature effectively revokes the will.[116]

It often happens that a testator wishes to vary the will. If the change is not a significant one, the best way to do so is by codicil. However, sometimes a testator will remove the relevant page from the will, insert the corrected page and have it executed. Is this effective? *Leonard v. Leonard*,[117] reproduced below, deals with this question.

LEONARD v. LEONARD
[1902] P. 243
Probate Division

The testator made his will in 1900. It consisted of five pages, but in the following years he had sheets one and two re-engrossed. All of the sheets were signed by

---

114 *Re Cowling*, [1924] P. 113, [1924] All E.R. Rep. 469.
115 *Re Shafner* (1956), 38 M.P.R. 217, 2 D.L.R. (2d) 593 (N.S.C.A.).
116 *Evans v. Dallow* (1862), 31 L.J.P. 128.
117 [1902] P. 243.

the testator and the same two witnesses. On the application for probate it was argued by some that the will should be admitted in its entirety or not at all, and by others that only sheets one and two should be admitted.

GORELL BARNES J.:

. . .

There are two questions to decide. The first is a question or questions of fact; the second, what is the law to be applied to the facts. Perhaps this question of law is in reality a mixed question of law and fact.

The questions of fact I have already determined. My view of the document before me is that the sheets 3, 4, and 5 are three of the original sheets of the will executed on June 16, 1900. I have already indicated that my view is formed partly from the evidence of the witnesses and partly from the evidence of the document itself, which, as pointed out by the law scrivener, has three cuts on the last three pages, shewing that they were originally fastened by means of those three cuts, while there are only two cuts on the pages 1 and 2. I have also found as a fact that the pages 1 and 2 are the pages signed by the deceased on or about December 9, 1901. Those findings of fact lead to the questions of law which have now been fully argued.

It is, I think, obvious that the deceased destroyed the first two pages of the will as it was originally executed, before the date when pages 1 and 2 as they now appear were signed by him and by the witnesses. That is I think, a fair inference to draw. What, then, has been the effect on the last three sheets of the destruction of the original first two sheets? The destruction, of course, revoked the operation of the two sheets destroyed - that is, of sheets 1 and 2 as they originally stood. I am of opinion that the question of the effect of that destruction on the last three sheets of the document must be decided according to the principles indicated in *Clarke v. Scripps*[118] and *In the Goods of Woodward*[119] the effect of which is neatly expressed in the passage cited by Mr. Russell from Theobald on Wills.[120]

Applying the principles to be gathered from those cases, I am of opinion from an examination of the last three sheets of this document, that they are practically unintelligible and unworkable as a testamentary document in the absence of the original sheets 1 and 2, and that the destruction of sheets 1 and 2 must be taken as having had the effect of destroying the validity of the whole will. The testator must be taken to have intended what his act would necessarily lead one to conclude as to his intention: having destroyed the earlier portions - pages 1 and 2 - he must have intended to revoke also the remaining portions - pages 3, 4, and 5. He did not intend these last three pages to be his operative will without doing something more. He intended to put two other sheets on to them. Up to that point the will was in my opinion, legally revoked.

---

118 2 Rob. 563.
119 L.R. 2 P. & M. 206.
120 5th ed., p. 48.

In December, 1901, he signed, and caused the witnesses also to sign, the first two sheets — pages 1 and 2 — of the document before me. Thereupon arises the question, What was the effect of that?

Here, again, I think there is ample authority for coming to a conclusion which is partly one of fact and partly of law.

The first authority on the point is *Ewen v. Franklin.*[121] The next is *Sweetland v. Sweetland,*[122] where, taking a similar view, Sir J.P. Wilde said:

> The first difficulty is, quo animo did the testator sign the fifth sheet? Ordinarily such a signature would be, I think, "intended to guard against other sheets being interpolated." So said Sir John Dodson in *Ewen v. Franklin.*[123] Certainly no one would, on the face of the will, conclude that it was intended as the final signature by which the testator's affirmation of the will was to be signified.

In that case, the fifth was not the last sheet. The will had been written on six sheets, and the testator had signed the first five, but had not signed the sixth. Another authority is *Phipps v. Hale,*[124] where Sir James Hannen specially referred to *Ewen v. Franklin.*

It becomes, therefore, a question whether, at the time the deceased in the present case signed and caused the witnesses to put their signature to these two pages (1 and 2), he did that as his will or part of his will, or simply to shew that they formed part of a will to which the signature at the end of the will was to give validity.

In my opinion those signatures were only put on the two pages in question to identify them, and to make them valid if the will was valid at the end. That was, unfortunately, an abortive act. The later sheets had no effect by themselves, and they had no effect to render the sheets 1 and 2 operative.

The result is that none of the sheets can be treated as a valid document of a testamentary character, and my judgment — unfortunate, I am afraid, for some of the parties — must be that this will must be pronounced against, and, if there is no other will, there will be an intestacy as to the whole of the deceased's estate.

. . .

Notes and Questions

1. For a case involving somewhat similar facts, but which did not involve a revocation, see *Re Ireland.*[125] Page two of the will had (probably because of an oversight) not been signed originally. Moreover, it had been typed at a different time and it was signed with a different pen. Nevertheless, it was admitted to probate.

2. What would have happened in *Leonard v. Leonard* if pages 3, 4 and 5 had been intelligible on their own?

3. What should the testator have done in *Leonard v. Leonard* in order to ensure that the entire will was valid?

---

121 (1855), Deane's Ecc. 7.
122 34 L.J. (P. & M.) 42; 4 Sw. & Tr. 6, 8.
123 *Supra.*
124 (1874), L.R. 3 P. & M. 166.
125 (1983), 44 B.C.L.R. 215, 15 E.T.R. 69, 147 D.L.R. (3d) 480 (C.A.), additional reasons at 47 B.C.L.R. 222, 15 E.T.R. 1, 147 D.L.R. (3d) 480 at 485.

4. In *Leonard v. Leonard*, Gorell Barnes J. stated at the beginning of his reasons: "This case is a remarkable illustration of the danger of testators meddling with their wills when once they have executed them." What can solicitors do as a practical matter to prevent this problem? Do they have any duty toward the beneficiaries in this respect?

5. The legislation only speaks of "burning, tearing or otherwise destroying" a will. The last of the triad must be read *ejusdem generis* with the first two. It follows, therefore, that when a testator merely draws a line through the dispositions in the will and writes on the back "All these are revoked," but keeps the will, the will is not revoked.[126] As James L.J., said in *Cheese v. Lovejoy:*[127]

> It is quite clear that a symbolical burning will not do, a symbolical tearing will not do, nor will a symbolical destruction.

And, quoting Dr. Deane in the lower court:

> All the destroying in the world without intention will not revoke a will, nor all the intentions in the world without destroying: there must be the two.

6. A testator executed his will in duplicate and subsequently destroyed one copy. Is the will revoked?[128]

7. A testatrix's signature on the will was obliterated, so that it was no longer apparent. Is the will revoked?[129]

8. If a testator revokes his will are any codicils thereto *ipso facto* revoked?[130] Consider the language of the statute in answering this question.

9. There is presumption that, if a will is last traced into the possession of the testator, but cannot be found after his or her death, it has been destroyed by the testator *animo revocandi.*[131] The presumption can be rebutted by appropriate evidence, such as destruction in an accidental fire.[132] The presumption does not apply, however, if the testator loses capacity after execution of the will,[133] for the testator cannot form the intent to revoke if his or her intellectual capacity and capacity for judgment are impaired.[134] In those circumstances, therefore, those who allege that it was destroyed while the testator was of sound mind must prove it.[135]

---

126 (1877), 2 P.D. 251 (C.A.).

127 *Ibid.*, at p. 253. See also *Re Mulholland and Van den Berg* (1915), 34 O.L.R. 242, 24 D.L.R. 785; *Bell v. Mathewman* (1920), 48 O.L.R. 364.

128 See *Re Anderson*, [1933] O.R. 131, [1933] 1 D.L.R. 581 (C.A.).

129 See *Re Adams (decd)*, [1990] 2 All E.R. 97 (Ch. D.).

130 *Black v. Jobling* (1869), L.R. 1 P. & D. 685; *Gardiner v. Courthope* (1886), 12 P.D. 14; *Re Formaniuk; Pitz v. Kasjau* (1963), 44 W.W.R. 686, 42 D.L.R. (2d) 78 (Man. C.A.).

131 *Kennedy v. Peikoff* (1966), 56 W.W.R. 381 (Man. C.A); *Re Weeks*, [1972] 3 O.R. 422, 28 D.L.R. (3d) 452; *Re Dreger* (1982), 13 E.T.R. 212, 38 A.R. 44 (N.W.T.S.C.); *Re Wherry Estate* (1991), 41 E.T.R. 146 (B.C.S.C.). If the testator did not have custody, the presumption does not arise: *Re Goudge* (1979), 26 N.B.R. (2d) 258, 55 A.P.R. 258 (Prob. Ct.); *Brimicombe v. Brimicombe Estate* (2000), 34 E.T.R. (2d) 14 (N.S.C.A.).

132 See *Re Perry* 56 O.L.R. 278, [1925] 1 D.L.R. 930 (C.A.).

133 *Re Broome* (1961), 35 W.W.R. 590, 29 D.L.R. (2d) 631 (Man. C.A.); *Re Whitelaw* (1985), 61 A.R. 96 (Q.B.).

134 *Re McGinn* (1969), 70 W.W.R. 159 (Alta. T.D.).

135 *Re Broome, supra.*

10. A will destroyed by the testator under a mistake of fact or law, or by mistake or accident, is not revoked.[136]

(iii) *By Another*

It often happens that the testator has left the will with another person for safekeeping. Thus, for example, wills are often left with the solicitor who prepared them. Suppose, then, that the testator wishes to revoke the will without making a new one. It would be a simple matter for the testator to instruct the solicitor to destroy the existing will. However, the statute requires that if another person destroys the will, it must be done in the presence of the testator and at his or her direction. *DeLack, Hickey and Camp v. Newton*,[137] reproduced below, deals with this issue.

DELACK, HICKEY AND CAMP v. NEWTON
[1944] O.W.N. 517
Ontario Surrogate Court
[County of Frontenac]

The testatrix made her will and asked a neighbour and her daughter to attest it, having told them that the document was her will, and they did so. The witnesses were unable to testify that they saw the testatrix execute the will, but thought that her signature was on it. The testatrix then sent the will to her sister in a sealed envelope, marked "Not to be opened until my death." Subsequently the testatrix made a new will and sent it to her sister with a letter, asking her to destroy the previous one. The sister, together with another sister, compared the two wills and testified that the testatrix had left all her property to the two sisters and a brother and that the only real difference between the two wills was a change in executors. The first sister then destroyed the original will.

When the brother and sisters tried to probate the second will, it was found that it was not validly executed. They then sought to establish the contents of the first will.

REYNOLDS SURR. CT. J.:

. . .

> [His Honour first discussed the law respecting proof of the contents of lost wills and, accepting the evidence of the witnesses, concluded that the contents of the first will were proved beyond peradventure. His Honour continued:]

The second question for determination is: Was the first will lawfully revoked? The requirements as to the revocation of a will are contained in s. 22 of The Wills Act.[138]

---

136 See, *e.g.*, *Re Thornton* (1889), 14 P.D. 82; *Re Southerden*, [1925] P. 177 (C.A.).
137 [1944] O.W.N. 517 (Surr. Ct.).
138 R.S.O. 1937, c. 164.

[His Honour quoted section 22 which is in substance the same as section 15 of the *Succession Law Reform Act*, reproduced above, and continued:]

Since the 1939 will, which contained a provision revoking former wills, has been held to have been improperly executed, and as the act of destruction of the first will was not done in the presence of the testatrix, the requirements of The Wills Act have not been complied with. The first will, if duly executed, therefore stands unrevoked.

It is in respect of this question of due execution that the real issue in the case is raised. I may state that there is practically no dispute as to the facts, and that the problem presented is only to apply the principles laid down in the decisions to which I will refer as to the effect of testimony of witnesses whose memories as to execution of a will are uncertain and imperfect.

. . .

In the case at bar, although neither witness states that the testatrix signed in her presence, acknowledgment of the will may be assumed by the fact that the testatrix asked the witnesses to sign a document which she said was the will. In Jarman on Wills,[139] it is said:

When the witnesses either saw or might have seen the signature, an express acknowledgment of the signature itself is not necessary, a mere statement that the paper is his will, or a direction to them to put their names under his, or even a request by the testator, or by some person in his presence, to sign the paper, is sufficient.

. . .

In this action, after carefully considering the evidence of the two witnesses, Mrs. Lewis and Mrs. Detler, I am of the opinion that there is nothing in their testimony which rebuts the presumption *omnia praesumuntur rite esse acta*. The cases show that the validity of execution does not depend upon the recollection of the attesting witnesses, and that the Court is entitled to infer that all due formalities were observed, and that what was intended to be done was done as it ought to have been done.

. . .

Notes and Questions

1. The testator's wife tore up her husband's will in a fit of temper when he was drunk. He treated it as a joke and did not make a new will.

Was the will revoked? If it was not, can the testator subsequently ratify the destruction?[140]

2. The testator made a holograph will in which he gave his estate to his friend, X. When X visited him, the testator gave X the document and asked him to take care of it for him. X took the document, but returned it the next day and, in the testator's presence, but not at his direction, tore the document in two and left the pieces on the table. The testator died

---

139 7th ed., p. 102.
140 See *Gill v. Gill*, [1909] P. 157.

two days later. The pieces of the will were found in a plastic shopping bag together with some garbage. X now wants to have the document probated. Can it be?[141]

5. ALTERATIONS IN A WILL

Testators often change their minds about testamentary provisions they have made and, if left to their own devices, may simply cross out an original provision and replace it with another. Such an alteration is not effective, however, unless it complies with the statutory requirements regarding alterations.[142] If the alteration is effective under the statute, the original provision is revoked.

There is a presumption that any apparent changes in a will were made after the will was executed.[143] Hence, the onus is on those who allege that the changes existed when the will was executed to prove the allegation.[144] The matter may be proved by any appropriate evidence,[145] including direct evidence of the testator's intention.[146]

In order to avoid any problems, the will should be retyped or, if that is inconvenient, the alterations made before execution should be executed and altered in accordance with the statute. The initials of the testator and the witnesses in the margin opposite the alteration suffice for this purpose.[147]

The statutory requirements regarding alterations are set out below.

A special problem arises when the alteration, although not signed and attested, obliterates the original words. In those circumstances the original words are effectively revoked. *Re Douglas Estate*,[148] reproduced below, deals with this issue.

SUCCESSION LAW REFORM ACT
R.S.O 1990, c. S.26

18. (1) Subject to subsection (2), unless an alteration that is made in a will after the will has been made is made in accordance with the provisions of this Part

---

141 See *Re Krushel Estate* (1990), 40 E.T.R. 129 (Ont. Gen. Div.).

142 In *Hubley v. Cox Estate* (1999), 31 E.T.R. (2d) 71 (N.S.S.C.) the court held that an alteration was ineffective because it was not executed in accordance with the statute. It was executed in the presence of only one witness. A second witness was later asked to execute the alteration, but the testatrix and the first witness did not first sign again.

143 *Law v. Law* (1989), 33 E.T.R. 183 (Ont. H.C.); *Re Scott* (1995), 8 E.T.R. (2d) 33 (Man. Q.B.); *Re Murphy Estate* (1999), 26 E.T.R. (2d) 167 (N.S. Prob. Ct.); *Re Brown* (1999), 27 E.T.R. (2d) 215 (Nfld. T.D.).

144 *Re East* (1923), 24 O.W.N. 394; *Re Thorne*, [1941] 1 W.W.R. 185, [1941] 1 D.L.R. 789 (Alta. T.D.); *Re Bowerman* (1978), 20 O.R. (2d) 374, 87 D.L.R. (3d) 597 (Surr. Ct.).

145 See, *e.g.*, *Gislason v. Gillis* (1988), 31 E.T.R. 6 (Man. C.A.), admitting the evidence of a document expert.

146 *Re Adamson* (1875), L.R. 3 P. & D. 253.

147 *Re Pattulla* (1955), 17 W.W.R. 667, 1 D.L.R. (2d) 237 (B.C.S.C.). See also the substantial compliance provisions in the Manitoba, Prince Edward Island and Saskatchewan statutes, discussed in the chapter on Formal Validity.

148 (1986), 25 E.T.R. 154 (Nfld. T.D.).

governing making of the will, the alteration has no effect except to invalidate words or the effect of the will that it renders no longer apparent.

(2) An alteration that is made in a will after the will has been made is validly made when the signature of the testator and subscription of witnesses to the signature of the testator to the alteration, or, in the case of a will that was made under section 5 or 6, the signature of the testator, are or is made,

  (a) in the margin or in some other part of the will opposite or near to the alteration; or

  (b) at the end of or opposite to a memorandum referring to the alteration and written in some part of the will.

Comparable Legislation

Probate Act, R.S.P.E.I. 1988, c. P-21, s. 73; *Wills Act*, R.S.A. 1980, c. W-11, s. 19; R.S.B.C. 1996, c. 489, s. 17; R.S.M. 1988, c. W150, s. 19; R.S.N.B. 1973, c. W-9, s. 18; R.S.N. 1990, c. W-10, s. 12; R.S.N.S. 1989, c. 505, s. 20; R.S.N.W.T. 1988, c. W-5, s. 12; S.S. 1996, c. W-14.1, s. 11; R.S.Y. 1986, c. 179, s. 11.

RE DOUGLAS ESTATE
(1986), 25 E.T.R. 154
Newfoundland Supreme Court
[Trial Division]

Clause 4 of the testator's will provided that if his wife predeceased him or died within 30 days after his death, all his property was to go to "my son, Leslie, if at the time of our deaths he needs the house in which to live, otherwise it is to be sold and the proceeds to" be divided equally among three named children. Prior to his death the testator had covered the quoted words with liquid paper correction fluid. He did not sign or initial the obliteration.

The executrix sought to prove the will, including the obliterated words on the ground that they were still legible.

STEELE J.:

. . .

[His Lordship set out in s. 12 of the *Wills Act*,[149] which is the same as the Ontario legislation in substance, and continued:]

I am concerned, therefore, with an obliteration that was an unexecuted alteration. The meaning of the term "apparent" becomes critical.

In ascertaining the meaning of s. 12 of our Wills Act, I have referred to the old English case of *Ffinch v. Combe*.[150] That was heard in the Probate, Divorce and

---

149 R.S.N. 1990, c. 401.
150 [1894] P. 191, 70 L.T. 695.

Admiralty Division of the Court before the President, Sir F.H. Jeune. The explanation of the section and the question posed is expressed in the following manner by the President:[151]

> The 21st section deals with obliterations, interlineations, or other alterations in the will made after the execution thereof. It might have been supposed that the Legislature would have provided that if it was clear that by such alteration the testator intended to bring about a partial revocation of his will, his intention should be carried out by his act of alteration. But that is not the provision which the Legislature has made. It is enacted that such alteration, whatever the intention of the testator in making it, shall be effectual only if the words or effect of the will before alteration be not apparent, and shall be wholly ineffectual if such words or effect be not apparent. *If, then, the words before alteration are apparent, they must be taken to form part of the testamentary disposition; but if they are not apparent, no extrinsic evidence can be admitted to show what in fact they were.* The difficulty in the present and in several cases which have been decided, is, What is the meaning of the word "apparent" within this section? (My emphasis added)

In *Ffinch v. Combe* reference is made to s. 21 of the *Wills Act, 1837*.[152] The language is sufficiently similar to s. 12 of our Wills Act that the two sections can be considered as being the same.

. . .

The alteration, not executed as required by the Wills Act, forces the question of whether the words before the alteration are "apparent". If the words are decipherable or apparent, they will be restored to the will and included in the will and grant of probate; if the words are not legible or apparent, extrinsic evidence cannot be adduced to establish what they were and the blank space remains, the will to be admitted to probate in that state.

. . .

A...concise meaning of the term "apparent" is found in Theobald, Wills:[153]

> **The test of being not apparent.** "Apparent" in section 21 means optically apparent on the face of the will itself. A word or phrase in a will is not apparent if an expert cannot decipher it by any "natural" means, such as holding the paper up to the light with a frame of brown paper around the portion attempted to be read or by using magnifying glasses. In determining whether a word is apparent it is not permissible to ascertain the word by the use of extrinsic evidence, or by physically interfering with the will by, for instance, using chemicals to remove ink-marks or removing a slip of paper pasted over the word, or by making another document, such as an infrared photograph. If the word can only be ascertained by these "forbidden" methods it is not apparent.

In the matter at hand I am satisfied that the original words cannot be deciphered; the effaced words are not legible. The obliteration by use of the liquid paper correction fluid is absolute and total. I find as a fact that the obliteration appearing in para. 4 of the testator's will is complete and that "the words or effect of the will before such alteration", are not apparent. That being so extrinsic evidence is not admissible to establish what the missing words may have been and probate of the will must proceed with a blank space in the place of the obliterated words.

---

151 At p. 695 L.T.
152 7 Will. 4 & 1 Vict., c. 26 (U.K.).
153 14th ed., 1982, at p. 64 (footnotes omitted).

Notes and Questions

1. As appears from *Re Douglas Estate*, it is not permissible to use artificial means to ascertain what was written beneath the obliteration. Thus, in *Re Itter*[154] the court refused to permit a handwriting expert to say what was underneath strips of paper pasted over the amounts of certain legacies. He was able to determine what was underneath only by making an infra-red photograph. In those circumstances, the court held, the original amounts were not apparent on the face of the instrument.

For the same reason, chemicals cannot be used[155] to render an obliteration apparent, or, indeed, any extrinsic evidence,[156] or physical interference with the document.[157]

2. In *Ffinch v. Combe*,[158] referred to in the *Douglas* case, the testator had pasted strips of paper over certain words. The will granted probate of the will without those words on the ground that they were no longer apparent. Subsequently, a writing expert discovered that by framing the obliterated words with opaque material and then holding the obliteration to the light, the obliterated words could be read. Persons who were not parties to the earlier proceedings then brought a new application to have the words in question admitted to probate. They were successful.

Would the executors be protected if they had already distributed the estate consequent upon the original grant of probate? Could the new beneficiaries recover from the ones to whom the property was distributed?

3. Since a holograph codicil is apt to change a formal will,[159] even though it is written on the will,[160] would a holograph alteration be effective to change a formal will?[161]

What is the difference between an alteration and a codicil?

4. A testator dictated changes to his will to X, who wrote them out at the end of the will. The testator then read the changes and wrote above them "Alterations to Will." He asked Y and Z to witness the alterations, but did not sign himself. Is the will, as amended, admissible to probate?[162]

5. A codicil made after a will has been altered without the necessary formalities makes the alterations valid.[163]

6. A holograph will is not "made" until the testator is satisfied with it, lays his or her pen down and puts the document away. Hence, if there is evidence that a holograph will

---

154 [1950] P. 130, [1950] 1 All E.R. 68.

155 *Re Hersford* (1874), L.R. 3 P. & D. 211.

156 *Townley v. Watson* (1844), 3 Curt. 761 at 764, 163 E.R. 893.

157 *Re Brasier*, [1899] P. 36; *Re Gilbert*, [1893] P. 183.

158 [1894] P. 191.

159 *Re Griffiths* (1969), 68 W.W.R. 1 (Sask. Surr. Ct.). Applied in *Olson v. Olson* (1988), 30 E.T.R. 243 (Sask. Q.B.).

160 *Re McLeod* (1964), 47 D.L.R. (2d) 370 (Alta. T.D.).

161 See *Re Schlee* (1976), 1 Alta. L.R. 93 (Surr. Ct.). And see *Re Manuel* (1960), 30 W.W.R. 516, 23 D.L.R. (2d) 190 (Alta. T.D.). For the effect of the substantial compliance provision in Manitoba (*Wills Act*, R.S.M. 1988, c. W150, s. 23), Saskatchewan (*Wills Act*, R.S.S. 1978, c. W-14, s. 35.1 [am. 1989, c. 66, s. 9]) and Prince Edward Island (*Probate Act*, R.S.P.E.I. 1988, c. P-21, s. 70), see *Re Pouliot; National Trust Co. v. Sutton,* [1984] 5 W.W.R. 765, 17 E.T.R. 225, 30 Man. R. (2d) 178 (Q.B.); Cameron Harvey, Comment, [1984] 7 E. & T.Q. 109; *Layeth Estate v. Gardiner* (1990), 39 E.T.R. 217 (Man. C.A.); Cameron Harvey, Annotation (1990), 39 E.T.R. 218; *Re Lang Estate* (1992), 45 E.T.R. 136 (Sask. Surr. Ct.); *Re Jensen Estate* (1993), 49 E.T.R. 114 (Sask. Q.B.).

162 *Re White (decd)*, [1990] 3 All E.R. 1 (Ch. D.).

163 *Re Sykes* (1873), L.R. 3 P. & D. 26.

is made at one sitting, the presumption in favour of validity is apt to validate alterations that appear in such a will.[164]

7. In provinces that have substantial compliance legislation, it may be possible to allow an alteration to be probated even if it was made, or was presumed to have been made after the will was executed.[165]

8. The testatrix's signature on the will was obliterated, so that it was no longer "apparent." What effect does this have on the will?[166]

6. CONDITIONAL REVOCATION

(a) Generally

Since a valid revocation depends in part upon the existence of an *animus revocandi*, it may be relevant to determine what the nature of the testator's intention was. It may have been absolute in the sense that the testator intended the document to be revoked no matter what the consequences, or the intention may have been conditional. There are three situations in which a revocation is conditional. These are discussed below:

(b) Testator Believes the Will is Void

If a valid will is destroyed because the testator believed at the time of the destruction that it was not a valid will, the will is not revoked, because the testator had no intention of destroying a valid testamentary document. *Giles v. Warren*[167] is an example. The testator destroyed his will by tearing it up when a friend told him that the will was not valid. After the friend departed, the testator retrieved the pieces and kept them in a safe place. The court held that the testator had no intention of revoking a valid will.

(c) Testator is Mistaken about the Facts or the Law

If a valid will is destroyed in circumstances in which the testator believes that he or she is revoking a valid will, but does so under a mistaken belief as to the facts or the law the will is not revoked. *Re Southerden*[168] illustrates this principle. The testator prepared a will prior to a trip out of the country, leaving all his property to his wife. One his return to England he destroyed the will in the mistaken belief that his wife would get all the property on his intestacy. That

---

164 *Currie v. Potter*, [1981] 6 W.W.R. 377, 12 Man. R. (2d) 396, 9 E.T.R. 170 (Q.B.).
165 See *Re Scott* (1995), 8 E.T.R. (2d) 33 (Man. Q.B.).
166 See *Re Adams (decd)*, [1990] 2 All E.R. 97 (Ch. D.).
167 (1872), L.R. 2 P. & D. 401.
168 [1925] P. 177 (C.A.).

belief was wrong in law, so the court held that the revocation was not effective. *Re Sorenson; Montreal Trust Co. v. Hawley*,[169] reproduced below, is similar.

RE SORENSON; MONTREAL TRUST CO. v. HAWLEY
(1982), 10 E.T.R. 282
Supreme Court of British Columbia

By her will, made in 1972, the testatrix gave 70% of the residue to her cousin, Mrs. Lillian M. Swan, if she survived her, failing which that part of the residue went equally to her husband's sisters, Mrs. Lillian Ivy Schioler and Mrs. Minnie Isabella Christensen, both of whom lived in New Zealand. Subsequently she wrote to her solicitor stating that both of her sisters-in-law had died, and that she, therefore, wanted to substitute her friend, Mrs. Gerda Hawley, for their names. The solicitor prepared a codicil to that effect which the testatrix executed.

In fact, while Mrs. Swan and Mrs. Christensen predeceased the testatrix, Mrs. Schioler survived her. The executor applied for directions.

VAN DER HOOP L.J.S.C.:

. . .

The first issue to determine is whether the codicil operates to revoke the original disposition in the will. Counsel for Mrs. Schioler referred to The Law Relating to Wills[170] where it is stated that "A revocation which is shown to be made upon a mistake either of fact or of law, and is considered by the Court not to be intended by the Testator except conditionally on the mistaken assumption being correct, is inoperative." That statement is based, in part, upon *Campbell v. French*,[171] which is summarized in the headnote as follows:

> Testator by his Will gave legacies to A. and B. describing them as grandchildren of C. and their residence in America: by a codicil he revokes these legacies; giving as a reason, that the legatees were dead: that fact not being true, they were held entitled upon proof of identity.

Loughborough L.C. stated:[172]

> It appears to me, there is no revocation; the cause being false: whether by misinformation or mistake is perfectly indifferent.

. . .

In *Re Wright Estate*[173] Embury J. adopted the principle set out in *Re Faris (No. 2)*[174] as:

---

169 (1982), 10 E.T.R. 282 (B.C.S.C.). See also *Re Keating* (1981), 46 N.S.R. (2d) 550, 89 A.P.R. 550 (Prob. Ct.).
170 W.J. Williams (3rd ed.) at 114.
171 (1797), 3 Ves. Jun. 321, 30 E.R. 1033.
172 At p. 1034 [E.R.].
173 (1937), 3 W.W.R. 452, at 454-5.
174 (1911), 1 Ir. R. 469.

> The true view (is) that a revocation grounded on an assumption of fact which is false takes effect unless, as a matter of construction, the truth of the fact is the condition of the revocation, or, in other words, unless the revocation is contingent upon the fact being true.
>
> . . .

In this case the basis for the revocation in the codicil was stated and I am satisfied from the wording and on the evidence presented that this basis was a condition for the revocation. I do not consider that, in so deciding, I am making a will for the testator, but rather I am carrying out the expressed intention of the testator. The bequest to Mrs. Hawley was to take effect only on the basis that Mrs. Schioler and Mrs. Christensen had died; Mrs. Schioler had not died, and the revocation was not intended to take effect in that event.

It is now necessary to consider the terms of the will, specifically to determine what is intended by the words "to such of my husband's sisters...as shall be living at the time of my decease in equal shares per capita..." Although the language leaves much to be desired, the intention to me seems clear: if both sisters survived the testatrix they are to share this portion of the residue equally, but if only one survives, she is to take the whole of the portion. This conclusion is supported by the words immediately following: "and in the event that my said husband's sisters shall *all* predecease me, then to The Salvation Army..." (The italics are mine.) I cannot conclude that the testatrix intended an intestacy if only one of her husband's sisters predeceased her. In Jarman on Wills[175] the author states: A gift to several named persons is not a gift to a class unless words of contingency are added; as where the gift is to A, B, C, and D, 'if living' and also:

> So if the gift is to such of the Testator's children as shall be living at the death of A, and A dies in the Testator's lifetime, this is a gift to a class; consequently the share of a child who survives A and dies in the Testator's lifetime does not lapse, and the children who survive the Testator take the whole.

Here Mrs. Schioler, the survivor, takes the whole, being in this case 70 per cent of the residue, and the executor is directed to distribute the estate accordingly.

. . .

(d) Dependent Relative Revocation

If a testator wishes to make a new will to replace an existing one and revokes the existing one in anticipation of making the new one, the revocation may or may not be effective. If the testator intends the revocation to be effective whether or not the new will is made, it is effective. But if the testator intends that the revocation shall not be effective unless and until the new will takes effect, the revocation is not effective. This is the doctrine of dependent relative revocation. It allows the old will to remain effective if the new one is not made or fails for

---

175 8th ed., vol. 1, at 449.

any reason, if you can show that the testator's intention was conditional upon the new will taking effect.

The doctrine also applies when parts of a will are revoked. Thus, a testator may revoke a gift in a will in anticipation of replacing it with a new gift in another testamentary instrument.

Re Service was a case of dependent relative revocation.[176] The testatrix had cut out three-quarters of page 2 of her will. The missing paragraph, III (c), contained legacies to nieces, nephews and a grandniece and a grandnephew of the testatrix amounting to approximately $50,000 in total. The executors were able to establish the contents of the missing paragraph from the copy of the will retained by the testatrix' solicitor. The original had always been in the testatrix' possession and it was highly unlikely that anyone other than she herself had mutilated the will. Apart from the bequests cut out, the will disposed of the residue by division among a number of charities. The estate presented the will for probate.

The court concluded that, since the testatrix was very fond of all her nephews and nieces and had no children herself, she did not intend to revoke the entire will. Further, the court held that she did intend to revoke the contents of the missing paragraph, but intended to substitute other provisions for the same beneficiaries. The court opined that she forgot or thought she had already done so. In other words, her intention to revoke was conditional upon the substituted provisions taking effect. Since they did not, the original provisions were restored.

The court was influenced by the fact that otherwise the will would only benefit one niece and a grandchild and disinherit all other nephews and nieces, including the executrix. As *Re Jones*,[177] reproduced below, makes clear, however, the doctrine is not applied automatically.

RE JONES
[1976] 1 Ch. 200, [1976] 1 All E.R. 593
Court of Appeal

The testatrix made a will by which she devised certain real property to the plaintiff and the plaintiff's sister, who were her nieces. Shortly before she died she attempted to instruct her solicitor to change the devise to the children of a nephew, one of the defendants. The solicitor was unavailable and the testatrix died without having been able to change the will. The will was found in a mutilated state among her papers. The devise to the nieces and other gifts had been cut out, as well as (on the other side of the page) the testatrix' signature and the attestation. The trial judge held that the will was mutilated because the testatrix intended to replace it with a new will. He pronounced in favour of the will on the basis of the doctrine of dependent relative revocation.

BUCKLEY L.J.:

. . .

---

176 [1964] 1 O.R. 197, 41 D.L.R. (2d) 480 (Surr. Ct.).
177 [1976] 1 Ch. 200, [1976] 1 All E.R. 593 (C.A.).

Where a testator mutilates or destroys a will, the questions which arise, I think, are these. (1) Did he do so with the intention of revoking it? He may have believed that it had been effectively revoked by some other means, but was mistaken. In those circumstances, he may have merely torn it up, thinking that it was no longer worth the paper it was written upon. For myself, in those circumstances, I should have thought the right inference to draw was that he did not intend to revoke it at all; he was merely disposing of what he thought was rubbish. He may have destroyed it or mutilated it without realising that the document was in fact his will, or he may have been under some other kind of misapprehension.

However, if the answer is that he did not destroy or mutilate it with the intention of revoking it, he cannot have revoked it, because section 20 of the Wills Act 1837,[178] so far as relevant, provides that a will shall be revoked by burning, tearing or otherwise destroying the same with the intention of revoking it. If there was no intention of revoking it, the act of destruction or mutilation will not effect a revocation.

If however, the answer to that question is that the testator did have a revocatory intention, the second question arises. (2) If he had an intention of revoking the will, was his intention absolute or qualified, so as to be contingent or conditional? If it was absolute, that is the end of the investigation, for the act takes effect as a revocation.

If, however, it was qualified, the further question which arises is, (3) What was the nature of the qualification? The testator's intention may have been dependent upon an intent to revive an earlier testamentary document founded on an erroneous belief that the cancellation of the later will would have that effect, as in *Powell v. Powell*,[179] or it may have been wholly and solely dependent upon an intention to displace it by some new testamentary disposition. An example of this may be taken to be *Dixon v. Treasury Solicitor*[180] where there was evidence that the testator thought that the cancellation of an earlier will was a necessary precondition of making a new one.

If the testator's intention is found to have been a qualified one, subject to some condition or contingency, the final question arises. (4) Has that condition or contingency been satisfied or occurred? If the condition or contingency to which the intention to revoke was subject has not been satisfied or occurred, the revocation is ineffective, if it has been satisfied or occurred, the revocation is effective.

The fact that at the time of the mutilation or destruction the testator intended or contemplated making a new will, is not, in my judgment, conclusive of the question as to whether his intention to revoke was dependent upon his subsequently making a new will. A testator who has made a will in favour of A may become disenchanted with A and decide not to benefit him. He may well at the same time decide that in these circumstances he will benefit B instead of A. It does not by any means follow that his intention to disinherit A will be dependent on his benefiting B, or making a will under which B could take.

---

178 7 Will. 4 & 1 Vict., c. 26.
179 (1866), L.R. 1 P. & D. 209.
180 [1905] P. 42.

If he were told that for some reason B could not or would not benefit under his new will, would the testator say, "In that case, I want my gift to A to stand," or would he say, "Well, even so, I do not wish A to benefit"? In the former case, his *animus revocandi* at the time of the destruction or mutilation of his will could properly be regarded as dependent on the execution of a new will, but not in the latter.

It is consequently necessary to pay attention to the circumstances surrounding the mutilation or destruction of the will to discover whether any intention that the testator then had of revoking the will was absolute or qualified, and if qualified, in what way it was qualified.

. . .

If, on the evidence, it is reasonable to infer that the mutilation was wholly and solely referable to her intention to make a new will, this was a case of conditional revocation or, as it is sometimes called, dependent relative revocation. If, on the other hand, it was referable wholly to her intention to cut out the plaintiff and her sister, it was not such a case, even if that intention was accompanied by an intention to make a new devise as soon as she could in favour of the children of her nephew James.

It seems to me, with deference to the judge, that his conclusion involves ignoring the evidence of the important conversations with the bank manager on September 23, 1970, when the testatrix complained, justly or unjustly, of the attitude of the plaintiff and her sister towards herself, and when she explained that she no longer intended to give the smallholding to them because they had acquired a property of their own and that she intended to give it to the children of her nephew Jim because he, Jim, had been very good to her.

Moreover, it is consistent, in my view, with the conversation with the testatrix's nephew William when she said on September 27, 1970, that she had not made a will. Of course, taken literally, that was not true, for she had made two wills in the course of her life, one in 1959, and her last will in 1965, but it seems to me much more consistent with the conversation that the testatrix should then have cancelled her last will with an intention to revoke it and should have been of the opinion that she had no will at that moment in force, than that she should have mutilated her will with the intention that that mutilation should not operate as a revocation unless and until she had made a new will.

There was no direct evidence of any belief by the testatrix that the destruction of her will was a necessary precondition of making an effective new will. Her last will had contained a revocation clause, by which she had revoked an earlier will, from which it is reasonable to infer in the absence of contrary evidence that she knew that an existing will could be effectively revoked by a revocation clause in a new will without any other form of cancellation.

If, as the judge held, she most probably defaced the will on September 23, 1970, this was three days before she was taken seriously ill. It was on September 27 that she felt that she was going to die. There is no ground for supposing that on September 23 she did not fully expect to see her solicitor within a week to make a new will. If her intention was merely to displace her existing will by another, what reason could she have had for mutilating the will on September 23?

With deference to the judge, it seems to me that the inference which most convincingly fits these facts is that the testatrix was not content that the revocation of her existing will should depend upon her making a new one, but that she wished and intended to achieve what she could, namely, the revocation of her existing will, there and then, and that this was her reason for mutilating it. This is not necessarily inconsistent with her having, at the same time, an intention to make a new will at the earliest opportunity devising "Dryslwyn" to the children of her nephew.

None of the findings of primary facts is disputed. I accept them without demur, but I differ from the judge in my opinion of the proper inference to draw from them. I would hold that by defacing her will on or about September 23 the testatrix intended there and then to revoke it and that this intention was not conditional or contingent on her making a new will.

[The concurring judgments of Roskill and Goff L.JJ., have been omitted.]

Notes and Questions

1. *Re Itter*[181] presents an interesting fact situation in which the court applied the doctrine. The testatrix had pasted strips of paper over the amounts of certain legacies in her will and had written new amounts on the strips. The alterations were not attested. It could not be determined what was underneath the strips except by infra-red photography and that is not permissible in determining whether the original amounts were still apparent. However, the court held that the testatrix intended that the old provisions should be revoked only if the new were effective. Since they were not, the doctrine of dependent relative revocation applied and the infra-red photographs were, therefore, admitted to determine what her original intention was.

2. *Bolton and Hess v. Toronto General Trusts Corporation*[182] is similar to *Re Jones*. The testator destroyed his will by burning it in the kitchen stove. Around the time of this act, he expressed the intention of making a new will. However, he did not do so during the remaining two years for his life. Did the doctrine of dependent relative revocation apply? If it did, the destroyed document would still be regarded as the testator's last will and a photocopy of it could be admitted to probate. The evidence fell short of establishing that the destruction of the will "was referable, wholly and solely, to an intention on the part of the testator to replace it by a new will."[183] It must be clearly demonstrated that the destruction depended upon the implementation of such intention; merely contemplating the making of a new will does not suffice. The court held that the act of destruction of the will was performed deliberately and *animo revocandi* with a resulting intestacy.

3. The court was more lenient in *Dwyer v. Irish*.[184] The testatrix had written "cancelled" on her will. She dated and signed this attempted revocation. Three months later she signed a typewritten will, but it was not witnessed. The doctrine of dependent relative revocation applied since the revocation by the deceased was conditional upon the new will being validly made. The later (purported) will was not valid, so that revocation of the first will failed.

181   [1950] P. 130, [1950] 1 All E.R. 68.
182   (1961), 29 D.L.R. (2d) 173 (Man. C.A.).
183   *Ibid.*, at p. 175.
184   (1985), 20 E.T.R. 98 (Nfld. T.D.). See also *Re Little Estate* (1998), 24 E.T.R. (2d) 317 (N.S.S.C.).

4. The testator made a will in 1967 in which he devised his real property to his nephew, D. In 1981 he purported to make another will, which contained the same devise. However, it did not satisfy the statutory formalities: the testator had signed in the presence of only one witness, who then signed his name, after which the testator had signed his name again, but only in the presence of the second witness, who then signed her name. The testator disappeared in 1987 in circumstances in which he was presumed to have died. The original of the 1967 will was not found. It was, however, last known to have been in the testator's possession. This attracted the presumption that a will is revoked by the testator when last traced to the testator's possession. Could the doctrine of dependent relative revocation be applied?[185]

5. A testator made three successive wills. Each left his house and contents and three-quarters of the residue to X. The second and third wills contained a revocation clause, revoking all previous wills. These wills made some changes in gifts to persons other than X. The testator asked X's husband to witness the third will. Can the gift to X be saved? If so, how?[186]

7. REVIVAL OF REVOKED WILLS

Sometimes a testator revokes a will with the intention of replacing the revoked will with a prior one and assumes that the revocation has that effect. In other words, by revoking the latest will, the testator assumes that the preceding will is thereby revived. This does not, in fact, occur, for section 19 of the *Succession Law Reform Act*, reproduced below, provides that a previously revoked will can be revived only in accordance with that section.[187] However, if the testator intended that the revocation of the latest will should only be effective in the event that the earlier one is revived, the doctrine of dependent relative revocation will save the latest will. The principle is discussed in *Re Ott*,[188] reproduced below.

The doctrine of revival, that is the doctrine which permits a revoked will to be revivified, should be distinguished from the doctrine of republication. Republication gives a will a new, later date. At common law this was done by re-executing the will, or by executing a codicil to the will, in both cases with the intention of confirming the contents of the will. The doctrine is important in that, if a will takes a later date because of republication, it can then be construed in accordance with any change in circumstances. Thus, if the will contains a gift "to the wife of X" and X has divorced his or her spouse and has remarried between the date of the original will and its republication, the new spouse will be allowed to take. Similarly, unattested alterations made to the will after its original execution can be validated by a republication. Section 6 of the former *Wills Act*[189] provided that

---

185 See *Valentine v. Whitehead* (1990), 37 E.T.R. 253 (B.C.S.C.).

186 See *Re Finnemore (decd)*, [1992] 1 All E.R. 800 Ch. D.).

187 See *Re Hodgkinson*, [1893] P. 339 (C.A.) which concerned an implied revocation. See also the substantial compliance provision in s. 23 of the Manitoba *Wills Act*, R.S.M. 1988, c. W150; s.70 of the *Probate Act*, R.S.P.E.I. 1988, c. P-21; and s. 35.1 of the *Wills Act*, R.S.S. 1978, c. W-14 [added by 1989, c. 66, s. 9].

188 [1972] 2 O.R. 5, 7 R.F.L. 196, 24 D.L.R. (3d) 517 (Surr. Ct.).

189 R.S.O. 1970, c. 499, rep. by *Succession Law Reform Act*, S.O. 1977, c. 40, s. 43 (1)(a).

every will re-executed, republished or revived by a codicil should be deemed to have been made at the time of re-execution, republication or revival. Although section 21 of the *Succession Law Reform Act*, reproduced below, contains a similar provision, it extends only to revival. Hence, as regards the law of republication, resort must now be had to the common law. You should note that the doctrines of republication and revival are based on a presumption that the testator intended to give a new date to the will. The doctrines do not, therefore, apply automatically, but depend upon the intention of the testator.[190]

SUCCESSION LAW REFORM ACT
R.S.O. 1990, c. S.26

19. (1) A will or part of a will that has been in any manner revoked is revived only,

  (a) by a will made in accordance with the provisions of this Part; or

  (b) by a codicil that has been made in accordance with the provisions of this Part,

that shows an intention to give effect to the will or part that was revoked, or,

  (c) by re-execution thereof with the required formalities, if any.

(2) Except when a contrary intention is shown, when a will which has been partly revoked and afterward wholly revoked is revived, the revival does not extend to the part that was revoked before the revocation of the whole.

. . .

21. When a will has been revived in the manner described in section 19, the will shall be deemed to have been made at the time at which it was so revived.

Comparable Legislation

Probate Act, R.S.P.E.I. 1988, c. P-21, s. 74; *Wills Act*, R.S.A. 1980, c. W-11, ss. 2(2), 20; R.S.B.C. 1996, c. 489, ss. 18, 20(1); R.S.M. 1988, c. W150, ss. 20, 22(1); R.S.N.B. 1973, c. W-9, ss. 19, 21(1); R.S.N. 1990, c. W-10, s. 13; R.S.N.S. 1989, c. 505, s. 21; R.S.N.W.T. 1988, c. W-5, ss. 2(1), 13; S.S. 1996, c. W-14.1, s. 20; R.S.Y. 1986, c. 179, ss. 2(1), 12.

RE OTT
[1972] 2 O.R. 5, 7 R.F.L. 196, 24 D.L.R. (3d) 517
Ontario Surrogate Court
[County of Hastings]

The testator made a will in December, 1966, by which he gave certain benefits to his wife. Thereafter differences arose between them and he made a second will

---

190 *Re Hardyman; Teesdale v. McClintock*, [1925] Ch. 287; *Re Heath's Will Trusts; Hamilton v. Lloyds Bank Ltd.*, [1949] Ch. 170, [1949] 1 All E.R. 199.

in March, 1970. They entered into a separation agreement and the testator then sent his wife a copy of the second will, stating that if she wished he would change it. His wife informed him that she preferred the will made in 1966. The testator then attended at his solicitor's office and, in the solicitor's presence, destroyed the 1970 will, declaring his belief that his will of 1966 would thereby again become effective. The solicitor informed him that he doubted that that was the case.

The testator's wife applied for probate of the 1970 will.

ANDERSON SURR. CT. J.:

. . .

The physical destruction of a will does not, in all cases, revoke the will. The destruction may be the result of an accident, or of various intentions. Therefore it is necessary to study the act done in the light of the circumstances under which it occurred, and the declaration of the testator with which it may have been accompanied. Unless it was destroyed *animo revocandi* it is not revocation.[191]

I am satisfied on the evidence of Mr. Follwell that the testator, William John Ott, on May 21, 1970, only destroyed the will dated March 23, 1970, believing that the said destruction would revive the earlier will, known in these proceedings as the Royal Trust will.

Dealing with Mr. Cass' contention that Mrs. Ott's evidence in relation to the testator's intention is hearsay evidence and is not to be accepted because she is an interested party, I think that the point made by Mr. Cass should bear careful consideration, and I would not find as a fact that Mr. Ott did not intend to revoke the will dated March 23, 1970, when he destroyed it on May 21, 1970, on her evidence alone, without corroboration.

I am of the view that her evidence is admissible on the question of intention, even although she is an interested party. It is the intention of the testator who destroys a will, which is vital in considering whether or not the destruction of the will is a revocation.

Mr. Follwell advised Mr. Ott that in his opinion the destruction of the will dated March 23, 1970, would not revive the earlier Royal Trust will, yet if Mr. Ott believed that the destruction by him of the March 23, 1970, will would have the effect of reviving the earlier will, whether or not in law that was so, then there was not an intention of revoking the 1970 will.

. . .

There can be no question in my mind that Follwell has related the events of the day and time exactly as he now remembers them. It might have been a little better if in addition to making the memorandum of the destruction of the will, Mr. Follwell had also made a note of the conversation which he had with Mr. Ott at that time, but in any event Mr. Follwell seems to be very clear in his recollection from Mr. Ott's conversation that the intention of Mr. Ott was, when he tore up his will of March 23, 1970, to revive the former will known as the Royal Trust

---

191 *Powell v. Powell* (1866), L.R. 1 P. & D. 209.

will, and under these circumstances I must find that the will of March 23, 1970, was not revoked.

Notes and Questions

1. *Re Ott* shows that it is impossible to apply the doctrine of conditional revocation in order to achieve a revocation of a revocation. In other words, once a will has been validly revoked, whether conditional or not, a prior will is not revived, even though it was the testator's intention to revive the former will by revoking the latter.[192] A will can only be revived by one of the methods set out in the statute.

2. T made a will in May. In October, he made a second will. Later, he expressed dissatisfaction with the October will. His niece told him that if he destroyed the October will, the May will would again take effect. Accordingly, he destroyed the October will. Should the October will be admitted to probate?[193]

3. The testator made a will in 1862, leaving all his property to his grandson. In 1864 he made a new will, revoking the previous one, in which he left everything to his nephew. In 1865 he got out both wills and read them over. He found that he preferred the 1862 will and stated that he wanted it to stand. Accordingly, he burned the 1864 will. The court applied the doctrine of dependent relative revocation and admitted the 1864 will to probate.

Is the doctrine appropriate in these circumstances? This was not a minor change of beneficiary as in some of the other cases, but a complete change of intention. By applying the doctrine, the testator's intention was completely defeated. Would it not be better to refuse probate of any will and let the testator die intestate, or should the law be changed to permit probate of the one intended to be revived, provided that the intention is clear?[194]

4. A testator made two successive wills. Later he made two codicils to the first will. The codicils confirmed "my said last Will and Testament" in all other respects. The effect of the codicils was to distort the meaning of the second will. Did the codicils revive the first will?[195]

5. A testator had made two attested wills, one in 1984, the other in 1989. The latter revoked the former. Subsequently, he wrote in his own hand on his solicitor's account, "Please follow will dated Feb. 23, 1984 and cancel all others." This was followed by his signature and the date. Did this revive the 1984 will?[196]

6. A testator's will was revoked by his marriage. Subsequently, he made a codicil to the revoked will. It showed that he thought the will was still effective. The codicil did not state that the will should be revived. Was it revived?[197]

7. The Alberta, British Columbia, Manitoba, New Brunswick, Northwest Territories and Yukon statutes[198] provide that every will re-executed, republished or revived by a codicil shall be deemed to have been made at the time of re-execution, republication or revival. Thus, unlike Ontario's s. 21, they extend also to re-execution and republication.

---

192 *Ibid.*

193 See *Re Janotta*, [1976] 2 W.W.R. 312 (Sask. Surr. Ct.).

194 *Powell v. Powell, supra.*

195 See *Re Chilcott*, [1897] P. 223; *Re Reade*, [1902] P. 75; *Re Squire Estate* (1989), 32 E.T.R. 106 (B.C.S.C.).

196 See *Morrison v. Owen* (1991), 44 E.T.R. 290 (Ont. Gen. Div.).

197 See *Re MacKinlay Estate* (1993), 50 E.T.R. 136 (N.S. C.A.), leave to appeal refused (1994), 2 E.T.R. (2d) 100 (S.C.C.).

198 *Wills Act*, R.S.A. 1980, c. W-11, s. 2(2); R.S.B.C. 1996, c. 489, s. 20(1); R.S.M. 1988, c. W150, s. 22(1); R.S.N.B. 1973, c. W-9, s. 21(1); R.S.N.W.T. 1988, c. W-5, s. 2(1).

8. There is a presumption that the testator has revoked a will last known to be in the possession of the testator if it cannot be found at the testator's death. Such a revocation does not revive an earlier will, unless the statute is complied with. However, the earlier instrument will be granted probate if it cannot be proved satisfactorily that the later instrument was properly executed and, by its terms, revoked the earlier instrument, either expressly, or because it was inconsistent with the earlier instrument.[199]

Further Reading

Palmer, "Dependent Relative Revocation and its Relation to Relief for Mistake" (1971), 69 Mich. L. Rev. 989.

---

199 *Cutto v. Gilbert* (1854), 9 Moo. P.C. 131, 12 E.R. 247. See also *Bell v. Matthewman* (1920), 48 O.L.R. 364; and *Hellier v. Hellier* (1884), 9 P.D. 237. And see *Macdonell, Sheard and Hull on Probate Practice*, 4th ed by Rodney Hull and Ian M. Hull (Scarborough: Carswell, 1996), 77.

8

RELATED MATTERS OF PROOF

1. INTRODUCTION

In this chapter we discuss several matters that may require proof or that may otherwise arise in an estate. They do not arise in every estate. Further, they are not closely related to each other. These matters include: proof of death in situations in which it is uncertain whether the person in question has died; proof of the contents of a will that has been lost; rules determining the formal and intrinsic validity of a will when it was made in another jurisdiction; and the power to appoint testamentary guardians and custodians of one's minor children.

2. PROOF OF DEATH AND RELATED MATTERS

(a) Generally

Sometimes a person is missing and has not been heard of for a long period of time. Questions may then arise about the preservation of his or her assets, the administration of the estate,[1] or the missing person's entitlement to share in another estate. Similarly, questions about another person's entitlement to share in the absentee's estate, to share in a third person's estate because of the absentee's possible death, or to share in insurance proceeds, pension benefits, or other rights arising because of the absentee's death may be raised. The law provides a number of different solutions to deal with these problems.

---

1 Obviously, the estate can only be distributed if the missing person is dead and the death must be proved: *cf.* Hebr. 9: 16, 17. In fact, the testator's death must be proved whenever a person seeks to represent the estate. In the normal situation (*i.e.*, when the deceased is not missing) the executors or administrators prove death in the application for probate or the application for administration [the "application for certificate of appointment of estate trustee" in both instances in Ontario] and the affidavit supporting the application.

(b) The Common Law

The first way in which the questions concerning a missing person may be dealt with is at common law. The law either draws inferences from the evidence adduced, or applies a presumption of death.

Proof of death by inference from the facts requires a determination that death as the explanation of the disappearance flows logically from the evidence. The conclusion that a person has died is a *prima facie* one and it can be rebutted by showing that there is another explanation for the disappearance, or that there was an impelling motive for the disappearance. The latter may exist if the person had family or financial difficulties, or was wanted for a crime.[2] The cases dealing with proof of death by inference from the facts usually involve a specific peril, such as a boating accident, or a storm. In those cases the inference may be raised within a short period of time after the disappearance. A specific peril is not a necessary prerequisite,[3] although in most situations in which there is no specific peril, it is preferable to rely on a presumption of death.

There is a presumption of law that a person is dead if he or she has been continuously absent from home for seven years and has not been heard from by those who would normally have received news from him or her if he or she were alive.[4] This presumption reverses the former presumption of continuance of life. It does not mean that a person who has not been absent for seven years is presumed to be alive.[5] Clearly, in order for the presumption to operate, the absence must be unexplained and inquiries must be made of the absentee's relatives and advertisements must normally be placed in newspapers circulated in places where the absentee might reasonably be expected to be.[6] If these requirements are satisfied, the presumption will be applied. A strong motive for disappearing can, however, rebut the presumption.[7] *Re Miller*[8] deals with the application of the presumption. However, it also concerns another matter, namely the question of the date of death. In many cases that question is not relevant, but it becomes material if it is necessary to determine whether the absentee has survived to a specific date for succession purposes. Proof of the date of death is not based on a presumption, but must arise by inference from the facts. The court may declare that the absentee was dead by a specified date,[9] or died on a specific date.[10] If the question of survivorship is relevant, it can be resolved either by proof of the date of death as just described, or by application of the relevant provincial commorientes legis-

---

2 See *Re Jewell and Metro Life Ins. Co.*, 19 W.W.R. 665, [1956] I.L.R. 1-242, 6 D.L.R. (2d) 213 (B.C.S.C.); *Re Kreutzweiser and Taylor*, [1946] O.W.N. 184 (Surr. Ct.).

3 *Re Small* (1924), 26 O.W.N. 388 (Div. Ct.).

4 *Re Phené's Trust* (1870), 5 Ch. App. 139; *Re MacGilchrist Estate* (1992), 46 E.T.R. 60 (Ont. Gen. Div.).

5 *Ibid.*

6 J.C. Shepherd, "Presumption of Death in Ontario" (1979), 4 E. & T.Q. 326 at pp. 338-9.

7 *Sheehy v. Robinson*, [1947] O.W.N. 121 (H.C.).

8 (1978), 22 O.R. (2d) 111, 92 D.L.R. (3d) 255 (H.C.), reproduced *infra*.

9 *Re Harlow* (1976), 13 O.R. (2d) 760, 72 D.L.R. (3d) 323 (C.A.).

10 *Re Kreutzweiser and Taylor*, *supra*.

lation.[11] The onus of proving death and the date of death may be important. If an inference of death is drawn from the evidence, the onus is throughout on the person who claims a right for which proof of death and, it may be, of the date of death, is necessary.[12] If the death is presumed, such a person has the onus of raising a *prima facie* case, whereupon it shifts to those denying the death to rebut the presumption.[13]

The difficulty with the question of proof of death is that, in the absence of statutory authority, a court cannot make a declaration that a person is dead except as incidental to its jurisdiction in other proceedings.[14] The reason is that such a declaration would bind not only the parties to the application, but all others who might have an interest in the question.

The question of proof of death most often arises in connection with an application for letters probate or letters of administration [application for certificate of appointment of estate trustee] of an absentee. In those circumstances the court does not, in fact, make a declaration that a person is dead, but only finds that sufficient evidence has been placed before it by the applicant to grant leave to the applicant to swear that the absentee is dead.[15]

In the exercise of its probate function, the court does not have jurisdiction to determine that a beneficiary predeceased the testator upon the application of another beneficiary who, if that fact were established, would be entitled to the deceased beneficiary's share in the estate.[16] In order to have that question determined, the beneficiary would have to bring an action against the personal representatives for payment of the entire amount. In that action the question can be determined. Alternatively, the beneficiary could apply to the court for the determination of the question under the Rules of Civil Procedure.[17]

Similarly, the question may be resolved on an application for payment of money out of court standing to the credit of an absentee beneficiary. The application would be brought by the person who becomes entitled to the money if the death of the absentee is established.[18] Other circumstances in which the question may be dealt with include in an application to quiet a title, as in *Re Miller*[19] and an action for spousal support in which the defendant alleges the invalidity of the marriage on the ground that the plaintiff was previously married and the plaintiff's previous spouse was not dead at the time of the marriage.[20] On the other hand,

---

11 We shall consider survivorship in a later chapter. In *Re Lay* (1961), 36 W.W.R. 414, 32 D.L.R. (2d) 156 (Man. Q.B.) the court applied survivorship legislation to determine the order of death of a husband and wife.
12 *Re Kreutzweiser and Taylor, supra*; *Re Aldersey*, [1905] 2 Ch. 181.
13 Shepherd, *supra*, at pp. 335, 341, 344.
14 *Re Irvin*, [1940] O.W.N. 372, [1940] 4 D.L.R. 736 (H.C.); *Re Hum Fong Shee*, [1967] 1 O.R. 220 (C.A.).
15 Susan E. Greer, "Recent Developments in Probate Practice", in Law Soc. of Upper Can. Special Lectures, 1980, *Recent Developments in Estate Planning and Administration*, p. 87 at pp. 97-8.
16 *Re Hum Fong Shee, supra*.
17 *Rules of Civil Procedure* (Ont.), R. 14.05(3).
18 *Re Harlow* (1976), 13 O.R. (2d) 760, 72 D.L.R. (3d) 323 (C.A.).
19 *Supra*.
20 *Homanuke v. Homanuke*, [1920] 3 W.W.R. 749, 13 Sask. L.R. 557 (C.A.).

the court cannot make a declaration that a person's spouse is dead merely to permit the applicant to remarry, since the question does not then arise incidentally to its jurisdiction in other proceedings.[21]

Unfortunately, the law is unclear on the rights of the absentee and any persons among whom his or her property has been distributed should the absentee reappear. It would seem clear that the absentee's personal representatives are protected in respect of any distributions of the absentee's property made in good faith.[22] However, apart from costs and expenses incurred in the administration of the property, the absentee may recover any part of the estate remaining in the hands of the personal representatives.[23] Moreover, the absentee may also, subject to the applicable limitation period, recover any part of the estate, or its value, from a beneficiary of the estate.[24]

(c) Special Statutory Provisions

The second way of dealing with issues surrounding missing persons is pursuant to a number of provincial and federal statutes. In particular circumstances, these statutes either presume a person to be dead or provide for a certificate by an official as proof of death.

The *Conveyancing and Law of Property Act*[25] raises a presumption of the death of a *cestui que vie* who remains out of Ontario, or absents himself or herself therefrom for the space of seven years, so that it cannot be ascertained whether the *cestui que vie* be alive or dead and no sufficient proof is made of the fact that he or she is alive. Moreover, a life tenant is presumed to be dead if the person entitled in remainder or reversion suspects that the life tenant's death is concealed by his or her guardian, trustee, spouse or other person and such person neglects or refuses to produce or show the life tenant before the court.[26]

The *Insurance Act*[27] permits an insurance company or a claimant to apply to the court for a declaration concerning the sufficiency of the evidence of death of the insured and the court may make a declaration that the evidence is sufficient to establish death. Moreover, if the insured has not been heard of for seven years, the insurance company or the claimant may apply to the court for a declaration that the insured should be presumed dead.[28] If the court is not satisfied that the evidence of death that has been furnished is sufficient, or that a presumption of death is established, it may direct that the matters in issue be tried in an action.[29]

---

21 *Re Mason*, [1943] 2 W.W.R. 243, [1943] 3 D.L.R. 810 (Sask.).
22 *Trustee Act*, R.S.O. 1990, c. T.23, s. 47(1). The section validates acts done by a personal representative under a grant of probate or letters of administration which is subsequently revoked because made erroneously.
23 *Ibid.*
24 *Ibid.*
25 R.S.O. 1990, c. C.34, s. 46.
26 *Ibid.*
27 R.S.O. 1990, c. I.8, s. 208.
28 *Ibid.*, s. 209.
29 *Ibid.*, s. 213.

You should note that a declaration under this legislation only binds the insurer making or who is a party to the application,[30] unless notice has been given to other insurers holding policies on the life of the insured.[31]

In addition, several federal pension statutes provide for a ministerial certificate deeming a contributor or beneficiary to be dead and stating the date of death, if the minister is satisfied beyond reasonable doubt of the death.[32] In some situations the certificate ceases to apply if the person returns.[33] The *Government Annuities Act*[34] permits the Governor General in Council to make regulations regarding proof of death for the purpose of that Act, while the *Pension Act*[35] defines "death" as including "death presumed for official purposes." Finally, the *Canada Shipping Act*[36] provides that in proceedings to recover a seaman's wages the ship on which the seaman sailed is deemed to have been lost with all hands if its last known call at port is more than twelve months ago, and the court is empowered to fix the date of death.

(d) Absentees

The third method of dealing with absentees is under the *Absentees Act*.[37] It makes provision for the administration of the assets of a person who is an absentee in order that they not be left to waste. An absentee is defined as a person who, having had his or her usual place of residence or domicile in Ontario, has disappeared, whose whereabouts is unknown and as to whom there is no knowledge whether he or she be alive or dead.[38] Upon the application of the Attorney General for Ontario, one of the next of kin, the spouse, a person of the opposite sex or the same sex with whom the alleged absentee was living in a conjugal relationship immediately before his or her disappearance, a creditor, or any other person[39] and upon proof that the person is an absentee, the Superior Court of Justice may declare the person to be an absentee[40] and may appoint a committee to administer

---

30 *Darling v. Sun Life Assur. Co.*, [1943] O.R. 26, 10 I.L.R. 1, [1943] 1 D.L.R. 316 (C.A.).

31 *Insurance Act*, R.S.O. 1990, c. I.8, s. 208; *Re Kreutzweiser and Taylor*, [1946] O.W.N. 184 (Surr. Ct.).

32 *Canadian Forces Superannuation Act*, R.S.C. 1985, c. C-17, s. 37; *National Defence Act*, R.S.C. 1985, c. N-5, s. 43; *Public Service Superannuation Act*, R.S.C. 1985, c. P-36, s. 33; *Royal Canadian Mounted Police Superannuation Act*, R.S.C. 1985, c. R-11, s. 21. A certification of death under the *National Defence Act*, *supra*, is treated as *prima facie* proof of death and the date of death for provincial purposes: *Evidence Act*, R.S.O. 1990, c. E.23, s. 51. See further J.C. Shepherd, "Presumption of Death in Ontario" (1979), 4 E. & T.Q. 326 at pp. 350-1.

33 *Canada Pension Plan Act*, R.S.C. 1985, c. C-8, s. 88; *Diplomatic Service (Special) Superannuation Act*, R.S.C. 1985, c. D-2, s. 13.

34 R.S.C. 1970, G-6, s. 13(e).

35 R.S.C. 1985, c. P-6, s. 3.

36 R.S.C. 1985, c. S-9, s. 211.

37 R.S.O. 1990, c. A.3. For similar legislation see: *Estates of Missing Persons Act*, R.S.B.C. 1996, c. 123; *Absentee Act*, R.S.S. 1978, c. A-3.

38 *Absentees Act*, R.S.O. 1990, c. A.3, s. 1.

39 *Ibid.*, s. 2(2), am. S.O. 1999, c. 6, s. 1.

40 *Ibid.*, s. 2(1).

his or her property.[41] The powers and duties of the committee are the same as those of a guardian appointed to administer the estate of an incapable person,[42] but the committee may, subject to the court's direction, spend money out of the estate in attempts to trace the absentee and to determine whether he or she is alive or dead.[43] You should note that the legislation only empowers the court to declare a person to be an absentee; the court can not make a declaration that a person is dead.[44] Nor does the legislation permit the court to apply the presumption of death, referred to above, in order to effect a distribution of the estate, or order payment of moneys out of court to the next of kin.[45]

If a person ceases to be an absentee, the court may so declare and vacate the order declaring him or her to be an absentee and appointing a committee. However, this does not affect anything done pursuant to the original order.[46]

(e) General Statutory Reform

The problems in respect of proof of death at common law have led to the enactment of presumption of death legislation in a number of provinces and the two territories. These statutes are based in whole or in part on the *Uniform Presumption of Death Act*[47] or a predecessor thereof.[48] They permit a declaration of death to be made *simpliciter* which has effect for all purposes and resolves most other problems that exist at common law.

RE MILLER
(1978), 22 O.R. (2d) 111, 92 D.L.R. (3d) 255
Supreme Court of Ontario
[High Court of Justice]

This case involved an application under the *Quieting Titles Act*, R.S.O. 1970, c. 396, and an application for the advice and direction of the court regarding the ascertainment of the persons entitled to an interest in certain lands.

CARRUTHERS J.:

. . .

---

41 *Ibid.*, s. 4.

42 *Ibid.*, s. 6, am. S.O. 1992, c. 32, s. 1. This means, *inter alia*, that an action for anything done by the absentee does not lie against the committee. Such an action must be brought against the absentee's personal representative: *Flynn v. Capital Trust Corp.* (1921), 51 O.L.R. 424, 62 D.L.R. 427, varied (1922), 52 O.L.R. 331, [1923] 3 D.L.R. 1144 (C.A.).

43 *Ibid.*, s. 7.

44 *Re Sell*, 56 O.L.R. 32, [1924] 4 D.L.R. 1115.

45 *Re Vaughan* (1921), 21 O.W.N. 215; *Re McFarlane* (1921), 19 O.W.N. 586.

46 *Absentees Act*, R.S.O. 1990, c. A.3, s. 3.

47 Uniform Law Conference of Canada, *Consolidation of Uniform Acts* (1978, as am.), p. 36-1, reproduced *infra*.

48 The statutes are: *Presumption of Death Act*, R.S.M. 1987, c. P120; R.S.N. 1990, c. P-20; S.N.B. 1974, c. P-15.1; R.S.N.S. 1989, c. 354; R.S.N.W.T. 1988, c. P-9; R.S.Y. 1986, c. 135; *Survivorship and Presumption of Death Act*, R.S.B.C. 1996, c. 444.

The object of the applications is really to determine whether Thelma Marie Coulter, the applicant, can be considered the absolute owner in fee simple of the lands and premises in question. In order to answer this question, it is necessary to determine whether one Wallace Miller can be found to have died prior to August 31, 1934. From the material filed in support of the application, it appears that in the month of November, 1910, Annie B. Wren conveyed the lands and premises in question to Walter James Miller and his wife, Nancy Miller, as tenants in common. Walter James Miller died in January of 1919, and by his will he devised all his will [sic] and personal property to his daughter, Alma May Miller. In addition to this daughter, Alma May Miller, Walter James Miller and Nancy Miller had a son, Wallace Miller, who disappeared in 1913 at the age of 19 years, and who was unmarried at that time. Nancy Miller died intestate in August of 1934, and there apparently has been no administration of her estate. Alma May Miller died in January, 1977, and by her will directed payment of her debts and small monetary legacies and then devised the remainder and residue of her estate to Thelma Marie Coulter, her cousin, the applicant herein.

The material also discloses that at the time of his disappearance, Wallace Miller had gone to the Toronto Islands by ferry boat. At that time he was an employee of the ferry service and the trip was being made on his day off. The police were informed and became involved in searching for Wallace Miller and their search and other searches which were carried out did not reveal the whereabouts of Wallace Miller.

From the material before me, it is clear that during a continuous period of seven years following his disappearance in 1913 and, in fact, during a continuous period from that time to the present, nothing has been heard of from Wallace Miller by those who, if he had been alive, would naturally have heard from him or of him. I am satisfied from reading the material filed in support of this application that following his disappearance, all due and appropriate inquiries having regard to the circumstances surrounding his disappearance were made to determine the possible whereabouts of Wallace Miller without success.

Under these circumstances then, from my understanding of the law, Wallace Miller can be presumed to have died some time within the period of seven years following his disappearance in 1913. Furthermore, because the period of his disappearance is, in fact, one of not less than seven years, I am able to presume that Wallace Miller died sometime within that period which commences with his disappearance and ends with the institution of these applications. Being able to arrive at this conclusion, however, does not in itself permit to decide the issue involved in these applications. I must be able to determine when during the period in question Wallace Miller died or, to be more specific, whether he died before August 31, 1934, the date of death of his mother.

Counsel for the Official Guardian takes the position that I am unable on these applications to determine when during the period in question Wallace Miller died. He submits that in order to do this I must refer to the Master the task of conducting an inquiry to determine this fact. He maintains that because the onus is upon the applicant to prove that Wallace Miller pre-deceased his mother, the applicant can, before the Master, adduce whatever evidence is available in this respect. Counsel for the Official Guardian, to support his position, referred me to the decision of Wells, J. (as he then was), in *Re Jones*,[49] where he said:[50]

> In my view on an application under Rule 600 I have no jurisdiction to make the declaration which is asked. It would appear to me that the questions asked in both *c* and *d* will be dealt with on the reference that I have already directed. The difficulty in which the trustees find themselves was solved in this way in *Re Bell*,[51] where such a declaration was made necessarily as incidental to the jurisdiction to ascertain the next-of-kin, by Lennox, Assistant Master. In dealing with the matter on appeal, Hogg J.A. said:[52]
>
>> With respect to the presumption that a person is dead, the rule which governs is laid down in the leading case of *Phené's Trusts, In re*[53] where it was said:
>>
>>> If a person has not been heard of for seven years, there is a presumption of law that he is dead; but at what time within that period he died is not a matter of presumption, but of evidence, and the onus of proving that the death took place at any particular time within the seven years lies upon the person who claims a right to the establishment of which that fact is essential.
>>
>> Sir James Stephen, in his Digest of the Law of Evidence[54] states the rule to be gathered from the *Phené's Trusts* case and the other cases cited by him to be:
>>
>>> A person shown not to have been heard of for seven years by those (if any) who if he had been alive would naturally have heard of him, is presumed to be dead unless the circumstances of the case are such as to account for his not being heard of without assuming his death; but there is no presumption as to the time when he died, and the burden of proving his death at any particular time is upon the person who asserts it.

I am not satisfied that anything would be gained by the institution at this time of an inquiry into an event which occurred more than 60 years ago. The material shows that the records of the police department for the year 1913 are no longer available. As I have noted above, the material indicates that inquiries made following his disappearance did not succeed in bringing forth any account or explanation for the disappearance of Wallace Miller. I think that a reference to the Master along the lines suggested by counsel for the Official Guardian should only take place when it appears to the Court that no due inquiries appropriate to the circumstances of its case have been conducted, and when there is present indication that such a reference might, having regard to the circumstances of that case, be fruitful. I do not believe that *Re Jones* should be interpreted as requiring a reference to be made and conducted, in any event. In this respect it is of interest to me to note that in two reported decisions dealing with an issue such as that

---

49 [1955] O.R. 837, [1955] 5 D.L.R. 213.
50 At pp. 842-3 O.R., p. 219 D.L.R.
51 [1947] O.R. 854, [1947] 1 D.L.R. 554.
52 At p. 861.
53 (1870), L.R. 5 Ch. 139.
54 10th ed. 1922, at pp. 115-6.

with which we are dealing here, no reference to the Master was made. I refer to *Re Watkins, Watkins v. Watkins et al.*[55] and *Re Harlow*.[56]

. . .

I do not accept the position of counsel for the Official Guardian that without a reference to the Master being conducted the Court, having accepted that the fact of death has been proved by the application of the presumption of death, is not able to determine when during the period of continuous disappearance in excess of seven years in length the death occurred. Arnup, J.A., in *Re Harlow*, said:[57]

It would seem to me incongruous that although there would have been ample evidence for a Court to declare in 1966 and 1967 that Donald Harlow was then dead, a Court could not make a declaration in 1975 that by 1966 Donald Harlow was dead.

. . .

In my view *Re Harlow* also stands for the proposition that once the fact of death is determined as having occurred before a certain date, whether by the application of the presumption of death or positive evidence, and such date is prior to the date of death of the person whose date of death is relevant, no uncertainty within the meaning of the *Survivorship Act*[58] exists and, accordingly, that Act has no application. Arnup, J.A., said:[59]

The fact of death may be proved by invocation of the presumption of death (as previously defined) just as readily as it can be proved by positive evidence of death.

. . .

In the present case then, I find that Wallace Miller died before 1934 and, accordingly, when his mother died in that year, she was survived only by her daughter Alma May Miller. I find, then, that Alma May Miller was the sole recipient of the estate of her mother Nancy Miller, which included her interest in the lands and premises known municipally as 263 Withrow Ave., Toronto. I further find that Thelma Marie Coulter is the only person having any estate right or interest in those lands and premises following the death of Alma May Miller.

. . .

UNIFORM PRESUMPTION OF DEATH ACT
Uniform Law Conference of Canada
Consolidation of Uniform Acts (1978), as am. p. 36-1

1. In this Act
(a) "court" means the (name of superior court of the jurisdiction);
(b) "interested person" means any person who is or would be affected by an order made under this Act and includes,

---

55 [1953] 2 All E.R. 1113.
56 (1976), 13 O.R. (2d) 760, 72 D.L.R. (3d) 323.
57 At p. 766 O.R., p. 329 D.L.R.
58 R.S.O. 1970, c. 454.
59 At p. 766 O.R., p. 329 D.L.R.

(i) the next of kin of the person in respect of whom an order is made or applied for, and

(ii) a person who holds property of the person in respect of whom an order is made or applied for.

2. (1) Where, upon the application of an interested person by originating notice of motion, the court is satisfied that

(a) a person has been absent and not heard of or from by the applicant, or to the knowledge of the applicant by any other person, since a day named;

(b) the applicant has no reason to believe that the person is living; and

(c) reasonable grounds exist for supposing that the person is dead, the court may make an order declaring that the person shall be presumed to be dead for all purposes, or for such purposes only as are specified in the order.

(2) An order made under subsection (1) shall state the date on which the person is presumed to have died.

(3) Any interested person may, with leave of the court, apply to the court for an order to vary, amend, confirm or revoke an order made under subsection (1).

(4) An order, or a certified copy thereof, declaring that a person shall be presumed to be dead for all purposes or for the purposes specified in the order is proof of death in all matters requiring proof of death for such purposes.

3. Where an order has been made declaring that a person shall be presumed to be dead for all purposes or for the purpose of distributing his estate, and the personal representative of the person presumed to be dead believes or there are reasonable grounds for him to believe that the person is not in fact dead, the personal representative shall not thereafter deal with the estate or remaining estate unless the presumption of death is confirmed by an order made under section 2(3).

4. (1) Where a person who is presumed to be dead is, in fact, alive, any distribution of his property that has been made in reliance upon an order made under section 2, and not in contravention of section 3, shall be deemed to be a final distribution and to be the property of the person to whom it has been distributed as against the person presumed to be dead.

(2) Where a person who is presumed to be dead is found by the court to be alive, the court may, upon the application of any interested person and subject to subsection (1), by order give such directions as the court considers appropriate respecting the property of the person found to be alive and its preservation and return.

5. Where a person who is presumed to be dead is in fact found to be dead, any distribution of his property that has been made in reliance upon an order made under section 2 shall be deemed to be a final distribution and to be the property of the person to whom it has been distributed as against any person who would otherwise be entitled if the order made under section 2 had not been made.

6. Any interested person may appeal an order made under this Act to the (*appropriate appellate court*).

Notes and Questions

1. What happens if a person stages a disappearance, the court declares the person presumed dead, but the person is subsequently discovered?

A Mr. Tidswell disappeared from his motorized sailboat on Lake Simcoe in July, 1970. He was thought to have fallen overboard and drowned, but his body was never recovered. A court order was obtained declaring him presumed dead and his wife and children received more than $70,000 under two life insurance contracts.

Tidswell went to the United States, remarried and applied for United States citizenship under a different name. His identity was discovered when American immigration officials asked the RCMP to run a fingerprint check. When Tidswell's name came up, he was ordered deported. Tidswell was reported to be making restitution to the insurance companies. A warrant was issued for his arrest in Canada on charges of fraud and public mischief.[60]

Further Reading

Roy J. Stewart, "Presumption of Death" (1988) 46 Advocate (Van.) 595.

David Norwood, "Dead Reckoning: Evidence and Proof of Death" (1996) 15 E. & T.J. 65.

J.C. Shepherd, "Presumption of Death in Ontario" (1979), 4 E. & T.Q. 326.

Susan E. Greer, "Recent Developments in Probate Practice", in Law Society of Upper Canada, Special Lectures, 1980, *Recent Developments in Estate Planning and Administration*, p. 87, at pp. 95-100.

D. Stone, "The Presumption of Death: A Redundant Concept?" (1981), 44 Mod. L. Rev. 516.

3. PROOF OF LOST WILLS

In the preceding chapters we considered various aspects of proving wills. In those chapters the testator's will was always in evidence. What happens if you know that the testator made a will, but it is not found at his or her death? It is often possible, despite the absence of a will, to prove its contents, due execution and the testator's capacity. The evidence of any person who has knowledge of the contents, a copy of the will and statements made by the testator before and after its execution are admissible for this purpose.[61]

Proof of execution and of the contents of the will are not sufficient by themselves, however. The propounder must usually also overcome the presumption of destruction *animo revocandi*.[62] However, the presumption only applies if the will was last known to be in the deceased's possession.[63]

---

60 Report in *The London Free Press*, Nov. 4, 1983, p. A13.

61 *Lefebvre v. Major*, [1930] S.C.R. 252, [1930] 2 D.L.R. 532.

62 See, *e.g.*, *Alston v. Wagar Estate* (1996), 10 E.T.R. (2d) 274 (Ont. Gen. Div.), in which the presumption was rebutted by notes found in the deceased's possession.

63 See *Re Flaman Estate* (1997), 18 E.T.R. (2d) 121 (Sask. Q.B.).

The leading case on the point is *Sudgen v. Lord St. Leonards*.[64] Lord St. Leonards' will could not be found after his death, but his daughter, Miss Sugden, had read it many times and was able to reproduce the bulk of its provisions, although some minor matters had slipped her mind. The court, being satisfied about the accuracy of the testator's testamentary intention, the honesty of the witness and her ability to recall the substance of the will, admitted her memorandum of the contents of the will to probate. In the course of his judgment, Sir George Jessel M.R. said that it would not matter that some legacies could not be given effect to since the testator's secondary intention was to leave his estate to his residuary legatee and effect should be given to his intention.[65]

These *dicta* were questioned in *Woodward v. Goulstone*,[66] in which the House of Lords refused to admit a will to probate upon parol evidence of its contents alone, holding that the evidence was not sufficiently reliable to act upon it.

That was also the problem in *Re Perry*.[67] It was clear that the will perished with the testatrix in a fire, so that the presumption of destruction *animo revocandi* did not arise. However, the conveyancer who prepared the will did not really recall the contents of the will. He remembered that one person was the residuary legatee and thought that certain other named persons were legatees of a number of legacies in specified amounts. However, he could not recall whether those legacies were contained in the testatrix' last will or in previous wills he had prepared for her. Thus, only the residuary gift was established. The court followed *Woodward v. Goulstone*[68] and its criticism of the *dicta* in *Sugden v. Lord St. Leonards*, and held that it would be improper to admit only the gifts of residue to probate.

Lefebvre v. Major,[69] reproduced below, is instructive in that it discusses all three aspects that must be proved when probate of a lost will is sought, namely, execution, contents, and no revocation.

Further Reading

Rodney Hull, "Contested Wills and Proof in Solemn Form" (1979-81), 5 E. & T.Q. 49, at 58-59.

LEFEBVRE v. MAJOR
[1930] S.C.R. 252, [1930] 2 D.L.R. 532
Supreme Court of Canada

The deceased, Alexandre Zotique Pigeon, was advised by his banker to have a will made. The banker referred him to an established Vancouver firm and, after the will had been prepared, the deceased attended there with his friend, Mr. Cyr,

---

64 (1876), 1 P.D. 154 (C.A.).
65 *Ibid.*, at p. 223.
66 (1886), 11 App. Cas. 469 (H.L.).
67 56 O.L.R. 278, [1925] 1 D.L.R. 930 (C.A.).
68 *Supra.*
69 *Supra.*

upon a Mr. Bourne. Bourne read the will to the testator in the presence of Cyr. Cyr testified that Bourne's partner was then called in, after which the deceased signed it and Cyr and the partner witnessed it.

The deceased and Cyr then went to the bank and left the will with the banker for safekeeping. The banker confirmed this. The deceased informed his sister in Ontario of the will and its contents, but she noticed that he had described himself by his nickname, "Peter," and expressed concern about its validity. for that reason, the deceased again attended upon Bourne with Cyr, having taken the will from the bank. The will was redrawn or corrected, there being no evidence on the point, and redeposited with the bank.

In 1924, Pigeon returned to Ontario and lived with his sister for a while, after which he bought his own property. The evidence was that he was throughout on good terms with his sister, to whom he left all his estate.

In 1925 Pigeon wrote to the banker stating that only requests for money signed by himself were to be honoured, not any signed by his brother-in-law, who was one of the executors. He asked that the will be sent to him and it was.

Shortly before he died in 1928, Pigeon told two independent witnesses that he had left all his estate to his only sister. His body was found in an advanced state of decomposition and, upon the undertaker's instructions, his bedding and clothes were burned. Thereafter a search was made for the will, but it was not found.

The executors, Cyr, and the sister and brother-in-law, sought to prove the will. They were successful at trial, but the Appellate Division of the Supreme Court of Ontario reversed.[70] The executors appealed.

ANGLIN J., delivered the judgment of the court:

. . .

Three questions are presented on the present appeal:

First — Was due execution of the alleged will established;

Second — Were its contents satisfactorily proved; and

Third — Does the evidence rebut the presumption of destruction by the testator *animo revocandi?*

. . .

[Cyr] is not asked where Pigeon placed his signature on the paper, nor whether DesBrisay was present and saw him sign it as well as himself, nor whether he and DesBrisay actually signed the will as witnesses, nor whether, if they signed it, they did so in the presence of the testator. In ordinary parlance, however, a man who says he witnessed the execution of a document means that he attested such execution by this signature; and that, I think, is a fair inference from this evidence. As to the observance of the statutory formalities, to which Cyr's attention was not specifically called, it is, I think, a reasonable assumption that they were duly observed, having regard to all the circumstances and especially to the fact that the will was carefully prepared by a competent solicitor and was executed in his office....While neither Mr. Bourne nor Mr. DesBrisay had any recollection of the circumstances, a charge is made in the books of the solicitors for the drawing of

---

70 (1929), 64 O.L.R. 43.

a will of Mr. Pigeon on the 22nd of November, 1923. We have no hesitation in finding the due execution of the will of November 22, 1923, to have been established.

. . .

While it would be more satisfactory had the circumstances of the making of the will of February 21, 1924, been adequately probed, it would seem to be not very material whether due execution of that will should or should not be regarded as having been established. Either it was or it was not duly executed. If it was, its contents, having been proved to be the same as those of the earlier will, are sufficiently established by proof of the contents of that will and the document to be admitted to probate would in that case be the will of February 21, 1924. If, on the other hand, the due execution and attestation of that document should be held not to have been sufficiently established, the will of November 22, 1923, would remain effective, even though it had been physically destroyed on the assumption that it had been duly replaced by the later will. Under such circumstances the doctrine of dependent relative revocation applies.[71]

It, therefore, seems to us not vital which document should be regarded as the last will of the testator. Either that of the 22nd of November, 1923, or that of the 21st of February, 1924, was a duly executed will; or perhaps both were so executed; and, the contents being identical except for the change in the testator's name, it does not seem to be very material which document should be admitted to probate.

As to the proof of contents, the evidence is absolutely clear and dependable. Not only are the contents stated by Zoel Cyr, who heard the will read, but they are also set forth in the testator's letter of the 2nd of March, 1924, to his sister; and this evidence is corroborated . . . .

. . .

There remains, therefore, only the difficulty presented by the presumption of revocation arising from the will, traced to the possession of the testator, not being forthcoming.[72] This is said by Cockburn C.J., in *Sugden v. Lord St. Leonards*[73] to be "*presumptio juris*, but not *de jure*, more or less strong" according to the circumstances such as the character of the testator and his relation to the beneficiaries, the contents of the instrument, and the possibility of its loss being accounted for otherwise than by intentional destruction on the part of the testator.

[His Lordship recited the facts on this point and continued:]

There can be no question upon this evidence that the document deposited with the bank in Vancouver in February, 1924, was forwarded to and was received by Peter Pigeon at Alexandria in May, 1925. It is this fact, coupled with the other fact that the will was not found amongst his papers, that gives rise to the presumption of destruction by the testator *animo revocandi*.

---

71 Jarman on Wills, 6th ed., pp. 148 *et seq.*
72 *Welch v. Phillips* (1836), 1 Moore P.C. 299.
73 (1876), 1 P.D. 154 at 217.

Reverting for a moment to the letter of the 3rd of May, 1925, the prohibition which it contains to the banker to pay money upon any paper bearing the signature of Mr. Lefebvre as well as Mr. Pigeon, is relied upon as suggestive of unpleasantness having arisen between him and the Lefebvre family. Whether any such inference would be open upon the document if standing alone, or whether the proper view is that taken by the learned trial judge, viz., that the testator, an ignorant and unlearned man, feared that the fact he had named Lefebvre as one of his executors might give that gentleman some present control of, or voice in, the disposition of moneys left by him with the bank and that he wished to guard against anything of the kind happening, is, perhaps doubtful. But, however that may be, any inference that could otherwise be drawn adverse to Mrs. Lefebvre, the testator's sister, is entirely overcome by the direct evidence in the record that there was at no time any interruption whatever of the friendly and affectionate relations subsisting between her and the testator. Moreover, to infer from this letter that the testator had destroyed his will *animo revocandi* at any time after its receipt by him on the 21st of May, 1925, is so utterly inconsistent with his statements made in April and May of 1928 to the independent witnesses...that it may safely be disregarded.

While the view taken by the learned trial judge of the interpretation proper to be placed upon the testator's letter of the 3rd of May to the banker may not be entirely correct, having regard to all the evidence it is at least less improbable than that suggested on behalf of the respondents.

[His Lordship recited the facts surrounding Pigeon's death and continued:]

That the testator regarded his will as of the highest importance and, there being no evidence of its deposit for safekeeping in the bank, or with a solicitor, or trust company, that he would quite likely have kept it near his person, not improbably in the pocket of his coat, or in his bed, is a fair inference from the testimony of the witness Zoel Cyr, who deposes to the great care he took of it in carrying it from the office of the solicitor to that of the banker and adds, very significantly, that he (Pigeon) thought the will a very important document and that it was not likely that he would be careless with it when it came into his possession; that "he wanted the will to be in a safe place." It is obvious that the will may have been inadvertently burned when the testator's personal effects were destroyed after his death. Having regard to this circumstance, and also to the facts that the will, as made, was eminently reasonable in view of the testator's affectionate feelings towards his only surviving sister, that there was no change in those feelings, as the evidence establishes, that the testator's intention to benefit his sister subsisted until within a few weeks of his death, as he declared to two independent and trustworthy witnesses, and lastly, to the simple character of the man himself, it seems highly improbable that he intentionally destroyed his will *animo revocandi*.

. . .

On the whole case we are convinced that the presumption of destruction by the testator *animo revocandi* is sufficiently rebutted and that the trial judge reached the correct conclusion when he directed that probate should be granted in accordance with the prayer of the petition of the executors. The observations of Sir James Hannon in the *Sugden* case[74] are much in point.

[The court allowed the appeal.]

Notes and Questions

1. As is apparent from the *Lefebvre* case, the executors of a lost or destroyed will must prove due execution of the will, just as in a case in which the will is prodcued. They may also have to prove capacity and knowledge of the contents. The main items of proof in a lost will case that differ from the normal case, therefore, are proof of the contents, and whether the presumption of destruction applies.

2. The standard of proof required to establish a lost will is the civil onus of a balance of probabilities only.[75]

3. A testatrix made her will in 1973, giving a legacy to a close friend, the income from the residue to the testatrix's daughter, who was confined in a mental institution, and the capital of the residue to a charity. She appointed a trust company as her executor. In 1979 she made a codicil confirming the will, but changing the executor to her friend. The trust company then sent her the 1973 will. In 1985 the testatrix referred to the will as "a good will." She died in 1986 in full possession of her faculties.

The testatrix was a widow and the daughter was her only child. At her death the codicil was found, but the will was not. However, the solicitor who drew it had kept a copy of it. What result?[76]

4. *Wagenhoffer v. Wagenhoffer Estate*[77] is another example. The testator had executed a will in 1969. The trial judge admitted evidence that showed the testator had made a later, properly executed, holograph will in 1981. This document, which was last seen in the possession of the testator, could not be found after his death. The trial judge was able to reconstruct its terms from the oral evidence of a person allegedly present when the will was made. On appeal, the court applied the presumption that the 1981 will was destroyed by the testator. The 1981 will had effectively revoked the 1969 will and destruction of the later will did not revive the 1969 document. Thus, the testator died intestate.

5. *Brimicombe v. Brimicombe Estate*[78] illustrates that the presumption of destruction can readily be overcome with appropriate evidence. While in hospital, the testatrix changed her will. She told a number of people about the change and that the will was kept in a sealed envelope marked "Last Will and Testament" in an unlocked box under her bed. When the testatrix died two years later, the executrix found only a copy of the will in the box and neither the executrix nor the solicitor could find the original. The solicitor did not recall whether the original will was ever given to the testatrix. The court held that the presumption was rebutted because the testatrix was very aware of the problems that would arise if she died intestate and expressed her clear intentions to her solicitor, her executrix

---

74 *Ibid.*, at pp. 202-3.

75 *Re Haverland; Haverland v. Farney*, [1975] 4 W.W.R. 673, 55 D.L.R. (3d) 122 (Alta. T.D.); *Scott v. Cresswell*, [1976] 3 W.W.R. 382, 56 D.L.R. (3d) 268 (Alta. C.A); *Re Hammond* (1982), 36 Nfld. & P.E.I.R. 69, 101 A.P.R. 69 (Nfld. Dist. Ct.); *Re Jones; Shaw and Brooks v. Stromme*, 16 W.W.R. 78, [1955] 5 D.L.R. 436 (B.C.S.C.); *Rules of Practice - Surrogate Court*, R.R.O. 1980, Reg. 925, s. 18.

76 See *Re Oliver Estate* (1987), 27 E.T.R. 35 (Ont. Surr. Ct.).

77 (1986), 22 E.T.R. 60 (Sask. C.A.).

78 (2000), 34 E.T.R. (2d) 14 (N.S.C.A.).

and others to ensure that she did not die intestate. Two prior wills of hers were not destroyed, which suggested that she did not destroy wills to revoke them. Further, if she intended to destroy the will, she would not have left the sealed envelope marked "Last Will and Testament" in the box. In any event, the evidence suggested that the original will was never in the testatrix's possession, in which case the presumption did not apply.

6. *Re Cole Estate*[79] is an interesting case on the issue of proof of the existence of the will and its execution, as well as its disappearance after the testator's death. On the evidence of one of the deceased's sisters and her daughters, which the trial judge believed, the will was executed while the deceased was in hospital. Although one of the witnesses had predeceased and the other had lost his memory, execution of the will was proved to the satisfaction of the court by other means. The sister and her daughters testified that they read the will the day after the funeral and that the will left everything to the sister, however, a brother took the will away with him, saying it was too old and no good. They never saw the will again. The brother testified that no will was ever found. The trial judge did not believe his evidence. The decision was affirmed on appeal.

7. If, in the course of a trial to establish the contents of a lost will, the parties reach a settlement, one party is not entitled to overturn the settlement after the will is discovered.[80]

4. CONFLICT OF LAWS RULES

It is common today for a testator to make a will in one jurisdiction and then to move to another, or, indeed, to move to several others in succession before death. Most of the testator's assets may be in the jurisdiction where he or she last resided, or they may be scattered all over the world. In these circumstances, which jurisdiction has power to deal with the administration of the estate? Also, what are the courts in that jurisdiction to do if the will was valid according to the place where the will was made, but is not valid according to the *lex fori*?

To answer these and other questions certain conflict of laws rules were developed, which are discussed below. In this respect, you should note two things. First, the conflicts rules are concerned both with the formal and the intrinsic validity of a will. Formal validity concerns such matters as capacity, manner of execution and number of witnesses, whereas the intrinsic or essential validity concerns the meaning and effect of the will. Unfortunately, it is not always easy to characterize an issue as one of formal or essential validity. Thus, for example, a foreign jurisdiction might permit a person between the ages of 18 and 21 to make a will, but insist that such a person's will be attested by two notarial witnesses. This might be a matter of form or essence, but the statutes incorporating the conflicts rules give no guidance on the question.

The second point to note is that under the conflicts rules the common law distinction between real and personal property is not used, but rather the civil law distinction between movables and immovables. The term "immovables" includes interests in land, plus leasehold interests. Therefore, it differs from the common law concept of real property in that it includes leasehold interests. The term "movables" comprises all other interests in personal property.

---

79 (1994), 4 E.T.R. (2d) 193 (N.S.C.A.).
80 See *Zimmer v. Zimmer* (1996), 13 E.T.R. (2d) 183 (Sask. Q.B.).

The excerpt from the Ontario Law Reform Commission's *Report on the Proposed Adoption in Ontario of the Uniform Wills Act*,[81] reproduced below, traces the history of the conflicts rules. It is followed by a commentary on the changes as subsequently adopted and by sections 34-41 of the *Succession Law Reform Act*,[82] which implement the recommendations of the Law Reform Commission.

ONTARIO LAW REFORM COMMISSION
REPORT ON THE
PROPOSED ADOPTION IN ONTARIO OF THE
UNIFORM WILLS ACT

(1968), pp. 14-18

CONFLICT OF LAWS

GENERAL

As a result of the increasing mobility of Canadians, problems frequently arise as to jurisdiction and choice of law in will matters.

This may be illustrated by the following example:

J was born of Italian parents in England, which was his domicile of origin. As a young man he emigrated to Manitoba, acquiring domicile there. He married a young lady from Quebec and made his will in that province. At that time he was a national of Italy. Later, he moved to Ontario where he spent the remainder of his working life. On his retirement, he decided to reside in Florida. He died domiciled there, although all his assets, consisting of both real and personal property were located in Ontario. J's son, who is the sole heir under the will, lives in Vancouver and would find it convenient to deal with his father's estate through the British Columbia courts. Two questions arise:

1. Which one or more of the seven territories mentioned above has jurisdiction to deal with the will?
2. Which of the seven systems of law should be applied by the court exercising jurisdiction?

These questions will be determined under the rules of private international law which are part of the laws of each province, as well as of the laws of Florida, Italy and England. Insofar as jurisdiction to admit a will to probate is concerned, the general rule is that the grant of probate will be made only if there is property of the deceased within the jurisdiction. Although it is possible for the law of a particular jurisdiction to permit the granting of probate where no such property is located, the obtaining of probate under such circumstances will be of no assistance as the jurisdiction where the property is located will normally require

---

81 Toronto, Ministry of the Attorney General (1968).
82 R.S.O. 1990, c.488.

probate to be granted there before the property can be dealt with. Thus, in the example above, for practical purposes, the will would have to be proved in Ontario.

The kind of problems that the courts may be concerned with in these situations are as follows:

(1) Did the testator have the capacity to make a will?
(2) Was the will formally valid? (i.e. Was it signed and witnessed as required?)
(3) What of the essential or intrinsic validity of the will? (i.e. Could the disposition under the will be effectually made?)
(4) How should the will be construed?

As the law dealing with these problems may vary from jurisdiction to jurisdiction, the question of choice of law is often a critical matter.

THE COMMON LAW

By the middle of the last century, two basic rules were firmly established in the common law insofar as both the formal and essential validity of wills are concerned:
(1) A will disposing of *immovable* property (i.e. interests in land) had to satisfy the law of the country in which the land was situated; and
(2) A will disposing of *movables* was governed by the law of the country in which the testator was domiciled at the date of his death.

Although a leasehold is regarded as personal, rather than real, property under the English common law, it is an immovable by the above classification. Consequently, in the example, the formal and essential validity of the Quebec will would have been determined in Ontario in the following way, until the first decade of this century (as will be seen later):
 (i) as to immovables, by the law of Ontario; and
(ii) as to movables, by the law of Florida.

The application of the above two rules has produced unfortunate results in some cases, particularly with regard to movables. For example, an Englishman, born and domiciled in England, made a will in that country. He subsequently changed his domicile to France where he died. Although his movables were located in England, the will was ineffective with respect to them as it did not comply with the formalities required by French law.

LORD KINGSDOWN'S ACT

To alleviate such hardships with respect to movables, the *Wills Act* of 1861[83] was enacted in the United Kingdom. This statute is sometimes referred to as *Lord*

---

83 24 & 25 Vict., c. 114.

Kingsdown's Act. A will would be formally valid under it if the requirements of any of the following jurisdictions were met:

A. *Where the will was made outside the United Kingdom,*
1. where the will was made;
2. where the testator was domiciled when the will was made; or
3. where the testator had his domicile of origin, if that place was part of His Majesty's dominions.

B. *Where the will was made in the United Kingdom,*
   the United Kingdom.

Thus a will would be formally valid if it met the requirements of any of the above places, or, if it met the requirements, as laid down by the common law rule of the place where the testator died domiciled.

The Act of 1861 had certain shortcomings:

1. It ignored the traditional private international law distinction between movables and immovables and expressly applied to "personal estate" thus bringing leaseholds within its ambit instead of leaving them where they should be as "immovables";
2. It only applied to wills made by British subjects; and
3. It made a pointless distinction between wills made in and outside the United Kingdom.

Criticism has also been levelled at the Act as it made relevant the domicile of origin, a place with which the testator might long ceased to have been connected. Despite these shortcomings, the statute remained in effect in the United Kingdom until it was replaced by the *Wills Act* of 1963.[84] This latter enactment was based on the 1961 convention on wills prepared by the Hague Conference on Private International law.

Ontario adopted *Lord Kingsdown's Act* in 1902,[85] with the exception of one provision. It made no reference to wills made in Ontario. It was therefore only remedial as to wills made outside Ontario. All the shortcomings of the British Act were contained in it. In 1910, the Ontario statutes dealing with wills were revised and consolidated into one enactment. The new *Wills Act*[86] included the 1902 statute and also the provision previously omitted dealing with wills made within the province. the Ontario version of *Lord Kingsdown's Act* remained the law of Ontario until 1954. It last appeared as section 19 of the *Wills Act* in the Revised Statutes of 1950.[87]

Applying the Ontario law as it existed from 1902 until 1954 to our example, the Quebec will would, insofar as it dealt with personal estate, be formally (but

---

84 C. 44 (U.K.).
85 By S.O. 1902, c. 18.
86 S.O. 1910, c. 57.
87 R.S.O. 1950, c. 426.

not essentially) valid if it met the requirements of the law of any of Florida (except as to leases), Quebec, Manitoba or England. However, this would only be the case if the will had been made by a British subject. The essential validity of the will insofar as it related to movables would still be governed by Florida law only. Since J, in our example, was an Italian national at the time he made the will, the formal validity of his will would not, of course, have been affected by the 1902 Ontario legislation and only Florida law would be relevant.

THE EARLY UNIFORM LEGISLATION AND ITS ADOPTION IN ONTARIO

Meanwhile, the Conference on Uniformity of Legislation in Canada had approved the 1929 *Uniform Act*. Part II of the *Uniform Act*, entitled "Conflict of Laws", consisted of a considerable revision and improvement of *Lord Kingsdown's Act*. The draft of that part of the *Uniform Act* was the work of Dean John D. Falconbridge, Q.C., of Osgoode Hall Law School. Dean Falconbridge produced a further improved revision in 1946 in a note in the Law Quarterly Review.[88] In 1951, the Ontario Commissioners to the Conference on Uniformity recommended that Dean Falconbridge's new revision be substituted for Part II of the 1929 *Uniform Act*. The Conference approved the substitution in 1953, making some slight modifications of Dean Falconbridge's new revision. The following year Ontario repealed the Lord Kingsdown provision in the *Wills Act* and replaced it with the new Part II of the *Uniform Act*.

The 1954 amendment[89] made the following improvements:

1. There was general clarification of the language of the statute;
2. There was codification of the two basic common law rules with regard to the choice of law in regard to the formal and essential validity of wills;
3. Leaseholds were to be treated as interests in land and not as personal estate;
4. No distinction was made between wills made in and outside of Ontario, the previous provision as to wills made outside the province being made applicable to all wills;
5. The new provisions were not confined to wills made by British subjects but were applicable regardless of the nationality of the testator;
6. There was codification of the common law principle that treats movables used in relation to land, such as the key to a house or title deeds, as immovables.

The statute, in dealing with the last point, made the provision apply to intestacies as well as wills, a matter which might have been more appropriately set out in *The Devolution of Estates Act*,[90] which governs intestate succession.

Applying the Act of 1954 to the example (thus assuming the will to have been made after July 1st, 1954) the following result is obtained. As British nationality was no longer a condition, the provisions now apply to J, and the will would be

---

88 "A Canadian Redraft of Lord Kingsdown's Act" (1946), 62 L.Q. Rev. 328.
89 S.O. 1954, c.105.
90 R.S.O. 1950, c. 103.

formally valid as to movables if the requirements of any of Florida, Quebec, Manitoba or England were met.

THE NEW UNIFORM LEGISLATION

Between 1959 and 1966, Part II of the *Uniform Act* was again under study by the Conference on Uniformity. This re-examination was undertaken as a result of a movement in England and Europe to improve and make uniform the laws relating to the formal validity of wills. In 1958, the United Kingdom Parliamentary Private International Law Committee recommended that *Lord Kingsdown's Act*, which was still in effect in England, be replaced with a more liberal statute and one that would be more generally in line with legislation in other European countries. At the same time the Hague Conference on Private International Law was preparing a multilateral convention on the subject. This was concluded in 1961 and subsequently ratified by Great Britain, but not Canada, since it is not a member of the Hague conference. In 1963, Great Britain enacted a new *Wills Act*[91] which implemented the report of the Private International Law Committee and the Hague Convention.

The Conference on Uniformity of Legislation in Canada completed their study in 1966 and in that year a new Part II of the *Uniform Act* was approved. The changes were:

1. The problem of *renvoi* was eliminated;
2. To the available determinants of the law governing the formal validity of wills as regards movables, there were added the law of the place where:
   (a) the testator had his habitual residence where the will was made;
   (b) the testator was a national when the will was made, if there was in that place one body of law governing the wills of nationals;
   (c) if the will was made on board a vessel or aircraft, the vessel or aircraft may be taken to have been most closely connected;
3. Insofar as a will revokes a former will, it would be formally valid as to movables if it conforms to any law by reference to which the revoked will would be treated as properly made;
4. Insofar as a will exercises a power of appointment, it would be formally valid as to movables if the making of the will conforms to the law governing the essential validity of the power;
5. The law of the domicile of origin was no longer included among the available determinants for establishing the formal validity of a will as to movables;
6. Where a law in force outside a province requires special formalities to be observed by particular testators or witnesses to have certain qualifications, such requirements would be treated by that province;
7. When determining whether a will conforms to the formal requirements of a particular law, regard would be had not only to that law at the time the will

---

91 1963, c. 44.

was made but to any subsequent alteration of that law which would make such a will valid.

All these changes had been contained in the United Kingdom *Wills Act* of 1963. Two significant provisions of the British statute were not followed by the Canadian Conference on Uniformity. The first of these made the law with respect to the formal validity of movables the same for immovables. If such a rule were adopted in Ontario, it could result that a holograph will, which is valid under Alberta law, could dispose of land in Ontario, when the internal law of Ontario imposes more formal requirements. This objection would be met if holograph wills were to receive recognition in Ontario, as this Report recommends. If the recommendation with regard to holograph wills is accepted, then the Commission further recommends that the law with regard to movables be made applicable to immovables.

The second provision of the British Act which was not considered suitable by the Canadian Conference on Uniformity was with respect to the use of the law of the place where the testator was a national at the time the will was made if that place was a state where there were two or more systems of internal law relating to the formal validity of wills. This would include such countries as Canada and the United States. Under the British statute, the courts would look, in the cases of these two countries, to the province or state with which the testator was most closely connected. The Conference felt that the British provision might prove difficult to apply and therefore did not include it in the *Uniform Act*.

The advantages of most of the changes adopted by the Conference are obvious. However, two require comment.

1. THE ELIMINATION OF RENVOI

The doctrine of *renvoi* requires that a reference to a law of a country means a reference to the whole of its law, including its private international law. Thus, if a judge in Ontario were hearing a case and was referred by Ontario law to the law of Italy and the Italian law refers it back to Ontario, the judge must apply Ontario law. The reference to the Italian law was to the whole of its law, not just its internal law. The application of the rules of Italian private international law resulted in a sending back or remission for the application of Ontario law. The doctrine becomes more complicated when a third country becomes involved. In the above example, in working out the law to be applied, the Ontario judge might find that the Italian law referred not back to the law of Ontario but to the law of England.

The doctrine of *renvoi* has been much criticized. (See, for example, Cheshire's Private International Law).[92] It is difficult to apply as it requires the judge seized of the matter to decide how the court of a foreign country would apply the private international law of that country. There may be further difficulties if the rules of the foreign country refer to the national law of the person concerned. What is

---

92 7th ed., 1965, at p. 55 *et seq*.

meant by "national law" is not clear, particularly with respect to countries which are federal in nature.

Furthermore, the doctrine may be objected to on principle. Instead of the law of the country seized of the particular matter determining the choice of law rule, the choice is made by the law of the foreign country. In addition, there are problems with respect to uniformity of results in applying the doctrine.

If the provisions of the *Uniform Act* are accepted, the doctrine is eliminated. When an Ontario judge is referred by Ontario law to the law of another country, he will be referred tothe internal law of that country only. The choice of law will have been made at that point.

The comments of Professor J.G. Castel of Osgoode Hall Law School on this subject are appropriate. He made these in a submission to the Conference on Uniformity and they are set out in the Proceedings of the 1966 meeting of the Conference.[93] He said:

> I support this change as it is intended to eliminate the problem of *renvoi*. Generally speaking, advocates of the theory of *renvoi* exclude from its sphere of application the manner and formalities of making a will. (Contra *Ross v. Ross*[94] on appeal from Quebec and many English cases.) On the other hand, as concerns the intrinsic validity and effect of a will, support will be found for the application of the conflict of laws rules of the place referred to by the forum on the ground that such an approach favours uniformity of distribution. In Canada, however, there are, to my knowledge, no reported decisions on this question.
>
> As an advocate of the "substantive reference" I believe that s.38(c) should be adopted. Furthermore, this provision is in conformity with the Hague Convention on the Conflict of Laws Relating to the Form of Testamentary Dispositions concluded on October 5, 1961, and the U.K. *Wills Act* of 1963[95] that implements the Hague Convention and gives effect to the Fourth Report of the Private International Law Committee[96] appointed by the Lord Chancellor. I am sure that Quebec would look favourably upon this disposition of the problem of *renvoi* as it relates to wills.

2. CHANGES AS TO CHOICE OF LAW

Domicile of origin has been dropped and, instead, nationality has been made a connecting factor. It is generally felt that domicile of origin is too remote a factor to be considered as relevant for choice of law. The Hague Convention of 1961 and the United Kingdom *Wills Act* of 1963 excluded it. The Conference on Uniformity agreed with this result. On the other hand, the nationality of the testator when he makes the will can well be taken to be a current connecting factor at that time. Both Dr. Castel and Professor Gordon C. Bale, of the Law Faculty of Queen's University, supported these changes, in comments quoted in the 1966 Uniformity Conference Proceedings.

The inclusion of the law of the place where the testator had his "habitual residence" when the will was made, in addition to that of his domicile at that time,

---

93 At pp. 131-132.
94 (1894) 25 S.C.R. 307.
95 *Supra.*
96 1958 Comnd. 491.

is intended to remedy deficiencies with respect to the meaning of domicile. Private international law has developed very technical rules with respect to the acquisition and loss of domicile, which at times produce unreal and unfortunate results.

Returning to the example given at the beginning of this Part..., a different result now will be reached if the 1966 *Uniform Act* were adopted in Ontario. In determining the formal validity of the will as to movables, the court would look to the law of Italy, Manitoba, Quebec and Florida.

CONCLUSION

The Commission considers that Part II of the Uniform Wills Act, as it was revised in 1966, is an improvement over the existing legislation and accordingly recommends its adoption. The Commission further recommends that, in the event its recommendation with respect to holograph wills is accepted, the law with regard to movables be made applicable to immovables.

SUCCESSION LAW REFORM IN ONTARIO
A.H. Oosterhoff (1979) pp. 48-9

The major changes made by the Act are the following:

(a) The *renvoi* problem has been eliminated. Under this doctrine it will be recaleld, a reference to the law of another country required that the whole of such law be referred to, including its law on the conflict of laws, and not just the internal law of such a country. When the law of such a country was considered it might have referred the matter back to the *lex fori*. Further difficulties could have resulted if a third country were involved and the law of the second country referred the matter to the law of such third country. To eliminate those and other difficulties the Ontario courts are now referred to the internal law of the first country only by section 36.[97]

(b) As regards the formal validity of wills respecting movables, the law of the testator's domicile of origin was dropped as a determinant.[98] On the other hand; the law of the following places was added as an appropriate determinant by section 37, *viz.*, where:

    (i) the testator had his habitual residence when the will was made;

    (ii) the testator was a national when the will was made, if there was in that place one body of law covering the wills of nationals;

    (iii) if the will was made on board a vessel or aircraft, [the place] the vessel or aircraft may be taken to have been most closely connected.[99]

---

97 For a succinct statement of the problems involved see the Ont. Law Ref. Comm. *Report on the Proposed Adoption in Ontario of the Uniform Wills Act* (1968), pp. 19-21.

98 *Ibid.*, at p. 21.

99 *Ibid.*, at p. 18.

As to the second addition, it will be noted that this cannot apply to a federal State such as Canada. The *Uniform Act*[100] contains an identical provision, although other jurisdictions such as the United Kingdom apply this determinant to both unitary and federal States. In the case of the latter, regard should be had to the province with which the testator was most closely connected.[101] The difficulty of application in the case of a federal State feared by the Conference of Commissioners for Uniformity of Legislation in Canada[102] is outweighed by the desirability of saving wills wherever made if they are valid under the law of such place.

(c) The following additional changes were recommended and made:

(i) Insofar as a will revokes a former will, it would be formally valid as to movables if it conforms to any law by reference to which the revoked will would be treated as properly made.[103]

(ii) Insofar as a will exercises a power of appointment, it would be formally valid as to the movables if the making of the will conforms to the law governing the essential validity of the power.[104]

(iii) The law of the domicile of origin was no longer included among the available determinants for establishing the formal validity of a will as to movables.

(iv) Where a law in force outside a province requires special formalities to be observed by particular testators or witnesses to have certain qualifications, such requirements would be treated as formal by the province.[105]

(v) When determining whether a will conforms to the formal requirements of a particular law, regard would be had not only to that law at the time the will was made but to any subsequent alteration of that law which would make such a will valid.[106]

The Ontario Law Reform Commission also recommended that if its recommendations respecting holograph wills were adopted the law with respect to the formal validity of immovables should be made the same as that for movables.[107] This change was implemented by the Act,[108] although it was not contained in the Commission's draft Bill.

---

100 Uniform Law Conference of Canada, *Uniform Acts of the Uniform Law Conference of Canada* (1978), p. 53-1.

101 *Report on the Uniform Wills Act, supra,* at p. 18; *Wills Act,* 1963 (U.K.), c. 44, s. 6(2).

102 *Report on the Uniform Wills Act, supra,* at p. 19.

103 *Ibid.,* s. 37(2)(b).

104 *Ibid.,* s. 37(2)(c).

105 *Ibid.,* s. 41(1).

106 *Ibid.,* s. 41(2).

107 *Ibid.* The point is that if the holograph will is not recognized in Ontario then if the law concerning formal validity with respect to land were the same as with respect to movables, a holograph will made in a place where it can be made, could validly dispose of land in Ontario. This was not possible heretofore, of course: *Re Dupont* (1966), 57 D.L.R. (2d) 109 (Ont. H.C.).

108 In the running heads of s. 37(1) and (2).

SUCCESSION LAW REFORM ACT
R.S.O. 1990, c. S.26

34. In sections 36 to 41,

(a) an interest in land includes a leasehold estate as well as a freehold estate in land, and any other estate or interest in land whether the estate or interest is real property or is personal property;

(b) an interest in movables includes an interest in a tangible or intangible thing other than land, and includes personal property other than an estate or interest in land;

(c) "internal law" in relation to any place excludes the choice of law rules of that place.

35. Sections 36 to 41 apply to a will made either in or out of Ontario.

36. (1) The manner and formalities of making a will, and its essential validity and effect, so far as it relates to an interest in land, are governed by the internal law of the place where the land is situated.

(2) Subject to other provisions of this Part, the manner and formalities of making a will, and its essential validity and effect, so far as it relates to an interest in movables, are governed by the internal law of the place where the testator was domiciled at the time of his or her death.

37. (1) As regards the manner and formalities of making a will of an interest in movables or in land, a will is valid and admissible to probate if at the time of its making it complied with the internal law of the place where,

(a) the will was made;

(b) the testator was then domiciled;

(c) the testator then had his or her habitual residence; or

(d) the testator then was a national if there was in that place one body of law governing the wills of nationals.

(2) As regards the manner and formalities of making a will of an interest in movables or in land, the following are properly made,

(a) a will made on board a vessel or aircraft of any description, if the making of the will conformed to the internal law in force in the place with which, having regard to its registration, if any, and other relevant circumstances, the vessel or aircraft may be taken to have been most closely connected;

(b) a will so far as it revokes a will which under sections 34 to 42 would be treated as properly made or revokes a provision which under those sections would be treated as comprised in a properly made will, if the making of the later will conformed to any law by reference to which the revoked will or provision would be treated as properly made; and

(c) a will so far as it exercises a power of appointment, if the making of the will conforms to the law governing the essential validity of the power.

38. A change of domicile of the testator occurring after a will is made does not render it invalid as regards the manner and formalities of its making or alter its construction.

39. Nothing in sections 34 to 42 precludes resort to the law of the place where the testator was domiciled at the time of making a will in aid of its construction as regards an interest in land or an interest in movables.

40. Where the value of a thing that is movable consists mainly or entirely in its use in connection with a particular parcel of land by the owner or occupier of the land, succession to an interest in the thing under a will is governed by the law that governs succession to the interest in the land.

41. (1) Where, whether under sections 34 to 42 or not, a law in force outside Ontario is to be applied in relation to a will, any requirement of that law that,

    (a) special formalities are to be observed by testators answering a particular description; or

    (b) witnesses to the making of a will are to possess certain qualifications,

shall be treated, despite any rule of that law to the contrary, as a formal requirement only.

(2) In determining for the purposes of sections 34 to 40 whether or not the making of a will conforms to a particular law, regard shall be had to the formal requirements of that law at the time the will was made, but account shall be taken of an alteration of law affecting wills made at that time if the alteration enables the will to be treated as properly made.

Comparable Legislation

Wills Act, R.S.A. 1980, c. W-11, Part 2; R.S.B.C. 1996, c. 489, Part 3; R.S.M. 1988, c. W150, Part II; R.S.N.B. 1973, c. W-9, Part II, am. 1997, c. 7, ss. 2-5; R.S.N. 1990, c. W-10, Part II; R.S.N.S. 1989, c. 505, ss. 15, 16; R.S.N.W.T. 1988, c. W-5, ss. 25-27; S.S. 1996, c. W-14.1, ss. 38, 39, 40; R.S.Y. 1986, c. 179, ss. 24-26.

Notes and Questions

1. Under the former conflicts rules a holograph will, executed without witnesses in Ontario by a testator born in Austria but domiciled in Ontario at the time the will was executed, was held to be valid insofar as it related to an interest in moveables situate in Ontario, because it was executed in accordance with the law in force at the time of its making in the place of the testator's domicile of origin. Holograph wills were not then recognized by Ontario law.[109]

2. You should note that the statute only directs the court to the law that should be applied in determining the validity of a will. It does not determine which court has jurisdiction to grant probate. However, the *Estates Act*[110] provides that the application shall be filed in the office of the court for the county or district in which the deceased had at the time of death a fixed place of abode, failing which, it shall be filed in the office of the court for the county or district in which the deceased had property at the time death, or, failing that, it shall be filed in any office of the Superior Court of Justice.

3. If proceedings for representation are commenced in courts in two different jurisdictions, both having power to deal with the matter, the court has power to stay the proceedings

---

109 *Re Bishop*, [1972] 1 O.R. 183, 22 D.L.R. (3d) 507 (C.A.).
110 R.S.O. 1990, c. E.21, s. 26.

and will do so if they are vexatious and oppressive.[111] However, it will not necessarily do so otherwise, even if the applicant in the domestic forum has brought proceedings in the foreign court contesting the proceedings there. It will not do so if it is likely that the deceased was domiciled in the foreign jurisdiction and had substantial assets there.[112]

4. The law of the deceased's domicile at the time of death determines the issue of testamentary capacity, not the law of the place where the will was made.[113]

5. You should note that the Ontario legislation refers to an interest in land and to movables. The reference to land is improper. The statute should have used the generally accepted term "immovables."

6. If a testator directs that a will shall be interpreted in accordance with the law of a specific jurisdiction, the court will give effect to the direction.[114]

7. A testator made a will in Quebec and then married. Then he and his wife moved to British Columbia and he died domiciled there. The question arose whether the will was revoked by his marriage. This depended on the question which law applied, since under Quebec law a will is not revoked by marriage, while it is in common law jurisdictions. The court held that the testator's matrimonial domicile governed the validity of the will and that the conflicts rules contained in the *Wills Act*[115] did not apply.[116]

8. *Granot v. Hersen Estate*[117] is an example of how the law of the *situs* for real property applies. The testator, who died domiciled in Ontario, made specific gifts to his son of property in Ontario and left the residue of his estate to his daughter. The residue included a condominium in Switzerland. Under Swiss law, which applied to govern succession to the condominium, forced heirship applied, giving the son a one-quarter interest in the condominium. The court held that the doctrine of election did not apply to require the son to elect between his entitlement under the will and his entitlement to an interest in the condominium. Thus, he could take both.

9. Because of continuing difficulties in applying the conflicts rules, the Hague Conference on Private International Law considered the issues again in the 1980s. The Conference promulgated the *Convention of 1 August 1989 on the Law Applicable to Succession to the Estates of Deceased Persons*.[118] Article 3 of the Convention provides that succession is governed by the law of the state in which the deceased was habitually resident at the time of death, if the deceased was then a national of that state, or if the deceased had been resident in that state for at least five years immediately before death. Article 5 permits a person to designate the law of a state to govern the succession of his or her estate. Article 7 provides that the law of the state determined in accordance with Arts. 3 and 5, governs: (a) the determination of the heirs, their shares, and the obligations imposed upon them by

---

111 *Re Page* (1981), 10 E.T.R. 247 (Ont. Surr. Ct.), one son of testator commencing proceedings for verification (probate) in Quebec where the testator made his will and died, other son subsequently bringing application for letters of administration in Ontario when the testator owned real estate.

112 *Re Zilberman; Chochinov v. Davis*, [1980] 4 W.W.R. 249, 6 E.T.R. 187 (Man. Surr. Ct.), affirmed 4 Man. R. (2d) 325, [1980] 5 W.W.R. 614, 7 E.T.R. 207, 113 D.L.R. (3d) 715 (C.A.), testatrix making will in Manitoba and subsequently making will in Israel and dying there, the second will being admitted to probate in Israel.

113 *Gillespie v. Grant* (1992), 46 E.T.R. 68 (Alta. Surr. Ct.).

114 *Re Barna Estate* (1990), 40 E.T.R. 89 (B.C.S.C.).

115 R.S.B.C. 1996, c. 489, s. 39(3).

116 See *Allison v. Allison* (1998), 23 E.T.R. (2d) 237 (B.C.S.C.).

117 (1999), 43 O.R. (3d) 421, 26 E.T.R. (2d) 221, 173 D.L.R. (4th) 227 (C.A.).

118 Hague Conference on Private International Law, 1989. See http:/www.hcch.net/e/conventions/menu32e.html.

the deceased, as well as other succession rights arising by reason of death, including court orders for the support of dependants; (b) disinheritance and disqualification by conduct; (c) any obligation to restore or account for gifts, advancements, or legacies; (d) the disposable part of the estate and restrictions on dispositions of property on death; and (e) the material validity of testamentary dispostions. Chapter III of the Convention addresses agreements about succession, such as an agreement arising from mutual wills. The balance of the Convention deals with more general provisions.

It is important to note that Art. 1 provides that the Convention does not apply to: (a) the form of dispositions of property on death; (b) the capacity to dispose of property on death; (c) issues pertaining to matrimonial property; and (d) property rights arising under will substitutes. The Convention abolishes scission, that is, the principle which applies one law (domicile) to movables, and another (*situs*) to immovables. Further, it replaces the concept of "domicile" with the concept of "habitual residence."[119] Perhaps for these reasons the Convention has not yet entered into force. Only three states have signed it, one of which has ratified it.[120]

Further Reading

Robert C. Dick, "Validity of Wills for Extraprovincial Assets" (1974), 1 E. & T.Q. 206.

J.A. Brulé, "Multiple Wills" (1979-81), 5 E. & T.Q. 200.

Margaret R. O'Sullivan, "The Role of Domicile and Situs in Succession Matters" (1996), 15 E. & T.J. 237.

Gareth Miller, *International Aspects of Succession* (Aldershot:, Ashgate Publishing Ltd., 2000).

5. TESTAMENTARY GUARDIANS AND CUSTODIANS

The former *Wills Act*[121] defined "will" to include the "devise of the custody and tuition of any child." The law was unclear on the existence of the right to appoint a testamentary guardian, however, since the enactment of the *Infants Amendment Act, 1923*.[122] In *Re Doyle*[123] the court held that such a right no longer existed, while in *Re McPherson Estate*[124] the court held that the right continued. The difficulty is that, at common law, parents did not have authority to appoint guardians for their children by will. Such a right was conferred upon the father

---

119 See Donovan W.M. Waters, Explanatory Report, Hague Conference on Private International Law, *Proceedings of the Sixteenth Session*, Tome II, *Succession to Estates - Applicable Law* (1989), p. 525 at 533ff.

120 See http://www.hcch.net/e/status/stat32e.html. For the status of all Hague conventions, see http://www.hcch.net/e/status/statmtrx.html.

121 R.S.O. 1970, c. 499, s. 1(e). For similar legislation see *Wills Act*, R.S.N.S. 1989, c. 505, s. 2(f).

122 S.O. 1923, c. 33, ss. 2(2), 6.

123 [1943] O.W.N. 119, [1943] 2 D.L.R. 315.

124 [1945] O.W.N. 533.

by statute in 1860.[125] A similar right was conferred on the mother in Ontario in 1886; it permitted her to appoint a guardian by will after the death of herself and her husband.[126] However these provisions were repealed by the 1923 Act.[127] It is probable that, despite the case law referred to, the right to appoint a guardian, therefore, rested solely with the surrogate court.[128]

The Ontario Law Reform Commission recommended in 1973 that the right to appoint a testamentary guardian be revived,[129] although it had earlier recommended otherwise.[130]

The *Succession Law Reform Act*[131] did not carry forward the old definition of "will," but redefined that term without a reference to testamentary guardianship. However, the right to appoint a testamentary guardian was revived in Ontario by section 61 of the *Children's Law Reform Act*,[132] set out below. The Act draws a distinction between custodianship, that is, the office of a person who has custody of a minor, and guardianship, that is, the office of a person who has been entrusted with the management of a minor's property. The two offices may be held by one person.

The Act further provides that, except as otherwise provided in it, the father and mother of a child are equally entitled to custody of the child;[133] that a parent of a child or any other person may apply to a court for an order respecting custody of a child;[134] that a court may appoint a guardian of the property of a child upon the application of a parent or any other person;[135] and that, apart from any court order or agreement between them, the parents of a child are equally entitled to be

---

125 *Tenures Abolition Act, 1660*, 12 Car. 2, c. 24, s. 8, which substituted testamentary guardianship for guardianship for nurture, which existed under feudal law. This right was enacted in Ontario by the *Infants Act(2)*, R.S.O. 1897, c. 340, s. 2, subsequently consolidated in *Infants Act*, R.S.O. 1914, c. 153, s. 3.

126 *Guardianship of Minors Act*, S.O. 1887, c. 21, s. 3.

127 *Supra*.

128 See *Minors Act*, R.S.O. 1980, c. 292 [rep. 1982, c. 20, s. 4(1)], s. 16. Similar legislation exists in some other provinces. However, statutes in some provinces specifically provide that the parents or surviving parent are the guardians of their infant children: see, *e.g.*, *Children's Law Act*, S.N.W.T. 1997, c. 14, s. 41; *Guardianship of Children Act*, R.S.N.B. 1973, c. G-8, s. 2(1). Moreover, some statutes permit the parents or surviving parent to appoint a guardian by deed or will: *Infants Act*, R.S.B.C. 1979, c. 196, s. 40; *Guardianship of Children Act* (N.B.), *supra*, s. 4; *Infants Act* (Sask.), *supra*, s. 24.

129 Ont. Law Reform Comm., Report on *Family Law Part, III, Children* (1973), at p. 188.

130 Ont. Law Reform Comm., Report on *The Proposed Adoption in Ontario of the Uniform Wills Act* (1968), at p. 24.

131 R.S.O. 1990, c. S.26, s. 1(1). For similar legislation, see *Probate Act*, R.S.P.E.I. 1988, c. P-21, s. 1(t); *Wills Act*, R.S.A. 1980, c. W-11, s. 1; R.S.B.C. 1996, c. 489, s. 1; R.S.M. 1988, c. W150, s. 1; R.S.N.B. 1973, c. W-9, s. 1; R.S.N.W.T. 1988, c. W-5, s. 1; R.S.S. 1978, c. W-14, s. 2; R.S.Y. 1986, c. 179, s. 1. The Newfoundland *Wills Act*, R.S.N. 1990, c. W-10 does not define "will".

132 R.S.O. 1990, c. C.12.

133 *Ibid.*, s. 20(1).

134 *Ibid.*, s. 21.

135 *Ibid.*, s. 47(1).

appointed by a court as guardians of the property of the child.[136] The Act also sets out the rights and duties of a guardian.[137]

CHILDREN'S LAW REFORM ACT
R.S.O. 1990, c. C.12

61. (1) A person entitled to custody of a child may appoint by will one or more persons to have custody of the child after the death of the appointor.

(2) A guardian of the property of a child may appoint by will one or more persons to be guardians of the property of the child after the death of the appointor.

(3) An unmarried parent who is a minor may make an appointment mentioned in subsection (1) or (2) by a written appointment signed by the parent.

(4) An appointment under subsection (1), (2) or (3) is effective only

(a) if the appointor is the only person entitled to custody of the child or who is the guardian of the property of the child, as the case requires, on the day immediately before the appointment is to take effect; or

(b) if the appointor and any other person entitled to custody of the child or who is the guardian of the property of the child, as the case requires, die at the same time or in circumstances that render it uncertain which survived the other.

(5) Where two or more persons are entitled to have custody of or to be guardians of the property of a child by appointors who die as mentioned in clause (4)(b), only the appointments of the persons appointed by both or all of the appointors are effective.

(6) No appointment under subsection (1), (2) or (3) is effective without the consent of the person appointed.

(7) An appointment under subsection (1), (2) or (3) for custody of a child or guardianship of the property of a child expires ninety days after the appointment becomes effective or, where the appointee applies under this Part for custody of the child or guardianship of the property of the child within the ninety-day period, when the application is disposed of.

(8) An appointment under this section does not apply to prevent an application for or the making of an order under section 21 or 47.

(9) This section applies in respect of,

(a) any will made on or after the 1st day of October, 1982; and

(b) any will made before the 1st day of October, 1982, if the testator is living on that day.

Comparable Legislation

Children's Law Act, R.S.N. 1990, c. C-13, s. 68; S.N.W.T. 1997, c. 14, ss. 43-50; S.S. 1990-91, ss. 30-33; *Domestic Relations Act*, R.S.A. 1980, c. D-37, ss. 48-50, as amended.

---

136 *Ibid.*, s. 48(1).
137 *Ibid.*, ss. 52-55.

Notes and Questions

1. The Act clearly states that parents have an equal right to the custody of their child.[138] It does not say that they have an equal right to the guardianship of the property of their child, but rather that they are equally entitled to be appointed by the court as guardians.[139] Does this mean that they are not otherwise, that is, by common law the child's guardians? If so, a parent's right to appoint a guardian of the property of his or her child conferred by section 62(2) is rendered nugatory.

2. While it is true that the Crown, as *parens patriae*, has a real interest in the welfare of children, does this legislation not carry state paternalism too far? Does the responsibility of parentage not automatically entail custody and guardianship of the property of the parents' infant children? If so, why should the state be allowed to reduce this responsibility to a "right" to custody and a "right" to be appointed guardians?

3. You should note that a testamentary appointment for custody of a child or guardianship of the child's property expires ninety days after it takes effect. In order for the custodianship, or guardianship, or both, to continue it is then necessary for the appointee to make application to the court for a permanent appointment under the Act.[140] Why should this be necessary after the parents of the child have carefully selected the proper person? An executor does not require a court appointment, although he or she often obtains probate for practical reason. Is this another example of overreaching by the state?

4. In those parts of Ontario where the Family Court has jurisdiction, proceedings under the Act must be commenced in that court.[141] When the Family Court doe not have jurisdiction in the geographical area, the Superior Court of Justice as well as the Ontario Court of Justice have jurisdiction to appoint a guardian of the property of a child.[142] The Superior Court of Justice has jurisdiction if the matter arises in a proceeding in respect of an estate.

---

138 *Ibid.*, s. 20(1).
139 *Ibid.*, s. 48(1).
140 *Ibid.*, s. 21 (custody), s. 47 (guardianship).
141 *Courts of Justice Act*, R.S.O. 1990, c. 43, s. 21.8, as amended.
142 *Children's Law Reform Act*, *supra*, s. 18(1), as amended.

PART IV

THE INTERPRETATION OF WILLS

9

CAPACITY OF BENEFICIARIES

1. INTRODUCTION

This chapter discusses the main situations in which the capacity of beneficiaries under a will may be called into question: illegitimacy, adoption, criminality, foreign beneficiaries and witnesses. There are other disabilities, such as non-charitable purpose trusts[1] and death before the testator. The latter topic is dealt with in a later chapter.

2. ILLEGITIMACY

At common law a person born outside marriage was *nullius filius* and could thus inherit from no one.[2] Hence, courts interpreted expressions such as "child," "grandchild," "issue," *etc.*, in wills to refer only to offspring born within marriage. The rules of interpretation allowed two exceptions in favour of persons born outside marriage, however, namely:

1. if it was impossible from the surrounding circumstances that any children born within the marriage could take under the gift; and
2. if it appeared from the language of the gift that children born outside the marriage were intended.[3]

---

1 In fact, non-charitable purpose trusts are now permitted to take in certain circumstances. See, *e.g.*, *Perpetuities Act*, R.S.O. 1990, c. P.9, s. 16.
2 *Re Stone, A.G. Can. v. A.G. Sask.*, [1924] S.C.R. 682 at 689, [1925] 1 D.L.R. 60, *per* Mignault J.
3 *Hill and Simmons v. Crook and Crook* (1873), L.R. 6 H.L. 265 at 282-3, *per* Lord Cairns L.C. See also *Re Brand*, [1957] O.W.N. 26, 7 D.L.R. (2d) 579 (H.C.); *Re Herlichka*, [1969] 1 O.R. 724, 3 D.L.R. (3d) 700 (H.C.); "Note" (1972), 50 Can. Bar Rev. 531; *Re McLaughlin* (1977), 16 O.R. (2d) 375, 1 E.T.R. 181, 78 D.L.R. (3d) 275 (H.C.); *Belanger v. Pester*, [1980] 2 W.W.R. 155, 6 E.T.R. 21, 2 Man. R. (2d) 283 (sub nom. *Re Horinek*) (Q.B.), grandchildren born outside marriage excluded; *Re Martin; Martin v. Cruise* (1978), 3 E.T.R. 91 (B.C.S.C.), surrounding circumstances showed issue born outside marriage intended to be included; *Re Jensen Estate* (1990), 37 E.T.R. 137 (B.C.S.C.), surrounding circumstances showed that the children of the testator's out-of-wedlock child were not intended to be included in a gift to "grandchildren."

The principle that a person born outside marriage could not inherit unless expressly named in the will, or included by implication, was meliorated somewhat in many jurisdictions for intestacies. Thus, for example, under section 28 of the *Devolution of Estates Act* a child born outside marriage or the child's issue could inherit from the child's mother if she left no issue born within marriage surviving her, and the mother could inherit from the child. A child born outside marriage could not inherit through its mother, however, so that, for example, if the mother's father died intestate and the mother predeceased her father, leaving no issue born within marriage surviving her and her father, the child born outside marriage could not share in the mother's father's estate.[5]

These rules were changed completely by the *Children's Law Reform Act*.[6] Sections 1 and 2 of this Act abolish the status of illegitimacy.[7] They are reproduced below.

Similar legislation is in force in some other provinces. The statutes declare that a reference in an instrument, statute or regulation to a person or group of persons described in terms of a consanguine or affine relationship, is to be construed to include a person or persons born outside marriage. Section 1(3) of the *Succession Law Reform Act*,[8] reproduced below, is representative.

As a result of these statutes, therefore, a person born outside marriage is able to inherit from both his or her parents and from their next of kin on their intestacy and under their wills, unless the wills provide otherwise.

The wills statutes of some of the other provinces also make provision for children born outside marriage. Generally, this is to the effect that a child born outside marriage shall be treated as if it were born to its mother within marriage, unless the will provides otherwise.[9]

The Nova Scotia intestacy legislation provides that a child born outside marriage shall be treated as if the child were the legitimate child of her or his mother.[10]

---

4 R.S.O. 1970, c. 129, rep. 1977, c. 40, s. 50(2).

5 *Re Walker*, [1954] O.W.N. 653.

6 R.S.O. 1990, c. C.12. For the application of this legislation when a child born outside marriage makes an application for support out of his or her father's estate, see *Re Ruby* (1983), 43 O.R. (2d) 277 (Surr. Ct.). The matter of support of dependants is discussed in a later chapter.

7 The legislation repealed the *Legitimacy Act*, R.S.O. 1970, c. 242, which legitimated children born outside marriage whose parents subsequently married. *Re Wright Estate* (1988), 30 E.T.R. 181 (Ont. H.C.), is an example. The testator made a will while that statute was in force in favour of a person who was legitimated. The gift took effect after the *Children's Law Reform Act* came into force. The court held the gift valid.

8 R.S.O. 1990, c. S.26.

9 *Wills Act*, R.S.A. 1980, c. W-11, s. 36; R.S.N.B. 1973, c. W-9, s. 33. There appears to be no similar legislation in British Columbia, or Nova Scotia. Even if legislation of this type was inapplicable, modern cases often favoured children born outside marriage on the ground that the legislation showed a change in public policy: *Re Hervey* (1961), 38 W.W.R. 12, 30 D.L.R. (2d) 615 (B.C.S.C.); *Re Stevenson* (1966), 66 D.L.R. (2d) 717 (B.C.S.C.); *Re Nicholls*, [1973] 2 O.R. 33, 12 R.F.L. 211, 32 D.L.R. (3d) 683 (H.C.). *Cf. Brule v. Plummer*, [1979] 2 S.C.R. 343, 4 E.T.R. 18, [1979] I.L.R. 1-1068, 94 D.L.R. (3d) 481.

10 *Intestate Succession Act*, R.S.N.S. 1989, c. 236, s. 16. For the effect of this kind of legislation, see *Manson v. Haynes*, [1979] 1 W.W.R. 542 (B.C.S.C.), holding that while a person born outside marriage can share in his or her intestate brother's or sister's estate, since the relationship between

This legislation has been held to be unconstitutional as infringing the equality guarantees of the *Charter*.[11] Hence, persons born outside marriage can also inherit on their father's intestacy. The section has not been repealed.

Two of the common law provinces still have legislation which legitimates children born before the marriage of their parents for all purposes of the law.[12] The legislation applies to valid and voidable marriages and, in certain circumstances, to void marriage as well. The effect of this legislation is to permit such children to inherit as if they were born within marriage.

CHILDREN'S LAW REFORM ACT
R.S.O. 1990, c. C.12

1. (1) Subject to subsection (2), for all purposes of the law of Ontario a person is the child of his or her natural parents and his or her status as their child is independent of whether the child is born within or outside marriage.

(2) Where an adoption order has been made, section 86 or 87 of the *Child Welfare Act* applies and the child is the child of the adopting parents as if they were the natural parents.

(3) The parent and child relationships as determined under subsections (1) and (2) shall be followed in the determination of other kindred relationships flowing therefrom.

(4) Any distinction at common law between the status of children born in wedlock and born out of wedlock is abolished and the relationship of parent and child and kindred relationships flowing therefrom shall be determined for the purposes of the common law in accordance with this section.

2. (1) For the purposes of construing any instrument, Act or regulation, unless the contrary intention appears, a reference to a person or group or class of persons described in terms of relationship by blood or marriage to another person shall be construed to refer to or include a person who comes within the description by reason of the relationship of parent and child as determined under section 1.

(2) Subsection (1) applies to,

(a) any Act of the Legislature or any regulation, order or by-law made under an Act of the Legislature enacted or made before, on or after the day this Act comes into force; and

(b) any instrument made on or after the day this Act comes into force.

---

them is traced through the mother, a child of the person born outside marriage cannot share in the estate, since the relationship would then be traced through the child's father.

11 *Canadian Charter of Rights and Freedoms*, s. 15(1). See *Surette v. Harris* (1989), 34 E.T.R. 67 (N.S. T.D.); *Re Tighe and McGillivray* (1994), 112 D.L.R. (4th) 201 (N.S.C.A.).

12 *Legitimacy Act*, R.S.A. 1980, c. L-11; *Family Maintenance Act*, R.S.N.S. 1989, c. 160, ss. 47-51. There was similar legislation in other provinces, but it was repealed as redundant consequent upon the legislative change of the status of children born outside marriage in those provinces.

Comparable Legislation

Children's Act, R.S.Y. 1986, c. 22, ss. 5, 6; *Children's Law Act*, S.N.W.T. 1997, c. 14, ss. 2, 3; S.S. 1997, c. C-8.2, ss. 40-42; *Child Status Act*, R.S.P.E.I. 1988, c. C-6, ss. 1, 2; *Family Maintenance Act*, R.S.M. 1987, c. F20, ss. 17, 18; *Family Services Act*, S.N.B. 1990, c. F-2.2, ss. 96, 97.

SUCCESSION LAW REFORM ACT
R.S.O. 1990, c. S.26

1.

. . .

(3) In this Act, and in any will unless a contrary intention is shown in the will, a reference to a person in terms of a relationship to another person determined by blood or marriage shall be deemed to include a person who comes within the description despite the fact that he or she or any other person through whom the relationship is traced was born outside marriage.

(4) Subsection (3) applies in respect of wills made on or after the 31st day of March, 1978.

Comparable Legislation

Children's Act, R.S.Y. 1986, c. 22, ss. 5, 6; *Child Status Act*, R.S.P.E.I. 1988, c. C-6, ss. 1, 2; *Family Maintenance Act*, R.S.M. 1987, c. F20, ss. 17, 18; *Family Services Act*, S.N.B. 1990, c. F-2.2, ss. 96, 97; *Intestate Succession Act*, R.S.A. 1980, c. I-9, s. 1(b) [added by 1991, c. 11, s. 3(1)]; *Wills Act*, R.S.M. 1988, c. W150, s. 35.

Notes and Questions

1. The *Children's Law Reform Act* makes detailed provisions for the establishment of parentage. Thus, for example, ss. 4 and 5 permits the court to make declaratory orders of paternity and maternity and s. 8 contains a statutory presumption of paternity.

2. The Act rendered otiose the *Legitimacy Act*,[13] which changed the status of children born outside marriage when their parents subsequently married, when the marriage of their parents was voidable and, in certain instances, when the marriage was void.

3. Because the legislation confers inheritance rights on persons born outside marriage, personal representatives are required to make reasonable inquiries to discover whether any persons born outside marriage might be entitled to share in an estate. This duty is set out in s. 23 of the *Estates Administration Act*.[14]

23. (1) A personal representative shall make reasonable inquiries for persons who may be entitled by virtue of a relationship traced through a birth outside marriage.

(2) A personal representative is not liable for failing to distribute property to a person who is entitled by virtue of a relationship traced through a birth outside marriage where,

---

13 R.S.O. 1970, c. 242 [rep. 1977, c. 41, s. 19].
14 R.S.O. 1990, c. E.22.

(a) the personal representative makes the inquiries referred to in subsection (1) and the entitlement of the person entitled was not known to the personal representative at the time of the distribution; and

(b) the personal representative makes such search of the records of the Registrar General relating to parentage as is available for the existence of persons who are entitled by virtue of a relationship traced through a birth outside marriage and the search fails to disclose the existence of such a person.

(3) Nothing in the section prejudices the right of any person to follow the property, or any property representing it, into the hands of any person other than a purchaser in good faith and for value, except that where there is no presumption or court finding of the parentage of a person born outside marriage until after the death of the deceased, a person entitled by virtue of a relationship traced through the birth is entitled to follow only property that is distributed after the personal representative has actual notice of an application to establish the parentage or of the facts giving rise to a presumption of parentage.

4. Presumably the personal representatives begin their search by making inquiries among members of the family about persons born outside marriage. They should also make a search of the records of the Registrar General. If these inquiries suggest that there are no such persons, the personal representatives have probably done all that is required. However, if the inquiries suggest that there may be a person born outside marriage, it may be necessary to advertise in any place where the child is reputed or thought to be, or to hire a private investigator. If this still does not produce results, it is possible to make application to the court under the Rules of Civil Procedure[15] to determine if there are missing heirs. The practice in that case is to direct a reference.[16] The Registrar General keeps a record of every court judgment or order confirming or making a finding of parentage.[17] Further, the names of the fathers and of children born outside marriage are cross-indexed.

5. Although the personal representatives are protected if they make the appropriate searches, the beneficiaries are not, since an heir born outside marriage can trace the property into their hands. Moreover, despite the wording of s. 23(3), a *bona fide* purchaser for value may not be protected if, for example, he or she takes a deed from the beneficiaries in whom the land has vested under the *Estates Administration Act*,[18] because an heir born outside marriage may not have joined in the deed. The same problem arises if the personal representative sells to a purchaser for the purpose of distribution on the basis that the majority of the beneficiaries representing not less then one-half of all the interests in property have concurred in the sale.[19]

6. Is there a limitation period with respect to the right to trace?[20]

7. To avoid the onerous searches required by the legislation and to avoid spurious claims by imposters, it has become common to insert a clause in wills which reverses the statutory change in status by providing that any reference to any person or persons in terms of a consanguine or affine relationship is deemed to refer to a person or persons born within marriage only.

---

15 *Rules of Civil Procedure* (Ont.), rule 14.05(3).

16 *Re Bell*, [1946] O.R. 854, affirmed at [1946] O.R. 854 at 859, [1947] 1 D.L.R. 554 (C.A.); *Re Jones*, [1955] O.R. 837, [1955] 5 D.L.R. 213.

17 *Children's Law Reform Act*, R.S.O. 1990, c. C.12, s. 14(1).

18 *Supra*, s. 9.

19 *Ibid.*, s. 17(2).

20 See A.H. Oosterhoff, *Succession Law Reform in Ontario* (Toronto: Canada Law Book Limited, 1979), at pp. 79-80.

8. In order for a child born outside marriage to take under a will that describes the child in common with others in terms of a consanguine relationship, or on a person's intestacy, there must, in fact, be a consanguine relationship, or an adoption order. *Re Darischuk Estate*[21] illustrates this point. The testator left property to his "grandchild," X, a person who was brought up by the testator's son and was treated by that son as his child. However, he was actually the child of a woman with whom the son had lived for a time. She had abandoned X, but the son had not adopted him. The court held that X was not entitled to share in the estate. Is the decision correct?

Further Reading

Malcolm S. Archibald, "Estate Administration After the Repeal of the Succession Duty Act", in Law Soc. of Upper Can. Special Lectures, *Recent Development in Estate Planning and Administration*, 1980, p. 63, at pp. 74-79.

A.H. Oosterhoff, *Succession Law Reform in Ontario* (Toronto: Canada Law Book Limited, 1979), pp. 5-9, 78-80.

3. ADOPTION

Under modern adoption legislation in force in all the common law provinces,[22] adopted children are treated for all purposes of the law as if they were born to the adoptive parent. The effect of this is that they can inherit from their adoptive parents and their kindred[23] and lose the right to inherit from their former parents and their kindred,[24] unless a will provides otherwise. Similarly, the adoptive parents and their kindred can inherit from the adopted child, whereas the child's former parents and kindred have lost their right to inherit from him or her. Clearly, it is possible to exclude any adopted person from one's will, either generally or specifically, and it is possible for a person who gave up his or her child for adoption to make provision for the child, or for the child to make a will in favour of his or her former parents and kindred.

The Ontario legislation, set out below, is very explicit. In particular, s. 158(4) makes it clear that it matters not when the adoption took place, before or after the section came into force and before or after the making of the will in question. This provision was necessary because of a series of cases which held that words such as "child" and "grandchild" in wills made before adoption legislation was enacted denote lawful offspring of a named person. Hence, if the testator made a will in favour of, for example, his or her grandchildren, and a child of the testator

---

21 [1986] 5 W.W.R. 542, 22 E.T.R. 181, 50 Sask. R. 8 (Surr. Ct.).

22 The statutes are listed below.

23 See, *e.g.*, *Barnes Estate v. Wilson* (1992), 45 E.T.R. 248 (Nfld. T.D.).

24 *Chauvin v. Rachow* (1988), 32 E.T.R. 157 (Ont. H.C.); *Oliphant v. Oliphant Estate* (1990), 38 E.T.R. 133 (Sask. Q.B.); *Re Matthews Estate* (1992), 44 E.T.R. 164 (Alta. Q.B.); *Canada Trust Co. v. Bowie* (1992), 46 E.T.R. 51 (Ont. Gen. Div.); *Re Schultz Estate* (1996), 16 E.T.R. (2d) 62 (B.C.S.C.); *Beck v. Hewitt* (1997), 17 E.T.R. (2d) 233 (Nfld. T.D.).

subsequently adopted a child, that child was excluded according to those cases. The modern legislation overrules these cases.[25]

The New Brunswick Act[26] permits the court to preserve the right of an adopted child to inherit from his or her former parents and kindred at the request of the former parents. Depending upon the wording of the relevant statute, an adopted child may also be able to seek an order for dependants' support from the estate of the child's original parent.[27] The Newfoundland Act provides that an adopted child becomes the child of his or her adoptive parents for all purposes and that the adoption order takes away legal rights from the natural parent.[28] It also provides that the status of an adopted child is as if it were born within marriage.[29]

CHILD AND FAMILY SERVICES ACT
R.S.O. 1990, c. C.11

158. (1) In this section, "adopted child" means a person who was adopted in Ontario.

(2) For all purposes of law, as of the date of the making of an adoption order,

(a) the adopted child becomes the child of the adoptive parent and the adoptive parent becomes the parent of the adopted child; and

(b) the adopted child ceases to be the child of the person who was his or her parent before the adoption order was made and that person ceases to be the parent of the adopted child, except where the person is the spouse of the adoptive parent,

as if the adopted child had been born to the adoptive parent.

(3) The relationship to one another of all persons, including the adopted child, the adoptive parents, the kindred of the adoptive parent, the parent before the adoption order was made and the kindred of that former parent shall for all purposes be determined in accordance with subsection (2).

(4) In any will or other document made at any time before or after the 1st day of November, 1985, and whether the maker of the will or document is alive on that day or not, a reference to a person or group or class of persons described in terms of relationship by blood or marriage to another person shall be deemed to refer to or include, as the case may be, a person who comes within the description as a result of an adoption, unless the contrary is expressed.

(5) This section applies and shall be deemed always to have applied with respect to any adoption made under any Act heretofore in force, but not so as to affect,

(a) any interest in property or right of the adopted child that has indefeasibly vested before the date of the making of an adoption order; and

(b) any interest in property or right that has indefeasibly vested before the 1st day of November, 1985.

---

25 *Re Fulton* (1978), 19 O.R. (2d) 458, 2 E.T.R. 89, 85 D.L.R. (3d) 291 (C.A.).
26 *Family Services Act*, S.N.B. 1990, c. F-2.2, s. 85(2)(c).
27 See, *e.g.*, *Hart v. Hart Estate* (1993), 1 E.T.R. (2d) 92 (N.S.S.C.).
28 *Adoption of Children Act*, R.S.N. 1990, c. A-3, s. 20(1)(b).
29 *Ibid.*, s. 27.

(6) Subsections (2) and (3) do not apply for the purposes of the laws relating to incest and the prohibited degrees of marriage to remove a person from a relationship that would have existed but for those subsections.

159. An adoption effected according to the law of another jurisdiction, before or after the 1st day of November, 1985, has the same effect in Ontario as an adoption under this Part.

Comparable Legislation

Adoption Act, R.S.B.C. 1996, c. 5, s. 37; R.S.P.E.I. 1988, c. A-4.1 [enacted 1992, c. 1], s. 42; S.S. 1989-90, c. A-5.1, ss. 18, 26; *Adoption of Children Act*, R.S.N. 1990, c. A-3, s. 20; *Child and Family Services Act*, R.S.M. 1987, c. C80, s. 61; *Children and Family Services Act*, S.N.S. 1990, c. 5, ss. 80, 97; *Children's Act*, R.S.Y. 1986, c. 22, ss. 5, 98; *Child Welfare Act*, S.A. 1984, c. C-8.1 [am 1988, c. 15, s. 35], ss. 65, 65.1; R.S.N.W.T. 1988, c. C-6, ss. 100-102; *Family Services Act*, S.N.B. 1990, c. F-2.2, s. 85(1), (2). See also *Wills Act*, R.S.M. 1988, c. W150, s. 35(2).

Notes and Questions

1. It has been held that the legislation permits a court to accept a foreign adoption order as *prima facie* valid, but it does not preclude the court from making a further adoption order.[30] Assuming that the adoption order appears to be made according to the law of the foreign state, does the section not require the court to accept it?

The issue arose in *Wende v. Strachwitz Estate (Official Administrator of)*.[31] An 82-year-old man and a 43-year-old woman had been living together in a marriage-like relationship for some years. The law of Germany prohibited them from marrying because of the difference in their ages. Consequently, he adopted her and left his estate to her. Then she moved to British Columbia, where she died intestate. Her (former) sister's child claimed the estate, but was faced with the argument that, because of the adoption, she was no longer related to her former aunt. The court held that the child could inherit and that, for policy reasons, the court should not recognize a foreign adoption the purpose of which was to allow a man and woman to live as husband and wife.

2. Persons who have not been adopted by their step-parent cannot inherit from the step-parent or the step-parent's relatives,[32] unless the will under which they claim, on proper construction permits it.

Philp Estate v. Greig et al.[33] illustrates this point. The testator left the residue of his estate equally to his grandchildren by a will made in 1983. He had three children, two of whom had six children between them. The third child, Charlotte, had a child, L, by her first marriage. Her second husband had two children, J and P. Charlotte tried to adopt them, to the testator's knowledge, but was unable to do so because the whereabouts of their former adoptive mother was unknown. The testator treated J and P as his grandchildren until 1976 when P became a ward of the state in another province. However, he continued to treat J as his grandchild. The solicitor who drafted the will kept a memorandum

---

30 *Re R. and G.* (1982), 139 D.L.R. (3d) 149 (Ont. Prov. Ct.).
31 (1998), 21 E.T.R. (2d) 282 (B.C.S.C.).
32 *Marcy v. Young* (1998), 20 E.T.R. (2d) 274 (Man. Q.B.).
33 (1987), 27 E.T.R. 17 (Ont. H.C.).

which referred to eight grandchildren. In the circumstances the court concluded that the testator intended J to share in the bequest.

In view of this case, consider again the decision in *Re Darichuk Estate*[34] referred to in Note and Question 8 in the preceding part. Which approach is correct?

Further Reading

A.H. Oosterhoff, *Succession Law Reform in Ontario* (Toronto: Canada Law Book Limited, 1979), at pp. 9-11.

4. HOMICIDE

(a) Generally

Under feudal doctrine, a person convicted of treason forfeited his or her lands and goods to the Crown and a person convicted of a felony lost his or her lands to the superior lord under the doctrine of escheat. In the latter situation this was because the tenant's blood was deemed to be attainted by the felony and that prevented the land from being inherited by the tenant's heir. Forfeiture and escheat for felony have been abolished.[35] It has been suggested that the modern rule of public policy that a person cannot benefit from his or her crime, takes the place of the old feudal doctrines in order to prevent a criminal from benefiting by his or her act.[36]

If this be so, it is relevant to determine what the policy behind the former doctrines was and whether that policy still holds, or whether there may be a different reason for denying benefits for a crime today. It is likely that the reason behind the old doctrines was simply to maintain order in society and it may well be that that is a sufficient purpose behind the new rules.

Unfortunately, the courts are not usually concerned with the reasons for the policy, but are content to state that it is repugnant to enforce rights which arise from crime.[37] The problem with this approach is that the policy may then be applied indiscriminately to cases where it ought not to be applied. For, as has

---

34 [1986] 5 W.W.R. 542, 22 E.T.R. 181, 50 Sask. R. 8 (Surr. Ct.).

35 In England by the *Act to Abolish Forfeitures for Treason and Felony*, 1870, 33 & 34 Vict., c. 23; in Canada by the *Criminal Code*, S.C. 1892, c. 29, s. 965, see now R.S.C. 1985, c. C-46, s. 6(1)(b).

36 Reppy, "The Slayer's Bounty — History of Problem in Anglo-American Law", in *Anglo-American Legal History Series: I*, No. 6 (1942), p. 15.

37 See, *e.g.*, *Cleaver v. Mutual Reserve Fund Life Assn.*, [1892] 1 Q.B. 147 at 156, *per* Fry L.J.; *Lundy v. Lundy* (1895), 24 S.C.R. 650 at 653. And see Norman M. Tarnow, "Unworthy Heirs: The Application of the Public Policy Rule in the Administration of Estates" (1980), 58 Can. Bar Rev. 582 at p. 584, repr. in (1981), 5 E. & T.Q. 376 at p. 379.

been said, "[P]ublic policy is...an unruly steed which should be cautiously ridden."[38]

It is, therefore, an important question how far the rule extends, to which crimes and what circumstances. Moreover, the question of proof of the crime in civil proceedings raises an important issue. We examine these questions in the following material.

The rule has been applied when one person kills another and the first person would otherwise have been entitled to life insurance proceeds,[39] social security benefits,[40] benefits under a will,[41] entitlement on an intestacy[42] and an interest as a surviving joint tenant.[43] The rule may also be applied to deny the slayer's application for probate of the deceased's will.[44]

The rule is not applied if the killer was insane,[45] but the law is unclear whether the rule is applicable in cases other than culpable homicide.

(b) Problems of Proof

It sometimes happens that, although it is clear that a crime has been committed, the slayer is not convicted. Clearly this is what occurs in a murder-suicide situation.[46] To ensure that the slayer does not inherit, the crime must nevertheless be proved in these circumstances, the onus being that applicable in civil cases.[47]

In most situations the slayer will have been convicted in criminal proceedings and the question then arises whether the conviction, or a possible guilty plea, or both, are admissible in evidence in the subsequent civil proceedings to determine the slayer's entitlement to share in the deceased's estate, or otherwise. *Hollington v. F. Hewthorn & Co., Ltd.*[48] held that a criminal conviction is not admissible in civil proceedings. In *Re Charlton*,[49] reproduced below, the court applied this rule and extended it to a guilty plea.[50]

---

38 *Gray v. Barr*, [1971] 2 Q.B. 554 at 581, [1971] 2 All E.R. 954 at 964, *per* Salmon L.J. A more familiar expression of the same import is: "Public Policy is a restless horse, and when once you get astride of it there is no knowing where it will carry you," attributed to Burroughs J., in a note in (1891), 7 L.Q. Rev. 306.

39 *Cleaver v. Mutual Reserve Fund Life Assn.*, *supra*.

40 *R. v. Nat. Ins. Comm.; Ex parte Connor*, [1981] 1 All E.R. 769 (Q.B.); *Re Gore*, [1972] 1 O.R. 550, 23 D.L.R. (3d) 534, [1972] I.L.R. 1-448 (H.C.). *Re Gore* is reproduced below.

41 *Lundy v. Lundy* (1895), 24 S.C.R. 650.

42 *Nordstrom v. Baumann*, [1962] S.C.R. 147, 37 W.W.R. 16, 31 D.L.R. (2d) 255; *Re Missirlis*, [1971] O.R. 303, 15 D.L.R. (3d) 257 (Surr. Ct.); *Re Gore*, *supra*.

43 *Schobelt v. Barber*, [1967] 1 O.R. 349, 60 D.L.R. (2d) 519; *Re Gore*, *supra*.

44 *In the Estate of Hall*, [1914] P. 1 (C.A.); *In the Estate of Crippen*, [1911] P. 108.

45 *Re Houghton; Houghton v. Houghton*, [1915] 2 Ch. 173; *Re Pitts; Cox v. Kilsby*, [1931] 1 Ch. 546; *Nordstrom v. Baumann*, *supra*.

46 As in *Re Missirlis*, *supra*, and *Re Gore*, *supra*.

47 *Re Missirlis*, *supra*, at O.R. 304; *Nordstrom v. Baumann*, *supra*, S.C.R. at 158, *per* Ritchie J.

48 [1943] K.B. 587, [1943] 2 All E.R. 35.

49 [1969] 1 O.R. 706, 3 D.L.R. (3d) 623 (C.A.), noted (1969), 19 U.T.L.J. 368.

50 The rule in *Hollington v. Hewthorn* has been repealed in England: *Civil Evidence Act, 1968* (U.K.), c. 64, ss. 11-13, but remains in force in Canada, although its abolition has been recom-

RE CHARLTON
[1969] 1 O.R. 706, 3 D.L.R. (3d) 623
Supreme Court of Ontario
[Court of Appeal]

The appellant, Oliver Robin Charlton, was charged with the non-capital murder of his wife, Tally Ann Charlton. After two days of trial, he pleaded guilty to manslaughter on the recommendation of his counsel, for reasons which appear in the judgment below. Mrs. Charlton died intestate, survived by her mother and a brother, as well as her husband. National Trust Company Limited was appointed the administrator of her estate and it brought a motion for the opinion, advice and direction of the court on the question whether or not the appellant was entitled to share in his wife's estate. On the return of the motion, the appellant asked the court to direct the trial of an issue to establish whether he was criminally responsible for the death of his wife and, thus, disentitled to share in her estate. King J., refused to make the order requested at first instance,[51] holding that the guilty plea was conclusive in the matter, although the result of the criminal trial, that is, the conviction, would not be admissible under the rule in *Hollington v. F. Hewthorn & Co. Ltd.*[52] His Lordship, therefore, held that Mr. Charlton was not entitled to share in his wife's estate. Mr. Charlton appealed.

JESSUP J.A., delivered the judgment of the Court:

. . .

In support of [the appellant's request for an order directing the trial of an issue] there was material filed which established that at the criminal trial law two reputable psychiatrists gave evidence that at the time of the killing the husband was in such a state of severe emotional shock that he had no control over his act. Both psychiatrists and a psychiatrist attending the trial on behalf of the Crown were of the opinion that the husband did not suffer from a disease of the mind and the defence being put forward prior to the plea of guilty to manslaughter was that of non-insane automatism. Counsel at the criminal trial for the husband accounted for the plea of guilty to manslaughter in these words:

> Once it became apparent at the trial that Mr. Charlton might receive a straight not guilty verdict, Mr. Justice Haines, the trial Judge, made known to me his feelings that it would be bad for the

---

mended: Alberta Institute of Law Research and Reform, *The Rule in Hollington v. Hewthorn*, Report No. 16, 1975, resulting in an amendment to the *Alberta Evidence Act*, R.S.A. 1980, c. A-21, s. 27; British Columbia Law Reform Commission, *Report on The Rule in Hollington v. Hewthorn*, 1977. See also *Uniform Evidence Act*, s. 80, in Uniform Law Conference of Canada, *Consolidation of Uniform Acts* (1978, as am.), p. 15-1 at p. 15-48. The Ontario Law Reform Commission has recommended the retention of the rule: *Report on the Law of Evidence*, 1976, ch. 6. However, in *Demeter v. Br. Pac. Life Ins. Co.*, 43 O.R. (2d) 33, 37 C.P.C. 277, [1983] I.L.R. 1-1689, 150 D.L.R. (3d) 249 (H.C.), the court held that the rule was never adopted in Ontario.

51 *Re Charlton*, [1968] 2 O.R. 96, 68 D.L.R. (2d) 216 (H.C.).
52 *Supra.*

administration of justice if a man who admittedly killed his wife went completely free. He further made known that he would direct the jury as strongly as possible that if they believed that Mr. Charlton was in a state of emotional shock when he killed his wife, then that condition amounted to temporary insanity and that their verdict should be not guilty by reason of insanity. While the Doctors, including Doctor White, a Psychiatrist, in attendance at the trial at the request of the Crown, were unanimously of the opinion that Mr. Charlton was not suffering from a disease of the mind and therefore was not insane, the position taken by the trial Judge certainly put the defence in a hazardous position. As Counsel for the defence I could not let Mr. Charlton, who was quite obviously of sound mind, run the risk of spending the rest of his life in a mental institution which would be the result of a not guilty but insane verdict. Accordingly, on my recommendation after two days of trial, Mr. Charlton pleaded guilty to manslaughter.

. . .

It is well settled law that one who has killed another by a criminal act cannot succeed to that other's property either under a will or under an intestacy. The rule is founded on public policy. Counsel for the respondents Mrs. John V. Cook and John Cook seeks to support the judgment of King, J., by advancing the proposition that the forfeiture resulting from the rule is simply the consequence of being declared in law to be a criminal. The brand of criminality being applied to Oliver Robin Charlton, counsel argues it, cannot avail him to establish that in fact the killing of his wife was not felonious. I find no support for that proposition in the authorities. Halsbury's Laws of England,[53] cites the New York State case of *Ellerson v. Westcott*,[54] as authority that the incapacity to take of a felonious killer does not depend on the trial or conviction of the beneficiary but on the fact of murder or manslaughter. In *Re Pollock*[55] and *Lloyd's Bank Ltd. v. Institute of Cancer Research*,[56] are both cases where the felonious killer was not allowed to take although there had been no conviction or even a charge laid. See also *In the Estate of G - (deceased).*[57] In my opinion, therefore, the incapacity of a felonious killer to take his victim's estate is not a form of forfeiture flowing from his conviction of a crime but a consequence of the felonious slaying itself.

In declining to consider the result of the criminal trial in reaching his judgment King, J., was applying the rule in *Hollington v. F. Hewthorn & Co., Ltd.*[58] that a conviction in a criminal trial is not admissible in a civil proceeding arising from the same facts because in the civil proceeding the conviction is *res inter alios acta*. However, he gave conclusive effect to the plea of guilty to manslaughter. If the result of a criminal trial is not conclusive in a subsequent civil proceeding arising from the same facts I can see no basis in principle and I find no authority that an admission or confession in the criminal trial is nevertheless conclusive in subsequent civil proceedings. It is undoubtedly evidence of very great weight but a plea of guilty like any admission, and notwithstanding its solemnity, is capable

---

53 3rd ed., vol. 1, p. 10.
54 (1895), 88 Hun's Reports (New York) 389.
55 [1974] Ch. 219.
56 [1964] 1 All E.R. 771.
57 [1976] 1 All E.R. 579.
58 [1943] 2 All E.R. 35.

of explanation.[59] The circumstances under which it is alleged the present plea was made may be capable of diminishing its otherwise overwhelming force.

In my opinion, therefore, the question of whether or not Oliver Robin Charlton feloniously killed his wife is a question of fact not necessarily concluded by his plea of guilty of manslaughter in her death. However, having regard to the circumstances of the case it is not capable of being decided on affidavit evidence. The appellant has raised a serious triable issue which cannot adequately be determined in summary proceedings.

In the result, I would set aside the judgment in appeal and direct that there should be the trial of an issue in which Oliver Robin Charlton as plaintiff alleges and Mrs. John V. Cook and John Cook as defendants deny that Oliver Robin Charlton was not criminally responsible for the death of Tally Ann Charlton and thus disentitled to share in her estate. The burden of proof is thus placed upon the appellant, and this is appropriate since the solemn plea of guilty to the offence of manslaughter entered by him makes out a *prima facie* case against him upon this issue. There should be the usual order for the delivery of pleadings and for production and discovery as in an ordinary action.

. . .

Notes and Questions

1. In the new trial directed in the *Charlton* case, could Charlton have succeeded on the basis of proof of temporary insanity, a defence not relied on in the criminal trial? Charlton apparently decided not to proceed with the new trial.[60]

2. In England the plea in cases such as *Re Charlton* is now the same as in Canada, that is, "not guilty by reason of insanity." Prior to 1965 it used to be "guilty, but insane". *Quaere* whether a guilty plea in such cases had any effect on the succession aspects in subsequent civil trials.

3. Since 1957, the plea "guilty (to manslaughter) through diminished responsibility" has also been available in England under the *Homicide Act, 1957*.[61] It would appear that the guilty plea does debar the slayer from inheriting in such a case.[62]

4. Is there not a danger that in the civil proceedings in which the claimant seeks to share in the deceased's estate after having been convicted of killing the deceased, a different result may be reached on the issue of criminal responsibility than in the criminal proceedings?

This problem came before Osler J., in *Demeter v. British Pacific Life Insurance Co.*[63] Christine Demeter was killed in 1973 and her husband Peter Demeter, was tried and convicted in a highly publicised trial of non-capital murder.[64] Peter owned three policies

---

59 *Cf.* Abbott, J., in *English and Laing v. Richmond*, [1956] S.C.R. 383 at 398, 3 D.L.R. (2d) 385 at 399.

60 See E.R. Alexander, "Note" (1969), 19 U.T.L.J. 368 at p. 375.

61 5 & 6 Eliz. 2, c. 11 (U.K.).

62 See *Re Giles*, [1972] Ch. 544, [1971] 3 All E.R. 1141.

63 43 O.R. (2d) 33, 37 C.P.C. 277, [1983] I.L.R. 1-1689, 150 D.L.R. (3d) 249 (H.C.).

64 See *R. v. Demeter* (1975), 6 O.R. (2d) 83, 19 C.C.C. (2d) 321 (H.C.), affirmed (1975), 10 O.R. (2d) 321, 25 C.C.C. (2d) 417 (C.A.), affirmed (sub nom. *Demeter v. R.*) [1978] 1 S.C.R. 538, 34 C.C.C. (2d) 137, 38 C.R.N.S. 317, 75 D.L.R. (3d) 251. An application to the Minister of Justice to re-open the case was refused.

of insurance on Christine's life, of which he was the beneficiary, and he brought actions against the three insurers to recover the proceeds.[65] The proceedings before Osler J., heard together, concerned applications by the three insurers for orders determining that the plaintiff was estopped by his conviction from again raising the issue of his criminal responsibility in the death of his wife and to dismiss the actions as an abuse of the process of the court. His Lordship held, *inter alia*, that the rule in *Hollington v. Hewthorn*[66] had not been adopted in Ontario, so that proof of Peter's conviction could be adduced in evidence. His Lordship further held that, in view of the solemn verdict of the jury, properly charged with respect to the burden of proof, the fact that proof must be beyond a reasonable doubt, the dismissal of the appeals, the refusal of the Minister of Justice to re-open the case, and the identity of the issues before the jury and in the civil actions, it would be a travesty of justice and would bring the administration of justice into disrepute if the proceedings were to go forward.[67]

5. If the decision of Osler J. in the *Demeter* case on the admissibility of a prior conviction is correct, would a prior acquittal also be admissible? The question arose in *Re Emele*,[68] a Saskatchewan case which predated *Hollington v. Hewthorn*.[69] The executor of an estate brought an application for the advice of the court on the question whether there should be a civil determination of the issue whether a beneficiary under a will, who had been acquitted of murdering her husband, the testator, had in fact murdered him. MacDonald J., opined that it "would be extremely bold for me to find the widow guilty of murder or manslaughter on affidavit evidence after the jury had acquitted her..."[70] and held that evidence of the acquittal was admissible and should be acted upon.

6. In view of the decisions in the *Demeter* and *Emele* cases, should a civil trial ever be allowed to determine disentitlement to benefits accruing as a result of the deceased's death, or are there circumstances in which such a trial may be appropriate? Was *Re Charlton* such a case?

7. If a killer has been found not guilty by reason of insanity, should a civil trial, in which his or her right to inherit is in question, or in which the question of insanity is raised, be allowed to go forward?[71]

8. In *Nordstrom v. Baumann*[72] the Supreme Court of Canada accepted the principle that it is within the jurisdiction of the civil courts to determine whether or not a claimant was

---

65 In earlier proceedings, *Demeter v. Occidental Life Ins. Co. of California* (1979), 23 O.R. (2d) 31, 9 C.P.C. 332, 94 D.L.R. (3d) 465 (H.C.), affirmed (1979), 26 O.R. (2d) 391, 12 C.P.D.C. 125, 102 D.L.R. (3d) 454 (Div. Ct.), applications by the defendant insurance companies to strike out jury notices were dismissed. Meanwhile, actions by the infant daughter of the Demeters claiming the proceeds of the policies as sole next of kin of her mother were dismissed on the ground that the daughter was not a party to the contract, that Christine had no legal or beneficial interest in the policies and that, therefore, the daughter had no enforceable equity: *Demeter v. Dom. Life Assur. Co.* (1981), 33 O.R. (2d) 839, [1981] I.L.R. 1-1450, 125 D.L.R. (3d) 708 (H.C.), affirmed (1982), 35 O.R. (2d) 560, 11 E.T.R. 209 (sub nom. *Demeter v. Occidental Life Ins. Co.; Demeter v. Br. Pac. Life Ins. Co.*), 132 D.L.R. (3d) 248 (C.A.).

66 [1943] K.B. 587, [1943] 2 All E.R. 35.

67 Osler J., followed *Hunter v. Chief Constable of the West Midlands Police*, [1982] A.C. 529, [1981] 3 All E.R. 727 (H.L.).

68 [1941] 2 W.W.R. 566, [1941] 4 D.L.R. 197 (Sask. K.B.).

69 *Supra*.

70 *Ibid.*, at p. 199.

71 *Moody v. Moody* (1982), 38 O.R. (2d) 773, 12 E.T.R. 92 (H.C.).

72 [1962] S.C.R. 147, 37 W.W.R. 16, 31 D.L.R. (2d) 255.

criminally responsible for the death of the deceased for the purpose of invoking the public policy rule.

(c) Nature of the Crime

In what circumstances should the rule of public policy be allowed to operate? The cases clearly establish that murder attracts the rule and *Re Charlton* presupposes that manslaughter falls in the same category. Some American cases hold that if the manslaughter is involuntary, the slayer is not debarred from taking any benefits accruing from the death.[73] You should note, however, that in some American states there are statutes which deal with the question and the decisions in those states often turn on an interpretation of the legislation.[74]

Much of the Anglo-Canadian jurisprudence suggests that it does not matter whether the killing was intentional or unintentional because the public policy rule insists that a person who kills another shall not benefit as a result.[75] If this were indeed the law, it would seem excessively harsh.[76] However, you should note that in all the cases that state the rule in this form there was an intentional killing and, hence, statements that any killing attracts the rule are *dicta* only. More recent *dicta* suggest a more lenient approach. In *R. v. National Insurance Commissioner*,[77] Lord Lane C.J., said:[78]

> [I]n each case it is not the label which the law applies to the crime which has been committed but the nature of the crime itself which in the end will dictate whether public policy demands the court to drive the applicant from the seat of justice. Where that line is to be drawn may be a difficult matter to decide....

In the *National Insurance Commissioner* case the applicant was denied a widow's allowance because she had deliberately and intentionally killed her husband.

That the nature of the crime is important is evidenced by a number of insurance cases which hold that the driver of a car, who has been held guilty of manslaughter, can nevertheless recover on a contract of insurance for his or her liability in

---

73 See, *e.g.*, *Legette v. Smith* (1955), 85 S.E. 2d 576 (S.C.), a husband unintentionally killed his wife while attempting to kill her lover was entitled to share in her intestacy; *Commercial Travelers v. White* (1966), 406 S.W. 2d 145 (Ky.); *Estate of Mahoney* (1966), 220 A. 2d 475 (Vt.), holding that only an intentional killing bars the slayer, whereas an unintentional killing does not.

74 See *Scott on Trusts*, 4th ed. by William Franklin Fratcher (Boston: Little, Brown and Company, 1989), §492; and see Wade, "Acquisition of Property by Wrongfully Killing Another - A Statutory Solution" (1936), 49 Harv. L. Rev. 715.

75 See, *e.g.*, *Cleaver v. Mut. Reserve Fund Life Assn.*, [1892] 1 Q.B. 147 at 156, *per* Fry L.J.; *Beresford v. Royal Ins. Co.*, [1938] A.C. 586 at 598-9, *per* Lord Atkin; *Re Giles*, [1972] Ch. 544 at 552, [1971] 3 All E.R. 1141; *Lundy v. Lundy* (1895), 24 S.C.R. 650 at 652, *per* Strong C.J.; *Re Charlton*, [1969] 1 O.R. 706 at 708-9, 3 D.L.R. (3d) 623 (C.A.), *per* Jessup J.A.

76 Even in Mosaic law a person who killed another unintentionally was allowed to flee to one of the cities of refuge. See Ex. 21:13; Num. 35:6-34.

77 [1981] 1 All E.R. 769 (Q.B.).

78 *Ibid.*, at p. 774.

respect of the death, when the death was not intentional.[79] The English Court of Appeal distinguished these cases in *Gray v. Barr*.[80] The insured brandished and fired a loaded shotgun to frighten another person and shot him accidentally. In the course of his judgment in that case, Salmon L.J., said:[81]

> I am not deciding that a man who has committed manslaughter would, in any circumstances, be prevented from enforcing a contract of indemnity in respect of any liability he may have incurred for causing death or from inheriting under a will or on the intestacy of anyone whom he has killed. Manslaughter is a crime which varies infinitely in its seriousness. It may come very near to murder or amount to little more than inadvertence....

In view of the majority of the American cases and the recent *dicta* set out above, therefore, it is arguable that a person should only be deprived from inheriting if he or she intended to kill the deceased.

Notes and Questions

1. An intention to bring about death is not a necessary element of the offence of criminal negligence,[82] although *mens rea* is, liability being determined by an objective assessment of the accused's conduct.[83] If a person has been convicted of criminal negligence in the death of another person, would the accused be debarred from sharing in the deceased's estate or from benefiting by the death in any other way?

2. Would the answer to question 1 be different if the death resulted, not from criminal negligence, but from dangerous driving? Death is not a constituent element of the latter offence.[84]

3. Would a wife, who deliberately sets fire to her house in which her husband is sleeping, in consequence of which he is asphyxiated, be entitled to share in his estate? Would it make any difference if she did not know that her husband was in the house, or that she thought he was elsewhere? In *Nordstrom v. Baumann*[85] the wife was allowed to take, because it was found that she did not appreciate the nature and quality of her act or know that it was wrong. However, it was admitted that if she was guilty of arson, she could not inherit.[86]

(d) The Limits of Disentitlement

As we have seen, if a person is not responsible for the crime in the sense that he or she does not understand the nature and quality of the act or know that it was

---

79 *Tinline v. White Cross Ins. Assn. Ltd.*, [1921] 3 K.B. 327; *James v. Br. & Gen. Ins. Co.*, [1927] 2 K.B. 311; *Hardy v. Motor Insurers' Bureau*, [1964] 2 Q.B. 745 (C.A.). Contrast *O'Hearn v. Yorkshire Ins. Co.* (1921), 51 O.L.R. 130, 67 D.L.R. 735 (C.A.).

80 [1971] 2 Q.B. 554, [1971] 2 All E.R. 954.

81 *Ibid.*, at Q.B. 581, All E.R. 964.

82 *Criminal Code*, R.S.C. 1985, c. C-46, s. 219. And see s. 220, causing death by criminal negligence, and s. 249, criminal negligence in operation of motor vehicle.

83 *R. v. Rogers*, 65 W.W.R. 193, [1968] 4 C.C.C. 278, 4 C.R.N.S. 303 (B.C.C.A.).

84 *Criminal Code*, *supra*, s. 249(4).

85 [1962] S.C.R. 147, 37 W.W.R. 16, 31 D.L.R. (2d) 255.

86 *Ibid.*, S.C.R. at 150, *per* Locke J.

wrong, in other words, if the slayer is insane, he or she is not disentitled from any benefits caused by the death.[87]

It may be difficult to prove insanity, however, particularly when the slayer commits suicide immediately after the killing.[88] In those circumstances, there is a presumption of sanity, the onus being on those claiming otherwise to prove it.[89] Apart from a murder-suicide situation, the onus rests on the slayer to prove insanity.[90]

Aside from the question of insanity, the question may arise whether the killer is absolutely and forever debarred from taking a benefit under the victim's estate, or whether there are circumstances in which he or she may succeed. This question is explored in *Re Gore*, set out below and the materials following that case.

RE GORE

[1972] 1 O.R. 550, 23 D.L.R. (2d) 534, [1972] I.L.R. 1-448
Supreme Court of Ontario
[High Court of Justice]

In 1971, Joseph Hector Gore went to his house in Thamesville and shot and killed his wife, Ruth Ann, his daughter, Christine Louise, who was eight years old, and his daughter, Laurie Anne, who was five years old, in that order, and then shot and killed himself. The evidence clearly established the order of the deaths and that the deaths were virtually instantaneous.

Joseph Hector and Ruth Ann owned the house as joint tenants. In addition Joseph Hector owned two contracts of life insurance on his life, one issued in 1962 and the other in 1968. The beneficiary under both contracts was his wife.

An application was brought to determine the order of the deaths and the distribution of the several estates.

OSLER J.:

. . .

At the time of her death Ruth Ann Gore was survived by her husband Joseph Hector Gore and by the two children already mentioned. It is well established that upon grounds of public policy a wrongdoer is prevented from benefiting personally by his act and hence, Joseph Hector Gore cannot share in the estate as on an intestacy. The persons entitled, therefore, were the only children, Christine Louise Gore and Laurie Ann Gore. At the time of the death of Christine Louise Gore the

---

87 See *Pub. Trustee of Man. v. Leclerc* (1981), 8 Man. R. (2d) 267, 123 D.L.R. (3d) 650 (Q.B.). But see *Moody v. Moody* (1982), 38 O.R. (2d) 773, 12 E.T.R. 92 (H.C.).

88 *Re Mason*, [1917] 1 W.W.R. 329, 31 D.L.R. 305 (B.C.S.C.): there was proof of the suicide's insanity.

89 *Re Pollock; Polock v. Polock*, [1941] 1 Ch. 219, [1941] 1 All E.R. 360; *Re Johnson*, [1950] 1 W.W.R. 263, 57 Man. R. 438, [1950] 2 D.L.R. 69 (K.B.); *Re Missirlis*, [1971] O.R. 303, 15 D.L.R. (3d) 257 (Surr. Ct.).

90 See *Re Pupkowski* (1956), 6 D.L.R. (2d) 427 (B.C.S.C.).

same principle prevents her father from sharing in her estate and hence her entire estate passed to her surviving sister Laurie Ann Gore.

Upon the death of Laurie Ann Gore, her father was disentitled and under the *Devolution of Estates Act*,[91] her estate would go to her next of kin in equal degree. These would normally comprise the three surviving grandparents, Mabel Roberts, maternal grandmother, Hector Gore, Sr., paternal grandfather and Bertha Gore, paternal grandmother of Laurie Ann Gore.

It was argued by counsel for Mabel Roberts that she was the only person entitled as next of kin of Laurie Ann Gore, his submission being that the heirs or next of kin of a person disqualified from inheriting because of his own wrongful act were likewise disentitled and could not be permitted to benefit. While it appears that there may be some support for that submission in what was said by Ritchie, J., in *Nordstrom v. Baumann*,[92] that dictum was unnecessary to the decision in that case. In any event, the claims of Hector Gore, Sr., and Bertha Gore under the *Devolution of Estates Act* are direct claims upon the estate of their granddaughter arising because of their relationship and not claims exercised through the estate of Joseph Hector Gore, the father. I am therefore of the opinion that the estate of Laurie Ann Gore must be divided between all three grandparents in the manner I have indicated.

As to the real property jointly held, I am in agreement with the views of all counsel that the judgment of Moorhouse, J., in *Schobelt v. Barber*,[93] is applicable to the present case. There the learned Judge held that the wrongdoer, then living, became a constructive trustee of the whole property subject to a beneficial interest in himself for an undivided one-half and as trustee for the next of kin of the deceased wife as to the other undivided one-half. While the principle that a wrongdoer must not profit from his crime remains applicable, that principle does not go so far as to work a forfeiture of rights already enjoyed by the wrongdoer at the time of the crime and hence, the real property in the present case is owned under a tenancy in common as to one-half by the estate of Joseph Hector Gore and as to one-half by the estate of Ruth Ann Gore.

In considering who is entitled to share in the estate of Ruth Ann Gore, of course, it is plain that the estate of her husband is not so entitled.

As to the two insurance policies, the beneficiary in each was Ruth A. Gore, wife of the life insured, and in each case, of course, she predeceased the insured, her husband Joseph Hector Gore, the owner of the policies.

In argument it was suggested that a distinction existed between a policy issued in 1962 and that issued in 1968. In the former case, the classification of preferred beneficiary was created by the *Insurance Act*,[94] and an insured could only alter or revoke the designation of beneficiary so long as the effect of so doing was merely to transfer or extend the benefits of the contract to another of the class of

---

91 R.S.O. 1960, c. 106 [repealed by 1977, c. 40, s. 50].
92 [1962] S.C.R. 147 at 156, 31 D.L.R. (2d) 255 at 262, 37 W.W.R. 16.
93 [1967] 1 O.R. 349, 60 D.L.R. (2d) 519.
94 R.S.O. 1960, c. 190.

preferred beneficiaries: see s. 171 as it then stood.[95] By 1968, the date of issue of the other policy, the right of an insured to designate a new beneficiary was no longer restricted by the requirement that he do so within the preferred class. In either case, the share of a beneficiary who dies before the maturity of the contract or before the life insured is payable to the insured or to his estate.

While there is little authority in our jurisdiction, there have been a number of discussions of this problem in the Courts of the United States of America and the conclusion seems there to have been reached that the rule prohibiting a person from profiting from his own wrong has no application in such a case.

> To say that the object of the murder was to accomplish what could be accomplished by the mere scratch of a pen carries its own refutation and leads to the conclusion that profit via the policy was not the object of the crime. The reason for the application of the rule failing, the rule cannot be invoked.[96]

Whether under the former or the latter legislation, Joseph Hector Gore could have divested his late wife, the named beneficiary, of her contingent right to the proceeds of the policies "by the mere scratch of a pen" and hence, it cannot be assumed that he murdered her for that purpose. A proper case for the application of the rule does not arise, the rule being based on the axiom that nothing should be done to encourage murder.

The only two cases binding upon me to which I was referred that would appear to suggest that there can be no relaxation of this rule were *Nordstrom v. Baumann*,[97] and *Deckert v. Prudential Ins. Co. of America*.[98] These are, however, distinguishable. In the former case the Supreme Court of Canada concerned itself with the procedural question as to whether under the Rules in force in British Columbia the Court in a civil proceeding can determine whether insanity existed so as to relieve a homicide of the taint of murder. In the latter case the Court of Appeal apparently acted upon the principle that a man may not be permitted to profit by his own criminal act. Profit and accretion is one thing but, as in the case of real property discussed above, forfeiture is another and in the circumstances of this case, read in the light of the applicable statute, to hold that the estate of the deceased Joseph Hector Grove was not entitled to the proceeds of the policies would work a forfeiture.

The answer to the final question must therefore be that the next of kin of Joseph Hector Gore are entitled to the proceeds of each of the said policies.

. . .

Notes and Questions

1. The *Insurance Act*[99] contains the following provision regarding the liability of an insurer to pay the insurance money if the insured commits suicide:

---

95 R.S.O. 1960, c. 190; later am. 1961-62, c. 63.
96 *Union Central Life Ins. Co. v. Elizabeth Trust Co. et al.*, 183 A. 181 at 185, *per* Berry, V.-C.
97 *Supra*, at p. 156 S.C.R., p. 262 D.L.R.
98 [1943] O.R. 448, [1943] 3 D.L.R. 747.
99 R.S.O. 1990, c. I-8.

165. (1) Where a contract contains an undertaking, express or implied, that insurance money will be paid if a person whose life is insured commits suicide, the undertaking is lawful and enforceable.

(2) Where a contract provides that in case a person whose life is insured commits suicide within a certain period of time the contract is void or the amount payable under it is reduced, if the contract lapses and is subsequently reinstated on one or more occasions, the period of time commences to run from the date of the latest reinstatement.[100]

2. While *Re Gore* holds that if the insured kills the beneficiary of the contract of insurance his or her estate is not disentitled to the proceeds, this is not always so. In *Deckert v. Prudential Insurance*[101] the insured killed the beneficiary and was subsequently executed for murder. The court held that the public policy rule precluded his estate from collecting the insurance proceeds. Of course, if the beneficiary kills the insured, he or she is unable to recover.[102]

3. Does it matter how or when the killer becomes entitled to the property?

(a) Suppose that X left property "to A for life, remainder to B," and B kills A. Should B be prevented from taking the property because B accelerated the vesting in possession by his or her own act? If so, does the law not, then, cause a forfeiture for a crime?[103]

(b) What if A devises property to B and C kills A. Can C inherit the property on B's death? Would it make any difference if B lacked the capacity to prevent C's inheriting the property because of minority or mental incompetency?

(c) What would be the result if A injures B and B dies of the injuries, but before B dies he or she makes a will leaving all his or her estate to A?[104]

4. In *Re Gore* the court held that the next of kin of Joseph Hector, that is, his parents, were entitled to share in their surviving granddaughter's estate along with her maternal grandmother, because they claimed, not as Joseph Hector's next of kin, but as the next of kin of the granddaughter. This accords with the dictum of Fry L.J., in *Cleaver v. Mutual Reserve Fund Life Association*,[105]

In a word, I think that the rule of public policy should be applied so as to exclude from benefit the criminal and all claiming under her, but not so as to exclude alternative or independent rights.[106]

---

100 For similar legislation see *Insurance Act*, R.S.A. 1980, c. I-5, s. 257; R.S.B.C. 1996, c. 226, s. 46; R.S.M. 1987, c. I40, s. 165; R.S.N.B. 1973, c. I-12, s. 149; R.S.N.S. 1989, c. 231, s. 190; R.S.P.E.I. 1988, c. I-4, s. 136; R.S.N.W.T. 1988, c. I-4, s. 86; R.S.Y. 1986, c. 91, s. 90; *Life Insurance Act*, R.S.N. 1990, c. L-14, s. 19; *Saskatchewan Insurance Act*, R.S.S. 1978, c. S-26, s. 150. See also *Beresford v. Royal Ins. Co.*, [1938] A.C. 586.

101 [1943] O.R. 448, 10 I.L.R. 158, [1943] 3 D.L.R. 747 (C.A.). See also *Standard Life Assur. Co. v. Trudeau* (1900), 31 S.C.R. 376; and see *Beresford v. Royal Ins. Co.*, *supra*: the insured committed suicide and the court denied recovery on the ground that the case was the same as if the insured had intentionally killed another.

102 *Demeter v. Br. Pac. Life Ins. Co.*, 43 O.R. (2d) 33, 37 C.P.C. 277, [1983] I.L.R. 1-1689, 150 D.L.R. (3d) 149 (H.C.).

103 See *Scott on Trusts*, 4th ed. by William Franklin Fratcher (Boston: Little, Brown and Company, 1989), §493.1.

104 See *Lundy v. Lundy* (1895), 24 S.C.R. 650 at 653.

105 [1982] 1 Q.B. 147 at 155.

106 To the same effect, see *Garbe v. Alberta (Public Trustee)* (1998), 24 E.T.R. (2d) 176 (Alta. Surr. Ct.). For an opposing view, see *Re Missirlis*, [1971] O.R. 303, 15 D.L.R. (3d) 257 (Surr. Ct.).

Suppose that X kills Y, a woman with whom he has been living, Z, who is Y's daughter, and himself. Under Y's will all her estate goes to her daughter and under Z's will everything goes to X. The order of death is as follows: Y, Z and X. Both X and Z are survived by different next of kin. Who is entitled to Z's estate?

5. *Re DWS (decd)*[107] affords another illustration of the difficulties that can arise. R was convicted of murdering his parents, F and M, both of whom died intestate. At the time of the murders, R had a two-year old son, T. R was precluded by the public policy rule from inheriting his parents' estates. T was not tainted by his father's actions. However, under the applicable intestacy statute[108] the issue of a child of an intestate could only take if the child had predeceased the intestate. T's claim was disputed by collaterals, who were entitled to take under the statute when an intestate left no issue. T argued that, because of the public policy rule, R should be treated as having predeceased his parents. The court held that the public policy rule did not require the court to treat R as having predeceased his parents for the purposes of the statute. Rather, the statute should be given its plain meaning. Since R had not predeceased his parents, T was, thus, not entitled to take. Further, the collaterals should be allowed to take on the basis that the issue, although in existence, were disabled from taking. If necessary, the words "capable of taking" after the words "no issue" who survived the intestate could be implied. Do you agree with this reasoning?

6. A husband, H, killed his wife, W, in 1956 and was convicted of manslaughter. He was the sole executor and beneficiary under her will. While H was in prison, his solicitor rented out the family home, registered in W's name and, after H's release, in 1960, he took possession of the home and lived there until his death in 1970. Thereafter, H's daughter (who was not W's daughter) remained in possession. W's administrator now seeks possession on behalf of W's next of kin. H and his daughter have satisfied the elements of adverse possession. Who is entitled?[109]

7. A husband and wife were joint owners of a contract of insurance on both their lives. They named "the survivor" as beneficiary. The husband murdered his wife and was convicted. He waived any rights he had under the contract. X was the wife's executor. Is X entitled to recover the proceeds from the insurer?[110]

8. In *Re Gore* the court held that Joseph Hector's interest in the jointly-owned house could not be forfeited, but that the public policy rule should operate to prevent an accretion to his estate. In the result, his estate became a constructive trustee of the entire interest as to a one-half beneficial interest for that estate and as to the other half for the estate of Ruth Ann. This seems a reasonable solution since the doctrine of survivorship is allowed to operate at law and the principle that a joint tenancy ought not to be severable by a criminal act is at least notionally honoured. Moreover, this solution does not effect a forfeiture of the killer's interest,[111] whereas the solution advocated by Scott, that the killer should only be entitled to retain a life interest in one-half of the property, does. Finally, the argument that there is a forfeiture of the killer's right to the entire property if he should survive the deceased, assuming that the latter died a normal death, may be answered by saying that the killer ended that right by his own act.[112]

---

107 [2000] 2 All E.R. 83 (Ch. D.).

108 *Administration of Estates Act 1925*, 15 & 16 Geo. 5, c. 23, s. 47(1)(1) (U.K.).

109 See *De Rocco v. Young* (1981), 31 O.R. (2d) 257, 9 E.T.R. 16 (sub nom. *Re Bradley*), 120 D.L.R. (3d) 169 (H.C.), reversed (1981), 37 O.R. (2d) 416, 11 E.T.R. 163, 130 D.L.R. (3d) 575 (C.A.).

110 See *Brisette v. Westbury Life Insurance Co.* (1992), 47 E.T.R. 109 (S.C.C.).

111 Abolished by the *Criminal Code*, R.S.C. 1985, c. C-46, s. 6(1)(b).

112 See also *Merkley v. Proctor* (1989), 33 E.T.R. 175 (Man. Q.B.).

9. Husband, wife and X are joint tenants of certain lands. Husband kills wife feloniously. How are the respective interests in the property to be determined?[113]

10. A married woman made a will leaving the residue of her estate to her husband, but if he should not survive her by 30 days, then to X. The husband killed his wife feloniously. Is X entitled to the residue?[114]

11. Suppose that a husband and wife enter into a suicide pact, but the husband survives, while the wife dies. Is the husband barred from sharing in his wife's estate?[115] Would the result be any different if both parties died and the order of death could be ascertained?[116]

12. In the past it was doubted that a killer could be prevented from inheriting from his victim's estate if the victim died intestate, because of the fact that succession in that case was entirely statutory.[117] However, it is now recognized that this makes no difference.[118] Would the killer also be debarred from applying for support out of the victim's estate as a dependant?[119]

13. An argument similar to that made with respect to intestacy was made in *R. v. National Insurance Commissioner; Ex parte Connor.*[120] A wife was convicted of the manslaughter of her husband and then applied for a widow's allowance under the *Social Security Act, 1975.*[121] It was argued that the Act was a self-contained code and since it did not specifically disentitle a widow in these circumstances, she should be allowed to succeed. However, the court held that the Act should be applied subject to the rules of public policy.

14. Parliament has modified the forfeiture rule in England. Under the *Forfeiture Act*[122] the court may make an order modifying the effect of the forfeiture rule which prevents a person who has unlawfully killed another from acquiring any interest in the latter's property if application is made within three months of the former's conviction.[123] The Act does not apply if the slayer is convicted of murder.[124]

15. What happens if a person is entitled to share in another's property under matrimonial property legislation but does not pursue that right and then kills the other person. Can the killer then make a valid claim for an on-death equalizing claim because of the original *inter vivos* entitlement?

The issue arose in *Maljkovich v. Maljkovich Estate.*[125] Mr. and Mrs. Maljkovich had two children, Rosemary and John. They separated in 1991 and, through their solicitors,

---

113 See *Rasmanis v. Jurewitch*, [1976] 1 N.S.W.R. 650 (C.A.).

114 See *Brisette Estate v. Brisette* (1991), 42 E.T.R. (Ont. Gen. Div.).

115 See *Whitelaw v. Wilson*, [1934] O.R. 415, 62 C.C.C. 172, [1934] 3 D.L.R. 554.

116 See *Dellow's Wills Trusts, Re Lloyds Bank* v. *Institute of Cancer Research*, [1964] 1 All E.R. 771. The case involved a killing and suicide in unusual circumstances.

117 *Re Houghton; Houghton v. Houghton*, [1915] 2 Ch. 173.

118 *Re Sigsworth; Bedford v. Bedford*, [1935] 1 Ch. 89; *Re Medaini*, [1927] 2 W.W.R. 38, 38 B.C.R. 319, [1927] 4 D.L.R. 1137 (S.C.); *Re Johnson*, [1950] 1 W.W.R. 253, 57 Man. R. 438, [1950] 2 D.L.R. 69; *Re Charlton*, [1969] 1 O.R. 706, 3 D.L.R. (3d) 623; *Re Missirlis*, [1971] O.R. 303, 15 D.L.R. (3d) 257.

119 See *Succession Law Reform Act*, R.S.O. 1990, c. S.26, Part V; *Cf. Re Johnson, supra*, in which the court held that the killer's estate was not entitled to dower benefits.

120 [1981] 1 All E.R. 769 (Q.B.).

121 C. 14, s. 24(1).

122 1982 (U.K.), c. 34.

123 *Ibid.*, s. 2(1), (3).

124 *Ibid.*, s. 5. For cases interpreting the Act, see *Re K., (decd)*, [1985] 2 All E.R. 833 (C.A.); and *Re Royse, (decd); Royse v. Royse et al*, [1984] 3 All E.R. 339 (C.A.).

125 (1995), 20 R.F.L. (4th) 222 (Ont. Gen. Div.), affirmed (1997), 33 R.F.L. (4th) 24 (Ont. C.A.).

began negotiating a settlement but they were unable to resolve matters. In 1993 Mr. Maljkovich killed his wife and Rosemary. He pleaded guilty to murder. Mrs. Maljkovich's will left her entire estate to her husband. Clearly, he was unable to take under her will. However, he filed an election under s. 6 of the *Family Law Act*[126] for an equalization of the spouses' net family properties. He argued that his right to an election was not forfeit, since nothing accrued to him as a result of the crime. This was because he was entitled to an equalization payment after the separation. The court disagreed. While Mr. Maljkovich was entitled to make an application for equalization after the separation pursuant to s. 5(1), that right was lost when his wife died. Thereafter he had a separate right under s. 6 to elect for an equalization in consequence of her death. However, since her death was caused by his criminal act, public policy precluded him from relying on s. 6. The court did not decide, but intimated that, in any event, Mr. Maljkovich's election was to take an equalization payment rather than to take under his wife's will. Since he was precluded from taking under her will, he should also be precluded from taking in lieu of the will by making an election against the will.

In *dictum* the court also opined that if Mr. Maljkovich had brought an application for equalization in consequence of the separation and the application had not been concluded when his wife died, his right was extinguished on his wife's death and he would then have to proceed under s. 6. This is surely wrong, since s. 7(2)(a) provides that an application based on s. 5(1) commenced before a spouse's death may be continued against the deceased spouse's estate.

16. Is the beneficiary disentitled if the deceased did not die by her criminal act but in the course of committing a crime himself? This issue arose in *Oldfield v. Transamerica Life Insurance Co. of Canada*.[127]

Mr. and Mrs. Oldfield had two children. They separated in 1995, but were not divorced. The agreed orally that he would not provide support, but would maintain certain life insurance coverage. Mrs. Oldfield was the beneficiary of the contracts of insurance. In 1996 Mr. Oldfield died in Bolivia. He was smuggling cocaine and had ingested 30 condoms filled with cocaine. One of them burst, causing cardio-respiratory arrest. The cause of his death was, therefore, his own criminal, albeit accidental act. The insurer argued that public policy absolved it from paying the face amount of the contract. The court disagreed. The beneficiary did not kill the insured and he did not kill himself in order to ensure that the beneficiary would receive the proceeds, so there was no intentional act involved.

Would the same argument hold if the insured died while driving a car under the influence of alcohol? Would it make any difference if the beneficiary was the estate of the insured?[128]

Further Reading

John L. Toohey, "Killing the Goose that Lays the Golden Eggs" (1958), 23 Aust. L.J. 14.

John W. Wade, "Acquisition of Property by Wrongfully Killing Another - A Statutory Solution" (1936), 49 Harv. L. Rev. 715.

T.G. Youdan, "Acquisition of Property by Killing" (1973), 89 L.Q. Rev. 235.

---

126 R.S.O. 1990, c. F.3.
127 (2000), 49 O.R. (3d) 737 (C.A.), affirming (1998), 43 O.R. (3d) 114 (Gen. Div.).
128 See *Mutual of Omaha Insurance Co. v. Stats*, [1978] 2 S.C.R. 1153.

Norman M. Tarnow, "Unworthy Heirs: The Application of the Public Policy Rule in the Administration of Estates" (1980), 50 Can. Bar Rev. 582, repr. (1981), 5 E. & T.Q. 376.

Ken Mackie, "Manslaughter and Succession" (1983), 62 Austr. L.J. 616.

5. FOREIGN BENEFICIARIES

When the Iron Curtain was still in place, it often happened that a Canadian who emigrated many years ago from Eastern Europe died testate or intestate and his or her beneficiaries or heirs were persons who resided behind the Iron Curtain. The immigrant wanted to benefit them, but was concerned that they might not get the money, or all of it, because the government of the country in which they resided might take all or part of it. To overcome that problem, the immigrant often made a will which directed the executors to send the estate to the testator's relations in the form of parcels containing consumable goods, or in which the testator gave the executors a discretion concerning the time and manner of payment. Unfortunately, this method did not usually work, since the testator gave the beneficiaries an absolute interest coupled with a discretion in the executors to send parcels, or to determine the time and manner of payment. The discretion was then held to be repugnant to the gift and the beneficiaries were able to call for immediate payment.[129]

In order to avoid this result, it was necessary to make the gift entirely dependent upon the discretion of the trustees, for example, by giving them the power to pay such sums to one or more of the beneficiaries as they may in their sole discretion determine and without an obligation to pay any beneficiary any amount.[130]

Section 20 of the *Estates Administration Act*[131] was enacted in Ontario in 1983[132] to deal with this problem. It prohibited personal representatives from distributing personal property worth more than $5,000 and money to foreign beneficiaries or their agents. The term "foreign beneficiary" was defined as a resident in a country designated by regulation made under s. 20. Gifts to foreign beneficiaries were made subject to the discretion of the court. The court could order that the property or money be distributed if it was satisfied that the claimant was indeed the foreign beneficiary to whom the property or money was given and that the gift would not be unduly depleted before it was received by the beneficiary. If the court was not satisfied of these matters, the subject matter of the gift, if property, would be held by the personal representative and, if money, would be paid into court until such time as the court ordered distribution.

---

129 See, *e.g.*, *Melnik (Melnyk) v. Sawycky* (1977), 2 E.T.R. 120, 80 D.L.R. (3d) 371 (Sask. C.A.); *Re Hordynsky* (1983), 13 E.T.R. 157, 23 Sask. R. 196 (Q.B.); *Re Chodak* (1975), 8 O.R. (2d) 671, 59 D.L.R. (3d) 35 (H.C.); *Re Pargaliauskas* (1979), 23 O.R. (2d) 502 (H.C.); *Re Czykalenko* (1983), 42 O.R. (2d) 631, 15 E.T.R. 3, 150 D.L.R. (3d) 68 (H.C.); *Re Lysiak* (1975), 7 O.R. (2d) 317, 55 D.L.R. (3d) 161 (H.C.).

130 *Ibid.*

131 R.S.O. 1990, c. E.22.

132 By S.O. 1983, c. 23, s. 1(1).

Notes and Questions

1. Does the legislation meet the need for which it was designed? Does it still have utility since the Iron Curtain no longer exists?

2. There appears to be no similar legislation in the other provinces.

3. The Lieutenant Governor in Council has not made any regulations under s. 20.

6. WITNESSES

(a) Generally

Testators and drafters of wills sometimes ask beneficiaries to attest the wills. This is especially true of homemade wills.[133] In a previous chapter we saw that such an attestation does not invalidate the will. However, the situation is potentially a fraudulent one and, therefore, traditionally, legislation has invalidated such gifts and continues to do so. More recent statutes, however, like the Ontario Act, have recognized that fraud or undue influence is not a necessary concomitant of such an attestation and, therefore, make provision for validating the gift. The Ontario legislation is reproduced below.

Difficulties may sometimes arise if the witness was not in the prohibited class when he or she signed the will, but subsequently becomes a member thereof, for example, by marriage to a beneficiary. Should the gift be held void in these circumstances? This question is explored in *Re Trotter*[134] reproduced below.

SUCCESSION LAW REFORM ACT

R.S.O. 1990, c. S.26

12. (1) Where a will is attested by a person to whom or to whose then spouse a beneficial devise, bequest or other disposition or appointment of or affecting property, except charges and directions for payment of debts, is thereby given or made, the devise, bequest or other disposition or appointment is void so far only as it concerns,

(a) the person so attesting;

(b) the spouse; or

(c) a person claiming under either of them,

but the person so attesting is a competent witness to prove the execution of the will or its validity or invalidity.

(2) Where a will is signed for the testator by another person in accordance with section 4, to whom or to whose then spouse a beneficial devise, bequest or other disposition or appointment of or affecting property, except charges and directions

---

133   Although not only homemade wills. See *Whittingham v. Crease & Co.*, 11 B.C.L.R. 398, [1978] 5 W.W.R. 382, 3 E.T.R. 97, 88 D.L.R. (3d) 353 (S.C.); *Ross v. Caunters*, [1980] Ch. 297; and other cases collected in Chapter 18, *infra*.

134   [1899] 1 Ch. 764.

for payment of debts, is thereby given or made, the devise, bequest, or other disposition is void so far only as it concerns,

(a) the person so signing;

(b) the spouse; or

(c) a person claiming under either of them,

but the will is not invalid for that reason.

(3) Despite anything in this section, where the Superior Court of Justice is satisfied that neither the person so attesting or signing for the testator nor the spouse exercised any improper or undue influence upon the testator, the devise, bequest or other disposition or appointment is not void.

(4) Where a will is attested by at least two persons who are not within subsection (1) or where no attestation is necessary, the devise, bequest or other disposition or appointment is not void under that subsection.

Comparable Legislation

Probate Act, R.S.P.E.I. 1988, c. P-21, ss. 64-67; *Wills Act*, R.S.A. 1980, c. W-11, ss. 13-15; R.S.B.C. 1996, c. 489, ss. 11-13; R.S.M. 1988, c. W150, ss. 12-14; R.S.N.B. 1973, c. W-9, ss. 12-14; R.S.N. 1990, c. W-10, ss. 7, 8; R.S.N.S. 1989, c. 505, ss. 12-13; R.S.N.W.T. 1988, c. W-5, s. 10; S.S. 1996, c. W-14.1, ss. 13-15; R.S.Y. 1986, c. 179, s. 9.

RE TROTTER
[1899] 1 Ch. 764
Chancery Division

The testator appointed his solicitor as one of his executors and trustees and directed that the solicitor should be entitled to all his professional charges for services rendered to the estate. The solicitor attested the will. Subsequently, the testator changed a bequest in his will by codicil. The solicitor did not attest the codicil. Later, the testator made a second codicil, again changing a provision in his will, but confirming his will and the first codicil in other respects. This codicil was again attested by the solicitor.

The question was whether the solicitor was entitled to charge for his services since he had executed the will and the last codicil.

BYRNE J.:

. . .

Had the matter rested on the will and first codicil alone, it is clear upon the authority of *Anderson v. Anderson*[135] that John Trotter would have been entitled, having regard to his attestation of the second codicil. The ground of decision in the case of *Anderson v. Anderson* was that, as had been held in *Allen v. Maddock*,[136]

---

135 L.R. 13 Eq. 381.
136 (1858) 11 Moo. P.C. 427.

the due execution by a testator of a codicil amounts to a republication of a former will, if the codicil refers to such former will, and that without any regard to the fact whether or not the paper referred to complied with the requirements of the law as to execution or attestation of such paper, and the Vice-Chancellor held that it would be as much beyond the provisions and the contemplations of the statute as it would be opposed to good sense and reason to hold that the codicil duly executed and attested had not the effect of republishing the will and making it a new and original disposition by the testatrix, at the date of the codicil, of the estate which she had dealt with by the will.

[His Lordship referred to a number of cases from which he deduced the following points of law:]

(1.) That a will invalid in itself may operate as a valid instrument when referred to and incorporated in or with a subsequent and validly-executed codicil. (2.) That a valid gift by will to a legatee is not rendered invalid by reason of his subsequently attesting a codicil, although the codicil has the effect of republishing and incorporating the will. (3.) That, although a gift by a valid will to an attesting witness is utterly null and void, such gift may be rendered effectual if the will is republished by a codicil referring to the will but not attested by the legatee. (4.) That the legatee must be able to point to an instrument giving him his legacy not attested by himself before he can establish his right to his legacy. Bearing in mind these principles, the question appears to be whether or not John Trotter can point to an instrument not attested by himself and giving him the benefit he claims. It cannot be to the will alone, for though a valid instrument it is utterly null and void so far as the disposition in his favour is concerned. But, just as had the original will been altogether void he would have been able to point to a codicil republishing and incorporating the whole of it, and as validating the whole of the dispositions intended to be made by the will, so in like manner I think he can point to the first codicil republishing and incorporating an instrument valid as to some of its dispositions, but invalid as to the dispositions in his favour, as being the instrument under which he claims. I think that the true view is that, where the original gift is by the operation of s.15 of the Wills Act utterly null and void, the will is pro tanto null and void, as it would have been, if unattested, null and void altogether; and that, just as in the latter case the whole will would, if referred to in a duly-executed and duly-attested codicil, operate in its entirety as from the date of the codicil, so where void in part as to its dispositions by reason of improper attestation, it will, so far as void, operate for the first time by the incorporation and republication effected by the due execution of the codicil. I think that John Trotter is entitled here to point to the first codicil as the instrument conferring upon him the benefit in question, inasmuch as that codicil incorporates the whole will, including the originally void disposition, and that this being so, . . . he has not lost this benefit by reason of his having subsequently attested the second codicil.

Notes and Questions

1. *Thorpe v. Bestwick*[137] illustrates the common law rule that applies when the witness subsequently becomes a member of the prohibited class. The testator devised a house to his niece. The will was attested by a Mr. Thorpe, who subsequently married the niece. Mr. and Mrs. Thorpe sought to establish the validity of the devise. The court held that the policy of the legislation is to prevent wills being proved by persons who benefit under them and their spouses. Thorpe was not in the prohibited category when he attested the will, so the devise was valid.

2. You should note that only the Ontario, Manitoba and Saskatchewan statutes confer a discretion on the court to validate a gift to a witness. The Ontario and Manitoba statutes are the only ones that address the question of attestation by an amanuensis, his or her spouse, or a person claiming under either of them.

3. A question that arises from time to time is whether an executor who attests a will is entitled to compensation if the will provides for compensation. The English cases hold that such compensation amounts to a gift and that the executor is precluded from taking it.[138]

It is more usual in Canada that the executor's compensation is not set out in the will. However most provincial Trustee Acts make provision for a statutory right of compensation. Thus, the Ontario *Trustee Act*[139] gives the judge passing the accounts of a trustee, personal representative, or guardian, power to award compensation, except when the allowance is fixed by the instrument creating the trust. A British Columbia court has held that the comparable provision under the British Columbia *Trustee Act*[140] does not amount to a bequest to the executor so that, when he or she executes the will, the statutory right to compensation is not destroyed.[141]

A provision in a will stipulating the amount of compensation to be paid the executors is an absolute limitation upon their allowances.[142] There is a presumption that a legacy to an executor is given in lieu of compensation, but the presumption is rebutted if the will provides otherwise.[143]

4. A testator provided in his will for the compensation to be paid to his executors and trustees. One of the witnesses was his solicitor. After the will was proved, one of the named executors and trustees died and the solicitor was appointed to replace him. Is the solicitor entitled to compensation?[144]

5. *Re Cumming*[145] examines the meaning of the expression "beneficial." The testator gave his house to his trustees to be put in perfect condition. Then they had to sell it "on a rental basis to X at the rate of $30 per month plus municipal taxes, for a period of three years." Thereafter a deed was to be delivered to X for an additional $10. The trial judge found the house to be worth $3500 which, together with the costs of repair, which were

---

137 (1881), 6 Q.B.D. 311.
138 *Re Barber* (1886), 31 Ch. D. 665; *Re Pooley* (1888), 40 Ch. D. 1, [1886-90] All E.R. Rep. 157 (C.A.).
139 R.S.O. 1990, c. T.23, s. 61(3).
140 R.S.B.C. 1996, c. 464, s. 90.
141 *Re Curry*, [1974] 1 W.W.R. 574, 41 D.L.R. (3d) 478 (B.C.S.C.).
142 *Re Robertson*, [1949] O.R. 427, [1949] 4 D.L.R. 319 (H.C.).
143 See, *e.g.*, *Re Stanley Estate* (1996), 13 E.T.R. (2d) 102 (Ont. Gen. Div.), in which the presumption was rebutted because the will gave legacies to the executrices in their "personal capacity."
144 See *Re Royce's Will Trusts; Tildesley v. Tildesley*, [1959] Ch. 626, [1959] 3 All E.R. 278 (C.A.).
145 [1963] 1 O.R. 625, 38 D.L.R. (2d) 243 (H.C.).

payable by the estate, made a total of $5300. The rent for three years would only be $1080. There was thus a beneficial gift to X and not a *bona fide* sale. Since Mrs. X drew the will and acted as a witness, the court held the gift to be void.

6. In *Re Bernard*[146] the court considered the effect of the legislation on a will by a status Indian. The wife of one of the beneficiaries had attested the will. The court held that the provincial *Wills Act*, which would have avoided the gift, did not apply to the deceased, because of the inconsistency between that Act and the *Indian Act*[147] and the *Indian Estates Regulations*,[148] which governed. Section 15 of the Regulations provide: "Any written instrument signed by an Indian may be accepted as a will by the Minister whether or not it conforms with the requirements of the laws of general application in force in any province at the time of the death of the Indian."

7. In *Re Campbell Estate*[149] the court considered the Saskatchewan equivalent of s. 12(3).[150] Two beneficiaries had attested the will and the executor's affidavit to the application for probate stated that in his opinion neither witness influenced the testator. The court held that this did not comply with the legislation, which expressly requires an application by the witnesses.

(b) Gift to Witness in Representative Capacity

It is also possible that the gift is made to the witness, not in his or her personal, but in a representative capacity. Is the gift void in these circumstances? *Ray's Will Trusts*,[151] reproduced below, deals with this issue.

RE RAY'S WILL TRUSTS
[1936] Ch. 520, [1936] 2 All E.R. 93
Chancery Division

The testator bequeathed the sum of £3000 in trust for his daughter, Agnes, for life, remainder as she should by will appoint. Agnes was a nun. By her will she appointed "the person, who at the time of my death shall be ... the abbess" of her convent "absolutely." Her will was attested by two other nuns. One of the attesting witnesses was the abbess at Agnes's death. The question was whether the abbess took the bequest beneficially or in trust for the convent.

CLAUSON J.:

. . .

[His Lordship noted that a testator can make three types of gift to a person who shall occupy a particular position in the society at the testator's death: (1) a beneficial gift; (2) a gift to be used for the purposes of the society; and (3) a gift to be divided equally

---

146 (1986), 29 D.L.R. (4th) 133.
147 R.S.C. 1970, (now R.S.C. 1985), c. I-5, ss. 45, 88.
148 C.R.C. 1978, c. 954.
149 (1990), 40 E.T.R. 82 (Sask. Surr. Ct.).
150 *Wills Act*, R.S.S. 1978, c. W-14, s. 12(2) [am. 1989-90, c. 66, s. 6].
151 [1936] Ch. 520, [1936] 2 All E.R. 93.

among the members of the society. Which type of gift is intended, depends upon the language of the will. It seemed clear that the gift in this case did not fall into the third class. His Lordship continued:]

There seems to be two alternatives. Is this a gift to a beneficiary which has to be dealt with as part of the funds which the beneficiary administers, or is it a gift to whoever may be the person, and that the testatrix could not possibly know, who happens to occupy the position either of abbess or acting abbess, for her own personal use. I will come in a moment to the consideration of the word "absolutely." But eliminating for a moment the word "absolutely," and considering the gift as being to the abbess, and realising that, according to the evidence, as the testatrix must well have known, the mere temporary absence of the abbess on business might leave someone described as vicaress, who would be acting as abbess of the convent, in other words that the personality of the legatee is one which is, so to speak, of no importance at all as compared with the office, I am driven to the conclusion that this is a gift to the official in respect of her office. And that, after all, is natural--to say that it is a gift to the official in respect of her office as an addition to the funds which it is her office to deal with as an administrator. In other words it is a gift to the abbess, *qua* abbess, for the purposes of the voluntary society, the convent.

As I think has been indicated in the argument, the real difficulty in this case is the use of the word "absolutely." "Absolutely" means free of a fetter of some kind. It is suggested that I ought to construe that word to mean that this person, this chance person who happens to be the recipient of this fund, is to have it for her own, although it is given to her only in respect of her office, it may be her quite temporary office, of vicaress or abbess. I cannot put such a meaning as that on the word "absolutely." I say the word "absolutely" has some meaning and I think it means this. I think it not only means that the recipient will obtain the full ownership, for the purposes indicated, of that which is given, but I think it also means that the recipient is to be free from any fetter which would bind her to keep the fund intact for the purposes of the community. It is really saying: "This is not to be fettered by the fact that it is to be an endowment and is to be a gift of income only. It is to go into the funds of the society and to be used without fetters for any purpose for which the funds of the society can be used." That gives a reasonable meaning to the whole matter and makes the whole will consistent, and produces such a testamentary disposition that, in the circumstances of the case, is exactly what one would imagine must be the disposition intended by the testatrix. I think the gift is a free and perfectly good one to the lady who was abbess at the death of the testatrix, that is Miss Barry, for the purposes of the convent, that is, as part of the property of the voluntary society.

Another point has been raised, which is this. As I have said, the will is attested by the lady who happens to be the lady who will be the hand to receive this gift. If she receives it as a trustee only, and I think she does receive it as a trustee only, the fact that she was an attesting witness to the will, can, on well settled authority, be no objection to the validity of the gift. But the two ladies who were the attesting witnesses were at the time of the execution of the will and both are now, members of the convent, and the argument is that, in so far as they form part of the community, the gift, according to my construction of it, will enure in some sense to their benefit. But does that circumstance afford any objection to the validity of the gift? If it does it must be because the circumstances come within the terms of the Wills Act, 1837.[152]

. . .

I do not see my way to hold that the attesting witness here obtained under the will, as I construe it, any such beneficial legacy or interest as to bring her within the terms of that section. The truth is that the gift is a gift to swell the community funds, to be administered for the benefit of the community. I do not think it is a fair construction of the section to treat the fact that an attesting witness may, as a member of the community, get some benefit in some shape or form out of the administration of the fund, as amounting to a legacy or gift by the will to such individual member . . .

Notes and Questions

1. For a lucid description of the various ways in which a gift to an unincorporated association may be construed, see *Re Recher's Will Trusts*.[153]

(c) Supernumerary Witnesses

Another problem arises when more than two witnesses attest the will and one of them is a beneficiary under the will. Modern legislation, such as s. 12(4) the Ontario Act, now addresses the question directly and validates the gift in these circumstances.

In jurisdictions which do not have legislation such as s. 12(4) of the Ontario Act, the case law is not entirely clear. The general rule appears to be that if the additional persons signed the will *qua* witnesses, they are precluded from taking.

An early Ontario case, *Little v. Aikman*[154] illustrates this point. The testator had devised certain land to Z. The will was signed by the testator in the presence of X, Y and Z and all three signed the will in the testator's presence as witnesses. The court held that Z did not, therefore, obtain title to the land.

Notes and Questions

1. *Kitcat v. King*[155] also illustrates the principle. The testatrix had left her residuary estate to A and B for life, remainder to C and D. By a subsequent codicil she took the life interest from A and B and gave it to C and D. The testatrix signed the codicil in the presence of A, B, C and D and they attested her signature. It was argued that C and D could nevertheless take and the court so held on the ground that they did not intend to

---

152 7 Will. 4 & Vict., c. 26, s.15.
153 [1972] Ch. 526, [1971] 3 All E.R. 401
154 (1868), 28 U.C.Q.B. 337.
155 [1930] P. 266.

attest as witnesses, but signed only to express their assent to the disposition of the property. This is an accepted rule of law; however, it only applies if the witnesses sign for that purpose and not at the request of the testator and it was probable that the testatrix asked C and D to sign. Moreover, there was no need for, nor indeed could, C and D give their consent to the disposition.

Contrast *Re Bravda*.[156] Two witnesses who took a beneficial interest under the will attested the testator's signature after two independent witnesses, "to make it stronger," at the request of the testator. The court held that the gift to them failed.

As a result of the *Bravda* case, the law was amended in England in 1968.[157]

2. By the *Statute of Frauds, 1677*[158] wills of real property had to be attested by at least three credible witnesses. If one of the witnesses or his or her spouse received a devise or a legacy under the will, the witness was no longer credible and the will was then void as regards the realty it purported to dispose of. The *Wills Act* of 1751[159] validated the attestation of the witness, but declared the gift void. However, it did not deal with gifts to the witness's spouse, so that if there was a gift to the witness's spouse the will was still invalid to the extent it disposed of real property.

The *Wills Act* of 1837[160] declared the attestation of the witness or his or her spouse to be valid, but the gift void. The Canadian statutes subsequently incorporated this provision.

You should note that some common law jurisdictions, especially in the United States, retain the requirement of three credible witnesses for wills of real property. Hence, it is common in the United States for a will to be attested by three witnesses.

3. If the will is entirely in the testator's hand and signed by the testator, but also witnessed by two beneficiaries, are the gifts to the witnesses void?[161] What would be the result if the will were a formal will so attested, but the testator in his own hand repeated the substance of the will and signed it?[162]

4. The Prince Edward Island statute has no provision concerning supernumerary witnesses.

---

156 [1968] 1 W.L.R. 479, [1968] 2 All E.R. 217 (C.A.).
157 *Wills Act, 1968*, c.28 (U.K.), s.1.
158 29 Car. 2, c.3, s.5.
159 25 Geo. 2, c.6, s.1, referred to in *Little v. Aikman, supra*.
160 7 Will. 4 & 1 Vict., c. 26, s.15.
161 See *Bertrand v. Lebrun* (1988), 32 E.T.R. 144 (Que. S.C.).
162 See *Lafrance v. Duval* (1988), 35 E.T.R. 124 (Que. S.C.).

10

GENERAL PRINCIPLES OF INTERPRETATION

1. SCOPE OF THIS CHAPTER

In this chapter we shall examine a number of different types of problems that can arise in the interpretation of wills. The chapter is concerned primarily with the general principles and rules of interpretation, the admissibility of evidence and the power to "correct" drafting errors and omission. In particular, we shall examine modern trends in construing wills, as well as proposals for and actual legislative reform.

We do not cover all aspects of construction in this chapter. In subsequent chapters we shall deal with more specific areas, such as the rules of construction relating to property disposed of by will, lapse, class gifts and vesting.

Further Reading

Hawkins and Ryder on the Construction of Wills, by E.C. Ryder (London: Sweet & Maxwell, 1965).

Mellows: The Law of Succession, 5th ed. by Clive V. Margrave-Jones (London: Butterworths, 1993), chapters 10 and 11.

Law Reform Commission of British Columbia, *Report on the Interpretation of Wills* (L.R.C. 58, November 1982).

Law Reform Committee (U.K.), *Nineteenth Report (Interpretation of Wills)* (Cmnd. 5301, May, 1973).

Julie Maxton, "Construction of Wills - A Need for Reform?" [1983] N.Z.L.J. (N.S.) 69.

C.H. Sherrin, "The Wind of Change in the Law of Wills" (1976), 40 Conv. 66.

Williams on Wills, 7th ed. by C.H. Sherrin, R.F.D. Barlow, and R.A. Wallington, assisted by L. Meadway (London: Butterworths, 1995), cc. 49 - 58.

Stan J. Sokol, *Mistakes in Wills in Canada* (Scarborough: Carswell, 1995).

2. JURISDICTION OF COURTS

(a) Generally

As we saw in the preceding chapters, it is the function of the court of probate, or of the superior court exercising its probate function in jurisdictions the courts of which have been amalgamated,[1] to determine whether a document, or several documents, constitute the will of the deceased, using such evidence as is admissible for the purpose, and to admit the will to probate, or to grant letters of administration with the will annexed. Once that has been done, the personal representative can proceed with the administration of the estate. However, it often happens that the meaning of the will is unclear and the personal representative needs the guidance of the court before he or she can proceed. If that is the case, he or she may bring the matter to the court of construction to have the will interpreted.

It is true that the court of probate also has an interpretative function. But that is limited to matters that fall within its jurisdiction, such as determining whether words were inserted in a will by mistake. Once it has concluded its duties, however, the task of interpreting the meaning of the will lies with the court of construction.

In jurisdictions in which one court has both probate and interpretative jurisdictions, the court sometimes fails to distinguish between the two jurisdictions. *Re Rapp Estate*[2] affords an example. The testatrix wished to have her existing will

---

1 In British Columbia, Manitoba, Newfoundland, the Northwest Territories, Ontario, Prince Edward Island, Saskatchewan and Yukon Territory, the superior court has probate jurisdiction as well as jurisdiction to interpret wills, but in the other common law provinces there continue to be two courts having testamentary jurisdiction, namely, the superior court and an inferior court, referred to as the surrogate court in Alberta and the probate court in New Brunswick and Nova Scotia. The relevant statutes are: Alta: *Judicature Act*, R.S.A. 1980, c. J-1, s. 6(1), Court of Queen's Bench; *Surrogate Court Act*, R.S.A. 1980, c. S-28, s. 9, The Surrogate Court of Alberta. B.C.: *Supreme Court Act*, R.S.B.C. 1996, c. 443, s. 9, Supreme Court of British Columbia; and see *Estate Administration Act*, R.S.B.C. 1996, c. 122, s. 1 — prior to 1990 the county court had concurrent jurisdiction up to a value of $25,000: *County Court Act*, R.S.B.C. 1979, c. 72, ss. 21, 38(a). Man: *Court of Queen's Bench Act*, S.M. 1988-89, c. 4, s. 32, Court of Queen's Bench; *Court of Queen's Bench Surrogate Practice Act*, R.S.M. 1987, c. C290, s. 6. N.B.: *Judicature Act*, R.S.N.B. 1973, c. J-2, s. 9(1), Court of Queen's Bench of New Brunswick; *Probate Court Act*, S.N.B. 1982, c. P-17.1, s. 2(1), Probate Court of New Brunswick. Nfld.: *Judicature Act*, R.S.N. 1990, c. J-4, s. 3, Supreme Court of Newfoundland; Part VI confers jurisdiction over probate and administration to the trial division of this court. N.W.T.: *Judicature Act*, R.S.N.W.T. 1988, c. J-1, ss. 3, 9, 10, Supreme Court of the Northwest Territories. N.S.: *Judicature Act*, R.S.N.S. 1989, c. 240, s. 4, Supreme Court of Nova Scotia; *Probate Act*, R.S.N.S. 1989, c. 359, s. 109, courts of probate. Ont.: *Courts of Justice Act*, R.S.O. 1990, c. C.43, ss. 2, 10, am. S.O. 1996, c. C.25, Part IV, s. 9(2), Superior Court of Justice. P.E.I.: *Supreme Court Act*, R.S.P.E.I. 1988, c. S-10, s. 2, Supreme Court of Prince Edward Island; s. 15(1) confers jurisdiction upon the Estates Division to deal with matters under the *Probate Act*, R.S.P.E.I. 1988, c. P-21, ss. 1, 2. Sask.: *Queen's Bench Act*, R.S.S. 1978, c. Q-1, s. 12(1), Court of Queen's Bench for Saskatchewan; *Queen's Bench (Surrogate Procedures) Amendment Act*, S.S. 1992, c. 62, confers probate jurisdiction on the Court of Queen's Bench. Yk.: *Supreme Court Act*, R.S.Y. 1986, c. 165, s. 4, Supreme Court of the Yukon Territory.
2 (1991), 42 E.T.R. 229 (B.C.S.C.).

redone. She wrote her instructions on a copy of the will. The notary public misconstrued the notes and drafted the new will with two errors, which were not drawn to the testatrix's attention. The first was that the shares of the residue were made contingent on the testatrix's sister predeceasing her; the second was the insertion of the number 18 instead of 16 for the number of shares. The evidence showed that these were, indeed, errors. The court permitted the will be rectified in a curious proceeding, described as an application to rectify the will before probate. The court then admitted the evidence and corrected the mistakes. Prof. Youdan has pointed out that this procedure is incorrect.[3] The court should have insisted on an application for probate. On the application the court, as court of probate, could have admitted the evidence (both direct and indirect evidence of the testatrix's intention) to strike out the errors. Then the court, as court of construction, should have interpreted the will, taking into consideration only indirect evidence of the testatrix's intention. In the circumstances, it would not have been difficult to determine what the testatrix intended.

The court of construction is normally the superior court of the province, although inferior courts are sometimes also given some jurisdiction in the area of construction. In any event, the court of construction takes the will as probated from the court of probate and, while any construction placed by the latter upon the will is not binding upon the former, the court of construction cannot review or reconsider matters that properly fall within the jurisdiction of the court of probate, except on appeal from that court.

In jurisdictions in which the superior court exercises the jurisdictions of both the court of probate and the court of construction, the two jurisdictions remain separate and distinct. It is to be hoped that the rules regarding the types of evidence that can be admitted for the purpose of probate and interpretation will be amalgamated. This should result in fewer inconsistent results and strained interpretations.[4]

A will that requires interpretation is normally brought before the court by the personal representative by application. In fact, any other person interested in the matter, such as the next of kin or a legatee, may bring such an application.[5] Although this is the normal way in which the matter comes before the court, a will may also be construed in the context of other actions or proceedings, such as a vendor and purchaser application brought to resolve a requisition respecting title to land.

(b) Function of the Court of Interpretation

The function of the court of construction in interpreting a will is to ascertain the true intention of the testator within the limits of the law. These limits prevent

---

3 T.G. Youdan, Case Comment (1991), 42 E.T.R. 229.
4 See on this point Brian MacIvor, "Admission of Extrinsic Evidence in Aid of the Interpretation of Wills" (1990), 39 E.T.R. 253.
5 See, *e.g.*, *Rules of Civil Procedure* (Ont.), R. 14.05 (3)(a),(d).

the court from indiscriminately admitting evidence of the testator's intention and of the circumstances surrounding the making of the will. Since it is the duty of the court to construe the document before it, it has traditionally been held that effect cannot be given to an intention which is neither expressed nor implied by the words of the will.[6] To do otherwise would render meaningless the requirement that a will must be in writing, and would involve the court in making a new will for the testator, something which courts have repeatedly said they will not do. As Viscount Simon L.C., stated in *Perrin v. Morgan*[7]

> ...the fundamental rule in construing the language of a will is to put on the words used the meaning which, having regard to the terms of the will, the testator intended. The question is not, of course, what the testator meant to do when he made his will, but what the written words he uses mean in the particular case — What are the "expressed intentions" of the testator.

It will be seen, however, that the modern approach to ascertaining the testator's intention is much more lenient. Nowadays courts are more willing to go outside the will to consider extraneous evidence as an aid in interpretation than they formerly were.

One aspect of this trend is the diminishing use of precedent in the interpretation of wills. At one time in the not too distant past, courts tended to rely heavily on what earlier cases had decided in the interpretation of other wills. This was particularly true in respect of technical expressions which had acquired a more or less fixed meaning in law. It will be appreciated, however, that this approach can often work to defeat the testator's intention, for language is not static. It changes its meaning with time and place and also as between different testators. The modern approach, therefore, is to disregard such precedents, or to use them with caution. In this connection, Laidlaw J.A. said:[8]

> The construction by the Court of other documents and decisions in other cases respecting the intention of other testators affords no assistance whatsoever to the court in forming an opinion as to the intention of the testator in the particular case now under consideration. Other cases are helpful only in so far as they set forth or explain any applicable rule of construction or principle of law.

Whether the courts take a strict or a lenient approach to the admission of extrinsic evidence and the use of precedent, they are guided by certain general principles and rules of construction in the interpretation of wills. These principles and rules will now be considered.

You should note that, if at the conclusion of the process of interpretation and after all relevant evidence has been admitted and the principles and rules of construction have been applied the disposition under consideration is devoid of meaning, or if its meaning cannot be ascertained, the disposition fails for uncertainty.

---

6 *Scale v. Rawlins*, [1892] A.C. 342 at 343-4 (H.L.), *per* Lord Halsbury L.C.

7 [1943] A.C. 399, [1943] 1 All E.R. 187 at 190 (H.L.).

8 *Re Burke*, [1960] O.R. 26 at 30, 20 D.L.R. (2d) 356 (C.A.), *per* Laidlaw J.A. See also *Re Coughlin* (1982), 36 O.R. (2d) 446 (H.C.).

3. PRINCIPLES AND RULES OF CONSTRUCTION

(a) General Principles

(i) *Generally*

In interpreting a will the court will often rely on certain general principles to guide them in determining the meaning of the words used. The main ones are discussed below. These principles do not really restrict the court in ascertaining the testator's meaning, but give it flexibility in interpretation.[9] Nevertheless, they do operate to attribute a fictional or presumed intention to a testator if the words and phrases used by him or her have left the intention doubtful and uncertain. If the testator's intention is clearly ascertainable, within the limits imposed by law on discovering that intention, there is no need to rely on any of the principles of construction,[10] for they are not rules of law, such as the rule against perpetuities, but yield to a contrary intention.

(ii) *The Whole Will to be Read in Context*

The first principle of construction is that the intention of the testator is to be collected from the will as a whole, read in its context. In other words, particular words and phrases are not to be read in isolation from the entire context.[11]

(iii) *Identical Words are Presumed to Have the Same Meaning*

A word, phrase, or expression may bear different meanings throughout a will and those meanings will be assigned to them if they can be ascertained by the nature of the subject matter, the context of the will, or extrinsic evidence.[12] It is presumed, however, that if a word or phrase is used with a clear meaning in one part of the will, it is intended to bear the same meaning elsewhere if it is repeated and its meaning there is uncertain.[13]

---

9 Law Reform Commission of British Columbia, *Report on the Interpretation of Wills* (L.R.C. 58, November, 1982), pp. 27-8.

10 *Singer v. Singer*, [1932] S.C.R. 44 at 49, [1932] 1 D.L.R. 284, *per* Newcombe J.; *Re Hammond*, [1934] S.C.R. 403 at 409, [1934] 2 D.L.R. 580, *per* Rinfret J.; *Re Browne*, [1934] S.C.R. 324 at 330, [1934] 2 D.L.R. 588, *per* Rinfret J.

11 *Crumpe v. Crumpe*, [1900] A.C. 127 at 130-3 (H.L.), *per* Earl of Halsbury L.C.; *Higgins v. Dawson*, [1902] A.C. 1 at 3 (H.L.), *per* Earl of Halsbury; *Marchuk v. Marchuk* (1965), 52 W.W.R. 652 (Sask. Q.B.); *Dobson Estate v. Dobson* (2000), 32 E.T.R. (2d) 62 (Ont. S.C.).

12 *Jestley v. National Trust Co.* (1994), 2 E.T.R. (2d) 239 (B.C.S.C.): the word "estate" had different meanings which varied with the context.

13 *Middlebro v. Ryan*, [1925] S.C.R. 10, [1925] 1 D.L.R. 589 at 593, *per* Anglin J.; *Re Birks; Kenyon v. Birks*, [1900] 1 Ch. 417 at 418 (C.A.), per Lindley M.R.

(iv) *Effect to be Given to All Words*

As a general principle, when interpreting an ambiguous or uncertain clause, the court will strive to give effect to all the words used by the testator, unless to do so would be contrary to the testator's plainly expressed intentions in other parts of the will.

An example of the application of this rule may be found in *Re Stark*.[14] In that case the testator had made a gift to his "nephews" and the court interpreted that word to include nephews of the half-blood. When he made his will the testator had only one nephew of the whole blood and the circumstances were such that it was unlikely that he would have any further nephews of the whole blood. In coming to this conclusion, Gale C.J.O, said:[15]

> ...then the use of the plural in mentioning the nephews can only have been for the purpose of including nephews of both the full and half-blood.

(v) *Ejusdem Generis*

The *ejusdem generis* rule operates to restrict the meaning of a general word included with words having a particular meaning to a meaning similar to the latter. Thus, for example, in *Re Resch's Will Trusts*[16] a bequest to a young boy of "my watches (other than my calendar watch), chains, studs and other personal jewellery," was held to be restricted to articles of masculine jewellery of small value and did not pass other valuable jewellery which the testator had received under his wife's will. Lord Wilberforce noted:[17]

> The word "other"...suggests an ejusdem generis interpretation: so do the references to chains and studs appear to indicate the meaning both of "personal" and of "jewellery". To suppose that so many other articles of a different character and of so different an order of value are casually and incidentally included under this general phrase seems contrary to the structure of the gift....

In order for the *ejusdem generis* principle to apply, the particular words must be of such a nature as to form a common class or genus.[18] The principle is not invoked if the context supports a broad meaning for the general words and it is normally excluded if its application would lead to an intestacy.[19]

---

14 [1969] 2 O.R. 881, 7 D.L.R. (3d) 313 (C.A.).
15 *Ibid.*, at p. 882.
16 [1961] 1 A.C. 514, [1967] 1 All E.R. 915 (P.C.).
17 *Ibid.*, at p. 551.
18 *Nat. Assn. of Local Government Officers v. Bolton Corp.*, [1943] A.C. 166, [1942] 2 All E.R. 425 at 433, 437 (H.L.), *per* Lords Wright and Porter, respectively.
19 *Re Johnston* (1970), 7 D.L.R. (3d) 256 (N.B.C.A.).

(vi) *General Versus Particular Intention*

If a testator expresses both a general and a particular intention with respect to a certain gift and the two are inconsistent, or the particular intention cannot be given effect to because of a rule of law, the court will give effect to the paramount general intention by disregarding, modifying or restricting the particular intention.[20]

Thus, in *Re Hopkins*[21] the testatrix owned a corporation which operated a private school. By her will she directed that her trustees should carry on the operation until such time as they could turn it over to a charitable educational foundation. In order that the foundation could continue to operate the school, she directed the trustees to transfer to it the operating assets of the corporation at the time of transfer, but continued:

> ...provided, however, that the said operating assets...shall be deemed not to include cash on hand or in banks or other depositories, term bank deposits or any other investments.

Such assets were to be retained by the corporation. The question arose whether school fees which were paid in advance were "operating assets" or "cash on hand". The court concluded that the testatrix's manifest general intention was to enable the foundation, when established, to carry on her work and it would not be able to do so effectively without a transfer to it of the operating assets. Of necessity, those assets included the monies held on account of prepaid school fees.

A somewhat more extreme example is afforded by *Re Harmer*.[22] A husband and wife made reciprocal wills and the testatrix survived her husband by several months. In her will she left her estate to her husband if he survived her and then provided:

> ...if my husband and I should both die under circumstances rendering it uncertain which of us survived the other, I declare that my will shall take effect as if my husband has predeceased me.

In that event her property was otherwise disposed of. However, she made no provision for the event which actually happened, that is, that she survived her husband. Normally, this would have meant that she would have died intestate. The court determined that her general intention was to dispose of her entire estate finally and completely. Hence, her particular intention, being incompletely expressed, could be disregarded.

A frequent application of the principle that the particular intention yields to the general if the two are inconsistent arises when the testator first disposes of an

---

20 *Kilby v. Myers*, [1965] S.C.R. 24, (sub nom. *Re Harmer*) 46 D.L.R. (2d) 501; *Re Hopkins* (1983), 39 O.R. (2d) 673, 13 E.T.R. 31, 141 D.L.R. (3d) 660 (C.A.); *Re O'Brien; Can. Permanent Trust Co. v. Murphy* (1976), 24 N.S.R. (2d) 45 (T.D.).

21 *Supra.*

22 *Supra.*

apparently absolute gift, followed by a gift over of what remains. If the two provisions cannot be reconciled,

> [t]he court has then to give such effect to the wishes of the testator as is legally possible, by ascertaining which part of the testamentary intention predominates and by giving effect to it, rejecting the subordinate intention as being repugnant to the dominant intention.[23]

It is submitted that in the "what remains" cases the courts are too ready to apply the repugnancy doctrine. In most of these cases it is quite apparent that what the testator intended to do was to give a life interest to the first beneficiary (often his or her spouse), coupled with a generous power to encroach on the capital, and to leave the remainder to the second beneficiary (usually his or her children). Such a gift would be perfectly valid and, had the testator been properly advised, or had he or she used more felicitous language, his or her intention would readily be given effect to. If, however, the intention is clear, it seems excessively legalistic not to give effect to it. Some cases have taken a lenient approach to such gifts.[24]

(vii) *Presumption against Intestacy*

If a will is fairly capable of two interpretation, one resulting in some or all of the property being incompletely disposed of and the other completely disposing of all of the testator's property, it is presumed that the testator intended to dispose of his or her entire estate and did not intend to die intestate in respect of the whole or any part of the estate. The presumption is especially strong if the testator has purported to dispose of all his or her property.[25]

> ...when a testator has executed a will in solemn form you must assume that he did not intend to make it a solemn farce—that he did not intend to die intestate when he has gone through the form

---

23 *Re Walker* (1925), 56 O.L.R. 517 at 522 (C.A.), *per* Middleton J.A. See also *Re Hornell*, [1945] O.R. 58, [1945] 1 D.L.R. 440 (C.A.); *Re Taylor*, 19 Sask. R. 361, [1982] 6 W.W.R. 109, 12 E.T.R. 177 (Surr. Ct.); *Re Freedman; Royal Trust Co. v. Freedman*, [1974] 1 W.W.R. 577, 41 D.L.R. (3d) 122 (Man. Q.B.); *Re Stanners*, [1978] 3 W.W.R. 70, 2 E.T.R. 107, 85 D.L.R. (3d) 368 (Sask. Q.B.); *Brown v. Schleyer* (1979), 27 N.B.R. (2d) 63, 60 A.P.R. 63 (C.A.).

24 See, *e.g.*, *Re Shamas*, [1967] 2 O.R. 275, 63 D.L.R. (2d) 300 (C.A.): *Huffman v. Nichols* (1979), 25 O.R. 521, 5 E.T.R. 59, 101 D.L.R. (3d) 365 (H.C.); *Re Hyslop* (1978), 3 E.T.R. 216 (Ont. H.C.). And see Gilbert D. Kennedy, "Comment" (1950), 28 Can. Bar Rev. 839; L.A. Sheridan, "Gifts over with Floating Subject-Matter: Estates, Powers, Repugnancy (and the Intention of the Testator)" (1977), 7 Man. L.J. 249. The *Administration of Justice Act 1982*, c. 53 (U.K.), s. 22, takes the opposite approach. It provides that when a testator gives an apparently absolute interest to his or her spouse, but by the same instrument purports to give his or her issue an interest in the same property, *prima facie* the gift to the spouse is absolute.

25 *Re MacDonnell* (1982), 35 O.R. (2d) 578, 11 E.T.R. 52 at 57-8, 133 D.L.R. (3d) 128 (C.A.), *per* Lacourcière J.A.; *Kilby v. Myers*, *supra*, footnote 16, at S.C.R. 28-9, *per* Ritchie J.; *Re Crone* (1969), 5 D.L.R. (3d) 317 at 326 (B.C.C.A.), *per* Bull J.A.; *Vickers v. Arbeau Estate* (1988), 31 E.T.R. 154 (N.B.Q.B.); *Ferguson v. Ferguson* (1992) 45 E.T.R. 36 (Man. C.A.); *Doyle v. Doyle Estate* (1995), 9 E.T.R. (2d) 162 (Ont. Gen. Div.), and see Archie J. Rabinowitz, Comment (1996), 16 E. & T.J. 17.

of making a will. You ought if possible to read the will so as to lead to a testacy, not an intestacy. This is a golden rule.[26]

However, if it clearly appears that the testator, in the circumstances which occurred, intended to leave some or all of his or her property undisposed of, or if he or she expressly so provides, an intestacy will ensue. The court will not give an unnatural or forced meaning to words in order to avoid an intestacy.[27]

> The inclination of Courts to lean against a construction which will result in intestacy is far from being a rule of universal application and is not to be followed if the circumstances of the case and the language of the will are such as to clearly indicate the testator's intention to leave his property or some part of it undisposed of upon the happening of certain events.

It appears to me, however, that when an individual has purported to make final disposition of all his "property both real and personal of every nature and kind and wheresoever situate", he is not to be taken to have intended to leave all that property undisposed of on the happening of certain events unless there are some very exceptional and compelling reasons for so holding.[28]

Further, if the testator has clearly considered who should receive certain property, but leaves part of it undisposed of, there will be an intestacy of that part. This is illustrated by *Huddart Estate v. Reid*.[29] The testatrix directed that a fund be established to produce annuities for her daughter and grandsons. She provided that when the last annuitant died the residue should be divided equally among her great-grandchildren, but failed to dispose of the income from the residue in the meantime. The court held that the income passed on an intestacy.

Howell v. Howell Estate[30] is another example. The testator's will, left all his estate to his wife if she survived him. Subject thereto, he directed that articles of domestic and household use be divided among the two sons of the marriage, but he did not dispose of the rest of the estate. His wife predeceased him. The two sons thought that they were entitled to the rest of the estate, but a son by a previous marriage successfully argued that the residue should be distributed as on an intestacy. The court held that the presumption against intestacy could not be used to overcome the fact that he failed to dispose of his estate other than articles of domestic or household use. The court noted that the presumption can only be used if the language of the will is ambiguous.

The presumption against intestacy is often invoked in the "money" cases, that is, cases in which the testator leaves "all the rest of my money" to a named person. Unless the word "money" is construed to mean "estate" the testator would usually

---

26 *Re Harrison; Turner v. Hellard* (1885), 30 Ch. D. 390 at 393 (C.A.), *per* Lord Esher, M.R.

27 *Re McEwen* (1967), 62 W.W.R. 277, 66 D.L.R. (2d) 87 at 92 (B.C.C.A.), *per* Tysoe J.A.; *Re Klein*, [1980] 1 W.W.R. 41, 21 B.C.L.R. 273, 7 E.T.R. 176 (C.A.); *Re MacDonnell, supra*, footnote 21; *Re Crago* (1976), 12 O.R. (2d) 356 at 360, 69 D.L.R. (3d) 32 (H.C.), *per* Galligan J.; *Melna v. Hall* (1999), 29 E.T.R. (2d) 274 (Man. Q.B.).

28 *Kilby v. Myers*, [1965] S.C.R. 24 at 28-9, (sub nom. *Re Harmer*) 46 D.L.R. (2d) 521, *per* Ritchie J.

29 (1991), 45 E.T.R. 50 (Ont. Gen. Div.).

30 (1999), 175 D.L.R. (4th) 318, 28 E.T.R. (2d) 168 (B.C.C.A.).

die partially intestate.[31] The courts will often so construe the word to prevent an intestacy. Thus, a residuary clause in a will giving "all the rest and residue of my bank accounts" was construed to dispose of the residue of the estate.[32]

(viii) *Presumption of Rationality*

A testator is entitled to be capricious in the disposition of his or her property and effect will be given to his or her intention so far as the law allows, if it is clearly expressed. Nevertheless, it is presumed that the testator did not intend capricious, arbitrary, unjust or irrational consequences to flow from his or her dispositions.[33] This presumption is frequently relied on in finding an error or omission which the court is willing to correct.[34]

(ix) *Presumption of Legality*

The traditional rule is that, in ascertaining the testator's intention, the will must be read initially without regard to the consequences of any rule of law. If on such a construction it turns out that a particular gift fails, for example, because of the rule against perpetuities, the court will not attempt to reinterpret the will in order to save the gift.[35]

However, if the will is ambiguous and one possible interpretation of the will appears to offend against a rule of law, while another possible construction which the will reasonably bears does not, the testator's intentions will be presumed to accord with the law.[36]

(x) *Presumption Against Disinheritance*

As a general rule, if the words of the will are ambiguous, the court will prefer a construction that will benefit the testator's heirs or immediate next of kin over

---

31 These cases are discussed later in this chapter.
32 *Re Stuart* (1983), 13 E.T.R. 74 (Ont. H.C.). See also *Re Parsons* (1979), 19 Nfld. & P.E.I.R. 531, 4 E.T.R. 189 (Nfld. C.A.); *Re Diver* (1962), 39 W.W.R. 612, 34 D.L.R. (2d) 667 (Alta. C.A.).
33 *Re Manning* (1978), 19 O.R. (2d) 257, 2 E.T.R. 195 at 206, 84 D.L.R. (3d) 715 (C.A.), *per* Houlden J.A.; *Re Dolands Wills Trusts*, [1970] Ch. 267 at 271-2, [1969] 3 All E.R. 713, *per* Buckley J.; *Re Allsop*, [1968] Ch. 39 at 47, [1967] 2 All E.R. 1056 (C.A.), *per* Lord Denning, M.R.
34 *Ibid.* And see *Re Freeman* (1975), 20 N.S.R. (2d) 644 at 659 (T.D.), *per* Dubinsky J.
35 *Hauck v. Schmaltz*, [1935] S.C.R. 478, (sub nom. *Re Hauck; Hauck v. Hauck*) [1935] 3 D.L.R. 691 at 693, *per* Lamont J.; *Re Schumacher* (1971), 20 D.L.R. (3d) 487 at 489 (Man. C.A.), *per* Dickson J., affirmed (1974), 38 D.L.R. (3d) 320 (S.C.C.); *Re Kirk*, [1956] O.W.N. 418, 2 D.L.R. (2d) 527 at 528 (H.C.), *per* Kelly J.
36 *Re Burke*, [1960] O.R. 26 at 32, 20 D.L.R. (2d) 356, *per* Laidlaw J.A.

one which favours more distant relatives or non-relatives.[37] However, if the intention of the testator is clearly expressed, the court will give effect to a provision that operates to disinherit an heir.

> Generally speaking, I feel that there is too much tendency on the part of those having potential rights to inherit or moral claims on the bounty of testators, to consider that those rights and claims should not be interfered with. While it is no doubt proper to guard against persons in such position being unlawfully deprived of their just rights and claims, it is equally important not to take away the prerogative of a person to dispose of his or her property as such person may wish.[38]

As between next of kin of equal degree it is presumed that an equality of distribution was intended and that the distribution is to be made *per capita*.[39]

(xi) *Last of Two Inconsistent Clauses Prevails*

The rule *cum duo inter se pugnatia reperiuntur in testamento ultimum* holds that if two inconsistent clauses appear in the same will or codicil[40] and it is impossible to reconcile the two clauses, the last one prevails. The rule is said to be based on the idea that the last clause is the last expression of the testator's intention and it should, therefore, be given effect to.[41] Thus, when a clause in a will gave a legacy of "one hundred pounds (£500)," it was held that a legacy of £500 was intended.[42]

However, if the inconsistency arises as a result of separate clauses in the will which give a single property to different beneficiaries, the beneficiaries will take as joint tenants, as tenants in common, or in succession, depending upon the nature of the property.[43]

If the application of the rule would result in an intestacy, the first gift will be preferred.[44] Moreover, the first gift prevails if the two gifts form part of the residue. In this case the two clauses are not regarded as irreconcilable, however. Rather,

---

37 *Re Gregory's Settlement and Will* (1865), 34 Beav. 600, 55 E.R. 767; *Coard v. Holderness* (1855), 20 Beav. 147, 52 E.R. 559.

38 *Re Spadafore*, [1950] O.W.N. 709 at 710 (H.C.), *per* Smiley J., affirmed [1951] O.W.N. 698 (sub nom. *Spadafore v. Prest*) (C.A.).

39 *Adams*, [1957] O.W.N. 568 (C.A.); *Re Alcock*, [1945] Ch. 264; *Re Verdonk* (1979), 7 E.T.R. 143 at 154-5, 106 D.L.R. (3d) 450 (B.C.S.C.), *per* Hinds L.J.S.C.

40 If one appears in the will and the other in the codicil, the latter impliedly revokes the former.

41 *Re Potter's Will Trust; Re Thompson Settlement Trusts*, [1974] Ch. 70.

42 *Re Hammond; Hammond v. Treharne*, [1938] 3 All E.R. 308. See also *Re Masoud* (1959), 16 D.L.R. (2d) 134 at 137, 141 (Ont. H.C.), *per* Wells J.

43 *Ridout v. Pain* (1747), 3 Atk. 486, 26 E.R. 1080; *Re Richardson* (1921), 20 O.W.N. 241 at 242, *per* Middleton J.; *Re Alexander's Will Trusts*, [1948] 2 All E.R. 111 at 113, *per* Roxburgh J.; *Re Bagshaw's Trusts* (1877), 46 L.J. Ch. 567, holding that the beneficiaries took the property in succession.

44 *Re Crombie; Crombie v. Cavanaugh* (1978), 23 N.B.R. (2d) 139 (T.D.); *Piper v. Piper* (1886), 5 N.Z.L.R. 135.

the second is seen as an ultimate gift of residue into which lapsed shares of residue and, if the context permits it, lapsed legacies will fall.[45]

Finally, it should be stressed that the rule is one of last resort, or a rule of despair[46] and the court will, if at all possible, try to reconcile the two clauses.[47]

(b) Specific Rules of Construction

(i) *Generally*

Specific rules of interpretation, as distinct from general principles, operate to fix an objective, arbitrary meaning upon certain common words or expressions. Their number is legion and, therefore, only some major examples will be referred to in this chapter. Others will be discussed in subsequent chapters.

Since these rules are rules of interpretation, they yield to a contrary intention expressed or implied by the will. In the past, the courts have often been reluctant to consider extrinsic evidence in order to find a contrary intention, however. This, it is submitted, is wrong. The object of interpretation is to ascertain the testator's intention and his or her intention should not be frustrated by the application of restrictive rules of admissibility of evidence and the application of rules of construction. The latter may be useful to save a gift from failing, but should only be used as a last resort.

The student should note that the rules can be avoided by proper drafting and should consider how the problems which arose in the following examples can be avoided by appropriate changes in language.

(ii) *Spouses*

A gift to a wife or husband *prima facie* refers to the lawful spouse of the testator,[48] or of the person named[49] when the will was made. A change in circumstances, such as a divorce or remarriage, does not alter the *prima facie* construction.[50] Statutes in some jurisdictions have, however, meliorated this rule in respect

---

45 *Re Iverson*, [1950] 2 W.W.R. 1021 at 1025 (Alta. T.D.), *per* Clinton J. Ford J.; *Re Gare; Filmer v. Carter*, [1952] Ch. 80 at 84, *per* Harman J.

46 *Re Potter's Will Trust*, [1974] Ch. 70 at 77, *per* Lord Greene M.R.

47 See, *e.g.*, *Re Burke*, [1960] O.R. 26, 20 D.L.R. (2d) 356 (C.A.); *Re Crombie* (1978), 23 N.B.R. (2d) 139 (T.D.).

48 *Re Bain*, [1953] O.W.N. 970 (H.C.).

49 *Re Cameron; Cameron v. Toronto Gen. Trusts Corp.*, [1940] O.R. 49, [1939] 4 D.L.R. 581 (C.A.).

50 *Re Brechin* (1973), 38 D.L.R. (3d) 305 (Alta. T.D.); *Re Marks*, [1945] O.W.N. 717, [1945] 4 D.L.R. 731.

of the testator's own divorce.[51] In addition, some statutes have redefined the term "spouse."[52]

Only if no one answering the description was alive at the time of the will, can the court consider extrinsic circumstances and allow a gift to a "wife," for example, to go to the woman with whom the testator was living.[53]

(iii) *Children and Grandchildren*

The word "children" *prima facie* means issue of the first degree. It excludes grandchildren and more remote issue, unless the context suggests otherwise.[54] The word does not include stepchildren, unless the testator has no children of his own, or the context suggests that he intends to include them, as in a gift to "our children" if the testator and his wife both had children by a prior marriage.[55] Illegitimate and adopted children are also excluded from the *prima facie* meaning. However, statutes have changed the rule in this respect.[56]

The word "grandchildren" *prima facie* means issue of the second degree, so that remoter issue are excluded, unless the testator intends to include them.[57]

---

51 See the discussion of this topic in the chapter on Revocation.

52 For example, the *Succession Law Reform Act*, R.S.O. 1990, c. S.26, s. 1(1), defines "spouse" to include a person who is legally married to another person, or who has entered into a void or voidable marriage with another person in good faith on the part of the person asserting a right under the Act. Section 1(2) provides that "marriage" includes a marriage that is actually or potentially polygamous if celebrated in a jurisdiction that recognizes such marriages. The statute does not provide that a person with whom the deceased was cohabiting is his or her spouse: *Ingram v. Fenton* (1987), 26 E.T.R. 193 (Ont. H.C.). However, persons who have cohabited together for not less than three years, or in a relationship of some permanence if they are the natural or adoptive parents of a child, are treated as spouses by s. 57 of the Act for the purpose of enabling a surviving partner to claim support out of the estate of the deceased partner. A same-sex partner is able to do so in similar circumstances by s. 57 as am. by S.O. 1999, c. 6, s. 61(2).

53 *Marks v. Marks* (1908), 40 S.C.R. 210.

54 *Re Bull* (1932), 41 O.W.N. 248 (C.A.); *Re Connolly*, [1935] 2 D.L.R. 465, 8 M.P.R. 448 (N.S.C.A.). See also *Re Sitter*, [1977] 2 W.W.R. 356 (Sask. Surr. Ct.); *Gray v. Beverley* (1989), 35 E.T.R. 168 (Ont. H.C.).

55 *Re Zehr*, [1944] O.W.N. 334, [1944] 2 D.L.R. 670 (H.C.); *Re Connolly* (1964), 47 D.L.R. (2d) 465 (N.S. T.D.). See also *Belanger v. Pester*, [1980] 2 W.W.R. 155, 2 Man. R. (2d) 283, 6 E.T.R. 21, (sub nom. *Re Horinek*) 108 D.L.R. (3d) 84 (Q.B.); *Re Hendrie*, [1969] 1 O.R. 673 at 688-90, 3 D.L.R. (3d) 590.

56 These changes are discussed in the previous chapter.

57 *Re Armstrong* (1918), 15 O.W.N. 148 (H.C.). Adopted grandchildren are included in the term "grandchildren," as discussed in the previous chapter. A person who was brought up by a child of the testator, but not adopted, and who was treated by the testator as his or her grandchild may fall within the description depending upon the court's view of the circumstances. *Cf. Re Darichuk Estate* (1988), 31 E.T.R. 3 (Sask. C.A.), person so brought up not included; and *Hickley v. Greig* (1987), 27 E.T.R. 17 (Ont. H.C.), persons included.

(iv) *Issue*

"Issue" *prima facie* means descendants to the remotest degree,[58] although it is often restricted in meaning, because of the context, to descendants of the first degree.[59]

The rule in *Sibley v. Perry*[60] is that when the word "issue" is used with reference to the parent of that issue, as in a gift "to my brothers and sisters, but if they predecease me leaving issue, then their respective shares shall go to their issue," it means "children."[61] The rule, perhaps more than others, is an arbitrary one and often operates to defeat the testator's intention. It ought, therefore, to apply only as a last resort, if at all.[62]

In *Weir Estate v. Weir*[63] the court interpreted the word "issue" to mean descendants. The testatrix left property to her children and then said, "and if any of my said children predecease me their issue if any is to take the parents share". The court held that the absence of the possessive apostrophe allowed it to interpret the word "parents" to mean that if a child of the testatrix predeceased her, that child's issue would take "the parents share." It followed, said the court, that the deceased child's share should be distributed *per capita* among the child's issue living at the testatrix's death, there being no indication that they were to take *per stirpes*.

(v) *Next of Kin*

The expression "next of kin" *prima facie* means the person or persons who are the testator's or named person's nearest blood relations. It does not mean the persons who would take on their intestacy, unless the context demands it. Thus, in a gift "to the next of kin of my son," if the son was survived by two sisters and nephews and nieces, only the sisters were entitled.[64]

---

58 *Kernahan Estate v. Hanson* (1990), 39 E.T.R. 249 (Sask. C.A.); *Adams v. Laursen* (1998), 23 E.T.R. (2d) 317 (B.C.S.C.).

59 *Fishleigh v. London & Western Trusts Co.* (1930), 39 O.W.N. 1, [1930] 4 D.L.R. 609 (P.C.). See also *Re Dover* (1983), 27 Sask. R. 198 (Q.B.); *Ridley v. McGimpsey* (1991) 43 E.T.R. 152 (B.C.S.C.); *Bicknell Estate v. McDougall* (1992), 48 E.T.R. 101 (B.C.S.C.).

60 (1802), 7 Ves. Jun. 522, 32 E.R. 211.

61 See *Re Le Blanc; Eastern Trust Co. v. Le Blanc* (1962), 33 D.L.R. (2d) 609, 47 M.P.R. 130 (N.S.S.C. [in banco]); *Re Sinclair*, [1963] 1 O.R. 335, 37 D.L.R. (2d) 103 (H.C.). See also *Re Verdonk* (1979), 7 E.T.R. 143, 106 D.L.R. (3d) 450 (B.C.S.C.); *Re Hudson* (1970), 14 D.L.R. (3d) 79 (N.S.T.D.).

62 See *Re Spencer*, [1974] 1 W.W.R. 509, 42 D.L.R. (3d) 127 (B.C.S.C.); *Re Tweedie*, [1976] 3 W.W.R. 1, 64 D.L.R. (3d) 569 (B.C.S.C.); *Re Deeley's Settlement*, [1974] Ch. 454, [1973] 3 All E.R. 1127.

63 (1998), 21 E.T.R. (2d) 277 (B.C.S.C.).

64 *Re Lally* (1917), 12 O.W.N. 242 (H.C.). And see *Re Wallis*, [1944] O.W.N. 255, [1944] 3 D.L.R. 223 (H.C.).

(vi) *Other Relatives*

"Family" *prima facie* means "children."[65] Hence, the word excludes a parent, especially a parent related by affinity, unless the parent is expressly included in the gift. Thus, a gift "to my brothers and their families," will exclude the widow of a deceased brother.[66]

"Nephews" and "nieces" includes brothers' and sisters' children of the whole and the half blood,[67] but excludes those related by affinity only, unless the context requires otherwise.[68] Thus, for example, extrinsic evidence may show that the testator regarded his sister's stepdaughter, whom she treated as her daughter, as his niece.

"Cousins" *prima facie* refers to first cousins only, that is, children of uncles and aunts,[69] whereas "second cousins" includes only those who have great-grand-parents in common with the testator.[70]

"Relatives," in its primary meaning, refers to the statutory next of kin who would take on an intestacy.[71]

(vii) *Legatees*

The word "legatees" strictly means only the persons to whom a pecuniary gift is made by will, but it is normally taken to include those to whom bequests of personalty are made as well. Nevertheless, it excludes devisees.[72] However, the distinction between legacies, bequests and devises is not as relevant today as it once was and, in any event, is not one that most testators appreciate. Hence, the rule has lost much of its force and should probably be disregarded.[73]

(viii) *Gifts to Two or More Persons*

If the testator makes a gift to two or more persons, the gift may be intended as a class gift or a gift *nominatim*. This issue is dealt with elsewhere.[74]

---

65 *Gibson Estate v. Ashbury College Inc.* (1999), 179 D.L.R. (4th) 577 (Ont. S.C.); *Creaghan v. Hazen* (1999), 32 E.T.R. (2d) 180 (N.B.Q.B.).

66 *Matheson v. Norman*, [1946] 3 W.W.R. 63, [1947] 1 D.L.R. 71 (B.C.S.C.). See also *Fenton v. Whittier* (1977), 26 N.S.R. (2d) 662 (T.D.); *Re Quaal*, [1920] 3 W.W.R. 117, 53 D.L.R. 592 (Sask. C.A.). See also *Re Barlow's Will Trusts*, [1976] 1 All E.R. 246; *Sloat v. Brunskill* (1987), 28 E.T.R. 39.

67 *Re Stark*, [1969] 2 O.R. 881, 7 D.L.R. (3d) 313 (C.A.); *Re Butt* (1986), 22 E.T.R. 120 (Ont. Surr. Ct.).

68 *Re Fisher*, [1959] O.W.N. 46 (H.C.).

69 *Re Powell*, [1956] O.R. 522, 5 D.L.R. (2d) 67 (H.C.).

70 *Re Masoud* (1959), 16 D.L.R. (2d) 134 (Ont. H.C.).

71 *Re Murray* (1915), 8 O.W.N. 463 (H.C.).

72 *Edwards v. Smith* (1877), 25 Gr. 159.

73 See, *e.g.*, *Re Stewart and Dunn* (1923), 24 O.W.N. 290 (H.C.).

74 In the chapter on Class Gifts.

The question may arise, however, whether the persons take as joint tenants or as tenants in common. At common law a gift to two or more persons was construed to mean that they took as joint tenants, but in equity the presumption is in favour of a tenancy in common and this presumption operates whenever the gift calls for a division, or an equal division, among the beneficiaries.[75] By statute, devises to two or more persons take effect as tenancies in common, unless a contrary intention is expressed.[76]

Another question that commonly arises is whether the beneficiaries take *per capita* or *per stirpes*. The *prima facie* rule is that they take *per capita*, unless the context directs otherwise.[77]

A gift "to A and B and C" typically suggests a stirpital distribution, there being two sets of beneficiaries, namely A on the one hand, and B and C on the other.[78]

On the other hand, a gift "to A and B and their children" *prima facie* means that they all take *per capita*.[79] Similarly, a gift "to A's next of kin," or "to A's heirs" normally results in the application of the *prima facie* rule, even though the beneficiaries are of different generations.[80]

A gift "to the children of A and B" if A and B are not married to each other, suggests a *per capita* distribution, especially if words of equal division are used.[81] However, the *prima facie* rule is ousted if there is a contrary intention either on the face of the will,[82] or as shown by the surrounding circumstances.[83]

Another question presented by the form of gift discussed in the preceding paragraph is whether the testator intended to benefit the children of A and the children of B, or whether he or she intended a gift to B and the children of A. The latter construction is normally preferred on the ground that if the testator had intended the former, he or she would have repeated the preposition "of" before the name "B."[84] Unfortunately, however, neither testators, nor, unhappily, their legal advisers, necessarily know or follow the strict rules of grammar, and, there-

---

75 *Clark v. Clark* (1890), 17 S.C.R. 376. See, *e.g.*, *Re Peters* (1967), 63 W.W.R. 180 (Man. Q.B.), a devise to three persons in equal shares; *Re Quebec* (1929), 37 O.W.N. 271 (H.C.), a devise to two persons jointly. This point is also discussed in the chapter on Lapse and Survivorship.

76 *Conveyancing and Law of Property Act*, R.S.O. 1990, c. C.34, s. 13; *Land Titles Act*, R.S.S. 1978, c. L-5, s. 242; *Law of Property Act*, R.S.A. 1980, c. L-8, s. 8; R.S.M. 1987, c. L90, s. 15; *Property Act*, R.S.N.B. 1973, c. P-19, s. 20; *Property Law Act*, R.S.B.C. 1996, c. 377, s. 11; *Real Property Act*, R.S.N.S. 1989, c. 385, s. 5; *Tenants in Common Act*, R.S.N.W.T. 1988, c. T-1, s. 1; R.S.Y. 1986, c. 168, s. 1.

77 *Re McNeil* (1959), 43 M.P.R. 357 at 359 (Nfld. T.D.), *per* Winter J.

78 *Hutchinson v. LaFortune* (1897), 28 O.R. 329 (C.A.).

79 *Re Grafton*, [1933] O.W.N. 526 (H.C.).

80 *Re Labatt* (1916), 11 O.W.N. 250 (H.C.); *Re McKenzie* (1917), 12 O.W.N. 159 (H.C.). But see *Re Bint* (1909), 1 O.W.N. 285 (H.C.), if a contrary intention was found in a gift to persons "who would be my natural heirs".

81 *Re Ottman; Ottman v. Ottman* (1961), 30 D.L.R. (2d) 485 (N.S. T.D.); *Re McNeil* (1959), 43 M.P.R. 357 (Nfld. T.D.); *Re Ollerhead* (1931), 40 O.W.N. 419 (H.C.).

82 As in *Re Parish*, [1964] 1 O.R. 353, 42 D.L.R. (2d) 212 (H.C.), involving a gift "equally among my brother, my sister, and the children of my deceased sister, namely A, B, C and D, and X", X being a friend of the testator.

83 *Re Ottman, supra.*

84 *Re Birkett; Holland v. Duvean*, [1950] Ch. 330, [1950] 1 All E.R. 316.

fore, the second interpretation should, perhaps, not be followed as a matter of course.[85]

If the gift takes the form "To A and the children of B" the *prima facie* construction is again that a *per capita* distribution is indicated. But a stirpital distribution may be suggested by the context, as when a testator leaves a share of residue to seven named persons and an eighth share "to the children of X, living at my death," if the first seven were blood relatives of the testator, while the eighth was not and his children were of a different generation.[86]

A gift "to A and B for life with remainder to their children" suggests a stirpital distribution, since A and B are not likely to die at the same time and their interests will, therefore, pass to their respective children at different times.[87] However, if distribution of the capital is to be postponed until both life tenants have died, the distribution is *per capita*.[88]

If the gift takes the form "to the issue of A," a *per capita* distribution is suggested, unless the context otherwise requires.[89] But, if the gift is "to A and B and if either or both predecease me then to their respective issue," a stirpital distribution is indicated.[90]

In gifts of the type discussed, the testator often makes it clear that he or she intends a stirpital distribution, but fails to make clear which generation should form the stocks or *stirps*. To solve this problem, the court must look at the language of the will, there being no *prima facie* rule of construction that supplies the answer.[91]

Thus, in one case the testator gave certain property equally to his two daughters for life, with remainder "among and between my grandchildren, *per stirpes*, in equal shares". It was held that the testator wanted to treat the daughters equally and, therefore, also their families. Hence, the stocks were formed by the daughters, with the result that the one child of one daughter took one share, while the three children of the other daughter shared the other.[92]

In another case, however, the testatrix directed that the residue of her estate be divided "in equal shares *per stirpes* among the issue of my brothers and sisters, A, B, C and D living at my death." The court held that, as the gift was not to the brothers and sisters, but to their issue, the stocks should be formed by their

---

85 See *O'Connor v. Perpetual Trustee Co.* (1975), 5 A.L.J. 47 (Austr. H.C.).

86 *Haidl v. Sacher*, 2 Sask. R. 93, [1980] 1 W.W.R. 293, 7 E.T.R. 1, 106 D.L.R. (3d) 360 (C.A.).

87 *Re Errington; Gibbs v. Lassam*, [1927] 1 Ch. 421.

88 *Re Rutherford* (1906), 7 O.W.R. 796 (H.C.); *Re Ianson* (1907), 14 O.L.R. 82 (H.C.).

89 *Re Rawlinson; Hill v. Withall*, [1909] 2 Ch. 36.

90 *Re Sibley's Trusts* (1887), 5 Ch. D. 494, [1874-80] All E.R. Rep. 250.

91 *Sidey v. Perpetual Trustees & Agency Co. of New Zealand Ltd.*, [1944] A.C. 194, [1944] 2 All E.R. 225 at 227 (P.C.), *per* Lord Simonds. See also *Re Sutherland* (1984), 29 Alta. L.R. (2d) 21, 16 E.T.R. 53, 52 A.R. 211 (Surr. Ct.).

92 *Re Karkalatos; Gettas v. Karavos*, [1962] S.C.R. 390, 34 D.L.R. (2d) 7. See also Carmen S. Thérien, "Hamel Estate v. Hamel: Should Will Drafters Abandon the Use of 'Issue per Stirpes'" (1999), 18 E.T. & P.J. 127, which comments on *Hamel Estate v. Hamel* (1995), 9 E.T.R. (2d) 315 (B.C.S.C.). She notes that the phrase "issue *per stirpes*" is generally clear, but that "children *per stirpes*" is contradictory.

children. Hence, the twelve living children each took a share and the issue of three children who predeceased the testatrix took the share of their parents.[93]

(ix) *Multiple Gifts*

A testator may make more than one gift to the same person by different instruments. This often happens when a will is modified by one or more codicils. *Prima facie* the donee is entitled to all the gifts. Hence, the presumption is that the gifts are cumulative. However, the presumption will be displaced if it is proved that the testator intended the gifts to be substitutionary.[94]

(x) *House and Contents*

A gift of a house "and the contents therein" normally means that the beneficiary is entitled to all choses in possession in the house, including a car in an adjoining garage.[95] The gift does not include choses in action. Those are not considered to be property in the house, but evidence of title to property elsewhere.[96] Nor does such a gift include cash in a cash box in the house.[97]

(xi) *Power of Selection*

A testator may sometimes give one property to one legatee and another of the same description to a second. The courts resolve the question which legatee receives which property in the following manner:

> A testator who has several properties, all having the same description, may by his will give one of them to a legatee, and leave the choice of that one to the legatee; and such a gift is clearly valid. And the fact that the legatee is to be able to select may appear either by express words used in the will, or by reasonable inference from it. And, *prima facie*, if the testator gives one of such properties to a legatee without saying more, then the reasonable inference is, that the testator intended the legatee to select; and this whether the fact appears on the face of the will that the testator had several such properties,...or whether the fact otherwise appears.... And I should myself be prepared to hold that, where a testator gives one of such properties to each of several legatees, then he intends (*prima facie*) to give the right of selection to the legatees according to the priority of the bequests. But in all these cases it is, of course, essential that the will should not shew that the testator was bequeathing any particular one of the properties to the legatee who desires to select,

---

93 *Re Montgomery*, [1973] 2 O.R. 92, 33 D.L.R. (3d) 48 (H.C.), noted (1973), 1 E. & T.Q. 3; *Re Simpson*, [1928] 3 D.L.R. 773 (S.C.C.); *Re McInnes*, [1958] O.R. 592 (H.C.); *Re Sitter Estate*, [1977] 2 W.W.R. 356 (Sask. Surr. Ct.); *Strittmatter v. Stephens* (1983), 40 O.R. (2d) 463 (H.C.); *Re Clark Estate* (1993), 50 E.T.R. 105 (B.C.S.C.).

94 *Russell v. Dickson* (1842), 2 Dr. & War. 133; *Henderson v. Fraser*, [1923] S.C.R. 23, [1923] 1 D.L.R. 636; *Jeffery Estate v. Rowe* (1989) 36 E.T.R. 217 (Ont. H.C.).

95 *Re Tremaine* (1929), 37 O.W.N. 186 (H.C.).

96 *Re Dixon Estate* (1990), 37 E.T.R. 268 (Sask. Surr. Ct.).

97 *Re McClean Estate* (1992), 47 E.T.R. 310 (Sask. Surr. Ct.).

for the selection by the testator is incompatible with the view that he intended the legatee to select. If a will shews that a testator intends to give a particular property to a legatee, and, owing to the testator having several properties answering the description in the will of the particular property given you are unable to say, either from the will itself or from extrinsic evidence, which of the several properties the testator referred to, then on principle the gift must fail for uncertainty, and the Court cannot, in order to avoid an intestacy, change the will, or construe it as giving to the legatee the option of choosing any one of the properties.[98]

Thus, when a testatrix owned a farm and directed her executor in one clause of her will to convey 30 acres thereof to her son, Joseph and in the next clause to convey 20 acres of it to her son, Thomas, Joseph was given the right to select whichever 30 acres he wished.[99]

A power of selection is personal to the beneficiary. Hence, at the latest, it must be exercised before his or her death.[100] However, in respect of real property, which, by statute, vests in the devisee within three years of the testator's death in Ontario, unless it is subject to an express or implied trust for sale, or unless it is required for the payment of debts and is protected by a caution,[101] the power of selection may have to be exercised before the three years have expired.[102]

(c) Statutory Rules

(i) *Generally*

In addition to the common law rules of construction, there is a number of statutory rules which codify or reverse the common law. Generally, they apply unless a contrary intention appears by the will. These rules are discussed briefly below, with the exception of those dealt with in later chapters. Reference is made only to the Ontario legislation, but the statutes in the other provinces contain comparable provisions.

(ii) *Disposition of Void Gift*

At common law a void, disclaimed or lapsed devise of real property devolved upon the heir at law, whereas a gift of personal property fell into residue in those circumstances.[103] Section 23 of the *Succession Law Reform Act*[104] now provides:

---

98 *Asten v. Asten*, [1894] 3 Ch. 260 at 262-3, *per* Romer J. And see *Re Knapton*, [1941] 1 Ch. 428, [1941] 2 All E.R. 573; and *Re Davison* (1979), 36 N.S.R. (2d) 152, 5 E.T.R. 103, 99 D.L.R. (3d) 81 (T.D.).

99 *Re Sapusak* (1984), 45 O.R. (2d) 584, 3 O.A.C. 234, 16 E.T.R. 197, 8 D.L.R. (4th) 158 (C.A.). See also *Re O'Brien; Can. Permanent Trust Co. v. Murphy* (1976), 24 N.S.R. (2d) 45 (T.D.).

100 *Boyce v. Boyce* (1849), 16 Sim. 476, 60 E.R. 959.

101 *Estates Administration Act*, R.S.O. 1990, c. 143, s. 9.

102 *Guild v. Mallory* (1983), 41 O.R. (2d) 21, 13 E.T.R. 218, 144 D.L.R. (3d) 603 (H.C.).

103 Ontario Law Reform Commission, *Report on the Proposed Adoption in Ontario of the Uniform Wills Act* (1968), p. 38. See further the chapter on Lapse and Survivorship.

104 R.S.O. 1990, c. S.26 (hereafter referred to without further citation).

23. Except when a contrary intention appears by the will, property or an interest therein that is comprised or intended to be comprised in a devise or bequest that fails or becomes void by reason of,

(a) the death of the devisee or donee in the lifetime of the testator; or

(b) the devise or bequest being disclaimed or being contrary to law or otherwise incapable of taking effect,

is included in the residuary devise or bequest, if any, contained in the will.

We shall discuss this section in greater detail in the chapter on Lapse and Survivorship.

(iii) *Devise of Real Property Includes Leaseholds*

Under Anglo-Canadian law a leasehold is regarded as personal property. However, most testators would assume that it is real property and intend that a leasehold interest should pass under a devise of real property. Hence, section 24 of the *Succession Law Reform Act* provides:

24. Except when a contrary intention appears by the will, where a testator devises,

(a) his or her real property;

(b) his or her real property in a place mentioned in the will, or in the occupation of a person mentioned in the will;

(c) real property described in a general manner; or

(d) real property described in a manner that would include a leasehold estate if the testator had no freehold estate which could be described in the manner used,

the devise includes the leasehold estates of the testator or any of them to which the description extends, as well as freehold estates.

(iv) *Gift Includes Property over Which Testator Has Power of Appointment*

At common law a general devise or bequest of property would not be apt to pass property over which the testator had a power of appointment. This is particularly inconvenient in respect of general powers of appointment which permit the testator to appoint to whomever he or she wishes. Moreover, if the general devise were not to carry such property it might, depending upon the terms of the power, be undisposed of. The statute has remedied this situation, but only, despite its broad language, as regards general powers. The expression "in any manner he thinks proper," refers only to the class of possible objects and, for this reason, it has been held that a special power[105] and a hybrid power[106] do not fall within the legislation. Of course, the property subject to such powers can be disposed of by will, but only if the testator shows that he or she intends to exercise it.[107] Section 25 of the *Succession Law Reform Act* provides:

---

105 *Re Penrose; Penrose v. Penrose*, [1933] Ch. 793. A special power is one which permits the testator to appoint among a described class of persons or among named persons.

106 *Re Byron's Settlement; Williams v. Mitchell*, [1891] 3 Ch. 474.

107 *Re Weston's Settlement; Neeves v. Weston*, [1906] 2 Ch. 620, [1904-7] All E.R. Rep. 174.

25. (1) Except when a contrary intention appears by the will, a general devise of,

(a) the real property of the testator;

(b) the real property of the testator,

   (i) in a place mentioned in the will, or

   (ii) in the occupation of a person mentioned in the will; or

(c) real property described in a general manner,

includes any real property, or any real property to which the description extends, which he or she has power to appoint in any manner he or she thinks proper and operates as an execution of the power.

(2) Except when a contrary intention appears by the will, a bequest of,

(a) the personal property of the testator; or

(b) personal property described in a general manner,

includes any personal property, or any personal property to which the description extends, which he or she has power to appoint in any manner he or she thinks proper and operates as an execution of the power.

(v) *Devise without Words of Limitation*

At common law a devise of real property without words of limitation conferred a life estate only,[108] whereas if words of limitation short of "and his heirs" were employed, the onus was on the devisee to show that the testator intended to pass the fee simple.[109] Since many testators were unaware of the technical form of words necessary to create a fee simple, the Legislature intervened and reversed the onus of proof. Section 26 of the *Succession Law Reform Act* now provides:

> **26.** Except when a contrary intention appears by the will, where real property is devised to a person without words of limitation, the devise passes the fee simple or the whole of any other estate or interest that the testator had power to dispose of by will in the real property.

(vi) *Meaning of "Heir"*

At common law, until Parliament conferred the power to make wills of land,[110] real property descended to the deceased's heir at law under the primogeniture rule, whereas personalty was distributed among his or her next of kin. By will, a testator can, of course, change the course of descent and distribution and, indeed, the law has long since been changed to abolish the privileged position of the heir and to require him or her to share in an intestacy with the other next of kin.[111] Since the meaning of the word "heir" has, therefore, changed significantly, section 27 of the *Succession Law Reform Act* provides:

---

108 *Doe d. Ford v. Bell* (1850), 6 U.C.Q.B. 527 (C.A.).

109 *Brennan v. Munro* (1841), 6 O.S. 92 (C.A.).

110 By the *Statute of Wills, 1540*, 32 Hen. 8, c. 1.

111 You should note that the legislation does not abolish the rule in *Shelley's Case* (1581), 1 Co. Rep. 93b, 76 E.R. 199, which is a rule of law and not a rule of construction, and holds that in a devise in the form "to A for life, remainder to his heirs" the words "his heirs" shall be construed as words of limitation and not as words of purchase, so that the ancestor, A, takes the fee simple. See *Re Rynard* (1980), 8 E.T.R. 185 (Ont. C.A.).

27. Except when a contrary intention appears by the will, where property is devised or bequeathed to the "heir" or "heirs" of the testator or of another person, the words "heir" or "heirs" mean the person to whom the beneficial interest in the property would have gone under the law of Ontario if the testator or the other person died intestate.

(vii) *Meaning of "Die without Issue"*

At common law a devise such as "to A, but if he dies without issue, to B," was construed to give A a fee tail, with remainder to B. In other words, the phrase "die without issue" was construed as an indefinite failure of issue or a failure of issue at any time in the future. A similar gift of personalty could confer the absolute interest upon A.[112] The rule was, however, abolished by statute and now operates to give A the fee simple in real property and the absolute interest in personalty, subject to defeasance in favour of B if A dies without issue surviving him.[113] Section 28 of the *Succession Law Reform Act* now provides:

28. (1) Subject to subsection (2), in a devise or bequest of property,
(a) the words,
(i) "die without issue",
(ii) "die without leaving issue", or
(iii) "have no issue"; or
(b) other words importing either a want or failure of issue of a person in his or her lifetime or at the time of his or her death or an indefinite failure of his or her issue,
mean a want or failure of issue in the lifetime or at the time of death of that person, and do not mean an indefinite failure of his or her issue unless a contrary intention appears by the will.
(2) This Part does not extend to cases where the words defined in subsection (1) import,
(a) if no issue described in a preceding gift be born; or
(b) if there be no issue who live to attain the age or otherwise answer the description required for obtaining a vested estate by a preceding gift to that issue.

(viii) *Devise to Trustee*

Sections 29 and 30 of the *Succession Law Reform Act* are designed to validate the titles of trustees if it is unclear from the will what interest the testator intended to give. These sections provide:

29. Except when there is devised to a trustee expressly or by implication an estate for a definite term of years absolute or determinable or an estate of freehold, a devise of real property to a trustee or executor passes the fee simple or the whole of any other estate or interest that the testator had power to dispose of by will in the real property.

---

112 Sir Robert Megarry and H.W.R. Wade, *The Law of Real Property* (5th ed., 1984), p. 536.
113 In order to avoid the inconvenience to A, who has to wait until his death to determine whether his interest will be absolute, the legislation was further amended in England to provide that it becomes absolutely vested as soon as any issue of A attains his majority: *Conveyancing Act, 1882*, 45 & 46 Vict., c. 39 (U.K.), s. 10, am. by *Law of Property Act, 1925*, 15 & 16 Geo. 5, c. 20 (U.K.), s. 134, and by *Family Law Reform Act, 1969*, c. 46 (U.K.), s. 1(3) and 1st Sched.

30. Where real property is devised to a trustee without express limitation of the estate to be taken by the trustee and the beneficial interest in the real property or in the surplus rents and profits,

    (a) is not given to a person for life; or

    (b) is given to a person for life but the purpose of the trust may continue beyond his or her life,

the devise vests in the trustee the fee simple or the whole of any other legal estate that the testator had power to dispose of by will in the real property and not an estate determinable when the purposes of the trust are satisfied.

(ix) *Undisposed of Residue*

At common law an executor was entitled to the residue of the estate if it was undisposed of.[114] It is unlikely that most testators intend this to happen. Hence, by statute, the executor is required to hold such residue upon resulting trust for those who would take on an intestacy.[115] Section 33 of the *Succession Law Reform Act* provides:

33. (1) Where a person dies having by will appointed a person executor, the executor is a trustee of any residue not expressly disposed of, for the person or persons, if any, who would be entitled to that residue in the event of intestacy in respect of it, unless it appears by the will that the person so appointed executor was intended to take the residue beneficially.

(2) Nothing in this section prejudices any right in respect of any residue not expressly disposed of to which, if this Part had not been passed, an executor would have been entitled where there is not any person who would be entitled to the testator's estate under Part II in case of an intestacy.

4. THE MEANING OF PARTICULAR EXPRESSIONS

(a) Generally

In the preceding part of this chapter the general principles and rules of construction were discussed. In this part some examples of how the courts proceed to interpret particular expressions will be given. In many respects these are but particular instances of the rules of construction.

(b) Prima Facie Meaning

When the court begins to interpret a will, it usually takes the words that the testator has used to have their ordinary, common or *prima facie* meaning, and may consult dictionaries for that purpose. This is not objectionable as a first step,

---

114 *Re Carville*, [1937] 4 All E.R. 464.

115 If the residue is given to the executors without an indication that they take in trust or beneficially, the statute does not apply, but the court must determine what the testator's intention is: *Re Gracey*, [1929] 1 D.L.R. 260 (Ont. C.A.); *Re Melvin*, [1972] 3 W.W.R. 55, 24 D.L.R. (3d) 240 (B.C.S.C.).

provided that the court does not stop there. It was, indeed, at one time the rule that the ordinary grammatical meaning of a word or expression governed and this was regarded as a

> rule of...universal application, which admits of no exception, and which ought never, under any circumstances, to be departed from.[116]

Fortunately, that is not the law today. It is now recognized that, although words may have a *prima facie*, or dictionary meaning, that meaning may not be the one intended by the testator. As Lord Denning observed (in dissent),

> It is very unlikely that he used a dictionary, and even less likely that he used the same one as you.[117]

It may be that the testator was inept in expressing himself or herself, or it may be that there are other common meanings to the words used. Whatever the reason, it is the testator's intention that must be ascertained, both from the context of the will and from the circumstances in which he or she wrote the will.

Perrin v. Morgan,[118] reproduced below, is concerned with the meaning of the word "money" and represents the modern approach to ascertaining the meaning of particular words and expressions. It is suggested that under the modern approach, while punctuation may be of assistance in ascertaining the meaning of a will, it is not by any means determinative and should, in appropriate cases be disregarded.[119]

PERRIN v. MORGAN
[1943] A.C. 399, [1943] 1 All E.R. 187
House of Lords

The testatrix, by a home-drawn will, left "all moneys of which I die possessed" to be shared among her nephews and nieces. Her estate included investments in excess of £33,000, cash in the bank of £389, some other cash, accrued dividends of £36, accrued rent of £82, an income tax repayment of £32, household goods of £62 and freeholds worth about £1800. If the word "moneys" were restricted to "cash" the nephews and nieces would only share about £840.

A long line of cases had defined "money" to mean not only cash on hand but also money in the bank and cash receivables, but the meaning so defined excluded investments and other personal and real property. The lower courts applied this definition. The nephews and nieces appealed to the House of Lords.

---

116 *Re Crawford's Trusts* (1854), 2 Drew. 230 at 233, 61 E.R. 707, *per* Kindersley, V.C.
117 *Re Rowland*, [1963] 1 Ch. 1 at 10, [1962] 2 All E.R. 837 (C.A.).
118 [1943] A.C. 399, [1943] 1 All E.R. 187 (H.L.).
119 *Cf. Re Patton*, [1971] 3 O.R. 85, 19 D.L.R. (3d) 497 (H.C.).

VISCOUNT SIMON L.C.:

. . .

My Lords, the fundamental rule in construing the language of a will is to put on the words used the meaning which, having regard to the terms of the will, the testator intended. The question is not, of course, what the testator meant to do when he made his will, but what the written words he uses mean in the particular case - what are the "expressed intentions" of the testator. In the case of an ordinary English word like "money", which is not always employed in the same sense, I can see no possible justification for fixing on it, as the result of a series of judicial decisions about a series of different wills, a cast-iron meaning which must not be departed from unless special circumstances exist, with the result that this special meaning must be presumed to be the meaning of every testator in every case unless the contrary is shown. I agree, of course, that, if a word has only one natural meaning, it is right to attribute that meaning to the word when used in a will unless the context or other circumstances which may be properly considered show that an unusual meaning is intended, but the word "money" has not got one natural or usual meaning. It has several meanings, each of which in appropriate circumstances may be regarded as natural. In its original sense, which is also its narrowest sense, the word means "coin". Moneta was an appellation of Juno, and the Temple of Moneta at Rome was the mint. Phrases like "false money" or "clipped money" show the original use in English, but the conception very quickly broadens into the equivalent of "cash" of any sort. The question: "Have you any money in your purse?" refers presumably to bank notes or Treasury notes, as well as to shillings and pence. A further extension would include not only coin and currency in the possession of an individual, but debts owing to him, and cheques which he could pay into his banking account, or postal orders, or the like. Again, going further, it is a matter of common speech to refer to one's "money at the bank", although in a stricter sense the bank is not holding one's own money and what one possesses is a chose in action which represents the right to require the bank to pay out sums held at the call of its customer. Sums on deposit, whether with a bank or otherwise, may be included by a further extension, but this is by no means the limit to the senses in which the word "money" is frequently and quite naturally used in English speech. The statement: "I have my money invested on mortgage, or in debentures, or in stocks and shares, or in savings certificates", is not an illegitimate use of the word "money" on which the courts are bound to frown, though it is a great extension from its original meaning to interpret it as covering securities, and, in considering the various meanings of the word "money" in common speech, one must go even further, as any dictionary will show. The word may be used to cover the whole of an individual's personal property — sometimes, indeed, all of a person's property, whether real or personal. "What has he done with his money?" may well be an inquiry as to the general contents of a rich man's will. Horace's satire at the expense of the fortune-hunter who attached himself to childless Roman matrons, has its modern equivalent in the saying: "It's her money he's after". When St. Paul wrote to Timothy that the love of money is the root of all evil, he was not warning him of the risks attaching to one particular kind of wealth, but was pointing to the dangers of avarice in general. When Tennyson's Northern Farmer counseled his son not to marry for money, but to go where money is, he was not excluding the attractiveness of private property in land. These wider meanings of "money" are referred to in some of the reported cases as "popular" meanings, in contrast to the "legal" meaning of the term, but for the purpose of construing a will, and especially a home-made will, a popular meaning may be the more important of the two. The circumstance that a skilled draftsman would avoid the use of so ambiguous a word only confirms the view that, when it is used in a will, the popular as opposed to the technical use of the word "money" may be important. I protest against the idea that, in interpreting the language of a will, there can be some fixed meaning of the word "money", which the courts must adopt as being the "legal" meaning as opposed to the "popular" meaning. The proper meaning is the correct meaning in the case of the particular will, and there is no necessary opposition between that meaning and the popular meaning. The duty of the court, in the case of an ordinary English word which has several quite usual meanings which differ from one another is not to assume that one out of several meanings holds the field as the correct meaning until it is ousted by some other meaning regarded as "non-legal", but to ascertain without prejudice as between various usual meanings which is the correct interpretation of the particular document.

I now turn to some of the reported cases, promising only that it seems to me a little unfortunate that so many of such cases should find their way into the books, for in most instances, the duty of a judge who is called on to interpret a will containing ordinary English words is not to regard previous decisions as constituting a sort of legal dictionary to be consulted and remorselessly applied whatever the testator may have intended, but to construe the particular document so as to arrive at the testator's real meaning according to its actual language and circumstances. It can rarely happen, I should suppose, that the interpretation of a word like "money" in one will provides a sure and certain guide to its meaning in another will, which is differently expressed.

[His Lordship referred to a number of cases which interpreted the word "money" strictly, and continued:]

Notwithstanding this long tradition I would urge the House to reject the view that, in construing a will, the court must start with a presumption in favour of a particular narrower meaning of the word "money" (though not, indeed, its narrowest meaning), and that, in the absence of contradictory context, the court is bound to apply this narrower meaning, even though the inference is that this is not what the testator really meant by the term. As I have already said, the word "money" has more than one meaning, and it is, in my opinion, a mistake to pick out one interpretation of the word and to call it the "legal" meaning or the "strict legal" meaning as though it had some superior right to prevail over another equally usual and not illegitimate meaning. The context in which the word is used is, of course, a main guide to its interpretation, but it is one thing to say that the word must be treated as having one particular meaning unless the context overrules that interpretation in favour of another and another thing to say that "money", since it is a word of several possible meanings, must be construed in a will in accordance with what appears to be its meaning in that document without any presumption that it bears one meaning rather than another. While disclaiming any idea of interpreting a document which is not before me, I should have thought that the mere fact that a will in a single sentence disposed of "all the money of which I die possessed" was a reason for interpreting "money" in a very wide sense, though there is no positive context.

In choosing between "popular" meanings, it seems to me that an interpretation which includes realty as well as personalty in the word "money" may often be going too far, though, of course, everything turns on the language and circumstances of the particular will. An amateur will-maker, though using the word "money" loosely, may be drawing a distinction between "my money" and "my land", and, indeed, may mean to include leaseholds as well as freeholds in the latter expression, if he owns both. In the present case, the testatrix owned no leaseholds, so the question whether "all moneys" would have include leaseholds does not arise. On the other hand, the will deals separately with the more important of the freeholds, and this circumstance goes to show that "all moneys" in this will does not include the omitted freeholds. If the expression were "all remaining moneys" it might have been different.

I have felt it right to deal with this case in the wider aspect, but before parting from it I must add that I am much disposed to share the view which I understand commends itself to some of your Lordships, that even if the so-called rule of construction were to be left standing, there are some indications in this will which might justify the application of the so-called rule being displaced by the language used and the circumstances of the case. The testatrix directed that "all moneys of which I die possessed" should be "shared by my nephews and nieces" as named. The testatrix held very considerable investments to which she makes no separate reference in her will. If the state of her property when she made her will was anything like what it was at her death, she must, therefore, either have deliberately intended to die intestate in respect of her stocks and shares and to leave these nephews and nieces to share in what happened to be the balance at her bank at the moment of her death and little else, or else she must have used the phrase "all moneys of which I die possessed" as covering her investments also. But whether or not these considerations would be sufficient to overthrow the presumption which has for so long been regarded as prima facie forcing the court to apply a narrower meaning, it is clear that, when the rule is rejected and the present will is given its natural construction free from the restraining use of a judicial dictionary, the appeal should succeed.

. . .

LORD ROMER:

My Lords, I take it to be a cardinal rule of construction that a will should be so construed as to give effect to the intention of the testator, such intention being gathered from the language of the will read in the light of the circumstances in which the will was made. To understand the language employed the court is entitled, to use a familiar expression, to sit in the testator's armchair. When seated there, however, the court is not entitled to make a fresh will for the testator merely because it strongly suspects that the testator did not mean what he has plainly said - that he was, in fact, one of those persons of whom Knight Bruce L.J. said that they spoke as if the office of language were to conceal their thoughts. In many of the cases to be found in the books the court is reported to have said that the construction it has put on a will has probably defeated the testator's intention. If this means, as it ought to mean, that the court entertains the strong suspicion to which I have just referred, no sort of objection can be taken to it, but if it means that the court has felt itself prevented by some rule of construction from giving effect to what the language of the will, read in the light of the circumstances in which it was made, convinces it was the real intention of the testator, it has misconstrued the will.

My Lords, I do not, of course, intend to suggest that well-settled rules of construction are to be disregarded. On the contrary, I think that they should be strictly observed, but they ought to be applied in a reasonable way. It is, no doubt, of great importance to lawyers and others engaged in the preparation of wills that they should have the certainty of knowing that certain well-known words and phrases will receive from the court the meaning that the court has for generations past attributed to them. Much confusion and uncertainty would be caused if this were not so. The rules of construction, in other words, should be regarded as a dictionary by which all parties, including the courts, are bound, but the court should not have recourse to this dictionary to construe a word or a phrase until it has ascertained from an examination of the language of the whole will, when read in the light of the circumstances, whether or not the testator has indicated his intention of using the word or the phrase in other than its dictionary meaning — whether or not, in other words, to use another familiar expression, the testator has been his own dictionary. I have thought it desirable to make these remarks, however elementary and obvious they may seem to be, as I have noticed in some of the reported cases on wills a tendency on the part of the court to pay more attention to the rules of construction than to the language of the testator.

[The concurring speeches of Lords Atkins, Thankerton and Russell of Killowen, have been omitted.]

Notes and Questions

1. *Perrin v. Morgan* has been applied on many occasions in Canada.[120]
2. Would a bequest of "all cash money available" include such investments as Canada Savings Bonds?[121]

---

120 See, *e.g.*, *Re Price*, [1955] O.W.N. 18, affirmed at 254 (C.A.); *Re Brooks* (1969), 68 W.W.R. 132, 4 D.L.R. (3d) 694 (Sask. Q.B.); *Re Stinson*, [1973] 1 O.R. 171, 30 D.L.R. (3d) 519 (H.C.); *Re Jones*, [1973] 2 O.R. 527, 34 D.L.R. (3d) 479 (H.C.); *Re Bahrychuk* (1978), 2 E.T.R. 140 (Man. Q.B.).
121 See *Re Bennett*, [1955] O.W.N. 211 (H.C.).

3. *Re Price*[122] shows that the word "money" may include real property. The testatrix, by her home-drawn will, gave 12 pecuniary legacies which totaled $47,500 and then provided, "If any money is left over it is to be divided between the Red Cross and the Hospital for Sick Children".

The testatrix' personal estate was valued at $28,444.04, of which $16,177.72 was deposited in a bank account, $21.98 represented cash on hand, $371.50 was in the form of an uncashed cheque and $11,872.84 was in the form of Dominion of Canada Bonds. In addition there were some other items of personalty of little value. Her real estate was worth more than $75,000. The court held that, in those circumstances, the testatrix intended to describe all her property, including the real estate when she spoke of any money being left over.

4. *Venczel v. Kovari*[123] is another example. A testatrix made her will without legal assistance. She left all her "personal monies" equally to her brothers and sisters and the residue equally to her husband of 48 years. She owned bank accounts, securities, investment certificates, and other investments. In light of the surrounding circumstances and the context of the will, the court held that "monies" should be given its popular meaning as moneys in the bank. It did not include securities. Otherwise there would be no residue and her husband would be disinherited, contrary to her intention.

5. In *Fekete Estate v. Simon*[124] the court held that the expression "all of my shares in the share capital of" certain corporations, included an interest in the corporations secured by shareholder loans made by the testator. Any other interpretation would have thwarted the testator's intention of making his wife the principal beneficiary of his will.

(c) Words Defined by the Testator

Although a word may have an ordinary, accepted meaning, the testator may give it a special meaning in his or her will. In other words, the testator may be supplying the court with the dictionary it is to use. In those circumstances there is usually little difficulty in construing the will. *Re Helliwell*,[125] reproduced below is of this type.

RE HELLIWELL
[1916] 2 Ch. 580
Chancery Division

The testator gave the residue of his estate in trust for his nephews and nieces, adding:

> And I declare that John Rushworth Feather, the son of my sister Mary Wright, and William Henry Hey, the son of my brother John Helliwell, shall be entitled to a share equally with my other nephews and nieces.

---

122 *Supra.*
123 (2000), 32 E.T.R. (2d) 137 (Ont. S.C.).
124 (2000), 32 E.T.R. (2d) 202 (Ont. S.C.).
125 [1916] 2 Ch. 580.

Mary Wright was the illegitimate daughter of the testator's mother who was born before her marriage to the testator's father. John was Mary's illegitimate son. William was the illegitimate son of the testator's lawful brother, John. The testator's mother had another illegitimate daughter, Sarah, who had died, survived by legitimate issue. All other beneficiaries and their parents were legitimate. The question was whether Sarah's children could share in the gift.

SARGANT J.:

. . .

Now, on looking carefully at the special words of inclusion here, it is, I think, fairly clear that the testator is intending in the case of John Rushworth Feather, as in the case of William Henry Hey, to cure the disqualifications due to an individual illegitimacy, and is not directing his mind to any disqualification due to the illegitimacy, in the former case, of the legatee's parent. The illegitimacy of Mary, as well as that of Sarah, was an old story which had been kept in the background during the whole of the testator's life, though he was no doubt aware of it. And it seems to me that he deliberately ignores it in this clause of his will, and speaks of Mary Wright as his sister in as full a sense as that in which he speaks of John Helliwell as his brother. Further, by directing that the two named persons, John Rushworth Feather and William Henry Hey, shall take with his *other* nephews and nieces, he impliedly recognizes them as included in his view as members of the class of nephews and nieces. Accordingly he is obviously using both the word "sister" in relation to the parent of a nephew, and the word "nephew" itself, in a sense going beyond the strict legal meaning of the word, and as including in the case of the word "sister" a natural sister, and in the case of the word "nephew" a son of a natural sister. Were the question here whether legitimate children of Mary Wright formed members of the class to take, there could be but little doubt that it should be answered in the affirmative. And when once the words "sister" and "nephew" are shown to be used in a wider or looser sense than their strict legal meaning, it is difficult to limit them to one of the two natural sisters and her children only, quite apart from the antecedent improbability that the testator here should be intending to include the illegitimate child of Mary while excluding the legitimate children of Sarah. The fact that the latter are not expressly mentioned may well be explained by the view I have adopted that the testator was only expressly attempting to cure personal illegitimacy.

In fine,...there is here in the will itself a context which shows that the testator is not using the words describing the class to take in their strict legal meaning, and it therefore becomes proper to consider, with the help of all the surrounding circumstances, what is the special sense in which he is using the words. And the cases of *In re Jodrell*,[126] and *In re Corsellis*[127] both tend to support the conclusion to which I have come, as tending to show that by treating or naming definite individuals as relations who are not strictly such, and by thereby indicating that

126 (1890) 44 Ch. D. 590, [1891] A.C. 304.
127 [1906] 2 Ch. 316.

he is using a word of relationship in a wider or looser sense than its strict sense, a testator may include in a general gift to relations of that class not merely the specially named individuals, but other persons who are in a corresponding position.

. . .

Notes and Questions

1. How far can the court go in ascertaining the testator's definition of a particular term? Can it go outside the will?

Atkinson's Will Trusts; Atkinson v. In re Hall[128] illustrates this issue. The testatrix gave her residuary estate to "such worthy causes as have been communicated by me to my trustees in my lifetime." Her solicitor, who was one of the trustees, prepared and signed a memorandum in which he related discussions held between the testatrix and himself when the will was prepared to the effect the testatrix wanted to benefit certain charities. He sent this to his co-trustees before his death. In addition, there was a letter from his firm which also explained the term "worthy causes" as meaning "charitable institutions and other institutions not strictly charitable".

Megarry V.C., held that while it is permissible to adduce evidence of the surrounding circumstances in which the will is made, or evidence of the habitual sense in which the testatrix used particular words, it is not permissible to adduce direct evidence of her intention. Hence, the memorandum and letter were inadmissible, with the result that the gift failed.

The case is complicated by two factors: first, this was not a case of an equivocation, that is, one in which there are two or more persons or objects to which the words used are equally applicable, and which is the only situation in which direct evidence of intention is traditionally admissible.[129] Second, there is a long line of cases which hold that a gift to objects, other than persons, is *per se* uncertain, unless the objects are charitable, and "worthy causes" is not charitable.[130] It would therefore, have been somewhat perverse for the Vice Chancellor to decide the case otherwise than he did. In principle, however, it ought not to matter how the testatrix' intention is ascertained, so long as the evidence is cogent, veracious and indubitable.[131]

2. If the testator belongs to a special group of persons, a word or expression that has a special meaning among the group can be ascertained from the surrounding circumstances. Thus, in *Re Van Lessen*[132] the court held that a bequest of "my collection of stamps...of the British Colonies..." included stamps not only of the British Colonies which then remained, but also of former colonies, which were then independent dominions. The testator was a philatelist and among philatelists the expression "British Colonies" had that extended meaning.

---

128 [1978] 1 W.L.R. 586, [1978] 1 All E.R. 1275.
129 Equivocation is discussed later in this chapter.
130 See, *e.g.*, *Chichester Diocesan Fund & Board of Finance (Inc.) v. Simpson*, [1944] A.C. 341, [1944] 2 All E.R. 60 (H.L.); *Brewer v. McCauley*, [1954] S.C.R. 645, [1955] 1 D.L.R. 415; *Re Albery*, [1964] 1 O.R. 342, 42 D.L.R. (2d) 201.
131 Law Reform Commission of British Columbia, *Report on the Interpretation of Wills* (L.R.C. 58, November 1982), pp. 18-25.
132 [1955] 1 W.L.R. 1326, [1955] 3 All E.R. 691.

(d) Terms of Art

Certain expressions have acquired a technical meaning in law, such as "and his heirs," "personal property," and a host of other terms. Traditionally, these have been assigned their restricted, legal meaning when used in a will, although the courts were always more lenient if the testator made his or her own will and had no legal training. More recently, the courts are more willing to assign another meaning to the technical terms if the context of the will requires it. *Re Cook*,[133] reproduced below, is concerned with the meaning of "personal estate."

RE COOK

[1948] Ch. 212, [1948] 1 All E.R. 231

Chancery Division

A husband and wife held title to their house as joint tenants. Section 36 of the *Law of Property Act 1925*,[134] which came into force on January 1, 1926, provided that they held title upon trust for sale after that date; thus the statute notionally converted the real property into personalty. After the husband's death, the wife made a will by which she gave "all my personal estate" to her nephews and nieces, and the question was whether the house passed under this bequest.

HARMAN J.:

The question to be decided is this: Did the trust for sale imposed by s. 36 come to an end on the husband's death? After that date there is no doubt that the entire interest in the property, both legal and equitable, became vested in the testatrix. It is said by Mr. Danckwerts for the Custodian of Enemy Property that, according to the ordinary and well-known rule in *In re Selous*[135] per Farwell J., the legal estate swallows up the equitable, that there is a merger between the two, and that from January, 1944, onwards the testatrix was merely the owner of this property and no trust could exist, because A cannot be trustee for A.

. . .

[Y]ou cannot have a trust existing when nobody is interested under it except the trustee, because nobody can enforce it and there is, in fact, no trust in existence.

I get some assistance also from s. 36, sub-s. 1 itself, because there are found the words "shall be held on trust for sale, in like manner as if the persons beneficially entitled were tenants in common". As soon as only one person is beneficially entitled there are no persons who would be tenants in common, because there is only one person interested. The phrase "persons beneficially entitled" must, as Mr. Freeman submitted to me, mean what it says, namely,

---

133 [1948] Ch. 212, [1948] 1 All E.R. 231.
134 15 & 16 Geo. 5, c. 20.
135 [1901] 1 Ch. 921.

"persons", in the plural, and therefore the sub-section does not apply as soon as there is but one person interested in the entirety of the property. Consequently, I hold that upon the death of the husband the testatrix became the absolute owner of this property and there was no trust for sale subsisting beyond that date.

. . .

If I am right so far, this property was at the time of her will and at the time of her death real estate to which she was entitled in fee simple. She had another property to which she was undoubtedly entitled in fee simple, and she had a small personal estate. It seems unlikely that she intended to dispose only of the personal estate in the lawyer's sense of that word and not to deal with the more substantial part of her property, namely, this house (in which she lived) and her other freehold house; but this is a case where a layman has chosen to use a term of art. The words "all my personal estate" are words so well-known to lawyers that it must take a very strong context to make them include real estate. Testators can make black mean white if they make the dictionary sufficiently clear, but the testatrix has not done so. It may well be that she thought "personal estate" meant "all my worldly goods"; I do not know. In the absence of something to show that the phrase ought not to be so construed, I must suppose that she used the term "personal estate" in its ordinary meaning as a term of art. Consequently, I hold that the testatrix only succeeded in disposing of what the lawyers would call her "personal estate" and she did not dispose of this house No. 16, Kirton Park Terrace, which therefore devolves as on an intestacy.

. . .

Notes and Questions

1. A testatrix gave a number of pecuniary legacies, followed by a gift of "all personal property owned by me" and a residuary clause. She owned no real property when she died. What passed under the gift of personal property?[136]

2. The testator was a farmer. He bequeathed the farm machinery to his son. He devised the farm to his wife for life, with remainder in one-half to his three daughters equally and in the other half to his son. He directed his executors to give his son "the first opportunity of purchasing" the half devised to his sisters after his mother's death. Does the son hold a right of first refusal or an option?[137]

5. PARTIAL INTESTACIES

A question that often arises in the context of partial intestacies is whether the next of kin are to be determined as of the date of the testator's death, or as of the

---

136 See *Re Davies Estate* (1989), 34 E.T.R. 249 (P.E.I. S.C.).
137 See *Allen v. Allen* (1994), 2 E.T.R. (2d) 276 (Sask. Q.B.).

date when the partial intestacy occurs. The *prima facie* rule, often referred to as the rule in *Bullock v. Downes*,[138] is that in the absence of a contrary intention appearing in the will, the next of kin are to be ascertained as at the death of the testator.

Many of the cases dealing with the question involve wills in which the testator directs that a part of the estate (if otherwise undisposed of) is to be distributed among his or her next of kin as on an intestacy.[139] If the testator expressly names the date upon which the next of kin are to be determined, there is no problem, but that is unusual.[140]

Other cases involve intestacies arising from the fact that the testator failed to dispose of part of the residuary estate,[141] from the operation of accumulations legislation,[142] because of lapsed gifts,[143] or because certain property does not pass under the will and comes into the estate at a later date.[144] In most of these cases the *prima facie* rule is applied, with the result that even, for example, the estate of a life tenant who died before the intestacy occurred, becomes entitled to share.[145] However, in *National Trust Co. v. Fleury*,[146] set out below, a contrary intention was found.

NATIONAL TRUST CO. v. FLEURY
[1965] S.C.R. 817, 53 D.L.R. (2d) 700
Supreme Court of Canada

The testator, Herbert W. Fleury, died, survived by his daughter, Marguerite Fleury. By paragraph 11(a) of his will he gave the residue of his estate upon trust to pay Marguerite an income of $5,000 *per annum* with a power to encroach on the capital in her favour. By paragraph 11(c) he then disposed of the corpus after her death by giving one-half equally to Marguerite's first cousins and the other half he directed to be distributed among such persons as would be entitled thereto as if he had died intestate.

On an application to construe the will it was held at first instance[147] that the next of kin should be determined as of the date of the testator's death. Hence,

138 (1860), 8 H.L.C. 1, 11 E.R. 627.
139 *Nat. Trust Co. Ltd. v. Fleury*, [1965] S.C.R. 817, 53 D.L.R. (2d) 700; *Re Hanson* (1978), 1 E.T.R. 280 (Ont. H.C.).
140 The testator specified the date as the date of distribution in *Fasken v. Fasken*, [1953] 3 D.L.R. 431 (S.C.C.).
141 *Re Martin; Proctor v. Downey* (1979), 4 E.T.R. 264 (Ont. C.A.).
142 *MacEachern and National Trusts Co. Ltd. v. Mittlestadt and Woodley* (1963), 46 W.W.R. 359, (sub nom. *Re McEachern*) 42 D.L.R. (2d) 587 (Alta. S.C.).
143 *Re Oswell* (1982), 11 E.T.R. 283 (Ont. H.C.).
144 *Re Jardine Estate* (1956), 17 W.W.R 197, 1 D.L.R. (2d) 225, further reasons at 18 W.W.R. 445, 3 D.L.R. (2d) 262 (Alta. C.A.).
145 See, *e.g.*, *ibid*; *Re Oswell* (1982), 11 E.T.R. 283 (Ont. H.C.); *Re Martin; Proctor v. Downey* (1979), 4 E.T.R. 264 (Ont. H.C.).
146 *Supra*.
147 [1964] 1 O.R. 377, 42 D.L.R. (2d) 402 (H.C.).

Marguerite would take the property. This was reversed on appeal.[148] The estate of Marguerite then appealed to the Supreme Court of Canada.

RITCHIE J.:

. . .

The learned Judge of first instance, Mr. Justice Hughes, decided that upon the true construction of the will, the testator intended that the fund should go to such persons as would have been entitled at the date of his death if he had died intestate and in so doing he relied upon the rule of construction which was stated by Lord Campbell L.C., in *Bullock v. Downes*[149] where he said:

> Generally speaking, where there is a bequest to one for life, and after his decease to the testator's next of kin, the next of kin who are to take are the persons who answer that description at the death of the testator, and not those who answer that description at the death of the first taker. Gifts to a class following a bequest of the same property for life vest immediately upon the death of the testator. Nor does it make any difference that the person to whom such previous life interest was given is also a member of the class to take on his death.

The late Marguerite Fleury was the only person entitled under the statute at the date of the testator's death and the result of applying the rule in *Bullock v. Downes* to the language of the present will is that her personal representative becomes entitled to the fund in question.

In the reasons for judgment delivered on behalf of the Court of Appeal by Schroeder, J.A., he has, however, found that the rule in *Bullock v. Downes* does not apply under the present circumstances and that the class of beneficiary is to be determined as at the date of the death of the life tenant so that the nephews and nieces of the testator are entitled to the fund.

. . .

I think that the true meaning of *Bullock v. Downes* is that described by Viscount Finlay in *Hutchinson v. National Refuges for Homeless and Destitute Children*,[150] where he says:

> *Bullock v. Downes* therefore decides that, prima facie, the next of kin are to be ascertained at the death of the testator, but, that if there is a sufficient indication to that effect in the words of the will, the time for ascertaining the class may be the time fixed by the will as the period of distribution. The question in this as in every other case of the kind must be whether there is in the will a sufficient indication that the period of distribution is the time at which the class is to be ascertained.

In the construction of wills, the primary purpose is to determine the intention of the testator and it is only when such intention cannot be arrived at with reasonable certainty by giving the natural and ordinary meaning to the words

---

148 [1964] 2 O.R. 129, 44 D.L.R. (2d) 393 (C.A.).
149 (1860), 9 H.L.C. 1 at 11, 11 E.R. 627.
150 [1920] A.C. 794 at 801-2.

which he has used that resort is to be had to the rules of construction which have been developed by the Courts in the interpretation of other wills. It is to be remembered that such rules of construction are not rules of law and that if their application results in attributing to the testator an intention which appears inconsistent with the scheme of the will as a whole, then they are not to prevail.

. . .

The whole scheme of the residuary clause in the present will appears to me to be predicated on the assumption that the testator's daughter would survive him and I agree with Schroeder, J.A., that he must also be deemed to have known that in that event she would be his only next of kin at the date of his death. This being the case, to interpret the terms of para. (11)(c) as being a gift of the income from "the remaining one-half" of the corpus to the daughter for life and after her death of the capital to the next of kin of the testator at the date of his death, is to attribute to the testator an intention to give his daughter a vested interest in this fund at his death. It appears to me, however, that such a construction runs contrary to the clear provisions of para. (11)(a) of the will whereby the testator expressly directed that this part of his estate was to be incorporated in a trust fund to be held by his trustees with direction to pay his daughter at least $5,000 a year from the income and if necessary from the capital and to the capital of which she could only otherwise have access if the trustees in their absolute discretion considered the sum of $5,000 annually to be insufficient for her proper support and maintenance. In my view this makes it apparent that the testator intended the whole of the corpus of his estate to be preserved intact during the lifetime of his daughter subject to the payments which the trustees were authorized to make. It seems to me that the result of applying the rule in *Bullock v. Downes* to this will is to ignore the carefully drawn provisions setting up this trust and to attribute to the testator the contrary intention to provide for his daughter in such manner as to enable her to obtain a substantial part of the fund for her own use absolutely without the exercise of any authority or discretion by the trustees and whether or not the whole fund produced an income of $5,000 a year.

In my opinion the inconsistency which results from the application of this rule to the language used in para. (11)(a) and (c) of the will is of itself a sufficient indication that the testator did not intend the ultimate beneficiaries under para. (11)(c) to be those entitled under the *Devolution of Estates Act*[151] at the date of his death, but rather that he intended one-half of the remainder of the corpus of his estate to be divided amongst the persons so entitled at the date of the death of his daughter. Such a construction does no violence to the language by which the trust fund was created under para. (11)(a) and is not inconsistent with the natural and ordinary meaning attributable to the words used in para. (11)(c).

For these reasons I am of opinion that the class entitled to the remaining one-half of the corpus of the estate is to be ascertained at the time of the death of Marguerite Fleury. I would therefore dismiss this appeal.

---

151 R.S.O. 1960, c. 106.

. . .

[Cartwright J., wrote a short concurring judgment. Martland J., concurred with Cartwright and Ritchie JJ. Spence J., concurred with Ritchie J. Judson J., dissented.]

Notes and Questions

1. T died testate, survived by his sister, S., and a mentally infirm daughter, D. By his will he left all his property in trust to pay a small allowance to S for life and to use the remaining income for the care and maintenance of D during her life. Any surplus income was to be accumulated until the death of the survivor of S and D, after which the capital was to be distributed as if the testator had died intestate. S died shortly after T. D survived T by sixteen years and died intestate. As of what date are T's next of kin to be ascertained?[152]

2. T died testate, survived by his widow, W, a daughter, D, a granddaughter, G, and two great-granddaughters, X and Y, daughters of G. By his will he gave all his estate upon trust to pay annuities to W, D and G and directed that after the death of the survivor of W and G the corpus was to be divided equally among G's children who should then be living. The annuities did not exhaust the income. Hence there was an implied direction to accumulate. However, the accumulation terminated 21 years after T's death by virtue of the *Accumulations Act*.[153] The income released as a result was, until the death of the survivor of W, D and G, therefore, undisposed of. The widow died before the 21 years were up. D and G are still living. Who is entitled to the undisposed of income?[154]

3. If a surviving spouse is given a life interest under the deceased spouse's will, a partial intestacy subsequently results and it is held that the *prima facie* rule applies, so that the spouse's estate is entitled to share in the partial intestacy, as of what date is the spouse's testamentary interest to be valued for the purpose of s. 45(3) of the *Succession Law Reform Act*?[155] Should it be valued at the testator's death, or at the spouse's death?[156]

4. A similar problem may arise under an *inter vivos* trust. For example, suppose that a trust confers on the income beneficiary the power to appoint the capital and provides that on default of appointment the capital shall be held in trust for the next of kin of the grandfather of the income beneficiary. Absent a contrary intention, the rule in *Bullock v. Downes* applies and the next of kin of the income beneficiary's grandfather should be determined as at the time of the grandfather's death.[157]

6. ADMISSIBILITY OF EVIDENCE

(a) Evidence of Surrounding Circumstances

There is a long-established tradition in the law of interpretation of wills that a court must initially construe a will without regard to any evidence other than the

---

152 See *Re Hanson* (1978), 1 E.T.R. 280 (Ont. H.C.).
153 R.S.O. 1990, c. A.5, s. 1(1), para. 4, (6) and its predecessors.
154 See *Re Martin; Proctor v. Downey* (1979), 4 E.T.R. 264 (Ont. C.A.).
155 Reproduced in the chapter on Intestate Succession.
156 See *Re Oswell* (1982), 11 E.T.R. 283 (Ont. H.C.). See also *Kotula Estate v. Kotula* (1995), 7 E.T.R (2d) 262 (B.C.S.C.).
157 *Canada Trust Co. v. Fasken* (1990), 37 E.T.R. 216 (Ont. H.C.), affirmed (1993) 49 E.T.R. 112 (Ont. C.A.).

will itself. Having concluded this exercise, the court then inquires whether there are subjects and objects in the outside world which match the description of those in the will and, if there are, that is the end of the matter. Evidence of surrounding circumstances showing that the testator intended something else is excluded.

Only if the words used in the will do not match external subjects or objects is there an ambiguity and the court may then consider evidence of surrounding circumstances at the time the will was made, such as the character and occupation of the testator; the amount, extent and condition of his or her property; the number, identity and relationship to the testator of his or her immediate family and other relatives; and the persons who comprised his or her circle of friends and any other natural objects of his or her bounty. The court may, therefore, as is often said, sit in the testator's armchair and look at the matter in the way the testator could have done when he or she made the will. Such evidence may then be used to attempt to resolve the ambiguity. Direct evidence of the testator's intention is inadmissible to resolve the matter, however, unless there is an equivocation.[158] If the ambiguity cannot be resolved, even with the use of evidence of surrounding circumstances, the gift in question fails for uncertainty.

The above is the strict constructionist, nineteenth century approach. Proponents of this approach argue that to go outside of the clear meaning of the language of the will would take the court beyond the construction of the document before it and engage the court in writing the testator's will for him or her. Thus in *Higgins v. Dawson*[159] the Earl of Halsbury L.C., stated:[160]

> My Lords, I have often said that to treat language with that violence and to say that you have arrived at the conclusion from external circumstances that the testator would have made a different disposition from what he has done if he had had the whole subject-matter in his mind, and, therefore, to construe his language differently, is not to construe or to interpret the language which the testator himself has used, but to make a will for him which you think he ought to have made if he had had the whole circumstances present to his mind.

It will be readily apparent that this approach is more likely than not to defeat the testator's intention and *Higgins v. Dawson*[161] is a perfect example of that.

In *Higgins v. Dawson* the testator owned some real property, plate, china, and two mortgages worth approximately £13,000. His will specifically disposed of the real estate, plate and china. He then set out a list of legacies totalling approximately £10,000. Then he gave "all the residue and remainder" of the mortgage debts, after payments of his debts and funeral expenses, to a charity. Extrinsic evidence showed that the testator had virtually no assets out of which to pay the legacies, except the two mortgages. Thus, it was probable that he intended the legacies to be satisfied out of the mortgage debts. In other words, he must have meant that "residue and remainder" of the mortgage debts meant "residue and remainder after paying the legacies and debts."

---

158 That is, a situation in which the description in the will applies equally to two or more persons or objects. This matter is discussed below.

159 [1902] A.C. 1 (H.L.).

160 *Ibid.*, at p. 6.

161 *Ibid.*

Unfortunately, on a strict reading of the will the expression "residue and re-mainder" referred to the amount remaining after the payment of debts and funeral expenses. Since the will was clear on its face, the House of Lords refused to consider the evidence relating to the nature and extent of the testator's property which suggested the other interpretation.

The Earl of Halsbury L.C., said in this respect:[162]

> I confess that it is to my mind absolutely amazing that any one can entertain the smallest doubt as to what those words mean. I have read the words by themselves because, in my view of the meaning of this instrument, they are by themselves. One does not doubt that, where you are construing either a will or any other instrument, it is perfectly legitimate to look at the whole instrument — and, indeed, you must look at the whole instrument — to see the meaning of the whole instrument, and you cannot rely upon one particular passage in it to the exclusion of what is relevant to the explanation of the particular clause that you are expounding. That is perfectly true as a general proposition; but I ask myself here what other words — what part of the will, what provision other than the one I am construing, reflects any light on, or gives the smallest interpretation to, the particular words which I am called upon to expound.

and again:[163]

> But when I come to look at the will itself, I must construe [the words "residue and remainder"] as they stand in the context, and in their grammatical meaning, and with reference to what is there said; and then it seems to me that the problem is solved without the smallest difficulty.

His Lordship accepted that it is quite permissible to ascertain whether the persons and objects described in the will exist and, to that extent, consider extrinsic evidence,[164] but refused to admit evidence that would have altered the meaning of the will.

Lord Davey said, in the same case:[165]

> My Lords, I have already said that the gift in this will does not, in my opinion present any difficulty of construction. No doubt the word "residue" is itself a relative term; but in this case the testator has himself told us the meaning in which he uses the word "residue", and the subject-matter with reference to which the word "residue" is used, namely, it is to be the residue of the mortgage debts, after the payment of debts and funeral and testamentary expenses. Am I to change my opinion of the meaning of those words, which I think very plain, because I know that at the time when he made his will the mortgage debts formed the bulk of his property? I think not. Nor do I think I ought to admit that consideration to influence my opinion merely because other persons as well qualified, or better qualified than myself, have attached a different meaning to those words. It may be that the testator may have been imperfectly acquainted with the use of legal language; he may not have understood the legal effect of making a specific gift or what a specific gift was, and he may have used language the legal interpretation of which does not carry out the intentions that he had in his mind. I do not know whether that is so or not. But, whether that be so or not, of this I am quite clear, that that fact should not induce the Court to put a meaning on his words different from that which the Court judicially determines to be the meaning which they bear.

---

162 *Ibid.*, at pp. 3, 4.
163 *Ibid.*, at pp. 4, 5.
164 *Ibid.*, at p. 5.
165 *Ibid.*, at p. 11.

A similar case is *The National Society for the Prevention of Cruelty to Children v. The Scottish National Society for the Prevention of Cruelty to Children*.[166] In that case the testator left a substantial gift to the N.S.P.C.C. There was an organization by that name, but it was an English society whose work was restricted to that part of the United Kingdom called England. On the other hand, the testator was domiciled and resident in Scotland; all his interests were Scottish; his money was invested there; and he left all his other property to Scottish charities. There was in fact an organization called The Scottish N.S.P.C.C. and in light of the testator's background, that was undoubtedly the society he wished to benefit. Nevertheless, the House of Lords held that the English society should receive the gift. Lord Dunedin expressed regret at this result,

> ...because I cannot help having the moral feeling that this money is probably going to the society to which, if we could have asked him, the testator would not have sent it.[167]

However, His Lordship felt unable to reach another conclusion. Earl Loreburn stated:[168]

> My Lords, I think the true ground upon which to base a decision in this case is that the accurate use of a name in a will creates a strong presumption against any rival who is not the possessor of the name mentioned in the will. It is a very strong presumption and one which cannot be overcome except in exceptional circumstances. I use as a convenient method of expressing one's thought the term "presumption". What I mean is that what a man has said ought to be acted upon unless it is clearly proved that he meant something different from what he said.

It was argued that there was an ambiguity because of the circumstances of the testator, but His Lordship thought that none had been raised and that the presumption had not been rebutted.

Lord Dunedin also did not think there was an ambiguity, since the name in the will matched that of an existing society. An ambiguity would arise, in His Lordship's view if there was no society which exactly matched the description used in the will and in that case the court may admit evidence of surrounding circumstances. His Lordship then stated:[169]

> Now, my Lords, we have gone into that inquiry. I do not myself put it so much as my noble and learned friend who has just spoken has done, as a presumption, but I put it thus: that here you have an accurate description of the one person and a description which is admittedly not quite accurate of the other. You must, I think, have positive evidence of some cogent sort to make you prefer the latter to the former. Such evidence unfortunately in this case I do not find.

The case suggests that the House may have been willing to look at the extrinsic evidence if it had been stronger. However, it is hard to imagine that any evidence could, indeed, have been stronger than was presented.

---

166 [1915] A.C. 207 (H.L.).
167 *Ibid.*, at p. 214.
168 *Ibid.*, at pp. 213-4.
169 *Ibid.*, at pp. 214-5.

The strict constructionist approach is not an appropriate one today. It is not the testator's objective intention that is relevant, but his or her subjective intention. Of the objective intention approach, Lord Denning M.R., said in dissent:[170]

> It seems to me that the fallacy in that argument is that it starts from the wrong place. It proceeds on the assumption that, in construing a will, 'It is not what the testator meant, but what is the meaning of his words'. That may have been the nineteenth-century view; but I believe it to be wrong and to have been the cause of many mistakes. I have myself known a judge to say: 'I believe this to be contrary to the true intention of the testator but nevertheless it is the result of the words he has used'. When a judge goes so far as to say that, the chances are that he has misconstrued the will.

The inadequacy of the objective or strict constructionist approach may be illustrated by the following example. A testator makes a will which says only, "All for mother." Extrinsic evidence will show that at the time he made his will he did, indeed, have a living mother, but also that he customarily referred to his wife as "mother." Should that evidence be disregarded? Of course it should not![171]

Canadian case law is replete with examples of a strict constructionist approach.[172] However, there are other cases, some quite old, which favour the more liberal, subjective approach to construction.[173] Under this approach the court admits evidence of surrounding circumstances immediately, that is, when it starts to interpret the will. In other words, it does not wait to sit in the testator's armchair until after it discovers that the will cannot be read sensibly without it. By sitting in the testator's armchair immediately, the court is better able to assign to the words used the meaning the testator intended them to bear.

Proponents of this approach stress that a will, by its very nature, is an expression of the testator's intentions and ought, therefore, to be interpreted as far as possible to reflect those intentions.

Haidl v. Sacher,[174] reproduced below, is the leading modern case adopting this approach.

Further Reading

Brian McIvor, "Admissibility of Evidence in Aid of the Interpretation of Wills" (1990), 39 E.T.R. 253.

---

170 *Re Rowland*, [1963] 1 Ch. 1 at 9-10; [1962] 2 All E.R. 837 (C.A.).
171 See *Thorn v. Dickens*, [1906] W.N. 54. In fact, the testator's mother was not living in that case, so the will created an ambiguity, which let in the extrinsic evidence.
172 See, *e.g.*, *Augur v. Beaudry*, [1919] 3 W.W.R. 559, [1920] A.C. 1010, 48 D.L.R. 356 (P.C.); *Re Warren* (1922), 52 O.L.R. 127 at 129 (H.C.), *per* Middleton J.; *Re Sheard* (1921), 49 O.L.R. 320 at 327, 58 D.L.R. 539 (C.A.), *per* Meredith J.A.; *Re McIntosh*, [1923] 2 W.W.R. 605 at 606 (Man. K.B.), *per* Dysart J.; *Tottrup v. Patterson*, [1970] S.C.R. 318 at 322, 1 W.W.R. 388, (sub nom. *Re Ottewell*) 9 D.L.R. (3d) 314 at 316, *per* Cartwright C.J.C.
173 *Marks v. Marks* (1908), 40 S.C.R. 210 at 212-3, *per* Idington J.; *Re Burke*, [1960] O.R. 26, 20 D.L.R. (2d) 356 (C.A.); *Re Waters* (1978), 21 O.R. (2d) 124, 89 D.L.R. (3d) 742 (H.C.).
174 2 Sask. R. 93, [1980] 1 W.W.R. 293, 7 E.T.R. 1, 106 D.L.R. (3d) 360 (C.A.).

HAIDL v. SACHER
2 Sask. R. 93, [1980] 1 W.W.R. 293, 7 E.T.R. 1
Saskatchewan Court of Appeal

The testator bequeathed the residue of his estate as follows:

3. I GIVE, DEVISE AND BEQUEATH all my property of every nature and kind whatsoever and wheresoever situate to my said Trustees upon the following trusts, namely...

(h) To deliver all the rest and residue of my Estate whatsoever and wheresoever situate including any property over which I may have a general power of appointment, to the following persons in equal shares, share and share alike:

    (i) Donnie Sacher
    (ii) Jerry Sacher
    (iii) Phyllis Haygarth
    (iv) Blair Luterbach
    (v) Florence Tischynski
    (vi) Elsie Luedtke
    (vii) Tillie Rothwell
    (viii) The Children of, Herbert Haidl, that may be living at the date of my death.

The four children of Herbert Haidl, entitled under clause 3(h)(viii) made an application to determine whether they were entitled to take *per capita* or *per stirpes*. At first instance[175] it was held they took *per stirpes*. The children appealed.

BAYDA J.A., delivered the judgment of the Court:

. . .

The circumstances of this case and the issues addressed to us on appeal call for a consideration, at the outset, of these questions: does the law require the "ordinary meaning" rule of construction to be applied to cl. (h) without admitting and taking into account any surrounding circumstances at all and that the meaning so ascertained shall prevail unless it is found that such an application produces a meaning which is unclear and ambiguous in which event such surrounding circumstances may then be admitted and looked at (procedure A)? Or, does the law require those surrounding circumstances to be admitted at the start and that the "ordinary meaning" rule of construction be applied in the light of those surrounding circumstances (procedure B)?

Before proceeding to answer these questions, I note two matters. First, there is no disagreement between the parties that the proper approach in construing the clause under scrutiny here requires the application of the "ordinary meaning" rule of construction as the initial step and that it should so be done in the light of the contents of the whole will. The disagreement lies in the role that the surrounding circumstances should play, if any, in the application of that rule. The second matter is that the term "surrounding circumstances" as used in these reasons refers only to indirect extrinsic evidence. It has no reference whatsoever to direct extrinsic evidence of intent, the admission of which is governed by a different set

---

175 2 E.T.R. 288, [1978] 5 W.W.R. 199.

of conditions. The former consists of such circumstances as the character and occupation of the testator; the amount, extent and condition of his property; the number, identity and general relationship to the testator of the immediate family and other relatives; the persons who comprised his circle of friends; and any other natural objects of his bounty.[176] An example of the latter is the instructions which the testator gave to his solicitor for the preparation of the will (as one finds, for instance, in *Reishiska v. Cody.*[177]

There is a distinct divergence in the authorities as to whether procedure A or procedure B, as I have termed them, is the correct approach in law. Procedure A has its origin in a literal, traditional, strict-constructionist stance or, to use the expression Lord Denning used in his dissenting judgment in *Re Rowland,*[178] in "the nineteenth-century view"; procedure B on the other hand in a liberal, "subjective-intention" stance.

It is desirable to briefly examine some of the English authorities on the point. Perhaps the most notable of the English authorities in support of procedure A is the House of Lords case of *Higgins v. Dawson.*[179]

> [His Lordship then considered *Higgins v. Dawson*, which has been discussed above, and continued:]

It has been suggested — by Lord Denning in his dissenting judgment in *Re Rowland* and by a Canadian legal writer, Feeney, The Canadian Law of Wills: Construction,[180] — that the rule in *Higgins v. Dawson* should no longer be accepted as stating the law in England, given the decisions of the House of Lords in *Nat. Society for the Prevention of Cruelty to Children v. Scotland Nat. Society for the Prevention of Cruelty to Children,*[181] and particularly *Perrin v. Morgan.*[182] In the following salient passage from his judgment in *Re Rowland,*[183] Lord Denning says (after dealing with and rejecting the "nineteenth-century" view):[184]

> ...in point of principle the whole object of construing a will is to find out the testator's intentions, so as to see that his property is disposed of in the way he wished. True it is that you must discover his intention from the words he used: *but you must put upon his words the meaning which they bore to him.* If his words are capable of more than one meaning, or of a wide meaning and a narrow meaning, as they often are, then you must put upon them the meaning which he intended them to convey and not the meaning which a philologist would put upon them. And in order to discover the meaning which he intended, you will not get much help by going to a dictionary. It is very unlikely that he used a dictionary, and even less likely that he used the same one as you. *What you should do is to place yourself as far as possible in his position, taking note of the facts and circumstances known to him at the time; and then say what he meant by his words.*

---

176 See Feeney, *The Canadian Law of Wills: Construction* (1978), p. 17.
177 (1967), 62 W.W.R. 581 (Sask. C.A.).
178 [1963] 1 Ch. 1 at 9, [1962] 2 All E.R. 837 (C.A.).
179 [1902] A.C. 1.
180 *Supra*, at p. 53.
181 [1915] A.C. 207 44 at 212, *per* Lord Loreburn.
182 [1943] A.C. 399, [1943] 1 All E.R. 187.
183 *Supra.*
184 At p. 10 Ch. (italics supplied).

All this follows, I think, from the case in the House of Lords of *Perrin v. Morgan* when Viscount Simon L.C. expressed it thus: 'the fundamental rule in construing the language of a will is to put on the words used the meaning which, having regard to the terms of the will, the testator intended'. Lord Atkin wholeheartedly agreed, saying: 'The sole object is, of course, to ascertain from the will the testator's intentions'. He clearly thought that by the decision of the House the old mistaken approach would be corrected. 'I anticipate with satisfaction', he said, 'that henceforth the group of ghosts of dissatisfied testators who, according to a late Chancery judge, wait on the other bank to the Styx to receive the judicial personages who have misconstrued their wills, may be considerably diminished'.

Lord Denning, in effect, rejects procedure A and adopts procedure B.

The issue as to whether procedure A or procedure B correctly states the present English law, it would seem, is not yet closed. A useful analysis of the *Rowland* and *Perrin v. Morgan* decisions and the effect each has had on changing "the nineteenth-century" approach is contained in an article by Michael Albery, Q.C., "Coincidence and the Construction of Wills."[185] In that learned writer's opinion, it can hardly be said that the *Perrin v. Morgan* decision has sounded the death knell of the 19th-century approach. After stating why Lord Denning's thesis does not accord with the authorities, Mr. Albery reaches the following conclusion:[186]

The proper object of inquiry on construction of a will is not then just the subjective meaning of the testator uncontrolled by his words nor the objective meaning of his words uncontrolled by any context, but rather the objective meaning of the words as used by the particular testator.

That conclusion, as a statement of the present English law, commends itself to me.

As for the Canadian authorities, the point seems to have been covered in three cases favouring procedure B. The first is the Supreme Court of Canada decision in *Marks v. Marks*.[187] In that case, the testator devised certain real property "to my wife". The testator had gone through a ceremony of marriage on two different occasions. Both women claimed to be the person referred to in the testator's will as "my wife". At the time of making his will, the testator had not, for many years, lived in a conjugal relationship with the appellant, the first woman. He had, however, for a number of years lived in a conjugal relationship with the second woman, the respondent, and was so living with her at the time of his death.

[His Lordship noted that while the majority agreed that the respondent was entitled to the property, they differed in their reasons. He continued:]

It is the reasons of Idington J. which most bear upon the point under discussion, that is, whether surrounding circumstances should be admitted and looked at from the outset. He said this:[188]

---

185 (1963), 26 Modern Law Rev. 353.
186 At p. 358.
187 (1908), 40 S.C.R. 210.
188 *Ibid.,* at pp. 212-13.

...it is claimed that there cannot be any one who can answer to that description "my wife" except the one person who may in law be decided to be such. I do not think the law so binds us.

Unless it does, I do not see why we should pervert the most obvious intention of this testator. *I think we are bound to read his language in light of all the circumstances that surrounded, and were known to him when he used it and give effect to the intention it discloses when so read.*

This proposition may seem to be in conflict with language that has been occasionally used by eminent authority. Expressions are here and there found to suggest that the will must first be read and if the particular language in question is free from ambiguity and in its primary or ordinary meaning consistent with all else in the will, no extraneous circumstances can be brought in evidence.

. . .

I am content to adopt and act upon the following language of Lord Cairns, in *Charter v. Charter*:[189]

The court has a right to ascertain all the facts which were known to the testator at the time he made the will, and thus to place itself in the testator's position in order to ascertain the bearing and application of the language he uses.

Idington J. leaves no doubt that the approach to be used is procedure B and not procedure A.

Similarly, in *Re Burke*,[190] Laidlaw J.A., with whom Morden J.A. concurred, appears to come down on the side of procedure B. He said:[191]

The Court is now called upon to construe a particular document and, at the outset, I emphasize what has been said before so frequently. The construction by the Court of other documents and decisions in other cases respecting the intention of other testators affords no assistance whatsoever to the Court in forming an opinion as to the intention of the testator in the particular case now under consideration. Other cases are helpful only in so far as they set forth or explain any applicable rule of construction or principle of law. Each Judge must endeavour to place himself in the position of the testator at the time when the last will and testament was made. He should concentrate his thoughts on the circumstances which then existed and which might reasonably be expected to influence the testator in the disposition of his property. He must give due weight to those circumstances in so far as they bear on the intention of the testator. He should then study the whole contents of the will and, after full consideration of all the provisions and language used therein, try to find what intention was in the mind of the testator. When an opinion has been formed as to that intention, the Court should strive to give effect to it and should do so unless there is some rule or principle of law that prohibits it from doing so. (The italics are mine).

[His Lordship referred to some other Canadian cases which seemed to favour the strict constructionist approach, and continued:]

In the end, it must be said that the Canadian authorities tend to put forward procedure B as the proper approach. After all, ascertaining the testator's true intention is the real and only purpose of the whole exercise. Hence, the learned

---

189 (1874), L.R. 7 H.L. 364 at 365 (italics supplied).
190 (1959), 20 D.L.R. (2d) 396 (Ont. C.A.).
191 At p. 398.

Chambers Judge, in the matter before us, did not err in admitting evidence of the testator's relationship to the beneficiaries named in his will, particularly those mentioned in cl. (h), as part of the surrounding circumstances in the light of which he then sought to interpret the testator's language by applying the "ordinary-meaning" rule.

. . .

It is reasonably plain...that, where the bequest is generally of the character found in the present case, there is a prima facie rule in favour of a per capita construction but such rule may be dislodged, by the surrounding circumstances, in favour of a per stirpital [*sic*] construction. The evidence here of the relationship of the beneficiaries to the testator, coupled with the manner in which the overall bequest in cl. (h) is framed, forcefully indicates that the testator was considering these beneficiaries not so much as individuals but by households.... The splitting up of the beneficiaries into eight subdivisions and putting those subdivisions into paragraphs numbered (i) to (viii) demonstrates quite graphically what the testator had in mind. The bequest so framed taken in conjunction with the circumstance that the children of Herbert Haidl grouped under para. (viii) are not related by blood to the testator and are not of the same generation as the beneficiaries named in paras. (i) to vii) (with the exception of the beneficiary named in para. (iv)) weighs heavily in favour of the per stirpital [*sic*] construction.

. . .

There is nothing in the surrounding circumstances that have been disclosed in the material before us to suggest that the children of Herbert Haidl should be placed on a better than a per stirpital [*sic*] footing.

In the result it must be said that the learned Chambers Judge did not err in arriving at a decision favouring the per stirpital [*sic*] construction. Accordingly, this appeal should be dismissed. There will be no costs other than the executors' on a solicitor-client basis to be paid out of the estate.

Notes and Questions

1. By and large, the trend of the Canadian cases since *Haidl v. Sacher* has been in favour of the subjective intention approach. Thus, for example, in *Re Hopkins*[192] the Ontario Court of Appeal reached its conclusion that school fees paid in advance were not "cash on hand" but "operating costs" "in the light of the manifest general intention of the testatrix [as displayed by the will] and the surrounding circumstances." The court also held that direct evidence of the intention of the testatrix, deposed to in a certain affidavit was inadmissible.

Re Coughlin[193] involved a gift of the testatrix' entire estate to her sister, her brother and a great-nephew "in equal shares, share and share alike to be theirs absolutely." This would normally create a tenancy in common, but the court construed it as creating a joint tenancy in light of the surrounding circumstances.

---

192 (1983), 39 O.R. (2d) 673, 13 E.T.R. 31, 141 D.L.R. (3d) 660 (C.A.).
193 (1982), 36 O.R. (2d) 446 (H.C.).

Similarly, in *Re Welsh; Re Thomson and Morrison*[194] the court used the subjective intent approach to determine that the testator used the word "income" in a special sense. His estate consisted largely of a substantial interest in a closely-held family corporation. He directed that the "income" from the estate be paid to his widow and to divide the residue of the estate among his children after her death. After the testator died, the assets of the corporation were sold, resulting in substantial capital surplus and this was paid out to the shareholders in the form of dividends (that is, free of income tax). It was held that the dividends were received as capital and not as income because the testator intended the value of his interest in the company to be the capital of his estate.

In *Re Davis*[195] the court also looked at the surrounding circumstances immediately. By clause 5 of his will the testator gave legacies to nephews and nieces and to the children of a deceased niece. By clause 7 he divided the residue among the nephews and nieces named in clause 5 in equal shares. The court held that the children of the deceased niece were also entitled to share in the residue.[196]

2. On the other hand, the court followed the traditional view in *MacCulloch v. Mac-Culloch.*[197] The court first construed the will itself to determine whether a yacht passed under a bequest of "all my articles of personal...use" and only looked at the evidence of surrounding circumstances because it felt compelled to do so by the cases. It concluded, properly, it is submitted, that the yacht, which was used mainly for commercial purposes, did not pass under the bequest, neither by looking at the will itself only, nor by also looking at the surrounding circumstances.

Similarly, in *Re Klein; Public Trustee of British Columbia v. Cochrane*[198] the court appears to have followed the objective approach. The testator left all his estate to his wife "to hold onto her, her heirs, executors and administrators, absolutely and forever." His wife having predeceased him, the question was whether the will created a substitutionary gift in favour of the wife's heirs.[199] The court held that it did not have that effect and, indeed, on a strict reading of the will, it did not. The court, moreover, felt bound by a Supreme Court of Canada decision in a very similar case[200] in which the Supreme Court relied upon the objective approach to construction. Hence, in *Re Klein*, the fact that the testator's wife had a son by a previous marriage with whom the testator had a close relationship and the fact that he did not change his will even though his wife died thirteen years before him did not change the interpretation. However, the court did not exclude such evidence. It said, in fact, that these circumstances were not sufficient to lead to a different conclusion.[201]

In *Tottrup v. Patterson*[202] Cartwright C.J., said:

---

194 (1980), 28 O.R. (2d) 403, 6 E.T.R. 257, 111 D.L.R. (3d) 390 (H.C.).

195 (1983), 15 E.T.R. 296, 51 A.R. 377 (Q.B.).

196 See also *Re Goldstein* (1984), 31 Alta. L.R. (2d) 80, 16 E.T.R. 212, 51 A.R. 341 at 344 (C.A.); *Re Flinton; Can. Trust Co. v. Banks*, [1981] 4 W.W.R. 549, 10 E.T.R. 236 at 246-7 (B.C.S.C.); *Cotherp v. Hall* (1989), 34 E.T.R. 86 (B.C.S.C.); *Lanois Estate v. Lanois* (1991), 43 E.T.R. 87 (Ont. Gen. Div.); See also *Re Bruce Estate* (1998), 24 E.T.R. (2d) 44 (Y.S.C.); *C.I.B.C. Trust Corp. v. Peebles* (1999), 180 D.L.R. (4th) 720, 30 E.T.R. (2d) 16 (Sask. Q.B.).

197 (1981), 8 E.T.R. 293 (N.S. T.D.), affirmed 9 E.T.R. 56n (N.S. C.A.).

198 [1980] 1 W.W.R. 41, 21 B.C.L.R. 273, 7 E.T.R. 176 (C.A.).

199 Substitutionary gifts are described in the chapter on Lapse and Survivorship.

200 *Tottrup v. Patterson*, [1970] S.C.R. 318, 1 W.W.R. 388, (sub nom. *Re Ottewell*) 9 D.L.R. (3d) 314.

201 *Re Klein, supra*, at E.T.R. 182, *per* Taggart J.A.

202 *Supra*, at S.C.R. 322.

In my opinion the duty of the court of construction is accurately stated in Theobald on Wills[203] as follows:

> What has to be done is first to construe the will. The meaning placed upon the language used as a result of this process cannot be altered by reference to the surrounding circumstances when the will was executed. The procedure is not — First ascertain the surrounding circumstances and with that knowledge approach the construction of the will, but first construe the will; if the meaning is clear surrounding circumstances cannot be looked at to throw a doubt upon that meaning or to give the will a different meaning.

In my view the meaning of the will is clear; it contains no patent ambiguity; if the facts surrounding its execution are considered they do not disclose a latent ambiguity and they are consequently irrelevant.

The *Tottrup* case was not referred to in *Haidl v. Sacher*.[204] Does this weaken that case, or can *Tottrup* be distinguished as decided on its peculiar facts?

3. A will listed various items of property, as well as the residue, but did not list any beneficiaries. Is extrinsic evidence admissible to show the identity of the intended beneficiaries?[205]

4. Although evidence of surrounding circumstances may be admissible, the evidence may not permit the court to come to a sensible interpretation of the will. In that event, the gift under consideration fails for lack of certainty.[206]

5. Evidence by witnesses present at the making and execution of the will regarding the testator's intention is not evidence of surrounding circumstances, but direct evidence of the testator's intention and is, thus, not admissible.[207] Evidence by the solicitor of what the testator intended will be also be excluded for the same reason.[208]

6. Some jurisdictions have enacted legislation which departs radically from the strict constructionist approach. Thus, the English *Administration of Justice Act 1982*[209] provides that insofar as any part of a will is meaningless, or its language is ambiguous on its face or is shown to be ambiguous in light of surrounding circumstances, all available evidence, including evidence of the testator's actual intention is admissible to assist in the interpretation of the will.

In Ireland, the *Succession Act, 1965*[210] provides:

> Extrinsic evidence shall be admissible to show the intention of the testator and to assist in the construction of, or to explain any construction in a will.

The Irish Supreme Court interpreted this section restrictively, however, in *Rowe v. Lowe*,[211] in which it held that, if a will is clear, unambiguous and without contradiction, the court may not receive evidence of the testator's intention. The court stressed the repugnancy between the formality requirements and allowing evidence of intention to be admitted without qualification or limitation.

---

203 12th ed., s. 417, p. 127.
204 *Supra.*
205 See *Re Omilusik Estate* (1988), 31 E.T.R. 144 (Alta. Surr. Ct.).
206 See *Re Olson Estate* (1988), 32 E.T.R. 75 (Sask. C.A.).
207 See *Rudaczyk Estate v. Ukrainian Evangelical Baptist Assocn. of Eastern Can.* (1989), 34 E.T.R. 231 (Ont. H.C.).
208 *Kernahan Estate v. Hanson* (1990), 39 E.T.R. 249 (Sask. C.A.).
209 C. 53 (U.K.), s. 21.
210 No. 27 (Ireland), s. 90.
211 [1978] I.R. 55 (S.C.).

7. In British Columbia, the Law Reform Commission has recommended:

Legislation should be enacted to provide that all relevant evidence, including statements made by the testator or other evidence of his intent, is admissible to determine the meaning the testator, when executing his will, attached to the words used therein.[212]

Moreover, the Commission was of opinion that the direct evidence thus admissible should not be restricted to evidence expressed when the will was made. However, it restricted the use of such evidence so as to prevent it being used to override the words used in the will, for otherwise a testator could alter his will orally.[213]

8. If the subjective intent approach is accepted, do the statutory rules of construction which operate absent a contrary intention in the will, have to be modified to include a reference to a contrary intention appearing from surrounding circumstances and, perhaps, expressions of intention? Or are these instances in which the need for certainty or policy considerations dictate that such evidence be excluded?[214]

9. A testator gave a number of legacies to various nieces and nephews, including legacies of £200, respectively, "to my grand-nephew Robert Ofner" and "to my grand-nephew Curt Ofner." He then gave the residue equally between all of the named legatees. He had only four grand-nephews, namely Alfred, Richard, Curt and Botho Ofner, the first two of whom were brothers. He had no grand-nephew, or any other relative, named "Robert Ofner."

When giving instructions for his will, the testator had given his solicitor a handwritten note which said: "To my grand-nephew Dr. Alfred Ofner of Prague £200 if he proves my will if not £100. To his brother Robert Ofner £100." Is the note admissible? If so, on what basis?[215]

10. A testatrix left the residue of her estate to be divided between her brother Walter Jeffery, his wife "and their daughter." However, Walter and his wife had five daughters. Extrinsic evidence showed that the testatrix was particularly fond of Phoebe, had wanted Phoebe to live with her permanently and had corresponded constantly with Phoebe and only occasionally with her sisters. In a previous will, the testatrix had left the residue equally between her brother "and his daughter Phoebe." What, if any, of this evidence is admissible?[216]

11. The testator left all his property "to my wife, Mary." Mary thought she was the testator's wife and was reputed so to be. However, the testator had committed bigamy in marrying her. The testator always referred to Mary as his wife. What result?[217]

12. A testatrix gave a legacy "to the two children (boy and girl) of William Cowan of Lake Johnston, Saskatchewan." The testatrix had moved from Saskatchewan in 1914 when William Cowan had two children (a boy and a girl), and it is probable that she knew them, since they were her cousins. Since then, however, William Cowan had four more children and it is unlikely that the testatrix knew them. She made her will in 1965 when all six children were living. What result?[218]

---

212 Law Reform Commission of British Columbia *Report in the Interpretation of Wills* (L.R.C. 58, November, 1982), p. 25.

213 *Ibid.*, at pp. 22, 24.

214 *Cf. ibid.*, at p. 38.

215 See *Re Ofner*, [1909] 1 Ch. 60, [1908-10] All E.R. Rep. 851 (C.A.).

216 See *Re Jeffery*, [1914] 1 Ch. 375. See also *Re Belliveau* (1973), 8 N.B.R. (2d) 152; *Charter v. Charter* (1874), L.R. 7 H.L. 364.

217 See *Re Smalley*, [1929] 2 Ch. 112 (C.A.).

218 See *Re Burgess* (1968), 64 W.W.R. 44, 67 D.L.R. (2d) 526 (B.C.S.C.).

13. The testator, a bachelor, gave specific bequests to 18 members of his family; the residuary clause read "Whats [*sic*] left divide among the [unclear word] as best you see how." The word resembled "adults." The surrogate court looked at the context of the entire will in light of surrounding circumstances. It held that even if the disputed word were "adults" it would be impossible to determine what the testator may have intended by its use; the residue of the estate, therefore, passed as on an intestacy.[219]

14. The testator left the residue of his estate "to my grandchildren." He was survived by three grandchildren: A was the legitimate child of her parents; B was legitimated by virtue of a statute which treats children born out of wedlock whose parents subsequently intermarry as legitimate; C, although illegitimate, was treated by statute as being legitimate for the purpose of the will. C was the child of the testator's son, S, and a woman with whom S lived for a time but to whom he was not married. The woman also had a child, D, whom S treated as his own. The woman abandoned C, D and S and S obtained custody of the two children. Is D entitled to share in the gift?[220]

15. Extrinsic evidence is admissible also to ascertain the testator's intention in respect of wills which purport first to give an absolute interest to a beneficiary and then to limit the interest and give what remains on the beneficiary's death to another beneficiary. It used to be common to strike the gift of "what remains" as repugnant to the absolute gift. Now it is more common first to ascertain the testator's intention from all admissible evidence and then to conclude that the testator meant to give the first beneficiary a life interest with, perhaps, a power to encroach, followed by a remainder to the second beneficiary.[221]

(b) Evidence of the Testator's Intention

Unless a statute provides otherwise, evidence of the testator's actual intention, such as statements made by him or her, a memorandum giving instructions for the will, or a prior will, is admissible only if there is an equivocation or, as it is more commonly called today, a latent ambiguity.

A latent ambiguity arises if the court finds that there is not one, but there are two or more subjects or objects of the gift to which the description in the will applies equally. A latent ambiguity may arise on the face of the will, or it may only come to light after the will has been read in light of the surrounding circumstances.[222]

There is, however, no latent ambiguity if a blank appears on the face of the will. That is a patent ambiguity and it raises the inference that the testator failed to complete his or her testamentary intention.[223]

---

219 See *Re Olson Estate* (1988), 29 E.T.R. 1 (Sask. Surr. Ct.), affirmed (1988), 70 Sask. R. 240 (C.A.).

220 See *Darichuk Estate v. Kotyk* (1988), 31 E.T.R. 3 (Sask. C.A.).

221 See, *e.g. Re Shamas*, [1967] 2 O.R. 275, 63 D.L.R. (2d) 300 (C.A.); *Bergman-Porter v. Porter Estate* (1991), 44 E.T.R. 218 (N.S.T.D.); *Cull Estate v. Cull Estate* (1993), 49 E.T.R. 132 (Nfld. T.D.).

222 See *Long v. Long* (1980), 23 Nfld. & P.E.I.R. 234 (Nfld. T.D.); *Re McMurdo; Gold v. Cameron* (1982), 14 Sask. R. 221 (C.A.); *Charter v. Charter* (1874), L.R. 7 H.L. 364.

223 *Re Lucey*, [1950] 2 W.W.R. 1167 (Sask. C.A.), reversed on other grounds [1951] S.C.R. 690,

A leading case on latent ambiguity is *Doe d. Gord v. Needs*.[224] The testator devised several properties to different persons among whom were "George Gord, the son of George Gord" and "George Gord, the son of John Gord." He also left property to "George Gord, the son of Gord." George, the son of George, claimed to be entitled under the last devise and offered evidence of declarations by the testator showing that he (George, the son of George) was intended. The defendant contended that this evidence was inadmissible.

The court held that the evidence was admissible, since the words "George Gord the son of Gord" was an equally accurate description of the two George Gords. In the result, George the son of George was entitled.

You should note that the will did not contain a blank before the last reference to "Gord." Had it done so, that would suggest that the testator had not yet made up his mind. There would then have been a patent ambiguity and direct evidence of the testator's intention would not have been admissible in such a situation. Of course, the ambiguity, being apparent on the face of the will was in a sense "patent," but not in the sense which would preclude admission of the evidence in question.

While a latent ambiguity or equivocation can arise the way it did in the *Gord* case, more often it arises after the court has interpreted the will by sitting in the testator's armchair. If, having done so, it finds that there is an ambiguity which is not an equivocation, the gift fails, but if there is an equivocation, direct evidence of the testator's intention is admissible.

The doctrine of equivocation requires that the description in the will be equally applicable in all its parts to two or more persons or objects. If that is not the case, direct evidence of intention is not admissible.

This point is illustrated by *Doe d. Hiscocks v. Hiscocks*.[225] The testator devised certain estates to his son John for life, with remainder "to my grandson John Hiscocks, eldest son of the said John Hiscocks." In fact, John Hiscocks, the father, had been twice married. By his first wife he had Simon, his eldest son; the eldest son of his second marriage was the defendant John Hiscocks. Hence, the devise did not apply equally to either Simon or John.

At trial, the testator's instructions for his will and certain declarations made by him were admitted in evidence. These showed that he had intended to benefit Simon and the trial court, therefore, declared in his favour.

On appeal, the decision was reversed. It was not a case of equivocation, because the description "my grandson John Hiscocks, eldest son of...John Hiscocks," was partly true of both grandsons, but in different ways: Simon was John's eldest son, whereas John was John's grandson.

Re Carrick,[226] reproduced below, further illustrates the rules.

[1951] 3 D.L.R. 717; *Re Diver* (1962), 39 W.W.R. 612, 34 D.L.R. (2d) 667 (Alta. C.A.); *Re Shapiro* (1979), 27 O.R. (2d) 517, 6 E.T.R. 276, 107 D.L.R. (3d) 133 (H.C.).
224 (1836), 2 M. & W. 129, 150 E.R. 698.
225 (1839), 5 M. & W. 363, 151 E.R. 154.
226 64 O.L.R. 39, [1929] 3 D.L.R. 373 (H.C.).

RE CARRICK
(1929), 64 O.L.R. 39, [1929] 3 D.L.R. 373
Supreme Court of Ontario
[High Court of Justice]

The testator bequeathed $3,000 to each of "the Protestant Orphan Boys' Home, Toronto" and "the Protestant Orphans Girls' Home, Toronto." No such organisations existed at the date of the will or the date of the testator's death. However, one institution known as the "The Girls' Home" was incorporated in 1863 and an institution known as "The Protestant Orphans' Home" was incorporated in 1851. They were amalgamated by statute before the date of the will as the "The Protestant Children's Homes."

Another institution, known as "The Boys' Home" on George Street was incorporated in 1861.

An affidavit of the testator's sister showed that the family referred to "The Boys' Home" as "The Protestant Boys' Home." The evidence further disclosed that the sister was interested in The Protestant Children's Homes; that the testator and his mother, on the other hand, were interested in The Boys' Home; that the testator was not interested in The Protestant Children's Homes; and that he stated to two persons that he had made a legacy of $3,000, to the Boys' Home on George Street.

There was no real dispute that the Protestant Children's Homes were entitled to the second legacy. The issue, therefore, was who was entitled to the first legacy.

WRIGHT J.

. . .

If this evidence is admissible, it would clearly shew the institution intended to be benefited by the testator, but the authorities are not in agreement as to whether extrinsic evidence of this nature is admissible to aid the Court in solving a difficulty such as that raised in the present case. The law appears to be that extrinsic evidence is admissible only to determine which of several persons or things was intended under an equivocal description. See Hawkins on Wills.[227] Are the descriptions here equivocal so as to admit the extrinsic evidence? In *Doe d. Hiscocks v. Hiscocks*[228] it would appear that the Court held that extrinsic evidence is admissible only if the meaning of the testator's words is neither ambiguous nor obscure and if the devise is on the face of it perfect and intelligible, but from some of the circumstances admitted in proof ambiguity arises. In *In re Clergy Society*[229] it was held that in the case of institutions bearing similar names, there being no society designated exactly as stated in the will, but several societies popularly called "clergy societies," there was an equivocal description; and in

---

227 2nd ed., p. 14.
228 (1839), 5 M. & W. 363.
229 (1856), 2 K. & J. 615.

Doe d. Allen v. Allen[230] it was held that description may be equivocal although the context favours one of the objects.

The last decision touching the point appears to be the judgment of Sargant J., in *In Re Ray*,[231] where...he says in part:[232]

> But then arises the question whether the evidence as to intention is admissible when the description in the will is equally applicable to two or more persons but imperfectly descriptive of each of them....In my opinion the evidence would be admissible.

In *Charter v. Charter*[233] Lord Cairns, in dealing with the question as to admissibility of extrinsic evidence, says:[234]

> The only case in which evidence of this kind can be received is where the description of the legatee, or of the thing bequeathed, is equally applicable in all its parts to two persons, or to two things.

It will be noted that the language used by Lord Cairns is "equally applicable," not "completely applicable."

Can it be said that the language used in the will under consideration describing the beneficiaries is equally applicable? Neither of them comes within the exact designation in the will, one being the Boys' Home and the other the Protestant Orphans' Home. It will be noted that in one description the word "Protestant" appears and not the word "Boys," whereas in the other the term "Boys" appears but not the word "Protestant." So it would appear that the description is equally applicable to either of these institutions. Applying the reasoning and principle of the decisions already referred to, I am of opinion that extrinsic evidence is admissible, and that the declarations of the intention of the testator, both before and after the dates of the wills, are admissible.

In addition, the Court has a right to consider the circumstances and the interest of the testator and his family in the Boys' Home, and the fact that so far as disclosed he had no connection with or interest in the other institution known as the Protestant Orphans' Home.

Having regard to all the evidence, and particularly the declarations of the testator, it is reasonably clear that the legacy was intended for the Boys' Home. I so hold.

> [His Lordship also was prepared to rely upon the presumption against a double legacy, which is to the effect that if a legacy in favour of a particular person is repeated and the amounts are the same, *prima facie* the legatee is entitled to one legacy only. On that basis, the first legacy could not also be given to the Protestant Children's Homes.]

---

230 (1840), 12 A. & E. 451.
231 [1916] 1 Ch. 461.
232 *Ibid.,* at p. 465.
233 (1874), L.R. 7 H.L. 364.
234 *Ibid.,* at p. 377.

Notes and Questions

1. *Re Gray*[235] followed *Hiscocks*.[236] The testator directed that the residue of his estate be divided equally between his brothers and sisters, but so that his brother John Norman Gray would receive a life interest only. The testator had no brother by that name, but he had a brother called John Gray and one called Norman Farquharson Gray. Direct evidence showing that the testator intended to refer to Norman was ruled inadmissible, because the description was not equally applicable to the two brothers. Note the effect of the decision: it removed the restriction of a life interest.

2. Although the *Hiscocks* case remains good law, the doctrine of latent ambiguity has been extended to a situation in which the description in the will applies with equal inaccuracy to two or more persons or objects.

Re Ray[237] illustrates the point. The testatrix left a parcel of real property to her niece Elizabeth Johnson, another parcel to her great nephew Richard Johnson, and a third to her great nephew Frederick Johnson.

The testatrix had no relatives named Johnson, but she did have a niece called Elizabeth Johnstone, who had three sons, Richard, Robert William and Joseph Francomb. Evidence that the testatrix intended to benefit Joseph Francomb Johnstone in respect of the third parcel of land was admitted, because the word "Frederick" applied equally to all three grand nephews.

An alternative approach to this case would have been for the court to reject the word "Frederick" as an incorrect description,[238] after which the latent ambiguity doctrine would also have applied.[239]

3. You should not suppose that it is always necessary to resort to direct evidence of the testator's intention to resolve a latent ambiguity.

Re Jackson[240] illustrates this. The testatrix gave her estate upon trust for sale and directed that the proceeds be held upon trust for her two brothers, two sisters and "my nephew Arthur Murphy" in equal shares. She had three nephews by that name, two being sons of her brothers, and one the illegitimate son of one of her sisters. The illegitimate nephew had married a legitimate niece of the testatrix, had managed the testatrix' affairs for some time and she was close to him. She did have some contact with the others as well, but one lived in Australia and the other, who lived in England, would get his father's share under the will, since the latter had predeceased the testatrix. On the basis of the evidence of surrounding circumstances the court was able to conclude that she intended to benefit the illegitimate nephew.

4. Evidence of the testator's intention is admissible only to resolve a latent ambiguity and for no other purpose.

This is evident from *Re Hill*.[241] The testator made a bequest of "Nola's watch and ring." The testator had left the watch and three rings in an envelope with the beneficiary for safekeeping. There was evidence that the testator intended the beneficiary to have all three rings, but the court refused to admit it, since it did not resolve the latent ambiguity. Evidence tending to show that he intended her to have a specific ring of the three would have been

---

235 [1934] O.W.N. 17 (H.C.).
236 (1839), 5 M. & W. 363, 151 E.R. 154.
237 [1916] 1 Ch. 461.
238 This approach is discussed below.
239 See also *Careless v. Careless* (1816), 1 Mer. 384, 35 E.R. 715, to the same effect.
240 [1933] Ch. 237, [1932] All E.R. Rep. 696.
241 (1978), 31 N.S.R. (2d) 265, 3 E.T.R. 261 (T.D.).

admissible. In the result, the court found that the beneficiary had a power of selection. Assuming that the evidence of the testator is cogent and veracious, is this result defensible or appropriate?

5. It has been shown that the distinction between an ambiguity which permits the court to sit in the testator's armchair (which includes the case of a patent ambiguity, that is, one in which a blank is left in the will), and a latent ambiguity in which direct evidence of intention is admissible, was not originally made to determine the nature of the evidence that should be admitted, but as a guide in pleading. Formerly, the courts refused to admit any evidence in the case of a patent ambiguity and facts supporting such evidence could not, therefore, be pleaded. However, courts did admit evidence of surrounding circumstances and evidence of the testator's intention in other cases. Hence, the distinction was used only to determine upon what issues evidence could be received.[242]

That being so, is there any need to continue to exclude evidence of the testator's intention in cases which do not raise a latent ambiguity? In other words, is there a rational basis for distinguishing between cases like *Gord*[243] and *Hiscocks*?[244]

6. Law reform in some jurisdictions and proposals for reform in others would admit evidence of the testator's intention in all or most circumstances. These were discussed earlier in this chapter.

7. Merely because direct evidence of the testator's intention is admissible, does not mean that it will be of assistance in interpreting a will. It may not resolve an ambiguity or be itself ambiguous. In that event, the gift will fail for uncertainty.[245]

8. You should note that evidence of the testator's intention is admissible to test certain equitable presumptions, such as the doctrine of satisfaction.[246]

7. DRAFTING ERRORS AND OMISSIONS

(a) Generally

The court of construction has a limited jurisdiction to "correct" omissions and errors and to reject incorrect descriptions in wills. This jurisdiction is discussed in the following material. The court does not actually correct, or rectify, the will. It interprets the will as probated and declares its meaning.

(b) Drafting Omissions

The court may "complete the testator's will" by supplying words that have been omitted if it is satisfied that an omission has occurred and it is able to

---

242 Thayer, *Evidence* (1898), pp. 424-6; Warren, "Interpretation of Wills - Recent Developments" (1936), 49 Harv. L. Rev. 686, at pp. 705ff.
243 (1836), 2 M. & W. 129, 150 E.R. 698.
244 (1839), 5 M. & W. 363, 151 E.R. 154.
245 See *Re Williams (decd), Wiles et al. v. Madgin et al.*, [1985] 1 All E.R. 964.
246 These are discussed in the next chapter.

discover what the testator meant.[247] It is not necessary that the court be able to discover the precise language the testator had in mind; it is sufficient if it is known that the testator intended to make a particular provision and what that provision was.[248]

Unfortunately there is a difference among the cases about the standard of certainty required before the missing words can be supplied.[249]

Re Craig[250] suggests a very strict standard. In that case the testatrix made various dispositive provisions, but failed to provide for the event that actually occurred, that is, that she survived her husband. The will gave everything to her husband if he survived her and to other persons if they both died in a common accident. The Ontario Court of Appeal held by a majority that the omission could not be corrected since it was unclear what her intention might have been in the events which actually happened. The result was that the testatrix died intestate. In the course of a short judgment for the majority, Mackinnon J.A., said:[251]

A Court should only tamper with and add to the words of a will, particularly one drafted by a solicitor, where it is perfectly clear that the testator has not accurately, or completely expressed his intention. In other words, a case which is almost beyond argument.

His Lordship continued:[252]

The testatrix could have had many contingencies in mind in the event she survived her husband, including the possible length of that survival, her needs and expenditures during that time, and her relationship to those who might assist or befriend her over that period.

To interpolate the words suggested [i.e., that the gift over should take effect if the testatrix' husband predeceased her at any time as well as if they both died in a common accident], is, in my view, to write a new will for the testatrix based on pure conjecture or speculation, and it is not a matter of necessary implication. It is far from clear to me that such interpolation would carry out her clear intentions as expressed in the will in the event of her husband predeceasing her, and I would be left very uneasy at the prospect of so doing.

---

247 *Re Follett*, [1955] 1 W.L.R. 429, [1955] 2 All E.R. 22 at 28 (C.A.), *per* Romer L.J.; *Re Miles* (1981), 9 E.T.R. 113 at 119-20 (Ont. H.C.), *per* Callaghan J.; *Re Freeman* (1975), 20 N.S.R. (2d) 644, (sub nom. *Central & Nova Scotia Trust Co. v. Freeman*) 58 D.L.R. (3d) 541 (T.D.); *Re Hicking; Central & Eastern Trust Co. v. Eaton* (1979), 40 N.S.R. (2d) 491, 6 E.T.R. 251 (T.D.).
248 *Re Whitrick*, [1957] 1 W.L.R. 884, [1957] 2 All E.R. 467 at 473 (C.A.), *per* Romer L.J.
249 Contrast, *e.g.*, *Re Whitrick, ibid.*, and *McLean v. Henning* (1903), 33 S.C.R. 305.
250 (1978), 42 O.R. (2d) 567, 2 E.T.R. 257, 149 D.L.R. (3d) 483 (C.A.).
251 *Ibid.*, at E.T.R. 261.
252 *Ibid.*, at p. 262.

Houlden J.A., who dissented, would have remedied the omission, relying upon *Re Whitrick*,[253] an almost identical case, in which Romer L.J., said:[254]

> The reason why I think it is reasonably clear that there has been an omission is that it would be capricious in the highest extreme to suppose that the testatrix intended her sisters and her nephew to take if she, the testatrix, and her husband died simultaneously, but that they were not to take if the husband predeceased her. One cannot see any shadow of reason for that.

Sellers L.J., said in the same case:[255]

> I cannot believe that the testatrix and her husband, in his turn, were both of them so playful, cynical or eccentric that they decided, by cl. (5) of their respective wills, to leave part of their estate to their relatives or friends only in the most highly improbable event of their both dying at the same time.

The majority, instead, followed the virtually identical case, *McLean v. Henning*[256] and distinguished *Re Harmer*[257] in which the Supreme Court of Canada had itself distinguished its earlier decision in the *McLean* case. The reason for the distinction was that in *Harmer* the testatrix had made a similar provision to that in *Craig* and *McLean*, but had added that in the event her husband and she died in a common accident her will should take effect as if her husband had predeceased her. That addition was sufficient for the Supreme Court in *Harmer* not to supply words in the will, but to conclude that the testatrix intended the gift over to take effect in any event.

It is submitted that the distinction is rather facile. The extra clause in the *Harmer* will is one that is commonly used in a provision providing against a common disaster and its purpose is not as was supposed in that case, but to prevent a claim by the husband's estate under a substitutionary gift.

A less strict test than that espoused in *Re Craig* is suggested by *Re MacDonald*,[258] which speaks of a "reasonable inference if not necessary implication," and *Hawkinson v. Hawkinson*,[259] which speaks of "reasonable certainty." The less strict test is exemplified in *Central & Nova Scotia Trust Co. v. Freeman*,[260] reproduced below.

---

253 [1957] 1 W.L.R. 884, [1957] 2 All E.R. 467 (C.A.).
254 *Ibid.*, at p. 473.
255 *Ibid.*
256 (1903), 33 S.C.R. 305.
257 [1965] S.C.R. 24, (sub nom. *Kilby v. Myers*) 46 D.L.R. (2d) 521.
258 (1956), 19 W.W.R. 468, 5 D.L.R. (2d) 175 at 180 (Alta. C.A.).
259 (1977), 4 B.C.L.R. 285, 1 E.T.R. 245, 80 D.L.R. (3d) 390 (S.C.). See also *Re Smith; Veasey v. Smith*, [1948] Ch. 49, [1947] 2 All E.R. 708 at 710 (C.A.).
260 (1975), 20 N.S.R. (2d) 644, 58 D.L.R. (3d) 541 (T.D.).

RE FREEMAN
(1975), 20 N.S.R. (2d) 644, 58 D.L.R. (3d) 541
sub. nom. Central & Nova Scotia Trust Co. v. Freeman
Nova Scotia Supreme Court
[Trial Division]

The testator, Gerald Morton Freeman, gave a life estate to his wife with a power to encroach and he directed that if his wife predeceased him or died within 30 days of his death, the property should go to other named beneficiaries. He did not provide for what should happen to the remainder if his wife survived him for more than 30 days, which is what happened.

An application was made to construe the will, the question being whether the testator died intestate as to the remainder, or whether to the other named beneficiaries could take in any event.

DUBINSKY J.:

> [His Lordship considered a number of cases which adhered to the strict rule that the court must not depart from the natural and ordinary meaning of the words of a will, unless the context justifies it. If the court were to do so, it would be speculating about the testator's intentions and would make a will for him or her.
> He also considered cases which held that the presumption against intestacy cannot override the clear words of a will, but can only be relied upon if the context allows it. His Lordship continued:]

[Counsel for the residuary legatees] cites three cases, the first of which is *Re Smith: Veasey v. Smith.*[261] In this case, a married woman by her will, having appointed her husband and the plaintiff, executors, and bequeathed specific and pecuniary legacies, including a legacy of chattels to her husband, provided that in the event of her husband predeceasing her or if surviving her, dying one calendar month of the date of her death, the executors were to hold the residuary estate in trust to be divided among a number of persons all relatives of the husband and three charities. The will contained no disposition of the residue in the event (which in fact happened) of the husband surviving the wife by more than one calendar month. The Court was called upon to decide whether there was an intestacy or alternatively that a gift in favour of her husband absolutely could be inferred.

Vaisey, J., said the following:[262]

> I start with this, that it is, in my judgment, very surprising that a lady who appoints her husband to be an executor and trustee of her will and bequeaths to him her personal chattels and was evidently on the best of terms with his relations as is shown from the alternative gifts to which I have referred - it is exceedingly surprising to find that she made no disposition at all of her estate either to him or to his relations in the event which happened of his surviving her for more than one calendar month. If I had read this will in draft and been asked whether I saw anything the

261 [1948] 1 Ch. 49.
262 At pp. 52-3.

matter with it, it would, I think, have leapt to the eye that there must have been some omission of a provision operating in the alternative, and I cannot possibly read this will without forming the conclusion that there has obviously been some omission, and the question is whether, having come to that conclusion, I am able to say what that omission is as a matter of necessity, that is to say,

> not natural necessity, but so strong a probability of intention, that an intention contrary to that which is imputed to the testator cannot be supposed.

I quote those words from *Wilkinson v. Adam*,[263] an old authority which is referred to in Hawkins on Wills.[264] I am asked, to speculate, not only on the question whether there has been an omission, but on the question whether I can say with reasonable certainty as a matter of necessary implication what the omission was. Now I feel reasonably sure that the omission was not a very large number of words, but probably of quite a few words, or possibly quite a short clause, and I have come to the conclusion that what the lady meant was that if her husband survived her sufficiently long to take charge of her estate he was to have it. I refer again to *Hawkins on Wills*, which quotes the following from the report of *Coryton v. Helyar*:[265]

> There is hardly any case where an implication is of necessity, but it is called 'necessary' because the court finds it so to answer the intention of the devisor.

Here I find without question an omission, and I think I am entitled, as a matter of necessary implication, in the sense in which those words are used in the quotation to which I have referred, to find that what has been omitted is a gift to the testatrix's husband.

Having come to that conclusion, I will now see whether the authorities justify me in giving effect to what I will not describe as speculation, but rather as a compelling conviction, that such was the nature of the error which has occurred. In the case of *Towns v. Wentworth*[266] Mr. Pemberton Leigh (who afterwards become Lord Kingsdown) used expressions which I think are very helpful in this connection. He says this:

> If the will shows that the testator must necessarily have intended an interest to be given which there are no words in the will expressly to devise, the court is to supply the defect by implication, and thus to mould the language of the testator, so as to carry into effect, as far as possible, the intention which it is of opinion that the testator has, on the whole will, sufficiently declared.
>
> In Jarman on Wills,[267] the matter is expressed thus:

> Where it is clear on the face of a will that the testator has not accurately or completely expressed his meaning by the words he has used, and it is also clear what are the words which he has omitted, those words may be supplied in order to effectuate the intention, as collected from the context.

I have not been informed whether that particular paragraph is in part of the original text of Jarman on Wills, but I think that it is an accurate statement of the law and of the principles which it is my duty to apply.

The second case referred to by this counsel is *Re Whitrick*.[268] Here, a testatrix by her will left her whole estate to her husband and then "in the event of my

---

263 (1812-13) 1 V. & B. 422.
264 3rd ed., at p. 8.
265 (1745), Cox. 340, 348.
266 11 Moo. P.C. 526.
267 7th ed., vol. 1, p. 556.
268 [1957] 2 All E.R. 467.

husband...and myself both dying at the same time" gave the whole of her estate on trust for three relations. The testatrix' husband predeceased her. The Court of Appeal comprised Lord Justices Jenkins, Romer and Sellers.

Lord Justice Jenkins said:[269]

> The question which we are asked to decide is whether there should be read into this will, by necessary implication, provision for the contingency of the husband dying in the testatrix' lifetime, so that the provisions of cll. (4) and (5) of the will take effect, or whether the court is constrained to confine itself to the actual language used in the will, in which case the provisions of cll. (4) and (5) cannot take effect, as on that view they are only limited to take effect in the event of both the testatrix and her husband dying at the same time, which event did not happen.
>
> The reading of words into a will as a matter of necessary implication is a measure which any court of construction should apply with the greatest caution. Many wills contain slips and omissions and fail to provide for contingencies which, to anyone reading the will, might appear contingencies for which any testator would obviously wish to provide. The court cannot re-write the testamentary provisions in wills which come before it for construction. This type of treatment of an imperfect will is only legitimate where the court can collect from the four corners of the document that something has been omitted and, further, collect with sufficient precision the nature of the omission.

His Lordship then referred extensively to *Re Smith*,[270] of which he approved. He then went on to say:[271]

> If the testatrix had simply made a will giving all her property to her husband absolutely and had made no other disposition, it is absolutely plain beyond possibility of argument that no court could there imply any gift in the event of the husband predeceasing the wife. It would be quite impossible to do that, because one could not say with certainty, if that was the form of the will, that she meant to make any other provision, nor could one say with certainty, or hazard a guess, what disposition the testatrix might have made had she made one. This case, however, is of a different character. The will begins with the absolute gift to the husband. Then the testatrix goes on to provide for a certain contingency, and the contingency provided for is, according to the express language used, that of the testatrix and the husband dying at the same time. Can one possibly believe that in making this alternative provision the testatrix really intended to make it operative only in the event of herself and her husband dying at the same time? That was an event extremely unlikely to happen.
>
> To my mind, it cannot be accepted for a moment that the words used, "in the event of my husband and myself both dying at the same time", comprise the whole of the contingency for which the testatrix intended to provide. It seems to me reasonably plain from the language and frame of the will that what the testatrix set out to do by cl. (3) and the subsequent clauses was to provide for the contingency of her husband not surviving her. The contingency of her husband not surviving her might take the form of the husband dying in her lifetime or of his failing to survive her by reason of his dying at the same time as the testatrix herself. It is reasonably plain that, in setting out to provide for the contingency of the husband not surviving her, the testatrix expressed imperfectly the contingency for which she intended to provide; and I think the court can say with sufficient certainty that the alternatives which she intended to provide for were the event of herself and her husband both dying at the same time or the event of his dying in her lifetime. That makes the will a sensible and complete disposition. In my view, although, as I have said, the court should be very sparing of implying words or reading words into a will, this is one of those rare cases where it is possible to say as a matter of necessary implication that there was

---

269 *Ibid.,* at p. 469.
270 *Supra.*
271 At pp. 471-2.

an intention to provide for the contingency which I have mentioned, and that through some mischance the necessary words were omitted.

[His Lordship also quoted from the judgments of Romer and Sellers L.JJ., which were referred to in the introductory material, and continued:]

The third case mentioned by Mr. Cowan is the Supreme Court of Canada case of *Re Harmer*.[272]

[His Lordship set out the headnote of this case (which was discussed above) and the quotation from the judgment of Ritchie J., reproduced above, and continued:]

I have carefully read and reread the will and particularly para. 7 of the third clause. I have tried to ascertain whether the trouble herein arose because of the accidental dropping of a line or two in that paragraph, that is to say, whether there has been some typographical mistake but I have not been successful in this regard. I should mention one small point that occurred to me as I read the paragraph. In the first part of the third clause, the testator left all his property *to his trustees* upon trust and in the first six paragraphs of that clause, he *directs his trustees* to do such and such. In the second line of para. 7 however, he uses the expression "*I* give and bequeath..." although in the fourth line thereof, he reverts to the original form of direction and says (presumably to his trustees) "*and* to divide the rest...". Although I am unable to put my finger on it, I have a strong feeling that some drafting error has crept into the document. (All italicizing is mine).

Irrespective of how it came about, there is no doubt whatsoever in my mind that there is an omission in the will. I find it passing strange — indeed, I find it incredible — that this testator, who from the other contents of the will...took such great care to dispose of his estate to named legatees, would intend an intestacy as to any portion thereof. It is most unreasonable, in my view, to say that he would intend to dispose of his assets as he did on his wife's death, but would want them to go by way of intestacy if she died, for example, 31 days or 60 days or 90 days or some longer period after his death. Moreover, it is to be remembered that he had two sisters, not one. Mrs. Ila Langille is a sister but in his will the testator only made provision for the other sister, Hazel Elizabeth Freeman. Is it to be said that it was his intention that if his wife survived him by more than 30 days, the sister Ila Langille who for reasons best known to the testator did not warrant the slightest mention in his will, should, on his wife's death, take one-half of his estate on intestacy? I do not think such a suggestion could ever be made.

The principle on which the Court acts in supplying by inference an omission in a document was well stated in the cases cited by Mr. Cowan and which I propose to follow. I would like to mention two more cases where the principle was set forth in language which I also adopt. In *Key v. Key*,[273] Knight Bruce, L.J., said:[274]

272 (1965), 46 D.L.R. (2d) 521, [1965] S.C.R. 24 (sub nom. *Kilbey et al. v. Myers et al*).
273 (1853), 4 De G.M. & G. 73, 43 E.R. 435.
274 At De G.M. & G. 84-5, 439 E.R 439.

In common with all men, I must acknowledge that there are many cases upon the construction of documents in which the spirit is strong enough to overcome the letter; cases in which it is impossible for a reasonable being, upon a careful perusal of an instrument, not to be satisfied from its contents that a literal, a strict, or an ordinary interpretation given to particular passages, would disappoint and defeat the intention with which the instrument, read as a whole, persuades and convinces him that it was framed. A man so convinced is authorized and bound to construe the writing accordingly.

Lord Kingsdown in *Towns v. Wentworth*[275] said:[276]

When the main purpose and intention of the Testator are ascertained to the satisfaction of the Court, if particular expressions are found in the Will which are inconsistent with such intention, though not sufficient to control it, or which indicate an intention which the law will not permit to take effect, such expressions must be discarded or modified; and, on the other hand, if the Will shows that the Testator must necessarily have intended an interest to be given which there are no words in the Will expressly to devise, the Court is to supply the defect by implication, and thus to mould the language of the Testator, so as to carry into effect, as far as possible, the intention which it is of opinion that the Testator has on the whole Will, sufficiently declared.

Keeping in mind the opinions expressed in the several cases cited earlier, I would construe para. 7 of the third clause to read as follows:

(7) Upon the death of my wife or on my death should my wife predecease me or die within thirty days of my death, I direct my Trustees to pay to my sister, Miss Hazel Josephine Freeman, 102 Glenelg Street West, Lindsay, Ontario, the sum of Fifty Thousand Dollars ($50,000.00) and to divide the rest and residue of my estate into twenty-three shares to be distributed as follows:

(Sub-paragraphs (a) to (o) to follow and to contain the same directions as to be found in the Will).

. . .

Notes and Questions

1. Which test is preferable, the strict one applied in *Re Craig*[277] or the more lenient one in the *Freeman* case? Does the fact that holograph wills are now allowed throughout Canada, with the probable attendant increase in errors and omissions in such wills, suggest a less stringent test?[278]

2. Prior to the adoption of the subjective intent approach to interpretation, the discovery of an omission and of the provision intended, was restricted to the will itself.[279] It remains uncertain whether the subjective intent approach extends to the finding of omissions, that is to say, whether surrounding circumstances may be considered in determining whether an omission has occurred. In *Re Krainyk Estate*,[280] Matheson J., held that the subjective intent approach is concerned with ascertaining the meaning of the words used by the

---

275 (1858), 11 Moore 526, 14 E.R. 794.
276 At Moore 543, E.R. 800.
277 (1978), 42 O.R. (2d) 567, 2 E.T.R. 257, 149 D.L.R. (3d) 483 (C.A.).
278 To the same effect as *Freeman*, see *Colthorp v. Hall* (1989), 34 E.T.R. 86 (B.C.S.C.); *Taylor v. Montgomery* (1990), 39 E.T.R. 49 (B.C.C.A.); *Re Vaughan Estate* (1990), 39 E.T.R. 305 (B.C.S.C.). To the same effect as *Craig*, see *Stock Estate v. Stock* (1990), 38 E.T.R. 290 (Ont. H.C.); *Nadeau v. Central Guarantee Trust Co.* (1993), 50 E.T.R. 159 (N.B. Prob. Ct.).
279 See, *e.g.*, *Re Whitrick*, [1957] 1 W.L.R. 884, [1957] 2 All E.R. 467 (C.A.); *Re Harmer*, [1965] S.C.R. 24, (sub nom. *Kilby v. Myers*) 46 D.L.R. (2d) 521.
280 (1982), 19 Sask. R. 414 (Surr. Ct.).

testator and has no relevance to the case of omitted words. However, in *Re Flinton*,[281] Legg J., in a *dictum*, favoured the use of extrinsic evidence for the discovery of omissions as well. Which is correct?

3. Do the existing principles of construction and, in the court of probate, powers of rectification operate adequately to give effect to the testator's intention in circumstances in which his or her intent is not adequately expressed in the will because of the drafter's misunderstanding, clerical errors, misdescription, inconsistency, ambiguity, failure to appreciate the significance of the words used, and failure to contemplate the possible future course of events?

Legislative reforms in England have broadened the jurisdiction of the court of probate to rectify a will in cases of clerical error and of failure by the drafter to understand the testator's intention.[282] This reduces the need of a court of construction to read words into a will to permit a sensible construction.

The Law Reform Commission of British Columbia recommends an extremely broad power of rectification. It favours a power in any court to rectify a will if it fails to carry out the testator's intention, as discovered from all relevant evidence, including evidence of actual intent, as a result of an error arising from an accidental slip or omission, a misunderstanding of the testator's instructions, a failure to carry out the testator's instructions, or a failure by the testator to appreciate the effect of the words used.[283]

Does the suggested power to rectify for failure by the testator to appreciate the effect of the words used involve the court in re-writing the testator's will, or is this justified by the policy consideration that the testator's intentions should not be frustrated merely because he or she no longer has the power to guard against events he or she did not anticipate?

In view of the fact that courts in recent years have been willing to find solicitors liable in negligence at the suit of disappointed heirs,[284] is a power to rectify for the drafter's errors necessary? Is it tantamount to providing statutory immunity for professional negligence?

4. In *Leir v. Public Trustee*[285] the court used a novel approach to solve an omission problem. The testator had failed to dispose of a share of the residue in the events which occurred. The trust of residue was, thus, uncertain. Accordingly, the court approved an agreement of the capacitated beneficiaries under the *Trust Variation Act*[286] by which the residuary share was divided somewhat contrary to the expressed wishes of the testator.

5. The testator expressly devised a part of his estate to one son, R, leaving a significant portion undisposed of. The testator had clearly indicated by his will that he did not wish his wife nor his six other children to share in the estate. Should the residue of the estate be distributed as on an intestacy, or should R take the entire estate?[287]

6. *Re Sherin*[288] also illustrates the court's willingness to cure an omission. The testator made a will which contained provisions which would apply if his wife predeceased him or failed to survive him for at least 30 days; it was silent as to the situation which actually

---

281 [1981] 4 W.W.R. 549, 10 E.T.R. 236 (B.C.S.C.).

282 *Administration of Justice Act*, c. 53 (U.K.), s. 20. See ch. 5, *supra*.

283 Law Reform Commission of British Columbia, *Report on the Interpretation of Wills* (L.R.C. 58, November, 1982), p. 50.

284 This matter is discussed later in this book.

285 (1983), 8 B.C.L.R. 92, 15 E.T.R. 241 (S.C.).

286 R.S.B.C. 1979, c. 413.

287 See *Re Sharpe* (1985), 18 D.L.R. (4th) 421 (Nfld. T.D.).

288 (1985), 18 E.T.R. 177 (Ont. H.C.).

occurred, namely that his wife survived him. By an earlier (revoked) will, which contained the same specific bequests made in the later will, he had provided that his wife would take the residue of his estate if she survived him. The court held that it was unreasonable to infer that the testator intended an intestacy. Having determined the intention of the testator, the court interpreted the will as if the clause in issue had included the words "upon the death of my wife, or upon my death...."

In contrast, in *Re Williams*[289] the court came to a different conclusion. The testatrix's will was silent as to the disposition of the residue of her estate if the husband were to survive her. The court stated that it "is not interpretation but conjecture as to what disposition she would have made, assuming inadvertence on her part, and assuming her attention had been directed to that inadvertence." The court was not satisfied that something was inadvertently omitted, nor what it was that may have been omitted. The court distinguished *Re MacDonell*,[290] since the Williams will did not demonstrate any patent ambiguity. Further, the court declined to follow the *Freeman*[291] and *Sherin*[292] cases, since they were decided in different circumstances and considered different wills. Consequently, the residue of the estate passed to the husband as an intestacy.

7. A testator left a life estate in his house to his wife, with remainder after his wife's death to his sister if she survived him and his wife by 10 days. He left the residue to his sister if she survived him by 10 days, with a gift over to her issue if she did not. The testator died first, followed 21 years later by the sister. The wife died 11 years after the sister. What happens to the house? Who gets the residue?[293]

8. A testator gave all his estate to his wife if she survived him. Subject to that gift, he directed that all articles of domestic and household use be divided between the two sons of the marriage. He failed to dispose of the rest of the estate if his wife predeceased him, which is what happened. The testator was also survived by a son of a previous marriage with whom he had had little contact. What happens to the residue of the estate?[294]

Further Reading

Ronald G. Hopp, "Correcting Omissions in Wills" (Annotation) (1978), 2 E.T.R. 257.
Stan J. Sokol, *Mistakes in Wills in Canada* (Scarborough: Carswell, 1995), ch. 9.

(c) Drafting Errors

In addition to its power to correct ambiguities and inconsistencies under the *falsa demonstratio* doctrine,[295] the court of construction has power to rectify errors contained in a will if the error is apparent and the actual intention of the testator is clear.[296]

---

289 (1985), 18 E.T.R. 188 (Ont. H.C.).
290 (1982), 35 O.R. (2d) 578 (C.A.).
291 (1975), 58 D.L.R. (3d) 541 (N.S.T.D.).
292 (1985), 18 E.T.R. 177 (Ont. H.C.).
293 See *Canada Trust v. Off Estate* (1999), 30 E.T.R. (2d) 185 (Ont. S.C.J.).
294 See *Howell v. Howell Estate* (1999), 175 D.L.R. (4th) 318, 28 E.T.R. (2d) 168 (B.C.C.A.).
295 Discussed below.
296 *Horton v. Horton* (1978), 2 E.T.R. 293, 88 D.L.R. (3d) 264 (B.C.S.C.); *Re MacDonnell* (1982),

Again, there appears to be a difference of opinion about the admissibility of extrinsic evidence for this purpose. *Re MacDonnell*,[297] reproduced below, suggests that such evidence is not admissible, whereas in *Re Ferguson Estate*[298] the court considered evidence of surrounding circumstances to find an error.

RE MACDONNELL
(1982), 35 O.R. (2d) 578, 11 E.T.R. 52, 133 D.L.R. (3d) 128
Supreme Court of Ontario
[Court of Appeal]

The testatrix, Ruth MacDonnell, died in 1973. By her will she gave various gifts to her sister Achsah Ena MacDonnell conditional upon her surviving the testatrix, including the use for life of the residence the testatrix and her sister owned as tenants in common and the income from the residue. Clause 3(f) of the will began "If and in the event that my sister...has predeceased me, then and in such event I make the following special bequests:..." and this was followed by 31 specific bequests of personal property, gifts of sums of money to named individuals and five other provisions. Subclause (37) then provided "All the rest and residue of my Estate I direct my Trustees to divide into three equal shares and to pay the shares..." to three named charities, but the last of these was conditional upon certain activity being carried on by that charity at the time of the death of the survivor of the testatrix and her sister.

The sister survived the testatrix and was her sole next of kin.

On an application for advice and directions, it was held at first instance that the gift of residue in clause 3(f)(37) took effect only if the sister predeceased the testatrix. Since she did not, there was an intestacy of the residue.

The charities appealed.

LACOURCIÈRE J.A., delivered the judgment of the Court:

. . .

With great respect to the learned Judge of first instance, I am unable to agree that the will shows the unambiguous intent to benefit the appellants only in the event that the testatrix's sister predeceased her and not otherwise. I am satisfied, on reading the will as a whole, that it was the clear intention of the testatrix to dispose of her entire estate, and that the Court of construction can give effect to this intention by deleting the parenthetical No. (37) which precedes the residuary clause and causes the ambiguity.

That the intention of the testatrix was to dispose of all her property can be determined by reading the will as a whole. She uses the words "...declare this to be and contain my only last will and testament" and "I give, bequeath all my

---

35 O.R. (2d) 578, 11 E.T.R. 52, 133 D.L.R. (3d) 128 (C.A.); *Re Raiter* (1979), 24 O.R. (2d) 603, 99 D.L.R. (3d) 183 (H.C.).
297 *Supra*.
298 (1980), 6 Sask. R. 316 (Q.B.).

estate both real and personal of whatsoever kind and wheresoever the same may be situate..." upon certain trusts. Thereafter, in cl. 3(c), the testatrix directs her trustees that her share of the premises then owned as tenant in common with her sister "shall fall into and form part of the residue of my estate" if certain events happen. There are other references on the part of the testatrix. The scheme of her will reveals an intention to dispose of all her property.... When that intention is clear, the Court will follow the construction which gives effect to it in preference to one which will result in partial or total intestacy....I must give effect to what has been called the "golden rule" of construction that I "...ought, if possible, to read the will so as to lead to a testacy, not an intestacy" per Lord Esher M.R. in *Re Harrison*[299] a rule which has been applied frequently in Ontario....

This is not to say that the above rule of construction is one [of] universal application; one should not strive to avoid an intestacy at all costs. The language of the will may sometimes be such as to lead to the inference that the testatorintended to leave part of his property undisposed of. I adopt the words of Ritchie J. In *Kilby v. Myers*.[300]

> [His Lordship reproduced the quotation from the judgment of Ritchie J., which is set out above, and which continued:]

> As was said by Lord Shaw in *Lightfoot v. Mayberry*,[301] a construction resulting in an intestacy "is a dernier resort in the construction of wills."

In the case at Bar, I find no compelling reason to conclude that the testatrix, by cl. 3(f)(37) of the will, intended to dispose of the residue of the estate only in the event that her sister predeceased her. To reach this conclusion, one would have to find that the testatrix intended an intestacy as to the residue of her estate if her sister survived her. The clear intention of the testatrix was to provide her sister with a life interest in the residue, with no power to encroach on the capital except for personal loans of capital in the event of severe illness or incapacity. The interpretation of the will urged upon us by the respondent would mean that the testatrix intended, by means of an intestacy, to leave the residue of her estate to her sister as her sole surviving heir-at-law, an intention clearly inconsistent with the life interest in the residue and with her stated declaration to dispose of all her estate.

I must therefore conclude that the insertion of the numeral 37 before the words "all the rest and residue of my estate..." was a clerical error which should be deleted to give full effect to the intention of the testatrix. Clause 3(f) provided for 36 "special bequests" in the event that the testatrix's sister had predeceased her. I agree with the appellant that sub-cl. 37 is not a bequest but a disposition of residue which is inconsistent with the rest of the will unless the numeral 37 is deleted completely. A Court of construction is bound to eliminate a numeral which is inconsistent with the general scheme of the will and frustrates the

---

299 (1885), 30 Ch. D. 390 at 394 (C.A.).
300 [1965] S.C.R. 24 at 28-29, 46 D.L.R. (2d) 521 at 524-5 (sub nom. *Re Harmer*).
301 [1914] A.C. 782 at 802.

intention of the testatrix. The learned author of Jarman on Wills,[302] makes it clear[303] that words and limitations may be transposed, supplied or rejected, where warranted by the immediate context, or the general scheme of the will.

In my opinion, if words can be rejected where warranted by the context and scheme of the will, so too can numerals be deleted.[304] It is true that there is no evidence of clerical mistake or oversight as in *Re Raiter*, but the reading of the present will as a whole supports the deletion more clearly than in *Re Raiter*.

There is one further compelling reason to reject the construction of sub-cl. 37 favoured by the Judge of first instance. The words contained in sub-cl. 3(f)(37)(iii) are clearly inconsistent with the introductory words of cl. 3(f). A bequest "if and in the event that my sister...had predeceased me" cannot logically introduce a direction to pay one share of the residue of the estate to the society described if the said society is carrying on specific work at the time of the death of the survivor of the testatrix and her sister. I do not think that it is necessary to resort to the rule of construction that in the event of two conflicting statements within a will, the latter statement prevails.[305] I would prefer to look upon this inconsistency as a further indication of the true intention of the testatrix that the residue of her estate be divided in three equal shares to be paid as directed at the time of the death of the survivor of herself and her sister. This can be achieved by deleting the numeral 37 from cl. 3(f).

. . .

Notes and Questions

1. A testatrix made a will in 1962 by which she devised three parcels of real property, A, B and C, to her son, and a fourth, D, to her daughter. In 1963 she sold parcel B to her son's company. Then, in 1964, she made a new will by which she purported to devise parcels A and B to her son and parcel D to her daughter. As a result, parcel C was undisposed of. Evidence of surrounding circumstances, namely, that the son had always worked on the family farm and had assisted his mother, is available. What result?[306]

2. A testatrix directed that the residue of her estate be divided into three equal shares and paid to her surviving children. When she made her will her three children were alive, but one predeceased her, leaving issue. Normally, because of the statutory anti-lapse provision,[307] the issue would take their deceased parent's share. However there is evidence of surrounding circumstances which shows that the testatrix intended only her two surviving children to take. What result?[308]

---

302 8th ed., 1951.
303 At p. 2071, para. XIX.
304 See *Re Raiter* (1979), 24 O.R. (2d) 633, 99 D.L.R. (3d) 183 (H.C.).
305 Jarman on Wills, p. 2069, para. VII.
306 *Re Ferguson Estate* (1980), 6 Sask. R. 316 (Q.B.).
307 See generally the chapter on Lapse and Survivorship.
308 *Horton v. Horton* (1978), 2 E.T.R. 293, 88 D.L.R. (3d) 264 (B.C.S.C.).

3. If a description in a will is wholly false, so that no object or subject matches it, the description will be rejected and evidence of surrounding circumstances may be admitted to ascertain the subject or object intended by the testator.[309]

Re Dyck Estate[310] illustrates this point. The testator was in receipt of royalty payments from Imperial Oil Ltd., which were paid into an account with the Canada Permanent Trust Co. By his will he disposed of the royalties "payable through the Winnipeg Trust Company." Since there was no such company, the court substituted the name "Canada Permanent Trust Co."[311]

(d) Rejection of Inaccurate Description

The maxim *falsa demonstratio non nocet, cum de corpore constat* permits the rejection of part of a description of an object or subject if part of the description is true and the other false. The false part will be disregarded if the true part describes the subject or object with sufficient certainty. Extrinsic evidence is admissible for this purpose.[312]

Thus, for example, in *Re Whitty*[313] the testator gave a legacy to his "sister Anastasia Cummings." He had no sister who bore that name, but he had a sister named Maria Cummings and a sister named Catherine Kelly to whom he had given a similar legacy. It was thus held that he intended to benefit Maria.

One aspect of the rule is exemplified by the maxim *veritas nominis tollit errorem demonstrationis* (the truth of a name prevails over the error of a reference). Thus, in one case the testator devised property to his wife Caroline. His wife's name was Mary, but he was living with Caroline and had gone through a form of marriage with her. It was held that Caroline was entitled.[314]

A subsidiary rule is *non accipi debent verba in demonstrationem falsam, quae competent in limitationem veram*, that is, words are not accepted as a false reference if they can be read as a true limitation of a general description.

Thus, in one case the testator devised one parcel of three described in a deed identified in the will. He then devised "the balance of the lands and premises in the aforesaid deed," but followed this immediately by a reference to the second parcel. The reference to the second parcel qualified and defined the general statement and could, therefore, not be rejected. Hence, the third parcel did not pass under the devise.[315]

The *falsa demonstratio* doctrine is discussed in *Re Beauchamp*,[316] reproduced below.

---

309 *Re Dyck* (1979), 26 A.R. 85, (sub nom. *Klassen v. Association for Retarded Children*) 11 Alta. L.R. 311 (Q.B.).
310 *Ibid.*
311 See also *Re Jennings* (1982), 41 Nfld. & P.E.I.R. 149, 119 A.P.R. 149 (Nfld. T.D.).
312 *Re Beauchamp* (1975), 8 O.R (2d) 2 at 4-5, 56 D.L.R. (3d) 644 (H.C.).
313 (1899), 30 O.R. 300 (H.C.).
314 *Pratt v. Mathew* (1856), 22 Beav. 328, 52 E.R. 1134.
315 *Re Fletcher* (1914), 31 O.L.R. 633, 19 D.L.R. 624 (C.A.).
316 *Supra.*

RE BEAUCHAMP
(1975), 8 O.R. (2d) 2, 56 D.L.R. (3d) 644
Supreme Court of Ontario
[High Court of Justice]

The will of the testator, Edgar Beauchamp, contained the following devises:

(III) (d) I leave a life estate to my said wife, Rita Beauchamp, in the home farm on Lot Sixteen (16) Concession 14, Township of Tiny, and of the contents therein.

. . .

   (f) I give, devise, and bequeath to my daughter Diane Robitaille the house and buildings on Lot Seventeen (17) Concession Thirteen (13), in the said Township of Tiny together with One (1) Acre of land surrounding the said house and buildings with a frontage of Two Hundred and Ten Feet (210') on the road.
   (g) I give, devise and bequeath to my son Michael Beauchamp the balance of the said Lot Seventeen (17), Concession Thirteen (13) for his own use absolutely.

When he made the will in 1972 the testator owned two parcels of land and lived with his wife on the "home farm" situated on Lot 17, Concession 13. The second parcel was Lot 14, Concession 13 and the testator's daughter, Diane Robitaille lived in a house on that parcel. In 1964 the testator placed the title to the home farm into his and his wife's names as joint tenants. She sold it after his death.

CORY J.:

. . .

The principles upon which a Court should proceed in a case such as this are set out in *Re Butchers*,[317] and may be summarized as follows:

1. Courts of construction have always attempted, where reasonably possible, having regard to the actual wording of the will, to give effect to every devise or bequest mentioned in the will and, in fact, to give some meaning and effect to all of the words in a will. They have leaned against allowing any expression denoting a gift to be totally ineffective or to fail because of misdescription, error in wording, lack of clarity or for any similar reason.

2. A will must be in writing and the intention of the testator should therefore be gathered from the written words expressed in that particular document together with any codicil thereto. It necessarily follows that the consideration of extrinsic evidence to contradict or add to the plain meaning of words used in the will have always been denied by Courts of construction. Such practice would effectively destroy the sanctity and legal effect of the will and would lend itself to all sorts of abuses whereby various witnesses might attempt to give evidence to the testator's intentions apart from or in opposition to his last will as gathered from a whole reading of the whole will.

---

317 [1970] 2 O.R. 589, 11 D.L.R. (3d) 519.

3. There are certain limited occasions when for specific purposes only, extrinsic evidence must be considered in attempting to interpret the testator's intentions as expressed in the will. One of these exceptions is based on the principle that it is the duty of the Court of construction in interpreting a will to put itself as much as possible in the testator's chair. The words of the will must be interpreted not only by a literal reading of it, but the Court must, when reading the will, have a knowledge of the circumstances surrounding the testator at the time of the making of the will and up to and until his decease. This principle applies to descriptions of recipients of the testator's assets and of the assets themselves.

4. There is also the right where there is a latent defect or ambiguity under the principle of *falsa demonstratio non nocet, cum de corpore constat*, to consider extrinsic evidence in order to attempt to resolve the ambiguity. A latent defect is by definition one which does not appear on the face of the will and is one which, therefore, can only be found to exist upon examining the will in the light of surrounding circumstances.

5. The three categories of cases where the principle of *falsa demonstratio* apply are as follows:

   (a) Where an object is described without sufficient certainty in the first place, additional words, which have no application to anything, may be rejected.

   (b) Where there is a complete description and the testator goes on to add words for the purpose of identifying or elaborating a previous description, these words, if consistent with the previous description, may be rejected.

   (c) Where there is one continuous description and there is something answering the part of it and something answering to the other part but the two together are inconsistent, the question is: which are leading words of the description? In the first class of cases under this head there is no repugnancy between the general terms and the particular super-added description; in the second and third class there is a repugnancy between two parts of a description.

It would appear that this is a proper case to consider extrinsic evidence of the circumstances of the testator at the time of the making of the will and up to and until his decease. As noted above, at the relevant times the testator owned only two parcels of land, namely, the "home farm" on Lots [*sic*] 17, Concession 13, in the Township of Tiny, and the other farm property on which was located the house occupied by the testator's daughter, Diane Robitaillie [*sic*], on Lot 14, Concession 13, Township of Tiny.

On looking at the will as a whole there is clearly a defect in cl. III(d). The leading words of that description must be "the home farm" and not the words "Lots [*sic*] 16, Concession 14". The description of "the home farm" is followed by restrictive words that are inconsistent with the prior description, and ought to be disregarded. Counsel for all contending parties agreed that if cl. III(d) was to be interpreted, then the "home farm" must be that parcel on Lot 17, Concession 13 where the testator lived and which he owned as a joint tenant with his wife Rita.

Assuming then, for a moment, rectification of cl. III(d) to have been made, it becomes apparent that the testator possessed only one other parcel of land. This, of course, was the parcel on which the house stood that was occupied by Diane Robitaillie [*sic*]. It would seem illogical to accept that in cl. III(f) the testator was referring to anything other than the remaining parcel of land he owned which would not be described as "the home farm".

In considering cl. III(f), the leading words must be those referring to "the house and buildings...together with one acre of land surrounding the said house and buildings with a frontage of 210 feet on the road", and not the description "Lot 17, Concession 13" which would appear to refer to the home farm.

Clause III(g) is inextricably bound up with cl. III(f). In cl. III(g) the testator bequeathed the balance of the parcel (with the exception of the one acre of land on which stood the house and buildings bequeathed to Diane Robitaillie [*sic*]) to his son Michael Beauchamp. This clause too must refer to the balance of the sole remaining parcel of land belonging to the testator at the time of making the will and at the time of his decease other than the "home farm".

It was submitted that cl. III(f) refers to property owned by the testator at the date of his death and, therefore, no extraneous evidence could be considered to ascertain what the intention of the testator was in using that specific description. To give effect to that argument would preclude both a consideration of the will as a whole and a consideration of the circumstances surrounding the testator at the time of making the will.

> [His Lordship accordingly held that Diane received the house and buildings plus one acre of land of Lot 14, Concession 13, and Michael received the rest of that lot].

Notes and Questions

1. A testatrix devised her house and the lot "on which it stands" to one daughter and the vacant lot to the south of it to another daughter and described the lots by number as well. However, the house encroached in the south lot. Is the *falsa demonstratio* doctrine available to solve the problem?[318]

2. A testator devised a parcel of land (Parcel 1), described as the southeast half of the northeast half of Lot 21, Concession 2, in the Township of Nassagaweya in the County of Halton to his brother and provided that "if the said 50 acre farm" was sold before his death the proceeds should be paid to his brother. The testator did not in fact own Parcel 1. He did own Parcel 2, an adjacent 50 acre farm which could be described as the northwest half of Lot 21, Concession 2. He had also formerly owned Parcels 3 and 4, adjacent to parcel 2, but these were sold before he made his will. Together, parcels 2, 3 and 4 had formed a 150 acre farm. Parcel 2 was not specifically disposed of by the will. Is the brother entitled to parcel 2?[319]

3. A testator devised "all my property...in Upper Blackville N.B. along the Howard Road, being on the north side of the Miramichi river..." to X. The testator owned a house on Howard Road on the north side of the river, but he also owned 150 acres south of the

318 See *Re Davidson* (1979), 25 O.R. 534, 101 D.L.R. (3d) 372 (H.C.).
319 See *Re Cargill* (1977), 17 O.R. (2d) 216, 1 E.T.R. 24, 79 D.L.R. (3d) 726 (H.C.).

river in the same municipality. Can the phrase "along the Howard Road, being on the north side of the Miramichi river..." be treated as an inaccurate description?[320]

4. Sometimes the *falsa demonstratio* doctrine can be used to create a latent ambiguity. This is shown by *In the Estate of Hubbock*.[321] The testator created a patent ambiguity by a gift "to my granddaughter   ." Direct evidence of his intention would not be admissible to fill in the blank. However, since the testator had three granddaughters, the court rejected the blank, so that the description was then equally applicable to all the granddaughters and direct evidence to the effect that the testator intended to benefit the eldest was admitted.

5. The testator devised the "East Half Sec. 4-53-11-W3rd," the "West Half Sec. 3-53-11-W3rd," and the "N.W. Quarter Sec. 3-53-11-W3rd" of his farm lands to his nephew. Consequently, he purported to dispose of the N.W. Quarter of section 3-53-11-W3rd twice. The testator also owned the N.E. Quarter of section 3-53-11-W3rd, but failed to devise it specifically, although the will did contain a residuary clause. The solicitor who drafted the will deposed that the testator had intended to devise all three parcels of his farm lands to his nephew. He submitted that the reference to the "northwest" rather than the "northeast" quarter was the result of a typographical or clerical error or misdirection. What result? Is the solicitor's extrinsic evidence admissible?[322]

---

320 See *Vickers v. Arbeau Estate* (1988), 31 E.T.R. 154 (N.B.Q.B.), affirmed (1990) 111 N.B.R. (2d) 124 (C.A.).
321 [1905] P. 129.
322 See *Re Phillips Estate* (1987), 27 E.T.R. 107 (Sask. Surr. Ct.).

11

TESTAMENTARY GIFTS

1. SCOPE OF THIS CHAPTER

In the previous chapter we discussed the general principles, rules of construction and major approaches to the interpretation of wills. In that context, we touched upon aspects of interpretation as they concern the property disposed of under wills. In this chapter we examine the principles of construction as they affect the disposition of property in greater detail.

First, we discuss the subject matter of testamentary gifts, that is, what a testator may dispose of by will. Then we discuss the several types of testamentary gift, followed by the rules of abatement and ademption. This is followed by a discussion of the statutory rule that a will is apt to dispose of all property owned by the testator at death that satisfies the description of the property in the will. Thereafter, we deal with the problems concerning the testamentary disposition of property sold, given away, or destroyed before death. Next we discuss the equitable rules of election and satisfaction and the rule against double portions. The chapter concludes with a consideration of the right of disclaimer.

Further Reading

Williams on Wills, 7th ed. by C.H. Sherrin, R.F.D. Barlow and R.A. Wallington, assisted by Suzannah L. Meadway (London: Butterworths, 1995), cc. 30-32, 37, 38, 41-44, 46, 59-64.

Mellows: The Law of Succession, 5th ed. by Clive V. Margrave-Jones (London: Butterworth & Co. (Publishers) Ltd., 1993), chapters 11, 31-33.

2. THE SUBJECT MATTER OF TESTAMENTARY GIFTS

What can a testator dispose of by will? The simple answer to this question is, anything he or she owns. However, that is inexact, because certain property that the testator owns ceases at death. Thus, for example, a testator cannot dispose of an interest in joint tenancy. While the testator owned it during his or her life, it ends at death and the interest passes to the surviving joint tenant or tenants. Similarly, if a testator is the owner of a life estate, the estate ends at death and the property then passes to the next person entitled in remainder or reversion. Yet another example is property in which the testator has a contingent interest and the contingency is personal to the testator. Thus, for example, if the testatrix was given Blackacre "when she marries" and she dies unmarried, she is unable to dispose of the property by his will. On the other hand, if the gift was to the testatrix "when John completes his book" and John, not yet having completed his book, is still living at the testatrix's death, the testatrix can dispose of the (as yet) contingent interest.

Clearly, a testator cannot dispose of more than he or she owns. This is illustrated by *Cherry v. Cherry Estate*.[1] A mother owned a home which was situate on an 80 hectare parcel of land. She and her two sons each owned a one-third interest in the parcel. By her will she left "any private dwelling owned by me at my death" to one of her sons. The court held that the son was entitled to the house and a four hectare parcel necessary to subdivide it out of the larger parcel.

It is important to note that a testator can only dispose of an interest in property. The interest must exist at the time of the testator's death, but it may be either a vested interest or a contingent (but continuing) interest. However, what the testator may not do is dispose of an expectancy or, as it is often referred to, a *spes successionis*. An expectancy is something that the testator hopes to receive but may not. The typical example of an expectancy is the hope of inheriting certain property. A child usually hopes to inherit some or all of his or her parents' property, either under their wills or on their intestacies. But the child has no right to the property and can, therefore, not count on receiving it. Thus, if the child dies before the parents, the child is unable to dispose of the expectancy.

In *Weinstein v. Weinstein (Litigation Guardian of)*[2] the court failed to appreciate and apply this very basic principle. Mrs. Weinstein had made an *inter vivos* trust which provided that on her death the corpus was to be paid to her estate to be distributed in accordance with her will. Her will left the residue of her estate equally to her grandchildren. She developed Alzheimer's disease and was placed in a nursing home. Her husband then made an application for an order equalizing their respective net family properties under the *Family Law Act*.[3] The court made

---

1 (1999), 26 E.T.R. (2d) 88 (B.C.S.C.).

2 (1997), 35 O.R. (3d) 229, 19 E.T.R. (2d) 52, 30 R.F.L. (4th) 116 (Ont. Gen. Div.). See Albert H. Oosterhoff, "Great Expectations: Spes Successionis" (1998), 17 E.T. & P.J. 181. An appeal of the decision to the Divisional Court was settled by the parties on June 29, 1999 (see Albert H. Oosterhoff, Comment (2000), 19 E.T. & P.J. 257, footnote 2).

3 R.S.O. 1990, c. F.3.

the order, which declared that Mr. Weinstein had a 50 percent interest in Mrs. Weinstein's trust and directed the trustees to pay one-half of the trust's assets to Mr. Weinstein. Mr. Weinstein then made a will in which he left legacies to his daughter and each of his five grandchildren and the residue to a charity. When he died, followed a year later by his wife, two of his grandchildren brought a motion to set aside the equalization order. Sheard J. granted the motion. In his opinion, the fact that Mrs. Weinstein lacked the mental competence to change her will meant that her will "in practical terms conferred on them what amounted to a vested interest. The grandchildren's entitlement was not a mere hope of succession. The result of [Mrs. Weinstein's] becoming afflicted by Alzheimer's disease was that the entitlement of her grandchildren was the same as if they were entitled to a remainder interest after life interests." Amazingly, his Honour said this despite an English case that was cited to him which clearly restated the principle that a beneficiary under a will has no interest in the property given by the will, but only a hope of succeeding to it, even if the testator is *in articulo mortis*.[4]

The *Weinstein* case may be contrasted with *Del Grande (Litigation Guardian of) v. Sebastian*.[5] Mrs. Del Grande was incapable of managing her affairs and Mrs. Sebastian, one of her daughter's, had been her attorney. However, the Public Guardian and Trustee was appointed statutory guardian and she obtained an order directing Mrs. Sebastian to pass her accounts. Mrs. Sebastian and the Public Guardian and Trustee reached a settlement on the issue whether the conveyance of a residential property to Mrs. Sebastian had been procured by undue influence. Mrs. Nicholson, another daughter, who had been granted intervenor status and who was the sole beneficiary under her mother's will, opposed the settlement and did not consent to it. On a motion for directions to determine whether Mrs. Nicholson's consent had the power to veto the settlement, Cullity J. held that she did not. Mrs. Nicholson was simply a beneficiary under her mother's will and, as such, she had no interest in the property being disposed of by the will until her mother died. Consequently, she had no property interest in the subject matter of the proceedings. The case, thus, reaffirmed the long standing rule that a beneficiary under a will only has an expectancy while the testator lives and that an expectancy is not property.

3. TYPES OF TESTAMENTARY GIFT

(a) Generally

We have seen[6] that, historically, three types of testamentary gift have been recognized, namely devises, which are gifts of real property, bequests, which are

---

4 That is, at the point of death. See *Re Midleton's Will Trusts; Whitehead v. Midleton (Earl)*, [1969] 1 Ch. 600 at 608.

5 (1999), 27 E.T.R. (2d) 295 (Ont. S.C.J.). See Albert H. Oosterhoff, Comment (2000), 19 E.T. & P.J. 257.

6 In chapter 1.

gifts of personalty, and legacies, which are gifts of money or money equivalents. Although the distinctions are not as important as before, they remain relevant in minor respects.

Legacies, bequests and devises are classified into four broad categories or types, mainly to assist the court in deciding whether or not a gift of property which has either ceased to exist in whole or in part, or which has come into existence since the will was made, should be effective. The four main classes are specific, general, demonstrative and residuary gifts. In addition, the cases often speak of a pecuniary legacy, that is, a gift of money, as distinct from a general legacy, which is a gift of property not specifically defined, such as stocks.

The distinction between these types of gift is important, in that it determines the order in which the property is available to pay the testator's debts and in that it decides whether a gift adeems or abates. A specific gift adeems when its subject matter is not in the estate at the testator's death. In that situation, subject to the will and to any statutory provisions to the contrary, the beneficiary will receive nothing. Abatement is the *pro rata* reduction of gifts when there are insufficient funds in the estate to pay the debts and gifts in full.

You should note that the above classification is somewhat inexact in respect of land and, hence, of devises. Formerly, devises were always thought of as specific, but today a devise can be general, specific or residuary.[7] It cannot be demonstrative.

Whether a gift is general, pecuniary, specific, demonstrative, or residuary, depends upon the intention of the testator as determined in part by the principles and rules of construction described in this chapter.

(b) General and Pecuniary Gifts

A general legacy is one payable out of the general assets of the estate. Thus, it is not a gift of an identified article owned by the testator, nor is it a direction to pay moneys out of a specific fund. Rather, it is a direction to the personal representatives to pay or transfer the assets described to the legatee.

A pecuniary legacy is a gift of money payable out of the general assets of the estate. A bequest of shares is *prima facie* general, as appears from *Re Millar*,[8] reproduced below.

RE MILLAR
60 O.L.R. 434, [1927] 3 D.L.R. 270
Supreme Court of Ontario
[Weekly Court]

The testator, Charles Millar, a Toronto lawyer, made the following gift by his will:

---

7 *Re Ridley; Nicholson v. Nicholson*, [1950] Ch. 415 at 421, [1950] 2 All E.R. 1.
8 60 O.L.R. 434, [1927] 3 D.L.R. 270 (C.A.).

> To each Protestant Minister exercising his clerical functions at an annual salary and resident in Toronto at the time of my death and to each Orange Lodge in Toronto I give one share of the O'Keefe Brewery Company of Toronto Limited.

The company named in the will had been incorporated in Ontario in 1892 with a share capital comprising preferred and common stock. After the will was made and before the testator's death, the company sold its assets to O'Keefe's Beverages Limited, a federally incorporated company in return for shares in the latter and the Ontario company changed its name to O'Keefe's Holding Company Limited. The latter, as the court found, was the company meant by the provision in the will. (The testator held an interest, through another holding company, in the federally incorporated company, but that was not in issue).

The shares of O'Keefe's Holding Company Limited were held by four persons when the testator died. The shares were not on the market, none having been sold for years. The testator did not own any of the shares.

The executors brought this application to construe the will.

MIDDLETON J.A.

. . .

The gift of these shares is thus seen to be a general legacy as distinguished from a special legacy.

If the clause quoted is alone looked at, the same result is reached.

> A gift of...shares of a particular description - if there is nothing on the face of the will to shew that the testator is referring to shares belonging to him - is a general legacy, though he may in fact possess the shares in question.[9]

A homely illustration may serve to make the situation plain - a testator directs his executors to give a watch to each of his twenty grandchildren. He may have a watch or he may have none, it is not likely that he has twenty, but this does not affect his gift. The duty is cast upon the executors of purchasing a watch for each grandchild.

To use the words of Lord Justice Kay in *In re Gray*,[10]

> ...a general legacy of this kind amounts in effect to a direction to the testator's executors to buy the shares or other property designated...if the legatee had a choice in the matter and said that he would rather not have shares, he would then take the amount of money which would have had to be expended in buying them.

In the case before Lord Justice Kay this principle could not be applied because the shares had ceased to be — and so no present value could be attached to them. That is not the case here — the shares exist and have a value — it may not be easy to ascertain value, but, as in all such matters, mere difficulty is of no importance, the value must be ascertained as nearly as may be.

---

9 Theobald on Wills, 7th ed., p. 148.
10 (1887), 36 Ch. D. 205, 211.

When it is said that the shares are not for sale, I understand that they are not for sale at a price which represents their value.

When shares that are usually bought and sold on the market are given, the money equivalent is the market price, and this the legatee may have. Nothing would be gained by the purchase by the executor at the market price and the transfer to the legatee of the shares bought, which he could elect to sell at once for the market price. The market price and value are identical.

But, when the thing given is not on the market, the actual value must be ascertained as nearly as possible. The owner who does not wish to sell may be induced to sell by the offer of some fancy price far in excess of the real value. This fancy price is not that which the legatee can demand.

A difficulty was suggested upon the argument by reason of there being two kinds of stock. It was said that this made the gift void for uncertainty. I do not think so. They may buy either preference or common as they think best in the interest of the estate, i.e., in the interest of the residuary legatee. The legatee cannot complain, because he is given no choice. What is offered to him is in compliance with the will.

To recur to my homely illustration. There are many kinds of watches — gold watches and silver watches, cheap watches and expensive watches. The grandchild cannot complain so long as he gets a watch. The executors are given a discretion, and when it is honestly exercised it is final.

. . .

Notes and Questions

1. For a case dealing with another aspect of Charles Millar's will, see *Re Millar*.[11]

2. As is apparent from *Re Millar*, if the testator does not own the assets disposed of by a general legacy, the legacy is, in effect, a direction to the personal representatives to acquire the assets, if they are available, and to give them to the legatee, unless the latter wishes to have the value of the assets instead.

3. As indicated in *Re Millar*, a legacy of stock is *prima facie* general. The presumption is not rebutted merely because the testator possessed the precise amount of stock or shares specified at the date of the will.[12]

> *Prima facie* a legacy of stock or of share is general, notwithstanding that the testator at the date of the will possessed the precise amount of stock or the precise number of shares. This rule, however, only furnishes a general guide to the construction of such bequests and necessarily yields to any other indications of the testator's intention appearing from the language used in his will, construed with reference to such circumstances as may legitimately be taken into account in arriving at its true meaning.[13]

Thus, in *Re Willcocks*[14] the testatrix bequeathed £948 3s. 11d. Queensland $3\frac{1}{2}\%$ inscribed stock to her father and £613 18s. 11d. Victoria $3\frac{1}{2}\%$ consolidated stock and £300

---

11 [1938] O.R. 188, [1938] 1 D.L.R. 65 (S.C.C.), reproduced earlier in this book.
12 *Re Willcocks*, [1921] 2 Ch. 327.
13 *Re Hawkins* (1922), 91 L.J. Ch. 486 at 488-9, *per* Lawrence J.
14 *Supra*.

Queensland 3% stock to her mother. When the testatrix made her will, she owned the exact amount of stock which she bequeathed to her parents. However, she later sold the stock and invested the proceeds in real estate. If the legacies were specific, they would have adeemed. But the court held that they were general only. The fact that the testatrix, in giving the residue of her estate to her husband, described it as "the remainder of *my* real and personal estate", did not show a contrary intention, since that is a typical expression used in the disposition of residue.

4. The context of the will and admissible evidence may show that the bequest was intended to take the form of a specific bequest.[15]

In *Re McLean; Larlee v. Earle*[16] the testator owned a substantial block of class A and class B shares in a limited company. By his will he made several individual bequests of those shares and then he bequeathed "the balance of my class B stock" in the Company. The individual bequests were not preceded by the possessive pronoun "my" and there was no disposition of the remaining class A shares. The court held that the use of the pronoun "my" rendered the bequest of the class B shares specific. It held, moreover, that it was unlikely that the testator intended one gift to be specific and one general. Hence, the bequests of the class A shares were also held to be specific. The result was that the bequests adeemed, since the testator had sold the shares before his death.

5. A direction to the executors to purchase an annuity for a beneficiary is normally a general legacy and the annuitant is entitled to demand that the money be paid to him or her instead. The fact that the testator provided that the annuitant may not have the value of the annuity in lieu is irrelevant and so is the fact that the testator provided for a gift over to the issue of the annuitant if he or she should die before all the benefits under the annuity are paid.[17]

The main exception to the general rule is that if the testator directs the trustees to purchase a Government of Canada annuity, the annuitant is required to take the annuity, since the *Government Annuities Act*[18] makes the property in an annuity purchased thereunder and the benefits arising therefrom inalienable.[19]

6. A gift of money in a named bank account, such as "my account in the Bank of Montreal" is a general legacy,[20] whereas a gift of a specific account, such as "my account no. 3789-271 in the Bank of Montreal at King and Bay Streets, Toronto" is a specific gift.[21] If the money is withdrawn from the account, the specific gift adeems, but not if the money is redeposited in another branch of the same or a different bank, unless it is put in a different name, such as a joint account.[22]

A gift of money to come from, or payable out of a particular account is a demonstrative legacy.[23]

---

15 See *e.g.*, *Re McLean* (1969), 1 N.B.R. (2d) 500, (sub nom. *Larlee v. Earle*) 4 D.L.R. 617 (C.A.); *Re Tetsall*, [1961] 1 W.L.R. 938, [1961] 2 All E.R. 801; *Re Rose*, [1949] Ch. 78, [1948] 2 All E.R. 971; *Re Fisher* (1924), 26 O.W.N. 295 (H.C.); *Re O'Connor*, [1948] Ch. 628, [1948] 2 All E.R. 270.

16 *Supra.*

17 *Lotzkar v. McLean* (1979), 15 B.C.L.R. 259, 6 E.T.R. 245 (S.C.).

18 R.S.C. 1970, c. G-6, s. 10(1) [not subsequently consolidated].

19 *Re Boxall; Jensen and Cunningham v. Wutzky*, [1946] 3 W.W.R. 413, [1947] 1 D.L.R. 66 (Sask. C.A.).

20 *Re Heilbronner*, [1953] 1 W.L.R. 1254, [1953] 2 All E.R. 1016.

21 *Re Ashdown*, [1943] O.W.N. 425, [1943] 4 D.L.R. 517 (C.A.).

22 *Ibid.* And see *Re Puczka* (1970), 73 W.W.R. 56, 10 D.L.R. (3d) 339 (Sask. Q.B.); *Re Brekken; Penn v. Burtness* (1977), 4 B.C.L.R. 211 (S.C.).

23 *Re Atkins* (1912), 3 O.W.N. 665, 21 O.W.R. 238, 3 D.L.R. 180 (H.C.).

(c) Demonstrative Gifts

A demonstrative gift is a gift of a specified amount or quantity which is directed to be satisfied *primarily* out of a particular fund or asset. A demonstrative legacy is treated as a specific legacy to the extent that it does not abate if the fund out of which it is payable is adequate to satisfy it, until the estate out of which the general legacies are payable is exhausted. If, however, the fund out of which the demonstrative legacy is payable has ceased to exist, the gift does not adeem, but is treated as a general legacy.[24] If the gift is to be paid *solely* out of a fund, it is a specific legacy.[25]

Re Webster; Goss v. Webster,[26] reproduced below, discusses the difference between specific and demonstrative legacies.

RE WEBSTER; GOSS v. WEBSTER
[1937] 1 All E.R. 602
Court of Appeal

The testator bequeathed the sum of £3,000 to his eldest son, "to be paid to him out of the share of my capital and loans in the business of Webster & Bullock." He directed that, provided his son should, within six months of the testator's death, be accepted by the remaining partners in the business as a partner, the legacy should not be withdrawn by the son until after the expiration of 12 months from the date of the testator's death.

The testator had been a partner in the firm. The partnership agreement provided that on the death or retirement of a partner, no allowance should be made to him or his estate for goodwill, but that otherwise the value of his share should be calculated in the usual way. The remaining partners had the right to liquidate the share of a retiring or deceased partner and to pay it in four equal quarterly instalments with interest at 5 per cent. In fact the testator owed about £2,000 to the firm. Moreover, it was possible that his interest did not amount to £3,000 and might amount to nothing at all.

On an application to construe the will, the judge at first instance held that the gift was specific. The son appealed.

LORD WRIGHT M.R.:

. . .

That being so [that is, that the testator's interest might be less than £3,000], the question has been raised whether the bequest is a demonstrative or a specific gift. Whether that is so is to be determined on a construction of the clause, with such help as any other part of the will may afford, and, in this case, the gift appears to me to be non-existent, but the clause has to be read as a whole. It may be convenient

---

24 *Walford v. Walford*, [1912] A.C. 658, [1911-13] All E.R. Rep. 950 (H.L.); *Re Tomlin*, [1945] O.W.N. 589 (H.C.); *Re Atkins, supra; Day v. Harris* (1882), 1 O.R. 147.

25 *Culbertson v. Culbertson* (1967), 60 W.W.R. 187, 62 D.L.R. (2d) 134 (Sask. C.A.).

26 [1937] 1 All E.R. 602 (C.A.).

here to refer to the judgment of SIR WILLIAM PAGE WOOD, V-C., in the case of *Paget v. Huish*.[27]

> These are, therefore, the three classes of gifts: First, a general gift, in which no special fund is pointed at for payment; secondly, a specific gift out of a particular fund alone; and, thirdly, a gift where a particular fund is pointed out as primarily applicable, but where the gift is not to fail by the failure of the particular fund. In this case I think there is a clear intention that the gift should take effect in any event, because, after bequeathing several legacies, the testator proceeds thus: "I give and devise the following annuities," specifying them, and then adds a declaration that these annuities shall be paid by the trustees out of the rents of the real estate thereby devised. Subsequently, there is a gift to the trustees of all the real estate and the residuary personal estate, upon trust, out of the rents of the realty to pay the annuities, and subject thereto to apply the real and residuary personal estate upon certain specified trusts. All this appears to me only to show that the testator, after making a positive gift, points out the particular fund which he desires to have first applied, and which he supposes to be adequate for the purpose. It is clear that he preferred that the gift should be satisfied out of the realty rather than the personalty; but the question now is, whether he preferred that it should fail altogether rather than be thrown upon the personalty. I think...that there is no indication of an intention that the gift was to fail on failure of the real estate.

Applying that here, I ask myself whether there is an indication of an intention that the gift was to fail on failure or insufficiency of the partnership interest. Now, the first words, "I bequeath to the said Frank Eric Webster the sum of £3,000," are, in themselves, obviously appropriate only to a specific gift. Then come the words:

> to be paid to him out of the share of my capital and loans account in the business of Webster & Bullock....

These words ought, I think, to be construed as meaning "to be paid to him primarily out of the share," and not as meaning "to be paid to him only out of the share of the capital and loans." That is very much on the same lines as the view expressed by PAGE WOOD, V-C., in the case to which I have just referred.

So far, I should think, and this was what the learned judge also thought, that the gift is clearly a demonstrative legacy. Then comes the remainder of the clause which I have read. Now, that does not, in my judgment, change the character of the gift; it provides for what is to happen in a particular contingency, which may or may not occur; in fact, it did not occur, but, if that contingency had occurred, then the payment of the legacy, or some part of it, might have to be postponed. In so far as it was to be paid only by being withdrawn from the partnership assets, it was to remain there until after the expiration of 12 months from the date of the death. That means that it was for the benefit of the partnership, and to that extent for the benefit of the son, because it only applies if he becomes a partner; and it would mean that, instead of the testator's interest being paid out in four quarterly instalments, it should remain unaffected for the whole period of 12 months. But, in my opinion, the addition of the purely conditional and hypothetical clause does

---

27 (1863), 1 Hem. & M. 663, at 671.

not change the character of the original words, which are clearly words appropriate to making a demonstrative gift.

[The concurring opinions of Romer and Greene L.JJ., have been omitted.]

Notes and Questions

1. For a Canadian case very similar to *Webster*, see *Day v. Harris*.[28]

2. A testator directed the payment of a legacy of $10,000 to be paid to his son out of the estate left to him by his mother. The testator had an absolute vested interest in the residue of his mother's estate, subject only to a life interest held by his father. What kind of legacy has the son been given?[29]

3. A legacy of $5,000 to be paid out of the proceeds of the sal of a farm which the testator directed to be sold is a demonstrative legacy. Hence, if the sale realizes less than the amount of the legacy, the legatee ranks with the general legatees for the balance of the $5,000.[30]

4. A testator directed his trustees "to hold in trust $15,000 of par value of the capital stock" of a certain company in which he was the largest shareholder and to pay the income thereon to his wife. This was followed immediately by a direction "to make over and assign" to the testator's adopted son "$10,000 worth of capital stock" of the same company.

The company had an issued capital of 250 shares of $100 par value each. The testator or his nominees owned 224 and his adopted son the other 26. Hence, unless further shares were issued (the authorized capital of the company being 500 shares), the testator held less than $25,000 (the total of the two gifts) par value of the company stock. At the testator's death, the paper value of the stock was $40.

Is the son's legacy specific, demonstrative or general? Depending upon the answer to that question, what is the son entitled to receive?[31]

(d) Specific Gifts

A specific testamentary gift is a gift of an identifiable property or object which the testator has described with sufficient particularity to distinguish it from his or her general estate. The fact that the testator did not own the asset described when he or she made the will does not make it a general gift.

A specific legacy is subject to ademption. That is, if the specific property given by will no longer exists at the testator's death, because it has been destroyed, sold, given away, or has otherwise disappeared, the subject matter of the gift is gone and the beneficiary receives nothing.[32] This rule has, however, been modified by statute in some jurisdictions and the implications of the statutory change will be discussed later in this chapter.

---

28 (1882), 1 O.R. 147.
29 See *Walford v. Walford*, [1912] A.C. 658.
30 See *Re Tomlin*, [1945] O.W.N. 589 H.C..
31 See *Re Warren* (1924), 54 O.L.R. 433 (H.C.). And see *Collins v. Collins* (1981), 34 Nfld. & P.E.I.R. 313, 95 A.P.R. 313 (Nfld. T.D.).
32 *Mountain v. Mountain* (1937) 12 M.P.R. 87 (P.E.I.); *Re Ross*, [1976] 3 W.W.R. 465 (B.C.S.C.)

A specific gift does not abate until the residue and the general estate out of which the general and, if necessary, the demonstrative legacies are to be paid, is exhausted.[33]

Culbertson and Culbertson v. Culbertson and Bieber,[34] reproduced below, discusses the distinction between specific and demonstrative gifts and what happens when the property which is the subject matter of a specific gift has ceased to exist.

Further Reading

Ralph E. Scane, "Specific Gifts: Some Problem Areas" (1982-84), 6 E. & T.Q. 217.

CULBERTSON v. CULBERTSON
(1967), 60 W.W.R. 187, 62 D.L.R. (2d) 134
Saskatchewan Court of Appeal

The testator gave 31 legacies in varying amounts to certain named persons and charitable organizations, totalling $24,750. These bequests were followed by this clause:

> I direct that each of the above legacies shall be paid out of the money realized from the sale of my farm lands and if the amount recovered from the sale of my farm lands should not be sufficient to cover the full amount of the said legacies, then each person shall take a proportionate share in accordance with the amount he would have received if the full amount of the legacies had been realized.

The testator owned 850 acres of farm land when he made his will, but sold them before he died under an instalment contract on which slightly more than $9,000 remained payable at his death. The proceeds received by the testator were deposited in his bank account with other moneys and, as a result of various deposits and withdrawals, had lost their identity.

The trial judge held that the legacies were demonstrative and that, the fund being insufficient to pay them in full, the legatees were entitled to receive the balance from the general assets of the estate. The residuary beneficiaries appealed.

MAGUIRE J.A., delivered the judgment of the court:

. . .

I think it is clear that if a bequest, general in form, but...in the nature of a specific legacy relating to a particular fund for payment, is to be declared a demonstrative legacy, the will must disclose: (1) That recourse for payment of the legacy is first to the fund; and (2) There is no expressed intention of the

---

33 *Lindsay v. Waldbrook* (1897), 24 O.A.R. 604; *Page v. Leapingwell* (1812), 18 Ves. 463, 34 E.R. 392.
34 (1967), 60 W.W.R. 187, 62 D.L.R. (2d) 134 (Sask. C.A.).

testator precluding satisfaction of the legacy out of some other property of the testator, if the particular fund proves inadequate.

. . .

With every deference to the learned chambers judge, I am of the opinion that the language used by the testator, given its natural and ordinary meaning, limits the payment of the legacies to the fund to be realized from the sale of his farm lands. To place upon the words of the testator an interpretation that he intended the legacies to take effect out of some other of his property if the fund proves inadequate would, in my opinion, defeat entirely his direct and specific instructions that the legacies abate if the fund should be deficient. In my view, by reading the two paragraphs together and giving to the language there its natural and ordinary meaning, the legacies constitute a bequest of the specific fund to be realized from the sale of the testator's farm lands to the amount of the bequests: If the fund should be deficient, the legacies would abate; if the fund exceeds the amount of the legacies, the excess would fall into residue. While the courts do not favour construing a bequest or devise in a will, as being specific when there is doubt, recourse cannot be taken to this rule of construction when, from the language of the will, the intention of the testator can be determined.

Payment of these legacies may, therefore, be made only from the fund designated by the testator. The portion of the sale proceeds received by the testator in his lifetime, having lost identity as such proceeds and thus as part of the designated fund, there remains only the balance of the sale price of the lands remaining payable at the testator's death, namely, $9,288.75, which may constitute the fund.

The further question remains, namely, whether the sale of these farm lands by the testator in his lifetime, adeemed all the legacies in question.

> [His Lordship held that, as the gift was not of the farm, but rather of the proceeds of its sale, there was no ademption, since the proceeds still existed to the extent that moneys remained payable under the instalment contract.]

The appeal is, therefore, allowed. The will is interpreted and construed as herein set forth. The 31 legacies referred to are payable out of the balance of said sale price of the farm lands, remaining payable at the death of the testator, and each shall abate, *pari passu*, as required.

. . .

Notes and Questions

1. Since a specific legacy is some property which has been identified with particularity to distinguish it from the general estate, a bequest of a bank savings certificate, identified by number and face value is specific. Hence, if the testator has cashed it, it adeems, even though he or she has replaced it with another certificate.[35]

---

35 *Re Hubert* (1975), 13 N.B.R. (2d) 257 (Q.B.).

2. The addition of the word "my" or similar possessive pronoun normally suggests that the gift is specific. Thus, a gift of "my piano" is specific.[36] Similarly, a gift of "my stock" is specific and not general.[37]

3. A direction by the testator to sell certain specific property and to pay a number of legacies out of the proceeds is normally a specific gift, unless the legacies are not payable solely out of the fund (in which case it would be demonstrative).[38] If aliquot portions of the fund or specific amounts are given to named legatees and the testator then purports to give any balance remaining in the fund to other legatees, the gifts to the latter are general.[39]

4. It is obvious that in order to be effective, a specific gift must describe the property correctly. Thus, for example, if a testator owns the majority of the shares in a family farming corporation but purports to devise "my farm" by his will, the gift is ineffective.[40] On the other hand, if the gift is a right of first refusal to purchase the testator's farm, but the mechanism to determine the value is defective, the court will substitute a workable mechanism.[41]

(e) Residuary Gifts

A gift of residue is a gift of that part of the testator's estate which he or she has not specifically disposed of. Hence, it includes all his or her property after pecuniary, general, demonstrative and specific gifts are satisfied. Gifts such as "the balance of my estate"[42] and "the rest of my estate"[43] are typical residuary gifts. So is a gift of "all my property," if no other gifts have been made.[44] A more restricted gift of residue such as "all the rest and residue of my estate, consisting of money, promissory note or notes, vehicles and implements" may be held to pass other property as well, such as a lapsed gift of real property, if the context supports such a construction.[45]

It sometimes happens that there is more than one residuary clause in the will. It may be clear, after construction, that one of them is intended to refer to the residue of certain property after specific gifts of that property have been satisfied and that the other is the general residuary gift. If so, effect will be given to the testator's intention.[46] However, if that construction is not possible, with the result that the two clauses are inconsistent, the last will be preferred as representing the

---

36 *Re Sikes*, [1927] 1 Ch. 364.
37 *Re McLean* (1969), 1 N.B.R. (2d) 500, (sub nom. *Larlee v. Earle*) 4 D.L.R. 617 (C.A.).
38 *Page v. Leapingwell* (1812), 18 Ves. 463, 34 E.R. 392; *Lindsay v. Waldbrook* (1897), 24 O.A.R. 604.
39 *Ibid.*
40 See *Re Lewis's Will Trusts, Lewis v. Williams*, [1984] 3 All E.R. 930.
41 See *Re Malpass (decd)*, [1984] 2 All E.R. 313.
42 *Re Lindsay* (1923), 25 O.W.N. 318.
43 *Re Achterberg* (1914), 5 O.W.N. 755.
44 *Hicks v. Snider* (1879), 44 U.C.Q.B. 486 (C.A.).
45 *Re Farrell* (1906), 12 O.L.R. 580. For a case in which the context did not permit such a construction, see *Re Brems*, [1963] 1 O.R. 122, 36 D.L.R. (2d) 218 (H.C.).
46 *Re Iverson*, [1950] 2 W.W.R. 1021 (Alta. T.D.).

final intention of the testator.[47] But, if a gift of residue lapses, the first gift will be preferred, since the lapsed gift will then fall into the ultimate gift of residue.[48]

Not only does all property which has not been specifically disposed of pass under a gift of residue, all specific gifts which fail because of lapse (that is, if the beneficiary predeceases the testator), perpetuities, the operation of the statutory restraints on alienation, or for any other reason, fall into residue,[49] in the absence of a contrary intention.

If the entire gift of residue fails, the property comprised in it passes on an intestacy. However, the courts are apt to apply the presumption against intestacy, if the will permits it, to prevent this from occurring.[50]

If part of a gift of residue fails, it goes out on an intestacy,[51] but here, again, the court may discern an intention on the part of the testator to dispose of his or her entire estate. Thus, if a testator purports to dispose of the entire residue by dividing it among a number of persons in stated proportions, but the proportions do not add up to a whole, there will not be an intestacy.[52] This is also the case if the testator purports to dispose of the entire residue among several persons and then provides that if any predecease the testator, that beneficiary's share shall fall back into residue.[53]

Notes and Questions

1. *Re Knight*[54] illustrates one aspect of the foregoing. The testator gave certain legacies and annuities, but he provided that if his estate should not be sufficient to pay them, they should be paid in a specific order, the first being the establishment of a trust fund of $25,000. The income on that fund was to be paid to his wife and after her death the capital was to fall into residue. The testator's son was entitled to the residue. The estate was sufficient to establish the $25,000 trust fund, but was insufficient to pay all of the other legacies and annuities. After the widow's death, the son claimed to be entitled to that sum. However, the court held that it did not form part of the residue but was available to pay the other legacies and annuities in accordance with the priorities set out in the will.[55]

2. A testator directed his trustees to divide the residue of his estate into 100 units. Then he disposed of 55 of the units, but failed to deal with the other 45. Later in the will he directed that if he had not disposed of all things to be disposed of, such things should fall into and form part of the residue. Is there an intestacy with respect to the 45 units?[56]

47 *Re Nolan* (1917), 40 O.L.R. 355.
48 *Ibid.*
49 *Re Smith* (1904), 7 O.L.R. 619; *Re Grenier* (1917), 12 O.W.N. 362.
50 *Re Archer* (1924), 27 O.W.N. 324; *Re Bingley* (1952), 7 W.W.R. (N.S.) 507 (Man Q.B.); *Re McKittrick*, [1933] 3 W.W.R. 536, 41 Man. R. 454, [1934] 1 D.L.R. 422 (C.A.).
51 *Re Walmsley* (1919), 15 O.W.N. 436; *Re East* (1923), 24 O.W.N. 394.
52 *Re Wilson's Will; Wood v. Wilson* (1935), 9 M.P.R. 572 (N.B.S.C.); *Re McArthur* (1952), 7 W.W.R. (N.S.) 182 (Alta. T.D.).
53 *Re Hanna*, [1937] O.W.N. 517; *Re Woodman; Patterson v. Nase* (1925), 52 N.B.R. 255.
54 [1938] O.W.N. 77, [1938] 1 D.L.R. 677 (C.A.).
55 See also *Re Rosar* (1975), 9 O.R. (2d) 447, 60 D.L.R. (3d) 615 (H.C.).
56 See *Sarkin v. Sarkin Estate* (1989), 36 E.T.R. 139 (B.C.S.C.).

4. ABATEMENT

Before any beneficiary under a will becomes entitled to any property the testator has given him or her, the testator's debts must be paid. If the estate is insolvent in that there are insufficient assets to pay all the debts, the creditors are entitled to the entire estate according to their priority or preference, the general creditors coming last and taking a *pro rata* share of what is left.

If there are sufficient assets to pay the creditors, but insufficient to pay all the gifts made by the will, some or all of the gifts may have to abate. Abatement is the *pro rata* reduction of the amounts or quantities of testamentary gifts when the estate is insufficient to pay the debts and gifts in full. Absent a contrary direction in the will, the order in which assets are liable to pay debts is determined by well-defined rules. The term "debts" in this context includes debts and liabilities of the testator, as well as funeral, testamentary and administration expenses.

The primary fund liable for debts is the residue and, by statute, residuary real and personal property are liable rateably for the payment of debts. Section 5 of the *Estates Administration Act*[57] provides:

> **5.** Subject to section 32 of the *Succession Law Reform Act*,[58] the real and personal property of a deceased person comprised in a residuary devise or bequest, except so far as a contrary intention appears from the person's will or any codicil thereto, is applicable rateably, according to their respective values, to the payment of his or her debts, funeral and testamentary expenses and the cost and expenses of administration.

The term "residue" as used in this context is the balance of the estate remaining after all other dispositions. Once the residue has been exhausted, the next category of legacies to abate is the general legacies, including pecuniary legacies.[59]

If the assets available to pay the general legacies are insufficient, the next category to abate rateably is the specific and demonstrative legacies.[60] The latter are treated as specific to the extent that the fund out of which they are payable is adequate. To the extent that it is not, they are treated as general legacies[61] and to that extent they abate with the general legacies and before the specific legacies.[62]

Because of the general rule, modified by statute only as regards residue,[63] that debts are, absent a contrary intention, payable primarily out of personalty,[64] devises, other than residuary devises, are the last category to abate.[65] In order to

---

57 R.S.O. 1990, c. E.22.
58 R.S.O. 1990, c. S.26 (hereafter referred to without further citation). Section 32 deals with a devise subject to a mortgage and provides that, absent a contrary intention, the property subject to the mortgage is primarily liable for the payment of the mortgage debt. The section is discussed later in this chapter.
59 *Re Church* (1906), 8 O.W.R. 228.
60 *Barton v. Cooke* (1800), 5 Ves. 461, 31 E.R. 682; *Re Anderson* (1912), 1 O.W.R. 217; *Re Pardo* (1926), 29 O.W.N. 425.
61 *Robinson v. Geldard* (1851), 3 Mac. & G. 735, 42 E.R. 442.
62 *Paget v. Huish* (1863), 1 H. & M. 663, 71 E.R. 291.
63 See *Estates Administration Act*, s. 5, reproduced above.
64 *Harmood v. Oglander* (1803), 8 Ves. 106, 32 E.R. 293.
65 *Re Siskin; Siskin v. Bogoch*, [1929] 1 W.W.R. 820, 23 Sask L.R. 626, [1929] 4 D.L.R. 1086.

cast the entire burden of the debts on the realty, moreover, it is necessary to show an intention to exonerate the personalty. A mere charge of the debts on the realty is insufficient to do so, for in that case the personalty will be used first to pay the debts and then the realty.[66]

While it is, therefore, a general principle that legacies within each category shall abate rateably as necessary, the testator can provide otherwise. Thus, in *Re Jost*[67] the testator established a number of trust funds and directed the payment of the income thereon to designated beneficiaries. One of the trusts was in favour of his nephew. A later clause in the will provided: "It is my will that no bequests be paid for three years after my demise except the half-yearly income to my nephew". It was held that the nephew's trust fund thereby received priority. The case also held that a gift of money to purchase land does not obtain priority but abates equally with the other general legacies.

The question whether the testator has evinced a sufficient intention to give priority to a legacy is discussed further in *Lindsay v. Waldbrook*,[68] reproduced below.

LINDSAY v. WALDBROOK
(1897), 24 O.A.R. 604
Supreme Court of Ontario
[Court of Appeal]

The testator, Robert Waldbrook, directed that his farm be sold. He then provided: "My executors shall first out of the said proceeds set apart the sum of two thousand dollars and invest the same...for the benefit...and maintenance and education of my grandson Robert J. Waldbrook." He then went on to direct that four other legacies in varying amounts be paid out of the proceeds to his three daughters and surviving son. The legacies to be paid out of the proceeds totalled $7,000. The farm having been sold, there was insufficient to pay the several legacies out of the proceeds. The executors brought this action to construe the will and it was held at trial by Armour C.J., that the grandson's legacy took priority over the others and did not, therefore, abate. Two of the testator's daughters appealed.

OSLER J.A.:

There are here five legacies payable out of a specific fund, consisting of the proceeds of the sale of one of the testator's farms, and the question is, the fund having turned out to be insufficient to pay them all in full, whether the first, which is that given to the testator's grandson, has priority over the others, or whether all should abate in proportion.

---

66 *Re Ovey* (1885), 31 Ch. D. 113.
67 15 M.P.R. 477, affirmed (1940) 15 M.P.R. 477 at 492, [1941] 1 D.L.R. 642 (N.S.C.A.), reversed on the issue of succession duties [1942] S.C.R. 54, [1942] 1 D.L.R. 81.
68 (1897), 24 O.A.R. 604.

On the face of this will I am unable to find anything which sufficiently indicates an intention on the part of the testator to place one legatee in a better position than the others.

It is well settled that the use of words directing a legacy to be paid "immediately," or "in the first place," or "out of the first moneys, etc.," or within a brief specified time after the testator's decease, is no evidence of an intention to give priority. The general rule is stated in many cases from Lord Hardwicke's time onwards, and may be quoted from Lord Justice Knight-Bruce's language in *Thwaites v. Foreman*:[69]

> *Prima facie* all bequests stand on an equal footing, and it lies upon those who assert the contrary to prove it. It is not sufficient that the words of the will should leave the question in doubt. They must positively and clearly establish that it was the intention of the testator that the bequests should not stand on an equal footing. Now, in considering whether such was the intention of the testator, we must recollect that words that are merely introductory cannot, generally, by themselves be held to direct any order of payment.

Then he quotes a passage...which is taken from the judgment of Lord Hardwicke in *Blower v. Morret*,[70] and has been frequently repeated, namely,

> Unless the testator tells you himself that he believes his assets to be insufficient you must attribute to him the notion that he has assets sufficient to satisfy all the bequests that he makes, and if you attribute that notion to him, you cannot well infer that he intended to make provision for an order of payment applicable only to the case of the assets being insufficient.
>
> . . .

In the present case the testator expressly contemplates the fund indicated as the source of payment of the legacies as being sufficient for the purpose, and there is no reason suggested in the will why the grandson, and son, and daughters, all of whom are equally subjects of the testator's bounty, should not all stand on the same footing. It was argued that the direction to invest the grandson's legacy made a difference; indicating an intention that it should have priority over the others, and I am informed that the judgement below proceeded upon the ground that this intention ought to be inferred, that the investment was directed to be made of a sum which the testator probably thought would be sufficient to produce a fund sufficient for the maintenance and education of the infant. I regret not to be able to adopt this view. I see nothing in the will which entitles me to say that the testator contemplated any particular sum as necessary or sufficient for maintenance. There is simply the gift with a direction which seems naturally to follow where the legacy is not payable until majority, and the income is to be applied towards maintenance and education during minority. The case appears to me quite different from that of *Gyett v. Williams*,[71] where the direction was to invest £2,000, part of the proceeds of the testator's estate, in the purchase of an estate to be held in trust for the legatee; followed by a disposition of *the residue*. Here the bequests

---

69 1 Coll. 409.
70 2 Ves. Sr. 420.
71 2 J. & H. 429.

to the son and daughters, except where the testator comes to deal with a possible surplus after payment of the five legacies, are not given as out of the residue of the fund produced by the sale, but simply out of the fund, and, apart from the direction to invest, in the same manner as the legacy to the grandson. As between these legacies and any other given by the will, these five no doubt have priority, but as between themselves it appears to me, with all respect, that the authorities require us to hold that in a deficiency of the fund, they abate.

[The concurring judgments of Burton C.J.O. and Maclennan J.A., have been omitted.]

Notes and Questions

1. You should note that if a testator directs the sale of property for a specific amount, or not less than a specific amount, and gives certain legacies out of the proceeds which are less in total than the amount specified, and then gives the balance of the proceeds to another legatee, the latter gift is also a specific legacy and abates *pro rata* with the others if the property is sold for less (with the court's approval) than stipulated by the testator.[72]

2. If the legacies are payable solely out of a specific fund, such as the proceeds of the sale of land, they are specific and, as *Lindsay v. Waldbrook*[73] holds, they must abate rateably among themselves if the fund is insufficient. Hence, it may be that general legacies payable out of other assets would take in priority to specific legacies in such circumstances.

3. A legacy to the testator's widow in lieu of dower, while general, takes priority over other general legacies, because it takes the place of something the widow was entitled to, so that she is not a volunteer.[74]

4. It seems that in Canada a legacy to the executors "for their trouble," although a general legacy, has priority over other general legacies and does not abate with them,[75] even though the legacy is more than what the executors might otherwise be entitled to demand.[76] The rule is otherwise in England.[77] The reason for the difference is that in Canada, as distinct from England, individual, as well as corporate executors are entitled by statute to remuneration.[78]

5. *Re Watt*[79] illustrates various principles that apply when there are debts. The testator specifically devised two parcels of real property, specifically bequeathed certain personal property, directed that a debt owing to him be forgiven, gave four general legacies and directed that an annuity be purchased for a beneficiary. The court held (a) that the general pecuniary legatees had no right to marshall as against the specific devisees, so that the latter's interest did not abate; (b) that the beneficiaries of the specific bequests also took their bequests without abatement; (c) that the debt, since it was forgiven, was not an asset of the estate and, thus, did not abate; and (d) that an annuity is a general legacy and, thus, its present value abates rateably with other general legacies.

---

72 See *Page v. Leapingwell* (1812), 18 Ves. 463, 34 E.R. 392.

73 *Supra*.

74 *Koch v. Heisey* (1894), 26 O.R. 87; *Re Lambertus* (1914), 6 O.W.N. 300; *Re Robinson*, [1939] O.W.N. 37; *Re Warren* (1924), 54 O.L.R. 433 (H.C.); *Re Cowan*, [1932] 1 W.W.R. 79, 40 Man. R. 221, [1932] 1 D.L.R. 771 (C.A.).

75 *Boy's Home of Hamilton v. Lewis* (1883), 4 O.R. 18.

76 *Anderson v. Dougall* (1868), 15 Gr. 405.

77 *Re White; Pennell v. Franklin*, [1898] 2 Ch. 217, [1895-9] All E.R. Rep. 229 (C.A.).

78 See *e.g.*, *Trustee Act*, R.S.O. 1990, c. T.23, s. 61.

79 [1958] O.W.N. 418 (H.C.).

6. It may be doubted that the forgiven debt in *Re Watt*[80] was no longer part of the estate. The forgiveness of a debt is usually treated as a specific legacy and, thus, not liable to abate before the general legacies are exhausted,[81] but, if necessary, the debt may have to be called in to pay for the testator's debts.

7. In contrast, a legacy given by a testator in satisfaction of a debt owed by him or her is a general legacy and, as such, is liable to abate with other general legacies.[82] What happens in such a case is that the legacy is usually substantially more than the debt. The creditor is then required to elect to take either the legacy or press his or her claim as a creditor. If he or she does the latter, the debt will be paid in full, but, if the former, it may not be.[83]

8. A testator provided for general legacies which exceeded the net value of his estate. Four of the legatees sought priority for their legacies on the basis that they had worked for wages but had not been paid by the testator. Three of the legacies were coupled with the words, "for years of work done for me, if I have not already paid him during my lifetime," while the words, "for faithful services in the past, if I have not already benefited him during my lifetime," were attached to the fourth. The other gifts were coupled with the words, "if I have not already benefited him/her during my lifetime." Did the testator intend that the four general legacies mentioned be paid in preference to those of the other general legatees or should all legacies abate together and proportionately?[84]

9. The equitable doctrine of marshalling of assets, referred to in *Re Watt*,[85] applies when there are two types of legacies and one is payable out of a specific fund, for example, when there are general legacies simpliciter and general legacies charged on land, but the estate is insufficient to pay all in full. In that case the general legatees simpliciter are entitled to marshall the assets so as to have the other legacies paid out of the land, while they are paid out of the personalty, with the result that both groups of legatees will receive something. Clearly as the *Watt* case holds, legatees cannot marshall as against specific devisees. The latter take the land itself, not money, and the same applies to specific bequests of personalty.[86]

10. A mere direction to the executors to pay death taxes is only a direction to them to perform their statutory duty. However, if the will makes it clear that a particular gift is to be free of tax, or that any taxes are to be paid out of a particular fund, the beneficiaries of the gifts thereby exonerated receive an additional pecuniary legacy and, if the assets of the estate are insufficient to pay all legacies in full, that additional legacy will abate with other general legacies.[87]

11. Testamentary gifts are not always paid immediately. This may be because the executors are dilatory in distributing the estate, or because payment is postponed due to a prior life interest or because of specific directions in the will. Beneficiaries are normally entitled to receive interest on their unpaid gifts. The interest begins to run after the executor's year, that is, one year after the testator's death, until they are paid.[88] The interest

---

80 *Ibid.*
81 *Re Wedmore*, [1907] 2 Ch. 277.
82 *Re Rispin* (1914), 35 O.L.R. 385, 27 D.L.R. 574 (C.A.).
83 See, however, *dicta* to the contrary in *Re Lawley; Zaiser v. Lawley*, [1902] 2 Ch. 799 (C.A.), affirmed [1903] A.C. 411 (H.L.).
84 See *Re Janzen* (1986), 23 E.T.R. 55 (Sask. C.A.).
85 [1958] O.W.N. 418 H.C..
86 *Cf. In re Cohen; Nat. Prov. Bank v. Katz*, [1960] Ch. 179, [1959] 3 All E.R. 740.
87 *Re McClintock* (1976), 12 O.R. (2d) 741 (Div. Ct.).
88 *Re Lord's Estate; Lord v. Lord* (1867), 2 Ch. App. 782.

is likely to be the current yield on authorized trust investments.[89] The interest is not a matter of the testator's bounty, but of fairness. Hence, it is not treated as an additional legacy and does not abate with it.[90]

The basic rule that beneficiaries are entitled to interest is subject to a number of exceptions. Thus, for example, specific bequests and legacies carry with it income earned on them from the date of death. Similarly, if a general legacy is charged on land and the will does not fix the time for payment, interest runs from the date of the testator's death. On the other hand, no interest will be payable if the testator directs otherwise and in certain other situations.[91]

12. Just as the residuary personalty bears the primary liability for debts in the absence of a statutory provision to the contrary, so it is primarily liable for the payment of legacies. Only if the testator has charged the legacies upon the residuary real property, or if the will treats the residue as a mixed fund of realty and personalty and directs that the legacies be paid out of it, can the real property be resorted to for this purpose.[92]

5. ADEMPTION

As we saw, ademption occurs when the property which is the subject matter of a specific gift, although in existence at the date of the will, is not in the testator's estate at his or her death. It may have been sold or given away by the testator, or it may have been lost, stolen, or destroyed. In the absence of statutory provisions to the contrary, if a specific gift has adeemed, the beneficiary receives nothing. This is true, again in the absence of statutory provisions to the contrary, even if the testator retains other property into which the property that was the subject matter of the gift has been converted. Thus, if the testator has received the proceeds of insurance for the destroyed property, owns property which he or she took in exchange, or holds a mortgage which he or she took back on a sale of the property, the beneficiary cannot claim them. *Re Hunter*,[93] reproduced below, discusses this point.

The testator may, of course, avoid this result by stating his or her intention to be that the beneficiary shall receive either the specific property or any property which replaces it. Thus, if a testator bequeaths certain specified securities belonging to him or her "or the investments representing the same at my death if they shall have been converted into other holdings," the legatee will be entitled to the proceeds from the sale of the securities received by the testator and held on deposit in the bank.[94]

---

89 See *Re Stekl; Lauer v. Stekl*, [1974] 6 W.W.R. 490, 47 D.L.R. (3d) 286 at 297 (B.C.C.A.), affirmed [1976] 1 S.C.R. 781, [1976] 2 W.W.R. 382, 16 N.R. 559, 54 D.L.R. (3d) 159n; *Re Lottman* (1978), 2 E.T.R. 1 at 16, *per* Wilson J.A., reversed on another point (sub nom. *Lottman v. Stanford*) [1980] 1 S.C.R. 1065, 6 E.T.R. 34, 107 D.L.R. (3d) 28, 31 N.R. 1.

90 *Re Wyles; Foster v. Wyles*, [1938] Ch. 313, [1938] 1 All E.R. 347.

91 For a good discussion of the right to interest in various circumstances, see Rosanne T. Rocchi and Michael W. Kerr, "Legacies: A Matter of Some Interest" (1997), 16 E. & T.J. 257, 305.

92 *Re Watson* (1922), 52 O.L.R. 387 at 389 (C.A.); *Re Thompson*, [1936] Ch. 676; *Re Carmichael*, [1944] O.W.N. 738, [1945] 1 D.L.R. 64.

93 (1975), 8 O.R. (2d) 399, 58 D.L.R. (3d) 175 (H.C.).

94 *Re Lewis's Will Trusts; O'Sullivan v. Robbins*, [1937] Ch. 118, [1937] 1 All E.R. 227.

Moreover, not all specific gifts adeem if they are generic in nature. This will be discussed in the next part. Nor is there an ademption if there is a mere change in name and form of the property only. This will also be discussed in the next part.

The inability of a specific legatee to claim property which represents and takes the place of the property which was given and the statutory changes modifying this inability are discussed later in this chapter.

RE HUNTER
(1975), 8 O.R. (2d) 399, 58 D.L.R. (3d) 175
Supreme Court of Ontario
[High Court of Justice]

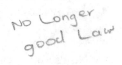

The testatrix devised and bequeathed her house and contents to certain beneficiaries. She died in a fire which destroyed those assets. The question arose whether the beneficiaries were entitled to the proceeds of the insurance. The beneficiaries were also the residuary beneficiaries. Apart from the insurance moneys, there was insufficient cash to pay the several legatees. The personal representative made application to the court to construe the will.

KEITH J.:

. . .

I am of the opinion that with respect to that part of the fund created by settlement of the loss with respect to the destruction of the contents of the house, namely, $6,600, the argument advanced by the Official Guardian must prevail, by reason of long-standing authority.

[His Lordship referred to a number of cases and continued:]

All of these cases dealt with chattels being destroyed in such circumstances that one could not tell whether a claim for insurance moneys arose before or after the death of the testator and hence, on the theory that the insurance claim arose simultaneously with the testator's death and before any legatee could be said to have acquired a vested interest in the chattels, the proceeds of such claims must go to the personal representatives and form part of the general estate and not be the property of the disappointed legatees.

. . .

Had the testatrix in this case sold the house before her death, I would have thought the devise of the house would have failed under the terms of this testatrix' will. In this connection it is to be noted that the four named devisees of the house were also the four residuary beneficiaries in equal shares, a circumstance that to my mind would militate against a finding that such a contrary intention appeared in the will as to prevent the law with respect to ademption being applicable.

. . .

I must find that the devisees of the real property in this case are not as such entitled to the proceeds of the insurance on the damaged house, but that such proceeds as well as the proceeds of the insurance on the contents of the house, are to be treated as personalty in the hands of the applicant available for the general purposes of the estate.

It was the applicant and the applicant only who in its capacity as personal representative of the testatrix, was entitled to enforce the insurance contract.

Such proceeds added to the other general personalty are available to pay the debts of the testatrix, funeral and testamentary expenses, and specific legacies.

Any surplus would, of course, fall into the residue.

. . .

Notes and Questions

1. Later in this chapter we shall see that the result in the *Hunter* case would now be different in Ontario and some other provinces by reason of statutory changes.

2. If the testator died first and then the property was destroyed, there would not be an ademption, but the beneficiaries would be entitled to the insurance monies.[95]

3. In Roman law ademption was not automatic. Rather, the court would inquire into the testator's intentions with respect to the property. In other words, an attempt was made to ascertain whether the testator intended the gift to adeem, or whether he or she wished the beneficiaries to have the value of the property if it no longer existed at the testator's death.

This approach was initially adopted by the English ecclesiastical courts, but as the courts of equity increased their jurisdiction in matters testamentary, the intent approach to ademption was frequently criticized as being "Productive of endless uncertainty and confusion."[96] As a result of this general dissatisfaction, the intent approach was abandoned in *Ashburner v. MacGuire*[97] in favour of the identity approach which prevails today. Under this approach, the question is simply whether the asset which is the subject matter of the specific gift still exists as such in the estate.

4. In view of the judicial trend in favour of ascertaining the testator's intention by the use of all appropriate evidence discussed in the previous chapter, should the identity approach to ademption be abolished and replaced with an intent approach? Recent cases show that some courts are willing to take this approach. This is particularly evident in cases in which the property has merely changed in name and form only and can be traced. This is discussed later in this chapter.

5. The statutory reforms introduced in some of the Canadian provinces dealing with this problem do not address the question. Instead, they are rather based upon a presumed intention of the testator.[98]

That is also the approach used in some of the American states. However, some of the legislation there goes further by providing that the specific legatee becomes entitled to the value of the gift which has been converted through sale, or expropriation, to the value of any insurance proceeds paid to the testator for destroyed property, or to the insurance proceeds themselves.[99]

---

95 *Durrant v. Friend* (1852), 5 DeG. & Sm. 343 at 346, 64 E.R. 1145, *per* Sir James Parker, V.C.

96 *Humphreys v. Humphreys* (1789), 2 Cox Eq. Cas. 184, 30 E.R. 85, *per* Lord Thurlow, L.C.

97 (1786) 2 Bro. C.C. 108, 29 E.R. 62.

98 These are discussed later in this chapter.

99 See, *e.g.*, Ore. Rev. Stat. § 112.385 (1969); Ky. Rev. Stat. § 394.360 (1970). And see the *Uniform Probate Code* (U.L.A.), (West Publishing Co., 1983), § 2-608.

6. What is the purpose of the ademption rule? Is it simply to produce certainty, or does it assume that, in the majority of cases, it is consistent with the actual intentions of testators? In either event, does the rule meet the goal?

Is the fact that a specific description of the property has been given a sufficiently strong indicator of the testator's probable intention so as to justify an irrebuttable presumption against a gift of the economic equivalent of the property? Should factors such as the testator's role in the disappearance of the original property, his or her opportunity to change the will, his or her dealings with the proceeds and his or her relationship to the specific and general and residuary beneficiaries, be considered in deciding whether the gift should adeem, or whether the beneficiary should receive the value of the gift?

7. Ademption typically occurs either by act of the testator, or by an event over which the testator has no control. The former occurs when the testator sells the subject matter of the gift or gives it away; the latter when the property is destroyed, expropriated, or stolen.

However, it may also happen that a representative of the testator disposes of property that is the subject of a specific testamentary gift. Should the ademption rule apply in those circumstances? For example, what if the testator has appointed an attorney to act for him or her and the attorney, in the legitimate exercise of his or her duties, disposes of property that is the subject matter of a specific testamentary gift. Does the gift adeem? Should it?

The Ontario *Substitute Decisions Act, 1992*,[100] which governs, *inter alia*, the appointment of attorneys for property, has made provision for this situation. Section 35.1 provides that a guardian and an attorney[101] of property shall not, subject to certain exceptions, dispose of property that they know to be subject to a specific testamentary gift in the incapable person's will. Further, s. 36(1) provides that the doctrine of ademption does not apply to property that is the subject of a specific testamentary gift and that a guardian or attorney disposes of. Rather, the beneficiary is entitled to receive the corresponding right in the proceeds of disposition from the residue. Section 36(2) provides that if the residue is insufficient, the right in the proceeds abates. Subsection (2) does not make it clear whether the gifts to all beneficiaries entitled to the residue abate *pro rata*, but the language suggests that beneficiaries of specific gifts, the property of which has been disposed of, take priority. In jurisdictions that have no similar legislation the courts may hold that a specific gift has adeemed if the attorney for the incapable testator disposes of it.[102]

---

100 S.O. 1992, c. 30 [am. 1994, c. 27, ss. 43(2), 62; 1996, c. 2, ss. 3 - 60; 1998, c. 26, s. 108], s. 36. To the same effect see: *Infirm Persons Act*, R.S.N.B. 1973, c. I-8, s. 18; *Wills Act*, R.S.M. 1988, c. W150, s. 24 [am. S.M. 1993, c. 29]; *Dependent Adults Act*, S.S. 1989-90, c. D-25.1, s. 34. See also *Mental Health Act 1959* (U.K.), c. 72, s. 107; and see Buist, "Persons under Disability: Dealing with Assets to be Disposed of by Will" (1956), 32 N.Z.L.J. 170. For an application of the legislation, see *Re Krawecki Estate* (1995), 8 E.T.R. (2d) 307 (Sask. Q.B.).

101 See *ibid.*, s. 38(1).

102 See, *e.g.*, Christina Walsh, "A Costly Application of Strict Statutory Construction: The Ohio Supreme Court's Interpretation of Ohio's Nonademption Statute, Revised Code Section 2107.501(B)" (1997), 28. U. Toledo L. Rev. 631; David A. Onega, "Hegel's Hobbled Heritage: The Ohio Supreme Court's Use of the Doctrine of Ademption to Prey on the Incompetent" (1997), 26 Capital University Law Review 201. Both articles comment on *In re Estate of Hegel*, 668 N.E. 2d 474 (Ohio, 1996), in which the Ohio Supreme Court held that there was an ademption when the attorney sold property that was the subject of a specific gift. The Code prevented ademption if the property was sold by a court-appointed guardian, but was silent on a sale by an attorney under a durable power of attorney.

Further Reading

John C. Paulus, "Ademption by Extinction: Smiting Lord Thurlow's Ghost" (1970-71) 2 Texas Tech. L. Rev. 195.

Richard L. Martin, "Ademption in New York: The Identity Doctrine and the Need for Complete Abrogation by Legislation" (1973-74), 25 Syracuse L. Rev. 978.

J. Bradley Schooley, "Ademption by Extinction in Indiana" (1978), 11 Indiana L. Rev. 849.

Mary Kay Lundwall, "The Case Against the Ademption by Extinction Rule: A Proposal for Reform" (1993-94), 29 Gonz. L. Rev. 105.

T.G. Youdan, Annotation (1982), 10 E.T.R. 118.

6. DATE FROM WHICH WILL SPEAKS

(a) The General Rule

Suppose that a testator devises "my real property in London, Ontario" to X. When he made the will the testator owned a house in London, but at death he no longer owns the house. However, the testator does own a condominium and a 50-hectare parcel of land which he intended to subdivide. Does the gift adeem, or does the property the testator owns at death pass under the gift? Would there be any difference if the testator bequeathed a specific property, such as "my house at 500 Richmond Street," or "my piano"?

The question is addressed by statute in the several provinces. The legislation provides in essence that, as regards dispositions of property, a will speaks as of the date of death, unless a contrary intention is indicated. Section 22 of the *Succession Law Reform Act*, reproduced below, states this rule. It derives from the English Act of 1837[103] and reverses the common law rule.

At common law a specific gift was apt to pass only the property comprised in it that was owned by the testator at the date of the will. After-acquired property of a similar nature would, therefore, pass under a gift of residue.

The questions raised above suggest that there are two types of specific gift, namely, one that is specific in nature, that is, one comprising of property which is by nature incapable of increase or decrease, and one that is generic in nature, that is, one in which the property can increase or decrease. The recognition of these subcategories to specific gifts assist the court in determining whether or not a gift does or does not adeem.

Re Rutherford,[104] reproduced below, affords an example of a generic gift.

---

103 *Wills Act 1837*, 7 Will. 4 & 1 Vict., c. 26, s. 24.
104 (1918), 42 O.L.R. 405 (H.C.).

SUCCESSION LAW REFORM ACT
R.S.O. 1990, c. S.26

22. Except when a contrary intention appears by the will, a will speaks and takes effect as if it had been made immediately before the death of the testator with respect to,

(a) the property of the testator; and

(b) the right, chose in action, equitable estate or interest, right to insurance proceeds or compensation, or mortgage, charge or other security interest of the testator under subsection 20(2).

Comparable Legislation

Probate Act, R.S.P.E.I. 1988, c. P-21, s. 76; *Wills Act*, R.S.A. 1980, c. W-11, s. 22(1); R.S.B.C. 1996, c. 489, s. 20(2); R.S.M. 1988, c. W150, s. 22(2); R.S.N. 1990, c. W-10, s. 15; R.S.N.B. 1973, c. W-9, s. 21(2); R.S.N.S. 1989, c. 505, s. 23; S.S. 1996, c. W-14.11, s. 21: R.S.N.W.T. 1988, c. W-5, s. 14(2); R.S.Y. 1986, c. 179, s. 14.

RE RUTHERFORD
(1918), 42 O.L.R. 405
Supreme Court of Ontario
[High Court of Justice]

The testator devised his "house and premises on Merton Street" to his widow for life or until she remarried, and thereafter to his children then living. He gave the residue of his estate to his widow absolutely.

At the date of the will the testator owned a house on Merton Street, built on a 20-foot frontage. Subsequently he acquired an additional 55 feet to the west, adjacent to the 20 feet, which he enclosed with the 20 feet and used as a garden and for a chicken house.

An application was brought to interpret the will. The widow argued that the 55 feet did not pass under the specific devise and that, therefore, she became entitled to it under the residuary clause.

MIDDLETON J.:

. . .

[Section 27 of the *Wills Act*] in effect provides that, unless from the will itself you can see that the testator did not intend after-acquired property to pass, it must be read as though he had executed it immediately before his death. In many cases this must result in imputing to the testator an intention which in fact he never had; but, on the other hand, the opposite rule would even more frequently result in defeating his intention. This is at once apprehended where the expression used is general, e.g., where there is a gift of "my house" or "my horse," and the testator had sold his house or his horse and had bought another. The wife to whom he had given his house or the son to whom he had given his horse would not easily understand why nothing was given because of the sale of the property owned at the will's date. So this statute established the rule, as put by one Judge, that the testator must be assumed to have read his will or carried it in his mind till shortly before his death, and to have refrained from any change because it expressed his intention at that time.

Now two things have been frequently found in wills which the Courts have taken as an indication of a contrary intention. When a testator speaks of that which he gives as that which he owns at the date of the will, clearly that and that alone is given, for the provision is not that the will must in all respects be regarded as made immediately before the death.

Then, when the will speaks of a specific thing, and is not general in its provisions, the thing given must be determined by the language used by the testator. Nothing else passes, for nothing else is given. In this way Judges, always slow to recognise by decision the desirability of reform, cut down the full meaning and effect of the statute. But it has always been held that when the thing given remains, and has been added to between the date of the will and the date of death, the whole property answering the description at the latter date will pass.

In re Willis,[105] is a striking example. The testator gave his "freehold house and premises at O. known as A. in which I now reside." He bought two additional plots, one contiguous to the house, one across the road, and used them in connection with the house. Both plots passed.

. . .

For these reasons, I find that the whole property on Merton street passed under the devise of the "house and premises on Merton street."

. . .

Notes and Questions

1. Section 20(2) of the *Succession Law Reform Act*, referred to in s. 22(b), is discussed later in this chapter. Only the Alberta and New Brunswick statutes contain a provision similar to s. 22(b).[106]

2. *Re Thompson*[107] affords another illustration of the problem. The testator directed that all his assets be converted and divided into four parts. He gave one of the parts to his son, James, and directed that a certain mortgage on real estate owed by the testator be paid out of James's part. Before his death, the testator refinanced the loan by paying it and granting a new mortgage to another person. On the question whether the mortgage should be paid by the whole estate or charged against James's part, the court held that it was payable out of James's part. The word "mortgage" is the same as "debt secured by mortgage." Hence, while the original mortgage was discharged, the debt, represented by the new mortgage, remained. The legislation was thus applied to a generic debt charged against property.

---

105 [1911] 2 Ch. 563.
106 *Wills Act*, R.S.A. 1980, c. W-11, s. 22(b), R.S.N.B. 1973, c. W-9, s. 21(2)(b).
107 (1919), 45 O.L.R. 520, 48 D.L.R. 457 (C.A.).

Is the construction placed upon the word "mortgage" by the court in *Re Thompson* correct? It is indeed true that that is what is probably meant when a person speaks of his or her mortgage. But does he or she not then speak of the debt secured by that specific mortgage rather than of whatever mortgage may exist on the property at his or her death? Since the new mortgage was used in part to retire the old one, the result probably accorded with the testator's intention. But would the result be otherwise if the old mortgage had been discharged and a new one given several years later?

3. *Thompson* indicates that when a specific thing is given which is incapable of increase or decrease, that is a sufficient contrary intention to take the case out of the statute.

Re Sikes[108] is to the same effect. The testatrix bequeathed "my piano." At the date of the will she owned a player piano, but sold it afterwards to the beneficiary's husband. She then bought a new electric motor player piano which she still owned at her death. It was held that the bequest constituted a sufficient contrary intention to take the case out of the Act, so that the gift adeemed.

There are two problems with this: (a) It is submitted that the will did not disclose a contrary intention. Rather, the object itself did. And (b) the question may be validly raised whether the result was likely to accord with the testatrix' intention. In any event, is a mortgage different from a piano?

4. *Goodlad v. Burnett*,[109] referred to in *Thompson*, is an example of a gift that was generic in nature. The testatrix bequeathed "my new three and a quarter per cent annuities." When she made her will she owned £3,101 worth of such annuities, but by the time of her death she had accumulated £17,010 worth of them. The annuities were clearly generic in nature and the court held that the words "my new" did not indicate a contrary intention, since they referred equally to what the testatrix owned at the date of her will as to what she might own at her death. Hence, the beneficiary was entitled to the whole amount.

5. Although the will speaks from death, the property may be valued at a later date. This is illustrated by *Re Udd*.[110] The testator gave his wife a life estate in the family home. He also gave certain legacies to be paid if his net estate should exceed $500,000. At the time of probate the estate was less than $500,000, but the family home increased in value during the 13 years the widow lived in it, so that, at her death the estate exceeded $500,000 in value. It was held that the date of valuation of the estate should, in the circumstances, be fixed as of the date of sale of the house.

6. You should note that section 22 applies only to the property disposed of by will. There is no similar statutory rule of construction respecting the description of persons. With respect to persons, the *prima facie* rule is that the person in existence at the date of the will who answers the description in the will takes the gift, even though the description subsequently becomes inaccurate. In other words, in respect of persons, *prima facie*, the will is interpreted as of its date and not as of the date of the testator's death.[111]

Section 17(2) of the *Succession Law Reform Act* has reversed this rule in respect of a dissolved marriage between the testator and his or her spouse.[112] However, if the gift is to a class of persons, the *prima facie* rule is that the membership of the class is to be ascertained

---

108 [1927] 1 Ch. 364.
109 (1855), 1 Kay & J. 341, 69 E.R. 489.
110 (1977), 16 O.R. (2d) 579, 78 D.L.R. (3d) 599 (H.C.), affirmed (1977), 84 D.L.R. (3d) 606 (C.A.).
111 *Re Hickman's Will Trusts*, [1948] Ch. 624, [1948] 2 All E.R. 303.
112 See the chapter on Revocation.

as of the testator's death, although, under certain circumstances, persons are allowed into the class after the testator's death.[113]

(b) A Contrary Intention

(i) *Generally*

As indicated in the preceding material, if a gift is made of a specific item which is incapable of increase or decrease, such as a piano, a horse, a car, *etc.*, the courts regard that as evincing a contrary intention to take the gift out of s. 22 of the *Succession Law Reform Act*. More generally, however, any language in the will which indicates that the testator intends to give only the property he or she owned at the date of the will has that effect.

Re Bird,[114] reproduced below, discusses the question of a contrary intention.

RE BIRD
[1942] O.R. 415, [1942] 3 D.L.R. 439
Supreme Court of Ontario
[Court of Appeal]

The testatrix bought Lot 57, Plan 184, Toronto, being 25 feet in width, on the north side of Mitchell Avenue in 1891. The cottage on this land was described for municipal purposes as 14 Mitchell Avenue.

She made her will in 1926 and by clause 6 she gave her son, William James Bird, the "House and premises 14 Mitchell Avenue, Toronto."

The city condemned the cottage in 1937 and the testatrix had it demolished and replaced with two semi-detached houses, which became known as 14 and 16 Mitchell Avenue. She died in 1942. Prior to her death she made an unattested codicil in which she purported to give both houses to her son.

On an application to interpret the will, Hope J., held that William James Bird was entitled to both houses. The residuary beneficiaries appealed.

RIDDELL J.A. (dissenting):

. . .

I think it may fairly be inferred that the testatrix intended both parcels to go to William James Bird, and I shall assume that such was the case. The difficulty in the way of the respondent is The Wills Act,[115] which reads:

> [His Lordship reproduced s. 26, which was the same in substance as the present legislation, and continued:]

---

113 See the chapter on Class Gifts, and see *Re Wood* (1982), 11 E.T.R. 104 (N.S. T.D.).
114 [1942] O.R. 415, [1942] 3 D.L.R. 439 (C.A.).
115 R.S.O. 1937, c. 164, s. 26(1).

Here, I find no contrary intention expressed in the will, of which we are furnished with a complete copy. Consequently, we must look at the will as though it had been executed at the time immediately before the death of the testatrix.

At that time, it is, I think, plain that the language employed covered only what is now known as No. 14; and it is always to be borne in mind that in interpreting a will, it is the legal meaning of the language employed that should govern.

This view would be strengthened if we were to admit as evidence (as to which I express no opinion) the document in which the testatrix plainly showed that the language of her will did not cover the two parcels — unfortunately, she took no steps to effect her intention to have both parcels go to William James Bird.

. . .

FISHER J.A.:

. . .

It is clear to my mind, the testatrix having by her will specifically described and identified the property she devised to her son, that notwithstanding the fact that the description at the date of death applied to part only of the property, the devise covered and included not only the land itself, but all the buildings thereon at the date of death, and further that even if there was a changed condition of the property subsequent to the making of the will, the changed condition satisfied the description of the property devised under the will.

Full support for this conclusion is, I think, to be found in *In re Evans; Evans v. Powell*.[116] In that case the testator by his will devised to his wife for life with remainder to his daughter, "house and effects" known as Cross Villa, situate in T. At the date of his will he was possessed of half an acre of ground with a house upon it, the premises being known as Cross Villa. Subsequently, upon a part of the ground separated from the rest by a hedge, he erected two semi-detached dwelling houses which he named "Ashcroft Villas." He died in 1908.

In that case it was held that, the testator having done nothing in reference to this property amounting to a revocation of the devise, and not having parted with any portion of the premises, the devise passed the whole of the property with all the erected buildings thereon, and that there was no intestacy.

Joyce J., in disposing of the *Evans* case referred to the following words of Lindley L.J. in *In re Portal and Lamb*:[117] "It [meaning section 24 of the English Wills Act] does not say that we are to construe whatever a man says in his will as if it were made on the day of his death." Hawkins on Wills,[118] on the authority of *In re Evans*, says: "A specific devise is not cut down by an alteration in the property made after the date of the will."...The Court, in construing a will such as this, is entitled to take into consideration the condition of things in reference to which it was made, and, where there exists a specific description, to consider

---

116 [1909] 1 Ch. 784.
117 (1885), 30 Ch. D. 50 at 55.
118 3rd ed., at p. 27.

all the circumstances relating to the property and material to identify the thing described; see Theobald on Wills.[119]

I am of opinion that a contrary intention within the meaning of s. 26(1) of The Wills Act, appears here from the fact that the testatrix has used the description, "14 Mitchell Avenue" to refer to the whole Lot 57. The description "14 Mitchell Avenue" meant the same to her as the description "Lot 57", and therefore the will must be read as if she had said "Lot 57".

If house No. 16 fell into the residuary estate, it would be due to the fact that the municipality had designated one of the semi-detached houses as No. 16, and not to the acts or the intention of the testatrix. Had a duplex house been built upon the property, and had the lower been designated as 14 and 14A and the upper 16 and 16A, I do not think that fact would alter or interfere with a devise of the whole property to the devisee under the will. If it did, it would lead to the ridiculous result that house No. 14 and the land thereunder would belong to one person and house No. 16, with no land thereunder, would belong to someone else.

. . .

[The judgment of Henderson J.A., who concurred with Fisher J.A., has been omitted.]

Notes and Questions

1. Which approach is correct, that of Riddell J.A., or that of Fisher J.A.? Why?

2. *Morrison v. Morrison*[120] also illustrates the problem. The testator devised all his "property on Hughson Street" to his brother, and all the rest of his property to his nephew. At the date of the will the testator owned the "Red Lion Hotel" on Hughson Street. Later he acquired three houses on the opposite side of the street from the hotel and unconnected with it. The majority of the court held that the nephew took the houses. The court came to this conclusion because of the residuary clause and the words in it, "which I shall be entitled to at my decease."

Do these words add anything to a residuary clause? Were these adequate reasons for the court to read the will as of its date, rather than as of the date of death?

3. By his will, a testator declared that all insurance policies on his life and owned by him and which were payable to his wife should be held in trust for his wife and children upon certain trusts. The testator owned five such policies when he made his will and at his death. However, he and his wife died in a common accident. Hence, by reason of the provisions of the *Insurance Act*[121] she was deemed to have predeceased her husband and the proceeds were payable to the husband. If, therefore, the will was found to speak from death, there were no policies of insurance "payable to my wife." Does the statute imposing a date of death construction apply?[122]

---

119 9th ed., p. 107.
120 (1885), 10 O.R. 303 (Div. Ct.).
121 R.S.A. 1980, c. I-5, ss. 263(1), 284.
122 See *Re Goldstein Estate* (1984), 51 Alta. R. 341 (C.A.).

(ii) *Use of temporal words*

In most cases, in order to avoid the operation of s. 22 of the *Succession Law Reform Act*, a testator will have to describe the property by referring to it as the property of a certain description he or she owns at the date of the will. Unfortunately, testators and their legal advisors often use words of time which are ill defined, such as "now" and "then." What do such words refer to, the date of the will or the date of death? *Re Forbes*,[123] reproduced below, examines this problem.

RE FORBES
[1956] O.W.N. 527, 3 D.L.R. (2d) 653
Supreme Court of Ontario
[Court of Appeal]

The testator, who had resided with a Mrs. Poore for a number of years, bought a house jointly with her on Dawson Street in Wiarton in 1942. A few years later he made his will in which he directed his executors to convey "the premises where I now reside in the town of Wiarton" to Mrs. Poore. Thereafter the testator conveyed his interest in this house to Mrs. Poore and he and Mrs. Poore signed a release at the same time in which they released each other from all claims that they might have against the other. Then the testator bought another house on McNaughton Street in Wiarton and he lived there until his death. Mrs. Poore did not live with him in this house, but visited him frequently.

On an application to interpret the will, it was held at first instance by Kelly J. that Mrs. Poore was entitled to the house on McNaughton Street. The other beneficiaries appealed.

HOGG J.A., delivered the judgment of the Court:

. . .

The sole question for determination is, therefore, whether or not a contrary intention is to be found in clause 1 of the said will which would denote that s. 26(1) of The Wills Act should be held not to apply to the devise.

. . .

Theobald on Wills,[124] expresses the following opinion:

Effect of the word "now" — On the other hand, the word "now" used in the description of property refers to the date of the will, and, if it is an essential part of the description, it limits the gift to property then belonging to the testator. If, on the other hand, such words as "now occupied by me," or the like, are merely added as an additional description not intended to cut down the generality of the earlier words, the devise will not be restricted to property belonging to the testator at the date of the will.

There are many cases to be found in the reports dealing with the meaning to be given to the word "now" as this word appears in various wills. In a comparatively

---

123 [1956] O.W.N. 527, 3 D.L.R. (2d) 653 (C.A.).
124 11th ed. 1954, p. 142.

recent case on the subject, that of *In re Whitby; Public Trustee v. Whitby*,[125] reference had been made in argument to a number of cases.

> [*Whitby* involved the following facts: The testator had given the residue of his personal property to his niece by codicil in 1939. A codicil in 1940 excepted from that bequest jewellery and other chattels "now deposited in safe custody" at a certain bank and gave them to other persons. Various items were deposited in the safety deposit box since 1940. It was held that the word "now" referred to the date of the 1940 codicil. The Master of the Rolls said:[126]
>
> > I cannot see why, when a testator has defined the objects to which he has referred both by time and by place, we should be forced to strike out from the will the reference to time as being an immaterial part of the description. Reading this simply as a piece of straightforward English I should have thought that the reference to time is just as essential a part of the description as the reference to place. The contrary view involves, in effect, striking out of this codicil the word "now."]

In *In re Horton; Lloyd v. Hatchett*,[127] which was referred to by the learned judge from whose order this appeal is taken, the words of the will under consideration, which pertained to certain property owned by the testator, were "now held by me as a customary tenant of the said manor, or otherwise", and it was held by Eve J. that the expression "now held by me" was an additional description of the property and not an essential part of such description. But Mr. Justice Eve also said in the course of his reasons for judgment that one of the questions to be considered was whether by reason of any context or any other provisions of the will it should be held that the testator intended by the word "now" to exclude an after-acquired interest from his devise. This view of the question is similar to that expressed by Lord Greene in the *Whitby* case.

I think that with reference to the will now before the Court, the...word "now" is, in my opinion, an essential part of the description of the property intended to be devised by clause 1 of the will of the late Mr. Forbes. It is my opinion that the testator was thinking of a particular time, namely, the date upon which he executed his will, just as he was thinking as well of a particular place.

It is also to be observed that although in clause 1 the testator used the word "now" he did not use this word in clause 2 with respect to the disposition of the balance of his estate; he there used the expression "at the date of my decease". To this difference in the language used by the testator, I think the observation of Mr. Justice Eve in the *Horton* case that the context or other provisions of the will must be considered in a determination of the meaning to be given to the word "now" is directly applicable. The contrasting dates signified by the word "now" and the phrase "at the date of my decease" manifest the respective dates as of which the subject-matter of the specific devise made by clause 1 and the residuary bequest in clause 2 are to be identified. This fact must be given due significance. I have concluded that it was the interest which the testator had in the residence

---

125 [1944] Ch. 210, [1944] 1 All E.R. 299.
126 At Ch. 215.
127 [1920] 2 Ch. 1.

on Dawson Street, in which he resided when he executed his will, which he intended to pass to the devisee named in clause 1 of the will and that such "contrary intention" is shown as to prevent the operation of s. 26(1) of the statute.

The appeal should be allowed.

. . .

Notes and Questions

1. Did the context really help the court in *Forbes*? What does the phrase "at the date of my decease" add to the residuary clause?

2. The problems which result from using ill-defined words of time are not restricted to gifts of property. They also arise in the descriptions of persons. Thus a gift in the following form: "to his children then living," may cause problems of construction in determining the members of the class. Thus, it may inadvertently exclude persons whom the testator intended to benefit; and the gift may be void in whole or in part for perpetuity. You are, therefore, well advised to avoid such temporal expressions or, if they are unavoidable, you should define them clearly.

(c) Change in Name and Form

(i) *Generally*

Suppose that a testator bequeaths "my 100 shares in ABC Ltd." and that he or she had those shares at the date of the will. Suppose, further, however, that ABC Ltd. thereafter reorganized its capital and split its stock two for one, so that the testator then owned 200 shares and continued to own them at death. Should the bequest adeem?

Alternatively, suppose that a testator bequeathed "my interest in Atlas Copiers Ltd." and that he or she owned a 25 per cent interest in that company at the date of the will. However, prior to the testator's death the shareholders of Atlas agreed to sell their shares to Xerox of Canada Ltd. and to take shares and notes in Xerox in return and that the testator owned those at death. Has the gift adeemed?

Re Britt,[128] reproduced below, discusses this issue.

RE BRITT
[1968] 2 O.R. 12, 68 D.L.R. (2d) 26
Supreme Court of Ontario
[Court of Appeal]

The testatrix, Yetta Britt, sold certain real property in 1959 and took back a first mortgage. Subsequently she made her will by which she directed that "all monies owing on a First Mortgage on the lands and premises situate at 52 1/2 St. Patrick Street, in the City of Toronto" be paid to her daughter, Freda Koskie, her

---

128 [1968] 2 O.R. 12, 68 D.L.R. (2d) 26 (C.A.).

three sons and a granddaughter in equal shares. Freda was named the residuary beneficiary.

The mortgagor defaulted and the testatrix instituted foreclosure proceedings. She obtained judgment on the covenant, fixed on a reference at $11,782 and, there being no redemption by the mortgagor, a final order of foreclosure.

The testatrix remained seised of the property until her death in 1967, without attempting to enforce the judgment on the covenant. It was then worth $17,000.

On an application to construe the will, Lieff J. held that the gift had not adeemed and that the five beneficiaries, therefore, each took a one-fifth interest in the property. Freda appealed.

LASKIN J.A., delivered the judgment of the Court:

. . .

It is well to note that the testatrix did not, in para. 5, dispose of either her mortgage or of all her interest in the property; she used the words "all monies owing on a first mortgage" of the particular property. Had the monies owing been paid off in her lifetime, it would be clear that the gift had been adeemed. Had she given the mortgage as such (instead of the money secured thereby) and final foreclosure had occurred in her lifetime, it would also be a proper conclusion that ademption resulted.[129]

. . .

Had the testatrix sold the property after the foreclosure, ademption would have resulted, even though she held an unrealized judgment on the covenant. Is the position any different where, at the date of her death, she still retains the property, even though, in view of its value, her executor (as he swore in an affidavit) has no intention of enforcing that judgment by the issue of execution?

To answer this question it is necessary to be clear about the difference between the mortgage debt and the mortgage security. They may be assigned to different persons, but a transfer of the security alone will also carry the debt because this is implicit in redemption by the mortgagor.[130] However, although this be so from the standpoint of the mortgagor, it does not follow that the holder of the security will necessarily succeed to the money charged upon it; he may be a trustee for others entitled to it.[131]

In the ordinary case of a mortgage to secure a loan, a contractual obligation of repayment was easily inferable despite the absence from the mortgage of a covenant to pay.[132] The inclusion of such a covenant converted a simple contract obligation into an obligation under seal. In either case, a mortgagee was not entitled, in equity, to have both the land and the money secured thereby. Thus, a sale of the property after foreclosure would preclude enforcement of the personal or covenant obligation of repayment. An attempt to enforce the obligation, either

---

129 See *Re Bridle* (1879), 4 C.P.D. 336, and *cf. Re Swick*, [1944] O.R. 420, [1944] 4 D.L.R. 55, where, however, a quitclaim for consideration followed after foreclosure proceedings were taken.

130 See Falconbridge, *Law of Mortgages*, 3rd ed., pp. 219-20.

131 See *Re Clowes*, [1893] 1 Ch. 214.

132 *Cf. Tomles v. Chandler* (1686), 2 Lev. 116, 83 E.R. 476.

by action after final foreclosure or by execution on a judgment on the covenant obtained in the foreclosure proceedings, would reopen the foreclosure if the mortgagee still retained the property.

Applying these propositions to the facts herein, it follows that because the mortgagee still retained the property at her death, the mortgage debt, although translated into a judgment on the covenant, remained enforceable by execution; in other words, it remained alive as a judgment debt. The question then becomes whether a bequest of a debt owing to a testator is adeemed where at his death it has become a money judgment.

I would answer this question in the negative, recognizing at the same time that we are dealing here with a specific bequest. I am prepared to accept the rule, going back to *Ashburner v. MacGuire*[133] that the intention of the testatrix is not a saving factor. But not every change affecting a specific legacy results in ademption. Where the change is in name or in form only but the specific thing given is substantially the same, it would be an over-refinement to find ademption.[134] That, in my view, is the case here. The judgment on the covenant is a step towards enforcement or collection of the debt; it itself remains outstanding, even though it is now in the form of a judgment.[135] It remains alive because the property by which it was secured is still in the creditor's hands and can be reconveyed if necessary. The fact that the executor has no intention of realizing on the personal judgment has no bearing on the issue of ademption.

I conclude, therefore, that para. 5 of the will remained an operative disposition to the extent of the money owing on the mortgage at the date of the death of the testatrix; that is, $11,782 and accumulated interest on the mortgage debt to January 11, 1967. The order of Lieff, J., should be affirmed in this respect, but it should be varied in respect of its apportionment of benefits. In place of the direction that each of the five beneficiaries is entitled to a one-fifth interest in the land, the order should direct that the foreclosed property vests in Freda Koskie as residuary beneficiary but charged with payment thereout of the sum above mentioned, to be divided in equal shares among the five persons of whom Freda Koskie is one.

. . .

Notes and Questions

1. A mortgagee who seeks to enforce a mortgage which is in default has a choice of three remedies: (1) foreclosure; (2) judicial sale; or (3) sale under the contractual power of sale. The testatrix in *Britt* opted for the first of these remedies.

When a mortgagee sues for foreclosure, he or she is seeking a judgment awarding the security (*i.e.*, the land) to him or her. However, in the typical foreclosure action a mortgagee seeks three things, foreclosure, possession and judgment on the covenant. The second of these is necessary to obtain possession if the land is to be retained. The third is a money judgment for the balance owing on the mortgage and it is an alternative to foreclosure. The choice of remedy is the mortgagee's and it can be exercised long after judgment.

---

133 (1786), 2 Bro. C.C. 108, 29 E.R. 62.
134 See *Re Slater*, [1907] 1 Ch. 665 at p. 672.
135 See Falconbridge, *op. cit.* at p. 723.

Typically, the mortgagor will be given an opportunity to redeem, which is rarely exercised. The mortgagee will then obtain a final order of foreclosure, which vests the land in him or her. Even after that the mortgagee can still proceed on the money judgment, however. But in order to be able to do so, he or she must be able to reconvey the land to the mortgagor, because payment of the judgment amounts to redemption and the mortgagee cannot have both the money and the security. Thus, once the mortgagee has sold the property, he or she can no longer proceed on the money judgment, since it is no longer possible to reconvey the land to the mortgagor.

2. Laskin J.A., noted in *Re Britt* that if the testatrix had given the mortgage instead of the monies secured by it (that is, the debt secured by the mortgage), there would have been an ademption. However, in *Re Thompson*[136] the court equated the word "mortgage" with "debt secured by mortgage." Are these two cases inconsistent?

3. *Re Slater*,[137] referred to in *Re Britt*, also illustrates the point. The testator bequeathed the interest arising from money invested in the Lambeth Waterworks Company. When he made his will he owned £1075 worth of £10 per cent stock in that company. However, before his death the company was taken over by, and its assets were vested in, the Metropolitan Water Board, pursuant to statute. The latter Board had jurisdiction over Metropolitan London. The testator received £3739 13 *s.* 2 *d.* worth of stock in the Board and he owned that stock at his death.

The court held that the bequest had adeemed in that there was more than a mere change in name and form in the property. Is that in accordance with the testator's intention?

4. A testator bequeathed "twenty-three of the shares belonging to me in the London and County Banking Company Limited" upon certain trusts. When he made his will, he owned 104 £80 shares in that bank. Thereafter the name of the company was changed to "The London County and Westminster Bank Limited". The capital was increased and new capital was issued. The old capital was split four for one and, thus, the testator received 416 new £20 shares, which he still owned at his death. Has the gift adeemed?[138]

5. A testatrix directed her executors to transfer the balance in a certain bank account to the capital of a trust fund of which X was the trustee. Later, she gave X a power of attorney over her affairs. X, being ignorant of the terms of the will, transferred the money from the account to another account in the same branch of the bank, which paid a higher rate of interest. Did the gift adeem?[139]

6. The testator bequeathed "all moneys held in my name in the X branch of the Y bank" equally to his children. Later he moved to a different community and transferred his account to the Z branch of the Y bank in that community. Has the gift adeemed?[140]

(ii) *Tracing*

It often happens that a testator directs the sale of certain property and then gives legacies out of the proceeds. However, before death the testator sells the property and puts the money in a bank account. Alternatively, the testator may make a gift

---

136 (1919), 45 O.L.R. 520, 48 D.L.R. 757 (C.A.).
137 [1907] 1 Ch. 665 (C.A.).
138 See *Re Clifford*, [1912] 1 Ch. 29.
139 See *Re Dorman (decd)*, [1994] 1 All E.R. 804 (Ch. D.).
140 Contrast *Re Holden Estate* (1945), 61 B.C.R. 493 (B.C.S.C.); *Koski v. Koski Estate* (1994), 3 E.T.R. (2d) 314 (S.C.C.).

of the money in a certain bank account and then later transfers the money to another account.

Has there been a change in name and form only in such situations and, if so, can the proceeds be traced? This question is discussed in *Re Cudeck*,[141] reproduced below.

RE CUDECK
(1977), 16 O.R. (2d) 337, 1 E.T.R. 17, 78 D.L.R. (3d) 250
Supreme Court of Ontario
[Court of Appeal]

The testator, by his will, made in 1973, bequeathed to his friend Marie Anne Dorinie "the proceeds of a Term Deposit of $28,000 principal plus interest," made with a certain bank in 1973. The testator owned such a term deposit when he made his will, but he cashed it on April 30, 1974 and the proceeds were credited to his account. On the same date he purchased another, which he cashed on July 29, 1974. Again, the proceeds were credited to his account. On that date he purchased another term deposit for $37,000 out of the account. He cashed it in October, 1974 and purchased a new one for $40,000. Thereafter, he executed a codicil to his will in which he declared his intention to give the $40,000 term deposit to his friend instead of the $28,000 one referred to in his will, and directed that the words "or at any time thereafter" be added to the date referred to in his will.

In January, 1975 the new term deposit matured and was credited to the testator's account. In August he bought a new one for $36,000, leaving a balance of $201.65 in the account. He cashed the $36,000 term deposit on September 12, 1975 and the principal and interest of $36,258.90 was credited to his account. However he withdrew it, together with another $200, on the same day, leaving a balance in the account of $1.15.

Also on September 12, 1975, the testator rented a safety deposit box at another bank. At his death, 37 one-thousand-dollar bills were found in the box together with a handwritten note in which testator purported to leave the contents of the box to his friend and directed that the note should be regarded as part of his will. Although signed by him, it was not attested.

On an application for advice and direction, the judge of first instance held that Marie Anne Dorinie was entitled to a gift in the amount of $36,000. The widow, who was the residuary legatee, appealed. Miss Dorinie cross-appealed.

MACKINNON J.A., delivered the judgment of the Court:

. . .

In my view the testator's intention is clearly set out in paragraph 4(e) of the will together with the codicil, and on the facts of this case the gift to Miss Dorinie was not adeemed. This is not a case where the judges will be confronted on the

---

141   (1977), 16 O.R. (2d) 337, 1 E.T.R. 17, 78 D.L.R. (3d) 250 (C.A.).

other side of the River Styx by an irate testator for distorting or frustrating his clear intention.

The words of the codicil quoted appear to be words of intention rather than of gift but they do extend the words of paragraph 4(e) so that it reads, after the codicil:

> To deliver over and pay to my friend, Marie Anne Dorinie, . . . *the proceeds* of a Term Deposit of $40,000,...said Term Deposit having been made on or about November 10th 1973, *or at any time thereafter* for her own use absolutely. [The italics are mine.]
>
> . . .

The gift in the instant case is of the *proceeds* of the term deposits as they may be from time to time, not of the term deposit itself. The words "at any time thereafter" were the means of determining the amount of the legacy, which, from the history of the testator's buying and selling of term deposits, can be seen to have had a fluctuating value. In my view, what was given here was a legacy in the amount realized from the term deposit last held. This legacy can only be lost if the testator has cashed the deposit and clearly appropriated the proceeds to himself. There are two decisions of the Supreme Court of Canada which are helpful here. In *Hicks v. McClure*,[142] a clause in the will directed the executors to sell a farm and divide "the proceeds" between the testator's two sons. The testator, after the execution of his will and before he died, sold the farm, taking back a mortgage as part payment. Duff J.[143] put the necessary question in the form in which it can be put in the instant case:

> Has the testator manifested his intention that his gift is not of the particular property only but of the proceeds of the property so long as the proceeds retain a form by which they can be identified as such?

The other members of the Court came to the same conclusion, and I would respectfully adopt the following words of Anglin J. as being apposite here:[144]

> *Morgan v. Thomas*,[145] shews that in a case such as this a broad and even a lax construction of the terms of the will should prevail if thereby effect will more probably be given to the testator's intention. That case and *Manton v. Tabois*,[146] establish that partial ademption owing to a portion of the property which is the subject of the devise being unavailable or to its identity having been lost will not prevent the devise taking effect as to so much of it as still forms part of the testator's available estate and can be fully identified.

> [His Lordship also referred to *Diocesan Synod of Fredericton v. Perrett*,[147] to the same effect, and continued:]

---

142 64 S.C.R. 361, [1922] 3 W.W.R. 285, 70 D.L.R. 287.
143 *Ibid.*, at p. 364.
144 *Ibid.*, at pp. 364-365.
145 (1877), 6 Ch. D. 176. (1877).
146 (1885), 30 Ch. D. 92. (1885).
147 [1955] S.C.R. 498, [1955] 3 D.L.R. 225.

[T]he proceeds did not lose their identity by being momentarily mingled in the testator's small bank account. The note of 12th September 1975, while it cannot itself be given testamentary effect, can, in my view, be used to trace and identify the proceeds given by the will and codicil, namely the $36,258.90. Like the Weekly Court Judge, I have no difficulty in finding that $36,258.90 of the $37,000 deposited in the safety deposit box was the proceeds of the term deposit cashed that same day. What the testator did was to "round" that amount to $37,000 so that he could deposit 37 one-thousand-dollar bills on 12th September. This is not a case of post hoc ergo propter hoc. There is no evidence from the executors, after an examination of all the estate records, that $36,258.90 of the $37,000 in the safety deposit box could have come from any other source but the $36,000 term deposit.

Mr. Sheard argued that the cases where the proceeds of sale have been traced and given to legatees have all been cases where the testator has, by his will, directed his executors to sell a specific part of his real estate and given specific directions for the disposition of the proceeds:[148]

With respect, I do not think there can be any distinction made between proceeds recovered from the dispositions of real or personal property. Further, the use of the words "to deliver over and pay...the proceeds..." implies a clear direction to sell, or to convert into cash, and to deliver that cash to Miss Dorinie. In my view the facts of this case fall clearly within the principles quoted from *Hicks v. McClure*,[149] and the Weekly Court Judge was right in his conclusion that the gift to Miss Dorinie had not been adeemed and the proceeds of the term deposit could be identified. I would, however, vary his judgment to include the interest received from the term deposit and direct that the total amount of $36,258.90 be paid out of the $37,000 found in the safety deposit box.

. . .

The appeal is accordingly dismissed and the cross-appeal is allowed to the limited extent noted.

. . .

Notes and Questions

1. *Re Cudeck* may be contrasted with *Re Stevens*[150] in which it was held that the proceeds of sale of real property, which the testatrix had bequeathed, could no longer be traced when they were paid into a bank account which already had a credit balance. Such a commingling stops the right to trace according to that case. Doull J., said in *Stevens*,[151] "the failure to keep such fund [the proceeds] separate from other funds involves such a change in the thing bequeathed that there is no longer anything upon which the gift can act." Further, Hall J., said[152] that the proceeds of sale were no longer identifiable once the

---

148 *Re Richmond*, [1939] O.W.N. 101 at 103.
149 *Supra*.
150 19 M.P.R. 49, [1946] 4 D.L.R. 322 (N.S.C.A.).
151 *Ibid.*, at D.L.R. 335.
152 *Ibid.*, at p. 333.

testatrix "had appropriated the whole account to her personal use without differentiating between money received from the sale and her other money."

It is submitted that the discussion in *Stevens* is correct, but rather for the reason that once there has been a commingling with other funds, there has been such a change in form that the property which is the subject matter of the specific gift no longer exists.

2. Tracing or, more accurately, following the property into its product does, indeed, become impossible at law once the funds which are sought to be traced become commingled with other funds in a bank account. In equity, tracing into a mixed fund is possible, but traditionally case law insisted that for tracing in equity to be possible there must be a fiduciary relationship, which does not exist between the testator and the beneficiary. It is questionable whether a fiduciary relationship is required before one can trace today,[153] but if it is, it is arguable that the *Cudeck* case was incorrectly decided, unless it could be argued that the moneys already in the account could be disregarded as *de minimis*.[154]

3. For a case to the same effect as *Re Stevens*[155] see *Re Rodd*.[156] A case similar to *Re Cudeck* is *Re Richmond*.[157]

4. New Brunswick[158] and the Northwest Territories[159] have enacted subsection 20(3) of the *Uniform Wills Act*[160] to overcome the problem of commingled proceeds. The section provides:

> Where the testator has bequeathed proceeds of the sale of property and the proceeds are received by him before his death, the bequest is not adeemed by commingling the proceeds with the funds of the testator if the proceeds are traced into those funds.

5. A testator bequeathed the money deposited in his account in a certain bank. Subsequently he transferred the money in the account plus some additional money to an account with another bank.

Has the bequest adeemed?[161] Would it make any difference if the testator closed his account and placed the money into a new joint account which he opened with another person?[162]

6. Does ademption of a specific bequest of a bank account occur if the account is closed and the monies are invested, not by the testator, but by someone acting on his or her behalf, such as the Public Trustee, appointed because of the testator's mental illness? In *Re Dupont;*

---

153 See *Oosterhoff & Gillese: Text, Commentary and Cases on Trusts*, 5th ed. by A.H. Oosterhoff and E.E. Gillese (Scarborough: Carswell, 1998), pp. 758ff.

154 *Cf. Moore v. Moore* (1860), 29 Beav. 496, 54 E.R. 720, in which an amount of £1 10s. already in the account was disregarded.

155 19 M.P.R. 49, [1946] 4 D.L.R. 322 (N.S.C.A.).

156 (1981), 10 E.T.R. 117 (P.E.I.S.C.). See also Youdan, Annotation, *ibid.*, at 118.

157 [1939] O.W.N. 101 (H.C.).

158 *Wills Act*, R.S.N.B. 1973, c. W-9, s. 20(3).

159 *Wills Act*, R.S.N.W.T. 1988, c. W-5, s. 14(3).

160 Uniform Law Conf., *Uniform Acts of the Uniform Law Conference of Canada* (1978, as rev.), p. 53-1

161 See *Re Brems*, [1963] 1 O.R. 122, 36 D.L.R. (2d) 218 (H.C.); *Re Puczka Estate* (1970), W.W.R. 56, 10 D.L.R. (3d) 339 (Sask. Q.B.).

162 See *Re Brekken; Penn v. Burtness* (1977), 4 B.C.L.R. 211 (S.C.). See also *Re Hubert* (1975), 13 N.B.R. (2d) 257, 13 A.P.R. 257.

Maynard v. Gosselin[163] the court held that the bequest does adeem in those circumstances, so long as the Public Trustee acts in good faith.

This rule has been reversed by statute in Ontario,[164] New Brunswick,[165] Manitoba[166] and Saskatchewan.[167] The legislation in those provinces preserves the rights of beneficiaries under the will to the proceeds.[168]

7. *Cudeck* indicates that courts are more willing today to have regard to the testator's intention. *Doyle v. Doyle Estate*[169] is another. The testator owned an incorporated business, Doyle Electric Ltd. In 1982 he made a will in which he authorized his trustees to sell his shares in the business as soon as possible after his death and to pay the proceeds in stated proportions to three family members, including 50 percent to his daughter. He left the residue of his estate to his wife. A year later, for income tax purposes, he caused the shares to rolled over into a holding company. Thereafter, he owned shares in the holding company, while the holding company held the shares in the business. Later, the testator caused the business to sell most of its business assets to his daughter and her husband. They incorporated a new company with the name Doyle Electric Ltd., while the testator changed the name of the original company to Theabush Investments Ltd. The testator died in 1991 without changing his will. The question was whether the gift of the shares in the original Doyle Electric Ltd. had adeemed. Greer J. held that it had not. She took a subjective approach to interpreting the will in order to ascertain the testator's intention and concluded that it was clear from the will that the testator intended to give his daughter one-half of his share capital. Further, there was no evidence that he intended to disinherit her. That would happen if the doctrine of ademption applied. Greer J. further held that the gift was in any event of the proceeds of sale of the shares, not a bequest of the shares themselves. Hence, the testator intended to confer a general economic benefit on the beneficiaries, rather than the shares themselves. She concluded that the shares had changed in name and form only and could be traced through the holding company into the shares the deceased owned in Theabush. Hence, the daughter was entitled to the proceeds of sale of one-half of the shares of Theabush.

The Court of Appeal affirmed, noting that it was clear from the will that the testator intended to leave one-half of his major assets to his daughter. In any event, the court held that the bequest was not a specific bequest, so that the doctrine of ademption did not apply. The court also confirmed that the bequest could be traced into the shares of Theabush.

Was it relevant that there was no evidence that the testator did not intend to disinherit his daughter? Such evidence could only arise after the will was made. Was the Court of Appeal correct in holding that the gift was not specific? Was it not the gift of aliquot

---

163 [1977] 6 W.W.R. 385, 1 E.T.R. 203, 79 D.L.R. (3d) 754 (Man. Q.B.). See to the same effect *Re Rodd* (1981), 10 E.T.R. 117 (P.E.I.S.C.).

164 *Substitute Decisions Act, 1992*, S.O. 1992, c. 30 [am. 1994, c. 27, ss. 43(2), 62, 1996, c. 2, ss. 3 - 60, 1998, c. 26, s. 108], ss. 35.1, 36.

165 *Infirm Persons Act*, R.S.N.B. 1973, c. I-8, s. 18.

166 *Wills Act*, R.S.M. 1988, c. W150, s. 24.

167 *Dependent Adults Act*, S.S. 1989-90, c. D-25.1, s. 34. See also *Mental Health Act 1959* (U.K.), c. 72, s. 107; and see Buist, "Persons under Disability: Dealing with Assets to be Disposed of by Will" (1956), 32 N.Z.L.J. 170.

168 For an application of the legislation see *Krawecki Estate, Re* (1995), 8 E.T.R. (2d) 307 (Sask. Q.B.).

169 (1995), 9 E.T.R. (2d) 162 (Ont. Gen. Div.), affirmed (1998), 22 E.T.R. (2d) 17 (C.A.). See Archie J. Rabinowitz, Comment (1999), 19 E.T. & P.J. 12.

portions of the proceeds of sale of specific property? Such gifts are considered to be specific according to cases considered earlier in this chapter.[170]

8. In *Re Thornton Estate*,[171] the Saskatchewan Surrogate Court took a different approach and applied the doctrine of ademption without regard to the testator's intention. The testator owned a number of farm properties. In 1976, on the advice of his accountant and lawyers, he transferred these properties to a corporation and took back shares in the corporation and a shareholder's loan. He did retain legal title to the properties to avoid having to pay land transfer taxes, a practice that was common. Ten years later, he made a will in which he purported to devise the several properties to named beneficiaries. The court held that the gifts were specific and that they had adeemed and fell into residue.

Considering that the testator still held effective ownership of the properties through his corporation, ought the court to have allowed the gift to be traced into the shares of the corporation? Note the difference between this case and *Doyle*. In *Thornton* the will was made after the transfer, whereas the reverse occurred in *Doyle*.

Interestingly, the law firm that did the legal work of transferring the properties to the corporation in 1976 also drafted the will in 1986. The disappointed beneficiaries sued the law firm for negligence and were successful.[172]

7. THE EQUITABLE DOCTRINE OF CONVERSION

(a) Generally

When a testator has devised or bequeathed specific property, but sells or otherwise disposes of the property before death, he or she has converted it into other property and, absent a remedial statutory provision, the gift adeems.[173]

It sometimes happens that the testator has not yet concluded the disposition of the property which is the subject matter of the gift, but has entered into an agreement to sell it. At his or her death, therefore, the property is still in the estate. Yet, apart from statute, the gift will adeem. Equity, which deems that as done which ought to be done, considers that in that case there is a notional conversion of the property into another kind of property.

The equitable doctrine is discussed in *Church v. Hill*,[174] reproduced below.

---

170 See *Lindsay v. Walbrook* (1897), 24 O.A.R. 604 (C.A.); *Culbertson v. Culbertson* (1967), 60 W.W.R. 187, 62 D.L.R. (2d) 134 (Sask. C.A.).

171 (1990), 85 Sask. R. 34 (Surr. Ct.).

172 See *Earl v. Wilhelm* (2000), 31 E.T.R. (2d) 193 (Sask. C.A.), leave to appeal refused (October 12, 2000), Doc. 27807 (S.C.C.).

173 *Nakonieczny v. Kaminski* (1989) 33 E.T.R. 219 (Sask. Q.B.), which permitted the beneficiary to trace the proceeds of sale, was, I submit, incorrectly decided.

174 [1923] S.C.R. 642, [1923] 3 W.W.R. 405, [1923] 3 D.L.R. 1045.

CHURCH v. HILL
[1923] S.C.R. 642, [1923] 3 W.W.R. 405, [1923] 3 D.L.R. 1045
Supreme Court of Canada

The testator, Arthur W. Church, devised Lot 15, Block 46, Edmonton, to his daughter Mary Hill. He directed that the balance of his property be divided equally between his daughters Amy Watson and Kate Joyce and his son Arthur Church.

In 1920 he entered into an instalment contract to sell Lot 15, Block 46 to one Lockerbie for $4,500. Five hundred dollars was paid immediately and the balance was payable in monthly instalments of $30 with interest at 8%. The testator died in 1921 with a substantial amount still owing under the agreement.

On an application to construe the will, the judge of first instance held that the gift to Mary Hill had adeemed. Her appeal to the Alberta Supreme Court, Appellate Division was successful. The residuary beneficiaries then appealed to the Supreme Court of Canada.

MIGNAULT J.:

. . .

In the Appellate Court Mr. Justice Stuart cited the well-known case of *Ross v. Watson*[175] as determining what are respectively the rights of the vendor and the purchaser under a sale agreement such as this. The question there was whether the purchaser, who had ceased his payments on account of non-fulfilment of representations (which were adjudged to be sufficient to absolve him from specific performance) had a lien on the property for the payments he had already made. The decision was that the purchaser had such a lien and it was clearly laid down by the Lord Chancellor, Lord Westbury, and by Lord Cranworth, who concurred with him, that where by an agreement of sale the ownership of an estate is transferred subject to the payment of the purchase price, every portion of the purchase money paid in pursuance of the agreement is a part performance and execution of the contract, and, to the extent of the money paid, does in equity finally transfer to the purchaser the ownership of a corresponding portion of the estate.

. . .

Lockerbie therefore, at the death of the testator, had acquired in equity, and to the extent of the purchase money paid by him, the ownership of a corresponding portion of the estate of the testator.

It will be said, and such was the reasoning of Mr. Justice Stuart, that the testator, at his death, had still a substantial interest in the property, to the extent at least of the purchase money still unpaid. But he could assert no such interest against Lockerbie if the latter continued, as he has done, to pay the purchase money as it becomes due. So long as the conditions of the agreement of sale were carried out, the vendor was entitled only to this purchase money, and the purchaser, on completing its payment, had the right to demand a conveyance. Had the vendor refused to make this conveyance, the purchaser would have been entitled to

---

175 (1864), 10 H.L. Cas. 672.

compel him to do so by an action for specific performance; and therefore the interest which the purchaser acquired under the sale agreement was certainly an interest which equity would recognize and one commensurate with the relief which equity would give by way of specific performance. *Howard v. Miller.*[176]

. . .

[T]he respondent, under the devise made to her, seeks to obtain the balance of the purchase money rather than an interest in the land itself, which interest the testator could not have asserted against Lockerbie so long as the latter fulfilled all the conditions of the promise of sale. The question now is whether this devise has become inoperative by reason of the sale of the devised property.

The legal position here can be stated as follows: By reason of the sale agreement, any interest in the property in question of the vendor as against the purchaser, and so long as the latter made the stipulated payments, was converted into a claim for the purchase moneys. What the testator devised to the respondent was the property itself. What he had at his death — and it is then that the will speaks — was the right to the price and not the property. The devise therefore fails because its subject matter no longer existed at the testator's death.

It does not appear to me to matter that in Alberta real estate has been assimilated to personal property, both going to the personal representative of the deceased. So long as Lockerbie is not in default, the respondent could not claim either from him or from the personal representative of the deceased the property itself, and the answer to any demand by her of the purchase money is that it was not given to her under the devise of the property.

I cannot therefore avoid the conclusion that the devise to the respondent entirely fails. But can the appellants claim the purchase moneys under the bequest to them of the balance of the testator's property? The answer should be in the affirmative if the bequest is a residuary bequest.

The language used, "the balance of my property to be divided equally between...." taken in connection with the declaration of the testator, "I give, devise and bequeath all my real and personal estate of which I may die possessed of in the manner following...." certainly indicates the intention that the appellants shall have everything except the property specifically devised to the respondent. They take therefore the residue of the estate, for the "balance" mentioned in the will is certainly what is known to the law as the "residue," both expressions having the same meaning. And the residue comprises this purchase price, so that it must go to the appellants.

That the testator ever contemplated that his youngest daughter, the respondent, would take nothing under his will, and that the price of the property he had left to her would go to his other children, or that he intended any such result, seems very doubtful. But the court cannot make a will for him or provide the respondent with an equivalent for the loss of the property which the testator had devised to her. Nothing would be more dangerous than to refuse to apply the settled rules as to the ademption of legacies because it may be conjectured that the result would

---

176 [1915] A.C. 318 at 326.

be contrary to the intention of the testator. *Dura lex*, it is true, *sed lex*, and the law must be applied.

Without therefore concealing my regret that this result cannot be avoided, I have come to the conclusion to allow the appeal with costs here and in the appellate court, payable out of the estate, and to restore the judgement of the learned trial judge.

[The other members of the Court concurred.]

Notes and Questions

1. If the gift is not of the property itself, but the testator directs that it be sold and certain legacies be paid out of the proceeds, the situation is different. If the testator then sells the property, there may be a problem in tracing the proceeds,[177] but, if he or she takes a mortgage back as security for part of the purchase price, the proceeds are, to that extent, still identifiable and the beneficiaries are entitled to the mortgage.[178]

2. *Dearden Estate v. Pittman*[179] affords another example of the problem. The testator, by a will made in 1970, gave his business and the land upon which it was situate, to his nephew. In 1986, the testator agreed to sell the business and the land. He died prior to the completion of the contract. In fact, the contract was never completed, since it was subject to true conditions precedent which were never satisfied. At issue was whether the contract of sale made by the deceased had adeemed the specific gift in the 1970 will. It was held that the doctrine of conversion applies only to a contract enforceable by and against the testator. Thus the gift was not adeemed.

It must not be supposed, however, that the doctrine of ademption does not operate on conditional contracts. It does, provided the conditions are fulfilled and the contract is completed after the testator's death.[180]

3. A testator devised his farm to his trustee upon trust to pay the income to his two sons for life. He directed that after their deaths the farm should be sold and the proceeds divided among his grandchildren, failing whom, among his nephews and nieces then surviving. The testator later sold the from himself under an instalment contract. No monies had been paid under the contract yet when he died. What result?[181]

4. T devised "whatever house and property I may own and may be using as a residence at the time of my death." T sold his house shortly before her death, subject to a mortgage back for part of the purchase price. What result?[182]

---

177 This is discussed in the preceding section.
178 See *Hicks v. McClure*, 64 S.C.R. 361, [1922] 3 W.W.R. 285, 70 D.L.R. 287. *Cf. Diocesan Synod of Fredericton v. Perrett*, [1955] S.C.R. 498, [1955] 3 D.L.R. 225. Of course, if the testator does not own the property, the gift will probably fail, even if the testator's company owned it: see *Wong v. Lee Estate* (1993), 49 E.T.R. 121 (B.C.C.A.).
179 (1987), 26 E.T.R. 111.
180 See *Re Sweeting (decd), Sweeting et al. v. Sweeting et al.*, [1988] 1 All E.R. 1016.
181 See *Public Trustee for Saskatchewan v. Montreal Trust Co. of Canada* (1989), 33 E.T.R. 292, 57 D.L.R. (4th) 742 (Sask. C.A.), and see A.H. Oosterhoff, Comment (1989), 9 E. & T.J. 191; Brian MacIvor, Case Comment, 33 E.T.R. 302.
182 See *Re Wilson Estate* (1989), 34 E.T.R. 121 (B.C.S.C.). See also the *Succession Law Reform Act*, s. 20(2), discussed below.

(b) Options

The equitable doctrine of conversion also applies when the testator has granted an option on the property which he or she has devised or bequeathed by will and the option is exercised after death. If it is exercised before death, there is an actual conversion.

Lawes v. Bennett,[183] held that when a person grants an option to another to purchase real property, and the option is exercised after the death of the optionor, the proceeds of sale are personalty and come to the optionor's estate as such and not as realty.

The rule, however, applies equally to an option on personalty. *Re Carrington*,[184] reproduced below, discusses the rule.

RE CARRINGTON
[1932] 1 Ch. 1, [1931] All E.R. Rep. 658
Court of Appeal

The testator made his will in 1911. By it he bequeathed certain shares he owned in a limited company to his sister, his niece and the wife of a nephew, and gave the residue of his estate to others. In 1927 the testator granted an option on the shares to X. He died in 1930 and one month later X exercised the option.

On an application to construe the will, the judge at first instance held that the bequests had adeemed. The specific beneficiaries appealed.

LORD HANWORTH M.R.:

. . .

The question is whether the specific bequests of these shares have been adeemed by the fact that the option has been exercised, with the result that the shares have been turned into money and no longer form part of the testator's estate.

. . .

In *Lawes v. Bennett*[185] there was an option given before the will was made, and it was exercised after the death of the testator. The words which have given rise to the difficulty are in the judgment of Lord Kenyon:[186]

When the party who has the power of making the election has elected, the whole is to be referred back to the original agreement, and the only difference is, that the real estate is converted into personal at a future period.

It is said that the meaning of those words was that Lord Kenyon was there treating the option as relating back to the date on which it was given, but I doubt whether that is the necessary inference from the words used. But in *Weeding v.*

183 (1785), 1 Cox Eq. Cas. 167, 29 E.R. 1111.
184 [1932] 1 Ch. 1, [1931] All E.R. Rep. 658 (C.A.).
185 1 Cox 167.
186 1 Cox 167, 171.

Weeding[187] we have a case practically on all fours with that which is before us. There the option was exercised after the death, and it was held that the property was converted from the date of the exercise of the option and passed to the residuary legatees. There is a difference between *Lawes v. Bennett* and *Weeding v. Weeding*, as *Weeding v. Weeding* was decided after the Wills Act, 1837,[188] had come into force, and under s. 24 of that Act a will now speaks from the death of the testator. It would seem that according to the decision in *Weeding v. Weeding* there was in the present case a conversion when the option took effect on February 18, 1930, of these shares into money, consequently that part of the testator's estate is money and the shares no longer form part of his estate, the result of which is that the specific legacies have been adeemed and the legatees are deprived of the shares, just as if the testator had sold the shares in his lifetime. It is too late to upset the reasoning in *Lawes v. Bennett* or to overrule *Weeding v. Weeding*. In 1894 Chitty J. in *In re Isaacs*[189] had to consider whether the principle in *Lawes v. Bennett* was applicable in the case of an intestacy, and, after going through the cases, he came to the conclusion that it was. He said

> I think the judgment in the case of *Townley v. Bedwell*[190] alone is a decision on the point, that the option does not operate completely to convert the property until it is exercised, because the rents in the interval after the testator's death go to the heir-at-law,

and he also said that he did not adopt the principle that the conversion related back to the date of the contract. Those cases were considered by the Court of Appeal in *In re Marlay*[191] and the three judges said that under this doctrine of conversion when the option was exercised at a later date the effect was not to be taken as from the date of the giving of the original option but from the date it was exercised.

. . .

One view appeared attractive — namely, that one might say with regard to personal property that as the option was not exercised till February 18, 1930, it was possible to hold that the shares were still part of the estate of the testator and that the specific bequests were effective even if subsequently to the testator's death they became money. In the course of the argument I put the case of a dividend on the shares arising before February 18, and suggested that the specific legatees might have been entitled to a portion of the dividend; but that view does not seem to be tenable having regard to what Warrington L.J. said in *In re Marlay*:[192]

> It is well settled that in such cases the rents and profits are payable to the heir or devisee, his heirs or assigns, until the happening of the event in question, and this I think can only be justified on

---

187 1 J. & H. 424.
188 7 Will. 4 & 1 Vict., c. 26.
189 [1894] 3 Ch. 506.
190 14 Ves. 590.
191 [1915] 2 Ch. 264.
192 *Ibid.,* at p. 281.

the footing that the land vests in him as land, and remains so vested until it shifts by the happening of the event.

It is plain then that the doctrine is that conversion does not take place at the date of the contract, but at the date when the condition is fulfilled which makes the contract effective. Then the interest shifts on the happening of that fulfilment.

. . .

Therefore after searching for means to carry out the intention of the testator it appears that it is not possible to do so for the reason that there has been at the date of the exercise of this option a conversion, and then there is necessarily an ademption of the shares. Therefore the shares, the subject-matter of the specific legacies, have been taken away and adeemed by being changed into money.

There is one further point — namely, whether the residuary estate has been specifically dealt with by the will or left so that there was an intestacy in respect of it. *In re Isaacs*[193] makes it plain that the principle of *Lawes v. Bennett* would still apply to an intestacy. *In re Marlay* approves and in effect follows that decision. I am therefore in the same position as Maugham J. was, and accordingly the appeal must be dismissed.

[Lawrence and Romer L.JJ., concurred.]

Notes and Question

1. *Lawes v. Bennett*[194] involved the following facts: The testator had granted a lease of certain real property with an option to purchase to X. Thereafter he made his will and devised all his real property to Y and his personalty to Y and Z. X exercised the option after the testator's death. The court held that upon the exercise of the option the real property was converted into personalty. Until it was exercised, however, Y, as devisee was entitled to the rents.[195]

You should note that in *Lawes v. Bennett* there was no ademption, since the devise to Y was not specific, but residuary.

2. In *Re Pyle*[196] the court held that the rule in *Lawes v. Bennett* did not apply. The testator made his will and devised certain real property to Z. Later he made a codicil by which he gave certain legacies and confirmed his will. On the same day he granted a lease with an option to purchase of the real property to X. X exercised the option after the testator's death.

The court held that, if a testator, knowing of the existence of a contract to purchase the property, afterwards devises it without referring to the contract, he or she intends that the devisee shall have the property or the proceeds. In the *Pyle* case, presumably the testator had the option in mind when he executed the codicil confirming his will and, thus, it was as though he made the devise afterwards.

---

193 [1894] 3 Ch. 506.
194 *Supra.*
195 *Re Marlay*, [1915] 2 Ch. 264 (C.A.).
196 [1895] 1 Ch. 724 (C.A.).

(c) The Effect of Republication

You will recall that the doctrine of republication operates so as to give a new date to a will, unless that is contrary to the testator's intentions.[197] Thus, if a testator re-executes his or her will or executes a codicil intending that it form part of the will, the will takes as its new date the date of re-execution or republication.

The doctrine may have the effect of avoiding the operation of the equitable doctrine of conversion. This was the case in *Re Pyle*.[198] *Re Reeves; Reeves v. Pawson*,[199] reproduced below, discusses the operation of the doctrine in this context.

RE REEVES; REEVES v. PAWSON
[1928] 1 Ch. 351, [1928] All E.R. Rep. 342
Chancery Division

The testator was the lessee of No. 1 Chesterfield Street, Mayfair, in London, under a seven-year lease which took effect September 29, 1917.

In 1921 the testator made his will and by a clause of the will he bequeathed to his daughter, Mrs. Pawson, "all my interest in my present lease" of the property. He gave his residuary estate equally to his daughter and two sons.

In 1923 the testator took a renewal of the lease for 12 years. Then, in 1926, he made a codicil to his will in which he made a certain bequest and confirmed his will.

The executors made an application to construe the will.

RUSSELL J.:

But for the fact that the testator executed a codicil to his will there is no doubt that the bequest to his daughter of "my present lease" would have only been a bequest of the lease that expired on September 29, 1924, but it is contended that by confirming his will by codicil on February 10, 1926, during the currency of the new lease, the testator has bequeathed that new lease to his daughter.

. . .

Put in another way the will and the codicil are treated as one document bearing the date of the codicil. Thus in *In re Smith*[200] the testatrix directed that:

No legacy given by this my will shall lapse by reason of the death of the legatee before me, but that the same shall take effect as if the death of such legatee had happened immediately after my death, and such legacy shall accordingly pass to the legal personal representative of such legatee.

In one of the codicils to her will the testatrix made a bequest to a person who predeceased her. All the codicils contained an express formal clause confirming

197 See the chapter on Revocation.
198 *Supra*.
199 [1928] 1 Ch. 351, [1928] All E.R. Rep. 342.
200 [1916] 1 Ch. 523.

in all other respects the testatrix's will. Sargant J. held that the clause applied to and saved the bequest in the codicil. He said:[201]

> It is well settled law that when a codicil expressly confirms a will the effect is, in the words of North J. in *In re Champion*,[202] "to bring down the date of the will to the date of the codicil, and to make the devise in the will operate in the same way in which it would have operated if the words of the will had been contained in the codicil of later date." This decision was affirmed in the Court of Appeal....[203] It is indeed urged here that the words "by this my will" point to a particular instrument of writing, namely, the will itself, and that therefore the saving clause is limited by its very terms to the legacies given by the will itself. But I think that this is too narrow a construction. In my view the will itself is alone named in the clause merely because at the time that was the only instrument containing the testatrix's testamentary dispositions. I cannot find in the phrase any intention to denote the particular instrument alone or to exclude from the application of the clause any legacies which should under codicils confirming the will form part of the testatrix's ultimate testamentary dispositions. The will being brought down to date by the confirming codicils and forming together with them one complete disposition, the legacies given by the codicils come, in my judgment, within the description legacies "given by this my will."
>
> . . .

Those are the modern authorities, and it is contended that they cannot apply to this case, because if the will be construed the expression "my present lease" can only refer to the old lease which has expired. It is true that if the testator in his will had bequeathed to his daughter, "my lease of No. 1 Chesterfield Street, Mayfair, dated September 25, 1917," the republication of his will by the codicil would not have given her any benefit, because the old lease had expired; but the testator has bequeathed to his daughter "my present lease," an expression that exactly fits the circumstances that existed at the date of the codicil. If I follow the principle laid down in *In re Champion*[204] and *In re Fraser*,[205] and applied in *In re Smith*[206] and *In re Hardyman*[207] and read this will and codicil as one document dated February 10, 1926, the date of the execution of the codicil, there is a bequest in favour of his daughter of "my present lease," the present lease being that dated December 31, 1923. Full effect can be given to that bequest, and the benefit of the lease passes to the testator's daughter under the testamentary disposition.

Notes and Questions

1. For a similar case see *Re Harvey; Public Trustee v. Hoskin.*[208]
2. You must not suppose that the doctrine of republication is a rule of law. It is rather a *prima facie* rule which yields to a contrary intention of the testator and to circumstances when his intention would be defeated.

---

201 *Ibid.,* at p. 530.
202 [1893] 1 Ch. 101.
203 *Ibid.*
204 *Ibid.*
205 [1904] 1 Ch. 726.
206 *Supra.*
207 [1925] Ch. 287.
208 [1947] Ch. 285, [1947] 1 All E.R. 349.

Re Maltby[209] illustrates the point. The testator had given the proceeds of certain policies of insurance on his life to his estate. By a subsequent *inter vivos* declaration he changed the beneficiary under the policies to his wife. Later he made a codicil to his will. It was held that the codicil did not republish the will, since, if it did, the testator's intention to benefit his wife would be defeated.[210]

3. A testator set up a testamentary trust for his daughter for life without power of anticipation during coverture. A subsequent statute abolished restraints in anticipation imposed on gifts to women. Thereafter the testator made a codicil to his will which did not refer to the gift to his daughter, but confirmed the will. Did the daughter take free of this restraint?[211]

4. The doctrine of republication can also be applied to the description of a beneficiary. This is illustrated by *Re Hardyman*.[212] The testatrix gave a legacy "in trust for my cousin, his children and his wife." The cousin's wife later died, to the testatrix' knowledge. Thereafter the testatrix added a codicil to her will and some years later the cousin remarried. It was held that the second wife was entitled to share in the legacy.

(d) Statutory Reforms

It will be apparent that the equitable doctrine of conversion is inconvenient and is more likely to defeat the testator's intention than not. Some provinces have, therefore, enacted legislation to meliorate its effects. Section 20(2) of the *Succession Law Reform Act*, reproduced below, is representative. The problems that remain with the legislation are discussed in *Re McLean*,[213] reproduced below.

SUCCESSION LAW REFORM ACT
R.S.O. 1990, c. S.26

20. (1) A conveyance of or other act relating to property that is the subject of a devise, bequest or other disposition, made or done after the making of a will, does not prevent operation of the will with respect to any estate or interest in the property that the testator had power to dispose of by will at the time of his or her death.

(2) Except when a contrary intention appears by the will, where a testator at the time of his or her death,

(a) has a right, chose in action or equitable estate or interest that was created by a contract respecting a conveyance of, or other act relating to, property that was the subject of a devise or bequest, made before or after the making of a will;

---

209 [1960] O.W.N. 473.
210 See also *Royal Trust Co. v. Shimmin*, 46 B.C.R. 237, [1932] W.W.R. 447 (S.C.), affirmed 47 B.C.R. 138, [1933] 3 D.L.R. 718 (C.A.).
211 See *Re Heath's Will Trusts*, [1949] Ch. 170, [1949] 1 All E.R. 199.
212 [1925] Ch. 287, [1925] All E.R. Rep. 83.
213 (1969), 1 N.B.R. (2d) 500, (sub nom. *Larlee v. Earle*) 4 D.L.R. 617 (C.A.)

(b) has a right to receive the proceeds of a policy of insurance covering loss of or damage to property that was the subject of a devise or bequest, whether the loss or damage occurred before or after the making of the will;

(c) has a right to receive compensation for the expropriation of property that was the subject of a devise or bequest, whether the expropriation occurred before or after the making of the will; or

(d) has a mortgage, charge or other security interest in property that was the subject of a devise or bequest, taken by the testator on the sale of such property, whether such mortgage, charge or other security interest was taken before or after the making of the will,

the devisee or donee of that property takes the right, chose in action, equitable estate or interest, right to insurance proceeds or compensation, or mortgage, charge or other security interest of the testator.

Comparable Legislation

(a) To section 20 (1)

Probate Act, R.S.P.E.I. 1988, c. P-21, s. 76; *Wills Act*, R.S.A. 1980, c. W-11, s. 21(1); R.S.B.C. 1996, c. 489, s. 19; R.S.M. 1988, c. W150, s. 21; R.S.N.B. 1973, c. W-9, s. 20(1); R.S.N. 1990, c. W-10, s. 14; R.S.N.S. 1989, c. 505, s. 22; S.S. 1996, c. W-14.11, s. 20(1); R.S.N.W.T. 1988, c. W-5, s. 14(1); R.S.Y. 1986, c. 179, s. 13.

(b) To Section 20 (2)

Wills Act, R.S.A. 1980, c. W-11, s. 21(2); R.S.N.B. 1973, c. W-9, s. 20(2); R.S.N.W.T. 1988, c. W-5, s. 14(2); R.S.N.S. 1989, c. 505, s. 32; S.S. 1996, c. W-14.11, s. 20(2).

RE McLEAN

(1969), 1 N.B.R. (2d) 500, (*sub nom.* Larlee v. Earle)

4 D.L.R. (3d) 617

Supreme Court of New Brunswick

[Appeal Division]

The testator, the Hon. A. Neil McLean, owned a large block of shares in Connors Bros. Limited. By his will, made in 1966, he bequeathed some of the class A and all of the class B shares to various members of his family. The rest of the class A shares fell into residue. In 1967, he and his brother, the other major shareholder, agreed to sell their shares to Loblaws's Groceteria Company Limited. He delivered some of his shares to that company and received a cheque for them which he deposited into his account with other funds. Subsequently he withdrew some moneys from the account. He died later in 1967, and thereafter the estate delivered the remaining shares to the purchaser and received payment therefor.

On an application to interpret the will, the judge of first instance held that the bequest had adeemed in part. Some of the beneficiaries appealed.

LIMERICK J.A.:

[His Lordship quoted the New Brunswick legislation which, in substance, is the same as the Ontario legislation. He also considered *Re Sutherland*[214] which applied the similar Alberta legislation to the sale of an interest in a partnership, which was the subject of a bequest, and on which a substantial sum was still owing at the testatrix' death. He continued:]

I have given considerable thought to the application of s. 20(2) of the *Wills Act* to this case for I realize if it does not apply the intention of the testator will be defeated. The section does not abolish ademption but provides for a substitute gift under certain circumstances.

The testator had at the time of his death the right to payment of the balance of the purchase price for all shares of both classes upon his delivery of the remainder. That was a single chose in action and was not severable. All the shares of the testator had to be delivered before he was entitled to payment of the purchase price. He could not deliver a portion and claim therefor. It was all or nothing. He could not deliver the number of shares specified in any specific bequest and demand payment therefor.

The difficulty that arises in applying s. 20(2) of the *Wills Act* to this case is that the testator had no separate rights or choses in action in respect to the shares comprised in each specific bequest, but only one right or chose in action which was in respect to all the shares which he agreed to sell. That chose in action was the right to receive the balance of the purchase price of the shares when all were delivered. To give those to whom the shares were specifically bequeathed the chose in action would mean they would receive approximately $1,000,000, when the value of their bequest was less than $600,000. Such an interpretation is unreasonable and must be rejected.

I have considered holding that, by reason of s. 20(2), those to whom specific bequests of shares were made and the legatees of the residue of the estate should take the chose in action, but as the subsection was enacted to give some relief from ademption, the words "devisee or donee of the...personal property" in the latter part of the subsection can refer only to a devisee or donee to whom a specific bequest is made, since a residuary devisee or donee is not prejudiced by ademption and particularly as the residue of the class A stock, not specifically bequeathed, goes not to the residuary legatees but to the executors, who may use the proceeds thereof to pay debts, succession duties and funeral expenses or other general bequests.

It was argued by counsel that the executors could collect in the debt or chose in action and allocate or proportion the proceeds between the specific legatees and the residue of the estate. The wording of the section precludes such a solution. The section substitutes the chose in action for the specific bequest, not the proceeds or any portion of the proceeds thereof. The chose in action is the right to

---

214 (1968), 67 D.L.R. (2d) 68, 63 W.W.R. 505 (Alta. S.C.).

bring an action for the debt. The executor's duty would be discharged by assignment of the debt and he would be under no obligation to expend estate moneys
to collect or sue for the debt. The same situation would exist as where a testator
specifically bequeathed a particular promissory note. The executors would fully
discharge their duties relating thereto by endorsing the note and delivering it, the
chose in action, to the legatee.

Counsel contended that s. 20(2) covers the situation where there is a right as
well as chose in action and advanced the argument that the specific legatees had
the right to be paid their legacies.

The word "right" as used in the section however refers to a right in the testator
not in the legatee.

The only right the testator had was to sue for or collect the total purchase price
and in this instance is synonymous with "chose in action".

The section is capable of a logical and reasonable interpretation as it stands
and the Court should not add words or strain the ordinary meaning of the words
used to extend the application of the section to situations not contemplated by the
wording used. To interpret the section as applying to other than the substitution
of the entire chose in action in lieu of one specific bequest would require use of
additional words read into the section or to be inferred.

We should not qualify, add to or rationalize a statutory provision of this nature
which deprives people (residuary legatees) of property rights created by common
law in order to enlarge or enhance the application thereof. We should adopt the
logical and reasonable interpretation of which it is capable without embellishment
or modification.

The legislation intended to deal only with the situation where the subject-matter
of a specific bequest was conveyed or agreed to be conveyed by a separate or
severable contract and the chose in action created by the contract is referable to
the subject-matter of the bequest solely and not intermingled with other assets.

The specific bequests of class A and class B shares of Connors Bros. Ltd. are
adeemed and s. 20(2) of the *Wills Act* does not apply in the circumstances before
us.

. . .

[The concurring judgment of Bridges C.J.N.B., has been omitted. Hughes J.A.,
concurred with Limerick J.A.]

Notes and Questions

1. Section 14 of the Newfoundland Act applies only to acts done after the re-execution
of a will.

2. Note that s. 20(1) of the *Succession Law Reform Act* does not alter the common law
rule that a gift of a mortgage adeems upon discharge of the mortgage during the testator's

lifetime.[215] Similarly, payment of a debt during the testator's lifetime will adeem a gift of the debt and part payment adeems it *pro tanto*.[216]

3. The New Brunswick and Northwest Territories legislation also contains a provision to meliorate the effects of the common law against following the proceeds of property into a mixed fund.[217]

4. The Alberta, New Brunswick, Northwest Territories and Saskatchewan provisions[218] comparable to s. 20(2) of the *Succession Law Reform Act* are not as extensive as that section. The former only apply to acts done by the testator after he or she made the will and do not apply to insured losses, nor to expropriation. Section 32 of the Nova Scotia Act only applies to a contract for the sale or conveyance of any real or personal property for which the testator was liable at death.

5. Is s. 20(2) of the *Succession Law Reform Act* adequate? What situations does it not apply to? Should it apply to them?

6. Is the decision in *Re McLean* reasonable? Does it accord with the intention of the legislation? Would a similar result obtain under the Ontario legislation?

7. You will appreciate that just as a testator can cause ademption by selling property subject to a specific gift, so can a substitute decision maker who acts on the testator's behalf. Thus, a committee or guardian appointed because the testator is incapable of managing property, or an attorney under a continuing power of attorney, may sell the property that is the subject matter of a testamentary gift. Some statutes that provide for substitute decisions contain an anti-ademption rule.[219] Legislation of this kind provides that the beneficiary's interest in the property is transferred to the proceeds. Presumably, however, the proceeds must still be traceable at the testator's death.

8. APPURTENANCES

Appurtenances are things that belong to another thing. They pass under a testamentary gift as part the other thing. Thus, for example, easements and rights of way which are necessary for the reasonable enjoyment of the property devised will pass with it.[220] Similarly, property that adjoins and is used in connection with the property devised normally passes with it. Thus, a devise of "my residence on Johnston Street" was held to include adjoining property which the testator had long used as a lawn and garden.[221] If, on the other hand the principal property is described more specifically, that is, by lot and plan number or by metes and

---

215 *Re Rally* (1911), 25 O.L.R. 112 (H.C.); *Re Ashdown*, [1943] O.W.N. 425, [1943] 4 D.L.R. 517 (C.A.).

216 *Re Shortts*, [1954] O.W.N. 481, [1954] 2 D.L.R. 817.

217 See *Wills Act*, R.S.N.B. 1973, c. W-9, s. 20(3); R.S.N.W.T. 1988, c. W-3, s. 15(3).

218 The statutory references are set out above.

219 See, *e.g.*, *Substitute Decisions Act*, S.O. 1992, c. 30 [am. 1994, c. 27, ss. 43(2), 62; 1996, c. 2, ss. 3 - 60; 1998, c. 26, s. 108] s. 36. To the same effect see: *Infirm Persons Act*, R.S.N.B. 1973, c. I-8, s. 18; *Wills Act*, R.S.M. 1988, c. W150, s. 24 [am. S.M. 1993, c. 29]; *Dependent Adults Act*, S.S. 1989-90, c. D-25.1, s. 34. See also *Mental Health Act 1959* (U.K.), c. 72, s. 107. For an application of the legislation, see *Re Krawecki Estate* (1995), 8 E.T.R. (2d) 307 (Sask. Q.B.).

220 *Schwann v. Cotton*, [1916] 2 Ch. 459 (C.A.), a water easement.

221 *Re MacFarlane*, [1947] O.W.N. 6 (H.C.); and see *Re Loblaw*, [1933] O.R. 764, [1933] 4 D.L.R. 264 (H.C.); *Re Richardson* (1930), 39 O.W.N. 208 (H.C.); *Bateman v. Bateman*, [1941] 3 D.L.R. 762, 16 M.P.R. 80 (N.B.Q.B.).

bounds, adjoining property will not pass under the devise.[222] A bequest of personal property at a specific place will carry all the personal property at that place,[223] unless the gift is restricted to certain items.[224]

9. REAL PROPERTY SUBJECT TO MORTGAGE

At common law, if a testator devised real property subject to a mortgage which he or she had created, or, if created by another, which the testator had assumed, the devisee was entitled to have the mortgage paid off out of the general personal estate.[225] On the other hand, if the testator had not created or assumed the mortgage, the devisee took the property subject to the mortgage.[226] These rules were changed by *Locke King's Acts*,[227] which provided that the devisee took the property subject to the mortgage. The substance of those statutes was accepted in Canada. Section 32 of the *Succession Law Reform Act*, reproduced below, is typical of the Canadian legislation.

The legislation is explained in *Re Hicknell; Perry v. Hicknell*,[228] also reproduced below.

SUCCESSION LAW REFORM ACT
R.S.O. 1990, c. S.26

32. (1) Where a person dies possessed of, or entitled to, or under a general power of appointment by his or her will disposes of, an interest in freehold or leasehold property which, at the time of his or her death, is subject to a mortgage, and the deceased has not, by will, deed or other document, signified a contrary or other intention,

(a) the interest is, as between the different persons claiming through the deceased, primarily liable for the payment or satisfaction of the mortgage debt; and

(b) every part of the interest, according to its value, bears a proportionate part of the mortgage debt on the whole interest.

(2) A testator does not signify a contrary or other intention within subsection (1) by,

(a) a general direction for the payment of debts or of all the debts of the testator out of his or her personal estate, his or her residuary real or personal estate or his or her residuary real estate; or

---

222 *Re Rogers* (1920), 47 O.L.R. 82 (H.C.).
223 *Re Tremaine* (1929), 37 O.W.N. 186 (H.C.).
224 *Re McMahan* (1924), 27 O.W.N. 146 (H.C.).
225 See *Re Anthony; Anthony v. Anthony*, [1893] 3 Ch. 498.
226 *Hepworth v. Hill* (1862), 30 Beav. 476, 54 E.R. 974.
227 *Real Estate Charges Act, 1854*, 17 & 18 Vict., c. 113; *Real Estate Charges Act, 1867*, 17 & 18 Vict. c. 69; *Real Estate Charges Act, 1877*, 40 & 41 Vict., c. 34.
228 (1981), 34 O.R. (2d) 246, 10 E.T.R. 288, 128 D.L.R. (3d) 63 (H.C.).

(b) a charge of debts upon that estate, unless he or she further signifies that intention by words expressly or by necessary implication referring to all or some part of the mortgage debt.

(3) Nothing in this section affects a right of a person entitled to the mortgage debt to obtain payment or satisfaction either out of the other assets of the deceased or otherwise.

(4) In this section, "mortgage" includes an equitable mortgage, and any charge whatsoever, whether equitable, statutory or of other nature, including a lien or claim upon freehold or leasehold property for unpaid purchase money, and "mortgage debt" has a meaning similarly extended.

Comparable Legislation

Wills Act, R.S.A. 1980, c. W-11, s. 37; R.S.B.C. 1996, c. 489, s. 31; R.S.M. 1988, c. W150, s. 36; R.S.N.B. 1973, c. W-9, s. 34; S.S. 1996, c. W-14.11, s. 34; R.S.N.W.T. 1988, c. W-5, s. 24; R.S.Y. 1986, c. 179, s. 23.

RE HICKNELL; PERRY v. HICKNELL
(1981), 34 O.R. (2d) 246, 10 E.T.R. 288, 128 D.L.R. (3d) 63
Supreme Court of Ontario
[High Court of Justice]

The testator, Patrick Joseph Hicknell, lived in a relationship of husband and wife with the applicant, Linda Perry, in his house at 6 Cheval Street, Cambridge, prior to his death. By his will he appointed his brother as his executor, left his house to Miss Perry and gave the residue equally to his two children. In the gift of the house, there was no reference to two existing mortgages on the house. The principal outstanding on these mortgages was $39,734.32 and $10,303.45 respectively. They had fallen into arrears after the testator's death and the mortgagees threatened foreclosure. The amounts necessary to bring them into good standing are $3,648.02 and $1,305.22, respectively.

Prior to his death the testator had taken out a life insurance policy for $10,000, the beneficiary being his estate. A "Family Income Benefit" rider was added to the policy by the testator in 1980 to provide $200.00 per month for 25 years after the testator's death in order to take care of the mortgage payments. The insurer paid the estate $9,708.88, being the face value of the policy less unpaid premiums.

Miss Perry brought this application for an order directing the executor to pay the mortgage arrears from the proceeds of the insurance policy.

GRIFFITHS J.:

. . .

In essence the section[229] provides that where a person devises his real property

---

229 *Succession Law Reform Act*, s. 32.

subject to a mortgage and the deceased has not "by will, deed or other document" signified a contrary intention then the devisee takes the real property subject to the mortgage.

It is common ground in this case that the will did not express a "contrary intention" and that the policy of life insurance including the family income rider makes no express reference to the mortgage or mortgage payments.

Counsel for the applicant submits that in the light of the oral discussion between the agent and the deceased in which the deceased expressed a clear intention that the additional insurance rider should serve to protect the mortgage coverage that I should consider the insurance policy and its rider as a "document" expressing a contrary intention.

While I have much sympathy for the applicant and can speculate that the deceased may well have intended the insurance policy rider of June 23, 1980 to provide protection against mortgage payments, I am not able to grant the applicant the relief claimed in view of the clear wording of s. 32 of The Succession Law Reform Act. Where s. 32 speaks of a contrary intention being signified by "other document", that intention in my view must clearly be expressed in the document itself.

The second submission of counsel for the applicant is that the executor was obliged in law to convey the dwelling house to the applicant-beneficiary with the mortgages in good standing. There was no default in the mortgages at the time of death and it is submitted that the executor had a duty to make all mortgage payments from the residue moneys in the estate and to keep the mortgages in good standing until the executor deed had been executed conveying the house to the applicant. That conveyance has not yet been effected.

Counsel for the applicant advises that he has been unable to find any authority in support of the above proposition. Section 22 of The Succession Law Reform Act provides, in effect, that in the absence of a contrary intention appearing in a will, the will speaks and takes effect "as if it had been made immediately before the death of the testator" with respect to the property of the testator. This section in my view provides that in the absence of an express contrary intention, the beneficiary is deemed to take a devise under the will effective at the time of death.

In my opinion the beneficiary acquired the same interest in the home as the testator at the time of death, namely the equity of redemption in the property, and the responsibility for mortgage payments thereafter fell on the beneficiary and was not a legal obligation of the estate....

The application is therefore dismissed.

. . .

Notes and Questions

1. The Nova Scotia, Prince Edward Island and Newfoundland statutes do not contain a provision similar to s. 32 of the *Succession Law Reform Act.*

2. *Re Cohen; National Provincial Bank Ltd. v. Katz*[230] also illustrates the operation of the legislation. The testator devised a house in trust for each of his two daughters and gave the residue in trust for his wife. The two houses, as well as four out of six houses forming part of the residue, were encumbered by a mortgage. The court held that, since the testator had given the two houses to his daughters by specific as opposed to a residuary devise, he had signified a contrary intention to take the case out of the English equivalent of section 32 of the *Succession Law Reform Act*.[231] Hence, the two houses given to the daughters were not liable to bear a proportionate part of the mortgage debt.

3. A testatrix agreed to purchase a house subject to a mortgage for 90% of the purchase price. She then executed a codicil to her will by which she left the house to her daughter. She died before completing the purchase. Does the daughter take the house subject to the mortgage?[232]

4. Section 32 of the *Succession Law Reform Act* applies to freehold and leasehold only. Hence, the beneficiary under a specific bequest of personalty, such as a business, is entitled to take the bequest free of any debts to which the property is subject, unless the testator directs otherwise.[233]

10.   THREE EQUITABLE DOCTRINES

(a)   The Doctrine of Election

There is a general principle of equity that a person cannot take a benefit under a will without confirming all its provisions.[234] Hence, if the testator gives his or her own property to a person, but also purports to give property that belongs to that beneficiary to a third person, whether purposely or by mistake, the beneficiary cannot take the gift and retain his or her own property. Instead, he or she is put to an election. The beneficiary may disclaim the gift and keep his or her own property, take the gift and transfer his or her own property to the third person, or take the legacy and keep his or her own property, but pay the value of the latter to the third person. A leading Canadian case on election is *Rosborough v. Trustees of St. Andrew's Church*.[235] The trustees had granted a mortgage on certain property to the testator. He assigned the mortgage to his son. Later the son became unsound of mind and was so found. Thereafter, the testator bequeathed the mortgage to the trustees of the church and left other property and moneys to trustees for the support and maintenance of his son. The committee of the son's estate made an application to determine the son's rights under the will. The court held that the doctrine of election applied and directed the committee to elect under and not against the will. In other words, the committee should elect to take the property and moneys left to trustees for the son and transfer the mortgage to the trustees

---

230 [1960] Ch. 179, [1959] 3 All E.R. 740.

231 *Administration of Estates Act 1925*, 15 & 16 Geo. 5, c. 23, s. 35.

232 See *Re Birmingham; Savage v. Stannard*, [1959] Ch. 523, [1958] 2 All E.R. 397.

233 See *Re Grisor* (1979), 26 O.R. (2d) 57, 5 E.T.R. 296, 101 D.L.R. (3d) 728 (H.C.); and see *Re Simpson*, 60 O.L.R. 310, [1927] 2 D.L.R. 1043.

234 *Codrington v. Codrington* (1875), L.R. 7 H.L. 854 at 861-2, *per* Lord Cairns (H.L.).

235 (1917), 55 S.C.R. 360, 38 D.L.R. 119.

of the church. The court directed the committee not to retain the mortgage and pay its value to the church.

The doctrine is explained further in *Granot v. Hersen Estate*[236] reproduced below.

Further Reading

Neville Crago, "Mistakes in Wills and Election in Equity" (1990), 106 L.Q. Rev. 487.
Elise Bennnett Histed, "Election in Equity: The Myth of Mistake" (1998), 114 L.Q. Rev. 621.

GRANOT v. HERSEN ESTATE
(1999), 173 D.L.R. (4th) 227
Ontario Court of Appeal

The testator, who was domiciled in Ontario, was survived by a daughter, a son, and the two children of a son who predeceased him. By clause III of his will he gave "all my property wheresoever situate" to his trustee and directed the trustee to pay $600,000 and to transfer a parcel of real property in Ontario to the son. By clause IV he directed the trustee to transfer the residue of his estate to his daughter. The residue included a condominium in Switzerland, thought to be worth between $600,000 and $800,000. Haley J., the judge of first instance, held the rights in the condominium were to be determined by Swiss law.[237] Under Swiss law forced heirship rights applied, giving the son a one-quarter interest, the daughter a one-half interest (one quarter in her capacity as the deceased's daughter, and one-quarter as the residuary beneficiary under the will), and one-eighth each to the two grandchildren. Her Honour then held that the doctrine of election applied, requiring the son to elect either the gifts to him under the will, or his rights under Swiss law. He appealed.

DOHERTY J.A. delivered the judgment of the court:

. . .

The Doctrine of Election

. . .

[9] Roland Hersen received two specific gifts in paragraph III of the will ($600,000 and the Powassan property). He is also entitled to a 1/4 interest in the Swiss condominium. That entitlement arose outside of the will, by the operation of Swiss domestic law.

[10] The applicability of the doctrine of election depends upon whether Roland Hersen's 1/4 interest in the Swiss condominium is "inconsistent with any provi-

---

236 (1999), 43 O.R. (3d) 421 (sub nom. *Re Hersen Estate*), 26 E.T.R. (2d) 221, 173 D.L.R. (4th) 227 (C.A.).
237 In accordance with s. 36(1) of the *Succession Law Reform Act*, R.S.O. 1990, c. S.26. The judgment at first instance is reported at (1998) 21 E.T.R. (2d) 153 (Ont. Gen. Div.).

sion of the will". If there is an inconsistency, Roland Hersen cannot take both under the will and under the Swiss law. If he elects to take the gifts provided in the will, he must forgo his rights in the condominium. If he chooses to take his interest in the Swiss condominium, his gifts under the will must be reduced by an amount equal to the value of his interest in the condominium ($150,000 - $200,000).[238] If Roland Hersen's interest in the Swiss condominium does not create any inconsistency with the provisions in the will, then he is entitled to take both the gifts under the will and his interest in the Swiss condominium.

[11] The 1/4 interest in the condominium given to Roland Hersen under Swiss law will be inconsistent with the terms of the will if Henry Hersen intended to give that interest in the condominium to someone other than Roland Hersen. That intention must be found in the language of the will either expressly or by necessary implication *[page232]* from the text of the will considered as a whole.[239]

[12] As the condominium is not referred to in the will, there can be no suggestion of an express intent to give Roland Hersen's 1/4 interest in that condominium to someone else. Haley J. found, however, that by necessary implication Henry Hersen intended to give the entire Swiss condominium to Lillian Granot as the residuary beneficiary in his will. In so holding, she relied on the opening words of paragraph III of the will, "I give all my property wheresoever situate", the gifts of specific property to Roland Hersen in paragraph III of the will, and the gift of the entire residue of the estate to Lillian Granot in paragraph IV of the will. Haley J. said:[240]

> Did the testator intend that the Swiss condominium pass under his will to his residuary beneficiary? Reading these two clauses together I am satisfied that they disclose the testator's intention to dispose of everything he owned by his will and that the words "wheresoever situate" cannot be dismissed as simply pro forma having regard to the actual existence of foreign property. The testator must be taken to know the extent of his assets but it is irrelevant as to whether or not he knew that his power to dispose of the foreign land was restricted by the Swiss law of forced heirship. I am satisfied that by "necessary implication" the testator was referring to the foreign land in the dispositions in his will. That being so we have the classic case of the testator disposing to Lillian an interest belonging to Roland and compensating Roland for the loss of his interest in the land by way of a cash legacy of $600,000 and a devise of other land. Therefore Roland is put to his election between his Swiss interest and his benefits under the will.

[13] On first impression, the conclusion of Haley J. is an attractive one. Counsel for the appellant has, however, assembled an impressive array of English and Canadian jurisprudence[241] which strongly supports his contention that the terms of this will cannot be construed as evincing an intention to give the entirety of the condominium to Lillian Granot, the residuary beneficiary. If those authorities

---

238 *Snell's Equity*, 29th ed. (1990), p. 504; *Cheshire and North Private International Law*, 12th ed. (1992), at p. 856.

239 *Graham v. Clark*, [1949] 2 W.W.R. 1042 at 1049, [1949] 4 D.L.R. 770 (Alta. C.A.).

240 (1998), 21 E.T.R. (2d) 153 at 165.

241 Counsel also relied on American texts. I will not refer to that authority. It is consistent with the English case law: see Atkinson, *Handbook of the Law of Wills*, 2nd ed. (1953), at p. 768; *Page on the Law of Wills*, vol. 5 (1960), at pp. 598-600.

control, the doctrine of election does not arise and Roland Hersen is entitled to both the interest in the condominium and the gifts given to him in the will.

[14] Counsel's review of the English authorities begins in the early years of the 19th century. Those cases reveal a strong resistance to the application of the election doctrine absent a clear expression of the testator's intention to dispose of property which *[page233]* the testator was not entitled to dispose of under the will.[242]

[The court discussed a number of these cases and continued:]

[20] In *Maxwell v. Maxwell*[243] the testator owned certain property in Scotland and England. Under the terms of his will, he devised to his trustees "all his [*sic*] real and personal estate whatsoever or wheresoever upon trust for his wife for life with the remainder for all of his children and their heirs". Under Scottish law applicable to the Scottish property, the will was ineffective and the Scottish property passed to the eldest son. As the eldest son was also a beneficiary under the will, it was contended that he was required to elect as between his rights under the Scottish law and his entitlement under the will. The Master of the Rolls rejected this contention holding that the general language of the devise to the trustees was not sufficient to reveal an intention by the testator to dispose of property which under the applicable foreign law belonged to his son.

[21] The House of Lords affirmed the finding that the eldest son was not required to elect stating:[244]

> It is said on the part of the other children, and denied on his part, that he must either give up the Scotch property for the purposes of the will, or take nothing under the will; the claim of the younger children being founded on the generality, the universality, of the language of gift contained in it. Nor can he gainsay that the Scotch property was part of the testator's estate, or that the will purports to give all his real and personal estate whatsoever and wheresoever. I apprehend, however, that, according to the principles or rules of construction which *the English law applies, if not to all instruments, at least to testamentary instruments liable to interpretation, as the will in question is, according to its principles and rules, the generality, the mere universality, of a gift of property, is not sufficient to demonstrate or create a ground of inference that the giver meant it to extend to property incapable, though his own, of being given by the particular act. If he has specifically mentioned property not capable of being so given, the case is not the same: as here, if the testator had mentioned Scotland in terms, or had not had any other real estate than real estate in Scotland, there might have been ground for putting the heir to his election.*
>
> The matter, however, standing as it does, we are, as it seems to me, bound to hold that the will before us does not exhibit an intention to give or to affect any property that the will was not adapted to pass.

[22] *Maxwell* is an important case. Not only is it confirmation of a line of authority by the highest appellate court in England, it is factually similar to our

---

242 *E.g.*, see *Greatorex v. Cary* (1802), 31 E.R. 1223 (Ch. H.C.); *Dummer v. Pitcher* (1833), 39 E.R. 944 (Ch. H.C.); *Usticke v. Peters* (1858), 70 E.R. 183 (Ch. H.C.); *Gibson v. Gibson* (1852), 61 E.R. 367 (Ch. H.C.); *Maxwell v. Maxwell* (1852), 51 E.R. 717 (Ch. Rolls Ct.), affirmed 42 E.R. 1048 (H.L.).

243 *Maxwell, ibid.*

244 *Ibid.*, at p. 1051, emphasis added.

case. In both *Maxwell* and this case, the alleged inconsistency between the will and the beneficiary's rights outside of the will arose by the operation of foreign law on part of the testator's property. Furthermore, in both cases, the party arguing for the *[page236]* application of the doctrine of election could only point to general language in the will to demonstrate the testator's intention to devise property which, by the application of foreign law, belonged to another who was also a beneficiary under the will.

[23] *Maxwell* is important for another reason. Lord Justice Knight Bruce, speaking for the Law Lords, candidly acknowledged that the decision that the eldest son need not elect might well be contrary to the testator's intention. He held, however, that absent a clear expression of that intention in the will, the court was restricted to interpreting the will in accordance with established general rules of construction to ensure consistency lest the interpretation of each will turn on the discretion of individual judges. I take his Lordship to mean that where the terms of the will are such that a determination of the testator's intention is a matter of speculation, it is better to decide those cases by established rules than by the surmises of individual judges.

. . .

[26] These old English authorities continue to reflect the state of the law in present day England.

> [The Court referred in particular to *Re Mengel's Will Trusts*[245] in which the facts were similar to the instant case. In *Mengel* Buckley J. noted that it is always more difficult to sustain a case of election when the testator has a partial interest in the property he or she purports to dispose of, than when the testator purports to dispose of property in which he or she has no interest at all. If the testator has some interest in the property, the court favours a construction that would make the testator deal only with that to which he or she was entitled. Further, His Lordship noted that a case of election will seldom be made out if the property is described only in general terms, whereas the case is easier to make out if the property is described specifically. The court continued:]

[32] The weight of the English authority clearly favours the appellant's position. On those authorities the language of this will does not demonstrate that Henry Hersen intended to dispose of Roland Hersen's interest in the Swiss condominium to Lillian Granot.

[33] The principles found in the English authorities have been adopted by Canadian courts. They have shown the same reluctance to invoke the election doctrine absent a clear intention on the face of the will to dispose of property in a manner inconsistent with the rights of another (who is also a beneficiary under the will) in that property. That intention has been found either in the express language of the will read as a whole or where the clear intention of the testator could not be carried out if the property interest of the other person were given effect. Like English courts, Canadian courts have held that general language in the residuary clause standing alone will not demonstrate an intention to dispose

---

245 [1962] 1 Ch. 791 (Div.).

of the property of another. Absent that intention, the doctrine of election does not arise.[246]

[34] Mr. Schnurr submitted that whatever the law in England may be, in Canada there is no hard and fast rule that the testator's intention to dispose of the property of another can never be inferred from general language in a residuary clause. He placed heavy reliance on *Re Mawson*.[247] In *[page 239] Mawson*, the testator and his wife were joint tenants of a property (the King Street property). When the testator died, his wife became the owner of the King Street property. In his will, the testator made extensive reference to the King Street property. He purported to give his wife a life interest in the King Street property (paragraph 1), he directed his trustee to pay the taxes and maintenance on the King Street property out of his estate (paragraph 10), and he directed that if his wife so requested, his King Street property could be sold and the proceeds used to produce additional revenue payable to his wife (paragraph 8). The wife was also given other specific gifts under the will. Paragraph 13, which included the residuary clause said:

> Upon the decease of my wife, Caroline Mawson, I direct my said executor and trustee to pay to my eldest sister, Grace Mawson, if she is then living, the sum of one thousand dollars out of the corpus of my estate, and I direct that the balance and residue of my estate then remaining is to be divided equally among such of my nephews and nieces as shall be living at the time of the decease of my wife, share and share alike.

[35] The wife argued that only the residuary clause disposed of property to persons other than herself and that the general language of that clause was not sufficient to demonstrate an intention by the testator to devise the wife's interest in the King Street property.

[36] Kelly J.[248] referred approvingly to the principle of construction that "general words will not, by themselves, be construed to include particular property not in fact belonging to the testator". He went on to hold, however, that those general words had to be examined in the context of the entirety of the will. The specific references to the King Street property in several paragraphs of the will made it clear that the testator intended his estate to include the King Street property. It was, therefore, property included in the phrase "the balance and residue of my estate" found in the residuary clause.

[37] I do not agree that *Mawson* breaks from the established line of authority. It appears to me, as I think it did to Kelly J., to be entirely consistent with previous authority. The testator's purported devise of a life interest in the King Street property to his wife, his direction that the taxes and maintenance on the King Street property be paid out of his estate and his indication that the proceeds from a sale of the property be invested to produce additional income for his *[page240]*

---

246 *E.g.*, see *Re Hurst* (1905), 11 O.L.R. 6 (Div. Ct.); *Re Hill*, [1951] O.R. 619, [1951] 4 D.L.R. 218 (H.C.); *Re Sullivan Estate*, [1951] 3 W.W.R. (N.S.) 363 (Alta. S.C.); *Graham v. Clark*, [1949] 1 W.W.R. 751, [1949] 3 D.L.R. 539 (Alta. S.C.), affirmed [1949] 2 W.W.R. 1042 at 1049, [1949] 4 D.L.R. 770 (Alta. C.A.); *Abbot v. Grant*, [1965] S.C.R. 268, 52 D.L.R. (2d) 313; *Re Baker* (1981), 10 E.T.R. 146 (Ont. H.C.) at 151.

247 [1939] O.W.N. 294, [1939] 4 D.L.R. 801n (H.C.)

248 *Ibid.*, at O.W.N. 297.

wife, are consistent only with an intention to include that specific property in his estate.

[38] The testator's intention to include the wife's interests in his devise is made all the more clear when it is recalled that the testator had absolutely no interest in the King Street property upon his death. The property belonged exclusively to his wife. Consequently, it could not be suggested that his extensive references to the King Street property in his will referred only to his interest in that property.

[39] Not only do I find *Mawson* to be consistent with prior authority, I can find nothing in that case which assists Lillian Granot's claim that the doctrine of election should apply in this case. In this will, there is no reference to the Swiss condominium. The contention that Henry Hersen intended to devise Roland Hersen's 1/4 interest in the Swiss condominium rests entirely on the general language of the opening paragraph of the will ("all my property wheresoever situate"), and the general language of the residuary clause. It is from that language and that language alone that the court is asked to infer that Henry Hersen intended to devise not only his interest in the Swiss condominium, but also the interest of Roland Hersen.

[40] Nor is the argument in favour of the applicability of the doctrine advanced by the fact that the will contains gifts of specific property to Roland. One can certainly infer from those gifts that it was the testator's intention that Roland Hersen should receive under the will that property specified in paragraph III of the will. That inference is, however, of no assistance in determining whether the testator intended to devise Roland Hersen's interest in the Swiss condominium as if it were his own.

. . .

[44] In summary, my review of the English and Canadian cases indicates that the following principles are applicable to the interpretation of this will:

• the doctrine of election applies only where the testator clearly intended to dispose of another's interest in property while at the same time making a gift to that person under his will;

• that intention must be made express or appear by necessary implication from the terms of the will;

• one starts from the premise that the testator only intended to dispose of his or her own property in the will; and

• general words in a will like "all my estate" or a residuary gift in general terms will not, standing alone, evince an intention to dispose of property or an interest in property which the testator was not entitled to dispose of in his will.

[45] Applying those principles, I am driven to the conclusion that Lillian Granot has failed to show that Henry Hersen intended to dispose of Roland Hersen's 1/4 interest in the Swiss condominium in his will. The doctrine of election has no

application and Roland *[page242]* Hersen is entitled to both the 1/4 interest in the Swiss condominium and the gifts under the will.

[46] In coming to that conclusion, I do not pretend to have divined Mr. Henry Hersen's true intention when he penned his will. I have no idea what he actually intended. Absent any solid indication of the testator's true intention in the words of the will, I, like previous courts, favour an interpretation which brings certainty and consistency. Those goals are best achieved by staying the course and applying the well-settled principles established over the last 200 years.

[The court allowed the appeal.]

Notes and Questions

1. In order for the doctrine of election to apply, several conditions must be satisfied. First, the property given to the beneficiary must in fact belong to the testator. Hence, the exercise by the testator of a power to appoint property does not attract the doctrine.[249] Second, the beneficiary must be able freely to alienate his or her own property. Hence, if the beneficiary is only a life tenant of his or her own property, the doctrine is excluded.[250] Third, the gifts must both be made by the same instrument, although if one gift is made by will and the other by codicil, the doctrine applies. But it would not apply if one gift were contained in a will and the other in a deed.

2. An election may be express or implied. An implied election occurs when the beneficiary, with knowledge of all the facts, takes the income from or attempts to deal with property given to him under the will.[251]

3. The testator's eldest son had for many years occupied a house owned by the testator. Years before his death, the testator wrote to this son, saying that if the son continued to pay the taxes and rent he would get title to the property if anything should happen to the testator and his wife. He added that this was all the son would receive when his parents died. The father's will left his estate to all his children. Is the son entitled to both the house and his share of his father's estate?[252]

4. A husband and wife owned two properties as joint tenants. She died first. Her will contained a gift to her husband and provided that any property she owned at her death should be held by her trustees for 10 years and then be distributed to named beneficiaries. Does the doctrine of election apply?[253]

5. *Bickley v. Bickley Estate*[254] is another case in which the doctrine of election did not apply. The testator owned US assets, the shares in a holding company, and other assets. Before he died, he transferred the US assets to himself and his wife as joint tenants. His will purported to divide the US assets among his wife and children. He left the residue equally to his wife and three children. After his death, his survivors obtained a consent judgment which held that the widow was entitled to 50 percent of the shares in the holding company under a constructive trust that arose at the time of incorporation. The judgment

---

249 *Bristowe v. Warde* (1794), 2 Ves. 336, 30 E.R. 660.
250 *Re Lord Chesham; Cavendish v. Dacre* (1886), 31 Ch. D. 466.
251 *Re Shepherd; Harris v. Shepherd*, [1943] Ch. 8, [1942] 2 All E.R. 584.
252 See *Shillabeer v. Diebel* (1979), 9 Alta. L.R. (2d) 112, 5 E.T.R. 30, (sub nom. *Re Shillabeer*) 18 A.R. 173 (T.D.).
253 See *Maw Estate v. Bush* (1999), 26 E.T.R. (2d) 184 (B.C.S.C.).
254 (1999), 29 E.T.R. (2d) 132 (Ont. S.C.J.).

also deemed the widow to have elected to take under the will for the purpose of the *Family Law Act*.[255] The court held that s. 6(4) of that Act, which says that when a spouse elects to take under the will she is also entitled to other property to which she is entitled because of her spouse's death, applied to entitle the widow to the US assets, since they were held in joint tenancy. However, the section did not apply to the shares held on constructive trust, since she was not entitled to them as a result of her husband's death. The doctrine of election did not apply, however. The husband's disposition of the shares should be taken as referring only to his shares and not those belonging to his widow. Consequently, she could take both her 50 percent shareholding under the constructive trust and the 20 percent of the residue.

(b) Satisfaction

Suppose that a testator is liable to X for a certain amount of money. Then the testator leaves X that amount of money as a legacy. Can X claim both as a creditor and as a beneficiary?

In circumstances such as these, equity presumes that the legacy satisfies the debt, provided that the debt precedes the will, the legacy is at least equal to the debt and is as advantageous to the creditor as the debt, the nature of the debt and the legacy are the same, and there is no contrary intention in the will. The doctrine is discussed in *Re Trider*,[256] reproduced below.

RE TRIDER
(1978), 2 E.T.R. 22, 84 D.L.R. (3d) 336
Nova Scotia Probate Court

The testatrix had been looked after for a number of years by Mrs. Weeks, her housekeeper-nurse, but she had not paid Mrs. Weeks for some time. By her will, the testatrix gave Mrs. Weeks a legacy. In citation proceedings brought to settle the claims of creditors, the registrar of probate allowed Mrs. Trider's claim for services at $7,800 and held, that this amount was in addition to the legacy.

The executors appealed.

O'HEARN J.:

. . .

[C]ounsel points out, there is a long standing rule that:

> If a testator dies, having bequeathed a pecuniary legacy to someone to whom he owed a sum of money, equity presumes that the legacy was given in satisfaction of the debt. Accordingly, unless evidence is available to rebut this presumption that the testator intended the legacy to pay the debt, the creditor cannot claim to be paid both the debt and the legacy.[257]

The executors further rely on the fact that the late Rachael B. Trider systematically increased the bequest to Mrs. Weeks in her series of wills, consisting of

---

255 R.S.O. 1990, c. F.3.
256 (1978), 2 E.T.R. 22, 84 D.L.R. (3d) 336 (N.S. Prob. Ct.).
257 Bailey, *Law of Wills*, (7th ed.), p. 151.

one in 1973 and four in 1974, the last of which admitted to probate was dated 19th November. Mrs Trider died on or about the 25th day of February 1975.

. . .

With respect to the doctrine of satisfaction and the presumption that a legacy is intended to pay a debt of the testator to the legatee, Mr. Jackson referred to Theobald on Wills,[258] which indicates that a direction in the will to pay debts and legacies rebuts the presumption. Several authorities are given in support of this....

From the cases cited it is clear that a direction in the will to pay either debts or legacies is something that prima facie takes the case altogether out of the rule and the presumption. It seems to follow from the authorities cited that once the presumption is rebutted, it is simply a matter of construction from the will and the evidence (to the extent that it can be applied to the construction of the will) whether it was the testator's intention to apply the legacy as payment of the debt or not.

. . .

Having considered the material on the file and the submissions of counsel and, in particular, the terms of the will, I have come to the conclusion that it was not the intention of the testatrix to have the legacy set off against any award that might be made against her estate, as the result of a claim by Mrs. Weeks for services, and that the award of the registrar and his subsequent determination of this particular question arising on the settlement is properly based on the law and the evidence, as well as on the terms of the will.

. . .

[The court dismissed the appeal.]

Notes and Questions

1. In determining whether or not the presumption of satisfaction applies, it seems that the court may admit direct evidence of the testator's intentions.[259]

2. A testator divorced his wife and in the divorce settlement agreed to pay her £3 per week every Monday. The payment was secured by transfer to the trustees of the settlement of real securities. By his subsequent will the testator gave his divorced wife "£3 a week as long as she remains unmarried." Has the legacy satisfied the debt?[260]

(c)   The Rule Against Double Portions

It is a rule of equity that if a testator has given a legacy or property of a substantial nature to a child and subsequently transfers the money or the property

---

258 (12th ed.), para. 1973.
259 See *Hoffman v. Dusko* (1982), 15 Man. R. (2d) 242 (Co. Ct.).
260 See *Re Haves; Haves v. Haves*, [1951] 2 All E.R. 928.

or the equivalent value thereof to that child, the legacy has been satisfied. This rule, often called the rule against double portions, is really a subrule of the doctrine of satisfaction. The rule is examined in *Re George's Will Trusts*,[261] reproduced below.

RE GEORGE'S WILL TRUSTS
[1949] Ch. 154, [1948] 2 All E.R. 1004
Chancery Division

The testator farmed two properties, the Glebe Farm, which he held in fee, and the Laurels Farm which he rented with his son, Ernest. Ernest was employed by his father. Another son, Robert, worked for a bank. By his will the testator gave the residue of his estate upon trust for sale and directed that the proceeds be divided, one-third to Robert and two-thirds to Ernest, but he gave an option to Ernest to purchase the farms at a fair value.

Subsequently, under emergency powers then in force, a governmental authority threatened to evict the testator because the farms were being poorly managed. As a result of an accommodation reached with the authority, the testator gave up management of the farms to Ernest, granting him a tenancy of the Glebe Farm and assigning the tenancy of the Laurels Farm. Moreover, he made a gift to Ernest of all the live and dead stock on the farm. After the testator's death, Ernest exercised the option.

JENKINS J.:

. . .

I may now proceed to consider whether on the facts and in the circumstances which I have stated the rule against double portions applies to the gift of live and dead stock to Ernest, or perhaps more accurately whether there is anything in those facts and circumstances to exclude the application of the rule. The principles on which the rule is based and applied are succinctly stated by Lord Greene M.R. in *In re Vaux*,[262] where he says:

> The rule against double portions rests upon two hypotheses: first of all, that under the will the testator has provided a portion and, secondly, that by the gift inter vivos which is said to operate in ademption of that portion either wholly or pro tanto, he has again conferred a portion. The conception is that the testator having in his will given to his children that portion of the estate which he decides to give to them, when after making his will he confers upon a child a gift of such a nature as to amount to a portion, then he is not to be presumed to have intended that that child should have both, the gift inter vivos being taken as being on account of the portion given by the will. When the word "portion" is used in reference to the gift inter vivos, it has a qualitative significance, in this sense, that it is not every gift inter vivos that will cause the rule to come into operation. If a testator gives to a child as pure bounty and by way merely of a present a sum of money, that will not have the character to cause the rule to come into operation. Similarly there may be various reasons why the testator should give property to a child. He may wish to free him

261 [1949] Ch. 154, [1948] 2 All E.R. 1004.
262 [1939] Ch. 465, 481.

from some embarrassment, or something of that kind. In cases of that sort upon the facts a gift may not be a portion at all, in which case, of course, the rule does not apply.

As appears from that passage...the first matter which must be made out is that both the gift by will and the gift inter vivos made by the testator to his child are gifts in the nature of portions. Once that essential condition is established, a presumption arises that the testator intended the provision inter vivos to be on account of the provision by will, but the presumption may be rebutted if the circumstances in which the gift inter vivos was made are such as to show that the testator did not intend the provision inter vivos to be on account of the provision by will.

It was not disputed before me that the provision made for Ernest by the testator's will in the present case was in the nature of a portion; it was, however, contended on his behalf that having regard to its character and the circumstances in which it was made the testator's gift inter vivos of the farming stock to Ernest was not in the nature of a portion at all, and alternatively that if this gift was in itself in the nature of a portion its character and the circumstances in which it was made were sufficient to rebut the presumption. The question of portion or no portion being necessarily to a great extent a question of the testator's intention, it is hardly possible to distinguish circumstances relied on as tending to show that the gift inter vivos was not in the nature of a portion at all from circumstances relied on as tending to rebut the presumption on the footing that it was in itself in the nature of a portion, and I do not propose to do so. First, as to the character of the gift of live and dead stock. I have no doubt that a gift by a farmer to his son of live and dead stock with which to set up in business as a farmer may be in the nature of a portion, and in the absence of circumstances tending to show the contrary would generally be regarded as such. In *Taylor v. Taylor*[263] Jessell M.R., mentioned the buying of the goodwill of a business for a son and giving him stock in trade as a typical instance of a portion. It was, however, contended that the difference in the character of the gift of live and dead stock from the provision made for Ernest in the present case was such as to rebut the presumption against double portions even if the circumstances were otherwise such as to raise it at all. Reference was made in the connexion to *In re Tussaud's Estate*[264] and *In re Jaques*.[265] The latter case is no doubt clear authority for the proposition stated in the headnote

that the presumption against double portions will not prevail where the testamentary portion and subsequent advancement are not ejusdem generis,

but the judgments of the Court of Appeal, as I understand them, further show that the proposition thus stated has no application where the "subsequent advancement" though not ejusdem generis with the testamentary provision is one on which a money value was set at the time it was made. In the present case I think that, having regard to the fact that the testator's live and dead stock formed part

---

263 (1875) L.R. 20 Eq. 155, 158.
264 (1878), 9 Ch. D. 363.
265 [1903] 1 Ch. 267.

of the assets which Ernest was to take in specie under the will in the event of his exercising the option under cl. 7, the gift inter vivos here was sufficiently ejusdem generis with the testamentary provision to prevent the exclusion or rebuttal of the presumption by reason of the difference in character between the two gifts. If I am wrong in that view, I think that in any case the difference in character is rendered immaterial by the circumstance that the live and dead stock was valued at the time of the gift inter vivos at 2,060*l.* 17*s.* 3*d.*, and can therefore be regarded for the present purpose as a gift of so much money.

Next, it was said that if the transaction of which the gift of the live and dead stock formed part was viewed as a whole, it would be found in truth to be no gift at all but simply part of a transaction under which Ernest took over certain assets and assumed certain liabilities.... I cannot accept this argument. I think Ernest must be regarded as receiving a fair quid pro quo, in the form of the testator's share of the Laurels tenancy and the tenancy of the Glebe Farm granted to him by the testator, for the liabilities in respect of rent, and so forth, which he undertook, and this is certainly the effect of the evidence. That leaves the whole of the 2,060*l.* worth of live and dead stock as pure gift, subject only to the question of the overdraft with which I will deal in a moment. It would to my mind be very strange if in a case where a father gave his son valuable live and dead stock, granting him at the same time a tenancy at a fair rent, of a farm on which to set up in business as a farmer, the son's liability for the rent would prevent the gift of the stock from being a gift, and, prima facie, a gift by way of portion. Further, I do not think the fact that a gift has an element of liability attached to it in itself prevents the gift from being a portion. It is rather "a matter to be taken into consideration in considering what the value of the gift was." See per North J. in *In re Vickers*,[266] a passage in his judgment which was not, I think, included in the disapproval expressed by the Court of Appeal in *In re Jaques*.[267]

Finally, it was urged that the testator's sole object here was not to benefit Ernest, but simply to placate the War Agricultural Committee. The testator did not want to make the farm over to Ernest or anyone else, but on the contrary was extremely reluctant to do so. He was forced to resign their management to somebody on pain of eviction, and entered into this transaction with Ernest merely to extricate himself from the difficulty in which he was placed and procure the withdrawal of the notices. Therefore, it is contended, the case is not one of portion at all, any more than a payment to meet a son's pressing debts is a portion, as to which see *In re Scott*.[268] I think this argument is a non sequitur. I am quite prepared to accept the assumption that but for the intervention of the committee the testator would have retained the farms with the live and dead stock upon them until he died, and only got rid of the farms and the stock under, in effect, the compulsion of the notices and the committee's insistence upon them. But why did he select Ernest as the recipient? Ernest was under no pressing financial difficulties calling for extraordinary assistance such as would not, on the authorities, be regarded as

---

266 (1888) 37 Ch. D. 525, 535.
267 [1903] 1 Ch. 267.
268 [1903] 1 Ch. 1.

in the nature of a portion. But Ernest was the testator's farmer son for whom the testator had made provision to the extent of two-thirds of his residuary estate with the option of taking the residue in specie (subject to a charge for Robert's one-third share to be quantified by means of a valuation of the whole) if he desired to carry on the testator's farm as (it is reasonable to suppose) the testator contemplated Ernest would in all probability wish to do. This is, I think, quite plainly the reason why Ernest was selected to take over the farms and receive the live and dead stock. Viewed in this light, I think the circumstances tend to reinforce rather than rebut the presumption. The testator being compelled to go out of farming and make provision for the future management of the farms to the satisfaction of the committee, did so by as it were anticipating his demise and putting Ernest in immediate beneficial possession of part of what he would in due course have taken under the testator's will. The attitude of the committee so far as I can see afforded no ground at all for increasing Ernest's provision at the expense of Robert, though it no doubt did afford good ground for putting Ernest into immediate possession of this part of the testamentary portion designed for him.

For these reasons I am of opinion that this is a case to which the rule against double portions applies with respect to the gift to Ernest of the live and dead stock.

. . .

In the result, therefore, I hold that the sum of 2,060*l*. 17*s*. 3*d*. (being the value of the live and dead stock at the date of the gift) less 151*l*. 17*s*. 3*d*. (being the amount of the overdraft at the same date) should be brought into account by Ernest in the ascertainment of the shares of the two sons in the testator's residuary estate.

Notes and Questions

1. If the portion or advancement was made before the will, it is presumed that the testator intended his or her child to have both. However, if the portion or advancement is required to be made by the testator under a covenant entered into before making the will and the nature of the covenant and the provision in the subsequent will are substantially the same, the gift in the will is presumed to have satisfied the covenant.[269]

2. The rule was held to apply in *Re Cameron*.[270] A testatrix left the residue of her estate equally to her four sons, who were the defendants in the action. Later she granted an enduring power of attorney to the first three defendants. Under s. 3(4) of the *Enduring Powers of Attorney Act 1985*[271] the attorneys had power to provide for and meet the "needs" of any person if the donor of the power might have been expected to do so. They paid a large sum to trustees to provide for the private education of the first defendant's son on the understanding that, as a portion, the payment would, by the rule against double portions, reduce *pro tanto* the first defendant's share in his mother's estate. After his mother died, the first defendant argued that his share should not be reduced. The court held that the payment was proper and that the rule applied. The court said that while the

---

269 *Lord Chichester v. Earl of Coventry* (1867), L.R. 2 H.L. 71 (H.L.).
270 [1999] 2 All E.R. 924 (Ch. D.).
271 C. 29 (U.K.).

rule requires that there be two portions that benefit the same person, a gift can be for a person's benefit even though he does not receive it. Thus, a gift to a grandchild can be regarded as a gift to the grandchild's parent. Because the gift operated *pro tanto* to discharge the first defendant's obligation to educate his son, the *inter vivos* gift and the testamentary gift should be treated as substantial provisions both of which were intended to benefit the first defendant. Thus, both were portions in favour of the first defendant and the rule applied.

11. DISCLAIMER

A beneficiary under a will and the next of kin on an intestacy cannot be compelled to accept the benefit to which they have become entitled.[272] The beneficiary may disclaim the gift either orally, by conduct, or in writing so long as he or she has not unequivocally accepted it.[273] A disclaimer of one gift under a will does not preclude a beneficiary from taking another, provided the two are not inextricably bound together.[274]

If a disclaimer is effective, the gift is void and its failure relates back to the testator's or intestate's death.[275] Hence if the gift is testamentary and specific, it falls into residue;[276] if residuary, it goes out on an intestacy.[277] If the disclaimer is of a share of an intestate estate, it has the effect of augmenting the shares of the other next of kin:[278] the disclaimed interest does not pass to the Crown as *bona vacantia*.[279]

It is unusual for a person to disclaim a gift, but he or she may wish to do so if it is made upon a condition which is unacceptable,[280] or which imposes onerous duties on him or her, or if the beneficiary is precluded by statute or otherwise from accepting the gift. It may be to the advantage of a beneficiary to disclaim a gift which is given upon an unacceptable condition, so that it will then fall into residue or go out on an intestacy if the beneficiary is also entitled to share in the residue or on the intestacy.

Montreal Trust Co. v. Matthews,[281] reproduced below, involved a gift to a charity which was disclaimed for tax reasons. The question then arose whether the gift should be applied *cy-près* to similar charitable organizations.

---

272 *Bence v. Gilpin* (1868), L.R. 3 Ex. 76 at 82, *per* Kelly C.B.
273 *Re Wimperis*, [1914] 1 Ch. 502; *Re Hodge*, [1940] Ch. 260.
274 *Re Hotchkys* (1886), 32 Ch. D. 408.
275 *Re McFaden*, [1937] O.W.N. 404 at 406.
276 *Re Backhouse*, [1931] O.W.N. 168.
277 *Re Metcalfe*, [1972] 3 O.R. 598, 29 D.L.R. (3d) 60.
278 *Re Scott; Widdows v. Friends of the Clergy Corp.*, [1975] 2 All E.R. 1033.
279 *Re Doornbos; Public Trustee v. Kelly* (1988), 31 E.T.R. 213 (N.W.T.S.C.).
280 *Ibid.*, McGill University disclaimed a gift to establish a medical scholarship restricted, *inter alia*, to Protestant males of good moral character.
281 [1979] 3 W.W.R. 621, 11 B.C.L.R. 276 (sub nom. *Re Jung; Montreal Trust Co. v. Matthews*) (S.C.).

MONTREAL TRUST CO. v. MATTHEWS
[1979] 3 W.W.R. 621, 11 B.C.L.R. 276
(sub nom. *Re Jung; Montreal Trust Co. v. Matthews*)
Supreme Court of British Columbia
[In Chambers]

The testator gave a bequest and the residue of his estate to the P.A. Woodward Foundation. That charity declined to accept the gift, however, because it could not accept outside donations for tax reasons. The executor brought an application for the opinion, advice and direction of the court.

ANDREWS J.:

. . .

[Counsel] agree that a disclaimer is refusal to accept an interest which has been bequeathed to the disclaiming party. The effect is to void the gift ab initio. Where an interest is disclaimed, it is as if it had never been acquired by the disclaiming party. Gifts which fail or are undisposed of are captured by the residuary gifts, or, if the residuary fails, an intestacy results. Where a residuary gift fails, there is a resulting trust in favour of the next of kin of the deceased.[282]

A disclaimer can be made by deed, writing, under hand only or even as a result of contract, as any document is admissible so that evidence of the disclaimer is available. A disclaimer may even be evidenced by conduct.[283]

A disclaimer once made is retroactive to the date of death of the deceased. A beneficiary who disclaims is refusing to acquire the property of another and the disclaimer operates so that in effect the property is never acquired.[284]

A disclaimer can be made at any time before the beneficiary has derived any benefit from the assets, but not afterwards.[285]

The position with regard to a disclaimer of an interest under a partial intestacy is the same as that where the disclaimer is of an interest under a total intestacy.[286]

The destination of the disclaimed income is determined solely by the intention of the settlor or testator or by the law governing distribution or intestacy. Where no contrary intention appears from the will, the disclaimed residue goes on an intestacy.[287]

On an intestacy, the next of kin are to be determined, prima facie, as of the date of the testator's death, unless there is sufficient indication in the will to some other effect.[288]

---

282 *Re Stuart* (1964), 47 W.W.R. 500 at 502 and 504 (B.C.); *Re Metcalfe*, [1972] 3 O.R. 598 at 600 and 602, 29 D.L.R. (3d) 60; 39 Hals. (3d) 946.

283 A.R. Mellows, *The Law of Succession*, 3rd ed., at p. 508; *Re Metcalfe, supra*, at O.R. 600.

284 *Re Metcalfe, supra*, at O.R. 600 and 602.

285 Mellows, *supra*, at p. 508.

286 *Ibid.*, at p. 229.

287 *Re Stuart, supra*, at p. 504.

288 *McEachern v. Mittlestadt* (1963), 46 W.W.R. 359 at 368, 42 D.L.R. (2d) 587 (sub nom. *Re McEachern*) (Alta. C.A.).

Counsel are further agreed, as I am, that the disclaimer here is accordingly valid resulting in an intestacy as to the residue, in which case the next of kin are entitled to the residue unless the testator can be said to have evidenced a general charitable intent so that a scheme cy-près is appropriate.

> [The Court went on to find that the will disclosed no general charitable intent so the gift could not be distributed cy-près to other charities. As a result this part of the estate went out on an intestacy].

Notes and Questions

1. In *Re Cranstoun's Will Trusts*[289] the court held that a disclaimer, if not made for value, can be retracted, provided no one has altered his or her position on the faith of it. Does this offend the principle that a disclaimer, once made, renders the gift void *ab initio*?

2. The right of disclaimer must be distinguished from the equitable doctrine of election which provides that, if a person accepts a benefit under a will, he or she must adopt the whole will, giving full effect to its provisions and must renounce every right inconsistent with it. Thus, a person cannot take both under and against a will. Hence if a testator leaves $1000 by will to B and also purports to give B's sailboat to X, B cannot take the legacy, unless B is prepared to give the sailboat to X.[290]

3. The marriage of H and W had broken down. They entered into a separation agreement under which W was given custody of the three infant children of the marriage and H agreed to pay a monthly sum for the maintenance of W and the children. H was in arrears under the separation agreement and W was on social welfare. H's father then died and left H a large sum of money. H disclaimed because he did not want W to get any part of the money. Moreover, he believed that X, his brother-in-law and the business head of the family firm, who, as residuary legatee under H's father's will, became entitled to the money disclaimed by H, was going to look after H's children. Is the disclaimer valid in these circumstances?[291]

4. Whether the interests of persons becoming entitled as a result of a disclaimer are accelerated, is a question of interpretation.[292] Unless the will provides otherwise, expressly or by implication, such interests accelerate.[293]

5. Interests accelerate not only because of disclaimer, but also for other reasons. Thus, for example, subsequent interests may accumulate because the testator (by mistake) revokes the prior interest in a later codicil.[294] So also, if the prior interest fails because the beneficiary witnessed the will, the subsequent interests accelerate.[295] This is so even though

---

289 [1949] Ch. 523, [1949] 1 All E.R. 871.

290 The doctrine of election is discussed earlier in this chapter.

291 See *Sembaliuk v. Sembaliuk*, [1985] 2 W.W.R. 385, 15 D.L.R. (4th) 303, 18 E.T.R. 23, 58 A.R. 189 (C.A.). Leave to appeal to Supreme Court of Canada refused Feb. 18, 1985.

292 *Re Flower's Settlement Trusts*, [1957] 1 W.L.R. 401, [1957] 1 All E.R. 462; *Re Hatfeild's Will Trusts; Hatfeild v. Hatfeild*, [1958] Ch. 469 at 475, [1957] 2 All E.R. 261, *per* Harman J.

293 *Re Coulson* (1977), 16 O.R. (2d) 497, 1 E.T.R. 1, 78 D.L.R. (3d) 435 (C.A.). See also *McGavin v. National Trust Co.* (1998), 22 E.T.R. (2d) 36 (B.C.C.A.), a trusts case in which the gift was to a person for life or until remarriage, with remainder to her son. She disclaimed with the intent that her son's interest would accelerate. The court held that the presumption of acceleration was not rebutted.

294 See *Lainson v. Lainson* (1854), 5 De G. M. & G. 754, 43 E.R. 1063.

295 See *Jull v. Jacobs* (1876), 3 Ch. D. 703.

the gift takes the form, "to X for life and after her death to Y." The words "after her death" are interpreted to mean "after the determination of X's life estate by whatever means." Thus, Y does not have to wait until X dies to enjoy the property.[296]

6. *Re Jacques*[297] discusses the question of a contrary intention sufficient to prevent acceleration. The testatrix directed that part of the residue of her estate be held in trust and the income thereon paid to her daughter for life. On the death of the survivor of the testatrix and the daughter, the capital of that part of the residue was to be paid to the testatrix's son if living at that date, with gifts over if not. The daughter disclaimed and it was suggested and not denied that she did so in order that her brother's interest would thereby accelerate and that he intended to give it to his sister. The court held that, while the disclaimer was effective, the son's interest did not accelerate. Acceleration would defeat the testatrix' intention of giving her son the corpus only if living at the specified date. In the result, the income passed as on an intestacy until the death of the daughter.

7. A testatrix directed her trustee to pay her husband $400 a month "until his death or remarriage, whichever occurs first." Then she directed the trustees, "upon the death of the survivor of me and my said husband," to divide the estate equally among her children "then alive." The will also provided that if the husband remarried, the residue was to be dealt with in the same manner as if he had died. The husband disclaimed after the testatrix died. Do the children's shares accelerate?[298]

8. Can a beneficiary disclaim part of a testamentary gift? For example, can a life tenant who has received income for some years disclaim the balance of the gift, or the income for one year?[299]

9. If the gift that follows after the disclaimed gift is a class gift, a question may arise about the membership of the class. Absent a contrary intention in the will, membership is determined in accordance with certain rules of construction known as the "class closing rules."[300] The rules may provide that membership of the class is determined on the death of the life tenant. If the life tenant disclaims and the gift to the class accelerates, does this accelerate the closing of the class as well?

The cases are divided on this question. Some hold that class closing is also accelerated;[301] others hold that it is not.[302] I submit that class closing and acceleration are two separate issues and both must be determined by reference to the testator's intention.

---

296 See *ibid.*, at 709, *per* Malins V.C.; *Lainson v. Lainson, supra*, at DeG. M. & G. 756-7, E.R. 1064, *per* Turner L.J.

297 (1985), 49 O.R. (2d) 623 (H.C.), varied (1986), 55 O.R. (2d) 534 (C.A.).

298 See *Brannan v. British Columbia (Public Trustee)* (1991), 41 E.T.R. 40, 56 B.C.L.R. (2d) 113 (B.C.C.A.).

299 See *Re Graydon*, [1942] O.W.N. 130, [1942] 2 D.L.R. 306; *Re Coulson, supra*.

300 These are discussed in the chapter on Class Gifts.

301 See *Re Johnson* (1893), 68 L.T. (N.S.) 20; *Wyndham v. Darby* (1896), 17 N.S.W.R. 272 (E.); *Re Crothers' Trusts*, [1915] 1 I.R. 53; *Re Chartres*, [1927] 1 Ch. 466; *Re Davies*, [1957] 1 W.L.R. 922, [1957] 3 All E.R. 52; and *Re Dawson's Settlement*, [1966] 1 W.L.R. 1456, [1966] 3 All E.R. 68.

302 See *Re Taylor*, [1957] 1 W.L.R. 1057, [1957] 3 All E.R. 56; *Re Kebty-Fletcher's Will Trusts*, [1969] 1 Ch. 339, [1967] 3 All E.R. 1076; and *Re Harker's Will Trusts*, [1969] 1 W.L.R. 1124, [1968] 3 All E.R. 1.

Further Reading

Mellows: The Law of Succession, 5th ed. by Clive Margrave-Jones (London: Butterworths, 1993).

Williams, Mortimer and Sunnucks on Executors, Administrators and Probate, 17th ed. by J.H.G. Sunnocks, J.G. Ross Martyn, and K.M. Garnett (London: Stevens & Sons, 1993), pp. 931, 940.

Maurice C. Cullity, "Post-Mortem Tax Planning: Renunciations, Disclaimers, Surrenders and Elections" (1998), 18 E.T. & P.J. 31.

12

LAPSE AND SURVIVORSHIP

1. INTRODUCTION

The doctrine of lapse is a rule of law. It states that a gift to a beneficiary who predeceases the testator fails or lapses. It will not pass to the beneficiary's estate. We will deal with the disposition of the lapsed gift below. The doctrine applies to gifts to any object, including corporations and charities. It also applies to powers of appointment. We discuss its application to these interests separately below.

The doctrine of lapse is subject to certain exceptions at common law, which we shall discuss. Moreover, modern wills statutes contain provisions to avoid the effects of lapse. We shall also discuss this legislation.

It is possible for a testator to avoid the effects of lapse by making a substitutionary, or alternative gift, by naming an alternative beneficiary to take if the first one should predecease him.

Lapse is inherent in a situation in which two persons die at the same time and either or both have left their property by will to the other. This type of situation involves the law of survivorship. It will be dealt with in the last part of this chapter.

Further Reading

H. A. J. Ford, "Lapses of Devises and Bequests" (1962), 78 L.Q. Rev. 88.

Feeney's The Canadian Law of Wills, 4th ed. by James MacKenzie (Toronto: Butterworths, 2000 (loose leaf)), c. 13.

Williams on Wills, 7th ed. by C.H. Sherrin, R.F.D. Barlow, and R.A. Wallington, assisted by Susannah L. Meadway (London: Butterworths, 1995), cc. 47, 70.

2. DISPOSITION OF LAPSED GIFT

Pass

At common law a lapsed devise of real property devolved upon the heir, whereas a gift of personal property which lapsed fell into residue.[1] In fact, this principle applied to all gifts that were void or otherwise failed.[2] The English *Wills Act, 1837*[3] assimilated the rule respecting real property to the rule concerning personal property. This legislation has been adopted in Canada. Section 23 of the *Succession Law Reform Act*,[4] reproduced below, is representative. It will be noted that that section, as distinct from the legislation it derived from, encompasses both real and personal property by reason of the definition of "property" in s. 1(1)(f) of the Act.

If there is no residuary gift, or if the gift was residuary, the property passes to the persons entitled on an intestacy.[5] *Re Stuart*,[6] reproduced below, deals with this point.

Further Reading

Laurie S. Redden, "Lapse of Testamentary Gifts of Residue" (1992), 11 E. & T.J. 244.

SUCCESSION LAW REFORM ACT
R.S.O. 1990, c. S.26

23. Except when a contrary intention appears by the will, property or an interest therein that is comprised or intended to be comprised in a devise or bequest that fails or becomes void by reason of,

(a) the death of the devisee or donee in the lifetime of the testator; or

(b) the devise or bequest being disclaimed or being contrary to law or otherwise incapable of taking effect,

is included in the residuary devise or bequest, if any, contained in the will.

Comparable Legislation

Probate Act, R.S.P.E.I. 1988, c. P-21, s. 77; *Wills Act*, R.S.A. 1980, c. W-11, s. 23; R.S.B.C. 1996, c. 489, s. 21; R.S.M. 1988, c. W150, s. 25; R.S.N.B. 1973, c. W-9, s. 22; R.S.N.S. 1989, c. 505, s. 24; S.S. 1996, c. W-14.11, s. 22; R.S.N.W.T. 1988, c. W-5, s. 16; R.S.Y. 1986, c. 179, s. 15.

---

1 *Wright v. Hall* (1724), Fort. 182, 92 E.R. 810.
2 This is discussed in the previous chapter.
3 7 Will. 4 & 1 Vict., c. 26, s. 25.
4 R.S.O. 1990, c. S.26 (hereafter referred to without further citation).
5 *Re Midgley; Barclays Bank Ltd. v. Midgley*, [1955] Ch. 576, [1955] 3 W.L.R. 119, [1955] 2 All E.R. 625.
6 (1964), 47 W.W.R. 500 (B.C.S.C.).

STUART RE
(1964), 47 W.W.R. 500
Supreme Court of British Columbia

By his home drawn will the testator gave 36 pecuniary legacies, including one to his niece, Annabelle Palmer. He then gave the residue equally among 13 named persons, including Annabelle Palmer. Annabelle predeceased him.

The executors brought an application for directions, *inter alia*, with respect to the lapsed share of residue.

The relevant legislation,[7] was virtually identical to section 23 of the *Succession Law Reform Act* set out above.

NEMETZ J.:

. . .

The English Act has substantially the same provision...[8]except that it deals only with real property and does not include any provision relating to personal property. The English decisions relating to lapsed devises, nevertheless, are relevant in considering the interpretation of our Act. 39 *Halsbury's Laws of England*[9] states:

> If there is no residuary devise or bequest, or if the gift which lapses or fails is of a share or interest in the general residue, the gift passes to those entitled on an intestacy.

And:[10]

> Property included in a residuary devise which lapses also passes as on an intestacy.

It is to be noted that *Halsbury* does not here distinguish between real property and personal property in its commentary. In addition, none of the United Kingdom cases cited in *Halsbury* to support the above propositions specifically interprets sec. 25 of their *Wills Act*.

. . .

It appears clear that a lapsed *specific* devise or bequest falls or is included in the residuary clause, if any, of a will. However, counsel before me have been unable to cite any case where a court has judicially considered the effect of sec. 22 of our *Wills Act* (or its counterpart in any other jurisdiction) in respect of lapsed *residuary* devises or bequests. Accordingly, I must now determine whether or not sec. 22 applies equally to lapsed devises and bequests in both *specific* and *residuary* bequests and devises.

Romer, J. in *Re Whitrod; Burrows v. Base*,[11] restates the general principle of law relating to lapsed gifts *vis-a-vis* the residual provisions of a will:

---

7 *Wills Act*, R.S.B.C. 1960, c. 408.
8 *Wills Act, 1837*, 7 Will. 4 & 1 Vict., c. 26, s. 25.
9 3rd ed., at p. 946.
10 *Ibid.*, at p. 949.
11 [1926] Ch. 118, 95 L.J. Ch. 205 at 121.

In Vaughan Hawkins on Wills,[12] that learned author, after referring to the general rule that a general residuary bequest carries lapsed and void legacies, continues:

> The comprehensive import of the word residue does not extend to a gift of the *residue* of that residue. Thus, if the testator gives £10,000 out of the residue of his personal estate to A., and the residue to B., and the bequest to A. fails, the gift to B. will not, it appears, in general carry the £10,000 bequeathed to A., which will therefore be undisposed of.

It was urged upon me by Mr. Johnson, counsel for some of the residuary beneficiaries, that, since sec. 22 makes no distinction between specific and residuary devises or bequests, Annabelle Palmer's portion of the residue should be distributed among the surviving residuary beneficiaries. However, it appears to me that in order to give effect to this argument, the legislature would have used words in sec. 22 similar to those appearing in sec. 30, e.g., "and in the case of a lapsed residuary devise or bequest, is divisible among the remaining residuary devisees and legatees."

Since the will does not dispose of Annabelle Palmer's lapsed share and since sec. 22 does not, in my view, provide for the disposition of lapsed *residuary* devises or bequests, her interest passes as on an intestacy.

. . .

Notes and Questions

1. The Newfoundland Act does not contain a provision similar to s. 23 of the *Succession Law Reform Act*.

2. The facts in *Re Shapiro*[13] were very similar to those in the *Stuart* case. The testator had disposed of the residue of his estate by giving defined portions thereof, expressed in percentages, to various beneficiaries. One of the beneficiaries, a niece, predeceased the testator. Montgomery J., held that the gift lapsed and went out as on an intestacy. However, His Lordship appears to have thought that Nemetz J., in *Stuart*, found that the naming of beneficiaries in the residuary clause amounted to an expression of a contrary intention under the legislation.[14] Nemetz J., of course, held quite the opposite.

3. In *Kossak Estate v. Kosak*,[15] the court considered a will which divided the residue equally among seven named beneficiaries, one of whom predeceased the testator. Doherty J. followed *Re Stuart* and *Re Shapiro*, holding that the lapsed gift of residue went out on intestacy.

4. Until recently, the Manitoba courts took a different approach, holding that a lapsed share of residue should be shared by the other residuary beneficiaries. That approach prevents intestacy.[16] However, the Manitoba Court of Appeal had since overruled those

---

12 3rd ed., p. 52.
13 (1980), 27 O.R. (2d) 517, 6 E.T.R. 276, 107 D.L.R. (3d) 133 (H.C.).
14 *Ibid.*, at p. 137.
15 (1990), 37 E.T.R. 235 (Ont. H.C.)
16 See, *e.g.*, *Pawlukewich v. Pawlukewich* (1986), 23 E.T.R. 37 (Man. Q.B.); *Cera v. Wolfe* (1986), 25 E.T.R. 68 (Man. Q.B.)

cases and adopted the orthodox view expressed in *Re Stuart* and other cases.[17]

It is interesting to note that the law of New York does provide that failed residuary gifts augment the shares of other residuary beneficiaries.[18]

5. *Doliphar Estate v. Stopar*[19] followed *Kossak*. The will left half of the residue to the testatrix's mother and divided the other half equally among 11 named persons. The mother predeceased the testator. Haley J. pointed out[20] that if the Manitoba approach were adopted difficulties would arise: the mother's half would have to be included in the residue again and would lapse again; then the same process would have to be repeated *ad infinitum*.[21]

6. A testator left one half of the residue of his estate to his wife and the other half, expressed in percentages, to four other persons. His wife predeceased him and he then made a codicil revoking "that part of my Will by which assets were bequeathed to" his wife, but confirming his will in all other respects. Does the half of the residue that went to the testator's wife go the other residuary beneficiaries, or does it go out on an intestacy?[22]

7. A contrary intention for the purpose of the legislation is normally expressed by an accruer clause. Thus, if a testatrix gives the residue of her estate upon trust as to one quarter each for her four daughters, A, B, C and D for life, with remainder to their respective issue, she is likely to add that if any of the daughters should die without issue their shares shall fall into and become part of the testatrix's residuary estate and be held and disposed of on the trusts declared for her other daughters and their issue. Such an accruer clause will prevent the share of a daughter dying without issue from being disposed of as on an intestacy.[23]

8. *Tribble Estate v. McGuire*[24] also illustrates a contrary intention. The testatrix divided the residue of her estate into six equal shares for distribution among six named persons. Then she said that if any of the named persons predeceased her, the number of residuary shares was to be reduced accordingly and the shares of the survivors augmented correspondingly.[25]

9. If a share of residue is given to two or more persons as joint tenants and one predeceases the testator, the remaining person or persons take the property by survivorship.[26]

10. If a gift is made of the remainder of a particular fund, whether the fund be of a specified part of the estate, or of the general residue, it is a question of construction whether the gift of the remainder will carry previous gifts out of the fund which have lapsed or have otherwise failed. If the gift of the remainder is construed as a gift of the mere balance of the fund after deduction of the sums previously given out of it, any of the latter which fail go out on an intestacy. But, if the gift of the remainder is construed as a gift of the

---

17 *Re Smith and Mackay* (1994), 116 D.L.R. (4th) 308, (sub nom. *Sparks v. Wenham*) 4 E.T.R. (2d) 147 (Man. C.A.).

18 See *Hammill Estate v. McDonell* (1994), 3 E.T.R. (2d) 300 (Ont. Gen. Div.).

19 (1990), 39 E.T.R. 120 (Ont. H.C.).

20 *Ibid.,* at p. 125.

21 See also *Re Redmond Estate* (1993), 50 E.T.R. 167 (Alta. Surr. Ct.), to the same effect.

22 See *Re Crago* (1976), 12 O.R. (2d) 356, 69 D.L.R. (3d) 32 (H.C.). *Cf. Re Forrest*, [1931] 1 Ch. 162; *Re Dunbar Estate* (1992), 49 E.T.R. 67 (N.B. Prob. Ct.).

23 See *Re Allan*, [1903] 1 Ch. 276 (C.A.).

24 (1993), 1 E.T.R. (2d) 69 (Ont. Gen. Div.).

25 See also *Hammill Estate v. McDonell* (1994), 3 E.T.R. (2d) 300 (Ont. Gen. Div.), in which the court also found a contrary intention.

26 *Morley v. Bird* (1798), 3 Ves. 629, 30 E.R. 1192; *Re Hutton* (1982), 39 O.R. (2d) 622, 11 E.T.R. 140 at 144, *per* Steele J., affirmed 39 O.R. (2d) 622n.

entire fund, subject only to the gifts made out of it to which effect can be given, the gift of the remainder carries any previous gifts out of the fund which have failed.[27]

Re Parnell; Ranks v. Holmes[28] illustrates the point. The testatrix directed that her trustees should stand possessed of the residue of her estate as a residuary trust fund and to hold aliquot portions thereof upon trust for various persons for life, with remainder to their issue. She then left "all the remainder of the residuary trust fund" in trust for another person. One of the beneficiaries of a portion of the residuary trust fund died a bachelor. It was held that the capital of the portion settled on him passed under the gift of the "remainder" of the residuary trust fund.

11. Surplus income from a specific fund set apart for the purpose of an annuity (after any applicable accumulation) falls into residue and does not go those entitled to the balance of the fund in the absence of a contrary intention.[29]

Further Reading

G.L. Certoma, "Particular Residue, True Residue or Specific Legacy" (1981) 55 Austr. L. J. 193.

3. ANTI-LAPSE LEGISLATION

(a) Generally

The doctrine of lapse is inconvenient and likely to be contrary to the testator's intention when he or she leaves a gift to a close relative. In such a case, the testator would probably want the heirs of that relative to take in the event that the primary beneficiary dies. Perhaps the testator believes that that will happen; perhaps he or she has not turned his or her mind to the matter at all. If the testator had thought about it, he or she would no doubt have named an alternative beneficiary to take. That being the likely intention, all the common law provinces have enacted legislation to achieve this result.

As indicated in the following material, there are basically two types of legislation. One derives from the English *Wills Act, 1837*,[30] and is designed actually to prevent lapse by letting the property pass through the estate of the primary beneficiary into that of the substituted beneficiary. The practical and interpretational difficulties generated by this legislation are explored below.[31] It is exem-

---

27 Hawkins and Ryder, *The Construction of Wills* (3rd ed., 1965), pp. 66-7.

28 [1944] 1 Ch. 107. *Cf. Re Bowman* (1975), 17 N.S.R. (2d) 76, 19 A.P.R. 76 (T.D.).

29 *Re Herman*, [1961] O.R. 25, 25 D.L.R. (2d) 93 (C.A.); *Re Struthers* (1980), 29 O.R. (2d) 616, 7 E.T.R. 307, 114 D.L.R. (3d) 492 (C.A.).

30 7 Will. 4 & 1 Vict., c. 26, s. 33. The *Administration of Justice Act 1982*, c. 53 (U.K.), s. 19 repealed and replaced s. 33 with one similar to the type now common in Canada, but restricts the preferred class to children and remoter descendants, and permits only their issue to take. The new section applies to class gifts.

31 In the excerpt from A.H. Oosterhoff, *Succession Law Reform in Ontario* (1979), pp. 41-44.

plified in the Nova Scotia legislation reproduced below. All of the other provinces at one time had similar legislation, but most have replaced it with the other type.

The other type derives from the *Uniform Wills Act.*[32] It does not, in fact, prevent lapse, but provides for statutory substitutionary beneficiaries. The Ontario legislation reproduced below is representative.

Re Wolson; Wolson v. Jackson,[33] reproduced below, explores the meaning of the phrase, an "estate or interest not terminable at or before" the death of the beneficiary.

WILLS ACT
R.S.N.S. 1989, c. 505

31. Where any person, being a child or other issue of the testator, to whom any real or personal property is devised or bequeathed for any estate or interest not determinable at or before the death of such person, dies in the lifetime of the testator leaving issue, and any such issue of such person are living at the time of the death of the testator, such devise or bequest does not lapse, but takes effect as if the death of such person had happened immediately after the death of the testator, unless a contrary intention appears by the will.

Comparable Legislation

Probate Act, R.S.P.E.I. 1988, c. P-21, s. 85.

SUCCESSION LAW REFORM ACT
R.S.O. 1990, c. S.26

31. Except when a contrary intention appears by the will, where a devise or bequest is made to a child, grandchild, brother or sister of the testator who dies before the testator, either before or after the testator makes his or her will, and leaves a spouse or issue surviving the testator, the devise or bequest does not lapse but takes effect as if it had been made directly to the persons among whom and in the shares in which the estate of that person would have been divisible,

   (a) if that person had died immediately after the death of the testator;

   (b) if that person had died intestate;

   (c) if that person had died without debts; and

   (d) if section 45 had not been passed.

---

32 Uniform Law Conf. of Canada, *Uniform Acts of the Uniform Law Conference of Canada* (1978, as rev.), p. 53-1.

33 [1939] Ch. 780, [1939] 3 All E.R. 852.

Comparable Legislation

Wills Act, R.S.A. 1980, c. W-11, ss. 34, 35; R.S.B.C. 1996, c. 489, s. 29; R.S.M. 1988, c. W150, s. 25.1; R.S.N.B. 1973, c. W-9, s. 32; R.S.N. 1990, c. W-10, ss. 18, 19; S.S. 1996, c. W-14.11, s. 32; R.S.N.W.T. 1988, c. W-5, s. 21; R.S.Y. 1986, c. 179, s. 20.

SUCCESSION LAW REFORM IN ONTARIO
A.H. Oosterhoff (1979), pp. 41-44

Anti-Lapse Provisions

Of the anti-lapse provisions contained in sections 35 and 36 of the former Act, only the latter is retained in a somewhat modified form. The former applied solely to estates tail and could thus be dropped. Section 36 of the former Act dates from 1959.[34] The section, despite its language did not in fact prevent a lapse; it merely named statutory substitutionary beneficiaries where the primary beneficiary died before the testator. Prior to the 1959 amendment, the Act[35] did in fact prevent a lapse in the circumstances set out in that legislation. Thus the property being given would pass to the deceased primary beneficiary's estate and thence out under that estate after payment of its debts, taxes, etc. The legislation created difficulties in that it involved a double succession and hence the property was subject to the claims of two sets of creditors and could be taxed twice.[36] There were interpretational difficulties as well. For example, the legislation deemed the beneficiary who predeceased the testator to have died immediately after the testator. The question whether he was notionally kept alive for all purposes connected with the distribution of the property comprised in the gift was not settled until 1945. The question is important in order to determine who the substitutionary beneficiaries would be: those alive at the testator's death or those alive at the actual death of the primary beneficiary. *Re Branchflower*[37] held that the next of kin of the deceased legatee were to be ascertained at the date of his death.[38] As indicated, section 36 had the effect of transmitting the property directly from the estate of the testator to the substitutionary beneficiaries described in the section. The section applied only where the gift was to a child, grandchild, brother or sister of the testator, it did not apply to class gifts, it required that the primary beneficiary must die before the testator, and it applied only when the deceased beneficiary left issue. By contrast, the *Uniform Act*[39] extends the class of primary

---

34 S.O. 1959, c. 108, s. 1.

35 *The Wills Act*, R.S.O. 1950, c. 426, s. 36.

36 Double taxation did not exist under the old *Dominion Succession Duty Act*, R.S.C. 1952, c. 89, rep. and sub. by the *Estate Tax Act*, S.C. 1958, c. 29: see *Toronto General Trusts v. M.N.R.* (1958), 15 D.L.R. (2d) 81 (S.C.C.); but the point was never settled with respect to the Ontario *Succession Duty Act*, R.S.O. 1970, c. 449.

37 [1945] 4 D.L.R. 559 (Ont. H.C.).

38 See also *Re Basioli; McGahey v. Depaoli*, [1953] Ch. 357, to the same effect.

39 *Uniform Wills Act*, Uniform Law Conf. of Can., *Uniform Acts of the Uniform Law Conference of Canada* (1978), p. 53-1.

beneficiaries to children "or other issue", applies to class gifts, provides that the section applies whether a person dies before or after the testator made the will, and makes provision for the case where the primary beneficiary died leaving either or both a spouse or issue him surviving.[40]

The Ontario Law Reform Commission recommended[41] that Ontario adopt only the provision respecting the death of the primary beneficiary leaving either or both a spouse or issue him surviving from the *Uniform Act* and section 31 of the Act so provides. This is an appropriate change since a surviving spouse would benefit if there were issue surviving. Hence there is no reason to exclude him or her if there are no issue surviving. In any event, in most cases the testator would want such spouse to benefit. Heretofore, it required a special clause in the will to achieve that effect, that is, if one were to rely solely on section 36 to effect a substitutionary gift. Such a spouse was, of course, not entitled to a preferential share under the legislation.[42]

The words "either before or after the testator makes his will" with respect to the time of death of the primary beneficiary are important. Without them the legislation could possibly be construed as applying only to cases where the primary beneficiary dies after the making of the will. For then it might be assumed that the testator simply made an error if, when he made his will, he made a gift to a relative who was already dead and that, therefore, there could not be a substitutionary gift either.[43] However, the adverbial phrase makes the meaning clear.

It is regrettable that the section has not been extended to class gifts, since very typical class gifts might be saved completely by carrying out the testator's intention fully if it were. For example, it is quite common to divide the residue of an estate among the children of the testator and then to provide for a substitutionary gift over to the spouse or issue or both of any children who have predeceased the testator. It is only upon failure of such spouse or issue that the share of the predeceased child is usually directed to go to the other members of the class who would, of course, have got that share automatically in the absence of such a substitutionary gift to the spouse or issue of the predeceased child.

---

40 Ont. Law Ref. Com. *Report on the Proposed Adoption in Ontario of the Uniform Wills Act* (1968), pp. 13-14.

41 *Ibid.*, pp. 14 and 41-2.

42 *Re Meunier* (1953), 36 D.L.R. (2d) 388, decided otherwise and the Act was amended accordingly by S.O. 1962-63, c. 144, s. 1.

43 For an odd case in which the issue was whether the testator had provided his own substitutionary beneficiaries, see *Re Marshall*, [1944] 3 D.L.R. 178 (Alta. C.A.). The case held that in the peculiar circumstances there presented the testator must have intended a substitutionary gift to the heirs of his brother who had died many years before the will to the knowledge of the testator. Clearly, the general rule would be otherwise. The case was distinguished in *Re Ottewell* (1970), 7 D.L.R. (3d) 358 (Alta. C.A.), affirmed 9 D.L.R. (3d) 314 (S.C.C.).

RE WOLSON; WOLSON v. JACKSON
[1939] Ch. 780, [1939] 3 All E.R. 852
Chancery Division

By his will, the testator, Solomon Wolson, gave a life interest in the residue of his estate to his wife, with remainder in one quarter of the residue to his three children, Ethel, Alec and Hilda at age 25. Ethel was married in 1930. She survived the testator, but died intestate in 1931 at age 24, survived by an infant daughter. The executrix brought this application to construe the will.

CROSSMAN J.:

. . .

Mr. Ungoed-Thomas, on behalf of G. O. Preiss and C. T. Preiss, has argued that s. 33 of the Wills Act, 1837, applies to a contingent interest and that, notwithstanding that Ethel Preiss died under twenty-five, the bequest to her of the share in question has taken effect in the manner provided by that section.

> [His Lordship quoted section 33, which is identical to section 30 of the Nova Scotia Act set out above, and continued:]

Mr. Ungoed-Thomas says that the share was bequeathed to Ethel Preiss for an interest not determinable at or before her death and therefore that it must under the section take effect as if her death had happened immediately after the testator's death, and that as if her death had happened immediately after the testator's death, she would have attained twenty-five, the bequest has taken effect in the manner provided by the section. Mr. Haylor and Mr. Buckley, who appear for parties interested in opposing this conclusion, contend that s. 33 does not apply to save a contingent interest which has already failed. In my judgment that contention is right. This is entirely a question of the construction of the section and I have to interpret what Parliament intended by the wording of the section. In my opinion the share in question, which was bequeathed to Ethel Preiss contingently on her attaining twenty-five, was bequeathed to her for an interest determinable at her death within the meaning of the section. Consequently, in my view the section does not apply to the interest at all. I think that the use in the section of the words "shall not lapse" shows that the purpose of the section was to provide against the effect of the death of a child in the lifetime of the testator, and not against the effect of death without attaining the age the attainment of which is a condition of the bequest. I hold, therefore, that the bequest has not taken effect in the manner provided by s. 33 of the Wills Act, 1837, and that there is an intestacy with respect to the share in question.

. . .

Notes and Questions

1. The Prince Edward Island Act differs from Nova Scotia's legislation in that, under the former, the property passes to the issue of the predeceased beneficiary *per stirpes* as

if the testator had died intestate with respect to the property and as if the beneficiary's issue were his only next of kin.

2. All of the statutes, except Ontario's, extend to "children or other issue."

3. The Newfoundland Act draws a distinction between "child or issue" and "brother or sister". With respect to the former, the statute takes effect if the beneficiary dies leaving issue who survive the testator; with respect to the latter, it operates only if the beneficiary leaves a child or children who survive the testator.

4. The statutes of most provinces apply not only to gifts to individuals, but also to persons who are members of a class. Thus, in most of the provinces if a gift is made "to my children" and one of them predeceases the testator leaving issue (or a spouse or issue, depending upon the particular legislation) the latter can take the share of the predeceased child. In contrast, in Ontario, Nova Scotia and Prince Edward Island, the share of the predeceased child would go to augment the shares of the other members of the class, in the absence of a contrary intention, in accordance with the principles of class gifts.[44] Should the legislation extend to class gifts?

5. The statutes in Alberta, Manitoba, New Brunswick, Newfoundland, Nova Scotia, Prince Edward Island, the Northwest Territories and the Yukon do not apply if the beneficiary leaves a spouse, but no issue, him or her surviving. The British Columbia statute does not permit the beneficiary's surviving spouse to take on the beneficiary's notional intestacy, however, if both issue of the beneficiary and his or her spouse survive. The Manitoba, Nova Scotia, New Brunswick, Northwest Territories and Yukon statutes do not preclude the beneficiary's surviving spouse from taking either a distributive or a preferential share. In the latter jurisdictions, therefore, it is likely that the surviving spouse would take a preferential share in the testator's estate in addition to what he or she might receive from the deceased spouse.[45] The present Ontario legislation also precludes the beneficiary's surviving spouse from taking a preferential share.

6. Several Canadian statutes still contain an anti-lapse section respecting estates tail and quasi estates tail,[46] even though the estate tail has been abolished in virtually all of the provinces.[47] The section typically provides that if a person, to whom real property is devised for what would have been an estate tail or in quasi entail,[48] dies before the testator, leaving issue who would inherit the estate if it existed, and the issue are living at the

---

44 Discussed in the next chapter. For a case holding that the anti-lapse provision does not apply to a class gift, see *Re Campbell Estate* (1998), 25 E.T.R. (2d) 169 (P.E.I., T.D.).

45 See *Re Meunier*, [1963] 1 O.R. 213, 36 D.L.R. (2d) 388 (H.C.). See also *Re Rake*, [1938] 1 W.W.R. 492, 45 Man. R. 616, [1938] 1 D.L.R. 191 (K.B.), to the same effect. *Re Meunier* was reversed in Ontario by S.O. 1962-63, c. 144, s. 1.

46 *Probate Act*, R.S.P.E.I. 1988, c. P-21, s. 84; *Wills Act*, R.S.A. 1980, c. W-11, s. 33; R.S.M. 1988, c. W150, s. 25.1 [re-enacted 1989 90, c. 44, s. 4]; R.S.N.B. 1973, c. W-9, s. 31; R.S.N.S. 1989, c. 505, s. 30; R.S.S. 1978, c. W-14 [1996, c. W-14.11], s. 31.

47 Although effectively abolished in Prince Edward Island, estates tail which still exist continue to exist until a deed by the tenant in tail is executed and registered: *Real Property Act*, R.S.P.E.I. 1988, c. R-3, s. 14.

Estates tail can still be created in Manitoba, in which the English *Fines and Recoveries Act, 1833*, 3 & 4 Will. 4, c. 74 is regarded as received law. Registration of a disentailing assurance is substituted for enrolment in Chancery: *Law of Property Act*, R.S.M. 1987, c. L90, s. 30(1).

48 A quasi entail is an estate created out of a life estate by utilizing the device of the estate *pur autre vie*. Thus, if A grants "to B and the heirs of his body for the life of C", B would hold in quasi entail. It was treated by analogy to the estate tail in much the same way as that estate: *Re Barber's Settled Estates* (1881), 18 Ch. D. 624 at 629. See also Challis, *The Law of Real Property* (3rd ed., 1911), pp. 362-3.

testator's death, the devise takes effect as if the primary beneficiary had died immediately after the testator. Since the language formerly apt to create an estate tail is nowadays construed as creating a fee simple in jurisdictions in which the former estate has been abolished,[49] the special legislation would seem unnecessary since the general anti-lapse provision would be applicable.

7. The Nova Scotia and Prince Edward Island statutes do not state that the legislation applies whether the primary beneficiary dies before or after the testator makes his will. If the testator leaves a gift to his brother in these jurisdictions, and the brother died before the will was made, leaving issue who survive the testator, does the gift lapse?[50]

8. The point considered in *Re Wolson; Wolson v. Jackson*[51] was also considered in *Re Nixey*.[52] In that case the testator left a legacy to his brother. The brother predeceased him, survived by a daughter, who survived the testator. It was held that the brother's daughter took the legacy. Counsel argued unsuccessfully that the phrase "not determinable" applied when a testator leaves to a person in the preferred class a percentage or fraction of his estate, the amount of which cannot be determined until after the testator's death.

The phrase, "not determinable at or before the death of such persons," or its equivalent, also appears on most of the other statutes. Is this issue relevant under a statute such as Ontario's, which does not contain this phrase?

9. It is currently unclear whether the definition of "spouse" in wills statutes and related family law legislation is unconstitutional because it is restricted to persons who are married to each other. As indicated elsewhere in this text, some cases have held that it is. This also has implications for the doctrine of lapse, since anti-lapse legislation provides that a gift that would otherwise have lapsed will, in certain situations, pass to the deceased beneficiary's intestate heirs.

The issue arose in *Re Lange Estate*.[53] The testator left his estate to his brother. His brother predeceased him, survived by three children and a common law spouse. The court held that the common law spouse did not qualify as the brother's spouse under the anti-lapse provision of the *Wills Act*,[54] but that she might have standing to challenge the constitutional validity of the definition of "spouse".

10. A testator left a legacy to his son. The son died shortly before his father, leaving his wife *enceinte*. After the testator's death the son's widow was delivered of a healthy daughter. Is the daughter entitled to take?[55]

11. A gift to a person in the preferred class named in the section under a general power of appointment does not lapse, assuming the other conditions of the legislation are satisfied.[56] However, a gift under a special power to such a person does lapse.[57]

---

49 See, *e.g.*, *Conveyancing and Law of Property Act*, R.S.O. 1990, c. C.34, enacted by S.O. 1956, c. 10, s. 1.

50 See *Re McCallum* (1924), 27 O.W.N. 169 (H.C.). See *contra Re Sheard* (1921), 49 O.L.R. 320, 58 D.L.R. 539 (C.A.); *Re Williamson* (1931), 40 O.W.N. 416 (H.C.).

51 [1939] Ch. 780, [1939] 3 All. E.R. 852.

52 (1972), 31 D.L.R. (3d) 597 (Man. Q.B.).

53 (1999), 30 E.T.R. (2d) 241 (Sask. Q.B.).

54 S.S. 1996, c. W-14.1, s. 22(1).

55 See *Elliott v. Joicey*, [1935] A.C. 209, [1935] All E.R. Rep. 578 (H.L.). The problem is avoided in some jurisdictions, which make specific reference to a posthumous child in their statutes: *Wills Act*, R.S.N. 1990, c. W-10, ss. 18(3), 19(3); *Wills Act, 1837*, 7 Will. 4 and 1 Vict., c. 26, s. 33(4)(b) [rep. and replaced by *Administration of Justice Act 1982*, c. 53 (U.K.), s. 19]. The Ontario *Succession Law Reform Act* avoids the problem by its definitions of "child" and "issue" in s. 1(1), which include posthumous children and issue.

56 *Eccles v. Cheyne* (1856), 5 K. & J. 676, 69 E.R. 954.

12. A testatrix gave all her estate to her daughter, Mary, who predeceased her, leaving a child, John, who also predeceased the testatrix. However, John was survived by his child, Lynn, who survived the testatrix. Does the gift lapse?[58]

13. A testatrix gave half the residue of her estate to her sister, but provided that if she should not survive the testatrix by 30 days then $1,000 was to be paid to the sister's husband unless he also failed to survive the testatrix by 30 days. The will did not dispose of the balance of the residue after payment of the $1,000 to the sister's husband. The sister predeceased the testatrix, but her husband and son survived the testatrix by more than 30 days. Is there a lapse?[59]

14. Anti-lapse legislation applies to residuary gifts as well, as illustrated by *Rothstein Estate v. Rothstein*.[60] The testatrix directed that the residue of her estate be divided into a number of shares equal to the total number of her children and grandchildren and paid to them. She had four children and four grandchildren. One of her children predeceased her, but died after the will was made. His two children survived and were, therefore, beneficiaries in their own right. The court held that they also were entitled to take their father's share under the legislation. The Saskatchewan legislation applies to class gifts, although the court was of opinion that the gift was not a class gift, since the shares of the children did not vest in the children in the same manner and at the same time as the shares of the grandchildren.

(b) Contrary Intention

The anti-lapse legislation applies only if the testator does not express a contrary intention in the will. A contrary intention is obviously expressed if he or she makes a substitutionary gift. Other relevant factors are considered in *Re Wudel; Moore v. Moore*,[61] reproduced below.

RE WUDEL; MOORE v. MOORE
(1982), 13 E.T.R. 25
Alberta Court of Queen's Bench

The testatrix, Maria Wudel, a widow, died in 1979, survived by four sons and three daughters. One daughter, Marion Bronson, predeceased her in 1961, survived by four daughters, who were living at the testatrix' death. By her will, made in 1977, the testatrix directed that the residue of the estate be divided as follows: 8% equally among her grandchildren living at her death, 28% equally among her sons, and 64% equally among her daughters. Then she provided that if any of her sons and daughters should die after the date of the will, but before her death, the portion that that child was entitled to should be divided equally among his or her children, and if any of the children should die leaving no children the portion that

---

57 *Freeland v. Pearson* (1867), L.R. 3 Eq. 658; *Holyland v. Lewin* (1884), 26 Ch. D. 266 (C.A.). See also part 5(a), *infra*.

58 *In the Goods of Packer* (1860), 1 Sw. & Tr. 523, 164 E.R. 842.

59 See *Gislason v. Gillis* (1988), 31 E.T.R. 6 (Man. C.A.).

60 (1996), 11 E.T.R. (2d) 125 (B.C.S.C.).

61 (1982), 22 Alta. L.R. (2d) 394, 13 E.T.R. 25 (Q.B.).

that child was entitled to should be divided among the testatrix's children alive at the time of her death.

An application was brought to construe the will.

CAWSEY J.:

[His Lordship quoted section 35 of the Alberta *Wills Act*,[62] which is similar to section 31 of the Ontario Act set out above, except that it applies to class gifts, and continued:]

Marion Bronson, as a daughter of the testatrix, Maria Wudel, who died in the lifetime of Maria Wudel and left issue living at the time of the death of Maria Wudel, is a person who falls within the provisions of s. 35(1) of the Wills Act.

The opening words of s. 35(1) are: "Except when a contrary intention appears by the will,..."

The question for interpretation by this Court is whether such a contrary intention is expressed in Maria Wudel's last will and testament.

Counsel for the applicants (executors) submitted that in construing a will the Court must read the will with the same knowledge of the surrounding facts and circumstances known to the testatrix at the time she executed her will. This is the "armchair principle" which permits the Court to look only at evidence as to the facts and circumstances as they existed at the time of the execution of the last will and testament and the Court is barred from receiving evidence as to subsequent events.

From the armchair of Maria Wudel on the 20th of August 1977, (the date of the execution of the will) she was a widow with three living daughters, four living sons and 14 grandchildren. The fourth daughter of Maria Wudel, Marion Bronson, had died 16 years prior to the execution of the will.

. . .

Reference is made to Re McNeill,[63] and Re Meredith.[64]

In both of these cases the testator had made a codicil after the death of two children in Re McNeill and one child in Re Meredith. In Re McNeill the residue of the estate was to be divided equally between brothers and sisters of the testatrix. A brother and sister predeceased the testatrix and the testatrix made a codicil in which she gave her deceased brother's share to that brother's only son. She did not make any provision for her deceased sister's only daughter. Section 19 of the Wills Act of Newfoundland[65] is similar to s. 35 of the Wills Act of Alberta. In Re McNeill counsel argued that the failure to mention the deceased sister's only daughter in the codicil was evidence of a contrary intention within the meaning of the Wills Act of Newfoundland. Hickman C.J. held that a specific bequest made to the nephew of the testatrix, such nephew being the only son of a deceased brother, did not by implication exclude her niece and therefore such omission of

---

62 R.S.A. 1980, c. W-11.
63 (1980), 25 Nfld. & P.E.I.R. 297, 6 E.T.R. 165, 109 D.L.R. (3d) 109, 68 A.P.R. 297 (Nfld. S.C.).
64 [1924] 2 Ch. 552.
65 R.S.N. 1970, c. 401.

any reference to the daughter of the deceased sister in the codicil did not constitute a contrary intention by the will which would exclude the operation of s. 19 of the Wills Act of Newfoundland.

In Re Meredith, the testator bequeathed a share of furniture and a legacy of 100 pounds to his only son and his residuary estate in equal shares between his five children by name including the son. The son died in the testator's lifetime, leaving children who survived the testator. After the death of the son, the testator made a codicil to his will and he recited that as his son had died and the legacy and share of the residue given to him by the previous will had lapsed, the testator would provide specifically for the two children of his deceased son. The Court held that as the testator believed the death of his son had caused the gifts of the legacy and the share of residue to lapse, his failure to make further disposition of the legacy and share of residue showed an intention to let them lapse and thereby "a contrary intention" appeared within the meaning of s. 33 of the Wills Act, 1837[66] of England. The Court also noted however, that if there had been no statement in the codicil as to the testator's belief that the gift had lapsed, a codicil leaving a specific legacy to two children of the deceased son would not be a contrary intention within the meaning of the section.

This last statement of the Court is clearly obiter because it is not dealing with the factual situation before the Court.

. . .

The whole will must be considered and not just isolated parts. When the will was drawn it must be accepted that Maria Wudel knew that her daughter, Marion, had predeceased her. However, she did not know what would happen between the date of her will and the date of death.

If one of Maria Wudel's other children had died between the execution of the will and the date of her death, the distribution with respect to that child would not be the distribution contemplated by s. 35 of the Wills Act since no provision is made for the spouse of such deceased child. This appears to be a clear intention on the part of Maria Wudel to oust the provisions of s. 35 of the Wills Act.

In Re McNeill the Court was dealing with the home-drawn holograph will and codicil. In the present case we are dealing with a will prepared by a solicitor. In Re McNeill the codicil was drawn after the death of a child of the testator and while a specific bequest was made to the issue of one child, no provision was made for the issue of another child. The will is therefore silent with respect to that other child, so no contrary intention appeared in Re McNeill.

In Re Meredith the codicil sets out that the son had died and that the testator believed that the share given to that son had lapsed and he then gave the two children of the deceased son each a legacy of 100 pounds. Lord Romer held that since the testator believed that the death of his son had caused the gifts of the legacy and share of residue to lapse, his failure to make further disposition of the legacy and share of residue showed an intention to let them lapse and thereby a contrary intention appeared within the meaning of s. 33 of the Wills Act 1837 so

---

66 7 Will. 4 & 1 Vict., c. 26.

as to prevent the application of that section. The remainder of Lord Romer's judgment is obiter.

I find that the testatrix has expressed a contrary intention in her will and that she intended to oust the provision of the Wills Act. This intention is shown by her bequest of 8 per cent of the residue of her estate to her grandchildren which indicates that she meant to treat all of her grandchildren equally. If the estate of Marion Bronson was to receive a share it would mean that the children of Marion Bronson are being preferred over other grandchildren and a reading of the will did not indicate that the testatrix had any such intention.

When Maria Wudel provided in her will for a scheme of distribution in the event that any of her children died between the date of the execution of the will and the date of her death, she proposed a scheme of distribution which was not in harmony with s. 35 of the Wills Act and this scheme of distribution is a further contrary intention appearing by the will.

There will be an order that s. 35 of the Wills Act has no application to the distribution of the residuary estate of Maria Wudel and the distribution of the estate of Maria Wudel is to proceed strictly within the terms of the will executed by Maria Wudel on the 20th of August 1977.

. . .

Notes and Questions

1. Remember that some of the statutes do not apply to class gifts. Section 31 of the *Succession Law Reform Act* is an example. Hence, the question that arose in *Re Wudel* would not arise under such legislation if the gift was to a class.

2. In *Re Wudell,* the court found the contrary intention to be implied from the gifts in the will and the surrounding circumstances.[67] Other cases, however, insist that the contrary intention must be express. *Doucette v. Fedoruk Estate*[68] is representative of the latter view. The deceased made unequal provision for the children of his deceased brothers and sisters. He also provided for a gift over in the residuary clause, but not in the clause giving a legacy to the person who predeceased the testator in respect of which the legislation was invoked. The Manitoba Court of Appeal held that those circumstances did not amount to a contrary intention. Further, the court held that an express contrary intention, such as the clause "if she survives me," is required. Which approach conforms best with the legislation?

3. A testatrix directed that the residue of her estate be divided "in three equal shares among my surviving children." The testatrix had three children when she made her will. One predeceased her, leaving issue who survived the testatrix. Do the deceased child's issue take?[69]

4. A testator left a large legacy to his son, S, but provided that if S should predecease him, the money should go to his daughter, D. S, in fact, did predecease the testator, but so did D. D left issue who survived the testator. Do D's issue take?

---

67 For a similar case, see *Walt Estate v. Williams* (1997), 18 E.T.R. (2d) 242 (B.C.S.C.).
68 (1992), 49 E.T.R. 199 (Man. C.A.).
69 See *Horton v. Horton* (1978), 2 E.T.R. 293, 88 D.L.R. (3d) 264 (B.C.S.C.).

5. It would seem that, if the gift is made to two or more persons within the preferred class as joint tenants, a contrary intention is expressed by the will. The surviving joint tenant or tenants would take the whole interest, to the exclusion of the issue of a joint tenant who has predeceased the testator.[70] What would be the result if the gift is to A and B as joint tenants (A and B being brothers of the testator) and both predecease the testator, either or both leaving issue?[71]

6. A testator left the residue of his estate in equal shares among his brothers and sisters, with a substitutionary gift to the children of any of his brothers and sisters who predeceased him. All of his brothers and sisters were living when the will was made, but two brothers died before the testator, survived by issue. The testator then made a codicil appointing another executor and confirming his will. Thereafter, the only child of one of the predeceased brothers died. The testator was survived by two sisters and the children of one predeceased brother.

What result?[72]

4. EXCEPTIONS TO LAPSE

(a) Joint Tenancy

A gift of property to two or more persons as joint tenants is a gift of the entirety and confers a right of survivorship. Hence, when one joint tenant dies his or her share accrues to the other or others; it does not go to his estate. This rule also applies to lapse. Thus, if a testator gives property to two or more persons as joint tenants and one predeceases him or her, the other takes the whole interest. This may appear somewhat strange, in that the interest does not vest in anyone until the testator's death. That principle is not offended, however. Rather, it is recognized that a gift in joint tenancy incorporates an alternative or substitutionary gift.

The situation is otherwise with respect to a tenancy in common. It does not, unless expressed, carry the right of survivorship. Hence, if a gift is made by will to two persons as tenants in common and one predeceases the testator, his or her interest lapses, unless the deceased falls within the preferred class named in the anti-lapse legislation.

At common law there was a presumption in favour of joint tenancies in order to preserve the lord's feudal rights. Hence, a gift "to A and B" was construed to give them a joint tenancy. Equity, however, favours equality and thus raises a presumption in favour of a tenancy in common which operates whenever a gift calls for a division, or an equal division among the grantees, donees or beneficiaries.[73]

---

70 *Re Cf. Gamble* (1906), 13 O.L.R. 299.
71 See *Re Butler; Joyce v. Brew,* [1918] 1 I.R. 394.
72 See *Re Hutton* (1982), 39 O.R. (2d) 622, 11 E.T.R. 140 at 143, affirmed 39 O.R. (2d) 622n.
73 *Clark v. Clark* (1890), 17 S.C.R. 376. See, *e.g., Re Peters* (1967), 63 W.W.R. 180 (Man. Q.B.) a devise to three persons in equal shares; *Re Quebec* (1929), 37 O.W.N. 271 (H.C.), a devise to two persons jointly.

By statute, devises to two or more persons take effect as tenancies in common, unless a contrary intention is expressed. Section 13 of the Ontario *Conveyancing and Law of Property Act*,[74] reproduced below is representative.

The distinction between join tenancies and tenancies in common is nicely illustrated in *Re Gamble*.[75] In that case the testator devised a farm to his sisters, Mary Ann and Catharine. It was clear that they were to take title as tenants in common. The testator also gave the residue of his estate to his two sisters. Catharine predeceased the testator. At the time the anti-lapse provision of the *Wills Act*[76] did not extend to brothers and sisters. The court held that Catharine's undivided half interest in the farm under the specific devise fell into residue under the equivalent of section 23 of the *Succession Law Reform Act*, set out at the beginning of this chapter. The residue then consisted of real and personal property. The court held, applying the predecessor of section 13 of the *Conveyancing and Law of Property Act*, that the real property was devised as a tenancy in common, but the personalty as a joint tenancy. Hence, Catharine's share of the residuary realty, including the lapsed share of the farm, lapsed and went out on an intestacy. However, the personalty went to Mary Ann as surviving joint tenant.

Re Coughlin,[77] reproduced below considers the question of a contrary intention.

CONVEYANCING AND LAW OF PROPERTY ACT
R.S.O. 1990, c. C.34

13. (1) Where by any letters patent, assurance or will, made and executed after the 1st day of July, 1834, land has been or is granted, conveyed or devised to two or more persons, other than executors or trustees, in fee simple or for any less estate, it shall be considered that such persons took or take as tenants in common and not as joint tenants, unless an intention sufficiently appears on the face of the letters patent, assurance or will, that they are to take as joint tenants.

(2) This section applies notwithstanding that one of such persons is the spouse or same-sex partner of another of them.

(3) In subsection (2),

"same-sex partner" means either of two persons of the same sex who live together in a conjugal relationship outside marriage;

"spouse" means,

(a) a spouse as defined in section 1 of the *Family Law Reform Act*, or

(b) either of two person of the opposite sex who live together in a conjugal relationship outside marriage.

---

74 R.S.O. 1990, c. C.34.
75 (1906), 13 O.L.R. 299.
76 R.S.O. 1897, c. 128, s. 36.
77 (1982), 36 O.R. (2d) 446, 12 E.T.R. 59 (H.C.).

EXCEPTIONS TO LAPSE   581

Comparable Legislation

Land Titles Act, R.S.S. 1978, c. L-5, s. 242; *Law of Property Act*, R.S.A. 1980, c. L-8, s. 8; R.S.M. 1988, c. L90, s. 15; *Property Act*, R.S.N.B. 1973, c. P-19, s. 20; *Property Law Act*, R.S.B.C. 1979, c. 340, s. 11; *Real Property Act*, R.S.N.S. 1989, c. 385, s. 5; *Tenants in Common Act*, R.S.N.W.T. 1988, c. T-1, s. 1; R.S.Y. 1986, c. 168, s. 1.

RE COUGHLIN
(1982), 36 O.R. (2d) 446, 12 E.T.R. 59
Supreme Court of Ontario
[High Court of Justice]

The testatrix died in 1978. By her will, made in 1974, she left her entire estate to her sister Mona Coughlin, her brother, Alonzo Coughlin and her great-nephew Gerard Grady, "in equal shares, share and share alike to be theirs absolutely."

The three persons named in the will had lived together with the testatrix (and another sister of the testatrix who died before the will was made) since 1956 as a common household, Gerard Grady having been raised by his great-aunts and great-uncle since he was one and a half years old.

Mona and Alonzo Coughlin predeceased the testatrix in 1977 and 1978, respectively. The testatrix' nearest relative was her nephew, Donald Coughlin, who visited the household approximately twice a year. An application was brought to interpret the will.

RUTHERFORD J.:

. . .

The starting point, and in a sense the sole duty of the Court in construing the wording of a will, is to determine the subjective intention of the testator.

. . .

In construing a will, furthermore, "the Court has the right to ascertain all the facts which were known to the testator at the time when he made the will, and thus to place itself in the testator's position at that time."[78]

. . .

This case raises a conflict between two rules of construction of wills: the rule that the will should be construed on the presumption that the testator did not intend to die totally or partially intestate, and the tendency of the law to lean towards a tenancy in common as opposed to a joint tenancy. If I find that the testatrix intended to benefit only the survivor of the three named beneficiaries, I must find that she intended to convey a joint tenancy. If I find she intended a tenancy in common, the result is that two of the bequests lapse and there is a partial intestacy with respect to two-thirds of her estate. These rules, I reiterate,

---

78 Mellows, *The Law of Succession* (3rd ed., 1977), p.167.

are to be used only if the intention of the testatrix is not manifest from the instrument in the light of surrounding circumstances.

In my view, I do not need to resort to these rules to interpret this will. My reading of para. 4 of the will convinces me that the testatrix intended that the residue of her estate pass to the survivor or survivors of the three named beneficiaries. The testatrix, with her brother, her sister and her great-nephew, formed a household which had existed at 291 Euclid Street, Peterborough, since 1956. To that household, Donald Coughlin was an outsider even though he was the nearest surviving blood relative, apart from her brother and sister, to the testatrix. I do not believe that the testatrix intended that Donald Coughlin, or any other person, should take the shares of her brother and sister, should they predecease her, leaving Gerard Grady as the sole survivor of the named beneficiaries.

This view is supported by the final words of the dispositive paragraph: "...to be theirs absolutely". These words denote an intention to dispose of the entire residue of the estate to the named beneficiaries and they imply a right of survivorship.

[His Lordship applied the presumption against intestacy, and continued:]

It was suggested to me on behalf of the applicant that the three named beneficiaries formed a class and that the making of a class gift expresses an intention to benefit the survivor(s) of the class.[79] A class gift, prima facie, is one where the beneficiaries are not only bound together by a common blood relationship, but are so described in the will. Here, the beneficiaries are separately named as personae designatae and they do not share a common relationship to the testatrix. The importance is, again, the subjective intention of the testatrix and I am convinced that her brother Alonzo, her sister Mona and her great-nephew Gerard formed a "class" in the mind of the testatrix, not in a strict legal sense but in the sense that they were the three people nearest to her in her day-to-day life. The fact that they were separately named and did not share a common blood tie to her is not controlling.

I am aware, as well, of the body of case law which favours a finding of a tenancy in common when words of distribution such as "in equal shares" and "share and share alike" are used. Those words are, in my view, not to be read in isolation and are modified and their meaning transformed by the words "to be theirs absolutely", which follow immediately after. The estate is thus left to the three named beneficiaries jointly, exclusively and finally....

[His Lordship, therefore, held that the entire residue passed to Gerard Grady.]

Notes and Questions

1. Newfoundland and Prince Edward Island do not appear to have legislation similar to s. 13 of the *Conveyancing and Law of Property Act*.

---

79 See Feeney, *The Canadian Law of Wills: Construction* (1978), pp. 132, 137.

2. *Re Couglin* does not indicate whether the estate consisted of real property, personal property or both. If it contained real property, the statutory presumption in favour of a tenancy in common would have applied to the gift of real property. Would that presumption have been rebutted on the facts? If the estate consisted solely of personal property, or to the extent that it consisted of personal property, there was an equitable presumption in favour of a tenancy in common because of reference in the gift to equality.

In light of existing case law, did Rutherford J. reach the correct decision on this point? Is the subjective intention of the testatrix relevant in determining such a technical point?

3. In his will the testator gave an undivided one-half of his property to his friend, H, and the remaining undivided one-half to his friend, R. He further provided that those two persons were the only ones who were to get his estate. H, who was 30 years older than the testator, predeceased him. What result?[80]

4. A testatrix left the residue of her estate, which consisted of real property, to her son and two daughters "to be theirs jointly in equal shares." She provided that if one or more of them should precease her, the residue should become the property "of the successor or successors of them." On an application to construe the will, the court held that the will created a tenancy in common because of the presumption in favour of a tenancy in common, the use of the words, "in equal shares," and the use of the words "successor or successors," rather than "survivor or survivors."[81] Do you agree?

(b) Gift in Fulfilment of Moral Obligation

There is an old rule that, if a testator makes a gift to discharge a moral obligation, and the beneficiary predeceases him, the gift does not lapse but passes to his estate.[82] It would appear that the ambit of this rule is not as wide as has sometimes been supposed, but is restricted to situations in which the gift combines a bounty and a legal, but unenforceable, obligation. The rule is explained in *Re Mackie*,[83] reproduced below.

RE MACKIE
(1986), 54 O.R. (2d) 784, 28 D.L.R. (4th) 571
Ontario Supreme Court
[High Court of Justice]

The testator made his will in 1981. He left his estate equally to his sister, Mary Poole, and his sister-in-law, Eleanor Harris. Eleanor died in 1984 and the testator died soon thereafter. The testator and his late wife had maintained a close relationship with Eleanor and her husband. Eleanor performed various household tasks for the testator's wife during her last illness and for the testator after his wife's death.

Mary, the executrix, brought an application to interpret the will.

---

80 See *Re Koleniec Estate* (1989), 31 E.T.R. 177 (Alta. Surr. Ct.).
81 See *Winchester v. McCullough* (2000), 31 E.T.R. (2d) 321 (N.B.Q.B.).
82 *Re Weir* (1923), 25 O.W.N. 149 (H.C.).
83 (1986), 54 O.R. (2d) 784, 28 D.L.R. (4th) 571 (H.C.).

EWASCHUK J.:

. . .

In general, where a beneficiary under a will predeceases the testator, the bequest to the beneficiary lapses, *i.e.*, it does *not* pass to the beneficiary's estate. The bequest instead falls into the residuary clause of the will; but, if the predeceasing beneficiary is also the residuary beneficiary, an intestacy results. In the present case, there is no residuary clause with the result that should a lapse occur an intestacy will necessarily also occur.

There is an exception to the rule that a bequest to a predeceasing beneficiary must lapse. That exception arises where the testator intends that the bequest to the beneficiary be irrevocable. This result may occur, for example, when the testator has a moral obligation to discharge a debt owed to the beneficiary by the testator or the testator's relatives. In effect, the testator by the particular bequest directs his executor to discharge the testator's moral obligation.

It is necessary to determine whether Robert Mackie, the testator, intended to give half of his estate irrevocably to Eleanor Harris, his sister-in-law, when he made his will. The will is obviously silent on that point and I could only make that determination by having regard to the testator's surrounding circumstances when he made his will.

. . .

I start my determination by construing the words used by the testator in writing his will. It is undoubted that it is the testator's subjective intention that must be ascertained. In this will, the testator says nothing about what should happen to Eleanor Harris' share should she predecease hi. It is my conclusion that the testator simply did not advert to this possibility and that it was natural not for him to do so since Eleanor Harris was more than 10 years younger than he was and in apparent good health when he made his will. In the natural course of events it was reasonable for the testator to expect that his younger sister-in-law would outlive him.

I must then determine whether the testator intended that his bequest to his sister-in-law be irrevocable in the sense that the bequest flowed from a moral obligation owed to her. In this regard, the leading Canadian case appears to be *Re McKay*.[84] In that case, the will provided that "the brothers are to receive more than the sisters in consideration of care and money given towards the support of our father for years". Two brothers predeceased their testatrix sister. The question then arose as to whether the estate [*sic*] of the two brothers took [*sic*] under the will because the testator [*sic*] intended the bequest [*sic*] to be irrevocable as arising from moral consideration or whether the bequests lapsed. In the result, Harrison J. held that the doctrine of moral obligation applied only to bequests discharging debts, legally enforceable or not, owed to persons predeceasing a testator. In his view, moral obligation standing alone, did not prevent a lapse.

---

84 (1949), 24 M.P.R. 267 (N.B.S.C.).

Counsel for Edward Harris, who would take if there is no lapse, commends to the court the case of *Re Inkster; Inkster v. Canada Trust Co. et al.*[85] In that case, the testatrix made a specific bequest to her nephew, who later predeceased her. The elderly and unmarried testatrix was close to and dependent on her nephew. From 1947 until his death in 1973, the nephew paid taxes, repaired, maintained and looked after the testatrix's property.

In the result, Solomon J. held that the gifts to the nephew were absolute and devolved to his estate on the testatrix's death notwithstanding that the nephew predeceased his aunt. I note that Solomon J. did not refer to any cases dealing with the moral consideration exception to the doctrine of lapse. In that regard, counsel for the testator's relatives has submitted that Solomon J.'s reasoning is unprincipled and constitutes a classic example of palm-tree justice.

I agree that a court must generally follow established precedent. In that regard, I prefer the reasoning of Harrison J. in *Re McKay*[86] to that of Solomon J. in *Re Inkster et al.*....[87]

It is my view that there is a need to confine situations where the moral obligation exception applies lest the exception swallow up and consume the general doctrine of lapse. It seems to me that it is generally arguable in most wills cases that a testator confers a testamentary gift on a beneficiary for some moral consideration, *e.g.*, for past friendship or kindness, or simply because of blood relationship.

Where a testator confers a testamentary gift on a beneficiary by reason of past friendship with, or kindness on the part of, the beneficiary, the testator is under no moral obligation to do so. The testator has a moral obligation to a beneficiary only when the beneficiary is owed a fixed debt by the testator or a relative of the testator. In the latter situation, the testator intends that the debt must be discharged, whether to the beneficiary or to the beneficiary's estate, since it is only morally proper to do so.

In non-debt situations, it is difficult to accept the notion that the testator would wish to reward the beneficiary's estate, and those persons that take from the beneficiary's estate, since whatever notional obligation the testator owed to the predeceasing beneficiary was more personal in nature than the payment of a fixed debt transmissible to the beneficiary's estate. In other words, this form of obligation is owed, if at all, only to the beneficiary and not to his or her estate.

In concluding that the bequest to Eleanor Harris has lapsed, I have not disregarded the presumption against intestacy and the equitable consideration that had the testator considered the situation it is probable that he would have wished his friend Edward Harris to take rather than his relatives from whom he had completely drifted apart over the years. It is simply not open to me to rewrite the testator's will to deal with a situation he did not contemplate happening.

---

85 (1979), 6 E.T.R. 94 (Man. Q.B.).
86 *Supra.*
87 *Supra.*

Result

The bequest to Eleanor Harris has lapsed by reason of her death prior to that of the testator.

. . .

Notes and Questions

1. The moral obligation exception has been applied to dispositions that were mere bounties. Thus, in *Re Lasham*,[88] it was applied when the testatrix gave all her estate to her husband on condition that he give certain legacies by will. He did so, but one of the legatees predeceased him. I submit that the rule does not extend this far.

2. In *Stevens v. King*[89] the principle was stated in rather wide terms, as a discharge of what the testator regarded as a moral obligation. The case concerned an overpayment of trust monies by a trustee to the testator. The older cases restrict the rule to the payment of debts discharged in the testator's bankruptcy[90] and of statute-barred debts.[91] In other words, traditionally the rule has been applied only to a debt that was formerly a legal obligation, but which is no longer enforceable, and if the testator indicates that he regards its payment as a moral obligation.

The principle in *Stevens v. King*[92] was, however, applied by Vaisey J., in *Re Leach's Will Trusts*.[93] In that case the testatrix recited in a codicil to her will that her deceased son was indebted to another person and directed her executors to pay the debt to that person. The ambit of the rule is, therefore, uncertain.

Further Reading

T.G. Youdan, Annotation, "The Doctrine of Lapse: The Ambit and Applicability of Common Law Exceptions" (1980), 6 E.T.R. 95.

(c) Class Gifts

The doctrine of lapse does not apply to class gifts, that is a gift to a group of beneficiaries who have a certain characteristic in common, such as "my children", "my nephews and nieces", etc. It is a principle of class gifts that, if a member of the class dies before the testator, the other members of the class take his share.[94] This principle may be obviated by the testator's giving a direction that the share of the member of the class who predeceases him or her shall go to others, such

---

88 (1924), 56 O.L.R. 137 (C.A.).
89 [1904] 2 Ch. 30, [1904-7] All E.R. Rep. 951. *Contra Re Brookman's Trust* (1869), 5 Ch. App. 182.
90 *Re Sowerby's Trusts* (1856), 2 K. & J. 630, 69 E.R. 935.
91 *Williamson v. Naylor* (1838), 3 Y. & C. Ex. 208, 160 E.R. 676.
92 *Supra.*
93 [1948] Ch. 232, [1948] 1 All E.R. 383.
94 *Re Jackson; Shiers v. Ashworth* (1883), 25 Ch. D. 162 at 164.

as the children of the deceased. This point is dealt with below. Of course, if all members of the class predecease the testator and there is no alternative gift, the gift will lapse.

It is sometimes difficult to determine whether the gift is really a class gift. However, a gift such as "to my children, A, B and C" is normally construed as not creating a class gift, but rather a gift to individuals *nominatim*, or as *personae designatae*.[95] If that construction prevails, and one of the named beneficiaries predeceases the testator, his or her gift lapses, unless there is an alternative gift, or unless the anti-lapse legislation applies.

As noted above, the anti-lapse legislation in several provinces applies to class gifts.

5. SPECIAL SITUATIONS

(a) Powers of Appointment

The doctrine of lapse applies to all powers of appointment,[96] so that, if the donee of the power (the person who is intended to make the appointment) dies before the testator (the donor of the power), the power of appointment lapses.[97] However, the lapse of the power does not cause a lapse of the gift to those who take under the testator's will in default of appointment.[98]

Thus, if a testator gives A the power to appoint certain property by will among A's brothers and sisters, but provides that, in default of appointment the property shall go to A's nephews and nieces, and A predeceases the testator, the power lapses. That means that it can no longer be exercised. But A's nephews and nieces will take the property.

An appointment made under a power of appointment will also lapse if the appointee predeceases the donee of the power. If the power is a general power, the property will fall into the residue of the donee's estate, or, if it is an appointment of the residue, will go out as on an intestacy.[99] Lapse may, however, be prevented by an alternative gift.[100]

---

95 This point will be discussed in the next chapter.
96 A power of appointment is an authorization by one person (the donor of the power) to another (the donee of the power, or appointor) to dispose of property belonging to the donor in favour of a third person or persons (the objects of the power). A person to whom an appointment is made is the appointee. A general power enables the donor to appoint to anyone, including himself or herself. Hence, it is virtually the equivalent of a gift of property to the donee. A special power is one which requires the donee to appoint among described persons or class of persons, of which the donee may be one. See generally *Oosterhoff & Gillese: Text, Commentary and Cases on Trusts*, 5th ed. by A.H. Oosterhoff and E.E. Gillese (Scarborough: Carswell, 1998), ch. 3.
97 *Jones v. Southall (No. 2)* (1862), 32 Beav. 31, 55 E.R. 12.
98 *Nichols v. Haviland* (1855), 1 K. & J. 504, 69 E.R. 558.
99 *Re Ladd; Henderson v. Porter*, [1932] 2 Ch. 219.
100 *Browne v. Hope* (1872), L.R. 14 Eq. 343; *Stevens v. King*, [1904] 2 Ch. 30.

If the power is a special power, the appointment normally lapses,[101] although lapse can be prevented by an alternative gift to other objects of the power.[102] The latter do not, of course, include the executors of such objects.[103] The appointment can also be saved if the appointees predecease the donee and by the gift of residue of the donee's estate other persons are appointed who are also objects of the power. This is only so, however, if the will discloses an intention to exercise the power in their favour as an alternative gift.[104] If the appointment fails by reason of lapse, the property falls back into the testator's estate.

If one of several objects of a power dies after the testator but before the donee, the power continues to be exercisable in favour of the survivors.[105]

(b) Dissolved Corporations

In as much as the doctrine of lapse applies to a gift to any person, it also applies to a corporation that has been dissolved before the testator's death. A company may cease to exist for failure to file annual returns. Most company statutes, however, contain provisions for reviving such a company.[106]

Montreal Trust Co. v. Boy Scouts of Canada (Edmonton Region) Foundation[107] illustrates what happens when the company is revived. The testator gave a share of the residue of his estate to the respondent company. It was struck off the register before his death, but was restored thereafter. The court held that, under the legislation, the revival dated back to the time the company was struck off. It held further that the provision in the legislation that the revival was without prejudice to the rights of third parties only applied to rights third parties acquired in dealing with the company and not to persons who might take the gift by reason of the operation of the doctrine of lapse. Hence, no lapse occurred.

(c) Charities

The doctrine of lapse also applies to gifts for charitable purposes. Thus, if the charitable purpose has ceased to exist before the testator's death, the gift will *prima facie* lapse.

The law favours gifts to charity and will give effect to such gifts whenever possible, even if it is impossible or impracticable to carry out the trust intended

---

101 *Freeland v. Pearson* (1867), L.R. 3 Eq. 658; *Re Susanni's Trusts* (1877), 47 L.J. Ch. 65; *Duke of Marlborough v. Lord Godolphin* (1750), 2 Ves. Sen. 61, 28 E.R. 41.
102 *Butcher v. Butcher* (1812), 1 Ves. & B. 79, 35 E.R. 31.
103 *Re Susanni's Trusts, supra.*
104 *Re Hunt's Trusts* (1885), 31 Ch. D. 308.
105 *Re Ware; Cumberlege v. Cumberlege-Ware* (1890), 45 Ch. D. 269 at 276.
106 See, *e.g.*, *Companies Act*, R.S.A. 1980, c. C-20, s. 206(1); *Canada Business Corporations Act*, R.S.C. 1985, c. C-44, s. 209(4); *Business Corporations Act*, R.S.O. 1990, c. B.16, s. 241(5)-(7).
107 [1978] 5 W.W.R. 123, 3 E.T.R. 1, 88 D.L.R. (3d) 99 (B.C.S.C.); Jones, Annotation, *ibid.*, at 2.

by the testator. However, in order to be able to do so in the case of a charity that ceased to exist before the testator's death, the court must find that the testator had a general charitable intention. If the testator has carefully selected a particular charity, it is unlikely that he or she will be found to have had a general charitable intention and, in that case, if the charity has ceased to exist before his or her death, the gift will lapse.[108] On the other hand, if the testator has indicated that he or she wants to advance some general charitable purpose, such as the advancement of education, and has merely added the name of a charity as a possible recipient of the money, he or she probably will be found to have had a general charitable intention. In that case, if the particular charity named has ceased to exist before the testator's death, the money will be applied *cy-près*, that is, to another charity or other charities as near as may be in purpose to the one suggested by the testator.[109]

If the charity to which the gift has been given ceases to exist after the testator's death, or if the trust then becomes impossible or impracticable to carry out, the gift can never lapse and the moneys are always applied *cy-près*, unless they have only been given to charity for a limited time.[110] You should note that many Canadian cases, although they do apply the *cy-près* doctrine in those circumstances, speak of the gift as lapsing after the testator's death. This usage is incorrect.

(d) Secret Trusts

A secret trust is a trust entered into between the testator and a beneficiary in which the beneficiary agrees to apply the money he or she will receive under the testator's will for the purpose or the persons designated by the testator.[111] If the beneficiary named in the will (the trustee) predeceases the testator, the gift will lapse, since the rights of the beneficiary under the trust depend upon the validity of the gift in the will. However, if the trustee survives the testator, but the trust beneficiary does not, the gift to the latter does not lapse since it is regarded as

108 *Re Harwood*, [1936] Ch. 285; *Re Spence*, [1979] Ch. 483, [1978] 3 W.L.R. 483, [1978] 3 All E.R. 92; *Re Allendorf*, [1963] 2 O.R. 68, 38 D.L.R. (2d) 459 (H.C.); *Re Hunter*, [1973] 3 W.W.R. 197, 34 D.L.R. (3d) 602 (B.C.S.C.); *Cox v. Pub. Trustee* (1983), 56 N.S.R. (2d) 657, 117 A.P.R. 657 (T.D.).

109 See generally *Oosterhoff & Gillese: Text, Commentary and Cases on Trusts*, 5th ed. by A.H. Oosterhoff and E.E. Gillese (Scarborough: Carswell, 1998), pp. 912ff. And see: *Re Voorhees* (1979), 4 E.T.R. 62 (Ont. H.C.); *Re Bezpalko; Pub. Trustee v. St. Anne's Orphanage* (1979), 11 Alta. L.R. (2d) 32, 6 E.T.R. 316, 27 A.R. 131, 106 D.L.R. (3d) 290 (Q.B.); *Re Jacobsen* (1977), 80 D.L.R. (3d) 122 (B.C.S.C.); *Re Roberts* (1981), 36 Nfld. & P.E.I.R. 234, 101 A.P.R. 234, 9 E.T.R. 156, 120 D.L.R. (3d) 74 (P.E.I.S.C.); *Re Buchanan Estate* (1996), 11 E.T.R. (2d) 8 (B.C.S.C.); *Walt Estate v. Williams* (1997), 18 E.T.R. (2d) 242 (B.C.S.C.).

110 *Fidelity Trust Co. v. St. Joseph's Vocational Sch. of Winnipeg*, [1984] 3 W.W.R. 429, 16 E.T.R. 221, 6 D.L.R. (4th) 644 (Man. Q.B.).

111 These trust are discussed in the chapter on the Nature of Testamentary Gifts.

having vested in him or her. Hence, the money will go to the trust beneficiary's estate.[112]

6. SUBSTITUTIONARY GIFTS

(a) Generally

Although the doctrine of lapse is a rule of law, it is quite permissible for a testator to avoid the effects of the rule by providing that if the beneficiary named should predecease him or her, the property shall go to someone else. In other words, the testator can make an alternative or substitutionary gift to take effect in those circumstances which would otherwise attract the doctrine of lapse. The testator may, in fact, provide for successive substitutionary gifts, such as, "To A, but if A predecease me, to B, and if B predecease me to C." Indeed, he or she may also make a substitutionary gift which differs from the statutory one provided by the anti-lapse legislation.

While a testator may avoid the effects of lapse, he or she can not avoid the doctrine of lapse. The difference is illustrated by *Re Greenwood; Greenwood v. Sutcliffe*.[113] The testatrix directed that her estate be sold and the proceeds divided among certain named persons. She declared that if her brothers, Booth and Joseph, her niece, Abigail, and her nephew, John, should die in her lifetime leaving issue who survived her, the benefits given to the beneficiary so dying "shall not lapse but shall take effect as if his or her death happened immediately after mine." Joseph and John both predeceased her, leaving issue who survived her.

The issue was whether the testatrix had tried to oust the doctrine of lapse by purporting to give the gifts to the estates of Joseph and John, or whether she had named Joseph's and John's heirs as substitutionary beneficiaries. The latter was permitted, but the former was precluded by law. The court held that, despite the words, "shall not lapse," the testatrix intended to make a substitutionary gift to the heirs of the primary beneficiaries. In the result, the gifts did not lapse.

A similar problem arose in *Re Cousen's Will Trusts; Wright v. Killick*,[114] reproduced below.

RE COUSEN'S WILL TRUSTS
[1937] Ch. 381, [1937] 2 All E.R. 276
Chancery Division

The testator, James Cousen, devised and bequeathed all the residue of his real and personal estate to his wife for life, and then upon trust for the children of his late uncle, Samuel Mann Cousen, who should be living at his death equally. He declared that if any child of his uncle should have predeceased the testator,

---

112   *Re Gardner*, [1923] 2 Ch. 230.
113   [1912] 1 Ch. 392.
114   [1937] Ch. 381, [1937] 2 All E.R. 276.

whether before or after the date of the will leaving issue living at the testator's death, the share which such child would have taken if he or she had survived the testator should be "held in trust for his or her personal representatives as part of his or her personal estate."

A child of Samuel Mann Cousen, Catherine Sarah Cousen Alcock predeceased the testator, intestate, survived by her daughter, Jane Wright, who survived the testator, and by her husband, William Alcock, who did not. William Alcock was his wife's personal representative and became entitled to her estate. By his will he gave certain property to his daughter, Jane Wright, which would have included everything he might have received under the testator's will.

The applicant was Catherine's personal representative. He applied to the court to determine whether the interest given to the children of Samuel Mann Cousen had lapsed.

FARWELL J.:

. . .

This question which I have now to determine is one, I think, of very considerable difficulty. It is quite plain that if there had been no provision, as there is here, for the event of one of the named persons predeceasing the testator and a substitutionary gift for the personal representative of that person, there must have been a lapse so far as that share is concerned and to that extent the estate would not have been disposed of, but the testator makes provision to prevent that event happening by providing that if such a person as the lady in question died in the lifetime of the testator, then the share which she would have taken if she had survived was to be held in trust for her personal representative as part of his or her personal estate.

. . .

[W]hen the testator in this case gave a share of residue in the events which have happened to Catherine Sarah Cousen or if she did not survive to her legal personal representatives, it was as though he had said:

In the event of Catherine Alcock predeceasing me then her share of the residue is to be held by her legal personal representatives on the same trusts on which they hold her personal estate but not so as to make it part of Catherine Alcock's estate but as though the words were written out in the Cousen Will and the property was held as part of the Cousen Estate to be distributed in accordance with the directions of the Cousen Will, which is by reference to the dispositions of Mrs. Alcock with regard to her own property.

. . .

In no sense does the share of residue which Mrs. Alcock would have taken if she had survived become part of her estate; it is part of the Cousen estate given to Mrs. Alcock's legal personal representatives to be held by them upon the same trusts as Mrs. Alcock's property was held, with the result...that there would be no further duty to be paid other than the duty on this legacy given under this will to the persons in question. It is not suggested, and could not be suggested, having regard to the authorities, that the legal personal representatives of Mrs. Alcock take beneficially; quite plainly they do not, they take as personal representatives, as trustees of her property, the share of the residue upon trust for the persons entitled.

That being so there then comes this difficulty. Mrs. Alcock, as I have said, predeceased the testator James Cousen. On Mrs. Alcock's death the person who became her legal personal representative and the person who became beneficially entitled to the whole of her estate was her husband, William Alcock. William Alcock did not survive the testator James Cousen. If, therefore, I read the gift in the will as though it were a gift to Mrs. Alcock if she was living at his decease, or, in the event of her death, to William Alcock her husband, he being the person, as she died intestate, beneficially entitled to her estate, it must follow, in my judgment, there is a lapse and that that portion of the estate of Cousen is undisposed of.

. . .

Under those circumstances, and bearing those principles in mind, the question here resolves itself into a question of construction of this particular will. The testator undoubtedly has endeavoured, and has succeeded up to a point, in avoiding the rule of lapse because he has provided that if the person or persons who would have taken directly under the will, that is in this case Mrs. Alcock, predeceased him, the benefit which that person would have taken is to go to that person's legal personal representative as part of his or her personal estate. The question then is: How are those last words to be read? In my judgment, according to the authorities to which I have referred, I must read them as a gift to Mrs. Alcock or, in the events which have happened, to the person who became entitled on Mrs. Alcock's death to her estate, that was her husband, William Alcock. William Alcock did not survive the testator, James Cousen, and since there is nothing in Cousen's will which provides against the lapse which must result if the person who is substituted for Mrs. Alcock as legatee predeceases the testator, it must follow that that portion of the estate of James Cousen has not been effectively disposed of.

. . .

Notes and Questions

1. *Re Ladd; Henderson v. Porter*[115] illustrates the principle that a testator cannot prevent the application of the doctrine of lapse itself. The testatrix made her will in express exercise of a power of appointment given to her under a marriage settlement and dealt only with the appointment. She appointed to her husband absolutely, "to the intent that this my will shall take effect whether I survive or predecease my husband". Her husband predeceased her. The court held that the gift lapsed. Clauson J., in interpreting the quoted words said:[116]

> I feel it is quite impossible so to construe these words as to give the will an effect which would save the residuary appointment for the benefit of the estate of the husband. If the words had been that the residuary gift was to take effect whether the testatrix survived or predeceased her husband,

---

115 [1932] 2 Ch. 219.
116 *Ibid.*, at pp. 225-6.

the matter, of course, would be much easier. But all that is said is that the will is to take effect whether she survives or predeceases her husband. I do not find it possible to spell out of those words an effective intention that her husband's estate should take the benefit of the bequest in case he were to predecease her.... What I do rely upon in deciding this case is that those words are not to my mind sufficiently clear to enable me to say that there is an effective gift in this will to the executors of the husband as part of his estate, so as to deprive those who would take on an intestacy of that which is the subject-matter of the suggested gift...

2. If the substitutionary beneficiary predeceases the testator as well as the primary beneficiary, the gift still lapses, as the *Cousen* case makes clear. If, however, the substitutionary beneficiary survives the testator, he or she will take the gift.[117]

3. If the beneficiary survives the testator, but dies shortly thereafter, there is no lapse, and the beneficiary's estate will take the gift, unless the gift is made subject to divestment. Thus, if a gift is made to X, "but if she should die before receiving the benefits given" by the will, then to Y, and X survives the testator, but dies before the end of the executor's year and before the property has been distributed, there is no lapse, since the property has vested in X, but it divests and goes to Y because of the contingency.[118]

4. It appears that republication does not avoid the doctrine of lapse. Hence, if a testator leaves a gift to X and X later dies, but the testator thereafter makes a codicil in which he or she does not refer to the gift to X, but does confirm the will, the gift to X lapses.[119] Of course, if the testator makes a substitutionary gift in the codicil, the substitutionary gift will take effect.[120]

(b) Words of Limitation or Substitution

There is a surprising number of cases in which the testator makes a gift in the following form: "To A, his heirs, executors and assigns." On the face of it, such a gift appears to give A an absolute interest, the words "his heirs, executors and assigns," being words of limitation. However, if A predeceases the testator, it is often argued that those words should be read as words of substitution, so that there is then a substitutionary gift to A's heirs. *Re Klein; Public Trustee of British Columbia v. Cochrane*,[121] reproduced below, discusses this issue.

---

117 *Re Main*, 30 M.P.R. 313, [1953] D.T.C. 1137 (N.B. T.D.); *Re MacDonald* (1956), 19 W.W.R. 468, 5 D.L.R. (2d) 175 (Alta. C.A.).

118 See *Re Ramsden; Borrie v. Beck*, [1974] 5 W.W.R. 554, 46 D.L.R. (3d) 758 (B.C.S.C.).

119 *Hutcheson v. Hammond* (1790), 3 Bro. C.C. 128, 29 E.R. 449; *Maybank v. Brooks* (1780), 1 Bro. C.C. 84, 28 E.R. 1000; *Re Hutton* (1982), 39 O.R. (2d) 622, 11 E.T.R. 140, affirmed 39 O.R. 622n.

120 *Re McNeill; Chancey v. Chancey* (1980), 25 Nfld. & P.E.I.R. 297, 6 E.T.R. 165, 109 D.L.R. (3d) 109 (Nfld. T.D.).

121 [1981] 1 W.W.R. 41, 21 B.C.L.R. 273, 7 E.T.R. 176 (C.A.).

RE KLEIN; PUBLIC TRUSTEE OF
BRITISH COLUMBIA v. COCHRANE
[1981] 1 W.W.R. 41, 21 B.C.L.R. 273, 7 E.T.R. 176
British Columbia Court of Appeal

The testator, who died in 1976, made his will in 1946. It left his entire estate to his wife, Violet, "to hold unto her, her heirs, executors, and administrators, absolutely and forever." The testator's wife predeceased him in 1963. There were no children of the marriage, nor did the testator have any known next of kin of the testator. The respondent was the testator's wife's son by a prior marriage. He had lived with the testator and his wife briefly about the time the will was made and had, by the time of the testator's death, formed a close relationship with the testator.

The respondent applied to have the will construed the will. Monroe J. held at first instance[122] that the will provided for a substitutionary gift in favour of the testator's wife's heirs, that is, the respondent. In effect, therefore, he read the gift as being, "to hold unto her, *or* her heirs...."

The Public Trustee appealed.

TAGGART J., delivered the judgment of the Court:

. . .

In my opinion, the construction of this will is governed in large part by the decision of the Supreme Court of Canada in *Re Ottewell; Tottrup v. Patterson.*[123]

. . .

Chief Justice Cartwright put the contention of the appellant in this way:[124]

The contention of the appellant is that the words with which the residuary clause concludes — "to hold unto him, his heirs, executors and administrators absolutely and forever" are words of substitution not of limitation. I can find no support for this submission in the numerous cases which were referred to in argument or in the text-writers....The words of the will with which we are concerned have long been held to be words of limitation, not of substitution. It is quite true that their insertion is no longer necessary to confer an absolute interest in realty and that, as Vaisey, J., pointed out in *Re McElligott*,[125] they are inapt in a bequest of personalty; but this circumstance does not alter their character or effect.

. . .

Turning, however, to the *Marshall*[126] case: I think that case is distinguishable upon its facts and, perhaps as well, upon the provisions of the will itself.

---

122 Sub nom. *Re Klein; Cochrane v. Royal Trust Co.* (1979), 5 E.T.R. 27 (B.C.S.C.).
123 [1970] S.C.R. 318, 71 W.W.R. 388, (sub nom. *Re Ottewell*) 9 D.L.R. (3d) 314.
124 At S.C.R. 316-7.
125 [1944] 1 Ch. 216 at 219.
126 *Re Marshall*, [1944] 3 D.L.R. 178, [1944] 2 W.W.R. 334 (Alta. C.A.).

[In *Marshall*, the testator gave one-fifth of the residue of his estate to each of his brothers, Matthew, Robert and Joseph, "their respective heirs, executors or administrators," one fifth to his sister, Lottie, "her heirs, executors or administrators," and one-fifth to the children of his deceased sister, Jennie.

Joseph died 43 years before the will was made, as the testator well knew, since he had killed him accidentally. Matthew died after the will, but before the testator. Both had children who survived the testator and they claimed their fathers' shares. They were unsuccessful at first instance, but Joseph's son appealed.]

Mr. Justice Ford in dealing with th[e] language [of the clause] said this:[127]

Grammatically the words "their respective heirs, executors or administrators" are to be read as if the word "or" preceded them; but, even if this is not the plain meaning of the words, the fact that the testator knew, when he made his will, that his brother Joseph was dead makes it hardly possible that, in respect at least to the gift to Joseph, he meant the gift to be other than substitutionary. If it were not so, he must be taken to have intended to make his gift ineffective. There is no ground for suggesting that he had any capricious or whimsical intention of going through the form of making a gift which the least intelligent of sane testators would know to be inoperative.

. . .

It will be apparent from my recital of the facts in the *Marshall* case that they differ decidedly from the facts of the case at Bar.

Here, at the time of the making of the will, there were extant the testator's wife and his stepson and, perhaps, other members of his family, none of whom, save only his wife, were mentioned by the testator in his will. I think it cannot be said in these circumstances that the mere fact of the existence of others who might have been mentioned in the will at the time of its making leads one irrevocably to the conclusion that the residuary clause as it appears in this will entitles those others to now come and claim a share in the will.

. . .

Having regard for the facts of the *Marshall* case, for the reference to it by Chief Justice Cartwright in the *Ottewell* case in the Supreme Court of Canada,...it seems to me that we are bound to follow the *Ottewell* case and distinguish the *Marshall* case in the same way.

One further word is necessary with respect to the reference by the trial judge to the presumption against an intestacy and to the possibility of an escheat. I have already adverted to the fact that there may or may not be an escheat in the case at Bar. That remains to be determined upon further inquiry being made by the trustee. However that may be, it seems to me, that in this case the presumption against an intestacy ought not to be raised.

[The court refused to apply the presumption against intestacy, because the will was not ambiguous, and continued:]

---

127 At W.W.R. 338.

For all of the reasons which I have given, I am of the view that the appeal must be allowed and the judgment below set aside.

. . .

Notes and Questions

1. For a similar type of case with the same result, see *Re Little*.[128]

2. The insertion of the disjunctive "or" before the phrase "his heirs, executors and assigns" is normally taken by modern cases to indicate a substitutionary gift both in respect of real property and personal property.[129] The conjunctive "and" may also have this effect, at least in respect of personal property.[130] However, the conjunctive normally has the effect of giving the named beneficiary the absolute interest, unless words such as "*per stirpes*" are added.[131]

3. Is the reasoning in *Re Klein* unduly technical? Should extrinsic evidence not be considered in view of the recent trend in Canadian law to ascertain the subjective intention of the testator?[132]

(c) Class Gifts

Although the doctrine of lapse does not apply to class gifts, substitutionary gifts are often used in class gifts as well. Thus, a testator may make a gift to his or her children and then say: "but if any of them predecease me leaving issue who survive me, their issue shall take their share per stirpes." There is no particular difficulty with such gifts unless one of the members of the class was already dead at the time the will was made. The issues raised by that situation may be conveniently dealt with at this point, particularly because several provinces extend their anti-lapse legislation to class gifts, as noted above.

If there is a gift to a class with a substitutionary gift to another or others in the event that a member of the class predeceases the testator, and one member of the class is already dead at the date of the will, it appears to be a question of interpretation whether the alternative beneficiary can take. The principle that a testator does not intend to make a gift to a person known to be dead is applied.[133] However, the principle can be displaced by appropriate language in the will. It seems that the alternative beneficiary will be able take if the gift is construed to be an original, or direct gift, although contingent upon the occurrence of the prescribed condi-

---

128 [1952] O.W.N. 732 (H.C.). And see *Re Taylor*, [1972] 3 O.R. 349, 28 D.L.R. (3d) 257.

129 *Re Whitehead; Whitehead v. Hemsley*, [1920] 1 Ch. 298, [1918-19] All E.R. Rep. 1170; *Re Kilvert; Midland Bank Executor & Trustee Co. v. Kilvert*, [1957] Ch. 388, [1957] 2 All E.R. 196; *Re Collishaw*, [1953] 3 D.L.R. 829 (N.S. T.D.); but see *contra Re Hayden; Pask v. Perry*, [1931] 2 Ch. 333, [1931] All E.R. Rep. 139.

130 See *Re Coulden*, [1908] 1 Ch. 320.

131 *Pearson v. Stephen* (1831), 5 Bligh (N.S.) 203, 5 E.R. 286.

132 See the chapter on General Principles of Interpretation.

133 *Sterling v. Navjord* (1989), 32 E.T.R. 237 at 239, *per* Southin J.A. (B.C.C.A.).

tion.[134] However, if the substitutionary gift is, in fact, treated as a substitutionary gift, the alternative beneficiary cannot take. In order to take he or she would have to have been able to point to a member of the class who would have taken but for his or her death and by definition a person who died before the will is made is not a member of the class.[135]

The issue is discussed in *Re Grasett*,[136] reproduced below.

RE GRASETT
[1973] 1 O.R. 361, 31 D.L.R. (3d) 153
Supreme Court of Ontario
[Court of Appeal]

The testator, Frederick Le Maitre Grasett died in 1930, having made his will in 1923. By the will, he gave certain life interests to his wife and son which were exhausted in 1968, when the son died. The testator gave the remainder interest, after the life estates:

> unto my brothers and sisters who shall be then living or in case of the decease of them or of any of them then to the child or children of each deceased brother or sister of mine in equal shares, but so that the child or children of any deceased brother or sister if more than one shall take only the share which the parent would have taken if living at the time of distribution.

The testator had three brothers and two sisters. Two brothers predeceased him without issue. The third brother, Arthur Wharton Grasett died in 1934, leaving issue (the Grasett family line). One of the two sisters, Henrietta Georgina Kingstone died in 1919, leaving issue (the Kingstone family line), while the other, Agnes Strachan Strathy, died in 1937, leaving issue (the Strathy family line).

On an application to interpret the will, it was held at first instance by Pennell J., that only the Grasett and Strathy lines were entitled to share and that the Kingstone line was excluded because Mrs. Kingstone died before the will was made.

The Kingstone family appealed.

McGILLIVRAY J.A., delivered the judgment of the Court:

. . .

The submission for the appellants is that the testator's use of the plural word "sisters" when he is presumed to have known that but one was alive makes it clear, as no original gift to the dead sister was contemplated, that the adoption of the plural term must have been to give effect to the claims of her children under

---

134 *Taylor Re*, [1972] 3 O.R. 349, 28 D.L.R. (3d) 257; *Re Grasett*, [1973] 1 O.R. 361, 31 D.L.R. (3d) 153 (C.A.); *Re Davison* (1979), 36 N.S.R. (2d) 152, 5 E.T.R. 103, 99 D.L.R. (3d) 81 (T.D.).

135 *Re Webster's Estate; Wigden v. Mello* (1883), 23 Ch. D. 737; *Re Earle's Settlement Trusts*, [1971] 1 W.L.R. 1118, [1971] 2 All E.R. 1188 (C.A.); *Mackintosh (or Miller) v. Gerrard*, [1947] A.C. 461 (H.L.).

136 *Supra.*

the "decease" portion of the clause. In effect the testator had made an original defeasible gift to living brothers and sisters but had in addition made, in the further provision, an original gift to the children of the Kingstone line.

This was the interpretation given to a similar clause in the case of *Loring v. Thomas*.[137] I deal with the case at some length to show the reasoning which underlay that interpretation....In her will the testator had made a bequest to children of named persons with a provision that, should the parent die in the testator's lifetime, his or her children would take that share. One of the intended original donees had in fact died prior to the making of the will and the question the Court was called upon to decide was whether the child of that person was entitled to share in the bequest. The Court held she was so entitled.

. . .

In the subsequent case of *Barraclough v. Cooper*,[138] Romer, L.J., followed the decision in the *Loring* case commenting that the construction which he had to consider could not be distinguished substantially from the *Loring* one....[H]e summarized the reasoning in the *Loring* case as follows:[139]

> In each case the original gift in the will in question is to a class of persons to be ascertained at the death of the testator, while the subsequent provision in favour of issue is not properly speaking a substitutional gift, but makes an addition to the class of persons taking under the original gift by reference to the issue of what I may call certain hypothetical persons.

The decision of the Court in *Barraclough* was affirmed on appeal to the House of Lords.[140]

It is, of course, the use of the word "sisters" which gives rise to the present litigation. Had it been "sister" there would have been none. It is a situation, however, which has arisen more than once in the past and the results are of interest. In *Theobald on Wills*[141] the learned author states:

> 900.(vii) *Children of parents dead at the date of the will.* When there is a gift to the members of a class for their lives, with remainder to their children, the death of a member of the class in the lifetime of the testator, after the date of the will, will not prevent his children from taking, but the children of members of the class dead at the date of the will will not take. On the other hand, if the gift is to the testator's brothers and sisters for their lives, with remainder to their children, and the testator has only one brother living at the date of the will, children of deceased brothers and sisters will take.

. . .

Turning then to consideration of the terms of this will I find them more consistent with the interpretation sought by the appellants than I do that of the respondents. In view of the fact that the testator is said to have been in full possession

---

137 (1861), 1 Dr. & Sm. 497, 62 E.R. 469.
138 [1908] 2 Ch. 121.
139 *Ibid.*, at p. 123.
140 [1908] 2 Ch. 121n.
141 12th ed., para. 900, p. 901.

of his faculties when the will was made it is a reasonable presumption, he having had two sisters, that he was well aware that one was dead. In that event he used the term "sisters" advisedly. Of course he was aware that one at least would not be living at the time of distribution but perhaps the others would not be either; and in fact they were not. Then he provided "in the case of the decease of them or any of them" to the children. How, one may ask, could this refer to any but brothers and sisters without qualification? It could not refer to a sister or brothers alive at the time of distribution for if they were alive at that time, there would be no share to descend. In any event I am satisfied that the term "sisters" associated as it was with "brothers" and followed by the "decease" clause was the testator's way of saying that he wanted the distribution to his nephews and nieces of parents who had not lived to inherit to be on the basis that all were included. I cannot bring myself to believe because he sought by the wording to benefit certain sisters and brothers if alive at time of distribution rather than their children that he intended (sisters having been mentioned) to restrict the balance of his gift to the children of some only of his deceased brothers and sisters. The testator was said to have been on excellent and friendly terms with the Kingstone children and no independent provision is made for them in the will. While one cannot speculate regarding that which might have been in the mind of the testator one cannot help but remark it would seem unlikely, in the absence of any apparent reason for so doing, that the testator would have deliberately followed the harsh course of excluding one whole group of his nephews and nieces.

Support is found for the view that there was an original gift to the children of Henrietta Kingstone in the testator's inclusion of the following words at the end of the trust clause:

> ...but so that the child or children of any deceased brother or sister if more than one shall take only the share which the parent would have taken if living at the time of distribution.
>
> If the testator had intended the children of his brothers and sisters to take by substitution only, as found at trial, the quoted provision was quite unnecessary. Children taking by substitution could only take that which would have been the share of the parent. If, however, an original gift to the children of a deceased sister was intended then the clause became necessary to ensure that they took *per stirpes* and not *per capita* with their surviving uncles and aunt. This will was prepared in the office of a well-known firm of solicitors. It may be thought unlikely that the provision would have been included had it not been required by reason of other provisions in the will.
>
> To give effect to the submissions for the respondents the Court would need to substitute the word "sister" for "sisters" and to say as well that the proviso at the end of the clause is superfluous. To give effect on the other hand to the interpretation sought by the appellant requires nothing to be deleted and no word to be changed. Every part of the clause is given significance. The only thing, in fact, that might cast any doubt on the appellants' interpretation would be the use of the words "in the case of the decease of them". It was the opinion of the learned trial Judge that these words could only import futurity. As a consequence they could only refer to brothers and sisters living when the will was made which restricted the original donees to that group. Decease of them in turn could only relate to those found to be in that group which excluded the Kingstone line.
>
> . . .
>
> For the reasons which I have stated I conclude that by the trust provision there was an original defeasible gift to those brothers and sisters living when the will was drawn and an original gift, as well, to the children of the Kingstone line.
>
> . . .

Notes and Questions

1. What would have happened if any of the Kingstone children had predeceased the testator? Would there be any difference if the case had arisen in a jurisdiction whose anti-lapse legislation extends to class gifts? What if the gift had been to the testator's children, with a substitutionary gift to their issue in such a jurisdiction?

7. SURVIVORSHIP

It sometimes happens that a testator and a beneficiary under the will, an intestate and his or her next of kin, an insured and the beneficiary under the policy of insurance, or two joint tenants, die in a common accident, or in circumstances in which it is uncertain who died first. Similarly, it may be uncertain whether a person who has been missing has predeceased the testator, intestate, insured, or joint tenant. Nevertheless, for the purpose of distributing the estate, or other property, it becomes necessary to determine the order of death.

At common law, it was necessary for a person claiming property in such circumstances to prove the order of death. In the case of a missing person, moreover, the claimant could not rely on the presumption of death after a seven-year absence, since the court does not presume that death occurred at a particular time, although it may infer that death occurred by a particular date from the evidence.[142] If the claimant was unable to establish the order of death, he or she would be unsuccessful, unless the will, if any, made specific provision for a common death situation. If it did not do so, the property of the deceased in a common death situation would be distributed as if each died simultaneously.[143]

Because the order of death could often not be proved and to remedy the hardship caused in these situations, the *Commorientes Act*[144] was passed in Ontario in 1940. It was subsequently renamed the *Survivorship Act*[145] and that Act was repealed and replaced by the *Succession Law Reform Act, 1977.*[146]

The *Survivorship Act*[147] provided that when two or more persons died at the same time, or in circumstances rendering it uncertain who died first, the deaths were presumed to have occurred in the order of seniority. This statutory presumption could be rebutted by contrary evidence,[148] but if it was not rebutted, its effect was that the younger person would inherit from the elder under the latter's will or on his intestacy.

---

142 *Re Harlow* (1976), 13 O.R. (2d) 760, 72 D.L.R. (3d) 323 (C.A.); *Re Miller* (1978), 22 O.R. (2d) 111, 92 D.L.R. (3d) 255 (H.C.).

143 *Wing v. Angrave* (1860), 8 H.L. Cas. 183, 11 E.R. 397; *Re Warwicker; McLeod v. Toronto Gen. Trusts Corp.*, [1936] O.R. 379, [1936] 3 D.L.R. 368; *Bennett v. Peattie* (1925), 57 O.L.R. 233 (C.A.); *Re Phillips and Can. Order of Chosen Friends* (1906), 12 O.L.R. 48; *Re Barber and Walker* (1919), 17 O.W.N. 215.

144 S.O. 1940, c. 4.

145 R.S.O. 1950, c. 382.

146 S.O. 1977, c. 40, Part IV; now R.S.O. 1990, c. S.26, Part IV.

147 Last consolidated R.S.O. 1970, c. 454 [am. 1972, c. 43].

148 See *Adare v. Fairplay*, [1956] O.R. 188, [1955] O.W.N. 950 (C.A.).

The Act was subject to section 36 of the *Wills Act*,[149] a provision avoiding the effects of lapse in certain circumstances, and to sections 190 and 268 of the *Insurance Act*.[150] These sections provided that, in the absence of a contrary provision in an insurance contract or declaration, in a common disaster situation the insurance moneys payable under a contract of life insurance and under a contract of accident and sickness insurance respectively, were to be paid as if the beneficiary had predeceased the insured.

Legislation of this type is in force in most of the common law provinces. The *Survivorship Act* of Alberta,[151] reproduced below, is typical of such statutes.

Survivorship statutes only apply if the order of death cannot otherwise be proved. It is, therefore, possible to prove the order of death to avoid the statutory presumption.

Adare v. Fairplay,[152] which involved a common death situation, is one case in which that occurred. Mr. and Mrs. Fairplay, aged 49 and 59 years, respectively, were found dead in their house in Toronto. They had died of carbon monoxide poisoning caused by a broken gas main in front of their house, as a result of which gas had filtered through the soil into the basement and then throughout the house. Mrs. Fairplay's administrator made an application for an order directing trial of an issue to determine which of the two died first. The order was made and it was found that Mr Fairplay died first, based on autopsies which established the onset of *rigor mortis* and on other evidence. The court held that the ordinary civil onus applied and that in the circumstances the statutory presumption of the *Survivorship Act*[153] did not apply.[154]

The statutory presumption can also be rebutted in cases involving a missing person if the court is prepared to find approximately when the missing person died.[155]

Despite the apparent simplicity of the survivorship legislation described above, it has led to difficulties. These arise out of the different operations of the survivorship legislation and the rules governing survivorship for insurance purposes. The problem is canvassed in *Re Topliss Estates*.[156] In that case a husband and wife died intestate in a common disaster. The husband was the elder and owned a policy of insurance of which his wife was the beneficiary. How should the insurance moneys be disposed of? Should they fall into the husband's estate under

---

149 R.S.O. 1970, c. 499. For the comparable provision see now *Succession Law Reform Act*, R.S.O. 1990, c. S.26, s. 31.

150 R.S.O. 1970, c. 224. See now *Insurance Act*, R.S.O. 1990, c. I.8, ss. 215 (reproduced *infra*) and 319.

151 R.S.A. 1980, c. S-31.

152 *Supra.*

153 R.S.O. 1950, c. 382.

154 For a similar case, but one in which the court was unable to determine the order of death, see *Sobiecki v. Bertsch Estate (Public Trustee of)* (1996), 14 E.T.R. (2d) 63 (B.C.S.C.). See further David Norwood "Dead Reckoning: Evidence and Proof of Death" (1995) 15 E. & T. J. 65.

155 *Re Harlow* (1976), 13 O.R. (2d) 760, 72 D.L.R. (3d) 323 (C.A.); *Re Miller* (1978), 22 O.R. (2d) 111, 92 D.L.R. (3d) 255 (H.C.).

156 [1957] O.W.N. 231, [1957] I.L.R. 1-262, 7 D.L.R. (2d) 719 (H.C.), affirmed [1957] O.W.N. 513, [1957] I.L.R. 1-279, 10 D.L.R. (2d) 654 (C.A.).

the insurance rule and remain there, or should they then go out to the wife's estate under the general survivorship rule on the assumption that the insurance rule was spent after it directed that the moneys should go to insured's estate? The Ontario courts in *Topliss* preferred the latter solution and it has also been adopted elsewhere.[157] However other cases have preferred the first,[158] although this approach has been criticized.[159]

The problem with the *Topliss* approach is that it is unfair to the next of kin of the spouse who is deemed to have predeceased the other, since the insurance moneys will go to the surviving spouse's next of kin, who may well be remote relatives. Only if the insured were the younger of the two would this be avoided.

Clearly, the problem is not restricted to cases involving insurance, for in all cases in which the statutory presumption applies, the next of kin of the younger person stands to benefit, unless the parties' wills provide otherwise.

To overcome these inequities, the survivorship rules contained in Part IV of the *Succession Law Reform Act* were enacted in Ontario in 1977.[160] The legislation, based on a new *Uniform Survivorship Act*,[161] is reproduced below. The substance of the legislation is that, in a common death situation, the property of each person is disposed of as if each survived the other. Moreover, with respect to property owned in joint tenancy or in a joint account and all the joint tenants die, they are deemed to hold the property as tenants in common, so that it will pass to their respective estates. If one or more joint tenants survive, of course, the Act has no application, since the survivor or survivors will take all. When insurance moneys are involved, they are to be paid out according to the unchanged insurance rules, after which the new survivorship rules apply. The new legislation also makes provision for substitute personal representatives, if the will makes provision for them, on the occurrence of a common death situation.

You should note that the statutory presumption is unchanged in this sense, that it remains possible to prove the actual order of death. Hence, *Adare v. Fairplay*[162] remains relevant under the present legislation.

You should also note that it is common in wills nowadays to provide expressly for substitute beneficiaries and personal representatives in the event that the first-named persons do not survive the testator for a specified period of time, such as sixty or ninety days. This can avoid having to prove the order of death in a common death situation. Moreover, in jurisdictions which tax estates, it avoids

---

157 *Re Currie* (1964), 44 W.W.R. 535, [1963] I.L.R. 1-112, 41 D.L.R. (2d) 666 (B.C.S.C.); *Re Cane* (1967), 63 W.W.R. 242, [1969] I.L.R. 1-222, 66 D.L.R. (2d) 741 (Man. Q.B.): *Re Fair* (1971), 2 N.S.R. (2d) 556, 17 D.L.R. (3d) 751 (C.A.).

158 *Re Law*, [1946] 2 W.W.R. 405, 13 I.L.R. 81, 62 B.C.R. 380, [1946] 2 D.L.R. 378 (S.C.); *Re Newstead*, 1 W.W.R. (N.S.) 528, [1951] 2 D.L.R. 302 (B.C.S.C.); *Re Biln* (1967), 59 W.W.R. 229, (sub nom. *Wolchina v. Biln*) 61 D.L.R. (2d) 535 (Alta. S.C.).

159 See Gilbert D. Kennedy, "Case and Comment" (1946), 24 Can. Bar Rev. 720; Kenneth B. Potter, "Comment" (1968-69), 7 Alta. L. Rev. 323.

160 By S.O. 1977, c. 40, Part IV, now R.S.O. 1990, c. S.26, Part IV.

161 Uniform Law Conference of Canada, *Consolidation of Uniform Acts* (1978, as am.), p. 46-1.

162 [1956] O.R. 188, [1955] O.W.N. 950 (C.A.).

double taxation, by ensuring that the property of the first to die does not first pass through the estate of the other for a relatively short period of time.

The doctrine of lapse is implicit in the statutory survivorship rules. It will be appreciated, therefore, that the statutory anti-lapse provision, discussed earlier in this chapter, may become relevant in survivorship situations. This issue is raised in the Problems below.

SURVIVORSHIP ACT
R.S.A. 1980, c. S-31

1. If two or more persons die at the same time or in circumstances rendering it uncertain which of them survived the other or others, the deaths are, subject to sections 2 and 3, presumed to have occurred in the order of seniority, and accordingly the younger is deemed to have survived the older.

2. When a statute or an instrument contains a provision for the disposition of property operative if a person designated in the statute or instrument

(a) dies before another person,

(b) dies at the same time as another person, or

(c) dies in circumstances rendering it uncertain which of them survived the other,

and the designated person dies at the same time as the other person or in circumstances rendering it uncertain which of them survived the other, then, for the purpose of that disposition, the case for which the statute or instrument provides is deemed to have occurred.

3. When a will contains a provision for a substitute personal representative operative if an executor designated in the will

(a) dies before the testator,

(b) dies at the same time as the testator, or

(c) dies in the circumstances rendering it uncertain which of them survived the other,

and the designated executor dies at the same time as the testator or in circumstances rendering it uncertain which of them survived the other, then, for the purpose of probate, the case for which the will provides is deemed to have occurred.

4. This Act is subject to sections 284 and 376 of the *Insurance Act* and section 320e of chapter 159 of the Revised Statutes of Alberta, 1955.

Comparable Legislation

Commorientes Act, R.S.P.E.I. 1988, c., C-12, s. 1; *Survivorship Act*, R.S.N. 1990, c. S-33; R.S.N.B. 1973, c. S-19; R.S.N.S. 1989, c. 454; S.S. 1993, c. S-67.1; R.S.N.W.T. 1988, c. S-16; R.S.Y. 1986, c. 167; *Survivorship and Presumption of Death Act*, R.S.B.C. 1979, c. 398.

SUCCESSION LAW REFORM ACT
R.S.O. 1990, c. S.26

55. (1) Where two or more persons die at the same time or in circumstances rendering it uncertain which of them survived the other or others, the property of each person, or any property of which he or she is competent to dispose, shall be disposed of as if he or she had survived the other or others.

(2) Unless a contrary intention appears, where two or more persons hold legal or equitable title to property as joint tenants, or with respect to a joint account, with each other, and all of them die at the same time or in circumstances rendering it uncertain which of them survived the other or others, each person shall be deemed, for the purposes of subsection (1), to have held as tenant in common with the other or with each of the others in that property.

(3) Where a will contains a provision for a substitute personal representative operative if an executor designated in the will,

(a) dies before the testator;

(b) dies at the same time as the testator; or

(c) dies in circumstances rendering it uncertain which of them survived the other,

and the designated executor dies at the same time as the testator or in circumstances rendering it uncertain which of them survived the other, then, for the purpose of probate, the case for which the will provides shall be deemed to have occurred.

(4) The proceeds of a policy of insurance shall be paid in accordance with sections 215 and 319 of *The Insurance Act*[163] and thereafter this Part applies to their disposition.

Comparable Legislation

Survivorship Act, R.S.M. 1987, c. S250; R.S.Y. 1986, c. 167; S.S. 1993, c. S-67.1.

INSURANCE ACT
R.S.O. 1990, c. I.8

194. (1) Where a beneficiary predeceases the person whose life is insured, and no disposition of the share of the deceased beneficiary in the insurance money is provided in the contract or by a declaration, the share is payable,

(a) to the surviving beneficiary; or

(b) if there is more than one surviving beneficiary, to the surviving beneficiaries in equal shares; or

(c) if there is no surviving beneficiary, to the insured or the insured's personal representative.

---

163 R.S.O. 1990, c. I.8.

(2) Where two or more beneficiaries are designated otherwise than alternatively, but no division of the insurance money is made, the insurance money is payable to them in equal shares.

. . .

215. Unless a contract or a declaration otherwise provides, where the person whose life is insured and a beneficiary die at the same time or in circumstances rendering it uncertain which of them survived the other, the insurance money is payable in accordance with subsection 194(1) as if the beneficiary had predeceased the person whose life is insured.

[The above sections appear in Part V of the *Insurance Act* and concern life insurance. For the comparable provisions respecting accident and sickness insurance, see ss. 267(2), 272].

Comparable Legislation

Insurance Act, R.S.A. 1980, c. I-5, ss. 263(1), 284; R.S.B.C. 1979, c. 200, ss. 147(1), 166; R.S.M. 1987, c. I40, ss. 171(1), 193; R.S.N.B. 1973, c. I-12, ss. 155, 177; R.S.N.S. 1989, c. 231, ss. 196, 218; R.S.P.E.I. 1988, c. I-4, ss. 142, 164; R.S.N.W.T. 1988, c. I-4, ss. 92, 114; R.S.Y. 1986 c. 91, ss. 96, 118; *Life Insurance Act*, R.S.N. 1990, c. L-14, ss. 25, 47; *Saskatchewan Insurance Act*, R.S.S. 1978, c. S-26, ss. 156(1), 177.

Notes and Questions

1. Section 62(2) of the *Succession Law Reform Act, 1977*[164] provides that the *Survivorship Act*[165] continues in force in respect of deaths occurring before 31 March 1978, the date the former Act came into force. What rules would apply to a case if it is uncertain whether the deaths occurred before or after that date?

2. A testator directed that his estate be divided equally among his four named children. One of the children predeceased him, leaving a spouse and issue surviving. What result?[166]

3. Section 55(1) of the *Succession Law Reform Act*, reproduced above, speaks of the property of each deceased, or any property of which he is competent to dispose. What rules would apply if property was given "to A for life, remainder to B if B survives A" and A and B die in a common disaster? Would the same result have obtained under the *Survivorship Act*,[167] which by s. 1(1) applied "for all purposes affecting the title to property"?

4. *Mandin Estate v. Willey*[168] is a strange case that seems to rob the legislation of its effect. A son killed his mother, stepfather and two sisters. The order of death was uncertain. He and his two sisters were all under age 18. The mother's will left her estate equally to her three children, to be paid to them when they reached age 18. The will did not contain a gift over if any of the beneficiaries died under age 18. The son was barred from inheriting

---

164 S.O. 1977, c. 40, not consolidated.
165 R.S.O. 1970, c. 454 [am. 1972, c. 43].
166 See *Tonon v. Vendruscalo* (1987), 25 E.T.R. 201.
167 *Supra.*
168 (1998), 28 E.T.R. (2d) 1, 160 D.L.R. (4th) 36 (Alta. C.A.).

the estate because of the public policy rule that prevents a criminal from benefiting by his criminal act. Consequently, the mother died intestate. She was survived by her mother and her former husband. The latter was the children's biological father. The question was whether the survivorship legislation caused the property to pass from the daughters to their father, or whether it should go the deceased's mother. The court held that, because of the wording of the legislation, the mother was entitled to the property. Section 1 of the *Survivorship Act*,[169] reproduced above, says that it is subject, *inter alia*, to s. 2. Section 2 provides that when a *statute* or instrument provides for the disposition of property operative if the person designated in the *statute* or instrument dies in a common death situation, then for the purpose of the disposition the case for which the *statute* or instrument provides is deemed to have occurred. Section 5 of the *Intestate Succession Act*[170] was such a statute in the court's opinion. It provides that if an intestate dies leaving no surviving spouse or issue, the estate goes to the intestate's parents in equal shares. While this argument is possible, it may be doubted if that was the intent of the legislation. The *Intestate Succession Act* is not concerned with common death and one would have thought that, therefore, it would only apply after the statute that is concerned with common death determines who survives. I suspect that the reference in section 2 to a *statute* was intended to refer to legislation such as the *Insurance Act*,[171] which does contain common death provisions.

Problems

The following problems can be approached under either type of statute. The persons involved are husband (H) and wife (W), and in some problems, daughter (D), and H's executor (E). The persons named in each problem die in a common accident. H is the elder or eldest. Unless otherwise stated, the order of deaths is unknown. What is the result in each?

1. H and W. Both died intestate.

2. H and W. Both died intestate. H owned insurance on his life of which W was the beneficiary.

3. H and W. They had reciprocal wills in which they gave their respective estates to the other.

4. H, W and D. D was married and was survived by her husband and a son. H left one-half of his estate to each of W and D by his will. W and D died intestate. H also owned insurance on his life of which W was the beneficiary.

5. H, W and D, but it was proved that D died first. D was married and was survived by her husband and a son. H left one-half of his estate to each of W and D by his will. W and D died intestate. H also owned insurance on his life of which W was the beneficiary.

6. H and W. They owned Blackacre as joint tenants.

7. H and E. In his will, H named another person as substitute executor in the event that E should predecease him.

---

169 R.S.A. 1980, c. S-31.
170 R.S.A. 1980, c. I-9.
171 R.S.A. 1980, c. I-5, ss. 263(1), 284.

Further Reading

A. H. Oosterhoff, *Succession Law Reform in Ontario*, (Toronto: Canada Law Book Ltd, 1979), at pp. 85-88.

Richard F. Double, "Practice Notes: Legacies, Survivorship and 'Mirror Wills' " (1997) 16 E. & T. J. 274.

David Norwood, "Dead Reckoning: Evidence and Proof of Death" (1995) 15 E.& T.J. 65.

13

CLASS GIFTS

1. INTRODUCTION

A testator who wishes to benefit more than one person may make separate gifts to each beneficiary, or one gift to the group of beneficiaries. It is often more convenient to give $1,000 to be shared equally by 10 persons than to give 10 separate gifts of $100 to each of the 10 persons. When the testator makes a gift to a group of persons, the gift may take one of three forms: (1) a sum of money to be shared by the named members of the group; (2) a sum of money to be shared by the members of the group described as a collective, such as "the children of A"; and (3) a sum of money to each member of a group. The first is a gift of to individuals; the second is a class gift; the third is a gift to individual members of a class. In this chapter we concentrate on the class gift.

A class gift is a convenient device, but it has its own problems of construction and operation. We shall first discuss the nature of class gifts. Second, we shall deal with the problem of identifying a class gift. Third, we shall outline the principles and rules of interpretation for determining the membership of a class.

Further Reading

Williams on Wills, 7th ed. by C.H. Sherrin, R.F.D. Barlow, and R.A. Wallington, assisted by Susannah L. Meadway (London: Butterworths, 1995), c. 66.

Feeney's Canadian Law of Wills, 4th ed. by James MacKenzie (Toronto: Butterworths, 2000 (loose leaf), c. 14.

Hawkins and Ryder on the Construction of Wills, by E.C. Ryder (London: Sweet & Maxwell, 1965), ch. 8.

A. James Casner, "Class Gifts - Effect of Failure of Class Member to Survive the Testator" (1947), 60 Harv. L. Rev. 751.

2. NATURE AND EFFECT OF A CLASS GIFT

In *Kingsbury v. Walter*[1] Lord Davey defined a class gift, as follows:

Prima facie a class gift is a gift to a class consisting of persons who are included and comprehended under some general description and bear a certain relation to the testator.

Hence, it is a gift to a body of persons, who are normally, although not necessarily, related to the testator. The body of persons is uncertain in number in the sense that it may increase or decrease before the testator's death or, indeed, thereafter, until the class closes. Thus, for example, a gift "to my brothers and sisters" will include, for the moment, all the testator's brothers and sisters living when he or she makes the will, but the class may decrease if any of them die and will increase if any are subsequently born.

Moreover, the amount that each member of the class will receive depends upon the ultimate number in the class. It also depends upon the proportions indicated by the testator. Thus, a gift of $50,000 "to my brothers and sisters," may indicate that the testator's sisters are to receive a double share.[2]

It follows, therefore, that if a member of the class predeceases the testator,[3] or is unable to take, for example, because he or she attests the will,[4] that person's share does not lapse, but goes to augment the shares of the other members. This statement is, however, subject to anti-lapse legislation in effect in several provinces which extends to class gifts.[5]

The effect of a class gift may be modified by a substitutionary gift. This is quite common. Thus, for example, a testator may give the residue of the estate equally to his or her children, but go on to provide that if a child should predecease the testator, that child's share shall go to his or her issue, if any, who survive the testator.[6] The problem that arises when a substitutionary gift is made in respect of a member of the class who died before the will was made has already been discussed.[7]

A class gift is treated differently than a gift to individuals for the purpose of the rule against perpetuities. This topic is discussed elsewhere.[8]

---

1 [1901] A.C. 187 at 192 (H.L.).

2 See *Jarman on Wills*, 8th ed. by Raymond Jennings, assisted by John C. Harper (London: Sweet & Maxwell Limited, 1951), p. 348; *Re Young; Payzant v. Armstrong*, [1927] 2 D.L.R. 1048, 59 N.S.R. 327 (T.D.).

3 *Re Creighton*, [1950] 2 W.W.R. 529, 58 Man. R. 362 (K.B.); *Re Jackson; Shiers v. Ashworth* (1883), 25 Ch. D. 162 at 164.

4 See *Re Brush*, [1942] O.R. 647, [1943] 1 D.L.R. 74 (H.C.), which considered this point, but held that the gift in that case was not a class gift.

5 This legislation is discussed in the preceding chapter.

6 See, *e.g.*, *Re Hutton* (1982), 39 O.R. (2d) 622, 11 E.T.R. 140 (H.C.), affirmed 39 O.R. (2d) 622n (C.A.).

7 In the preceding chapter.

8 See the chapter on Perpetuities and Accumulations, *infra*.

3. IDENTIFYING CLASS GIFTS

(a) A Class Gift or a Gift *Nominatim?*

There will be no difficulty in identifying a gift such as "to my children" as a class gift.[9] Other gifts are also readily identified as class gifts, although the scope of the gift may be a matter of interpretation. Thus, a gift to "my family" is a class gift and, if the testator has children, the members of the class are *prima facie* the children as a matter of interpretation.[10] Similarly, a gift of residue to be divided "equally among my nearest relations, named MacMurray" is a class gift.[11]

It is, however, common for testators to give aliquot portions of a sum of money or other property, or of the residue, to named individuals. In that case the gift is *prima facie* not a class gift, but a gift *nominatim* and the persons named take as *personae designatae*[12] even though they are also described collectively. Thus, for example, a gift "to my children, A, B and C," is not normally construed as a class gift, but rather as a gift to each of the named persons.[13]

Ultimately, whether a gift is construed as a class gift or as a gift *nominatim*, depends upon the testator's intention. Thus, in *Robinson v. Des Roches*[14] Saunders M.R., said:

> All these cases [referring to English and Canadian cases previously considered] have been decided on the question of the *intention* of the testator. Did the testator in the respective cases intend the gift to be an individual one? In that case if the beneficiary died in the lifetime of the testator the bequest will lapse. Or did he *intend* that it should operate as a class gift? In that case if one or more of the class died in the lifetime of the testator the gift goes to the survivors of the class. It is equally clear from those decided cases if the Court, putting itself in the same position as the testator occupied, with the same knowledge as the testator had when he was writing his will, comes to the conclusion that the gift, although expressed in the form of a gift to an individual but as a fact was *intended* to operate as a class gift, then there is no reason why effect should not be given to such intention.[15]

The traditional approach to this problem is exemplified by *Re Collishaw*.[16] In that case the testator gave a life interest in all his estate to his wife for life and

---

9 See, *e.g.*, *Re Campbell Estate* (1998), 25 E.T.R. (2d) 169 (P.E.I. T.D.), in which the court held that a residuary gifts "equally among my children, share and share alike," was a class gift.

10 See *Re Wilkie* (1906), 7 O.W.R. 473 (H.C.); *Creaghan v. Hazen* (1999), 32 E.T.R. (2d) 180 (N.B.Q.B.).

11 *Re MacMurray*, [1950] O.W.N. 681, [1950] 4 D.L.R. 440 (H.C.), the nearest relations in that case being the testator's brothers.

12 *Re James* (1919), 16 O.W.N. 87 (H.C.); *Re Bauman* (1910), 15 O.W.R. 423 (C.A.); *Re Cowan*, [1950] 1 W.W.R. 417 (Sask. K.B.), gift to beneficiaries mentioned earlier in the will; *Re Miller* (1925), 27 O.W.N. 385 (H.C.), division of estate equally between two named persons; *Re Murphy*, [1950] 4 D.L.R. 182, 25 M.P.R. 113 (N.S. T.D.), gift to named persons if they have children; *Stewart Estate v. Rodd Estate* (1994), 3 E.T.R. (2d) 195 (P.E.I. T.D.).

13 *Re Shannon* (1909), 19 O.L.R. 39 (C.A.); *Re Brush*, [1942] O.R. 647, [1943] 1 D.L.R. 74 (H.C.); *Re Griffith; Maritime Trust Co. v. Griffith*, [1951] 1 D.L.R. 551, 27 M.P.R. 181 (N.B. C.A.).

14 [1938] 3 D.L.R. 72, (sub nom. *Re Henderson*) 12 M.P.R. 596 (P.E.I.C.A.).

15 *Ibid.*, at D.L.R. 78-9.

16 [1953] 3 D.L.R. 829 (N.S. T.D.).

directed that the sum of $50,000 be paid to his sister, Lillian Brine, after his wife's death. However, he provided that if Lillian should die before his wife, the $50,000 should be paid

> in four equal shares — one share each, to her daughters Lucy and Louise, and one share to her son, John, and one share to the children of Charles A. Brine of Halifax, to be held in Trust for them, or their heirs, and not to be paid until the youngest is twenty-one years old.

The testator's wife died in 1952. Lillian Brine died in 1950. Her daughter, Louise Grant died in 1949, when she was more than 21 years old. Louise was survived by her husband and child. The court held that the use of the phrase, "four equal shares — one share each," the naming of the four children, the fact that three shares went to children of the testator's sister and the fourth share to grandchildren of the sister, and the use of the words of substitution, "or their heirs," indicated that the testator was not treating the beneficiaries as a class, but as individuals. Hence, Louise's interest, being vested, went to her estate.[17]

The distinction between a class gift and a gift *nominatim* is discussed further in *Re Snyder*,[18] reproduced below.

RE SNYDER
[1960] O.R. 107, 22 D.L.R. (2d) 71
Supreme Court of Ontario
[High Court of Justice]

The testator, James Snyder, died in 1921. His will was prepared by a fellow farmer on a stationers' form. The will, as construed by the court, devised one farm to the testator's son Dorwin Henry Snyder, for life, with remainder "to his two children Hugh James Snyder and Etta Florella Snyder if living." The testator devised another farm, again as construed by the court, to his wife and his daughter, "Laura Belle Snyder for life," with remainder to Dorwin for life and with further remainder "to his two children Hugh James Snyder and Etta Floretta Snyder if living." The residuary clause was not completed.

The testator's widow died in 1929. Etta died in 1947, having left her estate by her will to her brother Hugh and his wife. Laura died in 1954 and Dorwin died in 1957. His widow, the respondent, was his surviving executrix. Hugh made an application to interpret the will.

---

17 I submit that *Lindblom Estate v. Worthington* (1999), 30 E.T.R. (2d) 106 (Alta. Surr. Ct.) is wrong as the court should have followed the *Collishaw* approach. The testator purported to dispose of his estate in stated percentages to various named relatives. The court held that there was a commonality about the named beneficiaries because they were all extended family members who played a significant role in the testator's life. Hence, he intended to create a class gift, with the consequence that the shares of two beneficiaries who predeceased the testator accrued to the other beneficiaries.

18 [1960] O.R. 107, 22 D.L.R. (2d) 71 (H.C.).

SPENCE J.:

. . .

A much more difficult question arises upon the alternative submission of counsel for the respondents arising from the fact that Etta Florella Snyder, one of the two grandchildren and the sister of the applicant, died in 1947 prior to the death of her father, Dorwin Henry Snyder, and prior also to the death of her aunt, Laura Belle Snyder. Under such circumstances, does the whole of the estate go to the applicant Hugh James Snyder, or is there an intestacy as to the share of the estate, one-half in fact, which would have gone to Etta Florella Snyder had she survived the period of distribution? First, it would seem apparent on the actual language of both para. 1 and para. 3, that the ascertainment of the persons who are to take the remainder is only made upon the death of the survivor of the widow and the two children of the testator. In my view, the words "if living" repeated in both paragraphs, rule out any other conclusion. Such a view would appear to be also in accordance with the authorities.

. . .

Here there is no doubt that the class, if it is a class, is a small one composed only of two persons, the two grandchildren, the applicant and his late sister. Here also the two members of the alleged class are named. There is not, however, a simple naming of them with nothing more. In both para. 1 and para. 3 the actual words are: "To his children Hugh James Snyder and Etta Florella Snyder if living". Therefore, in addition to the names there are the words "to his two children" preceding the names and the most important words "if living" following the names. In Jarman on Wills[19] it is said:

> A gift to several named persons is not a gift to a class unless words of contingency are added: as where the gift is to A, B, C and D, "if living".

. . .

Here in paras. 1 and 3 of his last will the testator coupled the two grandchildren together in the words "his two children Hugh James Snyder and Etta Florella Snyder if living". In the fifth and sixth paragraphs of his will the testator also couples his two grandchildren together, using, however, in that case, the words "my two grandchildren" but returning in the last line of para. 6 to the designation "and his two children, Hugh James Snyder and Etta Florella Snyder" as those words follow the words "equally among my son Dorwin Henry Snyder"; and nowhere in the whole of the will is there any separation of the interests of the two grandchildren, Hugh James Snyder and Etta Florella Snyder, except in the words in para. 5, "providing that Dorwin will allow Etta Florella to live with my daughter Laura Belle until she is twenty-one years old". With that exception, not only are the two grandchildren named together on each occasion, but, on each occasion they are described as either "grandchildren" or "the children of my son". May

---

19 8th ed., vol. 1, p. 449.

such a small number as only two persons constitute a class when those two persons are named?

In *Re Miller*[20] Kelly J. considered a bequest in these terms "And if she died without living issue, the real estate to be equally divided between my said stepson John Miller and my stepdaughter Ada Dobson". When the testator executed his will and when he died he had only these two stepchildren. The gift to them was postponed to a life estate of his only daughter, and after his death and before the death of that daughter the stepdaughter Ada Dobson died. Kelly J. . . . said:[21]

> John Miller and Ada Dobson were included in the same general description and they bore the same relationship to the testator. They were, when he made the will, his only stepchildren. Moreover, there was no devise over in the event of the death of either of these stepchildren before that of Mary Jane. Considering all the circumstances, and, as far as possible, looking at the case from the position of the testator at the time he made the will, the learned Judge was of opinion that the testator's intention was that the stepchildren as a class, and not individually, should take the residuary real estate in the event of his only child (Mary Jane) dying without leaving living issue. The learned Judge could find no authority to the contrary applicable to the case in hand.

In *Re Brush*,[22] Urquhart J. was considering a case not of the death of one of the members of the alleged class prior to the period of distribution, but one in which two of the three daughters who allegedly formed the class had been witnesses to the will, and, therefore, the bequest to them was, the learned Judge held, barred under the provisions of s. 16 of the *Wills Act*.[23] The clause was very brief, reading: "Equally among my three daughters — Lina, Mabel and Beatrice". And there, as in the present case, the residual benefit clause read simply: "All the residue of my Estate not hereinafter disposed of I give devise and bequeath unto [blank]". Urquhart J. examined many cases but did not quote or refer to *Re Miller*. . . . [H]e said:[24]

> Having regard to the above authorities it seems to be that the testator in our case in planning his will had not in mind his three daughters as a class. If he had, he would have merely said "I give...to my daughters share and share alike," or something of that sort. In my opinion he had in his mind the three daughters as individuals, and the provision for them is the same as if he had said "I give to Lina, Mabel and Beatrice who are my three daughters".

I am forced to agree that the line is a very narrow one and perhaps one most difficult to ascertain. I have pointed out that in this will — that is the will under consideration in the present case — the names of the two grandchildren are always coupled and their interests are never separated. They are the only two grandchildren and they are the only children of the only son. Moreover, I attach a very considerable importance to the omission of the testator to complete the so-called residuary clause. It would seem that that clause appeared in some printed form which he had in hand when he was executing his will, by filling in the blanks. He

---

20 (1925), 27 O.W.N. 385.
21 *Ibid.*, at p. 386.
22 [1943] 1 D.L.R. 74, [1942] O.R. 647.
23 R.S.O. 1950, c. 426 (then R.S.O. 1927, c. 164, s. 16).
24 At O.R. 653.

had, prior to reaching that point on the paper, dealt with his real estate and with his personal estate and did so with some particular detail. It seems to me that a layman reaching that clause and failing to complete it, was expressing his view that he made a complete disposition of his estate and, therefore, there was no need to complete this residuary clause. It is significant that he thought of varying dates of death of his wife and sister on one hand, and his son on the other, and that he considered the grandchildren as being the last of his beneficiaries and, therefore, looked at them as a group, being sure that one of the other or both of them would survive any of the previous beneficiaries. This, therefore, is a case where I think the testator has pointed out to us that he was seeking to avoid any intestacy and had in his opinion made a complete disposition of his estate. I think that to hold now that one-half of the remainder should fall into intestacy would do serious damage to the intention of the testator.

Therefore, I have come to the conclusion that the gift to Hugh James Snyder and Etta Florella Snyder was, if not a true class gift, to quote the words of Maugham J. in *Re Woods; Wood v. Creagh*,[25] "in the technical sense, at any rate as a group of persons who have got to be living at the death of the testator in order to take any interest under the bequest", and that Etta Florella Snyder having died before the period of distribution, the whole of her interest goes to her brother, the applicant Hugh James Snyder.

. . .

Notes and Questions

1. Which of the two approaches is to be preferred, that in *Snyder*, or that in *Collishaw*?[26]

2. For a case similar to *Snyder*, see *Re Hutton*.[27] In that case the testator directed that the residue of his estate be divided equally among his brothers and sisters, A, B, C and D, but he provided that if any should predecease him, survived by a child or children who should survive the testator, the child or children would take his, her, or their deceased parent's share. A and B predeceased the testator, both leaving a child or children them surviving. However, B's only child also died before the testator.

The court held that the scheme of the will showed that the testator wanted to leave the entire residue to his brothers and sisters or their children. He thus created a type of class, with the result that the share of B (and his child) accrued to the other members of the class.

3. If the residuary clause provides for equal division among a list of named persons some of whom are unrelated to the testator and to each other, it is unlikely that the court will find that there was a class gift.[28]

4. A testator directed that the residue of his estate be held in trust for "my son A, my daughters, B, C, D and E, and such of my child or children, if any hereafter to be born as shall attain the age of twenty-one years or marry, in equal shares as tenants in common."

25 [1931] 2 Ch. 143.

26 [1953] 3 D.L.R. 829 (N.S. T.D.).

27 (1982), 39 O.R. (2d) 622, 11 E.T.R. 140 (H.C.), affirmed 39 O.R. (2d) 622n (C.A.).

28 *Re Stuart* (1964), 47 W.W.R. 500 (B.C.S.C.), one of 36 named beneficiaries in residuary clause predeceasing testator. See also *Re Griffith; Maritime Trust Co. v. Griffith*, [1951] 1 D.L.R. 551, 27 M.P.R. 181 (N.B.C.A.).

The testator had another son at the date of the will, F, but no other children were born to him. A, B, D and E predeceased him. What result?[29]

5. A testator divided the residue of his estate into seven equal shares, one share to be paid to each of the children of his late sister. He then named five of them but could not remember the names of the others. Moreover, he excluded any that were mentally ill. In fact, his sister only had six children, two being confined in a mental hospital. Who receives the residue?[30]

6. A testator had been married twice. He gave the residue of his estate, except the part he had received from his second wife, Mary, equally to his children A, B, C, D, E and F. The part he had received from Mary, he gave equally to D, E and F, who were his children by his wife, Mary. E was missing in action during World War I when the will was made, although the testator refused to believe him dead. Prior to the testator's death the War Office reported E as having been killed in action. Are these class gifts?[31]

7. Can a list of charities in a residuary clause qualify as a class?[32]

8. A testator directed that the residue of his estate be divided in equal shares among his children. Two of his five children predeceased him, leaving issue. Should the estate be divided into thirds for the surviving children, or are the estates of the deceased children also entitled?[33] Would the result have been different if the testator had named the children individually in the will?[34]

(b) Artificial Classes

Most class gifts are in favour of a group of persons who are described by a common characteristic, such as "my children," "my nephews and nieces," *etc*. However, it may be that the testator wishes to make one gift to two groups of persons which do not share the same characteristics and intends that it shall be a class gift. Thus, it may be that a testatrix wishes to provide for the children of her sister, Mary and the children of her sister, Evelyn, but not for her brother John's children. Hence, she cannot say "to my nephews and nieces." But she can make a gift in the following form: "To the children of Mary and the children of Evelyn equally."[35] It is a gift to a composite class, which is permissible. Alternatively, the testator could have made a separate gift to each of those classes.

It may also be that the testator wishes to benefit one person from one family and others in the same degree of relationship from another. Hence, he or she is

---

29 See *Re Jackson; Shiers v. Ashworth*, (1883), 25 Ch. D. 162 at 164.

30 See *Re Telfer*, [1964] 1 O.R. 373, 42 D.L.R. (2d) 327 (H.C.).

31 See *Re Whiston; Whiston v. Woolley*, [1924] 1 Ch. 122 (C.A.). Consider also the application of the rules respecting lapsed gifts in the preceding chapter. Contrast *Robinson v. Des Roches*, [1938] 3 D.L.R. 72, (sub nom. *Re Henderson*) 12 M.P.R. 596 (P.E.I.C.A.), in which one of the beneficiaries was also dead at the date of the will.

32 See *Montreal Trust Co. v. Boy Scouts of Can. (Edmonton Region) Foundation*, [1978] 5 W.W.R. 123, (1978), 3 E.T.R. 1 at 19-20, 88 D.L.R. (3d) 99 (B.C.S.C.).

33 See *Re Lightfoot* (1985), 19 E.T.R. 251 (Ont. H.C.).

34 See *Tonon v. Vendruscolo* (1987), 25 E.T.R. 201 (Ont. H.C.).

35 If the gift took the form: "To the children of Mary and Evelyn", other problems of construction arise (as well as problems relating to class gifts), which have been discussed in the chapter on General Principles of Interpretation.

trying to create an artificial class. The problems engendered by such an attempt are discussed in *Kingsbury v. Walter*,[36] reproduced below.

KINGSBURY v. WALTER
[1901] A.C. 187
House of Lords

The testator bequeathed certain property to Elizabeth Jane Fowler and the child or children of his sister Emily Walter at age 21 equally to be divided among them as tenants in common.

Elizabeth Jane Fowler was a few months short of her 21st birthday when the will was made. However she died two years before the testator, having attained age 21.

On an application to construe the will, North J., held that the gift to Elizabeth lapsed. The Court of Appeal reversed. A further appeal was then brought to the House of Lords.

LORD DAVEY:

. . .

The question, I agree, is whether a gift in this case to "Elizabeth Jane Fowler and the children of my sister Emily Walter" is what is called, by an expression well known in our law, a class gift. Prima facie a class gift is a gift to a class, consisting of persons who are included and comprehended under some general description and bear a certain relation to the testator....But it may be none the less a class because some of the individuals of the class are named. For example, if a gift is made "to all my nephews and nieces including A.", or if a gift is made "to C. and all other my nephews and nieces", each of those would be a class gift. *Stanhope's Case*[37] is an example: there the gift was to four named daughters and all his after-born daughters, and that was rightly, as I think, held to be a class gift. To the same effect is a case before Chitty J., *In re Jackson*,[38] where the gift was to five named individuals and all his other sons and daughters who should be born afterwards and attain the age of twenty-one years. Chitty J. held that that was a class gift, although the condition of attaining the age of twenty-one years was imposed upon the other children and not upon those who were named. He came to this conclusion upon the ground that it appeared from the evidence that those who were named had already attained the age of twenty-one years. That case seems to me to have a considerable bearing upon the case now before the House.

There may also be a composite class, such as, for instance, children of A. and children of B.: that would be a good class. On the other hand, a gift to A. and all the children of B. is, in my opinion, prima facie not a class gift, and I think that

---

36 [1901] A.C. 187 (H.L.).
37 (1859) 27 Beav. 201.
38 (1883) 25 Ch. D. 162.

has been so decided, and rightly decided, in...a case before Sir George Jessel of *In re Allen, Wilson v. Atter*.[39] There was in that case a direction "to divide equally amongst all the children of R.W., the child of W.W. and L. his wife, and A.W., the widow of J.W., share and share alike." It was held that this was not a gift to a class and that the share lapsed. I need not read the learned judge's judgment because it was read in the course of the argument, and it is present to your Lordship's minds.

My Lords, I think those cases were rightly decided, and I do not agree with the proposition which I understand to be laid down by Romer L.J., who says:

> In my opinion it is correct to say that a gift by will to a class properly so called, and a named individual such as A. equally, so that the testator contemplates A. taking the same share that each member of the class will take, is prima facie a gift to a class.

I think that that is contrary to the established authorities and to the principles applicable to this branch of the law.

But, my Lords, it is perfectly plain that a gift in the form which I have mentioned may be a class gift, if there is to be found in the will a context which will shew that the testator intended it to be a class gift. I think the same result may be arrived at if the Court, putting itself into the same position as the testator occupied, with the same knowledge as the testator had when he was writing his will, comes to the conclusion that the gift, although expressed in the form of a gift to an individual and the children of A., was intended to operate as a class gift. There is abundant authority for that proposition. I will only mention two cases, before Lord Romilly. The case of *Aspinall v. Duckworth*[40] appears to me to be exactly this case. It was a gift unto and equally amongst the testator's nephew A. and the children of his sister B. as tenants in common. Lord Romilly held that that was a gift to a class. It differs from this case only in one particular, namely, that the gift here is confined to those children who attain twenty-one.

My Lords, another principle which is, I think, established in this branch of the law is, that all the interests of members of the class must vest in interest at the same time. For instance, if there is a gift to A. for life and afterwards to B. and the children of C., the class must vest in interest at the death of the testator, although it is capable of enlargement by the birth of subsequent children of C. during the lifetime of the tenant for life. My Lords, it is, I conceive, on that ground that the other case to which I referred, namely, *Drakeford v. Drakeford*,[41] was decided. The learned judge, Lord Romilly, there said that the gift which he had before him in that case was not a class gift. It was in this form — a gift to A. for life, and at his death to be equally divided between his surviving children and the testator's niece Rosamond Willows. There, as your Lordships see, only those children who survived the tenant for life would have taken, whereas Rosamond Willows' interest would have become vested at the testator's death. On that ground Lord Romilly held that it was not a class. He says:

---

39 (1881) 29 W.R. 480.
40 (1866), 35 Beav. 307.
41 (1863) 33 Beav. 43, 48.

I have no doubt that if there be a gift to the children of A., and to my niece Rosamond, and to my niece Mary, and so on, that may be a class. But to make this one class it must be to this effect:

> I leave the whole of my funded property to my brother for his life, and at his death the property to be equally divided amongst his children and my niece Rosamond Willows, or such of them as shall survive the tenant for life

— making them all vested interests at the same time. [He says,]

> In all these cases the class would be ascertained at a particular period, and if one died there would be no lapse. But here Rosamond Willows is to take her share at all events; it is given absolutely to her, and the only persons to be ascertained are the children of the brother, and they are to be ascertained at his death

— not at the testators death. That appears to me to have been the ratio decidendi of that case, and being so it does not appear to me to be in conflict with the other decisions of that learned judge.

Now, my Lords, in this case it is a gift to Elizabeth Jane Fowler and the children of Mrs. Walter who shall attain the age of twenty-one years as tenants in common. It may be said, therefore, that in this case the gift to Elizabeth Jane Fowler was absolute whether she had attained the age of twenty-one years at the testator's death or not, whereas the gift to the children of Mrs. Walter would not vest in them until they attained the age of twenty-one. If it stood upon that bare fact alone, I should have been of opinion that North J.'s decision was right. But, my Lords, we have to look at the context, and, reading the whole of the will, I find that although Elizabeth Jane Fowler is not described as a niece in the gift itself, still in the previous part of the will the testator had appointed his "niece Elizabeth Jane Fowler" together with his wife executrix of his will, and he afterwards describes her as his "niece," and gives to her after his wife's death a messuage or tenement under the description of "my niece Elizabeth Jane Fowler". He also appoints her trustee of his will for various purposes. Elizabeth Jane Fowler was not indeed twenty-one years of age, but she was within a few months of attaining that age; and I think the testator treated her for the purpose of his will as if she had attained that age. In this respect it nearly resembles the case before Chitty J.

I do not at all deny that the case is very near the line; but I think there is enough in this will itself to shew that he gave the property to her as a niece, and that he makes a special class of nieces and nephews consisting of the only child of Mrs. Fowler and the children of his sister Mrs. Walter, and that it was intended to be a class gift to that special class, and I should so construe the will.

[The Earl of Halsbury L.C., and Lords Macnaghten, Brampton, Shand and Robertson concurred.]

Notes and Questions

1. A testator made a gift to his grandson, A, and continued, "or in case other sons should be born to my son, then to be equally divided between all the boys." Is this a class gift?[42]

2. A testator gave a life interest to A, his niece, with remainder "to the brothers and sisters of A and B, C and D." B and C were nephews of the testator. D was a stranger. What result?[43]

3. *Rothstein Estate v. Rothstein*[44] cited *Kingsbury* with approval. The testatrix divided the residue of her estate into a number of shares equal to the total number of her children and grandchildren and directed that one share be paid to each of them. She had four children and four grandchildren, but one of her children predeceased her, survived by two children. The court held that the gift was not a class gift, since the shares would not vest in the children in the same manner or at the same time as the grandchildren. Hence, the two children of the deceased child took their parent's share under anti-lapse legislation,[45] as well as their own shares.

(c) Description by Number

If a testator describes a class of persons by number, such as "to my three brothers," *prima facie* the gift is not a class gift, but a gift *nominatim*. Thus, in *Re Smith's Trusts*[46] the testator gave the residue of his estate, after a life interest, "to be equally divided between the five daughters" of A and B. Two of the daughters predeceased the testator. The court held that this was not a class gift, but rather a gift to the daughters as *personae designatae* and, therefore, the shares of the two deceased daughters lapsed.

On the other hand, if the testator clearly intends to benefit the persons as a class and not individually, effect will be given to his or her intention. A problem that sometimes arises, however, is that the number does not correspond with the actual members in the class. This problem is discussed in *Re Burgess*,[47] reproduced below.

BURGESS RE
(1968), 64 W.W.R. 44, 67 D.L.R. (2d) 526
Supreme Court of British Columbia

The testatrix was born in Saskatchewan and lived there until 1914 when she moved permanently to British Columbia. By her will she gave a legacy of $1,000 each "to the two children (boy and girl) of William Cowan of Lake Johnston, Saskatchewan." William Cowan was the testatrix' mother's brother, who home-

---

42 See *Re Chandler* (1889), 18 O.R. 105 (H.C.).
43 *Re Venn*, [1904] 2 Ch. 52.
44 (1996), 11 E.T.R. (2d) 125 (B.C.S.C.).
45 *Wills Act*, R.S.B.C. 1996, c. 489, s. 29.
46 (1878), 9 Ch. D. 117.
47 (1968), 64 W.W.R. 44, 67 D.L.R. (2d) 526 (B.C.S.C.).

steaded in Saskatchewan. Two children, a boy and girl, had been born to him when the testatrix left Saskatchewan in 1914. However, he subsequently had four more children. Hence, there were six children, both when the testatrix made her will and when she died.

An application was made to construe the will.

MACDONALD J.:

. . .

I refer firstly to *Newman v. Piercey*.[48] The facts were that the testatrix bequeathed "to each of the three children of Mrs. Walden, widow of William Walden, one hundred pounds". William Walden had died leaving a widow and three children, of whom one died in 1870 and two survived. His widow married again in 1858, W.J. Punter, and had six children by that marriage living at the date of the will which was 1873. The evidence proved that the testatrix knew of the second marriage and that there were children of that marriage but that she did not know their number and that she had not seen Mrs. Punter, formerly Mrs. Walden, for six years before the date of her will. It was held that the two children of this lady by William Walden were alone entitled and not her children by the second marriage. In his reasons Jessel, M.R., having found that it was these two children whom the testatrix intended to benefit, went on to say this:[49]

> That being my conclusion upon the evidence, is there any rule of law or any principle to be deduced from the decided cases which compels me to come to a different conclusion? If there were, I should do so most unhesitatingly, because it is no part of the duty of the Court to speculate or to discover what the intention of a testator is, except by legal means. Therefore, it is incumbent upon me to examine the authorities, and to see whether there is any such rule of law laid down by them. First of all, what is the rule? The rule cannot be stated more favourably, I think, than this: that where there is a gift to the children of any one, "children" means all the children, and it still means all the children, although the number of the children are specified, such as three children, four children, or five children, or whatever the number may be, unless there is some evidence to shew which of the children specified are meant....

The rule is also stated in the case of *Yeats v. Yeats*....[50]

> The principle on which this Court acts is well settled by authority. Where a testator gives a legacy between a class of persons, or separate and distinct legacies to each of a class, if the Court finds there are more of the class than those specified by the testator, it endeavours to find which of them were really meant; and if it is unable to discover them, then, in order that the legacy may not fail altogether, it infers or presumes that the testator intended to include all the class, notwithstanding the numerical error;

so that the principle is this, that the Court only resorts to striking out the number, which is a strong measure at all times with regard to a will or any other instrument, when it altogether fails to discover who is meant, that is, to discover who is meant both from the wording of the will and the extrinsic evidence, properly admissible.

---

48 (1876), 4 Ch. D. 41.
49 At pp. 46-7.
50 16 Beav. 170, 171.

. . .

Re Sharp; Maddison v. Gill[51] was a case where the Court found that a class gift had been intended and rejected the mistake in numbers. Cozens-Hardy, M.R., on appeal said this:[52]

> If, however, that is not the true construction, then it seems to me that by a long series of authorities, which are absolutely binding upon this Court, it is a plain case where you have a governing intention to benefit children — not, I agree, forming a class in the sense in which that word is frequently used in legal language, but children described as being the children of a certain person — coupled with a mistake in the number of those children; and under those circumstances the Courts have held, and as it seems to me in accordance with common sense, that the dominant intention to benefit the members so described must have effect given to it by rejecting the inaccurate enumeration.

> [His Lordship then referred extensively to a number of cases which examined the question whether a gift in which the beneficiaries are identified by number as well as a general description is a class gift or a gift *nominatim*. These cases included *Re Snyder*,[53] and two cases discussed in that case: *Re Brush*[54] and *Re Miller*[55]. His Lordship further referred to *Re Griffith Maritime Trust Co. v. Griffith*,[56] *Re Smith's Trusts*,[57] and *Re Stansfield*,[58] all of which held that a gift to a group of persons referred to by number is not a class gift. He continued:]

I return to the language of the particular will and the extrinsic evidence. When Miss Burgess moved away from Saskatchewan in February, 1914, two children had been born to William Cowan; Gladys Belle then 8 years of age, and William Henry at that time 6 years of age. It is reasonable to assume that the testatrix knew these cousins. But it is a question whether she had knowledge of the births of William Cowan's four other children, the first of which occurred in August, 1915. The material does not provide an answer. Emma Allan, with whom Miss Burgess lived for over a year after she retired, also a friend of the testatrix, swears in her affidavit that Miss Burgess frequently spoke of her early life in Moosomin, Saskatchewan, but she did recall any mention by her of the name of the Cowan family. The executor, a bank manager, whom the testatrix knew for over 40 years going back to the time when she taught him in school, swears that she never mentioned the Cowan family to him.

The will indicates that the testatrix had more information about some children she wished to benefit than she did about others. She named the four grandchildren of Mrs. Cartwright. She did not name her cousin, the son of her uncle Arthur Cowan. She did not name "the seven children of Leslie Somerton". She did not name or give the number of the children of Louise Burrows. The material shows

---

51 [1908] 2 Ch. 190.
52 *Ibid.*, at p. 193.
53 (1959), 22 D.L.R. (2d) 71, [1960] O.R. 107, reproduced above.
54 [1942] O.R. 647, [1943] 1 D.L.R. 74.
55 (1925), 27 O.W.N. 385.
56 [1951] 1 D.L.R. 551, 27 M.P.R. 181 (N.B.C.A.).
57 (1878), 9 Ch. D. 117.
58 (1880), 15 Ch. D. 84.

that apart from the children of William Cowan, the information set out in the will proved to be accurate.

Mr. Morris argued persuasively that Gladys Belle and William Henry were the two children of William Cowan that the testatrix had in mind because she must have known them before coming to British Columbia; she accurately described them as boy and girl; and it is reasonable to infer that she did not know the four children, the oldest of which was born after an eight-year interval from the birth of her cousin, William Henry. This submission is weakened, although not fatally, by the failure of the testatrix to name the two children. Looking at the will as a whole and having regard to the little extrinsic evidence, I am of the opinion that the testatrix did not know the names of her two cousins Gladys Belle and William Henry and did not know the name of her first cousin, the son of Arthur Cowan. Having acquaintance, or even closer relationship, some 40 years ago with two particular cousins whose names are forgotten, is an unlikely basis for preferring them to other cousins. My judgment of the question is that there was a dominant intention to benefit the children of William Cowan as a class rather than two of them specifically. The rule expounded in *Newman v. Piercey*[59] and *Re Sharp*, ...[60] as to rejection of a mistake in number should, therefore, be applied.

As to the law I just make this comment. The cases *Re Brush* and *Re Griffith* were stronger as indicating gifts to specified persons than is the present one. The beneficiaries were named. But in *Re Miller* and *Re Snyder*, notwithstanding that the beneficiaries were named, the dispositions were held to be class gifts. As for *Re Smith's Trusts* and *Re Stansfield* the beneficiaries were designated, and designated accurately by their numbers. Both Mallins, V.C., who decided the former, and Bacon, V.C., who decided the latter, considered that the effect was just the same as if the persons had been mentioned by name. The decisions are of no help in a case such as this where there is the question whether the testatrix knew how many children there were.

Notes and Questions

1. The gifts in *Re Burgess* and *Newman v. Piercey*,[61] referred to in that case, were not true class gifts, that is a gift of property to be divided among a described group, but rather a gift of a specified amount to each member of a described group. Nevertheless, the problem is the same for each type of gift.

2. In *Re Diver*,[62] there was a gift of $2,000 equally "to the two children of my niece." This was, therefore, a true class gift, but since the niece had three children, there was an error in the number of members. The court dealt briefly with the issue and followed *Newman v. Piercey*.[63]

---

59 (1876), 4 Ch. D. 41.
60 [1908] 2 Ch. 190 (C.A.).
61 (1876), 4 Ch. D. 41.
62 (1962), 39 W.W.R. 612, 34 D.L.R. (2d) 667 (Alta. C.A.).
63 *Supra*.

4. DETERMINING THE MEMBERSHIP OF THE CLASS

(a) Generally

In order to determine which members of the class are entitled to share in the gift, it must first be ascertained when the class closes. In the first instance, this must be determined by reference to the will itself, for the testator may direct when the class is to close, or which members of the class shall take. Thus, for example, a testator may provide for a life interest in favour of one person and then give the remainder to his or her children "then living." In such a case, only the children living at the life tenant's death are entitled to share in the gift and those who survived the testator but died before the life tenant are excluded.[64]

It often happens that the court cannot determine from the will when the class is to close. In that event it will apply certain rules of construction known as the class closing rules, or rules of convenience, which will be described below. These rules were adopted because of the administrative inconvenience in letting a class remain open indefinitely, that is, until the last member of the class is born or satisfies the criteria of the class, for until then the gift cannot be distributed.

The rules of convenience are only rules of construction, however, and should not be used if the testator's intention is clear.[65] Moreover, recent case law has stressed the duty of the court to mount a meaningful inquiry into a testator's intention before it considers the rules of convenience or any other rule of construction, such as the presumption in favour of earlier vesting.

Thus, in *Re Hanson*,[66] the testator made provision for his sister and his mentally infirm daughter for their respective lives out of the income of the estate. He also conferred a power to encroach on the capital for their benefit and directed that any surplus income should be added to the capital and invested until the death of the survivor of the sister and daughter. The testator provided for the payment of thirteen $1,000 legacies on the death of the survivor and directed that the residue of the estate should be distributed as if he had died intestate. He was survived by his sister, the mentally infirm daughter and another daughter. The sister died first and the second daughter died before the mentally infirm one. Osler J., said:[67]

It was submitted to me that the normal rule to be followed was that there was a presumption in favour of early vesting unless the contrary should be indicated in the will. In my respectful view, that puts the matter wrong way round. The primary rule, and one that must always govern the interpretation of wills, is that the intention of the testator must be ascertained, if possible, from an examination of the will itself together with those circumstances surrounding the making of the will which may properly be taken into consideration by the Court. It is only if the will itself is

---

64 See, *e.g.*, *Re Milne; Grant v. Heysham* (1887), 56 L.J. Ch. 543.

65 *Nat. Trust Co. v. Fleury*, [1965] S.C.R. 817, 53 D.L.R. (2d) 700 at 710, *per* Ritchie J. See, however, *Re Clifford's Settlement Trusts; Heaton v. Westwater*, [1981] Ch. 63, [1980] 1 All E.R. 1013, in which Megarry V.C., stated that the standard for excluding the class closing rules is high and that if an expression is capable of operating in conformity with the rules, they must be applied, even though some provisions in the will point to their exclusion.

66 (1978), 1 E.T.R. 280 (Ont. H.C.).

67 *Ibid.*, at p. 283.

ambiguous or does not make clear the intention of the testator that resort is to be had to rules and presumptions of the kind referred to.

His Lordship held that the terms of the will clearly indicated that the class of next of kin was to be determined as of the death of the mentally infirm daughter and that it was not necessary to refer to the rules of convenience. It was also held that the $1,000 gifts to two named legatees who had survived the testator, but died before the mentally infirm daughter lapsed and fell into residue.[68]

The question is discussed further in *Re Hyslop*,[69] reproduced below.

RE HYSLOP
(1978), 3 E.T.R. 216
Supreme Court of Ontario
[High Court of Justice]

The testator William Dodds Hyslop, who died in 1978, directed his trustees in clause 3(e) of his will to divide the residue of his estate in equal shares between his sons, Donald and Glen. Glen's share was to be invested and the income therefrom paid to Glen for life. On Glen's death, his share was to be divided in equal shares among his children.

The testator was survived by Donald and Glen, Glen's wife, and Glen's four children, three of whom had reached the age of majority.

An application was made to interpret the will.

The court held, *inter alia*, that Glen received a life interest only in one-half of the residue.

CRAIG J.:

. . .

Turning now to question 3, this is a gift to a class, the "children" of Glen Hyslop. The issue is whether the class closes on the death of the testator, William Dodds Hyslop, or at the time for distribution on the death of the life tenant, Glen Hyslop....

Two important points arise for consideration in answering question 3. Firstly, upon giving the words used their natural and ordinary meaning, is the intention of the testator reasonably certain? If the answer to that question is "yes" then that is the end of the inquiry because effect is then given to such intention. If the intention of the testator is not clear then it is necessary to turn to rules of construction. I will deal with the second point firstly because much argument was addressed to me as to what rule or rules of construction should apply if the intention of the testator is not clear.

---

68 To the same effect, see *Re Allan* (1983), 24 Sask. R. 144 (Q.B.); *Re Cairns*, [1972] 4 W.W.R. 322 at 325 (B.C.S.C.), *per* Wooton J.; *Re Ransome; Moberly v. Ransome*, [1957] Ch. 348 at 361, [1957] 1 All E.R. 690, *per* Upjohn J.
69 (1978), 3 E.T.R. 216 (Ont. H.C.).

In *Nat. Trust Co. v. Fleury*[70] the Supreme Court of Canada was called upon to interpret a will which provided for payment of income and some capital to a daughter of the testator during her lifetime with the remainder to his own next of kin. In the result the Court was able to give effect to the intention of the testator without resort to a rule of construction but the Court did state very clearly in that case that if the intention of the testator is not clear then prima facie the next of kin were to be ascertained at the date of the death of the testator.

I refer to the judgment of Mr. Justice Ritchie speaking for the majority,[71] where he stated as follows:

> I think that the true meaning of *Bullock v. Downes*,[72] is that described by Viscount Finlay in *Hutchinson v. National Refuges for Homeless and Destitute Children*,[73] where he says:
>
> > *Bullock v. Downes* therefore decides that, prima facie, the next of kin are to be ascertained at the death of the testator, but, that if there is a sufficient indication to that effect in the words of the will, the time for ascertaining the class may be the time fixed by the will as the period of distribution. The question in this as in every other case of the kind must be whether there is in the will a sufficient indication that the period of distribution is the time at which the class is to be ascertained.

In my view it is of importance to note that in the *Fleury* case and also in the case of *Bullock v. Downes*,[74] referred to therein, the Court was dealing with a class composed of next of kin of the testator and not of the life tenant as in the instant case. I say that because there are substantial authorities, some English and some Canadian, indicating that prima facie a gift over to children of the life tenant will keep the class open so as to let in all of those members coming into existence before the date of distribution. It may be that the *Fleury* case should be distinguished from the instant case.

. . .

I refer also to two Canadian cases decided, of course, before the *Fleury* case, *Re Duckworth*[75] and *Re McKee*.[76] In the *Duckworth* case Mr. Justice Wilson was called upon to interpret a will and to answer a question similar to question 3 herein. In that case he quoted and relied upon Hawkins on Wills[77]...referred to above, as follows:

> A devise or bequest of a corpus or aggregate fund to children as a class, where the gift is not immediate, vests in all the children in existence at the death of the testator, but so as to open and let in children subsequently coming into existence before the period of distribution.

---

70 [1965] S.C.R. 817, 53 D.L.R. (2d) 700.
71 At S.C.R. 828.
72 (1860), 9 H.L.C. 1.
73 [1920] A.C. 794 at 801.
74 (1860), 9 H.L.C. 1.
75 [1958] O.W.N. 236.
76 (1921), 21 O.W.N. 270.
77 (3rd ed.), p. 91.

The case goes on to indicate that all the children in existence at the testator's death take a vested interest subject to being partially divested in favour of children subsequently coming into existence during the life of the life tenant.

Having regard to these authorities, if it were necessary to resort to a rule of construction I would distinguish the facts of the *Fleury* case, which dealt with next of kin of the testator, and I would hold and apply the rule of construction that prima facie the class remains open until the date fixed for distribution; that is the death of Glen Hyslop. However, I do not feel it is necessary to resort to any rule of construction because giving the words of the will their natural, ordinary and grammatical meaning, it is my opinion that the intention of the testator is reasonably certain. The testator provided that the income from one-half of the residue would be paid to a son and on the son's death the corpus would be distributed among his, that is the son's children. In my view it is reasonably certain that the testator was referring to or looking at the son's children as of the time of distribution or putting it another way, it is reasonably certain from the words and the language used, that he did not intend to exclude any of the son's children that came into being after his death.

For these reasons and perhaps for greater certainty, my answer to question 3 is somewhat more extended than the question as framed anticipates. The answer to question 3 will be as follows:

> The children of Glen Hyslop in existence at the date of the death of the testator take an immediate vested interest in the remainder, being one-half of the residue, but the class remains open until the date of distribution, namely upon the death of Glen Hyslop so that any additional children of Glen Hyslop who come into existence at any time after the death of the testator shall be members of the class.

. . .

Notes and Questions

1. For a similar case see *Re Hudson*.[78] However, in that case the court applied the rules of construction.

2. A question often arises in the context of class closing about the ability or inability of a person to have children. The traditional rule is that the court will not make a presumption that a man is incapable of having children or that a woman is incapable of bearing children at any age, or hear evidence to that effect.[79] Equity will, however, give those administering an estate permission to distribute if it is clear that a woman is past the age of child bearing by reason of age or because of a medical condition[80] and the rule has also been waived in other respects for the purposes of administration and in special circumstances, although not before a woman reached age 54.[81]

---

78 (1970), 14 D.L.R. (3d) 79 (N.S.S.C.).

79 *Ward v. Van der Loeff*, [1924] A.C. 653; *Re Deloitte; Griffiths v. Deloitte*, [1926] Ch. 56; *Re G.* (1891), 21 O.R. 109 (H.C.); *Re Tinning* (1904), 8 O.L.R. 703 (H.C.).

80 *Inland Revenue Commissioners v. Bernstein*, [1960] Ch. 444 at 454, [1960] 1 All E.R. 697 at 702, *per* Danckwerts J., affirmed [1961] Ch. 399, [1961] 1 All E.R. 320 (C.A.).

81 See *Re Westminster Bank's Declaration of Trust*, [1963] 1 W.L.R. 820, [1963] 2 All E.R. 400n.

The rule, which was particularly strong for the purpose of the rule against perpetuities, has been abolished by statute in some jurisdictions, but only as regards perpetuities.[82]

There is no reason why the rule should not be abolished for all purposes today in view of the fact that reliable medical evidence proving inability to procreate is readily available.[83] *Quaere*, however, how one would deal with new fertilization techniques, such as *ex utero* embryo growth and storage of spermatozoa.

Getty v. Crow[84] may indicate a willingness on the part of the courts to approach this problem in a reasonable way. That case involved a 77-year old man who had been left a life estate in certain real property, with remainder to such of his children as should be living at his death. He wanted to sell the property and his children agreed to execute the deed to convey their interest, but the purchaser was concerned about possible unborn or adopted children. The man led evidence to prove that he could not sire further children because of ill health, and would not qualify to adopt any children. The court held that in this context it did not have to rely on mathematical certainty that the man was incapable of having further children, but could rely on moral certainty instead. The court was morally certain that the testator could have no further children, so that he and his existing children, between them, could convey the entire interest.

3. The class closing rules only apply to gifts of capital. They do not apply to gifts of income.[85]

(b) The Class Closing Rules

(i) *Immediate Gift to a Class*

When the gift to the class is immediate, *prima facie* the class closes at the testator's death and all persons who fall within the description of the class are members of the class and are entitled to share in the gift. All who are born thereafter are excluded. However, if there are no persons in existence who satisfy the description of the class at the testator's death, the class remains open until it closes naturally.[86]

Thus, in a gift, "to the children of A equally," if A has one child, X, who is alive at the testator's death and two, Y and Z, born thereafter, the rule operates so as to give the entire gift to X and to exclude Y and Z. If, on the other hand, X, Y and Z are all born after the testator's death, they each take one-third of the gift. The class closes naturally on A's death.

The rule is explained in *Re Charlesworth Estate*,[87] reproduced below.

You should note that the rule is not ousted merely because payment is postponed, otherwise than by a life interest or a direction to accumulate. Thus, if distribution is postponed until the youngest member of the class attains age 21,

---

82 See the chapter on Perpetuities and Accumulations, *infra*.

83 See *Re Westminster Bank's Declaration of Trust*, *supra*, at All E.R. 401, *per* Wilberforce J.

84 (1985), 52 O.R. (2d) 689, 38 R.P.R. 286, 21 E.T.R. 286 (Dist. Ct.).

85 See *Re Ward's Will Trusts; Ward v. Ward*, [1965] 1 Ch. 856, [1964] 3 All E.R. 442 (Ch. D.).

86 This rule is often referred to as the rule in *Viner v. Francis* (1789), 2 Cox Eq. Cas. 190, 29 E.R. 365.

87 [1996] 5 W.W.R. 578, 12 E.T.R. (2d) 257, 108 Man. R. (2d) 228 (Q.B.).

the rule still applies and excludes anyone born after the testator's death, unless no members of the class were then in existence.[88]

CHARLESWORTH ESTATE RE
(1996), 12 E.T.R. (2d) 257
Manitoba Queen's Bench

The testatrix left one-half of the residue of her estate to trustees in trust "for the children of my niece, LYNNE ARBEZ, and my nephew, WAYNE KINDRET, in equal shares." When the testatrix made her will, Wayne had one child and Lynne was pregnant with her first child. When the testatrix died, Wayne had two children and Lynne had one, but Lynne had her second child, Alaina, 16 1/2 months later. Lynne intervened in a motion to interpret the will and brought an application to vary the trust. Lynne and Wayne filed consents to the variation, as did a 16-year-old beneficiary. The other beneficiaries were too young.[89] There was no extrinsic evidence to help in the interpretation of the will. Thus, the issues before the court were whether the class of beneficiaries included Alaina and, if not, whether the trust should be varied to include Alaina as beneficiary.

BEARD J.:

. . .

III. Interpretation of the Will

[9] According to Thomas G. Feeney, from his text *The Canadian Law of Wills*,[90] the following rules would apply to the interpretation of this gift:

> 1. The controlling factor in construing a will is the intention of the testatrix when she executed the will, taking into account the circumstances in existence and known to that testatrix at that time.[91]

[10] The testatrix did not refer to any specific beneficiaries by name, but rather referred to "the children of my niece, LYNNE ARBEZ, and my nephew, WAYNE KINDRET." Given that Kindret had only one child and Arbez was pregnant with her first child at the date of the will, there is no indication as to whether the testatrix intended, by those words, to limit the gift to only those children in existence at the date she prepared the will, or to include children born after that date. Further, there is no direct extrinsic evidence to assist the court in determining her intention. Potentially, the class could remain open as long as there remains the potential for either Kindret or Arbez to have more children.

---

88 *Re Manners*, [1955] 1 W.L.R. 1096, [1955] 3 All E.R. 83; *Re Cairns*, [1972] 4 W.W.R. 322 (B.C.S.C.).

89 Surely, the 16-year-old was too young to consent, too?

90 Vol. 2 "Construction," 3rd ed. (Toronto/Vancouver: Butterworths, 1987).

91 *Ibid.*, p. 42.

2. Where the will and the circumstances of the case leave uncertain the time for ascertaining the members of a class, the courts rely on certain rules of convenience.[92]

[11] In this case, neither the will nor the uncontested information which has been placed before the court regarding the testatrix's circumstances at the date of the will provide further clarification as to when the testatrix intended the class of beneficiaries to close. Thus, I find that I must go on to rely on the rules of convenience to resolve this issue.

3. If the will provides for a direct or immediate gift with no provision as to the time of vesting, the class will close at the date of the testator's death, if there are *any* members of that class at that date, even though the date of payment to those beneficiaries may be postponed to a later date.[93]

[12] In this case, the rules of convenience would require that the class of beneficiaries be determined at the date of death of the testatrix. I am therefore in agreement with the executrix that the class of beneficiaries would, according to these rules, exclude Alaina as a beneficiary, as she was conceived and born after the death of the testatrix.

> [The court then went on to deal with the application to vary the trust under s. 59 of the *Trustee Act*.[94] It provides that the court may, on behalf of incapacitated beneficiaries, approve an arrangement to vary a trust that has been proposed by the capacitated beneficiaries. However, it may only do so if the arrangement appears to be for the benefit of the persons on whose behalf the court consents. The court held that the proposed variation was not contrary to the basic intention of the testatrix. It held further that, although there would be a clear financial detriment to three of the beneficiaries since their shares would decrease, there was a benefit in the form of "an enhancement of family well-being" in that each child would be treated equally and the two families would be treated equally. Finally, the court held that a prudent adult motivated not simply by selfish financial interests would be likely to accept the proposal. Accordingly, the court approved the variation.]

Notes and Questions

1. The *Charlesworth* case is unexceptional on the class closing issue. I submit, however, that it is wrong on the variation of trusts issue. The case law indicates that while family harmony and similar considerations are important aspects of "benefit," the court may not approve a variation unless there is also a financial benefit for the persons on whose behalf it approves the variation.[95]

2. A testatrix left the residue of her estate in trust to be used for the education of her late brother's great-grandchildren. When does the class close?[96]

---

92 *Ibid.*, pp. 160-161.
93 *Ibid.*, pp. 161 and 173 — Emphasis is mine.
94 R.S.M. 1987, c. T160.
95 See *Oosterhoff & Gillese: Text, Commentary and Cases on Trusts*, 5th ed. by A.H. Oosterhoff and E.E. Gillese (Scarborough: Carswell, 1998), pp. 276ff.
96 See *Long v. Long* (1979), 23 Nfld. & P.E.I.R. 234, 61 A.P.R. 234 (Nfld. T.D.).

3. A testator provided for the payment of annuities for his wife, two sisters and one other person for 20 years. At the end of that period, or upon the death of the last annuitant, whichever first occurred, he directed the trustees to pay certain legacies and to divide the income of the residue *per capita* among his grandchildren for 21 years, after which the capital of the residue was to be divided among the grandchildren then surviving *per capita*. When does the class close with respect to the gift of income; when with respect to the gift of capital?[97]

(ii) *Class Gift Postponed to Prior Interest*

If the gift to the class is postponed by a prior life interest or a direction to accumulate, *prima facie* the class closes on the death of the life tenant or at the end of the accumulation. All persons who fall within the description of the class who were living at the testator's death or who were born between that date and the death of the life tenant, or the end of the accumulation, are members of the class. If any of them die before the life tenant or the end of the accumulation, their estates take.[98]

However, if there are no persons who fall within the description of the class at the testator's death and none are born prior to the life tenant's death or the end of the accumulation, the class remains open until it closes naturally, to let in all members.

Thus in a gift, "To X for life, with remainder to the children of A equally," if A has one child, B, who is alive at the testator's death, and another, C, before X dies, the class closes at X's death. Any children born thereafter are excluded. It does not matter that both B and C predecease X, since their estates will take. If, B predeceased the testator and C is born after the testator's death and before X's death, B's estate will take nothing and C takes the whole gift. But if A had no children alive at the testator's death and none were born until after X's death, the class remains open to let in all of A's children. It will close naturally on A's death.

You should note that the gift vests in any persons who fall within the description of the class who are alive at the testator's death and who are born before the period of distribution, subject to partial divesting to let in new members.[99]

The rule is explained in *Latta v. Lowry*,[100] reproduced below.

The rule applies even though the life estate is determinable as, for example, in a gift "to A for life or until remarriage...," in which case, if the life estate is determined, the class closes at that time.[101]

The rule also applies if the subject matter of the gift is the reversion after a lease, but in that case the class will be left open until the later of the death of the

---

97 See *Re Roberts* (1978), 18 O.R. (2d) 387, 2 E.T.R. 74, 82 D.L.R. (3d) 591 (H.C.).

98 *Re Hudson* (1970), 14 D.L.R. (3d) 79 (N.S. T.D.).

99 *Ibid.*

100 (1886), 11 O.R. 517 (Ch. Div.).

101 *Re Warner*, [1918] 1 Ch. 368.

life tenant or the end of the lease,[102] unless the gift is residuary and merely includes the reversion with other property.[103]

LATTA v. LOWRY
(1886), 11 O.R. 517
Supreme Court of Ontario
[Chancery Division]

The testator, Francis Van de Bogart, died in 1829. By his will he gave certain real property to his son-in-law Emanuel Treadway for the life of Emanuel and his wife, Mary Ann, who was the testator's daughter. The remainder then went to Mary Ann's children in fee. Emanuel died in 1871 and Mary Ann in 1885.

At the date of the will Mary Ann had six children and two others were born after the testator's death. When she died only five survived, three having died between the date of the testator's death and her death, leaving issue.

A special case was brought to construe the will.

BOYD C.:

. . .

The rule laid down in *Hawkins* on Wills[104] appears to be substantiated by the authorities and is in these words:

> If real or personal estate be given to A for life, and after his decease to the children of B, all the children in existence at the testator's death take vested interest subject to be partially divested in favour of children subsequently coming into existence during the life of A.

See *Browne v. Hammond*;[105] *Middleton v. Messinger*.[106] The Court has arrived at this rule of construction impelled by the operation of two principles, *one* in favour of the early vesting of estates, and the *other* in favour of including all who come into being before the period of division: *Hutcheson v. Jones*.[107] By the terms of the will in this case the estate in remainder vested forthwith upon the testator's death in six children of his daughter then living and from time to time in the two subsequently born. The death of any child before the period of distribution does not affect the right of that child's representatives to claim the share of the one deceased. My opinion is therefore in favour of the estate being divided into eight parts and going to the living children and the representatives of the deceased children on that footing, and I so answer the case submitted.

Paradis v. Campbell[108] strongly urged for the plaintiffs, is not inconsistent with my conclusion. In that case the facts were different, for the child Henrietta had

---

102 *Harvey v. Stracey* (1852), 1 Drew. 73 at 123, 61 E.R. 379.
103 *Coventry v. Coventry* (1865), 2 Drew. & Sm. 470, 62 E.R. 699.
104 At p. 72.
105 1 Johns 212a.
106 5 Ves. 136.
107 2 Madd. 129.
108 (1883), 6 O.R. 632.

died not only before the period of division, but before the testator, so that the estate never vested in her, and could not therefore pass to her descendants.

Notes and Questions

1. What kind of life estate was given to the son-in-law in *Latta v. Lowry*?

2. A testator gave the income from the residue of his estate to his son and two daughters for life, with remainder

> equally among their issue, and should my son or daughter[s] leave no issue surviving, then in such event I give devise and bequeath that child's share to the survivor or to the issue in equal shares should a child of mine have died prior to the determination of whether the other child shall have had issue.

The three children survived the testator and at the latter's death each had children living. When does the class of issue close? Who are the "issue"?[109]

3. A testatrix devised a life estate in certain real property to her son, Joseph, and directed that the property should be sold on his death and the proceeds distributed among all her surviving children, or the issue of such children, including a share to the issue of her son Joseph. Nine of the testatrix' children, including Joseph, survived her. Five of these predeceased Joseph, leaving issue who survived Joseph; two survived Joseph; and one predeceased Joseph without issue.

When does the class close? Who are the members? Who are the "issue"? What proportions do the members take?[110]

4. Assuming that the rule applies, can a person who was adopted after the testator's death, but before the life tenant's death, share in a gift to a class if the legislation at the time of the adoption precluded his or her taking, but retroactive legislation enacted before the life tenant dies permits his or her taking, "but not as to divest any interest in property that has vested at the coming into force" of the legislation?[111]

5. A testator devised his farm to his two sons, A and B, for life, and "then to the issue of my said two sons." When is the class of issue to be determined? Who are the "issue"?[112]

6. The rule respecting postponed gifts to a class is subject to the Rule in *Bullock v. Downes*,[113] which provides that if the postponed class is composed of the testator's next of kin, as when the testator left the residue of his estate, "to A for life and then to the persons who would take as if I had died intestate," *prima facie* the class closes at the testator's death. This rule has already been examined.[114] It is commonly ousted by language displaying a contrary intention.[115]

---

109 See *Re Hudson* (1970), 14 D.L.R. (3d) 79 (N.S. T.D.). See also *Re Duckworth*, [1958] O.W.N. 236 (H.C.).

110 See *Re Hart*, [1979] 2 W.W.R. 413, 4 E.T.R. 290 (Sask. Surr. Ct.).

111 See *Re Woods; Can. Permanent Trust Co. v. Dearington* (1982), 11 E.T.R. 104, 133 D.L.R. (3d) 751 (N.S. T.D.).

112 See *Re Verdonk* (1979), 7 E.T.R. 143, 106 D.L.R. (3d) 450 (B.C.S.C.).

113 (1860), 9 H.L. Cas. 1, 11 E.R. 627.

114 In the chapter on General Principles of Interpretation.

115 See, *e.g.*, *Nat. Trust Co. v. Fleury*, [1965] S.C.R. 817, 53 D.L.R. (2d) 700; *Re Butler*, [1965] 2 O.R. 236, 50 D.L.R. (2d) 210 (C.A.); *Re Treble*, [1966] 2 O.R. 153, 56 D.L.R. (2d) 402 (C.A.); *Re Hyslop* (1978), 3 E.T.R. 216 (Ont. H.C.); *Re Johnston* (1982), 11 E.T.R. 244 (Ont. H.C.); *Re Martin* (1979), 3 E.T.R. 300 (Ont. H.C.).

(iii) *Class Gift Postponed by Condition*

The third rule of convenience, often referred to as the Rule in *Andrews v. Partington*,[116] really has two branches, since it applies to both immediate gifts to a class and class gifts postponed by a life estate or a direction to accumulate, but which is subject to a condition which is personal to the beneficiaries.

The rule provides that if there is a gift to a class when the members thereof have satisfied a condition, the class closes at the testator's death if a member of the class then in existence has satisfied the condition. If no one has, the class closes when the first member satisfies the condition. If the class gift is postponed by a prior interest or an accumulation, the class closes at the determination of that interest provided a member has then satisfied the condition. If no one has, the class closes when the first member satisfies the condition. Those persons who are in existence when the class closes but who have not yet satisfied the condition are potential members and are allowed to take if and when they do satisfy it. All others are excluded.

Thus, in a gift, "to the children of A when they marry," the class closes when the first member of the class marries. Hence, it will close at the testator's death if one of A's children who survived the testator is then married. All others then in existence are potential members who will take if and when they marry. All children of A who are born after the class closes are excluded. If no child of A who survived the testator is married at the testator's death, the class closes when the first one marries.

Similarly, in a gift "to X for life, remainder to the children of A at age 21," the class closes when the first child of A reaches age 21 and the life estate ends. Thus, if at X's death one child of A is 21, the class closes and others then in existence are potential members who will take if and when they reach that age. All children of A born after the class closes are excluded. It does not matter that a child of A reached 21 before X's death and then died before X; the class still closes at X's death. But if no child of A is 21 at X's death the class closes when the first one reaches that age.

The rule is an attempt to reconcile two inconsistent directions, namely, that the whole class should take and that the fund should be distributed amongst the class at a time when the whole class cannot be ascertained.[117] If there is no such inconsistency, the court will not apply the rule to close a class artificially.[118]

The rule applies even though no members of the class are living at the death of the life tenant or the end of the accumulation and none had previously satisfied the condition but died before that date. The class is then kept open only until the first person satisfies the condition.

---

116 (1791), 3 Bro. C.C. 401, 29 E.R. 610.

117 *Re Stephens; Kilby v. Betts*, [1904] 1 Ch. 322 at 328, *per* Buckley J.; *Re Wenmoth's Estate* (1888), 37 Ch. D. 266 at 269, *per* Chitty J., [1886-90] All E.R. Rep. 591.

118 *Re Kebty-Fletcher's Will Trusts; Pub. Trustee v. Swan*, [1969] 1 Ch. 339, [1967] 3 All E.R. 1076.

Thus in *Re Bleckly*[119] the testator gave a sum of money in trust to pay the income thereon to his daughter-in-law, Gette, while she remained his son's wife or widow, with remainder in trust for such of his son's children as should attain age 21. Two years after the testator's death the son's marriage to Gette was dissolved. There were no children of that marriage. The son then married Georgina, by whom he had two children, one of whom, Teresa, survived and became 21. It was held that the rule applied so as to close the class as soon as Teresa reached the age of 21.

The operation of the rule is explained in *Re Edmondson's Will Trusts; Baron Sandford of Banbury v. Edmondson*,[120] reproduced below.

RE EDMONDSON'S WILL TRUSTS;
BARON SANDFORD OF BANBURY v. EDMONDSON
[1972] 1 W.L.R. 183, [1972] 1 All E.R. 444
Court of Appeal

The testator, James Edmondson made his will and died in 1931. By his will he left one-fourth of the residue of his estate upon trust to pay the income therefrom to his son, later to become the first Baron Sandford, for life and thereafter in trust for such of the son's children as the son should by deed or will appoint. In 1948 Baron Sandford exercised the power to appoint by deed. By clause 1 of the deed he appointed to

> such of the children of [his] two sons...whenever born as being a son or sons shall attain the age
> of twenty one or being a daughter or daughters shall attain that age or marry as a single class and
> if more than one in equal shares.

By clause 2 the income was directed to be held for the two sons equally while they had no children. Clause 3 extended the statutory powers of maintenance and advancement to the trust. Clause 4 provided for a gift over to the two sons if the trusts in favour of their children should fail. By clause 5 the first Lord Sandford released his life interest.

In 1949 Lord Sandford conveyed certain freehold and leasehold properties to trustees on trust to retain or sell and by a contemporaneous settlement directed the trustees to hold the trust fund

> Upon trust for such of the children of [his] two sons...as being a son or sons shall attain the age
> of twenty one years or being a daughter shall attain that age or marry as a single class and if more
> than one in equal shares.

The two sons of the testator's son were John Cyril, the second Baron Sandford and Anthony James Kinghorn Edmondson. At the time of the exercise of the appointment, the second Baron Sandford had one daughter who was less than one year old and Anthony had no children. Thereafter the second Baron Sandford had three more children and Anthony had four children. All eight were still living,

---

119 [1951] Ch. 740, [1951] 1 All E.R. 1064 (C.A.).
120 [1972] 1 W.L.R. 183, [1972] 1 All E.R. 444 (C.A.).

the oldest being 23 years old and the youngest 13, three being over 21. Anthony had remarried and his second wife was only 30 years of age.

The second Baron Sandford and Anthony brought this application to interpret the will. It was held at first instance by Goulding J.[121] that the class closed, both for the purpose of the deed of appointment and the deed of settlement, on the date the eldest of the eight persons attained the age of 21.

The second Baron Sandford and Anthony appealed.

RUSSELL L.J., delivered the judgment of the Court:

· · ·

The first question concerns the appointment by the first Lord Sandford.

· · ·

We say at once that it appears to us that the question turns solely on the significance to be attached to the words 'whenever born' in the phrase in cl. 1 of the deed of appointment.... Neither side in our judgment could derive any support for its arguments from cll 2, 4 of 5 of the appointment. For the plaintiffs it was argued that the provision in cl 3 that 'the powers of maintenance and advancement implied by the Trustee Act 1925...shall apply to' the appointed funds, was inconsistent with the applicability of the rule, or at least gave some indication in that regard. We do not accept that. That clause is consistent equally with the class closing when the first member attained a vested interest (or, had it occurred later, the death of the life tenant appointor), and with the class remaining open until the death of the survivor of the appointor's two sons....

There are many reported cases on the applicability of this rule and the reasons for it. We do not think it necessary to recapitulate them. We believe that the question in this and other cases may be briefly thus stated: 'Is it clear from the language of the instrument in the circumstances in which that language is used that the rule is not applicable?' In the present case without the words 'whenever born' in cl 1 there is no doubt that the rule would apply. In the reported cases there are instances in which phrases descriptive of the class in apparently unlimited and general terms have been held not to exclude the rule, on the ground that they were capable of referring only to the period before the application of the rule would close the class. Among such phrases we find 'all the children...whether now born or hereafter to be born'; 'all and every the children of X'; 'the children of X as many as there might be'; 'all or any the children or child of X'. Goulding J.[122] considered that it would be too great a refinement to draw a distinction between such phrases (and in particular the phrase 'whether now living or hereafter to be born') and the words 'whenever born'. He described as tempting, and we think that in the end he succumbed to the temptation, to say that both phrases covered the future without any express limit and, therefore, why should the latter

---

121 [1971] 3 All E.R. 1121.
122 [1971] 3 All E.R. at 1128, [1971] 1 W.L.R. at 1660.

phrase disclose an intention to hold up the possibility of distribution of the shares of those with a vested interest?

We do not find this proposition thus tempting. In our view there is an important distinction between the two phrases. The former is a general phrase pointing towards the future and, therefore, to some time in the future. The phrase 'whenever born' is in our view a specific and emphatic phrase which in terms points to all time in the future. It is equivalent to 'at whatever time they may be born', and is limited only by the course of nature to the lifetime of the parents. If the phrase had been 'whenever in the lifetime of their respective parents born' there could be surely no doubt that the class was clearly defined as remaining open to membership by all grandchildren: just as was the case in *Scott v. Earl of Scarborough*[123] where the phrase was 'hereafter be born, during the lifetime of their respective parents'....If the phrase used was 'now born or hereafter at whatever time to be born' surely the rule would be excluded; and 'whenever born' is to our minds the precise equivalent. In summary the phrase 'born or hereafter to be born' is a general reference to the future without express limit in time and, therefore, consistent with a limit in time proposed by the direction for vesting and the rule. But 'whenever born' is a particular reference to the future expressly unlimited in time and, therefore, readily to be distinguished as inconsistent with a time limitation such as is imposed by the rule.

. . .

Accordingly in our judgment the rule in *Andrews v. Partington*[124] is excluded in the case of the appointment by the words 'whenever born' and the class will embrace all children of the sons whether born before or after the attainment by the first of a vested interest on 7th November 1968. On this aspect of the case the appeal will be allowed and an appropriate declaration substituted.

We turn now to the second part of the case.

[His Lordship described the settlement of 1949 and continued:]

The words 'whenever born' were absent. Prima facie, therefore, the rule applies and the class closed on 7th November 1968.

[Accordingly, the court dismissed the appeal on this point.]

Notes and Questions

1. A testator gave the residue of his estate to a number of objects for 21 years. Thereafter, he directed that two-fifths of the residue be held in trust for the child or children or remoter issue of his son, R, as R should appoint by will and in default of appointment in trust for all of R's children who being sons should attain age 21, or being daughters should attain that age or marry.

---

123 (1838), 1 Beav. 154.
124 (1791), 3 Bro. C.C. 401, [1775-1802] All E.R. Rep. 209.

The testator died in 1905. R had one son, A, who became 21 in 1916. In 1924 R released his power of appointment. In 1925 A died, having left his estate to R. The 21-year postponement ended in 1926. Does the rule apply?[125]

2. A testator, who died in 1918, left the residue of his estate upon trust for each of his nephews and nieces for life and after the death of a nephew or niece upon trust for the child or children of the niece or nephew, if male at age 21 and if female at that age or upon marriage.

One of the nephews, G, released his life interest to the trustee in 1960, to the intent that the income would be held upon the same trusts as if G were then dead. At that time G had two children, A and B. In 1963 A become 21. G is still living. Does the rule apply?[126]

3. A testatrix directed her trustees to hold certain property in trust and to use the income for the education of the children of her grandson, R. She directed that any income not used for that purpose should be accumulated until the youngest of R's children should attain age 21 and thereafter to hold the property and accumulated income upon trust for such of R's children as should then be living in equal shares.

R had a son, D, by his first marriage, who reached age 21. An infant daughter died unmarried. By R's second marriage there were no children. Is D entitled to the property?[127]

4. It will be apparent that a class gift postponed by a condition may readily infringe the rule against perpetuities. However, the class closing rules can save the gift if the class closes so as to exclude remote members. Although this matter will be dealt with in a later chapter,[128] it is useful at this point to see how this question is dealt with.

The issue arose in *Re Deeley's Settlement.*[129] In that case the settlor, in 1962, had directed that separate shares of a trust fund be held in trust for each of A, B and C for life and thereafter for their respective issue at age 21. At the date of the settlement A and B had children living or *en ventre sa mère*, but C did not. None was yet 21.

The court held that the word "issue" could not be read as children because there was not a sufficient context to do so. Hence, if the class closing rule applied, it would be possible for issue to take more than 21 years after the death of the life in being, that is, A, B and C in respect of the three classes. The court concluded that it would be absurd to take the word "issue" in its literal meaning and that, therefore, the testator intended only those persons to take who were born before the death of each life tenant and who survived the life tenant. Those persons would of course have to satisfy the age contingency if they had not already done so. All others were intended to be excluded. On that interpretation there was no perpetuity.

The *Deeley* case should, however, be contrasted with *Re Drummond's Settlement, Foster et al. v. Foster*[130] In *Drummond* the gift was to the testator's daughters and was similar to the one in *Deeley*, but continued with an accruer clause to the effect that if any of the testator's daughters died before taking a vested share, that share was to be divided among such of the daughters then living and the issue of any of them as should then be dead, the issue taking their parent's share on attaining age 21 or marrying under that age. The court held the accruer clause void for perpetuity.

---

125 See *Re Charters*, [1927] 1 Ch. 466.
126 See *Re Kebty-Fletcher's Will Trusts; Pub. Trustee v. Swan*, [1969] 1 Ch. 339, [1967] 3 All E.R. 1076.
127 See *Re Ransome; Moberly v. Ransome*, [1957] Ch. 348, [1957] 1 All E.R. 690.
128 See the chapter on Perpetuities and Accumulations, *infra*.
129 [1974] Ch. 454, [1973] 3 All E.R. 1127.
130 [1986] 3 All E.R. 45.

(c) Gifts to Each Member of a Class

If the gift is not a true class gift, but rather a gift of money to each member of a group of persons described by a common characteristic, another rule of convenience is applied. The rule in this case is that if there is an immediate gift of a separate amount to each member of a class, *prima facie* the class closes at the testator's death and only those then living are members or potential members. It matters not that the gift is postponed by a condition. Moreover, if no members or potential members of the class are living at the testator's death the class closes nevertheless.[131]

The reason for this strict rule is that there would be great inconvenience to the estate if it were otherwise, for if the class were kept open longer, the number of legacies might increase and the personal representatives could not distribute the estate until they knew the total amount required. This is not the case with a true class gift, since the total amount of such a gift is known.

Thus, if a testator gives $1,000 "to each of the children of A at age 21" and, at the testator's death, A has no children, the gift fails. If A has one child, B, who is 21, and another, C, who is 15, B can receive his or her legacy immediately, but C must wait until he or she becomes 21. Any afterborn children of A are excluded. Of course, if C dies before age 21, his or her share reverts to the estate; it does not go to augment B's share.

The rule is explained in *Re Bellville; Westminster Bank Ltd. v. Walton*,[132] reproduced below.

The rule, it is submitted, also applies when the legacies are postponed to a life interest. In other words, the class is then not kept open until the life tenant's death, for the inconvenience to the estate would be the same. However, the rule does not apply if the testator obviates the inconvenience by providing a fund, the income of which is to go to one person for life and thereafter aliquot portions thereof to his or her children at age 21.[133]

The rule also does not apply if the will evinces a contrary intention, as when the testator defers payment of the legacies until a future time, such as after the death of the life tenant.[134]

---

131 *Rogers v. Mutch* (1878), 10 Ch. D. 25.

132 [1941] Ch. 414, [1941] 2 All E.R. 629 (C.A.).

133 See *Defflis v. Goldschmidt* (1816), 19 Ves. 566, 35 E.R. 727; *Evans v. Harris* (1842), 5 Beav. 45, 49 E.R. 493.

134 *Ibid.*, and see *A.G. v. Crispin* (1784), 1 Bro. C.C. 386, 28 E.R. 1192; *Hawkins and Ryder on the Construction of Wills*, by E.C. Ryder (London: Sweet & Maxwell Limited, 1965), pp. 127-8.

RE BELLVILLE;
WESTMINSTER BANK LTD. v. WALTON
[1941] 1 Ch. 414, [1941] 2 All E.R. 629
Chancery Division

The testator, William John Bellville, who died in 1937, left a will in which he gave Mrs Audrey Belville, the wife of his nephew, Anthony Seymor Belville, £2,000 if she had another son born after the testator's death. Further, he directed that the sum of £10,000 be paid to any daughter of the Anthony and Audrey "who shall be born after the date of this my will but who shall be born before any further son born to my nephew Anthony Seymour Bellville."

Anthony and Audrey had three children, Belinda, Jeremy and Camilla, born in 1930, 1931 and 1939, respectively.

The executors brought an application to interpret the will. It was held at first instance by Farwell J. that only Belinda and Jeremy were entitled to their legacies. Camilla appealed.

LUXMOORE L.J, delivered the judgment of the Court:

. . .

We are unable to accept the view that, if the words of the gift "to any daughter or daughters of my nephew Anthony Seymour Bellville who shall be born after the date of my will" had stood alone, Camilla Audrey Bellville would be qualified to receive a legacy of 10,000*l*. That view is, we think, contrary to a long line of authority to which the attention of the learned judge was not called and which has established that the rule which (as is stated in Hawkins on Wills)[135]

> admits objects born after a testator's death and before the period of distribution to share in a bequest only applies when the total amount of the gift is independent of the number of objects among whom it is to be divided and is therefore not increased by the construction adopted. But a gift of a certain sum to each of a class of objects at a future period is confined to those living at the testator's death. Thus under a gift of 500*l* to all and every the children of A payable at 21 children born after the testator's death and before the eldest child attains 21 are included, if the gift be of 50*l* each to all and every the children of A payable at 21 the children living at the testator's death alone are entitled....The reason given is that in the latter case if after born children were admitted the distribution of the personal estate of the testator would have to be postponed till it could be ascertained how many legacies of the given quantity would be payable.

This passage was cited with approval by Jessel M.R. in *Rogers v. Mutch*....[136]

The rule, of course, does not apply when the inconvenience referred to by Mr. Hawkins in the passage quoted does not exist or is expressly contemplated by the testator....

It follows that, in our opinion, the correct method of construing the gift in the present case is to consider whether there is anything in the testator's will to

---

135 1st ed., p. 73.
136 10 Ch. D. 25, 27.

prevent the application of the rule, and that, if there is no sufficient indication of the testator's intention so to do, the duty of the court is to apply the rule....

> [The court held that there was nothing in the will to exclude the operation of the rule and concluded:]

[W]e are, therefore, of opinion that the rule applies to the present case and that the appellant, Camilla Audrey Bellville, is not entitled to the legacy in question. For these reasons we think the appeal fails and must be dismissed.

Notes and Questions

1. A testator gave legacies of $1,000 each to the children of his nephew, G, at age 21. At the testator's death G had several children, although none was yet 21. G's son, K, was *en ventre sa mère* at the testator's death, while his son, S, was born one year later. Are K and S each entitled to a legacy?[137]

2. By a codicil to her will a testatrix left a legacy of $5,000 to each of her grandchildren living at the date of the codicil "and any other grandchildren arriving later than" the date of the codicil, all to take at age 21. At the date of the codicil she had 5 grandchildren, all of whom survived her. One year after her death, A, another grandchild, was born. Is A entitled to a legacy?[138]

Further Reading

J.G. Riddall, "Developments in the Rule in Andrews v. Partington" (1970), 34 Conv. 393.

---

137 See *Re MacEwen*, [1963] 2 O.R. 490, 40 D.L.R. (2d) 152 (H.C.).
138 See *Rempel v. Braun* (1978), 3 E.T.R. 46 (Man. Q.B.).

14

VESTED AND CONTINGENT GIFTS AND VOID CONDITIONS

1. SCOPE OF THIS CHAPTER

In this chapter we discuss the abstruse learning of conditional gifts. In the first half of the chapter we shall consider first the distinction between vested and contingent interests and then the general principles and specific rules of construction used to determine whether an interest is vested or contingent. In the second half of the chapter we shall discuss conditions and limitations that are void for public policy, uncertainty and other reasons.

Further Reading

Edward H. Rabin, "The Law Favours the Vesting of Estates. Why?" (1965), 65 Col. L. Rev. 467.

Williams' Law Relating to Wills, 7 th ed. by C.H. Sherrin, R.F.D. Barlow, and R.A. Wallington (London: Butterworths,1995), chs. 34, 35, 93.

Hawkins and Ryder on the Construction of Wills, by E.C. Ryder (London: Sweet & Maxwell Limited, 1965), ch. 17.

Feeney's Canadian Law of Wills, 4th ed., loose leaf, by Thomas G. Feeney & James Mackenzie (Toronto: Butterworths, 2000), chs. 16, 17.

2. VESTED AND CONTINGENT GIFTS

(a) Background

There is perhaps no more recondite learning in the law of property generally and in the law of wills in particular than that concerning the law of vesting. The law in this area is replete with rules, exceptions to rules and exceptions to the exceptions. One of the reasons for the anfractuosity of the law in this area is that some rules derive from feudal common law; others, originally concerned with dispositions of personal property, find their origin in rules developed by the ecclesiastical courts while they had jurisdiction over testaments of personal property. The whole is overlaid with principles of equity, developed in Chancery when that court acquired jurisdiction over matters testamentary.

Moreover, many of the rules or exceptions thereto have developed because the courts were anxious to give effect to the intentions of particular testators. In contrast, other courts have adhered strictly to the received rules. These factors must be kept in mind when reconciliation of cases is sometimes difficult.

This is not to say that the situation is an acceptable one. In many respects the rules are a blot upon our jurisprudence and an affront to civilized society. However, it means that the law in this area can only be understood in its historical context. What is required in this area is a thorough reform designed to retain that which is good and to rationalize it, and to consign that which, while it may once have been relevant in a different age, is now spent to the dustbin.

(b) Meanings and Distinctions

(i) *Generally*

An interest may be either vested or contingent. In the context of wills contingent interests are often called executory, but there is no real difference between the two terms today, although they retain distinct meanings in the context of interests created by deed.

The term "vested" can mean either "vested in possession" or "vested in interest." The former means that the interest is presently being enjoyed by its owner and if it is vested in that sense, it is also vested in interest. "Vested in interest" refers to an interest that stands ready to fall into possession as soon all preceding interests have determined naturally. Unless the context indicates a different interpretation, the term "vested" means "vested in interest" and is used in that sense in this chapter.

An interest is vested if,
  (a) it is limited to a person who is
        (i) in existence, and
        (ii) ascertained, and
  (b) it is not subject to a condition precedent.

An interest is contingent if it does not satisfy one or more of these criteria, as in a gift, "to A for life, then to B for life, then to C absolutely when C attains the age of 21." In this example, the interests of A and B are vested, but C's interest is contingent. It will become vested if and when C attains the age of 21, that being the condition precedent C must satisfy before becoming entitled to the gift.

A condition precedent attached to a gift is a condition of its acquisition. Until it is satisfied, as in a gift "to A if she attains age of 25," the gift remains in suspense. Hence, it is also referred to as a "suspensive condition."

A condition subsequent, on the other hand, is a condition which goes to the retention of the gift. It is annexed to a gift that is vested and permits it to be divested if the event provided for in the condition occurs. Hence, it is also called a resolutive condition. Thus, in a gift, "to A, but if he ceases to use the land as a farm, the property shall revert to my estate," A has a vested interest, but he will lose the property if he uses it for a purpose other than a farm.

The distinction between vested and contingent interests is important in a number of respects, for example:

(1) The owner of a vested interest will receive the subject-matter of the gift automatically when all prior interests determine, while the owner of a contingent interest will receive nothing if he or she dies before the contingency is satisfied.

(2) A vested interest may accelerate if a preceding interest is destroyed; a contingent interest may not.

(3) Whether an interest is vested or contingent is important for the application of the rule against perpetuities.

(4) A contingent interest may not always be alienable.

(ii) *Types of Vested Interest*

(A) *Introduction.* Although an interest may be vested, it is not necessarily vested absolutely. It may be subject to divestment in whole or in part by the operation of a condition subsequent or for another reason. We may therefore distinguish the following three types of vested interest:

(B) *Absolutely or Indefeasibly Vested Interests.* These are interests that are vested at the testator's death and cannot be defeated. Thus, in a gift, "to A for life, remainder to B absolutely," B's remainder is vested indefeasibly. If he or she predeceases A, B's estate will take the interest. In contrast, in a gift, "to A for life, remainder to B for life, remainder to C absolutely," although C's interest is vested indefeasibly, B's is not, since it is a limited interest and B may not survive A to take it. It is, therefore, vested subject to complete divestment.[1]

(C) *Interests Vested Subject to Partial Divestment.* These are interests that are vested at the testator's death, but which may be defeated in part thereafter. This type of interest is common in class gifts which are postponed to a prior life interest and those which are subject to a condition. Even though one or more persons already qualify for the gift at the testator's death or when one satisfies the condition, other persons are let in before the class closes, that is, those who were born during the life tenancy or before the first person satisfies the condition and, in the latter case, who satisfy the condition themselves in due course.[2] To that extent, therefore the interests of those who originally qualified for the gift are divested.

---

1 American Law of Property, A. James Casner, Ed.-in-chief (Boston: Little, Brown, 1952-54), §§ 4.33, 4.35.

2 See the previous chapter.

Thus, in a gift, "to A for life, remainder to all her children at age 21," if A has a child, X, who is 21 at the testator's death and two other children who have not yet reached that age, Y and Z, X's interest is divested in part when Y and Z respectively reach age 21.

Gifts in default of appointment may be divested in whole or in part by the exercise of the power.[3]

(D) *Interests Vested Subject to Complete Divestment.* These are interests that are given in remainder and that are less than absolute interests, interests given in default of appointment and interests given upon a condition subsequent.

Thus, in a gift, "to A for life, remainder to B for life," B's interest is subject to complete divestment, since he or she may not survive A to take. If B's interest were absolute, such as a fee simple, or a comparable interest in personal property, it would be vested absolutely.

Similarly, in a gift, "to A for life, remainder to such of A's children as she shall appoint, but if she fails to appoint then to B," B's interest is construed as being vested subject to complete divestment if A appoints to her children.[4]

A gift, "to A for life, remainder to B absolutely, but if B does not marry, then to C," gives B a vested interest subject to complete divestment if B does not marry, in other words, if the condition subsequent, "if B does not marry," is fulfilled.

(iii) *Types of Contingent Interest*

There are certain contingent interests which operate at common law. These are called contingent remainders. They can nowadays only be created by grant[5] and can, therefore, be disregarded in this book. Other legal future interests, namely springing and shifting executory interests created by means of a deed to uses, which uses are executed by the *Statute of Uses*,[6] can also be disregarded since they can, today, also be created only by deed.[7]

Springing and shifting executory interests created under wills, although formerly legal if not established under a trust, are now all equitable[8] by virtue of the statutory trust imposed upon the personal representative by section 2 of the *Estates*

---

3 See *Henderson v. Eileen Henderson Trust* (1990), 38 E.T.R. 120 (Ont. H.C.).

4 See *ibid*. The case involved a gift of residue in trust for X for life, remainder equally to her children, but subject to the exercise by X of a power of appointment in favour of her issue and subject to a child or children dying before X leaving issue surviving X. Thus, the children's interests were defeasible in two situations.

5 See *Re Robson; Douglass v. Douglass*, [1916] 1 Ch. 116; and see generally Derek Mendes da Costa, Richard J. Balfour and Eileen E. Gillese, *Property Law: Cases, Text and Materials*, 2nd ed. (1990), ch. 16. *Re Crow* (1984), 48 O.R. (2d) 36, 17 E.T.R. 1, 12 D.L.R. (4th) 415 (H.C.), which holds otherwise, must be regarded as wrongly decided, since the *Robson* case appears not to have been cited to, or considered by, the court.

6 27 Hen. 8, c. 10 (1535).

7 Mendes da Costa and Balfour, *supra*, ch. 19.

8 *Re Robson, supra*.

Administrative Act.[9] Such interests, although equitable, nevertheless satisfy the criteria for all contingent gifts, namely, that they are limited to a person unborn or unascertained, or are subject to a condition precedent. Hence, in a gift, "to A when he marries," A's interest is contingent. Similarly, in a gift, "to all the children of A," the gift is contingent if A has no children as yet. So also, a gift of a house to X "if he wishes to live in it," followed by a direction for sale and division of the proceeds if he does not, is contingent.[10]

Interests created by will which are not contingent, but vested, are remainders and reversions. These interests are also equitable.

If the gift to one person is liable to be defeated by reason of an unfilled condition subsequent and the gift is then directed to go to another, the condition subsequent is a condition precedent to the latter's taking and his or her interest is often described as an executory gift over.

(c) General Principles of Vesting

(i) *Introduction*

The law has developed certain general principles of interpretation in relation to the question whether a gift is vested or contingent. These are particularizations of the general principle that the law favours vested gifts. Since these principles are commonly encountered, they are outlined below. They only apply if the testator's intention is unclear or ambiguous and do not operate so as to defeat a clearly expressed contrary intention.[11]

(ii) *Presumption in Favour of Early Vesting*

The law presumes that the testator intended the interest to vest at his or her death or at the earliest moment thereafter as is consonant with the terms of the will.[12] The reason for this presumption was aptly explained by Lord Seldon in the leading case, *Duffield v. Duffield:*[13]

---

9 R.S.O. 1990, c. E.22. The following are the comparable provisions in the other provinces: *Chattels Real Act,* R.S.N. 1990, c. C-11, s. 2; *Devolution of Estates Act,* R.S.N.B. 1973, c. D-9, s. 3; *Devolution of Real Property Act,* R.S.A. 1980, c. D-34, ss. 2, 3; R.S.S. 1978, c. D-27, ss. 4, 5; R.S.N.W.T., 1988, c. D-5, ss. 2, 3; R.S.Y. 1986, c. 45, ss. 2-3; *Estate Administration Act,* R.S.B.C. 1996, c. 122, ss. 77, 78; *Law of Property Act,* R.S.M. 1987, c. L90, s. 17.3(1)-(5) [added by 1989-90, c. 43, s. 14]; *Probate Act,* R.S.P.E.I. 1988, c. P-21, ss. 103, 104; *Real Property Act,* R.S.N.S. 1989, c. 385 , s. 1.

10 See *Davis Estate v. Thomas* (1990), 40 E.T.R. 107 (B.C.C.A.).

11 *Fast v. Van Vliet* (1965), 51 W.W.R. 65 at 77, 49 D.L.R. (2d) 616 (Man. C.A.), *per* Monnin J.A.; *Re Taylor,* [1972] 3 O.R. 349, 28 D.L.R. (3d) 257 at 259 (H.C.), *per* Lacourcière J.; *Re Carlson,* [1975] 5 W.W.R. 745 at 748, 55 D.L.R. (3d) 616 (B.C.S.C.), *per* MacFarlane J.

12 *Bickersteth v. Shanu,* [1936] A.C. 290, [1936] 1 All E.R. 227, [1936] 1 W.W.R. 644 (P.C.); *Re Duffield,* [1971] 1 O.R. 515, 16 D.L.R. (3d) 7 at 11 (H.C.), *per* Stark J.; *Re Taylor, supra,* at D.L.R. 259 (H.C.), *per* Lacourcière J.; *Re Down,* [1968] 2 O.R. 16 at 22, 68 D.L.R. (2d) 30

Whilst estates remain contingent, those in whom they are at a future time to be vested, have no interest in the estates, or the rents and profits of such estates.

Such estates must descend to the heir, if they are not given to any person to hold until the events happen, on which they are to become vested. This point is too clear to require any observation; indeed, it was not disputed at the bar. Testators who create contingent estates, often forget to make any provision for the preservation of their estates, and for the disposition of the rents and profits in the intermediate period, between their deaths and the vesting of their estates. In such cases, the estates descend to the heirs, who, knowing that they are to enjoy them only for a short period, and that they have obtained the possession of them from the inattention of, and not from the bounty of the testator, or from the mistake of the professional man who drew the will, will make the most that they can of them during the time that they remain theirs, regardless of any injury that the estates may suffer from their conduct. The rights of the different members of families not being ascertained whilst estates remain contingent, such families continue in an unsettled state, which is often productive of inconvenience, and sometimes of injury to them. If the parents attaining a certain age, be a condition precedent to the vesting estates by the death of their parents, before they are of that age, children lose estates which were intended for them, and which their relation to the testators may give them the strongest claim to.

The presumption applies to class gifts[14] as well as to gifts to individuals and other persons.[15] It is ousted, however, if the language of the will suggests a later date for vesting.[16]

(iii) *Presumption in Favour of Condition Subsequent*

If a condition is capable of being interpreted either as a condition precedent or as a condition subsequent and an interpretation as a condition subsequent is consonant with the will as a whole and is not contrary to the testator's intention, it will be construed as a condition subsequent. The reason is that the interest will then be vested, although subject to divestment, rather than contingent.[17]

Thus, in *Re Fulton*,[18] the testatrix devised her farm to her son, but went on to provide, "in the event of my son...dying without issue my...said farm shall be divided equally between all my children." It was held that, since the gift was not framed in terms strongly suggesting a condition precedent, the general principle should be applied and the condition should be construed as subsequent. Hence, the farm vested in the son is subject to divestment.

In contrast, a condition attached to the gift of a testator's estate to his grand-daughter that she come to Canada and make it her permanent home, was held to

---

(C.A.), *per* Laskin J.A., affirmed [1969] S.C.R. v; *Re Goian Estate*, 139 Sask. R. 29, [1996] 2 W.W.R. 614 (Q.B.).

13   (1829), 3 Bli. (N.S.) 260 at 330-1, 4 E.R. 1334, 1 Dow & Cl. 395, 6 E.R. 573 (H.L.).

14   *Re Prast* (1927), 32 O.W.N. 107 (H.C.); and see the previous chapter.

15   See, *e.g.*, *McDonell v. McDonell* (1894), 24 O.R. 468 (H.C.).

16   See, *e.g.*, *Keating v. Cassels* (1865), 24 U.C.Q.B. 314 (C.A.), devise to A and his wife for life and the survivor of them with remainder to their children or the survivors of them, vesting held to be postponed until death of surviving life tenant.

17   *Duffield v. Duffield, supra*; *Re Greenwood; Goodhart v. Woodhead*, [1903] 1 Ch. 749 at 755, [1900-3] All E.R. Rep. 332 (C.A.); *Sifton v. Sifton*, [1938] A.C. 656 at 676, [1938] 2 W.W.R. 465, (sub nom. *Re Sifton*) [1938] O.R. 529, [1938] 3 D.L.R. 577, *per* Lord Romer.

18   (1978), 19 O.R (2d) 458, 2 E.T.R. 89, 85 D.L.R. (3d) 291 (C.A.).

be a condition precedent.[19] Similarly, a gift of the testator's entire estate to three nephews provided they qualified by becoming residents of Canada, was held to be a condition precedent.[20]

(iv) *Presumption in Favour of Vested Interests*

This presumption, which is closely akin to the preceding two, is applicable particularly to remainders and gifts of residue. If a remainder is construed as contingent, not only will the person entitled to the remainder not take, but his or her issue will be excluded as well, since they would normally take via the estate of the person entitled to the remainder on his or her death.[21] Similarly, if the residuary gift is held to be contingent and it fails, there will be an intestacy.[22]

Thus, in *Re Smith*,[23] the testator made a gift to A for life, with remainder to A's children and a gift over to the children of any child of A who should die before the period of distribution. The court held that A's children who survived the testator took a vested remainder. Hence, since a child of A predeceased him without issue, his widow took his share, since the share was subject to divestment only if the child died before the period of distribution leaving issue.[24]

(v) *Presumption in Favour of Postponement of Enjoyment*

If it is possible to construe the language of a gift as merely postponing the right to enjoyment instead of postponing vesting, it will be so construed.[25] Thus, if the words of contingency can be used as meaning "subject to the interest previously limited," as when phrases such as "at the death" or "after the death" of the preceding beneficiary are construed, the subsequent beneficiary has a vested interest. He or she does not then have to survive the prior beneficiary in order to take, for the words merely indicate the time of enjoyment or possession of the gift.[26]

---

19 *Melnik (Melnyk) v. Sawycky*, [1978] 1 W.W.R. 107, 2 E.T.R. 120, 80 D.L.R. (3d) 371 (Sask. C.A.).
20 *Unger v. Gossen* (1996), 13 E.T.R. (2d) 194 (B.C.S.C.).
21 *Driver d. Frank v. Frank* (1814), 3 M. & S. 25 at 38, 105 E.R. 521, affirmed 8 Taunt. 468, 129 E.R. 465.
22 *Pearman v. Pearman* (1864), 33 Beav. 394 at 396, 55 E.R. 420.
23 61 O.L.R. 412, [1928] 1 D.L.R. 179 (C.A.).
24 See also *Re Brennan* (1978), 28 N.S.R. (2d) 411, 43 A.P.R. 411 (T.D.).
25 *Duffield v. Duffield* (1829), 1 Dow & Cl. 268 at 311, 6 E.R. 525.
26 *Re Leckie* (1921), 20 O.W.N. 478 at 479 (H.C.); *Re Lishman* (1920), 19 O.W.N. 365 (H.C.).

(vi) *Presumption in Favour of Indefeasible Interests*

While the courts prefer interests that are vested subject to divestment to contingent interests, they also prefer absolutely vested interests to those that are subject to divestment.

An example of this principle may be found in *Parkes v. Trusts Corp. of Ontario*.[27] In that case the testator devised a farm in trust for his grandson but, if he died before attaining age 21, the farm was to be transferred to his father. Since the father died before the grandson, the divesting condition could no longer occur and, therefore, although the grandson died before he became 21, nevertheless, it was held that his estate had become absolute.[28]

(d) Specific Principles of Vesting

(i) *Introduction*

The general principle in construing apparently contingent gifts is that all words importing futurity, whether conditional or merely temporal, make the gift *prima facie* contingent. Thus, a gift to a person "if," or "provided that," a specified event occurs, will be contingent. Similarly if words such as "at," or "upon" the occurrence of an event, or "when," "as," or "from and after" its occurrence are used, the gift will *prima facie* be contingent.[29] No distinction is drawn between conditional and temporal words, since the latter denote the time when the gift takes effect and are, thus, equivalent to words of condition.[30]

Thus, a gift, "to X when he attains the age of 25," is *prima facie* contingent[31] and a class gift, "to the children of X when they attain the age of 25 or marry" is also *prima facie* contingent.[32]

The *prima facie* principle is, however, subject to a contrary intention and, in view of the general principles regarding vesting discussed above, the courts readily find a contrary intention. In the following material, therefore, exceptions to the *prima facie* principle will be discussed.

(ii) *Gifts over on Death Generally*

(A) *The Rules in Edwards v. Edwards*. A testator will often purport to make a gift over or a substitutional gift on the death of the primary beneficiary, without specifying when the death must occur before the gift over takes effect. To solve

---

27 (1895), 26 O.R. 494 (H.C.).
28 See also *Re Clark Estate* (1993), 50 E.T.R. 105 (B.C.S.C.).
29 *Re Francis*, [1905] 2 Ch. 295; *Re Pfrimmer*, [1945] 2 W.W.R. 142, [1945] 3 D.L.R. 518 (Man. K.B.).
30 *Hanson v. Graham* (1801), 6 Ves. Jun. 239 at 243, 31 E.R. 1030, *per* Grant M.R.
31 *Re Francis, supra*.
32 *Leake v. Robinson* (1817), 2 Mer. 363, 35 E.R. 979.

the problem, certain rules of construction known as the rules in *Edwards v. Edwards*[33] were devised. These rules are as follows, the fourth rule being derived from *O'Mahoney v. Burdett*[34] which overruled the original fourth rule as stated in *Edwards v. Edwards*:

Rule 1: If there is an *immediate* gift to a person absolutely, with a gift over to another person in the event of the first person's death, *prima facie* the gift over is construed as a gift over only in the event of the first taker predeceasing the testator.

Thus, if the testator gives property "to A, and if A dies, to B," *prima facie* A's interest vests absolutely if he or she survives the testator. If A predeceases the testator, B takes a vested interest.

Rule 2: If there is a *postponed* gift to a person absolutely, with a gift over to another person in the event of the first person's death, *prima facie* the gift over is construed as a gift over only in the event of the death of the first taker during the lifetime of the testator or during the lifetime of the life tenant.

Thus, if the testator gives a legacy "to X for life, remainder to Y, but if Y dies, to Z," *prima facie*, Y takes a vested interest if he or she survives the testator, but it is subject to defeasance if Y dies before X. If Y survives X, his or her interest becomes absolute. But if Y predeceases the testator or survives the testator but predeceases X, Z takes a vested interest.

Rule 3: If there is an *immediate* gift, with a gift over on death coupled with an express contingency, *prima facie* the gift over will take effect whenever the death of the first taker occurs *and* the contingency is satisfied.

Thus, in a gift, "to A, but if she dies without leaving issue, to B," *prima facie* B will take only whenever A dies and the contingency is satisfied.

Rule 4: If there is a *postponed* gift, with a gift over on death coupled with an express contingency, *prima facie* the gift over will take effect whenever the death of the first taker occurs *and* the contingency is satisfied.

Thus, in a gift, "to X for life and then to A, but if A dies without leaving issue, to B," as in the third rule, *prima facie* B will take only whenever A dies and the contingency is satisfied.[35]

The rules are ousted if the will discloses a contrary intention. This is explored in *Re Brailsford*,[36] reproduced below.

RE BRAILSFORD
[1916] 2 Ch. 536
Chancery Division

The testator devised some real property upon certain trusts during the life of his widow, with remainder to his son, and with a gift over to the survivor of the son and the testator's daughter, "his or her heirs and assigns" if the son should

---

33 (1852), 15 Beav. 357, 51 E.R. 576, *per* Romilly M.R.

34 (1874), L.R. 7 H.L. 388, *per* Lord Cairns L.C.

35 Concerning the meaning of expressions such as "die without issue" generally, see the chapter on General Principles of Interpretation.

36 [1916] 2 Ch. 536.

die without issue him surviving. There was an alternative gift over to the son's child or children if the son should die leaving issue him surviving. The widow survived the testator, but predeceased the son. An application was made to interpret the will. At issue was whether the son's interest vested on the widow's death.

SARGANT J.:

. . .

This is a difficult case and very near the line. The question is whether the gift over following the gifts under which the children of the testator take is to be construed so as to apply generally to death leaving or not leaving issue at any time or is to be confined to a more limited period so as to apply only to death leaving or not leaving issue during the lifetime of the widow.

. . .

The two alternative events on which the gift over is to take effect are therefore absolutely exhaustive and comprise every possible contingency, and, that being so, the question is whether there is enough in those provisions of the will to exclude the *prima facie* rule laid down in *O'Mahoney v. Burdett*,[37] namely, that a reference to the death of a devisee or legatee coupled with a contingency must be construed as extending to the whole lifetime of the latter and is not to be limited to the lifetime of any prior person, in this case the lifetime of the widow.

. . .

It is contended in the present case that there is a sufficient expression of a contrary intention. It is said that the manifest intention is that there shall be a division of the property at the death of the widow. No doubt the property in question will in all probability be the only property of the testator and will be divided in this sense, that the real estate devised to the son will be handed over to him, although the other property may be retained by the trustees in order to carry out the trust for the separate use of the daughter. But on the whole I do not lay any great stress upon this view of the matter....

But a much more cogent reason for the contention is to be found in the fact that the property is expressly devised to the son, "his heirs and assigns," while if the two alternative gifts over are to be read as taking effect on the son's death whenever it occurs, the combined effect of the gifts over is to cut down what is prima facie an absolute interest to one which is in substance indistinguishable from a life estate. It is true that in point of law there is no objection to the gift of an estate in fee simple coupled with two executory devises which are exhaustive and provide for every event; but it is a curious intention to ascribe to the testator that where by marked words of limitation he has placed the devisee in the position of an absolute owner he should immediately afterwards reduce him practically to a position no better than that of a life tenant; and, bearing in mind that the

---

37 (1874), L.R. 7 H.L. 388.

presumption laid down in *O'Mahoney v. Burdett*[38] is only a prima facie presumption, I think that the marked use of words giving an estate of inheritance to the devisee is so far repugnant to a construction of the will which would reduce him practically to the position of a life tenant as to make it reasonable and proper for the Court to limit the time for the operation of the gifts over in such a way as to put the son in the position of being possibly entitled to become at some time during his life the absolute owner of the property.

. . .

In my own opinion this incompatibility between a definite devise in fee simple and the insignificance of the estate to which it would be reduced if the gifts over were held to operate at any time during the life of the devisee in fee simple is sufficient to exclude the prima facie rule laid down in *O'Mahoney v. Burdett*.[39]

Notes and Questions

1. A testatrix gave her husband her entire estate for life with remainder equally to her five children. She went on to provide that if any of the children should die without issue, that child or children's share should be divided among the other children then living, and if any of the children should die leaving issue, then the issue should take their parent's share. The testatrix was survived by her husband and the five children. The husband then died. Thereafter a daughter died survived by issue. Later a son died without issue. What result?[40]

2. A testator left all his estate to his widow for life and provided that after her death various properties and sums of money should be paid or transferred to his son and three daughters. He then provided that if any of the children should die without leaving legal issue, her, their, or his share should be divided equally between the survivor or survivors of the child or children so dying without leaving legal issue, as tenants in common and not as joint tenants. All four children survived the testator and his widow. Two died leaving issue and two without issue. When the second last child, a daughter, died without issue would her interest under the will go to her estate or to her surviving sister?[41]

(B) *The Rule in Doe d. Blomfield v. Eyre*. It sometimes happens that the gift over cannot take effect for some reason. In that event, *prima facie* the prior gift will nevertheless fail. This is the rule in *Doe d. Blomfield v. Eyre*[42] and it is discussed in *Re Archer*,[43] reproduced below.

---

38 *Supra*.
39 *Supra*.
40 See *Olivant v. Wright* (1875), 1 Ch. D. 346 (C.A.).
41 See *Re Roberts; Roberts v. Morgan*, [1916] 2 Ch. 42.
42 (1848), 5 C.B. 713, 136 E.R. 1058.
43 (1907), 14 O.L.R. 374 (H.C.).

RE ARCHER
(1907), 14 O.L.R. 374
Supreme Court of Ontario
[High Court of Justice]

The testator, William Archer, died in 1885. By his will he gave his wife Ann, a life interest in his entire estate, with remainder for life to Jane McArthur. The testator directed that at Jane's death his real estate was to go to her son, William, his heirs and assigns, but if he should die without issue before his mother, she was to receive a half interest in the real property absolutely and the other half interest was to go to the Presbyterian Church in Canada. At the time of the testator's death the gift to the Church was void for mortmain, although subsequent legislation had removed the Church's inability to hold land. There was no residuary clause.

Ann died in 1886 and William died in 1889, a minor.

RIDDELL J.:

. . .

Admittedly Jane McArthur had upon the death of the widow an estate for life, and there was also an estate in her son. This estate of the son, vested as it was, was liable to be divested upon his death in the lifetime of his mother. It is not disputed that the one moiety has been divested. Indeed, none of these propositions can be successfully disputed, in view of the authorities.

Whether there can ever be a case in which one moiety of an estate so vested may be divested, while the other moiety remains vested, I need not determine: see *Gatenby v. Morgan*.[44] The moiety in dispute cannot in any case be less liable to divestment than if it were the sole devise over; and it has been settled that a provision for divesting is not rendered of no avail by the fact that the gift over is void by the Statutes of Mortmain, though that gift be for all other purposes void: *Robinson v. Wood*.[45]

The leading case is *Doe d. Blomfield v. Eyre*.[46] In this there was an appointment to A., her heirs and assigns, but in case of the happening of an event (which did actually happen) then to B. B. was a person incapable of taking. It was held, nevertheless, in Cam. Scacc. that the estate was divested. Parke, B, giving the judgment of the Court,[47] says:

> If a testator were to devise to A.B. in fee, and to direct that, in the event of A.B. dying in the lifetime of J.S., the estate should go over to a charity, it surely is perfectly clear that, if A.B. died in the lifetime of J.S., he, A.B., or rather his heirs, would lose the estate....The estate of A.B. is in such case defeated, not by the giving over of the estate to the charity, but by the happening of the event on which the testator intended it should go over.

---

44 (1876), 1 Q.B.D. 685.
45 (1858), 6 W.R. 728, 27 L.J. Ch. 726.
46 (1848), 5 C.B. 713.
47 *Ibid.*, at p. 746.

And he adds:

> How she (*i.e.*, the settlor) would have disposed of it, if she had known that she could not give it in the mode proposed by her will, can only be matter of conjecture. One thing quite certain, is, that she has not expressed any intention, that in the events which have happened John (A.) should take; and, as he can only be entitled by virtue of an expressed intention in his favour, we think that he fails to establish any right.

This last remark is applicable to the case under consideration.

In *O'Mahoney v. Burdett*,[48] there was a gift of £1,000 consols to A. for life, after her death to her daughter B., "if B. should die unmarried or without children, the consols I here will to revert to C.," and D. was appointed residuary legatee. A. and C. died in the lifetime of the testatrix. B. entered into possession and died without children. It was held that the death of C. in the lifetime of the testatrix had no effect upon the divestment of the gift to B. upon her dying, and that, there being a lapse, the residuary legatee became entitled.

In *Hurst v. Hurst*,[49] certain property was given to trustees upon trust to permit H. to receive the rents for his lifetime, and after his death to convey to his children, with a proviso that if he charged or incumbered the property the gift to him should be absolutely forfeited, and the gift to the children at once take effect. He did incumber the estate, and it was held by Fry, J., and the Court of Appeal, that this had the effect of forfeiting the life estate of H., although H. had no children, so that there were no persons to take the gift over.

. . .

The decision in *Robinson v. Wood*[50] is directly in point; it seems to be in accord with previous authority, and not to have been questioned. I therefore follow it.

> [The Court then went on to hold that the gift over to the Presbyterian Church was void for mortmain, so that that half of the property went out on an intestacy, there being no residuary clause.]

Notes and Questions

1. The law of mortmain, referred to in *Re Archer*[51] formerly rendered devises of real property to charities, such as churches, void.[52]

2. The Rule in *Doe d. Blomfield v. Eyre*[53] does not apply if the will discloses a contrary intention, in other words, if the will makes it clear that the interest shall not divest unless the gift over is effective.[54]

---

48 1874), L.R. 7 H.L. 388.
49 (1882), 21 Ch. D. 278.
50 *Supra*.
51 (1907), 14 O.L.R. 374 (H.C.).
52 For a discussion of mortmain, see A. H. Oosterhoff, "The Law of Mortmain: An Historical and Comparative Review" (1977), 27 U. of T. L.J. 257.
53 (1848) 5 C.B. 713, 136 E.R. 1058.
54 *Crozier v. Crozier* (1873), L.R. 15 Eq. 282.

Re Rooke[55] illustrates the point. The testator gave a life interest in his estate to his wife and directed that after her death the estate should be sold and the proceeds divided equally between his brother and three sisters, whom he named. He went on to provide that if any of the brothers or sisters should predecease the testator's wife, his or her respective share should go to his or her respective issue. One sister survived the testator, but predeceased the widow without issue.

Harman J. held that the rule was ousted because of the substitutionary gift in favour of the issue of the primary donees. That was sufficient in his view to show an intention that the divesting of the deceased wife's sister's share not take place. In other words, he concluded that the testator only intended his brothers and sisters to be defeated if they died in the widow's lifetime leaving children them surviving. Is this reasoning convincing?

3. The rule in *Doe d. Blomfield v. Eyre*[56] also does not apply if the gift over is void for remoteness,[57] nor if the name of the proposed beneficiary is not inserted in the will.[58]

(iii) *Gifts over on Death under Specified Age*

An old rule, known as the rule in *Phipps v. Ackers*,[59] or the rule in *Edwards v. Hammond*,[60] provides that if there is a gift that is *prima facie* contingent upon the beneficiary attaining a specified age, but it is followed by a gift over if the beneficiary dies under that age, the contingency is to be construed as referring only to the time of payment. Hence, the gift will be construed as vested subject to divestment. Thus, a gift, "to X when she attains age 30, but if she dies before she reaches that age, to Y," is construed to give X a vested interest, subject to being divested in favour of Y if X dies before she becomes 30 years old.

That was the conclusion in *Phipps v. Ackers*,[61] in which the testator devised real property in trust to George Ackers when he should attain age 21, but if he should die under that age without lawful issue, the real property was to fall into residue. The House of Lords held that George took a vested interest subject to divestment if he died under age 21.

The rule was designed to avoid the destruction of legal remainders which would fail if they did not vest during the prior particular estate. However, it now applies to all remainders, both legal and equitable, to executory interests,[62] to gifts of personalty[63] and to class gifts.[64]

---

55 [1953] Ch. 716, [1953] 2 All E.R. 110.

56 *Supra.*

57 *Re Pratt's Settlement Trusts; McCullum v. Phipps-Hornby*, [1943] Ch. 356, [1943] 2 All E.R. 458.

58 *O'Mahoney v. Burdett* (1874), L.R. 7 H.L. 388 at 407, *per* Lord Selborne.

59 (1842), 9 Cl. & Fin. 583, 134 E.R. 453 (H.L.).

60 (1684), 3 Lev. 132, 83 E.R. 614.

61 *Supra.*

62 *Stanley v. Stanley* (1809), 16 Ves. Jun. 491, 33 E.R. 1071.

63 *Re Heath; Pub. Trustee v. Heath*, [1936] Ch. 259, [1935] All E.R. Rep. 677; *Re Barton; White v. Barton*, [1941] S.C.R. 426 at 429, [1941] 3 D.L.R. 653 at 656, *per* Kerwin J.; *Re Johnston*, [1945] 2 W.W.R. 324, [1945] 3 D.L.R. 213 (Man. K.B.).

64 *Re Turney*, [1899] 2 Ch. 739 (C.A.).

The rule is explained in *Re Barton*,[65] which is reproduced below.

RE BARTON
[1941] S.C.R. 426, [1941] 3 D.L.R. 653
Supreme Court of Canada

The testator, Willard Barton, bequeathed the sum of $7,000 to his grandson, Thomas Barton, when he should attain age 25. In the meantime the trustees were authorized to advance Thomas any income from the bequest as might be necessary for his maintenance and education. The testator provided, however, that if Thomas should die before the period of distribution leaving no wife or children him surviving, the gift should fall into residue, but if he should die before the period of distribution leaving a wife or children him surviving, the gift should be divided equally among them.

Thomas would not reach age 25 until 1944. An application was made to interpret the will.

KERWIN J.:

. . .

The question is whether the legacy of $7,000 vested in the grandson at the death of the testator, subject to being divested if he should die before attaining the age of twenty-five, i.e., going to his wife and child or children, or, failing them, falling into the residue of the estate. If this related to real estate, the question is settled by authority, *Phipps v. Ackers*,[66] and the reason for the rule is stated to be that if there is a gift over upon death under the stated age, the gift over shows that the first devisee is to take whatever interest the person claiming under the devise over is not entitled to, that is to say, the immediate interest.[67]

In *Bickersteth v. Shanu*,[68] the Judicial Committee saw no reason to doubt

> that the established rule for the guidance of the court in construing devises of real estate is that they are to be held to be vested unless a condition precedent to the vesting is expressed with reasonable clearness.

The same rule, I think, is a proper one to be applied in construing bequests of personal estate.

The rule in *Phipps v. Ackers* was held applicable to gifts of both realty and personalty, *Whitter v. Bremridge*,[69] and I agree with Farwell J. in *In re Heath*,[70] that the rule applies to personalty.

---

65 [1941] S.C.R. 426, [1941] 3 D.L.R. 653.
66 (1842) 9 Cl. & F. 583.
67 Halsbury, 2nd ed., vol 34, p. 381.
68 [1936] A.C. 290.
69 (1866) L.R. 2 Eq. 736.
70 [1936] 1 Ch. 259.

The order of the Court of first instance, affirmed by the Court of Appeal, declared:

> that the said Thomas Barton is entitled to receive on his attaining the age of twenty-five years interest upon the bequest to him in the said will contained of $7,000 to be computed at the legal rate of interest and commencing from the date of death of the testator, the said Willerton Barton, deceased, less such sums, if any as shall have been paid out in the meantime by the executrices for his maintenance and education.

I am satisfied that this is the correct order, and the appeal should be dismissed with costs.

[The concurring judgments of Hudson J. and of Davis J (with whom the other members of the court concurred) have been omitted.]

Notes and Questions

1. The rule is ousted by the expression of a contrary intention. Such an intention will be found if the age contingency is made part of the limitation and no specific persons are named, as in a gift, "to the children of A who attain age 21," with a gift over to another person. The difficulty in applying the rule in such circumstances is that until the contingency is satisfied, there is no one who answers the description of the beneficiaries and the gift cannot, therefore vest in anyone.[71]

2. A contrary intention will also be found if an additional contingency, which is personal to the beneficiary and unconnected with the determination of the prior estate, is added, as in a gift, "to X for life, remainder to Y if he is then alive, but if Y dies without issue, to Z, or if Y dies leaving issue, to her issue."[72]

3. A testator gave legacies of $30,000, to be paid with accrued interest to each of several named grand-nieces and grand-nephews alive at his death "when he or she respectively attains the age of twenty-five (25) years, subject always to the alternative disposition hereinafter provided if he or she fails to attain that age." The alternative disposition was that if any of the legatees should die before attaining age 25, his or her legacy should go to his or her issue, or if there should be no issue, then to his or her brothers and sisters living at his or her death. What result?[73]

4. A similar rule applies if the gift over is contingent not on the named beneficiary failing to meet the contingency, but on another person failing to meet a contingency specified in the will. Thus, in a gift "to the children of A at age 25, but if A dies without children him surviving, to B," A's first child takes an absolutely vested interest. If his interest were held to be contingent and if A had a child who died before age 25 after A, neither A's child nor B would be able to take since the contingencies are alternatives. To prevent the gift from failing completely, therefore, it is construed as giving A's child a vested interest.[74]

---

71 *Duffield v. Duffield* (1829), 1 Dow & Cl. 268 at 314, 6 E.R. 573, *per* Best C.J.; *Festing v. Allen* (1843), 12 M. & W. 279, 152 E.R. 1204; *Re Astor*, [1922] 1 Ch. 364 (C.A.).
72 See *Merchants Bank of Can. v. Keefer* (1885), 13 S.C.R. 515.
73 See *Re Jorgenson; Mearon v. Wall* (1982), 12 E.T.R. 112 (Man. Q.B.).
74 *Re Bevan's Trust* (1887), 34 Ch. D. 716, [1886-90] All E.R. Rep. 706.

(iv) *Gifts over on Death before Receipt*

If a gift over is made on the condition that the primary beneficiary die "before receiving his share" or words to that effect, the courts have consistently held that those words are to be construed as referring to death within the executor's year, the year following the testator's death traditionally being the period allowed the executors for administering and distributing the estate. This principle is discussed in *Re Stephens; Royal Trust Co. v. East*,[75] reproduced below.

ROYAL TRUST CO. v. EAST
[1978] 5 W.W.R. 444, 3 E.T.R. 55 (*sub nom*. Re Stephens)
Supreme Court of British Columbia

The testator, Lawrence Russell Stephens, who died in 1975, gave a life interest in his estate to his wife and directed his trustees to pay varying portions of the estate to seven named persons and organizations, including a 30% share to his friend Mrs. Freda Aylen provided she was still living at his death. He then went on to provide that if any of the primary beneficiaries should have died before distribution of the estate was about to take place, the shares of such beneficiaries should revert to the estate. The testator directed that any portions that reverted should be divided equally among five named persons.

The testator's wife died shortly after him, followed by Mrs. Aylen. At the latter's death the executors had not yet completed administration of the estate and were not, therefore, in a position to distribute the estate.

The executors brought an application to construe the will.

MACDONALD L.J.S.C.:

. . .

The Court is required to determine when the capital of the estate vested in beneficiaries who took after the life estate. The question arises, did it pass to the beneficiaries on the death of the testator, or on the death of his wife who had a life interest.

> [The court quoted extensively from *Browne v. Moody*,[76] which held that if an apparently contingent gift is postponed only to a prior interest and for no other reason, the interest vests at the testator's death. The court continued:]

On the authority of this decision, the Court would hold that under the will of the testator in this case, the capital of the estate would have vested in Freda Aylen on the death of the testator.

---

75 [1978] 5 W.W.R. 444, (sub nom. *Re Stephens*) 3 E.T.R. 55 (B.C.S.C.).
76 [1936] 3 W.W.R. 59, [1936] A.C. 635, [1936] 2 All E.R. 1695, [1936] O.R. 422, [1936] 4 D.L.R. 1 (P.C.).

Under the terms of the will the vesting was subject to divesting under the clause contained in para. 6(h) of the will. The question arises[:] is a devise of this nature valid?

. . .

In *Johnston v. Crook*[77] the facts were that a testator left a share of his estate to K. and G. but in case K. shall die before he shall actually have received the whole of his share and without leaving issue living at his decease, then in such case whether the same shall become due and payable or not, such part or parts as he shall not have actually received were to be paid to G. K. died unmarried without having received any share of the residue. In this case Jessel M.R. reviewed all the authorities up until that time and held that the gift over referred to above was a proper and legal devise. The decision of Jessel M.R. was followed by the Appellate Division of the Alberta Supreme Court in *Re Graham*.[78]

. . .

As far as the intent of the testator is concerned it seems clear enough that he wanted 30 per cent of the residue to go to Mrs. Aylen. However, if she died before distribution of the estate was about to take place then this 30 per cent of the residue was to go to the other five named beneficiaries. As to the certainty of the contingency or the condition subsequent, the words used by the testator in the will were "Should any of the primary or alternate beneficiaries named in this clause have died prior to the time when the division and distribution of moneys of my estate is about to be made". Freda Aylen died September 29th, 1976. At this point in time the executor had not as yet completed the administration of the estate to the point where he could divide and distribute....

This Court would hold that the vesting in Freda Aylen was not absolute, but subject to divestment in the event Mrs. Aylen were to die prior to the time the executors were about to distribute the estate. On the issue of whether the contingency or condition subsequent in the will has been expressed with certainty, counsel for the beneficiaries named under clause 6(h) of the will has cited a number of cases in which the words "before receiving payment", "before receiving benefits", "before final division", "before receiving their respective shares", have been held to mean "the end of the executor's year" or "completion in fact of the administration of the estate, whichever occurs first."

. . .

In *Re Chaston*[79] the testator had directed that in the case of the death of one of the testator' sons or daughters before the bequest made to them shall have been paid to him or her that there was to be a gift over. In the case before this Court the testator had directed that should Mrs. Aylen have died before the time when the estate was to be divided and distributed there was to be a gift over. In *Re*

---

77 (1879), 12 Ch. D. 639.
78 [1945] 3 W.W.R. 713, [1946] 1 D.L.R. 357 (Alta. C.A.).
79 (1881), 18 Ch. D. 218.

Chaston, Fry J. stated that he found the words "paid to them" referred not to the actual time of payment and receipt but to the time when payment ought to take place and held that this time was at the death of the party holding the life interest. He stated further that he dealt with a similar matter in *Collison v. Barber*,[80] where he had held that these words ought to be read as the period at which the division ought to have been made by the executors. I would hold that the words "prior to division and distribution of moneys of my estate" should be construed in the same manner the Court has construed the words "before receiving payment", "before final division", so that a definite date may be determined. In this case can I say that the division and distribution ought to have been made on the death of the life tenant?

> [His Lordship referred to *Hamilton v. Hart*[81] and other cases, which favoured the end of the executor's year, and continued:]

The Court is required to determine at what point in time the estate ought to be distributed. I would hold that in this case the Court could not rule that the date would be the date of the death of the testator's wife, the life tenant. I would hold that the point in time when this estate ought to be distributed would be at the end of the executor's year, or on completion in fact of the administration of the estate, whichever occurs first. In this case the estate was not about to be distributed, the administration of the estate had not been completed, and the end of the executor's year had not as yet been reached. I would find that the point in time when the estate ought to be distributed had not been reached and it would follow that under the terms of 6(h) of the will, Mrs. Aylen's share in this estate would revert to the testator's estate for distribution in equal amounts to the named beneficiaries in that clause.

> [It is interesting to note that Mrs. Aylen was advised that she had an indefeasibly vested interest in the estate on the death of Mrs. Stevens. Mr. Aylen alleged that, in consequence, she decided to discontinue kidney dialysis, knowing that that would result in her death. Mr. Aylen sought relief from forfeiture, but the court held that such relief was not available, since it was the testator's intention that governed. His Lordship continued:]

A reading of the will makes it clear that the testator intended that if Mrs. Aylen did not get the estate before she died, he wanted it to go to other named beneficiaries, and by implication not to the named beneficiaries or heirs of Mrs. Aylen.

. . .

Notes and Questions

1. A testatrix directed that her cottages be sold and the proceeds held in trust (after payment of debts and certain legacies) in four equal shares for her children. She directed

---

80 (1879), 12 Ch. D. 834.
81 [1919] 2 W.W.R. 164, 27 B.C.R. 101, 47 D.L.R. 231 (C.A.).

that the children should receive the income on their shares until they reached the age of 28. When a child reached that age he or she took the capital. However, she continued: "If any of my children predecease me or depart this life before receiving his or her share..." the share should be divided equally among the other children.

None of the children was 28 at the testatrix' death, but all reached that age thereafter. By agreement among them, the sale of the cottages was postponed. One of the daughters then died at age 33. Does the daughter's estate take?[82]

2. A will provided that if any of certain named residuary beneficiaries should die "before receiving the benefits given him or her by this my Will" his share should be divided among the survivors. One beneficiary died two days after the grant of probate and his share of the estate was neither received by him nor payable to him at the time of his death. What result?[83]

(v) Convenience of the Estate Rule

If a gift is *prima facie* contingent because of words of futurity, but the postponement is solely to let in a prior interest, it will be construed as vested at the testator's death.[84] A common situation is a gift, "to A for life, and after A's death to X." A's death is not really a contingency in this situation; it merely shows that X's estate is postponed until A's life estate has ended. Hence, X's interest vests *a morte testatoris*.

The rule, in effect says that the convenience of the estate requires that the two estates be enjoyed in succession.

The leading case on the rule is *Browne v. Moody*[85] which originated in Ontario. It is discussed in *Re Taylor*,[86] reproduced below, in which the rule was applied to a class gift.

The rule does not apply if the will discloses a contrary intention. This occurs, for example, if the gift is postponed until the marriage of, or the attainment of a specified age by, the beneficiary. The postponement is not then for the convenience of the estate, but for a reason personal to the beneficiary.[87] Furthermore, for the rule to apply, the postponement must be to a date which must occur, such as the death of a life tenant, and not to an uncertain event, such as marriage.[88]

---

82 See *Re Allan* (1981), 31 Nfld. & P.E.I.R. 510, 87 A.P.R. 510 (P.E.I.S.C.). See also *Re Hill* (1977), 1 E.T.R. 38 (Ont. H.C.); *Re Paterson* (1957), 65 Man. R. 127, 22 W.W.R. 38 (Q.B.).

83 *Re Ramsden; Borrie v. Beck*, [1974] 5 W.W.R. 554, 46 D.L.R. (3d) 758 (B.C.).

84 *Re Jobson* (1889), 44 Ch. D. 154.

85 [1936] A.C. 635, [1936] O.R. 422, [1936] 3 W.W.R. 59, [1936] 4 D.L.R. 1 (P.C.).

86 [1972] 3 O.R. 349, 28 D.L.R. (3d) 257 (H.C.).

87 *Re Astor*, [1922] 1 Ch. 364 (C.A.).

88 *Browne v. Moody, supra,* at O.R. 427, D.L.R. 5.

RE TAYLOR
[1972] 3 O.R. 349, 28 D.L.R. (3d) 257
Supreme Court of Ontario
[High Court of Justice]

The testator, Leonard Robert Taylor, died in 1966, a widower and without issue. By his will he gave the income from three-fifths of his estate to his sister-in-law, Norma Katherine MacGregor so long as she remained unmarried. In clause 9 he directed that after her death or marriage, the three-fifths of the estate should be converted into cash and divided equally between Norma, if married, and her sisters and brothers, or to the children equally of any of them who may be deceased. If any of the sisters and brothers had died without issue, the share of the deceased was to be equally divided among the surviving sisters and brothers.

Norma died in 1970, unmarried. One of her brothers, Keith Irving MacGregor, had died in 1942, leaving three children who survived both the testator and Norma. One of Norma's sisters, Lucy Elizabeth Walker, had died in 1944 and her one child died in 1963. Eight brothers and sisters of Norma were living at the testator's death, but two of them, Myrtle Rachel Window and Lyall William MacGregor, predeceased Norma, the first childless, the second leaving a widow and nine children.

The surviving executor brought an application for the advice and directions of the court upon the following questions:

1. Did shares in the residue of the testator's estate vest upon the testator's death under para. (9) of the will?
2. If the answer to Q. 1 is "no", did shares in the residue of the testator's estate vest upon the death of Norma Katherine MacGregor under para. (9) of the will?
3. Is the estate of the late Myrtle Rachel Window, who died without issue after the death of the testator, entitled to a share in the residue of the testator's estate?
4. Are the children of the late Keith Irving MacGregor, who predeceased the testator, entitled to a share in the residue of the testator's estate?
5. Is the share of the late Lyall William MacGregor in the residue of the testator's estate payable to his estate or to his children?

LACOURCIÈRE J.:

. . .

Questions 1 and 2

Questions 1 and 2 pose a common problem in the area of will construction of whether a remainder interest in the testator's estate vests upon his death or upon the death of the life tenant.

The problem is whether the class of sisters and brothers of the life tenant is to be ascertained at the testator's death or at the date of distribution, the death or marriage of the life tenant. The Court has a preference for early vesting, *i.e.*, at the date of death of the testator to facilitate estate administration, but this preference must give way if there is an intention otherwise in the will.

. . .

Upon consideration of all the provisions in the testator's will, it is my opinion that the testator intended shares in the residue of his estate to vest in interest upon his death, but that possession would be postponed for the benefit of the life tenant until her death or marriage. Upon reading paras. 4, 8, 9 and 13, it appears that the testator established a scheme of distribution which provided for an immediate one-fifth share to his sister at his death, an immediate one-fifth share to his niece and grandniece at his death, and an immediate vesting of a three-fifths share to his brothers and sisters-in-law at his death with possession and enjoyment postponed until the death or marriage of the life tenant. Paragraph 13 reads as follows:

> 13. Should my sister-in-law, Norma Katherine MacGregor, have predeceased me, then I direct that the three-fifths or whatever portion of my Estate remains for distribution, be divided among the surviving brothers and sisters-in-law who may be deceased, the children of the deceased having the share of their parent.

It reinforces a construction that the three-fifths share was vested in interest at his death, although not in possession, since, if the life tenant predeceased the testator, there was to be an immediate distribution to the same class.

The above interpretation is consistent with the rule of construction developed in *Browne v. Moody et al.*[89] and subsequent cases which applied that rule.... In *Browne v. Moody et al.*[90] their Lordships were construing a provision in a will which set up an investment fund, with the income payable to W during his lifetime, and on W's death to be divided among E, F, C and H. The obvious question was whether E, F, C and H acquired any vested interest in the fund on the death of the testatrix. Their Lordships held that they did for the following reasons:[91]

> Their Lordships observe in the first place that the date of division of the capital of the fund is a *dies certus*, the death of the son of the testatrix, which in the course of nature must occur sooner or later. In the next place, the direction to divide the capital among the named beneficiaries on the arrival of that *dies certus* is not accompanied by any condition personal to the beneficiaries, such as their attainment of majority or the like. The object of the postponement of the division is obviously only in order that the son may during his lifetime enjoy the income. The mere postponement of distribution to enable an interposed life-rent to be enjoyed has never by itself been held to exclude vesting of the capital.

The distinction between a present gift coupled with a postponement of the date of payment and a direction to pay at a future date without any words of present gift is no doubt an important distinction and is in certain circumstances an element in determining whether vesting *a morte testatoris* has or has not taken place, as where conditions of survivorship and the like are added to the direction to pay.

---

89 [1936] O.R. 422, [1936] 4 D.L.R. 1, [1936] A.C. 635 (P.C.).
90 *Supra.*
91 *Ibid.,* at O.R. 426-7, D.L.R. 5

But where there is a direction to pay the income of a fund to one person during his lifetime and to divide the capital among certain other named and ascertained persons on his death, even although there are no direct words of gift either of the life interest or of the capital, the rule is that vesting of the capital takes place *a morte testatoris* in the remaindermen. The principle is thus stated in Jarman on Wills:[92]

> Even though there be no other gift than in the direction to pay or distribute *in futuro*; yet if such payment or distribution appear to be postponed for the convenience of the fund or property, the vesting will not be deferred until the period in question. Thus, where a sum of stock is bequeathed to A. for life; and, after his decease, to trustees, upon trust to sell and pay and divide the proceeds to and between C. and D., or to pay certain legacies thereout to C. and D.; as the payment or distribution is evidently deferred until the decease of A., for the purpose of giving precedence to his life interest, the ulterior legatees take a vested interest at the decease of the testator.

This reasoning would appear applicable to the facts here. The date of the division of the three-fifths portion is a *dies certus*, the death or marriage of the life tenant. There are no other conditions imposed on the members of the class and the only object of the postponement of the division from a reading of paras. 9 and 13 would appear to be the enjoyment of the income by the life tenant during her lifetime or pre-marriage years. In *Re Simpson*,[93] Rose, C.J.H.C., considered the argument that *Browne v. Moody* should not apply because the remaindermen were named persons whereas in the clause in question (and in the present case) they represented a class. The learned Judge could see no reason why the description of the remaindermen as a class should be less effective than if they were named persons. Similar reasoning on this point was given by Pennell, J., in *Re Smoke*.[94]

Counsel for the Official Guardian and for certain of the remaindermen argued that the intention of the testator expressed in the will was that only those members of the class alive at the date of the death of the life tenant were to take a share in his estate. They alleged support for this interpretation in the language of the second sentence of para. 9 of the will which mentioned "surviving brothers and sisters", indicating an intention on the part of the testator that no member of the class should take an interest unless he survived the life tenant. Counsel also directed the Court's attention to the cases of *Re Treble*[95] and *Re Fleury*,[96] wherein it was held that the class was to be ascertained at the date of death of the life tenant. It is evident, however, that the facts and the nature of the dispositions in those cases were different from the facts and dispositions here. In my opinion, the above cases merely illustrate that in those particular situations the Court considered that the testator intended the class of beneficiaries to be determined at the date of death of the life tenant. Any ambiguity caused by the reference to

---

92 7th ed., p. 1377.
93 [1945] O.R. 169, [1945] 1 D.L.R. 678 (H.C.).
94 [1971] 3 O.R. 100 at 104, 19 D.L.R. (3d) 512 at 516 (H.C.).
95 [1966] 2 O.R. 153, 56 D.L.R. (2d) 402 (C.A.).
96 [1964] 2 O.R. 129, 44 D.L.R. (2d) 393, affirmed (sub nom. *National Trust Co. Ltd. v. Fleury et al.*) [1965] S.C.R. 817, 53 D.L.R. (2d) 700.

"surviving brothers and sisters" in cl. 9 is outweighed by the clear intention of the testator otherwise throughout the whole of the will to have the remainder interests vested at the date of his death.

Question 1 will therefore be answered in the affirmative with the result that it is unnecessary to answer question 2.

Question 3

Myrtle Rachel Window, a sister of the life tenant, survived the testator but died without issue prior to the death of the life tenant. On the basis of my finding on Q. 1 that shares in the residue of the testator's estate vested in interest upon the testator's death, this beneficiary took a vested interest since she survived the testator. However, a further problem is raised by the wording in para. 9 providing for the share of a beneficiary who died without issue to be divided among the survivors. The problem is whether the vesting that occurred upon the testator's death was an absolute one, or a vesting, subject to divestment, if the beneficiary predeceased the life tenant without issue. As a general rule, when shares in an estate have vested, the Court will lean against an interpretation that gives a divesting unless there are very clear words indicating that such was the intention of the testator: *Re MacInnes*.[97] In my opinion, the testator has set out his intention very clearly in para. 9 that, if a beneficiary died without issue, his share was divested.

. . .

Question 3 will be answered in the negative — the estate of the late Myrtle Rachel Window is not entitled to a share in the residue.

Question 4

At the time the testator drew his will, Keith Irving MacGregor, a brother of the life tenant, had been deceased for approximately 16 years. There is nothing to indicate in the will if the testator was aware that this class member was deceased. Generally, people leave bequests to persons alive at the date of their will, rather than to those deceased. However, para. 9 of the will refers only to "sisters and brothers", *or* "the children of any one of them who may be deceased" and raises the following possibilities. The testator may have been referring only to "sisters and brothers" living at the time of the making of his will, and therefore, children of any deceased brother refers only to children of a brother who was alive at that time and subsequently died; in that case, the children of Keith Irving MacGregor, a brother not alive at the date of the will, would be excluded. Alternatively, the testator may have intended that children of a deceased brother, referred to a brother who was deceased at the date of the will, as well as those alive at that date and who subsequently died; if so, the children of Keith Irving MacGregor would not be excluded.

If the language of the will is framed so generally as to be applicable both to a brother, living or deceased at the date of the will, the language in my opinion

---

97 [1958] O.R. 592 at 594, 15 D.L.R. (2d) 684 at 686-7.

should be construed as covering both situations. It must also be remembered that the relevant time is the death of the testator and not the date that the will was drawn. The question now is whether the testator has expressed any intention in the will that the children of class members who predeceased him should not share.

[His Lordship considered whether the gift to the issue of the predeceased brother was original or substitutionary, a question which was explored in an earlier chapter, and continued:]

There is support for interpreting "or" as "and" in para. 9 and para. 13 of the will where the testator provides for the residue of his estate to be divided among "surviving brothers and sisters-in-law *and* to the children of any of the brothers and sisters-in-law who may be deceased". It can be seen again that the testator has not made any distinction between "brothers-in-law" who were alive or deceased at the date of the will. It also appears that children of deceased brothers-in-law would be taking originally, rather than substitutionally.

[His Lordship referred to *Etches v. Etches*[98] and *Re Simpson*,[99] and continued:]

There does not appear to be any particular "magic" in the above cases for they all proceed on the same basis as to what was the intention of the testator from the language used, and found that it was more likely that the testator intended to import a gift in the first instance to class members as well as the issue of deceased members. The tendency towards such a construction appears to have been aided in such instances by the fact that the gift was in one sentence and the conjunction "and" was used. However,...the same construction may be applied even though the word "or" was used. It would also appear that, if there is any ambiguity as to the testator's intention and no express language in the will preventing the children of a class member who died in the testator's lifetime from taking, the Court will lean towards an interpretation that does not exclude such children.

Question 4 will be answered in the affirmative for the following reasons:

 (i) no distinction is made in the will between class members alive or deceased at the date of the will;
 (ii) "or" should be interpreted as "and" in these circumstances, especially in view of the wording of para. 13;
(iii) the testator intended to benefit brothers and sisters-in-law with an original gift; if he intended to benefit only brothers and sisters-in-law in the first instance, he would not have provided for those who died without issue to be divested; and
(iv) there is no indication in the will that the testator intended to benefit some of the children of brothers and sisters-in-law and not others.

---

98 (1856), 3 Drewry 441, 61 E.R. 971.
99 [1945] O.R. 169, [1945] 1 D.L.R. 678 (H.C.).

Question 5

Lyall William MacGregor, a brother of the life tenant, survived the testator, but died prior to the death of the life tenant, leaving issue surviving. On the basis of my holding on Q. 4 that there was an original gift to brothers and sisters-in-law and the children of any one of them who were deceased, it would follow that the vested interest this beneficiary took on the death of the testator should be payable to his estate (*i.e.*, personal representative). It would only be payable to his children if it could be argued that there was a divesting condition subsequent in favour of his children. This would mean that the word "or" meant "or" and implied a substitutionary gift to the children. As I have rejected such an interpretation previously, the answer to Q. 5 will be that the share of the late Lyall William MacGregor in the residue of the testator's estate is payable to his estate.

. . .

Notes and Questions

1. A testator gave his house to his daughter for life. He directed that on her death the house be sold and the proceeds distributed as part of the residue. He gave the residue equally to his children living at his death. The daughter lived in the house until her death. Is her estate entitled to a share of the residue?[100]

2. A testatrix gave the income from the residue of her estate equally to her children until the youngest should attain age 21 and thereafter to her husband for life. Upon the husband's death the residue was to be divided equally among the children *per stirpes*. All the children were 21 at the testatrix' death and the husband disclaimed his life interest. Are the children entitled immediately?[101]

3. A testator gave a life estate in the residue of his estate to his wife and directed his trustees, upon the death of his wife, to divide the residue equally among four named persons. Three of those predeceased the testator. The fourth survived the testator, but predeceased the life tenant. Does the fourth residuary beneficiary's estate take his share?[102]

4. A testator gave all his property to his wife for life, "and thereafter, to my living children, A, B, C and D, in equal shares." A survived the testator, but predeceased his mother. Is A's estate entitle to take?[103]

5. The convenience of the estate rule also applies if there are two or more successive life interests followed by a remainder "upon the death of" the last life tenant. Hence, unless the will discloses a contrary intention, the remainder vests on the death of the testator and the fact that the second life tenant predeceases the first is irrelevant.[104]

---

100 See *Wickens Estate v. Weiland* (1991), 45 E.T.R. 130 (Ont. Gen. Div.).

101 See *Strittmatter v. Stephens* (1983), 40 O.R. (2d) 463, 13 E.T.R. 127 (H.C.). See also *Re Clark Estate* (1993), 50 E.T.R. 105 (B.C.S.C.).

102 See *Re Oswell* (1982), 11 E.T.R. 283 (Ont. H.C.).

103 See *MacKay v. Nagle* (1988), 30 E.T.R. 191 (N.B.Q.B.); *McKeen Estate v. McKeen Estate* (1993), 49 E.T.R. 54 (N.B.Q.B.).

104 *Re Brennan* (1978), 28 N.S.R. (2d) 411, 43 A.P.R. 411 (T.D.).

(vi) *Postponed Payment*

It often happens that a testator gives a legacy or property to one of his or her children, or to another person, in apparently absolute form, but then goes on to provide that the money shall be paid or the property transferred to the beneficiary at some future time, such as the attainment of a specified age. The rule applied in such cases is that payment only is postponed, not vesting.[105] This will only be so, however, if the direction to pay is separate from the words of gift. If it is not, the gift is contingent. Thus a gift in the following form: "to A payable when she reaches age 30" is *prima facie* contingent. The principle was applied in the leading case, *Bickersteth v. Shanu*.[106]

In that case the testator devised several parcels of real property to his son and added in a separate clause, "These devises shall take effect upon my said son attaining the age of twenty-five years." The son did not reach that age until twelve years after the testator's death. He then brought action against the appellant executors to recover the rents they had collected on the properties during the twelve years. The Privy Council held that the words, "shall take effect," related to the time the devise took effect in possession and did not impose a condition precedent on the devise. Hence, the devise vested on the testator's death.

It would appear that the postponement does not have to be to an event that is certain to happen. Thus, in *Re Barrow*[107] a bequest with payment postponed until the beneficiary ceased to be under a disability was held to be vested.

The fact that the intermediate income is given to the beneficiary whose interest is postponed also makes the gift *prima facie* vested.[108]

If the gift is held to be vested, the Rule in *Saunders v. Vautier*[109] applies, which holds that a beneficiary who is *sui juris* and who is entitled to an absolutely vested gift is entitled to call for payment or transfer when he reaches the age of majority. This rule is dealt with in *Re Squire*,[110] reproduced below.

RE SQUIRE
[1962] O.R. 863, 34 D.L.R. (2d) 481
Supreme Court of Ontario
[High Court of Justice]

The testator devised certain real property to trustees in trust until his grandson, Edison Ashdon Squire, Jr. reached the age of 30 and then to convey the property to him. Until then the trustees were directed to invest the income from the rental of the property and to accumulate it and pay it to the grandson at age 30, unless

---

105 *Re Couturier, Couturier v. Shea*, [1907] 1 Ch. 470.
106 [1936] A.C. 290, [1936] 1 All E.R. 227, [1936] 1 W.W.R. 644 (P.C.).
107 (1980), 29 O.R. (2d) 374, 8 E.T.R. 169 (sub nom. *Barrow v. Partington*), 113 D.L.R. (3d) 184 (H.C.), varied 41 O.R. (2d) 144n, 129 D.L.R. (3d) 767n (C.A.), leave to appeal to S.C.C. refused 41 N.R. 536n.
108 *Re Williams*, [1907] 1 Ch. 180.
109 (1841), Cr. & Ph. 240, 41 E.R. 482.
110 [1962] O.R. 863, 34 D.L.R. (2d) 481 (H.C.).

he, after age 18, desired to pursue higher education, in which case the trustees could pay him up to $700 annually out of the current and accumulated income for that purpose. There was a similar devise of other property in trust for another grandson, Arthur Earl Squire.

The administrator with the will annexed brought an application for the opinion of the court upon certain questions, including whether the two grandsons became absolutely entitled to the two properties when they reached age 21, which they did, together with the accumulated income.

SCHATZ J.:

. . .

First of all it is necessary to determine whether the real property in question became vested in the devisees upon the death of the testator. Referring first to *Jarman on Wills*,[111] I quote the following:

> ...if a testator gives property to A absolutely, but directs his trustees to retain possession and accumulate the income for a certain number of years and then transfer the property and accumulations to A, the trust for accumulation is nugatory, and A is entitled to have the property transferred to him at once. Of course if the gift is contingent or defeasible, or if any other person may, by possibility, be interested in the trust, the principle does not apply.

And again on the same page:

> Again, if a testator gives property for the benefit of A absolutely (that is, without settling it on him for life, or providing for a gift over, or the like), and gives his trustees a discretion, or specific directions, as to the manner in which the property shall be held and applied for A's benefit, A takes it absolutely.

. . .

It is...clear from the authorities that the Courts lean towards an early vesting and I find in this will indications of the testator's intention which would be in support of following that policy. For example, the property in question is separated from the rest of the estate, also the intermediate income from the property is to be used or accumulated for the beneficiary, also there is no gift over in the event of death prior to attaining the specified age and also the fact that in para. 3 of the will, the two grandchildren who are the devisees under paras. 1 and 2 of the will are excepted from the class of grandchildren to share in the residue.

I refer also to the case of *Vawdry v. Geddes*[112] where the Master of the Rolls says:

> Where interim interest is given, it is presumed that the testator meant an immediate gift, because, for the purpose of interest, the particular legacy is to be immediately separated from the bulk of the property; but that presumption fails entirely when the testator has expressly declared that the legacy is to go over, in case of the death of the legatee before a particular period. I speak here of gifts of personal estate, and not of real estate.

---

111 8th ed., vol. 2, p. 882.
112 (1830), 1 Russ. & M. 202 at 208, 39 E.R. 78.

Here it is noted that the property is separate from the remainder of the estate and there is no gift over, and I conclude from *Bickersteth v. Shanu*[113] that the same rule applied to real estate.

On the other hand it is submitted by counsel for another beneficiary that there can be no vesting unless all the income is to be paid to the beneficiary. In this case the income is to be accumulated until the specified age, with the exception that an amount of $700 may be used for education and maintenance. I think it worthy of note, however, that the testator had in mind the possible deficiency in income for this purpose and provided for the use of capital therefor, thus indicating to me that in some circumstances the beneficiary would be entitled to all the income. Counsel in support of this said submission cites *Re Crothers*,[114] where Orde, J., states...[115] as follows:

> ...a gift which would be construed as contingent, because not expressed otherwise than by a direction to pay at some future time, is vested if the whole of the intermediate income is also given to the same legatee.

I do not, however, consider this authority for the contrary situation where only part of the income is given which as I have indicated does not necessarily apply to the will here being considered....On all these authorities I must therefore conclude that the gifts in paras. 1 and 4 of the will became vested in the respective devisees upon the death of the testator.

Having so found I therefore apply the principle expressed in *Saunders v. Vautier*,[116] which was followed and adopted in *Wharton v. Masterman*,[117] where Lord Davey says,[118] after stating the facts:

> This being so, the principle of *Saunders v. Vautier* would at once be applicable if this were the case of a gift to an individual. That principle is this: that where there is an absolute vested gift made payable at a future event, with direction to accumulate the income in the meantime, and pay it with the principal, the Court will not enforce the trust for accumulation in which no person has any interest but the legatee, or (in other words) the Court holds that a legatee may put an end to an accumulation which is exclusively for his benefit.

This seems to me to apply directly to the facts in this case and I note also that in the *Saunders v. Vautier* case the Lord Chancellor in reaching his conclusion also referred to the fact that the property was separated from the estate and that there was no gift over thus again making it similar to the facts of this case.

> [His Lordship, therefore, held that the two grandsons became entitled to a conveyance of the properties devised in trust for them when they became 21, together with the accumulated income.]

---

113 [1936] A.C. 291 at 298.
114 (1922), 22 O.W.N. 173.
115 *Ibid.*, at p. 174.
116 (1841), Cr. & Ph. 240, 41 E.R. 482.
117 [1895] A.C. 186.
118 *Ibid.*, at p. 198.

Notes and Questions

1. The principle of *Bickersteth v. Shanu*[119] applies even though there is a postponement, such as a trust for sale, to allow for the payment of debts.[120] However, the principle does not apply if the legacy is charged on land.[121]

2. A testator directed his executors to pay a substantial sum of money to X "upon his attaining the age of 23 years" and to pay $1,500 annually out of the corpus of the estate for X's proper education, maintenance and support until X reached age 23. Is the legacy vested or contingent?[122]

3. A testator left a large sum of money in trust for his grandson, the income from which was to be paid to him on a regular basis. He was to receive the capital when the grandson's daughter reached the age of 21. The residue of the testator's estate was distributed among several persons, with the grandson as the main beneficiary, subject to the same conditions. After the testator's death, but prior to the grandson's daughter attaining age 21, the grandson brought proceedings to terminate the trust and for payment of the trust funds immediately. What result?[123]

4. *Fast v. Van Vliet*[124] also illustrates the principle. The testatrix directed that her estate be divided into three equal shares and that a two-thirds' share be paid to her minor grandson upon attaining age 25. Another clause in the will provided that the trustee in his discretion could use the income and capital of the share of a beneficiary who was under age 21 for his or her maintenance and education, and for illnesses and other emergencies. When the grandson became 21, he applied to an order directing the trustee to pay him his two-thirds' share. The court held that the interest was contingent on the grandson attaining age 25, so the application was denied.

The correctness of the decision in *Fast v. Van Vliet* may be questioned. It would seem that the presumptive share of the beneficiary had been separated from the others and that the income from that share was to be applied for his benefit, albeit in the trustees' discretion. If that is the case, the share should be held to be vested. In other words, if the gift can be interpreted as giving each person in the class an aliquot share and as giving the trustees a discretion to apply the income from each share for the benefit of the legatee entitled to that share, the gift is vested.[125]

In contrast, if the gift is an undivided gift to a class and the trustees are given a discretion to apply the whole income to any one or more of the members, the gift of any member who has not satisfied the contingency is contingent.[126]

5. *R. v. Green*[127] followed *Fast v. Van Vliet.*[128] The testatrix directed her trustees to invest the residue of her estate and to use the income and capital therefrom in such amounts as they deemed advisable for the advancement and education of her children. Any income not so used was to be added to the capital. When the last child became 21, the residue of

---

119 [1936] A.C. 290, [1936] 1 All E.R. 227, [1936] 1 W.W.R. 644 (P.C.).
120 *Re Paterson* (1957), 65 Man. R. 127, 22 W.W.R. 38 (Q.B.).
121 *Taylor v. Lambert* (1876), 2 Ch. D. 177.
122 See *Re Waines*, [1947] 1 W.W.R. 880, [1947] 2 D.L.R. 746 (Alta. C.A.).
123 See *Whitman v. Hudgins* (1984), 19 E.T.R. 316 (N.S. C.A.).
124 (1965), 51 W.W.R. 65, 49 D.L.R. (2d) 616 (Man. C.A.).
125 See *Re Cairns*, [1972] 4 W.W.R. 322 (B.C.S.C.); *Perrot v. Davies*, (1877), 38 L.T. 52 (Ch.). And see *dicta* in *Re Barton; White v. Barton*, [1941] S.C.R. 426, [1941] 3 D.L.R. 653.
126 *Re Parker* (1880), 16 Ch. D. 44.
127 (1978), 2 E.T.R. 228, 89 D.L.R. (3d) 205 (Fed. T.D.).
128 *Supra.*

the estate was to be divided equally among the children then living. The court held that there was no gift to any of the children until the youngest attained age 21, since until then the estate was to remain one fund.

6. A testator left the residue of his estate in trust "for the education, maintenance and advancement of my son Christopher Roberts Carlson and to use such portion of income and/or capital" for that purpose as the trustees should think fit. When Christopher became 25, 90% of the residue was to be divided into two equal shares and one share was to be paid to each of Christopher and the testator's daughter, Janice. The remaining 10% was to be used to pay debts incurred by the testator's son, Paul. When do Christopher's and Janice's interests in the corpus of the residue vest?[129]

7. A testator gave the residue of his estate in trust,

> To hold the rest and residue of my estate in equal shares, one share for my son, JONATHON DAVID BETTER, and the other for my daughter, SANDRA BETTER, the share of each child to be paid out to such child upon the death of their mother, my wife, EDDIA BETTER, or upon such child marrying, whichever event shall first happen. If either child should predecease me or die before becoming eligible to receive his or her share, such share shall, subject to the same conditions, be paid to the surviving child.

The testator was survived by his widow and the two children. Both children are over the age of majority, but have not married. Are Jonathon and Sandra entitled to call for payment of their shares?[130]

8. A testator directed that the residue of his estate should be divided among his children when the youngest became 25 years old and, if the youngest died before that age, to divide his share among the testator's surviving issue. All the children have reached the age of majority, but the youngest is not yet 25. Can they call for a transfer of the residue?[131]

9. It will be apparent from the foregoing that the rule in *Saunders v. Vautier*[132] can be ousted by a gift of the intermediate income to another person, by a clear statement in the will that the beneficiary shall not receive the intermediate income, or by a gift over in the event that the primary beneficiary fails to satisfy the contingency. In the latter case the interest of the primary beneficiary is vested subject to divestment.

You should note, however, that the rule applies not only if one beneficiary is *sui juris* and solely entitled to the gift, but also if two or more beneficiaries between them are solely entitled to the property. Hence, in a gift, "to A to be paid to her at age 30 and if she dies under that age to B," A and B, if they can agree, can together demand the property once they have both reached the age of majority.[133]

10. The rule in *Saunders v. Vautier*[134] has been abolished in Alberta and Manitoba and replaced with a judicial discretion to terminate or vary a trust which would otherwise attract the rule.[135]

---

129 See *Re Carlson*, [1975] 5 W.W.R. 745, 55 D.L.R. (3d) 616 (B.C.S.C.).
130 See *Re Better* (1983), 14 E.T.R. 189 (Ont. H.C.).
131 See *Balkaran v. Davidson*, [1980] 4 W.W.R. 1 (Man. Q.B.). And see *Re Salterio* (1981), 14 Sask. R. 23, 11 E.T.R. 174 (C.A.).
132 (1841), Cr. & Ph. 240, 41 E.R. 482.
133 *Re Smith*, [1928] 1 Ch. 915.
134 *Supra.*
135 *Trustee Act*, R.S.A. 1980, c. T-10, s. 42; R.S.M. 1987, c. T160, s. 59.

(vii) *Gifts to Survivors*

If a gift is made to a group of persons, not necessarily a class, and the will provides that, if any one or more of the beneficiaries should die before they become entitled to the gift it will go to the survivor or survivors of them, the question also arises when the interest of the beneficiaries vests. The *prima facie* construction in such a case is that the gift vests at the time of distribution[136] and that time is determined in accordance with the class closing rules[137] if the gift is to a class.

The rule is explored in *Re Krause*,[138] reproduced below.

RE KRAUSE
(1985), 19 E.T.R. 92, 18 D.L.R. (4th) 631
Alberta Supreme Court
[Court of Appeal]

The testator, a bachelor, directed that the residue of his estate be divided "equally among my surviving brothers and sisters." At the time he made his will, one brother and five sisters were living. Before the testator died, one of the sisters, Theresa Dickau, died, survived by two children. On an application to interpret the will, it was held at first instance that the testator intended Theresa to share in the gift. Since there was no contrary intention, the anti-lapse provision[139] applied, so that her share was payable to her children.

The surviving brother and sisters appealed.

LIEBERMAN J.A. delivered the judgment of the court:

. . .

The Oxford English Dictionary defines "surviving" as: "That survives. a. Still living after another's death." The word has been considered judicially. In *Gee v. Liddell*[140] Lord Romilly M.R. considered a will in which the meaning of the word "survive" was in issue. He said:[141]

> ...and my opinion is, that the meaning of the word "survive" or "survivor" imports, that the person who is to survive must be living at the time of the event which he is to survive.

The learned author of *Theobald on Wills*[142] refers to the above case and says...:

> The word "survivors" is more usually employed to denote a class of persons who are to take, and in such cases it generally has its natural meaning, which is to outlive; that is to say, to be alive at

---

136 *Cripps v. Wolcott* (1819), 4 Madd. 11, 56 E.R. 613.
137 Discussed in the previous chapter.
138 (1985), 19 E.T.R. 92, 18 D.L.R. (4th) 631 (Alta. C.A.).
139 *Wills Act*, R.S.A. 1980, c. W-11, s. 35.
140 (1866), L.R. 2 Eq. 341.
141 *Ibid.,* at p. 344.
142 14th ed., at p. 677.

and after the happening of a particular event or the death of a particular person, which event or person the other is to survive.

This meaning is confirmed in *Re James's Will Trusts*,[143] where Buckley J. said...:

> There can be no doubt that, according to its proper meaning, the word "survive" means that he who survives the given event must be alive both at, and after, the time of that event.

The question that must be decided her is whether the word "surviving" in the context of the will before us refers to the date of the execution of the will or to the date of death of the testator.

In an Australian case, *Re Public Trustee v. Freeman; Lathbridge*,[144] the testatrix by her will provided:

> "I give devise and bequeath unto my husband...all my real and personal estate or in the event of his death prior to mine: to be divided between my surviving children equally". The husband and all children except one predeceased the testatrix.

Lowe J. said:[145]

> Uninstructed by authority I should not have thought that when a testatrix made a gift to "my surviving children", there was any real doubt as to what she intended. The testatrix knows, when she makes her will, what children she has, but she does not know and cannot know whether any and if so which of them will be living at her death. She is making plain that if all are living all will share in the gift: if one or more are not living that one or more will not share and if there is only one survivor that one only is to take.

In that case it was presumed that "surviving" referred to the death of the testatrix and not the execution of the will.

In *Re Horton*[146] the relevant facts are well set out in the headnote[147] which I quote:

> The testatrix in her will directed a division of the residue of her estate "in three equal shares among my surviving children". At the time the will was drawn the testatrix's three children were alive.

> Subsequently one of the testatrix's children predeceased her. An application for the interpretation of the will was made to determine whether the anti-lapse provisions of the Wills Act (B.C.) applied, in which case the issue of the testatrix's deceased child would share in the testatrix's estate, or whether the testatrix intended to benefit only those of her children which survived her.

Andrews J. interpreted the words "surviving children" to mean "my children who survive me" and not "my presently surviving children".

---

143 [1960] 3 All E.R. 744 at 747.
144 [1958] V.R. 366.
145 *Ibid.*, at p. 367.
146 (1978), 88 D.L.R. (3d) 264, 2 E.T.R. 293 (B.C.S.C.).
147 *Ibid.*, E.T.R. 293.

In my respectful view, the testator in the will before us clearly directed that the residue of the estate should be divided among his brothers and sisters *surviving at the time of his death*. Had he wanted to include his brothers and sisters who were living at the time of the execution of his will he could have done so by naming them or by using the phrase "presently surviving".

In view of my interpretation of the clause in question, s. 35(1) of the *Wills Act*[148] does not come into play because there was not devise or bequest to Theresa Dickau. Even if it were held that there was a devise or bequest to Theresa Dickau within s. 35, I am of the view that the clause in question clearly expresses the testator's intention that the gift to any brother or sister that predeceased him should lapse.

The appeal is allowed....

Notes and Questions

1. The question about the meaning of "survivorship" often arises in a gift of the type: "to A for life and then to my surviving brothers and sisters." As indicated above, *prima facie*, the members of the class must survive the life tenant in order to take under such a gift. However, the *prima facie* rule may be ousted by a contrary intention, as in *Re Hart*.[149] The testatrix devised certain real property to her son Joseph for life and directed that after his death the property be sold and the proceeds distributed "among all my surviving children, or the issue of such children, including a share to the issue of my son Joseph." Five children survived the testatrix, but predeceased Joseph, leaving issue who survived Joseph. Two children survived the testatrix and Joseph. One child survived the testatrix, but predeceased Joseph without issue. The court held that the words, "or the issue of such children," were words of substitution and evinced a contrary intention. Hence, the issue of those who predeceased Joseph took their parents' shares and those who survived Joseph took their shares directly. The child who predeceased Joseph was also not excluded. Her estate took.

2. If the reference to survivorship refers to survivorship among those who are entitled to the remainder themselves and not merely survivorship beyond the death of the life tenant, the survivor takes the entire gift even though he or she did not survive the life tenant.[150]

3. The conjunctive "and" in the phrase "the survivor and survivors of them" is normally construed as "or." However, this is not so if the beneficiaries take as joint tenants. In that case the last of the persons named takes the entire interest.[151]

4. A testator gave a life interest in the residue to his widow and then gave the corpus equally to three named cousins "or the survivor or survivors of them." The will went on to provide that if any of them failed to acquire "a vested interest," his share of the residue should be held on trust for the testator's next of kin. The three cousins survived the testator but predeceased the widow. Did the residue vest in them?[152]

---

148 R.S.A. 1980, c. W-11.
149 [1979] 2 W.W.R. 413, 4 E.T.R. 290 (Sask. Surr. Ct.).
150 *White v. Baker* (1860), 2 De G. F. & J. 55, 45 E.R. 542 (C.A.).
151 *Page v. May* (1857), 24 Beav. 328, 53 E.R. 382. See also *Re Taylor*, [1972] 3 O.R. 349, 28 D.L.R. (3d) 257 (H.C.); *Re Bowman* (1975), 17 N.S.R. (2d) 76 (T.D.).
152 *Re Stillman* (1965), 52 D.L.R. (2d) 601 (Ont. H.C.).

5. A testator gave a life interest in certain property to two named daughters. He directed that when they died the property was to be sold and the proceeds divided among certain of the testator's named children "share and share alike, or to the survivor or survivors or them." When the testator died, seven of the named children were alive; when the life tenants died only one named child was still living. Was the survivorship referable to the time of death of the testator or the time of distribution?[153]

(viii) *The Rule in Boraston's Case*

The rule in *Boraston's Case*[154] states that if real property is devised to a person when he or she attains a specified age and until that time the property is devised to another person, the first person takes an absolutely vested interest and the second a term of years. The rule was designed to save contingent remainders that would otherwise be destroyed.

The rule only applies to real property[155] and only if the words of futurity are temporal such as "when," or "at," not if they are conditional.[156] The rule is excluded if the intermediate interest is not limited to the time when the ulterior beneficiary attains the specified age, but is for a definite time.[157]

3. VOID CONDITIONS

(a) Introduction

A condition may be void for a number of reasons, including public policy, impossibility of performance and uncertainty. In this context a distinction must be drawn between conditions precedent and conditions subsequent.

The common law rule applicable to real property is that a condition precedent which is void for public policy, uncertainty, repugnancy to a prior gift, or illegality, renders the gift void.

The common law rule applicable to personalty, however, is that an illegal condition precedent renders the gift void only if the condition is *malum in se*; whereas, if the condition is *malum prohibitum*, the condition is void but the gift is valid.[158] Further, if the condition is only voidable and is avoided by the bene-

---

153 See *Hawkins Estate v. Pike* (1986), 22 E.T.R. 265 (Nfld. T.D.).

154 (1587), 3 Co. Rep. 19a, 76 E.R. 668.

155 Although it does apply to a devise which includes leaseholds and freeholds in the same gift: *James v. Lord Wynford* (1852), 1 Sm. & G. 40, 65 E.R. 18; and to a bequest of personalty which is directed to be converted into real property: *Snow v. Poulden* (1836), 1 Keen. 186, 48 E.R. 277.

156 *Doe d. Wheedon v. Lea* (1789), 3 T.R. 41 at 43, 100 E.R. 445, *per* Ashhurst J.

157 *James v. Lord Wynford, supra.*

158 The distinction is discussed below.

ficiary, is repugnant to the gift, is *in terrorem*,[159] or fails to operate, the gift is absolute and free of the condition, whether it is precedent or subsequent.[160]

A condition subsequent which is void, whether annexed to a gift of real or personal property, makes the gift absolute and free of the condition.

Because the law favours vested gifts and disfavours the divesting of gifts, the courts prefer a construction which will permit a gift to take effect. Hence, the courts have traditionally attempted to construe a condition as subsequent and, if it is subsequent, will readily strike down the condition for one of the above-mentioned reasons.

You should note that if the gift does not create a condition, but rather a determinable limitation as in a gift "to A so long as she lives apart from her husband," and the determining event is void for any of the reasons enumerated above, the entire gift will fail.[161]

(b) Public Policy

(i) *Generally*

A condition is contrary to public policy if it requires the beneficiary to do something which is contrary to the interests of society. Thus, a condition requiring the beneficiary to commit a crime, or other act prohibited by law[162] or by statute,[163] is void. So are conditions requiring the beneficiary to separate from his or her spouse,[164] preventing him or her from performing a public duty,[165] and conditions contrary to parental obligations.[166]

These principles are discussed in *Blathwayt v. Baron Cawley* ,[167] reproduced below.

---

159 This is also discussed below.

160 See *Williams' Law Relating to Wills*, 7th ed. by C.H. Sherrin, R.D.F. Barlow & R.A. Wallington, assisted by Susannah Meadway (London: Butterworths, 1995), pp. 339-41.

161 *Re Moore; Trafford v. Maconochie* (1888), 39 Ch. D. 116, [1886-90] All E.R. Rep. 187; *Re Moore; Royal Trust Co. v. Moore*, [1954] 3 D.L.R. 407 (B.C.S.C.), reversed on other grounds (sub nom. *Royal Trust Co. v. Moore*) [1955] 4 D.L.R. 313 (B.C.C.A.), reversed [1956] S.C.R. 880, (sub nom. *Moore v. Royal Trust Co.*) 5 D.L.R. (2d) 152.

162 *Mitchel v Reynolds* (1711), 1 P. Wms. 181 at 189, 24 E.R. 347; *Earl of Shrewsbury v. Scott* (1859), 6 Jur. 452 at 456.

163 *Re Brown; Brown v. Brown* (1900), 32 O.R. 323 (H.C.).

164 *Re Nurse* (1921), 20 O.W.N. 428; *Re Fairfoull* (1973), 41 D.L.R. (3d) 152 (B.C.S.C.), reconsidered 44 D.L.R. (3d) 765, affirmed [1974] 6 W.W.R. 471, 18 R.F.L. 165; *Re McBride* (1980), 27 O.R. (2d) 513, 6 E.T.R. 181, 107 D.L.R. (3d) 233 (H.C.); *McDonald v. Brown Estate* (1995), 6 E.T.R. (2d) 160 (N.S.S.C.).

165 *Re Beard; Reversionary & General Securities Co. v. Hall*, [1908] 1 Ch. 383; *Re Morgan; Dowson v. Davey* (1910), 26 T.L.R. 398. And see *Re Pape*, [1946] 3 W.W.R. 8, [1946] 4 D.L.R. 700 (Alta. T.D.).

166 *Clarke v. Darraugh* (1884), 5 O.R. 140 (H.C.); *Re Thorne* (1922), 22 O.W.N. 28 (H.C.).

167 [1975] 3 W.L.R. 684, [1975] 3 All E.R. 625 (H.L.).

Other types of condition which are contrary to public policy, such as conditions repugnant to the interest given, conditions in restraint of marriage and *in terrorem* conditions will be dealt with separately below.

BLATHWAYT v. BARON CAWLEY
[1975] 3 W.L.R. 684, [1975] 3 All E.R. 625
House of Lords

The testator, by his will, devised certain real property upon trust for Christopher Blathwayt for life, with remainder in tail male to his sons. If Christopher did not have issue, there was a further remainder to Justin Blathwayt (Christopher's younger brother) for life, with remainder to his first and other sons successively in tail male. There were final remainders over.

Clause 9 of the will provided that if any life tenant or tenant in tail in possession should "be a Roman Catholic...the estate hereby limited to him shall cease and determine and be utterly void and my principal estate shall thereupon go to the person next entitled...."

In 1939 (three years after the testator's death), Christopher became a Roman Catholic. In an application then made to the court, it was held that Christopher forfeited his life interest and, since he did not then have a son, Justin's interest was accelerated, subject to defeasance if Christopher had a son subsequently. In 1949 Christopher's son, Mark, was born and was baptised a Roman Catholic. In a further application to the court, it was held that Justin's interest was not defeated. When Mark attained his majority, he executed a disentailing assurance and assigned to Justin for life all the interest to which he was entitled under the settlement.

The advice of the court was then sought as to who would be entitled to the property on Justin's death. The lower courts held that the property would be held on the same trusts as they would have been held on if Christopher had died without issue. Mark appealed.

The House of Lords held (all of the Law Lords concurring) that the condition subsequent was valid. The House further held, Lords Wilberforce and Fraser of Tullybelton dissenting, that the property should be held during the balance of Christopher's life on the same trusts as would have arisen had he died without issue, and subject thereto on trust for Mark. The following extracts from the speech of Lord Wilberforce deal with the validity of the condition in the will.

LORD WILBERFORCE:

. . .

1. On the question whether the forfeiture clause, in so far as it relates to being or becoming a Roman Catholic is void for uncertainty, I am clearly of opinion that it is not. Clauses relating in one way or another to the Roman Catholic Church, or faith, have been known and recognized for many years both in Acts of Parliament...and in wills and settlements for it now to be possible to avoid them on this ground. I am of course aware that the present clause is a condition

subsequent (or resolutive condition) and I need not quarrel with the accepted doctrine of English law derived from Lord Cranworth's words in *Clavering v. Ellison*[168] which requires a greater degree of certainty in advance as to the scope of such conditions than is needed when the condition is precedent (or suspensive). I can respect this distinction for the purposes of this case without renouncing the right, which I conceive judges have, to judge the degree of certainty with some measure of common sense and knowledge and without excessive astuteness to discover ambiguities. The decisions which have been given, in relation to clauses as to Roman Catholicism, as well as those in which such clauses have passed scrutiny sub silentio, are, with rare exceptions, one way....The balance of authority is thus strongly in favour of validity and the contrary would be barely arguable but for the views expressed in this House in *Clayton v. Ramsden*.[169] The condition there was composite "not of Jewish parentage and of the Jewish faith". It was held by all members of the House that the first limb (and therefore on this ground the whole condition) was void for uncertainty and by four of their Lordships that the second limb was void on the same ground. Lord Wright took the opposite view on the second limb, as had Lord Greene M.R. delivering the judgment of the Court of Appeal.

My Lords, I have no wish to whittle away decisions of this House by fine distinctions; but accepting, as I fully do, the opinions of the majority of their Lordships as regards the religious part of this condition, I do not consider myself obliged, or, indeed justified, in extending the conclusion there reached, as to uncertainty, to other clauses relating to other religions or branches of religions. The judgment of Lord Greene M.R. in the Court of Appeal[170] contains a very full account of decisions relating to the Roman Catholic faith, to the Protestant religion and the Church of England...and the Lutheran religion... All of these cases must, from a reading of that judgment, and from their Lordships' own experience, have been present to their minds. The absence of any reference to them in the speeches in this House refutes any suggestion that a new general principle was being laid down as to the invalidity on ground of uncertainty of all subsequent conditions whatsoever relating to all varieties of religious belief. It confirms that the decision in *Clayton v. Ramsden*[171] was a particular decision on a condition expressed in a particular way about one kind of religious belief or profession. I do not think it right to apply it to Roman Catholicism.

2. Finally, as to public policy. The argument under this heading was put in two alternative ways. First, it was said that the law of England was now set against discrimination on a number of grounds including religious grounds, and appeal was made to the Race Relations Act 1968[172] which does not refer to religion and to the European Convention of Human Rights of 1950 which refers to freedom of religion and to enjoyment of that freedom and other freedoms without discrim-

---

168 (1859), 7 H.L. Cas. 707, 725.
169 [1943] A.C. 320, [1943] 1 All E.R. 16.
170 *In re Samuel; Jacobs v. Ramsden*, [1942] Ch. 1, [1941] 3 All E.R. 196.
171 [1943] A.C. 320, [1943] All E.R. 16.
172 C. 71 (U.K.).

ination on ground of religion. My Lords, I do not doubt that conceptions of public policy should move with the times and that widely accepted treaties and statutes may point the direction in which such conceptions, as applied by the courts, ought to move. It may well be that conditions such as this are, or at least are becoming, inconsistent with standards now widely accepted. But acceptance of this does not persuade me that we are justified, particularly in relation to a will which came into effect as long ago as 1936 and which has twice been the subject of judicial consideration, in introducing for the first time a rule of law which would go far beyond the mere avoidance of discrimination on religious grounds. To do so would bring about a substantial reduction of another freedom, firmly rooted in our law, namely that of testamentary disposition. Discrimination is not the same thing as choice: it operates over a larger and less personal area, and neither by express provision nor by implication has private selection yet become a matter of public policy.

The other and narrower branch of the argument is that first given modern currency by Parker J. in *In re Sandbrook, Noel v. Sandbrook*.[173] A condition "is bad which operates to restrain or forbid a man from doing his duty." This principle was applied to a condition applicable to a child during infancy, forfeiting his interest if he should "be or become a Roman Catholic or not be openly or avowedly Protestant"....[174]

My Lords, the force of the observations of Parker J. in *In re Sandbrook*, in relation to conditions applying to infants, may well be appreciated but is diminished to some extent at least by the doctrine evolved by the courts that, where an infant is involved, the time for choice as to compliance or non-compliance with the condition must be postponed until majority and a reasonable time thereafter.[175] In view of this sensible mitigation of the conditions, I do not find myself able to discern a rule of public policy sufficiently clear and definite for total invalidation of conditions of the kind now in question. To say that any condition which in any way might affect or influence the way in which a child is brought up, or in which parental duties are exercised, seems to me to state far too wide a rule. And even if the rule were confined to religious upbringing, I am unpersuaded that, in relation to landed estates in which family attitudes and traditions may be strong and valued by testators, and moreover which may often involve close association with one or another Church, public policy requires that testators may not prefer one branch of the family to another upon religious grounds. Certainly I should need much more concrete and positive reasons bearing upon the particular gift in question before I felt justified in nullifying the condition the testator has chosen to attach. After all, a choice between considerations of material prosperity and spiritual welfare has to be made by many parents for their children - and, one may add, by judges in infants' interests - and it would be cynical to assume that these cannot be conscientiously and rightly made....I would therefore reject all the appellant's arguments against the validity of the condition.

---

173 [1912] 2 Ch. 471, 477.
174 *In re Borwick*, [1933] Ch. 659.
175 See *In re May* and *In re May (No 2)*, [1932] 1 Ch. 99.

. . .

[The other Law Lords all agreed on this issue. Their concurring speeches have been omitted.]

Notes and Questions

1. If a condition subsequent requiring the beneficiary not to be married to a Roman Catholic is valid, would a similar condition precedent be valid? Would the condition be valid in either case if the reference was to the Jewish or another faith?[176]

(ii) *Restraints on Marriage*

A general restraint on marriage is *prima facie* void as being contrary to public policy, whether the condition be precedent or subsequent.[177] However, if the will shows that the testator did not intend to promote celibacy, but to provide for the person while single, or for some other lawful reason, the condition will be valid.[178]

Partial restraints on marriage, such as a condition against remarriage,[179] against marriage to a named person,[180] or against marriage without consent[181] are valid, provided they are reasonable in the circumstances.[182] *Re Goodwin*,[183] reproduced below, is a case of this type. This type of restraint may be subject to the *in terrorem* rule, however.[184]

RE GOODWIN
(1969), 3 D.L.R. (3d) 281
Supreme Court of Alberta
[Trial Division]

The testator gave one-half of his estate to his daughter-in-law, "provided she does not remarry," with a gift over in the event that she did remarry. The daughter-in-law remarried six months after the testator's death.

---

176 See *Re Tuck's Settlement Trusts; Pub. Trustee v. Tuck* [1978] 2 W.L.R. 411, [1978] Ch. 49, [1978] 1 All E.R. 1047 (C.A.), reproduced *infra*.

177 *Re Cutter* (1916), 37 O.L.R. 42, 31 D.L.R. 382 (H.C.).

178 *Re McBain* (1915), 8 O.W.N. 330 (H.C.).

179 *Re Deller* (1903), 6 O.L.R. 711 (H.C.); *Cowan v. Allen* (1896), 26 S.C.R. 292 at 313. But see *Re Tucker* (1910), 16 W.L.R. 172, 3 Sask. L.R. 473 (S.C.); *Re Muirhead*, [1919] 2 W.W.R. 454, 12 Sask. L.R. 123 (K.B.).

180 *Re Bathe; Bathe v. Pub. Trustee*, [1925] Ch. 377.

181 *Re Whiting's Settlement; Whiting v. De Rutzen*, [1905] 1 Ch. 96 (C.A.).

182 However, in *Desparts v. Petit* (1988), 34 E.T.R. 200 (Que. S.C.) the court held that such a clause infringes the Quebec *Charter of Rights and Freedoms*, because the widow in that case was in dire need and could not afford to remarry. Further, in *Béland-Abraham v. Abraham-Kriaa* (1989), 35 E.T.R. 118 (Que. S.C.) the court held that such clauses should always be treated as invalid because of the Quebec *Charter*.

183 (1969), 3 D.L.R. (3d) 281 (Alta. T.D.).

184 This rule is discussed below.

An application was made to construe the will, the question being whether the daughter-in-law had forfeited her interest.

RILEY J.:

. . .

The remarriage of Mrs. North (nee Goodwin) took place prior to the probate of the estate or prior, of course, to any distribution and accordingly Mrs. North (nee Goodwin) by such remarriage had already eliminated herself from any proposed distribution by virtue of such remarriage which occurrence was foreseen by the deceased and which occurrence he provided for in the terms of his will, and accordingly, pursuant to the said terms of his will Mrs. North (nee Goodwin) has divested herself of any interest whatsoever in the estate.

A distinction is of course drawn between a condition against marriage or requiring marriage with a particular person or a particular class of persons and a condition wherein the words used relating to marriage merely describe the interest to be taken by the donee. There is no prohibition to a gift to a donee so long as the donee remains unmarried for marriage may be the ground for which a gift is given or is revoked.

. . .

In the case of *Re Gilbert*,[185] the testator devised and bequeathed all his real and personal property to his widow "'subject to the proviso that, in the event that she should predecease me or remarry, I then bequeath all my property to...' his children in various shares set out in the clause."

. . .

It was held in this case that the personalty was an outright gift to the widow and that she had a fee simple in the real estate subject to the possibility of a right of re-entry in the children which might not be exercised if she did not remarry. However, if she should remarry then she would be divested of any interest which she may have with respect to the real estate.

. . .

In the case of *Re Jackson, Houston v. Western Trust Co.*,[186] the testator's will read in part that he gave the realty to his widow "so long as she remains my widow, and upon her remarriage..." The question here to be determined by the Court was whether or not the wife was left a life estate in the real property or a gift absolute subject to a defeasance on remarriage. It was held that there was an absolute gift of the real property subject to defeasance on remarriage only thus if she died without remarrying then the realty was hers absolutely and she could dispose of it in her own will.

---

185 [1959] O.W.N. 294.
186 [1940] 1 D.L.R. 283, [1940] 1 W.W.R. 65.

. . .

In the case of *Re Perrie*,[187] the following principles were laid down:

(a) If it is to the wife so long as she remains unmarried and if she dies without remarrying then it belongs to her estate.

(b) If it is to the wife during her widowhood then her right ceases either with her death or with her remarrying.

It does not matter that the donee is not a widow of the testator although historically the rationality for the rule allowing restraint against remarriages was the interest of his wife's widowhood....

The intention of the testator was only to provide for the daughter-in-law while she was in fact a widow and that upon her remarriage it was his intention to provide for his grandson on the basis that his daughter-in-law would then be provided for out of her subsequent remarriage.

The will does not avoid the "*in terrorem* rule" and in no sense is a restraint against marriage.

Even if Judith North (nee Goodwin) is entitled to the realty on the death of the deceased, it is divested upon the remarriage, and she is only entitled to the interest on the realty from the date of the death until the date of her remarriage meaning thereby from January 16, 1968, to July 27, 1968. The maxim *de minimis non curat lex* would seem to apply: see *Bechthold v. Osbaldeston*.[188]

. . .

Notes and Questions

1. A testator made a gift to his daughter provided she did not marry before age 28. Is the condition valid?[189]

2. A testator gave a gift to his son provided that he not marry "a relation by blood." Is the condition valid?[190]

3. *MacDonald* v. *Brown Estate*[191] shows that a gift to a person when she is widowed or divorced is not necessarily contrary to public policy. It depends on the testator's intention. The testator left property to a niece subject to her becoming "widowed or divorced from her present husband." The court held that the condition was not contrary to public policy, since the testator's intention was not to induce divorce but to provide for the niece in the event she should become widowed or divorced.

(iii) *In Terrorem Conditions*

An *in terrorem* condition is one that is imposed as a mere threat to induce the beneficiary to comply with it, but not so as to affect the gift. The rules respecting

---

187 (1910), 21 O.L.R. 100 at pp. 104-5.
188 [1953] 4 D.L.R. 783, [1953] 2 S.C.R. 177.
189 *Younge v. Furse* (1857), 8 De G. M. & G. 756, 44 E.R. 581.
190 *Re Lanyon; Lanyon v. Lanyon*, [1927] 2 Ch. 264, [1927] All E.R. Rep. 61.
191 (1995), 6 E.T.R. (2d) 160 (N.S.S.C.).

these conditions derive from the civil law via the ecclesiastical courts and, since those courts only had jurisdiction over testaments of personal property, they apply even now only to gifts of personal property,[192] and to gifts out of a mixed fund of real property and personal property.[193]

The *in terrorem* doctrine is normally applied to conditions, both precedent and subsequent, in partial restraint of marriage[194] and conditions prohibiting the beneficiary from disputing the will. *Kent and Christie v. McKay, Green, Royal Trust Corp. of Canada and Kent*,[195] reproduced below, is an example of the latter type.

The doctrine is normally avoided if there is a gift over, or a direction that the gift is to fall into residue on failure to fulfil the condition, since this indicates that the testator did not merely threaten the beneficiary but wanted to make a different disposition in the event the condition was not complied with.[196] A provision for the beneficiary whether the condition is complied with or not also avoids the doctrine.[197]

RE KENT
[1982] 6 W.W.R. 165, 13 E.T.R. 53,
38 B.C.L.R. 216, 139 D.L.R. (3d) 318
Supreme Court of British Columbia

The testator, Max Alexander Kent, left a will by which he gave his entire estate in trust for his wife and daughter and after the death of his wife upon two separate trusts for his two children for life, with remainder to their children.

The testator was concerned that his children might squander the estate if he gave them large amounts of money. Hence, he limited their interests to life estates and further provided in clause 9 that if any beneficiary should commence litigation in connection with any provision of the will, other than for interpretation thereof, or for the direction of the court in the course of administration, the benefits to which such beneficiary would have been entitled would cease and be revoked and fall into residue. Further, that if the beneficiary was also entitled to share in the residue, his or her share should be divided equally amongst the other beneficiaries.

The two children wished to seek further support out of the estate under the *Wills Variation Act*.[198] Hence they brought this application for an order declaring that an application for relief would not offend clause 9 and that clause 9 was void if it purported to do so.

---

192 *Bellairs v. Bellairs* (1874), L.R. 18 Eq. 510 at 515-6; *Reynish v. Martin* (1746), 3 Atk. 330, 26 E.R. 991.
193 *Re Hamilton* (1901), 1 O.L.R. 10 (H.C.); *Re Schmidt*, [1949] 2 W.W.R. 513, 57 Man R. 316 (K.B.).
194 *Reynish v. Martin, supra.*
195 [1982] 6 W.W.R. 165, 38 B.C.L.R. 216, 13 E.T.R. 53, 139 D.L.R. (3d) 318 (S.C.).
196 *Re Pashak*, [1923] 1 W.W.R. 873, [1923] 1 D.L.R. 1130 (Alta T.D.), actually in case involving a determinable interest.
197 *Re Nourse; Hampton v. Nourse*, [1899] 1 Ch. 63 at 71.
198 R.S.B.C. 1979, c. 435.

LANDER L.J.S.C.:

. . .

As to the first question, such application for relief under the Wills Variation Act is "litigation" within the meaning of para. 9 of the will. The term "litigation" encompasses the act of carrying on a legal proceeding.... A legal proceeding connotes the resolution by a judicial tribunal of an issue between two parties....

In the case at bar an application to the court under the Wills Variation Act would involve an issue between what is essentially two parties, the issue being whether the testator had made adequate provision for the maintenance and support of his children. The first question is answered in the affirmative. Therefore such an application under the Wills Variation Act being "litigation", and if para. 9 is valid, such an application by the petitioners would result in revocation of such benefits they might receive under the will.

The next consideration is to determine the validity of para. 9. The argument submitted by the petitioners is that it is not valid based on public policy grounds and these grounds are broken down into three distinct parts; they are:

1. That the provision attempts to deprive the Court of jurisdiction.

2. That the paragraph purports to grant the petitioners their interest on the condition that they will not dispute the will, and seeks to enforce that condition by threat. Such a condition in a will, imposed *in terrorem* is invalid at common law.

3. That the paragraph denies the petitioners their right to apply for relief under the Wills Variation Act.

As to the first ground, that if para. 9 had been inserted to deprive the petitioners of their right to apply to the courts to establish their existing legal rights, such a clause having this effect is contrary to public policy.[199] However, subject to the determination in the third ground, I have concluded that para. 9 does not have the effect of curtailing any action to enforce their legal rights. The very wording of the paragraph itself preserves to the petitioners certain rights to apply to the court. The petitioners are at liberty to commence proceedings for direction and interpretation, which is the case presently before the court.

. . .

As to ground two, that is the challenge made that para. 9 is a clause in terrorem, such a condition attached to a legacy of personalty may be void if made in such a manner. There are three criteria which must be met before the doctrine in terrorem is applicable:

(i) The legacy must be of personal property or blended personal and real property.[200]

---

199 See *Re Raven; Spencer v. Nat. Assn. for the Prevention of Consumption & Other Forms of Tuberculosis*, [1915] 1 Ch. 673; and *Re Bronson*, [1958] O.R. 367, 14 D.L.R. (2d) 51 (H.C.).
200 See *Re Hamilton* (1901), 1 O.L.R. 10; *Re Schmidt*, 57 Man. R. 316, [1949] 2 W.W.R. 513 (K.B.).

(ii) The condition must be either a restraint on marriage or one which forbids the donee to dispute the will.

(iii) The "threat" must be "idle"; that is the condition must be imposed solely to prevent the donee from undertaking that which the condition forbids. Therefore a provision which provides only for a bare forfeiture of the gift on breach of the condition is bad. However, if the donor indicates that he intended not only to threaten the donee but also to make a different disposition of the property to fix a benefit on another in the event of a breach of the condition, the "threat" is not "idle" and the condition is valid.[201]

In this instance there is no doubt that the legacies in this case contain personalty and, further, there is no doubt that the "condition" enjoins the petitioners from disputing the will.

In this instance is such a "threat" idle? Ordinarily if a provision which contains such a condition is followed by a gift over in the event of a breach of that condition, the condition is held to be valid.[202] While certain authorities question whether a gift over is always necessary, I have concluded in this instance that para. 9 of the testator's will creates a gift over. The words, "I direct that said benefits so revoked shall fall into and form part of the residue of my Estate" are sufficient to constitute a gift over for the purpose of meeting the in terrorem doctrine. Therefore the paragraph is valid and not subject to the doctrine, even if para. 9 does not completely deprive the court of jurisdiction. However, by depriving the petitioners of their right to apply for relief under the Wills Variation Act, para. 9 may be invalid as a provision which is contrary to public policy.

It is apparent that this "public policy" ground is not well known to the common law and indeed does not appear to have been argued in Canada, as indicated by the paucity of Canadian authorities. The only available reference is an Australian case, *Re Gaynor*.[203] In that case Gaynor's will contained a declaration which was similar to para. 9 and provided that if any beneficiary instituted any action to contest the will such beneficiary would forfeit all of his or her interest. In *Gaynor* the daughter of the testator wished to make an application under the provisions of the Administration and Probate Act, 1958,[204] which exists in the state of Victoria, Australia and is, as I understand it, virtually on all fours with the Wills Variation Act. In her application the daughter wished to contend that the testator had not made adequate provision for her proper maintenance and support. She applied for an interpretation of the clause and O'Bryan J. of the Supreme Court of Victoria held that the condition was void because it was imposed in terrorem. However, more importantly for our purposes, he also held the condition was void as it was opposed to public policy.

The learned judge reasoned that the dependent's [*sic*] relief legislation which the daughter sought to invoke was legislation imposed as a matter of public concern, and he states at p. 643 "...because it is a matter of public concern that

---

201 Feeney, *Canadian Law of Wills (Construction)*, vol. 2, 2nd ed. (1982), pp. 200-201.
202 Jarman on Wills, p. 1255.
203 [1906] V.L.R. 640.
204 (No. 6191), Pt. IV (Vict.).

they [dependents] [*sic*] should not be left without adequate provision for their proper maintenance and support..."

. . .

It cannot be denied with respect that the intent of the legislature in creating the Wills Variation Act is to ensure adequate maintenance and support for specified individuals. It is a matter of public policy that support and maintenance be provided for those defined individuals and it would be contrary to such policy to allow a testator to circumvent the provisions of the Wills Variation Act by the creation of such as para. 9. It is important to the public as a whole that widows, widowers and children be at liberty to apply for adequate maintenance and support in the event that sufficient provision for them is not made in the will of their spouse or parent. I have concluded that the intent of para. 9 was to prevent any such application. It is not necessary for the purposes of this decision to conjure up scenarios wherein inequitable and distressing results are created for a widow or children by being deprived of maintenance and support while an "undeserving" beneficiary takes under a will. Paragraph 9 therefore is void as against public policy. The petitioners shall have their costs of this application from the estate.

Notes and Questions

1. In *Re Goodwin*,[205] Riley J., held that the gift in that case did not offend the *in terrorem* doctrine. Why?
2. The doctrine does not apply to devises of real property,[206] legacies charged on freeholds, or bequests of personalty directed to be used to purchase land.[207]
3. A provision in a will which requires the resolution of any dispute concerning the will by binding arbitration is void, since it ousts the court from exercising its jurisdiction to interpret the will.[208]

Further Reading

Gerry W. Beyer, Rob G. Dickinson, and Kenneth L. Wake, "The Fine Art of Intimidating Disgruntled Beneficiaries with *In Terrorem* Clauses" (1998), 51 SMU L. Rev. 225.

(iv) *Conditions* Malum Prohibitum *and* Malum in Se

The distinction between conditions which are *malum in se* and those which are *malum prohibitum* also derives from the civil law and, therefore, also applies only to personalty and to a mixed fund of realty and personalty.[209] Unfortunately the

---

205 (1969), 3 D.L.R. (3d) 281 (Alta. T.D.). The case is reproduced above.
206 *Jenner v. Turner* (1880), 16 Ch. D. 188.
207 *Reynish v. Martin*, (1746), 3 Atk. 330, 26 E.R. 991.
208 See *Adams v. Adams*, [1892] 1 Ch. 369 (C.A.).
209 See *Bellairs v. Bellairs* (1874), L.R. 18 Eq. 510; *Reynish v. Martin* (1746), 3 Atk. 330, 26 E.R. 991; *Re Hamilton* (1901), 1 O.L.R. 10 (H.C.); *Re Schmidt*, [1949] 2 W.W.R. 513, 57 Man. R. 316 (K.B.).

distinction between these two types of condition has never been clearly defined. The cases usually refer back to *Sheppard's Touchstone* which defines these terms as follows: "anything which in its nature, is *malum in se*, as to kill a man, or the like; or *malum prohibitum*, being a thing forbidden of any statute or the like."[210]

While the distinctions are, thus, unclear, it is clear that a condition precedent *malum prohibitum* renders the gift absolute, while a condition precedent *malum in se* renders the condition and the gift void.[211]

Re McBride,[212] reproduced below, considers the distinction.

RE McBRIDE
(1980), 27 O.R. (2d) 513, 6 E.T.R. 181, 107 D.L.R. (3d) 233
Supreme Court of Ontario
[High Court of Justice]

The testator, John Donald McBride, died in 1979. By his will, made in 1974, he gave a life estate to his wife, with remainder in clauses 3(e) and (f) to three named charities equally if his son, Robert, should be married to Geraldine Gibbons, or to Robert if he should not be married to Geraldine.

Robert married Geraldine in 1973 and remained happily married to her. The testator never liked Robert's female companions and had always broken up his relationships with women, but Robert persisted with Geraldine, despite arguments from his father, according to Robert's affidavit.

Robert brought this application for advice and directions.

HENRY J.:

. . .

I have considered the language of paras. 3(e) and 3(f) of the will with care and find that on their face, the only reasonable view to take of the testator's intention is that he intended to promote the divorce of the spouses either as a result of one of them committing a matrimonial offence, or by collusion. The affidavit fortifies me in this conclusion and I find accordingly.

The condition is therefore void as being contrary to public policy. See *Re Fairfoull*,[213] and authorities therein cited.

As the conditions in both paragraphs, in my opinion, are directed towards the same end, namely the dissolution of the son's marriage, both are declared void.

Question 2 raises further issues. Although, as I have found the condition is void as being contrary to public policy, the gift does not fail if the reason for invalidity is malum prohibitum and not malum in se. While the distinction between the two

---

210 (8th ed., 1826), vol. 1, p. 123.
211 *Jarman on Wills*, 8th ed. by Raymond Jennings, assisted by John C. Harper (London: Sweet & Maxwell Limited, 1951), vol. 2, pp. 1457-8.
212 (1980), 27 O.R. (2d) 513, 6 E.T.R. 181, 107 D.L.R. (3d) 233 (H.C.), noted A.H. Oosterhoff (1980), 5 E. & T.Q. 97.
213 (1974), 41 D.L.R. (3d) 152 (B.C.S.C.), affirmed (sub nom. *Can. Permanent Trust Co. v. Bullman*), [1974] 6 W.W.R. 471, 18 R.F.L. 165 (B.C.S.C.) (further proceedings).

is somewhat obscure according to the scholars, I adopt the reasoning in *Re Fairfoull*..., where it was held that a testator's attempt to invade the sanctity of his son's marriage was malum prohibitum and that although the condition is void, the gift does not fail.

I am then urged by Mr. Eisen on behalf of the charities to recognize a principle found in the English cases that where a condition precedent (as distinct from a condition subsequent) is void an accompanying devise of real estate fails, his argument being, as I understand it, that any real property in the estate would then go to the charities under para. 3(e) if Robert McBride remains married to Geraldine. As is pointed out by the learned author of Sheard Canadian Forms of Wills,[214] however, this principle does not appear to have been adopted in Canada and he refers to the decision of the Ontario Court of Appeal in *Re Gross*[215] and *Re Going*.[216]

For that reason I do not consider the principle applicable here. I add moreover that there is no specific devise of real property in the will, there is no evidence that there is real property in the assets of the estate and in any event, as what is here concerned is residue, if the fund is mixed realty and personalty, in my opinion the rule to be followed is that relating to personalty, namely that the gift does not fail.

What then is the gift that is preserved? Reading paras. 3(e) and (f) together their combined effect reflects the testator's intention to disinherit his son if he is married to Geraldine but to pass the entire residue to him on the death of his mother if he is not. The object of the testator, as I see it, is to achieve dissolution of the marriage and not to deprive his son for any other reason or motive. He intends his son to inherit but seeks to terminate the marriage. When the condition fails the gift to Robert McBride is absolute; the charities were never intended to benefit except as a device to induce termination of the marriage.

In the result, therefore, Robert McBride will be entitled to the residue upon his mother's death, regardless of whether he is or is not then married to Geraldine.

The answer to Q.2 is therefore that the gift over to the charities will fail and the gift to Robert McBride under para. 3(f) be absolute.

As to Q.3, both conditions are conditions precedent because (assuming their validity) no gift is intended under either paragraph unless at the date of the death of the testator's widow, the defined state of the son's marriage exists. It is not a case where the gift takes effect subject to subsequent defeasance or condition, which is the essence of a condition subsequent.

. . .

Notes and Questions

1. I submit that *Re McBride* is of dubious authority. In the first place, the British Columbia case relied upon by the court, *Re Fairfoull*,[217] itself relied upon a number of

---

214   2d ed. (1960), pp. 261-63.
215   [1937] O.W.N. 88 (C.A.).
216   [1951] O.R. 147, [1951] 2 D.L.R. 136 (C.A.).
217   *Supra*, footnote 213.

cases which involved conditions subsequent, in which the issue is quite different. Second, the reference to Sheard, *Canadian Forms of Wills*[218] is incorrect, since that text states the opposite of what Henry J., stated in *McBride*. Sheard says that the English rule that a condition precedent annexed to a gift of personalty is void if the condition is *malum prohibitum*, but that the gift is valid, has not been adopted in Canada, but that in Canada the rule which also applies in England to real property, namely that a void condition precedent annexed to a devise of real property renders the devise void, is applied to conditions precedent annexed to personal property. Third, the two Ontario Court of Appeal cases, *Re Gross*[219] and *Re Going*[220] rejected the civil law rule, albeit in *dicta*.

Earlier cases in which the civil law rule was applied,[221] or adverted to[222] are, therefore, also of doubtful authority.

2. Assuming that the *malum prohibitum*, *malum in se* distinction is applicable in Canada, which of the following bequests are *malum prohibitum* and which *malum in se*?

(a) A condition calculated to bring about the separation of parent and child in the following form: "To such of A's children as attain the age of 30 and do not before attaining such age reside with A."[223]

(b) A bequest to A, "provided she accept a legacy to maintain the testator's grave," such a legacy being void for perpetuity (indefinite duration).[224]

(c) A bequest on condition that the legatee has, until vesting, been permitted to remain in her grandparents', rather than her parents', custody.[225]

(d) A bequest upon condition that the beneficiary is a member and adherent in good faith and standing in a Protestant Church.[226]

3. Should the distinction that exists between conditions precedent and subsequent annexed to gifts of personal property and those annexed to gifts of real property be abolished? If so, which regime should be adopted?

(v) *Repugnant Conditions*

A condition is repugnant to the interest granted if it interferes with or restricts the enjoyment of the property. Gifts which offend the rule in *Saunders v. Vautier*[227] fall into this category. So do restraints on alienation, discussed in *Re Collier*,[228] reproduced below. Attempts to interfere with the legal course of devolution also fall into this category, as will be seen from the notes and questions.

---

218 (2nd ed, 1960), pp 261-3. See now 4th ed. (1982), pp. 214-6.
219 [1937] O.W.N. 88 (C.A.).
220 [1951] O.R. 147, [1951] 2 D.L.R. 136 (C.A.).
221 *Re Hamilton* (1901), 1 O.L.R. 10.
222 *McKinnon v. Lundy* (1893), 24 O.R. 132 at 140, reversed 21 O.A.R. 560, reversed (sub nom. *Lundy v. Lundy*) (1895), 24 S.C.R. 650; *Re Patton; Patton v. Toronto Gen. Trusts Corp.*, [1930] A.C. 629, 636, [1930] 3 W.W.R. 1, [1930] 4 D.L.R. 321 (P.C.); *Re Starr*, [1946] O.R. 252, [1946] 2 D.L.R. 489 (C.A.); *Re Curran*, [1939] O.W.N. 191, [1939] 2 D.L.R. 803n (H.C.).
223 *Re Piper; Dodd v. Piper*, [1946] 2 All E.R. 503.
224 *Re Elliott*, [1952] Ch. 217, [1952] 1 All E.R. 145.
225 *Re Gross, supra*.
226 *Re Going, supra*.
227 (1841), Cr. & Ph. 240, 41 E.R. 482. This rule was discussed earlier in this chapter.
228 (1966), 60 D.L.R. (2d) 70, 52 M.P.R. 211 (Nfld. T.D.).

RE COLLIER
(1966), 60 D.L.R. (2d) 70, 52 M.P.R. 211
Newfoundland Supreme Court
[Trial Division]

The testator devised certain land to his nephew, or the nephew's children, or son, but directed that it should not be "sold, mortgaged or exchanged, or conveyed in any way, from the descendants of said family forever." The property was conveyed to the nephew subject to the proviso and when the nephew died, his estate proposed to sell it to someone outside the family. The nephew's executrix sought a declaration from the court that the proviso in the original will was void.

PUDDESTER J.:

. . .

The question I have to decide, therefore, is does the law permit a testator to annex to a devise of an absolute estate a condition that the devisee shall not alienate the property except to someone unnamed of a named class. I prefer to deal with the matter on this basis even though the condition as worded might be invalid on other grounds, that is, because it might not be possible to ascertain the "family" at a given time or because there is nothing said as to what is to happen to the property if it is alienated contrary to the condition, or because it restrains alienation for ever. In my opinion, without deciding the matter, the condition is void for uncertainty on each of those grounds.

. . .

In *Blackburn and Cox v. McCallum,*[229] where the person to whom the estate was devised was restrained from selling or encumbering it for a period of 25 years after the testator's death, the Supreme Court of Canada...held that a restraint which was void was not made good by putting a time limit on it. Mills, J.[230] states the principle in this way:

> Where property is given absolutely a condition cannot be annexed to the gift inconsistent with its absolute character, and where a devise in fee is made upon condition that the estate shall be shorn of some of its necessary incidents, as that...or that the proprietor shall not have the power to alien, either generally, or for a time limited, such conditions are void, because they are repugnant to the character of the estate.

In *Doherty v. Doherty*[231] it was held that a devise by a testator to his wife for life, with remainder to his sons and survivors of each, creates an estate in fee simple in favour of the sons upon the death of the life tenant; and that a condition in the will denying them the power to sell, mortgage or encumber their estate in any way except to one or more of the brothers, or to will it except to the devisee's

---

229 (1903), 33 S.C.R. 65.
230 *Ibid.,* at pp. 92-3.
231 [1936] 2 D.L.R. 180, 10 M.P.R. 286.

children, is inoperative as a restraint upon alienation because in a gift in fee simple no condition can be annexed not consistent with the absoluteness of the gift. And in *Re Malcolm*,[232] McRuer, C.J.H.C., held that a condition attached to a devise in fee simple as follows:[233]

> Upon and subject to the condition, however, that the said lands are not to be sold or mortgaged during the lifetime of my said two daughters or the survivor of them, except that one of my said daughters may convey the said lands to the other to be held on the terms hereinbefore set out.

was repugnant to the devise in fee simple since it deprived the daughters throughout their lives of fully enjoying the estate, and was therefore invalid. In those three Canadian cases reference was made to the four English cases I have already mentioned.

. . .

The test is one of repugnancy. The original rule was that you cannot annex to a gift in fee simple a condition which is repugnant to that gift. It has long been recognized that the right of alienation is a necessary incident to the fee simple....Indeed, the fundamental principle now adopted is

> that a condition, the effect of which would be to destroy or take away the enjoyment of the fee simple given is repugnant to the rights conferred on the holder of the fee,

to use the words of McRuer, C.J.H.C., in the *Malcolm* case.[234]

Frederick Collier's will gives to Eric Collier an absolute estate in the Forest Road property and then adds a condition which limits alienation of the property to a small class; a class which, at any given time, may be difficult to ascertain in any event, a class which, at any given time, for a variety of reasons, may not exist at all, but a class in which, nevertheless, must be found at any given time a person willing and financially able to enter into dealings about the property. If that condition is good, then Eric Collier is to all intents and purposes deprived for his whole life of his right to alienate the property and thus of full enjoyment of the property. In my view, both on principle and on authority, such a condition is repugnant to the absolute estate given to Eric Collier and as such is invalid.

. . .

Notes and Questions

1. In *Re Collier* the court noted that, while a total restraint on alienation is void, a partial restraint may be valid. With that in mind, are the following conditions void?

(a) A testatrix devised certain property to her husband, but provided that it should not be sold during her sister's lifetime and, if he predeceased the sister, it should be returned to her.[235]

---

232 [1947] 4 D.L.R. 756, [1947] O.W.N. 871.
233 *Ibid.,* at p. 757.
234 *Ibid.,* at p. 758.
235 *Cook v. Nova Scotia* (1982) 53 N.S.R. (2d) 87, 109 A.P.R. 87 (T.D.).

(b) A testator devised a farm to his wife for life and then to his son, Ivan, for life, with remainder to his son Allan. However, he provided that if Ivan wished to sell the farm he could do so with the consent of Allan or Allan's heirs. In that event Ivan and Allan or his heirs would each receive one-half of the residue of the estate, including the proceeds of the sale of the farm.[236]

(c) A testator devised real property "to my four sons in equal shares...this property to remain in the family, but if so desired any son or sons may buy the other shares."[237]

2. A large number of Canadian cases involves wills in which testators of East European extraction purport to make gifts to their relatives behind the Iron Curtain, but in order to ensure that those relatives actually receive the money, give the trustees a discretion to send it to them by way of parcels of consumable goods. Such attempts usually fail, the discretion of the trustees being held repugnant to the gift. They would succeed if the gift were entirely in the trustee's discretion.[238]

3. The rule against restraints on alienation also applies to deeds, but in that context an apparent condition is often construed as a covenant which, if breached, entitles the injured party to sue for damages only and not to forfeit the land.[239]

4. A testatrix and her husband owned their house in unequal shares as tenants in common. She devised her interest in the house to her husband "for his own use absolutely," but also provided that if the house was sold $25,000 was to be paid to her sister and $25,000 to her parents. Is the condition valid?[240]

5. A testator devised his house to his nephew "for his own use absolutely, provided and only in the event" that he reside in it for 10 years and that he should not encumber the property in any manner or use it as security for a loan during the 10 years. If the nephew did not use the property continuously as a home for 10 years, the house was to be sold and the proceeds divided among the testator's nephews and nieces equally. Is the condition against encumbrance void?[241]

6. A testator devised his house to his wife "for her own use absolutely," but provided that if she should sell it she was to pay half the proceeds to his son. Is the condition valid?[242]

7. Neither a right of first refusal nor an option given on property devised by the same will to another person is a restraint on alienation. The devise is simply subject to the other right.[243]

8. The repugnancy rule also applies to conditions which attempt to interfere with the legal course of devolution.

---

236 *Re Driscoll* (1983), 40 O.R. (2d) 744 (H.C.).

237 See *Wood v. Wood Estate* (1990), 37 E.T.R. 306 (N.B.Q.B.).

238 See, *e.g.*, *Re Hordynsky* (1983), 27 Sask. R. 196, 13 E.T.R. 157 (Q.B.); *Re Czykalenko* (1984), 42 O.R. (2d) 631, 15 E.T.R. 3, 150 D.L.R. (3d) 68 (H.C.); *Melnik (Melnyk) v. Sawycky*, [1978] 1 W.W.R. 107, 2 E.T.R. 120, 80 D.L.R. (3d) 371 (Sask. C.A.); *Hawryluk Estate v. Hawryluk* (1989), 34 E.T.R. 286 (Man. Q.B.).

239 See *Stephens v. Gulf Oil Can. Ltd.* (1975), 11 O.R. (2d) 129, 25 C.P.R. (2d) 64, 65 D.L.R. (3d) 193 (C.A.), leave to appeal to S.C.C. refused 11 O.R. 129n, 65 D.L.R. 193n; *Laurin v. Iron Ore Co.* (1977), 19 Nfld. & P.E.I.R. 111, 7 R.P.R. 137, 82 D.L.R. (3d) 634 (Nfld. T.D.); *B.C. Forest Products Ltd. v. Gay* (1978), 7 B.C.L.R. 190, 89 D.L.R. (3d) 80 (C.A.). See, however, *Trinity College School v. Lyons* (1995), 47 R.P.R. (2d) 95 (Ont. Gen. Div.), in which an option to purchase at a fixed price on the owner's death was held to be an unlawful restraint on alienation.

240 See *Re Johnson* (1985), 19 E.T.R. 260 (Alta. Q.B.).

241 See *Beadle v. Gaudette et al.* (1985), 21 E.T.R. 117 (B.C.S.C.).

242 See *Angus v. Angus Estate* (1989), 35 E.T.R. 170 (Ont. H.C.).

243 See *Allen v. Allen* (1994), 2 E.T.R. (2d) 276 (Sask. Q.B.).

In *Re Gee*[244] the testator, Gee Kee, by his will made in 1949, gave the residue equally to his four sons and two named grandsons, but provided that if his son Wing Leong Gee should die before his discharge as cured from any mental institution in which he might be confined, his share should go to the two grandsons. The court held that the condition was repugnant to the gift to Wing Leong Gee, because it interfered with the devolution of the property on his death, intestate, which was likely to happen. In other words, it is a principle of law that a contingent gift (the gift to the grandsons in this case) which is limited to take effect on the intestacy of the prior owner is void because it purports to alter one of the legal incidents of property. On Wing Leong Gee's death intestate, the law provides for the devolution of his property and the testator could not alter that law.

Is the rule followed in *Re Gee* a reasonable one in view of the fact that a testator may, without hindrance, provide for a substitutionary gift for other reasons, such as, for example, the death of the beneficiary without issue?[245]

(c) Conditions Impossible of Performance

A condition annexed to a gift of personal property which is based on an assumption of the existence of a state of facts which does not and cannot exist[246] has no effect and the beneficiary will take free of the condition.[247] However, if the testator clearly intends that the condition shall operate in any event, the condition is impossible to perform. Then, if the condition is precedent and if it was impossible at the date of the will or later becomes so by act of God or through circumstances beyond the control of the testator or the beneficiary, the gift fails.[248] In contrast, if the condition is subsequent, the gift becomes absolute and the condition is struck down.[249] These rules are discussed in *Re MacDonald*,[250] reproduced below.

The above rules derive from the civil law via the ecclesiastical courts and apply only to gifts of personalty. They do not apply to a devise of real property upon a condition precedent. If the condition is impossible in that case, the devise fails.[251] However, the same rules apply to real property as to personal property in respect of conditions subsequent.

---

244 (1973), 41 D.L.R. (3d) 317 (B.C.S.C.).
245 See Glanville L. Williams, "The Doctrine of Repugnancy" (1943), 59 L.Q. Rev. 343, at p. 354.
246 Such as a requirement that the trustees build a building and there are insufficient funds for the purpose: *Re Jones; Williams v. Rowlands*, [1948] Ch. 67, [1947] 2 All E.R. 716; *Re Down*, [1969] 2 O.R. 16 at 23, 68 D.L.R. (2d) 30 (C.A.), affirmed [1969] S.C.R. v. See also *Sifton v. Sifton*, [1938] A.C. 656, [1938] 2 W.W.R. 465, (sub nom. *Re Sifton*) [1938] O.R. 529, [1938] 3 D.L.R. 577.
247 *Yates v. University College, London* (1873), 8 Ch. App. 454 at 461, affirmed L.R. 7 H.L. 438.
248 *Egerton v. Earl Brownlow* (1853), 4 H.L. Cas. 1 at 120, 10 E.R. 359.
249 *Re Croxon; Croxon v. Ferrers*, [1904] 1 Ch. 252.
250 [1971] 2 O.R. 577, 18 D.L.R. (3d) 521 (H.C.).
251 *Re Turton*, [1926] Ch. 96, [1925] All E.R. Rep. 340.

RE MACDONALD
[1971] 2 O.R. 577, 18 D.L.R. (3d) 521
Supreme Court of Ontario
[Divisional Court]

The testator gave part of the residue of his estate to the Windsor Public Library Board, provided the house known as the "Baby House" had not been moved from its original foundation and provided the city of Windsor gave the executors the necessary assurance that the house would never be moved from it original foundation. The gift was to be used in collecting historical objects for showing and preservation in "Baby House." The executors were to seek the required assurance from the city after the death of the survivor of the testator and his wife and the city then had one year to comply. If it failed or refused to do so, the gift was to fall into residue.

The testator was a well-known historian who had given his collection of maps, documents and historical items to the Windsor Historical Sites Association to be placed in the Baby House, which was to be restored as a public museum. The house, which was one of the oldest, if not the oldest, brick dwelling still standing on either side of the Detroit River was transferred to the Association by the City of Windsor in 1940 upon a covenant that required the Association to return it to the City if it was unable to preserve it as a public museum. The testator was aware of these facts. The Windsor Public Library Board was authorized by the City to take over and maintain the building after its restoration.

The Board brought this application to interpret the will. The Public Trustee sought to have the gift declared invalid, *inter alia*, on the ground that the condition precedent respecting the assurance by the city could not be fulfilled.

LACOURCIÈRE J.:

. . .

The second objection can be disposed of on the basis of the following findings of fact and conclusions of law:

1. The condition precedent attaching to the gift to the Windsor Public Library Board that the City of Windsor gives necessary assurances that Baby House will never be removed from its foundations is impossible of performance.

2. The impossibility existed at the time the testator drew his will and has continued to exist to the present, and continues to exist.

3. The testator knew of the impossibility at the time he drew his will.

There are several reasons for this impossibility. First and foremost, the City of Windsor does not own the land in question and therefore is in no position to give any assurance as to its use. The covenant of re-grant should the land cease to be used as a museum does not alter this. Further, it is doubtful whether the city can give the type of assurance requested, and also whether there can ever be an adequate assurance given as to the use of real property for ever.

Macdonald must have been aware of the first ground of impossibility as he was a party to an agreement reciting who was the owner of the land, which agreement antedates the execution of his will, and had been president of the association which owned the historic Baby property.

As the gift in question was given subject to a condition which was at the time of its creation and to the knowledge of the testator impossible of performance, the condition must fail and the gift remains free of the condition. On these facts, the Windsor Public Library Board is to receive the 10% without any assurance being given.

The law in England is well settled on this point. It is summarized in *Williams on Wills*,[252] and is as follows:

> A condition precedent obviously impossible or a condition becoming impossible by operation of law before the date of the will, is repugnant and void and the gift remains.

This is a development from the civil law as the gift is one of personalty and has its roots deep in the common law.

. . .

The reasoning is that, when a testator grants a bequest subject to a condition which is impossible of performance, the dominant intent must be the gift, otherwise the clause is entirely ineffective. To intentionally draft into a will a clause which is void *ab initio* is an absurdity. Thus, unless it can be shown that the principal concern of the testator is the condition, and not the gift, the condition alone must fail.

. . .

In *Re Reeves*,[253] the only Ontario authority found, an apparently different result was reached. The testator left the residue of his estate to a named charity upon condition that the Government of Ontario waive the succession duties owing on his specific bequests. If the waiver were not given, the residue was to be divided among the testator's nieces and nephews. Riddell, J., found that the condition was impossible of performance as the Government had no power to waive the succession duties. He further found that the testator was unaware of this and concluded that, as the condition was not satisfied, the charity lost the bequest.

Re Reeves is distinguishable from the present facts in that the testator did not know of the impossibility. Had he so known, the tenor of his will was such that he would have left the residue outright to his nieces and nephews. In so far as the donative intent of the testator upon failure of the condition, the lack of knowledge of the impossibility is equivalent to the condition being possible and the Government consciously refusing to fulfil it.

On the present facts the testator must have known of the impossibility when he drafted the condition. Yet he still made the grant. It would be absurd to impute to him an intent to draft a totally ineffective clause in a document as solemn and important as his will when he had full knowledge of its ineffectiveness. In the absence of anything to the contrary, it must be that the gift for the benefit of an institution which he actively supported was paramount to the testator and so the

252 3rd ed. (1967), p. 270.
253 (1916), 10 O.W.N. 427.

condition must fail. The only reasonable interpretation that can be given the condition to enable the clause to have any effect when written is that, if at the death of the life tenant it is possible for the city to give the assurances, then it must give the assurance as a condition precedent to gift taking effect.

. . .

Notes and Questions

1. I submit that the civil law rule ought not to be applied to cases of impossibility, or indeed to any conditions in Canada. It is an anachronism that ought to be abolished. Nevertheless, as a matter of interpretation and of common sense, the result in the *Macdonald* case is surely appropriate.

2. A testator devised his house to trustees to permit his two named friends to occupy it for three years upon their undertaking to preserve it in its current state. After the three-year trial period the property would go to them absolutely upon them giving a similar undertaking. If they failed to do so, the property went to others. Is this a condition precedent or subsequent? Is it impossible of fulfilment?[254]

3. What happens if the condition becomes impossible of fulfilment by operation of law? This issue arose in *Ungar v. Gossen*.[255] A testatrix left her entire estate after a life interest to be divided among her three nephews, provided that, severally, they qualified by becoming residents in Canada within 15 years of the death of the testatrix. There was a gift over if they failed to qualify. The three nephews lived in the USSR until that state collapsed, after which they moved to Germany. However, they were unable to immigrate to Canada because they did not meet Canadian qualifications. The question, therefore, was whether the condition was void for impossibility. The court held that it was void and that the three nephews were entitled to the property.

(d) Uncertain Conditions

If a condition is uncertain in its meaning or operation, it is void and, if it is a condition precedent, the gift fails,[256] whereas, if it is a condition subsequent, the condition is struck down and the gift becomes absolute.[257] For this reason, the test of certainty is stricter for a condition precedent than for a condition subsequent. If the condition annexed to a gift is precedent, a beneficiary who claims the gift merely has to satisfy the court that he or she complies with the condition and not that it must be certain with respect to all possible claimants.[258] Hence, a condition precedent is struck down for uncertainty only if it is devoid of all meaning or is internally inconsistent or repugnant.[259]

---

254 *Re Cotton; Small v. Cotton* (1982), 13 E.T.R. 19 (B.C.S.C.).
255 (1996), 13 E.T.R. (2d) 194 (B.C.S.C.).
256 *Re Lysiak* (1975), 7 O.R. (2d) 317, 55 D.L.R. (3d) 161 (H.C.).
257 *Re Down*, [1969] 2 O.R. 16, 68 D.L.R. (2d) 30 (C.A.), affirmed [1969] S.C.R. v.
258 *Re Lowry's Will Trusts; Barclays Bank Ltd. v. United Newcastle-upon-Tyne Board of Governors*, [1967] Ch. 638, [1966] 3 All E.R. 955.
259 *Re Allen; Faith v. Allen*, [1953] Ch. 810, [1953] 2 All E.R. 898 at 900-1; *Re Mercer*, [1953] O.W.N. 765 (H.C.).

In contrast, in the case of a condition subsequent, the court must be able to determine "from the beginning, precisely and distinctly, upon the happening of what event it was that the preceding vested estate was to determine."[260]

These principles are discussed in *Re Tuck's Settlement Trusts; Public Trustee v. Tuck*,[261] reproduced below.

RE TUCK'S SETTLEMENT TRUSTS; PUBLIC TRUSTEE v. TUCK
[1978] Ch. 49, [1978] 2 W.L.R. 411, [1978] 1 All E.R. 1047
Court of Appeal

Sir Adolph Tuck was made a baronet in 1910. The title was hereditary in the male line. Sir Adolph was a Jew and he was anxious that the title should pass only to those of his successors who should be Jewish. Therefore, by a settlement in 1912 he gave substantial moneys to trustees in trust for "the Baronet for the time being if and when and so long as he shall be of the Jewish faith and be married to an approved wife" and be living with her, unless the separation was not caused by his fault. The settlement defined "approved wife" as follows:

"An approved wife" means a wife of Jewish blood by one or both of her parents and who has been brought up in and has never departed from and at the date of her marriage continues to worship according to the Jewish faith.

Moreover, the settlement provided:

As to which facts in case of dispute or doubt, the decision of the Chief Rabbi in London of either the Portuguese or Anglo German Community (known respectively as the Sephardim and the Ashkenazim Communities) shall be conclusive.

The baronet was entitled to the income of the fund for 18 months after the death of his approved wife, as well as to the income during the minority of an heir apparent born of an approved wife to maintain and educate the heir apparent.

An heir apparent over age 21 after the death of his "approved-wife" mother received £400 per annum, increased to one-third of the income when he married an approved wife and the current baronet was entitled to the balance of the income until he married a woman who was not an approved wife.

By clause 3(e) a baronet, while "a pervert from the Jewish faith...until he shall be received again formally into the Jewish faith," a bachelor, married to someone who was not an approved wife, separated from an approved wife by his own fault, or a widower under age 55 without male issue born of an approved wife and the approved wife had been dead for 18 months, was entitled to £400 per annum. The balance of the income went (subject to the provision for the heir apparent) as to

---

260 *Clavering v. Ellison* (1859), 7 H.L. Cas. 707 at 725, 11 E.R. 282, *per* Lord Cranworth, quoted by Laskin J.A. in *Re Down*, [1968] 2 O.R. 16 at 23, 68 D.L.R. (2d) 30 (C.A.). See also *Sifton v. Sifton*, [1938] A.C. 656, [1938] 2 W.W.R. 465, (sub nom. *Re Sifton*) [1938] O.R. 529, [1938] 3 D.L.R. 577.

261 [1978] 2 W.L.R. 411, [1978] Ch. 49, [1978] 1 All E.R. 1047 (C.A.).

one half in trust for the settlor and his heirs and as to the other half for Jewish charities.

Sir Adolph died in 1926. He was succeeded by his eldest son, Sir William, who married an approved wife. Sir William died in 1954 and was succeeded by his son, Sir Bruce. Sir Bruce was married to an approved wife by whom he had two sons. However, he divorced her in 1968 and married someone who was not an approved wife.

On an application to determine whether the settlement was void for uncertainty, it was held at first instance by Whitford J. that it was valid.

An appeal was then brought to the Court of Appeal.

LORD DENNING M.R.:

. . .

The issue of uncertainty

In making his submissions, Mr. Dillon used two phrases which have begun to fascinate Chancery lawyers. They are "conceptual uncertainty" and "evidential uncertainty." After a little probing, I began to understand a little about them. "Conceptual uncertainty" arises where a testator or settlor makes a bequest or gift upon a condition in which he has not expressed himself clearly enough. He had used words which are too vague and indistinct for a court to apply. They are not sufficiently precise. So the court discards the condition subsequent.

"Evidential uncertainty" arises where the testator or settlor, in making the condition, has expressed himself clearly enough. The words are sufficiently precise. But the court has difficulty in applying them in any given situation because of the uncertainty of the facts. It has to resort to extrinsic evidence to discover the facts, for instance, to ascertain those whom the testator and settlor intended to benefit and those whom he did not. Evidential uncertainty never renders the condition meaningless. The court never discards it on that account. It applies the condition as best it can on the evidence available.

This dichotomy between "conceptual" and "evidential" uncertainty was ... accepted by Lord Wilberforce in *In re Baden's Deed Trusts*.[262] I must confess that I find the dichotomy most unfortunate. It has led the courts to discordant decisions. I will give some relevant instances. On the one hand, a condition that a person shall "not be of Jewish parentage" has been held by the House of Lords to be void for conceptual uncertainty, at any rate in a condition subsequent:[263] and a condition that a person shall be "of the Jewish race" was held by Danckwerts J. to be void for conceptual uncertainty, even in a condition precedent.[264] The reason in each case being that the testator had given no information or clue as to what percentage or proportion of Jewish blood would satisfy the requirement. Is it to be 100 per

---

262 [1971] A.C. 424, 457.
263 See *Clayton v. Ramsden*, [1943] A.C. 320.
264 See *In re Tarnpolsk (decd)*, [1958] 1 W.L.R. 1157.

cent. or will 75 per cent. or 50 per cent. be sufficient? The words do not enable any definite answer to be given.

On this reasoning the condition in the Tuck settlement that an "approved wife" should be "of Jewish blood" would seem to be afflicted with conceptual uncertainty.

On the other hand, a condition that a person shall be "of the Jewish faith" has produced diverse views. Four out of five Law Lords thought that it was void for conceptual uncertainty, at any rate in a condition subsequent:[265] but Lord Wright thought it was sufficiently clear and distinct to be able to be applied....[266] I should range myself with Lord Wright. His view is supported by reference to the cases on other religions....The reason being in each case that evidence can be given of the tenets of that religion or faith so as to see if the person is or is not an adherent of it.

On this reasoning the condition in the Tuck settlement about "Jewish faith" would seem to be valid and not avoided for conceptual uncertainty.

In addition to those troubles, there is another distinction to be found in the cases. It is between condition precedent and condition subsequent. Conceptual uncertainty may avoid a condition subsequent, but not a condition precedent. I fail to see the logic of this distinction. Treating the problem as one of construction of words, there is no sense in it. If the words are conceptually uncertain — so as to avoid a condition subsequent — they are just as conceptually uncertain in a condition precedent — and should avoid it also. But it is a distinction authorised by this court in *In re Allen, decd.*[267] and acknowledged by Lord Wilberforce in *Blathwayt v. Baron Cawley.*[268]

I deplore both these dichotomies, for a simple reason and a good reason. They serve in every case to defeat the intention of the testator or settlor. The courts say: "We are not going to give effect to his intentions — because he has not expressed himself with sufficient distinctness or clearness." That assertion gives rise to argument without end as to whether his words were sufficiently clear and distinct: and whether the condition in which they occur was a condition precedent or a condition subsequent.

The Chief Rabbi's Clause

How is any testator or settlor to overcome these legal difficulties? And all the costs, expense and time expended in resolving them? Sir Adolph Tuck in this settlement said: "Let any dispute or doubt be decided by the Chief Rabbi." That seemed to him a good solution, and it seems to me a good solution. The Chief Rabbi should be able to decide — better than anyone else — whether a wife was "of Jewish blood" and had been brought up "according to the Jewish faith." But Mr. Dillon said that that was not an admissible solution. He submitted that, in a

---

265 See *Clayton v. Ramsden*, [1943] A.C. 320, 329, 334-335.
266 *Ibid.*, at p. 331.
267 [1953] Ch. 810.
268 [1976] A.C. 397, 424-425.

case where there was conceptual uncertainty (where the words were not clear enough for the court) it followed inexorably that they were not clear enough for a rabbi either....Alternatively he said that, by entrusting the decision of a rabbi instead of to the court, the settlor was ousting the jurisdiction of the court....

I cannot accept either of these submissions. Nor can I accept the decisions on which Mr. Dillon relies. All the cases on this subject need to be reconsidered in the light of *Dundee General Hospitals Board of Management v. Walker*.[269] A testator there gave money to a hospital provided that at his death it should not have been taken over by the state. He gave his trustees "sole and absolute discretion" to decide whether it had been taken over by the state. The House held that this entrusting to his trustees was perfectly valid....

I see no reason why a testator or settlor should not provide that any dispute or doubt should be resolved by his executors or trustees, or even by a third person.

[His Lordship illustrated this point by reference to the law of contracts, and continued:]

If two contracting parties can by agreement leave a doubt or difficulty to be decided by a third person, I see no reason why a testator or settlor should not leave the decision to his trustees or a third party. He does not thereby oust the jurisdiction of the court. If the appointed person should find difficulty in the actual wording of the will or settlement, the executors or trustees can always apply to the court for directions so as to assist in the interpretation of it. But if the appointed person is ready and willing to resolve the doubt or difficulty, I see no reason why he should not do so. So long as he does not misconduct himself or come to a decision which is wholly unreasonable, I think his decision should stand. After all, that was plainly the intention of the testator or settlor. He or his advisers knew that only too often in the past a testator's intentions have been defeated by various rules of construction adopted by the courts: and that the solution of them has in any case been attended by much delay and expense in having them decided by the courts. In modern times the courts have been much more sensible.... But still the testator may even today think that the courts of law are not really the most suitable means of deciding the dispute or doubt. He would be quite right. As this very case shows, the courts may get bogged down in distinctions between conceptual and evidential uncertainty: and between conditions subsequent and conditions precedent. The testator may want to cut out all that cackle, and let someone decide it who really will understand what the testator is talking about: and thus save an expensive journey to the lawyers and the courts. For my part, I would not blame him. I would give effect to his intentions. Take this very case. Who better to decide these question of "Jewish blood" and "Jewish faith" than a Chief Rabbi? The settlor mentions two Chief Rabbis. It is not necessary to ask both of them. Either one will suffice. I venture to suggest that his decision would be much more acceptable to all concerned than the decision of a court of law. I would let him decide it.

---

269 [1952] 1 All E.R. 896.

So it comes to this: if there is any conceptual uncertainty in the provisions of this settlement, it is cured by the Chief Rabbi clause. That was the view of Whitford J., and I agree with it. If the Chief Rabbi clause is inoperative, then I would so construe the settlement as to hold that there is no conceptual uncertainty. This is the view of Lord Russell of Killowen, whose judgment in a moment will be read. And I agree with it, too. In either case I would hold that the settlement is valid in all its provisions. I would, therefore, dismiss the appeal.

[Lord Russell of Killowen concurred. In his view the condition was a condition precedent and certain. "Of Jewish blood" meant "some Jewish blood" and the settlor had precluded the *reductio ad absurdum* argument that this might let in someone whose parents could only trace their Jewish blood to some remote ancestor by coupling that requirement with the requirement that the approved wife must practice her religion. His Lordship disagreed with Lord Denning on the validity of the distinction, as regards certainty, between conditions precedent and subsequent. He did not rule on the Chief Rabbi clause, since he found the condition certain.

Eveleigh L.J. also concurred. He agreed that "Jewish blood" meant "some Jewish blood" and that the condition was precedent. In his view, the Chief Rabbi clause did not oust the court's jurisdiction. Rather, the testator merely referred to the Chief Rabbi for the meaning of the term "Jewish faith." He was not directing the Chief Rabbi to supply a meaning for an uncertain term, for the term was certain.]

Notes and Questions

1. What are the differences between the three judgments in the *Tuck* case? Are they material? Which approach is preferable?

2. *Sifton v. Sifton*[270] is a leading case on uncertain conditions subsequent. The testator gave the residue of his estate in trust to pay his daughter out of the income "a sum sufficient to maintain her suitably until she is forty years of age," after which she would receive the whole income. However, the payments were to be made "only so long as she shall continue to reside in Canada."

While the daughter continued to reside in Canada, she spent 11 months abroad in 1934-5 to complete her education and proposed to travel and study abroad again in 1937. She applied to the court for advice and directions.

The Ontario Court of Appeal held that the condition was not uncertain, but that the interest would not be forfeited for temporary absences. On a *per saltum* appeal, the Privy Council reversed, holding that the condition was uncertain and, since it was a condition subsequent, the gift thus became absolute.

In the course of his opinion Lord Romer said:[271]

Their Lordships' attention was called during the arguments to numerous authorities in which the Court has been called upon to consider the meaning of the words "reside" and "residence," and the like. But these authorities give their Lordships no assistance in construing the present will. The meaning of such words obviously depends upon the context in which the words are used. A condition, for instance, attached to the devise of a house that the devisee should reside in the

---

270 [1938] A.C. 656, [1938] 2 W.W.R. 465, (sub nom. *Re Sifton*) [1938] O.R. 529, [1938] 3 D.L.R. 577 (P.C.).
271 *Ibid.*, at O.R. 540-1.

house for at least six weeks in a year can present no difficulty. In some contexts the word "reside" may clearly denote what is sometimes called "being in residence" at a particular house. In other contexts it may mean merely maintaining a house in a fit state for residence. It is plain, however, that in the present case the word "reside" means something different from either being in residence or merely maintaining a residence. No one can suppose that the testator intended either that his daughter should never leave Canada, or that so long as she maintained a residence in Canada she might spend the whole of her time abroad. He must have intended that, though Canada was to be her home in general, yet she was to be at liberty to leave Canada for some purposes and for some periods of time. Unfortunately, he omitted to define either the purposes or the periods. The result is that the majority of the Court of Appeal have found themselves unable to give any more precise direction than that the appellant may leave Canada for a limited period and for a purely temporary purpose, without being able to define either the word "limited" or the word "temporary." It necessarily followed that they, in common with Middleton J.A., were of opinion that the questions propounded in the trustees' notice of motion do not at present admit of categorical answers. Their Lordships are of the same opinion. But if the appellant's interest under the will is to be forfeited upon her "ceasing to reside in Canada," she has a right to have those questions categorically answered; and inasmuch as they cannot be so answered, the words, if constituting a condition subsequent, are void for uncertainty.

Does this approach come under the opprobrium heaped upon Chancery lawyers by Lord Denning in the *Tuck* case? Is the approach defensible? Is it the right approach?

3. A testatrix left her house to X and Y, but provided that if they did not wish to live in the house it was to be sold and the proceeds divided among several persons. Is this a condition subsequent? Is it certain?[272]

4. A testator devised his farm to his son, S, but so as to allow the testator's sister, M, to reside in the farm house for life and to pay her $300 per annum, and to allow his son, H, to live with M until age 21. When H attained age 21, he could farm the land with S, if he wished, in which case S would have to pay him wages. When H reached the age of 30 "providing he stays on the farm," the testator's entire estate was to be divided equally between the two sons. The testator further directed that the farm not be sold during M's life or until H attained age 30. What kind of conditions does the will contain? Are they certain?[273]

5. A testator devised all his property to one of his sons absolutely, provided that if another son should return to live there, "a lot of land of three acres along highway No. 2 be transferred to him." Is the gift void for uncertainty?[274]

---

272 See *Re McNally* (1979), 24 Nfld. & P.E.I.R. 531, 65 A.P.R. 531 (P.E.I.S.C.).
273 See *Re Down*, [1968] 2 O.R. 16, 68 D.L.R. (2d) 30 (C.A.), affirmed [1969] S.C.R. v. Applied in *H.J. Hayes Co. v. Meade* (1987), 29 E.T.R. 217.
274 See *Re Bernard* (1986), 29 D.L.R. (4th) 133 (N.B.Q.B.).

15

PERPETUITIES AND ACCUMULATIONS

1. SCOPE OF THIS CHAPTER

In this chapter we discuss the several rules against perpetuities and the rules against accumulations. The first half of the chapter contains a brief history of the law of perpetuities and a short discussion of the rule in *Whitby v. Mitchell*[1] and the rule against indefinite duration. This is followed by a detailed discussion of the common law rule normally called the rule against perpetuities,[2] at common law. This rule has been changed substantially in several of the provinces by statute and, therefore, the next portion of the chapter discusses the statutory changes. The second half of the chapter will deal with the rules against accumulations.

Further Reading

J.H.C. Morris and W. Barton Leach, *The Rule Against Perpetuities*, 2nd ed. (London: Stevens & Sons, 1962, with Supplement, 1964).

John Chipman Gray, *The Rule Against Perpetuities* (4th ed., 1942).

Ronald H. Maudsley, *The Modern Law of Perpetuities* (London: Butterworths, 1979).

William Franklin Fratcher, *Perpetuities and Other Restraints* (1954).

P.W. Hogg, "Ontario's Perpetuities Law" (1975), 2 E. & T.Q. 19.

Richard Gosse, *Ontario's Perpetuities Legislation* (No publication data, 1967).

W. Barton Leach, "Perpetuities in a Nutshell" (1938), 51 Harv. Law Rev. 638.

W. Barton Leach, "Perpetuities: The Nutshell Revisited" (1964-65), 78 Harv. L. Rev. 973.

J.H.C. Morris and H.W.R. Wade, "Perpetuities Reform at Last" (1964), 80 L.Q. Rev. 486.

---

1 (1889), 42 Ch. D. 494, affirmed (1890), 44 Ch. D. 85 (C.A.).

2 Since it is concerned with when an interest vest, the rule ought to be called the rule against remoteness of vesting.

Bertel M. Sparks, "Perpetuities Problems of the General Practitioner" (1955), 8 U. of Fla. L. Rev. 465.

2. HISTORY OF PERPETUITIES

The history of perpetuities is the history of the common law of property as it expresses itself in its bias in favour of the free alienability of property. Attempts by land owners to retain control over their property were curbed by such statutes as *Quia Emptores*[3] and the Statutes of Mortmain,[4] which respectively provided that a tenant could freely dispose of his or her interest in land and restricted conveyances to charitable organizations. Subsequent cases made it possible to bar entails, thereby again preventing a person from tying up his or her property for an indefinite period after death. All of these statutes and cases were, therefore, designed to prevent perpetuities. The rule in *Whitby v. Mitchell*,[5] which provides that a remainder to the issue of an unborn person after a limitation for life to that person is void was developed early on in the history of perpetuities to scotch attempts by the propertied classes to avoid the early statutes and cases against perpetuities.

When new executory interests were created which were not subject to destruction under the common law remainder rules after the *Statute of Uses*,[6] it became necessary to develop a new control against perpetuities in order to prevent such new interests from vesting at too remote a time. It was at that time that the rule which is usually called the rule against perpetuities, but which is, perhaps, more correctly called the rule against remoteness of vesting, was developed.

Farwell L.J. described the development of law of perpetuities as follows:[7]

Our Courts have from the earliest times set their face against the suspense or abeyance of the inheritance and have from time to time laid down various rules to prevent perpetuity. One of those is the rule that a preceding estate of freehold is indispensably necessary to support a contingent remainder;[8] another is the rule laid down in 1669 in *Purefoy v. Rogers*[9] that no limitation shall be construed as an executory or shifting use which can by possibility take effect by way of remainder; and another (and probably the oldest) was the rule in question forbidding the raising of successive estates by purchase to unborn children, i.e., to the unborn child of an unborn child. The modern rule arising out of the development of executory limitations and shifting uses, is what is now usually called the rule against perpetuities, namely, that all estates and interests must vest indefeasibly within a life in being and twenty-one years after. But this is an addition to, not a substitution for, the former rules.

---

3 18 Edw. 1, cc. 1, 2 (1290).
4 *Magna Carta* (1217), cc. 39, 43; (1225), 9 Hen. 3, cc. 23, 36; (1297), 25 Edw. 1, c. 1; *Provisions of Westminster* (1259), c. 14; *De viris religiosis*, 7 Edw. 1, stat. 2, c. 13; *Statute of Westminster II* (1285), 13 Edw. 1, cc. 32, 33; *Quia Emptores* (1290), 18 Edw. 1, c. 3; *Mortmain Act* (1299), 27 Edw. 1, stat. 2; (1306), 34 Edw. 1, stat. 3; (1391), 15 Ric. 2, c. 5.
5 *Supra.*
6 27 Hen. 8, c. 10 (1535).
7 *Re Nash; Cook v. Frederick*, [1910] 1 Ch. 1 at 7 (C.A.)
8 Co. Litt. 342b, Butler's note.
9 (1699), 2 Wms. Saund. (Ed. 1871), 768, 781-9.

The modern rule against perpetuities derives from the *Duke of Norfolk's Case*.[10] The rule, as it developed, was applied rigidly. Mathematical certainty was required in the application of the rule and the courts construed limitations in such a way as not to have any regard to the effect of the rule. In other words, a limitation would be construed according to its strict grammatical meaning and if that resulted in an offence against the rule, there was no recourse.

Although the rule originally applied only to interests in land, it did not take long for it to be applied to future interests in personalty as well. The historical rationale for the rule, therefore, was to facilitate free alienability of land and other property in the interests of the economy and society.

The need for the rule in modern society has been questioned because of the fact that, today, there are other means for preventing economic stagnation, including modern income and death taxes, dependants' support legislation and variation of trusts legislation. For this reason the Manitoba Law Reform Commission recommended abolition of the rule against perpetuities and the rules against accumulations[11] and this report has been implemented.[12]

On the other hand, it is arguable that the "the Rule against Perpetuities strikes a fair balance between the desires of members of present generations, and similar desires of succeeding generations, to do what they wish with property which they enjoy,"[13] and that, therefore, the rule should be retained. This argument can readily be supported by examples. Thus, for example, it can be supposed that most persons would think that a gift by a testator to his or her first-great-great grandchild at age twenty-five would be improper. It is for these and other reasons that the rule remains in effect in most common law jurisdictions.

3. THE RULE IN WHITBY v. MITCHELL

The rule in *Whitby v. Mitchell*,[14] also known as the old rule against perpetuities and the rule against double possibilities, provides that if a life estate in real property is limited to a person who is unborn when the instrument takes effect and a remainder is limited to his or her issue as purchasers, the remainder is void.

The rule applies only to legal and equitable contingent remainders in land. It does not apply to personalty nor to interests in land which has been directed to be sold.[15]

The following example illustrates how the rule operates:

A devise "to X for life, remainder to his issue for life, remainder to the issue of such issue in fee simple, provided that they are born within a life now in being and twenty-one years thereafter."

---

10 (1682), 3 Chan. Cas. 1, 22 E.R. 931, reversed (1683), 3 Chan. Cas. 53, 22 E.R. 963, restored (1685), 3 Chan. Cas. 54, 22 E.R. 963 (H.L.).

11 *Report on the Rules Against Accumulations and Perpetuities*, No. 49 (1982).

12 By the *Perpetuities and Accumulations Act*, R.S.M. 1987, c. P33, s. 3.

13 Lewis Mallalieu Simes, *Public Policy and The Dead Hand* (1955), p. 58.

14 (1890), 42 Ch. D. 494, affirmed (1890), 44 Ch. D. 85 (C.A.).

15 *Re Nash; Cook v. Frederick*, [1910] 1 Ch. 1 (C.A.); *Fonseca v. Jones* (1910), 21 Man. R. 168 at 184, 14 W.L.R. 148 at 162, affirmed 18 W.L.R. 259, 21 Man. R. 168 at 193 (C.A.).

Assuming that A has as yet no issue, the final remainder is void under the rule. You should note, however, that the rule against perpetuities is not infringed because of the proviso attached to the gift.

Contrast the following example:

A devise "to the grandchildren of X who are living at her death."

The gift to the grandchildren is valid even though X is living but has no children as yet, because the gift to the grandchildren is not limited to the unborn issue of an unborn person.

The rule has been abolished in those jurisdictions which have enacted modern perpetuities statutes.[16]

4. THE RULE AGAINST INDEFINITE DURATION

Although the rule against perpetuities applies to trusts for non-charitable purposes and, with some modifications, to charitable trusts, there is also an additional rule, the rule against indefinite duration, which strikes against interests that may last beyond the perpetuity period. The rule is, therefore, not concerned with remoteness of vesting, but with the duration of the interest. The rule does not apply to charitable trusts which, since they are beneficial to the public, are allowed to exist in perpetuity. It applies only to non-charitable purpose trusts. The period of the rule is the same as that for the rule against remoteness of vesting.

Non-charitable purpose trusts are trusts that benefit an object or purpose other than a person and that are not charitable.

A number of anomalous exceptions to the rule have been allowed in the past, such as testamentary trusts for the maintenance of monuments[17] and of the testator's animals.[18]

A gift to an unincorporated society for its purposes offends the rule,[19] unless the gift can be construed as an immediate gift,[20] as one for the present members of the association,[21] or as a gift to the association subject to its rules, which are

---

16 These are discussed below.
17 See, *e.g.*, *Trimmer v. Danby* (1856), 25 L.J. Ch. 424; *Re Hooper; Parker v. Ward*, [1932] 1 Ch. 38. See also Anne M. Werker, "Plots and Perpetuities" (1997), 16 E. & T. J. 295, who discusses changes to the *Cemeteries Act (Revised)*, R.S.O. 1990, c. C.4, which, as distinct from the old *Cemeteries Act*, R.S.O. 1990, c. C.3, s. 23, no longer contains a provision for the maintenance of graves and tombs as an exception to the rule against indefinite duration. The *Cemeteries Companies Act*, R.S.N.B. 1973, c. C-1, s. 24 contains provisions similar to s. 23 of the old Ontario statute.
18 *Lloyd v. Lloyd* (1852), 2 Sim. N.S. 255, 61 E.R. 338.
19 See *Lepage v. Communist Party of Canada* (1999), 209 N.B.R. (2d) 58 (Prob. Ct.), which held a gift to the unincorporated Communist Party to be void for offending the rule against indefinite duration.
20 *Re Price; Midland Bank Executor & Trustee Co. v. Harwood*, [1943] Ch. 422, [1943] 2 All E.R. 505.
21 *Cocks v. Manners* (1871), L.R. 12 Eq. 574.

regarded as a contract between the members, and which allow the members to dispose of the property as they wish.[22]

The rule against indefinite duration has been modified in those jurisdictions which have enacted modern perpetuities legislation.[23]

5. THE RULE AGAINST PERPETUITIES AT COMMON LAW

(a) Generally

The rule against remoteness of vesting, commonly called the rule against perpetuities, applies in all the common law jurisdictions of Canada, including those jurisdictions which have enacted modern perpetuities legislation. The statutes in those jurisdictions all continue the rule, except as modified by the legislation.

The rule has been variously defined, but the modern definition that is commonly used is the following:

> No interest is good unless it must vest, if at all, not later than twenty-one years after some life in being at the creation of the interest.[24]

(b) The Perpetuity Period

(i) *Generally*

Although the definition of the rule provides for a period of a life in being plus twenty-one years, *actual* periods of gestation, followed by live births, may extend the period. Thus, in the following example,

> a bequest, "to my children for life, remainder to my grandchildren who attain the age of twenty-one,"

if the testator has a posthumous child, A, A can be a life in being and take the life estate. If A leaves a posthumous child, B, B can take the remainder, even though his or her interest vests more than twenty-one years after the death of A, the life in being.

Since the perpetuity period commences with the creation of the interest, the period will commence at the date at the testator's death in the case of a will and at the date of delivery in the case of a deed.

---

22 *Re Lipinski's Will Trusts; Gosschalk v. Levy*, [1976] Ch. 235, [1977] 1 All E.R. 33; *Re Recher's Will Trusts; Nat. Westminster Bank Ltd. v. Nat. Anti-Vivisection Soc. Ltd.*, [1972] Ch. 526, [1971] 3 All E.R. 401.

23 As discussed below.

24 John Chipman Gray, *The Rule Against Perpetuities* (4th ed., 1942), §201.

Thus, in the following example,

> a gift "to X in trust for such of my grandchildren as attain the age of twenty-one years,"

the gift to the grandchildren is valid if it is a testamentary gift. The reason is that at the testator's death, all his or her children who are alive are lives in being. Therefore, all the grandchildren, if they satisfy the age contingency, must do so within a period of twenty-one years from the death of the last life in being.

In contrast, the gift to the grandchildren would fail if it were a gift *inter vivos*. The reason is that, in that case, the settlor may have further children after the delivery of the deed. Those children cannot be lives in being, because they were not living when the interest was created. It is, therefore, possible that grandchildren could take more than twenty-one years after the death of the last life in being.[25]

You should note that the common law rule is not concerned with what actually happens, but what may, by possibility, happen. Hence, the fact that all the grandchildren in fact take within the perpetuity period in the above example of the *inter vivos* gift is irrelevant. The possibility that some may take outside the period in the case of a gift *inter vivos* renders the entire gift void.

In the following example,

> a bequest "to A's grandchildren when they attain the age of twenty-one,"

the gift to the grandchildren is good if A predeceases the testator, because then those of his or her children who survive the testator are the lives in being and their children must take a vested interest, if at all, within the perpetuity period. If, however, A were still alive at the testator's death, the gift to the grandchildren would fail, since he could have further children who would not be lives in being, so that it would then be possible for their children to satisfy the contingency more than twenty-one years after the death of the last life in being.

(ii) *Lives in Being*

At common law any person who is alive at the creation of the interest can be a life in being, but he or she is only regarded as such if it is mathematically certain that the interest must vest during the life of that person plus twenty-one years. In other words, if there is no person within whose lifetime plus twenty-one years the interest must vest, there are no lives in being, because lives in being at common

---

25 Actually, in this situation there is no life in being, since there is no one who can save the gift. The settlor can not, nor can the settlor's children. Moreover, the settlor's children could not be measuring lives for their nephews and nieces in any event, but only for their own children, since they would only be relevant lives for the purpose of the latter. However, since this is a class gift, it has to be wholly valid. Since it is possible that the interests of some of the members of the class may vest outside the period, the entire gift fails.

law are only those which validate a gift.[26] Another view, but, it is submitted, an erroneous one, is that of Morris and Wade, who state that the common law lives in being are those persons whose lives "as a matter of causality...restrict the vesting period", but that only those persons whose lives "restrict [the vesting period] sufficiently to satisfy the Rule" can save the gift.[27]

Lives in being may be expressly named in the instrument, or they may be implied. If they are implied, they may be ascertained by asking the following question:

> Can I point to some person or persons now living and say that this interest will by the very terms of its creation be vested in an identified individual within twenty-one years after that person dies?[28]

An example of express lives in being is the following:

> "To such of my grandchildren as attain the age of twenty-one within twenty-one years of the death of the survivor of X, Y and Z."

Such a gift would be valid under the rule.

Although there is no theoretical limit to the number of lives that may be selected, there is a practical limit in that, if the number is so large that it becomes impractical to ascertain them, the limitation is void for uncertainty.[29] Thus, the following bequest,

> "to X to keep in repair my tomb for the longest period of time allowed by law, that is to say, until the period of twenty-one years from the death of the last survivor of all persons who shall be living at my death,"

was held void for uncertainty.[30]

This problem typically arises with the use of the so-called "Royal Lives" clauses, of which the following is an example:

> A trust for distribution among described family members living "at the expiration of 20 years from the day of the death of the last survivor of all the lineal descendants of Her Late Majesty Queen Victoria who shall be living at the time of my death."

That clause was held valid,[31] even though there were approximately 120 living descendants of Queen Victoria throughout the world at the time of testator's death

---

26 Ronald H. Maudsley, *The Modern Law of Perpetuities* (London: Butterworths, 1979), pp. 5, 42, 43, 88 ff., 94.

27 J.H.C. Morris and H.W.R. Wade, "Perpetuities Reform at Last" (1964), 80 L.Q. Rev. 486 at 497.

28 Bertel M. Sparks, "Perpetuities Problems of the General Practitioner" (1955), 8 U. of Fla. L. Rev. 465 at 470.

29 *Thellusson v. Woodford* (1805), 11 Ves. Jun. 112 at 145, 32 E.R. 1030 (H.L.), *per* Lord Eldon L.C.

30 *Re Moore; Prior v. Moore*, [1901] 1 Ch. 936 at 936-37.

31 *Re Villar; Pub. Trustee v. Villar*, [1928] Ch. 471, affirmed [1929] 1 Ch. 243 (C.A.).

in 1926. Testators have been warned that Queen Victoria clauses should no longer be used because they may be found to be uncertain.[32]

Two examples of implied lives in being are the following:

A bequest "to my grandchildren who attain the age of twenty-one."

A bequest "to the first of my descendants to tour Canada with X."

In the first example the lives in being are the testator's children and they render the gift automatically valid. Hence, this type of life in being may be called an "automatic life," since these persons are biologically involved in the outcome of the gift. In contrast, X, the life in being in the second example, is an "implicitly selected life" and he or she validates the gift.[33]

It has already been noted that a person conceived but unborn at the creation of the interest can be a life in being.

(iii) A Period in Gross

If no lives in being are expressed in the instrument and none are implied, the perpetuity period is a period in gross of twenty-one years.

Thus, in the following example,

a bequest, "to my issue who are living fifty years after my death,"

the gift to the issue is void, unless "issue" can be construed as "children."[34]

Similarly, the following gift,

a bequest of an annuity to a volunteer corps "on the appointment of the next Lieutenant-Colonel,"

is void, because the perpetuity period is a period in gross and a Lieutenant-Colonel might not be appointed for twenty-one years or more after the death or retirement of the existing commander.[35]

(iv) Some Examples

Since the common law rule insisted on certainty of vesting and disregarded probabilities, it operated so as to defeat many interests which looked innocuous at first glance. The following examples are illustrative.[36]

---

32 *Re Leverhulme; Cooper v. Leverhulme (No. 2)*, [1943] 2 All E.R. 274 at 281.

33 See generally Ronald H. Maudsley, *The Modern Rule of Perpetuities*, (London: Butterworths, 1979), pp. 92-4, 156-7.

34 *Speakman v. Speakman* (1850), 8 Hare 180, 68 E.R. 323.

35 *Re Lord Stratheden & Campbell; Alt v. Lord Stratheden & Campbell*, [1894] 3 Ch. 265. See also *Baker v. Stuart* (1897), 28 O.R. 439 (H.C.).

36 The titles are derived from W. Barton Leach, "Perpetuities in a Nutshell" (1938), 51 Harv. L. Rev. 638 at 643 ff, and W. Barton Leach, "Perpetuities: The Nutshell Revisited" (1964-65), 78 Harv. L. Rev. 973 at 992.

(A) *The "Fertile Octogenarian."* At common law it was conclusively presumed that a person was able to have children or procreate at any age.[37] Thus, in the following example,

a bequest, "to X for life, remainder to X's children for their lives, remainder to X's grandchildren,"

the remainder to the grandchildren is void even though X is a woman who is seventy years old at the testator's death, because X is conclusively presumed to be able to bear children until her death. Since such children would not be lives in being, the gift to the grandchildren could possibly vest more than twenty-one years after the death of the children who are living at the time of the testator's death.

In the following example,

a bequest, "to my wife for life or until her remarriage, remainder to the children of my brothers and sisters as shall attain the age of twenty-one,"

the gift to the children of the brothers and sisters fails even though the testator's father and mother are sixty-six years old when he dies, because they are conclusively presumed to be able to have further children who could not be lives in being for the purpose of the vesting of the gift to the testator's nephew and nieces. If, on the other hand, the testator's parents had predeceased him, the gift would be valid.

In order to avoid the problem in these examples, the gift should be limited to such of the children of X as were living at the testator's death in the first problem and to the children of such of the testator's brothers and sisters as were living at his death in the second.[38]

(B) *The "Precocious Toddler."* The problem with the "precocious toddler" is the opposite of the case of the fertile octogenarian. The following example illustrates the problem:

A bequest, "to A for life, remainder to such of her grandchildren living at my death or born within five years thereafter who shall attain the age of twenty-one." A was a widow, sixty-five years of age at the testator's death, with two children and a grandchild.

---

37 *Jee v. Audley* (1787), 1 Cox. 324, 29 E.R. 1186; *Ward v. Van der Loeff; Burnyeat v. Van der Loeff*, [1924] A.C. 653 (H.L.)

38 A perpetuity problem also exists with, what the late Prof. Barton Leach described as the "fertile decedent," that is, a person who deposits his sperm in a sperm bank, perhaps to fertilize a woman unborn at his death. Although the donor's resulting children would be illegitimate, they could inherit in a jurisdiction such as Ontario's which has abolished the status of illegitimacy. See generally W. Barton Leach, "Perpetuities in the Atomic Age: The Sperm Bank and the Fertile Decedent" (1962), 48 A.B.A.J. 942; Daniel M. Schuyler, "The New Biology and The Rule Against Perpetuities" (1967-68), 15 U.C.L.A. L. Rev. 420; and Robert J. Lynn, "Raising the Perpetuities Question: Conception, Adoption, 'Wait and See' and Cy Pres" (1963-64), 17 Vand. L. Rev. 1391.

The clause "or born within five years thereafter" made it possible that A might remarry and have another child who might have a child, all within five years of the testator's death.The gift was saved in *Re Gaite's Will Trusts; Banks v. Gaite*,[39] upon which the example is based, because, by statute, a marriage between persons either of whom was under the age of sixteen was void, so that a grandchild born within five years of testator's death would be illegitimate and, hence, unable to take. This beneficent solution is not, however, possible any longer in those jurisdictions that have abolished the status of illegitimacy.

(C) *The "Unborn Widow."* The problem in this case is illustrated by the following example:

> An *inter vivos* trust, "to pay the income to my son for life, after his death to pay the income to my son's widow for life, and then to pay the principal to my son's children then living."

The problem in this example is that the son's wife might die, or the marriage might be dissolved, and he might remarry a person unborn at the time of the creation of the interest. Then, if that person outlives the son by twenty-one years, the gift to the children of the son would be void.[40]

In order to avoid the problem, the son's widow should be named. Alternately the phrase "then living" should be deleted in order to make the interest of the children vested.

(D) *The "Magic Gravel Pit."* This problem is illustrated by the following example:

> The testator devised certain gravel pits to trustees "in trust to work my gravel pits until they are exhausted and then to sell them and divide the proceeds among my issue then living."

The gift to the issue fails because, although in actual fact the gravel pits were exhausted in six years, it was possible that they might not be exhausted for more than twenty-one years, the applicable perpetuity period, there being no lives in being, and in that case the gift would vest too remotely.[41]

In order to avoid the problem, the word "issue" could be changed to "children," express lives in being could be named, or the testator could direct that the gravel pits should be worked "for twenty-one years or until they are exhausted, whichever happens first."

If the gift is expressed to vest upon an "administrative contingency," such as "on the payment of my debts," "when my will is probated," "when my estate is realized," *etc.*, the contingency is usually construed to mean the date upon which the contingency occurs, or the end of the executor's year, whichever first happens.[42] In that case, the gift is valid.

---

39 [1949] 1 All E.R. 459.
40 *Re Curryer's Will Trusts; Wyly v. Curryer*, [1938] Ch. 952, [1938] 3 All E.R. 574.
41 *Re Wood; Tullett v. Colville*, [1894] 3 Ch. 381 (C.A.).
42 *Re Petrie; Lloyd's Bank Ltd. v. Royal Nat. Institute for the Blind*, [1962] Ch. 355, [1961] 3 W.L.R. 1348, [1961] 3 All E.R. 1067 (C.A.).

(c) The Application of the Rule to Various Interests

(i) *Class Gifts*

A class gift is either valid in its entirety, or fails in its entirety for perpetuity.[43] In the context of class gifts and perpetuities, a gift is, therefore, not vested until all the members of the class are ascertained and have satisfied any contingency personal to themselves and if the amount of their shares, both minimum and maximum, are ascertainable within the perpetuity period.

The following example will illustrate this principle:

> A testator devised property "in trust for A for life and, after his death, to his issue, but if he should die without issue, then to such of A's brothers and sisters as attain age twenty-five or marry." A died without issue. At the testator's death A had five living brothers and sisters. Two more were born before A's death and one thereafter.

In this case the whole gift is void, because it was possible at the time of the creation of the interest that further brothers and sisters might be born who might reach the age of twenty-five beyond the perpetuity period and the class does not close until the first member of the class attains the age of twenty-five. Any brother or sister born after the testator's death would have reduced the size of the share of the brothers and sisters living at the testator's death, so that the maximum size of the members' shares was not ascertainable within the period.[44]

It is apparent from the foregoing example, that the class closing rules, discussed in a previous chapter, may operate to save a class gift. Thus, in the foregoing example, if A had predeceased the testator and one of his brothers or sisters had reached the age of twenty-five or had married, the class would *prima facia* have closed at the testator's death. The brothers and sisters would then have been lives in being and their interests would clearly have vested within the period.

The same problems as in the foregoing example arise if the gift is to a composite class, as in the following example:

> A bequest, "to my wife for life with remainder to my children then living, the issue of any deceased child to take his or her parent's share at age twenty-four."

The problem with this kind of gift is that, if a child dies after the testator and before the death of the life tenant, leaving issue who were not living at the testator's death, the issue may take more than twenty-one years after the death of the last life in being, thereby increasing the shares of the other members of the class beyond the perpetuity period if any issue fail to attain the age of twenty-four.[45]

The problem only arises with composite classes, however, if the gift to the issue, as in the foregoing example, is construed as an original gift. If, on the other hand, it is construed as substitutional, it is possible to save the gift. Such a gift is

---

43 *Pearks v. Moseley* (1880), 5 App. Cas. 714 at 723 (H.L.), *per* Lord Selborne L.C.
44 *Leake v. Robinson* (1817), 2 Mer. 363, 35 E.R. 979.
45 *Hale v. Hale* (1876), 3 Ch. D. 643.

construed as substitutional and not as original if the gift to the parents is given upon a condition subsequent. The following example will illustrate this principle:

> A bequest "to my daughter for life, with remainder to all her children as shall attain the age of twenty-one, but if any die under that age leaving children who attain age twenty-one, such children shall take their parent's share."

In this case the interest of the children is construed as vested subject to divestment, because of the gift over on death under age. Hence, the interest of the daughter's children is valid, as well as the interest of the children of those of her children who were living at the testator's death. However, the interest of the children of the daughter's children whose parents were born after the testator's death is void, with the result that their parents' interests are indefeasibly vested.[46]

If the gift is split among sub-classes, instead of it being a gift to a composite class, the gift can be saved in respect of those persons whose interest must vest within the perpetuity period. Consider the following example:

> A bequest "to A for life, remainder to all his children for their lives, remainder as to the share of each child so dying, to his children." A had six children who were living at the testator's death and several who were born afterwards.

In this situation, the interests of those of A's children who were living at the testator's death are valid, while those of the children of after-born children are void. This is possible, because the gift to the children in each stock or family is independent of the gift to the children in another stock or family.[47]

If the gift is not a true class gift, but is, rather, a gift of property or a sum of money to each member of a class, the gifts are again independent of each other and, therefore, the gift to those persons whose interests must vest within the perpetuity period is valid, while the gift to those whose interest may not vest within the period is void. As in the case of true class gifts, the class closing rules should first be applied to determine whether the gift may be saved by the operation of those rules. The following example will illustrate the principle:

> A bequest of five hundred dollars, "to each child that may be born to either of the children of either of my brothers when they attain the age of twenty-one."

In this case the class closes at the testator's death, which will save the gift. Even if that were not so, however, the gift would be valid as regards any grandchildren of the brothers who were living at the time of the testator's death, whereas the interest of those who were born thereafter would be void.[48]

---

46 *Goodier v. Johnson* (1881), 18 Ch. D. 441 (C.A.).
47 *Cattlin v. Brown* (1853), 11 Hare 372, 68 E.R. 1319.
48 *Storrs v. Benbow* (1853), 3 De G. M. & G. 390, 43 E.R. 153.

(ii) *Powers of Appointment*

(A) *Generally.* The rule against perpetuities applies to powers of appointment in three ways. In the first place, it may strike down the power itself if it is exercisable beyond the perpetuity period. Second, an appointment made under the power may be invalid for perpetuity. Third, a gift in default of appointment may be struck down for offending the rule.

For the purpose of the rule against perpetuities, two types of powers are recognized, namely general and special powers of appointment. A general power is one in which the donee of the power may appoint by deed or will to anyone, including himself or herself, or to anyone except a named person.[49] A special power is one in which the donee cannot appoint to himself or herself, except with the consent of another. However, a power to appoint to anyone by will only, is treated as a special power in determining the validity of the power,[50] but as a general power for the purpose of determining the validity of an appointment made under the power.[51]

(B) *Validity of Power.* A general power is valid if the donee must be ascertainable within the perpetuity period and the power does not become void merely because the power can be or is in fact exercised outside the period.[52] Hence, if a general power exercisable by deed or will is given to the child of a living person, the power is valid, even though the child was unborn when the power was created.[53] In contrast, if the donee is the survivor of a class of unborn children of a living person, he or she may by possibility not be ascertained within the perpetuity period and, therefore, the power is void.[54]

A special power must be exercisable within the perpetuity period in order to be valid under the rule.[55] Thus, a power which is given to a living person, or which is exercisable only in favour of living persons, is valid,[56] whereas a power given to trustees which is exercisable in favour of unborn persons is void, since it is exercisable by successor trustees who were not living when the testator died.[57] It is, however, possible to sever such powers, so as to save the power vested in the present trustees, while holding a power vesting in their successors void.[58]

If a power is void, an appointment under it is also void,[59] but a gift over in default of appointment is not necessarily void.[60]

---

49 *Re Penrose; Penrose v. Penrose*, [1933] Ch. 793.
50 *Morgan v. Gronow* (1873), L.R. 16 Eq. 1.
51 *Rous v. Jackson* (1885), 29 Ch. D. 521; *Re Fasken*, [1961] O.R. 891, 30 D.L.R. (2d) 193 (H.C.).
52 *Morgan v. Gronow, supra; Re Fasken, supra.*
53 *Bray v. Hammersley* (1830), 3 Sim. 513, 57 E.R. 1090, affirmed (sub nom. *Bray v. Bree*), 2 Cl. & Fin. 453, 6 E.R. 1225 (H.L.).
54 *Re Hargreaves; Midgley v. Tatley* (1890), 43 Ch. D. 401 (C.A.).
55 *Re Abrahams' Will Trusts, Caplan v. Abrahams*, [1969] 1 Ch. 463, [1967] 2 All E.R. 1175.
56 *Re Albery*, [1964] 1 O.R. 342, 42 D.L.R. (2d) 201 (H.C.).
57 *Re Symm's Will Trusts; Pub. Trustee v. Shaw*, [1936] 3 All E.R. 236.
58 *Re De Sommery; Coelenbier v. De Sommery*, [1912] 2 Ch. 622.
59 *Re Fasken*, [1961] O.R. 891, 30 D.L.R. (2d) 193 (H.C.).
60 *Re Abbott; Peacock v. Frigout*, [1893] 1 Ch. 54.

(C) *Validity of Appointment*. With respect to general powers, the perpetuity period commences from the date of the appointment, because a general power is the equivalent of ownership in the donee of the power.[61] The validity of the appointment is then determined in the ordinary way.

In contrast, the perpetuity period runs from the date of creation of a special power, that is, the instrument which contains the power.[62] Hence, any dispositions made by the donee are valid only if they would be valid if made by the donor of the power. Nevertheless, by a curious leniency, the law permits a "second look" in this situation by permitting facts existing on the date the appointment is made to be taken into account. If the donee of the power exercises it in such a manner that the appointment offends the rule, the appointment fails, but if the appointment complies with the rule, the appointment is good. The reason for the "second look" is that it is impossible at the time the power is created to determine whether the rule will or will not be offended.[63]

The following example illustrates the operation of the "second look" doctrine:

> A bequest, "to A for life, remainder to such of A's issue as A shall appoint." A appoints to his children when they attain the age of twenty-four.

In the above example, the appointment will be valid if A's children were at least three years old when A made the appointment.[64]

(D) *Validity of Gifts in Default of Appointment*. A gift in default of appointment is treated as if had been made by the donee at the moment that the power expires or is released by the donee. The rules regarding the validity of an appointment respecting general and special powers then apply. The following example illustrates these principles:

> A bequest, "to my son for life, remainder to such of my son's children as he shall by deed or will appoint, and, in default of appointment as to one-half of the capital to my son's children when the youngest child attains the age twenty-one and as to the other half to such of my son's children as are living when the youngest attains age thirty-five." The son died without exercising the power, survived by four children, the youngest of whom was twenty-five.

In the above example, the gift in default of appointment was valid, because the youngest child had to attain the age of thirty-five, if at all, within the perpetuity period.[65]

Further Reading

J.H.C. Morris, "The Rule Against Perpetuities and the Rule in *Andrews v. Partington*" (1954), 70 L.Q. Rev. 61.

---

61 *Re Fane; Fane v. Fane*, [1913] 1 Ch. 404 (C.A.).
62 *Re Manning* (1978), 19 O.R. (2d) 257, 2 E.T.R. 195, 84 D.L.R. (3d) 715 (C.A.).
63 *Re Eliot* (1913), 24 O.W.R. 494, 11 D.L.R. 34 (H.C.); *Re Fasken, supra*.
64 *Wilkinson v. Duncan* (1861), 30 Beav. 111, 54 E.R. 831.
65 *Re Edwards*, [1959] O.W.N. 313, 20 D.L.R. (2d) 755 (H.C.).

A. James Casner, "Class Gifts - Effect of the Failure of Class Members to Survive the Testator" (1942), 60 Harv. L. Rev. 751.

(iii) *Contingent Remainders*

The rule against perpetuities does not normally avoid contingent remainders, since those interests either fail because of the common law remainder rules and ought, therefore, not be extended by the rule against perpetuities, or else they are valid under those rules in that they vest during the continuance of a prior particular estate.[66]

The rule does apply to contingent remainders, however, and if a contingent remainder is limited after a contingent remainder, the rule may avoid the gift. This is illustrated in the following example:

> A conveyance, "to A for life, then to any husband she may marry for life, with remainder to her children then living." A is unmarried.

The remainder to A's children may be valid under the common law remainder rules, since it may vest during the continuance of the prior life estate. However, since the remainder interest to the children may not vest within twenty-one years after A's death the rule against perpetuities is transgressed and the remainder is therefore void.[67] As has been noted previously, contingent remainders cannot, today arise under a will.[68]

(iv) *Legal Executory Interests*

The rule against perpetuities applies to legal executory interests. These are interests which arise under uses executed by the *Statute of Uses*,[69] or, formerly, executory devises which did not arise under a trust. As has been noted previously, legal executory interests cannot, today, be created under a will.[70] The following example is illustrative:

> A conveyance, "unto and to the use of X in fee simple, excepting and reserving a forty-foot strip commencing at a specified point and terminating at a road to be constructed by the purchaser, so as to give the vendor access to the road from other lands of the vendor."

The exception in the above example operates either at common law, in which case it is a limitation to commence in the future and, therefore, void under the

---

66 J.H.C. Morris and W. Barton Leach, *The Rule Against Perpetuities*, 2nd ed. (London: Stevens & Sons, 1962, with Supplement, 1964), p. 203.

67 *Whitby v. Von Luedecke*, [1906] 1 Ch. 783.

68 In the previous chapter. But see *Re Crow* (1984), 17 E.T.R. 1, 48 O.R. (2d) 36 (H.C.), to the contrary. That case appears to have been decided incorrectly, however.

69 27 Hen. 8, c. 10 (1535).

70 In the previous chapter. But see *Re Crow, supra*.

common law remainder rules, or under the *Statute of Uses*,[71] in which case it is void for perpetuity, because the road might not be constructed within the perpetuity period.[72]

(v) *Equitable Executory Interests*

Equitable executory interests also attract the rule against perpetuities;[73] indeed, this is the interest most commonly encountered today. Equitable executory interests are all contingent interests which arise under a trust, including statutory trusts created in respect of wills,[74] and any other contingent equitable interests. A typical example of an equitable executory interest is given in the following example:

> A bequest to trustees, "upon trust to pay the income to my wife for life and then to H for life and then upon trust to convey and transfer the capital to such son of M as should first attain the age of twenty-five years."

While the interest of H is equitable, it is a remainder and, therefore, vested. In contrast, the interest of the first son of M to attain the age of twenty-five years is contingent and, since it arises under a trust, equitable. It is, therefore, an equitable executory interest and is void for perpetuity.[75]

Trusts which are exercisable beyond the perpetuity period are also invalid, including, for example, a trust for sale.[76] However, if the trust for sale can be regarded merely as the machinery to facilitate division between the beneficiaries and the interests of those beneficiaries must vest during the perpetuity period, effect will be given to them, even though the trust for sale is void.[77]

(vi) *Rights of Entry for Condition Broken*

A right of entry for a condition broken is subject to the rule against perpetuities, except if the right of entry is reserved to a lessor.[78] The following is an example of the application of the rule in this situation:

> A testator devised land to a municipality for use as a public park, provided that if the corporation neglected or refused to keep the land and its surrounding fences in repair, the land was to revert to the testator's estate.

71　*Supra.*
72　*Savill Bros. Ltd. v. Bethell*, [1902] 2 Ch. 523 (C.A.).
73　*Re Ashforth; Sibley v. Ashforth*, [1905] 1 Ch. 535 at 545, *per* Farwell J.
74　*E.g.*, under the *Estates Administration Act*, R.S.O. 1990, c. E.22, s. 2.
75　*Re Finch; Abbiss v. Burney* (1881), 17 Ch. D. 211 (C.A.).
76　*Re Bewick; Ryle v. Ryle*, [1911] 1 Ch. 116.
77　*Re Daveron; Bowen v. Churchill*, [1893] 3 Ch. 421.
78　*Re Tyrrell*, [1907] 1 I.R. 292 at 298 (C.A.).

The above devise contains a condition subsequent[79] and, hence, gives a right of entry for condition broken to the testator's estate. Since it could, by possibility, be exercised beyond the perpetuity period, the right of entry is void and struck off.[80] The effect of the operation of the rule in these circumstances, therefore, is that the devise becomes absolute.[81]

(vii) Possibilities of Reverter

At common law the rule against perpetuities does not apply to possibilities of reverter, that is, the interest left in the grantor who conveys, or in the heirs of a testator who devises, a determinable fee simple.[82] The following example illustrates the point:

> A devise in 1849 to a church, "so long as they shall maintain and promulgate their present religious belief and faith and shall continue as a Church." The residue of the estate was given to X. The church ceased operations in 1939.

In the above example, a possibility of reverter was retained by the testator's estate and, since the rule against perpetuities did not apply, the possibility passed under the residuary clause.[83]

(viii) Gifts to Charity

The rule against perpetuities does apply to contingent gifts to charity, but with some modifications.

If the gift to the charity is upon a future contingent event which is, or may be, too remote, the gift is void. Thus, a gift of money for the training for the priesthood of a person from a particular church when a candidate comes forward is void.[84] This rule is, however, subject to the exception that if the testator has a general charitable intention, in the sense that he or she wishes to apply the gift to charity absolutely and forthwith, the gift is valid and it will be administered *cy près* until the testator's particular intention can be carried out.[85]

---

79 *Re Hollis' Hosp. Trustees and Hague's Contract*, [1899] 2 Ch. 540.
80 *Matheson v. Mitchell* (1919), 46 O.L.R. 546, 5 D.L.R. 477 (C.A.).
81 *Missionary Church, Can. East v. Nottawasaga* (1980), 32 O.R. (2d) 88, 120 D.L.R. (3d) 489 (H.C.).
82 *Re Tilbury West Pub. School Bd. and Hastie*, [1966] 2 O.R. 20, 55 D.L.R. (2d) 407, varied [1966] 2 O.R. 511, 57 D.L.R. (2d) 519 (H.C.); *Re Chambers' Will Trusts; Official Trustees of Charitable Funds v. Br. Union for Abolition of Vivisection*, [1950] Ch. 267; *Re McCormick* (1989), 34 E.T.R. 216 (Ont. H.C.). *Hopper v. Liverpool Corp.* (1943), 88 Sol. J. 213 (Lancaster, V.C. Ct.), which held otherwise, must be regarded as incorrectly decided.
83 *Brown v. Independent Baptist Church of Woburn*, 91 N.E. 2d 922 (1950, Mass. S.J.C.).
84 *Re Mander; Westminster Bank Ltd. v. Mander*, [1950] Ch. 547, [1960] 2 All E.R. 191. *Cf.*, *Re Odelberg Estate* (1970), 72 W.W.R. 567 (Sask. Surr. Ct.).
85 *Jewish Home for the Aged v. Toronto Gen. Trusts Corp.*, [1961] S.C.R. 465, 34 W.W.R. 638, 28 D.L.R. (2d) 48; *Re Mountain* (1912), 26 O.L.R. 163, 4 D.L.R. 737 (C.A.); *Re Pearse; Genn v. Pearse*, [1955] 1 D.L.R. 801 (B.C.S.C.).

If there is a gift over from a non-charity to a charity on a future event which may by possibility be beyond the perpetuity period, the gift over is void. A gift to a charity if a prior gift to unborn grandchildren at age twenty-five should fail, is void under this rule.[86]

If there is a gift over from a charity to a non-charity on a future contingent event which may be remote, the gift over is void and the gift to the charity becomes absolute, provided the property is given to the charity in perpetuity subject to a condition subsequent. The money is then distributed *cy près*. This rule was applied to a gift to establish a certain school subject to the proviso that if the government should thereafter establish a general system of education the gift should pass to the residuary legatees.[87] By contrast, if the property is not given in perpetuity, but is given over following a determinable fee or similar interest in personal property, the property results to the testator's estate under a resulting trust,[88] unless the gift over might possibly vest at too remote a time.[89]

If the gift over is from one charity to another on a future contingent event which may be too remote, the rule against perpetuities does not apply, because the property remains devoted to charitable purposes. Hence, in a gift of property to a municipality in trust for it poor inhabitants, with a gift over to another municipality in trust for a hospital if the first municipality should fail to carry out the trust, the gift over was held valid.[90]

(ix) *Administrative Powers and Trusts*

The rule applies to administrative powers and trusts, such as powers of sale and lease, if they can be exercised beyond the perpetuity period.[91] However, an administrative power is often construed as being exercisable only during the lifetime of a life in being, in which case it is valid.[92] Furthermore, even though an administrative power may be void, the beneficial interests under it will be valid if they must vest within the period.[93]

(x) *Ulterior Limitations*

If an interest is void for perpetuity, all limitations dependent upon it are also void. Thus, if a testator was given a power to appoint among his issue and he

---

86 *Re Mill's Declaration of Trust; Midland Bank Executor & Trustee Co. v. Mill*, [1950] 2 All E.R. 292 (C.A.).

87 *Re Bowen; Lloyd Phillips v. Davis*, [1893] 2 Ch. 491.

88 *Re Randell; Randell v. Dixon* (1888), 38 Ch. D. 213.

89 *Re Chardon; Johnston v. Davies*, [1928] Ch. 464.

90 *Christ's Hosp. v. Grainger* (1849), 1 Mac. & G. 460, 41 E.R. 1343. *Cf. Re Mountain, supra; Re Tyler; Tyler v. Tyler*, [1891] 3 Ch. 252 (C.A.).

91 *Ware v. Polhill* (1805), 11 Ves. Jun. 257, 32 E.R. 1087.

92 *Re Atkin's Will Trusts; Nat. Westminster Bank Ltd. v. Atkins*, [1974] 2 All E.R. 1.

93 *Goodier v. Edmunds*, [1893] 3 Ch. 455; *Meyers v. Hamilton Provident & Loan Co.* (1890), 19 O.R. 358 (C.A.).

appointed to his son, but if the son should have no child who should attain the age of twenty-five then to a named grandson, and the son and the grandson were unborn when the power was created, the gift to the grandson was void for perpetuity.[94]

Whether an ulterior limitation is expectant or dependent upon a prior limitation is a question of construction. In general, if the ulterior limitation commences with words such as "in default of," it is dependent, but if it commences with words such as "and then," it is not.[95]

6. THE RULE AGAINST PERPETUITIES UNDER STATUTE

(a) Generally

Several Canadian jurisdictions have enacted legislation to reform the rule against perpetuities in order to meliorate its strictness. The statutes commonly introduce the principle of "wait and see," which allows actual events to determine whether an interest is valid or void. In addition, the statutes correct some of the blatant traps which had arisen under the rule at common law.[96]

The several statutes abolish the rule in *Whitby v. Mitchell*[97] as redundant.[98] Moreover, they provide that the rule against perpetuities and the statutory restraints on accumulations do not apply to employee benefit trusts.[99] Similar legislation exists in some of the other provinces.[100]

It has already been noted that in Manitoba the rule against perpetuities has been abolished.[101]

Prince Edward Island has also enacted legislation respecting perpetuities. However, this legislation is quite short and substantially different from the others. It merely varies the perpetuity period to a life in being plus sixty years.[102]

All of the Canadian statutes retain the common law rule as modified by the statutes.[103] This, it is submitted, is unnecessary, at least if the statutes include as

---

94 *Re Brown and Sibly's Contract* (1876), 3 Ch. D. 156.
95 *Re Hubbard's Will Trusts; Marston v. Angier*, [1963] Ch. 275, [1962] 2 All E.R. 917.
96 The Canadian statutes are: *Perpetuities Act*, R.S.A. 1980, c. P-4 [am. 1992, c. 21, s. 47 (10)]; R.S.O. 1990, c. P.9 [am. 1999 c. 6, s. 54(1),(2)]; R.S.N.W.T. 1988, c. P-3; R.S.Y. 1986, c. 129; *Perpetuity Act*, R.S.B.C. 1996, c. 358. The several statutes are hereafter referred to without further citation.
97 (1889), 42 Ch. D. 494, affirmed (1890), 44 Ch. D. 85 (C.A.).
98 Alta Act, s. 21; B.C. Act, s. 2(2); Ont. Act. s. 17; N.W.T. Act, s. 18, Yukon Act, s. 21.
99 Alta. Act, s. 22; B.C. Act, s. 22; Ont. Act, s. 19; N.W.T. Act, s. 19; Yukon Act, s. 22.
100 *Trustee Act*, R.S.N.S. 1989, c. 479, s. 67; *Queen's Bench Act*, R.S.S. 1978, c. Q-1, s. 45, para 22; *Property Act*, R.S.N.B. 1973, c. P-19, s. 3 [am. 1997, c. 9, s. 3]. *Perpetuities and Accumulations Act*, R.S.N. 1990 c. P-7.
101 By the *Perpetuities and Accumulations Act*, R.S.M. 1987, c. P33, s. 3.
102 *Perpetuities Act*, R.S.P.E.I. 1988, c. P-3.
103 Alta. Act, s. 2; B.C. Act, s 2(1); Ont. Act, s. 2; N.W.T. Act, s. 3; Yukon Act, s. 2.

measuring lives all those that validate gifts under the common law rule, for the wait and see principle contains the common law rule.[104]

Of course, for the rule as modified to be attracted the interest must be contingent. If it is vested, the rule has no application.[105]

(b) The Wait and See Principle

The statutes provide that a limitation creating a contingent interest in property shall not be treated as void merely because the interest may possibly vest beyond the perpetuity period and that an interest that is capable of vesting either within or outside the period is presumptively valid until actual events establish either that it is incapable of vesting within the period, thus rendering it void, or that it is incapable of vesting beyond the period, in which case it is valid.[106]

The effect of the wait and see principle is that an interest which would be void as offending the rule at common law is now treated as valid for the time being and will be allowed to take effect if, in fact, it takes effect within the perpetuity period.

Thus, for example, it validates the "magic gravel pit" type of gift referred to above, and many others.

It is, however, not always necessary to rely upon the wait and see principle, since the statute also introduces specific remedies which cure other defects of the common law rule.

(c) The Perpetuity Period

Apart from special provisions for certain kinds of interests which will be mentioned below, the perpetuity period has not been altered by the Canadian legislation.

The British Columbia Act does, however, contain an alternative perpetuity period, namely a fixed period of eighty years. The Act provides[107] that an interest in property which expressly or by necessary implication must vest, if at all, not later than eighty years after its creation is valid.

The following is an example of a gift incorporating this provision:

---

104 Ronald H. Maudsley, *The Modern Rule of Perpetuities* (London: Butterworths, 1979), pp. 6, 109.

105 See *Baldiserra v. Baldassa* (1997), 18 E.T.R. (2d) 128 (B.C.S.C.). The testator directed that his trustees were to pay out the profits from his businesses from time to time, when they deemed that to be advisable, to certain named persons, and provided that on the death of any of them the otherwise payable to that person should be paid to his or her estate. The court held that the interest in the profits vested at the testator's death. Thus, the gift did not offend the rule as modified by the B.C. Act.

106 Alta. Act, ss. 3, 4(1); B.C. Act, ss. 4, 5(1); Ont. Act, ss. 3, 4(1); N.W.T. Act, ss. 4, 5(1); Yukon Act, ss. 3, 4 (1).

107 B.C. Act, s. 3(1).

A bequest, "to the first of X's children to travel to the moon within the perpetuity period of eighty years from my death."

You should note that, if the eighty-year perpetuity period cannot be implied from the gift, the wait and see principle applies to the normal perpetuity period.

The statutes retain the well-known perpetuity period of a measuring life plus twenty-one years.[108]

If no lives are expressed or implied by the instrument, the perpetuity period remains one in gross of twenty-one years,[109] or eighty years in British Columbia.[110] The wait and see principle applies to the period in gross. Thus, in the following example,

a bequest, "to the first person to walk around the world,"

the gift is valid if someone walks around the world within twenty-one years of the testator's death.

The commencement of the perpetuity period remains as it was at common law.

(d) Measuring Lives

(i) *Generally*

The Canadian statutes follow two models in the determination of who may be a measuring life in the application of the wait and see principle. One is the statutory list model, which has been enacted in Alberta, British Columbia and the Yukon; the second is the statutory formula model, which is in force in Ontario and the Northwest Territories.

It is submitted that the first of these is the correct approach, assuming that all necessary measuring lives are included, for then the fiduciary who must determine whether or not an interest is good or bad under the rule has simply to make a list of the appropriate measuring lives and keep track of them during the wait and see period. The statutory formula model is attended with a number of problems, as will appear from the discussion below.

(ii) *The Statutory List Model*

The British Columbia Act contains the following list;

---

108 Alta. Act, s. 5; B.C. Act, s. 6; Ont. Act, s. 6; N.W.T. Act, s. 7; Yukon Act, s. 5.
109 Alta. Act, s. 5(1)(b); Ont. Act, s. 6(3); N.W.T. Act, s. 7(3); Yukon Act, s. 5(1)(b).
110 B.C. Act, s. 6 (1)(b).

Determination of perpetuity period

10. (1) If section 9 applies to a disposition and the duration of the perpetuity period is not determined under section 7, 21 or 22, the perpetuity period must be determined as follows:
(a) if any persons falling within subsection (2) are persons in being and ascertainable at the commencement of the perpetuity period, the duration of the period, to the extent it is determined by a life in being, must be determined by reference to their lives and no others but so that the lives of any description of persons falling within subsection (2)(b) or (c) must be disregarded if the number of persons of that description is such as to render it impractical to ascertain the date of death of the survivor;

. . .

(2) The persons referred to in subsection (1) are as follows:
(a) the person by whom the disposition is made;
(b) a person to whom or in whose favour the disposition was made, that is to say,
  (i) in the case of a disposition to a class of persons, a member or potential member of the class,
  (ii) in the case of an individual disposition to a person taking only on certain conditions being satisfied, a person as to whom some of the conditions are satisfied and the remainder may in time be satisfied,
  (iii) in the case of a special power of appointment exercisable in favour of members of a class, a member or potential member of the class,
  (iv) if, in the case of a special power of appointment exercisable in favour of one person only, the object of the power is not ascertained at the commencement of the perpetuity period, a person as to whom all of the conditions are satisfied, or some of the conditions are satisfied and the remainder may in time be satisfied, and
  (v) in the case of a power of appointment, the person on whom the power is conferred;
(c) a person having a child or grandchild within paragraph (b)(i) to (iv), or a person any of whose children or grandchildren, if subsequently born, would by his or her descent, fall within paragraphs (b)(i) to (iv);
(d) a person who takes a prior interest in the property disposed of and a person on whose death a gift over takes effect;
(e) if
  (i) a disposition is made in favour of any spouse of a person who is in being and ascertainable at the commencement of the perpetuity period,
  (ii) an interest is created by reference to an event occurring during the lifetime of the spouse of a person who is in being and ascertainable at the commencement of the perpetuity period or during the lifetime of the survivor of them, or
  (iii) an interest is created by reference to the death of the spouse of a person who is in being and ascertainable at the commencement of the perpetuity period or the death of the survivor of them,
  the same spouse whether or not that spouse was in being or ascertainable at the commencement of the period.

This legislation may be explained by the following example:

A bequest, "to X for life, remainder to Y's grandchild at age twenty-one." When the testator dies, X is living, as are Y and his wife, their child P, P's wife and her parents, P's daughter and her husband, as well as her husband's father.

All of the above persons referred to, except the last, that is, the grandchild's husband's father, are measuring lives, and the section can be applied without difficulty. If, however, there are no grandchildren living at the testator's death, it is uncertain whether P is a measuring life. Similarly, if P was living at the testator's death, but had no child, it is uncertain whether P's wife and her parents can be measuring lives. It is probable, however, that these persons would be measuring lives, at least as soon as a person is born who is a grandchild of Y.

The following is a further example:[111]

> A bequest, "to the eldest son of X to marry." When the testator dies, X and his wife are living. So is X's mother-in-law and X's three sons, P, Q and R, all unmarried.

In this example, Q and R are not measuring lives, because neither is not the eldest son of X. Q only becomes a measuring life once P dies unmarried and R only becomes a measuring life when P and Q have both died unmarried.

The statutory list is not complete in that it does not include all possible lives in being which would have saved a gift at common law. Thus, an implied life, as in a gift, "to the first of my descendants to fly to the moon with X," which would be valid at common law, is not provided for by the statute.

(iii) The Statutory Formula Model

Ontario and the Northwest Territories use a statutory formula by means of which measuring lives are ascertained. The formula in the Ontario Act is as follows;

> **6.** (1) Except as provided in section 9, subsection 13(3) and subsections 15(2) and (3), the perpetuity period shall be measured in the same way as if this Act had not been passed, but, in measuring that period by including a life in being when the interest was created, no life shall be included other than that of any person whose life, at the time the interest was created, limits or is a relevant factor that limits in some way the period within which the conditions for vesting of the interest may occur.
>
> (2) A life that is a relevant factor in limiting the time for vesting of any part of a gift to a class shall be a relevant life in relation to the entire class.

The formula is sadly defective in that it is unclear who the measuring lives are intended to be. As noted earlier, the correct view at common law is that only those persons who validate a gift are lives in being, so that, if no person who is a potential life in being saves the gift, there are no lives in being. However, others suggest that at common law those persons are lives in being whose lives restrict the vesting period as a matter of causality and, although such lives were unhelpful at common law unless they saved the gift, they can be used under the statutory formula model.[112] It seems probable that the statutory formula model adopts that position, but restricts the list of measuring lives by insisting that only those lives may be included that limit or are a relevant factor that limit the period for vesting.

---

111 See M.J. Prichard, "Two Petty Perpetuity Puzzles" (1969), 27 Camb. L.J. 284 at 285-6.

112 J.H.C. Morris and H.W.R. Wade, "Perpetuities Reform at Last" (1964), 80 L.Q. Rev. 486 at 498. See generally Gosse, *Ontario's Perpetuities Legislation* (1967), pp. 23 ff.

On the other hand, section 6(2) broadens the common law list by including class members and their ancestors.

The following example illustrates how this model is likely to apply:

A bequest, "to the grandchildren of X when they marry." When the testator died, X and his wife were living, as were their two children, P and Q, and P's wife and her parents. P and his wife had one child.

Such a gift would be void at common law in its entirety. However, under the statutory formula model, it is likely that the measuring lives include X and his wife, in that they are the ancestors of the grandchildren, although it can not be said that they are relevant with respect to the time when the grandchildren marry. The same applies to P and his wife and Q, these being measuring lives under section 6(2). The grandchild is also a measuring life under section 6(2). However, the grandchild's mother's parents are probably not measuring lives, since they would not have been considered to be lives in being under the common law rule, as required by section 6(1) of the Ontario Act.[113]

The following is a further illustration:

A gift, "to X for life, remainder to Y's grandchildren living twenty-five years after the death of Y's children." When the testator died, X and Y and Y's husband were living and Y had one child, Z.

Z is included as a measuring life under section 6(2); however, Z is not in fact a measuring life because the interest in the grandchildren only vests twenty-five years after Z's death. X is probably not a relevant factor, because he does not limit the time of vesting. Y and her husband are relevant factors because the interest is limited to their grandchildren, although they have nothing to do with the time of vesting. If they are measuring lives, the gift will be valid if they live more than four years after the last of their children dies. It is, however, arguable that Y's husband will cease to be a measuring life when Y dies. Moreover, he is probably not a measuring life if Y were no longer living at the time of testator's death, since he would then have no relevance to the time of vesting.

(e) Specific Reforms

(i) *Generally*

The Canadian statutes have enacted specific reforms to deal with certain difficulties that arose under the common law rule and that proved to be traps for the unwary. In most cases the wait and see principle would save such gifts in any

---

113 See generally A.H. Oosterhoff and Gordon D. Cudmore, "Problems in Ascertaining Lives in Being Under Ontario's Perpetuities Act (On Limiting Lives and Relevant Factors)" (1977), 4 E. & T.Q. 119.

event, but the specific reforms will often make it unnecessary to rely upon that principle.

(ii) Capacity to have Children

The statutes provide that for the purposes of the rule against perpetuities a male is presumed to be able to have a child at age fourteen or over, but not under that age and a female is able to have a child at age twelve or over, but not under that age or over age fifty-five. In addition, evidence may be introduced to show that a living person can or is unable to have a child at a particular time.[114] These presumptions and rules avoid the "fertile octogenarian" and "precocious toddler" traps, previously described. The following example illustrates their operation:

> A bequest, "to X for life, remainder to such of her grandchildren living at my death or born within five years thereafter as shall attain the age of twenty-one." X is a widow sixty-five years old at the testator's death. She has two children and one grandchild at that time.

Since X is presumed to be incapable of having another child, the gift to the grandchildren is valid. Even if X were under age fifty-five, any child she might have would be incapable of having a child, and therefore, the gift to the grand-children would still be valid.

In these circumstances, therefore, it is not necessary to apply the wait and see principle. That principle would be applied if, for example, the woman in question who is the measuring life is under age fifty-five until she reaches that age.

The statutes provide that if a person has a child despite the presumptions, or if a child is subsequently adopted or becomes legitimate, the court may make an order to protect the rights of the child.[115]

(iii) Age Reduction

Many limitations failed under the common law rule because vesting was post-poned to an age greater than twenty-one. The Canadian statutes attempt to avoid the problem by providing for an age reduction in those circumstances.[116] The Ontario legislation is as follows:

> **8.** (1) Where a limitation creates an interest in [real or personal] property by reference to the attainment by any person or persons of a specified age exceeding twenty-one years, and actual events existing at the time the interest was created or at any subsequent time establish,
> (a) that the interest, would, but for this section, be void as incapable of vesting within the perpetuity period; but
> (b) that it would not be void if the specified age had been twenty-one years,

---

114 Alta. Act, s. 9(1); B.C. Act, s. 10(1); Ont. Act, s. 7(1); N.W.T. Act, s. 8(1); Yukon Act, s. 9(1).
115 Alta. Act, s. 9(2)-(4); B.C. Act, s. 10(2)-(4); Ont. Act, s. 7(2)(a); N.W.T. Act, s. 8(2)-(4); Yukon Act, s. 9(2) (4).
116 Alta. Act, s. 6(1); B.C. Act, s. 7(1); Ont. Act, s. 8(1); N.W.T. Act, s. 8(1); Yukon Act, s. 6(1).

the limitation shall be read as if, instead of referring to the age specified, it had referred to the age nearest the age specified that would, if specified instead, have prevented the interest from being so void.

The following example illustrates this provision:

A bequest, "to such of X's grandchildren as attain the age of twenty-five." At the testator's death, X, two of her children and a grandchild who was then five years old were living.

This gift would be void at common law in its entirety, since it is a class gift. X, her two children and the grandchild can, however, all be used as measuring lives under all of the Canadian statutes. If, however, all of them die three years after the testator, leaving two other grandchildren who are two and one years old, respectively, the wait and see principle will not allow the gift to vest within the period in respect of those two grandchildren. Hence, the vesting age in respect of them may be reduced to twenty-two. This age is arrived at by adding twenty-one to the age of the youngest grandchild when the wait and see principle can no longer be used.

The following example presents certain difficulties;

A bequest, "to the first grandchild of X to reach age thirty." When the testator died, X, X's two children and a grandchild aged five were alive.

Since the grandchild is a measuring life, it would not be not necessary to reduce his or her age. However, if that grandchild dies before age thirty, survived by two brothers and sisters, it is not clear what should be done under the Ontario and the Northwest Territories legislation. It might be that one should reduce the deceased grandchild's age retrospectively, or that one should reduce the oldest surviving grandchild's age and then, if that grandchild dies before reaching the reduced age, to reduce the younger grandchild's age. Alternatively, the ages of the two surviving grandchildren might have to be reduced. It is submitted that a staged reduction is called for under the statute.[117] You should note, incidentally, that the grandchildren's parents are not measuring lives under section 6(2) of the Ontario Act, since this is not a class gift.

The statutes of the other provinces provide that in this type of situation one age reduction should be made for all potential surviving beneficiaries. In other words, the age will be reduced to a common age for the two surviving grandchildren, whereas the grandchild who dies before satisfying the stated contingency will not take, even though he or she may have reached a greater age than his or her brothers and sisters.[118]

---

117 See A.H. Oosterhoff and Gordon D. Cudmore, *supra*.
118 Alta. Act, s. 6(2); B.C. Act, s. 7(2); Yukon Act, s. 6(2).

(iv) *Class Splitting*

While a class gift was wholly good or wholly bad under the common law rule, the several Canadian statutes permit the splitting of a class after the application of the wait and see principle and age reduction, if applicable, in order to exclude those persons whose interests do not vest in time.[119]

It should be remembered that the class closing rules may apply to close a class at an early date and thereby save the gift from the rule.[120] Hence, the class closing rules should be applied first, followed by the wait and see principle and the age reduction principle.

The Ontario legislation is as follows;

8.

. . .

(2) Where the inclusion of any persons, being potential members of a class or unborn persons who at birth would become members or potential members of the class, prevents subsection (1) from operating to save a limitation creating an interest in favour of a class of persons from being void for remoteness, such persons shall be excluded from the class for all purposes of the limitation, and the limitation takes effect accordingly.

(3) Where a limitation creates an interest in favour of a class to which subsection (2) does not apply and actual events at the time of the creation of the interest or at any subsequent time establish that, but for this subsection, the inclusion of any persons, being potential members of a class or unborn persons who at birth would become members or potential members of the class, would cause the limitation to the class to be void for remoteness, such persons shall be excluded from the class for all purposes of the limitation, and the limitation takes effect accordingly.

(4) For the purposes of this section, a person shall be treated as a member of a class if in the person's case all the conditions identifying a member of the class are satisfied, and a person shall be treated as a potential member if in the person's case some only of those conditions are satisfied but there is a possibility that the remainder will in time be satisfied.

This legislation may be illustrated by the following example:

A bequest, "to the grandchildren of A who marry." When the testator died, A, his three children, and two grandchildren, both unmarried, were alive. Later, three more grandchildren were born. Then the oldest grandchild married.

The class closing rules will not save this gift, since the class does not close until the first grandchild marries. A, his children and the two oldest grandchildren are all measuring lives, together with A's wife and the spouses of his children. The gift to the two oldest grandchildren will vest, if at all, during their lives and is therefore valid. The gift to the other grandchildren will be valid if they marry within twenty-one years after the death of the last of the measuring lives. If any of them do not marry within that time, they are excluded under the class splitting provision.

---

119 Alta. Act, s. 7; B.C. Act, s. 8; Ont. Act, s. 8(2)-(4); N.W.T. Act, s. 9(2)-(4), Yukon Act, s. 7.

120 These were discussed in the previous chapter and in connection with the common law rule earlier in this chapter.

(v) *The Unborn Spouse*

A gift in the following form,

"to A for life, then to her husband for life, remainder to such of their children as are then living,"
A being unmarried,

would be void at common law, because A might marry a man who might be
unborn at the testator's death. The Canadian statutes have solved this problem in
different ways. The statutory list model jurisdictions include the spouse as a
measuring life in their statutory lists,[121] whereas the statutory formula model
jurisdictions deem such a spouse to be a measuring life if the wait and see principle
does not otherwise save the gift.[122]

The Ontario legislation, which would save the above gift, is as follows:

9. (1) Where any disposition is made in favour of any spouse or same-sex partner of a person
in being at the commencement of the perpetuity period, or where a limitation creates an interest
in [real or personal] property by reference to the time of the death of the survivor of a person in
being at the commencement of the perpetuity period and any spouse or same-sex partner of the
person, for the purpose of validating any such disposition or limitation, that but for this section
would be void as offending the rule against perpetuities as modified by this Act, the spouse or
same-sex partner of such person shall be deemed to be a life in being at the commencement of
the perpetuity period even though such spouse or same-sex partner was not born until after that
time.

(2) For the purposes of subsection (1),
"same-sex partner" means a person of the same sex with whom the person is living in a conjugal
relationship outside marriage, if the two persons,
  (a) have cohabited for at least a year,
  (b) are together the parents of a child, or
  (c) have together entered into a cohabitation agreement under section 53 of the *Family Law
    Act*[123]
"spouse" means a person of the opposite sex,
  (a) to whom the person is married or
  (b) with whom the person is living in a conjugal relationship outside marriage, if the two
    persons,
    (i) have cohabited at least a year,
    (ii) are together the parents of a child, or
    (iii) have together entered into a cohabitation agreement under section 53 of the *Family
    Law Act*.[124]

---

121 Alta. Act, s. 5(2)(e); B.C. Act, s. 6(2)(e); Yukon Act, s. 5(2)(e).
122 Ont. Act, s. 9 [am. S.O. 1999, c. 6, s. 54(1)(2)]; N.W.T. Act, s. 10.
123 R.S.O. 1990, c. F.3 [am. 1999, c. 6, s. 25(23)].
124 *Ibid.*

(vi) *Cy-Près*

The statutory list model jurisdictions contain a salutary provision which allows the court to vary a gift so as to prevent failure for perpetuities if none of the other remedies included in the legislation save the gift.[125]
The British Columbia provision is as follows;

General *cy près* provision

> **13.** (1) If it has become apparent that, apart from the provisions of this section, a disposition would be void solely on the ground that it infringes the rule against perpetuities, and if the general intention originally governing the disposition can be ascertained in accordance with the normal principles of interpretation of instruments and the rules of evidence, on application to the court by an interested person, the disposition may be varied so as to give effect as far as possible to the general intention within the limits of the rule against perpetuities.
>
> (2) Subsection (1) does not apply if the disposition of the property has been the subject of a valid compromise.

(vii) *Order of Remedies*

The order in which the remedies provided by the statutes are to be applied are: the capacity to have children, wait and see, age reduction, class splitting, and the unborn spouse,[126] or *cy près*.[127]

(f) Application of the Statutory Rule to Various Interests

(i) *Powers of Appointment*

The several statutes modify the rule as it applies to powers of appointment in two ways, namely, by extending the wait and see principle to powers[128] and by defining general and special powers.[129]
The Ontario legislation is as follows;

---

125 Alta. Act, s. 8; B.C. Act, s. 9; Yukon Act, s. 8.
126 In Ont. and N.W.T. The statutes in these jurisdictions make this order clear from the language of the several sections.
127 Alta. Act, s. 11; B.C. Act, s. 12, Yukon Act, s. 11. These statutes give a list of the order in which the remedies are to be applied. The unborn spouse provision is not contained in them, since the unborn spouse is included in the list of measuring lives in those statutes.
128 Alta. Act, s. 4(2), (3); B.C. Act, s. 5(2), (3); Ont. Act, s. 4(2), (3); N.W.T. Act, s. 5(2), (3); Yukon Act, s. 4(2), (3).
129 Alta. Act, s. 13; B.C. Act, s. 14; Ont. Act, s. 10(2); N.W.T. Act, s. 11(2); Yukon Act, s. 13.

4.

. . .

(2) A limitation conferring a general power of appointment, which but for this section would have been void on the ground that it might become exercisable beyond the perpetuity period, is presumptively valid until such time, if any, as it becomes established by actual events that the power cannot be exercised within the perpetuity period.

(3) A limitation conferring any power, option or other right, other than a general power of appointment, which but for this section would have been void on the ground that it might be exercised beyond the perpetuity period, is presumptively valid, and shall be declared or treated as void for remoteness only if, and so far as, the right is not fully exercised within the perpetuity period.

. . .

11. (1) For the purpose of the rule against perpetuities, a power of appointment shall be treated as a special power unless,
   (a) in the instrument creating the power it is expressed to be exercisable by one person only; and
   (b) it could, at all times during its currency when that person is of full age and capacity, be exercised by the person so as immediately to transfer to the person the whole of the interest governed by the power without the consent of any other person or compliance with any other condition, not being a formal condition relating only to the mode of exercise of the power.

(2) A power that satisfies the conditions of clauses (1)(a) and (b) shall, for the purpose of the rule against perpetuities, be treated as general power.

(3) For the purpose of determining whether an appointment made under a power of appointment exercisable by will only is void for remoteness, the power shall be treated as a general power where it would have been so treated if exercisable by deed.

The following example illustrates the legislation:

A bequest, "to X for life, remainder to X's eldest son for life, remainder as X's eldest son may appoint after he marries." X was living at the testator's death, but had no son as yet.

Since the eldest son may not marry for more than twenty-one years after X's death, the power, which is a general power, would be void at common law. However, under the statute the power is presumed to be valid and will only become void if the eldest son has not exercised it within the perpetuity period, that is, during X's lifetime plus 21 years. Moreover, if he exercises the power within the perpetuity period, the appointment will be valid, provided that it is made within the perpetuity period and for this purpose the period begins to run from the date of the appointment.

The following is an example of a special power;

A bequest, "to X for life, remainder to X's children for their lives, remainder as the survivor of X's children may appoint among X's issue." At the testator's death, X was living but had no children.

The power and any appointment thereunder would be void at common law. However, under the statute the power is presumed to be valid and will in fact be valid if it is exercised within the perpetuity period, that is, within twenty-one years of the death of X. Moreover, any appointment made under the power will be valid to the extent that the interests vest during the perpetuity period which, in this case, runs from the date of the testator's death. For this purpose, wait and see, age reduction, class splitting, *etc.*, can be applied.

(ii) *Possibilities of Reverter and Rights of Re-entry for Conditions Broken*

The several Canadian statutes extend the application of the rule against perpetuities to possibilities of reverter and resulting trusts in real and personal property. It will be recalled that rights of entry for conditions broken were already subject to the rule at common law.[130]

The several statutes now apply the rule in the same way to all of these interests. However, the perpetuity period varies in the several statutes. Thus, it is a forty year period in Alberta and the Yukon,[131] whereas it is the normal perpetuity period of a measuring life plus twenty-one years, or eighty years if there are no measuring lives in British Columbia.[132] In Ontario and the Northwest Territories the period is twenty-one years if there are no measuring lives, or measuring lives plus twenty-one years to a maximum of forty years if there are.[133]

The Ontario legislation is as follows:

> **15.** (1) In the case of,
> (a) a possibility of reverter on the determination of a determinable fee simple; or
> (b) a possibility of a resulting trust on the determination of any determinable interest in real or personal property,
> the rule against perpetuities as modified by this Act applies in relation to the provision causing the interest to be determinable as it would apply if that provision were expressed in the form of a condition subsequent giving rise on its breach to a right of re-entry or an equivalent right in the case of personal property, and, where the event that determines the determinable interest does not occur within the perpetuity period, the provision shall be treated as void for remoteness and the determinable interest becomes an absolute interest.
>
> (2) In the case of a possibility of reverter on the determination of a determinable fee simple, or in the case of a possibility of a resulting trust on the determination of any determinable interest in any [real or personal] property, or in the case of a right of re-entry following on a condition subsequent, or in the case of an equivalent right in personal property, the perpetuity period shall be measured as if the event determining the prior interest were a condition to the vesting of the subsequent interest, and failing any life in being at the time the interests were created that limits or is a relevant factor that limits in some way the period within which that event may take place, the perpetuity period is twenty-one years from the time when the interests were created.
>
> (3) Even though some life or lives in being may be relevant in determining the perpetuity period under subsection (2), the perpetuity period for the purposes of this section shall not exceed a period of forty years from the time when the interests were created and shall be the lesser of a period of forty years and a period composed of the relevant life or lives in being and twenty-one years.

The following example illustrates how the Ontario legislation is applied:

---

130 As discussed earlier in this chapter.
131 Alta. Act, s. 19; Yukon Act, s. 19.
132 B.C. Act, s. 20.
133 Ont. Act, s. 15, N.W.T. Act, s. 16.

A devise, "to X so long as the land is used as a school during Y's lifetime and 21 years."

The devise creates a determinable fee, giving the testator's estate a possibility of a reverter. Under the statute, the possibility of a reverter is valid, so that the land reverts to the testator's estate if the land is no longer used as a school within Y's lifetime plus twenty-one years, to a maximum of forty years. If the land ceases to be used as a school after that time, the possibility of reverter becomes void and X acquires an absolute interest.

The following is a further example:

A devise, "to X provided that the land is not used for commercial purposes."

The devise in this example creates a fee simple upon condition subsequent and the testator's estate, therefore, retains a right of re-entry for condition broken. The latter interest is valid for a period of twenty-one years, entitling the estate to re-enter if the land is used for commercial purposes during that time. If, however, the use changes after that time, the right of re-entry becomes void and X acquires an absolute interest.

This result is inappropriate if the property or the money is given to a person in trust for charitable purposes upon a determinable event or a condition subsequent and, for this reason, some of the statutes provide that in that event, the interest of the trustee does not become absolute but the moneys are to be applied *cy près* to similar charitable purposes.[134]

(iii) *Interim Income*

At common law the interim income from a contingent gift, or the income from a gift to a minor could not be paid to the beneficiary, nor could the trustees make advances of capital to the beneficiary, except under the court's common law jurisdiction to vary a trust to allow maintenance payments.[135] In some provinces there are statutory powers of maintenance and advancement,[136] in others a statutory power of maintenance only;[137] yet other provinces make no provision for maintenance or advancement. A testator may, however, make express provisions for maintenance or advancement. Nevertheless, none of these powers can be exercised under the common law perpetuity rule if the interest is void under that rule.

Since an interest is now presumptively valid under the several perpetuities statutes, however, the statutes provide that the income is to be treated as income

---

134 Alta. Act, s. 19(3); B.C. Act, s. 20(2); Yukon Act, s. 19(3).
135 See, *e.g.*, *Re Wright*, [1954] O.R. 755, [1955] 1 D.L.R. 213 (H.C.).
136 *Trustee Act*, R.S.M. 1987, c. T160, ss. 31, 32; R.S.P.E.I. 1988, c. T-8, ss. 39, 40.
137 *Trustee Act*, R.S.A. 1980, c. T-10, ss. 33, 36; R.S.B.C. 1996, c. 464, ss. 24-26; R.S.N. 1990, c. T-10, s. 26; R.S.N.S. 1989, c. 479, s. 30; R.S.S. 1978, c. T-23, ss. 52-54; R.S.N.W.T. 1988, c. T-8, ss. 27, 28; R.S.Y. 1986, c. 173, ss. 30, 31; *Trustees Act*, R.S.N.B. 1973, c. T-15, s. 14 [subs. (1) re-en. 1986, c. 4; subs. (3) am. 1986, c. 4].

arising from valid contingent interests, unless it is otherwise disposed of.[138] Thus, in those jurisdictions in which there is a statutory power of maintenance, or if the testator has expressly given the income to the contingent beneficiary, the income can now be disposed of. If there is no express power of maintenance and no statutory power, the income must either be accumulated, or it will go out as on an intestacy.[139]

(iv) *Ulterior Limitations*

Ulterior limitations which are subject to, dependent upon or follow after a prior limitation that is void for perpetuity, are valid under the perpetuities legislation, provided that they do not, themselves, offend the rule. Moreover, the ulterior gift is allowed to accelerate unless, of course, it is itself subject to a contingency which is not yet satisfied.[140]

(v) *Administrative Powers*

The several Canadian statutes provide that administrative powers, such as powers to sell or lease, are not subject to the rule against perpetuities.[141]

(g) Modification of the Rule Against Indefinite Duration

The several statutes have also modified the rule against indefinite duration which applies to non-charitable purpose trusts, by permitting them to take effect for twenty-one years or such shorter period as the testator or settlor directs. However, the court may declare the trust void if it concludes that the result would more closely approximate the testator's or settlor's intention. At the end of the twenty-one year period the capital and any income not fully expended result to the estate.[142]

In order to take advantage of this provision, the non-charitable purpose trust must be "specific" and it has been held that a trust to a society for its "religious, literary and education purposes" is uncertain and, therefore not specific.[143] Presumably a trust to maintain a testator's animals, or his grave, would be specific.

---

138 Alta. Act, s. 12; B.C. Act, s. 13, Ont. Act, s. 5(2); N.W.T. Act s. 6(2); Yukon Act, s. 12.
139 See Terence Sheard, "Perpetuities — the New Proposed Act" (1966), 14 Chitty's L.J. 3 at 5.
140 Alta. Act, s. 13; B.C. Act, s. 14; Ont. Act, s. 10; N.W.T. Act, s. 11; Yukon Act, s. 13.
141 Alta. Act, s. 15; B.C. Act, s. 16; Ont. Act, s. 12; N.W.T. Act, s. 13; Yukon Act, s. 15.
142 Alta Act, s. 20; B.C. Act, s. 21; Ont. Act. s. 16; N.W.T. Act, s. 17; Yukon Act, s. 20.
143 *Re Russell; Wood v. R.*, [1977] 6 W.W.R. 273, 1 E.T.R. 285 (Alta. T.D.).

Problems

1. The following is a series of problems, principally concerning class gifts, which commonly occur. It is suggested that the student solve these problems in three stages, namely, determine (1) when the class closes; (2) whether the gift is void under the common law rule; and (3) if the gift is void at common law, whether the legislation saves the gift in whole or in part.

In each problem, when applicable, T is the testator, and A, B, C, *etc.*, are the first, second, and third members of the class.

Assume a gift of $10,000 to each of the classes in problems (a) to (k), a gift of $1,000 to each member of the class in problems in (l) and (m), and a gift of $1,000 to the beneficiary in problem (n).

   (a) "To the children of Y in equal shares."
      (i) Y predeceased T.
     (ii) Y survives T, and A is living at T's death.
    (iii) Y survives T, but A is not living at T's death.

   (b) "To the grandchildren of Y."
      (i) Y has predeceased T and A is living at T's death.
     (ii) Y has predeceased T, but A is born 30 years after T's death.
    (iii) Y survives T, and A is living at T's death.
    (iv) Y survives T, but A is born 35 years after T's death.

   (c) "To X for life, remainder to the children of Y in equal shares."
      (i) Y has predeceased T.
     (ii) Y survives T, and A is living at T's death.
    (iii) Y survives T, but A is born after T's death and before X's death.
    (iv) Y survives T, but A is born after T's death and X's death.

   (d) "To my widow, X, for life, and then to the children of my brothers and sisters in equal shares."
      (i) Y (brothers and sisters) have predeceased T.
     (ii) Y survives T, and A is living at T's death.
    (iii) Y survives T, but A is born after T's death and before X's death.
    (iv) Y survives T, but A is born after T's death and X's death.
     (v) Does it make any difference if T was survived by either or both his mother, M, and his father, F?

   (e) "To the children of Y who attain the age of 21." Assume first that Y predeceases T, then that he survives T.
      (i) A is 21 at T's death.
     (ii) A is 2 at T's death.
    (iii) A is 2 at Y's death.

   (f) "To the children of Y who attain the age of 30." Assume first that Y predeceases T, then that she survives T.
      (i) A is 30 at T's death.
     (ii) A is 2 at T's death.
    (iii) Y has no children yet.
    (iv) Y dies 20 years after T leaving A, aged 6, and B, aged 4.

(g) "To the children of Y when they marry." Assume first that Y predeceases T, then that he survives T.
   (i) A is married at T's death.
   (ii) A is not married at T's death.
   (iii) A marries after T's death, but before Y's death.
   (iv) A marries after T and Y have both died.
   (v) At T's death, Y is living and has two children, A and B, unmarried. After T's death, Y has a third child, C. All three children marry more than 21 years after Y's death.

(h) "To my sister, Y, for life and then to her children who attain the age of 21." Assume that Y survives T.
   (i) A is 21 at T's death.
   (ii) A is 21 at Y's death.
   (iii) A is unborn at T's death, but is 2 at Y's death.
   (iv) A is 2 at T's death.

(i) "To my sister, Y, for life and then to her grandchildren who attain the age of 25." Assume first that Y predeceases T, then that Y survives T.
   (i) A is unborn at T's death.
   (ii) A is 2 at T's death.
   (iii) A is 25 at T's death.
   (iv) A is 25 at T's death, and B is born after T's death but before Y's death.
   (v) As in (iv), but A and B died while C was only 1 year old.
   (vi) A is 3 at T's death.
   (vii) A was unborn at T's death, but A was 3 when Y died.
   (viii) A was unborn at T's death, but A was 3 and B was 2 when Y died.
   (ix) A was unborn at T's death, but A was 3 when Y died, and 2 years after Y's death B was born.

(j) "To A for life and then to such of A's children as attain age 25 and the children of such of them as shall die under age 25 leaving children who attain age 25, such children to take the share their parent would have taken." On T's death A is alive but has no children.

(k) "To A for life, then for A's children as they respectively attain age 21, but if any child of A dies under age 21 leaving children who attain age 21, such children shall take their parent's share."

(l) "To each of the children of X." Assume first that X predeceases T, then that he survives T.
   (i) A is unborn.
   (ii) A is living.

(m) "To each of the children of X who attain age 21." Assume first that X predeceases T, then that he survives T.
   (i) A is unborn.
   (ii) A is alive, but not yet 21 at T's death.
   (iii) A is 21, B is 15, and C is 5 years old.

(n) "To the first grandchild of X to attain age 30." X is alive at T's death; so are his children, Y and Z, as well as one grandchild, A, aged 5.

7. ACCUMULATIONS

(a) Introduction

An accumulation arises when income from a fund is put out at interest and is not distributed, but is added to the capital.

Statutory restrictions on accumulations of income came about as a result of the will of Peter Thellusson, who died in 1797. By his will he left the residue of his large estate in trust to accumulate the income during the lives of his sons, grand-sons and great-grandsons living at his death or born "in due time afterwards." On the death of the survivor, the corpus was to be divided into three parts, each of which was to be settled on the eldest lineal male descendants then living of the testator's three sons, who were required to adopt the testator's name. If there were no descendants, the corpus would pass to the Crown to reduce the national debt. The testator was survived by three sons and six grandsons, two of whom were *en ventre sa mère* at the time of his death. The House of Lords held the bequest valid.[144] However, the will raised a great public outcry, since it was calculated that the accumulated value of the estate would exceed £30 million. In fact, when the last life in being died in 1856, it turned out to be a relatively small amount, due to mismanagement and the cost of litigation, there being eight reported cases in respect of the will.[145] In answer to the public outcry the *Thellusson Act*[146] was passed, which imposed four possible periods during which income could be accumulated. Accumulations legislation in various common law jurisdictions is based on this original statute. In a number of jurisdictions, including Ontario, the permissible accumulation periods have subsequently been enlarged.[147]

The statute was regarded as received English law in Manitoba,[148] Alberta,[149] and Saskatchewan.[150] It was probably also received in Newfoundland, British Columbia and the Territories, but not in the Maritime provinces, because the reception dates in those provinces pre-date the statute.

---

144 *Thellusson v. Woodford* (1805), 11 Ves. 112, 32 E.R. 1030 (H.L.).
145 See J.H.C. Morris and W. Barton Leach, *The Rule Against Perpetuities*, 2nd ed. (London: Stevens & Son, 1962, with Supplement, 1964), pp. 266 ff.
146 *Accumulations Act*, 39 & 40 Geo. 3, c. 98 (1800).
147 *Accumulations Act*, S.B.C. 1967, c. 2; *Accumulations Amendment Act*, S.O. 1966, c. 2.
148 *Re Aikins Trusts* (1961), 35 W.W.R. 143 (Man. Q.B.).
149 *Re Burns* (1960), 32 W.W.R. 689, 25 D.L.R. 427 (Alta. C.A.).
150 *Re Fossum* (1960), 32 W.W.R. 372 (Sask. Q.B.).

The English Act was enacted or re-enacted in British Columbia,[151] Ontario[152] and New Brunswick.[153] However, it no longer applies to Alberta[154] and Manitoba[155] and the British Columbia Act has been repealed.[156]

In Prince Edward Island, accumulations are valid for the same period as the perpetuity period.[157]

It is submitted that the statutory restraints on accumulations are nowadays otiose in view of income and death taxes and ought, therefore, to be abolished.

As distinct from the rule against perpetuities, an accumulation which exceeds a permissible period is not void in its entirety, but is allowed to take effect for the appropriate period and the surplus income thereafter will either fall into residue or will go out on an intestacy, depending upon whether the accumulation is in respect of a specific gift or a gift of residue. On the other hand, an accumulation which extends beyond the perpetuity period is void under the common law rule.[158] Whether a direction to accumulate invokes the wait and see principle under the Ontario perpetuities legislation is questionable. Such a direction does attract the wait and see principle in Alberta and British Columbia.[159]

The statute applies both to a trust and to a power to accumulate,[160] as well as to an implied accumulation.

An accumulation is implied if the will bears such a construction,[161] but it cannot be implied if the interest given does not carry the intermediate income either expressly or by implication. An interest does not *prima facie* carry the intermediate income if it is a contingent or vested but deferred devise of real property, whether specific or residuary, but it does if it is a contingent gift of real and personal property which is blended.[162] A contingent specific bequest and a vested but deferred specific bequest do not carry the intermediate income, unless they are separated from the estate.[163] A vested residuary bequest which is deferred and a contingent residuary bequest which is deferred also do not carry the intermediate

151 *Accumulations Restraint Act*, R.S.B.C. 1897, c. 2, re-enacted as the *Accumulations Act*, S.B.C. 1967, c. 2.
152 *Accumulations Act*, R.S.O. 1897, c. 332. See now R.S.O. 1990, c. A.5, hereafter referred to without further citation.
153 *Property Act*, C.S.N.B. 1903, c. 152, ss. 2, 3. See now R.S.N.B. 1973, c. P-19, ss. 1, 2, hereafter referred to without further citation.
154 *Perpetuities Act*, R.S.A. 1980, c. P-4, s. 24.
155 *Perpetuities and Accumulations Act*, R.S.M. 1987, c. P33, s. 2.
156 *Perpetuity Act*, R.S.B.C. 1996, c. 358, s. 24.
157 *Perpetuities Act*, R.S.P.E.I. 1988, c. P-3, s. 1.
158 *Re Miller*, [1938] O.W.N. 118, [1938] 2 D.L.R. 765 (H.C.).
159 *Perpetuities Act*, R.S.A. 1980, c. P-24, s. 24(2); *Perpetuity Act*, R.S.B.C. 1996, c. 358, s. 24(1).
160 *Re Robb; Marshall v. Marshall*, [1953] Ch. 459, [1953] 1 All E.R. 920.
161 See, *e.g.*, *Re Baragar*, [1973] 1 O.R. 831, 32 D.L.R. (3d) 529 (H.C.); *Re Amodeo*, [1962] O.R. 548, 33 D.L.R. (2d) 24 (C.A.); *Re Struthers* (1980), 29 O.R. (2d) 616, 7 E.T.R. 307, 114 D.L.R. (3d) 492 (C.A.).
162 *Re Burton; Banks v. Heaven*, [1892] 2 Ch. 38.
163 *Re McGeorge; Ratcliff v. McGeorge*, [1963] Ch. 544 at 551, [1963] 1 All E.R. 519, *per* Cross J.

income,[164] but a vested residuary bequest that is subject to divestment does.[165] Finally, a contingent residuary bequest which is not deferred does carry the intermediate income.[166]

Under the statutory powers of maintenance in effect in several Canadian jurisdictions,[167] any income not used for the maintenance of an infant is accumulated and it would seem that the statutory restraints on accumulation do not apply in that case.[168] This is so also at common law if the infant has a vested interest in property.[169]

Further Reading

Ontario Law Reform Commission, *Report No. 1 (Perpetuities and Accumulations)* (1965): *Report No. 1A (The Perpetuities Act, 1965) (1966).*

Institute of Law Research and Reform (Alta.), *Report No.9 (The Rule in Saunders v. Vautier) (1972).*

Manitoba Law Reform Commission, *Report No. 49 (Report on the Rules Against Accumulations and Perpetuities) (1982).*

G. Boughen Graham, "Accumulations of Income" (1953), 17 Conv. (N.S.) 199.

S.J. Bailey, "Class-Closing, Accumulations and Acceleration" [1958] Cambr. L.J. 39.

(b) The Statute

ACCUMULATIONS ACT
R.S.O. 1990, c. A.5, am. S.O. 1993, c. 27, Sched.

1. (1) No disposition of any real or personal property shall direct the income thereof to be wholly or partially accumulated for any longer than one of the following terms:

1. The life of the grantor.
2. Twenty-one years from the date of making an *inter vivos* disposition.
3. The duration of the minority or respective minorities of any person or persons living or conceived but not born at the date of making an *inter vivos* disposition.
4. Twenty-one years from the death of the grantor, settlor or testator.

---

164 *Re Geering; Gulliver v. Geering*, [1969] Ch. 136, [1962] 3 All E.R. 1043.
165 *Re Hammond*, [1935] S.C.R. 550, [1935] 4 D.L.R. 209; *Watson v. Conant*, [1964] S.C.R. 312 (sub nom. *Re Watson*) 44 D.L.R. (2d) 346.
166 *Re Geering; Gulliver v. Geering, supra.*
167 *Trustee Act*, R.S.A. 1980, c. T-10, ss. 33, 36; R.S.B.C. 1996, c. 464, ss. 24-26; R.S.M. 1987, c. T160, ss. 31, 32; R.S.N. 1990, c. T-10, s. 26; R.S.N.S. 1989, c. 479, s. 30; R.S.N.W.T. 1988, c. T-8, ss. 27-28; R.S.P.E.I. 1988, c. T-8, ss. 39, 40; R.S.S. 1978, c. T-23, ss. 52-54; R.S.Y. 1971, c. T-5, ss. 32, 33; *Trustees Act*, R.S.N.B. 1973, c. T-15, s. 14 [subs. (1) re-en. 1986, c. 4; subs. (3) am. 1986, c. 4].
168 See *Mathews v. Keble* (1868), 3 Ch. App. 691 at 696.
169 *Ibid.*

5. The duration of the minority or respective minorities of any person or persons living or conceived but not born at the death of the grantor, settlor or testator.

6. The duration of the minority or respective minorities of any person or persons who, under the instrument directing the accumulations, would, for the time being, if of full age, be entitled to the income directed to be accumulated.

(2) The restrictions imposed by subsection (1) apply in relation to a power to accumulate income whether or not there is a duty to exercise that power, and such restrictions also apply whether or not the power to accumulate extends to income produced by the investment of income previously accumulated.

(3) The restrictions imposed by subsection (1) apply to every disposition or real or personal property, whether made before or after its enactment.

(4) Nothing in subsection (1) affects,

(a) the validity of any act done; or

(b) any right acquired or obligation incurred,

under this Act before the 6th day of September, 1966.

(5) No accumulation for the purchase of land shall be directed for any longer period than permitted under subsection (1).

(6) Where an accumulation is directed contrary to this Act, such direction is null and void, and the rents, issues, profits and produce of the property so directed to be accumulated shall, so long as they are directed to be accumulated contrary to this Act, go to and be received by such person as would have been entitled thereto if such accumulation had not been so directed.

2. Nothing in this Act extends to any provision for payment of debts of a grantor, settlor, devisor or other person, or to any provision for raising portions for a child of a grantor, settlor or devisor, or for a child of a person taking an interest under any such conveyance, settlement or devise, or to any direction touching the produce of timber or wood upon any lands or tenements, but all such provisions and directions may be made and given as if this Act had not been passed.

3. The rules of law and statutory enactments relating to accumulations do not apply and shall be deemed never to have applied to the trusts of a plan, trust or fund established for the purpose of providing pensions, retirement allowances, annuities, or sickness, death or other benefits to employees or to their widows, dependants or other beneficiaries.

Comparable Legislation

Property Act, R.S.N.B. 1973, c. P-19, ss. 1, 2.
See also *Perpetuities Act*, R.S.P.E.I. 1988, c. P-3, s. 1.

Notes and Questions

1. You will note that the legislation does not, by its terms, extend to a provision to pay debts, to raise portions or respecting the produce of timber or wood upon any lands.

2. A portion is a share set aside for a child out of property given to other persons. Is a trust to accumulate for the maintenance, education and support of the testator's issue the equivalent of raising of a portion?[170]

3. The statute does not apply to commercial transactions,[171] nor to corporations that direct an accumulation in an *inter vivos* settlement.[172]

(c) The Accumulation Periods

(i) *Generally*

A testator may not choose more than one of the periods permitted by the statute. If the testator's directions are unclear, the court will select the one that most closely approximates his intention.

Thus, in *Re Mulock Marriage Settlements*,[173] Sir William Mulock had directed that three-fifths of the property settled under three marriage settlements be accumulated, but that the accumulations "shall not continue for a longer period in any event than twenty-one years after the death of the Settlor." It was held that the first accumulation period only could be used, that is, for the life of the grantor, and any accumulations thereafter were void.

In the following materials examples of accumulations that are likely to arise in wills are given, that is, examples of periods 4, 5 and 6.

(ii) *Twenty-one Years from the Testator's Death*

The period of twenty-one years is appropriate if a testator directs that certain annuities be paid and that any surplus income not required for that purpose be accumulated during the lives of the annuitants and then distributed.[174] *Re Arnold*,[175] reproduced below is another example in which this period is appropriate.

RE ARNOLD
16 W.W.R. 129, [1955] 4 D.L.R. 535
Supreme Court of British Columbia

The testator died in 1952, a bachelor. By his will he directed that the residue of his estate be held in trust and the income thereon be paid to his only next of kin, his sister, Violet Arnold, and then to her husband for life. Thereafter, the

---

170 See *Re Davidson* (1926), 58 O.L.R. 597 (H.C.), affirmed 59 O.L.R. 643 (C.A.).

171 *Re A.E.G. Unit Trust (Managers) Deed; Midland Bank Executor & Trustee Co. v. A.E.G. Unit Trust (Managers)*, [1957] Ch. 415, [1957] 2 All E.R. 506.

172 *Re Dodwell & Co.'s Trust Deed*, [1979] Ch. 301, [1978] 3 All E.R. 738.

173 [1957] O.W.N. 453 (H.C.).

174 See *Re Benor*, [1963] 2 O.R. 248, 39 D.L.R. (2d) 122 (H.C.). And see *Re Major*, [1970] 2 O.R. 121, 10 D.L.R. (3d) 107 (H.C.); *Fasken v. Fasken*, [1953] 2 S.C.R. 10, [1953] 3 D.L.R. 431.

175 16 W.W.R. 129, [1955] 4 D.L.R. 535 (B.C.S.C.).

income was to be accumulated for six years. At the end of the six years three-fourths of the capital and accumulated income was to be paid to Angela Hollins, a cousin, while the other one-fourth of the income was to be accumulated for another twenty-five years. Then the income was to be paid to Angela Hollins for life, then to her husband for life and then to Angela's eldest son at age 30 for life, or failing a son, to her eldest daughter for life at age 30 or marriage. If Angela should die without issue, however, the income on the fourth share should be paid to another cousin, Mollie Burrows, for life, then to her husband for life and then to Molly's eldest son at age 30 for life, or failing a son, to her eldest daughter for life at age 30. The child of Angela or Molly who was the last income beneficiary was given a power to appoint the capital.

Violet died in 1954. Angela was then thirty-two years of age and had never been married. Mollie was thirty-four years old and married to Richard Burrows. They had two daughters, Fay and Caroline, who were six and three years old respectively. The latter were living when the testator died.

WHITTAKER J.:

. . .

The first question for consideration is whether the direction in the will for accumulating, adding to the capital and reinvesting one-quarter of the income for a period of 25 years (following a period of six years of accumulation of the whole income), 31 years in all from the date of death of Violet Arnold, violates the provisions of the *Accumulations Restraint Act*[176] and, if so, who will be entitled to receive said one-quarter of the income during the prohibited period, and the date of vesting thereof.

Any direction to accumulate income for a longer period than 21 years is void under the statute. The 21-year period begins to run from the date of death of the testator: *Kingsford, Canadian Law of Wills*;[177] *Webb v. Webb*.[178]

The testator died on September 11, 1952. The accumulation is therefore good only until September 12, 1973, commencing at the date of death of Violet Arnold, namely, April 6, 1954. But the total period of accumulation as directed by the will is until April 6, 1985, being 31 years from the date of Miss Arnold's death.

The direction to accumulate is not void in its entirely. It is good for 21 years from the testator's death, and thereafter is void for the remainder of the period during which the income is directed to be accumulated. Unless the accumulation during the void period is for the benefit of someone who has a vested interest therein, or unless there is in the will an express or implied disposition of accumulations made ineffective by the statute, the released income is to be dealt with as upon an intestacy.[179]

---

176 R.S.B.C. 1948, c. 5.

177 1913, p. 179.

178 (1840), 2 Beav. 493, 48 E.R. 1273.

179 *McDonald v. Bryce* (1838), 2 Keen. 276, 48 E.R. 634; *Green v. Gascoyne* (1865), 4 De G. J. & S. 565, 46 E.R. 1038; *Re Hammond*, [1935] S.C.R. 550; *Re Land*, [1939] O.W.N. 329; *Re Robertson*, [1939] O.W.N. 569.

The direction to accumulate the remaining three-fourths of the income for a period of 6 years from the death of Violet Arnold is valid, as it is well within the statutory period.

[His Lordship held that neither accumulation offended the rule against perpetuities, since the vesting of the gift of accumulated income was not postponed beyond that period. Rather, the property appointed pursuant to the power of appointment over the accumulated income would vest, if at all, during the life of Fay or Caroline Burrows. He continued:]

I am of the opinion, therefore, that the direction to accumulate is not entirely void, but only to the extent that it offends against the statute, that is, as to one-fourth of the income only, and only for the period from and including September 12, 1973, to April 6, 1985. The one-fourth income during the latter period will go as on an intestacy, and will vest in and be paid to the parties entitled as and when it is received.

[The Court went on to hold that the gift of income to Angela Hollins' eldest child was void for remoteness, but that the gift of income to Mollie Burrows, her husband and Mollie's eldest child was valid. Mollie's eldest child would, at age 30, have the power to appoint the corpus and, if she failed to do so, there would be an intestacy as to the corpus.]

(iii) *Duration of Minorities of Persons Living at Testator's Death*

The fifth period listed in the statute, namely, the duration of the minority or respective minorities of any person or persons living or *en ventre sa mère* at the death of the grantor, settlor or testator, is not always appropriate, even though the testator directs an accumulation for the duration of the minority of a living person. Thus, if a testator directs that income be accumulated until the youngest child of A becomes 25, and A has one child living at the testator's death, but there is a possibility of further children, a period of 21 years from the testator's death is more appropriate.[180] *Re Watt's Will Trusts; Watt v. Watt*,[181] reproduced below, is an example of how the fifth period operates.

RE WATT'S WILL TRUSTS; WATT v. WATT
[1936] 2 All E.R. 1555
Chancery Division

The testator directed an accumulation of the income of part of the residue of his estate, except for certain annual payments of income to his son Gerald, his wife and their children, during the minority of the children or child of Gerald, with power to apply the accumulations of any preceding year or years for any of

---

180 *Re Ransome; Moberly v. Ransome*, [1957] Ch. 348, [1957] 1 All E.R. 690.
181 [1936] 2 All E.R. 1555.

the purposes to which they might have been applied had they been income of the fund in the then current year. The capital and accumulated income were to be held for any child of children of Gerald who, being male attained age 21, or being female attained that age or married, and if more than one in equal shares.

The testator died in 1928. Gerald, his wife and three children, Kenneth, Francis and Harold, are still living. The children are now 22, 18 and 8.

BENNETT J.:

. . .

The direction to accumulate is a direction to accumulate the income of the whole of the Gerald Watt fund, except such part as may be required to provide for the annual payments that have to be made to or for the benefit of Gerald and his present wife and their children. The period for which accumulation is directed is during the minority of the children or child of Gerald. The children are not in terms confined to those living at the testator's death. The period in terms extends to the minority of any children of Gerald who may hereafter be born. Testators are not free to direct the accumulation of the income of property of which they die possessed for any period of time that to them may seem desirable. Their freedom in this respect is restricted by the provisions of the Law of Property Act, 1925,[182] s. 164.

> [His Lordship reproduced s. 164(1), which then contained only four periods. Those periods corresponded with periods 1, 4, 5 and 6, respectively, of the Ontario legislation set out above. He continued:]

It is settled that a testator may select only one of the four periods specified in sect. 164 (see LORD PARKER OF WADDINGTON in *Re Cattell*),[183] and when a question is raised whether or not the section has been breached the court has first to determine which of the four periods the testator has seemingly selected, determining that question by reference to the language employed and the facts of the case.[184] In the present will the choice is between the third period and the fourth. The first period is out of the case, and as regards the second the testator has not had in mind a period of years, but a period of time to be measured by the minority of children. In my judgment, the period which best fits with the language of the will and the facts of the case is the third. I reject the fourth for the reason that that period is the minority or the respective minorities of a person or of persons who, if of full age, would be entitled to the income directed to be accumulated. Under the testator's will the income of the whole fund is directed to be accumulated after some of those who may share in it have attained their majority. If the third period is, as I hold it is, the period the testator has selected, it is clear, in my judgment, that the section has been breached, for accumulation

---

182 15 & 16 Geo. 5, c. 20 (U.K.).
183 [1914] 1 Ch. 177.
184 *Jagger v. Jagger* (1883), 25 Ch. D. 729.

is not directed to be made during the minority of any child of Gerald living at the death of the testator. In terms the clause directs accumulation during the minority of any child of Gerald whenever born. Where the section has been breached the law is not that the direction is wholly void, but that there must be a curtailment of the period laid down by the testator to that one of the statutory periods which has to be applied. The answer to the first question asked by the amended originating summons is, in my judgement, that the direction to accumulate contained in clause 23 of the testator's will is valid and effectual so long as any child of Gerald living at the date of the testator's death is under the age of twenty-one years.

[The Court went on to hold that the class of beneficiaries remained open until the accumulation period ends, that is, when the last of Gerald's children, alive at the testator's death, attained the age of 21. Thus Kenneth was not yet entitled to call for his share, nor was he entitled to be paid the income from his expectant share.]

Notes and Questions

1. If money has been bequeathed to a minor, it cannot be paid until the minor attains the age of majority. Hence, subject to any prior interests and to any discretionary power of maintenance in the trustees or the court, the income must be accumulated, even though there is no direction to that effect.[185]

(iv) *Duration of Minorities of Persons Entitled to Income if of Full Age*

Under the sixth accumulation period it is possible to have successive accumulations, each accumulation ending when a beneficiary attains his or her majority. Moreover, it is not necessary that the beneficiaries be living at the testator's death. *Re Cattell; Cattell v. Cattell*,[186] reproduced below, explains the operation of this period.

RE CATTELL; CATTELL v. CATTELL
[1914] 1 Ch. 177
Court of Appeal

The testator, Thomas Cattell, devised his real property to his trustees for a thousand years upon trust to pay certain annuities to his wife and children, to pay £2,000 to each of his sons at age 25 and £5,000 for the children of each of his daughters who left children surviving her. The remainder, subject to certain powers of maintenance for infants, was given equally *per stirpes* to the children of his sons living at the testator's death or afterborn who, being sons should attain the age of 21 or, being daughters should attain that age or marry. Until the vesting

---

185 See, *e.g.*, *Re Delemere's Settlement Trusts; Kenny et al. v. Cunningham-Reid et al.*, [1984] 1 All E.R. 584 (C.A.).
186 [1914] 1 Ch. 177 (C.A.).

of the remainder interests, he directed that the surplus income (after payment of the annuities and portions) be accumulated and that the surplus of accumulations not applied to the remaindermen should fall into his residuary personal estate. The ultimate surplus income until the interests of the remaindermen vested was to be paid to any child or children (whether living at the testator's death or born afterwards) of any son or deceased son of the testator, and to the personal representatives of any deceased children (who if male attained age 21 and if female attained that age or married) of any son of the testator, but so that the income appropriated to a minor person should be accumulated during that person's minority and paid to that person when he or she attained the age of majority.

When the testator died in 1880, he was survived by his wife (who died in 1893), two sons, Thomas and Samuel (three others having predeceased him, unmarried) and several daughters. Thomas had one daughter who survived, namely Gladys, who was born in 1885.

Until Gladys' birth, the trustees had divided the income from the estate (after payment of the annuities and portions) between the two sons. In 1906 when Gladys turned 21, the trustees sought the advice of the court to determine whether they should now pay her the surplus income from the estate and whether the direction to accumulate during the minority of the sons' children was void because no child attained the age of 21 within 21 years of the testator's death. Neville J. held[187] that the direction to accumulate and the accumulations during Gladys' minority were valid. He further held that after she became 21, the trustees were to pay her the whole of the income until another child of a son should be born.

In 1912 Samuel's son, Frederick, was born and the trustees brought a further application to the court to determine the validity of the direction to accumulate. Swinfen Eady J. held, however, that the question had been properly answered by Neville J.

One of the testator's daughters, who had not been a party to the two earlier applications, appealed both orders with leave of the court. In the meantime, Samuel had had another child who was added as a party.

LORD PARKER OF WADDINGTON:

. . .

The difficulty arises in this case in regard to the fourth period. The first contemplates the case of a man who settles property otherwise than by will, in which case he may direct that the rents and profits be accumulated during his life. The settlor cannot direct an accumulation during his life and some further period. The second period contemplates an accumulation which is to commence from the death of the settlor, and includes the case of a settlor by will. No such accumulation is to go on for more than twenty-one years. Then the third alternative is a period - almost the same period of twenty-one years from the death of the settlor - during the minority or respective minorities of any person or persons "who shall be living or en ventre sa mère" at the time of the death of the settlor. That of course must

---

187 [1907] 1 Ch. 567.

be limited to twenty-one years, and some further period representing gestation in the case of a child yet unborn. Then there is the fourth alternative, which gives rise to the difficulty in the present case, and that is "or during the minority or respective minorities only of any person or persons who under the uses or trusts of the deed, surrender, will or other assurances directing such accumulations would for the time being, if of full age, be entitled unto the rents, issues and profits, or the interest, dividends or annual produce so directed to be accumulated." It is to be observed that this last alternative clause closely follows and seems to be contrasted with the alternative with regard to the minority or respective minorities of any person or persons who should be living or en ventre sa mère at the time of the death of the settlor. One would not therefore expect it to be limited (as contended by the appellant) to children living or en ventre sa mère at the settlor's death. Indeed if so limited it would in effect add nothing to the preceding alternative. The reason urged in support of the appellant's contention rests mainly on certain decisions which it is said we ought to follow and to which I will now refer.

[His Lordship referred to several cases and continued:]

In this state of the authorities I do not think we are bound to decide, with regard to the fourth alternative period, that it is limited to persons who are in existence or en ventre sa mère at the death of the testator, unless we are of opinion that his is the natural interpretation of the Act. In my opinion the fourth alternative period covers not only children who are born or en ventre sa mère at the death of the settlor, but children who are subsequently born, and I think the fact that the fourth alternative comes immediately after, and in contrast with, the third alternative, which refers only to born children, and children en ventre sa mère, at the time of the death of the settlor, points strongly to this conclusion.

Then we have a second argument advanced, that the children referred to are not children who would if of full age be entitled to the income directed to be accumulated, but are only those children who, if no accumulation had been directed, would be entitled to the income. Again I cannot see why we should not construe the words in their ordinary and natural meaning.

. . .

The question is would that child, if of full age, have been entitled to the income.

. . .

Then comes the last argument, which is an argument really on the presumed intention of the Act. It is said - and I think said with some truth - that in this case if we adopt the construction which allows a child who is not born at the death of the settlor to be one of the children during whose minority or respective minorities the accumulations are directed to be made, then we allow successive accumulations to be made of what practically, if not theoretically, is the same fund, which accumulations taken together may last for a considerable time. I think that may be true, but at the same time it is worth bearing in mind that though these periods may when added together amount to a considerable time, yet the periods in question are not really within the vice against which the Act is directed. Where a beneficiary is of full age a trust for accumulation operates to postpone his enjoyment, but in the case of an infant his inability to give a receipt would in any case postpone his enjoyment during his minority.... That is to say, the cases with which we are dealing not being within the vice of the Act, and there being nothing in the express words of the Act to prevent us giving effect to the old powers which were possessed by testators before the Act, there is no reason to construe the fourth alternative in any other way than I have suggested. It is well known that settlements are and have been drawn up on this footing. A testator may often direct a settlement of property upon A for life, and after his death upon his children on attaining twenty-one, and if he goes on to provide that during the minority or respective minorities of his children the income of the property shall be accumulated, it is only a clause in common form. I have never known any doubt to be thrown on the validity of such a clause, but if the appellant's contention prevailed its validity would be open to question. It seems to me, therefore, that Neville J. was right in his decision, and that this appeal ought to be dismissed.

[Lord Sumner and Warrington J. concurred]

(v) *Conclusion*

It is not always easy to determine which accumulation period the testator had in mind, as the foregoing cases show. Even if his or her intention can be determined, however, the period may not be appropriate on the facts. It is then up to the court to select the period that should be applied.

Further examples are found in the following problems.

Problems

1. Determine the appropriate accumulation period in the following situations.
   (a) A bequest to trustees, "to accumulate and reinvest the income therefrom during the life of X, and then to pay the capital and accumulated income to the eldest son of X living at his death."
   (b) A bequest, "to trustees to invest and accumulate the income until the first child of X attains the age of 21 and then to pay the capital and accumulated income to such child." X has no child at the date of the testator's death.

(d) Terminating the Accumulation

It sometimes happens that a testator directs an accumulation of the income from a fund for a certain period and then directs that the capital and accumulated income be paid to a person at an age beyond the age of majority. In that case the rule in *Saunders v. Vautier*[188] applies, which holds that if a person is *sui juris* and

---

188 (1841), 4 Beav. 115, 49 E.R. 282, affirmed (1841), 1 Cr. & Ph. 240, 41 E.R. 482.

solely interested in property which has been given him or her, the person can call for a conveyance or transfer of it when he or she reaches the age of majority.

Saunders v. Vautier, although often extended to other postponed gifts, was in fact a case involving an accumulation of the income of a specified fund and a direction to pay the accumulated income and the capital to a named beneficiary when he reached the age of 25. It was held that the beneficiary could call for the property and income at age 21.

The question whether the rule applies also arises in the context of a gift to charity. Thus, in *Wharton v. Masterman*[189] the testator made provision for certain annuities and directed that the surplus income be accumulated and that the capital and accumulated income be distributed among certain charities after the death of the last annuitant. Since the annuities were charged upon current income only, the charities were solely entitled to the surplus income and capital and it was, therefore, held that the rule applied, sufficient capital being set aside to pay the annuities.

If, however, the annuities are charged on the capital as well as the income, the rule does not apply.[190] *Re Burns*,[191] reproduced below, is an example of this situation.

RE BURNS
(1960), 32 W.W.R. 689, 25 D.L.R. (2d) 427
Supreme Court of Alberta
[Appellate Division]

Senator Patrick Burns, who died in 1937, gave the residue of his estate in trust to pay certain bequests and annuities and directed that his son's widow, Millicent, be paid a certain sum of money for life. The income was to be accumulated to pay the annuities until the death of the last annuitant and Millicent. Subject thereto, 60% of the income was to be paid to named beneficiaries; the other 40% was to be accumulated. On the death of the last annuitant or Millicent, 67% of the corpus was to be distributed to named beneficiaries while 33% was to be held in trust to pay the annual income to named charities.

Millicent gave up her interest under the will in return for a monthly payment for life. She survived all the annuitants and was still living in 1958 when the accumulation period expired (21 years after the testator's death).

On an earlier application, Egbert J., held[192] that the rule in *Saunders v. Vautier*[193] did not apply and that the capital could not, therefore be distributed until Millicent's death.

---

189 [1895] A.C. 186 (H.L.).
190 *Berry v. Geen*, [1938] A.C. 575 (H.L.); *Re Owens*, [1968] 1 O.R. 318, 66 D.L.R. (2d) 328 (H.C.).
191 (1960), 32 W.W.R. 689, 25 D.L.R. (2d) 427 (Alta. C.A.).
192 [1953] 1 D.L.R. 200.
193 (1841), 4 Beav. 115, 49 E.R. 282.

An application was then brought to determine what should happen to the 40% of the income which could no longer be accumulated. At first instance[194] it was held that the 40% of income released from accumulation went out on an intestacy.

An appeal was brought to the Appellate Division.

JOHNSON J.A.:

. . .

[His Lordship held that the *Thellusson Act*[195] applied in Alberta and continued:]

In the present case it is alleged that the persons who would take the income released by the *Accumulations Act* as next-of-kin are the same as the named beneficiaries of 67% of the trust estate, and that the rule in *Saunders v. Vautier*[196] would apply so as to prevent the operation of the *Accumulations Act*, as was the result in *Wharton v. Masterman.*[197]

In considering this argument, it is necessary to state the facts in the *Wharton* case. The testator, after giving certain legacies, bequeathed the residue of his personal estate to trustees upon trust to pay certain annuities. With a proviso (which is quite important) that if the annual income of the trust should not be sufficient for the payment of the annuities then the annuities would rateably abate. Any balance of income was to be accumulated until the death of the last annuitant when the trust, including the accumulation, was, after it had been reduced to cash, divided among certain named charities. The Court, applying the rule in *Saunders v. Vautier*, held that the direction to accumulate was ineffective and the *Accumulations Act* did not apply. It is interesting to note that in the subsequent action (reported sub nom. *Harbin v. Masterman*)[198] the Court set aside a sufficient sum to answer the annuities and paid out the balance of the accumulated income to the charities.

The appellants (the charities in the present case) ask us to hold that *Wharton v. Masterman* must be applied to this case. It is at least doubtful if this argument is open to the appellants. Egbert, J., in the judgment I have mentioned held that *Saunders v. Vautier* had no application to this will. That was, I think, a necessary part of the reasoning upon which his judgment is based and that decision has not been appealed. In *Wharton v. Masterman*, the court was applying *Saunders v. Vautier* to the facts of that case, and to permit the application of *Saunders v. Vautier* now would be to admit by the back door what has been rejected at the front.

However, if it is open to the appellants to rely upon *Wharton v. Masterman*, I am satisfied that the case does not apply to this will. I have pointed out that in that case the annuities were to be rateably abated if the annual income was not

194 15 D.L.R. (2d) 707.
195 39 & 40 Geo. 3, c. 98 (1800).
196 *Supra.*
197 *Supra.*
198 [1896] 1 Ch. 351.

sufficient to pay them. Neither the prior accumulation nor subsequent income were available to make good deficient annuities in any year. Prior accumulations as well as each subsequent year's surplus income therefore became free of any charge and because the income and capital went to the same persons, *Saunders v. Vautier* applied.

This, I think, was the opinion of the House of Lords when they were considering the subsequent case of *Berry v. Geen*.[199]

. . .

And in *Re Travis*[200] Lord Alverstone, M.R., said:

> But I think the real answer is that in *Wharton v. Masterman* the annuitants had no interest in the surplus income, and therefore there was no direction to accumulate except for the benefit of the persons who were to become ultimately entitled, and the principle of *Saunders v. Vautier* applied. The annuitants having no interest in the surplus income, the person entitled in remainder became entitled to it, and were, independently of the Thellusson Act, entitled to have the accumulations stopped and the property handed over to them.

. . .

In the present will there is no provision for abatement of annuities and, while there is also no provision that deficiency of income to satisfy the annuities each year are to be made good out of the accumulated or future income, such a provision is unnecessary. Romer, L.J., in *Re Coller's Deed Trusts*[201] said:

> But now take the case of a trust to pay an annuity out of the income of a trust fund without any subsequent indication being given that the annuity is in any case to be paid in full, and without any express words confining the annuity for any one year to the income of the year. Under such a trust the annuity is prima facie a continuing charge upon the income of the fund, and the annuitant, or his legal personal representatives after his death, will be entitled to have the income impounded until all arrears of the annuity are paid.

It is true that all the "annuitants" mentioned in the will are now dead. There is, however, Millicent Burns to be considered. The learned Chamber Judge, on a consideration of the language of the will, has held that the testator did not consider her to be an annuitant. At the testator's death she had, however, relinquished any rights she had under the will for $350 per month, which sum was later increased to $500 per month. These payments were charged against the income of the residue and could not be abated if the income were insufficient. Whether she is considered as an annuitant or not, she had a claim against the annual income and also a claim against accumulated and further income. It is quite immaterial that the income may be very much more than sufficient to satisfy her claim. (That was the case in *Berry v. Geen*).[202] She has therefore an interest in the income directed to be accumulated and *Wharton v. Masterman* does not apply. Even if the testator

---

199 [1938] A.C. 575.
200 [1900] 2 Ch. 541 at 548.
201 [1939] 1 Ch. 277 at 281.
202 *Supra*.

had set aside sufficient securities to satisfy Mrs. Burns' annual payments, her rights to call upon all the income of the estate to make good these payments would still subsist.

. . .

Having concluded that neither *Saunders v. Vautier* nor *Wharton v. Masterman* apply, it follows that because of the provisions of the *Accumulations Act* which have been quoted, the accumulation of income must cease as of February 24, 1958, and the released income, because there is no provision in the will to catch these released funds, goes as on intestacy, at least as to that portion which goes ultimately to the persons named in cl. 35.

> [His Lordship went on to hold that the 13.2% (that is, 33% of the 40%) of the income that would eventually have gone to the charities should be distributed annually *cy-près* there being a general charitable intent as to this part of the residue. Ford C.J.A., delivered a short concurring judgement. MacDonald J.A. concurred with Johnson J.A. Porter J.A. would have concurred but thought that the English Act was not in force in Alberta.]

Notes and Questions

1. The rule in *Saunders v. Vautier*[203] has been abolished in Alberta and Manitoba and replaced with a discretion in the court to terminate or vary a trust.[204]

2. The rule in *Saunders v. Vautier* also applies if the accumulation is directed for the benefit of a class of persons when they reach the age of majority, but is to last until the youngest member of the class reaches that age. Those members of the class who reach the age of majority can stop the accumulation of their presumptive share.[205]

3. A testator gave a sum of money in trust to pay an annuity to A for life and to accumulate the surplus income. After A's death the capital and accumulated income went to A's children at age 21. The annuity was charged on current income only. A was a woman 60 years of age and all her children were over 21. Can the children stop the accumulation?[206]

(e) Destination of Excess Income during Accumulation Period

If the testator directs the payment of limited income, such as an annuity, but fails to dispose of the surplus income, the question arises what should happen to the excess income during the accumulation period. This point is discussed in *Re Ellis; Canada Permanent Trust Co. v. Ellis*,[207] reproduced below.

---

203 (1841), 4 Beav. 115, 49 E.R. 282, affirmed (1841), 1 Cr. & Ph. 240, 41 E.R. 482.
204 This is discussed in the previous chapter.
205 *Hilton v. Hilton* (1872), L.R. 14 Eq. 468.
206 *Re Deloitte; Griffiths v. Deloitte*, [1926] Ch. 56.
207 [1982] 6 W.W.R. 353, 18 Sask. R. 342, 12 E.T.R. 205 (Q.B.).

RE ELLIS; CANADA PERMANENT TRUST CO. v. ELLIS
[1982] 6 W.W.R. 353, 12 E.T.R. 205, 18 Sask. R. 342
Saskatchewan Court of Queen's Bench

The testator made provision of $350 per month for his wife and directed that "the necessary funds" be provided to care for his retarded son, Lyle. He further directed that after Lyle's death any balance left over from the moneys set aside for his care should be paid as to one-half to "the mentally retarded fund" and as to the other half equally to his children, Murray and Marion. The latter two were also the residuary beneficiaries. Under a subsequent separation agreement the testator agreed to pay his wife $300 per month until her death or remarriage. The testator died in 1974.

After making certain applications to construe the will, the executors set up three funds, one to pay the income to the testator's widow under the separation agreement, the other to pay her the income under the will, and the third to provide maintenance for Lyle. In another application it was held that the will did not create an intestacy and that the "mentally retarded fund" was the Saskatchewan Association for the Mentally Retarded. In a subsequent appeal from a succession duty assessment it was held that the gift over on Lyle's death did not vest until his death.

This application was then brought to determine whether the surplus income in the three funds should be accumulated or whether it passed to the residuary beneficiaries.

GEREIN J.:

. . .

A reading of the will clearly indicates an intention on the part of the testator to provide for his widow, Margaret Ellis, and his son, Lyle Ellis, during their respective lifetimes. The testator obviously felt a primary responsibility to these persons and only a secondary responsibility to the residuary beneficiaries. This is understandable when one keeps in mind that Margaret Ellis was the spouse of the testator and Lyle Ellis is severely retarded and unable to provide for himself. It was only after these responsibilities had been met that the other two children were to benefit.

That the testator knew the difference between estate capital and estate income is evident from his specific direction that Margaret Ellis was to receive "(c) the balance as necessary from the income of my estate". Yet immediately thereafter in his will the testator does not make a similar distinction as to Lyle Ellis. It is my opinion that this was by design. The testator intended that a fund be set up for Lyle Ellis. In my view the testator intended that once his widow was provided for everything else, both capital and income, was to go into a fund to be used for Lyle "being taken care of". This being so, there was no reason to differentiate between capital and income. The executor was to have an absolute discretion as to the creation and management of the Lyle Ellis fund and there was no need to give any further directions particularly when the testator had no way of knowing the future needs of Lyle Ellis. This is unlike the situation of the widow. The testator had knowledge of the means and needs of the widow and could intelligently and reasonably forecast her future needs. The same could not be said in regard to Lyle Ellis, especially if it became necessary to place him in an institution.

I further note that the testator created two different sets of remaindermen. In the case of the Margaret Ellis will fund, they are Murray Ellis and Margaret Stotski. In the case of the Lyle Ellis fund, they are those two individuals plus the Saskatchewan Association for the Mentally Retarded. From this I conclude that the testator wanted to benefit the Saskatchewan Association for the Mentally Retarded, but only if all of the money was not required for Lyle Ellis. Thus, if I were to conclude that the income of the Lyle Ellis fund did not attach thereto I might effectively be defeating one of the indicated intentions of the testator. If I were to decide that the income, or the surplus income, of the Lyle Ellis fund was to immediately pass to the beneficiaries Murray Ellis and Marion Stotski, I would be bringing about the possible result that in the future, as a result of increased costs, there might not be sufficient funds to care for Lyle Ellis and there would be no benefit to accrue to the Saskatchewan Association for the Mentally Retarded. To do this would be to defeat the wishes of the testator.

From a reading of the will I conclude that it was the intention of the testator that all intermediate income, whether surplus or otherwise, would accrue to the respective funds. However, I come to this conclusion not only on the basis of the words contained in the will, but with the assistance of the canon of construction set out in *Wharton v. Masterman*,[208] wherein Lord Davey stated:

> When there is no express trust declared of the income of a trust fund, it follows the destination of, and is an accretion to, the fund from which it is derived (unless there be words excluding that implication).

This statement has been adopted in many cases including *Re Hammond*[209] and *Re Stevenson*.[210]

In my opinion the residuary beneficiaries to the Margaret Ellis will fund have a future vested interest. As stated earlier [because of the prior decision on this point], I decline to come to the same conclusion as to the Lyle Ellis fund. However, in my opinion the result is the same.

> [His Lordship noted that the English rule is vested gifts do not carry intermediate income, while contingent gifts do, whereas in Canada both gifts carry intermediate income, citing *Re Hammond*[211] and *Watson v. Conant*.[212] He continued:]

---

208 [1895] A.C. 186 at 198 (C.A.).
209 [1935] S.C.R. 550, [1935] 4 D.L.R. 209.
210 (1976), 12 O.R. (2d) 614, 69 D.L.R. (3d) 630 (H.C.).
211 *Supra*.
212 [1964] S.C.R. 312, 44 D.L.R. (2d) 396.

In the case of *Re Baragar*,[213] Lacourcière J. extensively reviewed the authorities and then formulated what I would call certain rules or guides. They are as follows:[214]

In my opinion, the following points can be drawn from the foregoing cases:

I. A direction to invest and accumulate surplus income generally indicates an intention to capitalize the income accumulated and convert it into capital in so far as a residuary trust fund is concerned: *Re Oliver, Watkins v. Fitton et al.*[215]

II. In those situations where the testator's will has dealt with the residue of his estate and has been construed as disposing of all his estate, the surplus income has been held to accrue to the capital fund of the residuary beneficiary's share for a period of 21 years from the death of the testator: *Re Hammond*[216] and *Re Watson*.[217] The Court will attempt to reach this result, especially where the testator's will indicates that the annuitant is to receive no more than the amount of his annuity from the estate, *i.e.*, the Court is reluctant to find an intestacy which would give the annuitant an interest that he was not intended to have.

(a) The Court will generally find in accord with the above intention an implied direction to accumulate the surplus income: *Re Hammond* and *Re Watson*.

(b) The provisions of the *Accumulations Act*, permit only an accumulation of surplus income for a period of 21 years after the testator's death at which time any further surplus income is distributed as on an intestacy to the testator's next of kin determined as of the date of the testator's death: *Re Hammond*; *Re Watson*; *Re Major*;[218] and *Re Owens*.[219]

III. In those situations where the testator's will has not been construed as disposing of all his estate, the surplus income has been distributed as on an intestacy to the testator's next of kin determined as of the date of the testator's death: *Re Amodeo*.[220]

IV. Residuary bequests have been categorized as contingent interests, vested indefeasible interests, vested defeasible interests and substitutionary interests. There appears to be an English rule that only contingent interests carry the intermediate income: *Re Oliver*;[221] *Re Gillett's Will Trusts*.[222] However, the results of the *Re Hammond* and *Re Watson* cases indicate that vested defeasible interests can carry intermediate income in Canadian jurisprudence, although certain comments in the *Re Amodeo* case which were not essential to the decision tended to support the English position. In any event the classification of the residuary interest is not of crucial significance.

In my opinion the case at Bar falls within the ambit of *Re Hammond, Watson v. Conant* and rule II above....

---

213 [1973] 1 O.R. 831, 32 D.L.R. (3d) 529 (H.C.).
214 *Ibid.,* at O.R. 844-5.
215 [1947] 2 All E.R. 162.
216 *Supra.*
217 *Supra.*
218 [1970] 2 O.R. 121, 10 D.L.R. (3d) 107 (H.C.).
219 [1968] 1 O.R. 318, 66 D.L.R. 328 (H.C.).
220 [1962] O.R. 548, 33 D.L.R. (2d) 24 (H.C.).
221 *Supra.*
222 [1949] 2 All E.R. 893.

A different situation exists as to the Margaret Ellis agreement fund. At the time the testator executed his will, the separation agreement did not exist and the testator obviously did not direct his mind to it. However, a reading of the agreement leads me to the conclusion that the provision for payment of $300 a month as contained therein constitutes a charge against the estate. Accordingly, the executor was correct in creating a fund to provide for payment of this liability. In my opinion, the establishing of this fund created a subsidiary trust. As well, the obligation is in the nature of an annuity. See *Re Cooper*[223] and *Re Wilson's Will*.[224] In Law of Trusts in Canada,[225] by D.W.M. Waters, the author states:

> If a small annuity is charged on a sizeable annual income, there is only the remotest chance that the income in any year will not be sufficient to meet the annuity, but the principle of law is that, unless the testator expresses a contrary intent, annuitants have an interest in past and future surplus income to make up any deficiencies of annuity payment that may occur in a bad year....

A similar statement is to be found in Williams on Executors and Administrators.[226] Thus, the income on this fund must accrue to it until the death of Margaret Ellis. In summary, my conclusion is that the income which is earned by each of the three funds accrues to the respective funds.

. . .

Notes and Questions

1. For a similar case see *Re Miles*.[227]

2. A testator directed that his estate should be converted and $100 per month be paid to his son from the income, or the capital if the income was insufficient, until the son's death or until the estate was depleted. On the death of the son the residue was divided equally between certain charities. The income was more than sufficient to pay the money to the son. What result?[228]

(f) Exceeding the Accumulation Period

If a direction to accumulate exceeds the permissible period, it must first be determined whether the direction exceeds the perpetuity period. Under the common law rule against perpetuities, the gift of the accumulated income and the direction to accumulate would both be void if the direction to accumulate was for a period which might exceed the period of the rule.

Under the Ontario *Perpetuities Act*, one can now wait and see and in the meantime income can be accumulated for the appropriate period of the *Accu-*

---

223 (1917), 88 L.J. Ch. 105.
224 11 W.W.R. (N.S.) 497, 62 Man. R. 81, [1954] 3 D.L.R. 161 (C.A.).
225 (1974), at 825.
226 13th ed., at p. 758.
227 (1981), 9 E.T.R. 113 (Ont. H.C.).
228 See *Re Miller; Can. Trust Co. v. St. Peter's Lutheran Church* (1981), 9 E.T.R. 37 (Ont. H.C.).

mulations Act. If the interest vests within the perpetuity period, the gift and the accumulation will be valid; if not, they are void.

If the direction does not violate the rule against perpetuities, but does exceed a permissible accumulation period, the accumulation is void only to the extent that it exceeds the period.

A question much litigated is who becomes entitled to the income released after the accumulation ends. This question is dealt with in *Re Struthers*,[229] reproduced below.

RE STRUTHERS
(1980), 29 O.R. (2d) 616, 7 E.T.R. 307, 114 D.L.R. (3d) 492
Supreme Court of Ontario
[Court of Appeal]

The testator directed that the income from the residue of his estate plus $4,000 a year from the capital be paid to his wife for life. Clause 3D, para. 4 of the will provided that on his wife's death the trustees had to set aside the sum of $75,000 and pay $5,000 per year or until the fund was exhausted to the testator's step-daughter, Geraldine. At Geraldine's death, the balance of the fund was to be divided among Geraldine's children, to be paid to them at age 21 and meanwhile the income of the share of each child was to be used for his or her benefit. The share of any child who died under age 21 accrued to the surviving children.

Clause 3D, para. 5 directed the trustees to divide the proceeds of the estate, after providing for the benefits theretofore conferred by the will, among the testator's grand-nieces who were living at his wife's death. If anyone had died in the meantime, her share passed to her children at age 21, together with accrued interest.

In clause 3D, para. 6, the testator directed that after Geraldine's death, whatever remained of the estate that had not been disposed of should be divided among his grand-nieces in the same manner.

The testator died in 1950, survived by his wife, his step-daughter Geraldine Rice and Geraldine's daughter, Kathleen, and his niece Marjorie and her three children, Betty, Patricia and Barbara. Geraldine had a second daughter, Patricia, in 1953. The testator's wife died in 1974.

On an application to construe the will it was held at first instance by R.E. Holland J., that the entire income from the $75,000.00 fund went to the grand-nieces and that, therefore, the *Accumulations Act* did not apply.

Geraldine and her two daughters appealed.

WILSON J.A., delivered the judgment of the Court:

. . .

In my view, the testator gave his stepdaughter a $5,000 annuity payable out of the fund without specifying whether it was to be a charge on income or capital or

---

229 (1980), 29 O.R. (2d) 616, 7 E.T.R. 307, 114 D.L.R. (3d) 492 (C.A.).

both. It is, however, common ground among counsel that at the time the testator made his will a $75,000 fund would not produce $5,000 a year. Counsel for the appellants submits that this is why the testator contemplated that the whole fund might be exhausted in paying the annuity. The corpus, he says, would have to be resorted to in order to make up any deficiency in the income. Counsel for the respondents has a different explanation. He argues that the testator contemplated that the fund would be consumed in payment of the annuity because he intended it to be paid wholly out of capital. Indeed, counsel for the respondents says that to characterize the $5,000 annual payment as an annuity is to prejudge the issue. He places great weight on the fact that the word "annuity" was not used by the testator. In my view, no significance attaches to the testator's failure to use the word. An annuity is simply a stream of payments, a fixed annual sum, and that seems to be what we have here. If the testator gives such a fixed annual sum but does not designate the source from which it is payable, then the law steps in to fill the vacuum.

I think this is a case to which the so-called "general rule" applies. Where there is a bequest of an annuity in general terms without its being specified whether the annuity is payable out of income or capital, then it is *primarily* payable out of income and *secondarily*, to the extent of any deficiency in income, out of capital.

. . .

I can find nothing in para. (4) of cl. 3(D) of Mr. Struthers' will to displace the general rule. I do not think the reference to the division of the "principal sum" into shares on the death of the annuitant evidences an intention on the part of the testator that the annuities were to be paid wholly out of capital. The testator might just as easily have directed the division of the corpus of the trust fund or, for that matter, of the trust fund simpliciter on the death of the annuitant. It would, in my opinion, take very clear and unambiguous language to make an annuity payable wholly out of capital, particularly where there is an investment power in the will and no disposition of the income of the fund on which the annuity is charged. The only issue therefore is with respect to surplus income, i.e., income earned on the fund in any year in excess of $5,000. I think the learned Judge erred in dealing with the destination of the entire income of the $75,000 fund in the answer to Q.4.

It is common ground among counsel that The Accumulations Act,[230] if it applies, would prevent any accumulation of income in the $75,000 fund since more than 21 years elapsed from the date of death of the testator until the life tenant died and the direction to set up the $75,000 fund was implemented....

I am of the view that, if para. (4) of cl. 3(D) of the will contains an invalid direction for the accumulation of surplus income, the surplus income earned on the fund since it was created cannot pass to the next-of-kin as upon an intestacy. It is the income of a specific fund and not the income of the residue itself. Surplus income of a specific fund falls into residue; surplus income of the residue passes

---

230 R.S.O. 1970, c. 5.

as upon an intestacy: see *Re Herman*;[231] *Re Major*.[232] I cannot accept Mr. Austin's submission that the $75,000 fund is part of the residue for purposes of the application of this principle. It is clear from a reading of cl. 3 of his will that the testator, in effect, created several "residues" of his estate. One "residue" was created in cl. 3(D) after the first group of pecuniary legacies were directed to be paid in cl. 3(C). His wife was given a life estate in that "residue". Another "residue" was created in cl. 3(D)(5) on the death of his wife after the payment of further legacies and the creation of the $75,000 fund. And finally on the death of his stepdaughter, Geraldine, "whatever remains of my estate" was disposed of in cl. 3(D)(6). Accordingly, while the $75,000 fund was directed to be set aside out of the "residue" in which the testator's wife had a life interest, and in that sense therefore it was part of *a* residue, it was not part of *the* residue, the "true" or "ultimate" residue of the testator's estate disposed of in paras. (5) and (6) of cl. 3(D) of the will. Accordingly, if an invalid accumulation of surplus income is directed in para. (4), the surplus income, in my view, falls to be distributed to the grandnieces under para. (5) or (6) of cl. 3(D) of the will.

But does the Act apply?

[Her Ladyship quoted the relevant portions of the Act and continued:]

It seems to me that, when one reads the will as a whole, it becomes quite clear that Mr. Struthers decided to provide for his stepdaughter Geraldine and her children to the extent of the $75,000 fund which he directed to be carved out of his estate for this purpose after the death of the life tenant. His stepdaughter's interest in the fund was to be restricted to $5,000 a year. The balance of the fund was to go to her children. Having provided in this way for that branch of his family, he then turned his mind to his grandnieces and made them the beneficiaries of the residue of his estate. I cannot persuade myself that the testator's intention was to make his stepdaughter and her children the beneficiaries of the capital only of the fund with the income being diverted over to his grandnieces. I think that had that proposition been put to him, he would have said, "No, no, my whole object is to set apart this fund for this group and the residue for the other group. My stepdaughter's children may not get very much because the fund may be completely eaten up by her annuity. But if there is anything left over, I want her children to have it." I think the testator thought of the possibility that his stepdaughter might die without leaving any children: she only had one at the time he made the will. So he provided for this eventuality in para. (6) of cl. 3(D). I think Mr. Hull is mistaken when he says that para. (6) must have been intended to pick up the income of the $75,000 fund because there is nothing else for it to "bite" on. Paragraph (6) opens with the words "after the death of my said stepdaughter..." and in my view is clearly designed to cover the contingency of his stepdaughter's dying without leaving children.

---

231 [1961] O.R. 25, 25 D.L.R. (2d) 93 (C.A.).
232 [1970] 2 O.R. 121, 10 D.L.R. (3d) 107.

Assuming I am right in what Mr. Struthers intended to accomplish to what extent is his intention frustrated by the law?

It appears to be well-settled that The Accumulations Act applies to *implied* directions and powers to accumulate as well as to *express* directions and powers.

[Her Ladyship referred to a number of cases on this point and continued:]

The fundamental question then is whether "the natural and necessary operation" of para. (4) of cl. 3(D) of Mr. Struthers' will is to produce an invalid accumulation. If it is, then the Act will apply. It seems to me that the paragraph does necessarily produce this result, given the fact that the testator's wife survived him by more than 21 years and that the fund, when created, produced more income than was required to pay the $5,000 annuity. If the fund had been created prior to the expiration of the 21-year period and earned surplus income, the surplus income would have formed an accretion to the fund itself since the remainder interests of the stepdaughter's children are contingent upon their being alive at the date of her death. Contingent remainder interests carry intermediate income earned during the period of lawful accumulation: *Bective v. Hodgson*;[233] *Re Taylor*;[234] *Re Gillett*.[235] Once, however, The Accumulations Act operates to put an end to the accumulation, the surplus income can no longer form an accretion to the fund but must, as directed in s. 1(6) of the Act, "go to and be received by such person as would have been entitled thereto if such accumulation had not been so directed."

. . .

I believe it is clear from the foregoing authorities that income cannot be accumulated in the $75,000 fund for the benefit of the stepdaughter's children because the period of lawful accumulation had already expired by the time the fund was created. The stepdaughter's children therefore have no interest in the surplus income.

Mr. Austin argued very strongly that the surplus income of the $75,000 fund should go to the testator's next-of-kin....

The difficulty I have with this submission is that it fails to distinguish *rules of law* from *rules of construction*. Rules of construction are designed to ascertain the intention of the testator when it does not emerge clearly from the language he has used. But rules of law apply whether the result will be consistent with his intention or not. It is a rule of law that the surplus income of a specific fund invalidly directed to be accumulated falls into residue. The testator does not intend that. Indeed, as Mr. Austin points out, this particular testator did not contemplate the existence of surplus income at all. I agree with Mr. Austin that the "residue" the testator intended to dispose of in para. (5) was the residue after the $75,000 fund had been set up. The intention which I think is relevant and which I have already mentioned is the testator's intention that the entire fund go to his step-

---

233 (1864) 10 H.L. Cas. 656, 11 E.R. 1181.
234 [1901] 2 Ch. 134.
235 [1950] 1 Ch. 102, [1949] 2 All E.R. 893.

daughter and her children. This is the intention which must be ascertained in the first instance, i.e., the intention of the testator without regard to the impact of any rule of law which may serve to defeat it....The testator's intention that his step-daughter and her children have the entire fund cannot be given effect to. The Accumulations Act has intervened. It is, in my view, inappropriate at that point to seek a fresh intention with respect to the destination of the surplus income released by operation of the Act. It is one thing to attribute to the testator, as Mr. Justice R.E. Holland did, in my respectful view mistakenly, an original intention to give the entire income of the $75,000 fund to the grandnieces under para. (5) as part of the residue: it is another thing entirely to attribute to him an intention as to the destination of surplus income released by operation of the Act, a circum-stance which he certainly did not envisage.

I appreciate that in some of the authorities dealing with the destination of surplus income the Courts appear to have engrafted a limitation on the rule of law based on the application of a rule of construction. They have said, in other words, that the surplus income of a specific fund falls into residue *unless a contrary intention appears in the will*. But these cases have to be carefully examined to see what they are dealing with. For example, the surplus income in *Re Wragg*,[236] *Re Amodeo*[237] and *Re Geering*,[238] was income earned during the lifetime of the annuitants in excess of the amount required to pay their annuities. There was no invalid direction, express or implied, to accumulate the surplus income. The question before the Courts was: the testator having omitted to deal with the surplus income, did he intend it to fall under the residuary clause or did he simply die intestate with respect to it? The language of the residuary clause had to be examined in order to find the answer. It was, in other words, essentially a question of construction. The presumption against an intestacy is frequently adverted to in such cases in aid of a liberal construction of the residuary clause.

The cases also have to be examined to determine whether the surplus income in issue is that of a specific fund or of residue or a share of the residue. As already pointed out, different principles apply depending on the answer to that question. *Re Hammond*,[239] *Re Amodeo*[240] and *Re Baragar*,[241] relied on by Mr. Austin for the next-of-kin, all involved surplus income of residue. And finally, they have to be examined to see whether the interest of the claimants can carry surplus income: are they contingent interests which at common law were held to carry intermediate income not otherwise specifically disposed of or are they vested interests, either vested absolutely and postponed only as to possession or vested subject to sub-sequent divestment, neither of which were capable at common law of carrying intermediate income: see *Re Gillett*....[242]

---

236 [1959] 2 All E.R. 717 (C.A.).
237 [1962] O.R. 548, 33 D.L.R. (2d) 24 (C.A.).
238 [1964] Ch. 136, [1962] 3 All E.R. 1043.
239 [1935] S.C.R. 550, [1935] 4 D.L.R. 209.
240 *Supra.*
241 [1973] 1 O.R. 831, 32 D.L.R. (3d) 529.
242 *Supra.*

I would respectfully adopt the reasoning of Chief Justice Porter in *Re Herman*.[243] In the will before him the testator had expressly excepted from the residuary gift the stock which yielded the surplus income released by operation of The Accumulations Act. The Chief Justice held that the surplus income fell into residue regardless.

> [Her Ladyship quoted from the judgment of the Chief Justice, including the following quotation from *Theobald on Wills*:[244]
>
>> If there is a residuary gift, and certain property is excepted from it which is disposed of by a later or earlier part of the will, or by a later will, the presumption is that the exception was made for the purposes of the particular disposition, and if that disposition fails the excepted property passes by the residuary gift.
>
> She continued:]

The judgment of this Court in *Re Baragar*[245] was strongly urged upon us by Mr. Austin as authority for the proposition that where a testator has not applied his mind to the possibility of surplus income, it should be held to devolve as upon an intestacy. *Re Baragar* did involve surplus income released by operation of *The Accumulations Act*. However, it is clearly distinguishable from the instant case in that the surplus income was the surplus income of shares of residue and not of a specific fund....

In my view, para. (4) of the testator's will contains an implied direction to accumulate the surplus income not required for the payment of the stepdaughter's annuity. The Accumulations Act applies to prevent that accumulation and the surplus income released by operation of the Act, being the income of a specific fund, falls into residue and passes to the testator's grandnieces under para. (5) of cl. 3(D) as and when earned during the lifetime of the stepdaughter. I tend to the view for the reasons already given that at this point it is not appropriate to seek the intention of the testator as to the destination of the surplus income but, if it is appropriate to make such an enquiry, I find no contrary intention which would prevent the surplus income from passing under para. (5). I would adopt the reasoning of Chief Justice Porter in *Re Herman*[246] and particularly the governing principle quoted by him from *Theobald on Wills*.[247] The testator in this case excepted the $75,000 fund from the gift of residue in para. (5) for purposes of disposing of it in para. (4). Part of that disposition having failed by operation of *The Accumulations Act*, the released income falls back into the residue.

I would allow the appeal.

. . .

---

243 [1961] O.R. 25, 25 D.L.R. (2d) 93 (C.A.).
244 11th ed., p. 220.
245 *Supra.*
246 *Supra.*
247 *Supra.*

Notes and Questions

1. A testator who died in 1957 established certain annuities for his widow, his daughter and his granddaughter and directed that after their deaths the residue should be divided equally among his great-grandchildren then living. The testator was survived by his widow, his daughter, his granddaughter and two great-granddaughters. The widow died in 1973. There was substantial surplus income after payment of the annuities. What result?[248]

2. A testator directed that $100 per month, or such greater sum as his executors saw fit, should be paid out of the income from his estate to his wife for life, with remainder equally to his children. The testator died in 1949. Although the income was insufficient for a time, there has been excess income since 1971, which has been accumulated. Who is entitled to the surplus income?[249]

3. *Adamson Estate v. McIntyre*[250] concerned a will in which the testatrix directed that the residue of her estate be set aside for the life of her sister and $150 per month be paid to her for life, out of income or capital. The trustees were given a discretion to encroach on the capital for the benefit of the sister. On the sister's death the residue was to divided among certain charities if they existed at the death of the sister. The testatrix died in 1973. At that time it was valued at $160,000. In 1997 it was worth $300,000, even though substantial encroachments had been made on the capital for the benefit of the sister over the years. On a previous application, the court directed that any excess income be capital-ized and added to the residue each year. The executors brought an application to determine who was entitled to the excess income not needed by the sister, who was over 90 years old and still going strong, since accumulation had to cease 21 years after the testatrix's death. The excess income was claimed by the charities and the next of kin. The court awarded it to the next of kin. Why was it not given to the charities?

---

248 See *Re Martin; Proctor v. Downey* (1979), 4 E.T.R. 264 (C.A.).
249 See *Re Hume,* [1983] 4 W.W.R. 728 (Sask. Surr. Ct.).
250 (1997), 16 E.T.R. (2d) 189 (Ont. Gen. Div.).

PART V

FAMILY PROTECTION

16

SPOUSAL RIGHTS

1. Scope
2. Matrimonial Property
3. The Family Law Act of Ontario
4. Legislation in Other Provinces
5. Other Rights

1. SCOPE

The traditional approach of the common law has been that a person has the right to dispose of his or her property at will. In fact, this "right" has never been an absolute. It was very much circumscribed early in the common law[1] and was regulated in other ways later. Thus, for example, the rule against perpetuities ensured that a person could not control his or her property beyond the grave for too long a period of time; it continues to do so. Further, the law of dower attempted to ensure that the testator's widow would be left some property.[2] Nonetheless, the right freely to dispose of one's property could and did work hardship upon those persons for whom, in the normal course of events, the testator ought to make provision, *viz.*, his or her dependants. For this reason, the Legislatures have enacted legislation designed to provide this kind of protection. One type of statute is dependants' support legislation which we shall discuss in the next chapter. Under it, a dependant for whom the testator has failed to make adequate provision can make application to the court for an order for support out of the estate. Another type is the modern matrimonial property legislation, which enables a surviving spouse in some provinces to make a claim against the deceased spouse's estate for a share of the matrimonial property. This type of legislation is the main focus of this chapter. We shall also briefly consider homestead legislation, which is in force in the western provinces.

2. MATRIMONIAL PROPERTY

Statutes reforming the law of matrimonial property were enacted in all of the Canadian common law jurisdictions in the 1970s and 1980s. These became nec-

---

1 See chapter 1.
2 Dower was the widow's right at common law to a life interest in possession in one-third of all the real property of which her husband died solely seised. By statute she also became entitled to a similar interest in all the real property to which her husband was beneficially entitled at his death. The widower had a similar, but not identical right, *viz.*, curtesy. It was a right to a life estate in all his wife's real property that she had not disposed of *inter vivos* or by will.

essary because the traditional ways in which property disputes between husband and wife were resolved under married women's property legislation,[3] at law and in equity[4] no longer worked well. Often, on a marriage breakdown, the spouse who did not have title received few or none of the assets acquired during the marriage. Further, there was a perception that husband and wife should be treated equally, so that the old rights of dower and curtesy, which applied to them unequally, should be abolished.

The statutes address primarily the division of assets on marital breakdown, but some permit application to be made on death as well. The importance of the latter kind of statute to estate planning and succession can be significant. The Ontario legislation, the *Family Law Act*,[5] and the Northwest Territories' legislation, the *Family Law Act, 1997*[6] are the most far-reaching. The relevant sections of Part I of the Ontario legislation are set out below.[7] Part I does not, in fact, permit a division of assets, but allows for an equalizing payment on breakdown of marriage and death. The effect of the legislation is explored in the text and the notes and questions following the statutory materials. The other statutes are listed and commented on briefly in part 4.

The several statutes are not identical, but, in substance, they all provide for deferred sharing of property, or for an equalization claim, upon marriage breakdown or, as noted, on death in some jurisdictions. The property to which they apply, however, differs from statute to statute. Some of the statutes apply only to those assets that are used for family purposes, while some apply to all assets owned by either spouse, save for stated exemptions. Further, all statutes confer upon both spouses equal rights of possession of the matrimonial home during marriage. Finally, the statutes, or related statutes, provide for support of spouses, cohabitees and other dependants and for domestic contracts whereby spouses and cohabitees may regulate their property and other rights.

Two points arise from this: (1) the right to share in matrimonial assets has so far been extended only to persons who are married to each other; and (2) same-sex partners were, until recently, not entitled to support under the statutes. The latter changed in Ontario because of *M. v. H.*[8] in which the Supreme Court of Canada upheld the right of a same-sex partner to support under the *Family Law Act* and held that the support provisions of that statute offended the equality provisions of the *Canadian Charter of Rights and Freedoms*. In consequence, Ontario amended[9] a large number of statutes to extend various rights to same-sex partners, including the *Family Law Act*, which now extends the right to support

---

3 Such as the *Married Women's Property Act*, R.S.O. 1970, c. 262.

4 By means of resulting and constructive trusts.

5 R.S.O. 1990, c. F.3 (enacted in 1986), hereafter referred to without further citation.

6 S.N.W.T. 1997, c. 18, Part III.

7 Part I is concerned with the division of family property.

8 (1999), 171 D.L.R. (4th) 577 (S.C.C.).

9 By *Amendments Because of the Supreme Court of Canada Decision in M. v. H. Act, 1999*, S.O. 1999, c. 6.

to same-sex partners. British Columbia made similar changes.[10] It is likely that similar changes will need to be made in other provinces. The amending legislation in neither province extended the right to share in matrimonial property or to an equalizing payment to opposite-sex and same-sex partners. However, the *Family Law Act*[11] of the Northwest Territories extends the right to an equalizing payment to persons who were cohabiting. The Act defines "cohabit" as "to live together in a conjugal relationship, whether within or outside marriage".[12] While it does not specifically address the issue, this definition could extend to same-sex partners.

The right of a cohabitee to a division of the couple's assets on a breakdown of the relationship was litigated in *Walsh v. Bona*.[13] The plaintiff sought a declaration that the definition of "spouse" in s. 2(g) of the *Matrimonial Property Act*[14] discriminated on the basis of marital status, contrary to s. 15(1) of the *Charter*, because it only included married persons. The Nova Scotia Court of Appeal agreed and declared s. 2(g) unconstitutional. It suspended the declaration for 12 months to allow the legislature to develop a new definition.[15] If this decision is upheld by the Supreme Court of Canada, it is likely that statutes permitting spouses to share in matrimonial and other assets, or their value on a breakdown of the relationship will have to be amended to extend the same right to partners of opposite-sex and same-sex. The materials below must be read subject to such possible developments.

3. THE FAMILY LAW ACT (ONTARIO)

(a) Introduction

As noted, the Ontario statute is the most far-reaching matrimonial property reform legislation. It applies to all assets acquired by the spouses during marriage, save for stated exceptions. The statute provides for a deferred equalization scheme on marriage breakdown and on death. The sections of this statute that are relevant to succession are set out below.

---

10 See *Definition of Spouse Amendment Act, 1999*, S.B.C. 1999, c. 29; *Definition of Spouse Amendment Act, 2000*, S.B.C. 2000, c. 24.
11 S.N.W.T. 1997, c. 18.
12 *Ibid.*, s. 1.
13 (2000), 186 D.L.R. (4th) 50 (N.S.C.A.).
14 R.S.N.S. 1989, c. 275.
15 To the same effect, see *Watch v. Watch* (1999), 182 Sask. R. 237 (Q.B.), holding that s. 5 of the *Matrimonial Property Act, 1997*, S.S. 1997, c. M-6.11, which permits a spouse to apply for order granting exclusive possession of matrimonial home, discriminates against common law spouses.

Further Reading

The Law Society of Upper Canada and the Canadian Bar Association - Ontario, Continuing Legal Education Joint Program, *The New Family Law Act for Solicitors* (Toronto, March 4, 1986), various articles.

Canadian Bar Association - Ontario, 1986 Annual Institute on Continuing Legal Education, *Wills & Trusts: Entering the New Era in Estate Planning and Administration* (Toronto, February 6, 7 and 8, 1986).

Canadian Bar Association - Ontario, 1987 Annual Institute on Continuing Legal Education, *Looking Toward the 1990's: Estate Administration; Will Drafting: Practical Solutions to Everyday Problems* (Toronto, February 7, 1987), various articles.

David C. Simmonds, "Wills Drafting and the Family Law Act, 1986," in The Law Society of Upper Canada, Continuing Legal Education Program, *Wills Drafting* (Toronto, April 29, 1987), p. D1, reprinted (1987), 2 Can. Fam. L.Q. 209.

Barry S. Corbin, "The Impact of Ontario's Family Law Act, 1986 on Estate Administration" (1985-86), 7 E. & T.Q. 208.

Wolfe D. Goodman, "Depletion of Net Family Property and Defeating a Spouse's Claim to an Equalizing Payment at Death" (1985-86), 7 E. & T.Q. 289.

Rodney Hull, Q.C., "The Effect of the Ontario Family Law Act, 1986 on Surviving Spouses and Estates of Deceased Spouses" (1986-88), 8 E. & T.Q. 20.

Glenn D. Feltham, "Estate Planning and the Family Law Act: A Guide for the General Practitioner" (1986-88), 8 E. & T.Q. 296.

Wolfe D. Goodman, Q.C., "Business Agreements and the Family Law Act" (1986-88), 8 E. & T.Q. 193.

Wolfe D. Goodman, "Proposed Amendments to the Family Law Act Dealing with the Death of a Spouse" (1994), 13 E. & T.J. 365.

Ontario Law Reform Commission, *Report on Family Property Law*, Toronto, 1993.

Berend Hovius and Timothy G. Youdan, *The Law of Family Property* (Toronto: Carswell, 1991).

Brian A. Schnurr, "Estate Matters and the Family Law Act: A Seven-year Retrospective (1993), 13 E. & T.J. 28.

Brian A. Schnurr, "Claims by Common Law Spouses and Same-Sex Partners Against Estates" (1996), 16 E. & T.J. 22.

(b) The Statute

FAMILY LAW ACT
R.S.O. 1990, c. F.3, am. S.O. 1999, c. 6, s. 25

1. (1) In this Act,

. . .

"spouse" means either of a man and woman who,

(a) are married to each other, or

(b) have together entered into a marriage that is voidable or void, in good faith on the part of a person relying on this clause to assert any right.

(2) In the definition of "spouse", a reference to marriage includes a marriage that is actually or potentially polygamous, if it was celebrated in a jurisdiction whose system of law recognizes it as valid.

. . .

4. (1) In this Part,

"court" means a court as defined in subsection 1(1), but does not include the Ontario Court (Provincial Division);

"matrimonial home" means a matrimonial home under section 18 and includes property that is a matrimonial home under that section at the valuation date;

"net family property" means the value of all the property, except property described in subsection (2), that a spouse owns on the valuation date, after deducting,

(a) the spouse's debts and other liabilities, and

(b) the value of property, other than a matrimonial home, that the spouse owned on the date of the marriage, after deducting the spouse's debts and other liabilities, calculated as of the date of the marriage;

"property" means any interest, present or future, vested or contingent, in real or personal property and includes,

(a) property over which a spouse has, alone or in conjunction with another person, a power of appointment exercisable in favour of himself or herself,

(b) property disposed of by a spouse but over which the spouse has, alone or in conjunction with another person, a power to revoke the disposition or a power to consume or dispose of the property, and

(c) in the case of a spouse's rights under a pension plan that have vested, the spouse's interest in the plan including contributions made by other persons;

"valuation date" means. . .

5. The date before the date on which one of the spouses dies leaving the other spouse surviving.

(2) The value of the following property that a spouse owns on the valuation date does not form part of the spouse's net family property:

1. Property, other than a matrimonial home, that was acquired by gift or inheritance from a third person after the date of the marriage.

2. Income from property referred to in paragraph 1, if the donor or testator has expressly stated that it is to be excluded from the spouse's net family property.

3. Damages or a right to damages for personal injuries, nervous shock, mental distress or loss of guidance, care and companionship, or the part of a settlement that represents those damages.

4. Proceeds or a right to proceeds of a policy of life insurance, as defined in the *Insurance Act*,[16] that are payable on the death of the life insured.

---

16 R.S.O. 1990, c. I.8.

5. Property, other than a matrimonial home, into which property referred to in paragraphs 1 to 4 can be traced.

6. Property that the spouses have agreed by a domestic contract is not to be included in the spouse's net family property.

(3) The onus of proving a deduction under the definition of "net family property" or an exclusion under subsection (2) is on the person claiming it.

(4) When this section requires that a value be calculated as of a given date, it shall be calculated as of close of business on that date.

(5) If a spouse's net family property as calculated under subsections (1), (2) and (4) is less than zero, it shall be deemed to be equal to zero.

5.

. . .

(2) When a spouse dies, if the net family property of the deceased spouse exceeds the net family property of the surviving spouse, the surviving spouse is entitled to one-half the difference between them.

. . .

(6) The court may award a spouse an amount that is more or less than half the difference between the net family properties if the court is of the opinion that equalizing the net family properties would be unconscionable, having regard to,

(a) a spouse's failure to disclose to the other spouse debts or other liabilities existing at the date of the marriage;

(b) the fact that debts or other liabilities claimed in reduction of a spouse's net family property were incurred recklessly or in bad faith;

(c) the part of a spouse's net family property that consists of gifts made by the other spouse;

(d) a spouse's intentional or reckless depletion of his or her net family property;

(e) the fact that the amount a spouse would otherwise receive under subsection...(2)...is disproportionately large in relation to a period of cohabitation that is less than five years;

(f) the fact that one spouse has incurred a disproportionately larger amount of debts or other liabilities than the other spouse for the support of the family;

(g) a written agreement between the spouses that is not a domestic contract; or

(h) any other circumstance relating to the acquisition, disposition, preservation, maintenance or improvement of property.

(7) The purpose of this section is to recognize that child care, household management and financial provision are the joint responsibilities of the spouses and that inherent in the marital relationship there is equal contribution, whether financial or otherwise, by the spouses to the assumption of these responsibilities, entitling each spouse to the equalization of the net family properties, subject only to the equitable considerations set out in subsection (6).

6. (1) When a spouse dies leaving a will, the surviving spouse shall elect to take under the will or to receive the entitlement under section 5.

(2) When a spouse dies intestate, the surviving spouse shall elect to receive the entitlement under Part II of the *Succession Law Reform Act*[17] or to receive the entitlement under section 5.

(3) When a spouse dies testate as to some property and intestate as to other property, the surviving spouse shall elect to take under the will and to receive the entitlement under Part II of the *Succession Law Reform Act*, or to receive the entitlement under section 5.

(4) A surviving spouse who elects to take under the will or to receive the entitlement under Part II of the *Succession Law Reform Act*, or both in the case of a partial intestacy, shall also receive the other property to which he or she is entitled because of the first spouse's death.

(5) The surviving spouse shall receive the gifts made to him or her in the deceased spouse's will in addition to the entitlement under section 5 if the will expressly provides for that result.

(6) Where a surviving spouse,

(a) is the beneficiary,

  (i) of a policy of life insurance, as defined in the *Insurance Act*,[18] that was taken out on the life of the deceased spouse and owned by the deceased spouse or was taken out on the lives of a group of which he or she was a member, or

  (ii) of a lump sum payment provided under a pension or similar plan on the death of the deceased spouse; and

(b) elects or has elected to receive the entitlement under section 5,

the payment under the policy or plan shall be credited against the surviving spouse's entitlement under section 5, unless a written designation by the deceased spouse provides that the surviving spouse shall receive payment under the policy or plan in addition to the entitlement under section 5.

(7) If a surviving spouse,

(a) elects or has elected to receive the entitlement under section 5; and

(b) receives payment under a life insurance policy or a lump sum payment provided under a pension or similar plan that is in excess of the entitlement under section 5,

and there is no written designation by the deceased spouse described in subsection (6), the deceased spouse's personal representative may recover the excess amount from the surviving spouse.

(8) When a surviving spouse elects to receive the entitlement under section 5, the gifts made to him or her in the deceased spouse's will are revoked and the will shall be interpreted as if the surviving spouse had died before the other, unless the will expressly provides that the gifts are in addition to the entitlement under section 5.

---

17 R.S.O. 1990, c. S.26.
18 *Supra*.

(9) When a surviving spouse elects to receive the entitlement under section 5, the spouse shall be deemed to have disclaimed the entitlement under Part II of the *Succession Law Reform Act*.[19]

(10) The surviving spouse's election shall be in the form prescribed by the regulations made under this Act and shall be filed in the office of the Estate Registrar for Ontario within six months after the first spouse's death.

(11) If the surviving spouse does not file the election within that time, he or she shall be deemed to have elected to take under the will or to receive the entitlement under the *Succession Law Reform Act*, or both, as the case may be, unless the court, on application, orders otherwise.

(12) The spouse's entitlement under section 5 has priority over,

(a) the gifts made in the deceased spouse's will, if any, subject to subsection (13);

(b) a person's right to a share of the estate under Part II (Intestate Succession) of the *Succession Law Reform Act*;

(c) an order made against the estate under Part V (Support of Dependants) of the *Succession Law Reform Act*, except an order in favour of a child of the deceased spouse.

(13) The spouse's entitlement under section 5 does not have priority over a gift by will made in accordance with a contract that the deceased spouse entered into in good faith and for valuable consideration, except to the extent that the value of the gift, in the court's opinion, exceeds the consideration.

(14) No distribution shall be made in the administration of a deceased spouse's estate within six months of the spouse's death, unless,

(a) the surviving spouse gives written consent to the distribution; or

(b) the court authorizes the distribution.

(15) No distribution shall be made in the administration of a deceased spouse's death [*sic*, estate] after the personal representative has received notice of an application under this Part, unless,

(a) the applicant gives written consent to the distribution; or

(b) the court authorizes the distribution.

(16) If the court extends the time for a spouse's application based on subsection 5(2), any property of the deceased spouse that is distributed before the date of the order and without notice of the application shall not be brought into the calculation of the deceased spouse's net family property.

(17) Subsections (14) and (15) do not prohibit reasonable advances to dependants of the deceased spouse for their support.

(18) In subsection (17), "dependant" has the same meaning as in Part V of the *Succession Law Reform Act*.[20]

(19) If the personal representative makes a distribution that contravenes subsection (14) or (15), the court makes an order against the estate under this Part and the undistributed portion of the estate is not sufficient to satisfy the order, the personal representative is personally liable to the applicant for the amount that

---

19 *Supra.*
20 *Supra.*

was distributed or the amount that is required to satisfy the order, whichever is less.

(20) On motion by the surviving spouse, the court may make an order suspending the administration of the deceased spouse's estate for the time and to the extent that the court decides.

7. (1) The court may, on the application of a spouse, former spouse or deceased spouse's personal representative, determine any matter respecting the spouse's entitlement under section 5.

(2) Entitlement under subsection... 5... (2)... is personal as between the spouses but,

. . .

(b) an application based on subsection 5(2) may be made by or against a deceased spouse's estate.

(3) An application based on subsection... 5... (2) shall not be brought after the earliest of,

. . .

(c) six months after the first spouse's death.

. . .

14. The rule of law applying a presumption of a resulting trust shall be applied in questions of the ownership of property between husband and wife, as if they were not married, except that,
   (a) the fact that property is held in the name of spouses as joint tenants is proof, in the absence of evidence to the contrary, that the spouses are intended to own the property as joint tenants; and
   (b) money on deposit in the name of both spouses shall be deemed to be in the name of the spouses as joint tenants for the purposes of clause (a).

Comparable Legislation

Family Law Act, 1997, S.N.W.T. 1997, c. 18, Part III.

(c) Scheme of the Statute

Part I of the Act gives spouses a right to make an equalizing claim on a breakdown of marriage and gives a surviving spouse the right to make a similar claim on the death of the other spouse. We are concerned only with the latter right in this chapter, but will refer also to cases decided in connection with other claims, since the law is often the same or similar.

Section 5(2) confers the right to make an equalizing claim on death, while s. 6 contains a code of the rights and obligations of the spouses and other interested parties when one spouse has died. The surviving spouse's primary right is his or her succession rights apart from the Act, but the spouse is given the right to elect within six months of the other spouse's death to make an equalizing claim. The surviving spouse must file the election and bring an application against the estate to claim an equalizing payment. If the claim is successful, the claimant's rights under the deceased's will cease, unless the will says otherwise. Similarly, if the deceased spouse died intestate the claimant loses the right to share on the intestacy.

Section 7 empowers the court, on the application of a spouse or the deceased spouse's personal representative, to determine any matter respecting the spouses' rights under s. 5. The remaining sections of Part I are concerned with procedural matters, including the kinds of orders the court may make. In the following materials we shall look at some of these provisions in greater detail.

The Act does not confer a right to property, but a right to a money payment. Thus, it does not divide the property of the spouses, but the value of the property.[21] Accordingly, the successful claimant becomes a simple creditor of the other spouse.[22]

Part I of the Act, therefore, is debtor-creditor legislation, but the spouses do not stand in a debtor-creditor relationship throughout the marriage. Their right to make a claim for an equalizing payment is an inchoate right that imposes no obligations and confers no rights until a triggering event, described in s. 5(1) - (3), occurs. Hence, during the marriage a spouse can give anything away, subject only to trust doctrines and s. 5(3). Consequently, a spouse cannot attack a gift made by the other spouse before a triggering event on the basis that the gift interfered with the debtor-creditor relationship between them, since there was then no such relationship.[23]

(d) Meaning of the Statute

(i) Entitlement

The basic scheme of Part I of the Act is to confer a right to equalize the assets of spouses. In regard to succession, this means that the surviving spouse is entitled to one-half the difference between the net family property[24] of the deceased spouse and the nfp of the surviving spouse, if the former is greater than the latter.[25]

Although the language of s. 7(1) is not entirely clear, it is clear that the estate of the deceased spouse does not have a right to bring an application for an equalizing payment.[26] The estate of the deceased spouse does have the right, on

---

21 *Berdette v. Berdette* (1991), 33 R.F.L. (3d) 113 (Ont. C.A.).

22 *Ibid.*; *Balyk v. Balyk* (1994), 3 R.F.L. (4th) 282 (Ont. Gen. Div.).

23 *Stone v. Stone* (1999), 46 O.R. (3d) 31, 29 E.T.R. (2d) 1 (S.C.J.), which holds otherwise and allows a surviving spouse to invoke the *Fraudulent Conveyances Act*, R.S.O. 1990, c. F.29, is wrongly decided. The spouse might successfully have sought an unequal division under s. 5(6).

24 Hereafter referred to as "nfp."

25 *Family Law Act*, s. 5(2).

26 *Rondberg Estate v. Rondberg Estate* (1989), 70 O.R. (2d) 146 (C.A.), affirming (1987), 8 R.F.L. (3d) 443 (Ont. H.C.).

an application by the surviving spouse, to argue, for example, that the equalization claim should be less than 50 percent.[27] Further, if a spouse has commenced an application based on breakdown of marriage, the estate of the applicant may continue the application.[28]

Notes and Questions

1. The drafting of the Act leaves a number of questions unanswered. The questions will have to be resolved by the courts over time. Some will be answered in cases involving applications on marriage breakdown, but others are peculiar to applications on death. For example, section 5(2) provides that the surviving spouse is "entitled" to the property specified. However, s. 7(1) appears to require an application to the court to determine the surviving spouse's entitlement. Similarly, section 7(2)(b) provides that the right is personal as between the spouses, but permits an application to be brought by or against a deceased spouse's estate.

2. Do the personal representatives have to continue an application for an equalizing claim brought by the deceased on the basis of breakdown of the marriage, or can they try to negotiate a settlement with the other spouse?[29]

3. Can a spouse who made an application on the basis of breakdown of marriage discontinue the claim after the other spouse dies, or is the estate of the deceased entitled to have the proceedings continue?[30]

4. If a spouse has not made an application for equalization on marriage breakdown and the other spouse then dies, the survivor must make application on death, so that the provisions of s. 6 apply. This can make a difference. For example, if the survivor was entitled to the proceeds of a contract of insurance on the deceased spouse's life and owned by the deceased, the survivor would not have to give credit for the proceeds on a marriage breakdown application but would have to do so on an after death application.[31]

(ii) *Unequal Division*

The Act confers an entitlement to equalization. However, the court has a discretion to award more or less than this amount if equalization would be unconscionable having regard to certain statutory criteria.[32] This is not a wide discretion, but very restricted. It does not confer a general power to do what is fair.[33] This is because the claimant must prove that equalization would be "un-

---

27 *Family Law Act*, s. 5(2).
28 *Ashton Estate v. Ashton* [1994] W.D.F.L. 355 (Ont. Gen. Div.), affirmed (December 10 1996) Doc. CA C18071 (Ont. C.A.).
29 See *Dunn v. Dunn Estate* (1994), 3 E.T.R. (2d) 220 (Ont. Gen. Div.).
30 See *Boychuk v. Boychuk Estate* (1993) 2 E.T.R. (2d) 81 (Sask. C.A.).
31 See *Panangaden v. Panangaden Estate* (1991), 42 E.T.R. 87 (Ont. Gen. Div.). See also *Maljkovich v. Maljkovich Estate* (1995), 20 R.F.L. (4th) 222 (Ont. Gen. Div.), affirmed (1997), 33 R.F.L. (4th) 24 (Ont. C.A.), in which the claimant killed his spouse and was precluded from electing to take under the Act.
32 *Family Law Act*, s. 5(6).
33 *Berdette v. Berdette* (1991), 33 R.F.L. (3d) 113 (Ont. C.A.).

conscionable." The courts have held that unconscionability is something that shocks the conscience of the court; it is different from "inequitable."[34]

Notes and Questions

1. If one spouse contributes a great deal more to the acquisition, preservation and maintenance of property than the other, can s. 5(6) be invoked?[35]

2. If the husband has incurred massive debts because of bad management and deliberately hid them from his wife, in consequence of which the family's financial security is threatened, would the wife be entitled to an unequal division?[36]

3. The court applied s. 5(6) in *Rivett v. Rivett Estate*.[37] Husband and wife held a number of bank accounts in their joint names. He had contributed most of the moneys. Without his knowledge, she withdrew most of the moneys and placed them in accounts and savings plans in her own name before she died. In consequence, her estate was a lot larger than his. She left most of her estate to her grandchildren. The court held that the husband was entitled to substantially more than one-half the difference between the two nfps, since equalization would be unconscionable.

4. The unequal division provision of s. 5(6) is a kind of anti-avoidance provision, but it does not permit a claw-back of assets disposed of with the intent to defeat the purpose of the legislation. The Ontario Law Reform Commission has recommended the adoption of a general anti-avoidance rule.[38]

(iii) *Spouse*

Section 1 of the Act defines the term "spouse" as follows:

"spouse" means either of a man and woman who,
(a) are married to each other, or
(b) have together entered into a marriage that is voidable or void, in good faith on the part of a person relying on this clause to assert any right.

It has been noted that the consequence of this definition may be that one spouse may have a right to an equalization payment, while the other does not. For example, if H is married but goes through a form of marriage with W and W does not know of H's existing marriage, H does not have equalizing rights, but W does.[39]

---

34 See, *e.g.*, *Skrlj v. Skrlj* (1986), 2 R.F.L. (3d) 305.
35 See *Berdette v. Berdette, supra.*
36 See, *Thompson v. Thompson*, [1994] W.D.F.L. 033 (Ont. Gen. Div.).
37 (1992), 45 E.T.R. 266 (Ont. Gen. Div.).
38 Ontario Law Reform Commission, *Report on Family Property Law* (Toronto, 1993), 99-100 (hereafter referred to as "OLRC Report," without further citation).
39 See James G. McLeod and Alfred A. Mamo, *Annual Review of Family Law 1994* (Scarborough, Ont.: Carswell, 1994), 247, citing *Lindmark v. Nielsen*, [1994] W.D.F.L. 777 (Ont. Gen. Div.).

(iv) *Property*

The legislation applies to property owned by the spouses on the valuation date, whether they were married before or after the Act came into force and whether the property was acquired before or after the Act came into force.[40]

Section 4(1) of the Act defines the term "property" very widely. The definition includes property over which the spouse has a power of appointment exercisable in favour of himself or herself and property disposed of by the spouse subject to a power to revoke. The power to appoint or to revoke may be exercisable by the spouse alone or in conjunction with another person.[41] The purpose of these provisions is to prevent depletion of the estate.

The definition also includes a spouse's interest in a pension plan when his or her rights have vested, and the spouse's interest for the purpose of the Act includes any contributions made by any other person.[42] The definition further includes any interest in property, present or future and vested or contingent.[43]

Notes and Questions

1. The courts have held that an interest under a trust, payment of which is postponed, or which is contingent upon a future event, is property and, if owned at the date of a person's marriage, forms part of that person's net family property. It is not excluded as property acquired by inheritance after the marriage under s. 4(2).1.[44] Do you think that is correct? When does the interest under the trust arise, when the trust is created, or when the property is paid to the beneficiary?

2. The Ontario Court of Appeal has held, correctly, I submit, that an income interest under a trust is property, even though it is inalienable. To the extent the interest is owned on the date of the marriage, it is deducted from the spouse's nfp under s. 4(1), "net family property," (b). To the extent that it is acquired after the marriage, it is excluded under s. 4(2).1.[45]

3. Does a beneficiary under a discretionary trust own property? Such a trust typically requires the trustees to distribute property (income or capital, or both), but gives them a power of selection among a class of beneficiaries. The following is an example:

> To my trustees in trust to distribute the annual income in such amounts and to such of my children as they shall in their absolute discretion think fit.

When trustees are given a power to encroach on the capital in favour of the life tenant, does the latter have a property interest in the capital? If so, how is its value determined?

4. The definition of "property" in s. 4(1) includes powers of appointment. Powers of appointment are different from discretionary trusts. A discretionary trust involves a power of appointment, but one that must be exercised. A power of appointment *per se* is a right

---

40 *Family Law Act*, s. 16.
41 *Ibid.*, s. 4(1), "property," paras. (a) and (b).
42 *Ibid.*, para. (c).
43 *Dawdy v. Dawdy*, [1994] W.D.F.L. 975 (Ont. Gen. Div.).
44 *Black v. Black* (1988), 66 O.R. (2d) 643 (H.C.).
45 See *Brinkos v. Brinkos* (1989), 34 E.T.R. 55 (Ont. C.A.).

to dispose of someone else's property: it does not involve a duty to dispose of it, unless it is made into a discretionary trust. Therefore, powers of appointment are not normally considered property. They are so treated in the definition to prevent evasion of the purpose of the Act. Does the definition go too far in clause (b), however? Suppose that X gave W a power to appoint property among her children, coupled with a power to revoke. Assuming that the power does not permit W to appoint to herself, why should the value of such property be included in her nfp? The Ontario Law Reform Commission has recommended that property should only be included under this clause if the spouse, alone or with another, has power to revoke a disposition or a power to consume or dispose of the property in favour of himself or herself.[46]

5. H was the adopted child of the testator's grandson. The testator left income from his estate to his great-grandchildren and H obtained a judgment in the courts of the testator's domicile holding that he was entitled to income from the estate. The will also provided that when the testator's last grandson died the capital would be distributed equally among the testator's surviving great-grandchildren. H was 64 years of age. The testator's only remaining grandchild was 87 years old. Does H have a property interest in the income, capital or both of the testator's estate? If so, what kind and how should it be valued?[47]

6. The interest of a beneficiary under an estate that has not yet been fully administered is not property.[48]

7. Jobs are not property;[49] neither are professional licences.[50]

(v) *Net Family Property*

Section 4(1) defines a spouse's nfp as all property owned on the valuation date, except excluded property, debts and liabilities, and after deducting property (other than the matrimonial home) owned on the date of the marriage less debts and liabilities calculated as of the date of the marriage.[51] This definition is complex, but becomes easy to understand by reference to the net family property statement reproduced below.

It is clear from the definition that the Act accords special treatment to the matrimonial home as the most valuable asset the spouses generally own. Further, Part II of the Act confers substantial rights of occupation on the spouse who does not hold the title to the matrimonial home. It is doubtful that the special treatment is needed for Part I. The Ontario Law Reform Commission has recommended that it be discontinued for Part I.[52] If this recommendation is adopted it will, at the very least, simplify the Act's definitions.

---

46 OLRC Report 86-89.

47 See *DaCosta v. DaCosta* (1992), 44 E.T.R. 196 (Ont. C.A.).

48 See *Gennaro v. Gennaro* (1994), 2 R.F.L. (4th) 179 (Ont. U.F.C.); and A.H. Oosterhoff, Case Comment, *ibid.*, at 184.

49 *Linton v. Linton* (1990), 1 O.R. (3d) 1, 30 R.F.L. (3d) 1, 41 E.T.R. 85 (C.A.).

50 *Caratun v. Caratun* (1992), 10 O.R. (3d) 385, 42 R.F.L. (3d) 113, 96 D.L.R. (4th) 404 (C.A.)

51 *Family Law Act, supra*, s. 4(1), "net family property."

52 OLRC Report 85.

When a spouse makes an application under s. 7 for an equalizing payment the spouse must file a financial statement[53] and a net family property statement.[54] If a spouse makes an application for equalization in divorce proceedings the same statements must be filed.[55] The other spouse is served with the statements and must then file his or her statements. The net family property statement is as follows:

FORM 69N
NET FAMILY PROPERTY STATEMENT
Rules of Civil Procedure, R.R.O. 1990, Reg. 194

(General Heading)
WIFE'S (*or* HUSBAND'S) NET FAMILY PROPERTY STATEMENT

Valuation Date _____ Statement Date _____

(Complete columns for both husband and wife, showing your assets, debts, etc. and those of your spouse.)

ITEM	HUSBAND	WIFE
1. Value of assets owned on valuation date *(by category with reference to the financial statements)*		
TOTAL 1.		
2. Value of debts and other liabilities on valuation date *(by category with reference the financial statements)*		
TOTAL 2.		

---

53 *Rules of Civil Procedure*, R. 70.04, Form 69K (or Form 69M if a claim for custody is made).
54 *Ibid.*. Form 69N.
55 *Ibid.*, R. 69.14.

ITEM	HUSBAND	WIFE
3. Net value of property, other than a matrimonial home, owned on date of marriage *(by category with reference to the financial statements)*		
TOTAL 3.		
4. Value of property excluded under subs. 4(2) of the *Family Law Act (by category with reference to the financial statements)*		
TOTAL 4.		
5. Net family property *(Total 1 minus Totals 2, 3, and 4)*		
	(Name, address and telephone number of solicitor or party)	

(vi) *Deductions*

The definition of nfp in s. 4(1) lists the deductions that may be made from the value of the property, other than excluded property listed in s. 4(2), that a spouse owns on the valuation date. These include (a) the spouse's debts and other liabilities and (b) the net value of property owned on the date of the marriage other than the matrimonial home.

A significant issue for the purpose of a claim on marriage breakdown is whether a spouse can claim a deduction for tax and disposition costs. The Ontario Court of Appeal has held that this may only be done if such costs are likely to be incurred in the foreseeable future.[56] If the costs are inherent in the asset it is also appropriate to claim them.[57]

---

56 *Starkman v. Starkman* (1990), 28 R.F.L. (3d) 208 (Ont. C.A.).
57 *Sengmueller v. Sengmueller* (1994), 2 R.F.L. (4th) 232 (Ont. C.A.).

Notes and Questions

1. It has been held that if a spouse's debts at the date of the marriage are greater than the spouse's assets, the negative value should be taken into account in calculating the spouse's nfp. In other words, it will increase the spouse's nfp.[58]

2. A cottage is not normally a matrimonial home and, if brought into the marriage, its value is deductible.[59]

3. If a spouse brings a matrimonial home into the marriage, but it is no longer used as the matrimonial home at the valuation date, the spouse can deduct its value.[60]

(vii) *Excluded Property*

The definition of nfp states that the value of the property mentioned in s. 4(2), if owned on the valuation date, is excluded from a spouse's nfp. Several kinds of property are mentioned, but they are defined in different ways.

The first and most often encountered exemption is gifts and inheritances received *after* the marriage. Those received *before* the marriage are deductions under s. 4(1). Note that the matrimonial home, if acquired by gift or inheritance, is not excluded. A gift to spouses jointly enables both to deduct their respective interests from their nfp calculations.[61]

Although the value of gifts and inheritances is excluded, income on such gifts or inheritances must be included in the spouse's nfp by reason of s. 4(2).2, unless the donor or testator provided otherwise. If that is not done, the donee spouse must apportion the value of the gift or inheritance between income and capital on the valuation date.[62]

Notes and Questions

1. Property which is acquired by purchase does not fall within the exemption of s. 4(2).1. Thus, if a father engages in an estate freeze to avoid gift tax and succession duty by transferring the common shares in his corporation to his son at fair market value, the son cannot argue that he received a gift of property from the father, *viz.*, control of the corporation and the subsequent increase in value of the shares.[63] This illustrates that tax related planning and family law related planning may well have different and conflicting objects.

2. The provision in s. 4(2).2 is awkward, although the intent of the legislation is clear: it is assumed that when you inherit income-producing property, you do not keep the

---

58 See *Jackson v. Jackson* (1986), 5 R.F.L. (3d) 8 (Ont. H.C.).

59 See *Best v. Best* (1993), 50 R.F.L. (3d) 120 (Ont. Gen. Div.), affirmed (1997), 31 R.F.L. (4th) 1, varied [1999] S.C.J. No. 40.

60 *Dearing v. Dearing*, [1993] W.D.F.L. 1615 (Ont. Gen. Div.).

61 *Gognavec v. Gognavec* (1996), 23 R.F.L. (4th) 395 (Ont. Gen. Div.).

62 See *Amaral v. Amaral* (1993), 50 R.F.L. (3d) 364 (Ont. Gen. Div.).

63 *Black v. Black* (1988), 66 O.R. (2d) 643 (H.C.). See also *Oliva v. Oliva* (1988), 12 R.F.L. (3d) 334 (Ont. C.A.); *Leslie v. Leslie* (1987), 27 E.T.R. 247 (Ont. H.C.); and *Cowan v. Cowan* (1987), 9 R.F.L. (3d) 401 (Ont. H.C.).

income separate from your other property. Hence, it would be difficult to account for that income so as to permit it to be exempt. But it is likely that the donors would wish the recipient spouse to keep the income as well as the capital and not have to account for it. For that reason, solicitors should recommend to their clients that they consider inserting a clause in their wills excluding the income from the nfp of the objects of their beneficence. Donors, of course, should consider making the same stipulation at the time they make a gift, but in most cases it will not occur to them. Is it appropriate to involve third parties in the property affairs of spouses in this way?

The exception does not help those who have already made absolute *inter vivos* gifts, nor testators who have died or who can no longer make another will.

Although the income on gifts and inheritances is dealt with in this manner, capital appreciation of the corpus of gifts and inheritances is not. A spouse who is minded to minimize his or her nfp should, therefore, invest gifts or inheritances in assets that are likely to appreciate in value and produce little or no income.

The Ontario Law Reform Commission has recommended that s. 4(2).2 be repealed and that all gains or losses in the capital value of an excluded asset, as well as income earned on the asset, should be included in the owner's nfp.[64]

3. While s. 4(2).1 speaks of gifts and inheritances acquired after marriage, clause 3, which speaks of a right to damages, is not so restricted. Does that mean that a spouse can claim damages paid before marriage as both a deduction under s. 4(1) and an exclusion under s. 4(2).3?[65]

4. Under s. 4(2).5, property into which property referred to in the earlier clauses of the section can be traced is also excluded property. It appears that the courts are applying the tracing rules developed for restitution purposes under this clause.[66] This is problematic, since those rules are intended to solve disputes between trustees and beneficiaries, and among beneficiaries *inter se*.[67]

(viii) *Valuation Date*

Section 4(1) defines "valuation date" for the purpose of after death claims as the date before one of the spouses dies leaving the other spouse surviving. This date was apparently chosen to ensure that the surviving spouse would be able to share in property jointly owned by the deceased spouse and a third person. On the death of the spouse, the third person would acquire title by survivorship. If the deceased spouse's property were valued at death, therefore, the interest in the jointly-owned property would no longer exist. This would leave the surviving spouse in a worse position than if he or she had made an application for equalization for marriage breakdown, for then the half interest of the other spouse would have been taken into account.[68]

---

64 OLRC Report, 77-8.
65 See *Mittler v. Mittler* (1988), 17 R.F.L. (3d) 113 (Ont. H.C.).
66 See, *e.g., ibid.*
67 For a summary of the law of tracing, see *Oosterhoff and Gillese, Text, Commentary and Cases on Trusts*, 5th ed. by A.H. Oosterhoff and E.E. Gillese (Scarborough: Carswell, 1998), ch. 13, part 3.
68 OLRC Report, 105.

However, the date before death choice causes a number of serious problems that would disappear if the valuation date were the date of death. The problems caused by that date can be solved in other ways. Three of the main problems caused by the valuation date are discussed in the following material.

First, it is unclear what valuation principles should be applied. For example, is the deceased spouse's life expectancy relevant?[69] This is significant if the spouse was suffering from a terminal illness. A person's life expectancy is taken into account by actuaries when they have to determine the present value of that person's life interest for other purposes. One would hope that, at least as regards such assets as life insurance and pensions, the courts will adopt limited hindsight since the valuation date precedes death by only a day.

The second problem is that the valuation date works inequity in many situations in that it requires the inclusion of property into the nfp of a deceased spouse that vanishes on death. That is the case with property owned jointly by the spouses and with pensions. The effect of the valuation date is that it increases the nfp of the deceased spouse and, in consequence, increases the equalizing claim of the surviving spouse unfairly. Further, this may cause difficulties to the estate of the deceased spouse in that it may not be able to pay an equalizing claim since the assets on which the claim is based will have disappeared. This problem would not exist if the Act required the assets of both spouses to be valued on the death of the first to die.

Suppose, for example, that the deceased's pension benefits comprise a large part of his or her estate. The value of the benefits must be included in that spouse's nfp, since they are valued the day before death. However, once the spouse has died, the value of the interest will not be paid out to the estate. Nevertheless, if the surviving spouse is entitled to a substantial claim, the money will have to be raised by the estate to pay it. This illustrates that the choice of valuation date in the case of death is improper and unworkable. It forces the estate to include property in the deceased spouse's estate that is non-existent.

The same difficulty arises if the spouses own property jointly. Then, each must add one-half of its value to their respective nfps. The addition will make no difference to the calculation, for the two half interests will offset each other. This is because of the rebuttable statutory presumption that when spouses own property jointly, that is *prima facie* proof that the parties intended so to own it[70] and, hence, to have an equal interest in it. Nevertheless, although the amounts are offset in the calculation, the surviving spouse benefits from it, since he or she will receive the entirety on the death of the other spouse. Further, the deceased's estate may have to pay an equalizing claim based on the half interest in property it no longer

---

69 Opinions are divided on this issue. *Cf.* Wolfe D. Goodman, "Defeating a Spouse's Claim under Part I of the Family Law Act, on the Death of the Other Spouse," in The Law Society of Upper Canada and the Canadian Bar Association - Ontario, Continuing Legal Education Joint Program, *The New Family Law Act for Solicitors* (Toronto, March 4, 1986), at 4, and Glenn D. Feltham, "Estate Planning and the Family Law Act: A Guide for the General Practitioner" (1986-88), 8 E. & T.Q. 296 at 317.

70 *Family Law Act*, s. 14.

owns. This again illustrates the inequity of making the valuation date the date before death, instead of at death.[71]

The third problem that the valuation date causes is the inability to deduct expenses and liabilities that are caused by death. Estate and funeral expenses are incurred in consequence of a person's death, but cannot be deducted if the valuation date is the day before death. Similarly, the estate may be liable to pay income tax by reason of deemed disposition of capital property on death. Logically, such a liability cannot be deducted from the value of the property the day before death.[72] There is now some case law on this point which has the effect of melioriating this harsh logic, however. It is discussed in the notes and questions below.

There is also a difficulty with property owned jointly by a spouse and a third person. If, for example, the husband owned Blackacre jointly with X and the husband predeceased his wife, the estate must include one-half of the value of Blackacre in his nfp. This is because his interest has to be valued the day before his death, at which time he had a perfectly valid half-interest. The fact that it disappears by operation of the law of survivorship the next day is not taken into account by the Act. But that is defensible in this situation. If the half interest were not included, the wife would have been worse off than if she had made a claim before her husband's death on the basis of breakdown of marriage.

If the legislation were changed to provide for a date of death valuation, the three problems mentioned above would disappear. There would, however, then be the problem that a spouse could arrange his or her affairs in such a way as to defeat the claims of the other spouse. For example, a spouse could take title to property with another person in joint tenancy. On the spouse's death, the other person would then take the entirety and leave the surviving spouse without a claim. But this result can be avoided by a "claw-back" provision.

The Ontario Law Reform Commission has recommended that the valuation date for on death claims be changed to the date of death and that the time of valuation be immediately after the death of the first spouse to die. The Commission has also recommended that the definition of "net family property" be changed to provide that property which the deceased was competent to dispose immediately before death, other than excluded property, should be included in the deceased's nfp, except to the extent it is otherwise included in the nfp of the surviving spouse. Further, it has recommended that pension and insurance benefits received by the surviving spouse in consequence of the deceased spouse's death should be included in the surviving spouse's nfp and excluded from the deceased's nfp.[73]

---

71 See Barry S. Corbin, "The Impact of Ontario's Family Law Act, 1986 on Estate Administration" (1986), 7 E. & T. Q. 208 at 224-5; Wolfe D. Goodman, "Depletion of Net Family Property and Defeating a Spouse's Claim to an Equalizing Payment at Death" (1986), 7 E. & T. Q. 289; Glen D. Feltham, "Estate Planning and the Family Law Act: A Guide for the General Practitioner" (1986-1988), 8 E. & T.Q. 296 at 314-26; Berend Hovius and Timothy G. Youdan, *The Law of Family Property* (Toronto: Carswell, 1991), 536.

72 See Brian A. Schnurr, "Estate Matters and the Family Law Act – A Seven-Year Retrospective," in *Family Law Conference 1993* (Scarborough, Ont.: Carswell, 1993).

73 OLRC Report 110.

Notes and Questions

1. If one spouse owns the matrimonial home jointly with a third person, the joint tenancy is deemed to have been severed immediately before the spouse's death.[74] In that situation, the half interest of the spouse must be included in his or her nfp, but it will be an asset of the estate, since it does not disappear by operation of the law of survivorship.

2. If the valuation date is changed to the date of death as recommended by the Ontario Law Reform Commission, s. 6(6) and (7) would be redundant. Section 6(6) requires a surviving spouse to give credit for life insurance benefits received under a contract of life insurance on the deceased's life and owned by the deceased, and for a lump sum pension benefit paid to the surviving spouse under a pension plan of which the deceased was a member. Section 6(7) permits the deceased's estate to recover life insurance and pension payments already made to the survivor in excess of the equalization entitlement.

3. In *Gregoric v. Gregoric*[75] the court held that a spouse could not require the other spouse to take after-tax profits into account if those profits were not known or foreseeable on the valuation date. However, *Gregoric* was an application based on marriage breakdown.

In *Bobyk v. Bobyk Estate*,[76] which was an application by a surviving wife, the court held that the liability of the deceased spouse for income tax arising from deemed dispositions immediately before death were deductible in determining the deceased's nfp. The liability existed in unquantified form before death and became quantified on death. Hence, while post-valuation date events can not be considered for the purpose of determining the value of property, they can be considered to determine the amount of deductions. However, the court also held that the cost of administering the estate could not be deducted in calculating the deceased's nfp: these did not exist on the valuation date, but only arose after his death.

(ix) *Additional Rights*

A testator may provide in his or her will that the gifts in the will to the testator's spouse are in addition to what that spouse is entitled to under the Act.[77]

The Act provides that the surviving spouse who elects to take under the will or on intestacy is also entitled to receive whatever other property he or she is entitled to because of the deceased spouse's death.[78] This refers to the property that a spouse might receive under will substitutes, such as property owned jointly with the deceased spouse.

There is no similar provision respecting the surviving spouse's rights to other property when he or she elects to take under the Act. The Act states that upon electing the surviving spouse's rights under the will are revoked, unless the will

---

74 *Family Law Act*, s. 26(1). This provision is discussed below. There is, however, no deemed severance of other property held by the deceased jointly with another person: *Cimetta v. Topler et al.* (1989), 68 O.R. (2d) 251 (H.C.).

75 (1990), 39 E.T.R. 63 (Ont. Gen. Div.).

76 (1993), 50 E.T.R. 186 (Ont. Gen. Div.).

77 *Family Law Act*, s. 6(5).

78 *Ibid.*, s. 6(4).

expressly says otherwise, and the rights on intestacy are deemed to have been disclaimed.[79]

The Act does make special provision for two kinds of will substitutes, *viz.*, the proceeds of a contract of insurance on the life of the deceased spouse which is owned by that spouse, and a lump sum payment provided under a pension or similar plan on the death of the deceased spouse. Such monies must be credited against the surviving spouse's entitlement, unless the deceased spouse declared in writing that the survivor should receive his or her rights under the Act, as well as the payment under the insurance contract or pension plan. Further, if the proceeds of insurance and pension payment exceed the amount of the survivor's entitlement under the Act, the deceased's personal representatives are entitled to recover the excess.[80] The proceeds of a contract of life insurance payable on the death of the insured are excluded property,[81] whereas rights under a pension plan are not.[82]

The deceased spouse must include the value of his or her interest under a pension plan (valued the day before his or her death) in his or her nfp, but the surviving spouse must also include any survivor benefit under the deceased spouse's pension in his or her nfp. However, only lump sum payments to the surviving spouse are apt to reduce that spouse's equalization claim.[83] In addition, the surviving spouse must include the value of his or her pension plan interest in his or her own nfp. It will be appreciated that the actuarial calculations can be horrendous.

Notes and Questions

1. Does s. 6(4) have any utility? This provision was considered in *Bickley v. Bickley Estate*.[84] The testator owned U.S. assets, the shares in a holding company which owned all the shares in an operating company, and other assets. Before he died, he transferred the U.S. assets to himself and his wife as joint tenants. His will purported to divide the U.S. assets among his wife and children and directed that the shares in the holding company be distributed one-quarter each to the widow and three children. After the testator's death, the beneficiaries obtained a consent judgment which held that the widow held 50 percent of the shares in the holding company under a constructive trust which arose at the time of incorporation. Further, the judgment deemed the widow to have elected to take under the will. The children brought an application for advice and directions in which they invoked the doctrine of equitable election which applies when a testator attempts to dispose of the assets of another person who is also a beneficiary.[85] If the doctrine applied, the widow would have to pay her 50 percent shareholding into the estate if she wished to take her interest in the residue. The court held that s. 6(4) entitled the widow to the U.S. assets, since they were held in joint tenancy. However, the section did not apply to the shares

---

79 *Ibid.*, s. 6(8),(9).
80 *Ibid.*, s. 6(6),(7).
81 *Ibid.*, s. 4(2).4.
82 *Ibid.*, s. 4(1), "property," para. (c).
83 *Ibid.*, s. 6(6)(a)(ii).
84 (1999), 29 E.T.R. (2d) 132 (Ont. S.C.J.).
85 The doctrine is discussed in Chapter 11, *supra*.

held on constructive trust for her, since the widow was not entitled to them because of her husband's death. The court then went on to hold that the doctrine of equitable election did not apply. Since the husband owned half of the shares, his disposition of the shares should be taken to refer only to his shares and not to his widow's. Consequently, she was entitled to both the 50 percent shareholding under the constructive trust and the 25 percent of the residue.

2. Does the absence in s. 6(8) and (9) of a provision similar to s. 6(4) mean that the surviving spouse's right to receive other property under will substitutes is also revoked?

3. Benefits under pension plans can vary greatly. However, pension plans must conform with legislation designed to protect employees and such legislation is in force in all the provinces. There is also federal legislation for employees under federal jurisdiction.

In Ontario, pension plans are governed by the *Pension Benefits Act*.[86] It provides that the normal form of pension benefit under Ontario pensions shall be a joint and survivor benefit if the former member of the plan has a spouse on the date the payment of the first instalment of the pension is due, and that the amount payable to the survivor of the former member and his or her spouse shall not be less than 60 per cent of the pension paid to the former member during the spouses' joint lives.[87] The Act also provides for other benefits, such as deferred pensions, ancillary benefits, and lump-sum pre-retirement death benefits, to the member's spouse.[88]

4. A surviving spouse is not precluded from making an application for dependants' support, whether he or she elects to take under the Act. However, if an election to take under the Act has been made, it is unlikely that an application for dependants' support will be required in most cases. In any event, the amount received under the Act would be a factor that the court would consider on the application.[89]

5. It would seem that a surviving spouse who is appointed executor of the will is not disentitled to act as such after making an election. Should a testator insert a clause in the will providing for a substitute executor to provide for this eventuality?[90]

(x) *Election*

In order to qualify for the entitlement, the surviving spouse must elect to take under the Act and file the election within six months of the deceased spouse's death in the office of the Estate Registrar for Ontario.[91] If this is not done, the surviving spouse is deemed to have elected to take under the will, the statutory rights on intestate succession, or both.[92]

There are two concerns about the right of election. The first is whether anyone can make the election on behalf of the surviving spouse. The second is whether it is possible to revoke an election.

---

86 R.S.O. 1990, c. P.8.
87 *Ibid.*, s. 44.
88 *Ibid.*, ss. 39, 40 and 48.
89 Dependants' support is discussed in the next chapter.
90 It may be noted that when a testator and his or her spouse subsequently divorce, the appointment of the spouse as executor is revoked, absent a contrary intention in the will: *Succession Law Reform Act*, R.S.O. 1990, c. S.26, s. 17(2).
91 *Family Law Act*, s. 6(10).
92 *Ibid.*, s. 6(11).

In *Rondberg Estate v. Rondberg Estate*[93] the court held that, since s. 7(2) makes the right of election personal as between the spouses, the surviving spouse's executor cannot make the election. The courts have also held that the committee of a spouse[94] and an attorney acting under a power of attorney[95] can make an election on behalf of the spouse. The distinction is defensible: in the case of the committee and the attorney the spouse is still alive and the election can, therefore, still be made; once the spouse is dead, the right to elect is also gone.

Whether a spouse may revoke his or her election is debatable. In *Re Bolfan Estate*[96] a surrogate court held that an election could not be revoked. The surviving husband elected for an equalization. Later he brought action to contest his wife's will for lack of capacity. The court held that he lacked standing to contest the will, since he had already made an election against it and the Act does not permit one to revoke one's election. Neither did the court have power to revoke it.

The court in *Bolfan* did not appear to be aware of the earlier case, *Re Van der Wyngaard Estate*.[97] The husband and wife were separated when she died. Under an earlier will she left him a substantial portion of the residue of the estate. However, she excluded him from her last will. He filed a caveat to contest the last will on the ground of lack of capacity, as well as an election under the Act. The wife's estate moved to strike the caveat, but was unsuccessful. The court held that the husband could elect to take under the Act in the event the last will should be declared valid, but to take under the first will if the last will should be found invalid. Thus, the election was a conditional election.

Notes and Questions

1. If a conditional election is possible, as in *Van der Wyngaard*, should a revocation of an election also not be possible?

2. Is *Van der Wyngaard* correct? Can you elect against a particular (*i.e.*, the last) will? Or should the husband have applied for an extension of time to file his election, *viz.*, after the validity of the last will had been decided?

3. Note that if a spouse fails to elect to take under the Act within the stipulated time, the spouse is deemed to take his or her succession rights apart from the Act. It is conceivable that you might want to change your mind later about a deemed disposition as well.

4. The Ontario Law Reform Commission has recommended that spouses should be able to revoke an election and a deemed election provided the court grants an extension of time, if necessary, and any assets remain in the estate.[98]

5. Is the limitation period long enough to permit an informed election to be made?

6. The Act provides that when a surviving spouse elects to take an equalizing payment under the Act his or her rights under the deceased's will or on the deceased's intestacy are lost. What happens if a spouse made a successful application for equalization based on

---

93 (1989), 70 O.R. (2d) 146 (C.A.), affirming (1987), 8 R.F.L. (3d) 443 (Ont. H.C.).
94 See *Ward v. National Trust Co.*, unreported (October 24, 1990), (Ont. Gen. Div.).
95 See *Anderson v. Anderson Estate* (1990), 74 O.R. (2d) 58, 27 R.F.L. (3d) 88 (H.C.).
96 (1992), 59 O.R. (2d) 195, 45 E.T.R. 23, 7 R.F.L. (3d) 81 (Surr. Ct.). See also T.G. Youdan, "Revocability of an Election under Part I of the Ontario Law Reform Act" (1992), 45 E.T.R. 29.
97 (1987), 7 R.F.L. (3d) 81 (Ont. Surr. Ct.).
98 OLRC Report, 116.

marriage breakdown and the other spouse then dies leaving a will made before the marriage breakdown under which the survivor receives property? Similarly, what happens if the deceased died intestate? Is the survivor entitled to share in the estate in those circumstances?[99]

7. What happens to the gifts to others under the will to the extent that the property comprised in them is not required to pay the equalization claim?

Stewart v. Stewart Estate[100] illustrates the point. A husband left the matrimonial home and contents to his wife for life, as well as a life interest in the residue. After the wife's death, the balance of the residue including the house and contents, was to be paid or transferred to the testator's daughter. However, if the daughter should die before the date of distribution, her share went to her issue or, failing issue, to named charities. The wife and daughter were named executrices. The wife elected under the Act and the executrices proposed to divide the estate equally between them. On a motion by the Public Trustee, the court held that the daughter's interest accelerated by reason of s. 6(7) which provides that if a surviving spouse elects against a will, the will is to be interpreted as if he or she predeceased the testator.

Is the decision correct? Would the same result obtain if the remainder had been limited to the daughter upon her marriage and she was not married?

8. If the surviving spouse makes an election under the Act, can he or she still act as personal representative of the deceased?[101]

9. A spouse who has lost the right to take under the deceased spouse's will cannot elect to take under the Act. The issue arose in *Maljkovich v. Maljkovich Estate*.[102] The husband and wife had separated and tried unsuccessfully to negotiate a division of their matrimonial property. Then the husband killed his wife. Under her will he was entitled to her entire estate. He brought an application for an equalization of the spouses' nfps and moved for a declaration that he was entitled to an equalization. The estate moved for an order dismissing the application. The court dismissed the husband's motion and granted the estate's motion. The court recognized that the husband could have brought an application for equalization following the separation under s. 5(1). However, that right was not exercised before his wife's death and expired with her, since s. 7(2) provides that the right is personal as between the spouses. Thus, the husband could not rely on s. 5(1) to make his claim, but could only rely on s. 5(2). Because of the public policy rule that a person is not allowed to benefit by his or her crime, the husband was not entitled to take under his wife's will. However, his right to make an election under s. 6 only arose because he murdered his wife. Hence, the public policy rule also precluded him from invoking the right to elect.

In *dictum* the motions judge suggested that if the husband had commenced his application based on the parties' separation before the wife's death the result would have been the same. This seems to be incorrect, since the right to bring such an application would be independent of his later criminal act. Thus, to deny recovery to the husband in those circumstances would amount to forfeiture, unless it could be shown that he deliberately, as part of a conscious plan, first made the application and then killed his wife.

---

99 OLRC Report, 117-8. Note that if the parties' marriage had been dissolved or declared a nullity, the gifts in the will would, unless a contrary intention was shown, be revoked by reason of s. 17(2) of the *Succession Law Reform Act*, R.S.O. 1990, c. S.26, and the survivor would also not be entitled to share on the deceased's intestacy.

100 (1989), 67 O.R. (2d) 321 (H.C.).

101 See OLRC Report, 119-20.

102 (1995), 20 R.F.L. (4th) 222 (Ont. Gen. Div.), affirmed (1997), 33 R.F.L. (4th) 24 (Ont. C.A.).

(xi) *Priorities*

The right under the Act has priority over: (a) all gifts in the will, unless the will was made pursuant to a contract for valuable consideration; (b) a person's right to share on the deceased's intestacy; and (c) an order for dependants' support, unless the order was in favour of a child of the deceased.[103] Thus, the claim of a dependent child has priority over the claim of a spouse.[104] The priority given to beneficiaries whose gifts are made pursuant to a contract is problematic. Section 6(13) is poorly drafted and its meaning is unclear. For example, the section does not state as of what date the value of the gift is to be determined: the date of the agreement or the valuation date under the Act.[105]

Although the Act does not say so explicitly, it seems clear that a spouse's right to equalization is inferior to the rights of creditors, since spouses are entitled to deduct debts from the value of their property. Thus, by inference, the creditors have priority. The Ontario Law Reform Commission has recommended that the Act provide expressly that the equalization obligation is a debt of the estate that ranks after the claims of all other creditors.[106]

(xii) *Burden of the Equalization Payment*

The Act does not say who should bear the burden of an equalization payment. This is a serious defect. It probably means that the normal rules for allocating debts in an estate will be applied. If there is a will those rules provide that the residue is used first to pay unsecured debts. If the residue is insufficient to pay the debts, the property comprised in general legacies, specific bequests and specific devises, will be used in that order. If the deceased died intestate, the real and personal property in the estate is applied rateably to pay unsecured debts.[107] But these rules can work serious hardship. For example, a testator may give specific property to one child and the residue to another. If the testator's spouse makes a successful application for equalization, the second child will bear the burden of paying it. So also, if the testator gave legacies to others, including, perhaps, charities, and the residue to the children, the children will lose if the spouse makes a successful application under the Act. The testator probably would not want this to happen, but unless there is a provision in the will stating the order in which assets should be used to pay the debts, it will happen.

The Ontario Law Reform Commission has recommended that the Act be amended to provide that: (a) all beneficiaries shall bear the burden rateably, unless the court determines that this would be inconsistent with the testator's intentions;

---

103 *Family Law Act*, s. 6(12), (13).
104 *Gaudet (Litigation Guardian of) v. Young Estate* (1995), 11 R.F.L. (4th) 284, 7 E.T.R. (2d) 146 (Ont. Gen. Div.).
105 See OLRC Report, 122-6. For a similar provision, see *Succession Law Reform Act*, R.S.O. 1990, c. S.26, s. 71.
106 OLRC Report 128.
107 See ch. 2, part 8.

(b) beneficiaries may apply to the court to allocate the burden otherwise than rateably; and (c) the court has power to make such an allocation if it is of the opinion that this would be consistent with the testator's intentions.

Notes and Questions

1. When the court makes an order of support in favour of a dependant under Part V of the *Succession Law Reform Act*[108] it has a discretion to charge the claim against the whole or any part of the estate.[109] This is a wider discretion than that proposed by the Ontario Law Reform Commission. Which is better?

(xiii) *Payment of Entitlement*

Section 9 of the Act, which has not been reproduced above, provides, *inter alia*, that the court may order a spouse to pay the other spouse the amount of the entitlement, or give security for an obligation imposed by the order. The court also has power to permit payment in instalments over a period not exceeding 10 years to avoid hardship, and it may direct that property be transferred to the other spouse in satisfaction of the equalization obligation.

Notes and Questions

1. It has been pointed out that the underlying premise of the Act is not to make a division of assets, but rather to make provision for an after tax and disposition costs cash payment to equalize the spouses' nfp's. Hence, subject to s. 10 (which permits the court to determine questions of title to property between spouses), the court should not use s. 9(1)(d)(i) (which permits the court to direct a transfer of property) to order that property be transferred in order to satisfy the equalization obligation if the spouse liable to make the payment is able to make it in cash.[110]

(xiv) *Duties of Personal Representatives*

The Act prohibits personal representatives from making distribution for six months after a spouse's death and after notification of an application by the surviving spouse has been received, unless the surviving spouse consents or the court otherwise orders.[111] Personal representatives are personally liable to the extent prescribed by the Act if they contravene these provisions.[112]

---

108 R.S.O. 1990, c. S.26.
109 *Ibid.*, s. 68(2).
110 *Heon v. Heon* (1989), 22 R.F.L. (3d) 273 (Ont. H.C.). See also *Hoar v. Hoar* (1993), 45 R.F.L. (3d) 105 (Ont. C.A.).
111 *Family Law Act*, s. 6(14), (15).
112 *Ibid.*, s. 6(19). See also OLRC Report, 120-1.

Notes and Questions

1. The Act says that executors may not distribute once they have received notice of an application. What if they distribute after they receive a letter from the surviving spouse's solicitors stating that they are in the process of filing an election pursuant to which the surviving spouse will elect to take under the Act? In *Paola v. Paola Estate*[113] the court held that the letter did not comply with s. 6(15). Only notice of an actual application will suffice. In this respect the decision is in conflict with the law on support of dependants which holds that a letter such as that sent by the surviving spouse's solicitors would have been sufficient notice to the estate to prevent distribution.[114] The limitations provisions in the two types of legislation are quite similar.

(xv) *Agreement to Exclude Act*

Spouses may, by domestic contract, agree to exclude property from their nfp.[115]

Notes and Questions

1. How would an agreement by husband and wife to leave their property by will in a particular way, in pursuance of which they make reciprocal wills, be regarded if the surviving spouse later made application under the Act? Such an agreement attracts the mutual wills doctrine.[116]

Similarly, would a secret trust, assumed by a legatee at the request of a spouse, take priority over the claim of the surviving spouse under the Act?[117]

(xvi) *Equalization and the Matrimonial Home*

We have seen that the matrimonial home is accorded special treatment under the Act. Thus, for example, it forms part of the definition of nfp and cannot be treated as excluded property. Further, Part II of the Act confers substantial rights of possession to the matrimonial home on the spouse who does not have title. Section 26(1) of the Act, which is in Part II, has special implications for an equalization under Part I. It provides:

> **26.** (1) If a spouse dies owning an interest in a matrimonial home as a joint tenant with a third person and not with the other spouse, the joint tenancy shall be deemed to have been severed immediately before the time of death.

---

113 (1997), 16 E.T.R. (2d) 142, 27 R.F.L. (4th) 418 (Ont. Gen. Div.). See also Barry S. Corbin, Comment (1997), 17 E.T. & P.J. 3.

114 See *Re Dentinger* (1981), 10 E.T.R. 6, 128 D.L.R. (3d) 613 (Ont. Surr. Ct.), discussed in the next chapter.

115 *Ibid.*, s. 4(2).6.

116 See *Oosterhoff & Gillese: Text, Commentary and Cases on Trusts*, 5th ed. by A.H. Oosterhoff and E.E. Gillese (Scarborough: Carswell, 1998), ch. 9, part 7(b).

117 See *ibid.*, ch. 9, part 7(a).

The intent of s. 26(1) is clear: it is to ensure that the surviving spouse will be able to receive credit for the half-interest in the property owned by the deceased spouse. Were it not for this provision, the third person would take the whole interest. But the provision's net is cast too wide. Although perhaps not intended, the section is not restricted to the situation in which the property is the matrimonial home of the spouses. If it is the matrimonial home of the third person, there is no need for a severance but, as worded, the provision would apply. It would also apply if the surviving spouse's equalization payment can be satisfied out of other property and if the surviving spouse does not elect for equalization but for his or her succession rights. In those circumstances, too, there is no need for a severance. For that reason, the Ontario Law Reform Commission has recommended that the section be amended to give the surviving spouse a lien against the property when necessary. If this recommendation is adopted, the surviving joint tenant will be able to keep the property after satisfying the lien.

Notes and Questions

1. *Whaley Estate v. Whaley*[118] illustrates the problems caused by the section. A father and daughter held joint title to property which later became the matrimonial home. The father's will left the residue of his estate to certain charities and did not refer to the matrimonial home. The widow made no claim under the Act for an equalization payment. If s. 26(1) were applied literally, the daughter would not be able to take the property by right of survivorship and the charities would take her father's 50 percent interest. The court held that it was not necessary to apply s. 26(1) literally in the circumstances, but that it should be read as if it applies only when the surviving spouse exercises the right to elect for equalization.

2. In *Fulton v. Fulton*[119] the Ontario Court of Appeal held that the section must be read literally. The husband owned property jointly with his son. When the husband remarried, the property became the matrimonial home. He died intestate and the court held that s. 26(1) had the effect of converting the joint tenancy into a tenancy in common, so that one-half the value of the property went to the husband's estate. In passing, the court noted that the section must be applied even if the equalization claim can be satisfied from other property. The court did not expressly overrule *Whaley*, but that would appear to have been the effect.

Problems

1. The following problems are simplified to illustrate specific aspects of the legislation. They assume that the parties did not bring any assets into the marriage and that they had no debts. In each problem, determine whether W should claim under the Act or under the will or intestacy, as the case may be.

(a) H died, survived by W and D, a daughter by a prior marriage. H left $800,000 nfp; W had $200,000 nfp. H and W's respective non-nfp's were negligible. H left $150,000 absolutely to W by his will and the rest to D.

---

118 (1993), 1 E.T.R. (2d) 59 (Ont. Gen. Div.).
119 (1994), 2 E.T.R. (2d) 113 (Ont. C.A.).

(b) As in problem (a), but H left $550,000 to D and the residue of his estate to a charity which had ceased to exist before his death and the rest to D. The gift to W was the same. The gift to the charity lapsed, resulting in a partial intestacy.

(c) As in problem (a), but H died intestate.

(d) As in problem (c), but H owned a policy of insurance on his life in the amount of $100,000, of which W is the beneficiary. The amount of the policy is in addition to H's other assets. H did not make a declaration to the effect that W should receive the proceeds of the policy in addition to her other rights under the Act.

(e) As in problem (d), but the insurance proceeds are payable to H's estate.

(f) As in problem (a), but H owned a pension of $600,000. W is entitled to a survivor benefit under the pension plan, consisting of a lifetime annuity of $20,000 per annum. Assume the present value of the annuity to be $200,000. The pension is in addition to H's other assets.

(g) As in problem (a), but H left his estate to W for life, with remainder to D. Assume that the present value of the life interest is $80,000.

(h) As in problem (a), but H received an inheritance of $200,000 after the marriage and bought the matrimonial home with it. This amount is comprehended in H's nfp as stated in problem 1. W received a gift of $100,000 from her parents after marriage. She invested this money in high income bearing securities and spent the income annually on family vacations.

(i) As in problem (a), but W's nfp consists of the matrimonial home which she inherited from her parents, while H's $800,000 is not nfp, but consists of $400,000 obtained in a personal injury settlement and $400,000 inherited money. He invested the former in non-income producing shares of a potentially lucrative business, while he used the income from the latter to set D up in business.

2. When H and W were married, he owned some investments worth $75,000, and had debts of $25,000. He was a widower and had a daughter, D, by his first wife. H lived in a house that became the matrimonial home. It was worth $100,000. W had a bank account which contained $5,000. She had no debts. After the marriage, H and W bought a cottage, taking title in their joint names. H later took title to Blackacre, another property, jointly with his brother. W's parents left her $500,000 after H and W's marriage. She invested this money wisely and reinvested the income every year.

H died this year in an automobile accident at age 55. He left $200,000 to W and the rest to D by his will. The value of H's assets the day before he died was as follows: the matrimonial home: $500,000; the half-interest in the cottage: $100,000; a policy of insurance on his life of which D was the beneficiary: $300,000; an interest under a pension plan of which W was the beneficiary: $200,000; the half interest in Blackacre: $300,000; and various investments: $500,000. His other assets were negligible, but he owed debts, including taxes, in the amount of $75,000.

The value of W's assets the day before H's death was as follows: investments: $700,000, of which $200,000 represented income earned on the original inheritance; her half interest in the cottage: $100,000; a bank account: $10,000; and a lump sum payment under H's pension: $25,000. Her other assets were negligible. Her debts were $10,000.

Calculate the parties' nfps and advise W.

4. LEGISLATION IN OTHER PROVINCES

The legislation in the other provinces in which a surviving spouse is allowed to make a claim under matrimonial property legislation after the other spouse's death is not as extensive as in Ontario and the Northwest Territories. As mentioned above, the Northwest Territories statute is very similar to Ontario's legislation, but applies also to cohabitees and cohabitees probably include same-sex partners.[120] The following is a summary of the legislation in the other provinces. It should be noted that all statutes confer a right to an order for an equal division of matrimonial assets, not a right to an equalization payment.[121] Moreover, the property to which each statute applies is usually defined by reference to the property used by the family for family purposes.

In Prince Edward Island[122] and Yukon Territory[123] the legislation does not apply after a spouse has died, but an application brought before death may be continued. The Prince Edward Island legislation is very similar to Ontario's but does not allow for an application to be made by a surviving spouse. The Yukon Act provides for equal division of family assets on marriage breakdown, but not on death.

Under Part 5 of the British Columbia *Family Relations Act*,[124] each spouse is entitled on marriage breakdown to an undivided half interest in the family assets as tenants in common. The court has power under s. 65 to vary the proportion if the division would otherwise be unfair. Part 6 of the Act makes provision for the division of pension entitlements.

The Alberta legislation permits an application for division of matrimonial property to be brought by a surviving spouse within six months after a grant of probate or administration in the estate of the other spouse, but only if the application could have been commenced immediately before death.[125] Thus, the application can only be made if there has been a breakdown of the marriage, divorce or annulment, or an attempted improvident gift or dissipation of the estate.[126] The court must have regard to any benefits the applicant received as a result of the death of the deceased spouse.[127] Further, an order made under the Act, takes precedence over the rights of beneficiaries of the deceased spouse's estate.[128] The right of a surviving spouse to make an application for dependants' support is expressly preserved.[129]

The Manitoba legislation is similar to Alberta's, in that it entitles an application to be made by a surviving spouse after the death of the other spouse, but only if a right to division of assets existed at the death of the other spouse, that is, if there had been a breakdown of the marriage.[130] The rights of a surviving spouse under the Act are in addition to that spouse's homestead rights[131] under the *Homesteads*

---

120 *Family Law Act*, S.N.W.T. 1997, c. 18, Part III.
121 The courts have a discretion to direct an unequal division in certain situations.
122 *Family Law Act*, S.P.E.I. 1995, c. 12, s. 7(2).
123 *Family Property and Support Act*, R.S.Y. 1986, c. 63, s. 18.
124 R.S.B.C. 1996, c. 128.
125 *Matrimonial Property Act*, R.S.A. 1980, c. M-9, s. 11.
126 *Ibid.*, s. 5.
127 *Ibid.*, s. 11.
128 *Ibid.*, s. 15.
129 *Ibid.*, s. 16.
130 *Marital Property Act*, R.S.M. 1987, c. M45 [am. 1992, c. 46], ss. 25, 28.
131 *Ibid.*, s. 44.

Act,[132] which gives the spouses rights of occupation in the homestead while both spouses are living and a life estate in the homestead to the survivor.

In contrast, the statutes in New Brunswick, Newfoundland and Nova Scotia are more like Ontario's in that these statutes permit an application for a division of the matrimonial property to be brought by a surviving spouse whether or not there has been a breakdown of the marriage. However, these statutes are unlike Ontario's in that they apply only to matrimonial property and do not provide for an equalizing payment, but for a division of property.

The New Brunswick Act requires the application to brought within six months of the death of the first spouse. On the application, the court must direct that the interest of the deceased spouse in the matrimonial home vest in the survivor. This right takes priority over the right to an equal division of the marital property.[133] Further, an order under the legislation takes precedence over the deceased's will and any dependants' support order.[134]

Payne v. Payne[135] illustrates the legislation. When he became ill, a husband conveyed his interest in the joint tenancy in the matrimonial home to his wife. The parties had been married for almost 35 years and the home had been purchased with jointly-owned funds. Shortly before she died, the wife sold the home and kept the proceeds. Her will left all her estate, which was comprised almost entirely of the proceeds of sale of the home, to her children from a prior marriage. After her death, her husband applied for an order transferring the proceeds of the home to him. The court held that this was not possible, since the proceeds of sale were not the same as the home. However, under s. 4(1) of the Act, the court ordered an unequal division of the matrimonial property to avoid inequity.

The Newfoundland Act provides that a surviving spouse may apply for a division of the matrimonial assets.[136] The surviving spouse's rights under the legislation are in addition to the right to inherit from the deceased spouse, but they are a factor to be taken into account on an application for dependants' support.[137]

In Nova Scotia, the surviving spouse must bring the application within six months after letters probate or letters of administration have been issued in the estate of the deceased spouse. The legislation provides that the surviving spouse's rights are in addition to his or her rights of inheritance from the deceased spouse.[138]

Re Fraser[139] illustrates how the legislation works. The deceased left the matrimonial home to his wife for life or until she no longer wished to reside in it. and the remainder of his estate to his daughter by a previous marriage. Mrs Fraser applied to have the matrimonial assets divided. The matrimonial home had been

---

132 S.M. 1992, c. 46.
133 *Leblanc v. Leblanc* (1984), 18 E.T.R. 160 (N.B.Q.B.). See also *O'Brien v. Johnson* (1990), 39 E.T.R. 129 (N.B.C.A.), leave to appeal to S.C.C. refused (1991), 41 E.T.R. 158n.
134 *Marital Property Act*, S.N.B. 1980, c. M-1.1, s. 4.
135 (1998), 159 D.L.R. (4th) 620 (N.B.C.A.).
136 *Family Law Act*, R.S.N. 1990, c. F-2 [am. S.N. 1997, c. 33], s. 21(1).
137 *Ibid.*, s. 21(2).
138 *Matrimonial Property Act*, R.S.N.S. 1989, c. 275, s. 12.
139 (1981), 25 R.F.L. (2d) 171, 130 D.L.R. (3d) 665 (N.S.T.D.).

sold pursuant to court order and the proceeds paid into court. Section 12(4) of the Act[140] provided that any right under the Act was in addition to the rights the surviving spouse had as a result of the death of the other spouse, whether those rights arise on intestacy or by will. The court granted Mrs. Fraser's application, holding that the legislation was clear and unambiguous.[141]

The Saskatchewan legislation enables a surviving spouse to bring an application within six months after the grant of probate or administration in the deceased spouse's estate. It provides that the surviving spouse's rights are in addition to his or her rights on the deceased's intestacy.[142] Further, an order transferring property to the surviving spouse under the Act has the effect of excluding it from the deceased's estate, but the court may direct that it remains part of the estate to safeguard the rights of the deceased's creditors.[143]

The Saskatchewan Court of Appeal has held that if a spouse makes an application for equal division of the matrimonial property because of marriage break-down, the applicant cannot discontinue the application without consent when the other spouse dies. The institution of the proceedings is a recognition of the right of the other spouse to a half interest in the matrimonial property and the estate of that spouse may continue to assert the right in the proceedings.[144]

5. OTHER RIGHTS

(a) Generally

A surviving spouse may have other rights in addition to a right to division of the matrimonial assets. These include rights under will substitutes, a right to bring application for support, and homestead rights. The first of these is dealt with elsewhere.[145] This right is restricted under the Ontario legislation, as discussed earlier in this chapter. We shall discuss the second right in the next chapter. We shall consider the third right presently, but we must first make reference to a spouse's right in the matrimonial home.

(b) The Matrimonial Home

Under matrimonial legislation in the several provinces, both spouses have an equal right to possession of the matrimonial home. However, the right is a personal one and ceases when the parties cease to be spouses. Thus, if one spouse has title

---

140 Then S.N.S. 1980, c. 9.
141 For a similar case, but in which the widow's application for division was unsuccessful, see *Re Levy* (1981), 25 R.F.L. (2d) 149, 131 D.L.R. (3d) 15 (N.S.T.D.).
142 *Matrimonial Property Act, 1997*, S.S. 1997, c. M-6.11, s. 30.
143 *Ibid.*, s. 35.
144 *Boychuk v. Boychuk Estate* (1993), 2 E.T.R. (2d) 81 (Sask. C.A.).
145 In the chapter on the Nature of Testamentary Dispositions.

to the matrimonial home, both have equal rights of possession, but upon divorce or death the right of the non-titled spouse ceases. It may, however, be continued after they cease to be spouses if a separation agreement or court order so provides. Hence, it is possible for a surviving spouse to have continuing possessory rights to the matrimonial home. The statutes typically provide that the parties may register a designation of a parcel of land as the matrimonial home. They also contain provisions prohibiting the titled spouse from alienating or encumbering the matrimonial home without the consent of the other spouse, but protect the *bona fide* purchaser for value without notice.[146]

(c) Dower, Curtesy and Homestead Rights

The traditional common law rights of dower and curtesy, as extended by statute, no longer exist in Canada. Dower was the right of a wife to a life estate in one-third of all the real property to which her husband died solely seised and, by statute, to which he died beneficially entitled. The right existed in inchoate form while the husband was alive and prevented him from alienating his real property without her consent or bar of dower, save in special circumstances. The right became consummate on the husband's death. Usually, however, the widow would elect to take her other rights on intestacy or under her husband's will, since those rights tended to be more valuable. Curtesy was the husband's right to a life estate in all of his wife's property which she did not dispose of by will. Neither right has existed in Newfoundland for many years. The two rights were abolished as part of the wholesale reform of matrimonial property reform that took place in Ontario and the Maritime provinces in the 1970s and 1980s.[147]

Dower and curtesy in the sense defined above were abolished in the Western Provinces at an early stage in their existence and replaced with a statutory dower or homestead right. The latter survived the matrimonial property reform of the 1970s and 1980s in those provinces. We shall now consider this right briefly.[148]

---

146 See *Family Law Act*, R.S.N. 1990 (am. S.N. 1997, c. 33), Part I: the Act confers a half-interest in the matrimonial home (or homes, since there may be more than one) on each spouse, title to be held in joint tenancy unless title was taken under a tenancy in common; *Family Law Act* (Ont.), Part II; *Family Law Act*, S.P.E.I. 1995, c. 12, Part II; *Family Law Act*, S.N.W.T. 1997, c. 18, Part IV; *Family Relations Act*, R.S.B.C. 1996, c. 128, ss. 5, 6(1)(d),(e), 77: the court is empowered to grant temporary exclusive occupancy rights; *Family Property and Support Act*, R.S.Y. 1986, c. 63 (am. S.Y. 1991, c. 11, s. 198; S.Y. 1998, c. 8), Part 2; *Marital Property Act*, R.S.M. 1987, c. M45, s. 6(2): the right is subject to an order under the *Family Maintenance Act*, R.S.M. 1987, c. F20, under s. 13(1) of which the court may award exclusive possession to one spouse; *Marital Property Act*, S.N.B. 1980, c. M-1.1, Part II: the proceeds of sale or expropriation are held in trust equally for both spouses; *Matrimonial Property Act*, R.S.A. 1980, c. M-9, Part 2; R.S.N.S. 1989, c. 275, s. 11; S.S. 1997, c. M-6.11, Part III.

147 See further Anger and Honsberger, *Law of Real Property*, 2nd ed. by A.H. Oosterhoff and W.B. Rayner (Aurora: Canada Law Book Inc., 1985), §§707-707.20, 708-708.2, 709.

148 See further, *ibid.*, §§710-710.15.

The statutory right is referred to variously as a dower right, a homestead right or a matrimonial property right, and the several statutes[149] define this right in different ways. Typically, the homestead is a parcel of land on which the dwelling occupied by the owner of the parcel as his or her residence is situate. The size of the parcel varies from province to province and with urban and rural locations. Except in British Columbia, the homestead is created by statute and does not, therefore, have to be registered. In British Columbia it must be registered.[150] Normally there is only one homestead, but in Saskatchewan any property that has been a homestead remains a homestead.[151]

The essence of the homestead right is that the surviving spouse receives a life estate in the homestead which takes priority over the deceased spouse's will. However, the definition varies from province to province and reference should be made to the several statutes for the exact definition of the right. In Alberta[152] the surviving spouse also receives a life estate in the personal property of the deceased that is exempt from seizure.

The homestead right is in addition to the surviving spouse's rights under the deceased's will or on the deceased's intestacy, but the surviving spouse may be required to make an election in the case of a will.[153] The surviving spouse's homestead right usually takes priority over dependants' support orders in favour of other dependants.[154] The right is in addition to the rights conferred by matrimonial property legislation.[155] The homestead right is lost if the spouse consents in writing to the disposition of the homestead, or releases his or her rights, or when the court dispenses with consent.[156]

---

149 *Dower Act*, R.S.A. 1980, c. D-38; *Land (Spouse Protection) Act*, R.S.B.C. 1996, c. 246; *Homesteads Act*, S.M. 1992, c. 46; S.S. 1989-90, c. H-5.1.

150 *Land (Spouse Protection) Act* (B.C.), *supra*, ss. 1, 2.

151 *Homesteads Act* (Sask.), *supra*, s. 2(c), 3, 4.

152 *Dower Act* (Alta.), *supra*, s. 23.

153 *Law of Property Act*, R.S.M. 1987, c. L90, ss. 9, 10. See, *e.g.*, *Ritchot v. Ritchot Estate* (1989), 33 E.T.R. 12 (Man. C.A.).

154 See, *e.g.*, *Family Relief Act*, R.S.A. 1980, c. F-2, s. 4; *Dependants Relief Act*, S.M. 1989-90, c. 42, s. 18.

155 *Matrimonial Property Act*, R.S.A. 1980, c. M-9, s. 28; S.S. 1979, c. M-6.1, ss. 16, 52; *Family Relations Act*, R.S.B.C. 1996, c. 128, s. 124(7).

156 *Dower Act*, R.S.A. 1980, c. D-38, s. 2; *Land (Spouse Protection) Act*, R.S.B.C. 1996, c. 246, s. 3; *Homesteads Act*, S.M. 1992, c. 46, s. 4; S.S. 1989-90, c. H-5.1, s. 5.

17

SUPPORT OF DEPENDANTS

1. INTRODUCTION

Freedom of testation has been a hallowed principle of Anglo-Canadian law for as long as wills and testaments have been allowed. This freedom was never an absolute, however. It was circumscribed by rules of public policy such as the rules prohibiting restraints on alienation, the several rules against perpetuities and the rule in *Shelley's Case*.[1] More recently various forms of death taxes have limited a testator's right to dispose of his or her property as the testator sees fit. Since 1900, legislation permitting dependants of a testator to seek support out of the estate has further restricted testamentary freedom. The purpose of this legislation is to provide support and maintenance to a person's dependants if the person was under a duty to provide support for them and failed to make adequate provision for them on death. An ancillary purpose is to relieve the state or other organizations from the obligation of providing support for such persons.

There are other ways in which these results can be achieved. The principal method is forced-share legislation, which requires that a certain proportion of a testator's estate go to his or her dependants. Legislation of this type is in force in some of the American states. The Canadian provinces, like the other common law jurisdictions have, however, opted for a type of legislation which vests a discretion in the court to determine whether the applicant is a dependant, whether the testator failed to make adequate provision for the applicant and, if so, how much the applicant should receive out of the estate.

Another method is to make provision for the surviving spouse by conferring on that spouse a right to an equalization payment. This was described in the previous chapter.

The first support of dependants statute was enacted in New Zealand in 1900.[2] Similar statutes were enacted in Alberta[3] and Saskatchewan[4] in 1910, British

---

1 (1581), 1 Co. Rep. 936, 76 E.R. 206.
2 *Testator's Family Maintenance Act*, 64 Vict., c. 20 (1900, N.Z.).
3 *Dependants' Relief Act*, S.O. 1929, c. 47.
4 *An Act to Amend the Devolution of Estates Act*, S.S. 1910-11, c. 13.

Columbia in 1920,[5] and Ontario in 1929.[6] The other provinces followed suit later. Today, support of dependants legislation, often referred to as dependants' relief and testator's family maintenance legislation, is in force in all Canadian common law jurisdictions. These materials concentrate on the Ontario legislation.

The modern Canadian statutes, although based on the *Uniform Dependants' Relief Act*,[7] differ in many respects from the English and Australasian statutes. Moreover, the legislation has been interpreted differently in the several commonwealth countries and the Canadian provinces. Hence you must be careful in applying cases from other jurisdictions.

You should note that while each province has a principal statute governing support of dependants, there may be other statutes that confer ancillary rights of support. Thus, for example, until recent reforms, in British Columbia the court had jurisdiction under ss. 1 and 76 of the *Estate Administration Act*,[8] to make a support order in favour of an intestate's "common law spouse,"[9] but this provision has now been repealed as redundant.[10] The court has jurisdiction under s. 111 of that Act to permit a surviving spouse who was separated from the deceased intestate spouse for not less than one year to share in the estate.[11]

The Ontario legislation was formerly contained in the *Dependants' Relief Act*,[12] but that statute was repealed by the *Succession Law Reform Act*.[13] Provisions for support are now contained in Part V of the latter Act.[14] The provisions in Part V were intended to mesh with the *inter vivos* support provisions contained in the *Family Law Reform Act*[15] and the statute which replaced it, the *Family Law Act*.[16] You should note that s. 34(4) of the latter Act provides that an *inter vivos* support order binds the estate of the payor unless the order states otherwise.[17] There are similar provisions in other jurisdictions.[18] It may also be possible to increase an *inter vivos* support order against the estate of a deceased spouse, even though the deceased tried to make alternative provision for the dependant by will.[19]

---

5 *Testator's Family Maintenance Act*, S.B.C. 1920, c. 94.

6 *Dependants' Relief Act*, S.O. 1929, c. 47.

7 Uniform Law Conference of Canada, *Uniform Acts* (1978, current revision), p. 11-1.

8 R.S.B.C. 1996, c.122.

9 The term is used restrictively. For an interpretation, see *Desjarlais v. McDonnel Estate* (1988), 31 E.T.R. 18 (B.C.C.A.); *McKelvie v. Heather* (1988), 31 E.T.R. 231 (B.C.S.C.); *Re Stout Estate* (1989), 33 E.T.R. 263 (B.C.S.C.); *Sudar v. McKay Estate* (1990), 36 E.T.R. 83 (B.C.S.C.); *Keddie v. Currie* (1991), 44 E.T.R. 61 (B.C.C.A.); *Wepruck v. McMillan Estate* (1993), 49 E.T.R. 209 (B.C.C.A.).

10 *Definition of Spouse Amendment Act, 1999*, S.B.C. 1999, c. 29, s. 9.

11 See *Law v. Tretiak* (1993), 50 E.T.R. 176 (B.C.C.A.).

12 R.S.O. 1970, c. 126 [am. S.O. 1973, c. 13, s. 1].

13 S.O. 1977, c. 40, s. 87.

14 Now R.S.O. 1990, c. S.26. This Act is hereafter in this chapter referred to without further citation.

15 S.O. 1978, c. 2, Part II, consolidated as R.S.O. 1990, c. 152.

16 S.O. 1986, c. 4, Part III, consolidated as R.S.O. 1990, c. F.3.

17 See also *Butler v. Butler Estate* (1990), 38 E.T.R. 93 (Ont. C.A.).

18 In British Columbia the order does not bind the estate unless it so provides. See *Despot v. Despot* (1992), 46 E.T.R. 169 (B.C.S.C.).

19 See *Will v. Thauberger Estate* (1991), 44 E.T.R. 266 (Sask. C.A.).

While some statutes allow common law spouses to apply for support, until recently this right was not extended to same-sex partners. The issue came before the Supreme Court of Canada in *M. v. H.*[20] A same-sex partner sought support *inter vivos* from the other partner after the relationship broke up. The court held that the *inter vivos* support provisions of the *Family Law Act*[21] infringed the equality provisions of the *Charter* because, while they allowed married persons and common law spouses to claim support, they did not allow same-sex partners to do so. As a consequence of the decision, Ontario amended a large number of statutes to include same-sex partners.[22] Among the statutes amended were the support provisions of the *Family Law Act* and the *Succession Law Reform Act*.

Case law in other provinces suggests that similar legislation will be forthcoming elsewhere. Thus, in *Grigg v. Berg Estate*[23] the court held that s. 2 of the British Columbia *Wills Variation Act*,[24] which permitted spouses to seek support by means of an order varying a will, infringed the right of a common law spouse to equal treatment under the *Charter*. The court read a definition that had not yet been enacted into the section to include common law spouses.

Subsequently, the British Columbia Legislature enacted the *Definition of Spouse Amendment Act, 1999*,[25] which permits same-sex partners and common law spouses to apply for support. That change was clarified by the *Definition of Spouse Amendment Act, 2000*.[26]

Further Reading

Rodney Hull, *Support of Dependants under The Succession Law Reform Act of Ontario* (1978).

A.H. Oosterhoff, *Succession Law Reform in Ontario* (1979), Part V.

A.H. Oosterhoff, "The Effect of Death on Familial Obligations" (1981), 23 R.F.L. (2d) 272.

A.H. Oosterhoff, "Some Aspects of Support of Dependants" (1983), 12 E.T.R. 197.

Macdonell, Sheard and Hull on Probate Practice, 4th ed. by Rodney Hull and Ian M. Hull (Scarborough: Carswell, 1986), c. 6.

Law Reform Commission of British Columbia, "Report on Statutory Succession Rights" (1983), chapter III — Dependant's Relief.

T.G. Youdan, "Status of a Dependant under Part V of the Ontario Succession Law Reform Act" (1986), 21 E.T.R. 303.

Leopold Amighetti, *The Law of Dependants' Relief in British Columbia* (Carswell, 1991).

Brian A. Schnurr and Suzan J. Woodley, "Dependant Support Proceedings" (1994), 14 E. & T.J. 159.

---

20 [1999] 2 S.C.R. 3, 171 D.L.R. (4th) 577.
21 R.S.O. 1990, c. F.3, Part III.
22 See *Amendments Because of the Supreme Court of Canada Decision in M. v. H. Act, 1999*, S.O. 1999, c. 6.
23 (2000), 31 E.T.R. (2d) 214, 186 D.L.R. (4th) 160 (B.C.S.C.)
24 1996, c. 490.
25 S.B.C. 1999, c. 29, ss. 17, 18.
26 S.B.C. 2000, c. 24, s. 13.

Brian A. Schnurr, "Claims by Common Law Spouses and Same-Sex Partners against Estates" (1997), 16 E. & T.J. 22.

2. THE APPLICATION

(a) The Court

An application for support in Ontario lies to the Superior Court of Justice.[27] The application is filed in the office of the court in the county or district in which the application for letters probate or letters for administration was, or ought to be, filed. That is the court office in the county or district in which the deceased had a fixed place of abode at the time of death or, if the deceased had no fixed place of abode, the court office in any county or district in which the deceased had property at the time of death or, if the deceased had no property in any county or district, any office of the court.[28]

(b) Procedure

A person seeking support does so by making application and the court may deal with an application by any dependant as an application on behalf of all dependants, so that the matter can be disposed of in one hearing and multiple proceedings can be avoided.[29]

Notice of the application must be served upon all interested persons,[30] including the deceased's personal representative[31] and, if the application is made by or on behalf of a patient in a psychiatric facility to which the *Mental Health Act*[32] applies or a resident in a facility to which the *Developmental Services Act*[33] applies, the Public Guardian and Trustee.[34]

Failure to give notice means that the application will be set aside.[35] However, the court has power to dispense with notice in appropriate cases.[36]

Applications may be dealt with on the basis of affidavit evidence alone,[37] but the more usual practice is to have a trial with *viva voce* evidence, since there are often serious disputes about the facts.[38]

---

27 *Succession Law Reform Act*, ss. 57 [am. S.O. 1999, c. 6, s. 61(6)], 58(1).
28 *Estates Act*, R.S.O. 1990, c. E.21, s. 7.
29 *Succession Law Reform Act*, s. 60.
30 *Ibid.*, s. 63(5).
31 *Ibid.*, s. 67(1).
32 R.S.O. 1990, c. M.7.
33 R.S.O. 1990, c. D.11.
34 *Succession Law Reform Act*, s. 74(2). Notice of the application for letters probate or letters of administration must also be served upon the Public Guardian and Trustee in those circumstances: *ibid.*, s. 74(1). Section 25(1) of the *Consent and Capacity Statute Law Amendment Act*, S.O. 1992, c. 32, renamed the "Public Trustee" the "Public Guardian and Trustee."
35 *Re Weir*, [1963] 1 O.R. 53 (C.A.).
36 *Succession Law Reform Act*, s. 63(6).
37 *Re Czajkowski*, [1963] 2 O.R. 513, 40 D.L.R. (2d) 270 (C.A.). You should note that s. 13 of the

(c) Limitation Period

The legislation provides that an application must be brought within six months of the grant of letters probate or letters of administration, but the court has a discretion to extend the time if any assets remain undistributed at the time of the application.[39] The purpose of the limitation period is to avoid delays in the administration and distribution of estates.[40] However, the courts have readily granted extensions of time, even if the application is brought long after the death of the deceased,[41] if that is equitable, having regard to the claims of all the parties.[42] An application to extend the time and the application for support are normally heard together.

The court has power to make an order suspending the administration of the estate upon the application of a dependant.[43] Moreover, once an application is made and notice thereof is served on the personal representative, distribution is stayed, as appears from s. 67 of the Act, reproduced below. The combined effect of the limitation period and s. 67 is discussed in *Re Dentinger*,[44] also reproduced in part below.

SUCCESSION LAW REFORM ACT
R.S.O. 1990, c. S.26

61. (1) Subject to subsection (2), no application for an order under section 58 may be made after six months from the grant of letters probate of the will or of letters of administration.

(2) The court, if it considers it proper, may allow an application to be made at any time as to any portion of the estate remaining undistributed at the date of the application.

. . .

67. (1) Where an application is made and notice thereof is served on the personal representative of the deceased, he or she shall not, after service of the notice upon him or her, unless all persons entitled to apply consent or the court otherwise

---

Evidence Act, R.S.O. 1990, c. 145, which requires corroboration in actions by or against estates, does not apply in applications for support: *Re Blackwell*, [1948] O.R. 522, [1948] 3 D.L.R. 621 (C.A.). But see *Re Ruby* (1983), 43 O.R. (2d) 277 (Surr. Ct.).

38 Applications for support are considered to be part of the "contentious business" of the surrogate court: *Re Jervas*, [1954] O.W.N. 48 (C.A.).

39 *Succession Law Reform Act*, s. 61.

40 *Maldaver v. Can. Permanent Trust Co.* (1977), 27 N.S.R. (2d) 248, 1 E.T.R. 41 (T.D.).

41 See, *e.g.*, *Re Bourne*, [1950] O.W.N. 807 (Surr. Ct.), a period of ten years; *Zaplotinsky v. Zaplotinsky* (1980), 14 Alta. L.R. (2d) 6, 8 E.T.R. 139 (Q.B.), application would have been granted after 25 years but for the fact that the estate was fully administered.

42 *Re Deis; Spicer v. Deis* (1983), 21 Sask. R. 328, 13 E.T.R. 88 (C.A.); *Re Stewart*, [1944] O.W.N. 380 (C.A.).

43 *Succession Law Reform Act*, s. 59.

44 (1981), 10 E.T.R. 6, 128 D.L.R. (3d) 613 (Ont. Surr. Ct.).

orders, proceed with the distribution of the estate until the court has disposed of the application.

(2) Nothing in this Part prevents a personal representative from making reasonable advances for support to dependants who are beneficiaries.

(3) Where a personal representative distributes any portion of the estate in violation of subsection (1), if any provision for support is ordered by the court to be made out of the estate, the personal representative is personally liable to pay the amount of the distribution to the extent that such provision or any part thereof ought, pursuant to the order or this Part, to be made out of the portion of the estate distributed.

Comparable Legislation

Dependants of a Deceased Person Relief Act, R.S.P.E.I. 1988, c. D-6, ss. 9, 13; *Dependants Relief Act*, R.S.N.W.T. 1988, c. D-4, ss. 8, 13; R.S.Y. 1986, c. 44, ss. 9, 14; *Dependants' Relief Act*, S.M. 1989-90, c. 42, ss. 6, 7; S.S. 1996, c. D-25.01, ss. 15-17; *Family Relief Act*, R.S.A. 1980, c. F-2 [am. 1984, c. 55, s. 20], ss. 15, 17; R.S.N. 1990, c. F-3, ss. 9, 14; *Provision for Dependants Act*, R.S.N.B. 1973, c. T-4 [renamed S.N.B. 1991, c. 62, s. 3(1)], ss. 8, 14; *Testators' Family Maintenance Act*, R.S.N.S. 1989, c. 465, ss. 9, 14; *Wills Variation Act*, R.S.B.C. 1996, c. 490 [am. S.B.C. 1999, c. 29, ss. 17, 18; S.B.C. 2000, c. 24, s. 13], ss. 3, 10, 12.

RE DENTINGER
(1981), 10 E.T.R. 6, 128 D.L.R. (3d) 613
Ontario Surrogate Court
[Bruce County]

The applicant was the deceased's second wife. He left her some property by his will, but the residue of his estate was left equally to his four children by his first marriage. The deceased's executrices were two of his daughters. They obtained probate on December 7, 1979. On January 16, 1980 the applicant informed the executrices' solicitor that she intended to make an application for support. Within the next three weeks the executrices distributed most of the property to themselves and the other two residuary beneficiaries. The applicant commenced proceedings for support on April 11, 1980, that is, slightly more than four months after probate was granted.

CARTER SURR. CT. J.:

In Gilles v. Althouse,[45] the Supreme Court of Canada had occasion to consider The Dependants' Relief Act of Saskatchewan.[46] There, as here, the estate had

---

45 [1976] 1 S.C.R. 353, 20 R.F.L. 41 at 43, [1975] 5 W.W.R. 549, 4 N.R. 36, 33 D.L.R. (3d) 410.
46 R.S.S. 1965, c. 128.

been fully distributed, and the Saskatchewan Court of Appeal[47] had concluded for that reason that no order for maintenance could be made. In a unanimous judgment, overruling the Saskatchewan Court of Appeal, delivered by Dickson J., the Court drew attention to ss. 15 and 16(1) of the Saskatchewan Act, which are similar to ss. 68 and 74(1),[48] of The Succession Law Reform Act. In that case, as here, the estate had been rapidly distributed. Unlike this case, prior to distribution and commencing proceedings the claimant had written a letter to the executrices, which they had interpreted as a disclaimer — quite the reverse of what we have here — where the intention of making a claim was transmitted to them. . . . Dickson J. writes:[49]

> Section 16 must be read with s. 15, the combined effect of which in my opinion is to inhibit an executor for a period of six months from distributing the assets of an estate if there is the possibility of an application under the Act; after six months the executor is free to distribute the estate unless and until he receives notice of an application under the Act. (The italics are mine).

Again at p. 360:

> At least until expiry of the six-month period Mrs. Gilles was a potential applicant under The Dependants' Relief Act. She did not effectively disclaim any rights which she might have under that Act. Executors or administrators have a duty not to distribute before the expiry of the limitation period if the possibility of an application for relief is hanging over the estate; if they do so they do so at their peril: see Re: Simson (deceased), Simson v. National Provincial Bank, Ltd. and Others.[50] (Author's italics).

I am of the firm view that these remarks of Dickson J. apply with equal force to s. 68(1) and s. 74(1) of The Succession Law Reform Act, and they apply with even more force in the case before me, as the solicitor for the applicant had advised the estate solicitor in writing of the applicant's intended claim before distribution was made.

> [Having already held that a lump sum award should be made to the applicant, His Honour, therefore, found the two executrices personally liable, jointly and severally, under what is now section 67(3) of the Act. Moreover, since the estate had already been distributed because of the precipitate action of the executrices and since the executrices and the other two children put forward a common position, the applicant's costs on a solicitor and client basis and on the Supreme Court scale were directed to be paid by the respondents.]

Notes and Questions

1. The *Dentinger* case also holds that the power of the personal representative to make advances to dependants who are beneficiaries under s. 67(2) requires that such advances be charged against the beneficiaries' shares and not against the entire estate as a debt.

---

47 (Sub nom. *Re Gilles*) [1973] 4 W.W.R. 561, 20 R.F.L. 41, 37 D.L.R. (3d) 635 (Sask. C.A.).
48 Now ss. 61 and 67(1).
49 At S.C.R. 358.
50 [1950] 1 Ch. 38.

2. In some provinces distribution is not merely stayed, but prohibited during the limitation period, whether or not notice of an application is served on the personal representative.[51]

3. What constitutes service of the notice upon the personal representative?

In *Re Gold*[52] an application for an extension of time was made and notice thereof was served on the estate's solicitors. They informed the executor and sole beneficiary who thereupon transferred the assets to himself. It was held that the service upon the solicitors and the executor's knowledge thereof was sufficient to stay distribution.

4. While the court has jurisdiction to add applicants to an existing application in appropriate circumstances, it cannot waive the limitation period to allow a potential applicant to bring an application, even though the executor knew of the potential claim within the limitation period.[53]

5. If the personal representatives have transferred the estate to themselves as beneficiaries during the limitation period, the court can make an order against the property in favour of dependants who make a claim within the period.[54] Can an order to extend the time and an order for support be made if the sole personal representative and sole beneficiary has distributed the estate to herself or himself after the expiration of the limitation period?[55]

6. If the executors are asked not to distribute, but do so and no stay of distribution is sought, what relief is available to the applicant?[56]

7. When is an estate fully distributed? In *Zaplotinsky v. Zaplotinsky*[57] the personal representative had delivered to all devisees completed transfers of their interests in the real property devised by the testator's will. The real property was the only remaining asset in the estate. The devisees had failed to register their transfers, so that title remained in the personal representative. The court held that none of the estate remained undistributed after the transfers had been delivered to the devisees.

If a portion of the estate is held in trust for the purpose of satisfying annuities or life interests, however, that portion remains undistributed.[58] Assets are undistributed if the executors retain possession and control of them.[59]

8. At common law, when one joint tenant dies, the title to the property vests in the survivor. By virtue of s. 72 of the *Succession Law Reform Act*, however, the capital value of the property is brought back into the estate for the purposes of s. 61(1) of the Act, if the application for support is brought within the specified time limit. Section 72 ceases to

---

51 *Dependants Relief Act*, R.S.N.W.T. 1988, c. D-4, s. 13; R.S.Y. 1986, c. 44, s. 14; *Dependants' Relief Act*, S.S. 1996, c. D-25.01, s. 17; *Family Relief Act*, R.S.A. 1980, c. F-2 [am. 1984, c. 55, s. 20], s. 15; *Provision for Dependants Act*, R.S.N.B. 1973, c. T-4 [renamed S.N.B. 1991, c. 62, s. 3(1)], s. 14.

52 (1975), 8 O.R. (2d) 694, 22 R.F.L. 280, 59 D.L.R. (3d) 58 (Surr. Ct.).

53 *Daye v. Holmes* (1987), 25 E.T.R. 161 (Ont. H.C.), a claim by a person alleging that she was the deceased's common law spouse who brought the application 16 months after the grant of probate.

54 *MacDonald v. MacKenzie Estate* (1989), 36 E.T.R. 176 (P.E.I. T.D.).

55 See *Re Brill*, [1967] 2 O.R. 586, 64 D.L.R. (2d) 478 (Surr. Ct.); *Schwartz Estate v. Schwartz* (1998), 21 E.T.R. (2d) 9 (Ont. Gen. Div.).

56 *Mazur v. Mazur*, 3 Man. R. (2d) 67, [1980] 3 W.W.R. 289, 7 E.T.R. 217, 109 D.L.R. (3d) 211 (C.A.), leave to appeal refused, 109 D.L.R. (3d) 211n.

57 (1980), 14 Alta. L.R. (2d) 6, 8 E.T.R. 139 (Q.B.).

58 *Maldaver v. Can. Permanent Trust Co.* (1977), 27 N.S.R. (2d) 248, 1 E.T.R. 41 (T.D.).

59 *Harvey v. Estate of Powell* (1989), 36 E.T.R. 100 (N.S. C.A.).

have effect outside this limitation period and the property is then considered to have been distributed, precluding an action under s. 61(2).[60]

9. If an application for support is brought by one dependant within the limitation period and disposed of, can another dependant make another application for support after the period has expired? The legislation provides that an application brought by any dependant, insofar as the limitation period is concerned, is deemed to be an application on behalf of all dependants.[61]

10. If notice of an application for letters probate or letters of administration must be served on the Public Trustee,[62] the latter has six months from the date of service within which to make an application.[63]

11. Since creditors take priority over beneficiaries, it would seem that personal representatives may continue to pay the debts and expenses of the estate even if distribution is stayed, unless the court orders that the administration of the estate, including the payment of debts and expenses, be suspended.[64]

12. *Blatchford (Litigation Guardian of) v. Blatchford Estate*[65] suggests that the limitation provisions in the Act must be read subject to those in the *Limitations Act*.[66] The deceased lived part of each year in Grenada with a woman and had a child by her. He died in 1994 and left nothing to the child. His sister was his executrix and she frustrated the mother's inquiries about the estate. In 1997 the mother learned of her son's right to make a claim under Part V and informed the executrix of the claim. The son brought the application in 1999 when he was 16. The executrix argued the preliminary issue that the claim was barred. The court held that the claim was not barred. Since the *Succession Law Reform Act* did not exclude application of the *Limitations Act*, s. 47 of the latter Act applied. It provides that the period within which a claim may be brought runs from the time the claimant reaches the age of majority. The court followed existing case law to the same effect, but it seems wrong, since s. 47 refers specifically to actions mentioned in ss. 45 and 46 and, thus, does not appear to have general application. However, the court was, in any event, willing to extend the time under s. 61(2) of the *Succession Law Reform Act*.

3. THE APPLICANT

(a) Generally

The class of dependants is quite large under the *Succession Law Reform Act*, as appears from s. 57, set out below. *Re Cooper*,[67] reproduced below, discusses the definition of "dependant."

Under the Ontario Act an application for support may be made by a dependant of a testator or intestate, or by a parent on his or her behalf.[68] In addition, an

---

60 *Re Dolan* (1983), 2 D.L.R. (4th) 379, 42 O.R. (2d) 677, 29 R.P.R. 255, 15 E.T.R. 124 (Div. Ct.).
61 *Succession Law Reform Act*, s. 60(2)(b).
62 *Succession Law Reform Act*, s. 74(1).
63 *Ibid.*
64 *Ibid.*, s. 59.
65 (1999), 45 O.R. (3d) 784, (sub nom. *B. (J.D.D.) (Litigation Guardian of) v. G. (J.E.)*) 29 E.T.R. (2d) 141 (S.C.J.).
66 R.S.O. 1990, c. L.15.
67 (1980), 30 O.R. (2d) 113, 7 E.T.R. 118, 115 D.L.R. (3d) 451 (Div. Ct.).
68 *Ibid.*, s. 58(2).

application for support may be made on behalf of a dependant by various social service agencies if they are providing an allowance or benefit towards the support of the dependant.[69] If a dependant is under a disability and an application is not made by a parent, the dependant may be represented by the persons specified in the *Rules of Civil Procedure*[70] or, when appropriate, by the dependant's attorney or guardian, or by the Public Guardian and Trustee under the *Substitute Decisions Act, 1992*.[71]

The definition of "dependant" differs significantly among the other provinces. Some provinces limit dependants to the surviving spouse and children, while others include parents, grandparents, and other relatives if they were actually dependent on the deceased. Cohabitees are treated as dependants under several statutes.[72] As indicated in the introduction to this chapter, it may be expected that all statutes will have to be amended to make cohabitees and same-sex partners dependants for constitutional reasons.

(b) Different Approaches to Claims for Support

Another significant difference among the provinces is that some provinces limit the entitlement of children to those under a specified age, typically age 16 or the age of majority and older children who are unable to earn a livelihood by reason of physical or mental disability, or other reason such as economic need[73] in some cases.[74] In the remaining jurisdictions all children of the deceased, of any age and whether disabled or not qualify as dependants.[75] Consequently, in the latter jurisdictions, adult children who are not disabled are often awarded support[76] on the basis that the testator's duty to make provision has not only legal, but also moral dimensions and extends to adult children.[77] Further, financial need is often not a

---

69 *Succession Law Reform Act*, s. 58(3) [rep. and re-enacted S.O. 1997, c. 25, Sched. E, s. 12(3)].

70 *Rules of Civil Procedure* (Ont.), R. 7.

71 S.O. 1992, c. 30 [am. S.O. 1994, c. 27, ss. 43(2), 61(1), (2), 1996, c. 2, ss. 3-60]. See also *Succession Law Reform Act*, s. 74(2).

72 *Dependants of a Deceased Person Relief Act*, R.S.P.E.I. 1988, c. D-6, s. 1; *Dependants Relief Act*, R.S.N.W.T. 1988, c. D-4, s. 1; R.S.Y. 1986, c.44, s. 14; *Dependants' Relief Act*, S.M. 1989-90, c. 42, s. 1; S.S. 1996, c. D-25.01, s. 2; *Provision for Dependants Act*, R.S.N.B. 1973, c. T-4 [renamed S.N.B. 1991, c. 62, s. 3(1)], s. 1.

73 See, *e.g. Zajic v. Chomiak Estate* (1990), 35 E.T.R. 177 (Man. Q.B.).

74 *Dependants of a Deceased Person Relief Act*, R.S.P.E.I. 1988, c. D-6, s. 1; *Dependants Relief Act*, R.S.N.W.T. 1988, c. D-4, s. 1; R.S.Y. 1990, c. 44, s. 1; *Dependants' Relief Act*, S.M. 1989-90, c. 42, s. 1; S.S. 1996, c. D-25.01, s. 2; *Family Relief Act*, R.S.A. 1980, c. F-2, s. 1.

75 *Family Relief Act*, R.S.N. 1990, c. F-3, s. 2; *Provision for Dependants Act*, R.S.N.B. 1973, c. T-4 [renamed S.N.B. 1991, c. 62, s. 3(1)], s. 1; *Testators' Family Maintenance Act*, R.S.N.S. 1989, c. 465, s. 2; *Wills Variation Act*, R.S.B.C. 1996, c. 490 [am. S.B.C. 1999, c. 29, ss. 17, 18; S.B.C. 2000, c. 24, s. 13], s. 2.

76 See, *e.g., Re Joudry Estate* (1989), 32 E.T.R. 227 (N.S.T.D.); *Black v. Keith Estate* (1989), 33 E.T.R. 97 (N.B.Q.B.); *Nulty v. Nulty* (1989), 35 E.T.R. 153 (B.C.C.A.); *Kaetler v. Kaetler Estate* (1990) 40 E.T.R. 97 (B.C.C.A.); *Tataryn v. Tataryn Estate* (1992), 47 E.T.R. 221 (B.C.C.A.), varied (1994), 3 E.T.R. (2d) 229, 116 D.L.R. (4th) 193 (S.C.C.); *Jones v. Jones* (1993), 1 E.T.R. (2d) 76 (N.S.S.C.).

77 *Landy v. Landy Estate* (1991), 44 E.T.R. 1 (B.C.C.A.).

prerequisite to an award,[78] although it is an important criterion.[79] Another important criterion is assistance provided to the deceased by the child,[80] as are estrangement between the parties[81] and the reasons assigned by the testator for failing to benefit specific children.[82]

In *Tataryn v. Tataryn Estate*,[83] the Supreme Court of Canada attempted to clarify the principles to be applied under the British Columbia Act. Justice McLachlin, who wrote the opinion for the court, stated that the Act confers a very broad power on the court to make orders that are just in the circumstances of each case and that conform to contemporary community standards. In her view, the Act is not designed to ensure maintenance for dependants who are in need, but allows redistribution of the capital of the estate if that is required to give effect to the testator's moral duty toward the dependants. The court has to have regard to the testator's legal and moral obligations in deciding whether to make an award. The former are those to which the testator was subject while living, such as the duty to support one's spouse and minor children; the latter requires the testator to leave a share of the estate to each member of the family if the size of the estate permits. Legal obligations take priority over moral obligations, so that a surviving spouse has priority over independent adult children. The case has been criticized for its lack of clarity and the excessive power it gives the courts to re-order estates.[84]

There are many cases in which a moral duty of the deceased is invoked.[85] Typically, this has resulted in awards in favour of adult, capacitated children who

---

78 See, *e.g.*, *Re Sleno* (1977), 78 D.L.R. (3d) 155 (B.C.S.C.); *Harvey v. Powell Estate* (1988), 30 E.T.R. 143 (N.S.T.D.), affirmed (1989), 36 E.T.R. 100 (N.S.C.A.); *Cowan v. Cowan Estate* (1990), 37 E.T.R. 308 (B.C.C.A.); *Brammal v. Brammal Estate* (1990), 40 E.T.R. 169 (B.C.C.A.); *Plut v. Plut Estate* (1991), 41 E.T.R. 49 (B.C.C.A.).

79 See, *e.g.*, *Bains v. Schaner* (1991), 41 E.T.R. 241 (B.C.S.C.).

80 See, *e.g.*, *Guzzo v. Catlin Estate* (1986), 23 E.T.R. 186 (B.C.S.C.), varied (1989), 33 E.T.R. 163 (B.C.C.A.).

81 See, *e.g.*, *Price v. Lypchuck Estate* (1987) 26 E.T.R. 259 (B.C.C.A.).

82 See *Bell v. Roy Estate* (1993), 48 E.T.R. 209 (B.C.C.A.).

83 (1994), 3 E.T.R. (2d) 229, 116 D.L.R. (4th) 193 (S.C.C.).

84 Leopold Amighetti, Comment (1995), 14 E. & T.J. 277; Robert C. Freedman and Carolyn L. Berardino, Comment (1995), 15 E. & T.J. 6; Faye L. Woodman, "Financial Obligations of Parents to Adult Disabled Children", Part II (1998), 17 E.T. & P.J. 221.

85 See *e.g.*, *Brauer v. Hilton; Wilson v. Hilton* (1979), 15 B.C.L.R. 116 (C.A.); *Re Bailey*, [1972] 1 W.W.R. 99 (B.C.S.C.), affirmed [1972] 3 W.W.R. 640 (B.C.C.A.), leave to appeal refused [1972] S.C.R. ix; *Re Jones* (1961), 36 W.W.R. 337, 30 D.L.R. (2d) 316 (B.C.C.A.), affirmed [1962] S.C.R. 273 (sub nom. *Re Jones: McCarwill v. Jones*), 37 W.W.R. 597, 32 D.L.R. (2d) 433; *Swain v. Dennison*, [1967] S.C.R. 7, 59 D.L.R. (2d) 357; *Re Willan* (1951), 4 W.W.R. (N.S.) 114 (Alta. S.C.); *Re Lawther*, [1947] 1 W.W.R. 577, 55 Man. R. 142, [1947] 2 D.L.R. 510 (K.B.); *Re Pfrimmer* (1968), 66 W.W.R. 574, 2 D.L.R. (3d) 525 (Man. C.A.), leave to appeal to S.C.C. refused D.L.R. *ibid.*, at 720 and [1969] S.C.R. x; *Barr v. Barr*, [1972] 2 W.W.R. 346, 25 D.L.R. (3d) 401 (Man. C.A.); *Beasley v. Willet* (1972), 4 N.B.R. (2d) 122, 23 D.L.R. (3d) 366 (Q.B.); *MacDonald v. MacDonald* (1980), 39 N.S.R. (2d) 573, 6 E.T.R. 302 (T.D.); *Corkum v. Corkum* (1976), 18 N.S.R. (2d) 501, 74 D.L.R. (3d) 700 (sub nom. *Corkum v. Hiltz*) (C.A.); *Re Blowers*; *Menrad v. Blowers* (1982), 16 Man. R. (2d) 288, 12 E.T.R. 218, 137 D.L.R. (3d) 309 (Q.B.); *Re Protopappas Estate* (1987), 25 E.T.R. 241 (Alta. Q.B.); *Walker v. Walker Estate* (1998), 23 E.T.R. (2d) 82 (N.S.S.C.); *Crerar v. Crerar Estate* (1998), 24 E.T.R. (2d) 1 (B.C.C.A.).

are not in need.[86] It is submitted that this is incorrect, for the statutes' purpose is not to give effect to the expectations of the deceased's children, or to create equality between them. The statutes do interfere with the freedom of testation, but not if there is no financial need. The cases do sometimes, but not always give effect to the reasons given by the testator for excluding a child, such as the child's abandonment of the family and choosing to live an immoral life style.[87] However, often estrangement between the deceased and the dependent child appears to be irrelevant, especially if the estate is large.[88]

Further Reading

Gordon Bale, "Palm Tree Justice and Testator's Family Maintenance — The Continuing Saga of Confusion and Uncertainty in the B.C. Courts" (1987), 26 E.T.R. 295.

Faye L. Woodman, "Financial Obligations of Parents to Adult Disabled Children", Part II (1998), 17 E.T. & P.J. 221.

Leopold Amighetti, "*Tataryn* v. *Tataryn Estate*" (1995), 14 E.T. & P.J. 277.

Robert C. Freedman and Carolyn L. Berardino, Comment (1995), 15 E. & T.J. 6.

(c) The Legislation

SUCCESSION LAW REFORM ACT
R.S.O. 1990, c. S.26, am. S.O. 1999, c. 6, s. 61

1. (1) In this Act,

"child" includes a child conceived before and born alive after the parent's death;

"grandchild" means the child of a child;

"issue" includes a descendant conceived before and born alive after the person's death;

"parent" means the father or mother of a child;

. . .

"spouse" means either of a man and woman who,

(a) are married to each other, or

---

86 See, *e.g.*, *Walker v. McDermott*, [1931] S.C.R. 94, [1931] 1 D.L.R. 662; *Re Osland* (1977), 1 E.T.R. 128 (B.C.S.C.); *Re Bartel; Bartel v. Holmes* (1982), 16 Man. R. (2d) 29, 14 E.T.R. 103 (Q.B.); *Re Dutka; Dutka v. Pullan* (1980), 7 Man. R. (2d) 211, 8 E.T.R. 282 (Q.B.); *Re Blowers; Menrad v. Blowers* (1982), 16 Man. R. (2d) 288, 12 E.T.R. 218, 137 D.L.R. (3d) 309 (Q.B.); *Morris v. Morris* (1982), 41 B.C.L.R. 239, 14 E.T.R. 35 (C.A.). See *contra Sloane v. Bartley* (1980), 7 Man. R. (2d) 222, 8 E.T.R. 207 , 119 D.L.R. (3d) 611 (C.A.); *Rutherford v. Rutherford* (1988), 29 E.T.R. 139 (B.C.S.C.); *Harvey v. Powell Estate* (1988), 30 E.T.R. 143 (N.S.T.D.), affirmed (1989), 36 E.T.R. 100 (N.S.C.A.); A.H. Oosterhoff, "Annotation" (1980), 7 E.T.R. 166; Gordon Bale, "Annotation" (1982), 14 E.T.R. 36.

87 *Kelly v. Baker* (1996), 15 E.T.R. (2d) 219 (B.C.C.A.).

88 *Walker v. Walker Estate* (1998), 23 E.T.R. (2d) 82 (N.S.S.C.); *Crerar v. Crerar Estate* (1998), 24 E.T.R. (2d) 1 (B.C.C.A.).

(b) have together entered into a marriage that is voidable or void, in good faith on the part of the person asserting a right under this Act;

. . .

(2) In the definition of "spouse", a reference to marriage includes a marriage that is actually or potentially polygamous, if it was celebrated in a jurisdiction whose system of law recognizes it as valid.

. . .

57. In this Part,
"child" means a child as defined in subsection 1(1) and includes a grandchild and a person whom the deceased has demonstrated a settled intention to treat as a child of his or her family, except under an arrangement where the child is placed for valuable consideration in a foster home by a person having lawful custody;
"cohabit" means to live together in a conjugal relationship, whether within or outside marriage;

. . .

"dependant" means,
   (a) the spouse or same-sex partner of the deceased,
   (b) a parent of the deceased,
   (c) a child of the deceased, or
   (d) a brother or sister of the deceased,
  to whom the deceased was providing support or was under a legal obligation to provide support immediately before his or her death;

. . .

"parent" includes a grandparent and a person who has demonstrated a settled intention to treat the deceased as a child of his or her family, except under an arrangement where the deceased was placed for valuable consideration in a foster home by a person having lawful custody;
"same-sex partner" means either of two persons of the same sex who have cohabited,
   (a) continuously for a period of not less than three years, or
   (b) in a relationship of some permanence if they are the natural or adoptive parents of a child.
"spouse" means a spouse as defined in subsection 1(1) and in addition includes either of a man and woman who,
   (a) were married to each other by a marriage that was terminated or declared a nullity, or
   (b) are not married to each other and have cohabited.
      (i) continuously for a period of not less than three years, or
      (ii) in a relationship of some permanence, if they are the natural or adoptive parents of a child.

Comparable Legislation

Dependants of a Deceased Person Relief Act, R.S.P.E.I. 1988, c. D-6, s. 1(a), (d); *Dependants Relief Act*, R.S.N.W.T. 1988, c. D-4, s. 1; R.S.Y. 1986, c. 44, s. 1; *Dependants' Relief Act*, S.M. 1989-90, c. 42, s. 1; S.S. 1996, c. D-25.01, s. 2(1)(a)-(c); *Family Relief Act*, R.S.A. 1980, c. F-2, s. 1(b), (d); R.S.N. 1990, c. F-3, s. 2(a), (c); *Provision for Dependants Act*, R.S.N.B. 1973, c. T-4 [renamed S.N.B.1991, c. 62, s. 3(1)], s. 1; *Testators' Family Maintenance Act*, R.S.N.S. 1989, c. 465, s. 1(a), (b).

RE COOPER
(1980), 30 O.R. (2d) 113, 7 E.T.R. 118, 115 D.L.R. (3d) 451
Supreme Court of Ontario
[Divisional Court]

The deceased died on March 31, 1978, the date on which the Succession Law Reform Act came into force. He was survived by the respondent, his former wife, from whom he was divorced in 1971, four adult children, of whom one was mentally incapacitated and who lived with her mother, and the applicant, Mrs. Hampton, with whom the deceased had been living in a relationship of man and wife for seven years ending with his death. The deceased had an "estate" of approximately $70,000. Slightly in excess of $50,000 went to the respondent under policies of insurance and a pension plan. The remainder would go to her and the four children. The deceased had not supported his former wife and children at any time since the divorce.

The deceased and the applicant each paid for their own personal expenses and clothes; the applicant paid the household expenses. The deceased also paid $50 into a joint bank account every two weeks, he being the sole contributor, from which furnishings were bought for their apartment. The deceased further paid the rent, while both parties bought items of furniture. Both the respondent and the applicant had small independent incomes.

Mrs. Hampton brought an application for support. At first instance the court held that she was not a dependant because the deceased was not providing support for her, since his contribution to their joint living expenses was less compared to his total income than hers compared to her total income. Further, the court held that the deceased was not under a legal obligation to support the applicant immediately before his death since she had not established a need. The applicant appealed.

GRAY J., delivered the judgment of the court:

. . .

In our view, the issue of support cannot be contingent on one person making a greater contribution than another and in sharing common expenses, a couple, married or not, are supporting each other. To find otherwise would have drastic consequences. Take for example, the situation in which a husband and wife were both working, earning the same amount of money, and contributing to all common expenses equally. On the basis that only the person who is contributing less (either less absolutely or less in comparison to his or her income) is being supported, neither of the husband or the wife in this example would be entitled to apply under s. 65.[89] This does not take into account the argument concerning "legal obligation" in the definition of "dependant" in the Act.

The extent to which the "wife" contributed to building up the estate against which she claims is a relevant factor in determining what is an adequate provision of her.[90] The statute also recognizes the right of the applicants to claim against the estate of a person to whom contributions were made by the applicant during the lifetime of the deceased.

[His Lordship quoted s. 69(1)(a) of the Succession Law Reform Act, and continued:]

The learned Judge found that Mrs. Hampton's contribution to the common expenses was a very significant factor in allowing Mr. Cooper to build up his estate and ironically as a result of this finding, he determined that Mrs. Hampton was disentitled to relief under the Act. . . .

In contrast to Mr. Cooper's improved capital position as a result of this cost sharing arrangement, Mrs. Hampton's financial position remained unchanged. . . .

In our opinion, the fact that the applicant has contributed to the welfare of the deceased to his or her own detriment is a factor which presumably, in these circumstances, should be taken into account in increasing the amount adequate for proper support under s. 65(1). It should not operate to defeat an otherwise valid claim under the Act.

The realities of modern life in which both partners in a marriage (or a common law relationship) often work and make financial contributions to the family have prompted many changes in the law culminating in the passing of The Family Law Reform Act, 1978[91] and The Succession Law Reform Act which both came into force on the day of Mr. Cooper's death. Obligations between common law spouses are now recognized. The support obligations between spouses and common law spouses are now mutual (s. 15 of The Family Law Reform Act, 1978).[92] Thus, the Legislature has recognized that these relationships are also economic partnerships to which both parties are expected to contribute.

Therefore, in this case Mrs. Hampton and Mr. Cooper, in sharing common expenses, were each contributing to the support of the other, but Mrs. Hampton's contribution was greater in relation to her income (and perhaps greater in absolute dollars) than was the contribution of Mr. Cooper.

The definition of "dependant" in s. 64[93] of the Act does not require that the applicant be actually dependent on the deceased. Rather "dependant" is a defined term in the Act with its own special meaning:

---

89 Now s. 58.
90 *Dowsett v. Dowsett*, [1948] O.W.N. 685; *Re Soroka* (1975), 10 O.R. (2d) 638, 25 R.F.L. 169, 64 D.L.R. (3d) 234 (H.C.).
91 S.O. 1978, c. 2.
92 See now *Family Law Act*, R.S.O. 1990, c. F.3, s. 31 [am. S.O. 1997, c. 20, s. 2].
93 Now s. 57.

[His Lordship set out section 64(d),[94] and continued:]

A reading of the section shows that one need not find "dependency" in the common sense of the word. The definition requires two things. First, it requires the person to be in a certain relationship to the deceased. This is set out in items (i) and (iv). Secondly, it requires that the deceased was either providing support or under a legal obligation to provide support to the person claiming to be a dependant immediately before death.

. . .

These two criteria in the wording of s. 64(d) are quite different and if the deceased was not providing any support to the applicant, nevertheless the applicant still falls within the definition of "dependant" if the deceased was under a legal obligation to provide support. Thus the section contemplates the applicant being a dependant within the meaning of the Act even where he or she was not actually dependent on the deceased for support. The definition of dependant in Part II of The Family Law Reform Act, 1978 also contemplates situations in which the applicant is not actually dependent on the person from whom support is being requested.

In any event, since Mrs. Hampton and Mr. Cooper were each contributing to common expenses, it may be said that each in his own way was dependent on the other in the ordinary meaning of the word. Mr. Cooper was dependent on Mrs. Hampton to provide the food and she in turn was dependent on him to pay the rent and other sundries.

Mr. Cooper was providing support to Mrs. Hampton immediately before his death. It is also true that Mrs. Hampton would qualify under the latter requirement of the second test in the definition of dependant because Mr. Cooper was under a legal obligation to provide for his common law spouse by virtue of s. 15 of The Family Law Reform Act, 1978.[95]

. . .

[T]he obligation springs from the relationship of the applicant and the deceased as spouses in s. 15. Once the obligation is established the Court may consider all the items in s. 69(1)(a) of The Succession Law Reform Act to determine what is an adequate provision for support of the applicant and it is at this stage of the proceedings under s. 65 of The Succession Law Reform Act that the needs and means of the parties ought properly to be considered.

We hold that Mrs. Hampton qualified as a dependant under s. 64[96] of The Succession Law Reform Act because she was the common law wife of the deceased who was being supported by the deceased at the time of his death. The fact that Mrs. Hampton was also supporting herself and contributing to the support of Mr. Cooper does not change this. In addition, there was a legal obligation on

94 Now s. 57 [part].
95 Now *Family Law Act*, R.S.O. 1990, c. F.3, s. 30 [am. 1999, c. 6, s. 25(3)].
96 Now s. 57.

the part of Mr. Cooper to provide for Mrs. Hampton under s. 15 of The Family Law Reform Act, 1978.

The learned trial Judge did not find Mrs. Hampton to be entitled to an order under s. 65 because he found that she was not a dependant within the meaning of s. 64. He did, however, determine that if she were found to be a dependant, he would have made an order in her favour for $15,000. The learned trial Judge considered under s. 69(1)(c) of the Act evidence of the deceased's reasons for not making adequate provision for a dependant.

> [His Lordship held that the trial judge erred in holding that the fact that the parties were not married showed that Mr. Cooper did not intend to bestow financial rights upon her, since both the Family Law Reform Act and the Succession Law Reform Act recognize the right of a common law spouse to make a claim for support against the common law partner, or his or her estate. He continued:]

In addition, it is an error in principle for a Judge to award an applicant less because she is a second wife. Galligan J. in *Re Duncan*[97] held that a second wife has every right to be adequately provided for. While Mrs. Hampton was not actually married to Mr. Cooper, it is submitted that this principle should also apply to "second" common law wives.

Secondly, the learned trial Judge concluded that in not making a will, Mr. Cooper intended to benefit his first wife and his retarded daughter, and intended that there be no provision for Mrs. Hampton on his death. With respect, this is not borne out by the evidence.

. . .

After a careful review of the evidence and the reasons for judgment, we have concluded that the applicant does qualify as a dependant, that the deceased did not necessarily intend to make no provision for the applicant and that in all circumstances the lump sum award should be fixed, as the learned trial Judge suggested, at $15,000, having in mind the disparity between the incomes and health of the applicant and the respondent. This also would appear to take into consideration the fact that the respondent has the care of the daughter, Janet.

An order will go that the sum of $15,000 be paid out of the assets of the net estate of the said William Theodore Cooper to the applicant, Roberta Joyce Hampton. The moneys payable to the respondent under the two insurance policies and the city of Toronto Pension Plan are to be charged to secure the payments hereunder.

The costs of the applicant and the respondent are to be paid on a solicitor and client basis out of the said estate forthwith after taxation thereof.

---

97 (1975), 11 O.R. (2d) 539, 24 R.F.L. 34, (sub nom. *Duncan v. Duncan*) 66 D.L.R. (3d) 603 (Div. Ct.).

Notes and Questions

1. Under s. 57, cohabitation for the requisite period appears to be the essence of a common-law relationship. It seems that this is so also in some other jurisdictions which permit a common-law spouse to make a claim. Hence, so long as the parties lived together and shared resources the survivor is a dependant, even though the deceased made it plain to the survivor that he had no intention of marrying her and introduced her publicly as his housekeeper.[98] If the parties lived together as husband and wife but had no romantic or sexual relationship, they also fall within the extended definition of "spouse."[99]

If the survivor has often stayed overnight at the deceased's apartment, if they have eaten most of their meals together and have had sexual relations, and if the deceased has publicly declared his intention to marry the survivor and occasionally introduced her as his wife, but they nevertheless maintained separate houses, is a common-law relationship established?[100]

2. As the *Cooper* case confirms, spouses are under a general legal obligation to provide support for each other in accordance with need, to the extent they are able to do so, which obligation is codified by the *Family Law Act*,[101] and this obligation extends to cohabitees. Common-law spouses are included in the definition of "spouse" and same-sex partners are treated the same way as common law spouses. Identical definitions of "spouse" and "same-sex partner" appear in s. 57 of the *Succession Law Reform Act*.[102] Parents have a similar obligation toward their unmarried minor children[103] and adult children have a like obligation toward their parents.[104]

In other cases, however, only actual support immediately before death, or a legal obligation imposed by court order will suffice to make a person named in s. 57 a dependant. This may present problems.

Would a gift to a "dependant" immediately before death entitle the dependant to support even if no other moneys had ever been given to him or her, or is continuity of provision over a period of time required? What if the deceased had been supporting a "dependant" for some time before death, but resolved no longer to do so one month before he or she died? Would it make any difference if the deceased had been providing support, but the state had, shortly before his or her death, assumed the obligation?[105]

3. The amount of support provided by the deceased may also be significant. Suppose that the deceased had been divorced and that he was ordered, in the decree, to pay his former wife support of one dollar per year. Would the deceased then have been under a legal obligation to provide support for her so as to enable her to make a claim?[106]

---

98 *Godden v. Cookson* (1981), 34 B.C.L.R. 263, 10 E.T.R. 270, 130 D.L.R. (3d) 553 (S.C.). The case was decided under ss. 1 and 76 of the *Estate Administration Act*, R.S.B.C. 1996, c. 122 (repealed by S.B.C. 1999, c. 29, s. 9), mentioned in the introduction to this chapter, under which the court could order that part of the estate of an intestate be retained for the support, *inter alia*, of the deceased's common law spouse. See also *Tuele v. Berton* (1984), 52 B.C.L.R. 384, 17 E.T.R. 117 (S.C.); *Renko v. Stevens (Estate)* (1998), 21 E.T.R. (2d) 1 (B.C.C.A.); *Naiker v. Naiker Estate* (1997), 19 E.T.R. (2d) 167 (B.C.C.A.).

99 See *Amatnieks v. Benkis Estate* (1992), 46 E.T.R. 204 (Ont. Gen. Div.).

100 See *Re Geiger* (1982), 11 E.T.R. 152 (Ont. Surr. Ct.).

101 R.S.O. 1990, c. F.3, s. 30 [am. 1999, c. 6, s. 25(3)].

102 *Ibid.*, s. 29 [am. 1999, c. 6, s. 25(2)].

103 *Ibid.*, s. 31 [am. 1997, c. 20, s. 2].

104 *Ibid.*, s. 32. See *Dolabaille v. Carrington (No. 2)* (1981), 34 O.R. (2d) 641 (Fam. Ct.).

105 See *Re Beaumont*, [1980] Ch. 444, [1980] 1 All E.R. 266.

106 See *Re Tothivan* (1982), 36 O.R. (2d) 410, 12 E.T.R. 248 (Surr. Ct.).

If an ex-spouse had received alimony payments until two years prior to the death of the deceased and both parties had previously agreed that the ex-spouse would have no further claim on the deceased's estate, can the ex-spouse succeed in an application for support as a dependant under s. 57 of the *Succession Law Reform Act*?[107]

If the parties agreed during their divorce trial that the husband's obligation to pay support would last for three years and he died during the three years, the order survives his death and is a continuing charge against his estate until the agreed-upon date for termination.[108] Unless the parties agree otherwise, or unless the divorce judgment made the support binding on the estate of the payor, however, the obligation to pay support ends at the payor's death.[109] In either case, since the deceased was providing support immediately before death, the applicant would be a dependant.

4. X, an adult, capacitated child lives with her mother and is provided with room and board in return for looking after her aged mother. X has an independent source of income. The value of her services exceeds the value of the room and board. Would X be entitled to make a claim as a dependant on her mother's death on the basis of *Re Cooper*?[110]

5. For approximately twenty years prior to his death, the testator had provided rent-free accommodation to his adult son. The son, who was left nothing in the will, brought an action under the *Succession Law Reform Act* alleging that the testator had not made adequate provision for his proper support. What result?[111]

6. Is a child of the deceased who was conceived but unborn at the time of the deceased's death a dependant under s. 57?[112]

7. Is a stepchild who had not been legally adopted considered a child of the testator within the meaning of the Act?[113]

8. The estate of a grandfather, who had shown no settled intention to treat certain of his grandchildren as his children and cut them out of his will, is not liable to support those grandchildren.[114]

9. What is the meaning of the word "spouse"? Does it include a widow or widower of the deceased who has remarried and who is supporting his or her new spouse?[115] Further, how many "spouses" might qualify as dependants at any one time? Suppose, for example that a man divorces his wife and is required to pay her support. He then remarries, but leaves his second wife and lives for the requisite period with another woman in a common law relationship. Could all three be his dependants?

10. Is a widow who had been granted small support payments under a decree nisi of divorce just prior to her husband's death, a "dependant" under the Ontario Act?[116] *Healy*

---

107 See *Re Taylor and Taylor* (1985), 53 O.R. (2d) 174, 21 E.T.R. 292 (Surr. Ct.).

108 *Brubacher v. Brubacher Estate (Trustee of)* (1997), 18 E.T.R. (2d) 296 (Ont. Gen. Div.).

109 *Schwartz Estate v. Schwartz* (1998), 21 E.T.R. (2d) 9 (Ont. Gen. Div.).

110 The fact situation is derived from Macdonell, Sheard and Hull, Probate Practice (3rd ed., 1981, by Rodney Hull, Q.C. and Maurice Cullity, Q.C.), pp. 132-3. And see *Re Wilkinson*, 7 Fam. Law 176, [1978] 1 All E.R. 221.

111 See *Re Trenton* (1987), 26 E.T.R. 209 (Ont. Surr. Ct.).

112 See *Succession Law Reform Act*, s. 1(1).

113 See *Naples v. Martin Estate* (1986), 23 E.T.R. 288 (B.C.S.C.). And see *Kennedy v. McIntyre Estate* (1987), 26 E.T.R. 128, (sub nom. *Re Kennedy and National Victoria & Grey Trust Co.*) 37 D.L.R. (4th) 70 (Man. Q.B.).

114 *Piggott Estate v. Piggott* (1998), 25 E.T.R. (2d) 12 (Ont. Gen. Div.).

115 See *Bailey v. Public Trustee*, [1960] N.Z.L.R. 741 (C.A.); *Re Cranston; Cranston v. Cranston* (1962), 40 W.W.R. 321 (Alta. T.D.).

116 See *Blago v. Aetna Life Insurance Co.* (1988), 30 E.T.R. 283 (Ont. Surr. Ct.).

v. Broadbent[117] is instructive in this regard. The estranged wife of the deceased applied for support as a "dependant" under the Act. The separation agreement stipulated that the deceased had no obligation to support his wife except to "maintain hospital and medical coverage under any current plan of the Ontario government." The deceased was not providing any support to his wife immediately prior to his death. The court held that, since the husband had reached the age of 65 before his death, the coverage in question was conferred upon the wife without any obligation his part, hence the wife was not receiving support from and was not a dependant of the husband.

11. Are the definitions of "dependant" and "spouse" in s. 57 of the *Succession Law Reform Act ultra vires* the provincial legislature to the extent that they permit a former spouse and children of the marriage to make an application for support even though a court has previously made a support order in their favour under the *Divorce Act?*[118] Does it make any difference whether the support order in the divorce decree is made binding on the estate of the spouse required to pay it, or whether it ends at death?[119]

12. Section 5(2) of the *Children's Law Reform Act*[120] provides that a declaration of parentage may only be made if both the child and the putative father are living. Does this preclude an application for support by a child born out of wedlock out of his father's estate?[121]

13. An application under the *Succession Law Reform Act* by a dependant against the estate of the testator does not survive the death of the applicant.[122] However, in British Columbia the estate of a dependant who has not brought an application for support is entitled to bring the application.[123]

14. What effect does the *Family Law Act*[124] have on applications for support?[125]

15. *Tataryn v. Tataryn,*[126] referred to in the introduction to this part, has been followed on many occasions. One example is *Glanville v. Glanville.*[127] A husband and wife had been married for many years when he died. Each had children from prior marriages. Neither had dependent children. His will left a life interest in the matrimonial home to her, with remainder to his children, and the personal estate to her. The court held that the will should not be varied, since the testator had considered both families and gave the wife and her family approximately 50 percent of the estate. Hence, the testator had fulfilled his legal obligations. However, since her pension and other income was reduced, contrary to expectations, the court directed that the remainder interest bear the cost of taxes, insurance and major repairs.

---

117 (1987), 25 E.T.R. 1 (Ont. C.A.).

118 *Divorce Act*, R.S.C. 1985 (2nd Supp.), c. 3, s. 15.

119 See *Re Burke* (1983), 36 R.F.L. (2d) 452 (Ont. Surr. Ct.).

120 R.S.O. 1990, c. C.12.

121 See *Re Ruby* (1983), 43 O.R. (2d) 277 (Surr. Ct.). See also *Re Bagaric and Juric* (1980), 29 O.R. (2d) 491, 114 D.L.R. (3d) 509 (H.C.), noted (1982), 60 Can. Bar Rev. 171; reversed (1981), 34 O.R. (2d) 288, 130 D.L.R. (3d) 768 (C.A.).

122 See *Golverk-Berger v. Berger Estate* (1986), 22 E.T.R. 195 (Ont. Surr. Ct.).

123 *Smith v. Bowen* (1989), 32 E.T.R. 185 (B.C.S.C.).

124 R.S.O. 1990, c. F.3.

125 See Rodney Hull, "The Effect of the Ontario Family Law Act, 1986 on Surviving Spouses and Estates of Deceased Spouses" (1988), 8 E. & T.Q. 20. Note that s. 34(4) of the Act provides that an *inter vivos* support order binds the estate of the payor unless the order provides otherwise. See also *Butler v. Butler Estate* (1990), 38 E.T.R. 93 (Ont. C.A.).

126 (1994), 3 E.T.R. (2d) 229, 116 D.L.R. (4th) 193 (S.C.C.).

127 (1998), 25 E.T.R. (2d) 258, 168 D.L.R. (4th) 332 (B.C.C.A.).

Similarly, if the spouses have reached an agreement about the division of their assets and have renounced any rights to each other's estates, including any claims for support, and if the survivor has adequate means of support, the court will not vary the deceased's will.[128]

Sawchuk v. McKenzie Estate[129] is another example. The testatrix left an estate of four million dollars, but left her only daughter a legacy of only $10,000. The daughter and her husband had a very modest income and lived in co-operative housing. The testatrix left most of her estate to her grandchildren, her step-grandchildren, and certain charities. The court varied the will, holding that the testatrix had disregarded the moral claim of her adult daughter and treated the daughter unfairly. She was awarded one million dollars.

In *Gow v. Gow Estate*[130] the court held that *Tataryn* applied to Alberta, and granted substantial amounts to a surviving husband on the wife's intestacy. I suggest that the case is wrong in applying *Tataryn*, since the legislation in Alberta is quite different than that in British Columbia.

4. THE ADEQUACY OF SUPPORT

Under the *Dependants' Relief Act*[131] the court could provide relief for a testator's dependants if it was satisfied that "adequate provision for the future maintenance" of the dependants had not been made by the testator.[132] In contrast, section 58(1) of the *Succession Law Reform Act*, reproduced below, speaks of "adequate provision for the proper support" of dependants. There is, therefore, an apparent change in emphasis from "maintenance" to "support". This is significant, because in cases under the former legislation the courts generally held that, save in exceptional circumstances, "maintenance" suggested financial assistance of a periodic nature.[133]

Moreover, while under the former statute the courts did take into account the dependants' accustomed standard of living, the cases suggest that the relief provided by the legislation did not entitle a dependant to a luxurious standard of living. Rather, if the court was satisfied that adequate provision for the dependants was not made it had to provide relief that would ensure a reasonable standard of living. They were thus not restricted to providing just a minimal amount, but neither would they be overly generous.[134] In contrast, courts in other jurisdictions and, hence, under different legislative regimes have generally taken a more liberal approach.[135]

The effect of the changed legislation in respect of these matters is addressed in *Re Davies*,[136] reproduced below. Reference should also be made to Part III of the

---

128 *Chutter v. Chutter Estate* (2000), 33 E.T.R. (2d) 67 (B.C.C.A.).
129 (2000), 31 E.T.R. (2d) 119, 184 D.L.R. (4th) 156 (B.C.C.A.).
130 (1999), 28 E.T.R. (2d) 197 (Alta. Surr. Ct.).
131 R.S.O. 1970, c. 126.
132 *Ibid.*, s. 2.
133 See, *e.g.*, *Re Duranceau*, [1952] O.R. 584, [1952] 3 D.L.R. 714 at 720 (C.A.), *per* Roach J.A.; *Re McCaffery*, [1931] O.R. 512 at 523, [1931] 4 D.L.R. 930 (C.A.), *per* Fisher J.A.
134 See, *e.g.*, *Re Duranceau*, *supra*, at D.L.R. 720.
135 See, *e.g.*, *Bosch v. Perpetual Trustee Co.*, [1938] A.C. 463 at 476-8, *per* Lord Romer (P.C.).
136 (1979), 27 O.R. (2d) 98, 6 E.T.R. 127, 105 D.L.R. (3d) 357 (Surr. Ct.).

Family Law Act[137] which contains very similar provisions for the *inter vivos* support of dependants.

Another question that concerns the court on an application for support is the basis of its jurisdiction. Obviously it rests solely in the statute. But does the statute require the court to take into account only economic considerations, or moral or ethical ones as well? An ethical standard was adopted by Edwards J., in *Re Allardice; Allardice v. Allardice*,[138] as appears from the following excerpt:

> It is the duty of the Court, so far as is possible, to place itself in all respects in the position of the testator, and to consider whether or not, having regard to all existing facts and surrounding circumstances, the testator has been guilty of a manifest breach of that moral duty which a just, but not a loving, husband or father owes towards his wife or towards his children, as the case may be. If the Court finds that the testator has been plainly guilty of a breach of such moral duty, then it is the duty of the Court to make such an order as appears to be sufficient but no more than sufficient to repair it.

The above quotation is often found in the Canadian cases and the approach there espoused has found acceptance in the Canadian courts, particularly in the western provinces.[139] In contrast, the Ontario courts, while paying lip service to the moral duty, have restricted their jurisdiction in the past to whether the testator made adequate provision for his or her dependants, as required by the statute.[140]

It would appear that the *Succession Law Reform Act* does not introduce a general ethical standard but restricts the court largely to an inquiry into the financial circumstances of the applicant. However, it cannot be denied that some of the factors the court must consider on an application for support have moral implications. The factors to be considered by the court and an application are set out in s. 62 of the Act, which is reproduced below.

Related to the question of the standard to be used by the court on an application is the question as of which date the adequacy of the provision of support should be measured. This question concerns both the court's jurisdiction to make an order and, once it has assumed jurisdiction on the ground that the deceased failed

---

137   R.S.O. 1990, c. F.3.

138   (1910), 29 N.Z.L.R. 959 at 972-3 (C.A.), affirmed [1911] A.C. 730 (P.C.).

139   See *e.g.*, *Brauer v. Hilton; Wilson v. Hilton* (1979), 15 B.C.L.R. 116 (C.A.); *Re Bailey*, [1972] 1 W.W.R. 99 (B.C.S.C.), affirmed [1972] 3 W.W.R. 640 (B.C.C.A.), leave to appeal to S.C.C. refused [1972] S.C.R. ix; *Re Jones* (1961), 36 W.W.R. 337, 30 D.L.R. (2d) 316 (B.C.C.A.), affirmed [1962] S.C.R. 273, (sub nom. *McCarwill v. Jones*) 37 W.W.R. 597, 32 D.L.R. (2d) 433; *Swain v. Dennison*, [1967] S.C.R. 7, 59 D.L.R. (2d) 357; *Re Willan* (1951), 4 W.W.R. (N.S.) 114 (Alta. S.C.); *Re Lawther*, [1947] 1 W.W.R. 577, 55 Man. R. 142, [1947] 2 D.L.R. 510 (K.B.); *Re Pfrimmer* (1968), 66 W.W.R. 574, 2 D.L.R. (3d) 525 (Man. C.A.), leave to appeal to S.C.C. refused 2 D.L.R. (3d) 525 at 720, [1969] S.C.R. x; *Barr v. Barr*, [1972] 2 W.W.R. 346, 25 D.L.R. (3d) 401 (Man. C.A.); *Beasley v. Willet* (1972), 4 N.B.R. (2d) 122, 23 D.L.R. (3d) 366 (Q.B.); *MacDonald v. MacDonald* (1980), 39 N.S.R. (2d) 573, 6 E.T.R. 302 (T.D.); *Corkum v. Corkum* (1976), 18 N.S.R. (2d) 501, 74 D.L.R. (3d) 700 (sub nom. *Corkum v. Hiltz*) (C.A.); *Re Blowers; Menrad v. Blowers* (1982), 16 Man. R. (2d) 288, 12 E.T.R. 218, 137 D.L.R. (3d) 309 (Q.B.); *Re Protopappas Estate* (1987), 25 E.T.R. 241 (Alta. Q.B.).

140   See, *e.g.*, *Re Hull Estate*, [1943] O.R. 778, [1944] 1 D.L.R. 14 at 19-20, *per* Laidlaw J.A. (C.A.); *Re McCaffery*, [1931] O.R. 512 at 517 (C.A.), *per* Roach J.A.

to make adequate provision for his dependants, the nature and amount of the award, the latter being within the court's discretion, but not the former.

Under the former legislation it was arguably the law that the court's jurisdiction was to be determined as of the date of the testator's death, since the question was whether the *testator* had or had not made adequate provision for his dependants. If that was the case, then the factors to be considered by the court[141] were relevant only in determining the quantum of the award. That result was supported by Laidlaw J.A., in *Re Hull Estate*,[142] who held that the judge of first instance lacked jurisdiction to make an award since the testator's widow's parlous financial circumstances arose after his death, whereas he had adequately provided for her by his will. *Dicta* in a later case suggest, however, that the factors to be considered by the court were to be used both to determine jurisdiction and quantum.[143]

The matter was never resolved in Ontario under the former legislation. You should note, however, that in the absence of statutory direction there are four possible dates which have been applied.[144] These are the date of the will,[145] the date of death,[146] the date of the application,[147] and the date of the hearing.[148] The first of these is clearly wrong, whereas the second was arguably the correct date under the former Ontario legislation.

The British Columbia Court of Appeal has held that the relevant date for determining the court's jurisdiction is the date of the testator's death, but in determining whether the testator has made adequate provision, the court should take into account circumstances reasonably foreseeable by the testator, as well as existing circumstances. Further, the court may have regard to moral and economic considerations, for the testator's duty has both aspects and both extend to adult children. However, if there has been a substantial change in circumstances between the date of the testator's death and the date of the trial, such as the death of a major beneficiary under the will, the court may take that into account.[149]

In Ontario the question has been laid to rest by s. 58(4) of the *Succession Law Reform Act*, reproduced below, which selects the date of the hearing. In any event,

---

141 *Dependants Relief Act*, R.S.O. 1970, c. 126, s. 7.
142 [1943] O.R. 778, [1944] 1 D.L.R. 14 at 20 (C.A.).
143 *Re Brill*, [1967] 2 O.R. 586, 64 D.L.R. (2d) 478 at 483 (Surr. Ct.).
144 See *Re Bowe*, [1971] 4 W.W.R. 234, 19 D.L.R. (3d) 338 (B.C.S.C.) which discusses the four possibilities. And see Bale, "Limitation on Testamentary Disposition in Canada" (1964), 42 Can. Bar Rev. 367 at 376-9.
145 *Re Hull*, [1943] O.R. 778, [1944] 1 D.L.R. 14 at 19-20, *per* Laidlaw J.A.
146 *Re Novikoff* (1968), 66 W.W.R. 164, 1 D.L.R. (3d) 484 (B.C.S.C.); *Re Bowe, supra*, footnote 81.
147 *Re Willan* (1951), 4 W.W.R. (N.S.) 114 (Alta. S.C.); *Re Calladine; Re Calladine and Farrar* (1958), 25 W.W.R. 175 (B.C.S.C.); *Re Martin* (1962), 40 W.W.R. 513, 36 D.L.R. (2d) 507 (sub nom. *Re Martin; Wilken v. Walker*) (Man. C.A.).
148 *Re Jones*, 49 B.C.R. 216, [1934] 3 W.W.R. 726 (S.C.); *Malychuk v. Malychuk; Traschuk v. Malychuk* (1978), 6 Alta. L.R. (2d) 240, 11 A.R. 372 (T.D.).
149 *Landy Estate v. Landy Estate* (1991), 44 E.T.R. 1 (B.C.C.A.); *Wagner v. Wagner Estate* (1991), 44 E.T.R. 24 (B.C.C.A.).

the question is no longer as important since the court can now vary earlier orders to take into account changed circumstances.[150]

SUCCESSION LAW REFORM ACT
R.S.O. 1990, c. S.26, am. S.O 1999, c. 6, s. 61

58. (1) Where a deceased, whether testate or intestate, has not made adequate provision for the proper support of his dependants or any of them, the court, on application, may order that such provision as it considers adequate be made out of the estate of the deceased for the proper support of the dependants or any of them.

. . .

(4) The adequacy of provision for support under subsection (1) shall be determined as of the date of the hearing of the application.

. . .

62. (1) In determining the amount and duration, if any, of support, the court shall consider all the circumstances of the application, including,

(a)   the dependant's current assets and means;

(b)   the assets and means that the dependant is likely to have in the future;

(c)   the dependant's capacity to contribute to his or her own support;

(d)   the dependant's age and physical and mental health;

(e)   the dependant's needs, in determining which the court shall have regard to the dependant's accustomed standard of living;

(f)   the measures available for the dependant to become able to provide for his or her own support and the length of time and cost involved to enable the dependant to take those measures;

(g)   the proximity and duration of the dependant's relationship with the deceased;

(h)   the contributions made by the dependant to the deceased's welfare, including indirect and non-financial contributions;

(i)   the contributions made by the dependant to the acquisition, maintenance and improvement of the deceased's property or business;

(j)   a contribution by the dependant to the realization of the deceased's career potential;

(k)   whether the dependant has a legal obligation to provide support for another person;

(l)   the circumstances of the deceased at the time of death;

(m)   any agreement between the deceased and the dependant;

(n)   any previous distribution of property made by the deceased in favour of the dependant by gift or agreement or under court order;

(o)   the claims that any other person may have as a dependant;

---

150 *Succession Law Reform Act*, s. 65.

(p)   if the dependant is a child,
     (i) the child's aptitude for and reasonable prospects of obtaining an education, and
     (ii) the child's need for a stable environment;

(q)   if the dependant is a child of the age of sixteen years of more, whether the child has withdrawn from parental control;

(r)   if the dependant is a spouse or same-sex partner,
     (i) a course of conduct by the spouse or same-sex partner during the deceased's lifetime that is so unconscionable as to constitute an obvious and gross repudiation of the relationship,
     (ii) the length of time the spouses or same-sex partners cohabited,
     (iii) the effect on the spouse's or same-sex partner's earning capacity of the responsibilities assumed during cohabitation,
     (iv) whether the spouse or same-sex partner has undertaken the care of a child who is of the age of eighteen years or over and unable by reason of illness, disability or other cause to withdraw from the charge of his or her parents,
     (v) whether the spouse or same-sex partner has undertaken to assist in the continuation of a program of education for a child eighteen years of age or over who is unable for that reason to withdraw from the charge of his or her parents,
     (vi) in the case of a spouse, any housekeeping, child care or other domestic service performed by the spouse for the family, as if the spouse had devoted the time spent in performing that service in remunerative employment and had contributed the earnings to the family's support,
     (vi.1) in the case of a same-sex partner, any housekeeping, child care or other domestic service performed by the same-sex partner for the deceased or the deceased's family, as if the same-sex partner had devoted the time spent in performing that service in remunerative employment and had contributed the earnings to the support of the deceased or the deceased's family,
     (vii) the effect on the spouse's or same-sex partner's earnings and career development of the responsibility of caring for a child,
     (viii) the desirability of the spouse or same-sex partner remaining at home to care for a child; and

(s)   any other legal right of the dependant to support, other than out of public money.

(2) In addition to the evidence presented by the parties, the court may direct other evidence to be given as the court considers necessary or proper.

(3) The court may accept such evidence as it considers proper of the deceased's reasons, so far as ascertainable, for making the dispositions in his or her will, or for not making adequate provision for a dependant, as the case may be, including any statement in writing signed by the deceased.

(4) In estimating the weight to be given to a statement referred to in subsection (3), the court shall have regard to all the circumstances from which an inference can reasonably be drawn as to the accuracy of the statement.

Comparable Legislation

Dependants of a Deceased Person Relief Act, R.S.P.E.I. 1988, c. D-6, ss. 2, 5; *Dependants Relief Act*, R.S.N.W.T. 1988, c. D-4, ss. 2(1), 6; R.S.Y. 1986, c. 44, ss. 2, 5; *Dependants' Relief Act*, S.M. 1989-90, c. 42, ss. 2(1), 10; S.S. 1996, c. D-25.01, ss. 3, 5(1), 6(1); *Family Relief Act*, R.S.A. 1980, c. F-2, s. 3(1)-(3); R.S.N. 1990, c. F-3, ss. 3(1), 5; *Provision for Dependants Act*, R.S.N.B. 1973, c. T-4 [renamed S.N.B. 1991, c. 62, s. 3(1)], ss. 2, 8; *Testators' Family Maintenance Act*, R.S.N.S. 1989, c. 465, ss. 3(1), 5; *Wills Variation Act*, R.S.B.C. 1996, c. 490, s. 2 [am. 1999, c. 29, s. 18].

RE DAVIES
(1979), 27 O.R. (2d) 98, 6 E.T.R. 127, 105 D.L.R. (3d) 537
Ontario Surrogate Court
[Judicial District of York]

The applicant and the deceased were married in 1969. They had both been married before and the deceased had a son by her first marriage. At the time of the marriage the applicant was 62 years of age. He sold his house and moved into his wife's house at 42 Galbraith Ave. For a while both were employed, but then the applicant retired. His wife continued to work up until two years before her death. The applicant paid most of his pension to his wife to pay for the expenses and upkeep of the home. The deceased died in May 1978 and left her entire estate to her son, naming him her sole executor. The value of the estate was approximately $146,000, $50,000 of which represented the value of the house and $5,500 of which represented one-half of the moneys in a joint account with the applicant.

At the date of the hearing the applicant received a pension of some $400 per month and had a bank account of approximately $82,000. Of that amount, $21,000 had been taken from joint accounts of himself and his wife to which he had contributed most of the money.

The applicant made an application for support. He sought to be allowed to remain in the house for the rest of his life.

DYMOND SURR. CT. J.:

> [Her Honour repeated the definition of "dependant" and the jurisdiction of the court to make an award from what are now ss. 57 and 58(1) the *Succession Law Reform Act* and ss. 1(b) and 2(1) of the *Dependants' Relief Act*, R.S.O. 1970, c. 126, set out or discussed above and continued:]

Thus the class of persons included as dependants has been widened and, in addition, the words "future maintenance" have been replaced by the words "proper support" and the same word, "support" is found in the definition of a dependant.

The Legislature has also made other changes of importance in that the matters into which the Court is to inquire at the hearing under the S.L.R.A. have been made more explicit on the one hand and broader on the other hand because evidence as to the reasons of the deceased for dispositions made in his will may be heard. Thus one must read carefully insofar as reliance upon previous case law in this province is concerned. It is my view that by the word "support" the Legislature has deliberately focused on a change from "maintenance". The word "support" does appear in legislation from other jurisdictions but usually with the word "maintenance". The Family Law Reform Act, 1978 (Ont.), c. 2,[151] it may be noted, has also gone away from the use of the words "maintenance" or "alimony".

Some examination of dictionary definitions of the word "support" may be helpful with definitions with respect to meanings unrelated to the question omitted:

> [Her Honour quoted from the Shorter Oxford English Dictionary, Black's Law Dictionary[152] and Stroud's Judicial Dictionary,[153] and continued:]

These definitions lead me to the conclusion that "support" as used in the S.L.R.A., includes not only furnishing food and sustenance and supplying the necessaries [sic] of life, but also the secondary meaning of giving physical or moral support. While the Ontario cases under The Dependant's Relief Act extended the meaning of "adequate provision for the further [sic] maintenance of a dependant", to a determination of the question "is the provision sufficient to enable the dependant to live neither luxuriously nor miserably, but decently and comfortably according to his or her station of life."[154] I am inclined to the view that the word "support" in the S.L.R.A. extends that meaning to include what might by some be considered as non-essentials or luxuries. For example, if a living husband had been accustomed to reading aloud to his wife whose sight had failed, it may well be that for her support, sufficient money should be provided to pay for a reader to substitute for that husband.

In the instant case I find that Mrs. Davies provided support for her husband by providing for him a home in which to live and by providing the services so often performed by a loving wife. Similarly he had been providing support for her by contributing financially to their living costs and by effecting repairs to the house and grounds. In my view each supported the other and, therefore, within the meaning of the S.L.R.A. each was dependant [sic] on the other. It is with that approach that I intend to proceed and I find that Mr. Davies was a dependant of the deceased.

It was made clear in the case of *Re Hull*,[155] that once one has found an applicant to be a dependant the next step is to decide whether the deceased by her will "has

---

151 Now the *Family Law Act*, R.S.O. 1990, c. F.3.
152 Rev. 4th ed. 1968.
153 *S.v.* "support".
154 *Re Duranceau*, [1952] O.R. 584, [1952] 3 D.L.R. 714 (C.A.).
155 [1943] O.R. 778, [1944] 1 D.L.R. 14 (C.A.).

made adequate provision for the proper support of her dependants or any of them". To determine this I have considered the matters outlined in s. 69[156] of the S.L.R.A. and I make the following findings of fact:

1. Mr. Davies has assets totalling just over $80,000 and is in receipt of pensions of about $400 monthly.

2. He is capable of providing maintenance for himself but is not capable of purchasing a home similar to the two-bedroom home in which he now lives and, were he to use all of his capital to purchase a similar home he would not be capable of maintaining himself in that home.

3. Mr. Davies is over 72 years of age and is alert but his physical prowess has diminished so that he no longer bowls and in addition he has some medical problem with his eyes.

4. His needs include living in the neighbourhood where he has lived for the past ten years close to his friends and acquaintances and in familiar surroundings.

5. He will never be able to find paid employment.

6. He was married to the deceased for more than nine years and there is no evidence that his relationship with her was anything but that of a loving husband.

7. He maintained the deceased's house, paid the taxes and utility charges and maintained his wife. She worked until about two years before her death and her earnings were hers to use as she would. The size of her estate may be indicative of her ability to save.

8. The deceased had also been supporting her son by giving him money from time to time, by paying him for work done on her home, probably by purchasing a cottage for him and by making gifts to him. It may well be that he too is a dependant within the meaning of the Act.

9. There was no obvious repudiation of the relationship of husband and wife.

10. At the time of her death the deceased owned her home, then valued at $50,000, a cottage valued at $35,000 which her son testified was held in trust for him and approximately $55,000 in her own name, excluding any joint accounts with her husband. The husband at that time owned in his own name approximately $60,000. There were joint accounts in the amount of approximately $20,000. It can then be seen that if the two pieces of realty are excluded, at the date of death of Mrs. Davies, she and her husband had close to equal assets. Mr. Davies had sold his home in order to move in with his wife and he kept the proceeds of that sale in his own account.

There was no evidence of any agreement between the deceased and her husband, nor was there evidence apart from his claim for the cottage of any real claim by the son who is an adult with grown children of his own. However the son is receiving some undefined disability pension and has, he swore, assets totalling only $2,000 and one assumes this is apart from the cottage which he maintained his mother was holding in trust for him.

Evidence was adduced that the testatrix had told her son in the spring before her death that her husband was provided for and there was also evidence from the husband that both he and his wife had expected that he would predecease his

---

156 Now s. 62.

wife who was younger than he and that to be forced to move from his home at 42 Galbraith Avenue would "break my heart".

I conclude from the facts to which I have referred that adequate provision for the proper support of Mr. Davies was not made because such adequate provision would include the right for Mr. Davies to occupy his wife's home as long as he is capable of living there, whether alone or with someone to look after him as he gets older and that to deprive him of that home would be to deprive him of the support which, under all the circumstances, would be adequate for him.

In reaching that conclusion I have been mindful of the adages under the older case law such as:

> The court should strive to give effect to the scheme of the testator and to his intentions as disclosed by the Will itself.[157]

and of the oft quoted words of Edwards J. in the case of *Re Allardice*[158] where he said:

> [Her Honour quoted the excerpt from this case,[159] reproduced above, and continued:]

In my view, in order to maintain the scheme of the will as far as possible, only the real property concerned should be kept from the son, the residuary legatee, and the applicant should continue to pay all of the carrying charges on the property and in addition should pay a sum sufficient to keep the real property in good repair. He has occupied the premises since the date of death of his wife, paying the carrying charges but, as I understand it, not having paid any money towards major repairs or depreciation. His assets are sufficient to enable him to contribute to the maintenance of the property so that the property will not be run down because of lack of repair during the applicant's lifetime, and so that the scheme of the will will not have to be disturbed by requiring additional moneys to be set aside for repairs on the property. To ensure this I have, in the order which I am making, included payment by the applicant towards the cost of major repairs.

> [Her Honour also required the applicant to pay municipal taxes and other local charges and the cost of insuring the premises.]

Notes and Questions

1. In *Davies* the court strove to maintain the scheme of the will. This is an accepted principle, also followed in other provinces.[160]

2. While the statutory provisions giving jurisdiction to make an award in the other provinces are very similar to s. 58(1) of the Ontario Act, there are differences which may affect the result. Thus, for example, the British Columbia and Saskatchewan statutes permit

---

157 *Re Schmidt*, [1952] O.R. 532, [1952] 4 D.L.R. 364 (C.A.).
158 (1910), 29 N.Z.L.R. 959 at 972 .
159 *Re Hull*, [1943] O.R. 778, [1944] 1 D.L.R. 14.
160 See, *e.g. Hutton v. Lapka Estate* (1991), 44 E.T.R. 231 (B.C.C.A.).

the court to make a provision which is "just and equitable in the circumstances." The British Columbia and Nova Scotia statutes extend only to testate succession.[161]

3. There is no provision comparable to s. 58(4) in the other statutes. Hence the date as of which the court's jurisdiction is to be determined and the relevant factors to be considered may be a moot point in the other provinces. In practice the date has been fixed judicially, the majority of the courts now taking the view that the date of the application is the correct one.[162]

4. Regarding the factors to be taken into account by the court, the Manitoba and British Columbia statutes do not address the question beyond allowing the court to accept evidence of the testator's reasons for making the dispositions he did. The Alberta, New Brunswick, Prince Edward Island, Saskatchewan, Northwest Territories and Yukon statutes expressly permit the court to admit such evidence as may be relevant. The Newfoundland and Nova Scotia statutes contain a list of factors to be considered, similar to, but less extensive than the list contained in the Ontario Act.

5. For a case interpreting s. 62 *seriatim*, see *Re Dentiger*.[163] In *Dentinger*, Judge Carter stated that he could not, under the statute, quantify the probability of future contingencies, such as loss of employment, because the matters listed in s. 62 have to be considered as of the date of the hearing. It has been stated, however, that the purpose of this statutory provision (s. 58(3)) is to prevent the matter from being decided on the basis of the deceased's moral duty when he died and not to fetter the court's discretion as regards future contingencies.[164] In any event Judge Carter said that common sense required him to take the present potentiality of such events occurring into consideration, bearing in mind the applicant's age.

Unforeseen future events can now be made the subject of a further order under s. 65. However, those that are foreseeable should probably be taken into account at the outset, since any order made in the future can only affect assets then remaining undistributed.

6. Was the happy marriage a relevant factor in *Dentinger* as Judge Carter stated? If not, what does the word "proximity" in s. 62(1)(g) mean? Consider the effect of s. 62(1)(r)(i), *i.e.*, conduct amounting to an obvious and gross repudiation of the relationship.

7. Is it relevant that an applicant who is a surviving spouse is entitled to, or has received an equalization payment under the *Family Law Act*[165] as a surviving spouse?

Statutes in some other provinces also provide for a division of matrimonial assets on death as well as on a breakdown of marriage.[166] Under the English legislation the court,

---

161 For the statutory references see *supra*.
162 See *Re Bowe*, [1971] 4 W.W.R. 234, 19 D.L.R. (3d) 338 (B.C.S.C.); *Re Hull*, [1943] O.R. 778, [1944] 1 D.L.R. 14; *Re Novikoff* (1968), 66 W.W.R. 164, 1 D.L.R. (3d) 484 (B.C.S.C.); *Re Willan* (1951), 4 W.W.R. (N.S.) 114 (Alta. S.C.); *Re Calladine; Re Calladine and Farrar* (1958), 25 W.W.R. 175 (B.C.S.C.); *Re Martin* (1962), 40 W.W.R. 513, 36 D.L.R. (2d) 507 (sub nom. *Wilken v. Walker*) (Man. C.A.); *Re Jones*, 49 B.C.R. 216, [1934] 3 W.W.R. 726 (S.C.); *Malychuk v. Malychuk; Traschuk v. Malychuk* (1978), 6 Alta. L.R. (2d) 240, 11 A.R. 372 (T.D.).
163 (1981), 10 E.T.R. 6, 128 D.L.R. (3d) 613 (Ont. Surr. Ct.).
164 Gordon Bale, "Annotation" (1982), 10 E.T.R. 7.
165 R.S.O. 1990, c. F.3.
166 *Family Law Act*, R.S.N. 1990, c. F-2, s. 21(1); *Marital Property Act*, S.N.B. 1980, c. M-1.1, s. 4; *Matrimonial Property Act*, R.S.N.S. 1989, c. 275, s. 12(1); S.S. 1997, c. M-6.11, s. 30; *Baker v. Baker Estate* (1992), 48 E.T.R. 261 (Alta. Q.B.), involved an application by a widow for a division of property based on marriage breakdown and an application for support. The court held that the application for division should be disposed of first, since any assets transferred to the applicant would then no longer form part of the deceased's estate.

in determining the quantum, may have regard to the provision the surviving spouse might reasonably have received on a termination of the marriage.[167]

8. Under s. 34(4) of the *Family Law Act*[168] an *inter vivos* order of support binds the estate of the person required to pay it, unless the order provides otherwise. Assuming that the order extends beyond the death of the person, what effect does it have on an application under the *Succession Law Reform Act*?

You should note that under s. 37 of the *Family Law Act* the court may discharge, vary or suspend any term of an order for support for, *inter alia*, a material change in the circumstances of the dependant or the respondent. Is the respondent's death a material change in circumstances?

9. Is the amount the applicant would have received on the deceased's intestacy a relevant factor in quantifying the award?[169]

10. The testator, a farmer, left all his estate to his wife absolutely, adding that it was his wish that she give each of the children a share as she may deem fit. There are five children, two of whom are minors at the testator's death. The family is a close one and it is likely that the widow will amply provide for the minor children's support. In these circumstances, should an award be made in favour of the minor children?[170]

11. X died intestate. He is survived by his widow and a daughter by a previous marriage who is a minor. All of the estate passed to X's widow, including the proceeds of certain insurance policies. Y is X's former wife. Under the decree *nisi* she was awarded maintenance of $1 per year and the daughter $40 per week. Y's income is approximately the same as X's was before his death. In these circumstances are Y and the daughter entitled to an award?[171]

12. Ought an award to be made in favour of a retarded child who is maintained at the expense of the state in a jurisdiction which does not have a provision similar to s. 58(3) of the *Succession Law Reform Act*, which allows a public agency to apply on behalf of a dependant to whom it is providing support?[172]

13. A testatrix and her husband had one child. They made reciprocal wills by which they left their respective estates to each other, but provided that if the other spouse predeceased, the child would receive $100,000, plus one-fifth of the residue. Would the child, who was 11 years old when her mother died, be successful on an application for support?[173]

14. The quantification of an award is not always easy, as appears from the above materials. In some cases it has been held that the amount to which the applicant would have been entitled to on an intestacy is appropriate.[174] However, that standard of measure-

---

167 *Inheritance (Provision for Family and Dependants) Act 1975*, c. 63, s. 3(2) (U.K.).
168 *Supra*.
169 See *Re Mannion* (1981), 11 E.T.R. 75 at 85, 127 D.L.R. (3d) 626 (Ont. Surr. Ct.), varied on another point, but expressly confirmed in this respect (1982), 39 O.R. (2d) 609, 13 E.T.R. 49 (Div. Ct.), affirmed (1984), 45 O.R. (2d) 339, 16 E.T.R. 190, 6 D.L.R. (4th) 758 (C.A.).
170 See *Public Trustee for Alta. v. Buchholz*, [1981] 1 W.W.R. 500, 8 E.T.R. 57, 116 D.L.R. (3d) 51 (C.A.).
171 See *Re Tothivan* (1982), 36 O.R. (2d) 410, 12 E.T.R. 248 (Surr. Ct.).
172 *Re Deis*; *Spicer v. Deis* (1983), 21 Sask. R. 328, 13 E.T.R. 88 (C.A.); *Re Cousins* (1951), 5 W.W.R. (N.S.) 289, 59 Man. R. 372 (K.B.); *Re Pfrimmer* (1968), 66 W.W.R. 574, 2 D.L.R. (3d) 525 (Man. C.A.); *Re Brousseau*, 7 W.W.R. (N.S.) 262, [1952] 4 D.L.R. 664 (B.C.S.C.); *Penty v. Mott* (1984) 6 D.L.R. (4th) 444 (B.C.S.C.).
173 See *Cameron v. Cameron Estate* (1991), 41 E.T.R. 30 (B.C.S.C.)
174 See, *e.g.*, *Re Jones* (1961), 36 W.W.R. 337, 30 D.L.R. (2d) 316, affirmed [1962] S.C.R. 273, (sub nom. *McCarwill v. Jones*) 37 W.W.R. 597.

ment has usually been rejected[175] and, it is submitted, properly so, since it does not necessarily measure the needs of the dependant accurately. The same objection, although with less force, may be made against the measurement supplied by the provision for the dependant in the testator's invalid will.[176] In one case, the value of the undistributed assets of the estate, which could pay 10% of the net value of the estate to each applicant, was used to quantify the award.[177]

An attractive solution is to employ actuarial evidence in determining the amount of the award if it is desirable that the estate be wound up and that a lump sum be set aside to provide income for a dependant. In those circumstances actuarial evidence of the dependant's life expectancy and the lump sum necessary to generate a specified income in constant dollars would be used.[178]

15. Would a widow who complained, not that she had been improperly provided for under her husband's will, but that the executors refused to exercise their discretion in her favour by increasing her benefits, be entitled to relief?[179]

16. With respect to s. 62(3), you should note that both oral and written statements of the deceased's reasons for the dispositions he has made are admissible. Hence, a statement in the will to this effect would be proper.[180]

Should a solicitor who is asked to advise a testator on the making of a will point out this possibility? Could the solicitor be held liable in negligence to the beneficiaries for failing to do so if, as a result, their share was reduced on a subsequent application for support?

5. ORDERS

(a) Introduction

The court has power to make several types of orders. These include suspensory orders which suspend the administration of the estate in whole or in part,[181] the main order making an award,[182] interim orders,[183] and variation orders.[184] In addition the court may give such further directions as are necessary to give effect to an order.[185] In this part we shall deal with interim orders, the content of the main order and variation orders.

---

175 *Re Hornett* (1962), 38 W.W.R. 385, 33 D.L.R. (2d) 289 (B.C.S.C.); *Re Mannion, supra.*

176 *Phipps v. Cartmill* (1980), 25 B.C.L.R. 222, 10 E.T.R. 137 (S.C.).

177 *Harvey v. Powell Estate* (1988), 30 E.T.R. 143 (N.S.T.D.), affirmed (1989), 36 E.T.R. 100 (N.S.C.A.).

178 This method was used in *Bates v. Bates* (1981), 9 E.T.R. 235 (B.C.S.C.), affirmed [1982] 4 W.W.R. 193, 11 E.T.R. 310 (B.C.C.A.).

179 See *Re Rankin*, [1951] O.W.N. 121 (C.A.).

180 See *Kelly v. Baker* (1996), 15 E.T.R. (2d) 219 (B.C.C.A.), in which the court refused to make an order in favour of an adopted son because of a statement in the will that the adopted son had been disinherited because he had abandoned the family and deliberately chosen an immoral life style.

181 *Succession Law Reform Act*, s. 59.

182 *Ibid.*, s. 58(1).

183 *Ibid.*, s. 64.

184 *Ibid.*, s. 65.

185 *Ibid.*, s. 69.

(b) Suspensory Orders

We have seen that the limitation provisions of the legislation effectively prohibit distribution by the personal representatives during the limitation period. Nonetheless, it may be desirable at times to obtain an order directing them not to distribute until a pending application for support is disposed of. Such a suspensory order is important if the estate includes property that is deemed part of the estate by virtue of s. 72 of the *Succession Law Reform Act*,[186] such as pension benefits and insurance proceeds. The order prevents the payors from making payments to the payees until the support application has been heard. Section 59 of the Ontario Act, set out below, confers the power to make suspensory orders.

SUCCESSION LAW REFORM ACT
R.S.O. 1990, c. S.26

59. On a motion by or on behalf of the dependants or any of them, the court may make an order suspending in whole or in part the administration of the deceased's estate, for such time and to such extent as the court may decide.

Comparable Legislation

Dependants of a Deceased Person Relief Act, R.S.P.E.I. 1988, c. D-6, s. 3; *Dependants Relief Act*, R.S.N.W.T. 1988, c. D-4, s. 2(2); R.S.Y. 1986, c. 44, s. 3; *Dependants' Relief Act*, S.M. 1989-90, c. 42, s. 3; *Family Relief Act*, R.S.A. 1980, c. F-2 [am. 1984, c. 55, s. 20], s. 3(4); R.S.N. 1990, c. F-3, ss. 3(2); *Provision for Dependants Act*, R.S.N.B. 1973, c. T-4 [renamed S.N.B. 1991, c. 62, s. 3(1)], s. 2(2); *Testators' Family Maintenance Act*, R.S.N.S. 1989, c. 465, s. 3(2).

Notes and Questions

1. A suspensory order cannot be made if the contract of insurance was made and the payment is payable in another jurisdiction to a beneficiary who resides out of the jurisdiction.[187]

2. Even though a suspensory order is in effect, the court may, by order, release part of the estate to particular beneficiaries. The court may do so if it is unlikely that the property so released will be needed to satisfy any support order.[188]

(c) Interim Orders

Under the former legislation the court had no power until 1973[189] to make an award pending the disposition of the main application. Since this may cause

---

186 This section is discussed below.
187 *Taylor v. Dolisie* (1991), 42 E.T.R. 57 (Ont. Div. Ct.).
188 See, *e.g.*, *Hecht v. Hecht Estate* (1990), 39 E.T.R. 97 (B.C.C.A.), leave to appeal refused (1994), 1 E.T.R. (2d) 75n (S.C.C.).
189 By S.O. 1973, c. 13, s. 3.

hardship to a dependant, some of the statutes now allow for the making of an interim order. Section 64 of the *Succession Law Reform Act* reproduced below is illustrative.

The basis for making an award under this section is discussed in *Re Pulver*.[190] The respondent made an application for support out of her deceased husband's estate. They had lived together for 17 years. She was 55 years old and of limited means. Probate of the will was contested on the grounds of incapacity and undue influence. Because of the delay, the respondent brought an application for interim support. The executors brought a motion for a stay until the disposition of the contestation of the will. Among others, they argued that the respondent was not a dependant, that she had released all her claims against the estate and that the testator was not domiciled in Ontario. The court dismissed the motion for a stay, holding that s. 64 should receive a fair and liberal interpretation consonant with its purpose. Hence, the balance of convenience favoured her application for an interim order, even though ultimately it might be determined that she was not entitled to support.

SUCCESSION LAW REFORM ACT
R.S.O. 1990, c. S.26

64. Where an application is made under this Part and the applicant is in need of and entitled to support but any or all of the matters referred to in s. 62 or 63 have not been ascertained by the court, the court may make such interim order under s. 63 as it considers appropriate.

Comparable Legislation

Dependants Relief Act, R.S.N.W.T. 1988, c. D-4, s. 17; *Dependants' Relief Act*, S.M. 1989-90, c. 42, s. 11.

Notes and Questions

1. For a case in which an interim order of support was made, see *Re Ruby*.[191] It was a case involving an application by a child of the testator born outside marriage. In that case, as in *Re Pulver*, probate of the will was delayed.

2. Section 19(3) of the *Family Law Reform Act*, discussed in *Re Pulver*, gave the court a wide discretion to grant interim support *inter vivos*. Compare this with the *Family Law Act*,[192] which lists the situations in which the court may make a interim order. Does this eliminate the discretion of the court?

---

190 (1982), 39 O.R. (2d) 460, 13 E.T.R. 1, 139 D.L.R. (3d) 638 (H.C.).
191 (1983), 43 O.R. (2d) 277 (Surr. Ct.).
192 R.S.O. 1990, c. F.3, s. 34(1)(a) - (k).

(d) The Content of Orders

As is apparent from ss. 63, 66 and 68 of the *Succession Law Reform Act*, reproduced below, the court has been given very wide powers to make such orders as will best achieve the appropriate support to the applicant. Sub-sections 63(5) and (6), which are not reproduced, require that notice be given to all persons interested in or affected by the order and empower the court to dispense with notice in appropriate cases.

Under the former legislation it was the practice of the courts to disturb the provisions of the will as little as possible. In other words, they strove to give effect to the testator's scheme and intention as disclosed by the will. This meant that not all of the estate would be charged with the award, but typically those parts of the estate which were not specifically disposed of and were not given to other dependants, such as the residue.[193] It would appear that cases under the new legislation continue to adhere to this policy.[194] Thus, in *Re Mannion*[195] the court directed that the widow be permitted to live in the matrimonial home until death or remarriage, the latter being a condition imposed by the testator on other benefits provided for her.

Under the former legislation it was also not common for the court to award a lump sum, since it was thought that the legislation's purpose was to provide maintenance for the dependants and that that could best be accomplished by periodic payments. Only if the latter would hold up administration unduly would a lump sum be awarded.[196] Under the current legislation it would seem that this inhibition is no longer felt, for lump sum awards have been made in several cases.[197] However the courts continue to recognize that a lump sum should not be given in such an amount as to provide the dependant with an estate, since the purpose of the legislation is to provide support only.[198]

The courts have also employed other powers given by the new legislation, such as the power to charge an award on part of the assets.[199]

---

193 *Re McCaffery*, [1931] O.R. 512 at 519, *per* Riddell J.A.; *Re Schmidt*, [1952] O.R. 532, [1952] 4 D.L.R. 364 (C.A.).

194 *Re Davies* (1979), 27 O.R. (2d) 98, 6 E.T.R. 127 at 135, 136, 105 D.L.R. (3d) 357 (Surr. Ct.); *Re Dentinger* (1981), 10 E.T.R. 6 at 30, 128 D.L.R. (3d) 613; *Re Mannion* (1981), 11 E.T.R. 75 at 84, varied (1982), 13 E.T.R. 49, affirmed (1984), 45 O.R. (2d) 339, 16 E.T.R. 190, 6 D.L.R. (4th) 758 (C.A.). See also *Bates v. Bates* (1981), 9 E.T.R. 235 at 244, affirmed [1982] 4 W.W.R 193.

195 *Supra*, at 11 E.T.R. 84.

196 *Re McCaffery*, [1931] O.R. 512 at 524, *per* Fisher J.A.; *Re Beyor*, [1949] O.W.N. 289, [1949] 2 D.L.R. 604 (C.A.); *Re Duranceau*, [1952] O.R. 584 (C.A.).

197 *Re Cooper* (1980), 30 O.R. (2d) 113; *Re Dentinger* (1981), 10 E.T.R. 6; *Re Tothivan* (1982), 36 O.R. (2d) 410; *Re Mannion* (1981), 11 E.T.R. 75, varied (1982), 13 E.T.R. 49, affirmed (1984), 45 O.R. (2d) 339 (C.A.).

198 *Re Mannion, supra*.

199 *Moores v. Hughes* (1981), 11 E.T.R. 213 (Ont. H.C.).

SUCCESSION LAW REFORM ACT
R.S.O. 1990, c. S.26, am. S.O. 1999, c. 6, s. 61(6)

63. (1) In any order making provision for support of a dependant, the court may impose such conditions and restrictions as the court considers appropriate.

(2) Provision may be made out of income or capital or both and an order may provide for one or more of the following, as the court considers appropriate,

(a) an amount payable annually or otherwise whether for an indefinite or limited period or until the happening of a specified event;

(b) a lump sum to be paid or held in trust;

(c) any specified property to be transferred or assigned to or in trust for the benefit of the dependant, whether absolutely, for life or for a term of years;

(d) the possession or use of any specified property by the dependant for life or such period as the court considers appropriate;

(e) a lump sum payment to supplement or replace periodic payments;

(f) the securing of payment under an order by a charge on property or otherwise;

(g) the payment of a lump sum or of increased periodic payments to enable a dependant spouse, same-sex partner or child to meet debts reasonably incurred for his or her own support prior to an application under this Part;

(h) that all or any of the moneys payable under the order be paid to an appropriate person or agency for the benefit of the dependant;

(i) the payment to an agency referred to in subsection 58(3) of any amount in reimbursement for an allowance or benefit granted in respect of the support of the dependant, including an amount in reimbursement for an allowance paid or benefit provided before the date of the order.

(3) Where a transfer or assignment of property is ordered, the court may,

(a) give all necessary directions for the execution of the transfer or assignment by the executor or administrator or such other person as the court may direct; or

(b) grant a vesting order.

(4) An order under this section may be made despite any agreement or waiver to the contrary.

. . .

66. The Court may at any time,

(a) fix a periodic payment or lump sum to be paid by a legatee, devisee or beneficiary under an intestacy to represent, or in commutation of, such proportion of the sum ordered to be paid as falls upon the portion of the estate in which he or she is interested;

(b) relieve such portion of the estate from further liability; and

(c) direct,

(i) the manner in which such periodic payment is to be secured, or

(ii) to whom such lump sum is to be paid and the manner in which it is to be dealt with for the benefit of the person to whom the commuted payment is payable.

. . .

68. (1) Subject to subsection (2), the incidence of any provision for support ordered shall fall rateably upon that part of the deceased's estate to which the jurisdiction of the court extends.

(2) The court may order that the provision for support be made out of and charged against the whole or any portion of the estate in such proportion and in such manner as to the court seems proper.

Comparable Legislation

Dependants of a Deceased Person Relief Act, R.S.P.E.I. 1988, c. D-6, ss. 6, 8, 10; *Dependants Relief Act*, R.S.N.W.T. 1988, c. D-4, ss. 5, 7, 9; R.S.Y. 1986, c. 44, ss. 6, 8, 10; *Dependants' Relief Act*, S.M. 1989-90, c. 42, ss. 9, 10; S.S 1996, D 25.01, ss. 6, 11; *Family Relief Act*, R.S.A. 1980, c. F-2 [am. 1984, c. 55, s. 20], ss. 5, 8, 9; R.S.N. 1990, c. F-3, ss. 5, 9, 11; *Provision for Dependants Act*, R.S.N.B. 1973, c. T-4 [renamed S.N.B. 1991, c. 62, s. 3(1)], ss. 4, 5; *Testators' Family Maintenance Act*, R.S.N.S. 1989, c. 465, ss. 6, 7, 8; *Wills Variation Act*, R.S.B.C. 1996, c. 490 [am. 1999, c. 29. ss. 17, 18; S.B.C. 2000, c. 24, s. 13], ss. 3, 4, 5.

(e) Change in Circumstances

Section 65 of the *Succession Law Reform Act*, reproduced below, confers upon the court jurisdiction to vary or discharge an order for maintenance. It would seem appropriate that there be such a power, since it is impossible to take account of all future contingencies at the outset.[200] Of course, if it is necessary to increase the award at a later date, this can only be done if part of the estate remains undistributed.

The jurisdiction of the court under this type of provision is discussed in *Maldaver v. Canada Permanent Trust Co. (No. 2)*.[201] Mrs. Maldaver, the testator's daughter, had been left $100 per week from the income of her father's estate by his will. On an application for support made five years previously, that amount had been increased to $170 per week.[202] Another daughter had received a similar amount under the will and had also applied for and received support under the original order. Mrs. Maldaver sought an increase in the award. The will directed that upon the death of the two daughters the residue was to be divided into three equal shares and held for the child or children then living of those two daughters and a third daughter. Section 6 of the *Testators' Family Maintenance Act*[203] was

---

200 The court did have power, prior to 1973, to permit an applicant to renew the application at a later date if the value of the assets was uncertain at the time of the application: *Re Rice Estate*, [1952] O.W.N. 465, [1952] 4 D.L.R. 846 (H.C.).

201 (1982), 53 N.S.R. (2d) 500, 12 E.T.R. 231 (T.D.).

202 *Maldaver v. Canada Permanent Trust Co.* (1977), 1 E.T.R. 41 (N.S.T.D.).

203 R.S.N.S. 1989, c. 303 [am. 1977, c. 18].

virtually identical to s. 65 of the Ontario Act set out below. The court dismissed the application. It held that under s. 6 the court cannot *increase* an order for support, since the adequacy of the provisions made by the testator should be determined on the basis of circumstances existing and reasonably foreseeable at the testator's death.

SUCCESSION LAW REFORM ACT
R.S.O. 1990, c. S.26

65. Where an order has been made under this Part, the court at any subsequent date may,
  (a) inquire whether the dependant benefitted by the order has become entitled to the benefit of any other provision for his or her support;
  (b) inquire into the adequacy of the provision ordered; and
  (c) discharge, vary or suspend the order, or make such other order as the court considers appropriate in the circumstances.

Comparable Legislation

Dependants of a Deceased Person Relief Act, R.S.P.E.I. 1988, c. D-6, s. 7; *Dependants Relief Act*, R.S.N.W.T. 1988, c. D-4, s. 6; R.S.Y. 1986, c. 44, s. 7; *Dependants' Relief Act*, S.M. 1989-90, c. 42, s. 14; S.S.1996, D-25.01, s. 20; *Family Relief Act*, R.S.A. 1980, c. F-2 [am. 1984, c. 55, s. 20], s. 6; R.S.N. 1990, c. F-3, s. 7; *Provision for Dependants Act*, R.S.N.B. 1973, c. T-4 [renamed S.N.B. 1991, c. 62, s. 3(1)], s. 6; *Testators' Family Maintenance Act*, R.S.N.S. 1989, c. 465, s. 7; *Wills Variation Act*, R.S.B.C. 1996, c. 490, s. 10.

Notes and Questions

1. Is the *Maldaver* case correct?[204]

2. Compare *Fox v. Grass*.[205] The testator's surviving common-law wife was awarded a monthly payment from his pension fund, pursuant to a support order under the *Succession Law Reform Act*. She died five years later and the original beneficiaries of the fund applied under s. 65 of the Act for an order to vary the original order so that they would receive the balance of the pension. In determining whether the wife's estate or the original beneficiaries should receive the money, the court considered that the original support order, which did not name any dependant of the wife, applied only to the wife, not to her estate. Thus the original order ceased to have effect upon her death. The court varied the original order to award the full payment of the pension to the original beneficiaries.

---

204 See Gordon Bale, Annotation (1982), 12 E.T.R. 231.
205 (1986), 22 E.T.R. 318 (Ont. Surr. Ct.).

6. PROPERTY SUBJECT TO AN ORDER

(a) Contracts to Leave Property by Will

If a person agrees to leave his or her property to another by will and carries out the agreement, the question might arise whether such property should be subject to an order for support. It is arguable that it should be to the extent that the testamentary disposition is made without consideration. Otherwise, this would be a method to evade the purpose of the legislation. Opinions under earlier legislation varied on this point.

In *Dillon v. Public Trustee of New Zealand*[206] the Privy Council held that the New Zealand support of dependants' legislation overrode a contractual obligation by a testator who had agreed to leave all of his farm lands to his children in return for their working the farm. The testator carried out the agreement. The basis for the decision was that the policy of the legislation was to provide support for dependants and the fact that beneficiaries under a will suffered from carrying out the policy was irrelevant.

In *Schaeffer v. Schuhmann*[207] the Privy Council reversed itself. In that case the testator, a widower, died at age 75, survived by seven children who were grown up and had moved out of the house. His will left $A200 to each of his four daughters and the residue of his $A98,700 estate equally to his three sons. Shortly before his death, the testator bought a house and hired the plaintiff as his housekeeper. He paid her wages for a couple of months, but then made a codicil to his will in which he left the house and contents to her if she should still be employed by him at his death, and he told her that thereafter he would not pay her any more wages. After his death, his daughters applied for support.

The Privy Council held that the support orders made at first instance could not be charged against the property left to the plaintiff pursuant to the valid *inter vivos* contract. The Board noted that the New Zealand legislature had changed its statute to overrule *Dillon* and concluded that valid contracts should not be overridden by the legislation unless the statute expressly permits it.

Section 71 of the *Succession Law Reform Act*, reproduced below, now deals specifically with this question.

Further Reading

Rodney Hull, "Contracts to Make Wills and Dependants' Relief Legislation" (1973-74), 1 E. & T. Q. 240.

William A. Lee, "Contracts to Make Wills" (1971), 87 L.Q. Rev. 358.

---

206 [1941] A.C. 294 (P.C.).
207 [1972] A.C. 572, [1972] 1 All E.R. 621, [1972] 2 W.L.R. 481 (P.C.).

SUCCESSION LAW REFORM ACT
R.S.O. 1990, c. S.26

71. Where a deceased,
- (a) has, in his or her lifetime, in good faith and for valuable consideration, entered into a contract to devise or bequeath any property; and
- (b) has by his or her will devised or bequeathed that property in accordance with the provisions of the contract,

the property is not liable to the provisions of an order made under this Part except to the extent that the value of the property in the opinion of the court exceeds the consideration therefor.

Comparable Legislation

Family Relief Act, R.S.A. 1980, c. F-2, s. 12; R.S.N. 1990, c. 124, s. 16; *Testators' Family Maintenance Act*, R.S.M. 1988, c. T50, s. 18; R.S.N.B. 1973, c. T-4, s. 16; R.S.N.S. 1989, c. 303, s. 15; *Dependants of a Deceased Person Relief Act*, R.S.P.E.I. 1988, c. D-6, s. 14; *Dependants' Relief Act*, S.S.1996, D-25.01 s. 15; R.S.N.W.T. 1988, c. D-4, s. 15; R.S.Y. 1986, c. 44, s. 15.

Notes and Questions

1. Does a beneficiary under a contract of the type referred to in section 71 have a remedy if the deceased has failed to carry out his contract, either by excluding the beneficiary from his will, or by dying intestate?

2. Assuming that the beneficiary under the contract does have a remedy if the contract is breached, would the judgment take priority over an order for support?

Suppose for example that a testator divorced his first wife. Under the separation agreement he agreed to pay her maintenance until her remarriage. He also agreed to keep her as beneficiary of certain insurance policies on his life and to give her half of his assets during his life or leave them to her by will. Both of them remarried and he then changed the beneficiary on the policies to his second wife, and a son. The testator borrowed against the insurance policies after separation, thus reducing their face value. He has left nothing to his first wife under his will. She brings action for breach of contract. The testator's second wife, who is also his executrix, seeks support. What result?[208]

(b) Evasion of Purpose of Legislation

The earliest forms of dependants' relief legislation enabled the courts to make an order only against the so-called probate estate, that is, the assets of the deceased subject to the control of the personal representatives. This could work severe hardship upon a dependant. Thus, for example, if the bulk of the property passing

---

208 See *Phillips v. Spooner*, [1979] 2 W.W.R. 473, 4 E.T.R. 178 (Sask. Q.B.), varied (1980), 7 E.T.R. 157 (Sask. C.A.).

on death consisted of the proceeds of insurance policies which were payable directly to a beneficiary, while there was very little in the probate estate and the latter went to other dependants, a dependant might not have a remedy.[209] Similarly, the deceased might denude his or her estate during his or her lifetime by gifts *mortis causa* or *inter vivos*,[210] or by other voluntary dispositions.[211] To prevent these forms of evasion, s. 72 of the *Succession Law Reform Act*, reproduced below, now deems such property to be part of the deceased's net estate. *Moores v. Hughes*,[212] reproduced below interprets this provision.

Further Reading

Harry W. McMurtry, "Group Life Insurance and the Succession Law Reform Act: Unfair Treatment" (1997), 16 E.& T.J. 193.

Barry S. Corbin, "Ontario Expands the Net for Dependants' Relief Claims" (2000), 20 E.T. & P.J. 1.

SUCCESSION LAW REFORM ACT
R.S.O. 1990, c. S.26, am. S.O. 1999, c. 12, Sched. B, s. 17

72. (1) Subject to section 71, for the purpose of this Part, the capital value of the following transactions effected by a deceased before his or her death, whether benefitting his or her dependant or any other person, shall be included as testamentary dispositions as of the date of the death of the deceased and shall be deemed to be part of his or her net estate for purposes of ascertaining the value of his or her estate, and being available to be charged for payment by an order under clause 63 (2)(*f*),

    (a) gifts *mortis causa*;

    (b) money deposited, together with interest thereon, in an account in the name of the deceased in trust for another or others with any bank, savings office, credit union or trust corporation, and remaining on deposit at the date of the death of the deceased;

    (c) money deposited, together with interest thereon, in an account in the name of the deceased and another person or persons and payable on death under the terms of the deposit or by operation of law to the survivor or survivors of those persons with any bank, savings office, credit union or trust corporation, and remaining on deposit at the date of the death of the deceased;

---

209 See, *e.g.*, *Kerslake v. Gray*, [1957] S.C.R. 516.
210 See, *e.g.*, *Dower v. Public Trustee* (1962), 38 W.W.R. 129, 35 D.L.R. (2d) 29 (Alta. T.D.), in which the testator made gifts of about one million dollars shortly before he died, leaving virtually no estate out of which his widow could obtain relief.
211 See, *e.g.*, *Re Collier* (1967), 65 D.L.R. (2d) 223 (Alta. C.A.), in which a wife transferred a large part of her estate in trust for herself for life with remainder to her children, so that there was little left for her husband.
212 (1981), 37 O.R. (2d) 785, 136 D.L.R. (3d) 516, 11 E.T.R. 213 (H.C.).

(d) any disposition of property made by a deceased whereby property is held at the date of his death by the deceased and another as joint tenants;

(e) any disposition of property made by the deceased in trust or otherwise, to the extent that the deceased at the date of his or her death retained, either alone or in conjunction with another person or persons by the express provisions of the disposing instrument, a power to revoke such disposition, or a power to consume, invoke or dispose of the principal thereof, but the provisions of this clause do not affect the right of any income beneficiary to the income accrued and undistributed at the date of the death of the deceased;

(f) any amount payable under a policy of insurance effected on the life of the deceased and owned by him or her;

(f.1) any amount payable on the death of the deceased under a policy of group insurance; and

(g) any amount payable under a designation of beneficiary under Part III.

(2) The capital value of the transactions referred to in clauses (1)(b), (c) and (d) shall be deemed to be included in the net estate of the deceased to the extent that the funds on deposit were the property of the deceased immediately before the deposit or the consideration for the property held as joint tenants was furnished by the deceased.

(3) Dependants claiming under this Part shall have the burden of establishing that the funds or property, or any portion thereof, belonged to the deceased.

(4) Where the other party to a transaction described in clause (1)(c) or (d) is a dependant, he or she shall have the burden of establishing the amount of his or her contribution, if any.

(5) This section does not prohibit any corporation or person from paying or transferring any funds or property, or any portion thereof, to any person otherwise entitled thereto unless there has been personally served on the corporation or person a certified copy of a suspensory order made under section 59 enjoining such payment or transfer.

(6) Personal service upon the corporation or person holding any such fund or property of a certified copy of a suspensory order shall be a defence to any action or proceeding brought against the corporation or person with respect to the fund or property during the period the order is in force.

(7) This section does not affect the rights of creditors of the deceased in any transaction with respect to which a creditor has rights.

Comparable Legislation

Dependants of a Deceased Person Relief Act, R.S.P.E.I. 1988, c. D-6 [am. 1978, c. 6, s. 64], ss. 19, 20; *Dependants' Relief Act*, R.S.N.W.T. 1988, c. D-4, ss. 19, 20; R.S.Y. 1986, c. 44, ss. 20, 21.

MOORES V. HUGHES
(1981), 37 O.R. (2d) 785, 136 D.L.R. (3d) 516, 11 E.T.R. 213
Supreme Court of Ontario
[High Court of Justice]

The testator died in 1979. He was married to the applicant, Gwen, in 1950 and there were two children of the marriage, now both adults. The parties separated in 1976 and were divorced in 1977. Under the separation agreement, which was incorporated into the decree *nisi*, the testator agreed to pay Gwen $800 per month in maintenance until his death. She was also permitted to remain in the matrimonial home until 1981, when it was to be sold and she was then to be paid $15,000. The testator married the respondent, Anne, soon after his divorce. They then moved to Regina and bought a home there. It was later sold by Anne. By his will the testator left half of his estate to Anne and the other half equally to his two children. The net probate estate, after payment of the $15,000 to Gwen (the house having been sold), was $40,000. Anne, however, also received approximately $365,000 under insurance policies, a pension plan and a joint bank account. Gwen was unable to work full-time because of mental illness. She had no substantial assets.

Gwen brought this application for support against the executor, the testator's brother-in-law, and against Anne. Gwen was awarded interim support by an order of Maloney J. Payments under that order were in arrears. It was not disputed that she was a dependant and that no provision was made for her support.

ROBINS J. (orally):

. . .

Deferring for the moment the amount of support that might be considered adequate in the circumstances, I turn to the question of what constitutes "the estate" of the deceased for the purpose of providing support for this dependant.

[His Lordship read portions of section 72 and continued:]

That section made a significant change in the law as it stood before the enactment of the Succession Law Reform Act. Certain specified transactions effected by a deceased before his death are now to be included as testamentary dispositions as of the date of death and deemed part of his net estate for the purposes of ascertaining its value and being available for the support of a dependant. Manifestly, the section was intended to ensure that the maintenance of a dependant is not jeopardized by arrangements made, intentionally or otherwise, by a person obligated to provide support in the eventuality of his death. It is designed to alleviate the hardship that can be visited on a dependant by causing money or property to pass directly to a beneficiary (donee or joint tenant) and not as part of the estate. Such transactions can, and often do, result in the amount passing in the estate being only a small percentage of the total sum passing upon the death of the deceased, as here where $40,000 is in the estate as against $365,000 outside it.

Turning then to the specific transactions in this case which it is contended should, under s. 72, be included as testamentary dispositions as of the date of Moores' death.

First, the deceased owned an insurance policy with Cuna Insurance Company under which the sum of $15,285.86 was paid to Anne after his death. That was clearly a policy covered by s. 72(1)(f) and must be included in the net estate for the purposes of ascertaining the value of the estate.

Second, the deceased was covered as an employee of The Co-Operators under a group life policy. Anne has received about $150,500 as the beneficiary of this insurance. The policy was issued by The Co-Operators Life Insurance Company as insurers and the policy holder is C.I. Management Group Limited, a company no doubt associated with The Co-Operators. This group policy covers the life of the employee and the amount payable is subject to increase based on the number of dependants of the employee. In this case, Moores was listed as having two dependants (as that term was intended for insurance purposes) his wife, Anne, and his son. The policy, it is of consequence to note, is convertible to an individual plan with The Co-Operators without medical evidence of insurability, within 31 days of termination of employment.

The argument is that it was not a policy owned by the deceased and accordingly is not to be included in his estate for present purposes. I cannot agree. In my view the policy falls within the intent of s. 72(1)(f) and its proceeds should be reflected in the estate. The meaning of words in a statute are to be gathered from the connection in which they are used. Here, the deceased could designate to whom the policy was to be paid; the policy was a benefit of his employment. In reality, he paid for the policy by his services to the company and he was entitled to convert to an individual plan without a medical on terminating his employment. As a practical matter the policy was held by the management company for the benefit of the group and the members of the group were the beneficial owners of the policy. I see no reason why this type of insurance should be excluded from the purview of s. 72(1)(f) and good reason why it should be included. To all intents and purposes the deceased "owned" this insurance and for the purposes of this type of legislation can be considered the owner of the policy insofar as his coverage is concerned.

This brings me to the pension plan in which the deceased was a participant as an employee of The Co-Operators. The sum of $174,500 was payable under the plan to Anne as his designated beneficiary. Like the group insurance, this plan was an employment benefit and Moores contributed to it over the many years he was with the company. The moneys payable under it are "payable under a designation of beneficiary under Part III" as provided for in s. 72(1)(g). Part III is entitled "Designation of Beneficiaries of Interest in Funds of Plans" and this plan is covered. The proceeds of the pension plan will be included as part of the estate of the deceased for the purposes of s. 72.

...

Anne held a joint bank account with the deceased from which she received $18,200 upon his death. The sum was contributed to the account by him and will be included in the estate under s. 72(1)(c).

...

It is argued that neither the insurance nor the pension plan proceeds can be included under s. 72 because of their distribution prior to these proceedings. The argument centres on the word "payable" in ss. (f) and (g) of s. 72(1). With deference, I can see no merit in that argument. It is evident that as a practical matter payments will be made (as they were here) shortly after, if not immediately as in the case of joint bank accounts, the death of the deceased. The insurance company, the trustees of a pension fund, a bank, or anyone paying or transferring funds or property covered by s. 72 is not prohibited from doing so and is freed of any liability unless there has been service made of a suspensory order enjoining such payment or transfer as provided for in s. 59 of the Act. The fact that no suspensory order was obtained, hardly an unlikely situation, does not render the proceeds unavailable. In short, the word "payable" includes "paid" for the purposes of this legislation.

Furthermore, the combined effect of s. 72 and s. 63(2)(f), together with s. 78(2) and s. 66, manifest the Legislature's intention to ensure the availability of such funds of property. In [sic] interpret these sections and the general scheme of the statute to enable the Court to trace funds or property included in s. 72 if necessary to persons to whom they may have been paid or transferred. If such authority is not present the aim of the Act can be frustrated simply because payment was made, as here, before the proceedings could conceivably have been instituted. No prejudice results from the payment because whether the funds are held by the insurance company or trustee or beneficiary, the result is the same. In each case it is available for inclusion in the net estate under s. 72.

In this case I propose to make a charging order only against the proceeds of the insurance or so much thereof as I consider necessary for the protection of the dependant. The pension plan has been converted to the income annuity in favour of Anne and to interfere with that at this time would involve serious tax ramifications. I would not want to jeopardize the tax deferral that has been effected by converting the pension plan proceeds into the registered annuity. If, however, I considered it necessary to do so, to give effect to s. 62, I would.

This brings me back to the question of what constitutes proper support in the circumstances. I have in mind, of course, the circumstances enumerated in s. 62 and have considered them insofar as they are relevant. These include the assets and means of the dependant which, as I have said, are non-existent here (save for the $15,000 she will be receiving out of the sale of the house); her capacity to provide for her own support; her age and physical and mental health, and her needs. I have also of course considered the duration of the dependant's relationship with the deceased. She was married some 26 years to the deceased and, with respect to the pension plan, it is evident that most of that was earned during

Moores' marriage to Gwen rather than to Anne which, regrettably, lasted only for about a year and a half. I place particular emphasis on s. 62(1)(a)(xiv)[213] which makes reference to "any agreement between the deceased and the dependant". In this case the deceased and his first wife, having the advice of counsel, agreed to a settlement of the financial matters between them and maintenance at the time of their divorce. No basis exists for impugning that agreement and while some evidence was led in this respect, it was not contended in argument that the agreement could be set aside. I consider the agreement made by the parties themselves as to what constituted adequate support at the time to be an important guidepost in determining proper support under the Succession Law Reform Act. I take into account also the position of the second wife, her responsibilities and her adequate financial circumstances as a result of this marriage. She is possessed of some assets aside from the benefits she received on Moores' death but they do not appear to be significant (aside from the house) and I do not consider them a factor in my considerations.

It was suggested by counsel for the applicant that the range to be awarded here is between $1,200 and $1,500 a month. That range appears to me to be reasonable and no argument was advanced suggesting that it is not. In the circumstances it is my view that a fair and just amount to fix for proper support is $1,300 per month. That together with the capital and the income on the $15,000 which Gwen will be receiving will put her in a position approximating the one she agreed to in 1977, having regard to the inflation and to her inability to obtain any rental income.

Anne will be receiving about $20,000 from the estate and the children about $10,000 each. Section 68 of the Act provides that the incidence of any provision for support shall fall rateably upon the deceased's estate but authorizes the Court to order that the provisions for support be made out of and charged against the whole or any portion of the estate in such proportion and such manner as to the Court seems proper. In the circumstances of this case I am satisfied that the interest of the children in the estate ought not to be charged and I direct the executor to make the payments to which they are entitled so soon as he is able to do so. I make that order for several reasons, not the least of which is that the award to the children is a small one. Also, Anne received an additional $75,000 on the group insurance policy as a result of the dependancy of one of the children who in fact has not been a dependant of hers. It seems to be equitable that the moneys payable to Anne be held subject to a charge for the purpose of securing the order that I have made.

[In the order directed to be issued, His Lordship further provided that the moneys should be paid to Gwen during her lifetime or until remarriage or until she should establish a permanent relationship with a man with whom she cohabits.]

---

213 Now s. 62(1)(m).

Notes and Questions

1. In *Moores v. Hughes* the court concluded that the group policy fell within the intent of the legislation, but apparently only because the deceased had effective control over it. Some cases followed *Moores*. Thus, in *Blaro v. Aetna Insurance Co.*,[214] the court held that a group life insurance policy under which the deceased was insured through his employment, was owned by the deceased. The employer paid all the premiums, but the employee was free to designate beneficiaries and could convert the policy to an individual life policy if employment ceased.[215]

However, other cases refused to follow *Moores*. *Re Urquhart Estate*[216] is an example. The deceased was insured under his employer's group insurance plan and had named his son beneficiary of the policy. The courts held that s. 72(1)(f) applies only to policies of insurance owned by the deceased: it did not apply in this case, because the policy was owned by the employer. One of the arguments relied on by the courts in *Urquhart* was that s. 173(1) of the *Insurance Act*[217] provides that when the insured designates a beneficiary, the insurance proceeds do not form part of the estate, so that s. 72 of the *Succession Law Reform Act* could not apply to the proceeds. However, *Dunn v. Dunn Estate*[218] resolved the conflict between the statutes. It held that the *Succession Law Reform Act*, as the special Act, overrides the *Insurance Act*, which is the general Act.

In consequence of the different opinions over the effect of s. 72(1)(f), Ontario added clause (f.1) to s. 72(1) in 1999. It extends the reach of s. 72(1) to group insurance. Is clause (f.1) problem-free?[219]

2. In *Smallman Estate v. Smallman Estate*,[220] the court considered s. 72(1)(g), regarding the designation of beneficiary under a pension plan. The testator's widow received a survivor's pension under his retirement plan. However, the plan left the award of the survivor's pension in the complete discretion of the pension committee. The court held that in those circumstances the pension did not accrue to her by her husband's designation and was, therefore, not deemed to be part of his estate.

3. Since an order can only be made in respect of property that remains undistributed, it is important for a dependant to ensure that those persons liable to pay third parties under insurance policies, pension plans and similar obligations which are deemed to be testamentary dispositions under s. 72 do not make such payments until the application for support has been disposed of. Section 59 of the Act, which enables the court to make a suspensory order, would not by itself achieve this result, since it is directed to the suspension of the probate estate. However, s. 72(5) appears to have the effect of preventing payment if such a suspensory order is served upon the payor. Presumably, therefore, it is necessary to obtain a suspensory order to prevent payment of obligations under insurance policies, pension plans and similar obligations. Notice of an application for support would

---

214 (1988), 30 E.T.R. 283 (Ont. Surr. Ct.).
215 See also *Barton v. Barton Estate* (1991), 42 E.T.R. 213 (Ont. Gen. Div.), to the same effect.
216 (1990), 38 E.T.R. 222 (Ont. H.C.), affirmed (sub nom. *Taylor v. Dolisie*) (1991), 42 E.T.R. 57 (Ont. Div. Ct.).
217 Now R.S.O. 1990, c. I.8.
218 (1992), 8 O.R. (2d) 95, 46 E.T.R. 115 (Gen. Div.), affirmed (1993), 49 E.T.R. 44 (Ont. Div. Ct.). The case was followed in *Roy v. Armstrong Estate* (1998), 21 E.T.R. (2d) 166 (Ont. Gen. Div.).
219 See Barry S. Corbin, "Ontario Expands the Net for Dependants' Relief Claims" (2000), 20 E.T. & P.J. 1.
220 (1991), 41 E.T.R. 86 (Ont. Gen. Div.)

not be sufficient. On the other hand, as *Moores v. Hughes* makes clear, the dependant can still reach the proceeds in the hands of the payee.

4. Although s. 72 deals specifically with gifts *mortis causa* and certain non-absolute gifts, it would seem that the purpose of the legislation can still be avoided by absolute gifts made shortly before death.

The Prince Edward Island, Northwest Territories and Yukon statutes have plugged this loophole by empowering the court to make a donee to whom a gift was made by the deceased within a specified period before death repay the estate such part thereof as may be necessary to make adequate provision for the dependants.[221]

5. The testator was twice married. By his will he left all his property to his second wife and appointed her his sole executrix. When he died he also held two parcels of real property in joint tenancy with his second wife. He had conveyed them to himself and his second wife without consideration. Beyond the limitation period specified in s. 61 of the *Succession Law Reform Act*, the testator's first wife made an application for support and claimed, *inter alia*, that the joint property can be made the subject of an order. What result?[222]

6. The legislation deems the capital value of a disposition by the deceased to the deceased and another person as joint tenants to be part of the estate. However, it does not permit the making of an order granting possession of the matrimonial home to the surviving spouse.[223]

7. It is inappropriate, on an application to determine a preliminary question of law, to ascertain whether the capital value of property held by a spouse in joint tenancy, which was acquired by the spouse as joint tenant with others and not disposed of by him prior to his death, is or is not deemed to be part of his net estate for the purpose of ascertaining the value of the estate and making it available to the charged under s. 72.[224]

However, in *Modopoulos v. Breen Estate*[225] the court held that s. 72 is not engaged when the property was acquired jointly by the deceased and another person, since there is then no disposition involved.[226] Section 72 only applies if the deceased owned the property and then transferred it to himself or herself and another person as joint tenants.[227]

8. Jurisdictions that have no similar legislation do not permit claimants to seek to have *inter vivos* transfers into joint tenancy set aside. The issue arose in *Hossay v. Newman*.[228] The testator had placed his major assets into joint tenancy before he died. After his death, his son brought an application to vary the will and sought to have the transfer set aside as a fraudulent conveyance under the *Fraudulent Conveyance Act*.[229] Only "creditors or others" can attack fraudulent transfers under this Act and the son did not fall into that category.

---

221 For the statutory references see *supra*.
222 See *Re Dolan* (1983), 43 O.R. (2d) 677 (Div. Ct.).
223 *Holland v. Clements Estate* (1988), 30 E.T.R. 93 (Ont. Surr. Ct.).
224 *Cimetta v. Topler, et al.* (1989), 68 O.R. (2d) 251 (H.C.).
225 (1996), 15 E.T.R. (2d) 128 (Ont. Gen. Div.).
226 As there was, for example, in *Holland v. Clements Estate* (1991), 43 E.T.R. 299 (Ont. Gen. Div.).
227 See also *Lamb (Litigation Guardian of) v. Lamb* (1998), 22 E.T.R. (2d) 294 (Ont. Gen. Div.), to the same effect.
228 (1998), 22 E.T.R. (2d) 150 (B.C.S.C.).
229 R.S.B.C. 1996, c. 163.

7. CONTRACTING OUT OF LEGISLATION

It sometimes happens that the deceased entered into an agreement with a dependant in which the dependant releases all claims upon the estate of the deceased. Is such an agreement valid so as to prevent the dependant from seeking support after the deceased's death?[230]

Under s. 63(4) of the *Succession Law Reform Act*[231] the court is given the discretion to make an order for support, even though the dependant has released or waived his or her right to support. In most cases, such a release or waiver would be contained in a domestic contract, that is, a marriage contract, a cohabitation agreement or a separation agreement. The *Family Law Act*[232] permits spouses and cohabitees to regulate, *inter alia*, their support obligations in such agreements. The court may set aside such an agreement while both parties are living only if the provision respecting support "results in circumstances that are unconscionable," if the dependant receives public support, or if there is default in support payments under the agreement.[233]

Although the *Succession Law Reform Act* does not contain a similar provision, the effect of s. 63(4) is perhaps stronger in that the court's discretion is wider than under the *Family Law Act*. The agreement is, however, a factor which the court must consider on an application for support.[234] It would seem that if, for example, a separation agreement provides that the husband is not required to support his wife during his lifetime, an order cannot be made under the *Succession Law Reform Act*, since he would not have supported or have been under a legal obligation to support her before his death and, hence, she would not be a dependant.[235]

The Yukon and Nova Scotia Acts expressly provide that a person cannot contract out of the legislation.[236] It has been held in New Brunswick that one can

---

230 Under the former legislation in Ontario it was always held that a person could not contract himself or herself out of the legislation, since the right to maintenance was a matter of public policy. See, *e.g.*, *Re Duranceau*, [1952] O.R. 584 (C.A.); *Re Carey*, [1940] O.R. 171 (C.A.); and *Smith v. Nat. Trust Co.* (1959), 15 D.L.R. (2d) 520 (Ont. H.C.).

There was one exception to that rule. This arose if a wife entered into a separation agreement under which she accepted a lump sum payment in lieu of all other claims against her husband. By her own act she had thereby forfeited her right to sue for alimony and, under section 9 of the *Dependants' Relief Act*, R.S.O. 1970, c. 126, she was thereby precluded from claiming relief. That section imposed a bar to relief if the wife was living apart from her husband at the time of his death in circumstances disentitling her to alimony: *Olin v. Perrin* [1946] O.R. 54; *Smith v. Nat. Trust Co.*, *supra*; *Re Stadnyk*, [1963] 1 O.R. 95 (C.A.). If the separation agreement called for periodic payments, the widow was not barred: *Re Carey, supra*.

231 Reproduced above.

232 R.S.O. 1990, c. F.3, ss. 52-54.

233 *Ibid.*, s. 33(4).

234 *Succession Law Reform Act*, s. 62(1)(m). See also *Goldhar v. Goldhar* (1985), 21 E.T.R. 189, 48 R.F.L. (2d) 1 (Ont. Div. Ct.), affirmed (1986), 21 E.T.R. xxxiii (Ont. C.A.); *Swire v. Swire* (1986), 23 E.T.R. 246 (Ont. Surr. Ct.); *Boulanger v. Singh* (1984), 16 D.L.R. (4th) 131.

235 See, *e.g.*, *Smith v. Henderson and Lane* (1985), 49 R.F.L. (2d) 351.

236 *Dependants Relief Act*, R.S.Y. 1986, c. 44, s. 17; and *Testator's Family Maintenance Act*, R.S.N.S. 1989, c. 303, s. 16(2).

contract oneself out of the legislation,[237] but cases in Alberta and Saskatchewan hold otherwise.[238] In British Columbia it appears that an agreement does not necessarily bar an application for support. The court must determine whether the dependant is in need when the testator dies. The testator's moral duty is assessed at that time. If the dependant is in need, the testator has failed to discharge his or her moral duty, even though the agreement was fair when made.[239]

Notes and Questions

1. Instead of an agreement entered into between the deceased and the dependant in which the dependant waives all claims against the estate, the deceased inserts a provision in his will to the effect that a benefit conferred by the will is revoked if the beneficiary commences litigation with respect to the will other than a proceeding to interpret the will or for the advice and directions of the court in the administration of the will. Would such a provision apply to an application for support? If so, is it valid?[240]

2. *Butts Estate v. Butts*[241] affords a good example of the court's jurisdiction to override a domestic contract. The husband agreed to pay his wife $500 per month for life. The parties intended their agreement to be final. However, when he died, he left an estate worth $700,000 and she was in want. The court held that she remained a dependant and that the support she had been receiving was inadequate. She was entitled to support of $1,500 per month, or a lump sum equivalent so that the estate and the deceased's Life Income Fund, payable to his third wife, would not be tied up for years into the future.

---

237 *Re Marquis* (1980), 30 N.B.R. (2d) 93 (Q.B.).
238 *Re Berube*, [1973] 3 W.W.R. 180, 12 R.F.L. 97, 34 D.L.R. (3d) 445 (Alta. C.A.); *Collard v. Collard* (1976), 28 R.F.L. 252 (Sask. Surr. Ct.); *Stepaniuk v. Koziol Estate* (1985), 24 E.T.R. 259.
239 See *Wagner v. Wagner Estate* (1991), 44 E.T.R. 24 (B.C.C.A.).
240 *Kent v. McKay*, 38 B.C.L.R. 216, [1982] 6 W.W.R. 165, 13 E.T.R. 53, 139 D.L.R. (3d) 318 (S.C.).
241 (1999), 27 E.T.R. (2d) 81 (Ont. Gen. Div.).

PART VI

SOLICITOR'S DUTIES AND RESPONSIBILITES

18

SOLICITOR'S DUTIES

1. Introduction
2. Taking Instructions for a Will
3. Duty of Care towards Beneficiaries

1. INTRODUCTION

Throughout this text we have examined a number of duties that solicitors owe to testators and others. In this chapter we shall focus on two such duties. The first is the duty that solicitors owe in taking instructions for a will. This is a broad duty, encompassing giving advice and ensuring that everything is done properly. Our concern in this chapter is the duty to ensure that the testator knows and understands the testamentary act, has capacity, and is not subjected to undue influence.

The second matter to be discussed is the duty of care that solicitors owe to beneficiaries. Traditionally, solicitors only owed a duty of care to the testator, but not the beneficiaries, since the solicitor did not contract with them. However, the modern law recognizes that solicitors owe a duty of care to beneficiaries as well.

2. TAKING INSTRUCTIONS FOR A WILL

(a) Introduction

The courts have, in many instances, had occasion to criticize the actions of solicitors in taking instructions for wills. The case law imposes an obligation on a solicitor to satisfy himself or herself that the testator has capacity, that the testator has knowledge and approval of the contents and that there is no apparent undue influence or fraud. This duty is particularly significant if the prospective testator is elderly or is apparently suffering from delusions or lack of capacity, if the instructions differ substantially from a previous will, and especially if the instructions are not received from the testator himself or herself.

(b) The Case Law

Of the solicitor's duty, Chancellor Boyd said in *Murphy v. Lamphier*:[1]

> A solicitor is usually called in to prepare a will because he is a skilled professional man. He has duties to perform which vary with the situation and condition of the testator. In the case of a person greatly enfeebled by old age or with faculties impaired by disease, and particularly in the case of one labouring under both disabilities, the solicitor does not discharge his duty by simply taking down and giving legal expression to the words of the client, without being satisfied by all available means that testable capacity exists and is being freely and intelligently exercised in the disposition of the property. The solicitor is brought in for the very purpose of ascertaining the mind and will of the testator touching his worldly substance and his comprehension of its extent and character and of those who may be considered proper and natural objects of his bounty. The Court reprobates the conduct of a solicitor who needlessly draws a will without getting personal instructions from the testator, and, for one reason, that the business of the solicitor is to see that the will represents the intelligent act of a free and competent person.

His Lordship continued:[2]

> [I]n drawing the will of one of considerably impaired or of doubtful capacity, the solicitor should regard himself as the professional *alter ipse* of his client, and seek to touch his mind and meaning and memory, to learn of the property to be dealt with and of the usual objects of his regard, as far as may be, by such questioning as shall elicit particulars, and thus to satisfy himself that he has done or tried to do all in his power to find out the real situation. Nor is it a counsel of perfection to suggest that a memorandum of results, apart from the formally expressed will, should be jotted down and preserved. The solicitor may in some perfunctory way go far enough to satisfy himself as to capacity, but it is to be remembered that his duty is to go far enough to satisfy the Court that the steps he took were sufficient to warrant his satisfaction.[3]

The solicitor's duty is further discussed in *Re Worrell*,[4] reproduced below.

RE WORRELL
[1970] 1 O.R. 184, 8 D.L.R. (3d) 36
Ontario Surrogate Court
[Simcoe County]

The testator's will left virtually the entire estate to his friends, Mr. and Mrs. Barfoot, their daughter and grand-daughter. Mr. Barfoot had prepared the letter of instructions which the testator signed. Barfoot took the letter to a solicitor who had never acted for the testator and who drafted the will with some changes from the instructions. He then gave it to Barfoot to have it executed.

The attesting witnesses, long-standing friends of the testator, testified that they believed the testator to be competent, that he had been conducting his affairs

---

1 (1914), 31 O.L.R. 287, 6 O.W.N. 238, affirmed (1914), 32 O.L.R. 19, 7 O.W.N. 45, 20 D.L.R. 906 (C.A.), at 31 O.L.R. 318-19.

2 *Ibid.*, at pp. 320-1.

3 See also *Re Seabrook; Dunne v. Dundas* (1978), 4 E.T.R. 135 at 158-60.

4 [1970] 1 O.R. 184, 8 D.L.R. (3d) 36 (Surr. Ct.).

competently and that he was very fond of the Barfoot family. The testator's physician also thought that the testator was competent to make a will.

There was no evidence that the will was ever read to the testator and only weak evidence that he ever read it.

The court concluded that the suspicious circumstances had not been removed and pronounced against the will.

CLARE SURR. CT. J.

. . .

I consider it necessary in this action to comment on the conduct of the solicitor who drew the will that is at issue. The solicitor impressed me as an honest, conscientious person, and yet on his own evidence he acted as set out hereunder:

(a) he prepared a will for a testator for whom he had never acted and whom he never saw and knew the testator concerned was 82 years of age and confined to a home for the aged,
(b) he drew the will without any knowledge of the size of the testator's estate or the nature of its assets,
(c) he drew the will leaving a substantial portion of the estate to the person who consulted him,
(d) he drew the will with changes from the original letter of instructions signed by the testator without any consultation with the testator,
(e) he handed the will to the beneficiary who had consulted him, to take out and have executed,
(f) he kept no docket entries or other records dealing with the matters in issue.

It seems incredible that a competent solicitor, the head of a respected law firm, would act in this manner. It seems even more incredible that he gave no indication in the witness-box which would indicate that he realized he had acted improperly.

The law as to a solicitor's duty in drafting a will has been set out many times, and I will deal with the solicitor's actions as set out above.

(a) *Jarman on Wills*,[5] deals with the responsibility of a solicitor in regard to wills and the editor, in a footnote, comments that these suggestions are reprinted verbatim from the original text so that they have been considered a proper guide to the profession for over 100 years. A portion only of the suggestions is set out:

FEW of the duties which devolve upon a solicitor, more imperatively call for the exercise of a sound, discriminating, and well-informed judgment, than that of taking instructions for wills. It frequently happens, that, from a want of familiar acquaintance with the subject, or from the physical weakness induced by disease, (where the testamentary act has been, as it too often is, unwisely deferred until the event which is to call it into operation seems to be impending), testators are incapable of giving more than a general or imperfect outline of their intention, leaving the particular provisions to the discretion of their professional adviser. Indeed, some testators sit

---

5 8th ed., pp. 2073-4, in app. A - "Suggestions to Persons Taking Instructions for Wills."

down to this task with so few ideas upon the subject, that they require to be informed of the ordinary modes of disposition under similar circumstances of family and property, with the advantages and disadvantages of each; and their judgment in the selection of one of these modes is necessarily influenced by, if not wholly dependent on, professional recommendation . . . .

[And][6]

To the preceding suggestions, it may not be useless to add, that it is in general desirable, that professional gentlemen taking instructions for wills should receive their instructions immediately from the testator himself, rather than from third persons, particularly where such persons are interested. In a case in the Prerogative Court[7] Sir J. Nicholl "admonished professional gentlemen generally, that where instructions for a will are given by a party not being the proposed testator, *a fortiori* where by an interested party, it is their bounden duty to satisfy themselves thoroughly, either in person, or by the instrumentality of some confidential agent, as to the proposed testator's volition and capacity, or in other words, that the instrument expresses the real testamentary intentions of a capable testator, prior to its being executed *de facto* as a will at all."

I would suggest that in this day of speedy methods of transportation there should be no occasion when a solicitor should prepare a will without receiving his instructions from the testator. It is certainly improper for a solicitor to draft a will without taking direct instructions from the testator and then not to attend personally when the will is executed. For example, a son of an old client might come to the solicitor's office and advise that his father, a widower, is in the hospital and wants a will leaving his whole estate equally among his children. In such circumstances, the solicitor might properly, for convenience, engross such a will and attend on the testator, but should — under no circumstances — say to the testator: "I understand you want a will leaving your property thus and so, and I have drawn such a will. Is this satisfactory?" This, especially with older people is a dangerous practice and the solicitor should, on attending the testator say: "I understand you want a will drawn and will you tell me how you wish your estate to go on your death." The asking of leading questions by a solicitor obtaining instructions from an elderly testator is a practice to be avoided. Too often the elderly person, if asked leading questions, will reply in the affirmative, but if simply asked "What property do you have?", or "How do you wish your estate to go on your death?", may exhibit complete lack of comprehension.

No better statement of the duties of a solicitor in drafting a will can be found than in the judgment of Chancellor Boyd in *Murphy v. Lamphier*:[8] "The Court reprobates the conduct of a solicitor who needlessly draws a will without getting personal instructions from the testator."

(b) Chancellor Boyd in the above cited case of *Murphy v. Lamphier* deals with the necessity for a solicitor to enquire as to the nature and extent of the testator's property. It seems clear that a solicitor who does not have this information is not in a position to properly advise the testator as to the incidence of estate tax or other problems of draftsmanship. As I have pointed out above, this realization of the extent of his assets is a further test of the competency of the testator.

---

6 *Ibid.*, p. 2077.

7 *Rogers v. Pittis* (1822), 1 Add. 30 at 46, 48, 162 E.R. 12.

8 (1914), 31 O.L.R. 287 at 318 to 321 inclusive, and in particular p. 319.

(c) Without the necessity of quoting authorities, it should be clear that a solicitor taking instructions from a major beneficiary under a proposed will rather than from the testator, should be at once alerted and should, in the language previously quoted from . . . Jarman, satisfy himself thoroughly that the instrument expresses the real testamentary intentions of a capable testator, prior to its being executed *de facto* as a will at all. In the case before us, the solicitor took no such precautions and to my mind when the beneficiary prepared a typewritten letter of instructions, the signature of the testator thereto in no way absolved the solicitor of his responsibilities.

(d) I simply cannot conceive how the solicitor can justify drawing a will not in accordance with the written instructions received from the testator. The solicitor acted after obtaining information from Mr. Barfoot, the beneficiary, and one cannot escape the conclusion that the solicitor, whether consciously or unconsciously, was taking instructions from Mr. Barfoot and ignoring the testator's written instructions which were his only connection directly with the testator.

(e) The fact that the solicitor handed the will, as engrossed, to the beneficiary to have executed is improper for the reasons set out in (a) above.

(f) I consider that any solicitor drawing a will should make full docket entries in regard to all details thereof. Especially is this so in the case of an elderly testator, and even more so in the circumstances in this case. Chancellor Boyd, in *Murphy v. Lamphier* said[9] "Nor is it a counsel of perfection to suggest that a memorandum of results, apart from the formally expressed will, should be jotted down and preserved." The practice of keeping solicitors' dockets may be falling into disuse, but in regard to testamentary matters they are essential. As was stated by Ferguson, J., in the recent case *Re Dingwall*,[10] "It is the most elementary of teaching in regard to the drafting of wills that the draftsman should preserve his notes of the testator's intentions." With no docket entries, the solicitor in this case was unsure as to whether he had recommended to Barfoot that he might get a letter from a doctor or somebody at the Simcoe Manor with regard to the capacity of the testator. I should point out that the solicitor rendered an account to Mr. Worrell in the amount of $30 for preparation of a will and power of attorney. This account is dated February 9, 1967 (ex. 5), and was paid by Mr. Worrell's cheque of the same date.

. . .

Notes and Questions

1. Is it ethical for a solicitor to refuse to draw a will for a person who in his or her opinion lacks capacity? Is that question for the solicitor to decide?[11]

2. A solicitor who knows the testatrix probably lacks capacity but nevertheless prepares the will without instructions from the testatrix "in anticipation of receiving instructions

---

9 *Ibid.*, at p. 321.
10 Unreported.
11 See *Banton v. CIBC Trust Corp.* (1999), 182 D.L.R. (4th) 486 at 495-6 (Ont. S.C.J.).

from her" and who takes part in propounding the will, is likely to have costs awarded against him or her on a solicitor and client basis.[12]

3. In *Wilson v. Kinnear*[13] solicitor had prepared a will for a testatrix which left her husband, a pensioner, with a life interest in a portion of her estate, at the discretion of the executors. When she read over the will, the testatrix ordered that it be altered to allow the husband to take his portion absolutely. Two previous wills of the testatrix named the husband sole beneficiary and executor. The day before the testatrix died, the solicitor was unable to visit her home to alter the will according to her wishes, but he took instructions over the telephone from X that the testatrix wished to revert to the original form and give the executors discretion over the husband's portion of the estate. X was the sister of the testatrix, in whose home the testatrix was staying, and was an executrix as well as a substantial beneficiary under the will. The solicitor sent his articled clerk to the testatrix's bedside. She signed the new will in the clerk's presence. The testatrix was in the final stages of exhaustion and had diabetes and gangrene. In restoring the judgment of the trial judge, who found undue influence on the part of the sister and rejected the will, the court stated, ". . . it was his [the solicitor's] imperative duty to make himself more than sure that the change was truly the wish of the testatrix, and not the will of someone else suggested to and impressed upon a dying woman."

4. Does a medical doctor who witnesses a will thereby warrant testamentary capacity?[14]

5. If a testator is old and infirm, should a medical doctor be asked, not only to satisfy himself or herself that the testator has capacity and understanding, but also to witness the will?[15]

6. A solicitor taking instructions for the will must obtain from the testator information about the testator's relatives and persons who have a moral claim on the testator's bounty. Further, the solicitor must find out the nature of the testator's property. However, it is not necessary that the solicitor know the exact value of the property.[16]

7. If there is concern about the testator's capacity arising partly from the fact that the testator is changing a former will substantially and disinheriting family members, it is wise to have an assessment done of his or her testamentary capacity. An assessment merely of the testator's capacity to manage property is not sufficient, as the capacity to manage property raises different concerns. Further, the person doing the assessment should be instructed to interview family members.[17]

8. Is it proper for the secretarial staff of a law firm to prepare a will and attend to its execution without the involvement of a lawyer?[18]

---

12 *Orleski v. Reid* (1985), 18 E.T.R. 305 (Sask. Q.B.), affirmed (1989), 31 E.T.R. 249 (Sask. C.A.).

13 [1925] 2 D.L.R. 641 (P.C.), reversing 24 O.W.N. 282, which reversed 22 O.W.N. 253.

14 See *Dougan v. Allan* (1914), 6 O.W.N. 713.

15 See *Re Simpson; Schaniel v. Simpson* (1977), 121 Sol. J. 224. And see Law Reform Committee (U.K.), *Twenty-Second Report (The Making and Revocation of Wills)*, Cmnd 7902 (May 1980), § 2.17-19.

16 *Piasta v. St. John's Cathedral Boys' School* (1989), 35 E.T.R. 139 at 148-9, *per* Monnin, C.J.M. (Man. C.A.). See also *Danchuk v. Calderwood* (1996), 15 E.T.R. (2d) 193 at 215-6 (B.C.S.C.).

17 See *Banton v. Banton* (1998), 164 D.L.R. (4th) 176, esp. at pp. 200-202, suppl. reasons *loc. cit.* at 244 (Ont. Gen. Div.). See also *Banton v. CIBC Trust Corp.* (1999), 30 E.T.R. (2d) 138, 148, 182 D.L.R. (4th) 486 (Ont. S.C.J.).

18 See *Vout v. Hay*, [1995] 2 S.C.R. 876, 7 E.T.R. (2d) 209, 125 D.L.R. (4th) 432. And see on this point Mary Louise Dickson, "Formalities of execution of will — Suspicious circumstances — Burden of proof " (1996), 15 E. & T.J. 308 at 311.

9. For an extreme example of a solicitor's egregious failure to meet her obligations in taking instructions, see *Ball v. Ball*.[19] The deceased has a history of mental illness, but the solicitor did not obtain medical advice about the deceased's capacity. She did not have a solicitor's file on the matter; had no written instructions or other evidence indicating that the content of the will, which left the estate to the deceased's niece, reflected the deceased's intention; and did not produce an earlier will which left the estate to the deceased's daughter. Further, the solicitor was herself a contingent capital beneficiary under the will.

10. *Mackenzie v. Mackenzie*[20] provides a striking contrast in the execution of solicitors's duties. It depicts one lawyer who punctiliously observed his obligations and prepared a proper will, and a second who exemplified a miserable failure to keep proper notes and to address issues of knowledge and approval, and undue influence. The first will was admitted to probate.

11. Solicitors should be particularly vigilant of testators who are illiterate or semi-literate. Often such persons go to great pains to hide the fact and this may cause problems if it is shown that they did not understand the meaning of the will. *Benson v. Sunderland*[21] involved an illiterate testatrix. The solicitor did not know about the illiteracy, but since the terms of the will were fully explained to the testatrix, the court was able to find that she knew and understood the contents.

Further Reading

Peter DeC. Cory, "A Whirl with Re Worrell" (1971), 5 L.S.U.C. Gazette 274.

Panel Discussion, "Wills and the Administration of Estates" (1953), 31 Can. Bar Rev. 353.

W.B. Williston, "Testamentary Capacity", in Law Society of Upper Canada Special Lectures (1963, Part I), *Mentally Disabled and the Law*, p. 89.

The Hon. Mr. Justice Stewart, "The Preparation and Presentation of Medical Proof", in Law Society of Upper Canada Special Lectures (1955), *Evidence*, p. 155, at pp. 175-8, 184-6.

Rodney Hull, "Obtaining Instructions for the Preparation of the Will" (1982), 6 E. & T. Q., 11.

Rodney Hull, "Relevant Considerations and Potential Consequences Pertinent to the Taking of Instructions for a Will or Estate Plan" (1980), 28 Chitty's L.J. 148.

J.A. Brulé "Will Planning and Drafting" in Law Society of Upper Canada Special Lectures (1980), *Recent Developments in Estate Planning and Administration*, p. 361.

Rodney Hull, "The Avoidance of Malpractice in Estate Planning and Administration" (1979), 5 E. & T.Q. 89.

Albert H. Oosterhoff, "Testamentary Capacity, Suspicious Circumstances and Undue Influence" (1999), 18 E. T. & P. J. 369, espec. at 392-5.

Albert H. Oosterhoff, "Consequences of a January/December Marriage: A Cautionary Tale" (1999), 18 E.,T. & P. J. 261.

Ian M. Hull, "Prior Wills and Testamentary Documents: Know When to Hold Them, Know When to Fold Them" (1997) 16 E.T.R. (2d) 94.

Heather A. Laidlaw, "Solicitor-Client Privilege: To Disclose or Not To Disclose . . . Even After Death" (1995),15 E.& T.J. 56.

---

19 (1996), 14 E.T.R. (2d) 309 (Ont. Gen. Div.).
20 (1998), 24 E.T.R. (2d) 260 (N.S.C.A,).
21 (1999), 26 E.T.R. (2d) 265 (Man. Q.B.).

Michael Silver, "Solicitor's Conflict of Interest and Breach of Duty Acting for Spouses in the Preparation of a Will" (1993) 13 E.T. & J. 111.

Mary Louise Dickson, "Conflicts in Estates" (1996) E. & T. J. 160.

3. DUTY OF CARE TOWARDS BENEFICIARIES

(a) Introduction

Until the middle of the twentieth century, the law of most jurisdictions denied recovery of damages to a beneficiary who failed to inherit because of the negligence of the solicitor who drafted the will. The reason for the denial was the doctrine of privity of contract. Thus, a solicitor was liable for negligence only to his or her client, that is, the person with whom the solicitor has contracted.[22] However, in 1958 the Supreme Court of California allowed a beneficiary's action for negligence.[23] Other jurisdictions have followed that lead.

The law of negligence has changed substantially in the last fifty years in Canada, England and other common law countries and, therefore, it is not surprising that actions by disappointed beneficiaries to recover from negligent solicitors should come before the courts in these jurisdictions.

The first non-American case was the British Columbia case, *Whittingham v. Crease & Co.*[24] It was followed by *Ross v. Caunters*[25] in England. *Ross v. Caunters* was followed in Australia,[26] and New Zealand.[27] *Ross v. Caunters* was also followed by the Court of Appeal in England in *White v. Jones*.[28] However, the House of Lords in that case based recovery on a different principle.[29]

(b) The Case Law

Many of the cases to date involve situations in which solicitors failed to observe well-known formal requirements of wills, with the result that beneficiaries lost the gifts intended for them. *Whittingham v. Crease*[30] is an example. The solicitor, having prepared the will in accordance with the testator's instructions, attended at the testator's home and read the will in the presence of the testator and the testator's son and the son's wife. The son was the main beneficiary under the will.

---

22 *Re Fitzpatrick*, 54 O.L.R. 3, [1924] 1 D.L.R. 981 (C.A.) *Hall v. Meyrick*, [1957] 2 Q.B. 455, [1957] 2 All E.R. 722 (C.A.).

23 See *Biakanja v. Irving* (1958), 49 Cal. 2d 647, 320 P.2d 16; followed in *Lucas v. Hamm* (1961), 56 Cal. 2d 283, 364 P.2d 685, cert. den. 368 U.S. 987.

24 [1978] 5 W.W.R. 45, 3 E.T.R. 97, 6 C.C.L.T. 1, 88 D.L.R. (3d) 353 (B.C.S.C.).

25 [1980] Ch. 297, [1979] 3 All E.R. 580.

26 *Watts v. Public Trustee*, [1980] W.A.R. 97 (S.C.).

27 *Gartside v. Sheffield Young & Ellis*, [1983] N.Z.L.R. 37 (C.A.).

28 *White v. Jones*, [1993] 3 All E.R. 481 (C.A.).

29 *White v. Jones*, [1995] 2 A.C. 207, [1995] 1 All E.R. 691 (H.L.).

30 *Supra.*

The solicitor asked the son's wife to attest the will and she did so. This rendered the gift to her husband void, by reason of s. 12(1) of the *Wills Act*,[31] as it would in most common law jurisdictions that do not have a statutory saving provision.[32] The court held that the solicitor was negligent. The mistake was not in respect of an esoteric point of the law of wills with which not every solicitor might be familiar; rather it was a point that any lawyer, indeed, any law student, knows or ought to know, namely, the effect of having a beneficiary or his or her spouse attest a will.

The British Columbia Supreme Court allowed recovery on the basis of the *Hedley Byrne*[33] principle. The principle of that case is that if a person seeks information from a person possessing a special skill and trusts that person to exercise due care, and if that person knew or ought to have known that reliance was being placed on his or her skill and judgment, then the skilled person owes a duty of care to the first person. Further, absent an express disclaimer of responsibility, the first person can recover damages for financial loss caused by the negligent misrepresentation, whether spoken or written, of the second person.

Ross v. Caunters[34] concerned a similar kind of situation. The defendant solicitors drafted the testator's will. The testator wrote to the solicitors, asking them to send the will to him and stating that he would sign it, have it witnessed and return it to the defendants. The defendants sent him the will with a covering letter giving instructions for its execution. These said, *inter alia*, that it should be signed by the testator at the end of the will in the presence of two witnesses who were not beneficiaries under the will. The plaintiff was a beneficiary under the will and her husband was one of the attesting witnesses. The effect of this was that the plaintiff's gift was void under s. 15 of the *Wills Act*.[35] The defendants failed to notice the problem when the will was returned to them, and it was not discovered until after the testator's death.

The plaintiff then brought action against the defendants for damages for the loss of her benefits under the will in that they failed to inform the testator about the statutory requirements, to check whether the will was properly executed, to notice that the gifts to the plaintiff would be void, and to inform the testator of the problem. The defendants admitted the allegations but denied liability on the ground that they only owed a duty of care to the testator and not to the plaintiff.

The court awarded damages to the plaintiff for the loss of the benefits the testator intended to confer on her by the will. The Vice Chancellor, Sir Robert Megarry, rejected the defendants' arguments that a solicitor, (1) is immune from an action in tort brought by the client, but can only be sued in contract; and (2)

---

31 R.S.B.C. 1960, c. 408.
32 See, for example, Ontario's *Succession Law Reform Act*, R.S.O. 1990, c. S.26, s. 12(3), which provides that a gift is not void if the court is satisfied that the person or the person's spouse attesting the will exercised any improper or undue influence upon the testator.
33 *Hedley Byrne & Co. v. Heller & Partners Ltd.*, [1964] A.C. 465, [1963] 2 All E.R. 575 (H.L.).
34 *Supra.*
35 7 Will. 4 & 1 Vict., c. 26 (1837).

can only be liable in negligence to his or her client, not to a third party. His Lordship stated:[36]

> In broad terms, a solicitor's duty to his client is to do for him all that he properly can, with, of course, proper care and attention. Subject to giving due weight to the adverb "properly", that duty is a paramount duty. The solicitor owes no such duty to those who are not his clients. He is no guardian of their interests. What he does for his client may be hostile and injurious to their interests; and sometimes the greater the injuries the better he will have served his client. The duty owed by a solicitor to a third party is entirely different. There is no trace of a wide and general duty to do all that properly can be done for him. Instead, in a case such as the present, there is merely a duty, owed to him as well as the client, to use proper care in carrying out the client's instructions for conferring the benefit on the third party. If it is to be held that there is a duty that is wider than that, that will have to be determined in some other case. The duty I hold to exist in the present case, far from diluting the solicitor's duty to his client, marches with it, and, if anything, strengthens it.

His Lordship noted: (1) the close proximity of the plaintiff to the defendants; (2) that this proximity was a product of the duty of care owed by the defendants to the testator; and (3) that to hold that the defendants were under a duty of care to the defendants would not impose an uncertain and unlimited liability, but a finite one to a finite number of persons, namely, one. He held that the defendants owed a duty of care to the plaintiff because it was obvious that if they were careless, she would suffer loss.

In discussing *Whittingham v. Crease & Co.*[37] his Lordship stated that the *Hedley Byrne*[38] doctrine could be used in this case because the beneficiary knew of the making of the will and the gift to her and relied on the solicitor to ensure that the will was efficacious. In similar circumstances, the court in *Whittingham* regarded the solicitor as having made an implied representation that the will was effective. The Vice Chancellor noted, however, that in many situations the beneficiary is not aware of the will and, therefore, places no reliance on the solicitor. In those situations, therefore, the *Hedley Byrne* principle can not be used, but the principle in *Donaghue v. Stevenson*[39] can. His Lordship concluded that a claim in negligence for economic loss can succeed not only under the *Hedley Byrne* principle, but can also be maintained under the *Donaghue v. Stevenson* principle. Finally, the Vice Chancellor held that there were no policy reasons precluding imposition of liability on the solicitor.

In *White v. Jones*,[40] which is reproduced below, the House of Lords rejected the approach used in *Ross v. Caunters*, but held that the principle in *Hedley-Byrne* could be extended to cover cases in which beneficiaries were unaware of the making of the will.

---

36   At [1980] Ch. 322, [1979] 3 All E.R. 599.
37   [1978] 5 W.W.R. 45 (B.C.S.C.).
38   [1964] A.C. 465 (H.L.).
39   [1932] A.C. 562 (H.L.).
40   [1995] 2 A.C. 207, [1995] 1 All E.R. 691 (H.L.).

WHITE v. JONES
[1995] 2 A.C. 207, [1995] 1 All E.R. 691
House of Lords

The defendants were a firm of solicitors and their managing clerk. In February 1986, the testator, Arthur Barratt, who was 78 years old, instructed the clerk to prepare a will disinheriting his two daughters, Carol (Mrs. White) and Pauline (Mrs. Heath). The testator wanted to cut them out of his estate because he and they had quarrelled. The firm prepared the will and the testator executed it in March 1986. In June 1986 the testator and his daughters were reconciled. The testator told his daughters what he had done and that he was about to rectify it. He sent a letter to the firm asking them to prepare a new will with a gift of £9,000 to each of the two daughters. The firm received the letter on July 17, but nothing was done until August 16, when the clerk asked the firm's probate department to prepare a will or codicil giving effect to the testator's instructions. The clerk went on vacation for two weeks on August 17. When he returned, he made arrangements to see the testator on September 17 to discuss the will and have it executed. The testator died on September 14. The two daughters brought this action for damages for negligence. The trial judge dismissed the action and the daughters appealed.

The Court of Appeal[41] followed *Ross v. Caunters*[42] and allowed the daughters' appeal. The defendants appealed to the House of Lords.

LORD GOFF OF CHIEVELEY:

. . .

The conceptual difficulties

[I]t has been recognised on all hands that *Ross v. Caunters*[43] raises difficulties of a conceptual nature, and that as a result it is not altogether easy to accommodate the decision within the ordinary principles of our law of obligations. . . .

It is right . . . that I should immediately summarise these conceptual difficulties. They are as follows:

(1) First, the general rule is well established that a solicitor acting on behalf of a client owes a duty of care only to his client. The relationship between a solicitor and his client is nearly always contractual, and the scope of the solicitor's duties will be set by the terms of his retainer; but a duty of care owed by a solicitor to his client will arise concurrently in contract and in tort.[44] But, when a solicitor is performing his duties to his client, he will generally owe no duty of care to third parties. Accordingly, as Sir Donald Nicholls V.-C. pointed out in the present case, a solicitor acting for a seller of land does not generally owe a duty of care to the

---

41 [1995] 2 A.C. 207 at 216, [1993] 3 All E.R. 481 (C.A.).
42 [1980] Ch. 297, [1979] 3 All E.R. 580.
43 *Ibid.*
44 See *Midland Bank Trust Co. Ltd. v. Hett, Stubbs & Kemp*, [1979] Ch. 384, [1978] 3 All E.R. 571, recently approved by your Lordships' House in *Henderson v. Merrett Syndicates Ltd.*, [1994] 3 W.L.R. 761, [1993] 3 All E.R. 506

buyer.[45] Nor, as a general rule, does a solicitor acting for a party in adversarial litigation owe a duty of care to that party's opponent.[46] Further it has been held that a solicitor advising a client about a proposed dealing with his property in his lifetime owes no duty of care to a prospective beneficiary under the client's then will who may be prejudicially affected.[47]

[T]he scope of the solicitor's duties to his client are set by the terms of his retainer; and as a result it has been said that the content of his duties are entirely within the control of his client. The solicitor can, in theory at least, protect himself by the introduction of terms into his contract with his client; but, it is objected, he could not similarly protect himself against any third party to whom he might be held responsible, where there is no contract between him and the third party.

In these circumstances, it is said, there can be no liability of the solicitor to a beneficiary under a will who has been disappointed by reason of negligent failure by the solicitor to give effect to the testator's intention. There can be no liability in contract, because there is no contract between the solicitor and the disappointed beneficiary; if any contractual claim was to be recognised, it could only be by way of a ius quaesitum tertio, and no such claim is recognised in English law. Nor could there be liability in tort, because in the performance of his duties to his client a solicitor owes no duty of care in tort to a third party such as a disappointed beneficiary under his client's will.

(2) A further reason is given which is said to reinforce the conclusion that no duty of care is owed by the solicitor to the beneficiary in tort. Here, it is suggested, is one of those situations in which a plaintiff is entitled to damages if, and only if, he can establish a breach of contract by the defendant. First, the plaintiff's claim is one for purely financial loss; and as a general rule, apart from cases of assumption of responsibility arising under the principle in *Hedley Byrne & Co. Ltd v. Heller & Partners Ltd.*,[48] no action will lie in respect of such loss in the tort of negligence. Furthermore, in particular, no claim will lie in tort for damages in respect of a mere loss of an expectation, as opposed to damages in respect of damage to an existing right or interest of the plaintiff. Such a claim falls within the exclusive zone of contractual liability; and it is contrary to principle that the law of tort should be allowed to invade that zone. Of course, Parliament can create exceptions to that principle by extending contractual rights to persons who are not parties to a contract. . . . But as a matter of principle a step of this kind cannot be taken by the courts, though they can redefine the boundaries of the exclusive zone, as they did in *Donaghue v. Stevenson*.[49]

The present case, it is suggested, falls within that exclusive zone. Here, it is impossible to frame the suggested duty except by reference to the contract between the solicitor and the testator — a contract to which the disappointed beneficiary is not a party, and from which, therefore, he can derive no rights. Second, the loss

45 See *Gran Gelato Ltd. v. Richcliff (Group) Ltd.*, [1982] Ch. 560, [1992] 1 All E.R. 865.
46 See *Al-Kandari v. J.R. Brown & Co.*, [1988] Q.B. 665, 672, [1988] 1 All E.R. 833 at 836, *per* Lord Donaldson of Lymington M.R.
47 See *Clarke v. Bruce Lance & Co.*, [1988] 1 W.L.R. 881, [1988] 1 All E.R. 364.
48 [1964] A.C. 465, [1963] 2 All E.R. 575 (H.L.).
49 [1932] A.C. 562.

suffered by the disappointed beneficiary is not in reality a loss at all; it is, more accurately, a failure to obtain a benefit. All that has happened is that what is sometimes called a spes successionis has failed to come to fruition. As a result, he has not become better off; but he is not made worse off. A claim in respect of such a loss of expectation falls, it is said, clearly within the exclusive zone of contractual liability.

(3) A third, and distinct, objection is that, if liability in tort was recognised in cases such as *Ross v. Caunters*,[50] it would be impossible to place any sensible bounds to cases in which such recovery was allowed. In particular, the same liability should logically be imposed in cases where an inter vivos transaction was ineffective, and the defect was not discovered until the donor was no longer able to repair it. Furthermore, liability could not logically be restricted to cases where a specific named beneficiary was disappointed, but would inevitably have to be extended to cases in which wide, even indeterminate, classes of persons could be said to have been adversely affected.

(4) Other miscellaneous objections were taken, though in my opinion they were without substance. In particular — (a) Since the testator himself owes no duty to the beneficiary, it would be illogical to impose any such duty on his solicitor. I myself cannot however see any force in this objection. (b) To enable the disappointed beneficiary to recover from the solicitor would have the undesirable, and indeed fortuitous, effect of substantially increasing the size of the testator's estate — even of doubling it in size; because it would not be possible to recover any part of the estate which had lawfully devolved upon others by an unrevoked will or on an intestacy, even though that was not in fact the testator's intention. I cannot however see what impact this has on the disappointed beneficiary's remedy. It simply reflects the fact that those who received the testator's estate, either under an unrevoked will or on an intestacy, were lucky enough to receive a windfall; and in consequence the estate is, so far as the testator and the disappointed beneficiary are concerned, irretrievably lost.

(5) There is however another objection of a conceptual nature, which was not adumbrated in argument before the Appellate Committee. In the present case, unlike *Ross v. Caunters* itself, there was no act of the defendant solicitor which could be characterised as negligent. All that happened was that the solicitor did nothing at all for a period of time, with the result that the testator died before his new testamentary intentions could be implemented in place of the old. As a general rule, however, there is no liability in tortious negligence for an omission, unless the defendant is under some pre-existing duty. Once again, therefore, the question arises how liability can arise in the present case in the absence of a contract.

· · ·

The impulse to do practical justice

Before addressing the legal questions which lie at the heart of the present case, it is, I consider, desirable to identify the reasons of justice which prompt judges

---

50 [1980] Ch. 297, [1979] 3 All E.R. 580.

and academic writers to conclude, like Megarry V.-C. in *Ross v. Caunters*, that a duty should be owed by the testator's solicitor to a disappointed beneficiary. The principal reasons are, I believe, as follows.

(1) In the forefront stands the extraordinary fact that, if such a duty is not recognised, the only persons who might have a valid claim (*i.e.*, the testator and his estate) have suffered no loss, and the only person who has suffered a loss (*i.e.*, the disappointed beneficiary) has no claim.[51] It can therefore be said that, if the solicitor owes no duty to the intended beneficiaries, there is a lacuna in the law which needs to be filled. This I regard as being a point of cardinal importance in the present case.

(2) The injustice of denying such a remedy is reinforced if one considers the importance of legacies in a society which recognises (subject only to the incidence of inheritance tax, and statutory requirements for provision for near relatives) the right of citizens to leave their assets to whom they please, and in which, as a result, legacies can be of great importance to individual citizens, providing very often the only opportunity for a citizen to acquire a significant capital sum; or to inherit a house, so providing a secure roof over the heads of himself and his family; or to make special provision for his or her old age. . . .

(3) There is a sense in which the solicitors' profession cannot complain if such a liability may be imposed upon their members. If one of them has been negligent in such a way as to defeat his client's testamentary intentions, he must regard himself as very lucky indeed if the effect of the law is that he is not liable to pay damages in the ordinary way. It can involve no injustice to render him subject to such a liability, even if the damages are payable not to his client's estate for distribution to the disappointed beneficiary (which might have been the preferred solution) but direct to the disappointed beneficiary.

(4) That such a conclusion is required as a matter of justice is reinforced by consideration of the role played by solicitors in society. The point was well made by Cooke J. in *Gartside v. Sheffield, Young & Ellis*,[52] when he observed:

> To deny an effective remedy in a plain case would seem to imply a refusal to acknowledge the solicitor's professional role in the community. In practice the public relies on solicitors (or statutory officers with similar functions) to prepare effective wills.

The question therefore arises whether it is possible to give effect in law to the strong impulse for practical justice which is the fruit of the foregoing considerations. For this to be achieved, I respectfully agree with the Sir Donald Nicholls V.-C. when he said[53] that the court will have to fashion "an effective remedy for the solicitor's breach of his professional duty to his client" in such a way as to repair the injustice to the disappointed beneficiary.

---

51 See *Ross v. Caunters*, [1980] Ch. 297, 303, [1979] 3 All E.R. 580 at 583, *per* Sir Robert Megarry V.-C.
52 [1983] N.Z.L.R. 37, 43.
53 See [1993] 3 W.L.R. 730,739.

Ross v. Caunters and the conceptual problems

In *Ross v. Caunters*, Sir Robert Megarry V.-C. approached the problem as one arising under the ordinary principles of the tort of negligence. He found himself faced with two principal objections to the plaintiff's claim. The first . . . was that a solicitor could not be liable in negligence in respect of his professional work to anyone except his client, his liability to his client arising only in contract and not in tort. This proposition Sir Robert rejected without difficulty. . . . The second, and more fundamental, argument was that, apart from cases falling within the principle established in *Hedley Byrne & Co. Ltd. v. Heller & Partners Ltd.*,[54] no action lay in the tort of negligence for pure economic loss. . . . Sir Robert . . . held that here liability could properly be imposed in negligence for pure economic loss, his preferred basis being by direct application of *Donaghue v. Stevenson*[55] itself.

It will at once be seen that some of the conceptual problems raised by the appellants in argument before the Appellate Committee were not raised in *Ross v. Caunters*.[56] Others which were raised plainly did not loom so large in argument as they have done in the present case. Thus the point founded on the fact that in cases of this kind the plaintiff is claiming damages for the loss of an expectation was briefly touched upon by Sir Robert[57] and as briefly dismissed by him, but (no doubt for good reason, having regard to the manner in which the case was presented) there is no further analysis of the point. It is however my opinion that, these conceptual arguments having been squarely raised in argument in the present case, they cannot lightly be dismissed. They have to be faced; and it is immediately apparent that they raise the question whether the claim properly falls within the law of contract or the law of tort. This is because, although the plaintiffs' claim has been advanced, and indeed held by the Court of Appeal to lie, in the tort of negligence, nevertheless the response of the appellants has been that the claim, if properly analysed, must necessarily have contractual features which cannot ordinarily exist in the case of a an ordinary tortious claim. Here I refer not only to the fact that the claim is one for damages for pure economic loss, but also to the need for the defendant solicitor to be entitled to invoke as against the disappointed beneficiary any terms of the contract with his client which may limit or exclude his liability; to the fact that the damages claimed are for the loss of an expectation; and also to the fact (not adverted to below) that the claim in the present case can be said to arise from a pure omission, and as such will not (apart from special circumstances) give rise to a claim in tortious negligence. Faced with points such as these, the strict lawyer may well react by saying that the present claim can lie only in contract, and is not therefore open to a disappointed beneficiary as against the testator's solicitor. . . .

---

54 [1964] A.C. 465, [1963] 2 All E.R. 575 (H.L.).
55 [1932] A.C. 562.
56 [1980] Ch. 297, [1979] 3 All E.R. 580.
57 *Ibid.*, at Ch. 322, All E.R. 599.

It must not be forgotten however that a solicitor who undertakes to perform services for his client may be liable to his client for failure to exercise due care and skill in relation to the performance of those services not only in contract, but also in negligence under the principle in *Hedley Byrne & Co. Ltd. v. Helter & Partners Ltd.*[58] on the basis of assumption of responsibility by the solicitor towards his client. Even so there is great difficulty in holding, on ordinary principles, that the solicitor has assumed any responsibility towards an intended beneficiary under a will which he has undertaken to prepare on behalf of his client but which, through his negligence, has failed to take effect in accordance with his client's instructions. The relevant work is plainly performed by the solicitor for his client; but, in the absence of special circumstances, it cannot be said to have been undertaken for the intended beneficiary. Certainly, again in the absence of special circumstances, there will have been no reliance by the intended beneficiary on the exercise by the solicitor of due care and skill; indeed, the intended beneficiary may not even have been aware that the solicitor was engaged on such a task, or that his position might be affected. Let me take the example of an inter vivos gift where, as a result of the solicitor's negligence, the instrument in question is for some reason not effective for its purpose. The mistake comes to light some time later during the lifetime of the donor, after the gift to the intended donee should have taken effect. The donor, having by then changed his mind, declines to perfect the imperfect gift in favour of the intended donee. The latter may be unable to obtain rectification of the instrument, because equity will not perfect an imperfect gift (though there is some authority which suggests that exceptionally it may do so if the donor has died or become incapacitated.[59] I for my part do not think that the intended donee could in these circumstances have any claim against the solicitor. It is enough, as I see it, that the donor is able to do what he wishes to put matters right. From this it would appear to follow that the real reason for concern in cases such as the present lies in the extraordinary fact that, if a duty owed by the testator's solicitor to the disappointed beneficiary is not recognised, the only person who may have a valid claim has suffered no loss, and the only person who has suffered a loss has no claim. . . .

. . .

[His Lordship noted that the problem was similar to that of transferred loss which arises principally in maritime law when a buyer of goods tries to enforce against a shipowner a remedy in tort in respect of loss of or damage to goods at the buyer's risk when the rights under the contract and the property have not yet passed to the buyer. Apart from statute, such a buyer has no remedy. His Lordship continued:]

In practical terms, part or all of the testator's estate has been lost because it has been dispatched to a destination unintended by the testator. Moreover, had a gift been similarly misdirected during the testator's lifetime, he would either have been able to recover it from the recipient or, if not, he could have recovered the

---

58 [1964] A.C. 465, [1963] 2 All E.R. 575 (H.L.): see *Midland Bank Trust Co. Ltd. v. Hett, Stubbs & Kemp*, [1977] Ch. 384.

59 See *Lister v. Hodgson* (1867), L.R. 4 Eq. 30, 34-35, *per* Romilly M.R.

full amount from the negligent solicitor as damages. In a case such as the present, no such remedies are available to the testator or his estate. The will cannot normally be rectified: the testator has of course no remedy: and his estate has suffered no loss, because it has been distributed under the terms of a valid will. In these circumstances, there can be no injustice if the intended beneficiary has a remedy against the solicitor for the full amount which he should have received under the will, this being no greater than the damage for which the solicitor could have been liable to the donor if the loss had occurred in his lifetime.

A contractual approach

It may be suggested that, in cases such as the present, the simplest course would be to solve the problem by making available to the disappointed beneficiary, by some means or another, the benefit of the contractual rights (such as they are) of the testator or his estate against the negligent solicitor. . . . Attractive though this solution is, there is unfortunately a serious difficulty in its way. The doctrine of consideration still forms part of our law of contract, as does the doctrine of privity of contract which is considered to exclude the recognition of a *jus quaesitum tertio*.

[His Lordship did not think it right to circumvent such a long established doctrine. He continued:]

The tortious solution

I therefore return to the law of tort for a solution to the problem. For the reasons I have already given, an ordinary action in tortious negligence on the lines proposed by Sir Robert Megarry V.-C. in *Ross v. Caunters*[60] must, with the greatest respect, be regarded as inappropriate, because it does not meet any of the conceptual problems which have been raised. Furthermore, for the reasons I have previously given, the *Hedley Byrne* principle cannot, in the absence of special circumstances, give rise on ordinary principles to an assumption of responsibility by the testator's solicitor towards an intended beneficiary. Even so it seems to me that it is open to your Lordships' House . . . to fashion a remedy to fill a lacuna in the law and so prevent the injustice which would otherwise occur on the facts of cases such as the present [because] if the solicitors were negligent and their negligence did not come to light until after the death of the testator, there would be no remedy for the ensuing loss unless the intended beneficiary could claim. In my opinion, therefore, your Lordships' House should in cases such as these extend to the intended beneficiary a remedy under the *Hedley Byrne* principle by holding that the assumption of responsibility by the solicitor towards his client should be held in law to extend to the intended beneficiary who (as the solicitor can reasonably foresee) may, as a result of the solicitor's negligence, be deprived of his intended legacy in circumstances in which neither the testator nor his estate will

---

60 [1980] Ch. 297, [1979] 3 All E.R. 580.

have a remedy against the solicitor. Such liability will not of course arise in cases in which the defect in the will comes to light before the death of the testator, and the testator either leaves the will as it is or otherwise continues to exclude the previously intended beneficiary from the relevant benefit. . . .

As I see it, not only does this conclusion produce practical justice as far as all parties are concerned, but it also has the following beneficial consequences.

(1) There is no unacceptable circumvention of established principles of the law of contract.

(2) No problem arises by reason of the loss being of a purely economic character.

(3) Such assumption of responsibility will of course be subject to any term of the contract between the solicitor and the testator which may exclude or restrict the solicitor's liability to the testator under the principle in *Hedley Byrne*. It is true that such a term would be most unlikely to exist in practice; but as a matter of principle it is right that this largely theoretical question should be addressed.

(4) Since the *Hedley Byrne* principle is founded upon an assumption of responsibility, the solicitor may be liable for negligent omissions as well as negligent acts of commission.[61] This conclusion provides justification for the decision of the Court of Appeal to reverse the decision of Turner J. in the present case, although this point was not in fact raised below or before your Lordships.

(5) I do not consider that damages for loss of an expectation are excluded in cases of negligence arising under the principle in *Hedley Byrne*, simply because the cause of action is classified as tortious. Such damages may in principle be recoverable in cases of contractual negligence; and I cannot see that, for present purposes, any relevant distinction can be drawn between the two forms of action. In particular an expectation loss may well occur in cases where a professional man, such as a solicitor, has assumed responsibility for the affairs of another; and I for my part can see no reason in principle why the professional man should not, in an appropriate case, be liable for such loss under the *Hedley Byrne* principle.

. . . Let me emphasise that I can see no injustice in imposing liability upon a negligent solicitor in a case such as the present where, in the absence of a remedy in this form, neither the testator's estate nor the disappointed beneficiary will have a claim for the loss caused by his negligence. This is the injustice which, in my opinion, the judges of this country should address by recognising that cases such as these call for an appropriate remedy, and that the common law is not so sterile as to be incapable of supplying that remedy when it is required.

Unlimited claims

I come finally to the objection that, if liability is recognised in a case such as the present, it will be impossible to place any sensible limits to cases in which

---

61 See *Midland Bank Trust Co. Ltd. v. Hett, Stubbs & Kemp*, [1979] Ch. 384, 416, [1978] 3 All E.R. 571, *per* Oliver J. and *Henderson v. Merrett Syndicates Ltd.*, [1994] 3 W.L.R. 761, 777, *per* Lord Goff of Chieveley.

recovery is allowed. Before your Lordships, as before the Court of Appeal, Mr. Matheson conjured up the spectre of solicitors being liable to an indeterminate class, including persons unborn at the date of the testator's death. [However, w]e are concerned here with a liability which is imposed by law to do practical justice in a particular type of case. There must be boundaries to the availability of a remedy in such cases; but these will have to be worked out in the future, as practical problems come before the courts. In the present case Sir Donald Nicholls V.-C. observed that, in cases of this kind, liability is not to an indeterminate class, but to the particular beneficiary or beneficiaries whom the client intended to benefit through the particular will. I respectfully agree, and I also agree with him that the ordinary case is one in which the intended beneficiaries are a small number of identified people. If by any chance a more complicated case should arise to test the precise boundaries of the principle in cases of this kind, that problem can await solution when such a case comes forward for decision.

Conclusion

For these reasons I would dismiss the appeal with costs.

LORD BROWNE-WILKINSON:

My Lords, I have read the speech of my noble and learned friend Lord Goff of Chieveley and agree with him that this appeal should be dismissed. In particular, I agree that your Lordships should hold that the defendant solicitors were under a duty of care to the plaintiffs arising from an extension of the principle of assumption of responsibility explored in *Hedley Byrne and Co. Ltd. v. Heller and Partners Ltd.*[62] In my view, although the present case is not directly covered by the decided cases, it is legitimate to extend the law to the limited extent proposed using the incremental approach by way of analogy. . . .

. . .

I am not purporting to give any comprehensive statement of this aspect of the law. The law of England does not impose any general duty of care to avoid negligent misstatements or to avoid causing pure economic loss even if economic damage to the plaintiff was foreseeable. However, such a duty of care will arise if there is a special relationship between the parties. Although the categories of cases in which such special relationship can be held to exist are not closed, as yet only two categories have been identified, *viz.* (1) where there is a fiduciary relationship and (2) where the defendant has voluntarily answered a question or tenders skilled advice or services in circumstances where he knows or ought to know that an identified plaintiff will rely on his answers or advice. In both these categories the special relationship is created by the defendant voluntarily assuming to act in the matter by involving himself in the plaintiff's affairs or by choosing to speak. If he does so assume to act or speak he is said to have assumed

---

62 [1964] A.C. 465, [1963] 2 All E.R. 575 (H.L.).

responsibility for carrying through the matter he has entered upon. In the words of Lord Reid in *Hedley Byrne*[63] "he has accepted a relationship ... which requires him to exercise such care as the circumstances require", i.e. although the extent of the duty will vary from category to category, some duty of care arises from the special relationship. Such relationship can arise even though the defendant has acted in the plaintiff's affairs pursuant to a contract with a third party.

I turn then to apply those considerations to the case of a solicitor retained by a testator to draw a will in favour of an intended beneficiary. As a matter of contract, a solicitor owes a duty to the testator to use proper skill in the preparation and execution of the will and to act with due speed. But as the speech of Lord Goff demonstrates that contractual obligation is of little utility. Breach by the solicitor of such contractual duty gives rise to no damage suffered by the testator or his estate; under our existing law of contract, the intended beneficiary, who has suffered the damage, has no cause of action on the contract.

Has the intended beneficiary a cause of action based on breach of a duty of care owed by the solicitor to the beneficiary? The answer to that question is dependent upon whether there is a special relationship between the solicitor and the intended beneficiary to which the law attaches a duty of care. In my judgment the case does not fall within either of the two categories of special relationships so far recognised. There is no fiduciary duty owed by the solicitor to the intended beneficiary. Although the solicitor has assumed to act in a matter closely touching the economic well-being of the intended beneficiary, the intended beneficiary will often be ignorant of that fact and cannot therefore have relied upon the solicitor.

However, it is clear that the law in this area has not ossified. [It has been recognized] that there might be other sets of circumstances in which it would be appropriate to find a special relationship giving rise to a duty of care [and] that the law will develop novel categories of negligence "incrementally and by analogy with established categories". In my judgment, this is a case where such development should take place since there is a close analogy with existing categories of special relationship giving rise to a duty of care to prevent economic loss.

The solicitor who accepts instructions to draw a will knows that the future economic welfare of the intended beneficiary is dependent upon his careful execution of the task. It is true that the intended beneficiary (being ignorant of the instructions) may not rely on the particular solicitor's actions. But, as I have sought to demonstrate, in the case of a duty of care flowing from a fiduciary relationship liability is not dependent upon actual reliance by the plaintiff on the defendant's actions but on the fact that, as the fiduciary is well aware, the plaintiff's economic wellbeing is dependent upon the proper discharge by the fiduciary of his duty. Second, the solicitor by accepting the instructions has entered upon, and therefore assumed responsibility for, the task of procuring the execution of a skilfully drawn will knowing that the beneficiary is wholly dependent upon his carefully carrying out his function. That assumption of responsibility for the task is a feature of both the two categories of special relationship so far identified in

---

63 *Ibid.*, at A.C. 486, All E.R. 583.

the authorities. It is not to the point that the solicitor only entered on the task pursuant to a contract with the third party (i.e. the testator). There are therefore present many of the features which in the other categories of special relationship have been treated as sufficient to create a special relationship to which the law attaches a duty of care. In my judgment the analogy is close.

Moreover there are more general factors which indicate that it is fair just and reasonable to impose liability on the solicitor. Save in the case of those rash testators who make their own wills, the proper transmission of property from one generation to the next is dependent upon the due discharge by solicitors of their duties. Although in any particular case it may not be possible to demonstrate that the intended beneficiary relied upon the solicitor, society as a whole does rely on solicitors to carry out their will making functions carefully. To my mind it would be unacceptable if, because of some technical rules of law, the wishes and expectations of testators and beneficiaries generally could be defeated by the negligent actions of solicitors without there being any redress. It is only just that the intended beneficiary should be able to recover the benefits which he would otherwise have received.

Further, negligence in the preparation and execution of a will has certain unique features. First, there can be no conflict of interest between the solicitor and client (the testator) and the intended beneficiary. There is therefore no objection to imposing on a solicitor a duty towards a third party there being no possible conflict of interest. Second, in transactions inter vivos the transaction takes immediate effect and the consequences of solicitors' negligence are immediately apparent. When discovered, they can either be rectified (by the parties) or damages recovered by the client. But in the case of a negligently drawn will, the will has no effect at all until the death. It will have been put away in the deed box not to surface again until the testator either wishes to vary it or dies. In the majority of cases the negligence will lie hidden until it takes effect on the death of the testator, i.e. at the very point in time when normally the error will become incapable of remedy.

In all these circumstances, I would hold that by accepting instructions to draw a will, a solicitor does come into a special relationship with those intended to benefit under it in consequence of which the law imposes a duty to the intended beneficiary to act with due expedition and care in relation to the task on which he has entered. For these and the other reasons given by my noble and learned friend Lord Goff of Chieveley, I would dismiss the appeal.

[Lord Nolan delivered a concurring speech. Lord Keith of Kinkel and Lord Mustill, in separate speeches, dissented.]

Notes and Questions

1. In *Hill v. Van Erp*[64] the Australian High Court also held that a disappointed beneficiary should be able to recover damages from a disappointed beneficiary. The case involved the

---

64 (1997), 188 C.L.R. 159.

common situation of a spouse of the beneficiary being asked to act as witness. Unfortunately, it is difficult to determine what the basis of the decision of the majority of the court was. None of them relied explicitly on *Hedley Byrne v. Heller*[65] and some rejected the notion of an assumption of responsibility by the solicitor to the beneficiary. Neither did the majority decide the case on the basis of a general concept of proximity. However, all were convinced that the policy factors mentioned in other cases favoured recovery. Which is the better approach: *Ross v. Caunters*, *White v. Jones*, or *Hill v. Van Erp*? Why?

2. Is a tortious remedy best suited to this kind of situation, or would a contractual one be better? For example, the law might give the disappointed beneficiary a remedy on the analogy of a contract for the benefit of a third party. This is possible in the United States where the privity rule has been abolished, but not in Canada and other common law jurisdictions. Case law in these latter jurisdictions precludes a third party beneficiary from suing on the contract.[66]

3. Is it relevant that the disappointed beneficiary does not have a property interest, but only a *spes successionis* at the time of the solicitor's negligence? Remember that the *spes* would have turned into a property interest on the testator's death but for the solicitor's negligence.[67]

4. In *Lucas v. Hamm*[68] the court held that a solicitor was not liable to the beneficiaries for failing to understand the anfractuosities of the rule against perpetuities and restraints on alienation.

What would a solicitor's liability be in the following situations:

(a) T asked her lawyer to make a will leaving all her estate to her two daughters and told the lawyer that she would shortly be remarrying. The solicitor failed to tell her that the will would be revoked on marriage[69] and failed to provide for that eventuality. T remarried and her husband became entitled to part of her estate on her death intestate.[70]

(b) A solicitor prepared a will for a client, but failed to ensure that there was a sufficient number of witnesses.[71]

(c) A solicitor prepared a will according to his client's instructions and sent it to him with correct instructions for its execution. The will was improperly executed and the testator's wife, when she realized it, called the solicitor, who told her that she would get the entire estate on her husband's death if he died intestate anyway, so that a new will was unnecessary. In fact, on the testator's death intestate, his widow received only one-half of the estate and her husband's next of kin took the other half.[72]

(d) A testatrix, aged 81, gave instructions to her solicitor to prepare a will leaving everything to her husband, aged 64. Nothing was left to the testatrix's step-children, although they were beneficiaries under previous wills. The testatrix's husband predeceased

---

65 [1964] A.C. 465 (H.L.).

66 See B.S. Markesinis, "An Expanding Tort Law — The Price of a Rigid Contract Law" (1987), 103 L.Q. Rev. 354.

67 See *Ross v. Caunters*, [1980] Ch. 297 at 321, [1979] 3 All E.R. 580; *cf. Watts v. Public Trustee of Western Australia*, [1980] W.A.R. 97 (S.C.); *contra Seale v. Perry*, [1982] V.R. 193 (S.C.); *White v. Jones*, [1995] 1 All E.R. 691, at 704-5, 711, *per* Lord Goff of Chieveley; *Hill v. Van Erp* (1997), 188 C.L.R. 159 at 179, *per* Dawson J.; Albert H. Oosterhoff, "Great Expectations: Spes Successionis" (1998), 17 E.T. & P.J. 181 at 192.

68 (1961), 56 Cal. 2d 283, 364 P. 2d 685, cert. den. 368 U.S. 987.

69 *Cf. Succession Law Reform Act*, R.S.O. 1990, c. S.26, ss. 15(a), 16.

70 See *Heyer v. Flaig* (1969), 449 P. 2d 161 (Cal. S.C.). *Cf. McAbee v. Edwards* (1976), 340 So. 2d 1167 (Fla. Dist. Ct.).

71 *Licata v. Spector* (1966), 225 A. 2d 28 (Conn. S.C.).

72 *Ward v. Arnold* (1958), 52 Wash. 2d 581, 328 P. 2d 164 (S.C.).

her and the testatrix's estate went to her nephews and nieces on her intestacy. Assuming that there was no discussion between the solicitor and the testatrix about any benefits to the step-children, can the solicitor be held liable to them?[73]

(e) A testator wanted to leave the residue of his estate equally to a number of named beneficiaries. The solicitor who drafted the will, so provided, but added the qualifier, "who survive me for a period of thirty days." Then he added, "If any of the above-named beneficiaries should not survive me for a period of thirty days, his or her share shall not lapse, but shall be paid to his or her respective estate." Some of the residuary beneficiaries predeceased the testator. The beneficiaries of their estates now want to receive their share of the residue. Are they entitled? If not, is the solicitor liable to them?[74]

5. Are solicitors under a duty to inform clients for whom they have made wills of any changes in the law so as to give the clients an opportunity to change their wills?

6. If a solicitor can be liable for negligence to disappointed beneficiaries under a will, can he or she also be liable to the disappointed donees of an *inter vivos* gift if, for example, the reason they are disappointed is that the solicitor negligently delayed preparing the deed so that the donor died before he or she could execute it?[75] What if the deed was improperly executed because of the solicitor's negligence and the donor destroyed it for that reason?

7. X instructed Y, a solicitor, to draft a document giving Z the right at any time to call on X in the future to pay Z a specified sum of money to enable Z to buy a house. Y drafted the document but, because of his lack of care and skill, the document did not give Z any rights against X. Y told Z that Z would receive the right in question when the document was executed, but also told her that he was acting solely for X and that Z should not rely solely on his (Y's) opinion. X later refused to carry out his promise. Is Y liable to Z?[76]

8. Instead of, or in addition to, an action against a negligent solicitor, should an action by the disappointed beneficiaries against those who received a windfall be allowed? What are the arguments for and against such an action?

9. How can a solicitor protect himself or herself from this kind of liability? Would an exclusionary clause in the contract with the client work? Would such a clause be upheld? Assuming that such a clause is valid, would it protect the solicitor against a disappointed beneficiary under the *Donaghue v. Stevenson* principle, or under *Hedley Byrne*?[77]

10. A solicitor prepared a will for a testator. The will devised a service station to C. Subsequently, the testator granted a lease of the service station to X for 21 years. Some years later, he retained the same solicitor to prepare an amendment to the lease to give X an option to purchase the service station for a fixed price after the death of the testator and his wife. When the testator died, the service station property was very valuable and X was proceeding to exercise his option.

---

73 *Sutherland v. Public Trustee*, [1980] 2 N.Z.L.R. 536 (S.C.).

74 To answer this question, you may wish to refer back to Chapter 12.

75 See *Seale v. Perry*, [1982] V.R. 193 at 224, *per* Murphy J. In *Young v. Ellis*, [1981] 2 N.Z.L.R. 547, a solicitor failed to implement instructions to change a will for one week and the testator died. Nothing turned on that fact, however. The court did not follow *Ross v. Caunters*, [1980] Ch. 297, [1979] 3 All E.R. 580, but approved *Whittingham v. Crease*, [1978] 5 W.W.R. 45, 3 E.T.R. 97, 88 D.L.R. (3d) 353 (B.C.S.C.). See further the *dicta* of Megarry V.C. in *Ross v. Caunters*, [1980] Ch. 297 at 322-3, [1979] 3 All E.R. 580 at 599-600.

76 See *Hemmens v. Wilson Browne*, [1993] 4 All E.R. 826 (Ch. D.).

77 See the *dicta* of Sir Donald Nicholls V.C. in *White v. Jones*, [1993] 3 All E.R. 481 at 490 (C.A.).

Would C have an action against the solicitor for breach of duty of care?[78] Would C have an action against the solicitor if the testator had asked the solicitor to make a new will giving the service station to X?[79]

11. Several months before her death a woman gave her solicitor instructions to commence divorce proceedings and to make a will benefiting her children. The will was not executed before her death and no equalization proceedings had been commenced because of delay on the part of the solicitor. Is the solicitor liable? Is the solicitor required to produce documents proving the deceased's intention, or are they privileged?[80]

12. A solicitor agreed to draft a will for a long-time acquaintance who insisted on giving a substantial gift to the solicitor. However, the solicitor refused to attend to its execution and insisted that the client obtain independent legal advice. The will was made shortly before the client's death, but the solicitor did not know the client was close to death. The client did not seek independent legal advice and the client died intestate. Should the solicitor have ensured that the will was executed? Is he liable to the other beneficiary under the will?[81]

13. The Saskatchewan Court of Appeal applied *White v. Jones* in *Earl v. Wilhelm*.[82] A farmer sold his farm properties to a corporation. Later he instructed his lawyer to prepare a will. The will purported to devise the farms to various persons. When the farmer died, the disappointed beneficiaries successfully sued the lawyer in negligence. He knew or should have known that the testator no longer owned the farms.

Carr-Glynn v. Frearsons[83] is a similar case. An elderly testatrix owned a parcel of land in joint tenancy with a nephew. She gave instructions to her solicitor to make a will devising the farm to another nephew and niece. The solicitor drafted the will, but informed the testatrix that her records indicated that property was held in joint tenancy and if that were so the joint tenancy should be severed. She suggested that the testatrix instruct her to obtain the deeds to check them. The testatrix did not respond to this suggestion, but came in to sign the will. The solicitor reminded her of the need to check the deeds. After the testatrix died and the property had passed to the co-owner by survivorship the niece sued the solicitor. The trial judge held that the solicitor had not breached her duty to the niece, if there was such a duty. The Court of Appeal disagreed and held that the solicitor should have ensured that a notice of severance was sent out at the time the will was signed, to ensure that the testatrix's intentions were carried out.

Of course, a mere allegation that the testatrix intended to benefit the plaintiff and that the solicitor was negligent in failing to carry out the testatrix's instructions is insufficient. The plaintiff must prove the case.[84]

14. If a solicitor is negligent in preparing a will for a person who lacks capacity and is being subjected to undue influence, and the beneficiaries under a former will are forced to contest the later will, are those beneficiaries entitled to recover the legal costs from the negligent solicitor?[85]

15. If a solicitor has failed to observe the duties of taking instructions for a will described in the preceding section and the will fails because the executors can not prove capacity,

---

78 See *Clarke v. Bruce Lance & Co. (a firm) et al.*, [1988] 1 All E.R. 364 (C.A.).

79 See the *dicta* of Sir Donald Nicholls V.C. in *White v. Jones*, [1993] 3 All E.R. 481 at 490 (C.A.), affirmed on different grounds [1995] 2 A.C. 207, [1995] 1 All E.R. 691.

80 See *Makhan v. McCawley* (1998), 22 E.T.R. (2d) 88 (Ont. Gen. Div.).

81 See *Smolinksi v. Mitchell* (1995), 8 E.T.R. (2d) 247 (B.C.S.C.).

82 (2000), 31 E.T.R. (2d) 193 (Sask. C.A.).

83 [1997] 2 All E.R. 614 (C.A.).

84 See *Walker v. Medlicott & Son*, [1999] 1 All E.R. 685 (C.A.).

85 See *Worby v. Rosser*, [1999] E.W.J. No. 3133 (C.A.).

is the solicitor liable to disappointed beneficiaries for negligence in failing to ascertain capacity? Did the solicitor's negligence cause the loss? Who has the onus of proving that the failure of the will was caused by the solicitor's negligence?[86]

16. There is American case law that suggests a solicitor should not be liable for delay in attending to the execution of will. *Radovich v. Locke-Paddon*[87] involved a lawyer who delayed in drafting a will for an elderly client who was suffering from cancer. He delivered the draft to her for review. She intended to discuss it with her sister first and never got back to the solicitor. She died with the will unexecuted. A disappointed beneficiary sued the lawyer. The court held that there was insufficient evidence of commitment to make the will or to benefit the plaintiff. The court felt that policy considerations militated against finding liability. Imposition of liability could improperly compromise the lawyer's undivided loyalty to the client, because it would create an incentive for the lawyer to exert pressure on the client to sign the will before due consideration by the client, in order to avoid possible liability to potential third party beneficiaries.[88]

Further Reading

Richard Jackman, "Solicitor's Liability for Negligence in the Drafting and Execution of a Will" (1971), 5 Ottawa L. Rev. 242.

Bonnie Leigh Rawlins, "Liability of a Lawyer for Negligence in the Drafting and Execution of a Will" (1983), 6 E. & T.Q. 117.

Rodney Hull, "The Avoidance of Malpractice in Estate Planning and Administration" (1979-81), 5 E. T.Q. 89.

Tony Weir, "*A Damnosa Hereditas*?" (1995) 111 L.Q. Rev. 357.

Rodney Hull, "A Current File With an Unsigned Will: A Loose Cannon in the Solicitor's Office" (1997) 17 E.T. & P. J. 31.

James C. Brady, "Solicitor's Duty of Care in the Drafting of Wills" (1995) 46 N. Ireland Q. 434.

Michael Silver, "Solicitor's Conflict of Interest and Breach of Duty Acting for Spouses in the Preparation of a Will" (1993), 13 E. & T.J. 111.

Jane Swanton and Barbara McDonald, "The Reach of the Tort of Negligence" (1997), 71 Australian L.J. 822.

Helen Roberts, "Liability of Solicitors to Disappointed Beneficiaries" (1997), 71 Australian L.J. 674.

Mark Lunney, "In Support of the Chancellor's Foot" (1998) 9 King's College L.J. 116.

---

86 See M.M. Litman and G.B. Robertson, "Solicitor's Liability for Failure to Substantiate Testamentary Capacity" (1984), 62 Can. Bar Rev. 457.

87 35 Cal. Rptr. 2d 573 (Cal. C.A., Sixth App. Distr., 1995).

88 See also *Krawczyk v. Stingle* (1988), 208 Conn. 239, 543 A. 2d 733; *Gregg v. Lindsay* (1994), 437 Pa. Super. 206, 649 A. 2d 935.

PART VII

PARA-TESTAMENTARY ACTIONS

19

SUBSTITUTE DECISIONS*

1. INTRODUCTION

In this chapter we shall consider certain kinds of actions that have become part of the typical estate practice but are not, themselves, testamentary. These actions are appointments of substitute decision-makers by clients.[1] Most commonly, substitute decision-makers are attorneys, appointed by powers of attorney. A power of attorney is a document that confers upon another (the attorney) an authority or power to act on behalf of the person granting the authority (the grantor or donor). A power of attorney serves as a document that an attorney may produce to verify his or her authority to act with third parties on behalf and in the name of the grantor of the power.

It has long been possible to appoint an attorney to make financial and property decisions on behalf of an individual while the individual is alive and retains mental capacity. But in the last number of years, people have become more concerned about what might happen to their property and themselves once they lose the mental capacity to make their own decisions. These concerns have become more pressing as our population ages. People are living longer, but sometimes compromised, lives. Newer legislation addresses these concerns. We shall consider the following Ontario statutes: *Substitute Decisions Act, 1992;*[2] *Health Care Consent Act, 1996;*[3] *Mental Health Act;*[4] and *Powers of Attorney Act.*[5] Whenever

---

* Written by Dawn Dudley Oosterhoff, RN, LLB, SJD (Cand.), Faculty of Law and Collaborative Program in Bioethics, University of Toronto.
1 "Substitute decision-maker" is the generic term identifying the individual specified by legislation, appointed by a board or court, or named in a power of attorney to make decisions on behalf of another person. It should never be assumed that the closest relation to a person is the substitute decision-maker by virtue of his or her relationship with the person.
2 S.O. 1992, c. 30.
3 S.O. 1996, c. 2, Sched. A.
4 R.S.O. 1990, c. M.7.
5 R.S.O. 1990, c. P.20.

possible and relevant, legislation from other provinces will be referred to.[6]

The law of substitute decisions is very much a work in progress. The provincial substitute decision-making laws are not perfect. Conflicting opinions abound as a result of untried legislation and continual evolution of complex family and care arrangements. However, despite the idiosyncrasies and blips, the legislation is effective in providing individuals with the opportunity to choose how their affairs shall be governed if they should become incapable.

Further Reading

Hy Bloom and Michael Bay, eds., *A Practical Guide to Mental Health, Capacity, and Consent Law of Ontario* (Toronto: Carswell, 1996).

M. Anne Bolton, "'The Vulnerable Persons Act': A Change for Manitoba" (1994), 14 E.T.J. 81.

Arthur Fish, "Making it Work: Practical Considerations in Drafting Continuing Powers of Attorney for Property" (1998), 17 E.T.P.J. 249.

Arthur Fish, "The Use and Abuse of Powers of Attorney for Personal Care" (1997), 17 E.T.P.J. 67.

Jeffrey Schnoor and Harold Dick, "Enduring and Springing Powers of Attorney" (1997), 17 E.T.P.J. 19.

Carmen S. Theriault, "Powers of Attorney – Some Fundamental Issues" (1999), 18 E.P.T.J. 227.

Sarita Verma, "Competency and Decision-Making Capacity" (1996), 29 Law Society Gazette 252.

2. HISTORY OF SUBSTITUTE DECISION-MAKING

In their simplest form, powers of attorney have been used for centuries in a variety of situations. It has been suggested that the idea of representation developed in the 13th century, deriving from the organization of royal courts where monarchs, who had so many affairs that they could not conduct them in person,

---

6 Alberta: *Powers of Attorney Act*, S.A. 1991, c. P-13.5 and *Personal Directives Act*, S.A. 1996, c. P-4.03; British Columbia: *Adult Guardianship Act*, R.S.B.C. 1996, c. 6, *Health Care (Consent) and Care Facility (Admission)* Act, R.S.B.C. 1996, c. 181, *Patients Property Act*, R.S.B.C. 1996, c. 349, *Power of Attorney Act*, R.S.B.C. 1996, c. 370, *Representation Agreement Act*, R.S.B.C. 1996, c. 405 (*n.b.*, not all sections of these Acts are in force); Manitoba: *Health Care Directives Act*, C.C.S.M. 1992, c. H27, *Powers of Attorney Act*, C.C.S.M. 1997, c. P97; New Brunswick: *Infirm Persons Act*, R.S.N.B. 1973, c. I-8, *Property Act*, R.S.N.B. 1973, c. P-19, ss. 56, 57, and 58.2; Newfoundland: *Enduring Powers of Attorney Act*, R.S.N. 1990, c. E-11, *Advance Health Care Directives Act*, S.N. 1995, c. A-4.1; Nova Scotia: *Powers of Attorney Act*, R.S.N.S. 1989, c. 352, *Medical Consent Act*, R.S.N.S. 1989, c. 279; Prince Edward Island: *Consent to Treatment and Health Care Directives Act*, S.P.E.I. 1996, c. 10, *Powers of Attorney Act*, R.S.P.E.I. 1988, c. P-16; Saskatchewan: *Health Care Directives and Substitute Health Care Decisions Makers Act, 1997*, S.S. 1997, c. H-0.001, *Powers of Attorney Act, 1996*, S.S. 1996, c. P-20.2. These several statutes are hereafter referred to without further citation.

assigned many of the royal tasks to representatives or agents.[7] In turn, other persons began to appear in the monarch's court by attorney. With commercial practices flourishing during the fourteenth and fifteenth centuries, trading companies necessarily acted through agents and the requirement that parties to legal acts must execute them in person yielded to practicalities, allowing agents or attorneys to act on behalf of another person for particular purposes.[8]

Until the late 1970s, Canadian substitute decision-making laws primarily provided for powers of attorney that were reserved for financial or property matters. These powers of attorney were predicated on the expectation that the grantor of the power of attorney would oversee the actions of the appointed attorney.[9] Because there was no structure to oversee the attorney's actions once the grantor was incapable of doing so, the law, in an attempt to protect the assets of the grantor, provided that the power of attorney failed upon the grantor's incapacity to manage his or her own affairs.

When an individual did become legally incapacitated, the state assumed responsibility for administering the individual's business affairs. Mental health legislation established a regime of public guardianship under which the state managed an incompetent's affairs unless a court appointed an individual or individuals (a "committee") in the place of the state. The applicable legislation only made provision for persons suffering total incompetence, that is, those who were subject to such an arrested or incomplete development of the mind that they required care, supervision and control for their own protection and protection of their property.[10]

Full guardianship was the only available means for making decisions on behalf of an incompetent individual, and the means were extreme. It was not possible for the incompetent person to maintain some control over his or her property or person, or even partake in the decision-making. As a result, the provisions addressed scenarios of severe dementia, for example, but did not deal with the more common scenarios of temporary, partial, or gradually declining incapacity.

Eventually, all provinces amended or introduced legislation, allowing a power of attorney to endure beyond the grantor's incapacity to manage his or her own property.[11] The changes made provision for a clause to be inserted into a power of attorney stating, "This power of attorney shall continue in effect despite any subsequent incapacity of mine." The positive effect of this "enduring power of attorney" was that a person could ensure that his or her financial affairs were taken care of privately even when the person was no longer capable of doing so. These private arrangements could provide the opportunity for personal, shared

---

7 Sir Frederick Pollock and Frederic F. Maitland, *History of English Law Before the Time of Edward I*, 2nd ed., vol. 2 (Cambridge: Cambridge University Press, 1968) at 227.

8 Sir William Holdsworth, *History of English Law*, 2nd ed., vol. 8 (London: Methuen & Co. Ltd., 1937) at 222-223.

9 It is for that reason that the grantor of the power was liable for the attorney's actions unless the attorney acted out of fraud or deceit.

10 H. Archibald Kaiser, "Mental Disability Law" in Downie & Caulfield, eds., *Canadian Health Law and Policy* (Toronto: Butterworths, 1999) at 236-238.

11 See, for example, *Powers of Attorney Act, 1979*, S.O. 1979, c. 107, ss. 4-12.

decision-making when the grantor of the power was not yet totally incapable. The problem was that, in many cases, there remained no efficient structure for overseeing the actions of the attorney once the grantor was incapable of overseeing them. This created opportunities for abuse of power. In addition, the amendment only affected decisions relating to property matters; personal care decisions were still not addressed.[12]

Substitute decision-making for personal care was governed by the traditions of the court's *parens patriae* jurisdiction, mental health legislation, and societal assumptions. As with incompetence for property matters, the legal system only addressed the needs of those requiring total care, but not the personal care needs of those suffering partial or declining incompetence. These decisions were left to be negotiated within the family unit in consultation with the responsible physician. And why not? The system worked effectively for years. Treatment options for each particular disease or illness were limited, value systems within a given society were fairly uniform, and family structures were uncomplicated. It was safe for physicians to assume that they knew their patients and the relevant clinical matters well enough to make the right recommendation to the right person. Choosing a substitute decision-maker was simply a matter of applying a physician's personal knowledge of the patient and the patient's family to the situation at hand.

In the latter half of the 20th century, the structure of health care and our society underwent a fundamental change. Specialists and health care practitioners other than physicians became responsible for many aspects of a patient's health care, and the realm of medicine expanded considerably to include numerous alternative courses of action. At one time, the choice of applicable treatment was limited to one or a few limited options, but now, advances in technology and medicine mean that, in many cases, numerous options or variations on an option are possible. Society's fabric is now woven with alternative family styles and a blend of cultures and religions not witnessed in this country before. In addition, traditional family structures have evolved to include remarriage, single-parent families, same-sex partnerships, and common-law relationships. Finally, the political emphasis on individual rights and rights theory prompted a demand for acknowledgement of patients' right to control the delivery of their own health care. In 1980, the courts affirmed this trend by ruling that, with few exceptions, medical treatment could not be given without voluntary, informed consent.[13] It was also at about this time that the Canadian Charter of Rights and Freedoms was introduced, making it clear that freedom, privacy, and autonomy were to be respected above all other values.

With the changes in health care and the politics affecting society's perception of rights regarding treatment decisions, the casual arrangements for substitute decision-making were no longer sufficient or effective. Some people attempted

---

12 "Personal care" refers to health care, nutrition, shelter, clothing, hygiene and safety. "Health care" can include treatment and admission to a hospital, psychiatric facility, or long-term or other care facility. Depending upon the circumstances, health care may also include home care or other services of assistance. See *Substitute Decisions Act*, s. 45.

13 *Hopp v. Lepp* (1980), 112 D.L.R. (3d) 67 (S.C.C.); and *Reibl v. Hughes* (1980), 114 D.L.R. (3d) 1 (S.C.C.).

to control the destiny of their health care futures by drafting advance directives, often called "living wills." These documents were an expression of people's wishes and desires for health care treatment should they be in a condition in which they could not make those wishes and desires clear themselves. Substitute decision-makers and health care professionals may have felt morally bound to adhere to such directives regarding treatment, but the laws of the time did not impose any legal obligation on a substitute decision-maker or health care provider to do so. Despite the early signals from the courts, advance directives generally remained nothing more than moral guides for a substitute decision-maker. Even if a substitute decision-maker veered from the directives, there was no reviewing body except perhaps an institution's ethics committee or an individual practitioner who might question the substitute decision-maker's actions.

Finally, in 1992, the Ontario provincial government responded to this confusing and inadequate patchwork of substitute decision-making laws by introducing new legislation and modifications to other, existing statutes.[14] The new regime:

(a) allows individuals to name who they want to make decisions for them should they become incapable of making decisions for themselves;

(b) allows individuals to express their wishes about how they want their property and themselves taken care of when they can no longer make those decisions; and

(c) creates a legal structure that governs almost all matters relating to substitute decision-making, including capacity assessments and the ability to oversee the actions of the named substitute decision-makers when the person is no longer capable of supervising the attorney's actions.

3. INCAPACITY AND SUBSTITUTE DECISION-MAKING

(a) Generally

At an earlier time, a person in a state of being incapable of making his or her own decisions could have been labelled an "imbecile," "idiot," "lunatic," or "of unsound mind," or something similar. In the more recent past, the designations "competent" and "incompetent" were used to denote whether a person was capable of making his or her own decisions. However, the competent/incompetent designation had a number of problems, most notably that only one or the other state was possible. A person was competent if he or she was of legal age without mental disability. Either a mental disability or lack of legal age resulted in a finding of incompetence. A finding of incompetence usually rendered the person incapable in law of making *any* decisions.

---

14 Other provinces have since followed suit with similar regimes. See, for example, Alberta, British Columbia, Manitoba, Saskatchewan, and Nova Scotia.

In keeping with the general trend to foster individual autonomy and preserve a person's own decision-making rights whenever possible, the Ontario *Substitute Decisions Act* and the *Consent to Treatment Act*[15] (the precursor to the *Health Care Consent Act*) introduced the concept of "capacity." The change in terminology was meant to signal a change in philosophy. Although capacity, like competence, is still a concept that seems to evade clear definition, the legislation does make a good attempt. More important, the scheme accommodates varying degrees of capacity and fosters a person's participation in decision-making to the extent of his or her ability.[16]

The legislative emphasis on assessing capacity relevant to "*a* decision"[17] in combination with the legislative directives to involve the capable person in decision-making as much as possible correlates with the modern clinical understanding of capacity. The modern concept of capacity is task and time specific, that is a person's capacity to make decisions may vary depending upon the complexity or type of decision, and the point in time at which a person is asked to decide. While the actual assessment of a person's capacity to make certain decisions may, at times, be sophisticated, the assessment will always be based on a development of the following two questions:

Does the person understand the information that is relevant to making the decision?

Does the person appreciate the reasonably foreseeable consequences of the decision being made?

On some occasions, the law requires that a person's age be considered in the determination of capacity. However, it is important to note that the occasions when age must be considered are limited. For the most part, age is a factor when other legal acts, which carry age restrictions themselves, are associated with the decision relevant to the assessment of capacity.[18]

Notes and Questions

1. It is to be assumed that people are capable of making their own decisions unless there are reasonable grounds for believing otherwise.[19]

2. The consideration of time in capacity assessments also includes time in a more protracted sense, represented by an individual's maturity.

3. Emotional volatility can negatively affect an individual's ability to make a decision. As a result, we tend to believe that the best decisions are a result of rational, non-emotional

---

15 *Consent to Treatment Act, 1992*, S.O. 1992, c. 31; repealed S.O. 1996, c. 2, s. 2(2).

16 Not all provinces have adopted this philosophy. See *Chipman v. Chipman* (1997), 19 E.T.R. (2d) 155 (B.C. C.A.), which indicates that varying degrees of capacity are not considered.

17 *Substitute Decisions Act*, s. 6 (emphasis added).

18 See, for example, ss. 4 and 5 of the *Substitute Decisions Act*, which require the grantor of a power of attorney and the attorney named in the power to be at least 18 years of age.

19 See *Substitute Decisions Act*, s. 2.

thought. Lately, however, bioethicists have begun to argue that while "understanding" may be a rational process, "appreciation" *requires* emotional engagement.[20]

4. In most situations, the person proposing treatment or assisting with the drafting of powers of attorney may assess an individual's capacity for the proposed purpose. However, professionals need to exercise caution and refrain from making an assessment of capacity for purposes outside of their professional realm. Only too often, lawyers, for example, willingly make determinations of capacity for the purpose of invoking a power of attorney for personal care, but would balk at making a determination of an individual's capacity to consent to a course of treatment. Yet, the determination in both situations is the same. In all cases, if a determination of capacity is beyond the professional realm of the person doing the assessment, recourse to a qualified professional or capacity assessor should be sought.

5. For a discussion of the relevance and potential impact of a capacity assessment upon a person and his estate, see *Banton v. Banton*.[21]

(b) Capacity to Grant and be Named in a Power of Attorney

The law does not designate a specific person for determining the capacity of a person to grant a power of attorney. If incapacity is suspected, the person assisting in the preparation of the power of attorney (*e.g.*, the lawyer) is responsible for ensuring the person is capable of granting the power. The *Substitute Decisions Act* specifies the information that must be understood by the grantor in order to be considered capable of granting a continuing power of attorney for property:

8. (1) A person is capable of giving a continuing power of attorney if he or she,

(a) knows what kind of property he or she has and its approximate value;

(b) is aware of obligations owed to his or his or her dependants;

(c) knows that the attorney will be able to do on the person's behalf anything in respect of property that the person could do if capable, except make a will, subject to the conditions and restrictions set out in the power of attorney;

(d) knows that the attorney must account for his or her dealings with the person's property;

(e) knows that he or she may, if capable, revoke the continuing power of attorney;

(f) appreciates that unless the attorney manages the property prudently its value may decline; and

(g) appreciates the possibility that the attorney could misuse the authority given to him or her.

---

20 See Louis C. Charland, "Appreciation and Emotion: Theoretical Reflections on the MacArthur Treatment Competence Study" (1998), 8 The Kennedy Institute Journal of Ethics 359-376; and the response by the co-author of the MacArthur Study, Paul Appelbaum, "Ought We To Require Emotional Capacity as Part of Decisional Competence?" (1998), 8 The Kennedy Institute Journal of Ethics 377-389. See also, Louis C. Charland, "Is Mr. Spock Mentally Competent?: Competence to Consent and Emotion" with commentaries and replies (1998), 5 Philosophy, Psychiatry and Psychology 67-86.

21 (1998), 164 D.L.R. (4th) 176 (Ont. Gen. Div.). See also Albert H. Oosterhoff, "Consequences of a January/ December Marriage: A Cautionary Tale" (1999), 18 E.P.T.J. 261.

In addition, the *Substitute Decisions Act* requires that a person be 18 years of age to grant a legally binding power of attorney.[22] The attorney (*i.e.*, the donee of the power) must also be 18 years of age[23] and capable of managing property.[24]

In contrast to powers of attorney for property, a grantor of a power of attorney for personal care in Ontario only has to be 16 years of age.[25] In addition to meeting the age requirement, the *Substitute Decisions Act* states:

> 47. (1) A person is capable of giving a power of attorney for personal care if the person,
> (a) has the ability to understand whether the proposed attorney has a genuine concern for the person's welfare; and
> (b) appreciates that the person may need to have the proposed attorney make decisions for the person.

The attorney named in a power of attorney for personal care must also be 16 years of age or older and capable of making personal care decisions.[26]

Often, when a lawyer assists a client with preparing a power of attorney for personal care, the lawyer also assists the client in preparing directions for the attorney, outlining the person's wishes with regard to treatment decisions ("advance directives"). Despite the fact that advance directives are often part of powers of attorney for personal care (or at least drafted at the same time), the capacity required for advance directives seems to be higher than that required simply to name an attorney for personal care.[27] Neither the *Substitute Decisions Act* nor the *Health Care Consent Act* clearly specify the determinants of capacity for the purpose of giving advance directives regarding personal care; however, s. 5 of the *Health Care Consent Act* read together with s. 4 of the same Act suggests that a person is capable of expressing wishes (and therefore, advance directives) with respect to treatment, admission to a care facility, or a personal assistance service if he or she,

> (a) understands the information that is relevant to making a decision about the treatment, admission, or personal assistance service, as the case may be; and,

---

22 *Substitute Decisions Act*, s. 4.

23 *Ibid.*, s. 5.

24 *Ibid.*, s. 12(1)(a).

25 *Ibid.*, s. 43.

26 *Substitute Decisions Act*, ss. 44, 46(5), and 53(1)(a). Note, however, that a parent under the age of 16 is presumed capable of making treatment decisions for his or her child. See *Health Care Consent Act*, s. 20(2).

    Other provinces maintain a consistent age requirement for all powers of attorneys and directives. For example, Alberta sets a minimum age of 18 years to grant a personal directive or act as an agent. See *Personal Directives Act*, ss. 3 and 12. The age requirement in British Columbia is 19. See *Representation Agreement Act*, ss. 1, 4, and 5(1)(a). In Manitoba, the donor of a health care proxy need only be capable of making his or her own personal care decisions, but the named proxy must be at least 18 years of age. See *Health Care Directives Act*, s. 12. Newfoundland's legislation is similar except that the substitute decision-maker must be 19 years of age. See *Advance Health Care Directives Act*, s. 3(2).

27 *Substitute Decisions Act*, ss.66 (2.1) and 67; and *Health Care Consent Act*, ss. 4, 5, 11.

(b) is able to appreciate the reasonably foreseeable consequences of a decision or lack of decision.

If the person's wishes or advance directives relate to treatment, the information that must be understood (under (a) above) is more complex, including:

(a) the nature of the treatment;
(b) the expected benefits of the treatment;
(c) the material risks of the treatment;
(d) the material side effects of the treatment;
(e) alternative courses of action; and,
(f) the likely consequences of not having the treatment.

Notes and Questions

1. A person is capable of managing property if he or she understands the information relevant to making a decision in the management of property and is able to appreciate the reasonably foreseeable consequences of making a decision.[28] Is this a high enough standard when assessing the capacity of an attorney who is making decisions on behalf of another person?

2. The capacity threshold for granting a power of attorney for personal care is quite low. What are the advantages of the low threshold? Are there risks?

3. Why would the standard for capacity to give advance directives be higher than the standard to name an attorney in a power of attorney for personal care?

4. For all but a few, specific medical treatments, Canadian law does not require that a person be of a specific age to be considered capable of making his or her own decisions. Rather, capacity to make treatment decisions is based upon the same two basic questions: Does the person understand the information relevant to the treatment? Does the person appreciate the consequences of the decision being made?[29] This is not to imply that assessing a child's capacity and applying the legislation is simple.[30]

5. Given that age is not relevant to a determination of capacity for the purpose of giving consent to treatment, why does the *Substitute Decisions Act* require that a person be 16 years of age or older to grant a power of attorney for personal care or specify binding advance directives for treatment?[31] In contrast, the Manitoba legislation simply states that if a person is capable of making health care decisions, the person is capable of giving directives regarding care.[32] The Newfoundland legislation is similar to Manitoba's, adding only that a person under the age of 16 does not benefit from a presumption of capacity.[33] Which legislative scheme is preferable?

6. Newfoundland's *Advance Health Care Directives Act*, s. 3(3) requires that the substitute decision-maker "indicate in writing his or her acceptance of the appointment." What are the advantages of this requirement?

---

28 See *Substitute Decisions Act*, s. 6.
29 See *Health Care Consent Act*, ss. 4 and 11.
30 See Rachel Urman, Bernard Dickens, and Christine Harrison, "Paediatric Health Care Physicians' and Surgeons' Views of Ontario's Health Care Consent Legislation" (1996), 4 Health Law J. 135.
31 See the *Health Care Consent Act*, ss. 4 and 21, and the *Substitute Decisions Act*, s. 43.
32 See *Health Care Directives Act*, s. 4(1).
33 See *Advance Health Care Directives Act*, ss. 3(1) and 7(c).

(c) Determining Incapacity for the Purpose of Invoking a Power of Attorney

Determining the loss of mental capacity to make property decisions can be determined according to instructions that the grantor specifies in his or her continuing power of attorney for property if such instructions were included. For example, the grantor may request that the attorney together with a close family friend determine the grantor's capacity to manage property. If the power of attorney for property states that it is only effective when the grantor becomes incapable, but the document does not state how incapacity is to be determined, then an assessor trained by the Public Guardian and Trustee's office, or a physician must determine mental capacity to manage property.[34]

The mechanism for determining capacity to make personal care decisions varies depending upon whether the decision is covered by the *Health Care Consent Act*, other legislation, or common law. Assessing capacity to make treatment decisions, which are covered by the *Health Care Consent Act*, occurs in a seamless fashion.[35] The health care practitioner proposing the treatment decision is responsible for ensuring that the patient has the requisite capacity to make the decision.[36] As with property decisions, the person needs to understand the information relevant to making a decision and appreciate the consequences of making the decision.

Notes and Questions

1. People whose capacity is fluctuating as a result of ageing or mental deterioration (for example, as a result of Alzheimer's disease) will demonstrate the requisite capacity to make some property decisions but not others. If the attorney's authority to act rests upon the person's incapacity, then in those cases, the attorney will make some decisions on behalf of the person, but not others.

2. Many physicians will balk when asked to assess a person's capacity to make property decisions. First, physicians are intimidated by any action that involves legal ramifications. Second, when physicians assess capacity, they do so under section 54 of the *Mental Health Act* and are reluctant to label their patients with the stigma of a determination of incapacity under mental health legislation.

3. All registered health care practitioners are considered qualified to make capacity assessments; however, if the practitioner does not feel comfortable doing the capacity assessment, he or she can easily refer the assessment to a more qualified practitioner. Many practitioners such as palliative care physicians, psychologists, and social workers have extensive experience in assessing a patient's ability to make treatment decisions.[37]

---

34 *Substitute Decisions Act*, s. 9(3).

35 "Treatment" is defined as "anything that is done for a therapeutic, preventive, palliative, diagnostic, cosmetic, or other health-related purpose." Treatment does not include assessment of capacity, the taking of a person's health history, admission to a hospital or other care facility, or a personal assistance service. See *Health Care Consent Act*, s. 2(1).

36 In Alberta, a person making an assessment of capacity must consult with a physician or psychologist. See *Personal Directives Act*, s. 9.

37 See *Health Care Consent Act*, ss. 2, 4, 10, and 11.

(d) Challenging a Finding of Incapacity

Prior to the current legislated regimes, a person who was found "incompetent" faced a complicated process of review in order to overturn the finding. Further, because of the "all or nothing" approach to competence, a person needed to demonstrate a full ability to understand and appreciate a range of decisions in order to reclaim an ability to make his or her own decisions. Ontario's *Substitute Decisions Act*, *Mental Health Act*, and *Health Care Consent Act* now make provisions for a simplified process of capacity review under one board: the Consent and Capacity Board. This Board can also hear certain other matters related to substitute decision-making. Because a challenge to a finding of incapacity is not typically part of an estate practice, this aspect of substitute decision-making is not discussed here.

4. POWERS OF ATTORNEY FOR PROPERTY

(a) Introduction

The legislative scheme of substitute decision-making is timely. Our lives are becoming more and more complex, and bureaucratic requirements are becoming more stringent in an attempt to protect individuals' privacy and interests. With our financial lives consisting of bank accounts, credit cards, debts, investments, leases, mortgages, utility payments, self-employment, support payments, and so on, one can hardly imagine life going on easily if cheques could not be written, bills paid, and decisions made. While some people may be able to manage without a power of attorney for personal care, few adults would be advised to forego a continuing power of attorney for property.

Often, it is assumed that all powers of attorney are continuing powers of attorney drafted under the *Substitute Decisions Act*. However, it must be remembered that the Ontario *Powers of Attorney Act*, while a skeleton of its former self, still remains in effect.[38] Under that Act, the option remains to draft and use general powers of attorney – those that are no longer effective once the grantor becomes incapable. Often referred to as "bank powers of attorney," general powers of attorney have been a staple of property management for many years. General powers are most often used today by and for corporations, or at the personal level for purposes of banking, investments, or selling real estate.

A continuing power of attorney, like the old enduring powers of attorney under the *Powers of Attorney Act*, is one that survives the incapacity of the grantor. According to the *Substitute Decisions Act*, a power of attorney will be continuing if it says so, or if it expresses the intention that the attorney may act on behalf of the grantor during the grantor's incapacity to manage property. Capable of being as flexible or as restrictive as the grantor directs, continuing powers of attorney

---

38 *Powers of Attorney Act*, R.S.O. 1990, c. P.20. There are similar statutes in the other provinces. See footnote 6, *supra*.

are powerful instruments that may cover all or only certain portions of a grantor's property. A continuing power of attorney's utility is limited only by the drafter's imagination and a few legal restrictions.

Notes and Questions

1. Because general powers of attorney are not valid once the grantor becomes incapable, the drafter of the general power may insert, for convenience, a clause directing that the authority given in the power of attorney may be exercised during the grantor's incapacity to manage property ("endurance clause"). While that may seem like a simple and harmless enough thing to do, the result may, in fact, be disastrous. According to s. 7 of the *Substitute Decisions Act*, a power of attorney is a continuing power of attorney if it expresses the intent that the power continues to be valid despite the grantor's incapacity. Therefore, should an endurance clause be inserted into a general power of attorney, the general power becomes a continuing power of attorney. Then, by virtue of s. 12 of the *Substitute Decisions Act*, any previous continuous powers of attorney for property are automatically revoked upon the execution of the new continuing power of attorney for property unless there is provision in the document for multiple continuing powers of attorney. Therefore, the general power with the endurance clause, while probably intended to be limited in application if not in time, has, in fact, revoked any other, broader, continuing power of attorney covering all of the grantor's assets.

2. In an English case, *Re X; X v. Y*,[39] the court concluded that a subsequent power of attorney did not automatically revoke a previous power of attorney unless the intent to revoke is conveyed by the grantor's words or conduct. Given the multiple uses of powers of attorney, often prepared and used by non-legally trained people, which system is preferable, that suggested by the English court or the Ontario legislation?

(b) Creation

The requirements for a valid continuing power of attorney for property are few; however, the options and alternatives regarding these few requirements are numerous. The legal requirements are simply a grantor capable of granting the power, a named attorney or attorneys, a statement that the attorney has the power to make property decisions on the grantor's behalf, the grantor's signature, the date, and the signature of two qualifying witnesses. A well-drafted power of attorney for property will also specify, if multiple attorneys are appointed, whether the attorneys function jointly, severally, or sequentially; indicate how capacity of the grantor will be assessed should that be relevant; and give clear directions on how the power is to be used.

The sections of the *Substitute Decisions Act* reproduced below specify the basic considerations for drafting powers of attorney for property.

---

39 [2000] 3 All E.R. 1004 (Ch. D.).

SUBSTITUTE DECISIONS ACT, 1992
S.O. 1992, c. 30

7. (1) A power of attorney for property is a continuing power of attorney if,

(a) it states that it is a continuing power of attorney; or

(b) it expresses the intention that the authority given may be exercised during the grantor's incapacity to manage property.

(2) The continuing power of attorney may authorize the person named as attorney to do on the grantor's behalf anything in respect of property that the grantor could do if capable, except make a will.

(3) The continuing power of attorney may name the Public Guardian and Trustee as attorney if his or her consent in writing is obtained before the power of attorney is executed.

(4) If the continuing power of attorney names two or more persons as attorneys, the attorneys shall act jointly, unless the power of attorney provides otherwise.

(5) If two or more attorneys act jointly under the continuing power of attorney and one of them dies, becomes incapable of managing property or resigns, the remaining attorney or attorneys are authorized to act, unless the power of attorney provides otherwise.

(6) The continuing power of attorney is subject to this Part, and to the conditions and restrictions that are contained in the power of attorney and are consistent with this Act.

(7) The continuing power of attorney may provide that it comes into effect on a specified date or when a specified contingency happens.

(7.1) The continuing power of attorney need not be in any particular form.

(8) The continuing power of attorney may be in the prescribed form.

. . .

9. (1) A continuing power of attorney is valid if the grantor, at the time of executing it, is capable of giving it, even if he or she is incapable of managing property.

(2) The continuing power of attorney remains valid even if, after executing it, the grantor becomes incapable of giving a continuing power of attorney.

(3) If the continuing power of attorney provides that it comes into effect when the grantor becomes incapable of managing property but does not provide a method for determining whether that situation has arisen, the power of attorney comes into effect when,

(a) the attorney is notified in the prescribed form by an assessor that the assessor has performed an assessment of the grantor's capacity and has found that the grantor is incapable of managing property; or

(b) the attorney is notified that a certificate of incapacity has been issued in respect of the grantor under the *Mental Health Act*.

10. (1) A continuing power of attorney shall be executed in the presence of two witnesses, each of whom shall sign the power of attorney as witness.

(2) The following persons shall not be witnesses:

1. The attorney or the attorney's spouse or partner.

2. The grantor's spouse or partner.

3. A child of the grantor or a person whom the grantor has demonstrated a settled intention to treat as his or her child.

4. A person whose property is under guardianship or who has a guardian of the person.

5. A person who is less than eighteen years old.

. . .

(4) A continuing power of attorney that does not comply with subsections (1) and (2) is not effective, but the court may, on any person's application, declare the continuing power of attorney to be effective if the court is satisfied that it is in the interests of the grantor or his or her dependants to do so.

Notes and Questions

1. The legislation does not set any restrictions on who may be appointed an attorney for property except that the attorney must be capable and at least 18 years of age.[40] While this wide latitude affords the grantor of the power the opportunity to exercise maximum control in naming his or her substitute decision-maker, it also subjects the grantor to risk if he or she makes an uninformed choice. This risk increases when a grantor chooses an attorney, not because of the attorney's skill at managing property, but because of the grantor's emotional ties to the attorney.

2. A continuing power of attorney, even though designed specifically to be effective during the grantor's incapacity, may come into effect at any time or upon the occurrence of any event before or at the time of the grantor's incapacity depending upon the grantor's wishes and needs. For a seamless transfer of power, some drafters recommend that the continuing power become effective upon execution, but to prevent abuse of the power, that the document be kept with the drafter (usually a lawyer) until the grantor indicates that the power should be released or some agreed upon event occurs. While this may seem to be a good solution, difficulties arise if the grantor is unexpectedly incapacitated, no one (except the lawyer) knows that the power of attorney exists, and the lawyer is not advised of the grantor's incapacity.

3. Various solutions have been proposed to resolve the tension between wanting the power to devolve upon the attorney as easily as possible while protecting the grantor from unscrupulous use of the power. For example, the power could contain instructions that incapacity will be determined by the attorney (or one of the attorneys) together with a member of the grantor's family, religious advisor, or other person who knows the grantor well. If adequate trust exists between the grantor and the attorney, there may be merit in having the power take effect upon execution so that the power can be used from time to time in a manner agreed upon by the grantor and attorney.

4. Manitoba's legislation attempts to resolve the dilemma of persuading third parties that a specified event – a condition precedent allowing the attorney to act – has occurred. Section 6 of the *Powers of Attorney Act* allows the donor of the power to name a declarant who can provide a written declaration that a specified event has occurred. The attorney may be named as the declarant. If a declarant is not named (or refuses to act), two physicians may make the declaration without invoking provisions in the mental health legislation.

---

40 See *Substitute Decisions Act*, ss. 5 and 12(1)(a).

5. Manitoba's *Power of Attorney Act* requires that the witnesses to an enduring power of attorney be from a list of specified professionals, notably legal or medical professionals.[41]

(c) Conditions and Restrictions

(i) *Introduction*

The conditions, restrictions, and directions contained in a power of attorney for property are critical. If no terms are specified, the attorney is authorized to "do on the grantor's behalf anything in respect of property that the grantor could do if capable, except make a will."[42] While that may be the intent of the grantor – that is, to grant the attorney full authority to manage the grantor's estate – the operation of certain laws may still circumscribe the attorney's authority or direct the attorney's actions to an undesired outcome. Provisions to address these possibilities can, and should, be included in the power of attorney.

(ii) *Compensation*

If the power of attorney does not say otherwise, an attorney is entitled to take annual compensation from the grantor's property at a prescribed rate.[43] Whether or not this is the grantor's intent, both the grantor and the named attorney should be aware that taking compensation raises the standard of care that the attorney must meet in managing the grantor's property. If uncompensated, the attorney is subject to the standard a "person of ordinary prudence would exercise in the conduct of his or her own affairs."[44] If compensated, the attorney must meet a higher standard of care, that of "a person in the business of managing the property of others."[45] Finally, if the grantor's intent is for the attorney to be compensated, the grantor may elect to specify the rate of compensation in the power of attorney.[46]

(iii) *Gifts, Donations, and Loans*

Without directions to the contrary, an attorney will be limited in distributing gifts and donations from the grantor's estate. Gifts and loans to friends and family

---

41 See *Powers of Attorney Act* (Man.), s. 11.

42 *Substitute Decisions Act*, s. 7(2). Not all provinces grant attorneys such latitude. For example, British Columbia restricts the attorney from engaging in certain activities unless the grantor of the power specifically grants the authority after consulting with a specified professional (usually a lawyer). See *Representation Agreement Act*, ss. 7 and 9.

43 *Ibid.*, s. 40.

44 *Ibid.*, s. 32 (7).

45 *Ibid.*, s. 32 (8).

46 *Ibid.*, s. 40 (4).

may be made only if the grantor indicated while capable that he or she would make or authorize such gifts and loans. Similarly, charitable gifts may only be made if there is evidence that the grantor made similar expenditures while capable or if the grantor authorizes those donations in the power of attorney. Even when gifts, loans, and donations are authorized in a power of attorney, the attorney is still subject to legislative restrictions, limiting the amount that may be used in this manner.[47]

(iv) Matrimonial Interests

Another obstacle an attorney might face unless specific provision is made in the power is the ability to dispose of or encumber any interest in a matrimonial home in which the grantor has a right of possession under Part II of the *Family Law Act*.[48] When disability strikes in a family, circumstances often require that a home be mortgaged or even sold. Yet the *Family Law Act* specifies that the right of possession of a matrimonial home is "personal as against the [other] spouse."[49] The question arises, then, whether an attorney acting as an agent can effect a transaction that negates a personal claim. Directions in the power authorizing the attorney to consent on behalf of the grantor to a disposal or encumbrance of a matrimonial interest will overcome this obstacle.[50]

(v) Investment in Mutual Funds

An attorney may also be limited by law in the types of investments and expenditures that can be made on behalf of the grantor. The *Trustee Act* now permits a trustee to invest in mutual funds;[51] however, according to the *Substitute Decisions Act*, the *Trustee Act* does not apply to an attorney.[52] In addition, the *Substitute Decisions Act* clearly states that an attorney is a fiduciary.[53] Therefore, unless the power of attorney says otherwise, an attorney will be subject to the common law limitations on investments that apply particularly to fiduciaries. These common law prohibitions include a prohibition on delegating authority, and investing in

---

47 *Ibid.*, s. 37.

48 R.S.O. 1990, c. F.3.

49 *Ibid.*, s. 19 (2).

50 See *ibid.*, s. 21(1). Saskatchewan legislation specifically prohibits a person acting under a power of attorney from signing the required consent. Instead, an application to the court for an order dispensing with the consent is required. See *The Homesteads Act, 1989*, R.S.S., c. H-51, ss. 6 and 11(1).

51 R.S.O. 1990, c. T.23, s. 27(3), as amended by *Red Tape Reduction Act, 1998*, S.O. 1998, c. 18, s. 16, proclaimed in force July 1999.

52 *Substitute Decisions Act*, ss. 32(12) and 38(1). Excluding an attorney from the provisions of the *Trustee Act* was meant to provide an attorney with wide latitude in managing the grantor's property, so it is ironical that a trustee now has more freedom with investments than an attorney.

53 *Substitute Decisions Act*, ss. 32(1) and 38(1).

mutual funds or discretionary investment accounts involves a delegation of authority.

Notes and Questions

1. In *Haslam v. Haslam*,[54] a committee was restricted from investing in mutual funds, even if the mutual funds were made up of investments authorised by the *Trustee Act*. The Court held that the use of mutual funds was an "abdication of responsibility" and an improper delegation of the function of making investment decisions because the trustee was no longer "free to follow or reject the advice of investment counsel."[55]

2. *Canada Trust Company v. Rutherford*,[56] involved the applicant trust company acting as the committee of the estate of a mentally incompetent individual. The issue was whether or not the committee was permitted to invest trust assets in a common trust fund. The Court held that all of the investments made by the common fund were permissible by statute and, furthermore, there was no abdication by the committee of its decision-making power because, in this case, the trust company was the committee and the investment decisions were those of the trust company.[57]

3. Delegation of authority will be authorized, and even expected, if the scope of the investments exceeds the attorney's expertise. However, the ultimate responsibility for the making of investment decisions remains with the attorney. The attorney may not delegate that function and must remain free to follow or reject the advice of investment counsel.[58]

(d) Exercise

(i) *Effectiveness*

A valid power of attorney for property is considered to be in effect when the original, signed document is in the hands of the attorney and the attorney, in accordance with any conditions or restrictions in the document, is acting on behalf of the grantor. As mentioned previously, the transfer of power from grantor to attorney can occur seamlessly if the grantor releases the document to the attorney and requests that the attorney begin acting. In this case, the attorney is able to assume more and more responsibility as the need arises, and eventually assume full control if the grantor becomes incapable of managing any of his or her property.

If the event triggering the transfer of power is not clear, the attorney cannot begin acting until the grantor is found incapable of making a property decision. In this case, the method of determining incapacity for authorizing the attorney to act is governed by the legislation reproduced below.

---

54 (1994), 3 E.T.R. (2d) 206 (Ont. Gen. Div.).
55 *Ibid.*, at p. 214.
56 (1995), 7 E.T.R. (2d) 270 (Ont. Gen. Div.).
57 See also *Central Guaranty Trust Co. v. Sin-Sara* (1995), 7 E.T.R. (2d) 273 (Ont. Gen. Div.).
58 See *Re Miller Estate* (1987), 26 E.T.R. 188 (Ont. Surr. Ct.).

SUBSTITUTE DECISIONS ACT, 1992
S.O. 1992, c. 30

9.

. . .

(3) If the continuing power of attorney provides that it comes into effect when the grantor becomes incapable of managing property but does not provide a method for determining whether that situation has arisen, the power of attorney comes into effect when,

    (a) the attorney is notified in the prescribed form by an assessor that the assessor has performed an assessment of the grantor's capacity and has found that the grantor is incapable of managing property; or

    (b) the attorney is notified that a certificate of incapacity has been issued in respect of the grantor under the *Mental Health Act*.

MENTAL HEALTH ACT
R.S.O. 1990, c. M.7

54. (1) Forthwith on a patient's admission to a psychiatric facility, a physician shall examine him or her to determine whether the patient is capable of managing property.

(2) A patient's attending physician may examine him or her at any time to determine whether the patient is capable of managing property.

(3) After an examination under subsection (1) or (2), the physician shall note his or her determination, with reasons, in the patient's clinical record.

(4) If the physician determines that the patient is not capable of managing property, he or she shall issue a certificate of incapacity in the approved form, and the officer in charge shall transmit the certificate to the Public Guardian and Trustee.

(5) If the circumstances are such that the Public Guardian and Trustee should immediately assume management of the patient's property, the officer in charge (or the physician who examined the patient, if the officer in charge is absent) shall notify the Public Guardian and Trustee of the matter as quickly as possible.

(6) This section does not apply if the patient's property is under guardianship under the *Substitute Decisions Act, 1992*.

(ii) *Duties of the Attorney*

The *Substitute Decisions Act* outlines the duties of attorney and other substitute decision makers for property and establishes a scheme of accountability.

SUBSTITUTE DECISIONS ACT, 1992
S.O. 1992, c. 30

32. (1) A guardian of property is a fiduciary whose powers and duties shall be exercised and performed diligently, with honesty and integrity and in good faith, for the incapable person's benefit.

(1.1) If the guardian's decision will have an effect on the incapable person's personal comfort or well-being, the guardian shall consider that effect in determining whether the decision is for the incapable person's benefit.

(1.2) A guardian shall manage a person's property in a manner consistent with decisions concerning the person's personal care that are made by the person who has authority to make those decisions.

(1.3) Subsection (1.2) does not apply in respect of a decision concerning the person's personal care if the decision's adverse consequences in respect of the person's property significantly outweigh the decision's benefits in respect of the person's personal care.

(2) The guardian shall explain to the incapable person what the guardian's powers and duties are.

(3) A guardian shall encourage the incapable person to participate, to the best of his or her abilities, in the guardian's decisions about the property.

(4) The guardian shall seek to foster regular personal contact between the incapable person and supportive family members and friends of the incapable person.

(5) The guardian shall consult from time to time with,

(a) supportive family members and friends of the incapable person who are in regular personal contact with the incapable person; and

(b) the persons from whom the incapable person receives personal care.

(6) A guardian shall, in accordance with the regulations, keep accounts of all transactions involving the property.

(7) A guardian who does not receive compensation for managing the property shall exercise the degree of care, diligence and skill that a person of ordinary prudence would exercise in the conduct of his or her own affairs.

(8) A guardian who receives compensation for managing the property shall exercise the degree of care, diligence and skill that a person in the business of managing the property of others is required to exercise.

(9) Subsection (8) applies to the Public Guardian and Trustee.

(10) A guardian shall act in accordance with the management plan established for the property, if the guardian is not the Public Guardian and Trustee, or with the policies of the Public Guardian and Trustee, if he or she is the guardian.

(11) If there is a management plan, it may be amended from time to time with the Public Guardian and Trustee's approval.

(12) The *Trustee Act* does not apply to the exercise of a guardian's powers or the performance of a guardian's duties.

33. (1) A guardian of property is liable for damages resulting from a breach of the guardian's duty.

(2) If the court is satisfied that a guardian of property who has committed a breach of duty has nevertheless acted honestly, reasonably and diligently, it may relieve the guardian from all or part of the liability.

33.1 A guardian of property shall make reasonable efforts to determine,

    (a) whether the incapable person has a will; and

    (b) if the incapable person has a will, what the provisions of the will are.

33.2 (1) A person who has custody or control of property belonging to an incapable person shall,

    (a) provide the incapable person's guardian of property with any information requested by the guardian that concerns the property and that is known to the person who has custody or control of the property; and

    (b) deliver the property to the incapable person's guardian of property when required by the guardian.

(2) For the purposes of subsection (1), the property belonging to a person includes the person's will.

(3) A person who has custody or control of any document relating to an incapable person's property that was signed by or given to the incapable person shall, on request, provide the incapable person's guardian of property with a copy of the document.

34. A guardian of property has power to complete a transaction that the incapable person entered into before becoming incapable.

35. When the Public Guardian and Trustee is the guardian of property for an incapable person who dies, he or she may, until notified of another person's appointment as personal representative, exercise the powers of an executor to whom the incapable person's property is given in trust for the payment of debts and the distribution of the residue.

35.1 (1) A guardian of property shall not dispose of property that the guardian knows is subject to a specific testamentary gift in the incapable person's will.

(2) Subsection (1) does not apply in respect of a specific testamentary gift of money.

(3) Despite subsection (1),

    (a) the guardian may dispose of the property if the disposition of that property is necessary to comply with the guardian's duties; or

    (b) the guardian may make a gift of the property to the person who would be entitled to it under the will, if the gift is authorized by section 37.

36. (1) The doctrine of ademption does not apply to property that is subject to a specific testamentary gift and that a guardian of property disposes of under this Act, and anyone who would have acquired a right to the property on the death of the incapable person is entitled to receive from the residue of the estate the equivalent of a corresponding right in the proceeds of the disposition of the property, without interest.

(2) If the residue of the incapable person's estate is not sufficient to pay all entitlements under subsection (1) in full, the persons entitled under subsection (1) shall share the residue in amounts proportional to the amounts to which they would otherwise have been entitled.

(3) Subsections (1) and (2) are subject to a contrary intention in the incapable person's will.

. . .

37. (1) A guardian of property shall make the following expenditures from the incapable person's property:

1. The expenditures that are reasonably necessary for the person's support, education and care.
2. The expenditures that are reasonably necessary for the support, education and care of the person's dependants.
3. The expenditures that are necessary to satisfy the person's other legal obligations.

(2) The following rules apply to expenditures under subsection (1):

1. The value of the property, the accustomed standard of living of the incapable person and his or her dependants and the nature of other legal obligations shall be taken into account.
2. Expenditures under paragraph 2 may be made only if the property is and will remain sufficient to provide for expenditures under paragraph 1.
3. Expenditures under paragraph 3 may be made only if the property is and will remain sufficient to provide for expenditures under paragraphs 1 and 2.

(3) The guardian may make the following expenditures from the incapable person's property:

1. Gifts or loans to the person's friends and relatives.
2. Charitable gifts.

(4) The following rules apply to expenditures under subsection (3):

1. They may be made only if the property is and will remain sufficient to satisfy the requirements of subsection (1).
2. Gifts or loans to the incapable person's friends or relatives may be made only if there is reason to believe, based on intentions the person expressed before becoming incapable, that he or she would make them if capable.
3. Charitable gifts may be made only if,
   i. the incapable person authorized the making of charitable gifts in a power of attorney executed before becoming incapable, or
   ii. there is evidence that the person made similar expenditures when capable.
4. If a power of attorney executed by the incapable person before becoming incapable contained instructions with respect to the making of gifts or loans to friends or relatives or the making of charitable gifts, the instructions shall be followed, subject to paragraphs 1, 5 and 6.
5. A gift or loan to a friend or relative or a charitable gift shall not be made if the incapable person expresses a wish to the contrary.
6. The total amount or value of charitable gifts shall not exceed the lesser of,
   i. 20 per cent of the income of the property in the year in which the gifts are made, and

ii. the maximum amount or value of charitable gifts provided for in a power of attorney executed by the incapable person before becoming incapable.

(5) The court may authorize the guardian to make a charitable gift that does not comply with paragraph 6 of subsection (4),

(a) on motion by the guardian in the proceeding in which the guardian was appointed, if the guardian was appointed under section 22 or 27; or

(b) on application, if the guardian is the statutory guardian of property.

(6) Expenditures made under this section shall be deemed to be for the incapable person's benefit.

38. (1) Section 32, except subsections (10) and (11), and sections 33, 33.1, 33.2, 34, 35.1, 36 and 37 also apply, with necessary modifications, to an attorney acting under a continuing power of attorney if the grantor is incapable of managing property or the attorney has reasonable grounds to believe that the grantor is incapable of managing property.

(2) An attorney under a continuing power of attorney shall make an application to the court to obtain the authority referred to in subsection 37(5).

(iii) *Termination*

Without exception, an attorney's power to act on behalf of the grantor ends with the grantor's death. An attorney's authority to act may also be terminated by the grantor (if the grantor is capable of revoking the power), by resignation, operation of law, or application to a court.

SUBSTITUTE DECISIONS ACT, 1992
S.O. 1992, c. 30

8.

. . .

(2) A person is capable of revoking a continuing power of attorney if he or she is capable of giving one.

. . .

11. (1) An attorney under a continuing power of attorney may resign but, if the attorney has acted under the power of attorney, the resignation is not effective until the attorney delivers a copy of the resignation to,

(a) the grantor;

(b) any other attorneys under the power of attorney;

(c) the person named by the power of attorney as a substitute for the attorney who is resigning, if the power of attorney provides for the substitution of another person; and

(d) unless the power of attorney provides otherwise, the grantor's spouse or partner and the relatives of the grantor who are known to the attorney and reside in Ontario, if,

(i) the attorney is of the opinion that the grantor is incapable of managing property, and

(ii) the power of attorney does not provide for the substitution of another person or the substitute is not able and willing to act.

(1.1) Clause (1) (d) does not require a copy of the resignation to be delivered to,

(a) the grantor's spouse, if the grantor and the spouse are living separate and apart within the meaning of the *Divorce Act* (Canada); or

(b) a relative of the grantor, if the grantor and the relative are related only by marriage and the grantor and his or her spouse are living separate and apart within the meaning of the *Divorce Act* (Canada).

(2) An attorney who resigns shall make reasonable efforts to give notice of the resignation to persons with whom the attorney previously dealt on behalf of the grantor and with whom further dealings are likely to be required on behalf of the grantor.

12. (1) A continuing power of attorney is terminated,

(a) when the attorney dies, becomes incapable of managing property or resigns, unless,

(i) another attorney is authorized to act under subsection 7 (5), or

(ii) the power of attorney provides for the substitution of another person and that person is able and willing to act;

. . .

(c) when the court appoints a guardian of property for the grantor under section 22;

(d) when the grantor executes a new continuing power of attorney, unless the grantor provides that there shall be multiple continuing powers of attorney;

(e) when the power of attorney is revoked;

(f) when the grantor dies.

(2) The revocation shall be in writing and shall be executed in the same way as a continuing power of attorney.

13. (1) If a continuing power of attorney is terminated or becomes invalid, any subsequent exercise of the power by the attorney is nevertheless valid as between the grantor or the grantor's estate and any person, including the attorney, who acted in good faith and without knowledge of the termination or invalidity.

Notes and Questions

1. An attorney must also maintain accounts of his or her management of the grantor's property. The attorney may be required, from time to time, to pass the accounts.[59] In Manitoba, the attorney *must* provide an annual accounting to the person named in the power, or if no one is named, then to the grantor's nearest relative.[60]

2. Spouses often name each other as attorney and share a joint bank account. Suppose a husband is the wage earner, the husband and wife have mortgaged their home, and each

---

59 See *Substitute Decisions Act*, s. 42.
60 See *Powers of Attorney Act* (Man.), s. 22.

has appointed the other as attorney under continuing powers of attorney for property. If it is the husband who becomes incapable, the wife will need to have access to the husband's financial resources to continue to pay the mortgage. Paying the mortgage, however, benefits both the husband (the grantor) and the wife (the attorney/fiduciary). Similarly, if the wife has no or very little income of his or her own, she may need to have access to her husband's finances in order to buy her own clothing and meet her own personal needs. These actions would benefit only the wife and not the husband. Do the wife's actions constitute a breach of her duty as her husband's attorney for property?

3. An attorney is prohibited from making a will on behalf of the grantor of the continuing power of attorney.[61] Does this prohibition include only the testamentary document that we know as a will, or does it also include will substitutes that dispose of property upon death without formal testamentary requirements? For example, can an attorney transfer the grantor's property into joint tenancy with right of survivorship or change beneficiary designations under an insurance contract or retirement plan? This matter is far from settled and subject to vigorous debate and uncertainty.[62]

4. The New Brunswick court, however, does have the authority to make, amend, and revoke wills for mentally incapable persons, or may direct the substitute decision-maker for property to do so, subject to the court's approval.[63]

5. A question that ought to be asked whenever an attorney proposes amending a beneficiary designation is, "Why?" An attorney is to manage the grantor's property for the grantor's benefit.[64] If changing a beneficiary designation has no effect upon the grantor – a likely result since the benefit will be realized by someone else after the grantor's death – then it would seem that the attorney has no *need* to so amend the designation. The act may not, therefore, be considered to be one carried out for the grantor's benefit and thus, would not be in the purview of an attorney's responsibilities.[65]

6. Some people like to include clauses in their powers of attorney outlining their wishes for a funeral or organ donation in the event of death. Would the attorney have the authority to carry out the grantor's wishes? See *Human Tissue Gift Act*.[66]

---

61 See *Substitute Decisions Act*, s. 7(2).
62 See *MacInnes v. MacInnes*, [1935] 1 D.L.R. 401 (S.C.C.); *Edwards v. Bradley* (1956), 2 D.L.R. (2d) 382 (Ont. C.A.); *Re Shirley* (1965), 49 D.L.R. (2d) 474 (Sask. Q.B.); *Hurzin v. Great West Life Assurance Co.* (1988), 29 E.T.R. 51 (B.C. S.C.); *Turner Estate v. Bezanson* (1995), 8 E.T.R. (2d) 169 (N.S. C.A.); *Moskoff v. Moskoff Estate* (1999), 34 E.T.R. (2d) 57 (Ont. S.C.J.); Ralph E. Scane, "Non-Insurance Beneficiary Designations" (1993), 72 Can. Bar Rev. 178; and Maxwell, "When is a Testamentary Instrument Not a Testamentary Instrument?" Case Comment (1996), 16 E.T.J. 7.
63 See *Infirm Persons Act*, ss. 3(4), 11.1, and 15(1); and Eric L. Teed and Nicole Cohoon, "New Wills for Incompetents" (1997), 16 E.T.J. 1.
64 See *Substitute Decisions Act*, s. 32(1).
65 But see *Patients Property Act*, R.S.B.C. 1996, c. 349, s. 18 and *Re Bradley* (1998), 25 E.T.R. (2d) 67 (B.C. S.C.) indicating that in British Columbia, if a substitute decision-maker for property is expected to manage property for the ultimate benefit of the incapable person and the family, the substitute decision-maker must also consider the estate. *Re Bradley* was overturned on appeal ((2000), 31 E.T.R. (2d) 16 (B.C. C.A.)) on the basis that the proposed distribution of the incapable person's property would leave the incapable person with an insufficient income should she recover and require more expensive care. The court did not dismiss the possibility that a substitute decision-maker could make decisions that would affect the testamentary disposition of an incapable person's property. See also *Re Goodman* (1998), 24 E.T.R. (2d) 194 (B.C. S.C.) and *O'Hagan v. O'Hagan* (2000), 183 D.L.R. (4th) 30 (B.C. C.A.).
66 R.S.O. 1990, c. H.20, s. 4, to be renamed the *Trillium Gift of Life Network Act*, S.O. 2000, s. 1, upon proclamation.

7. The *Substitute Decisions Act* does not state what standard will be expected of an attorney who is authorized to act on behalf of the grantor while the grantor is capable of managing his or her own property. Therefore, the general principles of the common law apply to the attorney in such a situation. *Banton v. Banton*[67] helped to clarify this matter. Elaborating on the role of an attorney, the Court stated:[68]

> An attorney for a grantor who has mental capacity to deal with property is merely an agent and, not withstanding the fact that the power may be conferred in general terms, the attorney's primary responsibility in such a case is to carry out the instructions of the grantor as principal. As an agent, such an attorney owes fiduciary duties to the grantor but these are pale in comparison with those of an attorney holding a continuing power when the grantor has lost capacity to manage property. In such a case, the attorney does not receive instructions from the grantor except to the extent that they are written into the instrument conferring the power. The attorney must make decisions on behalf of the grantor and, pursuant to sections 32 and 38 of the *Substitute Decisions Act, 1992*, he or she is a "fiduciary whose powers and duties shall be exercised and performed diligently, with honesty and integrity and in good faith, for the incapable person's benefit." The status of such an attorney is much closer to that of a trustee than an agent of the grantor.

8. British Columbia's legislation establishes a "monitoring" scheme to oversee an attorney's actions. An adult who appoints a substitute decision-maker (a "representative") must also appoint a monitor to oversee the representative's compliance with legislative requirements, or state in the power that a monitor is not required.[69]

(e) Precedent

SAMPLE CONTINUING POWER
OF ATTORNEY FOR PROPERTY

THIS CONTINUING POWER OF ATTORNEY FOR PROPERTY is given by [Grantor] of [Residence].

REVOCATION

I hereby revoke any prior power of attorney for property or any prior power of attorney that affects my property previously given by me.

APPOINTMENT

I appoint _____ [and _____] to be my attorney[s] for property [jointly, or jointly and severally] in accordance with the *Substitute Decisions Act, 1992*, S.O. 1992, c. 30. I will refer to my attorney or attorneys for property for the time being as my "Attorney."

---

67 (1998), 164 D.L.R. (4th) 176 (Ont. Gen. Div.).
68 *Ibid.*, at p. 239.
69 See *Representation Agreement Act*, ss. 12 and 20.

SUBSTITUTION

If the attorney I have appointed cannot or will not be my attorney because of refusal, resignation, death, mental incapacity, or removal by the court, I substitute _____ to act as my attorney for property with the same authority as the person s/he is replacing.

[I have appointed my Attorneys to act jointly. If one of my Attorneys is unavailable or cannot or will not be my attorney because of refusal, resignation, death, mental incapacity, or removal by the court, I authorize the remaining attorney to act solely. Written notification to any person by my remaining attorney of the inability or refusal of the other attorney to act shall be sufficient and conclusive evidence of the fact.]

AUTHORIZATION, INSTRUCTIONS, CONDITIONS, AND RESTRICTIONS

I authorize my Attorney to do on my behalf any and all acts in respect of property that I could do if capable of managing property, except make a Will, subject to the law and to any conditions and restrictions contained in this document.

Without restricting the generality of the above paragraph, but for greater certainty, I specifically provide my Attorney with the following powers:

Legal Representative: I authorize my Attorney to exercise all powers in my name as I would be able to exercise them had I chosen to exercise such powers myself, or had I legal capacity to exercise such powers. This, therefore, authorizes my Attorney to bind and secure information on behalf of my estate in respect of its dealings with any person. Without restricting the generality of the foregoing, I expressly constitute my Attorney as my "legal representative" for the purposes of Section 150(1)(d) and all other purposes of the *Income Tax Act*, R.S.C. 1985, c. 1 (5th Supp.) and authorize my Attorney to bind and secure information on behalf of my estate in respect of any matter involving the government of Canada or any institution, such as a bank, regulated by the government of Canada.

Family Law Act Consent: If my spouse wishes to dispose of or encumber any interest in a matrimonial home in which I have a right of possession under Part II of the *Family Law Act*, I authorize my Attorney in my name to consent, should my Attorney find it appropriate to do so, to the transaction as provided for in Section 21(1) of the Act.

Possession of Physical Property: I authorize my Attorney to take physical possession of all of my property, including property held in a safety deposit box, in safekeeping by others on my behalf, and held by others subject to some professional privilege, which privilege I waive for this purpose.

Review of Will: My Attorney shall be entitled to review my Will and demand delivery of a copy of my Will in order to be able to manage my estate in a manner that is sensitive thereto.

Testamentary Dispositions: My Attorney shall take such steps in the administration of my estate that will, in the judgment of my Attorney, facilitate the expeditious and cost-effective settlement of my estate consistent with any testamentary objectives I established while capable of doing so. I, therefore, authorize my Attorney to employ the assets of my estate consistent with this continuing power of attorney to, for example, create a joint property interest carrying a right of survivorship or establish a trust of which I am the principal life beneficiary. This authority [includes, or does not include] the right to change beneficiary designations previously made by me other than those made in my will.

Benefiting Others: My Attorney may manage my estate for:

my benefit;
the benefit of any person to whom I am under a legal obligation to provide a benefit, to the extent my Attorney considers it necessary to fulfil such legal obligation.

Other Powers of Attorney: From time to time, I may execute other powers of attorney for restricted purposes. The power granted in those powers of attorney, while effective, is a restriction on the power granted to my Attorney in this continuing power of attorney.

Investments: My Attorney may make any investments for my estate that my Attorney considers appropriate including units or other interests in any mutual funds, common trust funds, unit trusts or similar investments, and is not limited to those investments authorized by law for trustees. My Attorney shall not be liable for any loss that may happen to my estate as a result of any investment made by my Attorney in good faith.

Limited Power of Appointment: I hereby grant to my Attorney the power to appoint one or more attorneys or agents under him/her for any period of time, for an unlimited period of time, or from time to time for the limited purpose of managing my bank accounts, investment accounts, mutual funds, and/or similar investment matters. My Attorney may so appoint attorneys without in any way reducing or suspending my Attorney's own power of authority granted under this continuing power of attorney for property. My Attorney shall remain responsible for overseeing the actions of any appointed attorneys. My Attorney shall have discretion to revoke any such appointments.

COMPENSATION

I authorize my Attorney, and my Attorney has agreed, to accept [no] compensation for any work done by my Attorney pursuant to this continuing power of attorney.

AFFIRMATION

In granting this continuing power of attorney for property, I affirm that I am aware:

of the nature and extent of my property;

of the obligations I owe to my dependants;

that my Attorney will be able to do on my behalf any and all acts in respect of property that I could do if capable of managing property, except make a will, subject to the law and to any conditions and restrictions contained in this document;

that my Attorney must account for his/her dealings with my property;

that the value of my property administered by my Attorney may decline unless my Attorney manages it prudently;

that there is a possibility that my Attorney could misuse the authority given to him/her by this continuing power of attorney; and

that I may, while capable, revoke this continuing power of attorney.

DATE OF EFFECTIVENESS

This continuing power of attorney will come into effect [on the date it is signed and witnessed]. It is my intention and I so authorize my Attorney that this authority [may be exercised from that date forward, and] shall be exercised during any incapacity on my part to manage my property pursuant to sections 7 and 14 of the *Substitute Decisions Act, 1992*, S.O. 1992, c.30.

EXECUTION

Executed at [Place] this [Date] in the presence of both witnesses, each present at the same time.

In witness whereof, I have signed my name to this continuing power of attorney for property, written upon this page and initialled upon the preceding [#] pages.

)
)   [Grantor's Signature]
)

Witnesses

We are witnesses to this continuing power of attorney for property. The grantor of this continuing power of attorney for property has signed this document in the presence of both of us and we have each signed this document in the presence of the grantor and each other on the date shown in the paragraph above. Neither one of us is an attorney named in this continuing power of attorney for property; a spouse or partner of the named attorneys; a spouse, partner, or child of the grantor, or someone whom the grantor treats as his or her child; a person whose property is under guardianship or who has a guardian of the person; or a person under the age of 18 years.

_____	))))))	_____
[Witness's Signature] [Address of Witness]		[Witness's Signature] [Address of Witness]

5. ALTERNATIVE METHODS FOR MAKING DECISIONS ABOUT ANOTHER PERSON'S PROPERTY

(a) Introduction

Sometimes, individuals will become incapable of managing their own property but will not have granted a power of attorney for property. In these cases, other regimes under the *Substitute Decisions Act* can be utilized. These regimes include statutory guardians of property and court-appointed guardians of property.

(b) Statutory Guardian

A statutory guardian will be appointed in the following situations:

If a person who is a patient of a psychiatric facility is found to be incapable of managing property, the Public Guardian and Trustee becomes the person's statutory guardian of property.[70]

If a person is assessed by a capacity assessor as being incapable of managing property *and* there is no knowledge of an existing power of attorney for property or of a spouse or relative who intends to apply to the court to be appointed guardian of property, the Public Guardian and Trustee becomes the person's statutory guardian of property.[71]

---

70 *Substitute Decisions Act*, s. 15.
71 *Substitute Decisions Act*, ss. 16 and 22.

In both cases, the statutory guardianship can be terminated if a less restrictive course of substitute decision-making is available.

SUBSTITUTE DECISIONS ACT, 1992
S.O. 1992, c. 30

16.1 A statutory guardianship of property is terminated if,

(a) the incapable person gave a continuing power of attorney before the certificate of incapacity was issued;

(b) the power of attorney gives the attorney authority over all of the incapable person's property;

(c) the Public Guardian and Trustee receives a copy of the power of attorney and a written undertaking signed by the attorney to act in accordance with the power of attorney; and

(d) if someone has replaced the Public Guardian and Trustee as the statutory guardian under section 17, the statutory guardian receives a copy of the power of attorney and a written undertaking signed by the attorney to act in accordance with the power of attorney.

17. (1) Any of the following persons may apply to the Public Guardian and Trustee to replace the Public Guardian and Trustee as an incapable person's statutory guardian of property:

1. The incapable person's spouse or partner.

2. A relative of the incapable person.

3. The incapable person's attorney under a continuing power of attorney, if the power of attorney was made before the certificate of incapacity was issued and does not give the attorney authority over all of the incapable person's property.

4. A trust corporation within the meaning of the *Loan and Trust Corporations Act*, if the incapable person's spouse or partner consents in writing to the application.

(2) The application shall be in the prescribed form.

(3) The application shall be accompanied by a management plan for the property in the prescribed form.

(4) Subject to subsection (6), the Public Guardian and Trustee shall appoint the applicant as the incapable person's statutory guardian of property if the Public Guardian and Trustee is satisfied that the applicant is suitable to manage the property and that the management plan is appropriate.

(5) The Public Guardian and Trustee shall consider the incapable person's current wishes, if they can be ascertained, and the closeness of the applicant's relationship to the person.

(6) The Public Guardian and Trustee may refuse to appoint the applicant unless the applicant provides security, in a manner approved by the Public Guardian and Trustee, for an amount fixed by the Public Guardian and Trustee.

(7) If security is required under subsection (6), the court may, on application, order that security be dispensed with, that security be provided in a manner not

approved by the Public Guardian and Trustee, or that the amount of security be reduced, and may make its order subject to conditions.

(8) The Public Guardian and Trustee shall give the person appointed as statutory guardian of property a certificate certifying the appointment.

(9) The certificate is proof of the guardian's authority.

(10) The Public Guardian and Trustee may make an appointment under this section subject to conditions specified in the certificate.

(11) The Public Guardian and Trustee may certify that two or more applicants are joint statutory guardians of property, or that each of them is guardian for a specified part of the property.

(12) A person who replaces the Public Guardian and Trustee as statutory guardian of property shall, subject to any conditions imposed by the Public Guardian and Trustee or the court, manage the property in accordance with the management plan.

(c) Court-Appointed Guardian

A court-appointed guardian of property is a last resort when all other substitute decision-making options have failed or are unavailable.

SUBSTITUTE DECISIONS ACT, 1992
S.O. 1992, c. 30

22. (1) The court may, on any person's application, appoint a guardian of property for a person who is incapable of managing property if, as a result, it is necessary for decisions to be made on his or her behalf by a person who is authorized to do so.

(2) An application may be made under subsection (1) even though there is a statutory guardian.

(3) The court shall not appoint a guardian if it is satisfied that the need for decisions to be made will be met by an alternative course of action that,

(a) does not require the court to find the person to be incapable of managing property; and

(b) is less restrictive of the person's decision-making rights than the appointment of a guardian.

. . .

24. (1) A person who provides health care or residential, social, training or support services to an incapable person for compensation shall not be appointed under section 22 as his or her guardian of property.

(2) Subsection (1) does not apply to the incapable person's spouse, partner or relative or to the following persons:

. . .

2. The attorney for personal care.

3. The attorney under a continuing power of attorney.

(2.1) The court shall not appoint the Public Guardian and Trustee as a guardian under section 22 unless the application proposes the Public Guardian and Trustee as guardian and there is no other suitable person who is available and willing to be appointed.

(3) A person who does not reside in Ontario shall not be appointed as a guardian of property unless the person provides security, in a manner approved by the court, for the value of the property.

(4) The court may order that the requirement for security under subsection (3) does not apply to a person or that the amount required be reduced, and may make its order subject to conditions.

(5) Except in the case of an application that is being dealt with under section 77 (summary disposition), the court shall consider,

  (a) whether the proposed guardian is the attorney under a continuing power of attorney;

  (b) the incapable person's current wishes, if they can be ascertained; and

  (c) the closeness of the applicant's relationship to the incapable person.

(6) The court may, with their consent, appoint two or more persons as joint guardians of property or may appoint each of them as guardian for a specified part of the property.

25. (1) An order appointing a guardian of property for a person shall include a finding that the person is incapable of managing property and that, as a result, it is necessary for decisions to be made on his or her behalf by a person who is authorized to do so.

(2) An order appointing a guardian of property may,

  (a) require that the guardian post security in the manner and amount that the court considers appropriate;

  (b) make the appointment for a limited period as the court considers appropriate;

  (c) impose such other conditions on the appointment as the court considers appropriate.

(3) Clause (2) (a) does not apply if the guardian is the Public Guardian and Trustee or a trust corporation within the meaning of the *Loan and Trust Corporations Act*.

26. (1) The court may vary an order appointing a guardian of property under section 22 or substitute another person as guardian, on motion in the proceeding in which the guardian was appointed.

(2) A motion under subsection (1) may be made by the guardian, the applicant in the proceeding in which the guardian was appointed, or any person who was entitled under section 69 to be served with notice of that proceeding.

(3) Subsection 69 (2), subsections 69 (5) to (9) and section 77 apply, with necessary modifications, to a motion to vary an order.

(4) Subsection 69 (1), subsections 69 (5) to (9), subsection 70 (1) and section 77 apply, with necessary modifications, to a motion to substitute another person as guardian.

Notes and Questions

1. What are the advantages of a continuing power of attorney for property over statutory guardianship? Are there any disadvantages?

2. Courts will endeavour to preserve substitute decision-making regimes that are less onerous and more personal than the appointment of a court-appointed guardian.[72]

3. Should there be difficulties with a less onerous scheme of substitute decision-making, a court will necessarily intervene in order to protect the incapable person and the person's property. In that situation, a court will often have to choose between competing applicants for guardianship.[73]

4. The procedure for appointment of a court-appointed guardian is governed by Part III (ss. 67 to 77) of the *Substitute Decisions Act*.

6. POWERS OF ATTORNEY FOR PERSONAL CARE

(a) Introduction

While there are other alternatives for substitute decision-making for personal care, some easier than powers of attorney, the most flexible and personal option is, by far, a power of attorney for personal care. A power of attorney for personal care allows the grantor to name the person he or she chooses to make personal care decisions on his or her behalf when the grantor is no longer capable of making those decisions. The grantor can also include directions in the document about how those decisions should be made.

(b) Creation

(i) *Generally*

A well-drafted power of attorney for personal care will name who is to act as substitute decision-maker, specify how the attorney or attorneys are to act and how capacity of the grantor will be assessed when the time comes, and give clear directions on how the power of substitute decision-making is to be used. The legal requirements are minimal: a grantor capable of granting the power, a named attorney (or attorneys), a statement that the attorney has the power to make personal care decisions on the grantor's behalf should she be incapable of doing so, the grantor's signature, the date, and the signature of two qualifying witnesses.

---

72 *See Re Hammond Estate* (1998), 25 E.T.R. (2d) 188 (Nfld. T.D.) and *McGoey v. Wedd* (1999), 45 O.R. (3d) 300, 28 E.T.R. (2d) 236 (S.C.J.).

73 *See Public Guardian and Trustee v. Duggan* (1998), 121 O.A.C. 294 (C.A.), reversing (1998), 165 D.L.R. (4th) 713 (Gen. Div.) and Dawn Dudley Oosterhoff, "When 'Closest' Isn't Close Enough" Case Comment on Public Guardian and Trustee v. Duggan (Ont. Gen. Div.) (1999), 18 E.T. & P.J. 219, and "Case Comment on Public Guardian and Trustee v. Duggan (Ont. C.A.) (1999), 19 E.T. & P.J. 10.

The creation of a power of attorney for personal care is governed by the *Substitute Decisions Act.*

SUBSTITUTE DECISIONS ACT, 1992
S.O. 1992, c. 30

46. (1) A person may give a written power of attorney for personal care, authorizing the person or persons named as attorneys to make, on the grantor's behalf, decisions concerning the grantor's personal care.

(2) The power of attorney may name the Public Guardian and Trustee as attorney if his or her consent in writing is obtained before the power of attorney is executed.

(3) A person may not act as an attorney under a power of attorney for personal care, unless the person is the grantor's spouse, partner or relative, if the person,

  (a) provides health care to the grantor for compensation; or

  (b) provides residential, social, training or support services to the grantor for compensation.

(4) If the power of attorney names two or more persons as attorneys, the attorneys shall act jointly, unless the power of attorney provides otherwise.

(5) If two or more attorneys act jointly under the power of attorney and one of them dies, becomes incapable of personal care or resigns, the remaining attorney or attorneys are authorized to act, unless the power of attorney provides otherwise.

(6) The power of attorney is subject to this Part, and to the conditions and restrictions that are contained in the power of attorney and are consistent with this Act.

(7) The power of attorney may contain instructions with respect to the decisions the attorney is authorized to make.

(8) The power of attorney need not be in any particular form.

(9) The power of attorney may be in the prescribed form.

. . .

48. (1) A power of attorney for personal care shall be executed in the presence of two witnesses, each of whom shall sign the power of attorney as witness.

(2) The persons referred to in subsection 10 (2) shall not be witnesses.

(ii) *Ulysses Agreements*

In some circumstances, it may be appropriate for the grantor of a power of attorney for personal care to enter into a binding agreement with the attorney, limiting the grantor's ability to object to the attorney's actions once the grantor becomes incapable. These provisions, often referred to as Ulysses agreements, may be particularly helpful for persons who suffer episodic psychiatric disorders, the nature of which leads a person to deny the very treatment she needs to recover. Drafting such an agreement is anticipated by the *Substitute Decisions Act*:[74]

SUBSTITUTE DECISIONS ACT, 1992
S.O. 1992, c. 30

50. (1) A power of attorney for personal care may contain one or more of the provisions described in subsection (2), but a provision is not effective unless both of the following circumstances exist:

1. At the time the power of attorney was executed or within 30 days afterwards, the grantor made a statement in the prescribed form indicating that he or she understood the effect of the provision and of subsection (4).
2. Within 30 days after the power of attorney was executed, an assessor made a statement in the prescribed form,
   i. indicating that, after the power of attorney was executed, the assessor performed an assessment of the grantor's capacity,
   ii. stating the assessor's opinion that, at the time of the assessment, the grantor was capable of personal care and was capable of understanding the effect of the provision and of subsection (4), and
   iii. setting out the facts on which the opinion is based.

(2) The provisions referred to in subsection (1) are:

1. A provision that authorizes the attorney and other persons under the direction of the attorney to use force that is necessary and reasonable in the circumstances,
   i. to determine whether the grantor is incapable of making a decision to which the *Health Care Consent Act, 1996* applies,
   ii. to confirm, in accordance with subsection 49 (2), whether the grantor is incapable of personal care, if the power of attorney contains a condition described in clause 49 (1) (b), or
   iii. to obtain an assessment of the grantor's capacity by an assessor in any other circumstances described in the power of attorney.
2. A provision that authorizes the attorney and other persons under the direction of the attorney to use force that is necessary and reasonable in the circumstances to take the grantor to any place for care or treatment, to admit the grantor to that place and to detain and restrain the grantor in that place during the care or treatment.
3. A provision that waives the grantor's right to apply to the Consent and Capacity Board under sections 32, 50 and 65 of the *Health Care Consent Act, 1996* for a review of a finding of incapacity that applies to a decision to which that Act applies.

(3) A provision described in subsection (2) that is contained in a power of attorney for personal care is subject to any conditions and restrictions contained in the power of attorney that are consistent with this Act.

---

74 *Saskatchewan's Health Care Directives and Substitute Health Care Decisions Makers Act*, s. 5 also anticipates the use of a Ulysses contract.

(4) If a provision described in subsection (2) is contained in a power of attorney for personal care and both of the circumstances described in subsection (1) exist, the power of attorney may be revoked only if, within 30 days before the revocation is executed, an assessor performed an assessment of the grantor's capacity and made a statement in the prescribed form,

(a) indicating that, on a date specified in the statement, the assessor performed an assessment of the grantor's capacity;

(b) stating the assessor's opinion that, at the time of the assessment, the grantor was capable of personal care; and

(c) setting out the facts on which the opinion is based.

(5) No action lies against an attorney, a police services board, a police officer or any other person arising from the use of force that is authorized by a provision described in subsection (2) that is effective under subsection (1).

Notes and Questions

1. The grantor does not have to be capable of making decisions about his or her own personal care in order to grant a power of attorney. However, if the power of attorney for personal care contains any directions or instructions ("advance directives"), the grantor must be capable at the time of drafting of making those decisions.

2. The restrictions on who may be an attorney under a power of attorney for personal care are few: the attorney must be at least 16 years of age and capable of making personal care decisions. As a practical matter, should an attorney demonstrate more maturity than an average 16 year old? Does making treatment decisions for another person require more objectivity and equilibrium than a 16-year old might possess?

(c) Advance Directives

One of the most important reasons for granting a power of attorney for personal care, if not the most important reason, is the opportunity it affords the grantor to express any wishes or instructions he or she might have about treatment. Often, and mistakenly, referred to as "living wills," advance directives are guidelines that direct an attorney when making decisions on the grantor's behalf. Often, but not necessarily, advance directives form part of a power of attorney for personal care (acting as an equivalent to conditions and restrictions in a power of attorney for property). Directives for personal care decisions may be also be drafted in a separate document that accompanies a power of attorney for personal care, or exist as a separate document *without* an accompanying power of attorney for personal care. The directives may also be expressed orally or in any other manner. In all of these cases, the directives are binding.[75]

---

75 The Ontario legislation is unusual in permitting binding advance directives to be expressed orally or in some other manner (for example, on a Bliss Board – a communication device for those who lack the ability to speak). The legislation in Alberta, Manitoba, Newfoundland, and Prince Edward Island all specifically require advance directives to be in writing, signed, and witnessed.

Notes and Questions

1. How would you interpret the following directive?

I do not wish to have my life unduly prolonged by any course of treatment or any other medical procedure which offers no reasonable expectation of my recovery from life threatening physical or mental incapacity, except as may be necessary for the relief of suffering.

2. Poorly drafted advance directives can cause more problems than they were meant to address. In some cases, the problem is a result of health care practitioners falsely believing that advance directives are meant to be a replacement for direct communication between the patient and the practitioner. Rather, advance directives are meant to guide the substitute decision-maker in making decisions and communicating with the practitioner on the patient's behalf.[76]

3. Many lawyers are uncomfortable when assisting their clients with advance directives. This is understandable given that most lawyers are not medically trained. As well, a discussion of wishes regarding personal care takes the lawyer into a personal realm that few would wish to enter. One solution to this dilemma is to draft the power of attorney for personal care noting only conditions and restrictions that pertain to the legal use of the power. Clients can then be advised and encouraged to discuss wishes regarding personal care with their family members and physician, making note of their wishes and attaching those notes to the power of attorney. This course of action ensures that clients take full advantage of the benefits of a power of attorney for personal care but does not bind the lawyer into providing advice in an unknown realm. Lawyers can even go one step further by providing their clients with any one of the various tools available to guide individuals through the process of discerning their wishes regarding personal care.

4. There are any number of kits available for preparing advance directives or "living wills." Many of them are available on the Internet for free or for a small price. While some of these documents may prove useful in helping a person focus his or her thoughts, many are legally problematic and may inadvertently void a person's power of attorney for personal care.[77]

---

76 See Michael Gordon and Dan Levitt, "Acting on a Living Will: A Physician's Dilemma" (1996), 155 Canadian Medical Association Journal 893; Brian F. Hoffman and Anne-Marie Humniski, "Advance Direcctives: Principles, Problems, and Solutions for Physicians" (1997), 30 Annals of the Royal College of Physicians and Surgeons of Canada 169; and Peter A. Singer et al., "Reconceptualizing Advance Care Planning from the Patient's Perspective" (1998), 158 Archives of Internal Medicine 879.

77 For an example of the documents, both good and bad, that are readily available, see "The Living Wills Registry (Canada)" at www.sentex.net/lwr; The Joint Centre for Bioethics at www.utoronto.ca/jcb; "MED-DOCS online" at http://med-docs.com; D. William Molloy and V. Mepham, *Let Me Decide: The Health Care Directive that Speaks for You When You Can't* (Toronto: Penguin Books, 1992); M. Stephen Georgas, *Power of Attorney Kit: A Do-It-Yourself Guide* (Vancouver: Self-Counsel Press, 1998); and Linda L. Emanuel & Ezekiel J. Emanuel, "The Medical Directive: A New Comprehensive Advance Care Document" (1989), 261 Journal of the American Medical Association 3288, reprint (1990-91), 10 E.T.J. 134.

5. Clients may also want to include in their power of attorney conditions or restrictions other than advance directives. Examples of such restrictions include limiting the attorney's ability to act in certain circumstances until a confirmation of incapacity has been obtained. As well, some method of assessing the grantor's capacity may be advisable because a power of attorney for personal care only becomes effective upon the grantor's incapacity.

(d) Exercise

(i) *Effectiveness*

A power of attorney for personal care will only be effective if the grantor is incapable of making the personal care decision. The method of determining the grantor's incapacity – and hence, whether the attorney acts or not – depends upon the decision to be made and the legislation that addresses that particular decisions.

SUBSTITUTE DECISIONS ACT, 1992
S.O. 1992, c. 30

49. (1) A provision in a power of attorney for personal care that confers authority to make a decision concerning the grantor's personal care is effective to authorize the attorney to make the decision if,

(a) the *Health Care Consent Act, 1996* applies to the decision and that Act authorizes the attorney to make the decision; or

(b) the *Health Care Consent Act, 1996* does not apply to the decision and the attorney has reasonable grounds to believe that the grantor is incapable of making the decision, subject to any condition in the power of attorney that prevents the attorney from making the decision unless the fact that the grantor is incapable of personal care has been confirmed.

(2) A power of attorney that contains a condition described in clause (1) (b) may specify the method for confirming whether the grantor is incapable of personal care and, if no method is specified, that fact may be confirmed by notice to the attorney in the prescribed form from an assessor stating that the assessor has performed an assessment of the grantor's capacity and has found that the grantor is incapable of personal care.

(3) A power of attorney that contains a condition described in clause (1) (b) may require an assessor who performs an assessment of the grantor's capacity to consider factors described in the power of attorney.

(4) This section applies to powers of attorney given before or after the coming into force of section 32 of the *Advocacy, Consent and Substitute Decisions Statute Law Amendment Act, 1996.*

(ii) *Duties of the Attorney*

An attorney's duties are outlined in the *Substitute Decisions Act.*

SUBSTITUTE DECISIONS ACT, 1992
S.O. 1992, c. 30

66. (1) The powers and duties of a guardian of the person shall be exercised and performed diligently and in good faith.

(2) The guardian shall explain to the incapable person what the guardian's powers and duties are.

(2.1) The guardian shall make decisions on the incapable person's behalf to which the *Health Care Consent Act, 1996* applies in accordance with that Act.

(3) The guardian shall make decisions on the incapable person's behalf to which the *Health Care Consent Act, 1996* does not apply in accordance with the following principles:

1. If the guardian knows of a wish or instruction applicable to the circumstances that the incapable person expressed while capable, the guardian shall make the decision in accordance with the wish or instruction.

2. The guardian shall use reasonable diligence in ascertaining whether there are such wishes or instructions.

3. A later wish or instruction expressed while capable prevails over an earlier wish or instruction.

4. If the guardian does not know of a wish or instruction applicable to the circumstances that the incapable person expressed while capable, or if it is impossible to make the decision in accordance with the wish or instruction, the guardian shall make the decision in the incapable person's best interests.

(4) In deciding what the person's best interests are for the purpose of subsection (3), the guardian shall take into consideration,

(a) the values and beliefs that the guardian knows the person held when capable and believes the person would still act on if capable;

(b) the person's current wishes, if they can be ascertained; and

(c) the following factors:

1. Whether the guardian's decision is likely to,
   i.   improve the quality of the person's life,
   ii. prevent the quality of the person's life from deteriorating, or
   iii. reduce the extent to which, or the rate at which, the quality of the person's life is likely to deteriorate.

2. Whether the benefit the person is expected to obtain from the decision outweighs the risk of harm to the person from an alternative decision.

(4.1) The guardian shall, in accordance with the regulations, keep records of decisions made by the guardian on the incapable person's behalf.

(5) The guardian shall encourage the person to participate, to the best of his or her abilities, in the guardian's decisions on his or her behalf.

(6) The guardian shall seek to foster regular personal contact between the incapable person and supportive family members and friends of the incapable person.

(7) The guardian shall consult from time to time with,

(a) supportive family members and friends of the incapable person who are in regular personal contact with the incapable person; and

(b) the persons from whom the incapable person receives personal care.

(8) The guardian shall, as far as possible, seek to foster the person's independence.

(9) The guardian shall choose the least restrictive and intrusive course of action that is available and is appropriate in the particular case.

(10) The guardian shall not use confinement or monitoring devices or restrain the person physically or by means of drugs, and shall not give consent on the person's behalf to the use of confinement, monitoring devices or means of restraint, unless,

(a) the practice is essential to prevent serious bodily harm to the person or to others, or allows the person greater freedom or enjoyment.

(11) Nothing in this Act affects the common law duty of caregivers to restrain or confine persons when immediate action is necessary to prevent serious bodily harm to them or to others.

(12) The guardian shall not use electric shock as aversive conditioning and shall not give consent on the person's behalf to the use of electric shock as aversive conditioning unless the consent is given to a treatment in accordance with the *Health Care Consent Act, 1996.*

(13) Nothing in this Act affects the law relating to giving or refusing consent on another person's behalf to a procedure whose primary purpose is research.

(14) Nothing in this Act affects the law relating to giving or refusing consent on another person's behalf to one of the following procedures:

1. Sterilization that is not medically necessary for the protection of the person's health.

2. The removal of regenerative or non-regenerative tissue for implantation in another person's body.

. . .

(19) No proceeding for damages shall be commenced against a guardian for anything done or omitted in good faith in connection with the guardian's powers and duties under this Act.

67. Section 66, except subsections 66 (15) and (16), applies with necessary modifications to an attorney who acts under a power of attorney for personal care.

(iii) *Termination*

Without exception, an attorney's power to act on behalf of the grantor ends with the grantor's death. An attorney's authority to act may also terminated by the grantor (if she is capable of revoking his or her power), by resignation, operation of law, or application to the Consent and Capacity Board or court.

SUBSTITUTE DECISIONS ACT, 1992
S.O. 1992, c. 30

47.

. . .

(3) A person is capable of revoking a power of attorney for personal care if he or she is capable of giving one.

. . .

52. (1) An attorney under a power of attorney for personal care may resign but, if the attorney has acted under the power of attorney, the resignation is not effective until the attorney delivers a copy of the resignation to,

(a) the grantor;

(b) any other attorneys under the power of attorney;

(c) the person named by the power of attorney as a substitute for the attorney who is resigning, if the power of attorney provides for the substitution of another person; and

(d) unless the power of attorney provides otherwise, the grantor's spouse or partner and the relatives of the grantor who are known to the attorney and reside in Ontario, if the power of attorney does not provide for the substitution of another person or the substitute is not able and willing to act.

(1.1) Clause (1) (d) does not require a copy of the resignation to be delivered to,

(a) the grantor's spouse, if the grantor and the spouse are living separate and apart within the meaning of the *Divorce Act* (Canada); or

(b) a relative of the grantor, if the grantor and the relative are related only by marriage and the grantor and his or her spouse are living separate and apart within the meaning of the *Divorce Act* (Canada).

(2) An attorney who resigns shall make reasonable efforts to give notice of the resignation to persons with whom the attorney previously dealt on behalf of the grantor and with whom further dealings are likely to be required on behalf of the grantor.

53. (1) A power of attorney for personal care is terminated,

(a) when the attorney dies, becomes incapable of personal care or resigns, unless,

(i)   another attorney is authorized to act under subsection 46 (5), or

(ii) the power provides for the substitution of another person and that person is able and willing to act;

(b) when the court appoints a guardian for the grantor under section 55;

(c) when the grantor executes a new power of attorney for personal care, unless the grantor provides that there shall be multiple powers of attorney for personal care;

(d) when the power of attorney is revoked.

(2) A revocation shall be in writing and shall be executed in the same way as a power of attorney for personal care.

Notes and Questions

1. An attorney for personal care is also subject to the guidelines of the *Health Care Consent Act.* Most of the guidelines mirror those in the *Substitute Decisions Act.*[78]

2. A substitute decision-maker for personal care may find his or her decision-making challenged and reviewed if unable to substantiate his or her choices on behalf of the patient as based upon the incapable patient's previously expressed wishes or, if there are no wishes known, the patient's best interests.[79]

3. A substitute decision-maker for personal care must be capable of making personal care decisions in order to act.[80] Although the legislation contemplates replacement of an incapable substitute decision-maker,[81] the process for assessing the substitute decision-maker's capacity and replacing him or her, is not clear. If the substitute decision-maker voluntarily steps aside, the hierarchy of substitute decision-makers in s. 20(1) of the *Health Care Consent Act* will apply, or the Consent and Capacity Board may appoint a representative. If the substitute decision-maker resists replacement, a court application for appointment of a guardian will probably be necessary.

(e) Precedent

SAMPLE POWER OF ATTORNEY
FOR PERSONAL CARE

THIS POWER OF ATTORNEY FOR PERSONAL CARE is given
by [Grantor] of [Residence].

REVOCATION

I hereby revoke any prior power of attorney for personal care or any prior power of attorney that affects my personal care previously given by me.

APPOINTMENT

I appoint _____ [and _____] to be my attorney[s] for personal care in accordance with the *Substitute Decisions Act, 1992*, S.O. 1992, c. 30. I will refer to my attorney or attorneys for personal care as my "Attorney."

SUBSTITUTION

If the attorney I have appointed cannot or will not be my attorney because of refusal, resignation, death, mental incapacity, or removal by the court, I substitute

---

78 See *Health Care Consent Act*, ss. 6-7, 21-24, and 30.
79 See *M.(A.) v. Benes* (1998), 166 D.L.R. (4th) 658 (Ont. Gen. Div.) and *L.(L.) v. T.(I.)* (1999), 181 D.L.R. (4th) 125 (Ont. C.A.).
80 *Health Care Consent Act*, s. 20(2)(a).
81 See, for example, *ibid.*, s. 37(6.1).

_____ to act as my attorney for personal care with the same authority as the person s/he is replacing.

[I have appointed my Attorneys to act jointly. If one of my Attorneys is unavailable or cannot or will not be my attorney because of refusal, resignation, death, mental incapacity, or removal by the court, I authorize the remaining attorney to act solely. Written notification to any person by my remaining attorney of the inability or refusal of the other attorney to act shall be sufficient and conclusive evidence of the fact.]

CONTINUING POWER

It is my intention and I so affirm that this authority shall be exercised by my Attorney during any incapacity on my part to manage my personal care.

AUTHORIZATION

In the full knowledge that my Attorney will act in accordance with the wishes I have and will express, I authorize my Attorney to make on my behalf any decisions concerning my personal care, and to give or refuse consent on my behalf to any treatment to which the *Health Care Consent Act, 1996*, S.O. 1996, c.2, Sch. A applies.

REIMBURSEMENT FOR EXPENSES

All expenses incurred by my Attorney in carrying out his/her duties (including obtaining an assessment of my capacity, if required), shall be payable by me or my attorney for property out of my assets.

SPECIFIC INSTRUCTIONS

This power of attorney for personal care is subject to any advance directives that I have outlined, will outline in subsequent documents in the future, or express verbally. I trust my Attorney to use any such directives as guidelines wisely and with integrity, varying from my directives if, when applied to individual circumstances, they no longer reflect my underlying values and beliefs.

Values and Beliefs: [   ]

Tolerable or Acceptable "Quality of Life": [   ]

Unacceptable "Quality of Life": [   ]

Instructions Regarding Organ Donation and Research: In compliance with the *Human Tissue Gift Act*, R.S.O. 1990, c. H.20, section 4,[82] I declare that it is my

---

82 To be renamed the *Trillium Gift of Life Network Act*, S.O. 2000, c. 39, s. 1, upon proclamation by the Lieutenant Governor.

wish that my body or any part of it is [not] to be used after my death for the purpose of organ donation for transplant, research, or medical education.

Instructions Regarding Care of My Body after Death: I am aware that, legally, my Estate Trustee as appointed in my Will is responsible for making any decisions regarding my body after death. I request that my Attorney ensure that my Estate Trustee is aware of my wishes [namely _____.]

POWER OF APPOINTMENT

Limited Power of Appointment: I hereby grant to my Attorney the power to appoint one or more attorneys under him/her for any period of time, for an unlimited period of time, or from time to time for the limited purpose of substituting for my Attorney during his/her inability to act. My Attorney may so appoint attorneys without in any way reducing or suspending my Attorney's own power of authority granted under this power of attorney for personal care. My Attorney shall remain responsible for overseeing the actions of any appointed attorneys. My Attorney shall have discretion to revoke any such appointments.

COMPENSATION

I authorize my Attorney, and my Attorney has agreed, to accept [no] compensation for any work done by my Attorney pursuant to this power of attorney for personal care.

AFFIRMATION

In granting this power of attorney for personal care, I affirm that I am aware:

that my Attorney has a genuine concern for my personal welfare;

that my Attorney will be required and will be able to make personal care decisions on my behalf should I be unable to do so myself;

that my Attorney must be able to account for decisions made on my behalf;

that there is a possibility that my Attorney could misuse the authority given under this power of attorney for personal care; and

that I may, while capable, revoke this power of attorney for personal care.

DATE OF EFFECTIVENESS

This continuing power of attorney will come into effect upon my incapacity to manage my personal care myself. My incapacity to make decisions regarding treatment as defined by Section 2 of the *Health Care Consent Act, 1996*, S.O.

1996, c. 2, Sched. A shall be determined in accordance with that Act. [For all other purposes, my capacity to make decisions regarding my personal care shall be determined by my Attorney.]

EXECUTION

Executed at [Place] this [Date] in the presence of both witnesses, each present at the same time.

In witness whereof, I have signed my name to this power of attorney for personal care, written upon this page and initialled upon the preceding [#] pages.

)
)   [Grantor's Signature]
)

Witnesses

We are witnesses to this power of attorney for personal care. The grantor of this power of attorney for personal care has signed this document in the presence of both of us and we have each signed this document in the presence of the grantor and each other on the date shown in the paragraph above. Neither one of us is an attorney named in this power of attorney for personal care; a spouse or partner of the named attorneys; a spouse, partner, child of the grantor or someone who the grantor treats as his or her child; a person whose property is under guardianship or who has a guardian of the person; or, a person under the age of 18 years.

	)	
[Witness's Signature]	)	[Witness's Signature]
[Address of Witness]	)	[Address of Witness]
	)	

7. ALTERNATIVE METHODS FOR MAKING DECISIONS ABOUT ANOTHER PERSON'S PERSONAL CARE

(a) Persons Who Can Make Treatment Decisions

Should a person without a power of attorney for personal care be found incapable of making his or her own treatment decisions, the treatment decision often cannot be withheld until a board or court appoints a representative or guardian. Therefore, the *Health Care Consent Act* provides a prioritized list of substitute decision-makers to which a health care practitioner can refer when a decision needs to be made for an incapable patient.

HEALTH CARE CONSENT ACT, 1996
S.O. 1996, c. 2, Sched. A

20. (1) If a person is incapable with respect to a treatment, consent may be given or refused on his or her behalf by a person described in one of the following paragraphs:

1. The incapable person's guardian of the person, if the guardian has authority to give or refuse consent to the treatment.
2. The incapable person's attorney for personal care, if the power of attorney confers authority to give or refuse consent to the treatment.
3. The incapable person's representative appointed by the Board under section 33, if the representative has authority to give or refuse consent to the treatment.
4. The incapable person's spouse or partner.
5. A child or parent of the incapable person, or a children's aid society or other person who is lawfully entitled to give or refuse consent to the treatment in the place of the parent. This paragraph does not include a parent who has only a right of access. If a children's aid society or other person is lawfully entitled to give or refuse consent to the treatment in the place of the parent, this paragraph does not include the parent.
6. A parent of the incapable person who has only a right of access.
7. A brother or sister of the incapable person.
8. Any other relative of the incapable person.

(2) A person described in subsection (1) may give or refuse consent only if he or she,

(a) is capable with respect to the treatment;

(b) is at least 16 years old, unless he or she is the incapable person's parent;

(c) is not prohibited by court order or separation agreement from having access to the incapable person or giving or refusing consent on his or her behalf;

(d) is available; and

(e) is willing to assume the responsibility of giving or refusing consent.

(3) A person described in a paragraph of subsection (1) may give or refuse consent only if no person described in an earlier paragraph meets the requirements of subsection (2).

(4) Despite subsection (3), a person described in a paragraph of subsection (1) who is present or has otherwise been contacted may give or refuse consent if he or she believes that no other person described in an earlier paragraph or the same paragraph exists, or that although such a person exists, the person is not a person described in paragraph 1, 2 or 3 and would not object to him or her making the decision.

(5) If no person described in subsection (1) meets the requirements of subsection (2), the Public Guardian and Trustee shall make the decision to give or refuse consent.

(6) If two or more persons who are described in the same paragraph of subsection (1) and who meet the requirements of subsection (2) disagree about whether

to give or refuse consent, and if their claims rank ahead of all others, the Public Guardian and Trustee shall make the decision in their stead.

(7) Subject to subsection (8), two persons are spouses for the purpose of this section if they are of opposite sex and,

   (a) are married to each other; or

   (b) are living in a conjugal relationship outside marriage and,

      (i) have cohabited for at least one year,

      (ii) are together the parents of a child, or

      (iii) have together entered into a cohabitation agreement under section 53 of the *Family Law Act* .

(8) Two persons are not spouses for the purpose of this section if they are living separate and apart within the meaning of the *Divorce Act* (Canada).

(9) Two persons are partners for the purpose of this section if they have lived together for at least one year and have a close personal relationship that is of primary importance in both persons' lives.

(10) Two persons are relatives for the purpose of this section if they are related by blood, marriage or adoption.

(11) For the purpose of clause (2)(d), a person is available if it is possible, within a time that is reasonable in the circumstances, to communicate with the person and obtain a consent or refusal.

(b) Appointment of a Representative

If the incapable person, or any person concerned about the incapable person, is dissatisfied with the substitute decision-maker as selected under the legislation, the person may apply to the Consent and Capacity Board to have a representative appointed.

HEALTH CARE CONSENT ACT, 1996
S.O. 1996, c. 2, Sched. A

33. (1) A person who is 16 years old or older and who is incapable with respect to a proposed treatment may apply to the Board for appointment of a representative to give or refuse consent on his or her behalf.

(2) A person who is 16 years old or older may apply to the Board to have himself or herself appointed as the representative of a person who is incapable with respect to a proposed treatment, to give or refuse consent on behalf of the incapable person.

(3) Subsections (1) and (2) do not apply if the incapable person has a guardian of the person who has authority to give or refuse consent to the proposed treatment, or an attorney for personal care under a power of attorney conferring that authority.

(4) The parties to the application are:

  1. The incapable person.

  2. The proposed representative named in the application.

3. Every person who is described in paragraph 4, 5, 6 or 7 of subsection 20 (1).
4. The health practitioner who proposed the treatment.
5. Any other person whom the Board specifies.

(5) In an appointment under this section, the Board may authorize the representative to give or refuse consent on the incapable person's behalf,

(a) to the proposed treatment;
(b) to one or more treatments or kinds of treatment specified by the Board, whenever a health practitioner proposing that treatment or a treatment of that kind finds that the person is incapable with respect to it; or
(c) to treatment of any kind, whenever a health practitioner proposing a treatment finds that the person is incapable with respect to it.

(6) The Board may make an appointment under this section if it is satisfied that the following requirements are met:

1. The incapable person does not object to the appointment.
2. The representative consents to the appointment, is at least 16 years old and is capable with respect to the treatments or the kinds of treatment for which the appointment is made.
3. The appointment is in the incapable person's best interests.

(7) Unless the incapable person objects, the Board may,

(a) appoint as representative a different person than the one named in the application;
(b) limit the duration of the appointment;
(c) impose any other condition on the appointment;
(d) on any person's application, remove, vary or suspend a condition imposed on the appointment or impose an additional condition on the appointment.

(8) The Board may, on any person's application, terminate an appointment made under this section if,

(a) the incapable person or the representative requests the termination of the appointment;
(b) the representative is no longer capable with respect to the treatments or the kinds of treatment for which the appointment was made;
(c) the appointment is no longer in the incapable person's best interests; or
(d) the incapable person has a guardian of the person who has authority to consent to the treatments or the kinds of treatment for which the appointment was made, or an attorney for personal care under a power of attorney conferring that authority.

(c) Appointment of a Guardian of the Person

If the incapable person, or any person concerned about the incapable person, is dissatisfied with the person's attorney appointed in a power of attorney for personal care or with the representative appointed by the Consent and Capacity Board, an application to the court is required in order to have another substitute decision-maker named.

SUBSTITUTE DECISIONS ACT, 1992
S.O. 1992, c. 30

55. (1) The court may, on any person's application, appoint a guardian of the person for a person who is incapable of personal care and, as a result, needs decisions to be made on his or her behalf by a person who is authorized to do so.

(2) The court shall not appoint a guardian if it is satisfied that the need for decisions to be made will be met by an alternative course of action that,

(a) does not require the court to find the person to be incapable of personal care; and

(b) is less restrictive of the person's decision-making rights than the appointment of a guardian.

. . .

57. (1) A person who provides health care or residential, social, training or support services to an incapable person for compensation shall not be appointed under section 55 as his or her guardian of the person.

(2) Subsection (1) does not apply to the incapable person's spouse, partner or relative or to the following persons:

1. The incapable person's guardian of property.

2. The attorney for personal care.

3. The attorney under a continuing power of attorney for property.

(2.1) Subsection (1) does not apply to a person if the court is satisfied that there is no other suitable person who is available and willing to be appointed.

(2.2) The court shall not appoint the Public Guardian and Trustee as a guardian under section 55 unless the application proposes the Public Guardian and Trustee as guardian and there is no other suitable person who is available and willing to be appointed.

(3) Except in the case of an application that is being dealt with under section 77 (summary disposition), the court shall consider,

(a) whether the proposed guardian is the attorney under a continuing power of attorney for property;

(b) the incapable person's current wishes, if they can be ascertained; and

(c) the closeness of the applicant's personal relationship to the incapable person.

(4) The court may, with their consent, appoint two or more persons as joint guardians of the person or may appoint each of them as guardian in respect of a specified period.

Notes and Questions

1. The procedure for applying for a court-appointed guardian of the person is governed by Part III (sections 69 to 77) of the *Substitute Decisions Act*.

2. In an attempt to resolve conflicts about personal care decision-making quickly and keep the conflict out of court, the Ontario legislative scheme establishes a reviewing body, the Consent and Capacity Board. This Board may hear applications for the appointment of a substitute decision-maker, review findings of incapacity, provide directions if the incapable person's wishes are unclear, hear applications to depart from the incapable person's wishes, and review the actions of a substitute decision-maker if there is concern that the substitute decision-maker is not complying with his or her duties and obligations.[83]

3. The Consent and Capacity Board may grant permission for the substitute decision-maker to consent to treatment that the person declined in advance directives. The Board may not, however, authorize the substitute decision-maker to refuse consent to treatment that the incapable person requested.[84]

8. CONCLUSION

It is often said that *powers of attorney preserve one's decision-making rights in times of incapacity*. Unfortunately, that is a misstatement. Although the law of capacity has been modified by the introduction of legislation, the law has not been so modified as to grant a person the right to make his or her own decisions even while incapable. However, what the law does do, is attempt to keep decisions made on behalf of another person as similar as possible to what the incapable person would have decided could he or she have done so.

The primary responsibility for one's care and one's actions rests with each individual. As far as the law allows, individuals are free to make their own choices about personal care and use of their property. Daily, those choices involve ethical decisions that are based upon an informed conscience. Individuals are respected for their ability to make those informed choices – an ability that is the hallmark of "autonomy." However, once incapacitated, the choices and the ethical decisions become more difficult and, often, beyond an individual's grasp. Incapacitated people may be able to still exercise some choice, but the choices become limited.

By appointing someone who knows an individual well enough to make decisions on the individual's behalf, and by guiding that appointee/substitute decision-maker with directives that express the individual's informed conscience, the individual exercises his or her right to guide and inform choices made on his or her behalf (should that become necessary) and, in that way, preserves his or her dignity and autonomy. Once incapable, the actual decision-making may be beyond an individual's grasp, but the beliefs and value system that would once have informed his or her decision-making have been placed in the hands of a substitute decision-maker. In this way, the individual's ethical, spiritual, and philosophical beliefs are preserved to be used by the substitute decision-maker as guiding principles.

By keeping decision-making as close as possible to the person most strongly affected by the decisions, the dignity of each individual is preserved and his or her interests served effectively. To do otherwise and decide everything for another without giving due consideration to the needs and wishes of that person amounts

---

83 *See Health Care Consent Act*, ss. 32-37.1, 50-54.1, and 65-69.1. Part V of the Act (ss. 70-81) deals with the Board's administration. A similar review board is established under British Columbia's *Health Care (Consent) and Care Facility (Admission) Act*, Part 4, ss. 27-32.

84 *See Health Care Consent Act*, s. 36.

to paternalism and domination, and eventually becomes self-serving; that is, serving the needs of the substitute decision-maker.

INDEX

Informed side do not [...] clay [...] [...] intuition

intend do not -

This is [confused] owned by my dad
The am only holds it in [...] [...] [...] my
dad
declaration of Trust
in my name but the benefit owners are 50 d 50

LT   Vs   B[...]